BENSON *and* HEDGES
Cricket Year

SECOND EDITION

BENSON and HEDGES
Cricket Year
SECOND EDITION
September 1982 to September 1983

Editor: David Lemmon
Associate Editor: Tony Lewis

PELHAM BOOKS

First published in Great Britain by
Pelham Books Ltd
44 Bedford Square
London WC1B 3DU
1983

British Library Cataloguing in Publication Data
Benson and Hedges cricket year. – 2nd ed.
1. Cricket – Periodicals
796.35′8′05   GV911

ISBN 0–7207–1475–3

Filmset in Times and Univers by Filmtype Services Limited, Scarborough, North Yorkshire
Printed and bound in Great Britain by Blantyre Printing and Binding Company Limited, Glasgow

Editor's Note

The aim of *Benson and Hedges Cricket Year* is that the cricket enthusiast shall
be able to read through the happenings in world cricket, from each October
until the following September (the end of the English season). Form charts are
printed and a player's every appearance will be given on these charts, and date
and place allow those appearances to be readily found in the text.

The symbol * indicates 'not out' or 'wicket-keeper' according to the context
and the symbol † indicates captain.

The editor wishes to express his deepest thanks to VICTOR ISAACS, the
Hampshire C.C.C. scorer, for his corrections and advice in the preparation of
the English Counties form charts which appear at the end of this book.

Mr Isaacs is one of the country's leading statisticians, with particular
reference to limited-over cricket. His research and pursuit of accuracy are
renowned and we are deeply indebted to him.

Unless otherwise stated, all the comments and written material in the book
are the work of the editor who also compiles the statistics.

Foreword

Rain, Sun and Magnificent Memories

Probably the most significant element of the 1983 English cricket season was the weather, particularly as far as the Benson and Hedges Cup was concerned.

The wettest Spring in years meant we struggled to complete the early rounds. Many zonal round matches were called off and three days of continuous rain forced us to decide the Middlesex *v* Gloucestershire quarter-final on the toss of a coin.

Thankfully the competition ended on a sunny note. Glorious weather greeted the eventual finalists, Middlesex and Essex, and cricket enthusiasts were treated to one of the most exciting finals in the Cup's twelve-year history and another example of the marvellous uncertainty of the game. Essex looked the victors at tea, having reached 113 for one and needing only 84 more runs to clinch the title. But Middlesex fought back to win their first Benson and Hedges Cup trophy by just nine runs.

Readers of the Second Edition of the *Benson and Hedges Cricket Year* can re-live this memorable match through the words and pictures in the centre section, as well as other highlights of the 1982/83 first-class cricket season. India's victory in the Prudential World Cup; New Zealand winning every one of their eight home internationals and Transvaal's clean sweep in South Africa are just some of many achievements featured to remind you of a great cricketing year.

DEREK WILSON
Benson & Hedges Limited

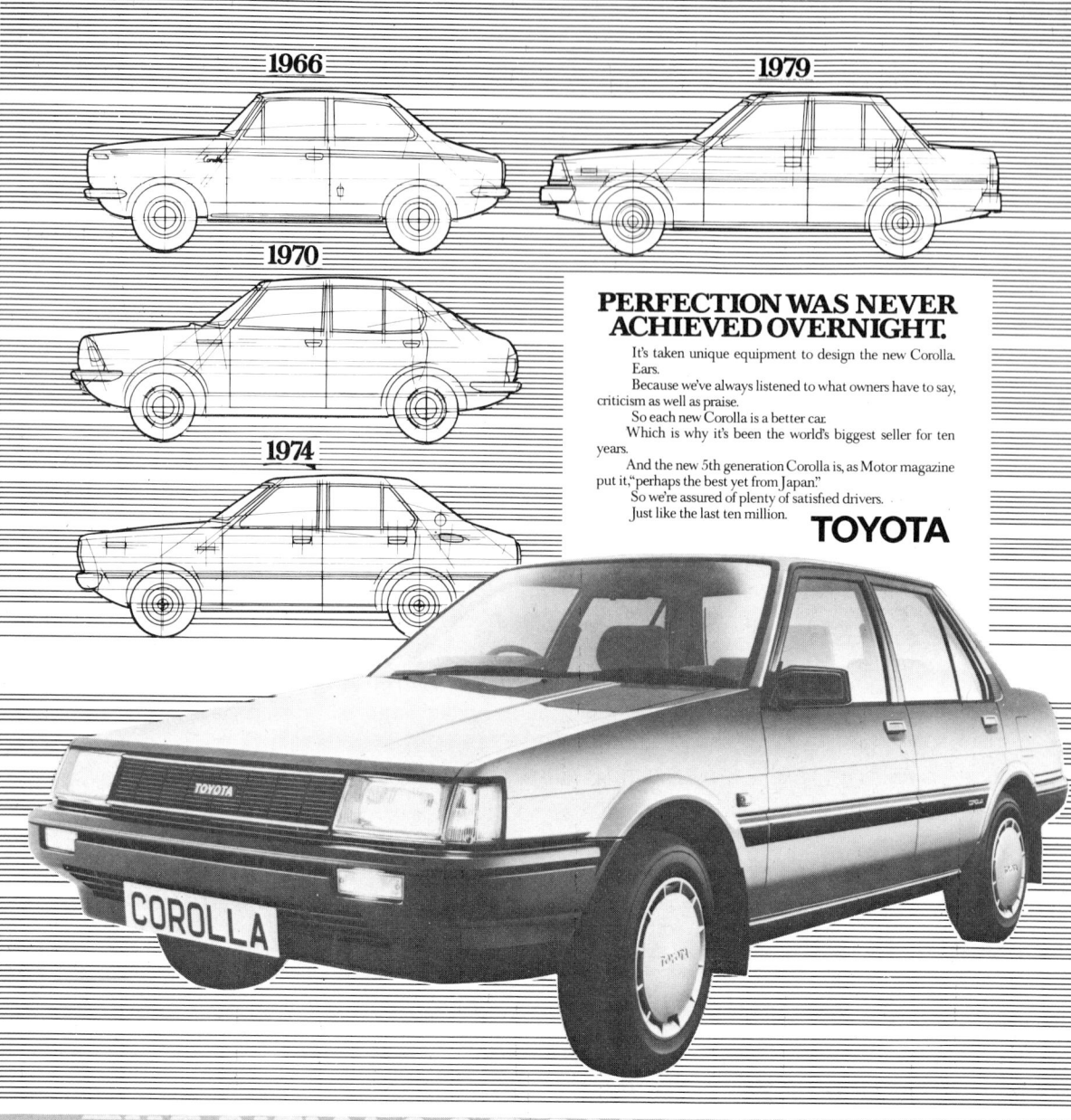

1966

1979

1970

1974

PERFECTION WAS NEVER ACHIEVED OVERNIGHT.

It's taken unique equipment to design the new Corolla.
Ears.

Because we've always listened to what owners have to say,
criticism as well as praise.

So each new Corolla is a better car.

Which is why it's been the world's biggest seller for ten
years.

And the new 5th generation Corolla is, as Motor magazine
put it, "perhaps the best yet from Japan."

So we're assured of plenty of satisfied drivers.

Just like the last ten million.

TOYOTA

COROLLA

THE NEW COROLLA. THE CAR THE WORLD MADE PERFECT

TOYOTA (GB) LTD., THE QUADRANGLE, REDHILL, SURREY RH1 1PX. TEL: REDHILL (0737) 68585.

Contents

How good is your cover?

Getting adequate insurance protection is a little like placing your field for a cricket match. You need to get just the right coverage in each vital area – not too much and certainly not too little. United Friendly Insurance, a name known to cricket supporters throughout the country* can provide insurance cover for many of your personal insurance needs – life assurance, fire, accident, home contents, house structure and travel insurances.

United Friendly is one of the country's largest home service insurance companies with 280 offices throughout the U.K., there's sure to be one near you – consult your Yellow Pages.

*In 1983 United Friendly Insurance sponsored the New Minor Counties Championship and supported the English Schools' Cricket Association Festival in Guildford.

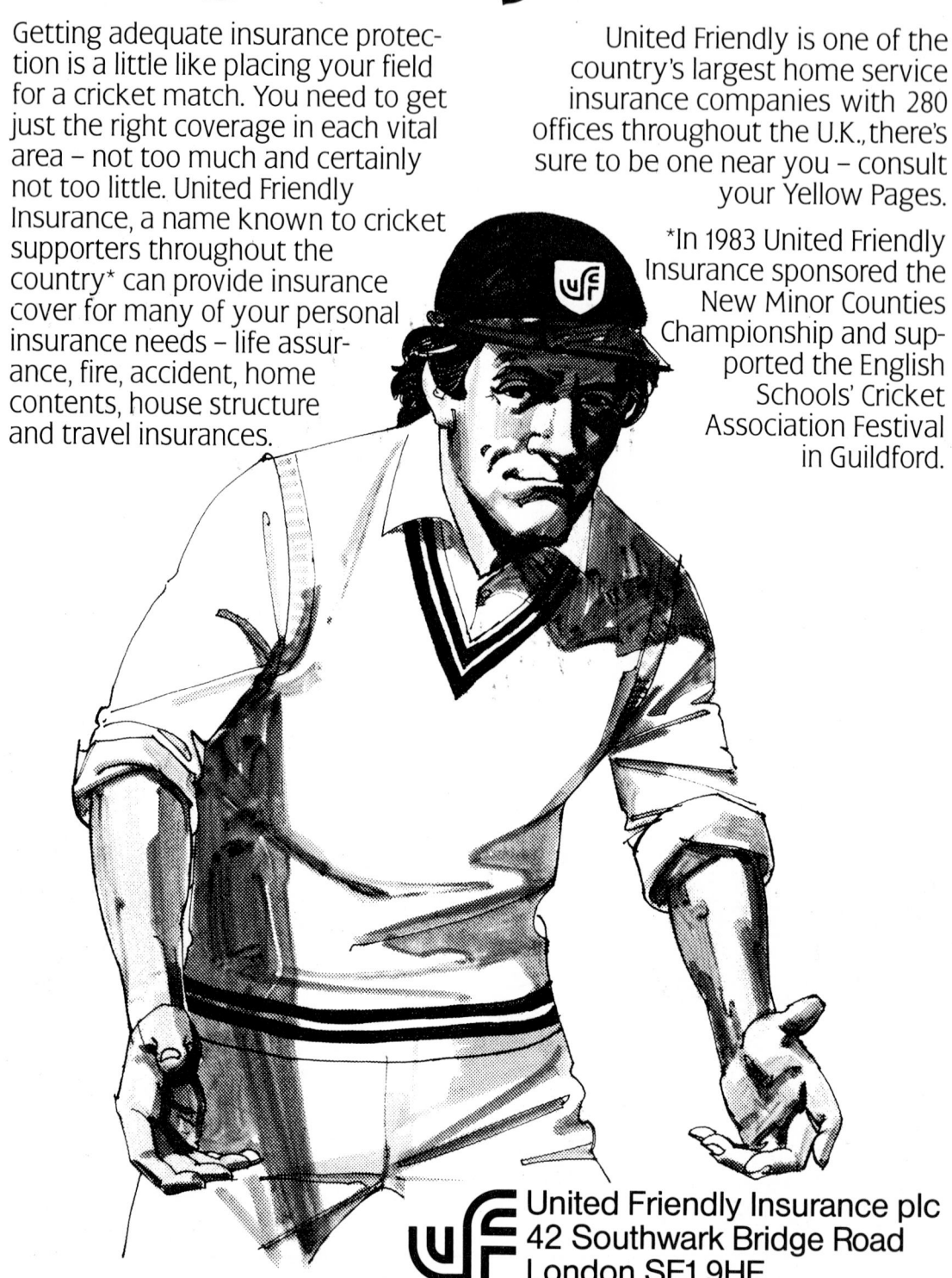

United Friendly Insurance plc
42 Southwark Bridge Road
London SE1 9HE

Brotherly Love

Sri Lanka in India
The Inaugural Test

Shastri and Kapil Dev. (Adrian Murrell)

Such is the growth of international cricket that it becomes increasingly difficult to determine where one cricket year ends and the next begins. While the English season of 1982 was still drawing to its close, India and Pakistan, who only a few days earlier had been engaged in Test series in England, were already entertaining touring sides in their own countries.

India's guests were Sri Lanka, the youngest of Test nations, and it is interesting to reflect that while it took India fourteen years to play her first ten Test matches, Sri Lanka will have attained that number within two years of becoming a Test-playing country, and that India herself engaged in twenty-one Test matches in just over eighteen months in 1981–83.

In another respect, Sri Lanka's short tour of India was symptomatic of the times in that it consisted of one Test match, three one-day internationals and one other one-day game. We are threatened by a surfeit of delights.

FIRST ONE-DAY INTERNATIONAL

With Gavaskar not yet considering himself fit enough for international cricket, Kapil Dev led an Indian side which was chosen specifically to meet with the demands of the limited-

Sandpeep Patil. Film star and cricketer. (Adrian Murrell)

Roger Binny whose all-round performances established him in the Indian side for the one-day internationals. (Adrian Murrell)

over game. So Srikkanth and Binny formed a new opening partnership, and the exciting, if undisciplined, Srikkanth provided an ideal start, hitting the ball firmly and eagerly to dominate the partnership of 62. The impetus given to the innings by the openers was maintained by the middle order, and later, a flurry from Kapil Dev and Yashpal Sharma, who added 68 for the sixth wicket, lifted India to a score which looked to be beyond the reach of Sri Lanka in the 46 overs to which the game had been reduced.

Sri Lanka made a dreadful start when they lost skipper Warnapura for nought and although there was some brave and determined batting, the skill of Doshi and the pace and accuracy of Kapil Dev assured India of success.

15 September 1982

at Delhi

Sri Lankans 241 for 7 (R.L. Dias 87, B. Warnapura 51)
Delhi 229 for 7

Sri Lankans won by 12 runs

In their only non-international match of the short tour the Sri Lankans gained an exciting victory over the Ranji Trophy holders. The Sri Lankan captain, Warnapura, had his solitary success with the bat in what proved to be his team's only win. The match was a 48-over contest.

FIRST ONE-DAY INTERNATIONAL: INDIA v. SRI LANKA
12 September 1982 at Amritsar

INDIA				SRI LANKA			
R. Binny	lbw, b de Mel	16		B. Warnapura†	b Madan Lal	0
K. Srikkanth	c John, b Warnapura	57		S.R. de S. Wettimuny	b Amarnath	43
D.B. Vengsarkar	c Ratnayeke, b D.S. de Silva	23		R.L. Dias	c Sharma, b Doshi	39
A. Malhotra	b Warnapura	40		L.R.D. Mendis	c Kapil Dev, b Doshi	33
S.M. Patil	lbw, b Ranasinghe	15		R.S. Madugalle	c Madan Lal, b Doshi	1
Kapil Dev†	st Goonatillake, b D.S. de Silva	49		A.N. Ranasinghe	c Binny, b Amarnath	35
Yashpal Sharma	not out	37		A.L.F. de Mel	c Madan Lal, b Doshi	1
M. Amarnath	c Wettimuny, b John	13		D.S. de Silva	b Kapil Dev	9
S.M.H. Kirmani*				H.M. Goonatillake*	not out	14
S. Madan Lal				J.R. Ratnayeke	not out	6
D.R. Doshi				V. John		
Extras	lb 4, w 11, nb 4	19		Extras	b 1, lb 5, w 2, nb 2	10
(46 overs)	(for 7 wickets)	269		(46 overs)	(for 8 wickets)	191

	O	M	R	W
de Mel	7	—	58	1
John	9	1	44	1
Ratnayeke	7	1	37	—
Warnapura	10	1	41	2
D.S. de Silva	10	—	49	2
Ranasinghe	3	—	21	1

	O	M	R	W
Kapil Dev	8	6	9	1
Madan Lal	8	2	24	1
Binny	6	—	33	—
Doshi	10	—	44	4
Amarnath	9	—	50	2
Patil	3	—	17	—
Vengsarkar	1	—	4	—
Malhotra	1	1	0	—

FALL OF WICKETS
1- 62, 2- 95, 3- 129, 4- 162, 5- 173, 6- 241, 7- 269

FALL OF WICKETS
1- 8, 2- 67, 3- 95, 4- 98, 5- 155, 6- 158, 7- 166, 8- 175

India won by 78 runs

SECOND ONE-DAY INTERNATIONAL

Sri Lanka could not have asked for a better performance from their batsmen when, after Warnapura had fallen to Kapil Dev at 10, Dias and Wettimuny added 170 for the second wicket. Dias became the first Sri Lankan batsman to score a century in a limited over international, and the later batsmen, particularly de Mel, hit hard in order to press home the advantage which had been gained.

Their efforts seemed as nothing, however, once Srikkanth began his assault upon the visitors' attack. He hit 13 fours in his innings of 95 which was scored off only 66 deliveries. Vengsarkar was content to play a supporting role in a second wicket stand of 134, but he, Malhotra and Patil continued to savage the Sri Lankan attack after Srikkanth had fallen to Warnapura, by far the best of the bowlers.

Having scored at just under seven runs an over, India won with more than nine overs to spare.

SECOND ONE-DAY INTERNATIONAL: INDIA v. SRI LANKA
15 September 1982 at Delhi

SRI LANKA				INDIA			
B. Warnapura†	lbw, b Kapil Dev	4		R. Binny	lbw, b John	10
S.R. de S. Wettimuny	c Srikkanth, b Binny	74		K. Srikkanth	c Mendis, b Warnapura	95
R.L. Dias	c Doshi, b Binny	102		D.B. Vengsarkar	c Warnapura, b Ratnayeke	53
L.R.D. Mendis	c Srikkanth, b Binny	10		A. Malhotra	not out	44
A.N. Ranasinghe	b Kapil Dev	20		S.M. Patil	c Dias, b G.R.A. de Silva	64
J.R. Ratnayeke	st Kirmani, b Madan Lal	2		Kapil Dev†	not out	1
R.S. Madugalle	c Kirmani, b Madan Lal	7		M. Amarnath		
A.L.F. de Mel	run out	28		Yashpal Sharma		
H.M. Goonatillake*	not out	4		S. Madan Lal		
G.R.A. de Silva	not out	6		S.M.H. Kirmani*		
V. John				D.R. Doshi		
Extras	b 2, lb 18	20		Extras	b 5, lb 8, nb 1	14
(50 overs)	(for 8 wickets)	277		(40.5 overs)	(for 4 wickets)	281

	O	M	R	W
Kapil Dev	10	—	41	2
Madan Lal	10	—	51	2
Binny	7	—	39	3
Patil	4	—	24	—
Amarnath	10	—	52	—
Doshi	5	—	34	—
Yashpal Sharma	4	—	16	—

	O	M	R	W
de Mel	2	—	23	—
John	5	—	44	1
Ratnayeke	8	—	48	1
G.R.A. de Silva	5.5	—	36	1
Ranasinghe	10	—	78	—
Warnapura	10	—	38	1

FALL OF WICKETS
1- 10, 2- 180, 3- 198, 4- 218, 5- 229, 6- 229, 7- 240, 8- 269

FALL OF WICKETS
1- 26, 2- 160, 3- 168, 4- 276

India won by 6 wickets

Srikkanth. His powerful hitting in the one-day internationals was the key factor in India's success. (Adrian Murrell)

Malhotra. Effective in the one-day internationals. (Adrian Murrell)

THE INAUGURAL TEST MATCH – INDIA v. SRI LANKA

With Gavaskar fit to return to lead India, the selectors decided to make Srikkanth twelfth man and so gave first Test caps to Rakesh Shukla, the Delhi all-rounder, and Jagdishlal Arun Lal, the West Bengal opening batsman, who had served a considerable apprenticeship as reserve to the Test side. Shukla had won acclaim in the Ranji Trophy final earlier in the year when he had taken 3 for 158 in the 63 overs he bowled and then shared in an unbeaten ninth wicket partnership of 118 with Peter which won the match for Delhi.

Warnapura had no hesitation in batting first when he won the toss. The visitors started badly, however, when both Warnapura and make-shift opener Goonatillake were dismissed with the score at 11. Their position would have been even worse had Kirmani not missed Dias before he scored. The wicket-keeper dived in front of Viswanath at first slip, but he could not hold the edged shot off Kapil Dev's bowling.

Having survived that chance, Dias joined with Duleep Mendis in a sparkling display of batting which brought 153 off 216 deliveries for the third wicket. Mendis was quite magnificent. His 105 came off only 123 balls faced and he

reached his hundred with a superb six over long-on off Doshi. In all, his innings lasted three hours and he hit 17 boundaries.

It was Dilip Doshi who brought about another Sri Lankan crisis when he took three wickets in seven deliveries as the score went from 203 for 3 to 204 for 6. It was Doshi's twenty-eighth Test match and when he had Ranatunga caught by Vengsarkar it was his hundredth Test wicket.

Somachandra de Silva and Madugalle added 77 in 84 minutes for the seventh wicket, and Sri Lanka ended the first day at 311 for 8.

The following day belonged entirely to India. They took the last two Sri Lankan wickets for the addition of 35 runs and then Gavaskar and Arun Lal began with a stand of 156 which ended shortly before tea when Arun Lal was bowled by de Mel for 60. Gavaskar went on to reach his twenty-fifth Test century, and India were 251 for 1 at the close.

Rain delayed the start of the third day until early afternoon. Gavaskar and Vengsarkar took their second wicket stand to 173 in 197 minutes before Vengsarkar was run out when attempting a quick single. Gavaskar was out when he tried to hit Somachandra de Silva for a huge six. His innings had lasted 400 minutes and included a six and twenty-four fours.

INAUGURAL TEST MATCH – INDIA v. SRI LANKA
17, 18, 19, 21, and 22 September 1982 at Madras

SRI LANKA

	FIRST INNINGS		SECOND INNINGS	
B. Warnapura†	c Sharma, b Madan Lal	4	c Sharma, b Dev	6
H.M. Goonatillake*	c Patil, b Dev	7	(10) c sub (Srikkanth), b Dev	0
R.L. Dias	c Arun Lal, b Doshi	60	c Gavaskar, b Shukla	97
L.R.D. Mendis	lbw, b Doshi	105	b Shukla	105
A. Ranatunga	c Vengsarkar, b Doshi	25	c Kirmani, b Doshi	15
R.S. Madugalle	c Madan Lal, b Doshi	46	c Patil, b Doshi	4
A.N. Ranasinghe	c Arun Lal, b Doshi	0	b Dev	77
D.S. de Silva	c Gavaskar, b Madan Lal	49	not out	46
J.R. Ratnayake	lbw, b Dev	23	(2) c Sharma, b Dev	6
A.L.F. de Mel	not out	18	b Doshi	12
G.R.A. de Silva	c Viswanath, b Dev	0	b Dev	14
Extras	b 4, lb 5	9	b 4, lb 5, w 1, nb 2	12
		346		394

INDIA

	FIRST INNINGS		SECOND·INNINGS	
S.M. Gavaskar†	c de Mel, b D.S. de Silva	155	(9) not out	4
J. Arun Lal	b de Mel	63	c Dias, b de Mel	1
D.B. Vengsarkar	run out	90	(1) c and b de Mel	5
G.R. Viswanath	c Warnapura, b D.S. de Silva	9	(6) lbw, b de Mel	2
S.M. Patil	not out	114	(3) run out	46
Yashpal Sharma	c Goonatillake, b de Mel	17	(5) not out	31
Kapil Dev	c Goonatillake, b Ratnayake	31	(4) c Goonatillake, b de Mel	30
S. Madan Lal	not out	37	(7) c and b D.S. de Silva	9
S.M.H. Kirmani*			(8) b de Mel	5
R.C. Shukla				
D.R. Doshi				
Extras	b 11, lb 8, w 2, nb 29	50	nb 2	2
	(for 6 wkts dec)	566	(for 7 wkts)	135

	O	M	R	W	O	M	R	W
Kapil Dev	22.5	2	97	3	24.3	3	110	5
Madan Lal	16	1	72	2	7	1	43	—
Doshi	30	8	85	5	38	4	147	3
Patil	2	—	13	—				
Shukla	22	4	70	—	27	5	82	2

	O	M	R	W	O	M	R	W
de Mel	28	2	133	2	14	—	68	5
Ratnayake	19	1	75	1	5	—	36	—
G.R.A. de Silva	17	2	78	—				
Warnapura	9	3	27	—				
D.S. de Silva	48	4	162	2	9	1	29	1
Ranasinghe	7	—	29	—				
Ranatunga	1	—	12	—				

FALL OF WICKETS
1- 11, 2- 11, 3- 164, 4- 203, 5- 204, 6- 204, 7- 281, 8- 304, 9- 346
1- 6, 2- 47, 3- 157, 4- 198, 5- 202, 6- 291, 7- 340, 8- 361, 9- 362

FALL OF WICKETS
1- 156, 2- 329, 3- 347, 4- 363, 5- 403, 6- 488
1- 3, 2- 16, 3- 78, 4- 90, 5- 94, 6- 125, 7- 130

Umpires: M.V. Gothaskar and Swarup Kishan

Match drawn

Sandeep Patil punished a tired attack to hit a brilliant century which contained thirteen fours and a six, and Gavaskar declared with a lead of 220 and ample time in which to bowl out Sri Lanka.

An Indian victory looked certain when both openers, Warnapura and Ratnayake, fell to Kapil Dev with only 47 scored, but already Roy Dias had begun to strike the ball in a positive and thrilling fashion. On the fourth evening, he and Mendis added 110 in 92 minutes, the runs coming at nearly four and a half an over. Dias hit 18 boundaries in his 97 which was scored off 108 deliveries. India were handicapped in that Kirmani was unable to keep wicket because of sunstroke and Yashpal Sharma took over behind the stumps.

On the last day, Mendis reached his second hundred of the match, a feat which only Sir Donald Bradman and Everton Weekes had previously accomplished against India, and Ranasinghe and Somachandra de Silva also batted well so that India were left to make 175 in 53 minutes and 20 overs to win the match.

India began poorly when they lost both openers, Arun Lal and Vengsarkar, for 16, but Patil and Kapil Dev gave a scent of victory with some powerful hitting and brisk running until

de Mel. Five wickets in the second innings of the Test match. The most dangerous of the Sri Lankan bowlers throughout the short tour. (Ken Kelly)

THIRD ONE-DAY INTERNATIONAL: INDIA v. SRI LANKA
26 September 1982 at Bangalore

SRI LANKA					
B. Warnapura†	lbw, b Kapil Dev				1
S.R. de S. Wettimuny	lbw, b Binny				18
R.L. Dias	c Doshi, b Kapil Dev				121
L.R.D. Mendis	b Doshi				23
R.S. Madugalle	run out				18
A.L.F. de Mel	b Doshi				25
J.R. Ratnayeke	b Madan Lal				1
D.S. de Silva	lbw, b Madan Lal				3
H.M. Goonatillake*	not out				8
R.J. Ratnayeke	not out				6
V. John					
Extras	b 1, lb 3, nb 5				9
(50 overs)	(for 8 wickets)				233

	O	M	R	W
Kapil Dev	10	2	41	2
Madan Lal	10	—	41	2
Amarnath	10	—	53	—
Binny	10	—	54	1
Doshi	10	—	35	2

FALL OF WICKETS
1- 2, 2- 48, 3- 106, 4- 157, 5- 193, 6- 198, 7- 208, 8- 222

INDIA					
R. Binny	run out				15
K. Srikkanth	b D.S. de Silva				92
D.B. Vengsarkar	c Dias, b de Mel				42
A. Malhotra	not out				27
Kapil Dev†	c J.R. Ratnayeke, b de Mel				15
Yashpal Sharma	not out				30
S. Madan Lal					
M. Amarnath					
S.M. Patil					
S.M.H. Kirmani*					
D.R. Doshi					
Extras	b 7, lb 1, w 3, nb 2				13
(39.2 overs)	(for 4 wickets)				234

	O	M	R	W
de Mel	8	1	58	2
John	9	—	33	—
Warnapura	2	—	15	—
R.J. Ratnayeke	7	—	38	—
J.R. Ratnayeke	3	—	25	—
D.S. de Silva	10	1	51	1
Dias	0.2	—	1	—

FALL OF WICKETS
1- 34, 2- 153, 3- 160, 4- 177

India won by 6 wickets

Patil was stranded at his partner's end and run out.

Sri Lanka now seized the initiative and with de Mel returning a career best 5 for 68, India lost 7 wickets in the chase for victory which ended with Yashpal Sharma and Gavaskar content to play out time and India forty runs short.

Sri Lanka came out of the game with much credit.

THIRD ONE-DAY INTERNATIONAL

In spite of another fine innings by Roy Dias, Sri Lanka lost the third and last one-day international of the series.

Dias saved Sri Lanka after Warnapura, who had won the toss and elected to bat, had once more been dismissed cheaply. Dias was twice dropped by Kapil Dev who had taken over the captaincy when Gavaskar again decided he was not fit for the rush of one-day cricket, but he batted with elegance and aggression and Sri Lanka owed him much.

The total of 233 seemed a reasonable one, but Srikkanth launched his customary attack on the bowling as he and Vengsarkar shared a second wicket stand of 119 which demolished the Sri Lankan bowling to such an extent that India moved to victory with nearly eleven overs to spare.

The Process of Maturing
is an Art to Be Learned

Pakistan's triumph against Australia

General view of Lahore Test Ground. (Adrian Murrell)

Once more the pressures of home and business deprived Australia of the services of Greg Chappell, and Kim Hughes was appointed to the unenviable task of leading the side on the tour of Pakistan. Hughes' record as a Test captain is not a good one, and it is doubtful if he is the best choice as Chappell's ultimate successor, but when Chappell declared himself unavailable the Australian selectors had no alternative but to return to Hughes.

No Test captain finds the visit to Pakistan less than very demanding and Hughes' task was not made easier when Lillee decided that he could not make the trip.

There were two interesting selections in the Australian party of fifteen, Greg Ritchie of Queensland and Wayne Phillips of South Australia. Both batsmen had earned selection by scoring heavily in the Sheffield Shield matches, but the choice of Phillips brought the number of opening batsmen in the side to four and left it with obvious weaknesses in the middle order and in spin bowling where Bright once more gained preference over more successful contenders.

Pakistan, under the leadership of Imran Khan, had a side of exciting potential. They had played some glorious cricket in England a few weeks earlier, and it was temperament rather than inferior ability which had deprived them of success in the Test series. Certainly, some of their leading players, notably Zaheer Abbas and Wasim Bari, had performed well below their capabilities, and there was also a need for support pace bowling for Imran Khan, but Imran had had a brief reign as Pakistan's captain and achieved much so that there was optimism that Pakistan cricket was on the eve of a golden period.

Rodney Marsh missed the first match of the tour, but he kept wicket as well as ever in a demanding series. (Adrian Murrell)

12, 13 and 14 September 1982

at Rawalpindi

Australians 327 for 9 dec (K.J. Hughes 101 not out, A.R. Border 59, G.M. Wood 50) and 166 for 8
B.C.C.P. Patron's XI 424 for 5 dec (Mansoor Akhtar 130, Masood Anwar 125, Haroon Rashid 94)

Match drawn

With Rodney Marsh's arrival in Pakistan delayed a week through family illness, Wayne Phillips kept wicket for the Australians in their opening match of the tour. The Patron's XI contained several of the party of 35 from whom Pakistan would select for the Test series so that Mansoor Akhtar, so highly rated in his own country, so vulnerable in England, wicket-keeper Saleem Yousuf, Haroon Rashid and skipper Iqbal Qasim all had hopes of impressing the selectors.

Iqbal Qasim was the most successful bowler on the first day when Australia dominated. There was a fine opening stand of 91 from Wood and Laird, and the score reached 163 before the second wicket fell. Uncertainty in the middle order saw Dyson, Sleep and Phillips all fail, but Hughes began the tour in regal style. In the penultimate over of the day, he hit pace bowler Zakir Khan for a six and three fours, and he reached his hundred with a straight six in the last over of the day.

Hughes declared over night, but on the second day the Australians fared badly. At 82, Shoaib Mohammad, son of the great Hanif, was caught at forward short-leg off Yardley, but Patron's XI reached 359 for 3 before the close. The

Australians dropped five catches and missed an easy run out while Phillips, who does not keep wicket for his state, failed to take a simple stumping chance. Alderman and Thomson wilted in the heat and only Border looked to bowl with any confidence and success.

Mansoor and Masood added 189 for the second wicket, Mansoor being stumped off the last ball before tea for 130. Haroon plundered quick runs and when the Australians batted again Wood was out for nought to Sikhander Bakht. Wickets fell regularly and the visitors were happy to draw a match which had gone against them from the beginning of the second day.

16, 17 and 18 September 1982

at Multan

Australians 277 (G.M. Ritchie 59, G.M. Wood 52, K.J. Hughes 50, Jalaluddin 5 for 70) and 124 for 3 dec
Pakistan Cricket Board XI 176 (Agha Zahid 64, Taslim Arif 51, G.F. Lawson 5 for 32, R.J. Bright 5 for 40) and 67 for 4

Match drawn

On a grassless pitch of uneven bounce in fierce heat, the Australians batted first and their innings was held together by Greg Ritchie who batted with enough assurance to suggest that he would be an asset to Australia in their search for a more stable middle order. The Board XI was handicapped when off-spinner Ilyas Khan was forced to leave the field with cramp, and the Australians closed the day on 251 for 8.

They added another 26 on the second morning before Jalaluddin captured the wickets of Ritchie and Lawson to bring him figures of 5 for 70. The Board XI began well, skipper Taslim Arif and Agha Zahid putting on 96 for the first wicket. Then Lawson and Bright brought about a remarkable collapse which saw ten wickets fall for 80 runs to give the Australians a first innings lead of 101. The only setback suffered by the Australians was when Wood was struck in the face while fielding at short-leg and had to retire from the match.

Led by Border and Hughes, the Australians reached 124 for 3 before declaring and they had a glimpse of victory when Callen and Lawson reduced the Board XI to 17 for 3, but Salim Malik and Rameez Raja stopped further alarms for the local side and the match was drawn.

FIRST ONE-DAY INTERNATIONAL

Whatever encouragement Australia may have derived from their having had the best of the draw with the Board XI and from the fact that Imran Khan withdrew from the Pakistan side for the first one-day international because he felt insufficiently fit was quickly dispersed by a fierce opening stand between Mohsin Khan and Mudassar Nazar.

Hughes won the toss and asked Pakistan to bat, but Mohsin, in particular, was quick to find his best form. He hit 15 fours and scored his 104 out of 169, but Pakistan's later batsmen failed to exploit the position that Mohsin, Mudassar and acting captain Zaheer had given them.

Laird and Wood gave Australia a fine start with a stand of 104, but off-spinner Tausif Ahmed dismissed both openers and Kim Hughes while only five runs were scored. Border and Dyson seemed to have set Australia back on course for victory, however, with a stand of 48. Then Jalaluddin, who had come into the side as a late replacement for Imran Khan,

had Border caught behind the wicket. In his next over, he bowled Marsh with his fourth ball, had Yardley caught behind by Wasim Bari with his fifth and bowled Lawson with his sixth to perform the hat-trick. There was no respite for the Australians who lost six wickets for 12 runs to leave Pakistan easy winners.

The Australian task had always seemed a little too demanding for the opening stand between Wood and Laird had occupied 24 overs so leaving the later batsmen to score 126 runs at the rate of nearly 8 runs per over.

FIRST TEST MATCH: PAKISTAN v. AUSTRALIA

Kim Hughes won the toss and rightly elected to bat first on a hard and true wicket. The Australians gave Greg Ritchie his first Test cap and decided to play only two pace bowlers, Lawson and Thomson, so that Alderman, who had come on the tour as the main strike bowler was omitted.

Like Australia, Pakistan chose to play two spinners, Iqbal Qasim, who had taken no part in the Tests in England, returning to the side to partner Abdul Qadir whose inclusion was criticised in the local press.

Australia began badly. In the third over of the day, Imran made a ball rear nastily at Wood who touched it to Wasim Bari behind the stumps. Australia never completely recovered from this mishap, and Pakistan never really relinquished their hold on the game. Laird and Dyson batted sensibly and seemed to be effecting a recovery until a dreadful misunderstanding five minutes before lunch saw Laird set off on a quick single to which his partner made no response. Mohsin Khan's return to the wicket-keeper left Laird stranded and he was run out by yards. The loss and the timing were equally bad for Australia.

Lunch was extended to one hour in keeping with the Pakistan government's request for an hour's national stop-

---

FIRST ONE-DAY INTERNATIONAL: PAKISTAN v. AUSTRALIA
20 September 1982 at Hyderabad

PAKISTAN				AUSTRALIA			
Mudassar Nazar	c Marsh, b Alderman	28		B.M. Laird	b Tauseef	44
Mohsin Khan	c Dyson, b Lawson	104		G.M. Wood	c Jalaluddin, b Tauseef	52
Zaheer Abbas†	c Wood, b Yardley	26		K.J. Hughes†	c Haroon, b Tauseef	2
Javed Miandad	not out	31		A.R. Border	c Bari, b Jalaluddin	24
Mansoor Akhtar	c Laird, b Thomson	8		J. Dyson	not out	30
Haroon Rashid	b Callen	4		R.W. Marsh*	b Jalaluddin	1
Tahir Naqqash	c and b Alderman	8		B. Yardley	c Bari, b Jalaluddin	0
Wasim Bari*	not out	5		G.F. Lawson	b Jalaluddin	0
Sikhander Bakht				I.W. Callen	b Sikhander	0
Jalaluddin				J.R. Thomson	c Zaheer, b Mohsin	1
Tauseef Ahmed				T.M. Alderman	not out	1
Extras	b 1, lb 6, nb 8	15		Extras	lb 6, w 8, nb 1	15
(40 overs)	(for 6 wickets)	229		(40 overs)	(for 9 wickets)	170

	O	M	R	W
Lawson	8	—	29	1
Alderman	8	—	63	2
Callen	8	—	32	1
Thomson	8	—	48	1
Yardley	8	1	42	1

	O	M	R	W
Sikhander Bakht	7	—	24	1
Tahir Naqqash	7	—	20	—
Jalaluddin	8	1	32	4
Mudassar Nazar	8	—	38	—
Tauseef Ahmed	8	—	38	3
Mohsin Khan	1	—	2	1
Mansoor Akhtar	1	—	1	—

FALL OF WICKETS
1- 82, 2- 160, 3- 169, 4- 180, 5- 191, 6- 202

FALL OF WICKETS
1- 104, 2- 106, 3- 109, 4- 157, 5- 162, 6- 162, 7- 162, 8- 164, 9- 169

Pakistan won by 59 runs

page in protest against the Beirut massacre, and Hughes and Dyson batted well for Australia throughout the afternoon, both reaching accomplished fifties, but Dyson was bowled by Iqbal Qasim shortly after tea.

Hughes was another Iqbal victim and Ritchie had time to hit only one four before he was taken at short-leg off Qadir's googly. Border and Marsh were all caution and Australia closed the day at 218 for 5.

The next morning the score moved steadily to 249 when Tahir Naqqash took 4 wickets in 8 balls with the second new ball. The last five Australian wickets added only 35 runs, and with Mohsin and Mansoor giving them a comfortable start, Pakistan had taken control of the match.

Mansoor fell to Thomson, but Haroon and Mohsin appeared to have negotiated all further problems when Mohsin was out, surprisingly, to the last ball of the day. The pair had added 125 when Mohsin played forward defensively at a ball from Jeff Thomson which spun back towards the batsman's stumps. Mohsin brushed the ball away with his hand and was given out handled ball.

The day had been marred somewhat by Lawson's reaction when he had an appeal rejected by umpire Mahboob Shah, but Lawson's and Australia's troubles became worse on the third day. Forty-five minutes play was lost through crowd disturbances which caused Hughes to lead his team off the field, the Australians dropped five catches – Lawson being the main sufferer, and the over-rate dwindled to under ten an hour in the afternoon. Haroon was out in the morning session and then Zaheer, who benefitted most from the dropped catches, and Javed moved slowly towards the

Australian total in the excessively hot weather. Both were ou[t] before the close, as was Imran, but Pakistan had gained a lead of 46.

Imran declared at lunch on the fourth day when Pakistan'[s] lead had been increased to 134. Mudassar, unable to ope[n] because of a bruised shin, held the later order together, and he and Abdul Qadir added a most valuable 51 for the ninth wicket.

It was Qadir who seized the centre of the stage in the afternoon session. Imran gained an early breakthrough when he dismissed Laird, and then he quickly introduced Qadir into the attack.

The leg-spin and googly bowler was used in a positive and aggressive role as five men clustered in close catching positions. He showed admirable control as he displayed his exciting variety of deliveries and mesmerized the Australian batsmen with his flamboyant artistry.

The Australians went from 20 for 1 to 73 for 7, Wood, Dyson, Hughes and Border all falling to Qadir, three of them inside seven overs. Marsh and Bright alone held firm and took the Australians to 123 for 7 by the close.

The end came before lunch on the last day and Abdul Qadir, the man whose selection had been criticised in the Karachi press, was named Man of the Match

SECOND TEST MATCH; PAKISTAN v. AUSTRALIA

Not unnaturally, Pakistan fielded an unchanged side after their overwhelming success in the first Test. Australia played leg-spinner Sleep in place of Bruce Yardley who had found

---

FIRST TEST MATCH – PAKISTAN v. AUSTRALIA
22, 23, 24, 26 and 27 September 1982 at Karachi

AUSTRALIA

	FIRST INNINGS		SECOND INNINGS	
G.M. Wood	c Bari, b Imran	0	c sub (Salim Malik), b Qadir	17
B.M. Laird	run out	32	c Mansoor, b Imran	3
J. Dyson	b Qasim	87	b Qadir	6
K.J. Hughes†	c Bari, b Qasim	54	(5) c Bari, b Qadir	14
A.R. Border	not out	55	(4) c sub (Salim Malik) b Qadir	8
G.M. Ritchie	c Haroon, b Qadir	4	b Qasim	17
R.W. Marsh*	b Tahir	19	lbw, b Imran	32
B. Yardley	c Javed, b Tahir	0	lbw, b Qadir	0
R.J. Bright	c Haroon, b Tahir	2	not out	32
G.F. Lawson	c Bari, b Tahir	0	run out	11
J.R. Thomson	st Bari, b Qadir	14	c Bari, b Qasim	18
Extras	b 4, lb 10, w 1, nb 2	17	b 2, lb 19	21
		284		179

	O	M	R	W	O	M	R	W
Imran Khan	23	3	38	1	12	5	17	2
Tahir Naqqash	16	3	61	4	7	3	17	—
Mudassar Nazar	13	—	33	—				
Abdul Qadir	21.4	1	80	2	26	7	76	5
Iqbal Qasim	26	10	55	2	21.5	6	48	2

FALL OF WICKETS
1- 0, 2- 71, 3- 169, 4- 202, 5- 211, 6- 249, 7- 249, 8- 255, 9- 255
1- 10, 2- 20, 3- 32, 4- 45, 5- 72, 6- 72, 7- 73, 8- 137, 9- 160

PAKISTAN

	FIRST INNINGS		SECOND INNINGS	
Mohsin Khan	handled ball	58	not out	14
Mansoor Akhtar	c Bright, b Thomson	32	(3) not out	26
Haroon Rashid	c Laird, b Yardley	82		
Javed Miandad	b Lawson	32		
Zaheer Abbas	c Marsh, b Lawson	91		
Mudassar Nazar	not out	52	(2) c Border, b Thomson	5
Imran Khan†	c Yardley, b Bright	1		
Tahir Naqqash	st Marsh, b Bright	15		
Wasim Bari*	b Bright	0		
Abdul Qadir	run out	29		
Iqbal Qasim	not out	2		
Extras	b 4, lb 8, w 1, nb 12	25	nb 2	2
	(for 9 wkts dec)	419	(for 1 wkt)	47

	O	M	R	W	O	M	R	W
Thomson	29	5	103	1	3	1	16	1
Lawson	39	10	93	2				
Bright	36	8	96	3	5	—	14	—
Yardley	23	2	98	1	3	1	9	—
Border	1	—	4	—				
Hughes					0.1	—	6	—

FALL OF WICKETS
1- 43, 2- 168, 3- 188, 4- 277, 5- 328, 6- 329, 7- 351, 8- 353, 9- 404
1- 5

Umpires: Khizer Hayat and Mahboob Shah

Pakistan won by 9 wickets

Dyson. One of Australia's few batting successes. 87 in the first innings of the first Test. (Adrian Murrell)

SECOND TEST MATCH – PAKISTAN v. AUSTRALIA
30 September, 1, 2, 4 and 5 October 1982 at Faisalabad

PAKISTAN

	FIRST INNINGS	
Mohsin Khan	c Marsh, b Lawson	76
Mudassar Nazar	c Hughes, b Border	79
Mansoor Akhtar	c Marsh, b Lawson	111
Javed Miandad	c Laird, b Lawson	6
Zaheer Abbas	b Sleep	126
Haroon Rashid	c Laird, b Lawson	51
Imran Khan†	not out	24
Tahir Naqqash	not out	15
Wasim Bari*		
Abdul Qadir		
Iqbal Qasim		
Extras	b 4, lb 1, nb 8	13
	(for 6 wkts dec)	501

	O	M	R	W
Thomson	23	5	79	—
Lawson	33	6	96	4
Sleep	36	3	159	1
Bright	41	15	107	—
Border	11	3	47	1

FALL OF WICKETS

1- 123, 2- 181, 3- 201, 4- 356, 5- 428, 6- 482

Umpires: Khizer Hayat and Mahboob Shah

Pakistan won by an innings and 3 runs

AUSTRALIA

	FIRST INNINGS		SECOND INNINGS	
B.M. Laird	lbw, b Qadir	8	c Mudassar, b Qadir	60
G.M. Wood	c Bari, b Mudassar	49	(7) c Bari, b Qasim	22
J. Dyson	c Mudassar, b Qasim	23	(2) c Qasim, b Qadir	43
A.R. Border	c Javed, b Imran	9	(3) c Haroon, b Qadir	31
K.J. Hughes†	c Imran, b Qadir	11	(4) lbw, b Qadir	7
G.M. Ritchie	run out	34	(5) not out	106
P.R. Sleep	lbw, b Imran	0	(6) c Mohsin, b Qadir	29
R.W. Marsh*	b Qadir	0	run out	8
R.J. Bright	c Haroon, b Qadir	0	c sub (Salim Malik), b Qasim	0
G.F. Lawson	c Zaheer, b Qasim	14	lbw, b Qadir	0
J.R. Thomson	not out	1	st Bari, b Qadir	11
Extras	b 8, lb 6, w 2, nb 3	19	lb 7, w 1, nb 5	13
		168		330

	O	M	R	W	O	M	R	W
Imran Khan	14	6	16	2	10	5	20	—
Tahir Naqqash	15	4	21	—	9	1	25	—
Abbdul Qadir	42	14	76	4	50.4	12	142	7
Iqbal Qasim	25	11	28	2	46	18	97	2
Mudassar Nazar	7	2	8	1	9	3	26	—
Zaheer Abbas					3	—	5	—
Javed Miandad					1	—	2	—

FALL OF WICKETS

1- 20, 2- 82, 3- 96, 4- 113, 5- 123, 6- 123, 7- 124, 8- 124, 9- 167

1- 73, 2- 125, 3- 133, 4- 162, 5- 218, 6- 290, 7- 309, 8- 309, 9- 310

Abdul Qadir. Eleven wickets in the second Test match and the tormentor of Australia in the series. (George Herringshaw)

neither form nor fitness after a bout of influenza.

Imran Khan won the toss and eagerly chose to bat. In a similar position in the first Test, Australia had frittered away the advantage that winning the toss had given them. Pakistan made no such mistake. In just over three hours, Mohsin and Mudassar put on 123 for the first wicket. The partnership was broken when Mohsin attempted to hook a Lawson bouncer and edged the ball to Marsh. Mansoor joined Mudassar and it looked as if another big stand was taking shape when Hughes introduced Border into the attack and Mudassar mishit him to mid-on.

Of the Australian bowlers, Lawson was by far the best. He alone, it seemed, was prepared to work untiringly on a wicket which gave help to none but the batsmen, and he was rewarded when he beat Javed Miandad with a slower ball in the final session. Pakistan had been restricted to three runs an over, but the close of play score, 232 for 3, did not bode well for Australia's chances.

The scoring rate increased considerably on the second day as Bright, Thomson and Sleep were treated contemptuously by the Pakistani batsmen. Mansoor Akhtar repaid the confidence shown in him with a chanceless maiden Test century. Although he became becalmed on 99 for nearly half an hour, his 111 was scored in only 2 hours, 43 minutes and contained 18 fours. Zaheer, who was twice dropped, was very slow to start, but quickened as his innings progressed. In one over from Peter Sleep, which cost 19 runs, he hit 2 of his 3 sixes. He also hit 12 fours and during the course of his innings

became the first Pakistani batsman to score 1000 runs in Test matches against Australia. The stand of 155 for the fourth wicket was a Pakistani record against Australia.

There were stolen runs against tired bowling at the end of the day when Pakistan declared at 501 for 6.

There were many who believed that Imran had been premature in his declaration, but as soon as he introduced Abdul Qadir into the attack he proved his critics wrong. Qadir bowled 36 of the 85 overs bowled on the third day, and from those 85 overs Australia scored only 141 for the loss of 8 wickets. Splendid as the Pakistan bowling was, it could not explain why the Australian batting was so dreadful. It was lacking in both application and technique. Qadir's leg-breaks and googlies teased and flustered leaden-footed batsmen throughout the day at the end of which he had taken the wickets of Laird, Hughes, Marsh and Bright at a cost of 72 runs.

In the final session of the day, the Australians lost 4 wickets for 1 run during one period when Border, having failed to score for an hour, fell to Imran and Sleep was leg before wicket first ball. Ritchie and Lawson took them to 141 for 8 before the close, and they survived for 80 minutes on the fourth morning, but then the agony began again.

Wood had stomach cramps and could not open in the second innings so that Dyson partnered Laird in a stand of 73. It was the highest stand of either Australian innings. It was ended by Qadir who took all four wickets that fell on the fourth day which closed with Australia at 176 for 4 struggling for survival.

Ritchie alone had seemed capable of reading Abdul Qadir's googly and he played positively from the start of his innings. Sleep partnered Ritchie in a stand of 56, and Wood looked solid until lunch on the last day when the score was 252 for 5, but in the afternoon 5 wickets fell for 40 runs in 6 overs and Pakistan had won the series.

Ritchie reached his hundred in what was only his second

Greg Ritchie looks thoughtful. He hit a maiden Test century in the second Test. (Adrian Murrell)

Test match. He was indebted to Marsh who sacrificed himself after a terrible muddle when the young Queenslander was on 96. It seemed as if Marsh's sacrifice would be in vain as Australia slipped to 310 for 9 with Ritchie still on 96, but he completed his century, which included three sixes and nine fours before Thomson was stumped off Qadir who had seven wickets and another Man of the Match award.

SECOND ONE-DAY INTERNATIONAL

For the second one-day international, Australia made two changes from the side which had just lost the second Test match, Alderman and Callen replacing the spinners Sleep and Bright. Pakistan left out the spinners, Abdul Qadir and Iqbal Qasim, and, except for Imran returning in place of Sikhander Bakht, they played the side that had won the first of the limited-over games.

Hughes won the toss and asked Pakistan to bat, and the slowness of their start seemed to vindicate his decision. Mudassar was out at 17 and Mohsin and Zaheer were just beginning to look settled when Mohsin called for a quick single only to be left stranded, amazed and very annoyed when his partner made no response.

Zaheer and Javed now began to accelerate, and soon Zaheer was thrashing the ball to all parts of the field. He was finally too adventurous against Border, but by then he had hit two sixes and thirteen fours in his 109. Imran and Javed continued the onslaught until the end of the innings.

Australia lost Wood, Dyson and Border for 73, but Laird and Hughes joined in a stand of 117, and they looked well capable of maintaining a rate of scoring that would bring victory.

80 were needed off the last ten overs, but some tight bowling by Imran and Tahir and the dismissal of Hughes ended any hopes that they had.

10, 11 and 12 October 1982

at Sialkot

Australians 283 for 4 dec (W.B. Phillips 92, J. Dyson 71 not out)
B.C.C.P. Invitation XI 169 for 7 (Wasim Raja 66, Rizwan-uz-Zaman 53)

Match drawn

With no play possible on the first day and 90 minutes play lost on the second day, there was never any likelihood of a result. Majid Khan put the Australians in, and Wayne Phillips hit a delightful 92 in just over 2½ hours. He hit a six and thirteen fours. Wood was forced to retire with cramp when he had made 38, but Dyson batted well and the first wicket did not fall until the score had reached 140.

The Invitation XI lost two wickets to Callen before a run was scored, but Rizwan-uz-Zaman and Wasim Raja added 109. There was a minor collapse when Bright took three wickets.

THIRD TEST MATCH: PAKISTAN v. AUSTRALIA

Both sides included a quick bowler at the expense of a slow left-arm bowler, Alderman playing his first Test of the series and Jalaluddin making his Test debut.

Imran won the toss and asked Australia to bat, which seemed a strange decision, but once more the Australians faltered. Wood and Laird gave them their best start of the series with a stand of 85, but then four wickets fell while 55 runs were scored and once more Australia had failed on a perfect pitch.

They plodded through the first day to end at 188 for 4 scored off 72 overs.

SECOND ONE-DAY INTERNATIONAL: PAKISTAN v. AUSTRALIA
8 October 1982 at Lahore

PAKISTAN					AUSTRALIA			
Mohsin Khan	run out		17		B.M. Laird	not out		91
Mudassar Nazar	lbw, b Thomson		7		G.M. Wood	b Jalaluddin		21
Zaheer Abbas	st Marsh, b Border		109		J. Dyson	c Imran, b Jalaluddin		11
Javed Miandad	not out		61		A.R. Border	b Tauseef		0
Imran Khan†	not out		29		K.J. Hughes†	c Mudassar, b Imran		64
Mansoor Akhtar					G.M. Ritchie	not out		4
Haroon Rashid					R.W. Marsh*			
Wasim Bari*					T.M. Alderman			
Tahir Naqqash					G.F. Lawson			
Jalaluddin					J.R. Thomson			
Tauseef Ahmed					I.W. Callen			
Extras	b 1, lb 6, w 1, nb 3		11		Extras	lb 10, w 4, nb 1		15
(40 overs)	(for 3 wickets)		234		(40 overs)	(for 4 wickets)		206

	O	M	R	W		O	M	R	W
Thomson	8	—	41	1	Imran Khan	8	1	38	1
Lawson	8	—	47	—	Tahir Naqqash	8	—	28	—
Alderman	8	1	29	—	Jalaluddin	8	1	33	2
Callen	8	1	50	—	Tauseef Ahmed	8	—	40	1
Border	8	1	56	1	Mudassar Nazar	6	—	40	—
					Zaheer Abbas	2	—	12	—

FALL OF WICKETS
1- 17, 2- 52, 3- 171

FALL OF WICKETS
1- 37, 2- 73, 3- 73, 4- 190

Pakistan won by 28 runs

THIRD TEST MATCH – PAKISTAN *v.* AUSTRALIA
14, 15, 16, 18 and 19 October 1982 at Lahore

AUSTRALIA

	FIRST INNINGS		SECOND INNINGS	
G.M. Wood	c Javed, b Qadir	85	(2) c Mudassar, b Jalaluddin	30
B.M. Laird	lbw, b Qadir	28	(1) lbw, b Tahir	6
J. Dyson	b Jalaluddin	10	lbw, b Tahir	51
A.R. Border	lbw, b Imran	9	st Bari, b Qadir	6
K.J. Hughes†	b Tahir	29	st Bari, b Qadir	39
G.M. Ritchie	lbw, b Imran	26	lbw, b Imran	19
R.W. Marsh*	c sub (Iqbal Sikander), b Imran	1	c Mudassar, b Jalaluddin	12
B. Yardley	c Haroon, b Jalaluddin	40	b Imran	21
G.F. Lawson	not out	57	c sub (Iqbal Sikander), b Imran	8
J.R. Thomson	lbw, b Jalaluddin	0	not out	5
T.M. Alderman	b Imran	7	c Zaheer, b Imran	0
Extras	b 5, lb 13, w 1, nb 5	24	b 4, lb 5, nb 8	17
		316		214

	O	M	R	W	O	M	R	W
Imran Khan	24.2	10	45	4	20	6	35	4
Tahir Naqqash	18	4	65	1	16	3	39	2
Mudassar Nazar	6	1	17	—	2	—	5	—
Jalaluddin	19	4	77	3	16	8	15	2
Abdul Qadir	37	7	86	2	35	7	102	2
Zaheer Abbas	2	—	2	—	1	—	1	—

FALL OF WICKETS
1- 85, 2- 120, 3- 140, 4- 140, 5- 197, 6- 202, 7- 203, 8- 264, 9- 264
1- 21, 2- 55, 3- 64, 4- 138, 5- 157, 6- 170, 7- 189, 8- 203, 9- 203

PAKISTAN

	FIRST INNINGS		SECOND INNINGS	
Mohsin Khan	b Border	135	lbw, b Lawson	14
Mudassar Nazar	lbw, b Lawson	23	not out	39
Abdul Qadir	c Laird, b Yardley	1		
Mansoor Akhtar	lbw, b Lawson	12	(3) not out	2
Javed Miandad	c Hughes, b Alderman	138		
Zaheer Abbas	c Yardley, b Alderman	52		
Haroon Rashid	c Ritchie, b Thomson	15		
Imran Khan†	not out	39		
Tahir Naqqash	not out	7		
Wasim Bari*				
Jalaluddin				
Extras	b 3, lb 13, w 2, nb 27	45	b 4, lb 5	9
	(for 7 wkts dec)	467	(for 1 wkt)	64

	O	M	R	W	O	M	R	W
Thomson	19	1	73	1	5	—	24	—
Lawson	35	4	91	2	7	1	21	1
Alderman	34	4	144	2	3	—	10	—
Yardley	27	6	102	1				
Border	4	1	12	1				

FALL OF WICKETS
1- 92, 2- 93, 3- 119, 4- 269, 5- 392, 6- 402, 7- 442
1- 55

Umpires: Javed Akhtar and Shakoor Rana

Pakistan won by 9 wickets

Hughes and Ritchie had batted doggedly at the end of the first day, but they and Marsh fell to Tahir and Imran early next morning and it was left to Lawson and Yardley to restore sanity to the Australian innings. They decided to attack the bowling so that even Imran who had conceded only twenty runs in his first 20 overs was shown to be human. They added 61 for the eighth wicket, and Lawson and Alderman put on a stubborn 52 for the last wicket.

Mohsin and Mudassar began briskly for Pakistan, scoring at 4 an over. Thomson lost all rhythm and kicked over the stumps in a petulant manner after being no-balled. Australia were not a happy side.

The courageous and persevering Lawson had Mudassar lbw before the close and nightwatchman Abdul Qadir fell to Yardley. Mansoor went early next day, but then Mohsin and Javed added 150 for the fourth wicket. Mohsin was out ten minutes before tea by which time the Australian out-cricket, three catches having been put down, was in disarray.

Mohsin hit 17 boundaries and when he departed Javed and Zaheer continued to pillage a limp attack which had been weakened by the absence of Thomson with a foot injury.

Javed reached his eighth Test century the next day. It was his third against Australia and included two sixes and thirteen fours. Australia dropped more catches, fielded poorly and conceded 45 extras. Imran's declaration must have come as a merciful act, but it meant that the Australian attack had failed to bowl out Pakistan during the entire series.

Bruce Laird. 91 not out in the second one-day international. (Adrian Murrell)

By the end of the fourth day, Australia were in tatters. Laird was lbw to Tahir, Wood was brilliantly caught by Mudassar and Border, for whom the series had been an unhappy one, was stumped as, like Hughes and others in the second Test, he failed to comprehend the bowling of Qadir. 66 for 3 at the close, and Pakistan poised to win the series 3 – 0.

Hughes and Dyson looked as if they might save the game on the last day when they took the score to 138, but Imran's men were not to be denied. Dyson fell to Tahir and after lunch Hughes swung an atrocious shot at Qadir and was stumped.

Still Australia had hope of saving the game, but Imran routed the tail after tea, and Pakistan were left needing 64 to win at three and a half runs an over. They scored them at more than four runs an over and Australia had lost every Test in a series for only the second time this century.

THIRD ONE-DAY INTERNATIONAL

It looked for the only time on the tour as if the Australian bowlers may have had the better of the Pakastani batsmen on a greenish wicket. Mudassar was bowled at 23, but play was halted after the eleventh over when Lawson was pelted with stones on the fine-leg boundary. The Australian players left the field and play was suspended for an hour. On the return, one over was bowled during which Ritchie became the target. The Australians left the field again, and the match was abandoned.

So the Australians left Pakistan with five losses and no victories in the nine matches that they played. It was a miserable record. It is easy to offer excuses for the Australian party – weather, diet, environment – but Kim Hughes, whose captaincy came in for much criticism, was honest in his appraisal. 'It took a lot of players a while before they admitted they

Kim Hughes. He worked hard, but once again his record as a Test captain was bad. He said that his side had failed to make the necessary adjustments to conditions in Pakistan. (Adrian Murrell)

THIRD ONE-DAY INTERNATIONAL: PAKISTAN v. AUSTRALIA
22 October 1982 at Karachi

PAKISTAN				AUSTRALIA	
Mohsin Khan	not out		25		W.B. Phillips
Mudassar Nazar	b Alderman		8		G.M. Wood
Zaheer Abbas	not out		5		K.J. Hughes[†]
Javed Miandad					A.R. Border
Mansoor Akhtar					G.M. Ritchie
Imran Khan[†]					J. Dyson
Wasim Raja					R.W. Marsh*
Wasim Bari*					G.F. Lawson
Tahir Naqqash					I.W. Callen
Jalaluddin					J.R. Thomson
Tauseef Ahmed					T.M. Alderman
Extras	b 1, lb 2, w 2, nb 1		6		
(12 overs)	(for 1 wicket)		44		

	O	M	R	W
Thomson	4	2	9	—
Lawson	2	—	7	—
Alderman	6	2	22	1

FALL OF WICKET
1- 23

Match abandoned owing to crowd disturbances

Australia in Pakistan 1982
First Class Matches

BATTING

	v. B.C.C.P. Patron's XI (Rawalpindi) 12-14 September		v. Pakistan Board XI (Multan) 16-18 September		First Test Match (Karachi) 22-27 September		Second Test Match (Faisalabad) 30 Sept.-5 Oct.		v. Invitation XI (Sialkot) 10-12 October		Third Test Match (Lahore) 14-19 October		Inns	NOs	Runs	HS	Av
G. M. Wood	50	0	52	—	0	17	49	22	38*	—	85	30	10	1	343	85	38.11
B. M. Laird	48	22	28	23	32	3	8	60			28	6	10	—	258	60	25.80
A. R. Border	59	21	6	38	55*	8	9	31	17	—	9	6	11	1	259	59	25.90
K. J. Hughes	101*	19	50	43	54	14	11	7	29	—	29	39	11	1	396	101*	39.60
J. Dyson	2	47	21	—	87	6	23	43	71*	—	10	51	10	1	361	87	40.11
P. R. Sleep	7	0					0	29	2*	—			5	1	38	29	9.50
W. B. Phillips	4	22							92				3	—	118	92	39.33
B. Yardley	24	12	14	—	0	0			—	—	40	21	7	—	111	40	15.85
R. J. Bright	5	1*	15	—	2	32*	0	0	—	—			7	2	55	32*	11.00
J. R. Thomson	11	7*			14	18	1*	11			0	5*	8	3	67	18	13.40
T. M. Alderman	—	—							—	—	7	0	2	—	7	7	3.50
G. M. Ritchie			59	15*	4	17	34	106*	14		26	19	9	2	294	106*	42.00
R. W. Marsh			11	—	19	32	0	8			1	12	7	—	83	32	11.85
G. F. Lawson			16	—	0	11	14	0			57*	8	7	1	106	57*	17.66
I. W. Callen			1*	—					—	—			1	1	1	1*	—
Byes	7	4	2	1	4	2	8		8		5	4					
Leg-byes	5	2	1	1	10	19	6	7	3		13	5					
Wides					1		2	1	3		1						
No-balls	4	9	1	3	2		3	5	6		5	8					
Total	327	166	277	124	284	179	168	330	283		316	214					
Wickets	9	8	10	3	10	10	10	10	4†		10	10					
Result	D		D		L		L		D		L						

Catches
7 — R. W. Marsh (ct 5/st 2)
6 — A. R. Border and B. M. Laird
2 — W. B. Phillips (ct 1/st 1), G. M. Wood, G. M. Ritchie, K. J. Hughes and B. Yardley
1 — J. R. Thomson, T. M. Alderman and R. J. Bright

† G. M. Wood retired hurt

BOWLING

	J. R. Thomson	T. M. Alderman	R. J. Bright	B. Yardley	A. R. Border	P. R. Sleep	G. F. Lawson	I. W. Callen
v. B.C.C.P. Patron's XI (Rawalpindi) 12-14 September	10–1–57–0	16–3–64–1	16–2–71–0	28–5–136–2	10–3–14–2	15–3–61–0		
v. Pakistan Cricket Board XI (Multan) 16-18 September			23–10–40–5 / 7–4–7–1	20–5–58–0	2–2–0–0		13.3–2–32–5 / 7–0–31–1	6–1–24–0 / 5–0–21–2
First Test Match (Karachi) 22-27 September	29–5–103–1 / 3–1–16–1		36–8–96–3 / 5–0–14–0	23–2–98–1 / 3–1–9–0	1–0–4–0		39–10–93–2	
Second Test Match (Faisalabad) 30 Sept.-5 Oct.	23–5–79–0		41–15–107–0		11–3–47–1	36–5–159–1	33–6–96–4	
v. Invitation XI (Sialkot) 10-12 October		15–5–42–1	9–4–28–3	18–7–40–1		5.2–1–27–0		9–2–15–2
Third Test Match (Lahore) 14-19 October	19–1–73–1 / 5–0–24–0	34–4–144–2 / 3–0–10–0		27–6–102–1	4–1–12–1		35–4–91–2 / 7–1–21–1	
	89–13–352–3 *av. 117.33*	68–12–260–4 *av. 65.00*	137–43–363–12 *av. 30.25*	119–26–443–5 *av. 88.60*	28–9–77–4 *av. 19.25*	56.2–9–247–1 *av. 247.00*	134.3–23–364–15 *av. 24.26*	20–3–60–4 *av. 15.00*

Pakistan *v.* Australia – Test Match Averages

PAKISTAN BATTING

	M	Inns	NOs	Runs	HS	Av	100s	50s
Zaheer Abbas	3	3		269	126	89.66	1	2
Mohsin Khan	3	5	1	297	135	74.25	1	2
Mudassar Nazar	3	5	2	198	79	66.00		2
Imran Khan	3	3	2	64	39*	64.00		
Mansoor Akhtar	3	5	2	183	111	61.00	1	
Javed Miandad	3	3		176	138	58.66	1	
Haroon Rashid	3	3		148	82	49.33		2
Tahir Naqqash	3	3	2	37	15*	37.00		
Abdul Qadir	3	2		30	29	15.00		

Also batted: Wasim Bari 0 (three Tests), Iqbal Qasim 2* (two Tests). Jalaluddin played in one Test but did not bat

PAKISTAN BOWLING

	Overs	Mds	Runs	Wkts	Av	Best	5/inn
Imran Khan	103.2	35	171	13	13.15	4/35	
Abdul Qadir	212.2	48	562	22	25.54	7/142	2
Iqbal Qasim	118.5	45	228	8	28.50	2/28	
Tahir Naqqash	81	18	228	7	32.57	4/61	
Mudassar Nazar	37	6	89	1	89.00	1/8	
Zaheer Abbas	6	—	8		—		

Also bowled: Jalaluddin 35 - 12 - 92 - 5; Javed Miandad 1 - 0 - 2 - 0

PAKISTAN CATCHES

11 - Wasim Bari (ct 7/st 4); 5 - Haroon Rashid; 4 - Mudassar Nazar; 3 - Javed Miandad and sub (Salim Malik); 2 - Zaheer Abbas and sub (Iqbal Sikhander); 1 - Mohsin Khan, Mansoor Akhtar and Imran Khan

AUSTRALIA BATTING

	M	Inns	NOs	Runs	HS	Av	100s	50s
G.M. Ritchie	3	6	1	206	106*	41.20	1	
J. Dyson	3	6		220	87	36.66		2
G.M. Wood	3	6		203	85	33.83		1
K.J. Hughes	3	6		154	54	25.66		1
A.R. Border	3	6	1	118	55*	23.60		1
B.M. Laird	3	6		137	60	22.83		1
G.F. Lawson	3	6	1	90	57*	18.00		1
B. Yardley	2	4		61	40	15.25		
J.R. Thomson	3	6	2	49	18	12.25		
R.W. Marsh	3	6		72	32	12.00		
R.J. Bright	2	4	1	34	32*	11.33		

Also batted: P.R. Sleep 0 and 29 (one Test), T.M. Alderman 7 and 0 (one Test)

AUSTRALIA BOWLING

	Overs	Mds	Runs	Wkts	Av	Best	5/inn
A.R. Border	16	4	63	2	31.50	1/12	
G.F. Lawson	114	21	301	9	33.44	4/96	
R.J. Bright	82	23	217	3	72.33	3/96	
J.R. Thomson	79	12	295	3	98.33	1/16	
B. Yardley	53	9	209	2	104.50	1/98	

Also bowled: P.R. Sleep 36 - 3 - 159 - 1; T.M. Alderman 37 - 4 - 154 - 2; K.J. Hughes 0.1 - 0 - 6 - 0

AUSTRALIA CATCHES

4 - B.M. Laird and R.W. Marsh (ct 3/st 1); 2 - B. Yardley and K.J. Hughes; 1 - G.M. Ritchie, R.J. Bright and A.R. Border

were there, had a job to do, for which they were being paid and got on with it. We didn't make the psychological adjustment we should have as professional sportsmen and that is why we struggled.'

It would also be fair to say that, under Imran Khan, Pakistan have reached a maturity which has at last made it seem possible that they will realise their great potential as an outstanding Test side.

Jeff Thomson reflects on a series which was very hard work for the Australian bowlers. (Adrian Murrell)

K. J. Hughes	Byes	Leg-byes	Wides	No-balls	Total	Wkts
	11	3		7	424	5
	14	6		2	176	10
	5	2		1	67	4
	4	8	1	12	419	9
				2	47	1
0.1–0–6–0	4	1		8	501	6
	8	5	1	3	169	7
	3	13	2	27	467	7
	4	5			64	1
0.1–0–6–0 —						

The Empire Strikes Back

England in Australia
England, Australia and New Zealand
in the Benson & Hedges World Series
Review of the England tour by Robin Marlar

England's destroyer Geoff Lawson. (Patrick Eagar)

Few England sides have departed on an overseas tour leaving their supporters feeling more disenchanted as to the composition and balance of the team than that which went to Australia in October, 1982. That the selectors, denied the services of Gooch, Boycott, Emburey and Les Taylor, faced a difficult task is unquestionable, but their policy and structuring was hard to determine from their selections for the Tests against India and Pakistan in 1982.

For much of the time, in the choice of Pringle, Marks and Ian Greig, who did not make the trip to Australia, there appeared to be a hankering after a golden past when the nucleus of the England side was composed of graduates and under-graduates from the universities of Oxford and Cambridge. Social changes have taken place which means that those times are no more and that the majority of the better younger cricketers are now at universities other than Oxford and Cambridge.

In the golden age of Fry, Warner and MacLaren, it was said that the best way to judge a cricketer was to see how he fared against the northern counties. This may not be a fair way of assessing him to-day, but one is equally sure that to judge a player on his performances for Cambridge on the benign wickets of Fenner's against county opposition which is mostly of second team standard is an insane guide to deciding that he is of Test quality.

Pringle is a likeable and unassuming young man, but it would have been better for him, and for English cricket, to have allowed him to prove himself in the county championship for a couple of seasons. It is there that cricketers are built, and broken. It is difficult to comprehend how he could have been selected before such as Gatting and Jesty who have proved themselves in that hard school. If it is argued that he was selected primarily for his potential as a quick bowler, then whatever happened to the aspirations we held for Allott and Dilley?

Gatting, Jesty and several others could also look complainingly at the choice of Cook whose record in 1982 had been meagre, but surely the most unjust of selections was that of Miller, Marks and Hemmings, three off-spinners, to the exclusion of both Phil Edmonds and Nick Cook who had taken 80 and 90 wickets respectively in 1982. The omission of both of these bowlers left the side without a front line bowler who could turn the ball from leg.

The choice of reserve wicket-keeper, too, was bewildering. With Bob Taylor now approaching his forty-second year, it was essential that the selectors should choose a wicket-keeper who could be seen as his natural successor in the Test side. Instead they selected Ian Gould, an eminently likeable man, not in the first dozen of county wicket-keepers. What Parks, David East, Richards, Downton or French must have thought of the way in which their art had been slighted, one cannot imagine. The fallacious argument was that Gould had been selected because of his quality as a batsman. French and Richards scored more runs at a higher average in 1982, and David East and Downton were only marginally below him. If a one-day wicket-keeper was being looked for, then Bairstow obviously had the greatest claims. It is very bemusing to read in every M.C.C. coaching publication that irrespective of all other considerations the best wicket-keeper must be chosen, and then to see this edict consistently violated by the establishment itself.

In the choice of Cowans, the selectors had sympathy and support. The selection of a comparatively unknown quick bowler as a shock tactic has history and past success to commend it.

If England left with their supporters showing little optimism over some of the selections, they were not totally without hope. We still had Botham and Gower and now Allan Lamb, and England did hold the 'Ashes'.

22, 23, 24 and 25 October 1982

at Brisbane

Queensland 297 for 9 dec (H. Frei 57, R.B. Phillips 55 not out, A.B. Henschell 50) and 435 for 5 dec (G.S. Chappell 126, K.C. Wessels 103, R.B. Kerr 65, A.B. Henschell 54)
England XI 372 (A.J. Lamb 117, D.I. Gower 100, A.B. Henschell 4 for 51) and 189 (A.B. Henschell 5 for 60)

Queensland won by 171 runs

England's tour of Australia began at Brisbane. The state side were without Ritchie and Border who were in Pakistan with the Australian team, but Greg Chappell was fit and eager to lead his side and, it was felt, was ready to reassert himself and reclaim the captaincy of Australia.

He gained first advantage when he won the toss and Queensland batted. Botham began wildly, but Willis who, as a captain, is an inspiring leader of the charge rather than a calm tactician bowled fast and straight, gained a little movement and was aggressive. Botham steadied, but Cowans and Pringle were disappointing. Nevertheless, with seven men out, including Chappell and the hard-hitting Henschell, Queensland had scored only 164, and England looked pleased.

It was then that Harry Frei came in. At the age of 31, the left-arm fast bowler, German born, was making his first-class debut because Thomson, like Border and Ritchie, was still in Pakistan. In 36 minutes, he hit 57, five sixes and five fours. Phillips hit a six and six fours in his unbeaten 55, and the pair added 75 in 36 minutes. Marks, who had Hohns taken at slip off the last ball of his first over in which he conceded a single, was hit for 38 in two overs.

Queensland declared at 297 for 9, and Cook was lbw to the first ball of the innings, but next day Gower and Lamb hit exciting centuries. Gower was at his most fluent, and Lamb hit belligerently off the front foot. Runs came briskly and the day belonged to the visitors who led by 75 on the first innings. The Queensland out-cricket was not helped by an injury to Phillips who was replaced behind the stumps by Broad.

The third day was misery for England. Pringle dropped both Wessels and Chappell who went on to reach centuries, and the English fielding in general looked vulnerable. The bowling looked positively short of talent and Marks, in particular, was brutally savaged by Chappell. The first wicket produced 152, and the second wicket stand between Broad and Wessels produced 70 in 68 minutes before Wessels mistimed a sweep off Miller and was caught at mid-wicket.

At tea the state side were 253 for 2, but shortly afterwards Miller lured Broad forward and Taylor pulled off a brilliant stumping. It was his 1,528th dismissal, his 168th stumping, and with it he broke John Murray's world record. It was England's one bright spot of the day.

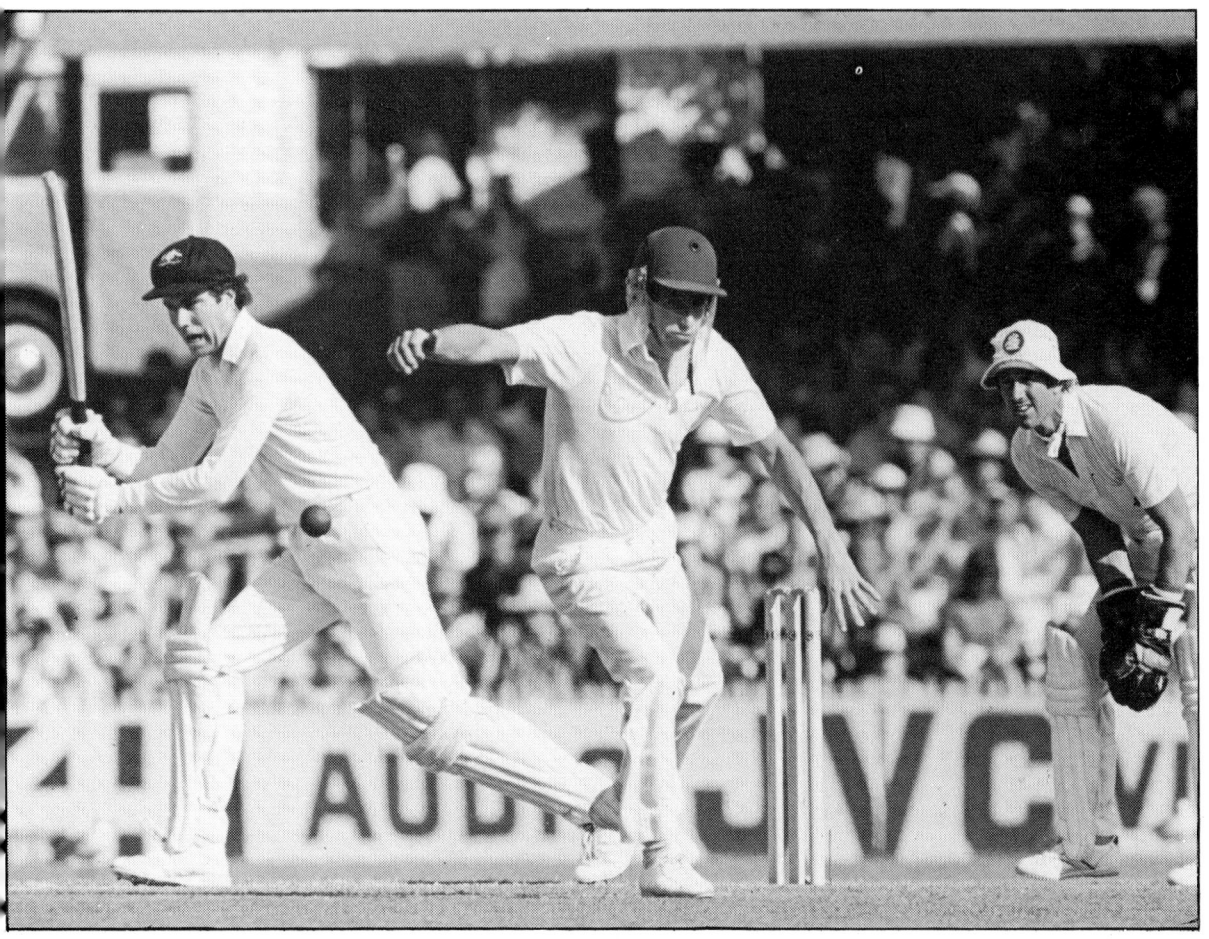

Power and elegance. Greg Chappell hits out during his innings of 117. (Adrian Murrell)

Chappell batted on for 45 minutes on the last morning and then set England to make 360 in 246 minutes and twenty overs. It was not an easy task, but it seemed unlikely that they would be beaten. They made the unhappiest of starts when Frei dismissed Fowler and Gower in his first two overs with only 4 scored. Cook batted stubbornly to score 39 in 162 minutes.

Queensland were without the injured Hohns, but Henschell's off-spin proved most effective and England struggled throughout the day. At tea, they were 163 for 5, and, seemingly, a draw was inevitable, but in the period after tea which began with Miller being lbw to Henschell's first ball 5 wickets fell for 26 runs, and Queensland had won by 171 runs.

It was the first time that Queensland had beaten an England touring side on an official Test tour although Harold Gilligan's below strength side had been beaten on their way to New Zealand in 1929–30.

It was not a happy start for England. The failure of their batting in the second innings and the ineptitude of the bowling were both worrying.

27, 28, and 29 October 1982

at Newcastle

Northern New South Wales 163 (R.B. McCosker 53, E.E. Hemmings 5 for 38, N.G. Cowans 4 for 46) and 166 (G. Arms 53, E.E. Hemmings 4 for 30)
England XI 305 (C.J. Tavare 157, D.I. Gower 56, S. Hatherall 5 for 37) and 27 for 0

England XI won by 10 wickets

England's morale was lifted somewhat by their victory over Northern New South Wales in a non-first-class fixture. The local side included McCosker, Holland and Gilmour, all rich in experience in Sheffield Shield cricket. Gilmour is best remembered for his mighty bowling deeds in the Prudential World Cup of 1975,

Hemmings and Cowans took 17 wickets between them in the match, and Chris Tavare hit 157, but took four hours to reach his first fifty. Tavare, on the evening of the first day, his twenty-eighth birthday, heard that he had been appointed captain of Kent, and he celebrated by batting for nearly six and a half hours and gaining useful practice. He was confronted mostly by the leg-spin of Holland who bowled 35 overs and by the off-spin of Steve Hatherall.

On the last evening, Cowans and Hemmings provided a

late burst which meant that England had 17 overs in which to score 25 runs. They got them in 9.4 overs.

31 October, 1, 2 and 3 November 1982

at Adelaide

England XI 492 for 9 dec (G. Miller 83, A.J. Lamb 78, E.E. Hemmings 60 not out, G. Cook 58, R.D. Jackman 50 not out) and 226 for 8 dec (P.R. Sleep 4 for 86)
South Australia 344 (D.W. Hookes 74, K.J. Wright 65 not out, P.R. Sleep 51, E.E. Hemmings 4 for 102) and 271 for 8 (A.M.J. Hilditch 79)

Match drawn

With the first Test match looming, England's batsmen gave another worrying display when, on the first day of the match against South Australia, they finished at 257 for 6. As the state side were without both Hogg and Garner, England's performance was all the more depressing, only Lamb and Cook showing any sort of form, but, like Tavare and Randall, failing to capitalise on a good foundation.

The second morning saw a revitalisation of the England batting. Miller and Gould added 103 in 32 overs for the seventh wicket, and then, with Miller once more failing when tantalisingly close to his century, Hemmings and Jackman joined in a stand of 112 in 25 overs, 69 minutes. Only Foster and Rhodes, in 1903–4, had previously shared a century last wicket stand for an England touring side in Australia.

England declared 90 minutes after lunch, and, by the close, they had captured four South Australian wickets, two of them to Hemmings, for 118.

Hookes, Sleep and Wright all denied England the next day, and it was left to Geoff Cook's very occasional left-arm spin to effect a breakthrough. Fowler, needlessly run out, and Cook were both out before the close, as were Tavare and Lamb, so that England's opening problem remained unsolved. In this match Fowler opened with Tavare with Cook at number 3.

Botham, who was leading England, set South Australia to make 375 in 4 hours, but it was England, through Hemmings and the improbable Cook, who came closest to victory. Hilditch reasserted himself with a fluent 79 off 89 balls, but the most memorable incident of the day was when Hookes recalled Botham who had been given out obstructing the field when he accidentally thwarted Wright who was attempting to catch him off off-spinner Harms.

5, 6, 7 and 8 November 1982

at Perth

Western Australia 167 (N.G. Cowans 4 for 33) and 197 (I.T. Botham 4 for 43)
England XI 156 (I.T. Botham 65, T.M. Alderman 5 for 63) and 209 for 9 (D.W. Randall 92, T.M.Alderman 5 for 67)

England XI won by 1 wicket

A cloudy morning and a pitch still damp from its preparation encouraged Bob Willis to ask Western Australia to bat when he won the toss in England's last game before the first Test.

He was rewarded with only one wicket before lunch, that of Laird, caught mis-pulling Pringle just before rain halted play for twenty minutes.

In the afternoon, Cowans assured himself of a Test cap when, in the space of 25 balls, he dismissed Wood, Shipperd, G. Marsh and Macleay at a personal cost of 6 runs. Aided by a strong breeze, he bowled at a lively and menacing pace and his performance was a great encouragement to England for whom Botham and Willis also bowled well so that the state side were dismissed with an hour and a half of the day remaining.

England began uncertainly against Lillee and Alderman. Tavare moved slowly to the second ball of Lillee's second over and was caught behind and Gower snicked to second slip off Alderman.

Fowler had batted resolutely on the first evening, but he was bowled third ball on the second morning. Lamb followed shortly after, and the only bright spot in a poor day for England was the batting of Botham and Miller. Miller was forced to retire hurt at 39 when he was hit on the hand by Lillee. England's last three wickets fell for one run and Western Australia had taken an unlikely lead of 11.

Cowans and Botham opened the England bowling in the second innings, and Botham quickly dismissed Laird, but Cowans bowled disappointingly short and the state side closed at 113 for 3.

They added only another 84 runs the next day when Botham, Willis and Cowans again bowled well and England were left to make 209 for victory. Tavare was again caught behind off Lillee for nought and Fowler failed so that England were left without an opening pair of form or substance for the first Test. Gower and Lamb added 52, but both were dismissed, as was Botham, and at 82 for 5, England faced defeat in three days.

Randall was dropped when 9. He hooked Lillee straight to Macleay at long-leg and a simple chance was missed. Pringle played on to Lillee, but the bails were not dislodged, and encouraged by these escapes and Lillee's retirement from the field, the two batsmen applied themselves positively to the task. Randall was impishly aggressive and by the close he was 68 and Pringle was 21, and England were only 41 short of victory.

Randall and Pringle took their partnership to 105 on the last morning before Pringle was out when attempting to hook Alderman. It was the first of four wickets that Alderman was to take in twenty deliveries at a cost of 7 runs.

At 201, Miller was caught at cover and in the same over Randall, after his splendid innings, was caught behind chasing a wide delivery. Cowans was total apprehension, but Willis and Taylor nudged the final five runs and England had won a close and morale-boosting victory, but one which left them with several problems on team selection still unsolved.

FIRST TEST MATCH: AUSTRALIA v. ENGLAND

There were some doubts in the days preceding the first Test match as to whether or not it would be played at Perth. A move in the Western Australian parliament to ban tobacco advertising threatened the venue of the match which was being sponsored by Benson and Hedges. Ultimately, the problem was resolved, and it made many ponder as to what would happen to sport and the arts in England, and

Yardley's hundredth Test wicket. Randall is caught by Wood.
(Patrick Eagar)

Australia, if the sponsorship of the tobacco companies were denied to them.

Of the team that had beaten Western Australia, Fowler lost his place, Cook being preferred as opening partner to Tavare. Hemmings was twelfth man as England played four seam bowlers.

Chappell won the toss and asked England to bat although it was not easy to understand why. Australia did not bowl well, but, in Lillee's fifth over, after 35 minutes of uncertainty, Cook fended a short ball into the hands of short leg. This was Australia's only success before lunch which was taken with England at 66 for 1.

Gower played most attractively, making 72 of the 95 runs added for the second wicket. He was superbly caught by Dyson diving full length at square leg.

Lamb started uneasily, fretting for his strokes, but he settled to play with confidence until well caught by Marsh when he edged a ball from Yardley, who bowled well throughout the day, onto his thigh and the wicket-keeper dived forward to grab the rebound.

Botham launched a violent attack on Lawson which produced 12 runs in 4 balls, but on the last ball of the over he was given out caught behind. The appeal was originally denied, but the square leg umpire indicated a catch and Botham was out although most felt that he had been very unfortunate. At the close of play, England were 242 for 4.

Chris Tavare was 66 not out. He had batted for six hours. At lunch, he was 20; at tea, 45. In the final 75 minutes of the day he failed to add to his score. He was missed at 31 and 41, but there were no other blemishes in an innings which, if not one to please an audience, was a stubborn response to what his side required of him. One wishes, however, that he were not cast eternally in this role, but it is better to remember Tavare's innings than the petulance of Lillee which marred the day.

Tavare and Randall extended their stand to one hundred the next morning, but the game was already ebbing to a draw on a perfect pitch. Randall struck the ball firmly. Dyson fielded finely. Yardley continued to bowl well, and it was his introduction to the attack which brought the end of Tavare twenty minutes before lunch, brilliantly caught by Hughes when he mis-hit a sweep. His 89 had occupied 466 minutes and he had faced 337 deliveries.

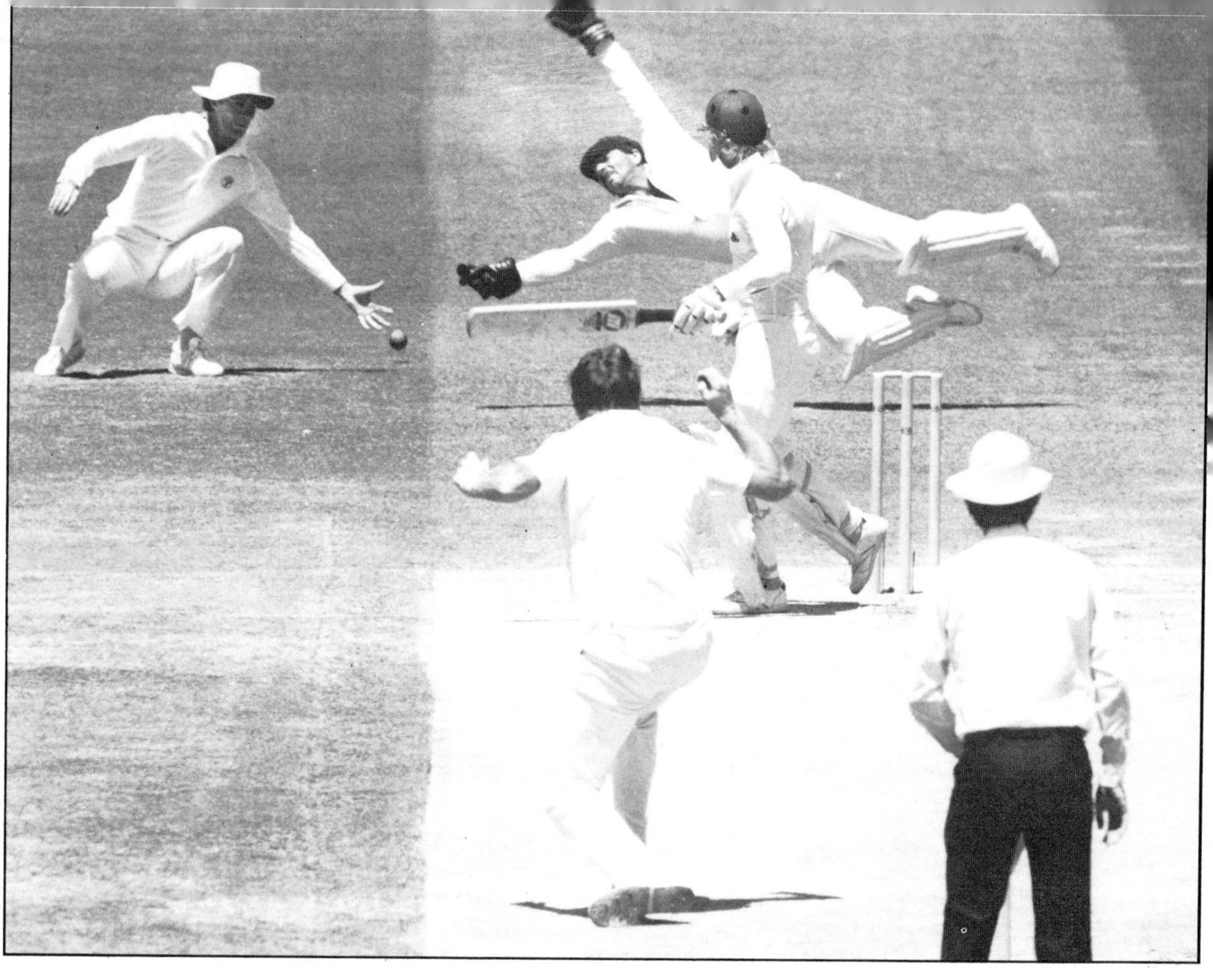

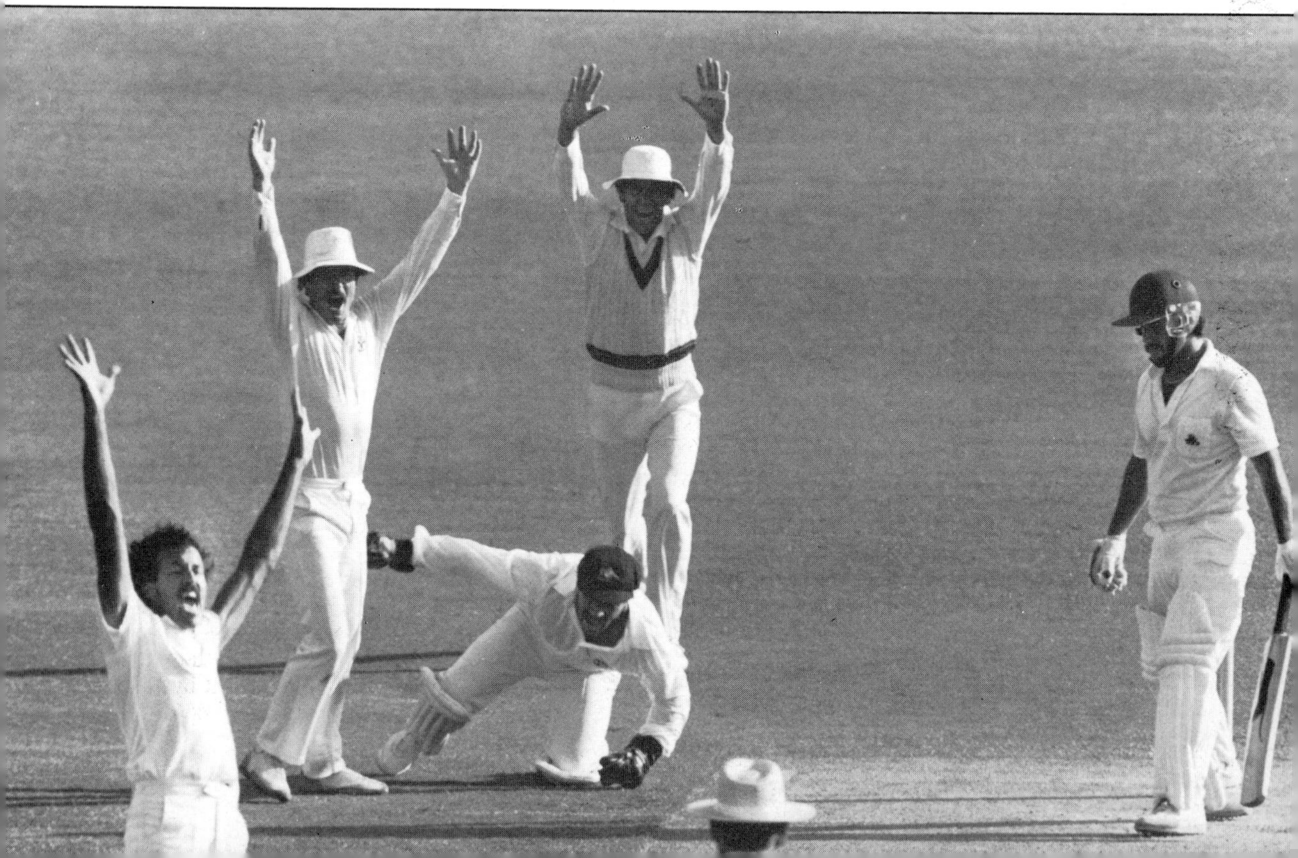

Miller and Taylor played Yardley most confidently. Pringle failed after half an hour of dither, and Willis smote well. England were out for 411, but Australia negotiated eleven overs without mishap. The sadly memorable incident of an unremarkable day was when England passed 400 and a group of drunken louts invaded the pitch. Players were angered and Alderman, having apparently been struck, chased one intruder and brought him down with a rugby tackle. In the process Alderman dislocated his shoulder, and his part in the Test match and the Australian cricket season was over. It was a sad day for cricket as the sickness pervading the western world made a further inroad into the noblest of games.

OPPOSITE ABOVE: *Rodney Marsh dives in vain, but not much eluded him during the series. His 28 catches set up a new wicket-keeping Test record.* (*Adrian Murrell*)

OPPOSITE BELOW: *On his way to the record. Allan Lamb is caught Marsh, bowled Yardley for 46.* (*Patrick Eagar*)

RIGHT: *Success for Lillee. Dismay for Pringle–bowled for nought.* (*Adrian Murrell*)

BELOW: *The malaise of mindless violence intrudes into the Test arena. Terry Alderman is carried from the field by his colleagues after dislocating his shoulder when tackling a loutish invader of the pitch. Alderman's season had ended.* (*Adrian Murrell*)

FIRST TEST MATCH – AUSTRALIA v. ENGLAND
12, 13, 14, 16 and 17 November 1982 at Perth

ENGLAND

Batsman	FIRST INNINGS		SECOND INNINGS	
G. Cook	c Dyson, b Lillee	1	c Border, b Lawson	7
C.J. Tavare	c Hughes, b Yardley	89	c Chappell, b Yardley	9
D.I. Gower	c Dyson, b Alderman	72	lbw, b Lillee	28
A.J. Lamb	c Marsh, b Yardley	46	c Marsh, b Lawson	56
I.T. Botham	c Marsh, b Lawson	12	b Lawson	0
D.W. Randall	c Wood, b Yardley	78	b Lawson	115
G. Miller	c Marsh, b Lillee	30	(8) c Marsh, b Yardley	0
D.R. Pringle	b Lillee	0	(9) not out	47
R.W. Taylor*	not out	29	(7) b Yardley	31
R.G.D. Willis†	c Lillee, b Yardley	26	b Lawson	0
N.G. Cowans	b Yardley	4	lbw, b Chappell	36
Extras	b 7, lb 9, w 2, nb 6	24	b 5, lb 11, w 2, nb 11	29
		411		**358**

	O	M	R	W	O	M	R	W
Lillee	38	13	96	3	33	12	89	1
Alderman	43	15	84	1				
Lawson	29	6	89	1	32	5	108	5
Chappell	3	—	11	—	2.3	1	8	1
Yardley	42.4	15	107	5	41	10	101	3
Border					7	2	21	—
Hookes					1	—	2	—

AUSTRALIA

Batsman	FIRST INNINGS		SECOND INNINGS	
G.M. Wood	c and b Willis	29	c Taylor, b Willis	0
J. Dyson	lbw, b Miller	52	c Cowans, b Willis	12
A.R. Border	c Taylor, b Botham	8	not out	32
G.S. Chappell†	c Lamb, b Willis	117	not out	22
K.J. Hughes	c Willis, b Miller	62		
D.W. Hookes	lbw, b Miller	56		
R.W. Marsh*	c Cook, b Botham	0		
G.F. Lawson	b Miller	50		
B. Yardley	c Lamb, b Willis	17		
D.K. Lillee	not out	2		
T.M. Alderman	absent hurt			
Extras	b 4, lb 1, w 1, nb 25	31	lb 1, nb 6	7
	(for 9 wkts dec)	**424**	(for 2 wkts)	**73**

	O	M	R	W	O	M	R	W
Willis	31.5	4	95	3	6	1	23	2
Botham	40	10	121	2	6	1	17	—
Cowans	13	2	54	—	3	1	15	—
Pringle	10	1	37	—	2	—	3	—
Miller	33	11	70	4	4	3	8	—
Cook	4	2	16	—				
Lamb					1	1	0	—

FALL OF WICKETS
1- 14, 2- 109, 3- 189, 4- 204, 5- 304, 6- 323, 7- 342, 8- 357, 9- 406
1- 10, 2- 51, 3- 77, 4- 80, 5- 151, 6- 228, 7- 242, 8- 292, 9- 292

FALL OF WICKETS
1- 63, 2- 76, 3- 123, 4- 264, 5- 311, 6- 311, 7- 374, 8- 414, 9- 424
1- 2, 2- 22

Umpires: A.R. Crafter & M.W. Johnson

Match drawn

The Australian first wicket realised 63 and the second wicket fell at 76 when Botham had Border, who had looked most uncertain, caught behind. It was Botham's 250th Test wicket and so it became a memorable match for him as he had reached 3000 runs in the first innings.

At one time Australia were 123 for 3, but Greg Chappell batted at his regal best and Hughes played brilliantly until he moved lazily down the wicket to Miller and lofted the ball to mid-off. They had added 141. England desperately needed another spinner in the side, a fact underlined by Pringle's sub-standard fielding and pedestrian bowling. Cowans, too, had an unhappy time. He bowled erratically and was handled with little sympathy. The England management and leadership seemed uncertain as to whether he was to be reckoned as a strike bowler or a stock bowler.

Chappell reached his twenty-first Test century, and his 117 which included two sixes and eleven fours came off 173 balls. It was majestic stuff. Hookes and Lawson hit fiercely on the fourth day and there was a plethora of no-balls from England, mostly from Willis. 333 for 6 at the end of the third day, Australia took a first innings lead of 13.

Cook again went quickly and Tavare, having spent 64 minutes at the wicket before scoring a run, batted another hour for 9 and then flashed wildly at Yardley to be caught at slip. Botham was bowled second ball by an inswinger and, at 80 for 4, England were in trouble. Lamb and Randall put on 71 and defeat became a more remote prospect.

Bob Taylor shared a stand of 77 with Randall, and it was this sixth wicket partnership that lasted until the final morning which put the game out of Australia's reach. There was

an alarm when Miller went for nought to the persevering Yardley, but Chappell unwisely confronted Pringle with pace instead of spin and the Essex player responded well to play by far his best innings in a Test match.

Randall reached a fine hundred and a Man of the Match award. His 115 included thirteen fours and lasted for just under four and a half hours. He faced 215 balls, and his innings, more than anything else, saved the game for England. Cowans hit a career best and surprised all of us, and Wood and Dyson both fell to Willis to leave England with a happy draw.

20, 21, 22 and 23 November 1982

at Sydney

England XI 240 (G. Cook 99, I.J. Gould 73, T.M. Chappell 4 for 23, M.J. Bennett 4 for 65) and 342 (C.J. Tavare 147, G. Cook 77, M.J. Bennett 5 for 123, M.R. Whitney 4 for 60)
New South Wales 250 for 9 dec (S.J. Rixon 57 not out, S.B. Smith 50) and 306 (P.M. Toohey 69, T.M. Chappell 61, J. Dyson 59, E.E Hemmings 5 for 101)

England XI won by 26 runs

Tavare is caught at slip by Chappell off Yardley in the second innings. (Patrick Eagar)

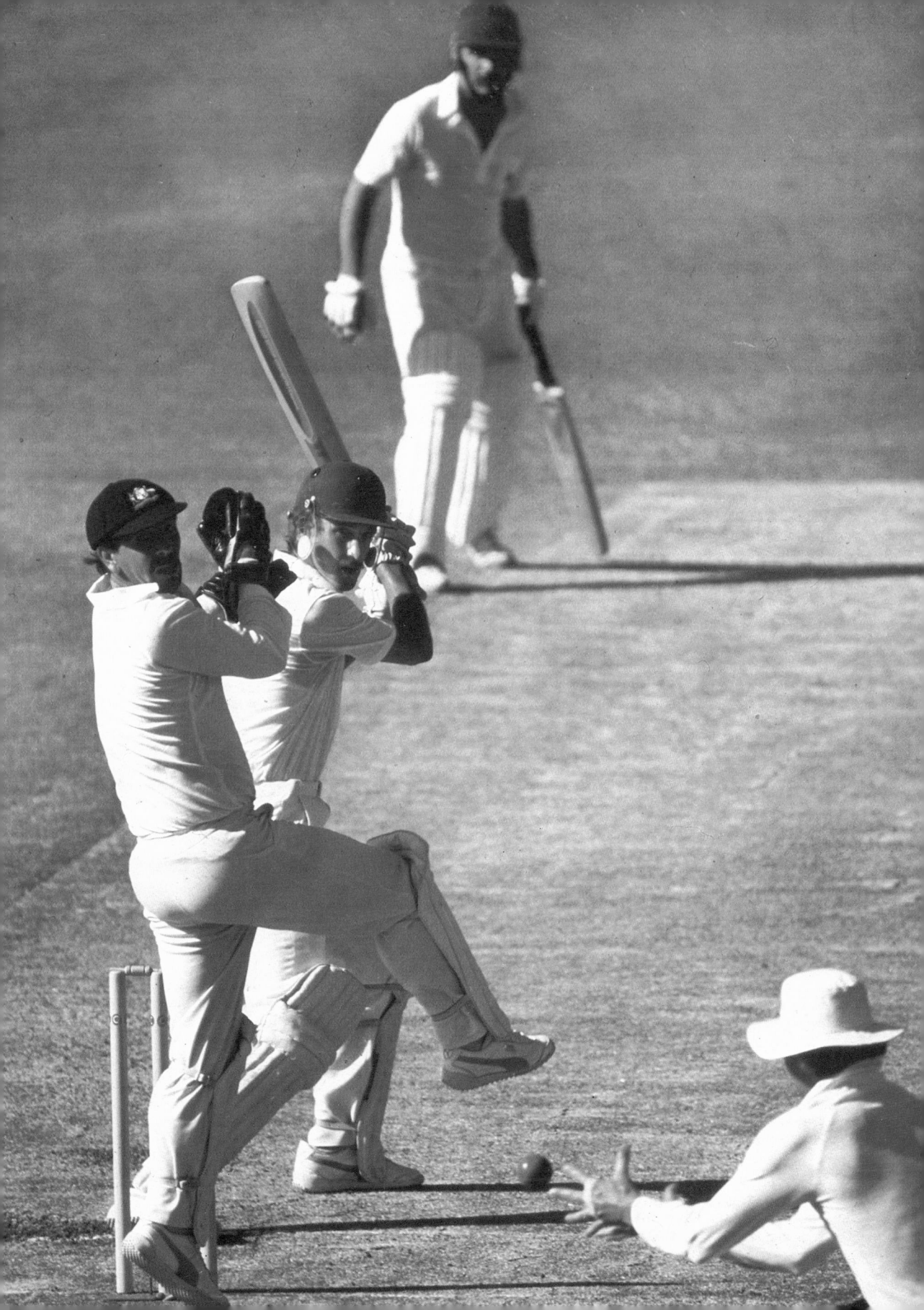

England included the five players who had not played in the Test match and although Gould and Marks could have had little hope of gaining a place in the side for the second Test, Jackman, Hemmings and Fowler were all looking to good performances which would enable them to force their way into the side. Willis had expressed his unhappiness at the way in which Pringle and Cowans had bowled at Perth, and there was a general feeling that it had been a mistake to leave out Hemmings. Jackman had bowled only 33 overs on the tour and had yet to take a wicket, but he could certainly do the job of stock bowler which England had lacked in Perth. Fowler, of course, was contending with Cook for the place as Tavare's opening partner.

It was Fowler who opened with Tavare, Cook dropping down to number three. Tavare monopolised the strike, but had scored only 3 when he edged Whitney to slip. Incomprehensibly, Fowler ducked under a medium pace full toss from Trevor Chappell and was ingloriously bowled. Gower was caught in the gully, Randall was caught in the covers, Pringle bowled and Marks caught behind off Lawson before the bowler left the field with an injured shoulder. 125 for 6.

Cook had had a nightmare beginning to his innings, but he ignored the lack of application around him and accumulated sensible runs. Sadly, he was out to a silly shot, an attempted sweep which ended in the hands of backward square-leg, when one short of his century. Gould gave excellent support with a pugnacious fifty, but England were out for 240, a very disappointing score. Trevor Chappell's medium pacers, which never looked dangerous, brought him 4 for 23, but it was slow left-arm bowler Murray Bennett who impressed most.

Before the close, Jackman bowled Chappell for his first wicket of the tour, and Cowans had McCosker caught behind. England's success with the ball did not continue on the second day when most of the state batsmen played miniature innings which took them to a ten-run lead. Steve Smith, who had played for Wanstead and Essex XI in 1982, was the most emphatic of the batsmen and looked an exceedingly promising player.

Fowler failed again, but Cook shared a second wicket stand of 135. Tavare's 147 was made in 351 minutes and he hit a six and twenty-one fours. Cook's solid 77 made certain that he would retain his Test place. Randall had a breezy knock, but the last seven England wickets fell for 33 runs to Bennett and Whitney, the left-arm opening bowler who had played for Australia as an emergency replacement in England in 1981.

McCosker was bowled by Cowans and England started the last day with the scent of victory in their nostrils. In the end, the victory was obtained, but it lacked conviction. At one stage New South Wales were 165 for 3, but they slipped 187 for 6. Dyson and Chappell added 90 for the third wicket before Dyson was caught behind by Taylor off Pringle. Taylor was fielding substitute for Gould, who was injured, and McCosker had permitted him to keep wicket.

A stand of 73 for the seventh wicket between Toohey and Bennett renewed the home side's hopes. Toohey hit a six and eight fours in his 91 minute innings, but he fell to Eddie Hemmings who took 5 for 101 and spun England to victory with only half of the last twenty overs remaining. An obstinate last wicket stand between Holland and Whitney was ended by Pringle.

SECOND TEST MATCH: AUSTRALIA v. ENGLAND

With Lillee undergoing an operation for the removal of fragments of loose bone from his right knee and Alderman incapacitated by his shoulder injury, Australia showed a revised attack, Thomson returning to Test cricket and Rackemann making his Test debut. Australia made one other change when they replaced Wood with Kepler Wessels, the South African born Queensland opener who formerly played for Sussex.

England, as expected, replaced Pringle with Hemmings, and, at the last moment, brought in Fowler for Cook who had a cracked rib, an injury sustained when batting against Botham in the nets.

Chappell again asked England to bat when he won the toss and his decision was fully justified by instant success. In Lawson's fourth over, Fowler dabbed at a ball outside the off stump and was caught in the gully. The next over from Lawson saw the end of Tavare, taken low at third slip. Lamb batted rather fretfully, but Gower seemed to be restoring the England innings until, on the last ball before lunch, he flicked lazily at Lawson and was brilliantly caught at backward short-leg by Wessels.

63 for 3 was not a happy lunch score for England, but in the early afternoon Lamb and Botham promised a recovery. They played forceful and confident strokes which made it all the more distressing when Botham drove loosely at Yardley and sliced the ball to deep point.

Eleven runs later Lawson delivered the most telling blows

Another one for Marsh. He catches Miller first ball off Lawson high above his head. (Adrian Murrell)

Yardley edges the ball between Tavare and Botham, but he survived to reach an invaluable 53. (Patrick Eagar)

of the match. After 166 minutes, 118 balls and ten fours, Lamb essayed a hook and was well caught by the leaping Marsh. Next ball was a bouncer to Miller. The batsman turned his head and the ball flew off the bat for Marsh to take above his head. 152 for 6. Lawson had 5 for 33 in 15 overs.

Randall hit five fours in his stay of just over an hour, but he never suggested that he would recapture the form of Perth and he provided the persevering and impressive Rackemann with his second Test wicket when he hooked to square leg. Taylor had already fallen at short square leg.

Willis fell to spin and play ended early when the skies darkened at the approach of a storm, but there was no delay the following morning when the England innings lasted only one more ball. Cowans edged Lawson to Marsh and the wicket-keeper took his 302nd catch in Test cricket. Lawson's six wickets had been achieved through fast bowling of high quality.

England fought back encouragingly when Botham bowled Dyson middle stump and the out of form Border turned a Willis bouncer to short-leg. Chappell and Wessels now took over, and the Australian captain reached a thrilling fifty inside an hour and a half before running himself out when he drove straight to cover and sauntered down the wicket. Hughes failed and Hookes played one of his run-a-minute innings before being adjudged caught behind. Marsh also fell

to Taylor when he tried to cut Botham and Australia, 171 for 6, were in some trouble.

Wessels had been batting with great determination and he now found an able partner in Yardley. Wessels inched closer and closer to his century, spending some forty-five minutes in the nineties. He should have been stumped by Taylor off Hemmings and celebrated by pulling the next ball for four to reach a hundred in his first Test innings. It had taken him 342 minutes. Australia had now gained the initiative and by the close they led by 27 runs.

That lead was increased to 122 the next day when Willis allowed Cowans only one over to add to the five he had bowled on Saturday morning. Wessels hit three fours in the over and Cowans was once more banished to the outfield. Wessels was last out, having batted for 463 minutes, faced 342 balls and hit seventeen fours. It was a mighty achievement.

Tavare and Fowler began England's second innings after lunch and, aided by dropped catches and a cascade of no-balls, they put on 54 for the first wicket in ten minutes under two hours. Bad light brought an early close with the score 71 for 1. The day ended unhappily with Thomson, who had bowled dreadfully in the first innings, being warned for intimidatory bowling by umpire Bailhache.

On the fourth day, however, Thomson became the Australian hero. In the pre-lunch session everything had gone England's way. Simple catches were dropped, Rackemann left the field with a groin strain and Fowler

found confidence grown from good fortune. Thomson's return brought the downfall of Gower just before lunch, and in the afternoon he took four more wickets while England advanced by 50. Yardley bowled tightly at one end while Thomson and Lawson bowled in three over spells from the other. Thomson's five wickets were claimed in three spells which cost 12 runs. One of his victims was Fowler, caught by Marsh off a steeply rising delivery down the leg side, after a plucky innings which lasted for 356 minutes. Miller and Hemmings survived the last 100 minutes of the day.

Their stand was ended by Lawson in the third over of the final morning, and the England innings closed with two controversial catches behind the wicket which gave Marsh six catches in the innings and nine in the match so equalling two Australian records. On consideration, the England innings was a bizarre affair, containing, as it did, 52 extras and eight dropped catches.

Eccentricities continued. Willis was no-balled eight times in his first two overs, Fowler dropped Wessels and Dyson retired hurt when he was hit on the shoulder.

LEFT: *Kepler Wessels. 162 on his Test debut. (Patrick Eager)*

BELOW: *Dyson fails in his spectacular attempt to catch Chris Tavare. Dyson was one of the outstanding fielders of the series. (Patrick Eager)*

OPPOSITE: *The victorious Australian team. (Adrian Murrell)*

SECOND TEST MATCH – AUSTRALIA *v.* ENGLAND
26, 27, 28, 30 November and 1 December 1982 at Brisbane

ENGLAND

	FIRST INNINGS		SECOND INNINGS	
C.J. Tavare	c Hughes, b Lawson	1	c Marsh, b Lawson	13
G. Fowler	c Yardley, b Lawson	7	c Marsh, b Thomson	83
D.I. Gower	c Wessels, b Lawson	18	c Marsh, b Thomson	34
A.J. Lamb	c Marsh, b Lawson	72	c Wessels, b Thomson	12
I.T. Botham	c Rackemann, b Yardley	40	(6) c Marsh, b Thomson	15
D.W. Randall	c Lawson, b Rackemann	37	(5) c Yardley, b Thomson	4
G. Miller	c Marsh, b Lawson	0	c Marsh, b Lawson	60
R.W. Taylor*	c Lawson, b Rackemann	1	c Hookes, b Lawson	3
E.E. Hemmings	not out	15	b Lawson	18
R.G.D. Willis†	c Thomson, b Yardley	1	not out	10
N.G. Cowans	c Marsh, b Lawson	10	c Marsh, b Lawson	5
Extras	lb 2, w 1, nb 14	17	b 8, lb 8, w 1, nb 35	52
		219		309

AUSTRALIA

	FIRST INNINGS		SECOND INNINGS	
K.C. Wessels	b Willis	162	b Hemmings	46
J. Dyson	b Bothar	1	retired hurt	4
A.R. Border	c Randall, b Willis	0	c Botham, b Hemmings	15
G.S. Chappell†	run out	53	c Lamb, b Cowans	8
K.J. Hughes	c Taylor, b Botham	0	not out	39
D.W. Hookes	c Taylor, b Miller	28	not out	66
R.W. Marsh*	c Taylor, b Botham	11		
B. Yardley	c Tavare, b Willis	53		
G.F. Lawson	c Hemmings, b Willis	6		
C.G. Rackemann	b Willis	4		
J.R. Thomson	not out	5		
Extras	b 2, lb 8, nb 8	18	b 2, lb 5, nb 5	12
		341	(for 3 wickets)	190

	O	M	R	W	O	M	R	W
Lawson	18.3	4	47	6	35.3	11	87	5
Rackemann	21	8	61	2	12.2	3	35	—
Thomson	8	—	43	—	31	6	73	5
Yardley	17	5	51	2	40.4	21	50	—
Chappell					6	2	8	—
Hookes					2	—	4	—

	O	M	R	W	O	M	R	W
Willis	29.4	3	66	5	4	1	24	—
Botham	22	1	105	3	15.5	1	70	—
Cowans	6	—	36	—	9	1	31	1
Hemmings	33.3	6	81	—	29	9	43	2
Miller	19.3	4	35	1	3	—	10	—

FALL OF WICKETS
1- 8, 2- 13, 3- 63, 4- 141, 5- 152, 6- 152, 7- 178, 8- 191, 9- 195
1- 54, 2- 144, 3- 165, 4- 169, 5- 194, 6- 201, 7- 226, 8- 285, 9- 295

FALL OF WICKETS
1- 4, 2- 11, 3- 94, 4- 99, 5- 130, 6- 171, 7- 271, 8- 310, 9- 332
1- 60, 2- 77, 3- 83

Umpires: R.C. Bailhache & M.W. Johnson

Australia won by 7 wickets

Australia on the way to victory. Kim Hughes slashes the ball to the boundary. Gower leaps for safety. Taylor looks on. (Patrick Eagar)

60 for 0 at lunch, Australia lost Border to the first ball of the afternoon, brilliantly caught at slip by Botham. Cowans bowled downwind and was very quick and hostile. He got a coveted first Test wicket when Chappell hooked him to Lamb. Wessels, too, was uneasy and fell to Hemmings, but Hookes unleashed a barrage of strokes, England dropped catches and Australia survived appeals and won with an hour to spare.

4, 5, 6 and 7 December 1982

at Melbourne

England XI 275 (D.I. Gower 88, R.J. Bright 5 for 81) and 324 for 7 dec (A.J. Lamb 108, D.I. Gower 88, R.J. McCurdy 4 for 70)
Victoria 295 (G.N. Yallop 69, D.R. Pringle 4 for 66) and 122 for 4 (M.D. Taylor 56 not out)

Match drawn

Yallop won the toss and asked England to bat on a grassy pitch. Bright bowled with commendable accuracy and tur-ned the ball enough to disconcert most English batsmen. Only Gower and Lamb shone in a gloomy day.

England bowled better than they had batted, especially Pringle and Miller, but the uneven Victorian batting still gained a slender lead.

Gower's second innings was sedate compared to his dazzling knock in the first, but he and Lamb added 189 in 212 minutes for the third wicket. Subsequently five wickets fell for 33 runs, including that of Lamb, stumped for a splendid 108.

There was never much hope of Victoria scoring the 305 they needed, nor of England bowling them out although Miller again bowled well. Drizzle and gloom brought an early close.

8 December 1982

at Horsham

Victorian Country XI 146 for 8
New Zealanders 186 for 5 (M.D. Crowe 77)

New Zealanders won by 7 wickets

In their first match of their short pre-Christmas tour, the New Zealanders batted on for the whole of their overs even though they had won the match.

Dean Jones of Victoria cuts Miller for 4. Gower again in the close catching position. Botham at slip. Gould keeping wicket. (Philip Tyson)

10, 11, 12 and 13 December 1982

at Melbourne

New Zealanders 301 for 9 dec (G.P. Howarth 102, B.A. Edgar 66) and 174 for 3 dec (J.F. Reid 58)
Victoria 230 for 5 dec (D.F. Whatmore 81) and 245 (J.M. Wiener 75, J.F.M. Morrison 4 for 62)

Match tied

The sad prelude to this exciting match was the news that Robin Bailhache had resigned from the Australian panel of Test umpires. Mr Bailhache, one of the most experienced and respected of Australian umpires, gave no reasons for his decision, but it was apparent that he felt that the pressures to which umpires are subjected at the top level had become unendurable.

In the first of their two first-class games the New Zealanders were indebted to the second wicket stand of 106 between Edgar and Howarth after the first day's play had been washed out. Yallop showed his determination to make up for lost time when he hit 38 off 31 deliveries, but it was Watts and Whatmore, with a stand of 99 in 127 minutes, who provided the backbone of the Victorian innings which Yallop declared overnight.

Howarth declared on the last day and set Victoria to make 246. The state side began well and a thrilling partnership of

68 in 52 minutes between Wiener, who hit ten fours, and Taylor for the fourth wicket made victory possible. Victoria needed only 6 runs to win with three wickets standing, but off the fifth ball of the final over, Callen was bowled by Snedden when he attempted to hit the one run needed for victory and the match was tied.

THIRD TEST MATCH: AUSTRALIA v. ENGLAND

'No captain who wins the toss and puts the other side in deserves to win the match, unless there are some very exceptional circumstances to be taken into his consideration.' So wrote A.G. Steel nearly eighty years ago, and Bob Willis may well have reflected on this statement as Australia reached 265 for 3 on the opening day and Greg Chappell hit his second century of the series. It was not as commanding as his innings in the first Test nor, indeed, quite as scintillating as his fifty in the second Test but, Wessels and Dyson having produced a solid start, Hughes and Chappell provided a formidable, and often elegant stand of 126.

In spite of his improved showing in the second innings at Brisbane, Cowans was omitted and Pringle returned to bowl an adequate quota liberally sprinkled with no-balls. Hogg returned to the Australian side for the injured Rackemann.

Nightwatchman Lawson went early, but most batsmen contributed a few and had Hughes not run himself out and the struggling Border not taken so much of the strike from the effervescent Hookes, Australia might well have reached 500. Hemmings bowled admirably in containment, Gower took two brilliant catches and Botham took four wickets and made three catches, his catching of Hookes off a sweep which the fielder first misjudged being remarkable.

Hogg struck a blow in his first over when Tavare was in no sort of position to deal with an outswinger and then Fowler fell to a good ball from Lawson. 21 for 2. Lamb and Gower moved to the close without further mishap.

They continued their stand of 119 into the following afternoon, but Gower was surprised by the second ball after lunch which bounced more generously than he had expected and took the edge of his bat. Botham looked solid and dependable, but Lamb swung at a ball from Lawson and in the flurry was given out caught behind to his obvious disbelief. Randall had his stumps knocked all over the place by a yorker second ball and Miller edged hard to gully. Chappell dived to take Taylor at slip, Botham went to a low catch at mid-wicket, Thomson bowled Hemmings and Willis. Seven wickets had gone down in 15 overs for 35 runs and England followed on 222 runs behind. It was a dismal display.

It became darker still for England when Tavare was caught bat and pad for nought, but Fowler and Gower survived and flourished to send England into the rest at 90 for 1.

RIGHT: *Kim Hughes in the middle of his glorious stand of 126 with Greg Chappell.* (*Patrick Eagar*)

BELOW: *Greg Chappell square cuts Miller for 4 on his way to his second century of the series.* (*Philip Tyson*)

OPPOSITE: *Lamb ducks under a Thomson bouncer. Thomson made an impressive return to Test cricket at Brisbane and consolidated his position in this Test.* (*Philip Tyson*)

THIRD TEST MATCH – AUSTRALIA *v.* ENGLAND
10, 11, 12, 14 and 15 December 1982 at Adelaide

AUSTRALIA

	FIRST INNINGS		SECOND INNINGS	
K.C. Wessels	c Taylor, b Botham	44	(2) c Taylor, b Botham	1
J. Dyson	c Taylor, b Botham	44	(1) not out	37
G.S. Chappell†	c Gower, b Willis	115	(4) not out	26
K.J. Hughes	run out	88		
G.F. Lawson	c Botham, b Willis	2	(3) c Randall, b Willis	14
A.R. Border	c Taylor, b Pringle	26		
D.W. Hookes	c Botham, b Hemmings	37		
R.W. Marsh*	c Hemmings, b Pringle	3		
B. Yardley	c Gower, b Botham	38		
R.M. Hogg	not out	14		
J.R. Thomson	c and b Botham	3		
Extras	lb 6, nb 18	24	nb 5	5
		438	(for 2 wickets)	83

	O	M	R	W	O	M	R	W
Willis	25	8	76	2	8	1	17	1
Botham	36.5	5	112	4	10	2	45	1
Pringle	33	5	97	2	1.5	—	11	—
Miller	14	2	33	—				
Hemmings	48	17	96	1	4	1	5	—

FALL OF WICKETS
1- 76, 2- 138, 3- 264, 4- 270, 5- 315, 6- 355, 7- 359, 8- 391, 9- 430
1- 3, 2- 37

ENGLAND

	FIRST INNINGS		SECOND INNINGS	
C.J. Tavare	c Marsh, b Hogg	1	c Wessels, b Thomson	0
G. Fowler	c Marsh, b Lawson	11	c Marsh, b Lawson	37
D.I. Gower	c Marsh, b Lawson	60	b Hogg	114
A.J. Lamb	c Marsh, b Lawson	82	c Chappell, b Yardley	8
I.T. Botham	c Wessels, b Thomson	35	c Dyson, b Yardley	58
D.W. Randall	b Lawson	0	c Marsh, b Lawson	17
G. Miller	c Yardley, b Hogg	7	lbw, b Lawson	17
R.W. Taylor*	c Chappell, b Yardley	2	(9) not out	3
D.R. Pringle	not out	1	(8) c Marsh, b Thomson	9
E.E. Hemmings	b Thomson	0	c Wessels, b Lawson	0
R.G.D. Willis†	b Thomson	1	c Marsh, b Lawson	10
Extras	lb 5, nb 11	16	b 7, lb 6, w 3, nb 15	31
		216		304

	O	M	R	W	O	M	R	W
Lawson	18	4	56	4	24	6	66	5
Hogg	14	2	41	2	19	5	53	1
Thomson	14.5	3	51	3	13	3	41	2
Yardley	21	7	52	1	37	12	90	2
Border					8	2	14	—
Hookes					3	1	9	—

FALL OF WICKETS
1- 1, 2- 21, 3- 140, 4- 181, 5- 181, 6- 194, 7- 199, 8- 213, 9- 213
1- 11, 2- 90, 3- 118, 4- 236, 5- 247, 6- 272, 7- 277, 8- 289, 9- 290

Umpires: R.A. French & M.W. Johnson

Australia won by 8 wickets

The Adelaide Oval. The beautiful setting of the third Test match. (Adrian Murrell)

Fowler failed to add to his overnight score and edged Lawson to Marsh. Lawson's accuracy, speed and hostility were making him the most feared of England's opponents. Lamb's stay was brief, but Botham joined Gower in a stand of sense and responsibility.

Gower batted beautifully, stroking the ball with languid charm and hooking, pulling and driving with such perfect timing as to surprise the field by the power with which the ball was hit. His 114 was his fifth Test hundred and lasted 370 minutes, a monument of concentration, but his sixteen fours testify as to his willingness to score runs when the opportunity presented itself.

Ten minutes before tea, Botham, who had batted with great restraint, was caught in two minds by Yardley as he tried to cut and he gave a simple catch to cover. His innings had lasted nearly three hours and his end signalled another horrendous England collapse. Their last six wickets went down for 68 runs.

The second new ball was the undoing. Gower played tiredly at a ball from Hogg and dragged it on to his stumps. Randall chased a very wide delivery to give Marsh a catch.

Miller was lbw to a shooter and Pringle was taken down the leg side. Hemmings was out for a 'pair' when he was caught at short leg, and Willis edged outside the off stump. Once more Lawson had been the principal cause of England's disintegration.

Needing only 83 to win, Australia lost Wessels before the close and nightwatchman Lawson the next morning, but it mattered little for the match was long since theirs and 6,000 people came to attend England's last rites on the final morning.

16 December 1982

at Sydney

New South Wales 239 for 8 (T.M. Chappell 89)
New Zealanders 223 for 7 (J.F.M. Morrison 63)

New South Wales won by 16 runs

A second wicket stand of 132 between Dyson and Trevor Chappell after McCosker had been bowled by Robertson on the first ball of the match set New South Wales on the way to victory in a fifty over match. New Zealand batted well under floodlights after losing Martin Crowe for 1. Morrison hit 63 in 80 minutes, but the tourists could never maintain the necessary scoring rate. 36 wides were called in the match, one of which, against Pascoe, caused the bowler to clash with the umpire, Michael Jay, so that the skipper had to intervene.

18, 19, 20 and 21 December 1982

at Bundaberg

Queensland 403 for 3 dec (K.C. Wessels 129, A.R. Border 104, R.B. Kerr 102) and 258 (R.B. Phillips 61)
New Zealanders 304 (G.P. Howarth 138, J.F.M. Morrison 62, C.G. Rackemann 5 for 47) and 221 for 7 (J.F.M Morrison 78 not out)

Match drawn

A run feast on the opening day saw Wessels score his fourth century of the season as he and Kerr put on 232 for the first wicket. Border gained much needed encouragement when he reached his hundred on the second morning, but New Zealand fought back strongly and Geoff Howarth played splendidly after 3 wickets had fallen for 52. He and Morrison added 122 for the fifth wicket.

Queensland went for quick runs in their second innings and looked as if they would force victory when Carl Rackemann again met with early success. New Zealanders were 67 for 4, but Reid and Morrison thwarted the Queensland attack.

This was the last of the New Zealander's four matches in the pre-Christmas tour. The object of the tour was to enable some of the less experienced to get a taste of competitive cricket in another country. Of the thirteen players on this trip, Robertson, B.R. Blair, Carrington, M.D. Crowe and Reid did not return with the full strength New Zealand party in January. Turner, Hadlee and Wright were among those not on the pre-Christmas tour.

18, 19 and 20 December 1982

at Hobart

Tasmania 273 (S.J. Reid 79, S.L. Saunders 53, G. Miller 4 for 63) and 131 for 5 dec (D.A. Smith 52 not out)
England XI 141 for 1 dec (G. Cook 73 not out, G. Fowler 63) and 264 for 4 (D.W. Randall 90 not out, G. Fowler 66, D.I. Gower 50 not out)

England XI won by 6 wickets

A dreadful day's cricket in windy conditions saw Tasmania score 187 for 6 in 6 hours off 92 overs on the Saturday, but Saunders hit more positively on the second morning. Reid faced 225 balls for his 79.

Fowler and Cook opened with 141 in 173 minutes, and Gower declared as soon as Fowler was caught off Clough.

Tasmania batted for two hours in the second innings, mostly against the bowling of Cook and Fowler who each took two wickets, and England were set to make 264 off 60 overs.

Tavare managed only 1 in 45 minutes, but Fowler hit 66 in 84 minutes with two sixes and nine fours. Randall and Gower then joined in an unbeaten fifth wicket stand of 99 in 73 minutes. Gower's 50 came off 43 deliveries and he hit a six and four fours.

22 December 1982

at Launceston

Tasmania 112
England XI 113 for 6 (I.T. Botham 56)

England XI won by 4 wickets

At the end of the third Test the morale of the England side had been low as heavy criticism of selection and performance was showered upon them. The positive approach to the match in Hobart, and the way in which victory was achieved, had certainly lightened the gloom which made the events at Launceston all the more distressing.

This fifty-over game was England's last match outside Tests and one-day internationals and it was played on an indifferent pitch where the ball lifted menacingly. An accurate spell by Jackman, who took three wickets, blunted the start of the Tasmanian innings and Marks took three wickets at the end. Holding hit two sixes and a four off Miller to give the Tasmanian score a much needed late boost.

The game was played under the rules which were to attend the Benson and Hedges World Series so that a new ball was allowed for each innings. A hard, shiny ball and a rough pitch were all the encouragement that Holding needed to bowl more quickly than he had done in Hobart. He dismissed Cook and Tavare again failed, caught behind off Holding, so that he had scored only 3 runs in his last 4 innings. 2 for 2, and one run later Randall was hit in the face from a rearing delivery by Holding. Wearing a helmet, but not a visor, Randall suffered facial injuries which were to keep him out of the fourth Test.

Not surprisingly, few of the English batsmen were at ease, but Botham and Gould thrived when Holding was withdrawn and added 71. Botham hit ten fours and a six in his fifty and his innings lasted only 44 balls. Both he and Gould were out, but England won a game which they came very close to losing.

It was announced that Trevor Jesty would be flying out to join the England party in view of the injury problems that they were suffering.

FOURTH TEST MATCH: AUSTRALIA v. ENGLAND

Not surprisingly, Australia were unchanged. For England, Cook replaced the injured Randall and Cowans returned for Hemmings. Consistent to a pattern established in the series, Chappell asked England to bat when he won the toss. He was quickly rewarded.

Fowler batted uneasily for twenty-five minutes before being caught at slip, a fate which Cook suffered an hour later. Gower was caught behind when he played back to Hogg shortly after lunch and England were 56 for 3. There was now a transformation to the England innings. Tavare drove and pulled with a certainty and power which he had shown at no other time on the tour. Lamb matched him in shots and runs and in 115 minutes before tea the pair put on 127 exciting runs.

The stand had become worth 161 in 147 minutes when Tavare swung unnecessarily at a wide ball from Thomson and was splendidly caught high to his left by Yardley in the

Melbourne. Fourth Test match. More than 64,000 people watched the first day's play. (Adrian Murrell)

gully. Tavare had hit fifteen fours and batted for just over 4 hours. He has not played better in a Test match.

Lamb had batted just over two and a half hours and hit thirteen fours when, ten runs after Tavare's dismissal, he swung Yardley to Dyson at deep mid-wicket. Sadly, the good work of Lamb and Tavare was now frittered away. The innings fell apart before the combined assault of Yardley's spin and Hogg's pace. The last seven wickets fell for 67 runs. It was a sad, and familiar story.

On the second morning Wessels and Dyson began steadily enough for Australia, but there was encouragement for England and Cowans when the West Indian was introduced into the attack with the ball only six overs old. Willis appeared to handle the bowler better than he had done in the second Test, and for England there was an exciting repayment.

Dyson had just slashed Cowans through the slips for four, but he was beaten for pace next ball and was lbw. Two men were posted deep for the hook when Chappell came in and he obliged by hooking the first ball high to Lamb, the squarer of the two. 55 for 2, Chappell on first ball. It was the tonic that England needed.

Willis squeezed the ball past Wessels' defence and, in the first over after lunch, Botham bowled the unhappy Border with an inswinger. 89 for 4, and for the first time in the series the advantage was with England.

Hughes had been fortunate to survive an lbw appeal from Botham, and Hookes had an equal stroke of fortune, but with a mixture of restraint from Hughes and belligerence from Hookes, they added 91 and Australia looked healthier.

HO B RUN FOW		RUN WKT		

DYSON	1	1	FOWLER
WESSELS	2	2	COOK
CHAPPELL	3	3	TAVARE
HUGHES	4	4	GOWER
BORDER	5	5	LAMB
HOOKES	6	6	BOTHAM
YARDLEY	7	7	MILLER
LAWSON	8	8	PRINGLE
HOGG	9	9	WILLIS
THOMSON	10	10	COWANS
MARSH	11	11	TAYLOR
WOOD	12	12	HEMMINGS

BENSON and HEDGES
When only the best will do.

2:19

SEIKO · MITSUBISHI ELECTRIC · SEIKO

Test cricket in the computer age. The new video scoreboard at Melbourne. (Patrick Eagar)

Hookes scored 53 off 69 balls before falling to Pringle whose introduction into the attack had been delayed. Marsh now joined Hughes in a stand of 81 and then Hughes whose innings had been nearly a quarter of an hour longer than Tavare's played on to Willis.

Marsh hit Miller for three fours in one over and was then bowled behind his legs by Willis. Miller was too accurate for the tail end, and with the last five wickets having fallen for 26 runs, Australia were out for 287 and England had achieved parity.

England began the third day in positive mood. Cook was more assured than in any previous Test innings and although it took Fowler 40 minutes and 34 deliveries to open his score, they put on 40 for the first wicket in under the hour. When Thomson came on Cook cut him for four, but next ball he was brilliantly caught in the gully inches from the ground by Yardley.

Tavare played forward half-heartedly to Hogg and was bowled. Gower flicked at Lawson on the leg side and was given out caught behind to his obvious displeasure. 45 for 3, and England's hopes sinking very quickly.

Fowler now played better than at any time on the tour. He attacked Yardley and when he hit him for three fours in one over he had passed fifty from 77 deliveries. Hit on the foot by a ball from Thomson, he needed both treatment and a runner. The delay and confusion over Gower coming out to act as runner broke concentration and both Fowler and Lamb were out in Hogg's next over. It was later revealed that Fowler had broken his right big toe in two places.

At 160, Miller was given lbw when he played back, but again he looked to have been unlucky in the decision. Botham mixed caution and extravagance, but while he lived, England hoped. Pringle proved an admirable partner. Like Fowler, he played his best innings of the tour. 193 for 6 at tea.

Botham appeared to be growing in belligerence and then he slashed wildly at Thomson and was caught at first slip. 201 for 7, and Australia now very much on top. But the England tail did not crumble. Taylor and Pringle concentrated initially on survival and then moved into the attack. After nearly an hour and a half 61 invaluable runs had been added before Taylor, turning his back on a lifter from Thomson, was given out lbw.

Pringle became Marsh's twenty-seventh victim of the series, a Test record for a wicket-keeper, but the last two wickets added 32 and Australia had two days in which to score 292 to win. On a wicket which was wearing and where the ball was coming through low, this was not an easy task.

Dyson began well, but Wessels, looking out of touch, was bowled off his pads by Cowans. Chappell was missed first ball by Cook, played uneasily and then tried to force Cowans through the off side only to be caught low down by the diving Gould who was fielding as substitute for Fowler. Dyson was taken at second slip, but Hughes and Hookes once more thwarted England.

Hookes had considerable good fortune. He was missed off successive half-chances when Miller was bowling and he received the benefit of the doubt when England thought he was lbw and caught behind. He responded by taking 15 off Willis in one over. Hughes and Hookes added 100 and then

ABOVE: *Miller is caught by Border off Yardley. The ball rebounded from Marsh's gloves. (Adrian Murrell)*

BELOW: *Hughes escapes in his first innings of 66. He edges Cowans, but Tavare just fails to make the catch. (Philip Tyson)*

ABOVE: *Botham is comfortably taken by Chappell off Thomson for 46. (Philip Tyson)*
BELOW: *Lawson leaps in appeal as he traps Miller l.b.w. (Philip Tyson)*

BELOW: *The tension of the final morning. Lamb and substitute Gould collide and Thomson escapes for a single when he should have been run out. (Adrian Murrell)*

LEFT: *An historical catch. Miller darts behind Tavare to catch Thomson off Botham and England have won by 3 runs. (Patrick Eagar)*

Allan Border is played back in to form and comes close to giving Australia an improbable victory. (Adrian Murrell)

Hughes was spectacularly caught by Taylor and Hookes was caught off a skier when he swung across the line at Cowans. Cowans, bowling with fire and fury, had Marsh and Yardley in the same over, and then he caught Lawson at long leg off Pringle. Bowling again, he had Hogg lbw. It was his day, six wickets for 69 and full of passion. 218 for 9 when Thomson joined Border who had been anonymous, and the game was as good as over.

Border had taken 40 minutes to get off the mark. He had been relegated to number six because he had lost form and confidence. Willis now produced a most extraordinary piece of captaincy. He set a totally defensive field for Border, pushing men right back on the boundary and allowing Border a single when he wanted it so that he could attack Thomson. The plan failed dreadfully. Border gained the upper hand and in the last forty-five minutes of the day – there was a brief stoppage for rain – 37 runs were added and Australia still had a chance of victory.

Willis continued with his tactics on the last morning when an estimated 20,000 people were admitted free to see 85 of the most dramatic minutes in Test history. Border pushed the ball and ran two where there should have been no single. Gould and Lamb collided in excitement when one, or both batsmen should have been run out, and Border and Thom-

FOURTH TEST MATCH – AUSTRALIA v. ENGLAND
26, 27, 28, 29, 30 December 1982 at Melbourne

ENGLAND

	FIRST INNINGS		SECOND INNINGS	
G. Cook	c Chappell, b Thomson	10	c Yardley, b Thomson	26
G. Fowler	c Chappell, b Hogg	4	b Hogg	65
C.J. Tavare	c Yardley, b Thomson	89	b Hogg	0
D.I. Gower	c Marsh, b Hogg	18	c Marsh, b Lawson	3
A.J. Lamb	c Dyson, b Yardley	83	c Marsh, b Hogg	26
I.T. Botham	c Wessels, b Yardley	27	c Chappel, b Thomson	46
G. Miller	c Border, b Yardley	10	lbw, b Lawson	14
D.R. Pringle	c Wessels, b Hogg	9	c Marsh, b Lawson	42
R.W. Taylor*	c Marsh, b Yardley	1	lbw, b Thomson	37
R.G.D. Willis†	not out	6	not out	8
N.G. Cowans	c Lawson, b Hogg	3	b Lawson	10
Extras	b 3, lb 6, w 3, nb 12	24	b 1, lb 9, nb 7	17
		284		**294**

	O	M	R	W	O	M	R	W
Lawson	17	6	48	—	21.4	6	66	4
Hogg	23.3	6	69	4	22	5	64	3
Yardley	27	9	89	4	15	2	67	—
Thomson	13	2	49	2	21	3	74	3
Chappell	1	—	5	—	1	—	6	—

FALL OF WICKETS
1- 11, 2- 25, 3- 56, 4- 217, 5- 227, 6- 259, 7- 262, 8- 268, 9- 278
1- 40, 2- 41, 3- 45, 4- 128, 5- 129, 6- 160, 7- 201, 8- 262, 9- 280

AUSTRALIA

	FIRST INNINGS		SECOND INNINGS	
K.C. Wessels	b Willis	47	(2) b Cowans	14
J. Dyson	lbw, b Cowans	21	(1) c Tavare, b Botham	31
G.S. Chappell†	c Lamb, b Cowans	0	c sub (Gould), b Cowans	2
K.J. Hughes	b Willis	66	c Taylor, b Miller	48
A.R. Border	b Botham	2	(6) not out	62
D.W. Hookes	c Taylor, b Pringle	53	(5) c Willis, b Cowans	68
R.W. Marsh*	b Willis	53	lbw, b Cowans	13
B. Yardley	b Miller	9	b Cowans	0
G.F. Lawson	c Fowler, b Miller	0	c Cowans, b Pringle	7
R.M. Hogg	not out	8	lbw, b Cowans	4
J.R. Thomson	b Miller	1	c Miller, b Botham	21
Extras	lb 8, nb 19	27	b 5, lb 9, w 1, nb 3	18
		287		**288**

	O	M	R	W	O	M	R	W
Willis	15	2	38	3	17	—	57	—
Botham	18	3	69	1	25.1	4	80	2
Cowans	16	—	69	2	26	6	77	6
Pringle	15	2	40	1	12	4	26	1
Miller	15	5	44	3	16	6	30	1

FALL OF WICKETS
1- 55, 2- 55, 3- 83, 4- 89, 5- 180, 6- 261, 7- 276, 8- 276, 9- 278
1- 37, 2- 39, 3- 71, 4- 171, 5- 173, 6- 190, 7- 190, 8- 202, 9- 218

Umpires: A.R. Crafter & R.V. Whitehead

England won by 3 runs

son seemed to have gained an historical victory for Australia when Botham began an over to Thomson with the home side needing only 4 for victory.

The first ball was short and swinging away. Thomson followed it and it flew off the edge of his bat straight into the hands of Tavare at second slip. And it bounced out again. But there was Miller running behind Tavare from first slip and catching the dropping ball. It was Miller's first catch of the series. It was the first time since 1902 that a side had won an England – Australia Test by a margin as small as three runs. And there had not been a Test before that with so close a margin.

What almost passed unnoticed as the crowds clamoured at the end of this glorious match which had kept alive England's very faint hopes of retaining the 'Ashes' was that when Botham had Thomson caught by Miller it was his hundredth wicket against Australia and that in his twenty-second Test against them, he had accomplished the fastest 'double' in the history of these matches.

LEFT: *To the victor the spoils. Man of the Match Cowans with treasured trophies.* (*Adrian Murrell*)

BELOW: *The controversial decision. Willis has thrown down the wicket and Dyson is given not out in the first over of the match.* (*Patrick Eagar*)

FIFTH TEST MATCH: AUSTRALIA v. ENGLAND

The euphoria that attended England's victory at Melbourne tended to obscure both the weaknesses in the side and the fact that England came close to losing a match that they should have won with ease. Nevertheless, in a series in which they had been outplayed for much of the time, England found themselves 1–2 down with one match remaining, a position far healthier than had looked possible a few weeks earlier.

An unchanged Australia won the toss and broke the tradition of the series by batting first. England had Randall back for the injured Fowler and Hemmings in for Pringle.

The first day was marred by rain and controversial umpiring decisions. Dyson seemed to have been run out by two feet in the opening over when Willis threw down the stumps, but he was given not out and was there at the end of the day when Australia were 138 for 2. Chappell was given out lbw to a doubtful appeal having earlier survived two confident ones and a dropped catch.

RIGHT: *Randall. Glorious determination until the last. (Adrian Murrell)*

BELOW: *An England hero. Eddie Hemmings during his innings of 95. A brave and resourceful cricketer. (Patrick Eagar)*

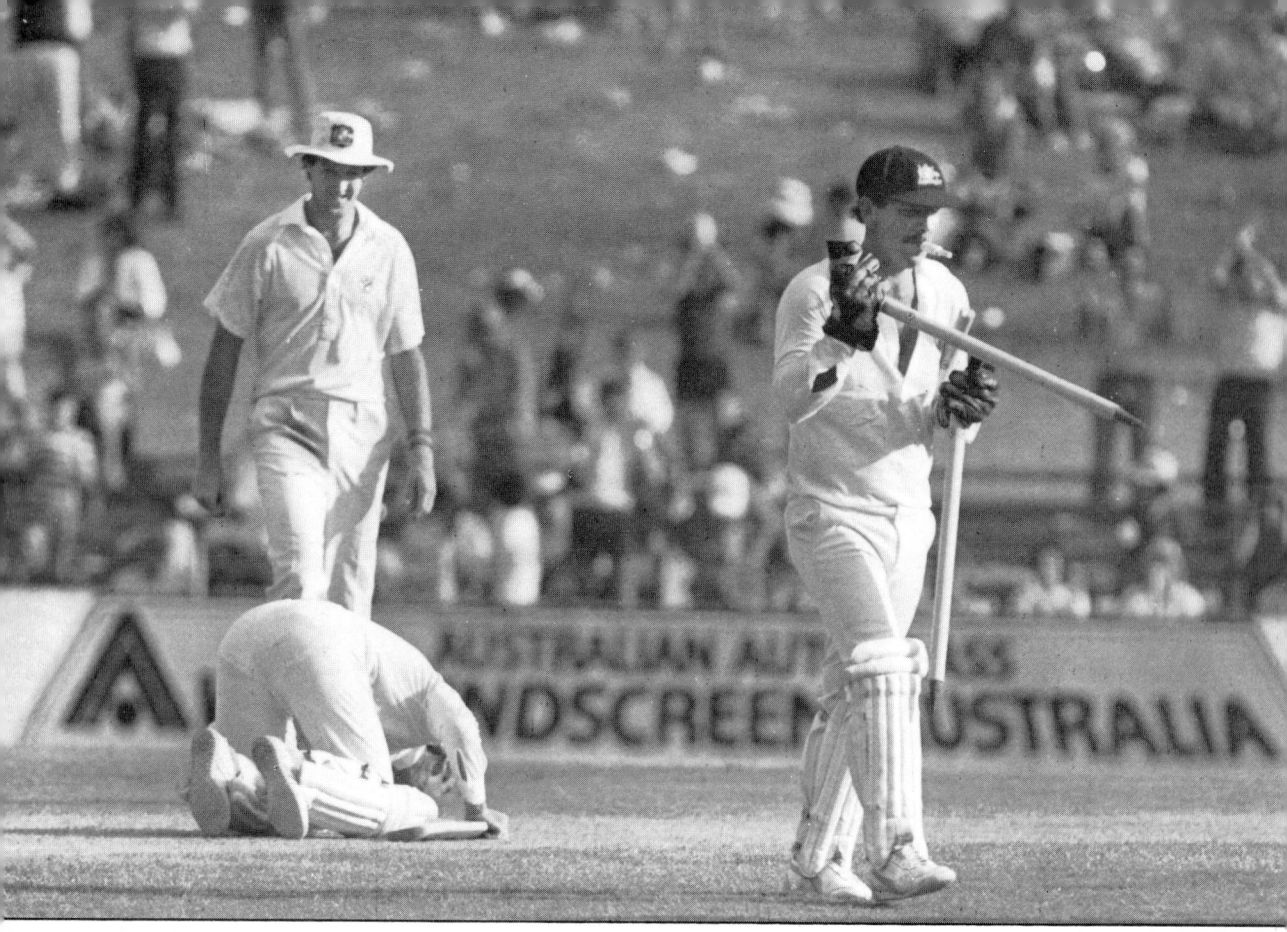

The last rites of a series. Rodney Marsh walks off with his trophies. Bob Taylor kisses the ground at Sydney. It was almost certainly the last Test match that he will play in Australia. (Patrick Eagar)

On the second day, the pitch gave a little encouragement to spin, but neither Miller nor Hemmings bowled well enough to exploit it. Chances were missed and Border, played back into form by England's tactics in the previous Test, held the side together when they threatened to disintegrate at 219 for 6. Yardley was confronted by spin when pace would have troubled him more – on his recall, Cowans bowled him in his second over – and Australia were out for 314 which, with time running out, made England's task difficult.

It became more difficult when Tavare played a grotesque shot and was bowled by Lawson, Cook gave first slip catching practice and Lamb played no stroke at an inslanted delivery from Lawson and was bowled. After seven overs England were 24 for 3. Three leading batsmen had been out to atrocious shots and misjudgement and the 'Ashes' were disappearing fast. Gower and Randall hung on bravely, and the next day they extended their stand to 122, the last 70 coming off 14 overs. Randall was particularly exhilarating, but he got all tangled up to Thomson and played on for a fine 70 which was made off only 90 deliveries.

Botham was very disappointing. He was dropped and then caught in the gully, and Gower, on what would have been the penultimate ball of the morning, drove flat-footed at a wide ball from Lawson and was caught breathtakingly by Chappell, the only slip.

169 for 6 at lunch with Taylor going shortly after to Thomson who had enjoyed another period of rejuvenation, England's faint hopes had been extinguished.

Miller and Hemmings were responsible for the score getting as high as 237.

England took two good catches to have Australia at 90 for 3 at the close and when Miller had Hookes lbw early on the fourth morning it seemed that the spinners might grasp the opportunity that had been given them. They did not. Not another wicket fell before tea and Hemmings and Miller were bitterly disappointing as Hughes and Border cut loose with a fine display of driving. Hemmings might have suffered less had he bowled round the wicket.

Border hit nine fours in an innings which lasted two and three quarter hours, and Hughes, who was at his thrilling best, hit three sixes and twelve fours in his hundredth Test innings which lasted for six and a quarter hours. Marsh hit lustily and England, needing 460 to win, had three overs before the close which was time enough to lose Cook.

The last day was one of those fading days of last rites for the series. Hemmings played a splendid knock and it was sad that this enthusiastic cricketer was denied the century which his courage had earned him. He hit six fours and batted for under four hours.

Yardley bowled for most of the day and Australia came closest to victory until Miller and Taylor got together at 261 for 7.

The 'Ashes' were back with Australia. Deservedly so.

FIFTH TEST MATCH – AUSTRALIA v. ENGLAND

2, 3, 4, 6 and 7 January 1983 at Sydney

AUSTRALIA

	FIRST INNINGS			SECOND INNINGS	
K.C. Wessels	c Willis, b Botham	19	(2) lbw, b Botham		53
J. Dyson	c Taylor, b Hemmings	79	(1) c Gower, b Willis		2
G.S. Chappell†	lbw, b Willis	35	c Randall, b Hemmings		11
K.J. Hughes	c Cowans, b Botham	29	c Botham, b Hemmings		137
D.W. Hookes	c Botham, b Hemmings	17	lbw, b Miller		19
A.R. Border	c Miller, b Hemmings	89	c Botham, b Cowans		83
R.W. Marsh*	c and b Miller	3	c Taylor, b Miller		41
B. Yardley	b Cowans	24	c Botham, b Hemmings		0
G.F. Lawson	c and b Botham	6	not out		13
J.R. Thomson	c Lamb, b Botham	0	c Gower, b Miller		12
R.M. Hogg	not out	0	run out		0
Extras	b 3, lb 8, w 2	13	lb 7, nb 4		11
		314			**382**

	O	M	R	W	O	M	R	W
Willis	20	6	57	1	10	2	33	1
Cowans	21	3	67	1	13	1	47	1
Botham	30	8	75	4	10	—	35	1
Hemmings	27	10	68	3	47	16	116	3
Miller	17	7	34	1	49.3	12	133	3
Cook					2	1	7	—

FALL OF WICKETS
1- 39, 2- 96, 3- 150, 4- 173, 5- 210, 6- 219, 7- 262, 8- 283, 9- 291
1- 23, 2- 38, 3- 82, 4- 113, 5- 262, 6- 350, 7- 357, 8- 358, 9- 382

ENGLAND

	FIRST INNINGS			SECOND INNINGS	
G. Cook	c Chappell, b Hogg	8	lbw, b Lawson		2
C.J. Tavare	b Lawson	0	lbw, b Yardley		16
D.I. Gower	c Chappell, b Lawson	70	(4) c Hookes, b Yardley		24
A.J. Lamb	b Lawson	0	(5) c and b Yardley		29
D.W. Randall	b Thomson	70	(6) b Thomson		44
I.T. Botham	c Wessels, b Thomson	5	(7) lbw, b Thomson		32
G. Miller	lbw, b Thomson	34	(8) not out		21
R.W. Taylor*	lbw, b Thomson	0	(9) not out		28
E.E. Hemmings	c Border, b Yardley	29	(3) c Marsh, b Yardley		95
R.G.D. Willis†	c Border, b Thomson	1			
N.G. Cowans	not out	0			
Extras	b 4, lb 3, nb 13	20	b 1, lb 10, w 1, nb 11		23
		237	(for 7 wickets)		**314**

	O	M	R	W	O	M	R	W
Lawson	20	2	70	3	15	1	50	1
Hogg	16	2	50	1	13	6	25	—
Thomson	14.5	2	50	5	12	3	30	2
Yardley	14	4	47	1	37	6	139	4
Border					16	3	36	—
Hookes					2	1	5	—
Chappell					1	—	6	—

FALL OF WICKETS
1- 8, 2- 23, 3- 24, 4- 146, 5- 163, 6- 169, 7- 170, 8- 220, 9- 232
1- 3, 2- 55, 3- 104, 4- 155, 5- 196, 6- 260, 7- 261

Umpires: M.W. Johnson & R.A. French

Match drawn

Australia v. England – Test Match Averages

AUSTRALIA BATTING

	M	Inns	NOs	Runs	HS	Av	100s	50s
K.J. Hughes	5	8	1	469	137	67.00	1	3
D.W. Hookes	5	8	1	344	68	49.14		4
G.S. Chappell	5	10	2	389	117	48.62	2	1
K.C. Wessels	4	8		386	162	48.25	1	1
A.R. Border	5	9	2	317	89	45.28		2
J. Dyson	5	10	2	283	79	35.37		2
B. Yardley	5	7		141	53	20.14		1
R.W. Marsh	5	7		124	53	17.71		1
G.F. Lawson	5	8	1	98	50	14.00		1
R.M. Hogg	3	5	3	26	14*	13.00		
J.R. Thomson	5	7	1	42	21	8.40		

Played in one Test:- G M Wood 29 and O; D.K. Lillee 2*; C.G. Rackemann 4; T.M. Alderman did not bat

ENGLAND BATTING

	M	Inns	NOs	Runs	HS	Av	100s	50s
D.W. Randall	4	8		365	115	45.62	1	2
D.I. Gower	5	10		441	114	44.10	1	3
A.J. Lamb	5	10		414	82	41.40		4
G. Fowler	3	6		207	83	34.50		2
E.E. Hemmings	3	6	1	157	95	31.40		1
I.T. Botham	5	10		270	58	27.00		1
D.R. Pringle	3	6	2	108	47*	27.00		
C.J. Tavare	5	10		218	89	21.80		2
G. Miller	5	10	1	193	60	21.44		1
R.W. Taylor	5	10	3	135	37	19.28		
N.G. Cowans	4	7	1	68	36	11.33		
R.G.D. Willis	5	9	3	63	26	10.50		
G. Cook	3	6		54	26	9.00		

AUSTRALIA BOWLING

	Overs	Mds	Runs	Wkts	Av	Best	5/inn
J.R. Thomson	127.4	22	411	22	18.68	5/50	2
G.F. Lawson	230.4	51	687	34	20.20	6/47	4
R.M. Hogg	107.3	26	302	11	27.45	4/69	
B. Yardley	292.2	91	793	22	36.04	5/107	1
G.S. Chappell	14.3	3	44	1	44.00	1/8	
D.W. Hookes	8	2	20	0	—		
A.R. Border	31	7	71	0	—		

Bowled in one Test: D.K. Lillee 71 - 25 - 185 - 4; T.M. Alderman 43 - 15 - 84 - 1; C.G. Rackemann 33.2 - 11 - 96 - 2

G.F. Lawson took eleven wickets in the second Test match.

ENGLAND BOWLING

	Overs	Mds	Runs	Wkts	Av	Best	5/inn
R.G.D. Willis	166.3	28	486	18	27.00	5/66	1
G. Miller	171	50	397	13	30.53	4/70	
N.G. Cowans	107	14	396	11	36.00	6/77	1
I.T. Botham	213.5	35	729	18	40.50	4/75	
E.E. Hemmings	188.3	59	409	9	45.44	3/68	
D.R. Pringle	73.5	12	214	4	53.50	2/97	
G. Cook	6	3	33	0	—		

Bowled in one Test: A.J. Lamb 1 - 1 - 0 - 0

AUSTRALIA CATCHES
28 - R.W. Marsh; 8 - G.S. Chappell and K.C. Wessels; 6 - B. Yardley; 4 - J. Dyson and A.R. Border; 3 - G.F. Lawson; 2 - K.J. Hughes and D.W. Hookes; 1 - G.M. Wood, D.K. Lillee, C.G. Rackemann and J.R. Thomson.

ENGLAND CATCHES
13 - R.W. Taylor; 9 - I.T. Botham; 5 - A.J. Lamb; 4 - D.I. Gower and R.G.D. Willis; 3 - D.W. Randall, N.G. Cowans and G. Miller; 2 - C.J. Tavare and E.E. Hemmings; 1 - G. Fowler, G. Cook and sub (I.J. Gould)

England Team in Australia 1982-3
First Class Matches

BATTING

BATTING	v. Queensland (Brisbane) 22-25 Oct. 1982		v. South Australia (Adelaide) 31 Oct.-3 Nov. 1982		v. Western Australia (Perth) 5-8 Nov. 1982		First Test Match (Perth) 12-17 Nov. 1982		v. New South Wales (Sydney) 20-23 Nov. 1982		Second Test Match (Brisbane) 26 Nov.-1 Dec. 1982		v. Victoria (Melbourne) 4-7 Dec. 1982		Third Test Match (Adelaide) 10-15 Dec. 1982		v. Tasmania (Hobart) 18-20 Dec. 1982		Fourth Test Match (Melbourne) 26-30 Dec. 1982		Fifth Test Match (Sydney) 2-7 January 1983	
G. Cook	0	39	58	5			1	7	99	77							73*	23	10	26	8	2
G. Fowler	9	0	10	12	14	2			12	14	7	83	5	31	11	37	63	66	4	65		
D. I. Gower	100	1			7	33	72	28	0	13	18	34	88	88	60	114	—	50*	4	3	70	24
A. J. Lamb	117	42	78	17	8	28	46	56			72	12	40	108	82	8			83	26	0	29
I. T. Botham	32	0	18	24	65	8	12	0			40	15	10	7	35	58			27	46	5	32
G. Miller	4	46	83	25*	39*	6	30	0			0	60	22	17*	7	17	—	30	10	14	34	21*
V. J. Marks	3	13							1	9			9	6			—	—				
D. R. Pringle	24	15*	16	9*	2	24	0	47*	1	1			0	7*	1*	9	—	—	9	42		
R. W. Taylor	37	9			2*	5*	29*	31			1	3			2	3*			1	37	0	28*
N. G. Cowans	0	1			0	1	4	36	0*	0	10	5			1	10			3	10	0*	
R. G. D. Willis	0*	0			1	1*	26	0			1	10*			1	10	—	—	6*	8*	1	
C. J. Tavare			29	38	0	0	89	9	3	147	1	13	18	35	1	0	—	1	89	0	0	16
D. W. Randall			31	47	14	92	78	115	11	48	37	4	30	4	0	17	—	90*			70	44
I. J. Gould			45	14					73	8			24	—								
E. E. Hemmings			60*	—					4	7*	15*	18			0	0					29	95
R. D. Jackman			50*	29					6	3			0*	—								
Byes	9	6	8	3			7	5	5	7	8		8	2		7	3	2	3	1	4	1
Leg-byes	20	8	6	2	3	4	9	11	13	4	2	8	3	2	5	6	2		6	9	3	10
Wides	1	2			1	4	2	2		2	1	1		1		3		1	3			1
No-balls	16	7			1	1	6	11	12	2	14	35	18	16	11	15			12	7	13	11
Total	372	189	492	226	156	209	411	358	240	342	219	309	275	324	216	304	141	264	284	294	237	314
Wickets	10	10	9	8	9†	1	10	10	10	10	10	10	10	7	10	10	1	4	10	10	10	7
Result	L		D		W		D		W		L		D		L		W		W		D	

Catches

18 — R. W. Taylor (ct 17/st 1) (includes one catch as sub.)	6 — G. Fowler, A. J. Lamb and D. R. Pringle
17 — I. T. Botham	5 — G. Miller, N. G. Cowans and V. J. Marks (including one as sub.)
11 — D. W. Randall	4 — G. Cook and C. J. Tavare
10 — I. J. Gould (ct 9/st 1) (includes one catch as sub.)	3 — E. E. Hemmings
9 — D. I. Gower	2 — R. D. Jackman
7 — R. G. D. Willis	

† G. Miller retired hurt

BOWLING

BOWLING	I. T. Botham	R. G. D. Willis	D. R. Pringle	N. G. Cowans	G. Miller	V. J. Marks	R. D. Jackman	E. E. Hemmings
v. Queensland (Brisbane) 22-25 October 1982	18-7-46-1 / 14-3-44-1	13-6-43-3 / 12-2-45-1	19-6-44-1 / 16-1-49-0	14-3-47-1 / 16-3-58-0	15-1-63-2 / 27-5-66-2	3-0-39-1 / 40-6-142-1		
v. South Australia (Adelaide) 31 Oct.-3 Nov. 1982	5-1-18-1 / 1-0-9-0		17-3-60-2 / 9-1-37-1		16-1-79-0		10-0-26-0 / 3-0-14-0	44.3-12-102-4 / 31-6-110-3
v. Western Australia (Perth) 5-8 November 1982	18-5-48-2 / 20-7-43-4	16.3-1-52-3 / 17-4-30-3	11-3-25-1 / 16-5-44-0	13-4-33-4 / 19.4-3-66-3				
First Test Match (Perth) 12-17 November 1982	40-10-121-2 / 6-1-17-0	31.5-4-95-3 / 6-1-23-2	10-1-37-0 / 2-0-3-0	13-2-54-0 / 3-1-15-0	33-11-70-4 / 4-3-8-0			
v. New South Wales (Sydney) 20-23 Nov. 1982			17-1-61-2 / 14.1-1-38-2	15-2-44-3 / 11-3-29-2		9-2-22-0 / 26-7-86-1	17-5-37-2 / 14-3-38-0	28-4-67-2 / 31-3-101-5
Second Test Match (Brisbane) 26 Nov.-1 Dec. 1982	22-1-105-3 / 15.5-1-70-0	29.4-3-66-5 / 4-1-24-0		6-0-36-0 / 9-1-31-1	19.3-4-35-1 / 3-0-10-0			31.3-6-81-0 / 29-9-43-2
v. Victoria (Melbourne) 4-7 December 1982	22.5-4-78-2 / 7-1-18-0		21-4-66-4 / 13-3-33-1		28-15-35-3 / 20-6-36-3	8-3-22-0 / 13-4-29-0	21-4-70-1 / 0.5-0-1-0	
Third Test Match (Adelaide) 10-15 Dec. 1982	36.5-5-112-4 / 10-2-45-1	25-8-76-2 / 8-1-17-1	33-5-97-2 / 1.5-0-11-0		14-2-33-0			48-17-96-1 / 4-1-5-0
v. Tasmania (Hobart) 18-20 December 1982			29.3-9-58-3 / 7-4-10-1	24-6-55-2 / 4-0-17-0	39-16-63-4 / 9-2-22-0	8-4-11-0	20-3-75-0 / 3-0-11-0	
Fourth Test Match (Melbourne) 26-30 Dec. 1982	18-3-69-1 / 25.1-4-80-2	15-2-38-3 / 17-0-57-0	15-2-40-1 / 12-4-26-1	16-0-69-2 / 26-6-77-6	15-4-44-3 / 16-6-30-1			
Fifth Test Match (Sydney) 2-7 January 1983	30-8-75-4 / 10-0-35-1	20-6-57-1 / 10-2-33-1		21-3-67-1 / 13-1-47-1	17-7-34-1 / 49.3-12-133-3			27-10-68-3 / 47-16-116-3
Totals	319.4-63-1033-29 av. 35.62	225-41-656-28 av. 23.42	263.3-53-739-22 av. 33.59	223.4-38-745-26 av. 28.65	325-95-761-27 av. 28.18	107-26-351-3 av. 117.00	88.5-15-272-3 av. 90.66	323-84-789-23 av. 34.30

	Inns	NOs	Runs	HS	Av
	14	1	428	99	32.92
	18	—	445	83	24.72
	19	1	821	114	45.61
	18	—	852	117	47.33
	18	—	434	65	24.11
	19	4	465	83	31.00
	6	—	41	13	6.83
	16	5	207	47*	18.81
	14	5	188	37	20.88
	13	2	70	36	6.36
	13	5	65	26	8.12
	19	—	489	147	25.73
	17	1	732	115	45.75
	5	—	164	73	32.80
	9	3	228	95	38.00
	5	2	88	50*	29.33

G. Cook	A. J. Lamb	G. Fowler	Byes	Leg-byes	Wides	No-balls	Total	Wkts
			3	1		11	297	9
			4	7	1	19	435	5
17–4–47–3			4	4		4	344	10
25–4–85–3			8	6	1	1	271	8
			1	5		3	167	10
			5	1		8	197	10
4–2–16–0			4	1	1	25	424	9
	1–1–0–0			1		6	73	2
				7		12	250	9
				10		4	306	10
			2	8		8	341	10
			2	5		5	190	3
			8	5		11	295	10
			3	1		1	122	4
				6		18	438	10
						5	83	2
			5	2		4	273	10
8–1–23–2		6–0–43–2	1	3		1	131	5
				8		19	287	10
			5	9	1	3	288	10
			3	8		2	314	10
				7		4	382	10
56–12–	1–1–	6–0–43–2						
178–8	0–0	av. 21.50						
av. 22.25	—							

7 January 1983

at Geelong

New Zealanders 292 (R.J. Hadlee 117, J.G. Wright 62)
Geelong 193 for 5 (C. Lynch 54)

New Zealanders won by 99 runs

In this 50-over warm up game the New Zealanders rallied from 130 for 6 thanks to Richard Hadlee's splendid hitting.

Benson & Hedges World Series

FIRST ONE-DAY INTERNATIONAL: AUSTRALIA v. NEW ZEALAND

A crowd of 45,137 watched the first of the Benson and Hedges World Series matches and saw Australia win with ease.

New Zealand were given a good start by Edgar and Wright who put on 84 in 16 overs, but the rest of the innings subsided quietly until Hadlee made a typical late flourish. Rackemann, replacing Yardley, was the most successful of the Australian bowlers.

Kim Hughes takes over as Australia's captain. When the Test series finished Greg Chappell asked to be relieved of the captaincy. (Adrian Murrell)

FIRST ONE-DAY INTERNATIONAL: AUSTRALIA v. NEW ZEALAND
9 January 1983 at Melbourne

NEW ZEALAND					AUSTRALIA			
J.G. Wright	c Dyson, b Rackemann	54			K.C. Wessels	b Snedden		79
B.A. Edgar	lbw, b Rackemann	38			J. Dyson	not out		78
G.P. Howarth†	c and b Rackemann	5			G.S. Chappell	c and b Snedden		3
J.J. Crowe	c Lawson, b Chappell	7			K.J. Hughes†	not out		7
J.V. Coney	c Marsh, b Rackemann	4			D.W. Hookes			
J.F.M. Morrison	c Marsh, b Thomson	10			A.R. Border			
P.N. Webb*	b Lawson	9			R.W. Marsh*			
R.J. Hadlee	run out	24			G.F. Lawson			
B.L. Cairns	c Hookes, b Lawson	7			R.M. Hogg			
M.C. Snedden	c Marsh, b Hogg	2			J.R. Thomson			
E.J. Chatfield	not out	0			C.G. Rackemann			
Extras	lb 9, w 7, nb 5	21			Extras	b 1, lb 11, w 3		15
(44.5 overs)		181			(46.4 overs)	(for 2 wickets)		182

	O	M	R	W			O	M	R	W
Lawson	7.5	1	28	2		Hadlee	9.4	2	36	—
Thomson	9	1	39	1		Chatfield	10	4	18	—
Hogg	8	—	32	1		Snedden	10	1	47	2
Rackemann	10	1	39	4		Cairns	8	1	30	—
Chappell	10	1	22	1		Coney	9	1	36	—

FALL OF WICKETS
1- 84, 2- 89, 3- 98, 4- 114, 5- 128, 6- 134, 7- 167, 8- 173, 9- 181

FALL OF WICKETS
1- 154, 2- 168

Australia won by 8 wickets

Hughes had replaced Chappell as Australia's captain and he asked New Zealand to bat first. Wessels and Dyson had a few uneasy moments against Hadlee, but they settled to put on 154 for the first wicket and decide the match. Dyson took the individual award.

New Zealand were handicapped by the absence of the injured Turner.

Benson and Hedges World Series

SECOND ONE-DAY INTERNATIONAL: AUSTRALIA v. ENGLAND

Another crowd of well over 40,000 saw England, poised for victory, throw away their chances with some limp middle order batting.

Marks and Jesty came into the England side, Jesty playing his first game since arriving in Australia, and Willis chose to field when he won the toss.

Botham alone of the England bowlers failed to contain the Australian batsmen. Marks and Miller bowled imaginatively. Marks, in particular, flighted the ball intelligently and troubled the batsmen. Jesty, too, bowled promisingly. He began with two prodigious wides, but then he pitched his away swinger right and Hughes fell for the bait. Hookes should have gone the same over, but Botham missed the hard chance.

Lawson raised Australian hearts with some good hitting, but 180 was not a good score.

Gower, pushed in to opening, played lazily and Tavare took ten overs to score 6, but Thomson was all over the place and it seemed that England must win in wides. Australia were plainly irritable, and so were the crowd.

Randall went at 53, but Lamb and Botham added 42 in ten overs before Botham was bowled playing back. Jesty played confidently and benefited when Dyson, blinded by the floodlights, dropped a dolly catch.

At 131 for 4, England were cruising to victory, then Thomson bowled Lamb, Jesty was insanely run out as soon as Miller arrived, and the last six wickets went down for 18 runs. It was a nightmare.

Benson and Hedges World Series

THIRD ONE-DAY INTERNATIONAL: ENGLAND v. NEW ZEALAND

England very much needed to win this match, but they lost in the most dramatic circumstances and after the first round of matches they were left pointless at the bottom of the table.

An opening stand of 87 in 25 overs again set New Zealand on the way to a good score and this time the middle order consolidated the position that Wright and Edgar had given them. Turner, playing for New Zealand for the first time in four years, hit 38 and Cairns lashed 36 in 4 overs. England fielded badly and bowled indifferently.

Tavare, Lamb and Jesty all failed to find their touch and when Jesty was out, 25 overs had gone and 92 runs had been scored so that a scoring rate of nearly six an over was needed in the second half of the innings.

Gower and Botham responded to the task with a stand of 98 in 15 overs. Gower was at his beautiful best and England were heading for victory. Botham was a little too adventurous and England needed 50 off the last 10 overs. When Gower was caught at mid-wicket after a splendid knock, England needed 17 from 3.

Marks and Taylor scampered and survived when Taylor should have been run out, but they needed nine off the last over. Marks needed to hit the last ball of the match for three. He swung, missed and Snedden jumped for joy as the stumps were knocked over.

SECOND ONE-DAY INTERNATIONAL: AUSTRALIA v. ENGLAND
11 January 1983 at Sydney

AUSTRALIA								ENGLAND							
J. Dyson	c Randall, b Marks					49		D.I. Gower	c Hookes, b Thomson					9
K.C. Wessels	b Cowans					18		C.J. Tavare	c Border, b Rackemann					6
G.S. Chappell	c Marks, b Botham					3		A.J. Lamb	b Thomson					49
K.J. Hughes†	c Taylor, b Jesty					0		D.W. Randall	b Rackemann					5
D.W. Hookes	b Marks					11		I.T. Botham	b Rackemann					18
A.R. Border	b Miller					22		T.E. Jesty	run out					12
R.W. Marsh*	c Taylor, b Miller					7		G. Miller	lbw, b Hogg					2
G.F. Lawson	not out					33		V.J. Marks	not out					7
J.R. Thomson	b Miller					8		R.W. Taylor*	lbw, b Chappell					2
R.M. Hogg	c and b Cowans					8		R.G.D. Willis†	c Marsh, b Chappell					0
C.G. Rackemann	b Willis					0		N.G. Cowans	b Chappell					4
Extras	lb 13, w 8					21		Extras	lb 12, w 17, nb 6					35
	(46.4 overs)					180			(41.1 overs)					149

	O	M	R	W			O	M	R	W
Willis	6.4	1	20	1						
Cowans	7	—	20	2		Lawson	8	1	33	—
Botham	7	1	41	1		Thomson	10	4	21	2
Jesty	6	—	23	1		Hogg	10	1	15	1
Marks	10	1	27	2		Rackemann	8	1	28	3
Miller	10	—	28	3		Chappell	5.1	—	17	3

FALL OF WICKETS
1- 26, 2- 33, 3- 36, 4- 77, 5-118, 6- 124, 7- 132,
8- 158, 9- 175

FALL OF WICKETS
1- 11, 2- 44, 3- 53, 4- 95, 5- 131, 6- 131, 7- 135,
8- 142, 9- 142

Australia won by 31 runs

LEFT: *Warren Lees appeals for run out against David Gower who was on 95.* RIGHT: *What can we do? Howarth, the New Zealand captain, and Lees console each other after Gower has been given not out. Gower went on to make 122, the first of his three centuries against New Zealand. (Adrian Murrell)*

THIRD ONE-DAY INTERNATIONAL: ENGLAND v. NEW ZEALAND
13 January 1983 at Melbourne

NEW ZEALAND				ENGLAND			
J.G. Wright	run out		55		D.I. Gower	c Turner, b Hadlee	122
B.A. Edgar	c Randall, b Marks		30		C.J. Tavare	run out	16
B.L. Cairns	c Miller, b Botham		36		A.J. Lamb	st Lees, b Coney	15
G.M. Turner	b Miller		38		T.E. Jesty	c Wright, b Coney	5
G.P. Howarth†	c Willis, b Botham		13		I.T. Botham	c Chatfield, b Snedden	41
J.F.M. Morrison	c Randall, b Botham		11		D.W. Randall	c Snedden, b Coney	8
R.J. Hadlee	c Botham, b Willis		24		G. Miller	c Turner, b Chatfield	2
J.V. Coney	not out		13		V.J. Marks	b Snedden	5
W.K. Lees*	run out		3		R.W. Taylor*	not out	5
M.C. Snedden					R.G.D. Willis†		
E.J. Chatfield					N.G. Cowans		
Extras	b 1, lb 10, w 5		16		Extras	lb 14, w 3, nb 1	18
(50 overs)	(for 8 wickets)		239		(50 overs)	(for 8 wickets)	237

	O	M	R	W			O	M	R	W
Willis	8	1	29	1		Snedden	10	—	34	2
Cowans	10	—	50	—		Chatfield	10	—	38	1
Jesty	3	—	11	—		Cairns	10	1	64	—
Botham	10	—	40	3		Hadlee	10	1	37	1
Marks	9	—	47	1		Coney	10	—	46	3
Miller	10	—	46	1						

FALL OF WICKETS
1- 87, 2- 100, 3- 137, 4- 164, 5- 188, 6- 205, 7- 231, 8- 239

FALL OF WICKETS
1- 42, 2- 80, 3- 92, 4- 190, 5- 205, 6- 221, 7- 223, 8- 237

New Zealand won by 2 runs

Benson and Hedges World Series

FOURTH ONE-DAY INTERNATIONAL: ENGLAND v. NEW ZEALAND

Both sides elected to play their reserve wicket-keepers in an attempt to strengthen batting line-ups, and Ian Gould opened with Tavare so allowing Gower to revert to number three.

Howarth asked England to bat when he won the toss and Gould and Tavare put on 26. Then came David Gower. He arrived in the ninth over of the innings and played one of the very greatest of innings ever seen in a limited-over international. His 158 was a record for the Benson and Hedges World Series competition and was made off 118 deliveries. He hit four sixes and eighteen fours.

He and Randall added 113 in 19 overs for the fifth wicket

FOURTH ONE-DAY INTERNATIONAL: ENGLAND v. NEW ZEALAND
15 January 1983 at Brisbane

ENGLAND				NEW ZEALAND			
I.J. Gould*	c Howarth, b Troup		15		J.G. Wright	c Randall, b Cowans	30
C.J. Tavare	b Cairns		24		B.A. Edgar	c Gould, b Botham	40
D.I. Gower	c sub (J.J. Crowe), b Snedden		158		G.P. Howarth†	c Jesty, b Marks	13
A.J. Lamb	c Cairns, b Hadlee		13		B.L. Cairns	c Gould, b Marks	12
I.T. Botham	c Webb, b Hadlee		0		G.M. Turner	c Jesty, b Botham	29
D.W. Randall	run out		34		J.V. Coney	st Gould, b Marks	13
T.E. Jesty	not out		4		P.N. Webb*	c Cowans, b Botham	4
G. Miller					R.J. Hadlee	b Willis	21
V.J. Marks					M.C. Snedden	run out	0
R.G.D. Willis†					G.B. Troup	c Botham, b Willis	39
N.G. Cowans					E.J. Chatfield	not out	0
Extras	lb 9, w 9, nb 1		19		Extras	lb 6, w 6	12
(50 overs)	(for 6 wickets)		267		(48.2 overs)		213

	O	M	R	W			O	M	R	W
Hadlee	10	1	44	2		Willis	9.2	1	30	2
Chatfield	10	3	44	—		Cowans	10	—	52	1
Snedden	10	—	76	1		Botham	9	2	47	3
Troup	7	1	38	1		Marks	10	2	30	3
Cairns	10	—	29	1		Miller	10	1	42	—
Coney	3	—	17	—						

FALL OF WICKETS
1- 26, 2- 89, 3- 114, 4- 116, 5- 229, 6- 267

FALL OF WICKETS
1- 43, 2- 75, 3- 100, 4- 100, 5- 148, 6- 148, 7- 150, 8- 150, 9- 213

England won by 54 runs

and the last four overs of the England innings produced 38 runs.

Wright and Edgar again gave their side a fine start and New Zealand reached 100 a ball earlier than England had done, but the task was too great and wickets fell leaving England victorious and the memory of Gower in all his glory.

Benson and Hedges World Series

FIFTH ONE-DAY INTERNATIONAL: AUSTRALIA v. ENGLAND

After the elation of Gower's mighty innings and the victory over New Zealand, England's performance at Brisbane against Australia was very disappointing.

Once more England had to rely on extras for a main source of run-getting as only Randall and Botham in a fifth wicket stand of 57 looked as if they were capable of presenting Australia with a significant target. Most of the other batting was bad and the running between the wickets was terrible, Gould and Miller both falling to run outs brought about by mental aberrations.

England bowled quite tightly and Botham looked hostile, deserving his three wickets. There was never any doubt that Australia would win and as if to emphasise their superiority, Hookes, Man of the Match, greeted Willis' return with a six and four fours in one over which duly finished the match.

Benson and Hedges World Series

SIXTH ONE-DAY INTERNATIONAL: AUSTRALIA v. NEW ZEALAND

Having swept all before them in the tournament, Australia suffered a surprise defeat in Sydney.

Put in to bat, New Zealand were 87 for 2 after 25 overs. After ten overs, four of which had been maidens, they had

Glenn Turner returns to the fold. Batting against England on his return to international cricket at Melbourne, January, 1983. (Adrian Murrell)

FIFTH ONE-DAY INTERNATIONAL: AUSTRALIA v. ENGLAND
16 January 1983 at Brisbane

ENGLAND				AUSTRALIA			
G. Cook	c Hookes, b Lawson	2		K.C. Wessels	c Gould, b Botham	19
I.J. Gould*	run out	2		J. Dyson	c Marks, b Botham	40
D.I. Gower	b Hogg	22		G.S. Chappell	c Jesty, b Botham	30
A.J. Lamb	c Marsh, b Thomson	19		D.W. Hookes	not out	54
I.T. Botham	c Hookes, b Rackemann	29		A.R. Border	not out	30
D.W. Randall	b Lawson	57		K.J. Hughes†		
T.E. Jesty	c Marsh, b Rackemann	0		R.W. Marsh*		
G. Miller	run out	4		G.F. Lawson		
V.J. Marks	b Thomson	3		J.R. Thomson		
R.G.D. Willis†	not out	7		R.M. Hogg		
N.G. Cowans	c Lawson, b Rackemann	0		C.G. Rackemann		
Extras	b 4, lb 12, w 13, nb 8	37		Extras	lb 9, w 2	11
(46.4 overs)		182		(41 overs)	(for 3 wickets)	184

	O	M	R	W		O	M	R	W
Lawson	10	2	23	2	Willis	7	1	31	—
Thomson	10	—	32	2	Cowans	9	1	35	—
Hogg	9	1	29	1	Botham	8	1	29	3
Rackemann	8.4	1	28	3	Miller	6	—	25	—
Chappell	9	1	33	—	Marks	10	—	46	—
					Jesty	1	—	7	—

FALL OF WICKETS
1- 2, 2- 10, 3- 54, 4- 71, 5- 128, 6- 138, 7- 143, 8- 165, 9- 178

FALL OF WICKETS
1- 41, 2- 95, 3- 98

Australia won by 7 wickets

SIXTH ONE-DAY INTERNATIONAL: AUSTRALIA v. NEW ZEALAND
18 January 1983 at Sydney

NEW ZEALAND			
J.G. Wright	c Marsh, b Hogg		1
B.A. Edgar	b Chappell		32
G.P. Howarth†	c Marsh, b Chappell		29
G.M. Turner	b Thomson		55
J.J. Crowe	run out		56
R.J. Hadlee	c Chappell, b Thomson		5
J.V. Coney	c Marsh, b Lawson		13
B.L. Cairns	c Border, b Hogg		2
P.N. Webb*	not out		10
E.J. Chatfield			
M.C. Snedden			
Extras	b 7, lb 10, w 6		23
(50 overs)	(for 8 wickets)		226

	O	M	R	W
Lawson	10	3	33	1
Hogg	10	2	32	2
Thomson	10	—	42	2
Rackemann	10	—	59	—
Chappell	10	—	37	2

FALL OF WICKETS
1- 7, 2- 65, 3- 93, 4- 159, 5- 167, 6- 191, 7- 194, 8- 226

AUSTRALIA			
J. Dyson	run out		11
K.C. Wessels	c Cairns, b Snedden		58
G.S. Chappell	c Webb, b Snedden		1
K.J. Hughes†	c and b Cairns		1
D.W. Hookes	run out		68
A.R. Border	c Hadlee, b Cairns		11
R.W. Marsh*	b Cairns		6
G.F. Lawson	run out		0
J.R. Thomson	b Cairns		0
R.M. Hogg	not out		3
C.G. Rackemann	lbw, b Hadlee		2
Extras	b 4, lb 9, w 5		18
(45.3 overs)			179

	O	M	R	W
Chatfield	10	1	47	—
Hadlee	8.3	2	19	1
Snedden	8	2	24	2
Cairns	10	4	16	4
Coney	9	—	55	—

FALL OF WICKETS
1- 27, 2- 28, 3- 29, 4- 145, 5- 163, 6- 169, 7- 169, 8- 169, 9- 176

New Zealand won by 47 runs

Rodney Hogg back in action. He played an important part in Australia's success with 16 wickets in the World Series. Here he is jubilant as Hadlee has just been run out in the first of the qualifying matches at Melbourne. (Adrian Murrell)

been 19 for 1. It was Turner and Crowe who, in their different ways, gave the innings its impetus and the last three overs produced 34 runs.

Wessels batted solidly, but New Zealand bowled well and suddenly things began to go wrong for Australia as Dyson and Wessels found themselves at the same end, Chappell was taken low down off an away swinger and Hughes was caught and bowled as Cairns followed through. After 25 overs, the score had advanced to 61 for 3, but then Hookes looked as if he would win the match for Australia off his own bat.

The breaking of the Wessels-Hookes partnership turned the game back to New Zealand. Wessels drove Coney back down the pitch and the bowler inadvertently deflected the ball onto the stumps with Hookes out of his ground. Border was out to a brilliant catch at short extra cover and everything fell apart for Australia.

Benson and Hedges World Series

SEVENTH ONE-DAY INTERNATIONAL: ENGLAND v. NEW ZEALAND

For the first time in the competition, the captain winning the toss decided to bat first, but New Zealand batted indifferently against some generally good seam bowling, prospering only against the spin of Miller and Marks who conceded 100 of the 179 runs scored from the bat.

Turner and Edgar put on 81 for the third wicket in 22 overs, the only substantial contribution of the New Zealand innings.

Fowler, playing his first game since his injury in the fourth Test, and Gower, with two successive centuries against New Zealand to his credit, were both out for nought. 10 for 2 in the eighth over.

There followed a scintillating stand between Tavare and Lamb which has rarely been bettered in a one-day interna-

Cricket by night. England v Australia at Sydney, January, 1983. (Adrian Murrell)

SEVENTH ONE-DAY INTERNATIONAL: ENGLAND v. NEW ZEALAND
20 January 1983 at Sydney

NEW ZEALAND		
J.G. Wright	c Randall, b Willis	9
B.A. Edgar	c Willis, b Cowans	74
G.P. Howarth†	c Miller, b Willis	1
G.M. Turner	c Gower, b Marks	37
B.L. Cairns	c Gower, b Miller	11
W.K. Lees*	b Botham	12
J.J. Crowe	run out	12
R.J. Hadlee	c Lamb, b Willis	15
J.V. Coney	c Miller, b Willis	6
M.C. Snedden	not out	2
E.J. Chatfield	lbw, b Botham	0
Extras	lb 17, w 3	20
(47.2 overs)		199

ENGLAND		
C.J. Tavare	not out	83
G. Fowler	c sub (Webb), b Chatfield	0
D.I. Gower	b Hadlee	0
A.J. Lamb	not out	108
I.T. Botham		
D.W. Randall		
G. Miller		
I.J. Gould*		
V.J. Marks		
R.G.D. Willis†		
N.G. Cowans		
Extras	b 1, lb 5, w 3	9
(42.4 overs)	(for 2 wickets)	200

	O	M	R	W
Willis	9	—	23	4
Cowans	10	1	26	1
Botham	8.2	—	30	2
Marks	10	—	49	1
Miller	10	—	51	1

	O	M	R	W
Hadlee	9	2	37	1
Chatfield	10	2	25	1
Cairns	8	2	31	—
Snedden	8.4	—	61	—
Coney	7	—	37	—

FALL OF WICKETS
1- 14, 2- 20, 3- 101, 4- 118, 5- 152, 6- 171, 7- 178,
8- 197, 9- 197

FALL OF WICKETS
1- 9, 2- 10

England won by 8 wickets

tional. In their first twelve overs together, they put on 37. In the next 23 overs, they added 153.

The match was decided in the forty-third over when Lamb hit Snedden for a straight six, two fours and a two and moved from 92 to 108 in the process.

It was the lift that England had desperately needed.

Benson and Hedges World Series

EIGHTH ONE-DAY INTERNATIONAL: AUSTRALIA v. NEW ZEALAND

Dropped three times and scoring only 2 in ten overs, John Wright went on to make 82 in the next 34 and win the Man of the Match award. He shared a first wicket stand of 83 with Edgar and a second wicket stand of 68 with Turner. The support batting was good throughout the innings and 246 was a commendable score.

Dyson was out in the seventeenth over with the score on 41 and Hookes was promoted presumably to quicken the pace, but he fell to a diving catch in the gully and Australia had a series of mishaps from that point.

Hogg ducked into a short pitched ball from Hadlee and had to have thirteen stitches in his ear. Thomson was reported as suffering from an ear and throat infection and Lawson had a strained thigh muscle.

Turner wanted to leave the field with a leg injury, but it was an hour before umpires could be persuaded that he had sustained the injury during the match.

Benson and Hedges World Series

NINTH ONE-DAY INTERNATIONAL: AUSTRALIA v. ENGLAND

A delayed start due to rain reduced the match to 37 overs, but it had little effect on the crowd of 84,153, a world record for a one-day match.

Australia welcomed back Lillee the indestructible and introduced Maguire to international cricket. Hogg played in spite of his thirteen stitches in an ear.

England started soundly with Botham and Tavare, but the day was dwarfed by a magnificent stand of 139 for the fourth wicket between Lamb and Randall. They were together for 23 overs and Lamb's second superb innings in three days saw him reach 94 off 76 balls. He suggested muscle and power in all that he did.

It seemed that England had scored enough runs to win the match, but we had reckoned without bowling which Willis was to describe as inept, lacking in ability and unprofessional.

Willis and Cowans began by bowling short and Border, who had been sent in instead of Wessels, plundered them mercilessly. He pulled Cowans for 24 in two overs and after the first four overs the Australian score was 41. There was now no need to hurry even though Chappell hit Botham for 21 in an over towards the close. It was a ghastly display by the England bowlers and what poor Allan Lamb, Man of the Match, must have thought one would not attempt to guess.

24 January 1983

at Canberra

New Zealanders 271 for 6 (J.J. Crowe 90, P.N. Webb 52)
A.C.T. 174 (J.V. Coney 4 for 32)
New Zealanders won by 97 runs

In this 50-over match, Crowe scored 90 off 89 deliveries.

EIGHTH ONE-DAY INTERNATIONAL: AUSTRALIA v. NEW ZEALAND
22 January 1983 at Melbourne

NEW ZEALAND				AUSTRALIA			
J.G. Wright	c Dyson, b Rackemann	84		K.C. Wessels	c sub (Coney), b Troup	62
B.A. Edgar	c Marsh, b Rackemann	32		J. Dyson	c Wright, b Snedden	21
G.M. Turner	lbw, b Thomson	31		D.W. Hookes	c Hadlee, b Cairns	1
R.J. Hadlee	c Wessels, b Rackemann	21		K.J. Hughes†	c Hadlee, b Troup	12
G.P. Howarth†	run out	30		G.S. Chappell	c Snedden, b Troup	37
J.J. Crowe	not out	20		A.R. Border	c and b Troup	5
B.L. Cairns	c Border, b Lawson	0		R.W. Marsh*	c sub (Webb), b Snedden	32
W.K. Lees*	not out	5		G.F. Lawson	lbw, b Hadlee	0
E.J. Chatfield				R.M. Hogg	retired hurt	0
M.C. Snedden				J.R. Thomson	c Crowe, b Chatfield	4
G.B. Troup				C.G. Rackemann	not out	0
Extras	b 4, lb 13, w 4, nb 2	23		Extras	lb 11, w 1, nb 2	14
(50 overs)	(for 6 wickets)	246		(44.1 overs)		188

	O	M	R	W		O	M	R	W
Lawson	10	2	27	1	Hadlee	8	2	21	1
Hogg	10	1	40	—	Chatfield	9	1	38	1
Rackemann	10	—	52	3	Snedden	7.1	1	12	2
Thomson	10	—	52	1	Troup	10	—	54	4
Chappell	10	—	52	—	Cairns	10	—	49	1

FALL OF WICKETS
1- 83, 2- 151, 3- 184, 4- 198, 5- 236, 6- 236

FALL OF WICKETS
1- 41, 2- 43, 3- 123, 4- 129, 5- 142, 6- 151, 7- 155, 8- 155, 9- 188

New Zealand won by 58 runs

Come on England! Bob Willis gives the rallying cry. Trevor Jesty, flown out to strengthen the side, is in the background. (Adrian Murrell)

New Zealand's spearhead – Richard Hadlee. Injury kept him out of the finals and his absence was a severe handicap to New Zealand. (Adrian Murrell)

NINTH ONE-DAY INTERNATIONAL: AUSTRALIA v. ENGLAND
23 January 1983 at Melbourne

ENGLAND				AUSTRALIA		
C.J. Tavare	c Lillee, b Rackemann		20	J. Dyson	run out	54
I.T. Botham	b Lillee		19	A.R. Border	run out	54
D.I. Gower	c Marsh, b Rackemann		6	D.W. Hookes	c Gower, b Cowans	50
A.J. Lamb	c sub (Macleay), b Lillee		94	K.J. Hughes†	c Miller, b Cowans	6
D.W. Randall	not out		51	G.S. Chappell	not out	32
I.J. Gould*	b Hogg		3	R.W. Marsh*	run out	8
T.E. Jesty	not out		1	K.C. Wessels	not out	5
D.R. Pringle				R.M. Hogg		
G. Miller				D.K. Lillee		
R.G.D. Willis†				J.N. Maguire		
N.G. Cowans				C.G. Rackemann		
Extras	lb 10, w 4, nb 5		19	Extras	lb 5, w 2, nb 1	8
(37 overs)	(for 5 wickets)		213	(34.4 overs)	(for 5 wickets)	217

	O	M	R	W		O	M	R	W
Hogg	7	—	36	1	Willis	6.4	1	29	—
Lillee	8	2	50	2	Cowans	6	—	46	2
Rackemann	8	—	41	2	Botham	7	1	45	—
Chappell	7	—	33	—	Pringle	7	—	47	—
Maguire	7	—	34	—	Miller	8	—	42	—

FALL OF WICKETS
1- 32, 2- 50, 3- 66, 4- 205, 5- 209

FALL OF WICKETS
1- 85, 2- 157, 3- 167, 4- 176, 5- 190

Australia won by 5 wickets

25 January 1983

at Canberra

A.C.T. 168
New Zealanders 169 for 4 (J.V. Coney 60 not out)

New Zealanders won by 6 wickets

New Zealanders won with nearly 8 of their fifty overs remaining.

26 January 1983

at Canberra

New Zealanders 189 for 8 (G. Irvine 4 for 23)
A.C.T. 48 for 6

Match abandoned due to rain

Benson and Hedges World Series

TENTH ONE-DAY INTERNATIONAL: AUSTRALIA v. ENGLAND

The match was reduced to 41 overs by afternoon rain and England looked in a poor position at 47 for 4, but Jesty and Randall restored some order to the England innings. Randall was not at his best, but it was Jesty who went first, bowled off his pads.

After the stoppage Randall ran himself out and Gould and Marks struck some brave blows, but, in the light of previous experience, few were optimistic about England defending a total of 207.

The lack of optimism was confirmed when Border began with another flourish and Jackman, playing his first game since Christmas, conceded 15 runs in his first over.

Jackman continued to be expensive, but Border was well caught and bowled by Willis. When Jackman found his rhythm he turned the game for England by dismissing Hughes, Chappell and Wessels in seven balls.

A brief recovery followed, but Marks and Hemmings took the last five wickets which fell for the addition of only 13 runs to give England their first victory over Australia in the series.

The win placed England level on points with New Zealand though they had played one game more. Australia led the table by two points.

Benson and Hedges World Series

ELEVENTH ONE-DAY INTERNATIONAL: ENGLAND v. NEW ZEALAND

England set a record for the competition when they scored 296 for 5. The record stood for some three hours as New Zealand gained a momentous victory with seven balls to spare.

Botham was out in the sixteenth over having scored 65 of the 75 made for the first wicket. Gower hit his third century against the New Zealanders in an innings which lasted only 85 balls. Jesty hit his first fifty for England off 34 balls. From their last twenty overs, England scored 165 runs. It was heady stuff.

To their credit, New Zealand showed no sign of wilting even when Jesty hit two sixes in the final over from Troup, nor when Wright was run out in the twenty-second over with 96 scored and Howarth and Turner also gone. 201 in 28 overs with the three best batsmen out – it was a daunting task.

Cairns came in at number five and he and Crowe hit 70 in 8 overs. They both fell at the same total, but New Zealand had the scent that anything was possible.

TENTH ONE-DAY INTERNATIONAL: AUSTRALIA v. ENGLAND
26 January 1983 at Sydney

ENGLAND				AUSTRALIA			
C.J. Tavare	c Marsh, b Thomson	14		J. Dyson	c Randall, b Botham	23
I.T. Botham	c Wessels, b Hogg	0		A.R. Border	c and b Willis	31
D.I. Gower	b Lillee	25		D.W. Hookes	b Marks	32
A.J. Lamb	lbw, b Lillee	0		K.J. Hughes†	c Gould, b Jackman	0
D.W. Randall	run out	47		G.S. Chappell	b Jackman	0
T.E. Jesty	b Maguire	30		K.C. Wessels	b Jackman	1
I.J. Gould*	c Wessels, b Hogg	42		R.W. Marsh*	b Hemmings	1
V.J. Marks	c and b Lillee	22		D.K. Lillee	b Hemmings	3
E.E. Hemmings	run out	3		J.R. Thomson	b Marks	7
R.D. Jackman	b Hogg	0		R.M. Hogg	not out	0
R.G.D. Willis†	not out	5		J.N. Maguire	c Lamb, b Hemmings	2
Extras	b 2, lb 4, w 9, nb 4	19		Extras	b 2, lb 2, w 3, nb 2	9
(41 overs)		207		(27.3 overs)		109

	O	M	R	W		O	M	R	W
Hogg	10	1	44	3	Willis	6	1	23	1
Maguire	8	—	42	1	Jackman	10	1	41	3
Lillee	8	—	34	3	Botham	2	—	13	1
Thomson	8	—	40	1	Marks	6	—	12	2
Chappell	7	—	28	—	Hemmings	3.3	—	11	3

FALL OF WICKETS
1- 8, 2- 45, 3- 47, 4- 47, 5- 101, 6- 157, 7- 197, 8- 201, 9- 201

FALL OF WICKETS
1- 40, 2- 72, 3- 73, 4- 73, 5-77, 6- 96, 7- 99, 8- 106, 9- 106

England won by 98 runs

ELEVENTH ONE-DAY INTERNATIONAL: ENGLAND v. NEW ZEALAND
29 January 1983 at Adelaide

ENGLAND			
C.J. Tavare	c Crowe, b Chatfield	16
I.T. Botham	b Chatfield	65
D.I. Gower	c Chatfield, b Troup	109
A.J. Lamb	run out	19
D.W. Randall	c Wright, b Snedden	31
T.E. Jesty	not out	52
I.J. Gould*	not out	1
V.J. Marks		
E.E. Hemmings		
R.D. Jackman		
R.G.D. Willis†		
Extras	lb 1, w 1, nb 1	3
(50 overs)	(for 5 wickets)	296

NEW ZEALAND			
G.M. Turner	b Willis	23
J.G. Wright	run out	30
G.P. Howarth†	b Jackman	3
J.J. Crowe	c Willis, b Botham	50
B.L. Cairns	c Gower, b Botham	49
J.V. Coney	not out	47
R.J. Hadlee	c Jesty, b Jackman	79
W.K. Lees*	not out	1
M.C. Snedden		
E.J. Chatfield		
G.B. Troup		
Extras	b 2, lb 7, nb 6	15
(48.5 overs)	(for 6 wickets)	297

	O	M	R	W
Hadlee	10	1	36	—
Cairns	10	1	45	—
Snedden	10	—	72	1
Chatfield	10	2	64	2
Troup	10	—	76	1

	O	M	R	W
Willis	9.5	2	43	1
Jackman	10	1	49	2
Jesty	8	—	52	—
Hemmings	6	—	49	—
Botham	8	—	61	2
Marks	7	1	28	—

FALL OF WICKETS
1- 75, 2- 86, 3- 121, 4- 204, 5- 278

FALL OF WICKETS
1- 26, 2- 33, 3- 96, 4- 166, 5- 166, 6- 287

New Zealand won by 4 wickets

England disintegrated. Hadlee and Coney began sensibly, but when they attacked England wilted. Catches were dropped in abundance throughout the innings. The bowling became ragged; the leadership disappeared in a mass of gesti-culations and voices. The Hadlee-Coney stand realised 121 in 18 overs. Willis brought himself back and bowled an over like something out of a horror film. There were two wides down the leg-side and 14 runs from the bat. That made it 18 needed off three overs.

Hadlee was caught on the mid-wicket boundary by Jesty who had maintained concentration and commitment in the field. Hadlee's 79 had been made from 64 balls. His judge-ment was superb and he was rightly named Man of the Match.

For England, triumph had turned to disaster, but it is better to remember this as one of the great, heroic wins of one-day cricket, and people at last had to accept that New Zealand were in Australia not just to make up the numbers.

Benson and Hedges World Series

TWELFTH ONE-DAY INTERNATIONAL: AUSTRALIA v. ENGLAND

England threw off the disappointment of the previous day and played with great determination to beat Australia for the second time.

Lawson returned to the Australian side and bowled very well, but there was application in the England batting which, once more, was buttressed by a stand between Gower and Randall. This time it produced 106 in 17 overs.

Australia were fined for not completing their fifty overs in the allotted time, and their batting, initially, was as laborious. Dyson took 60 balls to score 17. Hookes was tied down by Marks and England caught well and fielded well so that the issue was never really in doubt.

Benson and Hedges World Series

THIRTEENTH ONE-DAY INTERNATIONAL: AUSTRALIA v. NEW ZEALAND

New Zealand qualified for the final of the competition when they inflicted upon Australia their fifth defeat in six games.

Australia brought in Macleay for Wessels and slow left-arm bowler Hogan for Lillee. It was the first time in his international career that Lillee had been dropped. For the second day running the game was played in intense heat, and New Zealand's 199, built upon a fine innings from Turner, did not seem a big enough total to win the match.

This opinion was confirmed when Dyson and Border began with a stand of 64, but Howarth's leadership in terms of field placing and the response he got from his bowlers was excellent. Hughes, who had had a miserable series, was quickly frustrated and the last eight Australian wickets went down in 14 overs for 50 runs.

2 February 1983

at Northam

New Zealanders 221 for 5 (B.A. Edgar 62, J.F.M. Mor-rison 57, P.N. Webb 55)
Western Australia Country XI 163 for 4

New Zealanders won by 58 runs

Benson and Hedges World Series

FOURTEENTH ONE-DAY INTERNATIONAL: ENGLAND v. NEW ZEALAND

England needed to win this game to qualify to meet New Zealand in the final, but they found themselves opposed by both New Zealand and the weather.

TWELFTH ONE-DAY INTERNATIONAL: AUSTRALIA v. ENGLAND
30 January 1983 at Adelaide

ENGLAND				AUSTRALIA		
C.J. Tavare	b Hogg	18		A.R. Border	c Randall, b Willis	19
I.T. Botham	b Lawson	14		J. Dyson	c Lamb, b Hemmings	17
D.I. Gower	c Lillee, b Thomson	77		K.J. Hughes†	c Gower, b Marks	4
A.J. Lamb	b Hogg	2		D.W. Hookes	c Jesty, b Jackman	76
D.W. Randall	c and b Lawson	49		R.W. Marsh*	c Jackman, b Botham	7
T.E. Jesty	not out	22		G.S. Chappell	c Gower, b Jackman	33
I.J. Gould*	c Lillee, b Lawson	9		K.C. Wessels	b Botham	7
V.J. Marks	not out	10		G.F. Lawson	not out	28
E.E. Hemmings				J.R. Thomson	not out	12
R.D. Jackman				D.K. Lillee		
R.G.D. Willis†				R.M. Hogg		
Extras	b 1, lb 14, w 6, nb 6	27		Extras	b 6, lb 5	11
(47 overs)	(for 6 wickets)	228		(47 overs)	(for 7 wickets)	214

	O	M	R	W			O	M	R	W
Lawson	10	—	27	3		Willis	10	1	40	1
Lillee	10	—	50	—		Jackman	10	3	36	2
Hogg	9	1	25	2		Botham	7	—	49	2
Thomson	9	—	38	1		Hemmings	10	—	40	1
Chappell	7	—	45	—		Marks	10	1	38	1
Hookes	2	—	16	—						

FALL OF WICKETS
1- 25, 2- 62, 3- 70, 4- 176, 5- 178, 6- 200

FALL OF WICKETS
1- 27, 2- 89, 3- 97, 4- 149, 5- 161, 6- 167, 7- 189

England won by 14 runs

THIRTEENTH ONE-DAY INTERNATIONAL: AUSTRALIA v. NEW ZEALAND
31 January 1983 at Adelaide

NEW ZEALAND				AUSTRALIA		
J.G. Wright	c Border, b Thomson	15		J. Dyson	c Coney, b Chatfield	24
B.A. Edgar	b Macleay	18		A.R. Border	c Snedden, b Chatfield	41
G.M. Turner	c Hookes, b Thomson	84		D.W. Hookes	c Lees, b Hadlee	27
J.J. Crowe	c and b Hogan	14		K.J. Hughes†	c Wright, b Coney	6
B.L. Cairns	c Macleay, b Hogan	0		G.S. Chappell	c Lees, b Cairns	7
G.P. Howarth†	c Hughes, b Chappell	15		K.H. Macleay	lbw, b Hadlee	3
R.J. Hadlee	run out	8		R.W. Marsh*	c Hadlee, b Coney	15
J.V. Coney	c Marsh, b Thomson	5		G.F. Lawson	b Coney	7
W.K. Lees*	b Hogg	9		T.G. Hogan	run out	4
M.C. Snedden	not out	16		J.R. Thomson	b Cairns	3
E.J. Chatfield	not out	2		R.M. Hogg	not out	1
Extras	lb 8, w 2, nb 3	13		Extras	lb 13, w 2	15
(50 overs)	(for 9 wickets)	199		(44 overs)		153

	O	M	R	W			O	M	R	W
Lawson	10	3	20	—		Hadlee	7	1	15	2
Hogg	9	—	32	1		Cairns	10	—	41	2
Thomson	5	—	27	3		Snedden	7	1	16	—
Macleay	10	—	39	1		Chatfield	10	1	26	2
Hogan	10	—	42	2		Coney	10	—	40	3
Chappell	6	—	26	1						

FALL OF WICKETS
1- 23, 2- 64, 3- 95, 4- 95, 5- 144, 6- 156, 7- 170,
8- 171, 9- 195

FALL OF WICKETS
1- 64, 2- 76, 3- 103, 4- 112, 5- 116, 6- 116, 7- 141,
8- 148, 9- 149

New Zealand won by 46 runs

Asked to bat first, England struggled for survival in conditions which the New Zealand seam attack, Hadlee in particular, exploited to the full. In 15 overs, they were 37 for 3 and Gower had scored only 4 from the first 41 balls he received.

At 45 for 3 in 17.3 overs, a heavy storm brought play to a halt. The stoppage lasted four and a half hours and when play resumed in conditions still far from satisfactory England found that they had only another 33 balls in which to improve a meagre scoring rate. They slogged and fretted and New Zealand were left to make 89.

Turner was out to the first ball he faced and England took three fine catches, but there was never any doubt as to who would win the match.

FOURTEENTH ONE-DAY INTERNATIONAL: ENGLAND v. NEW ZEALAND
5 February 1983 at Perth

ENGLAND				NEW ZEALAND		
C.J. Tavare	c Lees, b Hadlee		0	J.G. Wright	c Tavare, b Willis	12
I.T. Botham	c Lees, b Hadlee		19	G.M. Turner	c Jackman, b Willis	0
D.I. Gower	not out		35	J.J. Crowe	c Botham, b Cowans	18
A.J. Lamb	c Crowe, b Snedden		7	J.V. Coney	not out	29
D.W. Randall	c Howarth, b Snedden		12	G.P. Howarth†	not out	26
T.E. Jesty	run out		0	J.F.M. Morrison		
I.J. Gould*	b Snedden		0	W.K. Lees*		
V.J. Marks	b Hadlee		2	R.J. Hadlee		
R.D. Jackman	not out		0	B.L. Cairns		
R.G.D. Willis†				M.C. Snedden		
N.G. Cowans				E.J. Chatfield		
Extras	b 3, lb 10		13	Extras	lb 1, w 3	4
(23 overs)	(for 7 wickets)		88	(20.3 overs)	(for 3 wickets)	89

	O	M	R	W		O	M	R	W
Hadlee	8	2	15	3	Willis	8.3	1	28	2
Cairns	5	—	21	—	Cowans	8	—	32	1
Snedden	6	1	25	3	Jackman	2	—	16	—
Chatfield	4	1	14	—	Botham	2	—	9	—

FALL OF WICKETS
1- 18, 2- 23, 3- 37, 4- 66, 5- 66, 6- 82, 7- 87

FALL OF WICKETS
1- 5, 2- 20, 3- 47

New Zealand won by 7 wickets

FIFTEENTH ONE-DAY INTERNATIONAL: AUSTRALIA v. NEW ZEALAND
6 February 1983 at Perth

AUSTRALIA				NEW ZEALAND		
G.M. Wood	c Wright, b Chatfield		25	G.P. Howarth†	b Hogg	8
S.B. Smith	c Webb, b Chatfield		28	J.G. Wright	c Marsh, b Chappell	33
K.J. Hughes†	b Morrison		21	G.M. Turner	c Marsh, b Lillee	30
A.R. Border	c and b Coney		2	J.J. Crowe	c Marsh, b Lillee	0
D.W. Hookes	b Hadlee		12	J.V. Coney	c Thomson, b Chappell	10
G.S. Chappell	b Snedden		24	P.N. Webb*	c Border, b Chappell	7
R.W. Marsh*	c Snedden, b Morrison		31	J.F.M. Morrison	not out	25
G.F. Lawson	b Snedden		8	R.J. Hadlee	c Marsh, b Hogg	5
J.R. Thomson	b Morrison		4	B.L. Cairns	run out	1
R.M. Hogg	not out		1	M.C. Snedden	c Thomson, b Lawson	25
D.K. Lillee	not out		0	E.J. Chatfield	b Lawson	0
Extras	b 9, lb 19, w 7		35	Extras	b 2, lb 6, w 8, nb 4	20
(50 overs)	(for 9 wickets)		191	(44.5 overs)		164

	O	M	R	W		O	M	R	W
Hadlee	5	2	7	1	Lawson	9.5	—	24	2
Cairns	6	—	20	—	Hogg	9	—	37	2
Snedden	10	1	41	2	Lillee	10	2	24	2
Chatfield	10	2	30	2	Thomson	8	—	24	—
Coney	10	—	22	1	Chappell	8	—	35	3
Morrison	9	—	36	3					

FALL OF WICKETS
1- 65, 2- 74, 3- 77, 4- 110, 5- 118, 6- 159, 7-183,
8- 188, 9- 191

FALL OF WICKETS
1- 9, 2- 61, 3- 61, 4- 81, 5- 92, 6- 108, 7- 123,
8- 125, 9- 162

Australia won by 27 runs

Benson and Hedges World Series

FIFTEENTH ONE-DAY INTERNATIONAL: AUSTRALIA v. NEW ZEALAND

Having led the table in the early stages, Australia arrived at the last match in the qualifying competition needing to win to reach the final. There was an emphatic reshaping of the Australian side with Wood returning for the first time since the first Test match and Steve Smith of New South Wales being brought in for his international debut. In 1982, Smith had played for Wanstead in the Richard Veneers League in Essex and had had an excellent season for his state. Dennis Lillee's return meant that Hogan was excluded from the team.

...ance Cairns seen here in action against England. His hitting was a feature of the competition and his 52 off 25 balls in the second final at Melbourne was an unforgettable demonstration of his power. (Adrian Murrell)

Howarth won the toss and asked Australia to bat, but the new opening pair denied New Zealand an early break-through by adding 65 runs in 16 overs. New Zealand were handicapped when Hadlee had to leave the field with a damaged hamstring after bowling only five of his quota of overs. This meant that New Zealand had to use a sixth bowler, the slow left-armer Morrison, but it was he who proved the most effective, drifting the ball into the right-hander and taking three wickets.

When he had Hughes playing on Australia were 118 for 5. Chappell and Marsh added 41, but Australia could not have been pleased with their final score.

Howarth went quickly, but Turner played a good innings and he and Wright took the score to 61 in 16 overs, but Lillee had Turner and Crowe caught behind off successive balls and as the middle order faltered, the advantage swung to Australia. Hadlee batted with a runner. Marsh took two more catches and was named Man of the Match. Morrison and Snedden put on thirty–seven for the ninth wicket in nine overs, but by then it was too late to stop Australia reaching the final.

Benson and Hedges World Series Qualifying Competition: Final Table

	P	W	L	pts
New Zealand	10	6	4	12
Australia	19	5	5	10
England	10	4	6	8

Benson and Hedges World Series
FIRST FINAL: AUSTRALIA v. NEW ZEALAND

Sadly, most of the cricket energy in between matches seemed to be geared towards insults being hurled between the sides, but when it came to the first final a truce appeared to have been declared and the most heated exchanges that took place were between Lillee and his captain over field placing.

None of the New Zealand front line batsmen could find his form. Turner scored 4 in 5 overs, and between them, Howarth, Edgar and Turner occupied 27 overs in scoring 25 runs. New Zealand were further handicapped by the absence of Hadlee. Coney and Morrison added 85 for the fifth wicket in 15 overs, but the New Zealand score never looked adequate.

Australia's task was made easier when interval rain reduced their target to 150 in 38 overs. Without Hadlee, New Zealand had little hope of containing them to this score and with Hughes finding form at last, the Australians won with just under seven overs to spare.

SECOND FINAL: AUSTRALIA v. NEW ZEALAND

For New Zealand the competition had gone on a little too long. Hadlee was flown back to New Zealand for treatment and Richard Webb flown out to replace him following good bowling in the domestic competitions. Australia left out Thomson, who had lacked discipline and direction in recent weeks, and brought in Macleay, the Western Australian all-rounder. 71,393 people attended the match.

Hughes won the toss and Wood and Smith began the Australian innings on a good wicket. In 25 overs they put on 140, a first wicket record for World Series Cricket. Wood's 91 came off 84 balls and, refusing to compromise when in sight of his century, he was out slogging at Coney.

BENSON AND HEDGES WORLD SERIES – FIRST FINAL: AUSTRALIA v. NEW ZEALAND
9 February 1983 at Sydney

NEW ZEALAND

Batsman	Dismissal	Runs
J.G. Wright	c Chappell, b Lawson	36
B.A. Edgar	b Thomson	12
G.M. Turner	lbw, b Lillee	4
G.P. Howarth†	c Marsh, b Chappell	9
J.V. Coney	not out	58
J.F.M. Morrison	b Lillee	35
W.K. Lees*	c Marsh, b Lawson	1
B.L. Cairns	c Lillee, b Hogg	9
M.C. Snedden	not out	2
E.J. Chatfield		
G.B. Troup		
Extras	lb 15, w 11, nb 1	27
(49 overs)	(for 7 wickets)	193

Bowler	O	M	R	W
Lawson	10	4	28	2
Hogg	10	2	24	1
Lillee	10	1	35	2
Thomson	10	—	42	1
Chappell	9	—	37	1

FALL OF WICKETS
1- 44, 2- 57, 3- 77, 4- 81, 5- 166, 6- 171, 7- 190

AUSTRALIA

Batsman	Dismissal	Runs
G.M. Wood	b Chatfield	12
S.B. Smith	b Cairns	10
K.J. Hughes†	c Coney, b Chatfield	63
A.R. Border	c sub (J.J. Crowe), b Chatfield	9
D.W. Hookes	not out	20
G.S. Chappell	not out	21
R.W. Marsh*		
G.F. Lawson		
D.K. Lillee		
J.R. Thomson		
R.M. Hogg		
Extras	b 4, lb 16	20
(31.1 overs)	(for 4 wickets)	155

Bowler	O	M	R	W
Troup	5	—	30	—
Cairns	8.1	—	27	1
Snedden	9	—	45	—
Chatfield	10	1	27	3
Coney	1	—	6	—

FALL OF WICKETS
1- 14, 2- 59, 3- 83, 4- 119

Australia won by 6 wickets (target reduced to 150 in 38 overs)

BENSON AND HEDGES WORLD SERIES – SECOND FINAL: AUSTRALIA v. NEW ZEALAND
13 February 1983 at Melbourne

AUSTRALIA			
G.M. Wood	b Coney		91
S.B. Smith	b R.J. Webb		117
K.J. Hughes†	c Lees, b Chatfield		12
A.R. Border	c and b Chatfield		11
D.W. Hookes	c Wright, b R.J. Webb		40
G.S. Chappell	c Wright, b Cairns		7
K.H. Macleay	run out		10
R.W. Marsh*	not out		3
G.F. Lawson	run out		3
D.K. Lillee			
R.M. Hogg			
Extras	b 1, lb 7		8
			—
(50 overs)	(for 8 wickets)		302

	O	M	R	W
R.J. Webb	9	1	47	2
Cairns	8	—	56	1
Chatfield	10	—	54	2
Snedden	7	—	47	—
Morrison	7	—	39	—
Coney	9	—	51	1

FALL OF WICKETS
1- 140, 2- 167, 3- 205, 4- 261, 5- 280, 6- 285, 7- 289,
8- 302

NEW ZEALAND			
J.G. Wright	c Marsh, b Hogg		3
G.M. Turner	c Marsh, b Lawson		1
G.P. Howarth†	b Lawson		3
J.J. Crowe	lbw, b Macleay		27
J.V. Coney	b Lillee		2
J.F.M. Morrison	b Lillee		2
W.K. Lees*	run out		3
B.L. Cairns	c Smith, b Lawson		52
M.C. Snedden	c Marsh, b Hookes		35
E.J. Chatfield	lbw, b Chappell		10
R.J. Webb	not out		6
Extras	lb 6, w 2, nb 1		9
			—
(39.5 overs)			153

	O	M	R	W
Lawson	8	3	11	3
Hogg	10	1	31	1
Lillee	7	3	29	2
Macleay	8	—	56	1
Chappell	5	1	15	1
Hookes	1.5	—	2	1

FALL OF WICKETS
1- 8, 2- 8, 3- 13, 4- 23, 5- 42, 6- 44, 7- 92, 8- 103,
9- 144

Australia won by 149 runs

Benson and Hedges World Series – Averages

AUSTRALIA BATTING

	M	Inns	NOs	Runs	HS	Av	100s	50s
S.B. Smith	3	3		155	117	51.66	1	
D.W. Hookes	12	11	2	391	76	43.44		4
G.M. Wood	3	3		128	91	42.66		1
J. Dyson	9	9	1	317	78*	39.62		1
K.C. Wessels	8	8	1	249	79	35.57		3
A.R. Border	12	11	1	235	54	23.50		1
G.S. Chappell	12	12	2	198	37	19.80		
G.F. Lawson	10	7	2	79	33*	15.80		
R.W. Marsh	12	9	1	110	32	13.75		
K.J. Hughes	12	11	1	132	63	13.20		1
R.M. Hogg	12	6	5	13	8	13.00		
J.R. Thomson	10	7	1	38	12*	6.33		
D.K. Lillee	6	2	1	3	3	3.00		
C.G. Rackemann	6	3	1	2	2	1.00		

Played in two matches: K.H. Macleay 3 and 10; J.N. Maguire 2
Played in one match: T.G. Hogan 4

AUSTRALIA BOWLING

	Overs	Mds	Runs	Wkts	Av	Best
G.F. Lawson	93.4	19	254	16	15.87	3/11
C.G. Rackemann	54.4	3	247	15	16.46	4/39
D.W. Hookes	3.5	—	18	1	18.00	1/2
D.K. Lillee	53	8	222	11	20.18	3/34
R.M. Hogg	111	10	377	16	23.56	3/44
J.R. Thomson	89	5	357	14	25.50	3/27
G.S. Chappell	93.1	3	380	12	31.66	3/17
K.H. Macleay	18	—	95	2	47.50	1/39
J.N. Maguire	15	—	76	1	76.00	1/42

Also bowled: T.G. Hogan 10 - 0 - 42 - 2

AUSTRALIA CATCHES
22 - R.W. Marsh; 5 - D.W. Hookes, A.R. Border and D.K. Lillee; 3 - K.C. Wessels and G.F. Lawson; 2 - J. Dyson, G.S. Chappell, J.R. Thomson and K.H. Macleay (one as sub.); 1 - K.J. Hughes, C.G. Rackemann, T.G. Hogan and S.B. Smith

NEW ZEALAND BATTING

	M	Inns	NOs	Runs	HS	Av	100s	50s
B.A. Edgar	8	8		276	74	34.50		1
G.M. Turner	11	11		332	84	30.18		2
J.G. Wright	12	12		362	84	30.16		3
J.V. Coney	11	11	4	200	58*	28.57		1
J.J. Crowe	9	9	1	204	56	25.50		2
R.J. Hadlee	10	9		202	79	22.44		1
J.F.M. Morrison	6	5	1	83	35	20.75		
M.C. Snedden	12	7	3	82	35	20.50		
B.L. Cairns	12	11		179	52	16.27		1
G.P. Howarth	12	12	1	155	39	14.09		
P.N. Webb	4	4	1	30	10*	10.00		
W.K. Lees	8	7	2	34	12	6.80		
E.J. Chatfield	12	6	3	12	10	4.00		

Played in four matches: G.B. Troup 39
Played in one match: R.J. Webb 6*

NEW ZEALAND BOWLING

	Overs	Mds	Runs	Wkts	Av	Best
R.J. Hadlee	85.1	16	267	12	22.25	3/15
J.F.M. Morrison	16	—	75	3	25.00	3/36
E.J. Chatfield	113	18	425	14	30.35	3/27
G.B. Troup	32	1	198	6	33.00	4/54
M.C. Snedden	102.5	7	500	15	33.33	3/25
J.V. Coney	68	1	310	8	38.75	3/40
B.L. Cairns	103.1	9	429	10	42.90	4/16

Also bowled: R.J. Webb 9 - 1 - 47 - 2

NEW ZEALAND CATCHES
7 - J.G. Wright; 6 - W.K. Lees (ct 5/st 1); 5 - M.C. Snedden 5, J.J. Crowe (two as sub.) and P.N. Webb (two as sub.); 4 - R.J. Hadlee and J.V. Coney (one as sub.); 3 - B.L. Cairns and E.J. Chatfield; 2 - G.M. Turner and G.P. Howarth; 1 - G.B. Troup

Benson and Hedges World Series – Averages

ENGLAND BATTING

	M	Inns	NOs	Runs	HS	Av	100s	50s
D.I. Gower	10	10	1	563	158	62.55	3	1
D.W. Randall	10	9	1	294	57	36.75		2
A.J. Lamb	10	10	1	326	108*	36.22	1	1
T.E. Jesty	9	9	4	126	52*	25.20		1
C.J. Tavare	9	9	1	197	83*	24.62		1
I.T. Botham	10	9		205	65	22.77		1
V.J. Marks	9	6	2	49	22	12.25		
R.G.D. Willis	10	3	2	12	7*	12.00		
I.J. Gould	8	7	1	72	42	12.00		
G. Miller	6	3		8	4	2.66		

Played in seven matches: N.G. Cowans 4 and 0.
Played in four matches: R.D. Jackman 0 and 0*.
Played in three matches: E.E. Hemmings 3.
Played in two matches: R.W. Taylor 2 and 5*.
Played in one match: G. Fowler 0, G. Cook 2, D.R. Pringle did not bat

ENGLAND BOWLING

	Overs	Mds	Runs	Wkts	Av	Best
R.D. Jackman	32	5	142	7	20.28	3/41
R.G.D. Willis	81	10	296	14	21.14	4/23
I.T. Botham	68.2	5	264	17	21.41	3/29
E.E. Hemmings	19.3	—	100	4	25.00	3/11
V.J. Marks	72	5	277	10	27.70	3/30
N.G. Cowans	60	2	261	7	37.28	2/20
G. Miller	54	1	234	4	58.50	3/28
T.E. Jesty	18	—	93	1	93.00	1/23

Also bowled: D.R. Pringle 7 - 0 - 47 - 0

ENGLAND CATCHES

7 - D.W. Randall; 6 - D.I. Gower; 5 - T.E. Jesty and I.J. Gould (ct 4/st 1); 4 - R.G.D. Willis and G. Miller; 3 - A.J. Lamb and I.T. Botham; 2 - R.W. Taylor, R.D. Jackman, N.G. Cowans and V.J. Marks; 1 - C.J. Tavare

Steve Smith continued the plunder. A firm, strong batsman, he cut viciously and beautifully and hit mightily off the front foot. He ran quickly and gave the constant impression of eagerness, pugnacity and reliability. His century was the first in the competition scored by a batsman other than an Englishman – Gower had hit three, Lamb one. It was reached in 163 minutes off 118 balls, and, included ten fours. With such a start, it was no surprise that Australia became the first side in the history of the tournament to reach 300 runs.

To follow the suffering they had endured in the field, New Zealand were now subjected to a splendid opening spurt by Lawson and Hogg. With Lillee and Macleay in a supporting role, the Australian bowling proved as dominant as their batting and after 17 overs New Zealand was 44 for 6.

Lance Cairns, who had been the great hitter of the tournament, now produced a final defiant flourish, one of utmost grandeur. In 34 minutes he faced 25 balls and scored 52 of the 59 added while he was at the wicket. He hit a four and six sixes, some of the mightiest ever seen on the Melbourne ground. It was a thrilling climax to a tournament which had gone on for rather a long time and it gave New Zealand a much deserved respectability.

Hughes was named man of the finals and Gower man of the tournament. Australia won with a great sense of panache at the end and one was only sorry that so much of the time this talented team seems to be embroiled in waging verbal warfare on and off the field. Cricket is the sufferer.

If one had to give a final award, it would go to New Zealand who proved to be the most consistent and disciplined of the three sides over the whole course of the competition.

A Review of England's Venture in Australia
by
ROBIN MARLAR
Cricket correspondent of The Sunday Times,
*secretary of the Cricket Writers' Club and
former captain of Sussex*

England, the oldest everything in organised sport, ought to give up centenaries altogether. That is if the England's team experience on the cricket field is a reliable guide. First there was the Melbourne Centenary Test Match, beautifully organised, but by Australians who proved themselves so closely in tune with history that their winning margin was exactly the same as it had been in that first match in ancient 1877. Then came the Lord's Centenary Test, said by some to be no more than a cynical pseudo-event for the raising of revenue. When MCC members, justifiably driven to distraction by the histrionics of non-playing umpires, so far forgot a century of Imperial history as to assault the said arbiters on the steps of the pavilion the last vestiges of Britain's moral ascendancy crashed to earth and joined the rubble of Empire and all those atlases painted red.

None of sound mind, therefore, set off from England to Australia for the grandiloquently named Centenary Ashes Series with anything but low hopes. Possibly sensing the future futility of England's competing in anything labelled a Centenary, the selectors cried out that they were undone by the exclusion of Gooch and large company because of the dreaded South African disease, and then chose a team which many critics felt guaranteed failure by its lack of balance. They cited the presence of three offspin bowlers and no left hander to support such condemnation. In the sense that most current Test teams contain three or four fast bowlers and just one spinner, this view seemed akin to saying that the most important feature of a boiled egg is its shell.

Certainly England were outbowled in the Series to come, but the group of offspinners had only walk-on parts, Hemmings and Miller taking together the same number of wickets, 22, as the Australian Yardley. But besides Yardley, Thomson's long swinging arm brought him 22 victims, whilst Lawson, the bowler of the series, took 34 wickets at 20 which ran him second only to Mailey in the bowlers' Hall of Fame, at least on a strict five match comparison. It was the comparison with England's two leading bowlers which was so revealing. Both Willis and Botham took 18 wickets, Willis at 27 apiece and Botham at an uncharacteristic 40. When England have done well in Australia, the bowlers have been decisive: Foster and Barnes, Larwood and Co, Statham and Tyson, even Snow, Willis and others in 70–71.

The Hill at Sydney. (Adrian Murrell)

England's selectors did commit one other howler. They chose an inadequate trio of opening batsmen, and whilst it is my belief that something could have been done on tour to recover from this error, by forcing an admittedly unwilling Lamb into that role. England twice had double figure opening partnerships in both innings, at Perth where they just made it with 14 and 10, and at Melbourne where the match was won.

Because of a foreshortened programme, the preliminary matches had to be used profitably. By the start of the first Test only Gower was looking better than ever. Nonetheless, Greg Chappell restored to the Australian captaincy by popular demand made an error in choosing to field on a perfect pitch and England ensured the draw they desperately needed by accumulating 411 in the first innings. This effort was built round a splendid example of patient and unruffled determination by Tavare, who sadly was only once to repeat his tally of 89. There was a nasty moment during the second innings when Lawson knocked over too many batsmen too quickly but Randall made 115 and in the end it was England who left the Indian Ocean behind them with feelings of both confidence and relief. The fact that Alderman had been seriously hurt during a pitch invasion caused the Australians not only the loss of a player but also to think harder about their policy of continuous beer sales on hot afternoons. England were also aware that Lillee, their scourge for many a year, had battled on when lame. It was no surprise when the great Australian bowler went under the knife: the surprise lay in the speed at which his knee recovered.

Apart from the changes forced on them the Australians brought in Wessels, their South African born left-handed opening batsman who had made such a grand impression on English cricket by his heavy scoring for Sussex. Shot out for too few by the reshaped Australian attack in which Lawson was now the acknowledged spearhead, England then suffered an innings of 162, comfortably the biggest in the series by Wessels. England cleared the lead on an improving pitch for the loss of only one wicket, but their old foe Thomson ripped the middle from their innings. With the pitch taking increasing spin, England's cause was not quite doomed and when Chappell, a century maker at Perth and run out for 53 in the first innings was caught cheaply hooking at Cowans there was an acute attack of Australian panic before Hughes most notably, and Hookes secured a home victory by seven wickets.

Adelaide, as ever the best wicket in Australia, would surely not yield a result. This would mean that England, who had defied the prediction of defeat at Perth, would go into the Christmas and New Year Tests with a chance of squaring the series and thus retaining the Ashes–provided nothing daft was done. However, for reasons which seemed sound at the time, Willis gave Australia first use of the perfect pitch. England's bowlers tried hard enough in their negative style, but Chappell hit a second hundred in the series in the city of his birth, his first on that amiable strip and Hughes only missed his by 12 runs and a silly run out as the Australians amassed 438. With the Australians bowling short and making the ball bounce only Lamb and Gower looked comfortable. The Australians had discovered their best attack by accident according to Willis, but England staged two sorry displays. The first lead to a follow on, which could have been saved incidentally by an absence of no-balls on the part of the England bowlers, and the second, which featured a gallant century by Gower, meant that the Australians needed only 83 for victory on the fifth and final day. As it had not rained in Adelaide for four years there was unlikely to be any heavenly intervention to save England. Nor, to be truthful, would that have been fair: the Australians had earned their victory. Effectively the series was theirs.

However, since England were last in Australia, Australia and, to a major extent, Chappell himself, had developed such an irrational hatred of the Melbourne pitch, that the leaders arrived looking for trouble which they inevitably found. It came in the form of an assault by Tavare which took them by surprise, since he had been firmly cast in the tradition of England stonewallers like Boycott before him.

England did not bowl as well as they might have but Wessels, Hughes, Hookes and for the first time for many Tests, Marsh all made runs and the Australians took a 3-run lead. Marsh, incidentally, had twenty-eight victims in the series and no one is likely to do better than that. Once again Fowler made top score in England's second innings and for once there was some solidity in the lower order. Australia were set to make 292 in the fourth innings on a wicket which was not wholly reliable without ever being either difficult or dangerous. Its tendency to keep low remained despite the relaying of half the square. Dyson, Hughes, Hookes and for the first time in the series, Border made runs but when the last man Thomson joined Border Australia still needed 74 for victory. Surely England could polish this one off before nightfall on the fourth day? But there were showers, and

ome highly spirited batting, and some pedestrian field plac-
ng and their pair went to bed with half their work done and
needing only 37 in the morning. The gates were opened but
no fewer than 18,000 came to watch what could have been a
single ball. Instead Border and Thomson produced one of
Test cricket's most gallant failures, Thomson succumbing to
a fumbled slip catch off Botham just three runs short of the
target. Tavare dropped the snick, but it bounced up behind
him and Miller was able to grab the rebound.

Throughout this fourth Test the standard of umpiring had
been deplorable. To the entire visiting contingent the fifth
and final Test at Sydney was ruined by a disgraceful decision
in the first session of play when Umpire Johnson, allegedly
Australia's best, failed to give out Dyson on a run out
decision before he had received a ball, the TV replay showing
the batsman a foot and a half short of his ground. He made
79. Hughes was Australia's top scorer with 89, and he too
was given the benefit of a doubt which none of the England
side would admit, this time off a bat and foot catch when he
had made but 17. Randall and Gower made 70 apiece for
England who conceded too big a lead to remain in serious
contention and when Hughes hit his century for the series in
the second innings, followed by another gritty effort from
Border, England knew that they could only bat for a draw.
Truth to tell, the offspinners had their chance here and were
not good enough to make the Australians both sweat and
suffer.

There were those who claimed that the series was close,
and that England had almost held on to the Ashes. The sheer
statistics of the matches prove the lie that this was so. The
evidence of the eyes was that the England party had with one
exception, under-achieved. Only Gower found glory. True,
Cowans enjoyed some glorious moments, especially with his
attack on Chappell at Melbourne and his six wickets there:
alas he was no Tyson. Willis kept the party going off the field,
but his own captaincy on it was noted more for absent-
mindedness than inspiration, although he offered perspira-
tion galore for the cause. The truth is that England always
seemed to be uphill and into the wind, a sure sign of the
weaker team.

In theory, the five day game and its disappointment was to
be forgotten as the team prepared for the one day campaign
against Australia and New Zealand. Organisationally the
programme was a huge success with large crowds at the Tests
and a one day average of well over 15,000. After a bad start,
England pulled up the table until they allowed a record-

*New Zealand confer as to what to do next. David Gower awaits
a new partner in the middle of his record breaking 158 at
Brisbane. (Adrian Murrell)*

breaking total of over 300 to be overhauled by New Zealand
at Adelaide where catches galore were spilled. After that the
drift was downhill as England lost its reputation as doughty
professional one-day cricketers. The team failed to qualify
for the final tough matches in which Australia won with some
ease. England hung about for almost a fortnight and then
completed the tour with a short one-day series in New
Zealand. That too was to end in defeat. Not since the
nineteenth century had the wheels come off on an England
tour in New Zealand. Then they were travelling by coach, not
with one!

Graham Yallop who broke the record for the number of runs scored in the Sheffield Shield. (Adrian Murrell)

With England and Australia engaged in a Test battle and New Zealand joining them after Christmas for the Benson and Hedges World Series, the Australian domestic season was once again overshadowed. It began while many of the leading players were still with the Australian team in Pakistan, but the fixture list showed more sense than in previous years when states were denied the use of their top players because of international calls.

Tasmania, now playing a full programme of matches, were strengthened by the arrival of Michael Holding and Roland Butcher, while Shield Holders South Australia were strengthened by the importation of Joel Garner.

15, 16, 17 and 18 October 1982

at Brisbane

South Australia 235 (R.J. Inverarity 63, D.W. Hookes 53, C.G. Rackemann 7 for 49) and 224 (D.W. Hookes 87, R.J. Zadow 87, C.G. Rackemann 4 for 58)
Queensland 178 (J. Garner 5 for 32) and 135 (R.J. Inverarity 5 for 56)

South Australia won by 146 runs
South Australia 16 pts, Queensland 0 pts

at Perth

New South Wales 502 for 6 dec (D.M. Wellham 136 not out, R.B. McCosker 84, P.M. Toohey 75, I.C. Davis 56, S.B. Smith 52) and 129 for 2 (R.B. McCosker 59)
Western Australia 428 (G. Shipperd 166, T.J. Zoehrer 104)

Match drawn
New South Wales 4 pts, Western Australia 0 pts

South Australia began their defence of their title with an emphatic win over Queensland in three days. In spite of magnificent bowling by Carl Rackemann, who had match figures of 11 for 107, South Australia recovered from 36 for 3 to reach 235, but this total was made to look very moderate as Queensland reached 132 for the loss of Wessels. Kerr's dour innings was then brought to an end and newcomer Garner carved his way through the middle order as the last nine wickets fell for 46 runs to give South Australia the surprise of first innings points.

Rackemann and Maguire had the visitors at 12 for 3 in their second innings, but Hookes and Zadow added 89 in 82 minutes for the fifth wicket. No other batsman reached double figures. When Queensland batted again Garner quickly dismissed both openers and the left-arm of John Inverarity proved too experienced for most of the remainder.

At Perth, McCosker and Davis began with a stand of 148, but the most exciting New South Wales' batting came from the determined Wellham, who hit a career best, and Toohey who hit 75 off 68 deliveries.

Greg Shipperd's patient career best of ten hours' duration nearly brought the home state the points, but he fell to a magnificent one handed catch by Rixon off Pascoe. Western Australia had been struggling at 182 for 6, but Tim Zoehrer joined Shipperd in a record seventh wicket partnership for the state. Zoehrer, who had never before reached fifty in first-class cricket, hit 104 in 332 minutes.

Carl Rackemann began the season with a career best 11 for 107 for Queensland against South Australia. (Adrian Murrell)

22, 23, 24 and 25 October 1982

at Sydney

Tasmania 351 (R.D. Woolley 88, S.L. Saunders 59, D.A. Smith 52, M.J. Bennett 4 for 55, R.G. Holland 4 for 100) and 94 for 3
New South Wales 133 (M.A. Holding 4 for 43) and 311 (R.B. McCosker 69, M.D. O'Neill 65)

Tasmania won by 7 wickets
Tasmania 16 pts, New South Wales 0 pts

at Adelaide

Victoria 260 (P.G. Sacristani 55, P.D. King 54, J. Garner 4 for 73) and 420 for 9 dec (G.N. Yallop 151, J.M. Wiener 73, B.C. Green 70)
South Australia 409 (D.W. Hookes 137, R.J. Inverarity 126, P.D. King 5 for 88) and 206 for 7 (D.W. Hookes 107, R.J. McCurdy 5 for 88)

Match drawn
South Australia 4 pts, Victoria 0 pts

Tasmania's new captain, Roger Woolley, shared a seventh wicket stand of 111 with Stuart Saunders to help his side to a creditable 351. The spinners Holland and Bennett were most effective for New South Wales, but they were let down in the field where several chances were missed.

Two wickets to Holding and one to Clough saw New South Wales at 3 for 2. They never completely recovered and were out for 133 so being forced to follow-on. McCosker, dropped three times, O'Neill and Rixon, who batted two hours for his 46, all strove to save the game for the home state, but both O'Neill and Rixon were foolishly run out and Tasmania were left to make 94 in 80 minutes. They accomplished their first Sheffield Shield victory over New South Wales with 5.4 overs to spare.

In Adelaide, Victoria recovered from 168 for 7 thanks to Graf, King and wicket-keeper Sacristani, but a stand of 212 for the fourth wicket between Hookes and Inverarity put South Australia well on top. Hookes' 137 came off 163 deliveries and contained two sixes and fourteen fours.

With Yallop and Wiener adding 141 for the second wicket, Victoria fought back dourly in their second innings, and the match appeared to be heading for the dullest of draws when Yallop's declaration demanded that South Australia score 272 in two hours. Either believing victory was possible or stung by the absurdity of the declaration, David Hookes opened the innings. He was out in the tenth over, caught by Green off McCurdy, but by that time South Australia were 128 for 2 of which he had scored 107. He had faced only 40 deliveries and had batted for only 55 minutes. His hundred was reached in 43 minutes off 34 balls, the fastest century ever recorded in Australia. A chart of his innings revealed that he had hit the ball to all parts of the ground. He hit three sixes (all on the leg side), eighteen fours, two threes, two twos and seven singles one of which was an overthrow by the stunned Victorian field.

29, 30, 31 October, and 1 November 1982

at Perth

Western Australia 232 (K.J. Hughes 67, S.F. Graf 3 for 53) and 358 for 7 dec (K.J. Hughes 130, B.M. Laird 99, S.F. Graf 5 for 95)
Victoria 194 (G.N. Yallop 84, K.H. Macleay 5 for 26, T.M. Alderman 5 for 62) and 319 for 7 (M.D. Taylor 69 not out, G.N. Yallop 58, G.M. Watts 56, B. Yardley 4 for 75)

Match drawn
Western Australia 4 pts, Victoria 0 pts

30, 31 October, 1 and 2 November 1982

at Launceston

Queensland 400 for 8 dec (A.R. Border 93, G.M. Ritchie 67, K.C. Wessels 65, R.B. Kerr 59) and 152 for 3 (A.R. Border 79 not out)
Tasmania 396 (D.A. Smith 81, R.D. Woolley 80, S.L. Saunders 79 not out, A.B. Henschell 5 for 82)

Match drawn
Queensland 4 pts, Tasmania 0 pts

Fine containing bowling on the opening day by Graf, Callen and Bright restricted Western Australia to 232, a total that would have been considerably smaller had chances offered by Kim Hughes, who otherwise batted well, been accepted.

Victoria looked certain to take first innings points with Yallop again in dominant form, but they collapsed after reaching 156 for 3, their last seven wickets going down to Alderman and Macleay for 38 runs.

David Hookes. The fastest century ever recorded in first-class cricket in Australia. He reached his hundred off 34 balls in 43 minutes for South Australia against Victoria. (Patrick Eagar)

Hughes continued his elegant aggression in the second innings and he and Laird shared a fourth wicket stand of 118. Hughes left Victoria a day in which to make 397, and the visitors reached 193 before the third wicket fell, but the task was always too much for them and Western Australia's hopes were ended by a brisk fifty from Mick Taylor.

In a consistent and solid batting performance, Queensland reached 400, but Tasmania, their spirits high after their victory over New South Wales, made a determined effort to win first innings points. Once more skipper Woolley gave the innings great substance and once more there was a late flourish from Stuart Saunders. Saunders and Blizzard added 55 for the ninth wicket, but Tasmania were still 34 short of the lead when Clough joined Saunders. He stayed while 29 were added and then was caught at slip by Chappell off Henschell, whose off-spin brought him five wickets.

6, 7, 8 and 9 November 1982

at Adelaide

South Australia 418 (W.M. Darling 98, R.J. Inverarity 77, D.W. Hookes 65, A.M.J. Hilditch 59, P.R. Sleep 52, M.R. Whitney 5 for 133, G.F. Lawson 4 for 77) and 235 for 7 dec (D.W. Hookes 60)
New South Wales 425 (R.B. McCosker 116, T.M. Chappell 92, D.M. Wellham 75, M.J. Bennett 59 not out, J. Garner 7 for 113) and 123 for 4 (J. Dyson 55 not out)

Match drawn
New South Wales 4 pts, South Australia 0 pts

Tom Hogan. A magnificent all-round performance for Western Australia against New South Wales at Sydney still left him on the losing side. (Adrian Murrell)

In a big-scoring match, the pace bowlers Lawson, Whitney and the great Joel Garner came out with great credit. The battle was always for first innings points and when New South Wales reached 317 for 3, they looked certain to claim them, but Garner took 4 for 11 in 17 balls to put the home side back in contention. His effort was in vain, however, for Bennett and Whitney added 45 for the last wicket to give the points to New South Wales.

McDonald's Cup

6 November 1982

at Hobart

Tasmania 147 (D.C. Boon 53)
Queensland 151 for 3 (K.C. Wessels 57 not out, A.R. Border 56 not out)

Queensland won by 7 wickets

7 November 1982

at Hobart

Victoria 272 for 2 (J.M. Wiener 94, G.M. Watts 85)
Tasmania 169 for 7

Victoria won by 103 runs

Tasmania made a quick exit from the competition when they lost their two matches on successive days. Border, who hit hard, and Wessels added an unbeaten 104 to win the first match, and, in the second, reduced to 45 overs by rain, Watts dropped on 0, and Wiener, thrashed 189 for the first wicket in 149 minutes, and Tasmania were never in the match.

12, 13, 14 and 15 November 1982

at St Kilda

Victoria 228 (G.M. Watts 61, M.A. Holding 6 for 66) and 272 for 8 dec (M.D. Taylor 85, D.F. Whatmore 74)
Tasmania 157 (R.J. Bright 5 for 38, R.J. McCurdy 4 for 52) and 40 for 1

Match drawn
Victoria 4 pts, Tasmania 0 pts

at Sydney

Western Australia 327 (T.G. Hogan 72 not out, B.M. Laird 55) and 197 (M.J. Bennett 5 for 39)
New South Wales 295 (D.M. Wellham 81, R.B. McCosker 60, T.G. Hogan 6 for 91) and 230 for 6

New South Wales won by 4 wickets
New South Wales 12 pts, Western Australia 4 pts

Victoria gained their first points of the season when, in spite of Michael Holding's fine bowling on the opening day, they headed Tasmania on the first innings. Tasmania had only themselves to blame as, after Smith and Ray had given them a useful start of 75, they crawled to destruction in strokeless indecision. Sacristani broke a knuckle on his left hand and Yallop took over behind the stumps and took four catches. Whatmore, Taylor and Yallop batted purposefully when Victoria went again, and Yallop left Tasmania 344 to make, but only 37 minutes play was possible on the last day.

A magnificent all-round display by Tom Hogan at Sydney failed to bring Western Australia victory. He hit 72 in 129 minutes and shared in a ninth wicket stand of 81 with David Boyd. Then he bowled his side to first innings points with his left-arm spin. The biggest stumbling block to the visitors was the last wicket pair of Holland (40) and Whitney (28 not out) who both reached career bests.

Western Australia's batting in the second innings was dreadfully slow as they prodded against the accuracy of Bennett and Holland. New South Wales were left four hours in which to make 230 and McCosker, Wellham, Chappell, Smith and Toohey kept the momentum going and won with time to spare.

McDonald's Cup

18 November 1982

at Sydney

New South Wales 166 (K.H. Macleay 4 for 15)
Western Australia 167 for 4

Western Australia won by 6 wickets

With the organisers still not quite settled as to how to organise the one-day competition, this was played as a day/

ight postscript to the Sheffield Shield game. New South Wales batted badly and only a wag by the tail helped them o 166, a score which the visitors passed with 15 balls to pare.

19, 20, 21 and 22 November 1982

at Brisbane

Victoria 151 (C.G. Rackemann 5 for 38) and 326 (G.N. Yallop 73, M.D. Taylor 66, J.M. Wiener 67)
Queensland 449 for 8 dec (R.B. Kerr 112, A.R. Border 99, K.C. Wessels 86, G.M. Ritchie 55) and 32 for 0

Queensland won by 10 wickets
Queensland 16 pts, Victoria 0 pts

20, 21, 22 and 23 November 1982

at Devonport

Western Australia 504 for 9 dec (K.J. Hughes 129, R.W. Marsh 110)
Tasmania 201 (S.L. Saunders 58, P.A. Blizzard 51, B. Yardley 5 for 41) and 184 (D.C. Boon 99, B. Yardley 5 for 68)

Western Australia won by an innings and 117 runs
Western Australia 16 pts, Tasmania 0 pts

Victoria struggled from the start of the match in Brisbane where they have not won since 1965. Queensland responded to a miserable 151 with an opening stand of 160 between Kerr and Wessels, and Ritchie and Border both hit well, Border's 99 coming off 116 balls before he was caught behind off Wiener. Victoria batted much better in their second innings, but they lost their last seven wickets for 89 runs, and with them, the match.

Centuries by Hughes and Rod Marsh put Western Australia in an unassailable position in Devonport, and after Lillee had removed both Tasmanian openers there was little resistance to the spin of Bruce Yardley. Lillee was forced to leave the field with his knee injury which was giving him considerable pain, but, in spite of Boon's valiant 99, Tasmania could not save the game, their last five wickets in the second innings going down for 15 runs. Boon was the fourth batsman to be caught close in by Wood off Yardley's bowling. The off-spinner finished with match figures of 10 for 109.

26, 27, 28 and 29 November 1982

at Adelaide

Queensland 267 (A.B. Henschell 71, R.M. Hogg 5 for 51, J. Garner 4 for 79) and 309 (A.B. Henschell 162, R.B. Phillips 50, R.M. Hogg 7 for 53)
South Australia 401 (M.D. Haysman 126, W.B. Phillips 92, K.J. Wright 52, H. Frei 4 for 106) and 158 for 8 (J.N. Maguire 4 for 70)

Match drawn
South Australia 4 pts, Queensland 0 pts

Sides depleted by Test calls were depleted further when South Australia suffered two dreadful injuries. On the first

Rodney Hogg. His splendid bowling for South Australia won him back his Test place. (Adrian Murrell)

day, Andrew Hilditch was struck in the face while fielding close in and had to have a broken jaw wired. On the second day, 'Rick' Darling was hit in the right eye by a ball from pace bowler John Maguire. It was a terrible blow and the injury had a sickening effect on the whole match. Darling was in hospital for five days. It was the fifth time in three seasons that he has been badly injured. Nevertheless Phillips and Haysman, on his first-class debut, led the home state to a comfortable first innings lead.

There was a maiden century for Brett Henschell in the second Queensland innings, and he and Phillips assured that South Australia would have to chase a target after Rodney Hogg had bowled superbly to destroy the early Queensland batting. Left to make 176 and ample time in which to score the runs, South Australia, without Darling and Hilditch, failed miserably and were thankful to hold on for a draw.

3, 4, 5 and 6 December 1982

at Perth

Queensland 52 (K.H. Macleay 5 for 12, W.M. Clark 4 for 21) and 261 (K.C. Wessels 128, T.G. Hogan 4 for 24)
Western Australia 406 (G.M. Wood 138, B.M. Laird 84, H. Frei 4 for 69)

Western Australia won by an innings and 93 runs
Western Australia 16 pts, Queensland 0 pts

at Sydney

South Australia 335 for 9 dec (W.B. Phillips 112, R.J. Inverarity 104, L.S. Pascoe 5 for 99) and 223 for 5 dec (W.B. Phillips 54, M.R. Whitney 4 for 70)
New South Wales 297 (R.B. McCosker 67, S.B. Smith 65, D.M. Wellham 55, J. Garner 4 for 61, R.M. Hogg 4 for 90) and 154 (S.J. Rixon 52, J. Garner 6 for 70)

South Australia won by 107 runs
South Australia 16 pts, New South Wales 0 pts

With Queensland fielding a full strength side and Western Australia without the injured bowlers, Lillee and Alderman, it seemed that the visitors would have the better of the contest, but such an idea vanished quickly on the first morning when Queensland were bowled out inside 29 overs. It was the veteran pace bowler Wayne Clark and the bright young newcomer Ken Macleay with his medium pace who destroyed Queensland for the second lowest score in their history.

Laird and Wood responded with an opening stand of 134, and from that point the match went entirely in favour of the home state. Wood's highest score of the season took him 493 minutes and he faced 409 deliveries, a marathon innings.

Apart from a brave century from Kepler Wessels, who batted with a leg injury, Queensland batted indifferently at the second attempt and the game was over in three days.

South Australia were 16 for 2 against New South Wales, but Phillips, so rich in promise, and the dependable John Inverarity added 145 to restore the innings. There were some late fireworks from Garner who then joined with Hogg in nagging away at the home side's batting.

South Australia scored briskly when they batted again in an attempt to give their bowlers time to bowl out the opposition. They had ample time, for with Garner taking six wickets, South Australia won with just under twelve overs remaining.

McDonald's Cup

8 December 1982

at Sydney

South Australia 195 for 9 (P.R. Sleep 61)
New South Wales 197 for 2 (T.M. Chappell 75 not out, R.B. McCosker 58)

New South Wales won by 8 wickets

Another day/night afterthought game in the patternless McDonald's Cup saw New South Wales stroll to victory through a second wicket stand of 113 between McCosker and Chappell. Dyson, Hookes, Lawson and Hogg were missing from the fixture which was thereby degraded. New South Wales reached their target with 29 balls to spare.

10, 11, 12 and 13 December 1982

at Brisbane

Tasmania 296 (D.C. Boon 115, S.J. Reid 54, J.N. Maguire 4 for 93) and 127 for 2 (D.C. Boon 57 not out)
Queensland 242 (T.V. Hohns 66, G.M. Ritchie 60)

Match drawn
Tasmania 4 pts, Queensland 0 pts

This match was ruined by the weather. David Boon scored 115 in 377 minutes to rescue Tasmania from 33 for 3. Boon batted well, but he was twice dropped off Maguire. At one time the Queensland skipper Trevor Hohns bowled ten maiden overs in succession. In spite of the efforts of Ritchie and Hohns, Queensland never really recovered from losing their first five wickets for 85 runs, and Tasmania took first innings points.

Qualifying Tables			
Group A	P	W	L	Pts
Queensland	2	2	–	4
Victoria	2	1	1	2
Tasmania	2	–	2	0
Group B	P	W	L	Pts
Western Australia	2	2	–	4
New South Wales	2	1	1	2
South Australia	2	–	2	0

17, 18, 19 and 20 December 1982

at Perth

South Australia 288 (M.D. Haysman 71, K.J. Wright 64, W.B. Phillips 58, W.M. Clark 4 for 47, D.K. Lillee 4 for 72) and 387 for 7 dec (D.W. Hookes 146, K.P. Harris 74, M.D. Haysman 53, W.M. Clark 5 for 125)
Western Australia 324 (K.J. Hughes 123, B. Yardley 65, G.R. Marsh 54, R.M. Hogg 5 for 88) and 209 for 6 (B.M. Laird 88 not out, J. Garner 4 for 43)

Match drawn
Western Australia 4 pts, South Australia 0 pts

18, 19, 20 and 21 December 1982

at Newcastle

New South Wales 316 for 9 dec (R.B. McCosker 124, D.M. Wellham 88) and 150 for 4 (R.B. McCosker 66 not out)
Victoria 90 (M.J. Bennett 4 for 9, G.F. Lawson 4 for 36) and 479 for 7 dec (M.D. Taylor 94, D.M. Jones 94, G. Miles 75, R.J. Bright 64 not out)

Match drawn
New South Wales 4 pts, Victoria 0 pts

Dennis Lillee returned to the Western Australian side only 24 days after undergoing an operation on his right knee. He proved his fitness and his unquenchable commitment to the game with four wickets including a spell of 3 for 12 in 18 deliveries. He seems indestructible.

He and Wayne Clark bowled out South Australia for 288, and, in an uneven batting display, the home state took first innings points. They owed much to Kim Hughes who was at his grandest. He and Bruce Yardley added 105 for the seventh wicket and took Western Australia into the lead.

On the third afternoon, David Hookes gave another of his astonishing displays of hitting as he and Harris added 188 in 32 overs between lunch and tea. Thereafter, the game always looked to be heading for a draw.

Dean Jones (Victoria). The batting of this young man was a bright light in a bleak season for Victoria. (Philip Tyson)

With skipper McCosker again in fine form and Dirk Wellham proving that he is now a better player than when first selected for Australia, New South Wales reached 316 against Victoria, McCosker and Wellham adding 181 in 224 minutes. Victoria then collapsed in inexplicable and humiliating fashion before Lawson and the slow left-arm of Murray Bennett who had the amazing figures of 14 overs, 10 maidens, 4 for 9.

Following-on, Victoria batted with great determination. Every batsman made a contribution and the game was saved. Most heartening was the stand of 124 for the fifth wicket between young batsmen Mike Taylor and Dean Jones. Miles also batted well.

McDonald's Cup

22 December 1982

at Perth

South Australia 157
Western Australia 158 for 8 (B.M. Laird 58)

Western Australia won by 2 wickets

South Australia batted most disappointingly and were all out in 43.3 overs. Laird and Clements gave Western Australia a sound start with a stand of 46, but then 4 wickets fell in 6 overs for 13 runs, with David Johnston doing the damage.

Laird and Rodney Marsh added 73 for the fifth wicket, but there followed another collapse as four wickets fell for 8 runs.

At 140 for 8, the match was in the balance, but Hogan and Boyd steered the home side to victory with 14 balls to spare. Boyd's 13 not out compensated for his earlier lapses when he sent down 12 wides and 2 no-balls.

1 January 1983

at Melbourne

Queensland 270 for 5 (A.B. Courtice 105, R.B. Kerr 86)
Victoria 257 (J.M. Wiener 51)

Queensland won by 13 runs

As both sides had already qualified for the semi-finals this match had little relevance, but Andrew Courtice and Rob Kerr batted finely in an opening stand of 178 in 138 minutes, 33 overs. The Victorian bowling and fielding were shoddy, but their batting was steady and they could have won had Yallop and Richardson not both been stupidly run out.

31 December 1982, 1, 2 and 3 January 1983

at Launceston

South Australia 330 (R.J. Inverarity 66, A.M.J. Hilditch 59, G. Bishop 55, W.B. Phillips 53, P.A. Blizzard 4 for 62) and 78 for 2
Tasmania 266 (S.J. Reid 55, R.O. Butcher 51, J. Garner 7 for 78)

Match drawn
South Australia 4 pts, Tasmania 0 pts

Batting solidly down the order, South Australia, who welcomed back Hilditch after injury, reached a strong position which was strengthened even more by the bowling of Joel Garner who was dominant yet again. There was no play at all on the third day because of rain and the match petered to a draw.

8, 9, 10 and 11 January 1983

at Brisbane

Queensland 394 (W.R. Broad 89, R.B. Phillips 56, T.G. Hogan 5 for 74) and 92 for 4
Western Australia 376 (G.M. Wood 74, G. Shipperd 64, A.L. Mann 56, A.B. Henschell 4 for 76)

Match drawn
Queensland 4 pts, Western Australia 0 pts

at Devonport

Victoria 153 (M.A. Holding 7 for 59) and 154 for 3 (G.W. Richardson 74 not out)
Tasmania 262 (S.L. Saunders 79 not out, R.J. McCurdy 5 for 98)

Match drawn
Tasmania 4 pts, Victoria 0 pts

Acting captain Bruce Laird won the toss and asked Queensland to bat, but in spite of Hogan's nagging accuracy, the home side reached a solid 394. The visitors responded well, but, in the main, their batting was very slow, and they failed by 18 runs to reach the Queensland score. After Western Australia's dogged batting there was never likely to be a battle for more than first innings points.

Rain hampered play on the last two days in Devonport to deny Tasmania a chance of victory. Michael Holding blasted out Victoria on the first day, but Tasmania, in their turn, struggled to 126 for 7, but Clough and Stuart Saunders put on 75 for the eighth wicket and gained the first innings points.

14, 15, 16 and 17 January 1983

at Melbourne

Victoria 500 for 8 dec (D.M. Jones 199, G.N. Yallop 69, J.M. Wiener 60, G. Miles 61)
Western Australia 336 (K.H. Macleay 100, G. Shipperd 79, R.J. McCurdy 5 for 94) and 265 for 6 (G. Shipperd 107)

Match drawn
Victoria 4 pts, Western Australia 0 pts

Victoria's twenty-one-year old right-handed batsman Dean Jones hit a magnificent maiden hundred in his fourth Sheffield Shield game. He was finally run out in a dreadful mix-up with Ray Bright, but he had batted for 338 minutes, faced 302 balls and hit 27 boundaries in his 199. Once past his 50, he cut loose with a dazzling array of shots and he and young wicket-keeper Miles shared a sixth wicket stand of 216 in 252 minutes.

Facing 500, Western Australia were encouraged by a maiden century from Ken Macleay who shared a fifth wicket stand of 155 with Shipperd. They could not save the follow-on, but Shipperd again batted resolutely and the match was drawn.

21, 22, 23 and 24 January 1983

at Brisbane

Queensland 110 and 291 (A.B. Courtice 74, T.V. Hohns 54 not out, A.B. Henschell 53, M.R. Whitney 5 for 93)
New South Wales 406 for 5 dec (S.B. Smith 119, R.B. McCosker 112, D.M. Wellham 93)

New South Wales won by an innings and 5 runs
New South Wales 16 pts, Queensland 0 pts

at Adelaide

South Australia 148 (P.M. Clough 6 for 53) and 447 for 7 dec (W.B. Phillips 161, A.M.J. Hilditch 109, M.D. Haysman 54, R.J. Inverarity 51)
Tasmania 336 (D.C. Boon 109, R.O. Butcher 53, A.T. Sincock 5 for 96) and 239 for 8 (D.A. Smith 72, P.R. Sleep 5 for 77)

Match drawn
Tasmania 4 pts, South Australia 0 pts

Queensland were bowled out for a miserable 110 on the first day, and then McCosker and Smith, who was opening for the first time, put on 218 for the first wicket to give New South Wales total dominance. Wellham and Matthews added

further to the rout, and, although Courtice batted stubbornly, Queensland never looked like saving the game and the match finished on the fourth morning.

Peter Clough's career best had South Australia struggling to a very poor 148 on the opening day in Adelaide. Tasmania took a firm grip on the game with fine innings from David Boon and Roland Butcher, who had been struggling for form, and they led by 192 on the first innings.

The Shield leaders faced defeat, but a sparkling second wicket stand of 198 between Phillips and Hilditch brought them right back into the match. Phillips was impressively aggressive, but Hilditch, so recently out of the game with a broken jaw, deserved every praise for his brave effort.

Set to make 260 to win in approximately 66 overs, Tasmania began well when David Smith and Mark Ray put on 111 for the first wicket, but then they lost their way against the leg-breaks of Peter Sleep and were happy to settle for a draw in this fine match.

28, 29, 30 and 31 January 1983

at Melbourne

New South Wales 562 for 7 dec (S.B. Smith 263, P.M. Toohey 104, G.R.J. Matthews 81 not out) and 166 for 2 dec (P.M. Toohey 72 not out, R.B. McCosker 66 not out)
Victoria 396 (M.D. Taylor 144, G.M. Yallop 109) and 314 for 8 (M.D. Taylor 88, G.N. Yallop 86, D.M. Jones 69)

Match drawn
New South Wales 4 pts, Victoria 0 pts

A brilliant innings by Steve Smith, the highest innings of the season in Australia, not only dominated the early part of the match, but earned him a place in the Australian side for the Benson and Hedges World Series Final and a place on the tour to Sri Lanka. For a young man who, before this season, had played in only five first-class matches with a highest score of 60, it was a remarkable achievement. Toohey and Matthews also batted well, but Victoria were handicapped when Shaun Graf broke down with injury.

Yallop and the ever-improving Taylor responded well for the home side who were eventually asked to make 333 to win. Yallop and Taylor again batted well, and Dean Jones gave further evidence of his class as Victoria recovered from 74 to 3 to come close to victory. They reached 291 for 5, but then lost 3 wickets for 8 runs, and a fine match ended with both sides just frustrated.

3 and 4 February 1983

at Melbourne

Victoria 220 for 6 dec (G.W. Richardson 90) and 336 for 4 (G.M. Watts 164, M.D. Taylor 93)
Sri Lankans 295 for 7 dec (L.R.D. Mendis 141)

Match drawn

6 February 1983

at Melbourne

Sri Lankans 211 for 9
Victoria 213 for 4 (G.W. Richardson 80 not out)

Victoria won by 6 wickets

Shepherd is caught and bowled by Gunasekera in Victoria's second innings of the opening match of Sri Lanka's tour. (Philip Tyson)

John appeals, unsuccessfully, for lbw against Richardson in the one-day match, Victoria v Sri Lankans. (Philip Tyson)

In the earlier matches, Richardson and Watts played fine innings for Victoria against the tourists.

8 February 1983

at Canberra

Sri Lankans 212 for 6 (S.R. de S. Wettimuny 50)
A.C.T. 153 (V. John 5 for 24)

Sri Lankans won by 59 runs

10, 11 and 12 February 1983

at Sydney

New South Wales 253 for 5 dec (P.M. Toohey 58, J. Dyson 52) and 104 for 3
Sri Lankans 207 for 9 dec (D.S. de Silva 65)

Match drawn

14, 15 and 16 February 1983

at Devonport

Sri Lankans 221 for 7 dec (E.R.N.S. Fernando 72) and 229 for 8 dec (R.J. Wijesuriya 74, J.R. Ratnayake 64 not out, W. Kirkman 4 for 44, P. Faulkner 4 for 55)
Tasmania 199 for 7 dec (R.D. Woolley 53 not out, R.J. Ratnayake 4 for 34) and 110 for 3

Match drawn

On their way to New Zealand, the Sri Lankans played a short five-match tour. Only the last two matches, against New South Wales and Tasmania, were first-class. The match in Sydney was brought to an abrupt end by a storm. In Devonport, Mithra Wettimuny and Fernando gave the Sri Lankans a good start with a stand of 60, but this was not built upon. Woolley declared 22 behind, but Dias failed to keep the game open and a dull draw resulted.

18, 19, 20 and 21 February 1983

at St Kilda, Melbourne

Victoria 132 (R.M. Hogg 4 for 31, P.R. Sleep 4 for 29) and 359 (G.N. Yallop 168, G.M. Watts 57)
South Australia 445 (D.W. Hookes 193, M.D. Haysman 153, R.J. McCurdy 6 for 73) and 47 for 3

South Australia won by 7 wickets
South Australia 16 pts, Victoria 0 pts

at Sydney

Queensland 402 (A.R. Border 165, R.B. Kerr 72, G.F. Lawson 4 for 102) and 195 (G.F. Lawson 4 for 59)
New South Wales 405 for 6 dec (T.M. Chappell 132, D.M. Wellham 124) and 193 for 6 (D.M. Wellham 50 not out)

New South Wales won by 4 wickets
New South Wales 16 pts, Queensland 0 pts

19, 20, 21 and 22 February 1983

at Perth

Western Australia 329 (K.H. Macleay 96, R.W. Marsh 52, P. Faulkner 4 for 86) and 242 for 6 dec (B.M. Laird 72, G.M. Wood 53 not out, P.A. Blizzard 4 for 70)
Tasmania 260 (D.C. Boon 59, R.O. Butcher 52) and 273 for 9 (S.L. Saunders 50, B. Yardley 5 for 117)

Match drawn
Western Australia 4 pts, Tasmania 0 pts

It was not a particularly successful summer for Merv Hughes, but here he has Andrew Hilditch caught behind by Miles for 6 in the second innings. (Philip Tyson)

On the opening day at St Kilda, Rodney Hogg's pace and Peter Sleep's spin routed Victoria for a paltry 132, with extras of 22 being the top score. Rod McCurdy and Merv Hughes fought back for Victoria with 4 wickets for 48 runs, but Hookes and Haysman changed the pattern of the game. They added 264 and, although having his thumb broken by a ball from McCurdy when on 97, Hookes went on to make 193, his 150 coming in under two hours off 96 deliveries. Haysman continued his prosperous season and South Australia led by 313 runs on the first innings.

Victoria faced a hopeless task, but Watts and Richardson gave them a start of 101 and Yallop played magnificently. Nevertheless, South Australia romped home before tea on the third day.

A commanding innings by Allan Border proved to be in vain as New South Wales hit 193 in 209 minutes to win a great match. Border, ably supported by Kerr, had taken Queensland to a big first innings score, but New South Wales topped them for the loss of only six wickets thanks to a splendid stand of 253 in 258 minutes for the fourth wicket between Wellham and Trevor Chappell.

Queensland batted disappointingly at the second attempt, the pace of Lawson and Pascoe proving too much for all but Border who, with 47, was again top scorer, and New South Wales won with a fine team display.

Ken Macleay provided the substance of the Western Australian innings against Tasmania. The visitors batted poorly and surrendered a first innings lead of 69. Eventually, they were given a target of 312 on the final day. They slumped to 115 for 5, but Saunders, Woolley, Faulkner and Blizzard saved them with solid innings. The main reason that Western Australia failed to clinch victory was that they put down seven catches in the innings.

25, 26, 27 and 28 February 1983

at Hobart

New South Wales 311 (D.M. Wellham 76, P.M. Clough 5 for 80) and 164 for 5 (R.B. McCosker 65 not out)
Tasmania 332 (R.D. Woolley 111 not out, D.A. Smith 56)

Match drawn
Tasmania 4 pts, New South Wales 0 pts

at Junction Oval, Melbourne

Queensland 536 for 4 dec (K.C. Wessels 249, R.B. Kerr 132, A.R. Border 80, G.M. Ritchie 58) and 188 for 8
Victoria 510 (G.N. Yallop 246, D.M. Jones 116, J.R. Thomson 4 for 85, T.V. Hohns 4 for 123)

Match drawn
Queensland 4 pts, Victoria 0 pts

at Adelaide

Western Australia 430 (G.M. Wood 111, K.J. Hughes 91, G. Shipperd 56, S.D.H. Parkinson 7 for 98)
South Australia 200 (T.G. Hogan 4 for 49) and 213 (M.D. Haysman 59, D.K. Lillee 4 for 29)

Western Australia won by an innings and 17 runs
Western Australia 16 pts, South Australia 0 pts

An even batting display saw New South Wales to 311 in Hobart, but Tasmania, rallied by a fine century from Roger Woolley, took the first innings points. Rain shortened the last day, but there was still time for the Tasmanian hero Clough, who had scored 10 at number 11 to help Woolley see his side past the visitors' score, to dismiss Dyson, Smith and Chappell with successive deliveries to perform the first hat-trick for Tasmania since they had been admitted to the Sheffield Shield.

At Melbourne, Yallop won the toss and asked Queensland to bat. Wessels and Kerr proceeded to score 388, the highest stand for any Queensland wicket since they were admitted to the Sheffield Shield in 1927–28. Wessels' 249 came off 285 deliveries and the partnership took only 323 minutes.

Victoria lost 4 wickets for 160, and then Dean Jones joined skipper Yallop in a stand of 270. Yallop went on to a career best 246 in 495 minutes and passed Bill Ponsford's Sheffield Shield record of 1217 runs which had stood since 1927–28. It should be emphasised that Ponsford's record was achieved in six matches, eight innings, while Yallop had played in ten matches and batted 18 times.

South Australia's defeat at the hands of Western Australia cost them a place in the Sheffield Shield Final. Wood and Shipperd added 142 for the visitors' second wicket and then Hughes batted with great majesty. Sam Parkinson performed nobly for South Australia, taking the last six wickets to fall and having a career best 7 for 98.

South Australia twice batted poorly against Lillee, Hogan and Yardley, and the chance of a place in the final was lost.

Sheffield Shield Final Table

	P	W	L	D	Pts
Western Australia	10	3	1	6	64
New South Wales	10	3	2	5	60
South Australia	10	3	1	6	60
Tasmania	10	1	1	8	32
Queensland	10	1	4	5	28
Victoria	10	–	2	8	8

Sheffield Shield Final

Western Australia needed only to draw to win the Sheffield Shield while New South Wales had to win to take the Shield for the first time in 17 years. New South Wales frittered away an opening stand of 110 and Yardley stemmed their advance with his accurate off-breaks. They finished the day at 266 for 8 and added only another 5 the next morning.

Western Australia appeared to be heading for a big lead, but Lawson bowled Hughes with a superb break back, and the last five wickets fell for 25 runs so giving New South Wales a lead of 12 runs. Sadly the latter part of the innings was marred by a clash between Rodney Marsh and Whitney which resulted in Whitney being fined.

New South Wales now moved to a position of strength, but having reached 218 for 4, they lost their last six wickets for 62 runs and the game was open again.

Western Australia needed 293 for victory, but they had a dreadful start, losing Wood at 3, Laird at 40 and Shipperd at 67. The bowling of Chappell and Lawson was decisive and though Hughes and Rod Marsh made notable contributions, the game was over by mid-afternoon on the fifth day.

McDonald's Cup Semi-Finals

12 March 1983

at Perth

Victoria 112 (D.L. Boyd 5 for 15)
Western Australia 115 for 7 (S.F. Graf 4 for 15)

Western Australia won by 3 wickets

SHEFFIELD SHIELD FINAL – WESTERN AUSTRALIA v. NEW SOUTH WALES

4, 5, 6, 7 and 8 March 1983 at Perth

NEW SOUTH WALES

	FIRST INNINGS		SECOND INNINGS	
R.B. McCosker†	c Boyd, b Yardley	71	lbw, b Macleay	44
J. Dyson	c Shipperd, b Yardley	57	c R. Marsh, b Yardley	10
S.B. Smith	c Hughes, b Yardley	3	(6) c R. Marsh, b Boyd	37
D.M. Wellham	c Laird, b Macleay	6	c R. Marsh, b Macleay	70
P.M. Toohey	lbw, b Clark	40	c Macleay, b Clark	26
T.M. Chappell	c Laird, b Hogan	10	(3) run out	33
G.R.J. Matthews	lbw, b Hogan	34	c Macleay, b Boyd	24
M.J. Bennett	c Wood, b Yardley	10	c R. Marsh, b Clark	9
S.J. Rixon*	c R. Marsh, b Clark	20	not out	10
G.F. Lawson	not out	7	b Clark	2
M.R. Whitney	c R. Marsh, b Clark	0	run out	0
Extras	b 3, lb 8, nb 2	13	b 8, lb 5, nb 2	15
		271		**280**

	O	M	R	W	O	M	R	W
Boyd	12	3	51	—	13.3	2	39	2
Clark	24	4	42	3	25	8	48	3
Macleay	22	7	45	1	21	3	64	2
Yardley	29	8	92	4	28	5	81	1
Hogan	16	7	28	2	12	2	33	—

FALL OF WICKETS
1- 110, 2- 123, 3- 142, 4- 149, 5- 188, 6- 216, 7- 237, 8- 243, 9- 271
1- 32, 2- 84, 3- 101, 4- 155, 5- 218, 6- 252, 7- 265, 8- 273, 9- 275

WESTERN AUSTRALIA

	FIRST INNINGS		SECOND INNINGS	
G.M. Wood	c Toohey, b Whitney	45	c Chappell, b Lawson	0
B.M. Laird	run out	24	lbw, b Whitney	15
G. Shipperd	lbw, b Lawson	10	c Toohey, b Lawson	48
K.J. Hughes†	b Lawson	66	c Toohey, b Lawson	55
G.R. Marsh	c Rixon, b Chappell	32	c Dyson, b Chappell	18
R.W. Marsh*	c Smith, b Whitney	36	c Dyson, b Lawson	58
D.L. Boyd	lbw, b Whitney	16	(10) not out	9
K.H. Macleay	st Rixon, b Chappell	1	(7) c Matthews, b Chappell	24
B. Yardley	not out	14	(8) c Rixon, b Chappell	8
T.G. Hogan	lbw, b Chappell	2	(9) lbw, b Lawson	0
W.M. Clark	b Whitney	3	c Whitney, b Chappell	0
Extras	b 2, lb 5, w 3	10	b 5, lb 1, nb 1	7
		259		**238**

	O	M	R	W	O	M	R	W
Lawson	22	6	58	2	28	10	52	5
Whitney	25.2	4	67	4	18	4	45	1
Chappell	16	5	32	3	20.5	6	45	4
Bennett	29	12	50	—	22	9	39	—
Matthews	20	9	42	—	18	4	50	—

FALL OF WICKETS
1- 70, 2- 76, 3- 105, 4- 183, 5- 200, 6- 234, 7- 235, 8- 247, 9- 256
1- 3, 2- 40, 3- 67, 4- 125, 5- 186, 6- 206, 7- 222, 8- 229, 9- 229

Umpires: P.J. McConnell and R.A. French

New South Wales won by 54 runs

at Brisbane

Queensland 205 for 9 (G.S. Chappell 71, G.M. Ritchie 69)
New South Wales 206 for 8 (S.B. Smith 59, G.S. Chappell 4 for 35)

New South Wales won by 2 wickets

On a very poor wicket in Perth which brought protests, both sides struggled and it took a typically belligerent 35 from Rod Marsh to turn the match in the home side's favour.

In Brisbane, New South Wales won with 13 balls to spare after Greg Chappell had turned in a fine all-round performance for the home state. Consistent batting helped New South Wales to victory.

The drought which had troubled eastern Australia broke with a deluge of rain which washed out the McDonald's Cup Final on 20 March. No suitable date could be fixed for a rematch and the final was held over until 1983–84 season, an unhappy end to a poor season for the competition which is still looking for a format and a place on the Australian cricket calendar.

First Class Averages

BATTING

	M	Inns	NOs	Runs	HS	Av	100s	50s
A.R. Border	11	20	5	1081	165	72.06	2	6
G.N. Yallop	12	22	1	1418	246	67.52	4	6
D.M. Wellham	13	23	5	1205	136*	66.94	2	10
D.W. Hookes	13	23	1	1424	193	64.72	4	9
K.J. Hughes	13	21	1	1280	137	64.00	4	7
T.J. Zoehrer	4	6	2	239	104*	59.75	1	
K.C. Wessels	12	23		1325	249	57.60	5	3
M.D. Hayman	7	14	2	684	153	57.00	2	4
R.B. McCosker	13	25	4	1153	124	54.90	3	9
D.M. Jones	7	11		603	199	54.81	2	2
G.R.J. Matthews	7	11	4	343	81*	49.00		1
M.D. Taylor	11	19	3	771	144	48.18	1	6
G. Shipperd	12	19	1	816	166	45.33	2	3
R.J. Inverarity	10	19	3	698	126	43.62	2	4
R.D. Woolley	12	16	3	551	111*	42.38	1	3
S.L. Saunders	12	15	3	498	79*	41.50		6
D.C. Boon	12	18	1	682	115	40.11	2	2
R.B. Kerr	12	22		876	132	39.81	3	3
G.S. Chappell	11	20	2	703	126	39.05	3	1
S.B. Smith	11	21	1	762	263	38.10	2	3
W.B. Phillips	9	18		680	161	37.77	2	4
B.M. Laird	11	18	1	622	99	36.58		5
G.M. Wood	11	18	1	610	138	35.88	2	2
J. Dyson	12	23	3	688	79	34.40		6
A.M.J. Hilditch	9	17	1	546	109	34.12	1	3
P.M. Toohey	11	19	2	568	104	33.41	1	3
M.J. Bennett	13	18	7	356	59*	32.36		1
K.J. Wright	11	19	4	455	65*	30.33		3
A.B. Henschell	12	19	1	543	62	30.16	1	4
D.F. Whatmore	8	15	1	410	81	29.28		2
T.V. Hohns	12	18	5	376	66	28.92		2
T.M. Chappell	13	24		633	132	28.77	1	2
G.R. Marsh	11	18		510	54	28.33		1
W.R. Broad	6	11		310	89	28.18		1
S.J. Reid	9	13	2	309	79	28.09		3
R.B. Phillips	12	20	6	391	61	27.92		4
J.M. Wiener	10	19		530	79	27.89		4
D.A. Smith	12	20	1	527	81	27.73		5
R.W. Marsh	13	20		538	110	26.90	1	3
S.C. Clements	4	6		158	45	26.33		
A.B. Courtice	6	11	2	234	74	26.00		1
W.M. Darling	6	11	1	253	98	25.30		1
R.O. Butcher	12	19	2	423	53	24.88		3
G.W. Richardson	7	12	1	273	74*	24.81		1
G.M. Watts	7	13		321	61	24.69		3

	M	Inns	NOs	Runs	HS	Av	100s	50s
G. Bishop	3	5		123	55	24.60		1
R.J. Bright	11	17	6	269	64*	24.45		1
P. Faulkner	4	5		122	47	24.40		
K.H. Macleay	12	18	1	407	100	23.94	1	1
G.M. Ritchie	9	16		382	67	23.87		4
C.L. Harms	7	13	2	259	46*	23.54		
B. Yardley	14	20	3	400	65*	23.52		2
A.L. Mann	4	6	1	117	56	23.40		1
M. Ray	9	15	1	327	39	23.35		
S.J. Rixon	13	20	3	393	57*	23.11		2
B.C. Green	6	11	1	227	70	22.70		1
P.R. Sleep	8	14	2	272	52	22.66		2
G.J. Miles	7	12	1	246	75	22.36		2
A.T. Sincock	7	10	5	106	40*	21.20		
M.A. Holding	9	11	2	187	47*	20.77		
P.A. Blizzard	10	14	3	227	51	20.63		1
R.J. Zadow	3	6		123	87	20.50		1
I.C. Davis	3	5		101	56	20.20		1
H. Frei	11	15		258	57	17.20		1
K.P. Harris	6	12	1	187	74	17.00		1
T.G. Hogan	11	16	2	228	72*	16.28		1
G.F. Lawson	11	15	3	190	50	15.83		1
S.F. Graf	6	11	1	155	48	15.50		
S.M. Small	7	10	1	136	44	15.11		
J. Garner	8	13	1	138	22	11.50		

(Qualification – 100 runs, average 10.00)
(also batted in one match – M.D. O'Neill 36 and 65)

BOWLING

	Overs	Mds	Runs	Wkts	Av	Best	10/m	5/inn
C.G. Rackemann	239.5	75	553	35	15.80	7/49	1	3
J. Garner	403.1	131	976	55	17.74	7/78	2	4
T.M. Chappell	192.5	52	482	27	17.85	4/23		
T.M. Alderman	137.2	36	353	18	19.61	5/65	1	3
G.F. Lawson	495.4	110	1368	65	21.04	6/47	1	5
J.R. Thomson	254.5	50	766	34	22.52	5/50		2
R.M. Hogg	401.5	85	1120	49	22.85	7/53	1	3
S.D.H. Parkinson	76.4	10	275	11	25.00	7/98		1
W.M. Clark	339.2	90	801	31	25.83	5/125		1
M.A. Holding	371.4	93	946	36	26.27	7/59		2
P.M. Clough	414.1	91	1089	41	26.56	6/53		2
T.G. Hogan	415.2	134	939	35	26.82	6/91		2
L.F. Balcam	98.1	20	279	10	27.90	3/50		
M.J. Bennett	507.5	203	1102	39	28.25	5/39		2
D.K. Lillee	343	103	907	32	28.34	4/29		
B. Yardley	705	237	1782	61	29.21	5/41	1	4
M.R. Whitney	427.5	85	1323	45	29.40	5/93		2
R.J. McCurdy	345.1	57	1326	45	29.46	6/73		4
P.J. Mancell	146	32	360	12	30.00	3/40		
S.F. Graf	151.2	38	427	14	30.50	5/95		1
L.S. Pascoe	264.1	41	878	27	32.51	5/99		1
P.R. Sleep	206.4	48	689	21	32.80	5/77		1
A.B. Henschell	321.5	90	832	24	34.66	5/60		2
P.A. Blizzard	275.4	60	841	24	35.04	4/62		
K.H. Macleay	349.3	90	912	26	35.07	5/12		2
J.N. Maguire	370	88	1019	28	36.39	4/70		
H. Frei	355.4	93	985	27	36.48	4/69		
R.J. Inverarity	291.5	80	733	19	38.57	5/56		1
P. Faulkner	140	20	436	11	38.63	4/55		
R.J. Bright	465	125	1199	31	38.67	5/38		2
I.W. Callen	267	57	823	21	39.19	3/69		
G.R.J. Matthews	192	60	455	11	41.36	3/65		
C.L. Harms	170.1	50	471	11	42.81	3/96		
T.V. Hohns	388.4	114	978	21	46.57	4/123		
A.T. Sincock	201	42	721	15	48.06	5/96		1
R.G. Holland	369.4	134	833	16	52.06	4/100		
M.G. Hughes	159.1	20	603	11	54.81	2/68		
S.L. Saunders	285.2	67	875	15	58.33	3/115		

Leading Fielders

61 R.W. Marsh; 42 R.D. Woolley (ct 40/st 2); 40 K.J. Wright (ct 36/st 4); 37 S.J. Rixon (ct 28/st 9) and R.B. Phillips (ct 35/st 2); 26 G.J. Miles (ct 24/st 2); 21 G.S. Chappell; 20 R.B. McCosker; 17 D.W. Hookes; 15 B.M. Laird; 14 K.C. Wessels; 13 J. Dyson and G.M. Wood; 12 R.O. Butcher, M.J. Bennett and K.H. Macleay; 11 A.R. Border, T.M. Chappell, P.G. Sacristani (ct 10/st 1) and T.G. Hogan; 10 G.M. Ritchie and B. Yardley

THE DOMESTIC SEASON IN AUSTRALIA 1982–83
by
FRANK TYSON

The year 1982–83 marked the ninetieth birthday of the Sheffield Shield. It was in 1891–92 that the third Earl of Sheffield sponsored and accompanied Dr W.G. Grace's England team on a tour of the Australian colonies. It was the only occasion that the 'Champion' of English cricket led an official Test tour 'down under' and to commemorate the event Lord Sheffield donated a sum of money to the Australian Cricket Council for the advancement of the game in its country. The gift was invested in a shield bearing the Sheffield and Australian coat of arms; a trophy which was contested by the leading Australian colonies for the first time in 1892–93. Because of the 'Two Great Interruptions' of 1914–19 and 1939–45, the Sheffield Shield has been competed for in only 81 Australian summers of the 91 which have passed since Lord Sheffield made his generous donation. Victoria won the first Shield in 1892–93; but since the genesis of the competition, the most consistent winner of the 46″ by 30″ plaque has been New South Wales who, before the 1982–83 season, had proved itself the premier cricketing state on 36 occasions.

At the beginning of October 1982, however, New South Wales had not won the Sheffield Shield for 13 years; an amazing lack of success when one considers the population superiority enjoyed by that state over the rest of Australia. Bobby Simpson last led the wearers of the light blue cap to victory in 1965–66. Norm O'Neill was still playing for New South Wales at the time and a young prodigy by the name of Doug Walters was just making his presence felt on both the first-class and international scenes. The 13 year hiatus in New South Wales' success story ended on 8 March 1983 in Western Australia when captain Rick McCosker led his men to a 54 run victory over the home side and took the Sheffield Shield back to Sydney with him.

Since New South Wales' previous triumph the competition had undergone a few experimental metamorphoses. The first innings bonus points system had been tried and jettisoned; Tasmania had been admitted to the ranks of the elite teams in 1977 on a part-time basis and had subsequently been elected to full membership in 1982. The most recent attempt to inject vitality and financial viability into a flagging competition, which was being stifled by an abundance of international fare, was the decision by the Australian Cricket Board to play a Cup Final knock-out game between the two top sides to determine the destination of the Sheffield Shield. Judged on the basis of figures, the latest essay to revive the competition met with a modicum of success. Interest in the lead-up game to the final between Western Australia and South Australia was lively and, when New South Wales met Kim Hughes' Perth side in the culminating stage of the tontine, 16,443 people turned up and paid $38,262 to watch. It was a gratifying vindication of an initiative made necessary by the growing number of touring sides which annually compete for a limited Australian spectator market. In 1982–83, for example, antipodean cricket watchers were tempted not only by the major attraction of the England and New Zealand representative sides, but also by the prospect of witnessing the most recent member of the Test match club, Sri Lanka, in action – to say nothing of such appetising titbits as the visit of a New Zealand second eleven, under the managership of the former England player, Martin Horton.

New South Wales thoroughly deserved its conquests of 1982–83. The experienced Rick McCosker led the side astutely. It was a competent all-round combination, endowed with a great depth of ability. Regular calls upon players for the Tests against England and the Benson and Hedges/World Series One-Day Internationals were fortunately confined to demands upon the services of opening batsman, John Dyson, and fast bowler, Geoff Lawson. Even when these two stars fell from the New South Wales firmament, there were always adequate replacements. Steve Smith, a cousin of Norman O'Neill, revealed the same stamp of authority in his stroke-making as that possessed by his distinguished predecessor. He was a more than adequate substitute for Dyson in the number one position, scoring 669 runs before he, predictably, was called up for national service. Whitney, the youthful veteran of two Tests in England in 1981, when he was summoned from Gloucestershire to replace the injured Lawson at Old Trafford and the Oval,

Geoff Lawson. His 5 for 52 in the second innings was a vital factor in bringing the Sheffield Shield to New South Wales for the first time in 17 years. (George Herringshaw)

was a major force in the New South Wales' attack, both when Lawson was at the other end and when he was absent. Whitney captured 33 wickets in the season at an average of just over 31 with his distinctly hostile left-arm medium-fast deliveries and showed, in such incidents as his clash with Rod Marsh in the Sheffield Shield final, that he had the fire in his belly necessary to the make-up of fast bowlers. In his unaccustomed role of second-string paceman, the ebullient Len Pascoe was still a potent enough force to capture 24 wickets at 33.83 – including a return of 5/99 in one South Australian innings. Trevor Chappell underlined the all-round worth which was later to gain him a berth in the Australian World Cup party by claiming 15 victims with his accurate medium-pace and supplementing this achievement with a 486 run batting aggregate and an average of 28.59. New South Wales' bowling find of the season, however, was the orthodox slow left-arm spinner, Murray Bennett whose 28 wickets cost him a remarkably economical 28 runs each; his form was such that the experienced wrist-spinner, Bob Holland, received few opportunities to display his prowess; even so the leg-spinner managed to further his team's quest for the Sheffield Shield with a contribution of 16 wickets. The real strength of the Sydney side, however, was to be found in an extremely solid and versatile batting line-up. Smith, Toohey, Dyson and Chappell all exceeded 500 first-class runs

Trevor Chappell. A good all-round season contributed much to New South Wales' success. (Adrian Murrell)

during the summer, whilst Dirk Wellham and Rick McCosker represented two-thirds of the Australian batsmen who surpassed the 1000 run milestone in Sheffield Shield competition. Both could count themselves unlucky not to catch the eye of the national selectors for the series against England. Wellham in particular was the epitome of reliability. The bespectacled middle-order batsman 12 times notched more than 50 – twice pressing on to the century mark – and registered 1033 Shield runs. Such stirling efforts gained th[e] Government Affairs Officer in the Esso Oil Company the captaincy of the Australian Under-25 team which toured Zimbabwe at the conclusion of the 1982–83 season.

The runners-up in the Shield, Western Australia, suffered far more at the hands of the Australian selectors than New South Wales. The demands upon the services of its players were not more frequent than those made upon players from other states; its Test and One-Day International representatives missed, on an average, only four State games. The barb in the tail of Test match honours for Western Australian players was that, when the calls came, they virtually decimated their team. In the course of the season Hughes, Marsh, Lillee, Yardley, Alderman, Wood, Macleay and Hogan were all asked to place national before parochial loyalties. Moreover, the fates were far from kind to Hughes' men. Terry Alderman, after recapturing the fine edge of form which eluded him during Australia's tour of Pakistan, appeared in only two games for his state before being cruelly sidelined by a shoulder injury, incurred during the shameful spectator hooliganism of Perth's first Test. At the time of his incapacitation, the medium-fast bowler had already reaped a promising harvest of 18 wickets in only two matches against Victoria and England. The injurious events of 1982 deprived Western Australia of its opening attack at one fell swoop. The damage to Dennis Lillee's right knee, caused by his successful herculean efforts to square the rubber against New Zealand early in the year, not only eliminated him from selection for the tour of Pakistan and made him a doubtful starter for the rubber against England, it also meant that he was a day-by-day proposition for the state selectors. After a recurrence of his injury during the first Test and a second operation, Australia's doyen fast bowler attempted a determined come-back but twice broke down in the course of matches against Tasmania and South Australia. Lillee appeared in six games for Western Australia, but, although he showed occasional glimpses of his greatness, he never found his true potency. His unavailability for the Shield final against New South Wales was crucial. The game was lost by only 54 runs and his bowling could have made all the difference.

Kim Hughes' contribution to the West Australian cause in 1982–83 won him the accolade of the Benson and Hedges' Sheffield Shield Cricketer of the Year Award, plus its accompanying rewards of a cheque for $2,000 and a gold tray and goblets. In the light of his less than 100 per cent attendance record at West Australian games, the honour was unexpected in many quarters and coloured, in some peoples' estimation, by his successes in the Tests against England. Nonetheless it was incontrovertible that when Hughes captained and batted for Western Australia, the benefits of his presence were usually reflected by success. But whilst a substantial proportion of Hughes' first-class run tally of 1280 were scored for his state, there were other batsmen whose

Bruce Yardley, 10 for 109, spun Tasmania to defeat at Devonport. (Adrian Murrell)

scoring efforts were directed more exclusively towards fulfilling the Shield ambitions of the Perth side. The dogged Greg Shipperd nudged and deflected his way to an aggregate of 599 runs at an average of 49.93. Bruce Laird, passed over for the Test team, had to content himself with 571 runs for Western Australia. Most of Graeme Wood's 610 runs were collected in the cause of his local team whilst the two Marshes, Graeme and Rodney, both exceeded the 500 run mark in the first-class arena. Australia's young hopeful all-rounder, Ken Macleay, enjoyed a moderate Shield season of 352 runs and 22 wickets, but on occasions proved to be a real match-winner with his gentle, medium-pace swingers. Lillee's sporadic appearances on the cricket field yielded him 22 Shield victims but the bulk of Western Australia's bowling burden was shouldered by the veteran paceman, Wayne Clark, and the spinners, Yardley and Hogan, who appropriated 25, 34 and 32 wickets respectively in the course of the summer. The slow bowlers strove manfully to paper over the cracks in the Western Australian attack created by adverse fortune and injury. The fact that they did not succeed completely was no reflection on their ability; in the final analysis the Shield went to the team with the stronger fast bowling reserves.

At the outset of 1982–83, South Australia's avowed intention was to extend its reign as the country's premier side for another season and to win at least five more Sheffield Shields before the end of the decade. David Hookes' Adelaide-based eleven came very close to attaining its first objective and might conceivably have brought off the coup – if it had not played for the safe draw which would have taken it into the final in its last game against Western Australia. Having won the toss, Hookes mistakenly opted to send Hughes' side into bat and, as a result, suffered the indignity of losing the game by an innings. The saga of South Australia's eventual frustration was a classical case of a side depending too often on too few players. The dynamic hitting of Hookes brought him 967 runs for his state at an impressive average of 74.38 and a grand total of 1424 first-class runs for the season. Inverarity was once more a major reason for his team's accumulating 60 Sheffield Shield points from its 10 fixtures. The former skipper of Western Australia fell just one run short of a 700 run aggregate and proved his double worth by taking 19 vital wickets with his seemingly innocuous left-handed spinners. The tall, bespectacled left-handed opener, Wayne Phillips, returned from his tour of Pakistan in the complacent frame of mind which is not unusual amongst young players to whom success has come early. Not surprisingly his form declined in direct proportion to the relaxation of his concentration and he was finally dropped from the South Australian eleven. Jolted back to reality, Phillips, to his credit, applied himself with renewed vigour and before the coming of autumn had scored 670 runs and won himself a place in the Australian Under-25 team to tour Zimbabwe. His South Australian team-mate, Michael Haysman, accompanied Phillips on that tour after what had been for Haysman a meteoric rise through the ranks of Australian cricket. Haysman did not play in South Australia's first three encounters of the summer against Queensland, Victoria and New South Wales. He came into the side for the second match against Queensland when David Hookes was called away on Test duty and he compiled a century on his first appearance at the crease for his state. By the end of the Shield competition, the correct, upright right-hander had 684 runs to his credit at an average of 57 and was on the plane to Zimbabwe.

The names of Hookes, Inverarity, Phillips and Haysman ended the recital of South Australia's major batting successes. Hilditch, the former New South Wales opener, contributed 429 runs to the cause of his adopted state, but he was handicapped for part of the season by a broken jaw, sustained whilst fielding against Queensland. Another foreigner, former West Australian and wicketkeeper, Kevin Wright, chipped in with 352 runs, but no other batsman contributed more than 250. All-rounder Peter Sleep proved a grave disappointment, notching only 212 runs and capturing an expensive 14 wickets with his leg-spinners. It was scarcely the form one expected of an Australian touring player.

The pattern of South Australia's reliance on the few in batting was duplicated in the bowling sphere. Its cosmopolitan, international fast spearhead of Joel Garner and Rodney Hogg enjoyed a marvellously rewarding season. In spite of his Test duties, Hogg still found the energy and speed to defeat 38 batsmen from other states. The West Indian import of the year, Garner, was even more successful overthrowing 55 victims, before returning to the West Indies for the Tests against India. Unfortunately for Hookes' side, Gar-

Joel Garner. 55 wickets in the Shield, 10 of them in the victory over New South Wales in Sydney 3-6 December. (Adrian Murrell)

ner's departure proved untimely for it coincided with South Australia's last two games – including the vital clash against Western Australia. Garner's absence was decisive. The South Australian selectors brought in the left-handed speedster, Sam Parkinson, for the all-important game and Garner's replacement performed heroically, taking 7/98 in Western Australia's only innings. But it was not enough and, deprived of the tall West Indian's ability to tie up an end for virtually scoreless hours, Hookes' men were unable to prevent their opponents from amassing a mammoth 430 first innings total. For the lack of a bowler a match, and possibly the Shield, were lost.

Australia's northernmost state, Queensland, was plagued with the identical problems which afflicted the most occidental member of the Sheffield Shield. Greg Chappell, Keppler Wessels, Allan Border, Carl Rackemann, Jeff Thomson and John Maguire were frequent absentees from Queensland matches. In one important respect, however, the Brisbane side was more advantageously placed than Western Australia: it possessed the most promising brood of young cricketers in the country. There are no more accomplished apprentice Test batsmen in Australia than Greg Ritchie, Rob Kerr, Brett Henschell and Andrew Courtice. The bowling side of the picture was more sombre. Deprived of the services of Thomson, Rackemann and Maguire, deputy skipper Trevor Hohns, had to fall back on the honest medium-pace of Frei, Twible and Mainhardt, in consequence his fast attack lacked penetration. The surprising facet of Queensland's performance in 1982–83 was that even when the side was

at full strength, its results were far from flattering. Sou Australia vanquished the full might of Chappell's tea outright, as did New South Wales; Western Australia on dismissed them for 52 and won by an innings and 93 runs ar even the lowly Tasmania held them to a draw, losing narrov ly on the first innings, in Launceston. Such unlooked-f disappointments meant that Queensland's inaugural Shiel victory proved once more elusive.

The batting successes of the banana state were Borde Wessels and Kerr, all of whom topped the 600 run mark Shield matches. Greg Ritchie, the solitary century-maker Australia's 1982 disastrous series against Pakistan, neve found his touch and tried the selector's good-will an patience with an aggregate of 349, an average of 24.93 an a highest score of 67. He was in excellent company, for Gre Chappell's record for his state was even worse. He eked ou a mere 148 runs in eight innings at a mean figure of 18.50: a aggregate which was precisely 39 runs less than that medium-pace bowler, Harry Frei. Frei, moreover, warrante his retention in the eleven by capturing 20 wickets, four les than the leading Queensland wicket taker, Maguire and thre less than the side's most effective strike force, Ca Rackemann, whose 23 victims cost him an economical 11.9 runs each. The absence of a regular match-winning bowle however, was reflected in the fact that Queensland's wicket were bought at the expense of 35.90 runs each – the secon worst run rate in the competition.

Tasmania's first year as a fully-fledged member of th Sheffield Shield brotherhood was an extremely satisfyin experience. It produced 28 points and the fourth position i the Championship; a merited status, earned by dint of firs innings victories over Queensland, Victoria, South Australi and New South Wales plus the bonus of the island state' first-ever outright win over the team which eventually wo the Shield. Tasmania had the unique gratification of no allowing New South Wales a single point from the two matches it played against the premier team, plus the rewar of gaining 20 points from the dual experience. Such result would not have been possible, had the Apple Island's attack not benefited from the fiery catalyst of the fast bowling o West Indian Michael Holding, one of the two importe professional players permitted the junior member of th Sheffield Shield by the Australian Cricket Board. It would b too simplistic, however, to attribute Tasmania's coming-of age in senior ranks solely to the influence of Holding and it other overseas recruit, England's West Indian county player Roland Butcher. Butcher, in fact, laboured unsuccessfully on Australian wickets for most of the season and contributed only an unimpressive 363 runs at an average of 27.92 to his team's outstanding achievements. By comparison with Butcher, David Boon, Roger Woolley, Stuart Saunders and David Smith, played far greater roles in posting the respectable totals which Tasmania regularly scored against first-class attacks. This quartet all registered more than 400 Shield runs, with Saunders, Boon and Woolley averaging more than 40 per innings. The 22 year-old number three batsman, Boon, was particularly effective. He was the only Taswegian to surpass the 500 run mark and his efforts earned him the just reward of a berth in the Australian Under-25 team to Zimbabwe in March 1983. He proved to be one of the outstanding batsmen in Dirk Wellham's party and seems destined for greater things in senior ranks. The Tasmanian

:ipper Roger Woolley's feats were the equal of Boon's. His ¦1 runs came at the rate of 40.08 per innings and included ¹ unbeaten 111 against the New South Wales Test attack of awson, Pascoe, Whitney and Trevor Chappell. He ¹pplemented these runs with a fine season behind the umps, catching 31 and stumping 2 opponents. It was an all-¹und display which won him the right to substitute for ¹ustralia's regular 'keeper', Rod Marsh, on the autumn tour ¹ Sri Lanka. Nor were Tasmanian bowlers inferior to their ¹ainland counterparts. Right-handed speedster, Peter ¹lough, rivalled the effectiveness of Holding, equalling the ¹est Indian Test bowler's tally of 36 victims and taking five ¹ickets or more in an innings against South Australia and ¹ew South Wales. The rangy paceman, was well supported ¹y the medium-pace left-handed swing bowling of Phil ¹lizzard, whose rewarding summer brought him 24 wickets ¹ a cost of 31.38. Importantly, Woolley's men played as a ¹nit; this fact was exemplified by the determined ¹ontributions of leg-spin bowler, Stuart Saunders, who ¹eldom batted above the number eight position, yet in spite ¹f his limited opportunities, notched five half-centuries: a ¹atting consistency which he complemented with 12 wickets ¹rom 234 overs.

The once mighty Victoria finished the season as wooden ¹poonists of the Sheffield Shield competition for the second ¹uccessive time. The competition was only two months old ¹hen the rumour was bruited abroad in the media that the ¹tate selectors were dissatisfied with the captaincy of the Test ¹atsman, Graham Yallop, and were investigating the ¹ossibility of attracting the South Australian star, David ¹Iookes, to Melbourne to replace the man who once before ¹ad been summarily deposed by the capricious Victorian ¹egime. It was incongruous treatment of an individual who ¹vas apparently doing everything within his power as a player ¹o alleviate his team's growing humiliation and who, in the ¹ourse of the season, broke Bill Ponsford's 55 year-old Shef-¹ield Shield record aggregate of 1217 runs. Yallop's leader-¹hip certainly left a great deal to be desired, but there was no ¹uestioning his intrinsic worth as a batsman who notched ¹our of the seven centuries acquired by Victorian batsmen ¹nd who almost doubled the number of runs scored by any ¹f the players under him. It was also hard to appreciate how ¹he Victorian selectors could blame him for the repeated ¹ailure of his side's batting in its first innings: pathetic ¹isplays of irresolution which five times produced sub-200 ¹otals and once, against New South Wales, saw the Mel-¹ourne side humbled for 90. The only occasions on which ¹Yallop's batsmen exceeded the 300 mark at their first batting ¹attempt was when their skipper contributed a century or a ¹double hundred to their collective score. The southern selec-¹tors appeared unable to decide what constituted a Shield ¹player and in the span of six months experimented with 22 ¹players – including three wicket-keepers and 10 batsmen. ¹Seasoned performers such as Dav Whitmore who gathered ¹410 runs from his limited opportunities and bowlers like ¹Shaun Graf, who captured nine wickets in Victoria's away ¹game against a strong West Australian side, were whimsic-¹ally discarded after short lapses of form. Young batsmen ¹Peter Davies and Brad Green and all-rounders, Peter Cox ¹and Peter King, basked only briefly in the sun of the selec-¹tors' favour before receiving their congé. King scored 54 and ¹15 not out in his first game against South Australia, as well

Graham Yallop hits a leg-side boundary in his innings of 246 which took him past Bill Ponsford's 55-year old Sheffield Shield record of 1217 runs. (Philip Tyson)

as taking 5/88 in one innings; he received one more chance and was then handed his walking papers! Against this back-ground of indecision and uncertainty, it was small wonder that the Victorian side lacked confidence; it was even less to be wondered at that it lost seven matches on the first innings as well as one game outright and gathered only eight points from its season's efforts.

The summer was not a total loss, however, for the southern side. The burgeoning talents of the young batsman, Dean Jones, gained national acclaim when he plundered centuries off the West Australian and Queensland bowlers: hundreds which boosted his Shield aggregate to 567, his average to a commendable 63.00 and won him a place in Dirk Wellham's team to Zimbabwe. Mick Taylor's 641 runs included one century against New South Wales in Melbourne as well as five fifties and stamped him as one of the few reliable batsmen on the shifting Victorian scene. A dispirited Julien Wiener also collected 395 runs but at a less than impressive average of 26.33; by the end of the season he had made himself unavailable for selection for personal reasons. On the bowl-ing side of the coin, only two individuals captured more than 20 wickets for Yallop's team. The 22 victims of the left-handed spinner, Ray Bright, proved to be expensive pur-chases at more than 40 runs each. The broad-in-the-beam speedster, Rod McCurdy, was far more parsimonious and penetrative. His hostile, inslanting deliveries yielded him 38 Shield victories at a cost of 29.42 each and won him inclusion in the touring Australian Under-25 team. The former Test speedster, Ian Callen, was a disappointment. He was seldom

Dean Jones cuts a four during his innings of 116 for Victoria v Queensland. (Philip Tyson)

fully fit and rarely able to strike a consistent line and length. His 17 wickets were bought for 36.94 runs each: an exorbitant price for a bowler who had toured Pakistan with Hughes' team only six months previously. The former Australian one-day all-rounder, Shaun Graf, began the season well, but a serious back injury drastically curtailed his summer activities and he had to content himself with 14 wickets at just over 30 runs each. All in all it was a season to forget for Yallop's team and the continuation of the captaincy squabble throughout the ensuing autumn makes it almost certain that next summer will still be a wintry period for Victorian cricket.

Rick McCosker's New South Welshmen began their march towards Shield honours in unimpressive vein, winning one but losing two of its first five encounters: matches which also yielded two first innings decisions in favour of the Sydney side. Its first points came from its opening game against Western Australia in Perth: a high scoring clash in which the New South Wales batsmen mauled the home attack to the tune of 6/502 before declaring. McCosker and Ian Davis opened the visitors' assault with a stand of 148 in 171 minutes and their destructive work was continued by Wellham and Toohey who contributed a joint 114 runs. Wellham's eventual tally was an unbeaten 136: a total which was augmented by half-centuries from the bats of McCosker, Toohey, Davis

and Smith. In reply the home side began confidently and reached the comfort of 2/163, before losing four wickets in the space of 17 runs and 31 minutes to the variegated pace of Bennett and Skilbeck. Greg Shipperd and wicket-keeper Tom Zoehrer restored the game to an even keel with a record West Australian seventh wicket partnership of 204 – Zoehrer registering his maiden first-class century in the process. Rick McCosker also achieved a notable first in the game: his first unfortunate victims in Shield cricket, Zoehrer and Lillee. Even McCosker's fine flurry of form with the ball however could not tip the scales decisively and the game gasped its last with the visitors 2/129 in their second innings.

McCosker's hopes for Shield glory received a severe setback when Tasmania visited Sydney and returned to Hobart with a seven-wicket victory and 16 points under its belt. Never before had the Apple Islanders defeated New South Wales in a Shield match. Woolley's men showed the host team that they meant business by opening the game with a respectable first innings total of 351: a score to which Smith, Woolley and Saunders each subscribed 50 or more. Fast bowlers Clough and Holding thereupon carved a swathe through the New South Wales batsmen, dismissing them for 133 and subjecting them to the indignity of following on. The Sydneysiders never really recovered from losing their first three batsmen for two runs. They did, however, improve their performance at the second attempt. McCosker benefited from being missed three times to make 69 invaluable runs and a two hour partnership between Mark O'Neil and wicket-keeper Steve Rixon all but salvaged their team's attered reputation. They both committed run-out hara-kiri and their indiscretion left Tasmania 94 runs to score in 20 minutes and 20 overs: a task which it duly accomplished with more than five overs to spare. In retrospect, New South Wales had only themselves to blame for conceding this game, for they fielded and caught deplorably during Tasmania's first innings.

The Adelaide encounter with South Australia proved to be another run-feast. Hookes' men began their knock as though they intended to score 1000. Hilditch and Darling added 130 for the second wicket, paving the way for Hookes, who strode to the wicket to lambast 65 runs in 52 balls and bolster his side's tally with an 85 run fourth wicket partnership with John Inverarity. Hookes' knock was electrifying for it included four sixes in five deliveries, plus an additional seven fours. In all, 52 of his eventual 65 runs eventuated from boundaries. Visions of truly mammoth South Australian first innings total, faded, however, as its last six wickets surrendered for only 53 runs. In the final analysis, South Australia regretted sacrificing its middle and lower order batsmen. New South Wales never gave up hope of attaining its 419 target. McCosker blazed the trail by scoring 69 for the first wicket with Dyson in a mere 75 minutes and then proceeded to advance his team's cause further with a 115 partnership with Trevor Chappell. After the New South Welsh skipper had departed for a blameless 116, Chappell combined with Dirk Wellham to reduce his side's deficit by 131 and together they took the total to 317 before Joel Gar-

ner set the Sydney side back on its heels by snatching 4/11 in 17 deliveries. Undeterred, Bennett and Whitney steered their team to first innings points with a last wicket stand of 45. Hookes slammed 60 in South Australia's second innings of 7/235, but McCosker was not tempted by the proposition of scoring 229 in 34 overs and the contest faded into a no-contest.

Western Australia batted like tortoises in Sydney, with Laird taking 195 minutes over 55 runs. Hogan consolidated the later phases of the innings with 72 in just over two hours and thanks to his stand of 81 with fast bowler Boyd, the Perth side accumulated a relatively substantial 327 total. New South Wales began its reply confidently and at 1/118 was heading for a first innings lead. Then the orthodox left-handed spinner, Hogan, struck, capturing 6/91 and sending McCosker's men back to the pavilion for 295. The slow bowler's good work was completely dissipated however, when Western Australia collapsed against Hogan's counterpart in the opposing team, Murray Bennett, who captured 5/39 to bundle out the Westerners for 197. Set to score 230 in 191 minutes for victory, the home team were at one stage ahead of the clock at 2/100: Toohey and Smith improved the situation even more with a fourth wicket partnership of 39 in only 24 minutes. Then Wayne Clark captured 3 wickets for two runs in 14 balls and the match was once more in the melting pot. Toohey, however, stuck to his guns and his 46 enabled New South Wales to emerge the victor from a tense finish.

When Hookes brought his men to Sydney it was New South Wales' turn to taste defeat. Batting first, the Adelaide side experienced an early setback when two wickets fell with

John Inverarity. His enthusiasm was as unquenchable as ever. (Philip Tyson)

Wayne Phillips, one of Australia's most exciting young batsmen is bowled by Rod McCurdy in the Victoria v South Australia game 18-21 February. (Philip Tyson)

only 16 runs on the board. Phillips and Inverarity then defied the rampant Pascoe to augment their team's total by 145. Inverarity was dropped three times and profited from his good fortune to record 104: his twenty-sixth first-class century. The left-handed Phillips, finding the form which had eluded him early in the season, out-scored the former West Australian skipper by eight runs and together they were mainly instrumental for South Australia reaching the respectability of 335. When McCosker, Smith and Wellham took their side to within 112 runs of their opponents' total with only three wickets down, it appeared that the Sydneysiders would take first innings points. Hogg and Garner, however, had other ideas and seven wickets tumbled for 64 against the disparate Test pace duet. In its second innings South Australia raced to 5/223 in 250 minutes before declaring. The home batsmen in their second innings had no answer to Garner as he swept aside all opposition to capture six wickets and finish with match figures of 10/131. Rixon scored 52 in a total of 154, but when the home side's last wicket fell, it still needed 108 runs for victory.

McCosker was again in the mood to score a hundred when his side encountered the dejected Victorians in Newcastle. His 124 and Wellham's 88 enabled their side to reach 9/316 before declaring and then humiliating the opposition for a paltry 90. The contrasting pace of Lawson and Bennett was responsible for the Victorian discomfiture, Lawson taking 4/36 and the spinner, Bennett, returning the remarkable figures of 4/9. It was hard to recognise the Victorian side which followed on as the same eleven which had earlier failed so dismally with the bat. Mike Taylor and the youthful Dean Jones each notched 94 and, with wicket-keeper Miles reaching 75 and Bright 64 not out, Yallop was able to declare at 7/479. New South Wales made no attempt to chase the 254

runs it needed for victory and, when stumps were down, were 4/150, McCosker having been once more successful with 6

A journey northward to Brisbane brought New South Wales the reward of a victory in the space of three days by an innings and 5 runs. The left-handed paceman Whitney and leg-spinner Holland each captured three cheap wickets in Queensland's meagre first innings of 110. Opening batsman Rob Kerr and skipper Trevor Hohns contributed 80 of that score and the remaining nine members of their team could only manage a joint 28 runs. When McCosker and Steve Smith opened proceedings for the visitors with a stand of 218, Queensland's outright defeat was already written large on the wall. McCosker went on to record his 26th first class century and Smith his first in his initial essay at opening the innings. Wellham and Matthews pushed the Brisbane side further into the slough of defeat with a fifth wicket partnership of 133 before McCosker called his batsmen in with the scoreboard showing 5/406. Queensland's resistance in its second innings was more substantial, but it still fell within the token category. Courtice, Hohns and Henschell each passed the fifty mark but could not prevent the inevitable, which came with their team's score standing at 291 Whitney's speed rewarded him with an innings return of 5/9. and match figures of 8/126.

Smith followed his maiden Shield century against Queensland with a double hundred against Victoria in his second game in the opening position. New South Wales amassed 437 on the first day of its match against Victoria in Melbourne Smith was not one of the four batsmen dismissed and at close of play was 227: a total which included 116 runs scored in the last two hours of an eventful day. After having lost 2/37 to the bowling of Graf, who subsequently left the field with a badly injured back, the Sydney side went on to reach 7/562 with Smith and Toohey contributing 241 for the fourth wicket. Victoria made a spirited reply of 396 with Taylor and Yallop both reaching three figures. It followed up this substantial effort with 8/314 in its second knock, after New South Wales had declared a second time at 2/166. The game cluded innings of 263 from Smith, 104 from Toohey, 144 om Taylor and 109 from Yallop, plus half-centuries from e bats of Wellham, Matthews, McCosker, Taylor, Yallop d Jones. Not surprisingly this welter of runs resulted in a awn game.

New South Wales completed the double over Queensland th a victory by four wickets in Sydney in mid-February. e exciting win came with just under three overs to spare, ter the home-side had been set 193 runs to score in 209 inutes. It was a meritorious triumph since Queensland ccumulated a substantial 402 in its first innings and ap-ared to be in an invincible position. But in reply to Allan order's 165, Wellham and Trevor Chappell each scored a n' and McCosker's men passed their demanding target th four wickets in reserve. Fast bowler Geoff Lawson tore e heart out of the Queensland batting when the visitors ent to the crease again: his 4/59 restricted Chappell's men an unimpressive 195, with Border top-scoring again with 7. The chase was on; and when Wellham and Chappell dded 66 in quick time for the fourth wicket, the fate of the risbane side was sealed.

Tasmania sprang a surprise on its New South Welsh sitors in Hobart Town by taking first innings points off em, when every indication pointed to a probable home side efeat. Every batsman in the Sydney side except Whitney ached double figures, but none save Wellham built on their romising starts. McCosker's team, nonetheless, recorded a mfortable 311 total in its first innings and, when Woolley's de collapsed to be 7/193, the visitors appeared to be virtu-ly assured of four points. Woolley, however, played a cap-in's innings and his unbeaten 111, combined with dogged arguard actions from Faulkner, Blizzard and Clough abled the locals to edge past their distinguished guests. hen New South Wales batted again more shocks awaited . Fast bowler, Peter Clough, took Tasmania's first hat-trick Sheffield Shield cricket, boosting his tally of first-class ickets for the season to a local record of 40. McCosker revented further alarms with a solid 65 not out and when e contest petered out in a draw, New South Wales were a cure 5/164.

The inaugural final of the Sheffield Shield was a hard-fought atch between two well-matched and seasoned competitors. Vestern Australia enjoyed a home ground advantage but is did not prevent New South Wales from carrying off the onours by a decisive – but far from comfortable – margin f 54 runs. Batting first, the visitors were at one stage 110 ithout loss and well on the way to the victory which it eeded to clinch the championship. After McCosker's 71 and Dyson's 57, however, there was no substance to the New outh Wales batting and the innings closed at 271. The vital elivery in Western Australia's first knock was the Lawson all which cut back from outside Hughes' off stump to bowl im, when the Australian skipper had scored 66 and looked ke going on to greater deeds. Subsequently the host side lost s last five wickets for a paltry 25 runs on the third day, to ive its opponents a 12 run advantage on the first innings. Vellham was the major contributor to the New South Welsh econd innings but, in spite of the right-hander's defiant 70, is side could only better its earlier effort by nine runs, losing s last batsmen for 99. A final target of 293 proved to be eyond the capabilities of the West Australian batsmen when hey went to the crease a second time. Lawson's pace again

claimed the prize scalp of Hughes for 55 and the lanky speed-ster finished the match with seven victims. Trevor Chappell's medium-pace yielded 7/77 in the game, whilst Whitney's aggression brought him five wickets and an on-field altercation with Rodney Marsh, which cost the bowler a $50 fine for violating the players' behaviour code. In view of the $18,000 prize money which fell to the lot of New South Wales as winners of the Shield, it is to be doubted that the penalty caused Whitney any financial embarrassment.

Whilst New South Wales was probably the most admirably balanced and consistent team in the 1982–83 Shield competition, it was at a disadvantage at the beginning of the five-day final game. Its opponents from Perth, with a four point lead in the table, had only to draw the contest to ensure that the trophy went West. The first four of Western Australia's eventual 64 points came from its second game against Victoria, when, after drawing its initial encounter with New South Wales, it vanquished Victoria on the first innings by 38 runs. On the opening day of this Perth clash, the home side was restricted to 232 in its first innings by some excellent swing bowling from the medium-fast Graf, who was rewarded by match figures of 9/148. Hughes' men were fortunate to reach the double century mark, for their captain was dropped twice in scoring 67 and, thanks to the largesse of the Victorian fieldsmen, was permitted to add 91 for the fourth wicket in company with Geoff Marsh. At one stage, when Victoria were 3/156 and Yallop had scored 84 off 121 deliveries, it appeared certain to gain first innings points. Amazingly the visitors squandered their advantage and lost their last seven batsmen for 38 runs, five of them to the parabolic swingers of the medium-pace Macleay, who captured 5/26 after Alderman had dismissed the top five players in the Victorian order. Skipper Kim Hughes was again the man of the Western Australian batting when his side went in again; he notched 130, adding 118 in tandem with Laird for the fourth wicket, before declaring to leave Victoria to score 397 for victory on the last day. The visitors declined the challenge and were 2/193 when the umpires called time.

A loss to New South Wales by four wickets ensued, before Hughes took his men south to crush Tasmania by an innings and 177 and gain a maximum of 16 points from their game in the northern port of Devonport. The Taswegians were outclassed. By the end of the second day of the game, Western Australia had amassed 9/504 declared and had made early inroads into the home team's batting. Hughes compiled his second hundred of the season and was aided and abetted by Rod Marsh, who contributed 110 to the common cause. Lillee sent the Tasmanian openers, Smith and Ray, back to the pavilion in his opening spell before being compelled to retire by a recurrence of his knee injury. The work which the fast bowler left undone was completed by off-spinner Yardley, whose 10 wickets in the game cost him only 109 runs. The only resistance in Tasmania's first innings of 201 came from the bats of tail-enders Saunders and Blizzard whose eighth wicket partnership of 96 was a record for their state. When it batted again, Tasmania fared even worse, being dismissed for 184. David Boon played a remarkable knock of 99; more than half of the runs scored by his side. His association with captain Roger Woolley realised 72: but the last five Tasmanian wickets fell for an insignificant 15 runs as Western Australia cruised to an easeful victory.

Having tasted success in Devonport, Hughes' men apparently craved for more and they returned to Perth where they vanquished Queensland, again by the impressive margin of an innings. The game proved an outstanding triumph for the local side's second-string pace bowlers, Wayne Clark and Ken Macleay. Together they demolished the full might of a Queensland batting line up which included Wessels, Chappell, Border, Kerr, Ritchie and Henschell, in just over a session for a miserly 52 runs! Clark and Macleay won themselves the excellent figures of 4/21 and 5/12 respectively. Then, as if to prove the wicket blameless, Wood and Laird began the Western Australian response with a partnership of 134; the left-handed Wood eventually grafted his way to 138, being dropped once en route, but still providing the cornerstone on which his side's 406 total was founded. Queensland's second attempt was a one-man band, but it was better. Kepler Wessels defied a leg injury to eke out 128 runs before being ninth out for 128. Once Macleay removed Greg Chappell, however, the left-handed South African expatriate received little support from his other Queensland colleagues. Ten batsmen contributed precisely 122 runs as their side descended to the depths of defeat by an innings and 93 runs.

Dennis Lillee attempted his second come-back of the season when he played in Perth against South Australia, 24 days after a further operation on his right knee. The fast bowler captured 4/72 on the first day: figures which included a spell of 3/12 in 18 balls. Phillips, Haysman and Wright fought back for South Australia, each notching half-centuries in a total of 288. Clark stifled hopes of a more substantial score by taking the last four wickets cheaply, only to see his side slump immediately to 3/48. Hughes came to the rescue once more with an inspired 123 and assisted Geoff Marsh to add 108 for the fourth wicket. He then combined with Yardley to advance his side's total by a further 105 for the seventh wicket and give the Perth side a 36 run advantage on the first innings. David Hookes was the Messiah of the South Australian second knock. He made 118 of his eventual tally of 146 in the afternoon session of the third day and his 188 run association with Harris enabled him to close the innings at 7/387. Faced with the problem of survival in the final phases of the match, Western Australia hung on to be 6/209 at stumps, opener Laird proving the main stumbling block in the path of the South Australian bowlers and remaining unbeaten on 88. Garner added the figures of 4/43 to his previous analysis of 3/87, but Hogg was unable to reproduce the form which yielded him 5/88 in his first stint at the bowling crease.

Western Australia's ship of shield hopes became becalmed in the doldrums when it gleaned only four points from its next three matches. Laird, deputising for Hughes in Brisbane, won the toss and sent Queensland in, only to see his gamble misfire as the home batsmen scored steadily throughout the first day. Slow bowler, Tom Hogan, pulled Laird's chestnuts from the fire by taking 5/74, including the wickets of both openers and the promising Ritchie. The spinner was powerless, however, to prevent Hohn's men accumulate a respectable 394 runs. The Perth side plodded in pursuit of this total, Laird and Clements providing the solid prologue for a dogged 74 from Test opener, Graeme Wood, who on this occasion, went in at number three. Shipperd carried on in the same vein when Wood departed, taking 410 minutes over 64 runs and adding 92 with leg-spinner Tony Mann for the seventh wicket. The slowness of the visitors'

innings lost them the day and they fell 18 runs short of taki first innings points. There was only time for Hogan to add further three wickets to his match return and for Queensla to score 4/92 before the game died to a close.

Victoria collected four of its season's eight points whe Hohn's Laird's men stopped off in Melbourne on the return journey to Perth. On a flawless M.C.G. wicket, Vi toria's exciting middle-order discovery of the year, Dea Jones, scored runs at will before he was run out, attemptin his two hundredth run. He was well supported by sixties fro Yallop, Wiener and wicket-keeper, Geoff Miles, and t home side compiled 500 runs before closing with six wicke down. Western Australia replied with a spirited 336, a rounder Macleay contributing a precise hundred and t consistent Shipperd 79. Victorian paceman, McCurdy, aga showed a glimpse of the form which was to win him a pla in the national Under 25 side by capturing 5/94 and w instrumental in enabling Graham Yallop to enforce t follow-on. Shipperd was again well to the fore when his si batted a second time; his 107 foiled the home team's bid f outright victory and steered the Perth side into the sa waters of a 6/265 total.

Western Australia won its first points of 1983 in Perth February 22 when Tasmania crossed the Nullabor Plain do battle at the W.A.C.A. ground. The four points which gained on that occasion could and should have been 16, fo when stumps were drawn, Tasmania were well short of t home team's aggregate with their last batsmen still at t crease after having survived an unlikely five overs. Batti first, the full-strength local side lost its first four wicke including that of Hughes, for a modest 112. Macleay an Shipperd restored matters with a fifth wicket partnership 128, before Shipperd was dismissed three runs short of h half-century by Faulkner. Macleay appeared poised to regi ter his second hundred in as many games, when he to became a Faulkner victim when he was a mere boundary h away from his goal. Three of Peter Faulkner's eventual fo wickets came in the space of 19 balls and at a cost of five ru and enabled the visitors to restrict the locals to a 329 run fir innings total. When Tasmania batted it found runs hard come by, in spite of the encouragement which its batsme received from the Western Australian fieldsmen, wh dropped seven catches in the match. David Boon's 59 wa flawed by two missed chances, but he persevered and with t assistance of one of the rare half-centuries which came fro the bat of the English import, Roland Butcher, in 1982-8 took Tasmania to within 69 runs of its opponents' score. I its second innings Western Australia sped to 1/125 befo Blizzard reined the home batsmen in by taking 4/8 in 24 ball Laird's 72 and Wood's undefeated 53, however, enable Hughes to declare with 6/242 on the board, thus setting h opponents the challenge of 312 runs on the final day of th game. Tasmania were never in the hunt and declined rapidl to 6/115 in the face of the varied skills of Lillee, Clark an Yardley. Once again, however, Hughes' fieldsmen let hi down; Reid was dropped four times in scoring 42 and h hung on tenaciously as the tail-end batsmen, Saunder Faulkner and Blizzard saved the game for Woolley. Saun ders completed a fine double of 47 and 50 with the bat an was undoubtedly the individual who denied Wester Australia the extra 12 points which would come from a outright triumph.

The clear-cut victory which eluded Western Australia in its game against Tasmania came its way in its crucial clash with South Australia in Adelaide: an encounter which eliminated the home side as a Sheffield Shield contender. Hookes' men had only themselves to blame for their failure at the last hurdle. In the first instance, the home side, knowing that a draw was sufficient to gain them a finals place, played defensively and sent Western Australia in to bat after having won the toss. They then compounded their initial error by dropping Wood at 12 off a mistimed hook, and the left-hander went on to remind the bowlers of that blunder for a further 79 runs. Shipperd combined with the opener to add 142 for the second wicket: a stand which was consolidated by a century partnership between Hughes and Andrews for the fifth wicket. Western Australia were ultimately dismissed for 430, with South Australia's left-handed paceman Sam Parkinson capturing 7/98. When South Australia batted, Lillee set the local supporters back on their heels by trapping Harris lbw in his first over. The spin duet of Yardley and Hogan then chipped in with a joint seven wickets and Hughes was able to ask Hookes to bat again. The unfortunate South Australians fared little better in their second attempt, being dismissed for 213, to lose by an innings and 17 runs. Only Haysman and Sleep showed any stomach for their side's rearguard action, scoring 59 and 40 respectively and taking the total from 106 to 192 for the sixth wicket. Lillee captured seven wickets in the game, but suffered the double misfortune of straining a ligament in his already damaged knee and being reported for rudeness towards the South Australian spectators. This thick slice of misfortune resulted in the fast bowler missing the Shield final and being fined to boot.

South Australia's defeat at the hands of Western Australia was a bitter pill to swallow for a team which had set its sights on a half-a-dozen Shield premierships in the decade. It was all the more galling in the light of the consistent and victorious showing which Hookes' side had made throughout the season. It began well in Brisbane by dismissing an undepleted Queensland team twice for sub-200 totals and winning by 146 runs. Speedster Rackemann was in fine fettle when South Australia took first strike. Only Inverarity and Hookes were able to counter the blond paceman's bounce and movement and reach the half-century mark; Rackemann captured 7/49 in South Australia's first innings which ended suddenly at 235. Then it was Queensland's turn on the rack. The tall West Indian, Joel Garner, with the backing of Hogg and off-spinner Chris Harms, reduced the home batsmen to a state of tentative uncertainty and sent them all on their way back to the pavilion for 179. Batting a second time, South Australia failed by 11 runs to overhaul its first innings score, and the local players with only 282 runs to score and plenty of time in which to do it, must have felt confident of victory. Confidence, however, went before their fall. Garner shot out Kerr and Wessels, before Inverarity stepped into the breach with his left-handed spinners to complete the discomfiture of Chappell's side with a return of 5/56; an analysis which turned the Queensland second innings into a rout of 135 runs. Garner's figures for the three day game were 7/64, but the victory was primarily a resounding triumph of team spirit, with Hookes, Inverarity, Hogg, Garner, Zadow and Harms all making substantial contributions with either bat or ball.

Victoria's visit to the Adelaide Oval caused the cricket record book to be re-written as David Hookes became the Percy Fender of 'Down Under' by scoring the fastest 100 by an Australian and the quickest century registered anywhere in the world in terms of balls faced. In his side's second innings, Hookes went to the wicket piqued by what he regarded as an unjust declaration on the part of Victorian skipper, Yallop. He then proceeded to lambast the bowlers to all quarters of the ground. He raced into three figures in just 43 minutes off 34 deliveries and was dismissed after scoring 107 in 55 minutes off 40 balls. In spite of Hookes' fireworks, the game was inconclusive with Victoria recovering from a poor initial effort to record 9/420 in its second knock. Taking first strike, the Melbourne side slumped to 6/109 against the lifting pace of Garner. All-rounder, Shaun Graf, led a minor recovery, reaching 48 after 73 minutes at the crease and combining with wicket-keeper Sacristani to advance Victoria's score by 59 runs for the seventh wicket. Sacristani and fast bowler, King each contributed fifties to their side's eventual tally of 260. Hookes and Inverarity quickly made the Victorian players aware of the fact that their effort was not good enough. The captain and former skipper of South Australia notched 136 and 126 respectively and in tandem advanced the score by 212 for the fourth wicket. Faced with a deficit of 149, Victoria made a better fist of its second batting attempt. Yallop stroked the ball superbly for 151 but did little to enhance his reputation as a fair captain when he declared to leave South Australia the impossibility of scoring 272 in two hours to win. But at least Yallop's insensitive closure provoked Hookes into giving the Adelaide spectators an unforgettable display of hitting.

After conceding four points to New South Wales in Adelaide, South Australia exacted the identical tribute from Queensland on the same ground. Deprived of six players by Test calls, the Brisbane team only managed 267 in its first knock, Henschell being its lone star with a valiant 71. He had to contend with the pace of Hogg and Garner who appropriated nine of the ten wickets to fall. South Australia replied with 401, with opener Phillips occupying the crease for only two hours to score 92. But the real star of the Adelaide side was the elegant right-hander Michael Haysman, who was the replacement for David Hookes, absent on Test duty in Brisbane. Endowed with an immense amount of time in which to play his strokes, the stylish 21 year-old made his effortless way to an impressive 126 in his first match; it was the complete vindication of the ability which was already obvious when, at the age of 19, he recorded a double century for the South Australian Colts. Queensland gave every indication of performing as badly with the bat in its second innings as it had in the first. Three men were out with only 24 on the board, before Henschell mounted a slashing counter-attack which took him into three figures in 145 minutes and ultimately to 162. He and opener Kerr compiled a joint 157 for the fourth wicket and it was thanks largely to their resistance that South Australia were set the challenge of scoring 176 in about 55 overs. In the final analysis 56 overs were bowled and, astonishingly, the side failed to score at only three runs per over.

By the time that South Australia travelled to Launceston to meet Tasmania, it had recorded another outright victory at the expense of New South Wales and lost on the first innings against Western Australia. Rain washed out the third day of the game against Woolley's Taswegians and it was therefore not surprising that the match was limited to a first

New South Wales 1982-3
First-Class Matches

BATTING

BATTING	WA (Perth) 15-18 Oct I	II	Tas (Sydney) 22-25 Oct I	II	SA (Adelaide) 6-9 Nov I	II	WA (Sydney) 12-15 Nov I	II	England XI 20-23 Nov I	II	SA (Sydney) 3-6 Dec I	II	Victoria (Newc.) 18-21 Dec I	II	Qld (Brisbane) 21-24 Jan I	II	Victoria (Melb.) 28-31 Jan I	II	Sri Lankans 10-12 Feb I	II	Qld (Sydney) 18-21 Feb I	II
R. B. McCosker	84	59	1	69	116	30	60	21	3	1	67	5	124	66*	112	—	6	66*	8	45*	8	9
I. C. Davis	56	17	0	14															14	—		
T. M. Chappell	16	30*	1	16	92	0	15	42	1	61	37	5	7	—	16	—	8	22	40*	2	132	35
S. B. Smith	52	21*			2	13	1	40	50	3	65	32	0	14	119	—	263	1			15	18
D. M. Wellham	136*	—	37	16	75	6*	81	42	23	38	55	11	88	9	93	—	56	72*	35	—	124	50*
P. M. Toohey	75	—	14	21	24	16	16*	—	17	69	0	14	28	0	3	—	104	—	58	2*		
S. J. Rixon	27	—	11	46	0	—	19	0	57*	7	11	52	20	25*	—	—	1	—	14		18	10
M. J. Bennett	30*	—	21*	23	59*	—	20	21*	10	29	31	6	4	—	—	—	4	—	24		6*	6*
L. S. Pascoe	—	—	2	15							5	5	0	—								
A. J. Skilbeck	—	—	0	0																		
M. R. Whitney	—	—			10	—	28*	—	5*	7	0*	0*										
M. D. O'Neill			36	65																		
R. G. Holland			3	9*	10	—	40	—	0	17*	1	0					5*	—				
J. Dyson					15	55*			43	59			4	18					52	—	35	21
G. F. Lawson					0	—			22	1			16*	—								
G. R. J. Matthews							4	1							49*	—	81*	—	26*	—	40*	15
E. S. Gordon							1	—														
G. Spring											1	10										
Byes	3	1			2		5	2			2	8	4				11	1			1	5
Leg-byes	12	1	3		8	2	3	7	7	10	9	1	(25)	6	10		14	1	(20)	(17)	3	7
Wides	1		1	1	1	1	1				1				1						3	
No-balls	10		3	3	11	1	6	8	12	4	13	4			8		9	3			23	19
Total	502	129	133	311	425	123	295	230	250	306	297	154	316	150	406		562	166	253	104	405	193
Wickets	6	2	10	10	10	4	10	6	9	10	10	10	9	4	5		7	2	5	3	6	6
Result	D		L		D		W		L		L		D		W		D		D		W	
Points	4		0		4		12		—		0		4		16		4		—		16	

Catches

37 – S. J. Rixon (ct 28/st 9)	8 – J. Dyson and P. M. Toohey	4 – L. S. Pascoe
20 – R. B. McCosker	7 – S. B. Smith and M. R. Whitney	3 – I. C. Davis
12 – M. J. Bennett	6 – D. M. Wellham	2 – E. S. Gordon
11 – T. M. Chappell	5 – R. G. Holland, G. F. Lawson and G. R. J. Matthews	1 – A. J. Skilbeck and M. D. O'Neill

BOWLING

	L. S. Pascoe	A. J. Skilbeck	M. R. Whitney	T. M. Chappell	M. J. Bennett	R. B. McCosker	R. G. Holland	G. F. Lawson
v. Western Australia (Perth) 15-18 October, 1982	39.4–11–109–3	35–11–87–2	29–6–74–0	15–6–26–1	52–25–74–2	14–4–28–2		
v. Tasmania (Sydney) 22-25 October, 1982	33–8–112–2 10.2–0–45–2	14–1–47–0 3–0–11–0		8–2–17–0	40.1–22–55–4		54–22–100–4 7–0–33–1	
v. South Australia (Adelaide) 6-9 November, 1982			32–3–133–5 21–7–62–2	16–5–52–1 4–0–14–0	18–7–60–0 4–1–22–0		22–4–86–0 34–10–65–3	29.4–7–77–4 25–5–58–2
v. Western Australia (Sydney) 12-15 November, 1982			22–7–68–2 8–3–27–1	5–1–12–0 4–1–10–1	29.2–16–47–3 36–23–39–5		36–12–98–2 44.4–22–59–1	
v. England XI (Sydney) 20-23 November, 1982			19–4–73–1 27.3–6–60–4	8.1–1–23–4 11–3–21–0	21–5–65–4 44–13–123–5		7–3–19–0 38–8–123–0	15–4–30–1
v. South Australia (Sydney) 3-6 December, 1982	28–5–99–5 12–3–44–1		25–3–92–2 20–6–70–4	2–1–6–0	10.5–6–34–2 7–0–27–0		11–7–16–0 22–4–51–0	
v. Victoria (Newcastle) 18-21 December, 1982	9–2–16–1 34–3–123–0		8–2–22–1 24–6–94–0	10–3–17–2	14–10–9–4 47–18–97–2	2–0–9–0		15.2–6–36–4 40–5–120–3
v. Queensland (Brisbane) 21-24 January, 1983		7–1–21–1 6–1–16–0	10.3–0–33–3 39–11–93–5	5–1–21–2 11.4–4–17–1	14–6–33–0		11–6–16–3 37–17–53–0	
v. Victoria (Melbourne) 28-31 January, 1983	28–3–98–3		23–2–98–2 7–2–14–1	17.1–5–40–3 21–3–87–3	19–8–31–1 31–6–102–2		23–14–40–0 23–5–74–2	
v. Sri Lankans (Sydney) 10-12 February, 1983	19–1–66–3		15–0–54–2	10–3–20–1	14.3–3–42–2			
v. Queensland (Sydney) 18-21 February, 1983	17.3–1–60–1 10.4–1–32–3		19–1–30–0 16–4–40–2	4–2–8–0	37–7–108–2			36–6–102–4 19–2–59–4
v. Tasmania (Hobart) 25-28 February, 1983	23–3–74–3		19.3–4–74–3	4–0–14–1	18–6–45–1			35–8–89–2
v. Western Australia (Perth) 4-8 March, 1983			25.2–4–67–4 18–4–45–1	16–5–32–3 20.5–6–45–4	29–12–50–0 22–9–39–0			22–6–58–2 28–10–52–5
	264.1–41–878–27 av. 32.51	65–14–182–3 av. 60.66	427.5–85–1323–45 av. 29.40	192.5–52–482–27 av. 17.85	507.5–203–1102–39 av. 28.25	16–4–37–2 av. 18.50	369.4–134–833–16 av. 52.06	265–59–681–31 av. 21.96

v. Tasmania (Hobart) 25-28 February, 1983		v. Western Australia (Perth) 4-8 March, 1983		Inns	NOs	Runs	HS	Av
13	65*	71	44	25	4	1153	124	54.90
				5	—	101	56	20.20
12	0	10	33	24	2	633	132	28.77
13	0	3	37	21	1	762	263	38.10
76	6*	6	70	23	5	1205	136*	66.94
		40	26	19	2	568	104	33.41
28	17	20	10*	20	3	393	57*	23.11
43*	—	10	9	18	7	356	59*	32.36
15	—			6	—	42	15	7.00
				2	—	0	0	—
0	—	0	0	9	4	50	28*	10.00
				2	—	101	65	50.50
				9	3	85	40	14.16
22	14	57	10	13	1	405	59	33.75
44	—	7*	2	7	2	92	44	18.40
24	45	34	24	11	4	343	81*	49.00
				1	—	1	1	1.00
				2	—	11	10	5.50
	5	3	8					
13	4	8	5					
5								
3	8	2	2					
311	164	271	280	.				
10	5	10	10					
	D	W						
	0	—						

E. S. Gordon	G. R. J. Matthews	G. Spring	Byes	Leg-byes	Wides	No-balls	Total	Wkts
			5	3		22	428	10
			6	8	1	5	351	10
				4		1	94	3
			2	3		5	418	10
			5	5		4	235	7
7-2-53-2	22-8-37-1			5	2	5	327	10
-3-16-0	13-7-27-2		8	7		4	197	10
			5	13		12	240	10
			7	4	2	2	342	10
		33-9-76-0		4		8	335	9
		6-1-23-0	2			6	223	5
				(7)			90	10
			1	12	1	5	479	7
	13-7-17-1			1	1		110	10
	29-8-65-3		5	7		2	291	10
	18-3-60-0		8	11		10	396	10
	4-0-14-0		10	12	1		314	8
	6-1-14-1			(11)			207	9
	25-5-63-2		3	10		18	402	10
	18-4-49-1		1	2	2	10	195	10
	6-4-17-0			8	1	10	332	10
	20-9-42-0		2	5	3		259	10
	18-4-50-0		5	1		1	238	10
23-5–	192-60–	39-10–						
9-2	455-11	99-0						
v. 34.50	av. 41.36	—						

innings decision. When the visitors batted first, four batsmen – Inverarity, Phillips, Hilditch and Bishop – subscribed fifties to their side's eventual tally of 330. Only two Tasmanians – Reid and Butcher – emulated their achievements as the island batsmen floundered against the rearing deliveries of the accurate Garner. The West Indian speedster sent seven batsmen back to the dressing-room at a personal cost of 78 as the home team fell 64 runs short of its target for first innings points. Then the rains came, leaving only the remnant of a match – just enough time for South Australia to notch 2/78 in its second innings.

David turned the tables on Goliath when the Taswegians returned South Australia's visit. In Adelaide, it was Tasmania who emerged from the contest with the points. Fast bowler and former New South Welshman, Peter Clough, had a field day, returning career best figures of 6/53 in the home state's inadequate first innings total of 148. The islanders then rubbed salt in their hosts' wounds by reeling off a substantial reply of 336 runs. Boon's powerful forearms and crisp strokes yielded him a century and, with the support of Butcher's 53, he advanced the Tasmanian score by 92 before the fifth wicket fell. Andrew Sincock proved an admirable stand-in for Rodney Hogg by taking 5/96. South Australia did much better when it tried its luck a second time. The dominating Phillips opened the innings with a bang, dispatching the ball to all parts of the Adelaide Oval and helping Hilditch – now fully recovered from a broken jaw sustained in the course of the Queensland game – to add 198 for the second wicket. Phillips departed after contributing 161 glorious runs, but Hilditch went on to record 109 and find other partners in Inverarity and Haysman, both of whom topped the fifty mark. Taunted with the task of scoring 260 in 66 overs Tasmania set off at a rattling pace and openers Smith and Ray posted 111 runs on the scoreboard in no time at all. Sleep's leg-spinners halted the gallop however, bringing him five wickets and causing Tasmania to settle for a draw with its score standing at 8/239.

Wresting full points off Victoria in Melbourne was like taking candy off a child for Hookes' South Australians. So superior were the wearers of the red, yellow and black caps that the game was won with a day and a session's play unused. On a pitch which gave fast man Rodney Hogg a great deal of encouragement, Victoria was bundled out for 132. It does not bear thinking about how many the home side would have scored if Garner had not already returned home to the West Indies. South Australia also began shakily and lost 4/48 before Hookes strode to the wicket to put an end to the uncertainty about which side was going to win the game. The powerful left-hander literally tore the Victorian attack apart. At the end of the first day's play, Hookes was an unbeaten 181, having rocketed to his hundred in 91 minutes and 75 balls and to 150 in 21 more deliveries. Speedster McCurdy broke Hookes' thumb when he was 97 but this merely spurred him on to greater efforts and he was dismissed when he was only seven runs short of his double century. Haysman also donated a hundred to his side's massive 445 aggregate and he was far from overshadowed by Hookes. His 153 was a model of elegance, accomplishment and steely control and together he and Hookes took 262 runs off the suffering Victorian bowlers during their fifth wicket partnership. McCurdy stuck to his fast bowling task manfully and was rewarded with the figures of 6/73. The strongly

Queensland 1982-3
First-Class Matches

Match column key:

- M1 — v. South Australia (Brisbane), 15-17 October, 1982
- M2 — v. England XI (Brisbane), 22-25 October, 1982
- M3 — v. Tasmania (Launceston), 30 Oct.-2 Nov., 1982
- M4 — v. Victoria (Brisbane), 19-22 Nov., 1982
- M5 — v. South Australia (Adelaide), 26-29 Nov., 1982
- M6 — v. Western Australia (Perth), 3-5 December, 1982
- M7 — v. Tasmania (Brisbane), 10-13 Dec., 1982
- M8 — v. New Zealanders (Bundaberg), 18-21 Dec., 1982
- M9 — v. Western Australia (Brisbane), 8-11 January, 1983
- M10 — v. New South Wales (Brisbane), 21-24 January, 1983
- M11 — v. New South Wales (Sydney), 18-21 February, 1983

BATTING

Batting	M1	M2	M3	M4	M5	M6	M7	M8	M9	M10	M11
K. C. Wessels	39 12	14 103	65 12	86 —		0 128		129 16			25 39
R. B. Kerr	48 8	7 65	59 12	112 —	16 48	7 13	0 —	102 33	36 12	49 28	72 15
W. R. Broad	36 8	20 45			32 14		16 —		89 37	9 4	
G. S. Chappell	1 5	40 126	30 —	19 —		19 28					17 29
A. B. Henschell	0 25	50 54	21 0*	6 —	71 162	1 0	10 —		44 —	3 53	10 4
R. J. Lawrence	19 48	1 6*			11 1						
T. V. Hohns	4 2	17 —	11* —	30 10*	18 21	10* 5	66 —	28	21 —	31* 54*	38 4
R. B. Phillips	14 13	55* 5*	15 —	5* 19*	8 50	1 1	6 —	61	56 12*	9 11	23 9
I. N. Gallagher	3 3										
C. G. Rackemann	0 8	11 —	16* —	2* —				3			
J. N. Maguire	1* 0*	10* —	— —		2 0*	0 7*	10 —		3	5 —	7* 0*
H. Frei		57 —	16 —	0 —	13 2	4 18	41 —	14	26 —	1 20	1 30
A. R. Border			93 79*	99 —		1 23		104* 30*			165 47
G. M. Ritchie			67 46	55 —		5 5	60 —	24 9	12 0	0 1	0 3
J. R. Thomson				— —		0 22					13 0
A. B. Courtice					25 0		9 —		21* 37	39 22	0 74
C. B. Smart					34 0						
S. Beattie					10* 0						
M. A. Gaskell							10 —				
M. S. Mainhardt							0* —	5			
G. S. Trimble										48 5*	1 10
P. W. Twible										4* —	0 11
M. Maranta											— 11
Byes	1	4	1		10 1		1	7 3	1 2	5	3 1
Leg-byes	3	3 7	5 3	12 2	9 3	1 6	9	2 8	8 2	1 7	10 2
Wides		1 1		5 1				2	1 5	1	2
No-balls	9 3	11 19	1	18	8 7	3 5	2	14 9	2	2	18 10
Total	178 135	297 435	400 152	449 32	267 309	52 261	242	403 258	394 92	110 291	402 195
Wickets	10 10	9 5	8 3	8 0	10 10	10 10	10	3 10	10 4	10 10†	10 10
Result	L	W	D	W	D	L	D	D	D	L	L
Points	0	—	4	16	0	0	0	—	4	0	0

Catches 37 – R. B. Phillips (ct 35/st 2) 10 – G. M. Ritchie 8 – T. V. Hohns and A. B. Henschell 6 – K. C. Wessels
12 – G. S. Chappell 9 – R. B. Kerr and W. R. Broad (one as sub.) 7 – A. R. Border and H. Frei 2 – R. J. Lawrence

† M. Maranta (12th man) was allowed to bat in the second innings when J. N. Maguire was called to the Australian side.

BOWLING

Match	C. G. Rackemann	J. N. Maguire	G. S. Chappell	T. V. Hohns	I. N. Gallagher	W. R. Broad	A. B. Henschell	H. Frei	A. R. Border
v. South Australia (Brisbane) 15-17 October, 1982	23-8-49-7 / 24.3-7-58-4	24-2-78-1 / 21-5-50-3	5-0-13-0 / 6-3-8-0	14-7-24-1 / 13-4-31-0	8-2-30-1 / 15-4-33-1	7-1-17-0			
v. England XI (Brisbane) 22-25 October, 1982	20-6-61-2 / 12-5-35-0	20-6-48-2 / 12-5-28-2		28-5-90-0			6-0-29-2 / 12.2-3-51-4	19-4-76-2 / 15-7-31-3	
v. Tasmania (Launceston) 30 October-2 November, 1982	39-13-86-4	33-11-73-1	4-3-2-0	35-12-78-0			34.2-10-82-5	16-3-42-0	3-1-12-0
v. Victoria (Brisbane) 19-22 November, 1982	18.3-5-38-5 / 28-6-43-3		1-0-12-0 / 7-1-23-0	32.3-10-89-3			7-3-24-1 / 10-3-39-0	8-2-30-1 / 19-9-25-2	
v. Western Australia (Adelaide) 26-29 November, 1982		39-11-127-1 / 28-5-70-4		27-6-51-3		4-0-17-0 / 7-2-17-1	16-2-46-0	35.1-8-106-4 / 21-4-64-1	
v. Western Australia (Perth) 3-5 December, 1982		19-3-46-1	15-3-31-3	49-16-122-1			35-18-49-0	29.1-5-69-4	
v. Tasmania (Brisbane) 10-13 December, 1982		34-10-93-4 / 6-1-12-1		26.1-15-26-3		10-2-22-1	17-6-51-1 / 16-6-26-0	28-7-66-2 / 10-5-25-0	
v. New Zealanders (Bundaberg) 18-21 December, 1982	20-6-47-5 / 21.3-8-40-3			17.2-2-70-2 / 22-8-60-2			16-2-58-1 / 13-4-27-0	19-2-59-1 / 20-7-44-1	1-1-0-0
v. Western Australia (Brisbane) 8-11 January, 1983		29-8-66-1		24-10-43-0			47-16-76-4	37-16-75-2	
v. New South Wales (Brisbane) 21-24 January, 1983		29-5-80-2		28-4-70-0		2-0-5-0	27-10-66-1	30.2-5-98-2	
v. New South Wales (Sydney) 18-21 February, 1983		30-8-93-3	1-0-1-0 / 9-1-43-0	32-8-101-2			12-1-43-0 / 2-0-16-0	23-5-61-0 / 7-0-28-1	3-0-9-0
v. Victoria (Junction Oval) 25-28 February, 1983		29-4-104-0		40.4-7-123-4			33-4-89-0	19-4-86-1	
Totals	206.3-64-457-33 av. 13.84	370-88-1019-28 av. 36.39	54-12-115-3 av. 38.33	388.4-114-978-21 av. 46.57	23-6-63-2 av. 31.50	30-5-78-2 av. 39.00	321.5-90-832-24 av. 34.66	355.4-93-985-27 av. 36.48	7-1-21-0 av. —

† W. M. Darling retired hurt; A. M. J. Hilditch absent injured a P.W. Twible 31.4-10-82-3 b P.W. Twible 20-4-73-0

(Junction Oval) 25-28 February, 1983

		Inns	NOs	Runs	HS	Av
49	22	15	—	939	249	62.60
32	2	22	—	876	132	39.81
		11	—	310	89	28.18
		10	—	314	126	31.40
—	28	19	1	543	162	30.16
		6	1	86	48	17.20
—	6	18	5	376	66	28.92
—	18*	20	6	391	61	27.92
		2	—	6	3	3.00
		6	2	40	16*	10.00
—	1*	13	8	46	10*	9.20
—	15	15	—	258	57	17.20
80	43	11	3	764	165	95.50
58	37	16	—	382	67	23.87
—	—	4	—	35	22	8.75
5*	2	11	2	234	74	26.00
		2	—	34	34	17.00
		2	1	10	10*	10.00
		1	—	10	10	10.00
		2	1	5	5	5.00
		4	1	64	48	21.33
		3	1	15	11	7.50
		1	—	11	11	11.00

	6
7	2
	1
5	5
36	188
4	8
D	
4	

– A. B. Courtice, M. A. Gaskell, G. S. Trimble, C. B. Smart and J. R. Thomson

J. R. Thomson	S. Beattie	M. S. Mainhardt	Byes	Leg-byes	Wides	No-balls	Total	Wkts
				8		16	235	10
				5	1	9	224	10
			9	20	1	16	372	10
			6	8	2	7	189	10
				7		14	396	10
6–24–1			1	5	2	15	151	10
–1–74–2			3	11	3	16	326	10
		7–0–39–0	2	2		11	401	8†
			1	5		1	158	8
6–76–1			2	5		6	406	10
		13–2–40–0	3	5	2	10	296	10
		13–2–38–0		1		3	127	2
		12–2–44–1	1	7		18	304	10
		8–0–20–1	8	5	2	15	221	7
			8	10		16	376	10a
				10	1	3	406	5b
5–7–70–1			1	3		23	405	6
–4–26–3			5	7	3	14	193	6
3–4–85–4				6		17	510	10
27–28–	7–0–	46–6–						
55–12	39–0	142–2						
v. 29.58	—	av. 71.00						

built speedster and Graham Yallop were the only bright spots in an otherwise mediocre Victorian display. When the home side batted a second time its skipper emulated his counterpart in the South Australian team and completely dismembered the opposing attack. Yallop's punishing knock of 168 compelled South Australia to go to the wicket a second time: it experienced little difficulty, however, in knocking off the required 37 runs for victory for the loss of three wickets. Sadly after its moral-boosting defeat of Victoria, South Australia was doomed to ultimate disappointment. Five days later it met its Philippi at the hands of Western Australia in Adelaide.

One outright victory, three first innings wins and 28 points constituted the factual resumé of Queensland's 1982–83 season. It was indicative of the northern state's poor summer that 20 of its points were won at the expense of Victoria, the bottom team in the Shield ladder. After losing its initial encounter against South Australia in Brisbane in mid-October, Chappell's side travelled to Launceston, determined to redeem its pawned reputation against Tasmania. It succeeded in its ambitions – but only just! Batting first, the visitors began well and Wessels and Kerr were not separated until the scoreboard showed Queensland to be 95. Border carried on the good work with a competent 93, increasing his team's total by 107 for the fifth wicket. Four individuals contributed fifty or more to the Queensland cause and Greg Chappell was able to declare at 8/400. Tasmania opened with a sound 58 run association between Ray and Smith, but subsequently lost Ray, Boon, Small and Butcher for the addition of a further 66 runs. As he was destined to do so often in the course of the summer, Roger Woolley played a responsible captain's role; his 80 ensured that, by the time that the eighth wicket fell, his side had progressed to 312. Then Saunders and Blizzard batted with great determination to add a further 55 for the ninth wicket, before Blizzard and Clough became the fourth and fifth victims of off-spinner Henschell, leaving Saunders marooned on 79 not out and Tasmania a frustrating five runs short of a first innings victory. The domination of bat over ball continued in Queensland's second innings with the visitors compiling 3/152 and the left-handed Border completing a sound double with an undefeated 79.

Victoria's unenviable 17 year-old record of failure in Brisbane continued when it visited the northern capital in mid-November to lose by 10 wickets and give Queensland its only outright victory of the season. Yallop's side began its fixtures as it was destined to continue, failing miserably with the bat in its first innings. Rackemann's fast-medium pace completely bemused the southern players and they trooped to and from the pavilion in a constant despondent procession, gathering only 151 runs en route. The Queensland openers, Kerr and Wessels, bettered this total themselves and came within 21 runs of the first wicket record of Bill Brown and Rex Rogers – established in 1938–39 – before they were separated. Kerr's fourth Shield century was reinforced by Border's 99, 86 from Wessels and 55 from Ritchie, as the home side amassed 8/449 declared. Victoria improved when it was given a second chance. Yallop notched 73, Wiener 67 and Taylor 66 in an effort which realised 326; but it was a case of too little, too late, and Queensland knocked off the 32 runs required for victory without loss.

Flushed with success, a depleted Queensland departed on

South Australia 1982-3
First-Class Matches

BATTING

BATTING	v Queensland (Brisbane) 15-17 October, 1982	v Victoria (Adelaide) 22-25 October, 1982	v England XI (Adelaide) 31 Oct.-3 Nov., 1982	v New South Wales (Adelaide) 6-9 November, 1982	v Queensland (Adelaide) 26-29 Nov., 1982	v New South Wales (Sydney) 3-6 December, 1982	v Western Australia (Perth) 17-20 Dec., 1982	v Tasmania (Launceston) 31 Dec. 1982-3 January, 1983	v Tasmania (Adelaide) 21-24 January, 1983	v Victoria (St. Kilda) 18-20 February, 1983	v Western Australia (Adelaide) 25-28 February, 1983
W. M. Darling	26 5	10 11	39 23	98 5	17* —					15 4	
K. P. Harris	1 1	9 0					22 74	5 20*	21 17		0 17
A. M. J. Hilditch	7 8	42 0*	38 79	59 45	— 4			59 26	0 109	2 6	20 42
R. J. Inverarity	63 2	126 15*		77 21	8 20	104 46*	8 0	66 —	21 51	0 15*	37 18
D. W. Hookes	53 87	137 107	74 39	65 60		35 42	10 146			193 —	32 0
R. J. Zadow	4 87	5 8	11 8								
K. J. Wright	9 4	33 30	65* 38	0 49*	52 0	0 49*	64 22	31* —	0 —	8 —	1 0
C. L. Harms	23 4	21 3	22 46*	28 11	12 42	3 —	14 30*		0 —	17 10	
J. Garner	14 0	7 19		10 8*	12 13	22 —	6 —				
R. M. Hogg	7 7	0 —		3* —	1* 0*	— —	0* —			13 —	17* 9
A. T. Sincock	4* 4*	8* —	24 6*	8 —					2 —	40* —	5 5
W. B. Phillips			5 5	8 15	92 30	112 54	58 10	53 13	7 161	4 1	42 10
P. R. Sleep			51 9	52 7	23 18	2 13		13 —	28* 10*	0 —	6 40
R. C. Christensen			3 2					0 —			
M. C. Dolman			0 —								
M. D. Haysman					126 9	45 6	71 53	29 14*	21 54	153 10*	34 59
D. A. Johnston					43 15*	0* —	2 2*	0 —			
I. R. McLean						0 5					
G. A. Bishop							9 31	55 —	19 9		
S. H. Parkinson									7 —	0 —	0 3*
Byes		— 5	4 8	2 5	2 1	2 —	5 —	5 4	3 3	1 —	3 3
Leg-byes	8 5	6 7	4 6	3 5	2 5	4 —	4 10	9 —	1 19	8 7	3 6
Wides		1 1	— 1	1 —			2 3	1 1		1 —	
No-balls	16 9	4 —	4 1	5 4	11 1	8 6	13 6	4 —	1 4	9 2	1 —
Total	235 224	409 206	344 271	418 235	401 158	335 223	288 387	330 78	148 447	445 47	200 213
Wickets	10 10	10 7	10 8	10 7	8† 8	9 5	10 7	10 2	10 7	10 3	10 10
Result	W	D	D	D	D	W	D	D	D	W	L
Points	16	4	—	0	4	16	0	4	0	16	0

Catches 40 – K. J. Wright (ct 36/st 4)
14 – D. W. Hookes
8 – P. R. Sleep, R. J. Inverarity and M. D. Haysman
7 – W. B. Phillips
6 – A. M. J. Hilditch
5 – C. L. Harms and A. T. Sincock
4 – K. P. Harris
3 – J. Garner, R. M. Hogg and G. A. Bishop
2 – D. A. Johnston and R. J. Zadow
1 – W. M. Darling, R. C. Christensen and sub.

† W. M. Darling retired hurt, A. M. J. Hilditch absent injured

BOWLING

v. Queensland (Brisbane) 15-17 October, 1982
19-7-44-2 24.1-12-32-5 14-5-27-2 9-1-26-1 8-1-36-0
13-6-27-2 13-4-32-2 4.1-0-17-1 14-4-56-5

v. Victoria (Adelaide) 22-25 October, 1982
20.1-4-38-2 28-5-73-4 14-4-38-1 14-5-48-0 18-9-50-2 3-1-8-1
21-6-62-1 30-9-81-2 29-9-71-2 41-7-116-3 18-3-77-1 2-1-6-0

v. England XI (Adelaide) 31 October-3 November, 1982
32-11-79-1 30-4-105-0 12-2-33-2 27-6-84-1 34-9-89-3
28-6-96-3 7-2-22-0 1-0-1-0 6-1-15-0 29-11-86-4

v. New South Wales (Adelaide) 6-9 November, 1982
20-1-73-0 46-14-113-7 8-1-28-0 25.5-6-65-1 21-3-69-2 12-3-30-0
9-2-29-0 12-1-57-4 1-1-0-0 1-0-13-0 6-1-20-0

v. Queensland (Adelaide) 26-29 November, 1982
27.2-7-51-5 31-4-79-4 11-7-8-0 16-4-38-0 12-1-38-1
18-3-53-7 23.4-5-63-2 12-2-46-1 11-2-33-0 21-3-89-0

v. New South Wales (Sydney) 3-6 December, 1982
32-6-90-4 39-18-61-4 5-1-13-0 12-2-28-0 12-2-34-1
15-4-42-2 20.1-7-70-6

v. Western Australia (Perth) 17-20 December, 1982
25.5-4-88-5 32-11-87-3 4-0-25-0 10-3-16-0 1-0-12-0 5-1-16-1
10-1-27-1 23-11-43-4 9-4-23-0 31-11-72-1 3-0-18-0

v. Tasmania (Launceston) 31 December, '82-3 January, '83
33.1-16-78-7 23-8-51-2 14-3-37-1 3-0-30-0

v. Tasmania (Adelaide) 21-24 January, 1983
23-10-44-0 32-13-51-2 31-8-96-5 20.4-5-64-2 21-4-58-
25-4-63-1 6-0-18-2 8-0-41-0 20-4-77-6 6-0-25-0

v. Victoria (St. Kilda) 18-20 February, 1983
12-2-31-4 7-1-35-1 10-3-29-6 5-1-15-1
21-4-67-2 14-5-38-1 21-4-73-3 19-4-75-0 16.5-2-7

v. Western Australia (Adelaide) 25-28 February, 1983
31-2-96-1 32-8-77-1 31-7-104-1 3-1-12-0 27.5-3-9

Totals
294.2-59-818-38 av. 21.52
403.1-131-976-55 av. 17.74
170.1-50-471-11 av. 42.81
291.5-80-733-19 av. 38.57
201-42-721-15 av. 48.06
29-4-103-3 av. 34.33
47-10-136-2 av. 68.00
206.4-48-689-21 av. 32.80
76.4-10-275-11 av. 25.00

a M. C. Dolman 15-3-72-2   b M. D. Haysman 5-2-12-0

Inns	NOs	Runs	HS	Av
11	1	253	98	25.30
12	1	187	74	17.00
17	1	546	109	34.12
19	3	698	126	43.62
15	—	1080	193	72.00
6	—	123	87	20.50
19	4	455	65*	30.33
13	2	259	46*	23.54
13	1	138	22	11.50
10	5	57	17*	11.40
10	5	106	40*	21.20
18	—	680	161	37.77
14	2	272	52	22.66
3	—	5	3	1.66
1	—	0	0	—
14	2	684	153	57.00
6	3	62	43	20.66
2	—	5	5	2.50
5	—	123	55	24.60
4	1	10	7	3.33

		1	3		9	178	10
			3			135	10
		1	1		3	260	10
			3		4	420	9
3-2-4-0	2-0-12-0	8	6			492	9a
		3	2		1	226	8
		2	8	1	11	425	10
	1-0-1-0		2		1	123	4
	7-1-26-0	10	9		8	267	10
	6-2-14-0	1	3		7	309	10
	26-8-47-1	2	9		13	297	10
		8	1	1	4	154	10
	21-3-72-2	9	17		10	324	10
	8-3-13-0		9	1	3	209	6
	16-3-56-0		5		9	266	10
		1	5	1	16	336	10
		4	8		3	239	8
		1	13		8	132	10
		4	13	1	9	359	10
		9	9	8	5	430	10b

3-2-	3-0-	84-20-
4-0	13-0	228-3
—	—	av. 76.00

its southern tour at the end of November. It returned pale with disappointment, for, even though it was reinforced by its Test players for the match against Western Australia, it failed to gain a point from eight day's play, losing on the first innings against South Australia and being annihilated by an innings by the Perth side. Nor were brighter days around the corner when Woolley's Taswegians flew north to do battle in Brisbane. Not only did rain mar the match, but, in the course of the play which was possible, Tasmania proved themselves the better team. The island side began its first innings unconvincingly losing its first three batsmen for 33. David Boon then stepped into the role of the man of the hour. Benefiting from two missed catches he occupied the crease for just over six hours to compile 115 runs and guide his side to the respectability of 296. His main support came from all-rounder Reid who helped him to boost the total with a fourth wicket stand of 92. In reply Queensland lost Kerr without a run on the board and then crumbled to a parlous 5/85. The out-of-form Ritchie came to the rescue with an invaluable 60 before being foolishly run out. All of Queensland's hopes for a first innings ascendancy were finally dashed when Hohns was bowled by Holding for 66. With a 54 run lead, Tasmania went to the crease again and was 2/127, with Boon on 57 not out, when the rains returned and drew a convenient curtain over Queensland's discomfiture.

The rot really set in after the northern team's first innings loss to Tasmania. Four points from its home game against Western Australia were small consolation for successive outright defeats against New South Wales by an innings and five runs and by 4 wickets. Only the whipping boy of the Shield competition, Victoria, provided any measure of consolation for Chappell's men as the season died to a fall – and even then the solace came in the shape of an enormous score and first innings points rather than the more welcome alternative of a decisive victory. Yallop won the toss and, at the prompting of the Victorian selectors, asked Wessels to have the first use of a perfect wicket at the St Kilda Ground: an oval which at this stage of the summer was substituting for the Melbourne Cricket Ground which was being refurbished for the following season. The enormity of the failure of Yallop's gamble can be gauged from the fact that at close of play on the first day, the visitors had scored 2/434 off 99 overs. Kerr and Wessels began the batting mayhem by despatching the four specialist bowlers on whom the Victorian selectors exclusively pinned their hopes to all sections of the ground, to the tune of 388 in 323 minutes. Their partnership was the highest by any pair of Queensland batsmen since the state joined the Sheffield Shield competition in 1926. Enormous beginnings culminated in a mammoth conclusion, and when Wessels closed his team's innings, 536 runs were on the board for the loss of only four wickets. The acting skipper himself subscribed 249 of those runs in 340 minutes off 285 balls, scoring 36 boundaries in the process. Victoria were on a collision course with outright defeat when Watts, Richardson, Green and Taylor were all dismissed with only 160 on the board. It was then that Yallop and his young lieutenant, Dean Jones, dug in. Once their beach-head was established, the left and right-handed duet launched a ferocious assault upon the Queensland bowlers, doing unto others what had been done to themselves when Queensland batted. They were together for 270 runs, just failing by one run to break the Victorian record for the fifth wicket. Yallop, aware of the

Tasmania 1982-3
First-Class Matches

Match columns (each cell shows both innings where played):

1. v. New South Wales (Sydney) 22-25 October, 1982
2. v. Queensland (Launceston) 30 Oct.-2 Nov. 1982
3. v. Victoria (St. Kilda) 12-15 Nov. 1982
4. v. Western Australia (Devonport) 20-23 Nov. 1982
5. v. Queensland (Brisbane) 10-13 Dec. 1982
6. v. England XI (Hobart) 18-20 Dec. 1982
7. v. South Australia (Launceston) 31 Dec. 1982-3 Jan. 1983
8. v. Victoria (Devonport) 8-11 January, 1983
9. v. South Australia (Adelaide) 21-24 January, 1983
10. v. Sri Lankans (Devonport) 14-16 February, 1983
11. v. Western Australia (Perth) 19-22 February, 1983

BATTING

Batsman	NSW (Syd)	Qld (Lau)	Vic (StK)	WA (Dev)	Qld (Bris)	Eng XI (Hob)	SA (Lau)	Vic (Dev)	SA (Adel)	Sri L (Dev)	WA (Perth)
D. A. Smith	52 27	81 —	37 19	2 11	1 6	5 52*	40 —	0 —	23 72	25 3	0 15
M. Ray	3 23	33 —	33 12*	1 17				24 —	36 39	14 25	11 32
D. C. Boon	27 5	16 —	29 0*	4 99	115 57*	46 16	28 —	7 —	109 15	31 —	59 11
S. M. Small	44 13*	0 —	2 —				36 —	0 —	27 12		2 0
R. O. Butcher	29 21*	17 —	11 —	35 4	15 21*	0 7	51 —	31 —	53 3	13 40	52 0
R. D. Woolley	88 —	80 —	7 —	20 33	7 —	14 3*	27 —	35 —	16 21	53* —	18 18
P. J. Mancell	0 —	23 —	5 —	6 1	8 —	1 —					
S. L. Saunders	59 —	79* —	2 —	58 4	17 —	53 7	11 —	79* —	1 27*	— —	47 50
M. A. Holding	16 —	11 —	9 —	8 0	47* —	6 —	0 —	39 —	16* 35		
P. A. Blizzard	13 —	31 —		51 2*	7 —	31 13	2 —	0 —	9 0*		4 46*
P. M. Clough	0* —	4 —	1* —	0* 2	4 —	1* —	2* —	23 —	6 —		0* 0*
P. Faulkner			2 —							32 —	25 47
S. J. Reid				10 0	54 —	79 —	55 —	2 —	17 0	9* 19*	8 42
I. R. Beven					1 39	26 28	0 —				
N. J. Allanby										18 19*	
W. Kirkman										0 —	
Byes	6		4 7	3	3	5 1		4	1 4		9 3
Leg-byes	8 4	7	6		4 5	2 3	5	5	5 8	(4) (4)	9 5
Wides	1		5	1	2 1			1	1		1
No-balls	5 1	14	4 2	5 4	10 3	4 1	9	12	16 3		16 3
Total	351 94	396	157 40	201 184	296 127	273 131	266	262	336 239	199 110	260 273
Wickets	10 3	10	10 1	10 10	10 2	10 5	10	10	10 8	7 3	10 9
Result	W	D	D	L	D	L	D	D	D	D	D
Points	16	0	0	0	4	—	0	4	4		0

Catches
42 – R. D. Woolley (ct 40/st 2)
12 – R. O. Butcher
8 – P. A. Blizzard and M. Ray
7 – S. M. Small and D. C. Boon
5 – S. L. Saunders and S. J. Reid
3 – M. A. Holding, D. A. Smith and P. M. Clough
2 – P. Faulkner and I. R. Beven
1 – sub. (N. J. Allanby)

BOWLING

Match	M. A. Holding	P. M. Clough	P. A. Blizzard	S. L. Saunders	P. J. Mancell	M. Ray	P. Faulkner	I. R. Beven	S. J. Reid
v. New South Wales (Sydney) 22-25 October, 1982	24-5-43-4 / 24-6-54-1	9.1-2-19-3 / 23-7-41-3	4-1-8-0 / 4-0-8-0	21-5-51-1 / 46.2-12-115-3	6-4-4-1 / 31-7-57-0	4-3-1-1 / 19-8-19-1			
v. Queensland (Launceston) 30 October-2 November, 1982	33-9-93-2 / 4-0-12-0	31-5-83-0 / 13-1-33-1	17-2-75-3 / 9-2-24-1	30-4-105-2	13-3-14-1 / 8-1-29-1	5-0-23-0 / 13-0-51-0			
v. Victoria (St. Kilda) 12-15 November, 1982	26.5-5-66-6 / 34-11-70-2	17-5-45-0 / 21-7-44-3		13-4-38-0 / 12-0-30-0	18-7-40-3 / 25-3-60-2	1-1-0-0	13-0-36-1 / 13-0-53-0		
v. Western Australia (Devonport) 20-23 November, 1982	43-12-114-2	29-3-85-1	35-6-118-2	16-6-55-0	21-2-78-3	13-3-37-0			
v. Queensland (Brisbane) 10-13 December, 1982	25-8-56-3	17-2-42-1	18.1-6-48-3	19-5-60-1	8-3-10-0			3-1-12-1	
v. England XI (Hobart) 18-20 December, 1982	12-2-19-0 / 9-2-24-0	9.5-2-24-1 / 15-2-87-2	13-2-56-0 / 9-2-33-0	1-0-2-0 / 14-1-76-1	7-1-35-0 / 7-1-33-1				1-0-3-0
v. South Australia (Launceston) 31 Dec., 1982-3 January, 1983	31-10-82-2 / 7-1-25-1	16-3-55-1 / 2-0-5-0	23-8-62-4 / 12-2-34-1	12-0-63-0 / 3-0-9-0				27-14-49-2	
v. Victoria (Devonport) 8-11 January, 1983	22.5-5-59-7 / 29-7-79-2	14-3-42-1 / 19-6-35-1	15-3-46-2	14-6-17-0	10-7-15-0	3-3-0-0			
v. South Australia (Adelaide) 21-24 January, 1983	16-3-52-3 / 31-7-98-1	16-3-53-6 / 30.3-1-107-2	9-0-38-1 / 26-8-70-1	23-3-73-1		22-3-70-1			1-0-3-0
v. Sri Lankans (Devonport) 14-16 February, 1983		16-4-41-2 / 11-2-23-0		20-5-50-2 / 16-7-35-0			12-1-35-0 / 23-5-55-4		1-0-1-0 / 1-0-6-0
v. Western Australia (Perth) 19-22 February, 1983		25-10-53-3 / 18-5-49-2	19.3-4-66-2 / 27-5-70-4	11-2-53-0		21-7-56-0 / 19-2-48-0	25-4-86-4 / 10-0-56-0		
v. New South Wales (Hobart) 25-28 February, 1983		37.4-10-80-5 / 24-8-43-3	21-3-68-0	5-2-15-2 / 13-4-30-2		16-4-32-0 / 4-1-4-0	27-5-78-2 / 17-5-37-0		
Totals (overs-mdns-runs-wkts)	371.4-93-946-36	414.1-91-1089-41	275.4-60-841-24	285.2-67-875-15	146-32-360-12	140-35-341-3	140-20-436-11	30-15-61-3	4-0-13-0
Average	av. 26.27	av. 26.56	av. 35.04	av. 58.33	av. 30.00	av. 113.66	av. 38.63	av. 20.33	av. —

a R. O. Butcher 4-1-9-0

v. New South Wales (Hobart) 25-28 February, 1983		Inns	NOs	Runs	HS	Av
56	—	20	1	527	81	27.73
24	—	15	1	327	39	23.35
8	—	18	1	682	115	40.11
		10	1	136	44	15.11
20	—	19	2	423	53	24.88
11*	—	16	3	551	111*	42.38
		7	—	44	23	6.28
4	—	15	3	498	79*	41.50
		11	2	187	47*	20.77
18	—	14	3	227	51	20.63
10	—	13	7	53	23	8.83
16	—	5	—	122	47	24.40
14	—	13	2	309	79	28.09
		5	—	94	39	18.80
32	—	3	1	69	32	34.50
		1	—	0	0	—

```
8
1
10
332
10
  D
4
```

D. A. Smith	N. J. Allanby	W. Kirkman	Byes	Leg-byes	Wides	No-balls	Total	Wkts
				3	1	3	133	10
			7	3		7	311	10
			1	5		1	400	8
				3			152	3
			1	1		1	228	10
			6	6		3	272	8
			5	10		2	504	9
			1	9	2	2	242	10
			3	2			141	1
3-0-4-0			3		1		264	4
			5	9	1	4	330	10
			4		1		78	2
			4	2			153	10
			4	4			154	3
			3	1		1	148	10
			3	19		4	447	7
	16-6-38-2	16-3-52-1	(4)				221	7
-1-14-0	10-2-37-0	19-6-44-4	(6)				229	8a
			1	5	1	8	329	10
			1	11	5	2	242	6
		6-1-17-1		13	5	3	311	10
	9-2-33-0		5	4		8	164	5
.3-1-	41-11-	35-9-						
8-0	125-3	96-5						
—	av. 41.66	av. 19.20						

fact that a mere century would not save his side, applied himself with a vengeance and, driving superbly to all quarters of the ground, progressed royally to his maiden double century in Shield cricket. En route to his eventual 246 the left-hander passed Bill Ponsford's record of 1217 runs in Shield cricket. The immensely promising Jones recorded his second first-class hundred of the season before being run out, as he was in his previous knock of 199 against Western Australia. Significantly, no other Victorian player could do better than 25; it was therefore perhaps as well that they were not put to the test a second time and that the match eventuated in a draw with Queensland a pointless 8/188 in its second innings.

Tasmania began its first full schedule of Sheffield Shield matches with a bang and no apologetic whimpers. Woolley's side disposed of the eventual premier side, New South Wales, by seven wickets in its first game in Sydney. Losing on the first innings against Queensland by a mere four runs, it might easily have added a further four points to its aggregate had its batsmen not failed dismally in their clash with Victorian bowlers, McCurdy and Bright. The Apple Island bowlers performed with great credit when they took the field at St Kilda. West Indian fast man, Michael Holding mowed a swathe through the Victorian opposition, capturing 6/66 and restricting the home batsmen to a moderate 228; a total which might have been substantially less had it not been for a third wicket partnership of 68 between Watts and Whatmore. The last five Victorian wickets tumbled for 51 runs and Tasmania appeared to be well on top when its openers, Smith and Ray, cruised with little apparent difficulty to 75. Caution proved to be the undoing of Woolley's men. They spent five hours painstakingly collecting 138 of their eventual 157 runs; en route they lost their last ten wickets for 82 runs, slow left-handed spinner, Ray Bright capturing 5/38 and paceman, Rod McCurdy 4/52. Deputising for the injured Sacristani behind the stumps, Victorian captain, Graham Yallop, took four catches in the Tasmanian innings. When the home team batted again it improved on its first showing. Whatmore and Taylor's efforts for the fourth wicket added up to 154, and in spite of the fact that Victoria subsequently lost 5/23, Yallop was able to declare at 8/272, leaving the visitors the task of knocking off 344 to win. They were denied the opportunity of responding to the challenge by rain which reduced the last day to a 37 minute affair.

The return game between the two sides was also marred by rain – but not before Tasmania had reversed the earlier decision in Melbourne and taken first innings points. Holding repeated his earlier triumph at St Kilda in Devonport, returning match figures of 9/138 and bringing his tally of Victorian victims in two games to 17. The fast bowler's 7/59 analysis in the Melbourne team's first knock restricted it to an inadequate 153 runs: a total which, when Tasmania were a precarious 6/81 in reply, appeared sufficient to win the day for the mainlanders. Seventh and eighth wicket stands of 49 and 75 between fast bowler Clough and Woolley and between Clough and Saunders, however, turned back the tide of defeat. A last wicket partnership of 61 between Holding and Saunders carried the Tasmanian score to 262, but by the time that they came together Victoria were a beaten side. Opener Richardson's 74 not out in Victoria's second innings helped to cancel out his side's 109 run deficit and carry it into the lead. Soon afterwards the heavens opened, denying the home team the outright victory which was a distinct possibility.

Victoria 1982-3
First-Class Matches

BATTING

BATTING	v. South Australia (Adelaide) 22-25 October, 1982	v. Western Australia (Perth) 29 Oct.-1 Nov. 1982	v. Tasmania (St. Kilda) 12-15 Nov., 1982	v. Queensland (Brisbane) 19-22 Nov. 1982	v. England XI (Melbourne) 4-7 December, 1982	v. New Zealanders (Melbourne) 10-13 Dec., 1982	v. New South Wales (Newcastle) 18-21 Dec. 1982	v. Tasmania (Devonport) 8-11 January, 1983	v. Western Australia (Melbourne) 14-17 January, 1983	v. New South Wales (Melbourne) 28-31 January, 1983	v. South Australia (St. Kilda) 18-20 February, 1983
J. M. Wiener	2 73	35 44	4 28	11 67	49 8	3 75	5 26	33 6	60 —	1 0	
G. M. Watts	0 0	25 56	61 2	16 2		45 25					13 57
G. N. Yallop	28 151	84 58	8 47	20 73	69 24*	38 33	15 38	23 13	69 —	109 86	18 168
P. J. Davies	29 27	3 38									
B. C. Green	14 70	10 2	45 7	37* 14		1 5					
P. J. Cox	20 47										
S. F. Graf	48 18	9 24	22 5	5 12				7 —		4 1*	
P. G. Sacristani	55 2	2* 6	18* —								
P. D. King	54 15*	0 —									
R. J. McCurdy	5* 9		0 6	4 4	0	15	0	4*	13*	2 10*	3 4
J. D. Higgs	0 1*										0 0
M. D. Taylor		5 69*	13 85	2 66	2 56*	34* 38	21 94	1 —	5 —	144 88	15 13
R. J. Bright		11 6*	9 2*	6 0	36 —	— 0*	5 64*	27 —	44* —	2 5	16 11
I. W. Callen		0 —	8 1*	1 12*	3* —	— 21	0* —	2 —	16 —		
D. F. Whatmore			37 74	26 43	0 2	81 13	16 22	24 39*	11 —	15 7	
R. Templeton				0 0	40 —						
G. F. Richardson					31 27		3 46	0 74*	1 —	5 22	7 48
D. M. Jones						36 0	8 94	20	199 —	37 69	17 7
L. F. Balcam					5 —		— 0	3 1*			
G. J. Miles						15* 0	7 75	6 14	61	48 3	4 8
M. G. Hughes										0* —	0* 14*
D. Shepherd											17 2
Byes	1	2 4	1 6	1 3	8 3	10	1	4 4	2	8 10	1 4
Leg-byes	1 3	5 10	1 6	5 11	5 1	5 8	(7) 12	2 4	11	11 12	13 13
Wides		2 1		2 3					1		1
No-balls	3 4	1 1	1 3	15 16	11 1	8 2	5		8	10	8 9
Total	260 420	194 319	228 272	151 326	295 122	230 245	90 479	153 154	500	396 314	132 359
Wickets	10 9	10 7	10 8	10 10	10 4	5 10	10 7	10 3	8	10 8	10 10
Result	D	D	D	L	D	Tie	D	D	D	D	L
Points	0	0	4	0	0		0	0	0	0	0

Catches
26 – G. J. Miles (ct 24/st 2)
11 – P. G. Sacristani (ct 10/st 1)
9 – G. N. Yallop and G. M. Watts
8 – R. J. Bright and R. Templeton (ct 6/st 2)
7 – D. F. Whatmore
5 – J. M. Wiener, M. D. Taylor and D. M. Jones
4 – B. C. Green
3 – S. F. Graf and R. J. McCurdy
2 – G. F. Richardson and P. J. Davies

BOWLING

BOWLING	R. J. McCurdy	P. D. King	S. F. Graf	D. M. Jones	J. D. Higgs	B. C. Green	G. N. Yallop	I. W. Callen	R. J. Bright
v. South Australia (Adelaide) 22-25 October, 1982	23-2-95-2 / 12-0-88-5	28-5-88-5 / 2-0-38-0	23-5-74-1 / 10-0-67-2		10-1-46-0	4.3-1-16-1	5-2-10-0		
v. Western Australia (Perth) 29 October-1 November, 1982		9-2-44-0 / 11-0-47-1	23-9-53-4 / 34.2-8-95-5			4-1-6-0 / 4-0-17-0	3-0-17-0	21-3-69-3 / 19-5-71-1	28.5-12-4 / 32-9-97-4
v. Tasmania (St. Kilda) 12-15 November, 1982	22-7-52-4 / 5-1-10-0		10-2-14-0					17-2-34-1 / 6-1-21-0	28.5-12-3 / 0.4-0-0-1
v. Queensland (Brisbane) 19-22 November, 1982	25-3-93-0		26-6-77-0 / 2-0-9-0			12-5-18-1		28-6-105-2 / 2-0-13-0	39-11-110
v. England XI (Melbourne) 4-7 December, 1982	10-1-58-0 / 20-3-70-4							20-8-53-2 / 26-9-71-1	30-7-81 / 27-4-83-1
v. New Zealanders (Melbourne) 10-13 December, 1982	28-13-52-2 / 9-0-29-1					8-4-15-0 / 4-0-12-0	1-1-0-0	20-6-50-1 / 8-1-21-0	34-10-89 / 16-2-56-1
v. New South Wales (Newcastle) 18-21 December, 1982	17-1-56-1 / 3-0-26-1				5-1-17-0			28-5-81-3 / 11-0-36-2	26-2-74-1 / 9-4-22-1
v. Tasmania (Devonport) 8-11 January, 1983	24.1-3-98-5		19-5-30-1				1-0-10-0	29-6-83-3	22-12-18
v. Western Australia (Melbourne) 14-17 January, 1983	28-5-94-5 / 21-5-72-1				5-1-10-0		2-0-11-0	27-4-87-2 / 5-1-28-0	22.4-6-58 / 35-16-37
v. New South Wales (Melbourne) 28-31 Jan., 1983	20-2-88-1 / 17-2-87-1		4-3-8-1		8-0-43-0 / 1-0-3-0		8-0-36-2		35-6-141 / 4-0-20-0
v. South Australia (St. Kilda) 18-20 February, 1983	18.3-3-73-6 / 6.3-1-21-2				18-0-115-0		11-1-40-1		27-1-102
v. Queensland (Junction Oval) 25-28 February, 1983	20-1-127-1 / 16-4-37-3			4-0-19-0	20-2-90-0 / 10-1-24-2	7-0-35-0	11-0-44-1 / 2-1-3-0		26-5-77 / 22-6-61-2
Totals	345.1-57-1326-45 av. 29.46	50-7-217-6 av. 36.16	151.2-38-427-14 av. 30.50	23-2-92-0 av. —	58-4-275-2 av. 137.50	43.3-11-119-2 av. 59.50	44-5-171-4 av. 42.75	267-57-823-21 av. 39.19	465-125-1199-31 av. 38.67

a P. J. Cox 25-3-69-1

b G. M. Watts 1-0-3-0; M. D. Taylor 0.5-0-4-0

c M. D. Taylor 1-0-4-0; D. F. Whatmore 1-0-1-0

d M. D. Taylor 2-0-7-0; D. F. Whatmore 2-2-0-1 and 2-0-10-0

e G. M. Watts 2-1-6-0

v. Queensland (Junction Oval) 25-28 February, 1983	Inns	NOs	Runs	HS	Av
	19	—	530	75	27.89
19 —	13	—	321	61	24.69
46 —	22	1	1418	246	67.52
	4	—	97	38	24.25
22 —	11	1	227	70	22.70
	2	—	67	47	33.50
	11	1	155	48	15.50
	5	2	83	55	41.50
	3	1	69	54	34.50
25 —	16	4	104	25	8.66
0 —	5	1	1	1*	0.25
20 —	19	3	771	144	48.18
25* —	17	6	269	64*	24.45
	10	4	64	21	10.66
	15	1	410	81	29.28
9	3	—	40	40	13.33
16	12	1	273	74*	24.81
	11	—	603	199	54.81
5 —	4	1	9	5	3.00
0 —	12	1	246	75	22.36
	4	3	14	14*	14.00
	2	—	19	17	
6					
17					
510					
10					
D					
0					

— L. F. Balcam, P. D. King, I. W. Callen, M. G. Hughes and sub (S. Maddocks)

J. M. Wiener	M. G. Hughes	L. F. Balcam	Byes	Leg-byes	Wides	No-balls	Total	Wkts
			6	1		4	409	10a
			5	7	1		206	7
			1	7		9	232	10
			3	6	2	3	358	7
			4	6	5	4	157	10
			7			2	40	1
-0-19-2			12	5		18	449	8
			2	1			32	0b
-0-4-0		21.5-7-50-3	8	3		18	275	10
-2-29-1		16-4-50-0	2	2	1	16	324	7
		17.2-1-53-3	4	10	3	25	301	9
		13-1-41-1	1	10		4	174	3
-0-4-0		23-5-59-3	(25)				316	9
-0-7-0		7-2-26-0	4	6		8	150	'4c
-3-11-1			4	5	1	12	262	10
-1-18-0	19-2-60-0		1	8	1	9	336	10
3-5-23-0	21-4-68-2			5	1	3	265	6d
7-3-66-1	35-5-136-2		11	14		9	562	7
	13-1-51-1		1	1		3	166	2
	16-0-98-2					8	9	445	10
	6-0-15-1		1	7	1	2	47	3
	31.1-1-132-2			7		5	536	4
	18-7-43-1		6	2	1	5	188	8e
59-14-81-5	159.1-20-603-11	98.1-20-279-10						
av. 36.20	av. 54.81	av. 27.90						

Sincock fails to hold a caught and bowled chance offered by Yallop who went on to make 168. Wright is the wicket-keeper and Inverarity is at slip. Victoria v. South Australia. (Philip Tyson).

The remainder of Tasmania's programme produced an outright loss to Western Australia in Devonport and five draws, two against South Australia and one each against Western Australia, New South Wales and Queensland. These results could hardly be described as a grand climax to the season. But Woolley's men must have derived a warm glow of satisfaction from the fact that in three of the inconclusive matches they took first innings points from Queensland, South Australia and Western Australia: a catalogue of talents which included the two Sheffield Shield finalists. All in all, the Cinderella state of the Australian domestic competition had every reason to be well satisfied with its first full season in senior ranks. Woolley, Boon, Clough and Saunders clearly demonstrated that they were the stuff of which Test players are made. The advances made by Tasmania's cricketers were significant enough for them to more than hold their own in elite company – even after the departure of Michael Holding to play in the West Indies – India Test series.

The satisfaction of Tasmanian cricket administrators with the way in which their players acquitted themselves in Sheffield Shield matches was not replicated across Bass Strait at Cricket House in Melbourne. Seldom has Victoria experienced such a disastrous season as it did in 1982–83. It had to wait for its first points until its third game against Tasmania, losing on the first innings in the interim to South and Western Australia. Another two months, Christmas and New Year had gone by before Yallop's men enjoyed the sweet taste of success again. In the meantime they had lost outright to Queensland and trailed on the first innings against New South Wales and Tasmania. Moreover, its minor defeat of Western Australia was only a temporary reprieve and was followed by a thrashing at the hands of South Australia and no points from its clashes with New South Wales and Queensland. It was small wonder that the Victorian administrators began casting around at the conclusion of the summer for some solution to their dilemma. The fact that they looked for an impossible salvation to one man – South Australia's David Hookes – suggested, however, that they had not come to grips with the magnitude of the malaise in Victorian ranks and that their approach to the problem was far too simplistic.

Western Australia 1982-3
First-Class Matches

BATTING

Column key (each cell shows 1st and 2nd innings):
- A = v. New South Wales (Perth) 15-18 October, 1982
- B = v. Victoria (Perth) 29 Oct.-1 Nov., 1982
- C = v. England XI (Perth) 5-8 November, 1982
- D = v. New South Wales (Sydney) 12-15 Nov. 1982
- E = v. Tasmania (Devonport) 20-23 Nov. 1982
- F = v. Queensland (Perth) 3-5 December, 1982
- G = v. South Australia (Perth) 17-20 Dec. 1982
- H = v. Queensland (Brisbane) 8-11 January, 1983
- I = v. Victoria (Melbourne) 14-17 January, 1983
- J = v. Tasmania (Perth) 19-22 February, 1983
- K = v. South Australia (Adelaide) 25-28 February, 1983

Player	A	B	C	D	E	F	G	H	I	J	K
G. R. Marsh	33 —	39 42	0 21	37 17	37 —	45 —	54 25	28 —	0 12	40 30	
S. C. Clements	30 —			20 45				28 —	2 33		
G. Shipperd	166 —	0 20	20 39	12 18	39 —	44 —	9 5	64 —	79 107	47 33*	56 —
M. F. Wolfe	39 —										
C. S. Serjeant	2 —			16 18							
K. H. Macleay	5 —	23 —	2 28	26 26	49* —	4 —	0 0	15 —	100 0	96 7	1 —
A. L. Mann	0 —			34 8				56 —	4 15*		
T. J. Zoehrer	104 —			17 27*				36 —	31 24*		
D. K. Lillee	0 —	5 —	26 1		22* —		4* —		0* —	5 —	19 —
W. M. Clark	19* —			5 0		4* —	9 —	2* —	0* —	0* —	4* —
G. D. Thomson	0 —										
B. M. Laird		2 99	11 1	55 13	25 —	84 —	13 88*	26 —	30 37	21 72	6 —
G. M. Wood		11 4	31 25		20 —	138 —	0 4	74 —	30 28	7 53*	111 —
K. J. Hughes		67 130	20 37		129 —	29 —	123 38			22 4	91 —
R. W. Marsh		3 23	25 29		110 —	8 —	8 28			52 7	27 —
B. Yardley		47* 9*	8 0		48 —	27 —	65 —		11 —	4 17	5 —
T. G. Hogan		14 17	15 1	72* 6	1 —	7 —	3 8*	1 —	30 —	20 —	31 —
T. M. Alderman		4 —	0* 1*								
D. L. Boyd				21 0	7 —	3 —			12 —		
W. Andrews											48 —
Byes	5	1 3	1	8 5	2		9 8		1	1 1	9
Leg-byes	3	6	5 5	5 7	10	5	17 9	10	8	5 11	9
Wides		7 2	1	2				1	1 1	1 5	8
No-balls	22	9 3	3 8	5 4	2	6	10 3	16	9 3	8 2	5
Total	428	232 358	167 197	327 197	504	406	324 209	376	336 265	329 242	430
Wickets	10	10 7	10 10	10 10	9	10	10 6	10	10 6	10 6	10
Result	D	D	L	L	W	W	D	D	D	D	W
Points	0	4			16	16	4	0	0	4	16

Catches
- 33 – R. W. Marsh
- 15 – B. M. Laird
- 13 – G. M. Wood
- 12 – K. H. Macleay
- 11 – T. G. Hogan
- 9 – G. Shipperd and T. J. Zoehrer (ct 6/st 3)
- 5 – G. R. Marsh (inc. one as sub.)
- 4 – K. J. Hughes, D.L. Boyd (inc. two as sub.) and B. Yardley
- 3 – S. C. Clements, C. S. Serjeant and W. M. Clark
- 2 – D. K. Lillee and T. M. Alderman
- 1 – M. F. Wolfe, A. L. Mann and W. Andrews

BOWLING

(each cell shows 1st innings / 2nd innings figures, O-M-R-W)

Match	D. K. Lillee	W. M. Clark	G. D. Thomson	K. H. Macleay	A. L. Mann	T. M. Alderman	B. Yardley	T. G. Hogan	D. L. Boyd
v. New South Wales (Perth) 15-18 October, 1982	37-11-118-2 / 9-1-42-1	36-10-91-1 / 6-1-22-0	20-2-117-0 / 7-1-33-0	40-16-85-2 / 9-3-20-1	27-9-65-1				
v. Victoria (Perth) 29 October-1 November, 1982	20-10-29-0 / 27-6-88-1			15.5-5-26-5 / 21-5-51-0		26-9-65-5 / 22-3-74-2	13-2-42-0 / 28-10-75-4	7-0-22-0 / 2-0-15-0	
v. England XI (Perth) 5-8 November, 1982	20-7-53-3 / 22-5-64-3			9-3-23-0 / 12-1-42-1		24-6-63-5 / 22.2-3-67-5	4-0-13-0 / 7-1-27-0		1.1-1-0-1
v. New South Wales (Sydney) 12-15 November, 1982		3-0-10-0 / 9.4-0-38-2		15-3-29-0 / 11-2-34-0	37-8-107-2 / 12-1-56-1			46-14-91-6 / 23-5-71-3	9.3-1-43-1 / 5-1-14-0
v. Tasmania (Devonport) 20-23 November, 1982	7-0-13-2			18-5-48-1 / 18-6-29-1			31.4-15-41-5 / 44-24-68-5		19-2-64-2 / 6-2-11-0
v. Queensland (Perth) 3-5 December, 1982		14-7-21-4 / 12-3-34-1		6.4-1-12-5 / 18-5-55-2					8-4-15-1 / 12-0-44-1
v. South Australia (Perth) 17-20 December, 1982	25-6-72-4 / 12-0-58-0	22.4-4-47-4 / 33-2-125-5		15-4-56-0 / 13-2-82-2			32-8-93-2 / 26-15-41-1		
v. Queensland (Brisbane) 8-11 January, 1983		35-11-76-1 / 7-4-8-1		33-6-72-1	20-1-81-2 / 10-3-22-0			42.3-18-74-5 / 15-6-27-3	19-3-75-1 / 8-1-26-0
v. Victoria (Melbourne) 14-17 January, 1983		48-15-113-2		23-6-64-0	15-0-63-1		51-18-132-3	40-12-102-1	
v. Tasmania (Perth) 19-22 February, 1983	26-7-57-3 / 27-13-45-2	24-10-42-2 / 14-5-37-1		12-0-44-0 / 6-3-8-0			31-18-34-3 / 39-11-117-5	20-7-49-2 / 16-7-54-1	
v. South Australia (Adelaide) 25-28 February, 1983	21-2-54-3 / 19-10-29-4	7-0-11-0 / 19-6-36-1		8-3-18-0 / 3-1-5-2			24-8-62-3 / 25-3-71-3	19.4-5-49-4 / 29-11-55-0	
v. New South Wales (Perth) 4-8 March, 1983		24-4-42-3 / 25-8-48-3		22-7-45-1 / 21-3-64-2			29-8-92-4 / 28-5-81-1	16-7-28-2 / 12-2-33-0	12-3-51-0 / 13.2-3-39-2
Totals	242-78-722-28 av. 25.78	339.2-90-801-31 av. 25.83	27-3-150-0 av. —	349.3-90-912-26 av. 35.07	121-22-394-7 av. 56.28	94.2-21-269-17 av. 15.82	412.4-146-989-39 av. 25.35	415.2-134-939-35 av. 26.82	111.5-20-382-8 av. 47.75

a G. Miller retired hurt   b M. Laird 1-1-0-0   c W. Andrews 1-0-7-0

v. New South Wales (Perth) 4-8 March, 1983		Inns	NOs	Runs	HS	Av
32	18	18	—	510	54	28.33
		6	—	158	45	26.33
10	48	19	1	816	166	45.33
		1	—	39	39	39.00
		3	—	36	18	12.00
1	24	18	1	407	100	23.94
		6	1	117	56	23.40
		6	2	239	104	59.75
		8	2	82	26	13.66
3	0	11	6	46	19*	9.20
		1	—	0	0	—
24	15	18	1	622	99	36.58
45	0	16	1	581	138	38.73
66	55	13	1	811	130	67.58
36	58	13	—	414	110	31.84
14*	4	13	3	259	65	25.90
2	0	16	2	228	72*	16.28
		3	2	5	4	5.00
16	9*	7	1	68	21	11.33
		1	—	48	48	48.00
2	5					
5	1					
3						
	1					
259	238					
10	10					
L						
—						

Ken Macleary. A fine all-round season and 100 for Western Australia v. Victoria at Melbourne. (Adrian Murrell)

S. C. Clements	M. F. Wolfe	G. R. Marsh	Byes	Leg-byes	Wides	No-balls	Total	Wkts
			3	12	1	10	502	6
	1-0-6-0	1-0-4-0	1	1			129	2
			2	5	2	1	194	10
			4	10	1	1	319	7
			3	1			156	9a
			4	4	1		209	9
			5	3	1	6	295	10
			2	7		8	230	6
					1	5	201	10b
			3	4		4	184	10
			1			3	52	10
			6			5	261	10
			5	4	2	13	288	10
				10	3	6	387	7
			1	8	5	2	394	10
4-2-5-0			2	2			92	4
1-0-5-0			2	11		8	500	8
			9	9		16	260	10
			3	5	1	3	273	9
			3	3			200	10
			3	6	1		213	10c
			3	8		2	271	10
			8	5		2	280	10
5-2-10-0	1-0-6-0	1-0-4-0						
—	—	—						

The Victorian despondency was not an Australia-wide phenomenon in 1982–83. The Australian Cricket Board was far more sanguine than it had been previously about the future of the Sheffield Shield. The concept of a final to decide the winner of the competition appeared to have far more spectator appeal than the preceding league format. It is worth noting however, that one financially viable match does not guarantee the profitability of a whole programme of Shield games. The attempt of Victoria to lure David Hookes to Melbourne with promises of payment also highlighted the future possibility of players who earn substantial sums in international cricket demanding commensurate rewards for their services in Shield games. Without subsidisation from the Test match coffers, professionalism in the lower echelons of the game is an impossibility in Australia. State games simply do not generate enough income. Thus, whilst the Sheffield Shield cricket, seen through rose-tinted spectacles, may be considered to be in a healthier state in 1982–83 than it was in preceeding years, it is still far from out of the financial woods. Its existence will hinge upon the growth or decline of professionalism amongst the ranks of Australian players. It is not too hard to visualise that the schism which has emerged in England between club and professional county players will develop in this country at the stage when the cricketer is promoted to national ranks. Such a differentiation can only have a deleterious effect on the standard of play at the lower level.

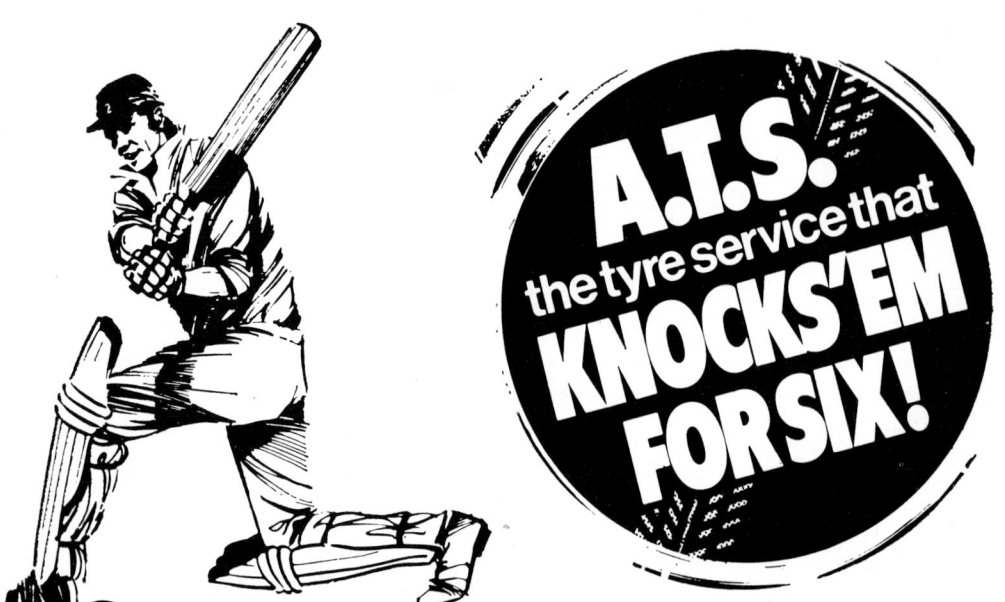

SECTION E
The Record Breakers

The Indian Tour of Pakistan
The six Test Series
and four one-day internationals

Imran Khan. Inspiring captain. Dashing batsman.
Forty wickets in the Test Series. (Adrian Murrell)

Having soundly thrashed the Australians, Pakistan received the Indians with optimism. In their ten-week tour India were to play six Test matches and four one-day internationals, an unenviable task against a side as strong and so confident in success as Pakistan.

27 November 1982

at Quetta

Baluchistan Governor's XI 170 for 7 (Mohsin Khan 70)
Indians 174 for 6

Indians won by 4 wickets

Gavaskar asked the home side to bat first on a very cold day, but Mohsin Khan and Mudassar Nazar opened with a stand of 73. Mohsin was in particularly fine form and hit three leg-side sixes before being brilliantly caught by Gavaskar off the left-arm spinner Shastri.

The strong Governor's side, all current Test players with the exception of Wasim Raja, failed to capitalise on the fine start and India were left a target of 171 in their 35 overs. Their chances of victory looked slim, however, when they collapsed to 118 for 6, but Mohinder Amarnath and Yashpal Sharma shared an unbeaten stand of 56 to win the game with four balls to spare.

For India, it was an encouraging start: for Pakistan, it was a warning against complacency.

29 and 30 November, 1 December 1982

at Sahiwal

B.C.C.P. XI 282 for 5 dec (Saleem Malik 124 not out, Ashraf Ali 66 not out, Ejaz Faqih 51 not out) and 211 for 4 dec (Ejaz Faqih 100 not out, Rameez Raja 73 not out, R.J. Shastri 4 for 80)
Indians 249 for 2 dec (D.B. Vengsarkar 100 not out, J. Arun Lal 76) and 86 for 3

Match drawn

An interesting Board XI led by Ejaz Faqih lost 4 wickets for 25 runs on the opening day, three of them to Madan Lal. One of Madan Lal's victims was Qasim Umar, the opening batsman who had scored prolifically in the Quaid-e-Azam Trophy. Saleem Malik and Ejaz Faqih rescued the home side with a stand of 116 in 134 minutes, and then Malik and Ashraf Ali added an unbeaten 141. Ashraf Ali hit ten fours in his 66 and Saleem Malik, dropped on ten, hit sixteen fours in his 124 not out.

Ejaz declared overnight and the Indians responded well. Srikkanth went off with his usual flourish, and Arun Lal and Vengsarkar added 114 in 125 minutes for the second wicket. Vengsarkar reached a composed and confident century and Kapil Dev declared 33 runs behind.

By the end of the day, the game had swung dramatically in favour of the Indians. Shastri having taken 3 wickets for 1 run in 25 deliveries. He improved on this the next morning when B.C.C.P. XI were 42 for 4. Shastri having taken all four wickets for 10 runs. The next two hours and forty minutes saw the game wrenched from India's grasp by Rameez Raja

and Ejaz Faqih who added 169.

Set to make 245 in two hours and twenty minutes, the Indians lost 3 for 35 and settled for a draw.

FIRST WILLS ONE-DAY INTERNATIONAL: PAKISTAN v. INDIA

A new international cricketing venue, the Municipal Stadium at Gujranwala, witnessed a splendidly contested match in which Pakistan maintained their winning way in exciting style.

Gavaskar put Pakistan in, and his decision seemed fully justified when, at the half-way point in their innings, Pakistan had scored only 56 for the loss of Mohsin, Mudassar and Zaheer, but Javed and Imran engaged in a fierce fourth wicket stand of 111. Imran hit four fours and a six before being bowled by Kapil Dev, and Javed went on to complete his hundred in 114 minutes with twelve fours and a six. He was named Man of the Match.

India began badly, Imran removing Gavaskar and Srikanth in successive overs. Vengsarkar and Amarnath added 71 before Vengsarkar was run out by Mansoor Akhtar. Patil was caught at deep mid-wicket off Mudassar, who came in for some punishment, Kapil Dev hitting him for one mighty six.

Imran returned to bowl a containing spell, but it was Jalaluddin who made victory certain when he had Kapil Dev

Mansoor Akhtar. (George Herringshaw)

FIRST ONE-DAY INTERNATIONAL: PAKISTAN v. INDIA

3 December 1982 at Gujranwala

PAKISTAN			
Mohsin Khan	b Madan Lal		5
Mudassar Nazar	run out		20
Zaheer Abbas	c Kapil Dev, b Madan Lal		10
Javed Miandad	not out		106
Imran Khan[†]	b Kapil Dev		49
Mansoor Akhtar	not out		21
Wasim Raja			
Ejaz Faqih			
Tahir Naqqash			
Wasim Bari*			
Jalaluddin			
Extras	b 1, lb 6, w 6		13
(40 overs)	(for 4 wickets)		224

	O	M	R	W
Kapil Dev	8	1	42	1
Madan Lal	8	—	39	2
Amarnath	8	1	20	—
Sandhu	8	—	55	—
Shastri	6	—	41	—
Patil	2	—	14	—

FALL OF WICKETS
1- 5, 2- 25, 3- 49, 4- 160

INDIA			
S.M. Gavaskar[†]	lbw, b Imran		1
K. Srikkanth	c Wasim Bari, b Imran		6
D.B. Vengsarkar	run out		39
M.B. Amarnath	c Tahir, b Jalaluddin		51
S.M. Patil	c Mohsin, b Mudassar		4
Kapil Dev	c Mansoor, b Jalaluddin		15
Yashpal Sharma	not out		56
S.M.H. Kirmani	not out		27
S. Madan Lal			
R.J. Shastri			
B.S. Sandhu			
Extras	b 1, lb 3, w 5, nb 2		11
(40 overs)	(for 6 wickets)		210

	O	M	R	W
Imran Khan	8	—	38	2
Jalaluddin	8	2	36	2
Tahir Naqqash	8	—	31	—
Ejaz Faqih	8	—	38	—
Mudassar Nazar	7	—	50	1
Zaheer Abbas	1	—	6	—

FALL OF WICKETS
1- 2, 2- 13, 3- 84, 4- 100, 5- 120, 6- 121

Pakistan won by 14 runs

caught at short mid-on and Amarnath taken superbly, one-handed at mid-off, by Tahir in the same over.

5, 6 and 7 December 1982

at Rawalpindi

Indians 255 for 3 dec (J. Arun Lal 84, S.M. Gavaskar 84, G.R. Viswanath 50 not out) and 307 for 8 dec (K. Srik-kanth 135, S.M. Patil 70)
B.C.C.P. Patron's XI 322 for 5 dec (Zaheer Abbas 108, Saleem Malik 105) and 8 for 2

Match Drawn

In their last match before the first Test, the Indians batted well on the opening day against another strong side. Gavaskar, batting at number three, joined Arun Lal in a second wicket stand of 152, and then Viswanath completed a welcome, if uneasy fifty before the declaration.

Masood Anwar fell to Maninder before the close, but on the second day, Saleem Malik scored his second century against the Indians, a patient one which confirmed his place in the Pakistan side for the first Test, and Zaheer hit five sixes and nine fours in his sparkling innings of 108, his ninety-ninth first-class century. Saleem and Zaheer shared a fourth wicket stand of 113 before Zaheer was stumped by Yashpal Sharma, keeping wicket, off Doshi.

India, 116 for 1, had regained the lead before the close, Srikkanth was 55 not out. The next morning Srikkanth batted brilliantly. He and Patil added 205 for the second wicket, and Krishna Srikkanth hit five sixes and seventeen fours in his 135, a magnificent innings which could not win him a place in the Test side. The Indians lost 5 for 68 after lunch before Gavaskar declared, but, with Mansoor and Masood both out cheaply, bad light ended play.

FIRST WILLS TEST MATCH: PAKISTAN v. INDIA

The decision of the Pakistan Board of Control to sell the Test series to a private contractor for sixteen million rupees proved to have a most unhappy beginning. The contractor's decision to raise admission charges to nearly double the normal cost resulted in only 7,000 people watching the first day's play when, in the past, for a Pakistan – India Test, one would have expected a capacity crowd of 50,000.

Gavaskar won the toss and asked Pakistan to bat, a rather surprising decision. With Abdul Qadir injured, Pakistan fielded an all seam attack.

Mohsin and Mudassar started briskly on a pitch which did not seem to have suffered from the two days of rain which had preceded the match. Mudassar was caught at slip a quarter of an hour before lunch which was taken with Pakistan at 91 for 1. After lunch, Pakistan became bogged down by some accurate bowling and when play ended early through bad light only 170 had been scored from 66 overs, only 7 of which had been spin by Doshi.

The second day showed a transformation in the Pakistan batting. Mohsin was out for 94, 360 minutes, ten fours, after sharing a fourth wicket stand of 112 with Zaheer. Zaheer then dominated the rest of the innings with a series of glorious strokes, cuts, drives and pulls rattling to the boundary in an exquisite stream. His innings lasted for 334 minutes, and his 215 was made out of 321 scored while he was at the wicket. He hit two sixes and twenty-three fours with his perfect timing. He reached his ninth Test hundred and it was also his hundredth hundred in first-class cricket. He is the first Pakistani to have achieved this feat. Sadly, this glorious day of batting and Zaheer's historical achievement was watched only by a few spectators as people once more refused to pay the high admission charges. A hurriedly arranged press conference after the close of play witnessed the

Dilip Doshi. 5 for 91 in the first Test, but he lost form and favour and we may well have seen the last of him in Test cricket. (Adrian Murrell)

organisers announce that tickets would be sold at half price for the last three days.

In all, on the second day, Pakistan scored 315 runs in 323 minutes, and 139 runs came in the two hours between lunch and tea.

Rain ruined the third day's play which ended at lunch with India on 87 for 0. They comfortably avoided any threat of being asked to follow-on as they reached 306 for 6 on the fourth day in spite of some superb fast bowling by Imran. Sarfraz, too, bowled well, but Tahir and Jalaluddin were very wayward and were severely punished by Patil and Amarnath. In one over, Patil hit Jalaluddin for 20 including a mighty hook for six and three fours. The Pakistan outcricket was far below the standard it had reached in the series against England and Australia and a few chances were missed.

As the game petered to a draw on the last day it was brightened by the performance of Mohsin Khan. In two and three quarter hours, he scored 101 not out. He hit ten fours and a six (off Doshi over long-on) and when he had scored 84 he became the first Pakistani batsman to score 1,000 runs in Test cricket in a calendar year. It was his fourth century in nine Tests and his third in succession at the Qaddafi Stadium, Lahore.

SECOND WILLS ONE-DAY INTERNATIONAL: PAKISTAN v. INDIA

For the third time in eleven days Zaheer Abbas took a century off the Indian bowling, and Mohsin Khan brought his total in three innings against the Indians to 312 for once

FIRST TEST MATCH – PAKISTAN v. INDIA
10, 11, 12, 14 and 15 December 1982 at Lahore

PAKISTAN

	FIRST INNINGS		SECOND INNINGS	
Mohsin Khan	c Amarnath, b Madan Lal	94	not out	101
Mudassar Nazar	c Gavaskar, b Dev	50	c Arun Lal, b Doshi	17
Mansoor Akhtar	c Gavaskar, b Dev	3	not out	14
Javed Miandad	c Gavaskar, b Madan Lal	17		
Zaheer Abbas	b Doshi	215		
Saleem Malik	b Madan Lal	6		
Imran Khan†	c Madan Lal, b Doshi	45		
Wasim Bari*	c Arun Lal, b Doshi	12		
Tahir Naqqash	st Kirmani, b Doshi	20		
Sarfraz Nawaz	c Amarnath, b Doshi	18		
Jalaluddin	not out	1		
Extras	lb 3, nb 1	4	lb 3	3
		485	(for 1 wicket)	135

INDIA

	FIRST INNINGS	
S.M. Gavaskar†	c Bari, b Sarfraz	83
J. Arun Lal	c Mudassar, b Imran	51
D.B. Vengsarkar	c Mudassar, b Imran	3
G.R. Viswanath	c Bari, b Imran	1
M.B. Amarnath	not out	109
S.M. Patil	run out	68
Kapil Dev	c Bari, b Sarfraz	9
R.J. Shastri	lbw, b Jalaluddin	7
S.M.H. Kirmani*	c Bari, b Jalaluddin	10
S. Madan Lal	c Saleem, b Sarfraz	7
D.R. Doshi	b Sarfraz	0
Extras	b 2, lb 11, nb 18	31
		379

	O	M	R	W		O	M	R	W
Kapil Dev	39	3	149	2		8	2	27	—
Madan Lal	27	2	101	3		5	1	10	—
Amarnath	23	5	59	—		3	1	5	—
Doshi	32.5	6	91	5		15	2	57	1
Shastri	22	3	81	—		14	1	33	—
Gavaskar						1	1	0	—

	O	M	R	W
Imran Khan	27	8	68	3
Sarfraz Nawaz	31.5	11	63	4
Jalaluddin	34	10	93	2
Tahir Naqqash	29	6	114	—
Mudassar Nazar	3	1	10	—

FALL OF WICKETS
1- 85, 2- 100, 3- 126, 4- 238, 5- 250, 6- 367, 7- 438, 8- 447, 9- 478
1- 55

FALL OF WICKETS
1- 105, 2- 111, 3- 123, 4- 188, 5- 294, 6- 305, 7- 322, 8- 348, 9- 375

Umpires: Amanullah Khan & Mahboob Shah

Match drawn

Zaheer Abbas. 215 in the first Test. His hundredth hundred.
The first Pakistani to reach this goal. (Adrian Murrell)

out. For Pakistan cricket, it was another momentous day.

Imran Khan won the toss and Mohsin and Mudassar opened before a capacity crowd. There was a terrible mix up between the pair when the score was 41 and Mudassar was run out. In the next 27 overs, Mohsin and Zaheer scored 205 runs, a record for any wicket for a limited-over international. When Zaheer was finally out, slogging wildly at Kapil Dev, he had scored 118. His fifty came in 51 minutes and his hundred was scored in 96 minutes off 72 balls. In all, he hit ten fours and four sixes, one each off Amarnath, Shastri, Doshi and Yashpal Sharma, and faced 86 balls in 116 minutes. If overshadowed, Mohsin still batted with that elegant positivity that makes him such a joy to watch. He hit nine fours and a six in his 179 minutes at the crease and faced 120 balls.

The Indians contributed to their own defeat by twice dropping each batsman, and their faint hopes of winning receded further when Jalaluddin bowled both openers, and Ejaz removed Amarnath. Vengsarkar and Patil played a courageous and often brilliant partnership of 109, and Patil was in thunderous form, crashing three fierce sixes and taking 19 from one over by Sikhander Bakht. Surprisingly, it was Zaheer's occasional off breaks which accounted for both Vengsarkar and Patil whose innings had lasted for only 73 minutes. From the 60 deliveries he faced, he hit seven fours as well as his three sixes.

The inspiration that Patil had given to India could not be sustained and the last seven overs of their innings produced only 21 runs.

Pakistan joy. A common picture in the series. (Adrian Murrell)

SECOND ONE-DAY INTERNATIONAL: PAKISTAN v. INDIA
17 December 1982 at Multan

PAKISTAN						INDIA			
Mohsin Khan	not out			117		K. Srikkanth	b Jalaluddin		8
Mudassar Nazar	run out			12		J. Arun Lal	b Jalaluddin		6
Zaheer Abbas	b Kapil Dev			118		D.B. Vengsarkar	c Sikhander, b Zaheer		37
Javed Miandad	not out			3		M.B. Amarnath	c Mansoor, b Ejaz		6
Mansoor Akhtar						S.M. Patil	c Javed, b Zaheer		84
Imran Khan†						Kapil Dev†	b Mudassar		35
Wasim Raja						Yashpal Sharma	c and b Mudassar		16
Ejaz Faqih						S.M.H. Kirmani*	not out		16
Wasim Bari*						R.J. Shastri	not out		3
Sikhander Bakht						B.S. Sandhu			
Jalaluddin						D.R. Doshi			
Extras	b 1, lb 10, w 2			13		Extras	lb 10, w 3, nb 2		15
(40 overs)	(for 2 wickets)			263		(40 overs)	(for 7 wickets)		226

	O	M	R	W			O	M	R	W
Kapil Dev	8	—	42	1		Imran Khan	8	4	14	—
Sandhu	8	—	28	—		Jalaluddin	4	—	31	2
Amarnath	6	—	46	—		Ejaz Faqih	8	—	50	1
Doshi	8	1	58	—		Mudassar Nazar	7	—	40	2
Yashpal Sharma	6	—	45	—		Sikhander Bakht	8	1	50	—
Shastri	4	—	31	—		Zaheer Abbas	4	—	23	2
						Mansoor Akhtar	1	—	3	—

FALL OF WICKETS
1- 41, 2- 246

FALL OF WICKETS
1- 14, 2- 17, 3- 34, 4- 143, 5- 162, 6- 190, 7- 205

Pakistan won by 37 runs

18, 19 and 20 December 1982

at Multan

Punjab Governor's XI 132 (Qasim Umar 55, Maninder Singh 6 for 35, L. Sivaramakrishnan 4 for 46) and 215 for 4 (Qasim Umar 120, Shoaib Mohammad 82, Maninder Singh 4 for 49)
Indians 328 for 9 dec (R.J. Shastri 93, K. Srikkanth 64, S.M. Gavaskar 50, Iqbal Sikander 4 for 72)

Match drawn

Fourteen wickets fell on a turning wicket on the opening day of the match. The home side were bowled out for 132 and the Indians closed at 95 for 4. The star performers for the tourists were the teenage spinners, slow left-arm Maninder Singh and right-arm leg-break bowler Sivaramakrishnan.

The early impetus to the Indian innings again came from Krishna Srikkanth who hit ten fours and two sixes in his 93-minute innings, but it was spirited batting from the middle order which gave India the advantage. Gavaskar and Shastri added 77 for the sixth wicket, and Shastri batted for 238 minutes before being caught behind off Iqbal Sikander when 7 short of his century. He hit seven fours.

It seemed that India would win, but on the last day, Qasim Umar and Shoaib Mohammad, who had scored 23 on the second evening, batted through all three sessions to raise their opening stand to 208. Qasim hit his sixth century of the season, his patient and invaluable innings lasting 323 minutes. Shoaib was out seven minutes before Qasim after an equally determined innings, and the Governor's XI had a fright at the end when the seventeen-year old Maninder Singh took 4 wickets in 20 deliveries to finish with match figures of 10 for 84. For India, his destructive burst came too late to force victory.

The game had originally been scheduled for Bahawalpur and had been shifted to Multan only the day before it was due to commence. Wasim Raja took over the captaincy of the Governor's side when Majid Khan withdrew and must have doubted his wisdom in batting first on the initially treacherous pitch.

SECOND WILLS TEST MATCH: PAKISTAN v. INDIA

With prices reduced to normality, the crowds flocked back to witness a great triumph for Pakistan. Each side made a change from the first Test. Abdul Qadir, recovered from his foot injury, replaced Tahir Naqqash, and for India, Maninder Singh took the place of Ravi Shastri. At 17 years, 193 days, Maninder became the youngest player to represent India in a Test match.

Imran won the toss and showed his knowledge of the relaid square when he asked India to bat. In his third over, Imran began a decline from which India never totally recovered. Gavaskar went for an unwise single and Imran swung round from his follow-through to hit the stumps from fifteen yards with Gavaskar stranded. The next ball Vengsarkar touched to Mohsin at slip and India were 10 for 2.

Viswanath batted with a lack of certainty, but he survived until Abdul Qadir began to weave his magic spells. Viswanath was caught behind and Amarnath and Patil went in quick succession so that India were 70 for 5.

Arun Lal had stood resolutely while disasters were happening at the other end and he now gave sturdy support to Kapil Dev who, typically, chose the aggressive way out of trouble, attacking Abdul Qadir fiercely. Arun Lal had batted for three and a quarter hours when he fell to Sarfraz. Kapil Dev's innings ended 35 runs later. He had batted for only 84 minutes and hit a six and twelve fours in the 53 deliveries he

Wasim Bari. His enthusiasm remains undiminished. He had an outstanding series. (George Herringshaw)

Dilip Vengsarkar. He hit three fifties in the series, but by his high standards, his form was disappointing. (Adrian Murrell)

aced. His fifty had been reached off 34 balls. Following the dismissal of Kapil Dev, the last four wickets added only 4 runs.

Pakistan had to change their batting order. As Mudassar was ill, Mansoor opened with Mohsin, but both openers and Saleem Malik fell to Madan Lal with only 18 on the board. Zaheer and Javed took Pakistan to the close of 57 for 3 without further alarms. 13 wickets had fallen on the first day while 226 runs had been scored.

On the second day, the complexion of the game changed completely. Javed and Zaheer took their stand to 110 before Javed was unluckily bowled off his pads. Mudassar, still troubled with a sore throat, joined Zaheer in a sumptuous record stand of 213. It bettered the previous Pakistan fifth wicket record against India by 58 runs. Mudassar played admirably in a support role and his courageous and often pugnacious innings lasted for 294 minutes, but the day really belonged to the glorious Zaheer. Once more he displayed the full range of strokes, exquisitely timed and never anything but elegant. He became the first Pakistan batsman to score a thousand runs in Tests against India and his was the hundredth century scored for Pakistan in Test cricket. It was a magnificent achievement and in its accomplishment, it destroyed the Indian attack which ended in total disarray. Zaheer's innings lasted for 328 minutes and he faced 246 balls, hitting twenty-three fours. It was a greater innings than his double century at Lahore, for it changed the course of the

match. When Zaheer came to the wicket the score was 18 for 3; when he was out it was 341 for 5.

Mudassar had useful stands with Imran and Wasim Bari before, like Zaheer, he fell to Kapil Dev, the most successful of the Indian bowlers.

India, trailing by 283 on the first innings, batted with a greater sense of determination at the second attempt, but it was Abdul Qadir who achieved the first breakthrough when he had Arun Lal lbw with his googly.

India seemed to have overcome this loss and to be heading for safety when, after tea on the third day, Imran Khan produced one of the fiercest, finest and most devastating spells of fast bowling ever seen in Test cricket. On a wicket which gave him no undue help, he took five wickets in twenty-five deliveries while he conceded three runs. When he bowled Viswanath he became the first Pakistan bowler to take 200 wickets in Test cricket. It was his forty-fifth Test match and he once more staked his claim to be considered as the greatest of Pakistan's Test captains. From 102 for 1, India went to 118 for 7 by the close, the victims of ferocious fast bowling which left them floundering helplessly.

Vengsarkar and Madan Lal made a spirited reply on the fourth morning, scoring at a run a minute in their stand of 83, and then, twenty minutes before lunch, Imran produced another spell of destruction which ended the match. It was his second spell of the morning, and he took the edge of Vengsarkar's bat for Wasim Bari to make the catch. Manin-

SECOND TEST MATCH – PAKISTAN v. INDIA
23, 24, 25 and 27 December 1982 at Karachi

INDIA

	FIRST INNINGS		SECOND INNINGS	
S.M. Gavaskar[†]	run out	8	b Imran	42
J. Arun Lal	lbw, b Sarfraz	35	lbw, b Qadir	11
D.B. Vengsarkar	c Mohsin, b Imran	0	c Bari, b Imran	79
G.R. Viswanath	c Bari, b Qadir	24	b Imran	0
M.B. Amarnath	lbw, b Imran	5	lbw, b Imran	3
S.M. Patil	c Javed, b Qadir	4	b Imran	0
Kapil Dev	c and b Sarfraz	73	(8) b Imran	1
S.M.H. Kirmani*	c Mohsin, b Qadir	11	(7) c Saleem, b Qadir	1
S. Madan Lal	not out	3	not out	52
Maninder Singh	lbw, b Qadir	0	lbw, b Imran	0
D.R. Doshi	b Imran	0	b Imran	0
Extras	lb 4, nb 2	6	b 1, lb 3, w 1, nb 3	8
		169		**197**

	O	M	R	W	O	M	R	W
Imran Khan	12.2	6	19	3	20.1	4	60	8
Jalaluddin	10	2	28	—	7	2	31	—
Sarfraz Nawaz	16	2	49	2	10	2	23	—
Abdul Qadir	15	3	67	4	23	3	75	2

FALL OF WICKETS
1- 10, 2- 10, 3- 48, 4- 55, 5- 70, 6- 130, 7- 165, 8- 168, 9- 168
1- 28, 2- 102, 3- 108, 4- 112, 5- 112, 6- 113, 7- 114, 8- 197, 9- 197

Umpires: Khizar Hayat & Shakoor Rana

PAKISTAN

	FIRST INNINGS	
Mohsin Khan	c Amarnath, b Madan Lal	12
Mansoor Akhtar	c Kirmani, b Madan Lal	0
Saleem Malik	c Kirmani, b Madan Lal	3
Javed Miandad	b Amarnath	39
Zaheer Abbas	lbw, b Dev	186
Mudassar Nazar	c Kirmani, b Dev	119
Imran Khan[†]	c Amarnath, b Dev	33
Wasim Bari*	c Arun Lal, b Doshi	30
Abdul Qadir	b Dev	0
Sarfraz Nawaz	lbw, b Dev	13
Jalaluddin	not out	0
Extras	b 2, lb 6, w 2, nb 7	17
		452

	O	M	R	W
Kapil Dev	28.4	3	102	5
Madan Lal	23	1	129	3
Doshi	18	1	68	1
Maninder Singh	23	2	67	—
Amarnath	17	1	69	1

FALL OF WICKETS
1- 6, 2- 15, 3- 18, 4- 128, 5- 341, 6- 397, 7- 427, 8- 427, 9- 452

Pakistan won by an innings and 86 runs

der Singh was comprehensively lbw first ball to give him a 'pair' on his Test debut, but Doshi saved the hat trick only to have his stumps knocked over by the first ball of Imran's next over. He had finished with 8 for 60, just failing to beat the record he had set up with his 8 for 58 against Sri Lanka earlier in the year.

Imran had become the first man to capture ten wickets in a Pakistan-India Test in Pakistan. India had been beaten by an innings and 86 runs, the biggest margin ever achieved in the matches between these traditional rivals, and they had been beaten with well over a day to spare. Their saving light on the final morning had been the gallant flourish of Madan Lal, 52 not out, 50 of them (a six and eleven fours) in boundaries, but not even that hitting could stop Imran and his men.

THIRD WILLS ONE-DAY INTERNATIONAL: PAKISTAN v. INDIA

India were somewhat fortuitous to beat Pakistan in the third one-day international. A morning drizzle had cut the contest to 33 overs an innings, but Pakistan made a massive 252 for 3. India went for the runs bravely, but bad light brought play to a close when they were 193 for 4 from 27 overs. As the Pakistan score had been 175 for 2 after 27 overs, India were declared the winners with a scoring rate of 7.14 to Pakistan's 6.48. One doubts, however, that with two new batsmen at the crease India would have managed ten runs an over for the remainder of their innings.

Pakistan recovered from the loss of Mohsin Khan in the

Mohinder Amarnath. Three hundreds in the series. India outstanding batsman. (Adrian Murrell)

first over through a stand of 69 for the second wicket between Mudassar and Zaheer. The real feast for the capacity crowd came in the third wicket stand of 158 between Javed and Zaheer, both of whom hit centuries. Dropped at 71, Zaheer reached his hundred off 79 balls and, in all, hit a six and eight fours before being caught at deep square-leg off another mighty hit. Javed was even more impressive. He hit seven fours and six sixes, and, in one spell, took 40 off Kapil Dev in two overs. The third wicket stand lasted for only 142 minutes and appeared to have won Pakistan the match.

India responded well, however, and Srikkanth hit Imran for sixes over square-leg and long-leg and two crashing fours in the Pakistani captain's fourth over. Imran conceded only three runs in his other four overs. Gavaskar and Srikkanth put on 57 for the first wicket before Srikkanth fell to Shahid Mahboob who was making his debut in international cricket.

The fast-medium Mahboob had begun nervously with a wide, but his first real delivery had Srikkanth caught at mid-off. The first wicket stand had lasted 7 overs, and Gavaskar and Patil maintained a fierce rate of scoring when they added 115 for the second wicket.

Mudassar, brought late into the attack, removed both Patil and Kapil Dev to check the flow of runs, but then the game was brought to its premature close.

THIRD WILLS TEST MATCH: PAKISTAN v. INDIA

India fielded a side unchanged from the second Test, Viswanath holding off the strong challenge that Srikkanth had made for his place. Pakistan made one change. It had been intended that Tahir should replace Jalaluddin, but Tahir's elder brother died on New Year's Day and he withdrew from the side so that Sikhander Bakht returned to the Pakistan side.

Imran won the toss and put India in on a pitch which

Syed Kirmani. In the third Test he did not concede a bye in the Pakistan innings of 652. (Adrian Murrell)

THIRD ONE-DAY INTERNATIONAL: PAKISTAN v. INDIA
31 December 1982 at Lahore

PAKISTAN						INDIA						
Mohsin Khan	c and b Dev			0		S.M. Gavaskar†	c Mansoor, b Tahir				69	
Mudassar Nazar	c and b Shastri			24		K. Srikkanth	c Zaheer, b Shahid				39	
Zaheer Abbas	c Srikkanth, b Amarnath			105		S.M. Patil	c Raja, b Mudassar				51	
Javed Miandad	not out			119		Kapil Dev	lbw, b Mudassar				8	
Wasim Raja	not out			1		Yashpal Sharma	not out				4	
Mansoor Akhtar						M.B. Amarnath	not out				1	
Imran Khan†						D.B. Vengsarkar						
Ejaz Faqih						S.M.H. Kirmani*						
Tahir Naqqash						R.J. Shastri						
Wasim Bari*						S. Madan Lal						
Shahid Mahboob						B.S. Sandhu						
Extras	lb 1, w 2			3		Extras	lb 8, w 11, nb 2				21	
(33 overs)	(for 3 wickets)			252		(27 overs)	(for 4 wickets)				193	

	O	M	R	W			O	M	R	W
Kapil Dev	7	—	73	1		Imran Khan	5	2	23	—
Madan Lal	7	—	35	—		Tahir Naqqash	6	—	42	1
Sandhu	7	—	52	—		Shahid Mahboob	7	—	55	1
Shastri	7	—	39	1		Ejaz Faqih	7	—	39	—
Amarnath	5	—	50	1		Mudassar Nazar	2	—	13	2

FALL OF WICKETS
1- 1, 2- 70, 3- 228

FALL OF WICKETS
1- 57, 2- 172, 3- 185, 4- 192

Umpires: Shakoor Rana & Khizar Hayat

India won on faster scoring rate

seemed to threaten no danger to the batsman, but Arun Lal was dismissed in the second over of the day and by the seventh over, Gavaskar and Vengsarkar had also been dismissed.

Viswanath, very much playing for his place, survived some awkward moments, but he and Mohinder Amarnath added 60 valuable runs before Mudassar Nazar, so often Pakistani's remover of stubborn obstacles, clipped Amarnath's off stump to leave India 95 for 4 at lunch.

Viswanath was bowled shortly after lunch, but in the next hour Patil and Kapil Dev added 68, and India reached 200 in 210 minutes. The stand was reaching threatening proportions when Imran returned to trap Kapil Dev lbw and Patil's brilliant knock ended fifteen runs later. Kirmani and Madan Lal stopped any threat of collapse and an entertaining first day closed with India 334 for 7.

The next day, Kirmani and Madan Lal extended their eighth wicket stand to 122, an Indian record in Tests against Pakistan, before Imran Khan dismissed them both giving five or more wickets in an innings of a Test match for the fourteenth time, a Pakistani record.

In the first hour and a half of their innings, Pakistan lost three wickets for 79, but once more India were overwhelmed by the brilliance of Javed and Zaheer. By the end of the day, Pakistan were 255 for 3 and Zaheer had completed his sixth century against the tourists as well as becoming the highest scoring Pakistani in Test cricket, having overtaken Majid Khan's aggregate of 3931 runs.

The third day saw Javed and Zaheer raise their fourth wicket stand to 287, a Pakistan record for any wicket against

India. They both fell to Madan Lal shortly before lunch when he took the new ball. Javed went first, having hit three sixes and ten fours in his 276-minute innings. Zaheer spooned a catch to Kirmani after 264 minutes at the wicket during which he hit a six and twenty-three fours and confirmed that he now had no superior in international cricket.

There was to be no respite for India. Another record stand followed, this time between Saleem Malik and Imran Khan 207 for the sixth wicket in three and a quarter hours. Imran reached his fifty when he pulled the ball out of the ground and he hooked Kapil Dev into the crowd to reach his hundred. His explosive innings contained five sixes, and he became Maninder Singh's first victim in Test cricket when he was caught by Madan Lal. Saleem became the fourth Pakistan batsman to score a century, boldly hitting his way through the nineties and reaching the hundred with his fourteenth four. 594 for 6 at the close and Pakistan batted on into the fourth day.

The rest day was much welcomed by India who returned to the fray and took the four remaining wickets for the addition of 58 runs. Abdul Qadir played a chirpy knock and Kapil Dev finished with a valiant 7 for 220.

India were soon facing defeat when they lost three wickets for 48 runs in half an hour, but Gavaskar and Mohinder Amarnath batted with great tenacity to take them to 181 for 3 by the close so giving hope that they could survive the last day and save the game.

But it was not to be. Amarnath went early on the last morning, Patil shortly after and wickets fell regularly to the Pakistan pace attack. Imran again captured five wickets and

---

THIRD TEST MATCH – PAKISTAN v. INDIA
3, 4, 5, 7 and 8 January 1983 at Faisalabad

INDIA

	FIRST INNINGS		SECOND INNINGS	
S.M. Gavaskar†	c Saleem, b Imran	12	not out	127
J. Arun Lal	b Sarfraz	0	c Zaheer, b Sarfraz	3
D.B. Vengsarkar	lbw, b Imran	6	lbw, b Imran	1
G.R. Viswanath	b Mudassar	53	c Javed, b Sarfraz	9
M.B. Amarnath	b Mudassar	22	lbw, b Imran	78
S.M. Patil	c Bari, b Imran	84	b Imran	6
Kapil Dev	lbw, b Imran	41	c Sikhander, b Sarfraz	16
S.M.H. Kirmani*	lbw, b Imran	66	c Bari, b Sikhander	6
S. Madan Lal	c Saleem, b Imran	54	lbw, b Sarfraz	10
Maninder Singh	c Mohsin, b Qadir	6	lbw, b Imran	2
D.R. Doshi	not out	2	b Imran	4
Extras	b 6, lb 8, w 4, nb 8	26	b 1, lb 9, nb 14	24
		372		286

	O	M	R	W	O	M	R	W
Imran Khan	25	3	98	6	30.5	12	82	5
Sarfraz Nawaz	23	4	95	1	33	11	79	4
Sikhander Bakht	13	1	66	—	9	3	41	1
Mudassar Nazar	12	2	39	2	11	3	27	—
Abdul Qadir	12.3	1	48	1	11	1	33	—

PAKISTAN

	FIRST INNINGS		SECOND INNINGS	
Mohsin Khan	c Kirmani, b Dev	4	not out	8
Mudassar Nazar	c Kirmani, b Dev	38	not out	2
Mansoor Akhtar	c Kirmani, b Dev	23		
Javed Miandad	c Gavaskar, b Madan Lal	126		
Zaheer Abbas	c Kirmani, b Madan Lal	168		
Saleem Malik	b Dev	107		
Imran Khan†	c Madan Lal, b Maninder	117		
Wasim Bari*	c Kirmani, b Dev	6		
Sarfraz Nawaz	c Gavaskar, b Dev	4		
Abdul Qadir	not out	38		
Sikhander Bakht	b Dev	9		
Extras	lb 10, nb 2	12		0
		652	(for no wkt)	10

	O	M	R	W	O	M	R	W
Kapil Dev	38.4	3	220	7				
Madan Lal	28	5	109	2				
Doshi	29	2	130	—				
Amarnath	16	1	68	—				
Maninder Singh	20	3	103	1				
Gavaskar	2	—	10	—				
Arun Lal					1.1	—	6	—
Vengsarkar					1	—	4	—

FALL OF WICKETS
1- 6, 2- 17, 3- 22, 4- 82, 5- 122, 6- 220, 7- 235, 8- 357, 9- 370
1- 27, 2- 28, 3- 48, 4- 193, 5- 201, 6- 227, 7- 236, 8- 261, 9- 282

FALL OF WICKETS
1- 4, 2- 66, 3- 79, 4- 366, 5- 367, 6- 574, 7- 595, 8- 599, 9- 612

Umpires: Mahboob Shah & Shakeel Khan

Pakistan won by 10 wickets

joined Botham as the all-rounder who has scored a cen-
ury and taken ten wickets in a Test. An innings defeat was
aved, but the game was won by Pakistan half an hour before
a.

Whilst all around him fell Gavaskar battled on for over
even hours to score his twenty-sixth Test century, the first
ndian to carry his bat through a completed Test innings. It
as an innings of courage, determination and dignity.

India had one other hero. Wicket-keeper Syed Kirmani
id not concede a bye in Pakistan's innings of 652 and took
ve catches, the first person to take five catches in an innings
a an India-Pakistan Test match.

0, 11 and 12 January 1983

t Peshawar

Jorth West Frontier Province Governor's XI 255 for
dec (Haroon Rashid 133, Shoaib Mohammad 71) and
86 for 2 dec (Wasim Raja 102 not out, Ejaz Faqih 100 not
ut)

ndians 292 for 5 dec (S.M. Patil 137, D.B. Vengsarkar
00 not out) and 253 for 6 (M.B. Amarnath 84, K. Srikanth 67)

ndians won by 4 wickets

Desperately in need of a boost to their morale, the Indians
ad a most depressing first day when, helped by several
dropped catches, Haroon Rashid and Shoaib Mohammad
shared a second wicket stand of 220 and helped the home side
o a score of 255 for 3. Haroon reached his hundred in three
ours.

The tourists began disastrously. Arun Lal was run out
vithout a run on the board, Srikkanth was bowled two runs
ater and then another mix-up saw Yashpal Sharma run out.
They were thankful for the bad light which ended play 20
minutes early with the score at 15 for 3.

Viswanath was out for the addition of one run the next
morning, but then Patil joined Vengsarkar and when he was
but just over two hours later he had scored 137 chanceless
uns and the score was 227. There were twenty fours and a
ix in Patil's blistering innings, and Vengsarkar reached a
nore sedate century to give the Indians an unexpected lead
of 37. Shoaib was out before the close.

The last day provided some sensational cricket for the
crowd of 10,000. Wasim Raja and Ejaz Faqih were unbeaten
after a third wicket stand of 206 and both reached centuries.
Haroon Rashid declared leaving India 83 minutes plus 20
overs in which to make 250.

The Indians went for the runs from the start and scorned
danger as they maintained a scoring rate of more than seven
runs an over which ended with Viswanath driving the winning boundary with eleven balls to spare. It was a much
needed win.

FOURTH WILLS TEST MATCH: PAKISTAN *v.* INDIA

Each side showed two changes from the teams that had been
fielded at Faisalabad. India brought in Balwinder Sandhu for
his Test debut in place of Madan Lal who was flown back to
India with an injured heel and Krishna Srikkanth replaced

Jagdish Arun Lal. Pakistan included Haroon Rashid in place
of Mansoor Akhtar and Iqbal Qasim in place of Sikhander
Bakht. Haroon was rather fortunate to be preferred ahead of
Qasim Umar who had had a splendid season and had been
twelfth man in the second and third Tests.

Imran won the toss and, not surprisingly, elected to bat. In
an hour and a half, Mohsin and Mudassar put on 60 and then
Sandhu celebrated his first Test by having Mohsin lbw and
celebrated further by bowling Haroon first ball. Another
wicket did not fall until eight minutes before the close of the
second day. By that time Javed and Mudassar had added
451, a Test record for the third wicket, 81 runs better than the
previous record set up by Compton and Edrich against South
Africa in 1947. The young Pakistani batsmen equalled the
record Test partnership for any wicket held by Bradman and
Ponsford. The stand ended when Mudassar misjudged the
flight of a ball from Doshi and was caught at cover. His
innings had lasted just short of ten and a half hours and he
had hit a six and twenty-one fours. It was his highest score
in a Test match.

515 for 3 at the close, Pakistan batted on for an hour on
the third morning and then declared. Javed Miandad was left
on 280 not out. He had batted for six minutes over ten hours
and hit a six and nineteen fours, and his innings was second
only to Hanif Mohammad's 337 against the West Indies in
1957–58 in Pakistan's Test history.

In 50 minutes batting before lunch, India lost Srikkanth
and were 24 for 1 at the interval. Twenty-two minutes after
the resumption disaster struck for India when Gavaskar was
caught behind off Imran. It heralded a collapse as Imran

Madan Lal. His injury was a grievous blow to India. (*George Herringshaw*)

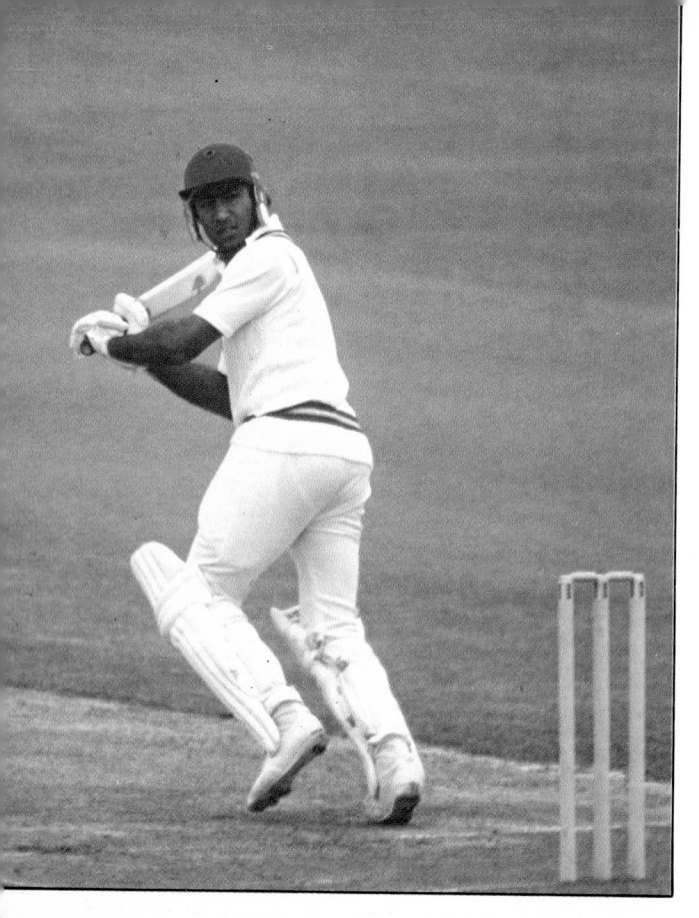

dismissed Viswanath, playing in his eighty-fifth consecuti Test so equalling Gary Sobers' record, Vengsarkar, Kap Dev and Kirmani within the next half hour. At tea, Ind were 100 for 7.

Amarnath, the most improved player in the Indian sid and Sandhu added 59 for the eighth wicket before Amarna was smartly stumped off Iqbal Qasim. Then Manind helped Sandhu in a stand of 53 for the ninth wicket. Sandh was finally bowled by Sarfraz for 71, but with bat and ball h had had a splendid Test debut.

India were out for 189, Imran's pace and lift on a pit which gave him no help again being the prime cause of the destruction. Next morning they followed-on and they batte doggedly all day. Srikkanth was lured into an unwise hoo early on and perished on the boundary, but Gavaskar an Mohinder Amarnath added 125. They both fell to goo catches off Iqbal Qasim, but Viswanath and Vengsark: gave hope of saving the match when they batted to the clo at 198 for 3.

The hopes were shattered in the first over of the last da when Viswanath was lbw to Sarfraz. The fight had now gor out of the Indians as Sarfraz produced a fine spell of swin bowling and they were all out shortly before lunch, havin scored 75 runs for the loss of the last 7 wickets in the morn ing.

India announced that Sekhar would be joining them as

LEFT: *Mudassar Nazar and Javed Miandad. Their partnersh of 451 for the third wicket in the fourth Test was a recor Mudassar hit 721 runs in the series. (Adrian Murrell)*

OURTH TEST MATCH – PAKISTAN v. INDIA

4, 15, 16, 18 and 19 January 1983 at Hyderabad

AKISTAN

	FIRST INNINGS	
ohsin Khan	lbw, b Sandhu	24
udassar Nazar	c Maninder, b Doshi	231
aroon Rashid	b Sandhu	0
ved Miandad	not out	280
aheer Abbas	not out	25
aleem Malik		
mran Khan†		
asim Bari*		
arfraz Nawaz		
bdul Qadir		
bal Qasim		
Extras	b 9, lb 12	21
	(for 3 wkts dec)	581

	O	M	R	W
apil Dev	27	2	111	—
andhu	33	7	107	2
marnath	15	—	64	—
laninder Singh	50	10	135	—
oshi	41	9	143	1

ALL OF WICKETS
- 60, 2- 60, 3- 511

Umpires: Javed Akhtar & Khizar Hayat

INDIA

	FIRST INNINGS		SECOND INNINGS	
S.M. Gavaskar†	c Bari, b Imran	17	c and b Iqbal	60
K. Srikkanth	lbw, b Sarfraz	2	c Saleem, b Imran	5
M.B. Amarnath	st Bari, b Iqbal	61	c Imran, b Iqbal	64
G.R. Viswanath	lbw, b Imran	0	lbw, b Sarfraz	37
D.B. Vengsarkar	c Bari, b Imran	4	not out	58
Kapil Dev	b Imran	3	b Sarfraz	2
S.M.H. Kirmani*	b Imran	1	lbw, b Sarfraz	0
S.M. Patil	c Imran, b Sarfraz	2	c Imran, b Qadir	9
B.S. Sandhu	b Sarfraz	71	c Imran, b Qadir	12
Maninder Singh	not out	12	lbw, b Sarfraz	4
D.R. Doshi	lbw, b Imran	1	b Imran	14
Extras	b 1, lb 7, nb 7	15	b 1, lb 1, nb 6	8
		189		273

	O	M	R	W	O	M	R	W
Imran Khan	17.2	3	35	6	24.4	14	45	2
Sarfraz Nawaz	19	4	56	3	30	4	85	4
Abdul Qadir	11	2	35	—	26	7	77	2
Iqbal Qasim	9	1	48	1	31	9	58	2

FALL OF WICKETS
1- 3, 2- 44, 3- 44, 4- 52, 5- 61, 6- 65, 7- 72, 8- 131, 9- 184
1- 8, 2- 133, 3- 134, 4- 201, 5- 203, 6- 203, 7- 223, 8- 249, 9- 254

Pakistan won by an innings and 119 runs

OURTH WILLS ONE-DAY INTERNATIONAL: AKISTAN v. INDIA

ndia included Sekhar in their side in place of Doshi. Sekhar
ad arrived in Karachi only the night before.

Gavaskar won the toss and decided to bat. Srikkanth
atted for more than two hours for his 48 which included five
ours. He shared a first wicket stand of 41 with Arun Lal and
third wicket stand of 66 with Yashpal Sharma, but there
as a distinct lack of urgency and commitment about the
ndian innings and Pakistan were left a comparatively easy
ask.

They lost an early wicket to Sandhu, the best of the Indian
owlers, but Zaheer showed from the start that this was to
e another day when he would dominate the play. He
eached his fifty in 51 minutes off 35 balls and when he
eached his century in 131 minutes off 94 balls Mudassar was
6 not out.

Zaheer faced 99 deliveries in his 138-minute stay and hit
hree sixes and eleven fours. It was his seventh hundred of the
eason against the Indians and his sixth in one-day interna-
ionals, a number which places him as the outstanding bats-
nan in limited-over international cricket.

Mashin Khan. (Adrian Murrell)

FOURTH ONE-DAY INTERNATIONAL: PAKISTAN v. INDIA
21 January 1983 at Karachi

INDIA				PAKISTAN			
K. Srikkanth	c Tahir, b Ejaz	48		Mohsin Khan	lbw, b Sandhu		
J. Arun Lal	b Sarfraz	16		Mudassar Nazar	not out		6
M.B. Amarnath	b Sarfraz	8		Zaheer Abbas	c Amarnath, b Sandhu		1
Yashpal Sharma	c Imran, b Sarfraz	27		Javed Miandad	not out		
Kapil Dev	c Mansoor, b Imran	20		Mansoor Akhtar			
S.M. Gavaskar†	c Raja, b Imran	23		Wasim Raja			
D.B. Vengsarkar	not out	22		Imran Khan†			
S.M.H. Kirmani*	not out	1		Tahir Naqqash			
B.S. Sandhu				Ejaz Faqih			
Maninder Singh				Wasim Bari*			
T.A. Sekhar				Sarfraz Nawaz			
Extras	lb 12, w 16, nb 4	32		Extras	lb 10, w 3		1
(40 overs)	(for 6 wickets)	197		(35 overs)	(for 2 wickets)		19

	O	M	R	W			O	M	R	W
Imran Khan	8	3	15	2		Kapil Dev	5	1	11	—
Tahir Naqqash	8	1	38	—		Sandhu	7	—	38	2
Mudassar Nazar	8	1	30	—		Sekhar	4	—	19	—
Sarfraz Nawaz	8	1	31	3		Srikkanth	2	—	27	—
Ejaz Faqih	8	—	51	1		Yashpal Sharma	8	—	39	—
						Maninder Singh	8	—	47	—
						Gavaskar	1	—	4	—

FALL OF WICKETS
1- 41, 2- 54, 3- 120, 4- 124, 5- 162, 6- 192

FALL OF WICKETS
1- 9, 2- 179

Umpires: Mahboob Shah & Khizar Hayat

Pakistan won by 8 wickets

FIFTH WILLS TEST MATCH: PAKISTAN v. INDIA

India introduced Sekhar to Test cricket and brought in Yashpal Sharma for Patil who was injured. Pakistan brought Majid Khan back to Test cricket.

Gavaskar won the toss and asked Pakistan to bat first on a damp pitch. Kapil Dev gained early success when he took the wickets of Mohsin Khan and Majid Khan in quick succession, but Javed Miandad, flamboyantly, and Mudassar Nazar, more introverted, put on 148. Zaheer failed for the first time in the series, and at the end of a dour day in which India's poor outcricket was brightened only by Kapil Dev's bowling and in which the batting was disappointing, Pakistan were 224 for 5, Mudassar 99 not out.

Mudassar reached his third century of the series the following morning and carried his bat through the innings for 152 so emulating the feat of his father, Nazar Mohammad, who carried his bat for 124 in the first meeting of the countries at Lucknow in 1952–53.

The Pakistan innings ended 45 minutes after lunch when Kapil Dev took three wickets in five balls to finish with 8 for 85, a career best performance and a splendid piece of bowling.

India lost Gavaskar and Srikkanth for 41 and appeared to be in danger of wilting when Amarnath and Yashpal Sharma rallied them.

Their stand was extended to 190 the next day so establishing a new Indian third wicket record against Pakistan. Only seven balls were bowled before lunch because of bad light and play ended 50 minutes early. Amarnath reached a splendid hundred and looked by far the most confident and assured of the Indian batsmen in the series. He was caught behind when Imran took the second new ball. After that came gloom and rain and no play was possible on the last two days.

Kapil Dev. An untiring bowler. Twenty-four wickets in th[e] series left him far ahead of India's other bowlers. (Adria[n] Murrell)

Yashpal Sharma. Found form late on the tour. (Adrian Murrell)

FIFTH TEST MATCH – PAKISTAN v. INDIA
23, 24, 25, 27 and 28 January 1983 at Lahore

PAKISTAN

FIRST INNINGS

Mohsin Khan	c Srikkanth, b Dev	7
Mudassar Nazar	not out	152
Majid Khan	c Kirmani, b Dev	0
Javed Miandad	c Viswanath, b Maninder	85
Zaheer Abbas	c Kirmani, b Dev	13
Saleem Malik	b Maninder	6
Imran Khan†	c Kirmani, b Dev	20
Wasim Bari*	c Amarnath, b Dev	8
Sarfraz Nawaz	c Sharma, b Dev	26
Abdul Qadir	b Dev	0
Iqbal Qasim	lbw, b Dev	0
Extras	lb 6	6
		323

	O	M	R	W
Kapil Dev	30.5	7	85	8
Sandhu	21	2	56	—
Sekhar	20	2	86	—
Maninder Singh	32	7	90	2

FALL OF WICKETS

1- 22, 2- 26, 3- 174, 4- 191, 5- 202, 6- 244, 7- 276, 8- 323, 9- 323

Umpires: Khizar Hayar and Javed Akhtar

INDIA

FIRST INNINGS

S.M. Gavaskar†	lbw, b Imran	13
K. Srikkanth	b Qadir	21
M.B. Amarnath	c Bari, b Imran	120
Yashpal Sharma	not out	63
D.B. Vengsarkar	not out	1
G.R. Viswanath		
Kapil Dev		
S.M.H. Kirmani*		
B.S. Sandhu		
Maninder Singh		
T.A. Sekhar		
Extras	b 6, lb 5, w 1, nb 5	17
	(for 3 wickets)	**235**

	O	M	R	W
Imran Khan	18	5	45	2
Sarfraz Nawaz	23.2	9	46	—
Abdul Qadir	16	1	63	1
Majid Khan	1	—	4	—
Mudassar Nazar	11	1	41	—
Iqbal Qasim	12	3	19	—

FALL OF WICKETS

1- 29, 2- 41, 3- 231

Match drawn

SIXTH WILLS TEST MATCH: PAKISTAN v. INDIA

Wasim Raja was recalled to the Pakistani fold and Shastri came back to the Indian side as an opening batsman.

Gavaskar won the toss and India occupied all but half an hour of the first two days in making their best score of the series. Shastri achieved a maiden Test century in an innings which lasted more than eight hours. He was stumped off leg-spinner Abdul Qadir so providing Wasim Bari with his two hundredth dismissal in Test cricket. The Indian wicket-keeper Kirmani had reached a landmark of his own with 2000 runs in Test cricket.

The third and fourth days' play belonged to Mudassar. He shared an opening stand of 157 with Mohsin and a second wicket stand of 112 with Javed. He reached his third century in succession against India and his fourth of the series, joining Bradman, Fingleton, Weekes and Gavaskar with this achievement. With 761 runs in the series, he established another Pakistan record.

Sadly, crowd disturbances and pitch invasions brought play to an end two and a half hours early. Imran declared overnight and India began their second innings on the last morning, the stoppage and some tedious batting having already made a draw inevitable.

Ravi Shastri. Unsuccessful with his bowling, Shastri was recalled to the side for the sixth Test and hit a maiden Test Century. (Associated Sports Photography)

SIXTH TEST MATCH – PAKISTAN v. INDIA
30, 31 January, 1, 3 and 4 February 1983 at Karachi

INDIA

	FIRST INNINGS		SECOND INNINGS	
S.M. Gavaskar†	c Bari, b Tahir	5	b Imran	67
R.J. Shastri	st Bari, b Qadir	128	c Bari, b Imran	17
M.B. Amarnath	c Bari, b Imran	19	not out	103
Yashpal Sharma	c Bari, b Imran	9	not out	19
D.B. Vengsarkar	c and b Tahir	89		
G.R. Viswanath	b Mudassar	10		
S.M.H. Kirmani*	c Zaheer, b Sarfraz	18		
Kapil Dev	lbw, b Imran	33		
B.S. Sandhu	not out	32		
T.A. Sekhar	not out	0		
Maninder Singh				
Extras	b 13, lb 9, nb 28	50	b 10, w 3, nb 5	18
	(for 8 wkts dec)	393	(for 2 wkts)	224

	O	M	R	W	O	M	R	W
Imran Khan	32	11	65	3	16	3	41	2
Sarfraz Nawaz	41	10	92	1	14	4	45	—
Tahir Naqqash	24	7	69	2	8	1	28	—
Abdul Qadir	23	3	86	1	14	2	42	—
Mudassar Nazar	15	4	30	1				
Wasim Raja	1	—	1	—	5	2	12	—
Zaheer Abbas					8	2	24	—
Mohsin Khan					1	—	3	—
Javed Miandad					2	—	11	—

PAKISTAN

	FIRST INNINGS	
Mohsin Khan	lbw, b Dev	91
Mudassar Nazar	lbw, b Dev	152
Javed Miandad	c Kirmani, b Sandhu	47
Zaheer Abbas	c Amarnath, b Shastri	43
Wasim Raja	run out	10
Imran Khan†	not out	32
Wasim Bari*	c Kirmani, b Sandhu	12
Sarfraz Nawaz	not out	6
Saleem Malik		
Abdul Qadir		
Tahir Naqqash		
Extras	b 5, lb 12, w 1, nb 9	27
	(for 6 wkts dec)	420

	O	M	R	W
Kapil Dev	33	2	137	2
Sandhu	28.2	4	87	2
Sekhar	14	1	43	—
Maninder Singh	16	3	49	—
Shastri	22	1	62	1
Amarnath	5	1	15	—

FALL OF WICKETS
1- 47, 2- 86, 3- 109, 4- 178, 5- 218, 6- 267, 7- 316, 8- 393
1- 43, 2- 150

FALL OF WICKETS
1- 157, 2- 269, 3- 342, 4- 362, 5- 371, 6- 411

Umpires: Khizar Hayar and Javed Akhtar

Match drawn

Pakistan *v.* India – Test Match Averages

PAKISTAN BATTING

	M	Inns	NOs	Runs	HS	Av	100s	50s
Zaheer Abbas	6	6	1	650	215	130.00	3	
Mudassar Nazar	6	8	2	761	231	126.83	4	1
Javed Miandad	6	6	1	594	280*	118.80	2	1
Imran Khan	6	5	1	247	117	61.75	1	
Mohsin Khan	6	8	2	341	101*	56.83	1	2
Saleem Malik	6	4		122	107	30.50	1	
Abdul Qadir	5	3	1	38	38*	19.00		
Sarfraz Nawaz	6	5	1	67	26	16.75		
Wasim Bari	6	5		68	30	13.60		
Mansoor Akhtar	3	4	1	40	23	13.33		

Played in two Tests - Tahir Naqqash 20; Jalaluddin 1 and 0*; Iqbal Qasim 0
Played in one Test - Sikhander Bakht 9; Haroon Rashid 0; Majid Khan 0;
Wasim Raja 10

PAKISTAN BOWLING

	Overs	Mds	Runs	Wkts	Av	Best	5/inn
Imran Khan	223.2	69	558	40	13.95	8/60	4
Sarfraz Nawaz	241.1	61	633	19	33.31	4/63	
Iqbal Qasim	52	13	125	3	41.66	2/58	
Abdul Qadir	151.3	23	526	11	47.54	4/67	
Mudassar Nazar	52	11	147	3	49.00	2/39	
Jalaluddin	51	14	152	2	76.00	2/93	
Tahir Naqqash	61	14	211	2	105.50	2/69	

Also bowled: Sikhander Bakht 22 - 4 - 107 - 1; Zaheer Abbas 8 - 2 - 24 - 0;
Majid Khan 1 - 0 - 4 - 0; Wasim Raja 6 - 2 - 13 - 0; Mohsin Khan 1 - 0 - 3 - 0;
Javed Miandad 2 - 0 - 11 - 0

PAKISTAN CATCHES

7 - Wasim Bari (ct 15/st 2); 5 - Saleem Malik; 4 - Imran Khan; 3 - Mohsin
Khan; 2 - Mudassar Nazar, Zaheer Abbas and Javed Miandad; 1 - Sarfraz
Nawaz, Sikhander Bakht, Iqbal Qasim and Tahir Naqqash

INDIA BATTING

	M	Inns	NOs	Runs	HS	Av	100s	50s
Yashpal Sharma	2	3	2	91	63*	91.00		1
M.B. Amarnath	6	10	2	584	120	73.00	3	3
B.S. Sandhu	3	3	1	115	71	57.50		1
R.J. Shastri	2	3		152	128	50.66	1	
S.M. Gavaskar	6	10	1	434	127*	48.22	1	3
S. Madan Lal	3	5	2	126	54	42.00		2
D.B. Vengsarkar	6	9	2	241	89	34.42		3
S.M. Patil	4	7		173	84	24.71		2
Kapil Dev	6	8		178	73	22.25		1
J. Arun Lal	3	5		100	51	20.00		1
G.R. Viswanath	6	8		134	53	16.75		1
S.M.H. Kirmani	6	8		113	66	14.12		1
K. Srikkanth	2	3		28	21	9.33		
Maninder Singh	5	6	1	24	12*	4.90		
D.R. Doshi	4	7	1	21	14	3.50		

Played in two Tests - T.A. Sekhar 0*

INDIA BOWLING

	Overs	Mds	Runs	Wkts	Av	Best	5/inn
Kapil Dev	205.1	22	831	24	34.62	8/85	3
S. Madan Lal	83	9	349	8	43.62	3/101	
D.R. Doshi	135.5	20	489	8	61.12	5/91	1
B.S. Sandhu	82.2	13	250	4	62.50	2/87	
Maninder Singh	141	25	444	3	148.00	2/90	
R.J. Shastri	58	5	176	1	176.00	1/62	
M.B. Amarnath	79	9	280	1	280.00	1/69	
S.M. Gavaskar	3	1	10	0	—		
T.A. Sekhar	34	3	129	0	—		

Also bowled: J. Arun Lal 1.1 - 0 - 6 - 0; D.B. Vengsarkar 1 - 0 - 4 - 0

INDIA CATCHES

14 - S.M.H. Kirmani (ct 13/st 1); 6 - M.B. Amarnath; 5 - S.M. Gavaskar;
3 - J. Arun Lal; 2 - S. Madan Lal; 1 - Maninder Singh, K. Srikkanth, G.R.
Viswanath and Yashpal Sharma

Imran dismissed both Gavaskar and Shastri so becoming the first all-rounder to take 40 wickets and score 200 runs in a Test series, a series which he had dominated in so many ways and which he had shaped by his vibrant leadership and unquenchable endeavour.

There was one last consolation for India when Mohinder Amarnath completed his third century of the series. Unquestionably, he had been India's outstanding player of the tour and had his team-mates been able to show the same application that he and Kapil Dev had shown, they might have fared better on the tour.

For Pakistan, the series had been another triumph. In twelve Tests under Imran, they had won 7, lost 2 (both in England) and drawn 3. It was a most impressive record, and one of which Pakistan, and Imran, could be proud.

Viswanath walks away. He played in all six Tests, but with very little success. A distinguished Test career is near its end. (Patrick Eagar)

Indians in Pakistan 1982-3
First Class Matches

Match columns (left to right):
1. v. B.C.C.P. XI (Sahiwal) 29 Nov.–1 Dec. 1982
2. v. B.C.C.P. Patron's XI (Rawalpindi) 5–7 December 1982
3. First Test Match (Lahore) 10–15 December 1982
4. v. Punjab Governor's XI (Multan) 18–20 December 1982
5. Second Test Match (Karachi) 23–27 December 1982
6. Third Test Match (Faisalabad) 3–8 January 1983
7. v. N.W.F.P. Governor's XI (Peshawar) 10–12 January 1983
8. Fourth Test Match (Hyderabad) 14–19 January 1983
9. Fifth Test Match (Lahore) 23–28 January 1983
10. Sixth Test Match (Karachi) 30 Jan.–4 Feb. 1983

BATTING

BATTING	Sah 1	Sah 2	Raw 1	Raw 2	1T 1	1T 2	Pun 1	Pun 2	2T 1	2T 2	3T 1	3T 2	NWFP 1	NWFP 2	4T 1	4T 2	5T 1	5T 2	6T 1	6T 2
K. Srikkanth	33	20	8	135			64	—					2	67	2	5	21	—		
J. Arun Lal	76	6	84	17	51	—	10	—	35	11	0	3	0	6						
D. B. Vengsarkar	100*	28*			3	—	4	—	0	79	6	1	100*	26*	4	58*	1*	—	89	—
G. R. Viswanath	25*		50*	5	1	—	16	—	24	0	53	9	4	4*	0	37			10	—
M. B. Amarnath		23*		20	109*	—			5	3	22	78	27*	84	61	64	120	—	19	103*
S. Madan Lal		3			7	—			3*	52*	54	10								
R. N. Kapil Dev					9	—			73	1	41	16			3	2			33	—
R. J. Shastri					7	—	93	—											128	17
S. M. H. Kirmani					10	—	27	—	11	1	66	6			1	0			18	—
Maninder Singh									0	0	6	2			12*	4				
L. Sivaramakrishnan				1			21*	—												
S. M. Gavaskar			84	11*	83	—	50	—	8	42	12	127*			17	60	13	—	5	67
S. M. Patil				70	68	—	0	—	4	0	84	6	137	33	2	9				
M. Yashpal Sharma					25	—	0	—							2	13	63*	—	9	19*
B. S. Sandhu				6			7	—					5		71	12			32*	
D. R. Doshi				5*	0	—			0	0	2*	4			1	14				
T. A. Sekhar																			0*	
Byes	10	2	2	2			16			1	6	1	11	1	1	1	6		13	10
Leg-byes	5	2	(29)	3		11	4		4	3	8	9	4	12	7	1	5		9	
Wides		1					9		1	4							1			3
No-balls		1	7	18			7		2	3	8	14	5	2	7	6	5		28	5
Total	249	86	255	307	379		328		169	197	372	286	292	253	189	273	235		393	224
Wickets	2	3	3	8	10		9		10	10	10	10	5	6	10	10	3		8	2
Result	D		D		D		D		L		L		W		L		D		D	

Catches
17 — S. M. H. Kirmani (ct 15/st 2)
8 — S. M. Gavaskar
6 — M. B. Amarnath
5 — J. Arun Lal
3 — G. R. Viswanath and Maninder Singh
2 — S. Madan Lal, R. N. Kapil Dev and Yashpal Sharma (ct 1/st 1)

BOWLING

Match	R. N. Kapil Dev	S. Madan Lal	M. B. Amarnath	Maninder Singh	R. J. Shastri	L. Sivaramakrishn	K. Srikkanth	B. S. Sandhu
v. B.C.C.P. XI (Sahiwal) 29 November–1 December 1982	11-1-48-1	15-6-37-3 / 4-1-7-0	4-1-15-0 / 2-0-10-0	19-2-63-0 / 26-8-47-0	29-9-33-1 / 29-6-80-4	13-0-67-0 / 14-2-59-0	1-0-6-0	
v. B.C.C.P. Patron's XI (Rawalpindi) 5-7 Dec. 1982			8-2-36-0 / 2-1-3-1	21-2-85-2		11-0-70-0		12-4-44-1 / 3-1-4-1
First Test Match (Lahore) 10-15 Dec. 1982	39-3-149-2 / 8-2-27-0	27-2-101-3 / 5-1-10-0	23-5-59-0 / 3-1-5-0		22-3-81-0 / 14-1-33-0			
v. Punjab Governor's XI (Multan) 18-20 Dec. 1982				24-7-35-6 / 33-14-49-4	26-6-46-0	20.2-5-46-4 / 28-5-62-0	5-1-19-0 / 2-0-3-0	12-2-27-0 / 12-2-36-0
Second Test Match (Karachi) 23-27 Dec. 1982	28.4-3-102-5	23-1-129-3	17-1-69-1		23-2-67-0			
Third Test Match (Faisalabad) 3-8 Jan. 1983	38.4-3-220-7	28-5-109-2	16-1-68-0	20-3-103-1				
v. North West Frontier Province Governor's XI (Peshawar) 10-12 January 1983			7-4-21-0 / 7-2-23-0	17-1-51-1 / 26-5-87-0		8-0-44-0	1-0-5-0 / 4-0-28-0	14-5-58-1 / 15-3-47-1
Fourth Test Match (Hyderabad) 14-19 Jan. 1983	27-2-111-0		15-0-64-0	50-10-135-0				33-7-107-2
Fifth Test Match (Lahore) 23-28 January 1983	30.5-7-85-8			32-7-90-2				21-2-56-0
Sixth Test Match (Karachi) 30 January-4 February 1983	33-2-137-2	5-1-15-0		16-3-49-0	22-1-62-1			28.2-4-87-2
Totals	216.1-23-879-25 *av.* 35.16	102-16-393-11 *av.* 35.72	109-19-388-2 *av.* 194.00	307-64-861-16 *av.* 53.81	142-26-335-6 *av.* 55.83	94.2-12-348-4 *av.* 87.00	13-1-61-0 —	150.2-30-466-8 *av.* 58.25

a G. R. Viswanath 2-0-12-0   b D. B. Vengsarkar 1-0-4-0   c D. B. Vengsarkar 5-0-21-0

Inns	NOs	Runs	HS	Av
10	—	357	135	35.70
12	—	299	84	24.91
14	6	499	100*	62.37
14	3	238	53	21.63
14	4	738	120	73.80
6	2	129	54	32.25
8	—	178	73	22.25
4	—	245	128	61.25
9	—	140	66	15.55
6	1	24	12*	4.80
2	1	22	21*	22.00
13	2	579	127*	52.63
10	—	413	137	41.30
7	2	131	63	26.20
6	1	133	71	26.60
8	2	26	14	4.33
1	1	0	0*	—

— D. B. Vengsarkar, D. R. Doshi, R. J. Shastri, K. Srikkanth and L. Sivaramakrishnan

Rashid Khan (George Herringshaw)

D. R. Doshi	S. M. Gavaskar	T. A. Sekhar	J. Arun Lal	Byes	Leg-byes	Wides	No-balls	Total	Wkts
				7	5	4	3	282	5
					2			211	4
8–0–71–2				9	6		1	322	5
				1				8	2
32.5–6–91–5					3		1	485	10
5–2–57–1	1–1–0–0				3			135	1
					4	1		132	10
					6		1	215	4a
8–1–68–1				2	6	2	7	452	10
29–2–130–0	2–0–10–0				10		2	652	10
			1.1–0–6–0					10	0b
22–5–53–1				10	11		2	255	3
5–7–39–1			5–0–23–0	4	9		5	286	2c
41–9–143–1				9	12			581	3
		20–2–86–0			6			323	10
		14–1–43–0		5	12	1	9	420	6
190.5–32–652–12 av. 54.33	3–1–10–0 —	34–3–129–0 —	6.1–0–29–0 —						

Annus Mirabilis

The Season in New Zealand
The Sri Lankan team in New Zealand
One-Day International against England
Review of New Zealand's fine year by Don Cameron

Martin Crowe who won his way back into the Test side. (Adrian Murrell)

Enthusiasm for cricket has never been as high in New Zealand as it is at present. The successes of the national side have stimulated an interest throughout the land and the competition for places in the provincial sides is keener than it has ever been.

Glenn Turner was not the only player to return to his native land after years of exile. Jeff Crowe returned from Australia where he had played five seasons for South Australia in the Sheffield Shield, and Alan Stimpson returned to New Zealand after three years abroad, but, although he won selection for the Northern Districts' squad, he did not play in any of the matches.

There were absentees. Glenn Bateman and Bryan Ritchie were unable to play for Canterbury at the start of the season because of business commitments, and, sadly, 'Jock' Edwards was to miss the season because of a broken leg he had sustained while playing football. Brian McKechnie stated that he would not be available and Cran Bull, having been dropped from the captaincy of Canterbury, was left out of the side altogether. Richard Hadlee was named as Canterbury's captain, but as he would be spending most of the season with the New Zealand side in Australia, Richard Leggat would, in effect, lead the side.

Canterbury welcomed back Craig Thiele, the pace bowler who had missed most of the previous season through injury,

and there were rumours that Dayle Hadlee was anxious t return to first-class cricket at the age of thirty-five, his bac injury hopefully a thing of the past.

Carl Dickel, a thirty-six year old leg-spinner and physic education teacher, returned to first-class cricket with Otag He had last played for Otago in 1972 and his last game o first-class cricket was for Canterbury in 1975. Dickel's retur underlined what is, perhaps, the weakest part of the game i New Zealand, the lack of encouragement given to spinner at international level. There was some criticism that the sele tors, in naming the 'experimental' side for the pre-Christma tour of Australia, had found no place for Boock, Joh Bracewell or Gray and had concentrated the attack in th hands of five pace bowlers.

With Turner and Lees going to Australia, Barry Milbur returned as captain and wicket-keeper of Otago while oth wicket-keepers contending for places were Nigel Scott an Paul Kelly for Auckland and Paul Rutledge, an excitin young prospect, and Ash Hart for Canterbury where th position was wide open.

Of the many overseas players coaching in New Zealan Richard Hayward, the former Hampshire batsman, an Robin Dyer of Warwickshire were available for Centra Districts, and Kevan James of Middlesex and Tony Pigott c Sussex were available for Wellington.

On the eve of the season, Robert Anderson, the Centra Districts and former New Zealand opener, announced hi retirement from first-class cricket.

Peter Webb loses his off-stump, but at the beginning of the season he scored so well that he was to finish top of the averages. His form faded on the tour to Australia. (Adrian Murrell)

Shell Trophy

27, 28 and 29 December 1982

at Wellington

Northern Districts 266 (S.R. Gillespie 59, E.J. Cha field 6 for 76) and 258 for 7 dec (A.D.G. Roberts 79 n out, B.L. Cairns 77 not out)
Wellington 267 for 3 dec (B.A. Edgar 146) and 10 for

Match drawn
Wellington 3 pts, Northern Districts 1 pt

at Auckland

Otago 285 (B.R. Blair 61, G.M. Turner 55, R.N. Hoski 55, W.K. Lees 50) and 140 (M.C. Snedden 5 for 50, J.G Bracewell 4 for 37)
Auckland 277 (M.D. Crowe 119, P.N. Webb 59, S.L Boock 5 for 79) and 152 for 2 (P.N. Webb 76 not out)

Auckland won by 8 wickets
Auckland 11 pts, Otago 4 pts

at Christchurch

Central Districts 212 (R.J. Hadlee 4 for 40) and 14 (R.J. Hadlee 6 for 43)
Canterbury 202 (D.A. Stirling 4 for 34) and 131 (D.F O'Sullivan 5 for 64)

Central Districts won by 23 runs
Central Districts 16 pts, Canterbury 0 pts

At Basin Reserve, Morrison asked Northern Districts to ba and the probing bowling of Pigott and Chatfield had them i me trouble, but debutant opening batsman Lindsay rocker played soundly and attractively for his 48, and when orthern slumped to 166 for 7, Gillespie hit bravely and the st three wickets produced 100.

Edgar was soon in majestic form for the holders and he nd Ormiston added 139 for the second innings. Morrison as able to declare as soon as Wellington passed the visitors' tal, and they looked sure of forcing victory when Northern ere 92 for 6 and 146 for 7, but Cairns then joined Roberts nd hit a typically lusty 77 out of 112 so that the match was awn, both sides losing a point for slow over-rate.

Jeff Crowe was overshadowed by brother Martin as Auck- nd swept to victory over Otago. He hit a fine century, an nswer to the selectors who had omitted him from the New ealand tour party for the Benson and Hedges World Series. e was well supported by Peter Webb, but Auckland still iled to take first innings points.

Otago had launched an early attack on the home bowling rough Glenn Turner, but they lost his services through jury on the second day. They were perplexed by the pace f Snedden and the off-spin of their former team-mate John racewell, and Auckland were left needing 149 to win. purred by Peter Webb, named Man of the Match, they ored the runs at three an over for the loss of Franklin and eid.

67 for 6, Central Districts recovered to reach 212. Aber- art and O'Sullivan effected a similar recovery in the second nings when 83 for 8 was transformed into 132 for 9, 144 all ut.

In spite of Hadlee's magnificent bowling, 10 for 103, the rst time he had taken 10 wickets in a match for Canterbury, entral Districts gained a splendid victory. O'Sullivan bow- d unchanged in the second innings. His left-arm spin being ontrasted by the pace of Stirling and Robertson proved too uch for Canterbury who were beaten by 23 runs.

Richard Hadlee was named Man of the Match for his all- ound performance for the losing side. When he had Ian mith lbw in the second innings it was his 750th wicket in rst-class cricket, and earlier in the innings he had captured is 200th wicket for Canterbury.

Martin Snedden, a consistent bowler and increasingly reliable batsman.

hell Cup

0 December 1982

t Wellington

Vellington 110 for 8
Iorthern Districts 80

Vellington won by 30 runs

t Rangiora

Canterbury 139 for 6
Central Districts 140 for 6 (A. Blain 57 not out)

Central Districts won by 4 wickets

t Auckland

Auckland 269 for 9 (J.F. Reid 71, P.N. Webb 57, M.D. Crowe 52)
Otago 203 (W.L. Blair 108, M.C. Snedden 4 for 25)

Auckland won by 66 runs

The matches at Wellington and Rangiora were curtailed to 33 overs an innings by the weather. On a difficult pitch, Wellington fared badly against Gillespie, Roberts and Cairns, but Northern Districts fared even worse when they set out to score the meagre 111 needed for victory. Crocker, John Wright and Howarth were all out with only 9 scored, and the side never effectively recovered against some fine seam bowling by Steve Maguiness who had 3 for 19 and the personal award. He was well supported by Kevan James, Coney Cederwall and Chatfield, and Wellington won with surprising ease.

Chasing 140, Central Districts were 24 for 4, but an heroic innings from exciting young batsman-wicket-keeper Tony Blain brought them victory with nine balls to spare.

There was an equally heroic innings at Auckland, but this time the batsman, Wayne Blair, finished on the losing side.

A second wicket stand of 128 between Peter Webb and John Reid, the enigma of New Zealand cricket, helped to lift Auckland to a formidable 269 from their fifty overs, Martin Crowe again batting well.

Otago were 36 for 3 against Troup and Stott and then Wayne Blair laid about the bowling with some pugnacious shots. The left-hander shared a stand of 69 with Warren Lees (27), but no-one else could make twenty and Auckland won comfortably, Snedden mopping up the tail in accomplished fashion.

Shell Trophy

1, 2 and 3 January 1983

at Tauranga

Otago 90 (S.M. Carrington 4 for 3) and 246 (C. Dickel 56, B.G. Cooper 5 for 40)
Northern Districts 370 (J.M. Parker 78, M.J.E. Wright 72 not out, B.L. Cairns 58, S.L. Boock 5 for 99)

Northern Districts won by an innings and 34 runs
Northern Districts 16 pts, Otago 0 pts

at New Plymouth

Central Districts 218 (S.J. Gill 53) and 209 (P.S. Briasco 59, E.J. Chatfield 5 for 69)
Wellington 424 for 7 dec (R.W. Ormiston 179, J.V. Coney 93, P.J. Holland 52) and 4 for 0

Wellington won by 10 wickets
Wellington 16 pts, Central Districts 0 pts

at Auckland

Canterbury 165 (M.C. Snedden 7 for 49) and 150 (J.G. Bracewell 4 for 40)
Auckland 282 (T.J. Franklin 66, J.G. Bracewell 61) and 34 for 0

Auckland won by 10 wickets
Auckland 16 pts, Canterbury 0 pts

John Parker, Northern Districts v Otago. A mature and consistent performer, but the selectors seem to think his Test days are over. (Norman Smith)

Mark Carrington, who had not had a successful tour Australia with the 'experimental' side, roared back to for with a devastating opening spell of 4 for 0 from which Ota never recovered. Otago had been ill-prepared for the start the season through lack of match practice and they we hampered further by injuries. This meant that Carl Dicke return to first-class cricket saw him used as an emergen opening batsman. He was one of Carrington's victims in t first innings, but he played a very brave knock in the seco innings when his colleagues succumbed to the quickish, f off-spin of Barry Cooper whose 5 for 40 was a career best. F had previously bowled only occasionally for Northe Districts and before this game had only four first-cla wickets to his credit.

Northern Districts batted solidly against the mainly sp attack and Parker and wicket-keeper Mike Wright gave tl innings the substance needed to force victory.

Wellington showed that they had no intention of reli quishing the Shell Trophy when they put Central Distric firmly in their place. The pace of Chatfield and the mediu pace of Brian Cederwall were too accurate for the Centr batsmen, but there was a maiden fifty from Scott Briasco

The innings of the match, however, came fro Wellington's twenty-seven year old Ross Ormiston who h his maiden first-class century in his home town. Ormisto whose innings was studded with fluent cover drives none which seemed to leave the ground an inch, reached thousand runs in first-class cricket in the course of his i nings. Not surprisingly, he took the Man of the Mat award.

There was another career best performance at Aucklar where Martin Snedden took 7 for 49 on New Year's day set Canterbury on the way to defeat inside two days. Snedd took three wickets in the second innings so taking 10 wicke in a match for the first time in his short, but impressive caree

John Bracewell showed his all-round quality as Aucklar moved to the top of the table and Canterbury suffered the second defeat in two matches.

Shell Cup

4 January 1983

at Tauranga

Northern Districts 194 (J.M. Parker 54)
Otago 148 (B.L. Cairns 4 for 19)

Northern Districts won by 46 runs

at Auckland

Canterbury 150 (R.M. Carter 51, M.C. Snedden 5 f 19)
Auckland 151 for 3 (P.N. Webb 70)

Auckland won by 7 wickets

at Wanganui

Central Districts 221 (S.J. Gill 55, J.R. Wiltshire 54 n out)
Wellington 229 for 4 (B.A. Edgar 128 not out)

Wellington won by 6 wickets

The weakened Otago side suffered another defeat at the hands of Northern Districts for whom Parker's batting and Lance Cairns' bowling were dominant factors. Carl Dickel (40) and Bruce Blair (37) gave Otago early hope that they could achieve a win, but they slipped from 110 for 4 to 148 all out with 4.5 overs unused.

Canterbury received further embarrassment from Auckland who beat them with more than 20 overs to spare. Canterbury reached 118 for 4 thanks mainly to ex-Northants player Carter, but then Martin Snedden brought about a collapse as he took five of the last six wickets which fell, and Canterbury were all out in the forty-seventh over for 150.

Peter Webb made a storming start for Auckland which gave him the personal award and made victory a formality.

Wellington joined Auckland with two victories when a splendid innings from Bruce Edgar dominated the match and brought the visitors victory with more than five overs to spare. It was Edgar's second century in four games for Wellington before his departure with the New Zealand side.

Central Districts were 68 for 5, but Wiltshire and Steve Gill added 74 to make Wellington's task more difficult.

Shell Trophy

6, 7 and 8 January 1983

at Napier

Central Districts 363 (I.D.S. Smith 145, M.H. Toynbee 100, M.D. Crowe 5 for 69) and 179 for 3 dec (R.A. Pierce 94)
Auckland 259 (T.J. Franklin 107, J.F. Reid 67, D.R. O'Sullivan 5 for 82) and 275 (A.J. Hunt 61, M.D. Crowe 57, J.F. Reid 54, D.C. Aberhart 6 for 55)

Central Districts won by 8 runs
Central Districts 15 pts, Auckland 0 pts

at Hamilton

Canterbury 150 (S.M. Carrington 4 for 23, C.W. Dickeson 4 for 49) and 313 for 6 (V.R. Brown 118 not out)
Northern Districts 273 (C.M. Kuggeleijn 85, J.M. Parker 57)

Match drawn
Northern Districts 4 pts, Canterbury 0 pts

at Alexandra

Wellington 380 (R.H. Vance 112, E.J. Gray 69) and 70 for 3
Otago 160 (A.C.S. Pigott 5 for 47) and 286 (B.R. Blair 106, A.C.S. Pigott 5 for 93)

Wellington won by 7 wickets
Wellington 16 pts, Otago 0 pts

Wellington's win at Alexandra moved them to the top of the Shell Trophy table. They owed much to Bob Vance who hit a maiden century in first-class cricket and, with Evan Gray and skipper Ervin McSweeney, made possible a substantial first innings score by the defending champions.

Tony Pigott tore through the Otago batting and the home side were forced to follow-on. They looked certain to be beaten by an innings, but Bruce Blair, coming in at 92 for 4, lashed the ball to all parts of the field in typical fashion and Wellington had to bat again.

Wellington's first innings total was the highest recorded in a first-class match at Molyneux Park, Alexandra. The match also marked the reappearance in first-class cricket of Grant Cederwall and the first time that he and his brother Brian had appeared together in a first-class match. Richard Pither reappeared for Wellington after an absence of six years. He had previously played one first-class match.

The Man of the Match award went to Tony Pigott for his 10 for 140.

At Napier, Central Districts inflicted the first defeat of the season on Auckland and ousted them from second place. Nothing looked less likely than a Central victory when Ian Smith joined Matthew Toynbee at 88 for 5. Smith, who had lost his Test place because of his disappointing batting, and Toynbee both hit maiden centuries and shared a sixth wicket partnership of 220, a record sixth wicket partnership for Central Districts and the highest stand ever recorded at McLean Park.

Auckland battled back well with a second wicket stand of 145 between Reid and Franklin who hit a maiden first-class century and emphasised his rich promise as an opening batsman. Auckland saved the follow-on and then Roger Pierce led Central's bid for victory with a fine 94.

Set to make 284, Auckland made a great effort to sustain the pace needed to win the match and Reid, Martin Crowe (who had earlier taken a career best 5 for 69) and Alan Hunt all batted well. The visitors reached 269 for 6 and looked set to win, but Denis Aberhart's accurate medium pace proved decisive. The last four wickets fell to him as 6 runs were scored and Central Districts won a splendid game by 8 runs.

Canterbury remained pointless after their drawn game with Northern Districts who had looked to be moving to a decisive victory until Vaughan Brown's century.

The combination of Carrington's pace and Dickeson's left-arm spin had destroyed the first Canterbury innings, and Chris Kuggeleijn led Northern Districts to a big lead which would have been bigger but for Brown's late 3 for 31.

Shell Cup

9 January 1983

at Napier

Central Districts 111
Auckland 115 for 1 (A.E.W. Parsons 57 not out)

Auckland won by 9 wickets

at Alexandra

Otago 263 for 7 (B.R. Blair 76, R.N. Hoskin 58)
Wellington 110 (C. Dickel 4 for 28)

Otago won by 153 runs

at Hamilton

Northern Districts 248 for 8 (B.G. Cooper 93, A.D.G. Roberts 52, C.H. Thiele 4 for 47)
Canterbury 247 (P.J. Rattray 52)

Northern Districts won by 1 run

Auckland maintained their unbeaten record when they over-whelmed Central Districts at Napier to win with nearly twenty-one overs to spare. John Bracewell had 3 for 19 in his ten overs and took the Man of the Match award. Martin Crowe again showed his development as a medium pace bowler with the wickets of Pierce and Snook.

Wellington lost ground on Auckland when they were sur-prisingly completely outplayed by Otago. Bruce Blair gave another belligerent display with the bat which made many wonder why he was not with the New Zealand side in Australia. Carl Dickel had Wellington in a state of unease with his leg-breaks and he was well supported behind the stumps by Barry Milburn.

The outstanding match of the round was at Hamilton where Dayle Hadlee reappeared in the Canterbury side and, although not taking a wicket, bowled with commendable accuracy. It was Craig Thiele, however, who had Northern Districts struggling at 13 for 2, but Barry Cooper then played a magnificent innings which, with help from Roberts and Parker, lifted the home side to an impressive 248 from their fifty overs.

Dempsey and Rattray began Canterbury's reply with a stand of 68. Everybody contributed a little, but there were two mid-order stumbles which meant that Canterbury's last pair came together with 21 still needed for victory. A brave stand with much scampering from hits and leg-byes ended with Hart run out off the last ball of the innings and Canter-bury beaten by one run.

Shell Trophy

13, 14 and 15 January 1983

at Christchurch

Canterbury 255 (D.W. Stead 81) and 20 for 0
Wellington 104 (V.R. Brown 7 for 28) and 167 (V.R. Brown 4 for 28)

Canterbury won by 10 wickets
Canterbury 16 pts, Wellington 0 pts

at Gisborne

Auckland 365 for 6 dec (T.J. Franklin 136, J.F. Reid 68, J.G. Bracewell 54 not out) and 219 for 5 dec (M.D. Crowe 108)
Northern Districts 218 (J.M. Parker 91) and 241 for 7 (A.D.G. Roberts 79, C.M. Presland 60 not out)

Match drawn
Auckland 4 pts, Northern Districts 0 pts

Martin Crowe forces the ball away for Auckland against Northern Districts. Mike Wright is keeping wicket. Crowe's consistent form and aggression won him back his international place. He is New Zealand's most exciting prospect for the future. (Norman Smith)

at Dunedin

Otago 396 for 6 dec (B.R. Blair 143, G.J. Dawson 67, I.A. Rutherford 62)
Central Districts 244 (S.J. Gill 107) and 128 for 3 (P.S. Briasco 57)

Match drawn
Otago 4 pts, Central Districts 0 pts

Canterbury provided the sensation of the season when they scored their first points in either competition with an emphatic victory over reigning champions and Trophy leaders, Wellington.

A hard hit 81 from David Stead had helped Canterbury to a first innings of 255 against the steady seam attack of James, Maguiness and Carter, but Wellington were completely routed by the off-spin of Vaughan Brown and they lost their last nine wickets for 48 runs. Brown's 7 for 28 was a career best (he took only two wickets in 1981–82) and he followed it with 4 for 28 in the second innings to give him more than ten wickets in a match for the first time.

Wellington's defeat did not dislodge them from the top of the table for Central Districts failed to take any points at Dunedin where there was no play on the first day. Bruce Blair then launched one of his devastating attacks on the bowling, and, having scored at 4 an over, Otago declared at 396 for 6.

Central Districts were 131 for 7 before Steve Gill confirmed his great advance as a batsman with a splendid maiden century. It did not save the follow-on, but Central Districts were immune from defeat.

Making his debut for Otago was Kassem Ibadulla, son of 'Billy' Ibadulla.

A stalwart innings by John Parker, Northern Districts' acting captain, saved the follow-on after Trevor Franklin's second century in successive matches, a career best 136, had boosted Auckland to 365 for 6, a record for the Harry Barker reserve at Gisborne.

When Auckland batted again, Martin Crowe hit his second hundred of the season and Reid declared, leaving Northern Districts a mighty 367 to win. At 134 for 6, they looked well beaten, but Craig Presland, playing his first first-class match, joined veteran Andrew Roberts in a stand of 73 to save the match. Presland finished on 60 not out which, with his first innings 3 for 96, constituted a highly satisfactory debut.

Shell Cup

16 January 1983

at Gisborne

Northern Districts 306 for 2 (B.G. Cooper 97 not out, J.M. Parker 96 not out, M.J.E. Wright 50)
Auckland 309 for 8 (A.T.R. Hellaby 80, J.G. Bracewell 66)

Auckland won by 2 wickets

at Christchurch

Canterbury 245 for 7 (D.W. Stead 67 not out, R.M. Carter 54)
Wellington 219 (E.B. McSweeney 59)

Canterbury won by 26 runs

Trevor Franklin's consistent batting won him a place in the New Zealand team to tour England. This untypically awkward shot against Otago led to his downfall–caught Lees. (Mark Baker)

at Oamaru

Central Districts 253 (J.R. Wiltshire 80, J. Wilson 4 for 46)
Otago (W.L. Blair 58, D.A. Stirling 4 for 36)

Central Districts won by 15 runs

It was a round of remarkable records. Northern Districts became the first side to score 300 in a limited-over game in New Zealand, but their record lasted only for half a day as Auckland passed their score with four balls of their fifty overs remaining. Mike Wright set a record with five catches behind the wicket, and Craig Presland set an unenviable record when he took 2 for 93 in his 10 overs, the most expensive bowling in limited-over cricket in New Zealand.

Auckland's brilliant win was made possible by all-rounder John Bracewell's fierce 66 from his number one batting place and Tom Hellaby's forceful 80 when his side threatened to flag, but the victory was finally accomplished by McIntyre and Stott who scored the last 42 runs for the ninth wicket.

Auckland's win meant that they had qualified for the final, but the other finalist would not be known until after the last round of matches. David Stead with 67 and 1 for 16 in 10 overs inspired Canterbury's surprise win over Wellington, their second in three days, and Central Districts moved level with Wellington and Northern Districts when David Stirling blunted Otago's innings after Rutherford and Wayne Blair set them on course for a win with an opening stand of 104.

Wiltshire and Robertson had added 84 for Central's fifth wicket, and in the course of the innings Barry Milburn had emulated Mike Wright's feat with five catches behind the wicket.

Shell Trophy

20 and 21 January 1983

at Christchurch

Canterbury 99 (R.J. Webb 4 for 33) and 117 (C. Dickel 5 for 22)
Otago 256 (B.R. Blair 70, V.R. Brown 6 for 55)

Otago won by an innings and 40 runs
Otago 16 pts, Canterbury 0 pts

21, 22 and 23 January 1983

at Palmerston North

Central Districts 295 (I.D.S. Smith 111, P.S. Briasco 53) and 239 for 6 dec (P.S. Briasco 52, R.T. Hart 51)
Northern Districts 214 (B.G. Cooper 55, D.J. White 54 not out, G.K. Robertson 4 for 57) and 322 for 6 (R.D. Broughton 122, J.M. Parker 69)

Northern Districts won by 4 wickets
Northern Districts 12 pts, Central Districts 4 pts

at Wellington

Auckland 153 (J.G. Bracewell 60 not out, B.J. Maguiness 4 for 28) and 178
Wellington 390 (E.B. McSweeney 130, R.H. Vance 61, P.J. Holland 56)

Wellington won by an innings and 59 runs
Wellington 16 pts, Auckland 0 pts

Canterbury's successes came to an abrupt end when Otago beat them inside two days in Christchurch. The rejuvenated Richard Webb continued his impressive form when he, Brendon Bracewell and Abernethy shot out Canterbury for 99 in the first innings, and he bowled well in the second innings when Carl Dickel had his best return, his leg-breaks earning 5 for 22.

A solid start by Rutherford and Wayne Blair was consolidated by some powerful shots from Bruce Blair as Vaughan Brown threatened to take charge, and Otago's 256 was enough to force an innings victory, their first win of the season.

Wellington moved into a 16-point lead at the top of the table when they equalled their biggest ever win over northern rivals, Auckland, at the Basin Reserve. It was the Wellington seam attack which twice troubled Auckland and only two good innings from John Bracewell saved the visitors from a bigger defeat.

Vance and Holland shared a second wicket stand of 84 which put Wellington on top. The real impetus to the innings, however, came from Ervin McSweeney, the wicketkeeper whose batting strongly recommended him for a place in the New Zealand side. He hit a maiden century and took

Wellington to a first innings lead of 237 which proved far too big a deficit for Auckland to overcome.

The match at Palmerston North was one of the great games in Shell Trophy history.

Central Districts were 11 for 3, 148 for 7, before Ian Smith hit his second century of the season, scoring 111 out of 20 as the score mounted to 295 all out.

Northern Districts, in their turn, were struggling badly until middle order contributions from Cooper, Roberts and White meant that Northern trailed only by 81 on the first innings.

Central failed to press quickly enough for runs when they batted again, and their 239 for 6 declared was a somewhat grim affair against some tight spin bowling from Dickeson and Cooper. The feature of the Central second innings was three catches by substitute Chris Kuggeleijn.

Northern Districts were asked to make 321 to win at more than three an over. At 17 for 2 the task looked impossible. Roger Broughton, who had not found a place in the Northern side in 1981–82 when Howarth, John Wright and the rest were available, began cautiously, but soon he blossomed into playing some powerful drives and reached a maiden century, and the first century of the season by a Northern Districts batsman. Skipper Parker shared a stand of 139 with him, and good knocks by Roberts and White allowed the visitors to pull off a remarkable victory. Their 322 was the highest score that Northern Districts had ever made in the fourth innings.

Shell Cup

23 January 1983

at Christchurch

Otago 208 (A.J. Farrant 4 for 51)
Canterbury 210 for 8 (R.J. Webb 4 for 34)

Canterbury won by 2 wickets

24 January 1983

at Wellington

Wellington 232 for 6 (P.J. Holland 53, R.H. Vance 52)
Auckland 193 (J.F. Reid 55, S.J. Maguiness 4 for 26)

Wellington won by 39 runs

at Palmerston North

Northern Districts 226 for 8
Central Districts 176 (S.J. Scott 4 for 42)

Northern Districts won by 50 runs

Canterbury's win over Otago had no influence on the competition as both sides had already failed to qualify for the final.

Wellington inflicted the first Cup defeat on Auckland and so kept alive their own chances of meeting Auckland in the final. Their victory was founded on an opening stand of 106 between Bob Vance and Peter Holland and some brisk late hitting by Gray. The Auckland batting could never come to

Robert Vance in action for Wellington against Auckland. In spite of another fine season, Vance could not find a place in the New Zealand side.

terms with the Wellington seam attack and the home side always looked to be winners.

Wellington, however, did not qualify for the final. Northern Districts' victory over Central Districts gave them the same number of points as Wellington, and as they had a superior runs per wicket average over Wellington, they took second place.

Lindsey Crocker batted well for Northern, scoring 46 in an opening stand of 84 with Mike Wright and being top scorer in the match. Crocker took the individual award which was a little hard on Steve Scott who had destroyed the Central Districts' middle order with four wickets which had reduced them to 117 for 8.

One who could feel equally aggrieved was Wellington's wicket-keeper captain Ervin McSweeney. He took six catches in the Auckland innings so establishing a New Zealand record for limited-over cricket, beating the record that had been set up by Wright and Milburn in the previous round, but the Man of the Match award went to Vance. It pays to be a batsman wherever you are in the world.

Shell Cup – Final Positions

	P	W	L	Pts
Auckland	5	4	1	8
Northern Districts	5	3	2	6
Wellington	5	3	2	6
Central Districts	5	2	3	4
Canterbury	5	2	3	4
Otago	5	1	4	2

Auckland and Northern Districts qualified for the final.

Shell Trophy

28 and 29 January 1983

at Invercargill

Otago 282 (I.A. Rutherford 96, R.N. Hoskin 57, D.W. Stead 7 for 99)
Canterbury 106 (S.L. Boock 4 for 34) and 89 (K. Ibadulla 5 for 22, S.L. Boock 4 for 45)

Otago won by an innings and 97 runs
Otago 16 pts, Canterbury 0 pts

29, 30 and 31 January 1983

at Hamilton

Central Districts 392 (I.D.S. Smith 143, G.K. Robertson 96, P.S. Briasco 52, C.W. Dickeson 4 for 84) and 218 for 6 dec (R.T. Hart 54, D.J. White 4 for 89)
Northern Districts 292 (D.J. White 66, A.D.G. Roberts 65) and 202 for 9 (D.A. Stirling 4 for 23)

Match drawn
Central Districts 4 pts, Northern Districts 0 pts.

at Auckland

Wellington 238 and 269 for 5 dec (E.B. McSweeney 61 not out, E.J. Gray 53 not out)
Auckland 224 (M.D. Crowe 100, T.J. Franklin 50, A.C.S. Pigott 4 for 38, E.J. Gray 4 for 100) and 159 for 5

Match drawn
Wellington 4 pts, Auckland 0 pts

Although Wellington failed to force victory over Auckland, they maintained their comfortable lead at the top of the Shell Trophy table. Solid and even batting saw Wellington to 238, but two young Auckland men of great promise, Mark Greatbatch and Trevor Franklin, responded with an opening stand of 77. When Greatbatch was bowled by Gray, John Cushen, making a return to first-class cricket after an absence of two years, was sent in as night-watchman.

Cushen batted throughout the rest of the innings, scoring 30 not out, the highest score he had made in his 45 first-class matches, and surviving while 147 runs were added.

His fourth wicket stand with Martin Crowe realised 113, Crowe scored 100. Six wickets fell for 7 runs, and then Cushen and Tracy added 15 for the last wicket. Pigott took three wickets in four balls, but was denied the hat-trick which has never been performed at Eden Park.

In the match at Queen's Park, Invercargill, Otago won in two days. A second wicket stand of 97 for the second wicket between Rutherford and Hoskin was the foundation of an Otago innings which did not look big enough to win the match, but after Gully and Dempsey had put on 32 for Canterbury's first wicket, they lost their last nine wickets for 61, 44 of them from Paul McEwan. Stephen Boock, the forgotten man of New Zealand cricket, was the main destroyer, but Carl Dickel's leg-breaks brought him 3 for 0 in 4.2 overs, only the third time that such a feat has been achieved in New Zealand.

When they batted again Canterbury fared even worse, Bob Carter scoring 38 out of their total of 89. Boock again bowled well, but chief honours went to young Kassem Ibadulla who took five wickets in the innings in what was only his second first-class game. He had also scored 30 not out and could be very happy with his part in Otago's victory which put them second in the table.

Central Districts were 117 for 7 when Gary Robertson joined Ian Smith. They shared a record eighth wicket stand of 173, and with O'Sullivan contributing 33 at number ten, Central Districts reached 392.

Northern Districts batted solidly and there was a mid-innings boost from Roberts and White, who added 85 for the sixth wicket, but the home side still trailed by 100 on the first innings.

Central Districts set Northern 319 to make at three an over in their second innings, but the home side struggled from the start and only the defiance of Presland and Carrington at the end saved them from defeat.

Shell Trophy

2, 3 and 4 February 1983

at Auckland

Northern Districts 352 (M.J.E. Wright 115, J.M. Parker 71) and 219 for 5 dec (J.M. Parker 56 not out)
Auckland 287 for 7 dec (A.J. Hunt 68 not out) and 27 for 9 (M. Greatbatch 80)

Match drawn
Northern Districts 4 pts, Auckland 0 pts

at Nelson

Central Districts 417 for 6 dec (P.S. Briasco 95, R.A. Pierce 89, M.H. Toynbee 66 not out, R.T. Hart 53, J.F. Wiltshire 52) and 143 for 5 dec
Canterbury 199 (D.W. Stead 81, D.R. O'Sullivan 4 for 57) and 324 (P.J. Rattray 133, P.E. McEwan 50, S.J. Gi 4 for 28)

Central Districts won by 37 runs
Central Districts 16 pts, Canterbury 0 pts

4, 5 and 6 February 1983

at Lower Hutt

Otago 181 (B.R. Blair 90, G.J. Dawson 54, B.W. Cederwall 4 for 34) and 197 (R.N. Hoskin 77, A.C.S. Pigott 4 for 47)
Wellington 224 (J.B. Boyle 76, B.P. Bracewell 4 for 44) and 155 for 4

Wellington won by 6 wickets
Wellington 16 pts, Otago 0 pts

Wellington's victory over Otago assured them of at least sharing top place in the Shell Trophy table. The Man of the Match was Brian Cederwall whose right-arm medium pace brought match figures of 7 for 74.

Otago's first innings was entirely dependant upon Bruce Blair and Garth Dawson, the only batsmen to reach double figures, who added 124 for the fourth wicket after which Otago lost their last seven wickets for 37 runs.

Vance and Justin Boyle gave Wellington a good start, but Brendon Bracewell and Carl Dickel restricted the home side to a lead of 43. It proved decisive as Tony Pigott and Brian Cederwall again made batting uncomfortable, and Wellington moved easily to the 155 that they needed for victory.

Roger Pierce and Ronnie Hart had an opening partnership of 132 for Central Districts against Canterbury, a record for the province. Scott Briasco then hit a career best 95 and Central moved to a massive 417 for 6 declared.

O'Sullivan's slow left-arm spin and Robertson's pace condemned Canterbury to follow-on in spite of a brave knock from David Stead, but, somewhat surprisingly, Wiltshire decided not to enforce the follow-on and Central Districts accumulated quick runs.

Canterbury were asked to make 362 to win, a daunting task. Thanks to a magnificent maiden century by Peter Rattray, Canterbury looked as if they would achieve the impossible. They reached 322 for 5, and then lost their last five wickets for 2 runs. Steve Bateman was run out for 0, his fifth 'duck' in a row, and Ian Smith caught Rutledge off Gill for the last wicket, the New Zealand 'keeper's hundredth dismissal in first-class cricket.

There was a maiden hundred at the Eden Park number two ground where Mike Wright scored 115 and shared a Northern Districts record third wicket stand against Auckland of 131 with John Parker. Parker reached 4,000 runs for the province and, in the same match, Andy Roberts passed the 5,000 runs mark.

Set 285 to win, Auckland made a valiant attempt and were greatly indebted to young Mark Greatbatch who hit 80 in his second first-class match. Auckland needed to score at well over four runs an over, and they continued to press for runs even though wickets fell. When Sean Tracy joined John Reid, who had gone in at number ten, Auckland were still 19 short of victory with one wicket to fall, and neither side managed to clinch victory in a fine game.

SHELL CUP FINAL: AUCKLAND v. NORTHERN DISTRICTS

A fine innings by Roger Broughton gave Northern Districts an initial impetus which was carried on by John Parker and only faltered in the late mad scramble for runs when the nagging accuracy of Cushen and Stott proved a hindrance to any attempt to raise the tempo.

Trevor Franklin and Mark Greatbatch gave Auckland a sound start which ended when Greatbatch was run out. John Bracewell then joined Franklin in a stand of 81, and Franklin and the effervescent Martin Crowe took the score to 188 before both were out in successive overs.

The highlight of the Northern outcricket had been the brilliant fielding of Steve Scott and he was rewarded with a second wicket when he bowled Steve Adams, but by then Auckland were only 3 short of victory. Alan Hunt ended Northern dreams when he drove the first ball of the last over for 4.

Shell Trophy

11, 12 and 13 February 1983

at Christchurch

Northern Districts 175 (C.M. Presland 52, D.R. Hadlee 4 for 58) and 269 (M.J.E. Wright 73, V.R. Brown 4 for 50)
Canterbury 255 (D.W. Stead 51, C.M. Presland 4 for 47, S.J. Scott 4 for 66) and 190 for 7 (P.J. Rattray 63, A.D.G. Roberts 4 for 45)

Canterbury won by 3 wickets
Canterbury 16 pts, Northern Districts 0 pts

at Dunedin

Otago 234 for 7 dec (B.R. Blair 72, J.A.J. Cushen 4 for 67) and 211 for 5 dec (W.L. Blair 65, L.W. Stott 4 for 75)
Auckland 159 (M.D. Crowe 55, R.J. Webb 4 for 36) and 198 for 2 (T.J. Franklin 101 not out)

Match drawn
Otago 4 pts, Auckland 0 pts

SHELL CUP FINAL: AUCKLAND v. NORTHERN DISTRICTS
6 February 1983 at Eden Park, Auckland

NORTHERN DISTRICTS				
M.J.E. Wright*	b Cushen			3
R.D. Broughton	c Stott, b McIntyre			52
J.M. Parker†	c Hunt, b Stott			77
B.G. Cooper	st Kelly, b McIntyre			16
A.D.G. Roberts	b M.D. Crowe			4
D.J. White	c M.D. Crowe, b Cushen			38
C.W. Dickeson	c M.D. Crowe, b Cushen			2
S.J. Scott	b Cushen			8
C.M. Presland	c Greatbatch, b Stott			1
S.M. Carrington	run out			2
K. Treiber	not out			0
Extras	lb 7			7
(49.2 overs)				210

	O	M	R	W
Cushen	10	1	38	4
Stott	9.2	—	29	2
M.D. Crowe	7	1	42	1
J.G. Bracewell	3	—	19	—
McIntyre	10	2	29	2
Adams	10	—	46	—

FALL OF WICKETS
1- 4, 2- 81, 3- 123, 4- 139, 5- 195, 6- 196, 7- 206, 8- 208, 9- 210

AUCKLAND				
T.J. Franklin	lbw, b Scott			76
M. Greatbatch	run out			7
J.G. Bracewell	b Roberts			42
M.D. Crowe	b Roberts			54
A.J. Hunt	not out			14
S. Adams	b Stott			8
A.T.R. Hellaby	not out			0
P.J. Kelly*				
J.M. McIntyre†				
L.W. Stott				
J.A.J. Cushen				
Extras	b 3, lb 7, w 1			11
(49.1 overs)	(for 5 wickets)			212

	O	M	R	W
Carrington	5	—	20	—
Treiber	9.1	2	36	—
Presland	4	—	16	—
Scott	9	1	38	2
Dickeson	10	1	41	—
Roberts	10	—	30	2
Cooper	2	—	20	—

FALL OF WICKETS
1- 29, 2- 110, 3- 188, 5- 208

Auckland won by 5 wickets

at Wellington

Wellington 129 (G.K. Robertson 4 for 42) and 227 for 4 (J.B. Boyle 67, R.W. Ormiston 60 not out, R.H. Vance 52)

Central Districts 259 (R.T. Hart 52, S.J. Gill 51, G.N. Cederwall 4 for 47)

Match drawn
Central Districts 4 pts, Wellington 0 pts

With most of the last day lost to rain, the match at Basin Reserve was drawn and Wellington took the Shell Trophy for the second year running. They had laboured badly against Robertson and Stirling and finished 130 behind on the first innings when Hart made his fourth fifty in as many matches. Then Justin Boyle and Bob Vance put on 112 for Wellington's first wicket in the second innings, remarkably the first century opening partnership ever recorded in matches between these two teams.

Canterbury won an encouraging victory over Northern Districts in a match full of incident. It marked the return of Dayle Hadlee to first-class cricket and the reappearance of Glenn Bateman who replaced cousin Steve for Canterbury. The Bateman cousins have appeared in a total of 36 first-class matches, but never together in the same side.

Hadlee marked a fine return with 4 for 58 in the first innings and then scored a valuable 43, second top score, as Canterbury grasped a first innings lead. He had much to do with inspiring Canterbury's second win of the season.

The match at Carisbrook, Dunedin, saw Ken Rutherford, the seventeen-year old brother of Ian, and Steve Adams make their first-class debuts. Few players can have had an unhappier debut than Adams. Batting at number six, he had his jaw broken by a rising ball from Richard Webb.

There were two more good knocks from Bruce Blair, and one from brother Wayne, but Trevor Franklin played the innings of the match when Otago looked as if they might force a victory. He dominated the bowling in impressive style.

The match was remarkable for the fact that when it was known that Richard Webb would be required for the Benson and Hedges World Series finals as replacement for the injured Richard Hadlee, Bruce Abernethy took his place in the match and, although a substitute, was allowed to bat and bowl. In effect, his batting was not needed, but he did bowl 19.5 overs. The same thing had happened in both England and Australia when Small of Warwickshire and Maguire of Queensland were called to join their national sides.

Shell Trophy Final Table (1982 positions in brackets)

	P	W	L	D	1st Inns Lead	Pts
Wellington (1)	8	4	1	3	6	71
Central Districts (6)	8	3	2	3	6	59
Otago (5)	8	2	4	2	5	44
Northern Districts (2)	8	2	1	5	3	35
Canterbury (4)	8	2	5	1	2	31
Auckland (3)	8	2	2	4	2	31

(all sides except Otago had one point deducted for slow over-rate)

OPPOSITE *Derek Randall gets in a tangle in the first one-day international at Eden Park, Auckland. Warren Lees who had a fine year behind the stumps looks on.* (*Mark Baker*)

FIRST ONE-DAY INTERNATIONAL: NEW ZEALAND v. ENGLAND

England had not played a match for nearly three weeks when they arrived in New Zealand for a three-match one-day series against the host country who had returned proud, if a little battered, from their performances in Australia.

New Zealand were greatly handicapped by the absence of both Richard Hadlee and John Wright through injury, but such is their team-spirit that the loss of two of their most important players did not seem to trouble them in the slightest.

England laboured on a slow wicket. It wrecked Botham's timing and though he hit Cairns for one six, he was never himself, and he perished when he attempted a shot that the pace of the pitch did not allow. Gower, on the other hand, once more adapted quickly to the conditions. He did not bat as well as he had done in Australia, but it was the merit of his maturity that he was able to acquire 84 runs through application and a little luck while others floundered.

The most important stand of the England innings was between Gower and Randall for the fourth wicket which produced 64 runs in 15 overs. Randall was bowled as he tried to give himself room to cut, and then, as if by habit, England went from 104 for 3 to 115 for 7. Marks saved them from total disgrace by staying with Gower while 53 were added.

Gower got a top edge as he attempted to pull Snedden and he was caught at square-leg. Had New Zealand accepted chances that he had given when 22 and 39, England would have not sighted the 184 that they finally achieved from their 50 overs.

Turner announced immediately that New Zealand were in search of victory. It was his first appearance in international cricket in New Zealand for six years and he celebrated by hitting the last three balls of Willis' opening over to the boundary. 50 came up in 11 overs. 100 was on the board in 22 overs.

Edgar went to a tumbling catch by Jackman, who had announced that he was to retire from cricket at the end of the tour, and Cairns came in at number three as a gesture to the capacity crowd of 41,000 and hit a couple of sixes.

Turner's 50 had come off 54 balls, but he needed 75 balls for his last 38. Nevertheless, although Turner and Crowe were out within two runs of each other, there was never any doubt as to who would win, and victory was achieved with 21 balls left.

19, 20 and 21 February 1983

at Christchurch

Sri Lankans 167 (C.H. Thiele 6 for 45) and 214 (R.S. Madugalle 81, G.C. Bateman 6 for 66)
Canterbury 344 for 8 dec (D.R. Hadlee 109 not out, R.I. Leggat 83, P.J. Rattray 62, R.J. Ratnayake 4 for 101) and 38 for 2

Canterbury won by 8 wickets

FIRST ONE-DAY INTERNATIONAL: NEW ZEALAND v. ENGLAND
19 February 1983 at Auckland

ENGLAND							NEW ZEALAND						
C.J. Tavare	b Cairns				11		G.M. Turner	c sub (Cowans), b Willis					88
I.T. Botham	c Morrison, b Chatfield				12		B.A. Edgar	c Jackman, b Miller					35
D.I. Gower	c Morrison, b Snedden				84		B.L. Cairns	c Lamb, b Botham					19
A.J. Lamb	run out				0		J.J. Crowe	lbw, b Botham					15
D.W. Randall	b Chatfield				30		J.V. Coney	not out					9
T.E. Jesty	c Coney, b Chatfield				1		G.P. Howarth†	not out					14
I.J. Gould*	lbw, b Cairns				3		J.F.M. Morrison						
G. Miller	lbw, b Morrison				3		W.K. Lees*						
V.J. Marks	not out				23		M.C. Snedden						
R.D. Jackman	b Cairns				4		E.J. Chatfield						
R.G.D. Willis†	not out				1		R.J. Webb						
Extras	lb 10, w 2				12		Extras	b 1, lb 4, nb 2					7
(50 overs)	(for 9 wickets)				184		(46.3 overs)	(for 4 wickets)					187

	O	M	R	W			O	M	R	W
Webb	10	—	30	—		Willis	10	1	39	1
Cairns	10	2	28	3		Jackman	8.3	—	38	—
Snedden	8	1	35	1		Botham	8	—	40	2
Chatfield	10	—	27	3		Marks	10	1	30	—
Coney	2	—	17	—		Miller	10	—	33	1
Morrison	10	1	35	1						

FALL OF WICKETS
1- 17, 2- 40, 3- 40, 4- 104, 5- 106, 6- 110, 7- 115,
8- 168, 9- 176

FALL OF WICKETS
1- 101, 2- 129, 3- 164, 4- 166

New Zealand won by 6 wickets

The beginning of Sri Lanka's tour of New Zealand was lost in the excitement of the victory over England, and it is difficult to imagine a more unhappy start to the tour. On the opening day they lost skipper Duleep Mendis when he was hit on the hand by the first ball he received and was forced to retire with a broken finger. The splendid bowling of Craig Thiele saw Sri Lanka dismissed for 177, but with Canterbury at 128 for 6, it seemed as though the visitors might snatch a first innings lead.

Sri Lanka had to wait another three hours for their next wicket, however, as Dayle Hadlee and skipper Richard Leggat added 186. Hadlee, thirty-five years old, in his second come-back match, scored the first century of his career. It was his 105th first-class match, a mighty achievement.

73 for 4 at the close of the second day, the Sri Lankans faced an innings defeat, but some fine batting by Ranjan Madugalle withstood the pace and movement of Glenn Bateman, who, like Thiele, had a career best six wickets.

Rumesh Ratnayake had a fierce four overs at the beginning of Canterbury's second innings, but the issue was never in doubt.

23 February 1983

at New Plymouth

Minor Associations 184 for 9 (J.M. Parker 81)
Sri Lankans 187 for 5 (R.S. Madugalle 64 not out)

Sri Lankans won by 5 wickets

Sri Lankans won their first match of the tour with two and a half of their fifty overs remaining. Fernando and Sidath Wettimuny put on 68 for the first wicket after which Madugalle again showed his class. The match was marred by

the accident to young all-rounder Craig Presland who broke his ankle in trying to take a catch on the boundary.

24 February 1983

at Wanganui

Sri Lankans 216 (R.L. Dias 50)
Minor Associations 220 for 5 (J.M. Parker 91 not out, S.J. Gill 64)

Minor Associations won by 5 wickets

Winning with exactly an over to spare, Minor Associations gained their revenge and owed much to John Parker, named Man of the Match for the second time, who shared a stand of 88 with Gill.

SECOND ONE-DAY INTERNATIONAL: NEW ZEALAND v. ENGLAND

Trevor Jesty had been taken ill during the first match and was confined to bed. Pringle replaced him. Wright returned to the New Zealand side and batted at number four in place of Crowe.

The game was virtually decided in the first session. Turner, who hit at everything, and Edgar put on 152 in 29 overs for the first wicket before Edgar was run out by Randall.

Cairns came next and he clubbed 44 off 31 deliveries in the style which is cherishably his own.

Willis bowled Turner, 94 off 94 balls, and Cairns in successive overs, but at 214 for 3, New Zealand had no care. Jackman and Willis apart, England bowled dreadfully and fielded indifferently.

Tavare batted firmly, but there was not the big start that was necessary if victory was to become remotely possible for

---

SECOND ONE-DAY INTERNATIONAL: NEW ZEALAND v. ENGLAND
23 February 1983 at Wellington

NEW ZEALAND					ENGLAND			
G.M. Turner	b Willis		94		C.J. Tavare	c Howarth, b Chatfield		32
B.A. Edgar	run out		60		I.T. Botham	c Lees, b Cairns		15
B.L. Cairns	b Willis		44		D.I. Gower	c and b Chatfield		2
J.G. Wright	b Miller		30		A.J. Lamb	b Coney		7
J.V. Coney	not out		31		D.W. Randall	c Howarth, b Morrison		16
G.P. Howarth†	c Botham, b Jackman		10		I.J. Gould*	c Wright, b Coney		14
J.F.M. Morrison	b Botham		8		G. Miller	b Cairns		46
W.K. Lees*	not out		3		V.J. Marks	c Snedden, b Webb		27
M.C. Snedden					D.R. Pringle	b Webb		11
E.J. Chatfield					R.D. Jackman	b Cairns		9
R.J. Webb					R.G.D. Willis†	not out		2
Extras	lb 9, w 4, nb 2		15		Extras	lb 6, w 5		11
(50 overs)	(for 6 wickets)		295		(44.5 overs)			192

	O	M	R	W		O	M	R	W
Willis	9	—	54	2	Snedden	10	1	37	—
Jackman	10	2	38	1	Cairns	10	—	38	3
Pringle	7	—	57	—	Webb	7.5	—	27	2
Miller	10	—	51	1	Chatfield	7	1	28	2
Marks	7	—	34	—	Coney	5	—	17	2
Botham	7	—	46	1	Morrison	5	—	34	1

FALL OF WICKETS
1- 152, 2- 192, 3- 214, 4- 250, 5- 275, 6- 287

FALL OF WICKETS
1- 20, 2- 37, 3- 52, 4- 60, 5- 83, 6- 106, 7- 162, 8- 170, 9- 182

New Zealand won by 103 runs

England, and when Gower was caught and bowled by the diving Chatfield when he played too soon and got a leading edge, the massive crowd could sit back and enjoy their heroes' triumph.

THIRD ONE-DAY INTERNATIONAL: NEW ZEALAND v. ENGLAND

England's sad tour of Australasia came to a miserable end when they were beaten by New Zealand for the third time in a week.

Cowans replaced Pringle in the England side. Jeff Crowe returned to the New Zealand side in place of Webb. Hadlee was fit, but he could not find a place as it was felt that he should be rested in view of the Tests against Sri Lanka.

New Zealand won first use of the pitch and Turner and Edgar opened in front of a crowd of 31,000. The England disaster started when Gould missed a straightforward chance offered by Edgar in the third over when the batsman had scored 2. One could have little sympathy for an England management who chose to leave out a wicket-keeper of Taylor's calibre in favour of a stopper who might scramble a few runs. Edgar and Turner added 64.

Gould made some recompense by stumping Wright, but Cairns then made his customary assault, hitting Miller for four and for two sixes out of the ground in the same over. Cairns fell to Jackman, and Miller and Marks then bowled intelligently to reduce New Zealand to 156 for 8. At this point Snedden, who was to be voted Man of the Match, joined Morrison in a stand of 55 in the last eight overs which, as well as lifting the New Zealand score to respectable heights, cast gloom and frustration on England.

Gloom continued when Gould made a terrible hash of trying to hook Snedden's second ball and the ball lobbed off his glove to Turner at slip. In his next over Snedden pushed

Ewen Chatfield. The most dependable of New Zealand's bowlers. (Norman Smith)

THIRD ONE-DAY INTERNATIONAL: NEW ZEALAND v. ENGLAND
26 February 1983 at Christchurch

NEW ZEALAND					
G.M. Turner	lbw, b Botham				34
B.A. Edgar	b Marks				32
J.G. Wright	st Gould, b Marks				2
B.L. Cairns	c Marks, b Jackman				21
J.J. Crowe	lbw, b Jackman				18
J.V. Coney	run out				30
G.P. Howarth†	lbw, b Miller				8
J.F.M. Morrison	not out				24
W.K. Lees*	c Botham, b Cowans				2
M.C. Snedden	not out				31
E.J. Chatfield					
Extras	lb 5, w 3, nb 1				9
(50 overs)	(for 8 wickets)				211

	O	M	R	W
Cowans	10	3	55	1
Willis	10	1	35	—
Botham	5	1	17	1
Marks	10	2	31	2
Miller	7	1	32	1
Jackman	8	1	32	2

FALL OF WICKETS
1- 64, 2- 70, 3- 93, 4- 103, 5- 126, 6- 152, 7- 153, 8- 156

ENGLAND					
I.J. Gould*	c Turner, b Snedden				0
C.J. Tavare	b Snedden				4
D.I. Gower	c Wright, b Chatfield				53
A.J. Lamb	c Chatfield, b Morrison				37
I.T. Botham	c and b Morrison				3
D.W. Randall	b Coney				2
G. Miller	c and b Chatfield				7
V.J. Marks	b Cairns				1
R.D. Jackman	b Cairns				5
R.G.D. Willis†	c Coney, b Morrison				6
N.G. Cowans	not out				1
Extras	lb 6, w 1, nb 1				8
(40.1 overs)					127

	O	M	R	W
Snedden	7	3	14	2
Cairns	7	—	13	2
Chatfield	8	2	26	2
Coney	10	—	42	1
Morrison	8.1	—	24	3

FALL OF WICKETS
1- 0, 2- 8, 3- 94, 4- 103, 5- 105, 6- 114, 7- 114, 8 -116, 9- 125

New Zealand won by 84 runs

a good ball through Tavare's defence and England were 8 for 2.

Gower, inevitably, and Lamb batted well and there seemed a chance that they would restore England's pride, but the intrusion of four drunks onto the pitch did not help concentration and Lamb was caught at mid-on.

A further interruption caused Gower to become very angry, Botham to pacify him and Howarth to announce that he would lead his team from the field if the game were disturbed again. Howarth has god-like standing in New Zealand at present and his words were obeyed.

Botham, who had not been fully fit for some weeks, was caught and bowled after taking 24 balls to make 3. Gower was caught on the square-leg boundary and the side collapsed. From 103 for 3, they went to 127 all out. New Zealand had won the series 3–0, and England wondered how they would ever put the pieces together again.

26, 27 and 28 February 1983

at Auckland

Auckland 198 (A.T.R. Hellaby 62, R.J. Ratnayake 5 for 50) and 186 for 5 (M.D. Crowe 70 not out)
Sri Lankans 328 (S.R. de S. Wettimuny 105, R.S. Madugalle 64, J.G. Bracewell 4 for 56)

Match drawn

Only a partnership of 82 between Parsons and Hellaby saved Auckland on the opening day when Rumesh Ratnayake, at nineteen the youngest member of the Sri Lankan party, took five wickets in an innings in a first-class match for the first time.

The Sri Lankans took a first innings lead of 130 thanks to a fine hundred by Sidath Wettimuny who hit thirteen four in an innings lasting 264 minutes. Madugalle also batte well.

Martin Crowe defied Sri Lanka at the second attempt s denying them victory and enhancing his own chances of recall to the national side.

FIRST ONE-DAY INTERNATIONAL: NEW ZEALAND v. SRI LANKA

On a wicket which Geoff Howarth later criticised as bein unfit for a one-day international, New Zealand struggled t 183 for 8, the hitting of Lance Cairns being decisive in th closing stages. Young Rumesh Ratnayake was again th most impressive of the Sri Lankan bowlers.

Hadlee demonstrated his return to fitness with an openin burst which demoralised the Sri Lankans who helped t bring about their own downfall with some bizarre runnin between the wickets.

FIRST TEST MATCH: NEW ZEALAND v. SRI LANKA

Play was delayed until after lunch on the first day and ende twenty minutes early because of bad light, but New Zealan did little to lighten the gloom as they struggled against a sean attack which exploited the conditions well and had the hom side in trouble at 171 for 7. Lees joined Coney and by th close 40 had been added.

Sri Lanka were never again to reach the heights that the had attained after they had put New Zealand in on that firs day. They had arrived at the Test with only twelve fit player two of whom were the wicket-keepers in the party, and no the tide turned against them completely as Lees and Cone took the score to 250 before Coney was run out by a direc

FIRST ONE-DAY INTERNATIONAL: NEW ZEALAND v. SRI LANKA
2 March 1983 at Dunedin

NEW ZEALAND			
G.M. Turner	b John	18
B.A. Edgar	c de Alwis, b de Mel	3
J.G. Wright	b R.J. Ratnayake	45
J.J. Crowe	lbw, b J.R. Ratnayake	5
J.V. Coney	b R.J. Ratnayake	15
G.P. Howarth†	b R.J. Ratnayake	11
B.L. Cairns	b John	37
R.J. Hadlee	b John	11
M.C. Snedden	not out	13
W.K. Lees*	not out	7
E.J. Chatfield		
Extras	lb 10, w 4, nb 4	18
(50 overs)	(for 8 wickets)	183

	O	M	R	W
de Mel	9.3	2	36	1
John	10	4	28	3
R.J. Ratnayake	10	—	30	3
J.R. Ratnayake	10	—	45	1
D.S. de Silva	10	1	20	—
S.R. de S. Wettimuny	0.3	—	6	—

SRI LANKA			
S.R. de S. Wettimuny	run out	15
E.R.N.S. Fernando	c Turner, b Hadlee	0
M. de S. Wettimuny	b Hadlee	2
Y. Goonasekera	run out	23
R.S. Madugalle	run out	3
D.S. de Silva†	b Chatfield	18
A.L.F. de Mel	lbw, b Hadlee	1
J.R. Ratnayake	c Snedden, b Coney	14
R.G. de Alwis*	not out	13
R.J. Ratnayake	c Coney, b Howarth	15
Extras	b 2, lb 10, w 2	14
(50 overs)	(for 9 wickets)	118

	O	M	R	W
Hadlee	8	3	9	3
Cairns	10	6	10	1
Snedden	9	1	25	—
Chatfield	10	4	8	1
Coney	10	1	42	1
Howarth	2	—	10	1
Wright	1	1	0	—

FALL OF WICKETS
1- 26, 2- 26, 3- 50, 4- 99, 5- 113, 6- 124, 7- 150, 8- 165

FALL OF WICKETS
1- 1, 2- 7, 3- 39, 4- 46, 5- 62, 6- 65, 7- 85, 8- 85, 9- 118

New Zealand won by 65 runs

Somachandra de Silva bowling his tantalising leg-breaks. He is watched by umpire Fred Goodall and batsman Warren Lees. De Silva's brave leadership when Mendis was injured could not save Sri Lanka from five defeats at the hands of New Zealand. RIGHT Sridath Wettimuny, the soundest of the Sri Lankan batsmen. He alone showed the ability to cope with the New Zealand seam attack. (Norman Smith)

had been added, and all that remained to be seen was whether Lees, whose batting weighed against him with the selectors, could reach a maiden Test hundred, but he was bowled by de Silva for 89.

The Wettimuny brothers began well with a pleasant stand, but Mithra Wettimuny was caught behind off Cairns who also bowled Fernando, the first ball he had faced in Test cricket. The New Zealand pace attack used the conditions to full advantage, and at the close, Sri Lanka were hanging on at 141 for 8, still four runs short of saving the follow-on.

The follow-on was not saved in spite of Sidath Wettimuny's valiant innings as he joined that select group who have carried their bats through the innings of a Test match.

With the ball now swinging grotesquely, Sri Lanka had little hope of saving the match and though Hadlee failed to take a wicket, New Zealand won the match inside three days, their quickest ever victory in a Test match.

FIRST TEST MATCH: NEW ZEALAND v. SRI LANKA
4, 5 and 6 March 1983 at Lancaster Park, Christchurch

NEW ZEALAND

FIRST INNINGS

G.M. Turner	c de Alwis, b John	32
B.A. Edgar	c M. Wettimuny, b J.R. Ratnayeke	39
J.G. Wright	b R.J. Ratnayeke	13
G.P. Howarth†	c Gunasekera, b J.R. Ratnayeke	0
J.J. Crowe	run out	12
J.V. Coney	run out	84
R.J. Hadlee	b John	12
B.L. Cairns	c M. Wettimuny, b R.J. Ratnayeke	3
W.K. Lees*	b D.S. de Silva	89
M.C. Snedden	c sub (S.A.R. Silva), b J.R. Ratnayeke	22
E.J. Chatfield	not out	10
Extras	lb 14, w 2, nb 12	28
		344

	O	M	R	W
R.J. Ratnayeke	31	8	125	2
John	12	2	45	2
J.R. Ratnayeke	31	9	93	3
D.S. de Silva	22.5	10	41	1
Jeganathan	5	2	12	—

FALL OF WICKETS
1- 59, 2- 93, 3- 93, 4- 93, 5- 137, 6- 139, 7- 171, 8- 250, 9- 292

Umpires: F.R. Goodall and D.R. Kinsella

SRI LANKA

	FIRST INNINGS		**SECOND INNINGS**	
S.R. de S. Wettimuny	not out	63	(2) lbw, b Cairns	
M. de S. Wettimuny	c Lees, b Cairns	17	(1) c Leeds, b Snedden	
E.R.N.S. Fernando	b Cairns	0	b Cairns	4
Y. Goonasekera	c Lees, b Cairns	4	c Turner, b Cairns	
R.S. Madugalle	run out	34	c Lees, b Snedden	2
D.S. de Silva†	c Lees, b Hadlee	7	b Chatfield	5
J.R. Ratnayeke	run out	0	lbw, b Cairns	
R.G. de Alwis*	c Turner, b Hadlee	0	c Hadlee, b Snedden	
S. Jeganathan	lbw, b Cairns	6	b Chatfield	
R.J. Ratnayeke	c Coney, b Hadlee	1	c Howarth, b Chatfield	
V. John	lbw, b Hadlee	0	not out	
Extras	b 2, lb 7, nb 3	12	b 1, lb 6, w 5, nb 1	1
		144		**17**

	O	M	R	W	O	M	R	W
Hadlee	13.3	3	33	4	22	12	27	—
Snedden	10	1	30	—	23	6	48	3
Cairns	15	6	49	4	20	7	47	4
Chatfield	15	4	20	—	16.5	3	40	3

FALL OF WICKETS
1- 49, 2- 49, 3- 55, 4- 104, 5- 121, 6- 129, 7- 133, 8- 141, 9- 144
1- 14, 2- 26, 3- 46, 4- 95, 5- 108, 6- 124, 7- 133, 8- 168, 9- 170

New Zealand won by an innings and 25 runs

SECOND TEST MATCH: NEW ZEALAND v. SRI LANKA

New Zealand fielded an unchanged side. Sri Lanka changed wicket-keepers which meant that each of their twelve fit men had played in a Test. Only one hour's play was possible on the first day when Howarth won the toss and Sri Lanka batted, menaced by the New Zealand seam attack and a ring of close fielders. Both the Wettimuny brothers had been taken in the slips before the close when the score was 34.

Fernando was out to the first ball of the second day and when Goonasekera was out at 48 a collapse seemed to have begun, but with great patience Madugalle and de Silva restored their side's fortunes. They reached a century partnership in 137 minutes and both reached hard earned fifties. The stand had increased to 130 in 204 minutes when Madugalle was slow to start for a run and Edgar's sharp throw beat him. Apart from Ravi Ratnayeke the tail offered little once de Silva had fallen to Chatfield, and Sri Lanka were out for 240, leaving New Zealand twenty minutes batting before the close.

Gleefully, the Sri Lankans captured the wicket of Turner, caught off an extravagant hook, and Bruce Edgar went early next morning. Then John Wright had his nose broken from a flier by Rumesh Ratnayeke, an incident which upset the young bowler as much as it did the batsman.

John Wright, a mature player of world class. (Adrian Murrell)

Howarth and Crowe saw New Zealand haltingly into the afternoon when Vinothan John became the second Sri Lankan to take five wickets in a Test innings. Some good catching in the gully by Goonasekera off John's intelligent bowling, and some loose cutting were New Zealand's downfall. At tea they were 145 for 7.

Wright came in at the fall of the eighth wicket, reached his thousand runs in Test cricket and was out. Sri Lanka made their crucial lapse when they dropped Cairns on 0, and again on 18. He smashed the ball about in typical fashion, scored 45, and New Zealand, trailing by only 39, were back in the game.

By the close Hadlee and Snedden had swung the match totally in New Zealand's favour, dismissing both openers and night-watchman Silva with only 13 scored. Sri Lanka limped to 26 by the close.

A delayed start and interruptions destroyed the flow at the start of the fourth day, but Goonasekera and Fernando dragged the score to 57 before Goonasekera was caught behind off Chatfield's first delivery. This heralded a collapse. The bowlers swung the ball, the batsmen played and touched and Lees gathered the catches. 57 for 3. 93 all out. New Zealand needed 133 to win and had four sessions in which to get the runs.

They were 62 for the loss of Turner at the end of the fourth day. Although they lost Howarth, Crowe and Coney the next morning, the runs came briskly and Hadlee finished the

National hero. Lance Cairns waves 'Excalibur' and another ball is deposited in the crowd. (Mark Baker)

SECOND TEST MATCH: NEW ZEALAND v. SRI LANKA
11, 12, 13, 14 and 15 March 1983 at Basin Reserve, Wellington

SRI LANKA

	FIRST INNINGS		SECOND INNINGS	
S.R. de S. Wettimuny	c Cairns, b Hadlee	8	c Coney, b Hadlee	9
M. de S. Wettimuny	c Coney, b Snedden	6	c Cairns, b Snedden	0
E.R.N.S. Fernando	c Wright, b Hadlee	12	c Lees, b Snedden	12
Y. Goonasekera	c Lees, b Cairns	13	(5) c Lees, b Chatfield	23
R.S. Madugalle	run out	79	(6) c Lees, b Hadlee	13
D.S. de Silva†	lbw, b Chatfield	61	(7) c Lees, b Snedden	0
S.A.R. Silva*	c Lees, b Chatfield	8	(4) c J. Crowe, b Hadlee	0
J.R. Ratnayeke	not out	29	(10) c sub (M. Crowe), b Chatfield	1
S. Jeganathan	c Lees, b Chatfield	5	c Lees, b Chatfield	0
R.J. Ratnayeke	b Snedden	12	(8) b Hadlee	12
V. John	c Wright, b Chatfield	0	not out	8
Extras	b 1, lb 5, nb 1	7	b 5, lb 10	15
		240		93

	O	M	R	W	O	M	R	W
Hadlee	25	9	47	2	17	5	34	4
Snedden	24	5	56	2	17	7	21	3
Chatfield	26.5	7	66	4	12	5	15	3
Cairns	20	5	53	1	7	2	8	—
Coney	5	2	11	—				

FALL OF WICKETS
1- 14, 2- 14, 3- 34, 4- 48, 5- 178, 6- 191, 7- 194, 8- 220, 9- 239
1- 0, 2- 12, 3- 13, 4- 57, 5- 61, 6- 61, 7- 78, 8- 81, 9- 83

NEW ZEALAND

	FIRST INNINGS		SECOND INNINGS	
G.M. Turner	c Goonasekera, b John	10	b J.R. Ratnayeke	29
B.A. Edgar	c John, b R.J. Ratnayeke	10	not out	47
J.G. Wright	c de Silva, b R.J. Ratnayeke	14		
G.P. Howarth†	c S. Wettimuny, b de Silva	36	(3) c Silva, b John	1
J.J. Crowe	c Silva, b R.J. Ratnayeke	36	(4) b R.J. Ratnayeke	11
J.V. Coney	c Goonasekera, b John	2	(5) c Goonasekera, b de Silva	17
R.J. Hadlee	c Goonasekera, b John	30	(6) not out	17
W.K. Lees*	c Goonasekera, b John	0		
B.L. Cairns	c de Silva, b John	45		
M.C. Snedden	lbw, b R.J. Ratnayeke	5		
E.J. Chatfield	not out	2		
Extras	b 4, lb 3, w 3, nb 1	11	lb 11, nb 1	12
		201	(for 4 wkts)	134

	O	M	R	W	O	M	R	W
R.J. Ratnayeke	24	5	81	4	15	—	46	1
John	25.2	9	60	5	8	2	38	1
J.R. Ratnayeke	14	3	36	—	8.1	4	20	1
D.S. de Silva	9	5	13	1	6	1	18	1

FALL OF WICKETS
1- 12, 2- 33, 3- 104, 4- 107, 5- 141, 6- 141, 7- 145, 8- 163, 9- 169
1- 59, 2- 62, 3- 81, 4- 116

Umpires: S.J. Woodward and I.C. Higginson

New Zealand won by 6 wickets

match by hitting Ravi Ratnayeke for a straight, high six.

Shortly after the second Test match with Sri Lanka, the New Zealand team, under the inspiration of captain Geoff Howarth, flew to Australia to play a one-day international in Sydney, the receipts to go to the relief fund for the victims of the gigantic bushfire.

Whether this will count as an 'official' or 'first-class' one-day international is not certain, but the scores were as follows.

17 March 1983

at Sydney, Australia

New Zealand 138 for 8 (M.D. Crowe 66)
Australia 124 (E.. Chatfield 4 for 20)

New Zealand won by 14 runs
The match was reduced to 35 overs. Trevor Franklin, replacing Glenn Turner, made his debut in international cricket, and Whitney played his first one-day international for Australia. A stand of 93 between Coney and Martin Crowe was the highlight of the match.

SECOND ONE-DAY INTERNATIONAL: NEW ZEALAND *v.* SRI LANKA

The Sri Lankans tour of New Zealand closed with two one-day internationals. At Napier, the consistency of the New Zealand pace attack was again too much for Sri Lanka who slumped to 105 for 7. They were rescued by de Silva and Ravi Ratnayeke who added 56, but this only gave a mark of respectability. Turner and Wright launched a brisk assault on the bowling and the brothers Crowe, together in the New Zealand team for the first time, finished the match with a sparkling stand of 87.

The triumphant return. Glenn Turner clips a boundary during his brilliant innings of 140 in the third one-day international against Sri Lanka. (Mark Baker)

SECOND ONE-DAY INTERNATIONAL: NEW ZEALAND *v.* SRI LANKA
19 March 1983 at Napier

SRI LANKA					
S.R. de S. Wettimuny	b M.D. Crowe				20
E.R.N.S. Fernando	run out				0
E.G. de Alwis*	b Cairns				12
Y. Goonasekera	c Turner, b M.D. Crowe				11
L.R.D. Mendis†	c Hadlee, b Chatfield				11
R.S. Madugalle	b Cairns				7
D.S. de Silva	not out				37
A.L.F. de Mel	c Coney, b Chatfield				19
J.R. Ratnayeke	c M.D. Crowe, b Snedden				27
R.J. Ratnayeke	not out				1
V. John					
Extras	b 10, lb 11, nb 1				22
	(50 overs)	(for 8 wickets)			167

	O	M	R	W
Hadlee	10	3	22	—
Snedden	10	2	25	1
Cairns	10	2	25	2
Chatfield	10	—	43	2
M.D. Crowe	10	—	30	2

FALL OF WICKETS
1- 5, 2- 25, 3- 51, 4- 51, 5- 63, 6- 76, 7- 105, 8- 161

NEW ZEALAND		
G.M. Turner	c R.J. Ratnayeke, b John	2?
B.A. Edgar	c Madugalle, b J.R. Ratnayeke	?
J.G. Wright†	hit wkt., b de Silva	3?
J.J. Crowe	not out	4?
M.D. Crowe	not out	4?
J.V. Coney		
R.J. Hadlee		
B.L. Cairns		
W.K. Lees*		
M.C. Snedden		
E.J. Chatfield		
Extras	b 1, lb 4, w 3, nb 7	1?
	(36.4 overs) (for 3 wickets)	168

	O	M	R	W
de Mel	4	—	27	—
John	10	3	31	1
R.J. Ratnayeke	6.4	—	17	—
J.R. Ratnayeke	7	—	39	1
de Silva	6	1	28	1
Goonasekera	3	—	11	—

FALL OF WICKETS
1- 32, 2- 56, 3- 81

New Zealand won by 7 wickets

THIRD ONE-DAY INTERNATIONAL: NEW ZEALAND v. SRI LANKA
20 March 1983 at Auckland

NEW ZEALAND		
G.M. Turner	c J.R. Ratnayeke, b R.J. Ratnayeke	140
B.A. Edgar	c de Mel, b Goonasekera	52
B.L. Cairns	b R.J. Ratnayeke	18
J.G. Wright	b S. Wettimuny	45
R.J. Hadlee	c J.R. Ratnayeke, b de Mel	9
J.J. Crowe	not out	17
M.D. Crowe	not out	7
G.P. Howarth†		
W.K. Lees*		
M.C. Snedden		
E.J. Chatfield		
Extras	b 3, lb 10, w 3	16
(50 overs)	(for 5 wickets)	304

	O	M	R	W
de Mel	10	1	65	1
R.J. Ratnayeke	10	—	50	2
J.R. Ratnayeke	5	—	41	—
D.S. de Silva	10	—	46	—
Jeganathan	10	—	49	—
Goonasekera	3	—	24	1
S.R. de S. Wettimuny	2	—	13	1

FALL OF WICKETS
1- 132, 2- 158, 3- 230, 4- 176, 5- 279

SRI LANKA		
S.R. de S. Wettimuny	run out	31
E.R.N.S. Fernando	b Cairns	36
Y. Goonasekera	c Turner, b Cairns	35
L.R.D. Mendis†	c Wright, b Cairns	7
R.S. Madugalle	not out	30
D.S. de Silva	b Cairns	1
A.L.F. de Mel	c Hadlee, b M.D. Crowe	16
J.R. Ratnayeke	not out	13
R.G. de Alwis*		
S. Jeganathan		
R.J. Ratnayeke		
Extras	b 2, lb 15, w 1, nb 1	19
(50 overs)	(for 6 wickets)	188

	O	M	R	W
Hadlee	7	2	18	—
Snedden	7	—	22	—
Cairns	10	2	23	4
M.D. Crowe	10	1	51	1
Chatfield	10	—	47	—
Wright	2	—	2	—
Edgar	2	—	5	—
J.J. Crowe	1	—	1	—
Turner	1	1	0	—

FALL OF WICKETS
1- 55, 2- 110, 3- 111, 4- 118, 5- 123, 6- 165

New Zealand won by 116 runs

THIRD ONE-DAY INTERNATIONAL: NEW ZEALAND v. SRI LANKA

Howarth returned to lead New Zealand in the final match of the season which turned out to be another total triumph so leaving New Zealand with a season in which they had won every one of the six one-day internationals and both the Tests in which they played, a record unique in modern cricket.

The last match was a personal triumph for Glenn Turner who hit a brilliant 140, shared another devastating century opening stand with Edgar and put New Zealand into a position of invincibility.

Colonel Frank Rennie, Chairman of Rothmans Sports Foundation, presents the Rothmans Cup to Geoff Howarth after New Zealand's triumph over England. (Norman Smith)

Auckland 1982-3
First Class Matches

BATTING	v. Otago (Auckland) 27-29 December 1982		v. Canterbury (Auckland) 1-2 January 1983		v. Central Districts (Napier) 6-8 January 1983		v. Northern Districts (Gisborne) 13-15 January 1983		v. Wellington (Wellington) 21-23 January 1983		v. Wellington (Auckland) 29-31 January 1983		v. Northern Districts (Auckland) 2-4 February 1983		v. Otago (Dunedin) 11-13 February 1983		v. Sri Lankans (Auckland) 26-28 February 1983	
T. J. Franklin	17	0	66	22*	107	23	136	—	5	34	50	35	57	5	6	101*		
P. N. Webb	59	76*	17	10*														
J. F. Reid	2	38	10	—	67	54	68	7	4	21	1	22*	33	11*				
J. J. Crowe	4	34*	23	—														
J. G. Bracewell	4	—	61	—	3	16	54*	36	60*	44	0	7	40	20	18	46	3	29
M. C. Snedden	29	—	32	—														
A. T. R. Hellaby	34	—	39	—	0	0	41	9*	0	21			0	16	2	0	62	8
L. W. Stott	0	—	10*	—	2	0	—	—	1	2*	2	—	—	5	6*	—		
G. B. Troup	4*	—	0	—											0	—		
N. A. Scott	0	—																
M. D. Crowe	119	—	6	—	33	57	6	108	27	19	100	30	46	35	55	25*	0	70*
P. J. Kelly			9	—	8	19	10*	—	2	0	0	9*	12	36	0	—	0	—
A. E. W. Parsons					0	29	3	19	40	17							42	11
A. J. Hunt					25	61	33	26	2	4	0	27	68*	41	5	—	15	16
J. M. McIntyre					1*	4*	—	—	4	5	1	—			23	—	31*	—
S. Tracy					0	1	—	—	4	3	5	—	—	0*				
J. A. J. Cushen											30*	—	0*	5	4	—	17	—
M. Greatbatch											28	28	8	80	11	10	4	36
S. Adams															7*	—		
I. Fisher																	6	10*
Byes		1		1	3			5	1		5		9	1	8	5	2	2
Leg-byes	2		3	1	3	9	11	7		8			8	10	10	8	9	4
Wides	2			1		1				1			3	1			4	
No-balls	1	3	6		7	1	2	2		3	1	1	3	6	4	3	3	
Total	277	152	282	34	259	275	365	219	153	178	224	159	287	272	159	198	198	186
Wickets	10	2	10	0	10	10	6	5	10	10	10	5	7	9	9†	2	10	5
Result	W		W		L		D		L		D		D		D		D	
Points	11		16		0		4		0		0		0		0		—	

Catches

23 – P. J. Kelly (ct 21/st 2)	4 – T. J. Franklin and L. W. Stott
8 – J. F. Reid	3 – J. J. Crowe, M. C. Snedden, J. M. McIntyre and sub (W. P. Fowler)
6 – J. G. Bracewell and A. J. Hunt	2 – P. N. Webb, S. Adams and A. E. W. Parsons
5 – A. T. R. Hellaby, M. D. Crowe and S. Tracy	1 – N. A. Scott

† S. Adams retired hurt

BOWLING	G. B. Troup	M. C. Snedden	L. W. Stott	J. G. Bracewell	A. T. R. Hellaby	M. D. Crowe	J. F. Reid	S. Tracy	J. M. McIntyre
v. Otago (Auckland) 27-29 December 1982	17–4–56–3	20–2–68–1	22–6–77–3	19.2–7–29–3	6–2–17–0	5–0–15–0			
	9–3–27–0	19.1–6–50–5	3–2–6–0	23–11–37–4		2–1–5–0			
v. Canterbury (Auckland) 1-2 January 1983	12–3–33–2	24.1–9–49–7	17–6–40–1	11–6–21–0					
	6–1–23–0	12–2–50–3	15–6–25–2	25.1–13–40–4			1–0–7–0		
v. Central Districts (Napier) 6-8 January 1983			23–7–48–0	29–3–81–3	14–3–41–1	23–3–69–5		19–4–69–1	32–6–37–0
			29–11–46–2	9–0–41–0		2–1–4–0		7–0–31–0	29–11–45–1
v. Northern Districts (Gisborne) 13-15 January 1983			22–6–48–2	10.3–1–46–1		20–8–45–3		14–4–54–3	6–1–19–1
			17–6–31–2	23–3–77–1		5–2–19–0	4–1–14–0	15–2–42–2	26–9–46–2
v. Wellington (Wellington) 21-23 January 1983			49–18–105–2	27–9–72–2	12–3–41–0	14–5–31–3		28–6–80–1	17–7–37–2
v. Wellington (Auckland) 29-31 January 1983			9.3–4–16–3	32–7–97–3			1–0–3–0	17–3–66–2	18–8–21–1
			13–4–27–1	40–16–89–2			4–1–11–0	16–3–64–1	23–15–17–1
v. Northern Districts (Auckland) 2-4 February 1983			33–13–81–1	25–9–58–1	14–4–42–1		4–2–5–1	15–4–53–1	
			33–8–84–3	30–8–71–1				9–0–37–1	
v. Otago (Dunedin) 11-13 February 1983			26–6–51–0	25–8–74–1	2–0–2–0				4–0–21–1
			49–22–75–4	49–18–75–1					7–2–25–0
v. Sri Lankans (Auckland) 26-28 February 1983	25–8–53–3			22.4–7–56–4	7–3–15–0	9–2–32–1			17–8–28–0
	69–19–192–8 av. 24.00	75.2–19–217–16 av. 13.56	360.3–125–760–26 av. 29.23	400.4–126–964–31 av. 31.09	55–15–158–2 av. 79.00	80–22–220–12 av. 18.33	14–4–40–1 av. 40.00	140–26–496–12 av. 41.33	179–67–296–9 av. 32.88

a S. Adams 3–0–11–0   b I. Fisher 18–5–45–1

	Inns	NOs	Runs	HS	Av
	15	2	664	107	51.07
	4	2	162	76*	81.00
	13	2	338	68	30.72
	3	1	61	34*	30.50
	16	2	441	61	31.50
	2	—	61	32	30.50
	14	1	232	62	17.84
	9	3	28	10*	4.66
	3	1	4	4*	2.00
	1		0	0	—
	16	2	736	119	52.57
	12	2	105	36	10.50
	8	—	161	42	20.12
	13	1	323	68*	26.91
	7	3	69	31*	17.25
	6	1	13	5	2.60
	5	2	56	30*	18.66
	8	—	205	80	25.62
	1	1	7	7*	—
	2	1	16	10*	16.00

	J. A. J. Cushen	A. J. Hunt	T. J. Franklin	Byes	Leg-byes	Wides	No-balls	Total	Wkts
				2	13		8	285	10
				9	4		2	140	10
					9		13	165	10
				3	1		1	150	10
				9	4	1	4	363	10
				4	6	1	1	179	3
					4		2	218	10
				5	6		1	241	7
				15	4		5	390	10
	4–11–26–1			3	5		1	238	10
	1–17–0	6–1–15–0	3–1–10–0	10	6		3	269	5
	2–7–76–3	6–1–16–0		8	5		8	352	8
	–0–10–0			3	9		5	219	5
	6–7–67–4						8	234	7a
	1–18–0			4	11		3	211	5
	0–2–57–1	12–5–23–0		11	13		5	338	10b
	07–29–	24–7–	3–1–						
	71–9	54–0	10–0						
	v. 30.11	—	—						

First Class Averages

Batting	M	Inns	NOs	Runs	HS	Av	100s	50s
P.N. Webb	2	4	2	162	76*	81.00		2
B.A. Edgar	4	7	3	263	146	65.75	1	
J.V. Coney	4	4		224	93	56.00		2
I.D.S. Smith	7	8		446	145	55.75	3	
M.D. Crowe	9	16	2	736	119	52.57	3	3
E.B. McSweeney	8	9	3	314	130	52.33	1	1
B.R. Blair	8	13		680	143	52.30	2	4
T.J. Franklin	8	15	2	664	107	51.07	3	3
B.L. Cairns	4	5	1	183	77*	45.75		2
R.W. Ormiston	8	13	2	502	179	45.63	1	1
D.J. White	4	7	2	227	66	45.40		2
J.M. Parker	8	14	1	560	91	43.07		5
R.H. Vance	7	12	1	462	112	42.00	1	2
M.H. Toynbee	7	9	2	293	100	41.85	1	1
A.D.G. Roberts	8	14	3	453	79*	41.18		3
M.J.E. Wright	8	14	1	486	115	37.38	1	2
R.T. Hart	4	7		260	54	37.14		4
P.S. Briasco	8	15	1	519	95	37.07		6
W.K. Lees	4	6		214	89	35.66		2
S.J. Gill	6	10	2	282	107	35.25	1	2
G.J. Dawson	8	13	2	357	54	32.45		2
J.G. Bracewell	9	16	2	441	61	31.50		3
C.M. Presland	5	8	2	188	60*	31.33		2
J.F. Reid	7	13	2	338	68	30.72		3
R.D. Broughton	6	11		335	122	30.45	1	
E.J. Gray	8	13	2	333	69	30.27		1
R.N. Hoskin	7	11		321	77	29.18		3
G.K. Robertson	8	12	3	258	96	28.66		1
R.J.Hadlee	4	7	1	171	46	28.50		
A.J. Hunt	7	13	1	323	68*	26.91		2
V.R. Brown	8	15	1	375	118*	26.78	1	
W.L. Blair	8	13	1	321	65*	26.75		1
P.J. Rattray	9	18	1	454	133	26.70	1	2
G.M. Turner	3	5		133	55	26.60		1
D.W. Stead	9	16		417	81	26.06		3
M. Greatbatch	4	8		205	80	25.62		1
R.A. Pierce	8	15		382	94	25.46		2
J.G. Wright	4	5		125	43	25.00		
J.B. Boyle	5	9		223	76	24.77		2
P.J. Holland	6	10	1	219	56	24.33		2
R.I. Leggat	9	16	3	315	83	24.23		1
J.J. Crowe	4	6	1	120	36	24.00		
J.R. Wiltshire	8	15	4	246	52	22.36		1
D.R. O'Sullivan	8	9	1	178	42	22.25		
I.A. Rutherford	8	13		285	96	21.92		2
P.E. McEwan	6	11	1	218	50	21.80		1
D.A. Stirling	8	11	4	147	47	21.00		
A.E.W. Parsons	4	8		161	42	20.12		
G.P. Howarth	4	6		110	45	18.33		
C. Dickel	6	9	2	128	56	18.28		1
L.M. Crocker	8	14		254	48	18.14		
B.W. Cederwall	8	9	1	145	34	18.12		
A.T.R. Hellaby	8	14	1	232	62	17.84		1
I.R. Snook	5	10		178	37	17.80		
R.T. Latham	4	7		121	49	17.28		
D.C. Aberhart	5	8	2	100	40*	16.66		
D.A. Dempsey	6	12	1	179	42	16.27		
B.G. Cooper	8	14		212	55	15.14		1
B.P. Bracewell	8	13	3	146	36*	14.60		
R.M. Carter	7	14	1	184	45	14.15		
P.J. Kelly	8	12	2	105	36	10.50		

(Qualification 100 runs, average 10.00)

Bowling	Overs	Mdns	Runs	Wkts	Av	Best	5/inn
R.J. Hadlee	152.5	54	277	23	12.04	6/43	1
V.R. Brown	202.2	64	452	30	15.06	7/28	2
M.C. Snedden	149.2	38	372	24	15.50	7/49	2
E.J. Chatfield	189.5	66	389	25	15.56	6/76	2
B.W. Cederwall	177	43	284	17	16.70	4/34	
C. Dickel	116.1	35	272	16	17.00	5/22	1
A.C.S. Pigott	196.4	56	581	33	17.60	5/47	2
R.J. Webb	165.4	50	397	22	18.04	4/33	

Canterbury 1982-3
First Class Matches

BATTING

BATTING	v. Central Districts (Christchurch) 27-29 Dec. 1982	v. Auckland (Auckland) 1-2 Jan 1983	v. Northern Districts (Hamilton) 6-8 Jan 1983	v. Wellington (Christchurch) 13-14 Jan 1983	v. Otago (Christchurch) 20-21 Jan 1983	v. Otago (Invercargill) 28-29 Jan 1983	v. Central Districts (Nelson) 2-4 Feb 1983	v. Northern Districts (Christchurch) 11-13 Feb 1983	v. Sri Lankans (Christchurch) 19-21 Feb 1983
D. A. Dempsey	2 11	19 14				11 0	23 42	30 5	0 22*
D. W. Stead	2 23	9 21	16 45	81 —	18 14	5 0	81 13	51 24	14 —
V. R. Brown	33 14	15 28	6 118*	34 —	1 31	0 2	12 44	16 21	
R. M. Carter	6 3	4 17	28 45	12 1*	1 10	8 38		11 0	
R. T. Latham	5 0	0 29	49 20	18 —					
P. J. Rattray	47 7	28 1	4 41	20 19*	11 0	0 1	2 133	3 63	62 12
R. I. Leggat	45 36	0 1	17 16	27 —	2 12*	0 5*	15 18	22 16*	83 —
R. J. Hadlee	21 26	46 19							
S. N. Bateman	7 0	14 14	7 0*	0 —	5* 0	0 0	0 0		
P. D. Rutledge	0 0			8* —	1 11	0* 3	10 0		
C. H. Thiele	2* 0*	0 1	1* —	2 —	17 0		4* 0*	1* —	— —
A. W. Hart		8* 0*	10 —					25 1*	12 —
D. J. Boyle			2 7		4 7				0 —
A. J. Nuttall			3 —	32 —	3 3				
P. E. McEwan				1 —	24 19	44 2	22 50	9 39	6 2*
J. Gully						20 6	0 5		22 0
A. J. Farrant						7 18	6 0		
D. R. Hadlee								43 11	109* —
G. C. Bateman								13	— —
Byes	4 3	— 3	2 8		5 1	4 6	3 9		3 2
Leg-byes	15 5	9 1	4 11	5	1 5	4 8	11 8	24	4 12
Wides			1 1		2 1	1	1	3 2	5
No-balls	13 3	13 1	1 1	14	4 3	3	9 2	4 1	17 1
Total	202 131	165 150	150 313	255 20	99 117	106 89	199 324	255 190	344 38
Wickets	10 10	10 10	10 6	10 0	10 10	10 10	10 10	10 7	8 2
Result	L	L	D	W	L	L	L	W	W
Points	0	0	0	16	0	0	0	16	—

Catches

14 — A. W. Hart (ct 13/st 1)
10 – P. D. Rutledge (ct 8/st 2)
7 – P. E. McEwan
6 – R. T. Latham, V. R. Brown and D. W. Stead
5 – C. H. Thiele
4 – R. J. Hadlee and R. M. Carter

BOWLING

BOWLING	R. J. Hadlee	C. H. Thiele	S. N. Bateman	R. M. Carter	D. W. Stead	V. R. Brown	A. J. Nuttall	R. I. Leggat	D. R. Hadlee
v. Central Districts (Christchurch) 27-29 December 1982	23-8-40-4, 25-6-43-6	19.1-4-50-2, 11-1-27-1	18-5-52-2, 13-0-26-2	6-2-9-0	15-5-40-2, 16-5-39-1	4-2-4-0, 7-5-6-0			
v. Auckland (Auckland) 1-2 January 1983	27.2-11-53-3	20-6-65-2	13-3-66-1	4-1-13-0	23-4-55-2	9-1-21-2, 4-1-7-0		4-0-22-0	
v. Northern Districts (Hamilton) 6-8 January, 1983		23-4-63-1	26-9-35-2	10-3-25-0	27-6-47-1	17.1-5-31-3	21-9-45-1	6-1-14-1	
v. Wellington (Christchurch) 13-14 January 1983		10-3-19-1, 10-1-35-0	12-7-28-0, 10-5-23-3	7-3-12-1	4-3-3-1, 21-7-40-3	18.2-12-28-7, 13.5-5-28-4	14-8-22-0		
v. Otago (Christchurch) 20-21 January 1983		19-3-63-1	18-3-58-0	4-1-15-0	15.4-4-41-2	20-6-55-6	7-2-6-0		
v. Otago (Invercargill) 28-29 January 1983			19-7-33-2		48.1-17-99-7	40-12-72-0		11-3-28-1	
v. Central Districts (Nelson) 2-4 February 1983		13-3-37-2, 15-3-46-3	10-1-63-0, 7-0-29-0		40-18-91-1	34-8-107-2, 7-0-31-1		13-2-39-1	
v. Northern Districts (Christchurch) 11-13 Feb. 1983		10-2-33-2, 14-3-41-0			9.4-2-28-2	4-0-12-1, 24-7-50-4			19.2-6-58, 12-1-41
v. Sri Lankans (Christchurch) 19-21 February 1983		17.5-5-45-6, 14-1-56-2			9-3-26-0				12-6-17, 11-4-19
	75.2-25– 136-13 *av.* 10.46	196-39– 580-23 *av.* 25.21	146-40– 413-12 *av.* 34.41	31-10– 74-1 *av.* 74.00	228.3-74– 509-22 *av.* 23.13	202.2-64– 452-30 *av.* 15.06	42-19– 73-1 *av.* 73.00	34-6– 103-3 *av.* 34.33	54.2-17– 135-7 *av.* 19.28

a R. T. Latham 1-0-2-0
P. J. Rattray 0.5-0-1-0

† L. R. D. Mendis retired hurt, absent hurt

	Inns	NOs	Runs	HS	Av
	12	1	179	42	16.27
	16	—	417	81	26.06
	15	1	375	118*	26.78
	14	1	184	45	14.15
	7	—	121	49	17.28
	18	1	454	133	26.70
	16	3	315	83	24.23
	4	—	112	46	28.00
	13	2	47	14	4.27
	9	2	33	11	4.71
	11	6	28	17	5.60
	6	3	56	25	18.66
	5	—	20	7	4.00
	4	—	41	32	10.25
	11	1	218	50	21.80
	6	—	53	22	8.83
	4	—	31	18	7.75
	3	1	163	109*	81.50
	1	—	13	13	13.00

Bowling cont'd	Overs	Mdns	Runs	Wkts	Av	Best	5/inn
M.D. Crowe	80	22	220	12	18.33	5/69	1
G.C. Bateman	71.2	15	210	11	19.09	6/66	1
D.C. Aberhart	126.5	41	309	16	19.31	6/55	1
S.L. Boock	290	127	604	30	20.13	5/79	2
B.L. Cairns	116.4	34	289	14	20.64	4/47	
D.A. Stirling	203.3	55	552	25	22.08	4/23	
B.G. Cooper	87.2	24	226	10	22.60	5/40	1
D.W. Stead	228.3	74	509	22	23.13	7/99	1
A.D.G. Roberts	118	40	257	11	23.36	4/45	
C.H. Thiele	196	39	580	23	25.21	6/45	1
S.M. Carrington	171	41	456	17	26.82	4/3	
E.J. Gray	241.5	95	596	22	27.09	4/100	
B.P. Bracewell	224	56	603	22	27.40	4/44	
S.J. Maguiness	250	102	469	17	27.58	4/28	
S.J. Gill	110.4	31	287	10	28.70	4/28	
G.K. Robertson	234	47	720	25	28.80	4/42	
C.M. Presland	170.3	46	497	17	29.23	4/49	
L.W. Stott	360.3	125	760	26	29.23	4/75	
J.G. Bracewell	400.4	126	964	31	31.09	4/37	
D.R. O'Sullivan	403	120	950	30	31.66	5/64	2
C.W. Dickeson	261.1	80	748	23	32.52	4/49	
S.N. Bateman	146	40	413	12	34.41	3/23	
S. Tracy	140	26	496	12	41.33	3/54	

(R.J. Hadlee, V.R. Brown, M.C. Snedden and A.C.S. Pigott each took ten wickets in a match upon one occasion)

(Qualification - 10 wickets)

Leading Fielders

27 – E.B. McSweeney (ct 25/st 2); 23 - P.J. Kelly (ct 21/st 2); 22 - B.D. Milburn; 20 - I.D.S. Smith (ct 19/st 1); 18 - W.K. Lees; 14 - A.W. Hart (ct 13/st 1); 12 - L.M. Crocker and M.J.E. Wright; 10 - P.D. Rutledge (ct 8/st 2); 8 - J.F. Reid, B.W. Cederwall and A. Blain (ct 7/st 1) (inc. one catch as substitute)

John Morrison, a surprising choice, and an equally surprising success. Randall in the field. Morrison said that he was betrayed by the selectors when omitted from the side to tour England.

	G.C. Bateman	A.J. Farrant	D.A. Dempsey	Byes	Leg-byes	Wides	No-balls	Total	Wkts
					10		7	212	10
					3			144	10
					3		6	282	10
				1	1			34	0a
				5	3		5	273	10
				11	3			104	10
				14	3	1	1	167	10
				5	8	1	4	256	10
		12-5-18-0	6-3-14-0	16	2			282	10
		19-5-57-0		(23)				417	6
			9-2-29-1		7		1	143	5
–6-50-3				3	7	2	10	175	10
2-23-1			21-6-67-3	7	6	2	4	269	10
–5-71-1			5-2-14-0	9	5	1	5	167	9†
2-2-66-6			12-6-27-0	8	4		8	214	9†
2-15-		31-10-	53-19-						
0-11		75-0	151-4						
19.09		—	av. 37.75						

– J. Gully, R. I. Leggatt, P. J. Rattray and S. N. Bateman

– A. J. Nuttall and D. A. Dempsey

– D. J. Boyle, D. R. Hadlee, G. C. Bateman and A. J. Farrant

Central Districts 1982-3
First Class Matches

BATTING

	v. Canterbury (Christchurch) 27-29 Dec. 1982		v. Wellington (New Plymouth) 1-3 January 1983		v. Auckland (Napier) 6-8 January 1983		v. Otago (Dunedin) 14-15 January 1983		v. Northern Districts (Palmerston N.) 21-23 January 1983		v. Northern Districts (Hamilton) 29-31 January 1983		v. Canterbury (Nelson) 2-4 February 1983		v. Wellington (Wellington) 11-13 February 1983		*Inns*	*NOs*	*Runs*	*HS*	*Av*
I. R. Snook	33	14	28	1	28	10	2	37	4	21							10	—	178	37	17.80
R. A. Pierce	6	6	7	13	3	94	29	7	2	46	0	31	89	29	20	—	15	—	382	94	25.46
P. S. Briasco	4	32	20	59	8	49*	0	57	53	52	52	9	95	12	17	—	15	1	519	95	37.07
J. R. Wiltshire	6	2	41	41	1	0*	11	10*	12	0*	8	29*	52	0	33	—	15	4	246	52	22.36
A. Blain	7	4	29	10	19	—											5	—	69	29	13.80
S. J. Gill	0	2	53	0			107	—			0	22*	37*	10	51	—	10	2	282	107	35.25
I. D. S. Smith	34	0			145	—	11	—	111	—	143	—	2	—	0	—	8	—	446	145	55.75
G. K. Robertson	32	7	22*	8	32*	—	6	—	24	15	96	5	—	9*	2	—	12	3	258	96	28.66
D. C. Aberhart	40*	29	0	1	1	14	1	—	14*	—							8	2	100	40*	16.66
D. R. O'Sullivan	20	42	0	23	1	—	23	—	36	—	33	—	—	—	0*	—	9	1	178	42	22.25
D. A. Stirling	13	3*	1	1*	7	—	0*	—	4	37	1*	33	—	—	47	—	11	4	147	47	21.00
M. H. Toynbee			5	35	100	—	43	7*	8	—	27	—	66*	—	2	—	9	2	293	100	41.85
R. T. Hart									0	51	8	54	53	42	52	—	7	—	260	54	37.14
R. E. Hayward											0	24	0	33*	10	—	5	1	67	33*	16.75
Byes			6	6	9	4		1			3	3			5						
Leg-byes	10	3		7	4	6	4	6	(27)	(17)	19	6	(23)	7	5						
Wides			1	1	1	1					1	1			3						
No-balls	7		5	3	4	1	7	3			1	1		1	12						
Total	212	144	218	209	363	179	244	128	295	239	392	218	417	143	259						
Wickets	10	10	10	10	10	3	10	3	10	6	10	6	6	5	10						
Result	W		L		W		D		L		D		W		D						
Points	16		0		15		0		4		4		16		4						

Catches
20 – I. D. S. Smith (ct 19/st 1)
8 – A. Blain (ct 7/st 1) (including one catch as sub.)
7 – R. A. Pierce and G. K. Robertson
4 – J. R. Wiltshire and M. H. Toynbee (including one as sub.)
3 – I. R. Snook, D. C. Aberhart, R. T. Hart, S. J. Gill and P. S. Briasco
2 – D. R. O'Sullivan
1 – R. E. Hayward, D. A. Stirling and sub (Perkins)

BOWLING

	D. A. Stirling	D. R. O'Sullivan	G. K. Robertson	D. C. Aberhart	S. J. Gill	I. R. Snook	M. H. Toynbee	P. S. Briasco
v. Canterbury (Christchurch)	19–5–34–4	36–15–55–3	14–1–50–1	16–8–21–1	7–3–8–1	2–0–2–0		
27-29 December 1982	11–1–34–2	32–10–64–5	16–7–14–2	4.3–1–8–1				
v. Wellington (New Plymouth)	17–5–31–0	29–9–68–0	22–4–76–1	25–8–69–3	15–3–41–0		16–1–64–0	10–2–39–0
1-3 January 1983	0.2–0–4–0							
v. Auckland (Napier)	14–3–37–1	44.3–15–82–5	17–3–52–2	16–4–36–1				7–1–15–0
6-8 January 1983	13–1–61–1	13–0–73–1	13–0–67–0	15.2–0–55–6			1–0–8–0	
v. Otago (Dunedin)	16–5–67–1	25–3–88–1	17–6–46–1	19–7–54–1	13–1–66–2		3–1–9–0	9–3–25–0
14-15 January 1983								
v. Northern Districts (Palmerston	19–5–67–3	20–7–48–1	23–7–57–4	13–4–26–1				
North) 21-23 January 1983	6–3–11–1	41–8–125–2	16–2–42–1	18–9–40–2			21–5–89–0	
v. Northern Districts (Hamilton)	20–4–63–2	38.3–11–83–3	17–3–52–2		13–3–40–1		14–3–29–0	2–0–8–0
29-31 January 1983	9–4–23–4	29–16–37–2	13–3–33–1		13–4–28–1		21–8–44–0	6–2–8–0
v. Canterbury (Nelson)	11.4–5–28–2	29–9–57–4	14–1–56–3		7–3–17–0		9–1–17–0	
2-4 February 1983	17–4–38–0	35–6–111–1	17–3–76–2		12.4–3–28–4		9–1–47–1	
v. Wellington (Wellington)	11.3–3–26–3	4–2–3–0	17–5–42–4		14–5–31–1			
11-13 February 1983	19–7–28–1	27–9–56–2	18–2–57–1		16–6–28–0		10–3–25–0	
	203.3–55–552–25 *av.* 22.08	403–120–950–30 *av.* 31.66	234–47–720–25 *av.* 28.80	126.5–41–309–16 *av.* 19.31	110.4–31–287–10 *av.* 28.70	2–0–2–0 —	104–23–332–1 *av.* 332.00	34–8–95–0 —

A MEMORABLE YEAR
by
DON CAMERON
New Zealand's leading cricket writer

The surge of interest in New Zealand cricket toward the end of the 1981–82 season, when Eden Park squeezed in 43,000 for a one-day international against Australia, and later almost the same number in total for a test victory over Chappell's men, seemed to reach close to the high-water mark.

These vibrant events, following New Zealand's entry the season before into the televised extravaganza of one-day cricket in Australia, bred an astonishing interest in cricket throughout New Zealand. It did not seem possible that the re-awakened public interest could be increased; rather the problem was how to sustain the flood of interest created in those two astonishing summers.

Yet those surges of interest starting in early 1981 now seem almost like ripples compared with the tidal-wave of public enthusiasm which washed over New Zealand cricket last summer.

Some of the New Zealand players became instant folk-heroes, whether it was Lance Cairns with his enormous six-hitting bat, or Richard Hadlee either hitting stumps or sixes. Glenn Turner came home like the prodigal son and was immediately ushered toward the fatted calf. The question whether Geoff Howarth would score runs in keeping with his reputation (which, sadly, he did not always do) was balanced by the hero-worship which his leadership attracted.

Everyone felt the impact. Administrators had to set limits on the crowds for some of the one-day internationals, schools and clubs desperately searched about trying to find grounds to accommodate the thousands of youngsters who wanted to start playing the game. Sports-goods shops suddenly found their shelves stripped of bats, pads and anything else to do with cricket. Cricket-writers suddenly found themselves the target for doting letters from elderly ladies which usually started … 'I am 72 years old and have never taken much interest in cricket before, but …'

It all became a mad, merry and slightly giddy experience, this New Zealand season of 1982–83. For which we can thank, in equal measure, the development of an increasingly-proficient New Zealand side and, with a touch of the cap toward Kerry Packer, the heady mixture of one-day cricket and live television.

There has always been a latent, ground-root interest in cricket within New Zealand, sustained occasionally by a victory or a proud performance. Little wonder, then, that the swell of support grew to such size, for the first time New Zealanders almost became sated with the success of their cricket team.

From the first week in January to the middle of March New Zealand played no fewer than nineteen one-day internationals and two five-day Tests. They won 13 of the one-dayers (four over Australia, six from England, three against Sri Lanka) and lost six (four to Australia, two to England) and took both home Tests against Sri Lanka.

Twelve of the one-dayers were in Australia during the Benson and Hedges World Series Cup contest, in which New Zealand qualified first ahead of Australia and England in the ten-match preliminary series, and then lost 0–2 to Australia in the finals.

Two years previously New Zealand had also qualified for the BHWSC finals (India were eliminated) but lost to Australia in the finals which launched the hysteria of the under-arm bowl by Trevor Chappell at the Melbourne Cricket Ground. So New Zealand competing, and winning, in Australia was not exactly a novelty, and the expedition had a subdued start when the New Zealanders were clearly beaten in the first match by Australia.

The interest picked up when New Zealand stole a last-ball win over England, 239 to 237, in their second match, but then David Gower slaughtered the New Zealanders at Brisbane. With Australia winning three in succession, and England having the firepower of Gower and Allan Lamb, there came the strong feeling that New Zealand might finish third in a three-horse race. But suddenly New Zealand cracked the Australian armour at Sydney, did it again at Melbourne, and the three teams went to Adelaide for the crucial three games in the contest.

On a blisteringly hot Saturday afternoon England scored 296 for five, again with Gower in masterly form, and as they clustered around their television sets that evening New Zealanders moped about for defeat in this match – and very likely in the preliminary series – seemed certain. But with a mixture of gritty, cool-headed batting and some lamentable England fielding, the New Zealanders topped the record England score with four wickets and seven balls to spare.

R. A. Pierce	R. E. Hayward	R. T. Hart	Byes	Leg-byes	Wides	No-balls	Total	Wkts
			4	15		13	202	10
			3	5		3	131	10
-1-8-1			3	8		17	424	7
							4	0
-1-24-0			3	3		7	259	10
				9	1	1	275	10
			4	15	7	15	396	6
-1-2-1				(14)			214	10
				(15)			322	6
-0-4-0	1-1-0-0		2	10	1		292	10
-2-12-0		1-0-12-0	1	3		1	202	9
	2-2-0-0		3	11	1	9	199	10
-0-5-0			9	8		2	324	10
0-5-8-2			8	6		5	129	10
-0-11-0	3-1-4-0		5	6	3	4	227	4
4-10-	6-4-	1-0-						
4-4	4-0	12-0						
. 18.50	—	—						

Northern Districts 1982-3
First Class Matches

BATTING

BATTING	v Wellington (Wellington) 27-29 Dec. 1982 (1)	(2)	v Otago (Tauranga) 1-3 Jan 1983 (1)	(2)	v Canterbury (Hamilton) 6-8 Jan 1983 (1)	(2)	v Auckland (Gisborne) 13-15 Jan 1983 (1)	(2)	v Central Districts (Palmerston North) 21-23 Jan 1983 (1)	(2)	v Central Districts (Hamilton) 29-31 Jan 1983 (1)	(2)	v Auckland (Auckland) 2-4 Feb 1983 (1)	(2)	v Canterbury (Christchurch) 11-13 Feb 1983 (1)	(2)	Inns	NOs	Runs	HS	Av
L. M. Crocker	48	0	32	—	33	—	39	19	10	10	15	8	8	12	0	20	14	—	254	48	18.14
J. G. Wright	20	43	35	—													3	—	98	43	32.66
G. P. Howarth	45	9	19	—													3	—	73	45	24.33
B. G. Cooper	16	2	9	—	21	—	14	4	55	18	0	29	10	9	25	0	14	—	212	55	15.14
J. M. Parker	12	3	78	—	57	—	91	8	3	69	39	27	71	56*	1	45	14	1	560	91	43.07
A. D. G. Roberts	15	79*	38	—	7	—	1	79	39	49*	65	11	29	19*	0	22	14	3	453	79*	41.18
M. J. E. Wright	23	20	72*	—	25	—	6	24	13	1	37	31	115	45	1	73	14	1	486	115	37.38
B. L. Cairns	0	77*	58	—													3	1	135	77*	67.50
S. R. Gillespie	59	10	1	—	0	—											4	—	70	59	17.50
S. M. Carrington	8	—	16	—	0*	—	20	—	0	—	1	5*			23	15	9	2	88	23	12.57
K. Treiber	1*	—			31	—											2	1	32	31	32.00
C. W. Dickeson			1	—	0	—	18	7*	20	4*	15*	0	21*	—	0	1	11	4	87	20	12.42
C. M. Kuggeleijn					85	—	9	2									3	—	96	85	32.00
R. D. Broughton			1	—			8	26	1	122	37	22	40	49	18	11	11	—	335	122	30.45
C. M. Presland							6	60*	0	—	0	46*	17	—	52	7	8	2	188	60*	31.33
N. D. Pollock							0*	—									1	1	0	0*	—
D. J. White									54*	34	66	13	15	—	33*	12	7	2	227	66	45.40
S. J. Scott									5	—	4	5	5*	12	0	44*	7	2	75	44*	15.00
Byes	1	6	2		5			5			2	1	8	3	3	7					
Leg-byes	13	5	5		3		4	6	(14)	(15)	10	3	5	9	7	4					
Wides											1				2	2					
No-balls	5	4	4		5		2	1				1	8	5	10	6					
Total	266	258	370		273		218	241	214	322	292	202	352	219	175	269					
Wickets	10	7	10		10		10	7	10	6	10	9	8	5	10	10					
Result	D		W		D		D		W		D		D		L						
Points	−1		16		4		0		12		0		4		0						

Catches
12 – M. J. E. Wright (ct 10/st 2) and L. M. Crocker
6 – B. G. Cooper, J. M. Parker, S. J. Scott, R. D. Broughton, C. M. Kuggeleijn (inc. 3 as sub) and S. M. Carrington (inc. one as sub)
5 – C. W. Dickeson
4 – G. P. Howarth
3 – A. D. G. Roberts and C. M. Presland
2 – B. L. Cairns
1 – J. G. Wright, S. R. Gillespie and D. J. White

BOWLING

BOWLING	S. M. Carrington	B. L. Cairns	K. Treiber	S. R. Gillespie	A. D. G. Roberts	S. J. Scott	C. W. Dickeson	B. G. Cooper	D. J. White
v. Wellington (Wellington) 27-29 December 1982	22-7-50-0	26-5-54-0	20-5-44-1	19-2-75-1	11-3-21-0				
	5-2-5-0	1.3-1-0-0	3-2-2-0						
v. Otago (Tauranga) 1-3 January 1983	7-6-3-4	9.5-0-39-3		12-3-24-2	4-2-12-1				
	15-5-36-1	17.2-8-39-2		8-1-35-0	2-0-8-0		29-10-67-2	24-11-40-5	
v. Canterbury (Hamilton) 6-8 January 1983	14-6-23-4		8-1-25-0	17-3-36-2	4-1-4-0		22.3-8-49-4	1-0-6-0	
	23-2-70-1		18.4-3-59-0	21-4-48-1	5-3-5-1		27-7-74-2	13-4-22-1	
v. Auckland (Gisborne) 13-15 January 1983	24-5-70-1				4-1-11-0		18-5-53-0	9-2-23-0	
	6-0-32-1						12.1-1-55-2	7-0-20-0	
v. Central Districts (Palmerston North) 21-23 January 1983	10-1-37-2				17-3-50-2	20-6-59-1	12-4-43-1	8.2-3-22-2	1-0-4-0
					14-3-30-3	16.3-5-53-1	22-11-48-0	13-4-27-0	2-1-2-1
v. Central Districts (Hamilton) 29-31 January 1983	15-4-41-2				13-5-42-0	25.3-6-80-1	28-12-84-4	3-0-24-0	8-3-35-1
	5-1-17-0					5-2-5-0	27.3-9-87-2		24-4-89-0
v. Auckland (Auckland) 2-4 February 1983			20-3-58-2		11-7-7-0	17-5-47-0	21-4-58-2		6-1-27-0
			4-0-15-1			4-2-8-0	28-3-99-3	9-1-42-2	11-1-64-4
v. Canterbury (Christchurch) 11-13 February 1983	22-2-66-1				12-4-22-0	30.1-7-66-4	8-2-23-1		
	3-0-6-0				21-8-45-4	13-2-46-1	6-4-8-0		
	171-41-456-17	54.4-14-132-5	73.4-14-203-4	77-13-218-6	118-40-257-11	131.1-35-364-8	261.1-80-748-23	87.2-25-226-10	52-10-221-6
	av. 26.82	*av. 26.40*	*av. 50.75*	*av. 36.33*	*av. 23.36*	*av. 45.50*	*av. 32.52*	*av. 22.60*	*av. 36.83*

a G. P. Howarth 5-2-17-0   b G. P. Howarth 2-0-6-0   c C. M. Kuggeleijn 4-1-14-0   d M. J. E. Wright 4-0-32-0

A vast wave of pride and euphoria swept over the country, ...art from the proprietors of one Sunday newspaper who ...ith a two-and-a-half hour time gap with Adelaide) had ...it out their first edition with huge headlines and story ...king of a disastrous New Zealand loss, and did not have ...ne to cover their error with a second-edition victory issue. The whole country seemed delightfully, deliciously ...lirious with these cricketers who could achieve the imposs-...le, and the enormous eruption of sheer joy was carried over ...the Monday when in even hotter temperatures the New ...aland bowlers clawed down Australia for 153 when they ...re bowling against the moderate total of 194.

Those two incredible wins put New Zealand into the finals ...and they confirmed this with a win over England at Perth ...hen the game was ridiculously fore-shortened by rain – but ...hile their adoring supporters back home were still in rap-...res those two wins at Adelaide were to represent the New ...ealanders' peak for the tour.

Australia re-organised their side, especially in the develop-...ent of a lively opening style by Graeme Wood and Steve ...mith, and were clearly superior to New Zealand, minus an ...jured Richard Hadlee, in the two finals.

Still Howarth's men came home to a heroes' welcome, and ...o find that their approaching three one-day internationals ...gainst England had stirred up fantastic interest. It did not ...atter that New Zealand had lost the BHWSC finals, nor ...at England were spluttering along on three cylinders, with ...ost of their large party wishing that their long tour was ...ready over.

Everyone wanted to see their New Zealand team play; ...ell, almost everyone. Mindful of the problems caused by the ...3,000 crowd for the Australia match at Eden Park the year ...efore, Auckland officials set a 41,000 limit for Eden Park. ...n Wellington the Basin Reserve crowd would be held to ...bout 18,000, at Lancaster Park to 31,000. Never before had ...ew Zealand officials had to peg down the size of their ...ricket crowds, and such was the fever that on the day that

Bob Willis' men arrived for the three one-day internationals came the news that all three grounds had been sold out.

Howarth, now almost established as the guru of New Zealand cricket, made the interesting point that the one way his players could repay the support and loyalty of their home followers would be to win well against England. Which they did, in spades.

On a slow tiresome pitch at Eden Park only Gower, with 84, showed any dedication to the cause, England's total of 184 was far too modest, Turner scored a dazzling 88, put on 101 for the first wicket with Bruce Edgar (35), Cairns turned up with a couple of the now obligatory sixes and New Zealand cruised home with six wickets and three and a half overs to spare.

This was the start of the triumphal New Zealand progress through another sweeping victory at Wellington, with Turner scoring 94 in a total of 295 for six, and England finished limply at 192. On a dodgy pitch at Christchurch the margin was smaller – New Zealand 211, England 127, but still convincing enough. As the last of the trials and tribulations of their long expedition England managed to lose their last eight wickets for 33 runs, and this against a bowling attack of Martin Snedden, Cairns, Ewen Chatfield, Jeremy Coney and that most mysterious of left-arm spinners, John Morrison.

Everything that New Zealand attempted turned to gold, whereas Willis was still poking round in the ashes of defeat. In a week 90,000 New Zealanders had seen their heroes win three times, and the New Zealand Cricket Council happily went off to the bank with a profit of about £75,000.

At about the same time Sri Lanka had started their first tour of New Zealand, which very quickly became an ill-starred venture. In their first match they lost Duleep Mendis, their captain and senior batsman, who suffered a broken finger from the first ball he received on tour. A week or so later Roy Dias, their second-ranked batsman, broke a thumb while fielding.

Even though the New Zealand side was showing signs of wear and tear they won easily the first one-dayer, and then the first Test by an innings in three days. Sri Lanka fought much harder in the second Test, affected by rain and bad light in Wellington, but still lost by six wickets in a little more than 18 hours playing time.

But there was still time for another peak. As Howarth tossed and turned in bed the night before the first one-dayer against England at Eden Park bush-fires were ravaging parts of South Australia and Victoria. So Howarth came up with the notion that New Zealand should play Australia in a day-night match at Sydney, with all the proceeds going to the Bushfire Appeal.

It was a masterly stroke by Howarth, the match was fitted in between the second Sri Lankan Test and the Saturday–Sunday one-dayers which were to mark the end of the Sri Lankan tour. Rain in Sydney almost ruined the bush-fire match, the game was played on a wet and tricky pitch, Martin Crowe came bounding back to international cricket with 62, and New Zealand won handily.

Then, as the final flourish of this magical season, New Zealand beat Sri Lanka easily in the one-day match at Napier and on the next day, at Auckland, won again – this time scoring 304. The total was really of academic interest in the context of that game for Sri Lanka have still to learn the art

N. D. Pollock	C. M. Presland	R. D. Broughton	Byes	Leg-byes	Wides	No-balls	Total	Wkts
			4			2	267	3a
				2	1		10	0
			3	3	1	5	90	10
			7	4		4	246	10b
			2	4		1	150	10
			8	11	1	1	313	6c
-2-98-2	29.3-8-96-3			11	1	2	365	6
-3-38-2		4-0-28-0	5	7		2	219	5d
	16-4-53-2			(27)			295	10
	24-4-62-1			(17)			239	6
	14-6-62-2		3	19	1	1	392	10
	6-1-9-0		3	6	1	1	218	6
	20-3-67-2		9	8	3	3	287	7
	9-4-26-1		1	10	1	6	272	9
	29-12-47-4			24	3	4	255	10
	23-4-75-2		3	4	2	1	190	7
-5-	170.3-46-	4-0-						
6-4	497-17	28-0						
34.00	av. 29.23	—						

Otago 1982-3
First Class Matches

BATTING	v. Auckland (Auckland) 27-29 Dec. 1982		v. Northern Districts (Tauranga) 1-3 January 1983		v. Wellington (Alexandra) 6-8 January 1983		v. Central Districts (Dunedin) 14-15 January 1983		v. Canterbury (Christchurch) 20-21 January 1983		v. Canterbury (Invercargill) 28-29 January 1983		v. Wellington (Lower Hutt) 4-6 February 1983		v. Auckland (Dunedin) 11-13 February 1983		Inns	NOs	Runs	HS	Av
I. A. Rutherford	9	18	0	18	4	4	62	—	39	—	96	—	6	2	12	15	13	—	285	96	21.92
G. M. Turner	55	7															2	—	62	55	31.00
B. R. Blair	61	0	3	21	27	106	143	—	70	—	0	—	90	39	72	48	13	—	680	143	52.30
W. L. Blair	6	27	19	16	46	21	35	—	29	—	13	—	2	22	20	65*	13	1	321	65*	26.75
R. N. Hoskin	55	10	0	39			38	—	5	—	57	—	4	77	33	3	11	—	321	77	29.18
G. J. Dawson	11	12	28*	10	16	28	67	—	17	—	28	—	54	16	31*	39	13	2	357	54	32.45
W. K. Lees	50	22	21	32													4	—	125	50	31.25
B. Abernethy	3	2	2	32	0	4			40	—	0	—	8	0	—	—	10	—	91	40	9.10
S. L. Boock	3*	14	0	6	6	2	—	—	0	—	21	—	2*	3	18*	—	11	3	75	21	9.37
B. P. Bracewell	9	8	1	0*	17	36*	5	—	25	—	0	—	8	5	22	10*	13	3	146	36*	14.60
R. J. Webb	0	5*			1*	5			0*	—			0	2	—	—	7	3	13	5*	3.25
C. Dickel			1	56	16	8	5*	—	11	—	10	—	0	21*			9	2	128	56	18.28
P. W. Hills			3	1													2	—	4	3	2.00
R. Jones					4	45											2	—	49	45	24.50
B. D. Milburn					1	18	—	—	2	—	9	—	1	1			6	—	32	18	5.33
K. Ibadulla							—	—			30*	—			1	—	2	1	31	30*	31.00
K. Rutherford															17	13	2	—	30	17	15.00
Byes	2	9	3	7	3	3	4		5		16		3	2	4						
Leg-byes	13	4	3	4			15		8		2		1	5	8	11					
Wides			1		1	1	7		1												
No-balls	8	2	5	4	18	5	15		4				2	2	3						
Total	285	140	90	246	160	286	396		256		282		181	197	234	211					
Wickets	10	10	10	10	10	10	6		10		10		10	10	7	5					
Result	L		L		L		D		W		W		L		D						
Points	4		0		0		4		16		16		0		4						

Catches
22 – B. D. Milburn
6 – G. J. Dawson
5 – W. K. Lees, I. A. Rutherford, R. N. Hoskin and B. Abernethy
4 – S. L. Boock and B. P. Bracewell
3 – K. Ibadulla
2 – G. M. Turner, C. Dickel, W. L. Blair, B. R. Blair, and K. Rutherford
1 – P. W. Hills and sub (B. Wilson)

BOWLING	R. J. Webb	B. P. Bracewell	B. Abernethy	S. L. Boock	B. R. Blair	R. N. Hoskin	I. A. Rutherford	W. L. Blair	K. Rutherford
v. Auckland (Auckland)	26–11–33–2	36–10–94–1	19–6–45–0	37.5–16–79–5	9–3–21–1				
27-29 December 1982	8–1–26–1	16–4–37–0	7–3–20–0	15–6–44–1	4–0–12–0	1.5–0–1–0	1–0–1–0	0.2–0–5–0	
v. Northern Districts (Tauranga)		15–1–51–1	10–2–32–1	45.3–20–99–5	6–0–37–1				
1-3 January 1983									
v. Wellington (Alexandra)	26.3–3–82–3	29–3–85–2	29–6–90–3	38–18–73–0	9–3–19–1				
6-8 January 1983	9–2–30–2	3–0–15–0	1–0–2–0	3–0–12–0					
v. Central Districts (Dunedin)	18–4–49–3	15–2–62–3		10.5–4–40–3	10–3–23–0				
14-15 January 1983	3–1–13–0	8–3–21–0		28–16–40–2	4–2–10–1				
v. Canterbury (Christchurch)	13.5–4–33–4	12–2–27–3	15–6–27–3	14–5–20–2	1–0–3–0				
20-21 January 1983	12–6–20–2	12–2–37–1	2–0–5–0						
v. Canterbury (Invercargill)		4–1–14–0	7–1–17–1	19–11–34–4					
28-29 January 1983		4–3–1–0	6–4–7–1	20–8–45–4					
v. Wellington (Lower Hutt)	18.2–4–50–1	19–7–44–4	15–5–44–0	24–9–38–1	2–1–1–0				
4-6 February 1983	10–3–25–0	15–5–36–3	7.4–3–14–0	11–5–26–1					
v. Auckland (Dunedin)	21–11–36–4	21–9–36–2	19.5–4–72–0	18.5–7–36–2	6–0–23–0				7–1–13–1
11-13 February 1983		15–4–43–2		5–2–18–0					
	165.4–50–397–22	224–56–603–22	138.3–40–375–9	290–127–604–30	51–12–149–4	1.5–0–1–0	1–0–1–0	0.2–0–5–0	7–1–13–1
	av. 18.04	av. 27.40	av. 41.66	av. 20.13	av. 37.25	—	—	—	av. 13.00

a G. J. Dawson 0.1–0–2–0   † S. Adams retired hurt

f one-day cricket. But the New Zealanders still took some pleasure from scoring 304, for it topped by two runs the 302 which Australia had scored against them in the second HWSC final at Melbourne, and became the highest one-day score of this giddy Australasian summer.

But where, after all the froth and bubble had subsided, did all this leave New Zealand cricket in terms of playing strength? It is one thing to win a string of one-day internationals, or to take two soft Test wins against an out-of-luck side such as Sri Lanka. It is another thing to attract enormous public interest in the fizz and pop of one-day matches, and still maintain that support in the sterner contests of five-day tests. But at the very least the New Zealand cricketers of 1982–83 have re-awakened interest in cricket, and have attracted thousands more youngsters to the playing of the game – and thousands more adults into becoming involved in some manner or another.

And the mad, merry season has left New Zealand with a solid core of very experienced players who know how to win, and a decidedly interesting bunch of younger men who are not all that far away from international class.

The batting will, for the next year or two, be built round John Wright, Bruce Edgar, Glenn Turner (provided he is available), Geoff Howarth and Jeremy Coney. The bowling will be based on Richard Hadlee, who might be coming into the autumn of his career, Martin Snedden, Lance Cairns and Ewen Chatfield, who now has the confidence of knowing that he can remove test-class batsmen. These nine players started the season as the basis of the side and really not one of them showed any decline, apart from Howarth whose batting technique has acquired some flaws, but who remains the obvious leader.

Turner was seldom out of the news during the summer, whether it be conjecture about his availability, praise of his sublime batsmanship, being the butt of ill-mannered criticism from the Australian captain Kim Hughes, or making

himself available for the Prudential World Cup, but not the subsequent test tour of England.

New Zealanders had not seen Turner bat for his country since 1977, and he had played only occasionally for Otago since. So his batting was a revelation to many of us. He played so many memorable innings, some of them annoyingly brief, others of the purest class such as his 88 and 94 in consecutive matches against England in one-day matches at Auckland and Wellington. It was hard to reconcile memories of the methodical, acquisitive Turner of the early 1970s with this flamboyant fellow whose batting has become a vehicle for his own entertainment. He gave the final signature to the season with his century in the final one-dayer against Sri Lanka at Auckland (after being dropped from a simple chance at six) and afterward said that after a flourishing progress into the 70s he had worked on to a century 'because it seemed to matter to some people'.

The old Turner arguments arose when he stated that he would only be available for the World Cup, and did not want to play the test tour of England. But this time there was no rancour. Turner has now taken on employment as a sports officer with the University of Otago, and part of his duties include surveys of sporting facilities and their use in Otago and Southland, which is a very wide parish. Another of his thoughts was that he had stepped down from Worcestershire because he did not want to face the long grind of an English county season – and that he would have been committing himself to five months of similarly hard labour if he had been available for both the World Cup and the England tour. But the obvious reason is that Turner now prefers the colour and flourish (and the ability to entertain himself, and thus others) in the one-day game. The long drawn-out process of test cricket does not offer the same appeal.

There was the comment from people in high NZCC places that Turner must be available for all the English tour, and not just the World Cup. Ten or fifteen years ago this argument, based on emotion, might well have become fact. But the practicalities of modern cricket swayed the issue in Turner's favour. He is one of the finest one-day batsmen in world cricket and therefore he could not be excluded from the World Cup simply because he chose not to be available for the later tour of England. And every ringing blow from that massive bat of his leant weight to Turner's argument.

A handful of decidedly interesting players gravitated round the basic group of nine players mentioned a few paragraphs back. Some of them made significant progress, others slipped back.

Two of the latter were Gary Troup, the tall left-arm medium-fast bowler, and Peter Webb, the jaunty little right-hand batsman. Troup, who had looked such a good prospect against the West Indians four seasons before, never quite adjusted to the demands of limited-over bowling. He became the easiest target for the batsmen (in an attack based very much on economical operation) and this did his confidence no good at all. Webb was taken as a batsman who had some basic ability as a wicket-keeper, and thus appeared to be a better one-day prospect than Warren Lees, whose batting is a thing of puckish moods. Webb played one or two useful low-order innings in Australia, but the emergence of Hadlee and Cairns as one-day all-rounders did not give Webb the chance to develop in the pressure-cooker atmosphere of one-day cricket.

P. W. Hills	C. Dickel	K. Ibadulla	Byes	Leg-byes	Wides	No-balls	Total	Wkts
				2	2	1	271	10
			1			3	152	2a
–2–36–0	31–4–104–2		2	5		4	370	10
	11–1–15–1			12		4	380	10
	3–1–3–1		2	3	1	2	70	3
	11–3–38–1	6–1–21–0		4		7	244	10
	11–5–22–0	6–2–12–0	1	6		3	128	3
			5	1	2	4	99	10
	10.5–5–22–5		1	5	1	3	117	10
	4.2–4–0–3	11–1–30–2	4	4		3	106	10
		17.2–7–22–5	6	8			89	10
	23–10–40–3		2	8	1	9	224	10
	11–2–28–0		2	4		7	155	4
		10–3–16–0	8	10		4	159	9†
		4–0–26–0	5	8		3	198	2
–2–	116.1–35–	54.2–14–						
–0	272–16	127–7						
	av. 17.00	av. 25.40						

Wellington 1982-3
First Class Matches

BATTING	v. Northern Districts (Wellington) 27-29 Dec. 1982		v. Central Districts (New Plymouth) 1-3 January 1983		v. Otago (Alexandra) 6-8 January 1983		v. Canterbury (Christchurch) 13-14 January 1983		v. Auckland (Wellington) 21-23 January 1983		v. Auckland (Auckland) 29-31 January 1983		v. Otago (Lower Hutt) 4-6 February 1983		v. Central Districts (Wellington) 11-13 February 1983		Inns	NOs	Runs	HS	Av
R. H. Vance	26	3*			112	—	32	41	61	—	14	31	42	33	15	52	12	1	462	112	42.00
B. A. Edgar	146	4*	17	0*													4	2	167	146	83.50
R. W. Ormiston	44		179		25	0	0	30	26	—	45	26	20	42*	5	60*	13	2	502	179	45.63
E. J. Gray	35*		25		69	6	8	17	24	—	45	53*	33	7	1	10	13	2	333	69	30.27
J. F. M. Morrison	10*		0														2	1	10	10*	10.00
J. V. Coney			93														1	—	93	93	93.00
E. B. McSweeney	—	—	4*	—	47	—	5	8	130	—	27	61*	0	—	32*	—	9	3	314	130	52.33
B. W. Cederwall	—	—	26	—	28	15*	0	1	34	—	20	—	18	—	3	—	9	1	145	34	18.12
A. C. S. Pigott	—	—	—	—	35	—	—	—	24	—	21	—	1	—	7	—	5	—	88	35	17.60
S. J. Maguiness	—	—	—	—	7*	—	11	4	6	—	0	—	7*	—	5	—	7	2	40	11	8.00
E. J. Chatfield	—	—	—	—	—	—	—	—	—	—	—	—	—	—	—	—	—				
P. J. Holland	—	—	52	4*	4	—	—	—	56	—	45	29	1	7	17	4	10	1	219	56	24.33
K. D. James	—	—	0*	—	—	—	11	16*									3	2	27	16*	27.00
S. B. Cater	—	—	—	—	12	—	3*	20									3	1	35	20	17.50
R. J. Pither	—	—	—	—	14	13*	9	4									4	1	40	14	13.33
G. N. Cederwall	—	—	—	—	11	28	3	0							6	—	5	—	48	28	9.60
J. B. Boyle							8	7	1	—	0	26	76	27	11	67	9	—	223	76	24.78
T. Ritchie									4	—	8	24	6	26*	8	16*	7	2	92	26*	18.40
B. Rule									0*	—	4*	—	0	—			3	2	4	4*	4.00
Byes			3			2	11	14	15		3	10	2	2	8	5					
Leg-byes	4		8		12	3	3	3	4		5	6	8	4	6	6					
Wides			2				1	1					1			3					
No-balls	2	1	17		4	2		1	5		1	3	9	7	5	4					
Total	267	10	424	4	380	70	104	167	390		238	269	224	155	129	227					
Wickets	3	0	7	0	10	3	10	10	10		10	5	10	4	10	4					
Result	D		W		W		L		W		D		W		D						
Points	3		16		16		0		16		4		16		0						

Catches

27 – E. B. McSweeney (ct 25/st 2)
8 – B. W. Cederwall
7 – R. H. Vance and R. W. Ormiston
6 – E. J. Gray
5 – T. Ritchie (including one as sub)
4 – J. V. Coney, S. J. Maguiness and G. N. Cederwall (including one as sub)
3 – A. C. S. Pigott and J. B. Boyle (including one as sub)
2 – J. F. M. Morrison and P. J. Holland
1 – E. J. Chatfield and K. D. James

BOWLING	A. C. S. Pigott	E. J. Chatfield	S. J. Maguiness	E. J. Gray	B. W. Cederwall	J. F. M. Morrison	J. V. Coney	K. D. James	P. J. Holland
v. Northern Districts (Wellington) 27-29 December 1982	25-6-70-2 / 6-2-23-2	31.1-9-76-6 / 34-15-61-1	29-12-60-2 / 17-3-56-2	11-6-20-0 / 1-0-17-0	5-1-21-0 / 13-3-39-1	4.3-1-27-0	1-1-0-0 / 4-0-20-1		
v. Central Districts (New Plymouth) 1-3 January 1983			26.3-14-42-3 / 27.3-9-69-5	15-7-29-1 / 8-6-6-0	28-13-58-2 / 26-15-51-2	1-0-4-0	12-6-20-1 / 8-4-18-0	8-1-30-2 / 7-3-13-0	11-2-23-0 / 2-0-10-0
v. Otago (Alexandra) 6-8 January 1983	17.4-8-47-5 / 21-4-93-5		12-8-18-1 / 26-11-40-0	17-7-37-3 / 26.5-4-84-2	9-3-27-1				
v. Canterbury (Christchurch) 13-14 January 1983			35-13-62-3	6-1-18-0 / 5-1-3-0	10-2-17-1			16.5-3-52-3	
v. Auckland (Wellington) 21-23 January 1983	16.4-2-51-3 / 24-8-53-3		17-7-28-4 / 20-8-36-2		2-0-14-0 / 9.5-1-42-3		7-1-20-1 / 6-4-7-0		
v. Auckland (Auckland) 29-31 January 1983	19-7-38-4 / 7-1-30-0		20-9-34-1 / 6-1-23-1		50.5-20-100-4 / 7-3-16-1		9.5-1-12-0 / 4-0-10-1		8-1-17-0 / 7-1-19-1
v. Otago (Lower Hutt) 4-6 February 1983	18-5-65-2 / 18-8-47-4		16-6-31-0 / 15-5-26-0		10.2-4-23-3 / 21-11-53-1		16-8-34-4 / 16-8-40-3		12-6-12-0
v. Central Districts (Wellington) 11-13 February 1983	24.2-5-64-3		14-6-20-0	20-9-50-1	12-4-32-2				3-0-21-0
	196.4-56-581-33 av. 17.60	119.1-47-248-15 av. 16.53	250-102-469-17 av. 27.58	241.5-95-596-22 av. 27.09	117-43-284-17 av. 16.70	5.3-1-31-0 av. —	25-11-58-2 av. 29.00	31.5-7-95-5 av. 19.00	43-10-102-2 av. 51.00

a R. J. Pither 10-2-21-0
R. J. Pither 4-3-1-0
5.1-3-7-0

b R. H. Vance 1-1-0-0
R. W. Ormiston 6-0-26-1
J. B. Boyle 2-0-19-0

Much to everyone's surprise John Morrison was recalled, the ripe age of 35, for the short shake-down tour of [A]ustralia in December – a tour designed to put several can-[di]dates for the later major tour under the microscope. Mor-[ris]on batted very well on that short tour (as did Howarth [wi]th two first-class centuries) and so could not be left out of [th]e major tour. After a quiet start Morrison became a [de]cidedly useful player. His low-order batting was solid and [se]nsible, and his left-arm slow bowling became an interest-[in]g, if scarcely potent, part of the bowling pattern. Even on [th]e most helpful of pitches Morrison is a very modest spinner [of] the ball, so on Australian pitches his deviation from the [pi]tch was minimal. But he could drift the ball, he was acc-[ur]ate, he did not offer the batsman any help in getting power [in]to a stroke. So to many people's amusement, including his [ow]n, Morrison bowled some economical spells, and [oc]casionally fiddled out good batsmen.

He held his place for the one-dayers against England in [N]ew Zealand, but was not wanted in the Tests. Nor was he [c]hosen for the tours of England, a fact that annoyed Mor-[ri]son so much he stated publicly that he had been 'betrayed' [b]y the selectors. It was a hard word to use, and one that [s]uggests that Morrison will not be required by the national [se]lectors of the future.

However, if the decline of Troup and Webb and the [d]iscarding of Morrison were the minuses of the season, the [p]lusses were rather more numerous.

Jeff Crowe, a former New Zealand secondary schools' [c]aptain, had spent five years playing cricket in and for South [A]ustralia with so much success he seemed to be heading for [a] place in the Australian team. When this door seemed to [c]lose, Crowe returned to Auckland, and in several early club [in]nings looked every bit as good a batsman as his Adelaide [r]eputation would suggest.

However a broken thumb interrupted his progress, he was [n]ot selected (on the basis that none of the selectors had seen him bat for years) for the preliminary tour of Australia, but gained a place in the fourteen-man side for the BHWSC expedition. Crowe played several solid innings, but never often enough to command a permanent place. He played in the Tests against Sri Lanka, again without scoring heavily, although he played a longish hand for a very valuable 36 in the first innings of the second Test when the other batsmen looked decidedly rusty.

Then Crowe finished with a flourish in the one-day internationals against Sri Lanka, and won himself the tour of England. He looks a batsman of decided promise, is an accurate fielder, and has a very mature attitude. All he requires now is the breakthrough of a big innings at international level.

When the New Zealand team to tour Australia was announced it was relayed over the public address system to the Aucklanders playing on the Eden Park No 2 ground, which, incidentally, has now developed into one of the best non-Test playing areas in New Zealand. The list did not contain Martin Crowe, Jeff's young brother, who had just scored a century for Auckland, and who was visibly shaken by hearing the news on the field.

Martin had made his test debut against the Australians the summer before as a nineteen-year-old, but had a tough baptism against Dennis Lillee and Jeff Thomson, and was a sadder, if wiser, young man afterward. The national selectors, Frank Cameron, John Guy and Don Neely, worked on the theory that Martin was at a stage in his career when a recipe of one-day internationals in Australia was not required. It would be better for him to remain at home, play eight three-day and five one-day matches for Auckland, and to rebuild the confidence shattered by the Australians the previous summer.

Martin may have succeeded in Australia, but it was still a perceptive piece of selection, or non-selection. He remained with Auckland, scored three centuries, worked on his medium-fast bowling when a heel injury allowed, and finished the summer with 666 runs in first-class matches, average just over 50. Then the selectors worked Martin back into the New Zealand squad as twelfth man, played him in the Bushfire game at Sydney, where he scored 62 on a devilish wicket, and took wickets as well.

The following weekend Martin, mostly in partnership with his brother Jeff, played two healthy innings against Sri Lanka, and was an obvious choice for England. Martin is no stranger to English conditions, for he spent one season on the ground staff at Lord's, and last season in league cricket. A tall, strapping young man, he has promise of being a strong batsman, and his medium-fast right-arm bowling is developing to the point that he can almost be classed as an all-rounder.

Like Martin Crowe, four other players who were to win the tour of England made big strides forward while the top players were in Australia.

Ian Smith went to Australia in 1980–81 as Lees' understudy as wicket-keeper and took over when Lees injured a hand. Last summer Smith's keeping seemed to develop some rough edges, and Lees regained his place. New Zealand selectors still prefer their wicket-keepers to score runs, so Smith did just that in the Shell Trophy matches, scoring centuries in three consecutive games, and those were feats which the national selectors could not ignore.

G. N. Cederwall	S. B. Cater	B. Rule	Byes	Leg-byes	Wides	No-balls	Total	Wkts
			1	13		5	266	10
			6	5		4	258	7
			6		1	5	218	10
			6	7	1	3	209	10
4–20–0	9–3–16–0		3		1	18	160	10
1–12–0			3		1	5	286	10a
–3–41–0	19–5–44–3			5	1	14	255	10
							20	0
		11–3–36–2	1			3	153	10
		11–3–32–2		8			178	10
		3–0–16–0	5		1		224	10
		2–0–15–0				1	159	5b
		4–0–22–0	3	1		2	181	10
		8–3–10–0	2	5		2	197	10
–5–47–4			5	5	3	12	259	10
–10–	28–8–	39–9–						
0–4	60–3	131–4						
30.00	av. 20.00	av. 32.75						

Sri Lankans in Australasia, 1983
First Class Matches

BATTING

	v. NSW (Sydney) 10-12 Feb		v. Tasmania (Devonport) 14-16 Feb		v. Canterbury (Christchurch) 19-21 Feb		v. Auckland (Auckland) 26-28 Feb		First Test Match (Christchurch) 4-6 March		Second Test Match (Wellington) 11-15 March		Inns	NOs	Runs	HS	Av
S. R. de S. Wettimuny	9	—			8	22	105	—	63*	7	8	9	8	1	231	105	33.00
M. de S. Wettimuny	0	—	31	24	16	18	9	—	17	5	6	0	10	—	126	31	12.60
R. G. de Alwis	42	—			0	8			0	3			5	—	53	42	10.60
R. L. Dias	15	—	27	25	40	5							5	—	112	40	22.40
L. R. D. Mendis	15	—			0*	—							2	1	15	15	15.00
R. S. Madugalle	35	—	24	9	30	81	64	—	34	23	79	13	10	—	392	81	39.20
D. S. de Silva	65	—			26	17	15*	—	7	52	61	0	8	—	243	65	34.71
J. R. Ratnayeke	5	—	22*	64*	9	26			0	7	29*	12	9	3	174	64*	29.00
S. Jeganathan	10	—	14	74	12	14*	27	—	6	8	5	0	10	1	170	74	18.88
A. L. F. de Mel	0*	—					12	—					2	1	12	12	12.00
V. John	—	—			6*	3	0	—	0	3*	0	8*	7	3	20	8*	5.00
E. R. N. S. Fernando			72	19			27	—	0	46	12	12	7	—	188	72	26.85
Y. Goonasekera			27	7			7	—	4	8	13	23	7	—	89	27	12.71
S. A. R. Silva			0	0			43	—			8	0	5	—	51	43	10.20
R. G. C. E. Wijesuriya			—	1									1	—	1	1	1.00
R. J. Ratnayeke			—	—	0	0	0	—	1	0	12	1					
Byes	1		2		9	8	11		2	1	1	5					
Leg-byes			4	3	5	4	13		7	6	5	10					
Wides				1		1			5								
No-balls	10				5	8	5		3	1	1						
Total	207		221	229	167	214	338		144	175	240	93					
Wickets	9		7	8	9†	9	10		10	10	10	10					
Result	D		D		L		D		L		L						

† L. R. D. Mendis retired hurt, absent hurt

Catches
9 – S. A. R. Silva (inc. one as sub)
8 – Y. Goonasekera
6 – R. G. de Alwis
3 – D. S. de Silva, S. Jeganathan and J. R. Ratnayeke
2 – A. L. F. de Mel, R. S. Madugalle and M. de S. Wettimuny
1 – E. R. N. S. Fernando, R. G. C. E. Wijesuriya, S. R. de S. Wettimuny and V. John

BOWLING

	A. L. F. de Mel	V. John	J. R. Ratnayeke	D. S. de Silva	S. Jeganathan	M. de S. Wettimuny	R. J. Ratnayeke	Y. Goonasekera
v. New South Wales (Sydney) 10-12 February	12-1-49-1 / 6-0-24-0	14-1-41-1 / 12-2-27-1	6-1-12-0 / 6-1-20-2	22-3-70-1	22-5-58-2 / 10-3-16-0	1-0-3-0		
v. Tasmania (Devonport) 14-16 February		15-4-52-0 / 12-2-37-2	16-3-34-4 / 4-0-13-0		16-4-38-0 / 6-2-11-0	5-3-6-0	19-12-34-2 / 10-4-39-1	4-0-17-1
v. Canterbury (Christchurch) 19-21 February		14-3-55-2 / 3.1-0-20-0	7-1-27-0	25-9-80-1	19-6-45-0		29-2-101-4 / 4-0-16-2	
v. Auckland (Auckland) 26-28 February	17-9-36-2 / 5-0-13-0	11-3-15-1 / 9-3-31-1		17-5-45-1 / 27-8-44-2	8-2-28-0 / 13-2-35-1	1-0-6-0 / 4-2-9-0	23-10-50-5 / 8-1-32-1	12-3-16-0
First Test Match (Christchurch) 4-6 March		12-2-45-2	31-9-93-3	22-10-41-1	5-2-12-0		31-8-125-2	
Second Test Match (Wellington) 11-15 March		25.2-9-60-5 / 8-2-38-1	14-3-36-0 / 8.1-4-20-1	9-5-13-1 / 6-1-18-1			24-5-81-4 / 15-0-46-1	
	40-10-122-3 av. 40.66	135.3-31-421-16 av. 26.31	92.1-22-255-10 av. 25.50	128.5-41-311-8 av. 38.87	99-26-243-3 av. 81.00	11-5-24-0 —	163-42-524-22 av. 23.81	16-3-33-1 av. 33.00

Evan Gray, the tallish Wellington left-arm spinner and middle-order batsman, has several times been regarded as international material, especially for a longish tour. He was again consistent in Shell Trophy matches, and won a place in a New Zealand B team which made a tour of Australia in February–March, playing three-day second class matches in country centres. The main aim of the tour seemed to be the finding of an up-and-coming fast bowler, and four were chosen – Sean Tracy, a burly young Aucklander, Derek Stirling and Gary Robertson of Central Districts and, after Mark Farrington withdrew through injury, Brendon Bracewell, who has never quite realised the youthful potential he showed in England in 1978.

This was a less than satisfactory tour for the opposition was of modest quality, the match arrangements often second-rate, and none of the faster bowlers leaped to the head of the queue. But Gray did, bowling consistently and effectively for 40 wickets, leading the averages, and winning a place in the England tour.

Similarly John Bracewell, Brendon's brother and a genuine off-spinner of the ball, was not required in Australia, but left to work his passage with his new province, Auckland. Bracewell, used to quick success on the turning pitches at Carisbrook, had a rather modest bowling season with Auckland, but his batting developed so well he scored just over 400 runs, average in the high 30s, and regained his New Zealand place for the tour.

One of the most distinctive of the new faces is that of Trevor Franklin, the tall, young opening batsman who was called in from the B team tour of Australia as an opening batsman in the Bushfire match at Sydney, without conspicuous success for he started his New Zealand career with a nought.

Franklin is close to 6ft 6in, slim, and with a lantern jaw and serious face which makes him look older than his twenty-one years. He is also a very good striker of the ball, predictably at his best from the front foot. He started with Auckland in the 1981–82 season by scoring a handful of moderate scores, most of them coming quickly for he went eagerly for his shots. After scoring heavily in league cricket Franklin ran into a bad patch early last season, and it seemed as if the bowlers had worked out his style, gave him nothing to drive, and let him destroy himself. However, perhaps the main problem was that he kept bobbing his head up and down as the bowler approached. Somewhere Franklin found the solution and he had a very good year for Auckland, with three centuries, 664 runs and, most important of all, a substantial score in every game.

So the development of Jeff and Martin Crowe and Franklin as batsmen of international potential has been one of the most heartening aspects of the New Zealand season. The progress made by Smith, Gray and Bracewell gives New Zealand much more bowling and wicket-keeping scope. The great need now is the development of one or two genuinely fast strike bowlers who can start to take over the Richard Hadlee role.

Tracy made his debut and may well be the quickest prospect. Stirling, a very big young man, and Robertson have possibilities, although they lack the classical action of the really fast bowler. Sadly, injuries may prevent Brendon Bracewell from developing genuine speed.

On the horizon there is other talent. Ervin McSweeney, who led Wellington to victory in the Shell Trophy in Morrison's absence, could develop into a really good batsman-wicket-keeper. John Reid, the elegant Auckland left-hand batsman who already has a Test century in his locker, was left behind by the one-day mania, and did not have his best season with Auckland. Still, Reid still looks a batsman of test-match technique.

Bruce Blair, the Otago left-hander, did not survive the preliminary tour of Australia, but finished off the season for Otago with scores of 106, 143, 70, 0 and 90.

As mentioned earlier Wellington retained the Shell Trophy by once again producing a consistent team effort. Auckland, the early favourite, started promisingly with two wins, but dropped out of sight over the next six games. However, Auckland were invariably an effective one-day side, and duly won the one-day Shell Cup final.

And, as a tail-piece, it should be noted that age does not wither the really good players.

During the summer the minor associations in New Zealand compete, on a challenge basis, for the Hawke Cup, which has been in existence since 1911. Usually the cup rests in some smaller centre – Nelson has had a long career as cup champions – for long periods of time, and comes into the news only when it moves. Last season Northland, bolstered by the forty-two-year-old Bob Cunis, the former New Zealand medium-fast bowler, and Brian Dunning, forty-three and who had played for New Zealand in one-day matches, sallied south and won the cup.

Twice Northland were in batting trouble – especially against North Canterbury whose bowling was headed by the forty-five-year-old off-spinner Frank Rapley – and twice Dunning scored centuries from No 7 to hold the cup in Whangarei. But then a team of youngsters from Hawkes Bay (for David O'Sullivan, the former Hampshire and New Zealand left-arm spinner was only thirty-nine) went north, this time Dunning could only score 60 not out, and Hawkes Bay won on the first innings by 40 runs or so.

So there was something for everyone in this marvellous New Zealand cricket summer of 1982–83 – the season when the New Zealand team realised they were good enough to win, and just kept on winning.

R.G.C.E. Wijesuriya	Byes	Leg-byes	Wides	No-balls	Total	Wkts
	2	2		16	253	5
—1–20–0		1	2	14	104	3
		3		1	199	7
		2		2	110	3
	2	12	5	17	344	8
		1		1	38	2
	2	9	3	4	198	10
	2	4			186	5
		14	2	12	344	10
	4	3	3	1	201	10
		11		1	134	4
—1–20–0						

SECTION G
The Indian Season

The Ranji Trophy, The Duleep Trophy,
The Irani Cup and the Gopalan Trophy

Sanil Gavaskar. (A.S.P.)

With the demands of Test cricket so great, performances in the domestic season in India become more important than ever with trips to Pakistan and West Indies to be won by those who gave good accounts of themselves. It was the deeds of players like Sekhar, Sandhu and Gaekwad in the Duleep and Ranji Trophies which influenced the selectors in their choices, in the case of Gaekwad an enforcement of the view that his Test career was not over.

Duleep Trophy

Quarter Final

2, 3 and 4 October 1982

at Brabourne Stadium, Bombay

Central Zone 172 (G. Sharma 51, Maninder Singh 4 for 66) and 152 (S. Khandkar 54, Maninder Singh 5 for 48, Kirti Azad 4 for 39)
North Zone 425 (Yashpal Sharma 134, R.N. Kapil Dev 89, Gursharan Singh 72, S.C. Khanna 64)

North Zone won by an innings and 101 runs

Semi-Finals

8, 9, 10 and 11 October 1982

at Wankhede Stadium, Bombay

West Zone 313 (R.G. Borde 89, S. Keshwala 56 not out,

B.S. Sandhu 56, R.J. Shastri 51, T.A. Sekhar 5 for 66) an[d]
231 for 8 dec (L. Siveramakrishnan 5 for 63, M.D. Gunja[...]
retired hurt 69)
South Zone 273 (G.R. Viswanath 56, A. Jabbar 52, B.S[.]
Sandhu 6 for 86) and 86 for 3

Match drawn. West Zone won on first innings.

at Brabourne Stadium, Bombay

North Zone 664 for 5 dec. (M.B. Amarnath 207, Kirt[i]
Azad 156, A. Malhotra 139, R. Shukla 77)
East Zone 161 (H. Gidwani 54, R. Shukla 4 for 31[,]
Maninder Singh 4 for 48) and 201 (J. Arun Lal 68, H[.]
Gidwani 58, Maninder Singh 5 for 53)

North Zone won by an innings and 302 runs

DULEEP TROPHY

In 1981–82, North Zone had lost the quarter final matc[h]
with South Zone on the toss of a coin, two and a half day[s]
of the match at Trivandrum having been lost to rain. Thi[s]
season the triumph of North Zone, led by Kapil Dev, wa[s]
total, their win in the final by 8 wickets being their closes[t]
match in the tournament. Their success owed much to th[e]
fine batting of Yashpal Sharma and Mohinder Amarnat[h]
and to the splendid left-arm spin bowling of Maninder Sing[h]
who took 18 wickets at 14.16 runs each in the first tw[o]
matches, but, ironically, did not take a wicket in the fina[l]

DULEEP TROPHY FINAL: NORTH ZONE v. WEST ZONE
14, 15, 16 and 17 October 1982 at Wankhede Stadium, Bombay

WEST ZONE

	FIRST INNINGS		SECOND INNINGS	
A.D. Gaekwad	lbw, b Madan Lal	2	c Sharma, b Madan Lal	104
G.A.M.H. Parkar	c Azad, b Madan Lal	26	c Shukla, b Madan Lal	11
S.M. Gavaskar†	c Azad, b Kapil Dev	1	(4) c Azad, b Madan Lal	67
A.V. Mankad	b Kapil Dev	44	(6) b Madan Lal	1
D.B. Vengsarkar	c Azad, b Madan Lal	1	(3) c Chauhan, b Dev	50
R.J. Shastri	b Madan Lal	5	(5) run out	30
R.G. Borde	lbw, b Madan Lal	3	(8) run out	0
S. Keshwala	lbw, b Madan Lal	0	(7) c Sharma, b Madan Lal	5
B.S. Sandhu	b Amarnath	10	b Kapil Dev	13
S. Gudge	c and b Valson	37	not out	4
Z.A. Parkar*	not out	20	c Amarnath, b Kapil Dev	0
Extras	b 7, lb 5, nb 3	15	b 13, lb 10, nb 6	29
	penalty runs	4	penalty runs	16
		168		330

	O	M	R	W	O	M	R	W
Kapil Dev	18	6	37	2	31.5	4	97	3
Madan Lal	25	9	59	6	25	7	63	5
Valson	12.2	3	24	1	9	1	37	—
Amarnath	7	1	18	1				
Maninder Singh	5	1	6	—	17	4	45	—
Shukla	3	1	5	—	6	1	14	—
Kirti Azad					8	—	29	—

FALL OF WICKETS
1- 14, 2- 15, 3- 65, 4- 72, 5- 84, 6- 86, 7- 87, 8- 96, 9- 113
1- 43, 2- 123, 3- 237, 4- 272, 5- 273, 6- 291, 7- 291, 8- 304, 9- 314

NORTH ZONE

	FIRST INNINGS		SECOND INNINGS	
C.P.S. Chauhan	c Gaekwad, b Sandhu	0	not out	63
R. Shukla	c Gaekwad, b Shastri	31	b Shastri	19
A. Malhotra	c and b Shastri	76	c Z. Parkar, b Shastri	18
M.B. Amarnath	run out	80	not out	67
Yashpal Sharma*	c Borde, b Shastri	83		
Kirti Azad	b Shastri	4		
Gursharan Singh	lbw, b Shastri	0		
R.N. Kapil Dev†	c Keshwala, b Shastri	39		
S. Madan Lal	c Keshwala, b Gudge	8		
S. Valson	c Borde, b Shastri	0		
Maninder Singh	not out	0		
Extras	b 2, lb 3, nb 3	8	lb 2, nb 1	3
		329	(for 8 wickets)	170

	O	M	R	W	O	M	R	W
Sandhu	22	11	76	1	13	5	18	—
Keshwala	20	5	56	—	2	1	5	—
Shastri	49.3	10	105	7	20	7	37	2
Gudge	22	6	52	1	14	2	60	—
Borde	5	1	7	—	8		29	—
Mankad	9	3	25	—	7	1	14	—
Gavaskar					1	—	4	—

FALL OF WICKETS
1- 0, 2- 70, 3- 143, 4- 232, 5- 239, 6- 243, 7- 299, 8- 311, 9- 328
1- 25, 2- 49

North Zone won by 8 wickets

IRANI CUP: DELHI v. REST OF INDIA
21, 22, 23 and 24 October 1982 at Delhi

DELHI

	FIRST INNINGS			SECOND INNINGS	
C.P.S. Chauhan	c Parkar, b Sandhu	8		lbw, b Sandhu	26
R. Lamba	b Doshi	93		b Sandhu	46
Gursharan Singh	b Shastri	94		st Parkar, b Sivarama	18
M.B. Amarnath†	c Malhotra, b Doshi	127		c Gavaskar, b Shastri	52
Kirti Azad	c Shastri, b Sandhu	32		st Parkar, b Shastri	36
R. Shukla	lbw, b Sandhu	29		(7) c Parkar, b Sivarama	5
S. Madan Lal	c Parkar, b Sandhu	12		(6) b Arun Lal	0
S.C. Khanna*	b Sandhu	0		c and b Sivarama	0
R. Peter	c Srikkanth, b Doshi	3		st Parkar, b Doshi	46
S. Valson	c Srikkanth, b Doshi	14		lbw, b Sivarama	2
Maninder Singh	not out	1		not out	5
Extras		16			12
		429			**258**

	O	M	R	W	O	M	R	W
Sekhar	23	4	74	—	11	2	27	—
Sandhu	30	8	110	5	11	3	34	2
Srikkanth	1	—	4	—				
Doshi	29.2	11	66	4	13.1	4	31	1
Sivaramakrishnan	22	1	97	—	30	3	127	4
Shastri	21	6	62	1	23	12	27	3

FALL OF WICKETS
1- 32, 2- 172, 3- 268, 4- 337, 5- 385, 6- 400, 7- 404, 8- 407, 9- 415
1- 67, 2- 78, 3- 124, 4- 187, 5- 187, 6- 194, 7- 194, 8- 202, 9- 209

REST OF INDIA

	FIRST INNINGS		SECOND INNINGS	
K. Srikkanth	st Khanna, b Maninder	83	c Maninder, b Valson	110
J. Arun Lal	lbw, b Valson	5	(3) st Khanna, b Maninder	82
A. Malhotra	lbw, b Maninder	67	(5) not out	116
S.M. Patil	c Amarnath, b Maninder	0	b Azad	41
S.M. Gavaskar†	b Maninder	0	(2) c Lamba, b Maninder	28
R.J. Shastri	lbw, b Shukla	29	st Khanna, b Amarnath	26
B.S. Sandhu	st Khanna, b Maninder	20	not out	0
T.A. Sekhar	c Chauhan, b Shukla	12		
L. Sivaramakrishnan	not out	20		
Z.A. Parkar*	c Chauhan, b Maninder	0		
D.R. Doshi	c Maninder, b Shukla	11		
Extras		20		21
		267	(for 5 wickets)	**424**

	O	M	R	W	O	M	R	W
Madan Lal	8	3	44	—	7	4	10	—
Valson	13	1	56	1	5	—	52	1
Amarnath	4	—	15	—	6	—	40	1
Peter	2	—	8	—				
Maninder Singh	28	10	66	6	38.2	3	180	2
Shukla	16	1	44	3	14	—	70	—
Kirti Azad	9	4	14	—	13	2	51	1

FALL OF WICKETS
1- 16, 2- 123, 3- 125, 4- 125, 5- 199, 6- 203, 7- 220, 8- 240, 9- 240
1- 143, 2- 145, 3- 193, 4- 359, 5- 418

Rest of India won by 5 wickets

where Madan Lal bowled quite magnificently.

West Zone, who won the Trophy in the previous season, were somewhat fortunate to reach the final. They were 201 for 9 in the semi-final with South Zone, but Keshwala and Sandhu then added 112 for the last wicket. It was a decisive stand as the match was decided on the first innings where West Zone had a lead of 40.

IRANI CUP

The Irani Cup Match, named after the late Mr Z.R. Irani who was treasurer to the Board of Control for Cricket in India for over three decades, was played between the Ranji Trophy holders and the Rest of India. 162 runs behind on the first innings, Rest of India won a remarkable victory when they reached their target of 421 for the loss of only five wickets. Once more, the young spinner Maninder Singh was most impressive, and there was some equally fine bowling by Sivaramakrishnan, the leg-break bowler, who was to become the youngest player to represent India. Srikkanth, Malhotra and Arun Lal all batted magnificently as Rest of India scored runs at five an over to win the match.

Kapil Dev who led North Zone to success in the Duleep Trophy matches. (George Herringshaw)

THE RANJI TROPHY

North Zone

14 and 15 October 1982

at Srinagar

Jammu and Kashmir 129 (S. Talwar 5 for 21) and 135 (S. Talwar 5 for 51)
Haryana 246 (D. Sharma 102, R. Chadha 50) and 19 for 1

Haryana won by 9 wickets
Haryana 9 pts, Jammu and Kashmir 0 pts

20 and 21 October 1982

at Srinager

Punjab 273 (R. Handa 117, A. Kaul 5 for 74)
Jammu and Kashmir 97 (D. Chopra 7 for 32) and 140 (A. Ajaz 59, D. Chopra 7 for 52)

Match drawn
Punjab 5 pts, Jammu and Kashmir 3 pts

5, 6 and 7 December 1982

at Chandigarh

Haryana 301 (A. Malhotra 155, M. Prabhaker 5 for 88) and 64 for 0.
Delhi 366 (R. Shukla 163 not out)

Match drawn
Delhi 5 pts, Haryana 3 pts

at New Delhi

Punjab 386 (R. Handa 72, Y. Dutt 66, D. Chopra 62) and 128 for 5
Services 291 (B. Ghosh 134)

Match drawn
Punjab 5 pts, Services 3 pts

9, 10 and 11 December 1982

at New Delhi

Delhi 180 and 209 for 2 (R. Lamba 107 not out, C.P.S. Chauhan 76)
Punjab 313 (Y. Dutt 104, R. Shukla for 75)

Match drawn
Punjab 5 pts, Delhi 3 pts

10, 11 and 12 December 1982

at New Delhi

Haryana 481 for dec (A. Malhotra 228, M.B. Amarnath 100 not out)
Services 160 and 294 (Sudhakarrao 88, Ratandas 59, A. Jha 53, C. Sharma 5 for 59)

Haryana won by an innings and 27 runs
Haryana 9 pts, Services 0 pts

15, 16 and 17 December 1982

at New Delhi

Services 164 (A.K. Sethi 57, Kirti Azad 5 for 47) and 22? (P. Sur 110)
Delhi 297 (Gursharan Singh 60, R. Shukla 53) and 89 fo 1

Delhi won by 9 wickets
Delhi 8 pts, Services 0 pts

18, 19 and 20 December 1982

at Chandigarh

Punjab 208 (Balkar Singh 74) and 250 for 8 (Amarji Kapyee 120 not out, S. Talwar 5 for 58)
Haryana 313 (R. Jolly 88 not out, Amankumar 65, A Malhotra 60)

Match drawn
Haryana 5 pts, Punjab 3 pts

at Jammu

Jammu and Kashmir 132 and 84
Delhi 150 (A. Kavl 7 for 54) and 67 for 3

Delhi won by 7 wickets
Delhi 8 pts, Jammu and Kashmir 0 pts

24, 25 and 26 December 1982

at Jammu

Services 81 for 9 dec (M. Iqbal 6 for 35) and 326 (C Vijay 98, Ratandas 51, A. Kavl 5 for 110)
Jammu and Kashmir 328 (V. Sharma 92, P. Akhtar 55, A. Jha 5 for 115) and 73 for 6

Jammu and Kashmir won by 4 wickets
Jammu and Kashmir 8 pts, Services 0 pts

North Zone Table

	P	W	L	D	Pts
Haryana	4	2		2	26
Delhi	4	2		2	24
Punjab	4			4	18
Jammu and Kashmir	4	1	2	1	11
Services	4		3	1	3

West Zone

20, 21 and 22 November 1982

at Kolhapur

Bombay 370 (K. Mokashi 80, S. Hattangadi 69) and 145 for 3 dec
Maharashtra 279 (M.D. Gunjal 77, R. Thakkar 8 for 102) and 112 for 4 (S.B. Nimbalkar 69)

Match drawn
Bombay 5 pts, Maharashtra 3 pts

at Baroda

Gujarat 184 (P. Desai 58, S. Hazare 5 for 47) and 162 (J. Bakrania 71, S. Hazare 6 for 46)
Baroda 390 for 6 dec (A.D. Gaekwad 225, R.V. Hazare 63)

Baroda won by an innings and 44 runs
Baroda 9 pts, Gujarat 0 pts

27, 28 and 29 November 1982

at Baroda

Maharashtra 180 (M.D. Gunjal 59) and 187 (R. Punawala 52, R.B. Bhalekar 65 not out)
Baroda 253 (A.D. Gaekwad 64) and 115 for 1 (A.D. Gaekwad 81 not out)

Baroda won by 9 wickets
Baroda 8 pts, Maharashtra 0 pts

28, 29 and 30 November 1982

at Surat

Gujarat 146 (K. Bhrahmbhatt 59, S. Keshwala 5 for 48) and 259 (J. Bakrania 100, B. Mistry 64)
Saurashtra 225 (S. Keshwala 62, A. Patel 59) and 185 for 7 (K. Chauhan 51, J. Pandya 5 for 47)

Saurashtra won by 3 wickets
Saurashtra 8 pts, Gujarat 0 pts

4, 5 and 6 December 1982

at Bombay

Bombay 243 (G.A.M.H. Parker 52, S. Hazare 5 for 29) and 101 for 0 (L. Rajput 64 not out)
Baroda 337 for 7 dec (A.D. Gaekwad 144, R.V. Hazare 77, R.Y. Deshmukh 51)

Match drawn
Baroda 5 pts, Bombay 3 pts

at Surendranagar

Saurashtra 262 (K. Chauhan 79, K.D. Ghavri 58, R. Daniel 6 for 60) and 158
Maharashtra 223 and 198 for 5 (R.B. Bhalekar 83 not out)

Maharashtra won by 5 wickets
Maharashtra 8 pts, Saurashtra 0 pts

11, 12 and 13 December 1982

at Bombay

Gujarat 101 (R. Thakkar 6 for 25) and 196 (P. Desai 55, J. Bakrania 51)
Bombay 363 for 2 dec (R. Mankad 138 not out, A.V. Mankad 121 not out, L. Rajput 54)

Bombay won by an innings and 66 runs
Bombay 9 pts, Gujarat 0 pts

at Baroda

Saurashtra 233 and 118 for 2 (S. Keshwala 63 not out)
Baroda 401 for 8 dec (A.D. Gaekwad 135, A.S. Bhansali 100 not out, S. Parikh 52)

Match drawn
Baroda 6 pts, Saurashtra 3 pts

18, 19 and 20 December 1982

at Jamnagar

Bombay 388 for 7 dec (A.V. Mankad 74, R. Mankad 72, S.V. Nayak 65, S. Hattangdi 52) and 107 for 0 (S. Hattangdi 59 not out)
Saurashtra 353 (H. Joshi 67, B. Jadeja 56, N. Jadeja 52, R. Kulkarni 5 for 99)

Match drawn
Bombay 5 pts, Saurashtra 3 pts

at Nasik

Gujarat 337 (K. Bhrahmbhatt 100, B. Mistry 70) and 171 for 4 (J. Desai 67)
Maharashtra 462 for 6 dec (R.B. Bhalekar 126, P. Pradhan 110, M.D. Gunjal 77, M. Dixit 50)

Match drawn
Maharashtra 5 pts, Gujarat 3 pts

West Zone Table

	P	W	L	D	Pts
Baroda	4	2		2	28
Bombay	4	1		3	22
Maharashtra	4	1	1	2	16
Saurashtra	4	1	1	2	14
Gujarat	4		3	1	3

Central Zone

20, 21 and 22 November 1982

at Nagpur

Vidarbha 296 (R. Pankule 72, R.S. Hans 5 for 66) and 148
Uttar Pradesh 384 (A. Bambi 109 not out, V. Chopra 91) and 61 for 1

Uttar Pradesh won by 9 wickets
Uttar Pradesh 9 pts, Vidharba 0 pts

27, 28 and 29 November 1982

at Bhopal

Madhya Pradesh 304 (S. Ansari 56, S. Gulrezali 50) and 256 for 6 dec (Sanjivrao 105, S. Joshi 50, R. Pankule 5 for 61)
Vidarbha 160 (J. Rathod 73) and 198 (S. Phadkar 62, A. Patel 5 for 64)

Madhya Pradesh won by 202 runs
Madya Pradesh 8 pts, Vidarbha 0 pts

3, 4 and 5 December 1982

at Gorakhpur

Vidharba 170 and 318 (V. Telang 155)
Railways 291 (A. Burrows 91, Vedraj 51) and 200 for 5 (R. Vats 65)

Railways won by 5 wickets
Railways 8 pts, Vidharba 0 pts

4, 5 and 6 December 1982

at Sagar

Madhya Pradesh 256 (Sanjivrao 139 not out) and 271 for 6 (Mohammad Hassan 79 not out, S. Deshmukh 60)
Rajasthan 409 for 9 dec (K.R. Gattani 100, P. Sharma 55)

Match drawn
Rajasthan 5 pts, Madhya Pradesh 3 pts

9, 10 and 11 December 1982

at New Delhi

Railways 196 (A. Burrows 62) and 342 for 2 dec (R. Vats 178 not out, N. Churi 88, A. Burrows 68)
Madhya Pradesh 135 and 274 for 9 (R. Talwar 74, R. Dave 54)

Match drawn
Railways 5 pts, Madhya Pradesh 3 pts

at Hinghanghat

Vidarbha 153 and 212 (V. Telang 64, S. Hedaoo 52 not out, Vivekbhan Singh 8 for 64)
Rajasthan 221 (P. Shastri 120 not out, S. Takle 5 for 46) and 150 for 5

Match drawn
Rajasthan 5 pts, Vidarbha 3 pts

14, 15 and 16 December 1982

at Jaipur

Rajasthan 377 (P. Sharma 115, P. Shastri 51, D. Mahan 55, S. Shastri 50, S. Joshi 53)
Railways 139 and 168 for 3 (R. Vats 85)

Match drawn
Rajasthan 5 pts, Railways 3 pts

at Agra

Madhya Pradesh 195 (G. Sharma 5 for 54) and 257 (Mohammad Hassan 85, A. Gupte 58)
Uttar Pradesh 385 for 7 dec (Sekhar Anand 120 not out, G. Sharma 78) and 68 for 1

Uttar Pradesh won by 9 wickets
Uttar Pradesh 9 pts, Madhya Pradesh 0 pts

19, 20 and 21 December 1982

at Allahabad

Uttar Pradesh 504 for 7 dec (A. Mathur 201 not out, Sekhar Anand 114)
Railways 318 (M.I. Ansari 82, U. Dastane 62, Aslam A. 55) and 232 for 7 (U. Dastane 78 not out, S. Hyder Ali 52 not out)

Match drawn
Uttar Pradesh 6 pts, Railways 3 pts

24, 25 and 26 December 1982

at Udaipur

Uttar Pradesh 158 and 293 for 5 (A. Bambi 128, G. Sharma 57 not out)
Rajasthan 246 (D. Mahan 53)

Match drawn
Rajasthan 5 pts, Uttar Pradesh 3 pts

Central Zone Table

	P	W	L	D	Pts
Uttar Pradesh	4	2		2	30
Rajasthan	4			4	20
Railways	4	1		3	19
Madhya Pradesh	4	1	1	2	14
Vidarbha	4		3	1	3

East Zone

4, 5 and 6 December 1982

at Dibrugarh

Assam 196 (M. Kakoti 57) and 108 for 4
Bihar 260 for 2 dec (Subrata Das 129, H. Gidwani 89 not out)

Match drawn
Bihar 5 pts, Assam 3 pts

10, 11 and 12 December 1982

at Dibrugarh

Assam 100 and 154 (H. Praharaj 6 for 29)
Orissa 184 (C. Biswal 51) and 71 for 0

Orissa won by 10 wickets
Orissa 8 pts, Assam 0 pts

11, 12 and 13 December 1982

at Krishnagar

Bihar 138 and 193 for 8 (S. Roy 83 not out, M. Ghosh 6 for 64)
Bengal 323 for 6 dec (P. Roy 109, Raja Venkat 60, Probir Chail 58 not out)

Match drawn
Bengal 5 pts, Bihar 3 pts

17, 18 and 19 December 1982

at Patna

Bihar 334 (D. Augustus 110, S. Saba Karim 70, S. Sahu 5 for 121)
Orissa 262 for 7 (A. Jayaprakash 73, K. Dubey 54, S. Mahalik 58)

Match drawn
Bihar 2 pts, Orissa 2 pts

at Dibrugarh

Bengal 248 for 2 dec (Palas Nandy 140, P. Roy 75)
Assam 122 and 28 for 5

Match drawn
Bengal 5 pts, Assam 3 pts

23, 24 and 25 December 1982

at Asansol

Orissa 271 (B.K.R. Patnaik 96, H. Praharaj 74, A. Bhattacharji 5 for 75) and 205
Bengal 231 and 26 for 0

Match drawn
Orissa 5 pts, Bengal 3 pts

East Zone Table

	P	W	L	D	Pts
Orissa	3	1		2	15
Bengal	3			3	13
Bihar	3			3	10
Assam	3		1	2	6

South Zone

4, 5 and 6 December 1982

at Bangalore

Karnataka 377 for 8 dec (M.R. Srinivas Prasad 106, R. Sudhakar Rao 56, J. Abhiram 52 not out, B. Vijayakrishna 51) and 155 for 5 dec
Andhra 274 (K.B. Ramamurthy 106, B. Vijayakrishna 7 for 85) and 141 (B. Vijayakrishna 5 for 28)

Karnataka won by 117 runs
Karnataka 8 pts, Andhra 0 pts

at Secunderabad

Tamil Nadu 373 (P.S. Moses 120, R. Madhavan 96, B. Reddy 53, S.N. Yadav 6 for 111) and 50 for 3
Hyderabad 469 for 9 dec (V. Paul 156 not out, K.A. Qayyum 135)

Match drawn
Hyderabad 5 pts, Tamil Nadu 3 pts

10, 11 and 12 December 1982

at Kothagudem

Hyderabad 347 for 4 dec (V. Mohanraj 122, V. Paul 67 not out, M.V. Narasimha Rao 57)

Kerala 112 (C. Sridhar 5 for 31) and 221 (V. Hariharan 56, S.N. Yadav 6 for 49)

Hyderabad won by an innings and 27 runs
Hyderabad 8 pts, Kerala 0 pts

14 and 15 December 1982

at Venkatagiri

Andhra 362 (G.A. Pratapkumar 69, K.V.S.D. Kamraju 59)
Kerala 132 and 102 (K. Chandrasekhar 6 for 28)

Andhra won by an innings and 127 runs
Andhra 9 pts, Kerala 0 pts

18, 19 and 20 December 1982

at Bangalore

Karnataka 217 (J. Abhiram 70) and 203 for 3 dec (R.M. Binny 111 not out)
Hyderabad 156 (R. Bhatt 6 for 55) and 119 for 6

Match drawn
Karnataka 5 pts, Hyderabad 3 pts

at Madras

Tamil Nadu 398 for 9 dec (V. Sivaramakrishnan 104, P. Vijayakumar 101 not out, A. Jabber 66)
Andhra 144 (S. Venkataraghavan 7 for 44) and 156 (R. Madhavan 5 for 32)

Tamil Nadu won by an innings and 98 runs
Tamil Nadu 9 pts, Andhra 0 pts

24, 25 and 26 December 1982

at Madras

Karnataka 186 (S. Viswanath 55) and 231 for 2 (R.M. Binny 69, M.R. Srinivas Prasad 59, S. Viswanath 67 not out)
Tamil Nadu 376 for 9 dec (C.S. Sureshkumar 146, P. Vijayakumar 57, V. Sivaramakrishnan 52)

Match drawn
Tamil Nadu 6 pts, Karnatka 3 pts

8, 9 and 10 January 1983

at Pulghat

Kerala 211 (S. Ramesh 53) and 136 (T.A. Sekhar 9 for 54)
Tamil Nadu 343 for 4 dec (C.S. Sureshkumar 162, A. Jabber 83, V. Sivaramakrishnan 61) and 4 for 0

Tamil Nadu won by 10 wickets
Tamil Nadu 9 pts, Kerala 0 pts

21 and 22 January 1983

at Kozhikode

Kerala 126 and 135 (R.M. Binny 5 for 52)
Karnataka 221 for 6 dec (R.M. Binny 62) and 41 for 0

Karnataka won by 10 wickets
Karnataka 9 pts, Kerala 0 pts

Sandeep Patil (Bombay) (A.S.P.)

22, 23 and 24 January 1983

at Guntur

Andhra 164 (M.V. Narasimha Rao 5 for 46) and 213 for 9 dec (M.N. Ravikumar 87, Prasanakumar 81, M.V. Narasimha Rao for 71)
Hyderabad 321 for 7 dec (V. Paul 86, K.A. Qayyum 58, M.V. Narasimha Rao 51, Azharudin 55) and 57 for 2

Hyderabad won by 8 wickets
Hyderabad 8 pts, Andhra 0 pts

South Zone Table

	P	W	L	D	Pts
Tamil Nadu	4	2		2	27
Karnataka	4	2		2	25
Hyderabad	4	2		2	24
Andhra	4	1	3		9
Kerala	4		4		0

Pre-Quarter Finals

29, 30, 31 January and 1 February 1983

at Baroda

Rajasthan 281 and 230 for 6 dec (Vivekbhansingh 104 not out, S. Mudkavi 52)
Baroda 558 (N.Y. Satham 131, A.S. Bhansali 116, A.D. Gaekwad 82, Vivekbhansingh 6 for 45)

Match drawn
Baroda won on first innings

at Madras

Uttar Pradesh 351 (S. Khandkar 191, S. Venkataraghavan 5 for 134) and 269 (S. Khandkar 76, A.G. Mathur 56 not out, S. Venkataraghavan 5 for 110)
Tamil Nadu 449 (S. Srinivasan 148 not out, N.P. Manhavan 125, V. Sivaramakrishnan 54, R.S. Hans 6 for 125) and 172 for 6

Tamil Nadu won by 4 wickets

Quarter-Finals

11, 12, 13 and 14 February 1983

at Bombay

Bombay 500 for 9 dec (A.V. Mankad 150 not out, S. Hattangdi 141, S.V. Nayak 90, R.V. Mankad 52)
Orissa 96 and 153 (R. Thakkar 5 for 34)

Bombay won by an innings and 255 runs

at New Delhi

Tamil Nadu 229 (A. Jabbar 87 not out, K. Srikkanth 58, R. Shukla 5 for 24) and 306 for 8 (C.S. Sureshkumar 110, S. Srinivasan 67)
Delhi 559 (Kirti Azad 186, Rajinder Singh 74, R. Shukla 57, R. Lamba 52)

Match drawn
Delhi won on first innings

at Faridabad

Haryana 279 (A. Bhattacharji 5 for 67) and 190 (Ashwinkumar 66, D. Sharma 50, D.R. Doshi 6 for 78)
Bengal 145 (C. Sharma 5 for 70, S. Talwar 5 for 29) and 253 (Raja Vekat 73, S. Talwar 6 for 96)

Haryana won by 71 runs

at Baroda

Karnataka 128 (D. Pardeshi 7 for 33) and 179
Baroda 63 (B. Vijayakrishna 6 for 17) and 130 (R. Bhatt 7 for 57)

Karnataka won by 114 runs

Semi-Finals

25, 26, 27 and 28 February 1983

at New Delhi

Haryana 78 (R.M. Binny 8 for 22) and 125 (R. Bhatt 7 for 24)
Karnataka 230 (R.M. Binny 54)

Karnataka won by an innings and 27 runs

at New Delhi

Bombay 494 (S. Hattangdi 92, G.A.H.M. Parkar 141, R.V. Mankad 76, A.V. Mankad 65)
Delhi 338 (S.C. Khanna 143, R. Kulkarni 8 for 111) and

16 for 6 (M. Prabhakar 86, Kirti Azad 75, R. Thakkar 5 for 3)

Match drawn
Bombay won on first innings

The Ranji Trophy Final

The Ranji Trophy Final was once more a high-scoring game with the trophy going to the side that led on the first innings. Facing a total of 534, Karnataka found themselves at 526 for when Bhatt joined Vijayakrishna. The number eleven defended stoutly while Vijayakrishna scored the runs necessary to take Karnataka into the lead and eventually the stand realised 25. Karnataka owed much to the fine all-round cricket of Roger Binny who steadied the side with Abhiram after a mid-order collapse had seen five wickets fall for 68 runs.

There were some fine performances earlier in the competition. Sekhar took 9 for 54 for Tamil Nadu against Kerala, a career best, the best performance by a Tamil Nadu

bowler, and the tenth best bowling performance in the history of the competition. In the four West Zone matches for Baroda, Anshuman Gaekwad scored 649 runs at an average of 162.25, but, perhaps, the best performance of all was by Jammu and Kashmir. When they beat Services by 4 wickets at the end of December, it was the first time that they had won a Ranji Trophy match since joining the competition in 1959–60.

Gopalan Trophy Match

at Colombo

Sri Lanka Board President's XI 450 (L.R.D. Mendis 189, A.L.F. de Mel 100 not out, B. Kumar 4 for 106) **Tamil Nadu** 258 (S. Sivaramakrishnan 74, V. Kumar not out) and 75 for 3 (S. Sivaramakrishnan 58 not out)

Board XI won on first innings

In view of later events, this match, played on 22, 23 and 24 January 1983, had a deep and sad significance this year.

RANJI TROPHY FINAL: BOMBAY v. KARNATAKA
11, 12, 13, 14 and 15 March 1983 at Wakhede Stadium, Bombay

BOMBAY

	FIRST INNINGS		SECOND INNINGS	
S. Hattangdi	c Sudhakar, b Binny	13	c Binny, b Abhiram	3
J. Singhani	c Jayaprakash, b Binny	78	c Sudhakar, b Khanwilkar	0
R.V. Mankad	c Srinivasa, b Abhiram	14	c S. Viswanath, b Khanwilkar	23
S.M. Patil	b Vijayakrishna	48	not out	121
G.A.H.M. Parkar	c S. Viswanath, b Bhatt	60	c S. Viswanath, b Abhiram	7
C. Pandit*	c S. Viswanath, b Khanwilkar	157	not out	33
A.V. Mankad†	c Srinivasa, b Binny	13		
S.V. Nayak	c Srinivasa, b Bhatt	67		
R. Kulkarni	c G. Viswanath, b Bhatt	40		
S. Shetty	not out	22		
R. Thakkar	c G. Viswanath, b Bhatt	0		
Extras	b 3, lb 7, w 2, nb 10	22	ib 4, nb 2	6
	penalty runs	0		20
		534		213

KARNATAKA

	FIRST INNINGS		SECOND INNINGS	
M. Srinivasa Prasad	lbw, b Kulkarni	29	c Pandit, b Kulkarni	2
S. Viswanath*	c Pandit, b Shetty	92	b Shetty	77
A.V. Jayaprakash	c and b Thakkar	89	lbw, b Shetty	10
R.M. Binny	c Hattangdi, b Thakkar	115	c Singhani, b Thakkar	45
G.R. Viswanath†	lbw, b Shetty	3	c Pandit, b Shetty	20
B.G. Patel	c Pandit, b Kulkarni	18	not out	4
Sudhakar Rao	c Parkar, b Kulkarni	9		
J. Abhiram	c A. Mankad, b Nayak	69	(7) not out	11
R. Khanwilkar	b Kulkarni	32		
B. Vijayakrishna	lbw, b Kulkarni	42		
R. Bhatt	not out	0		
Extras	b 10, lb 19, w 1, nb 7	37	lb 6, nb 4	10
	penalty runs	16		0
		551	(for 5 wickets)	179

	O	M	R	W	O	M	R	W
Binny	43	12	119	3				
Khanwilkar	34	4	116	1	11	3	51	2
Jayaprakash	5	2	8	—				
Abhiram	11	1	43	1	8	—	48	2
Vijayakrishna	37	5	86	1	4	1	39	—
Bhatt	52.4	15	121	4	4	—	49	—
Sudhakar Rao	10	2	19	—				

	O	M	R	W	O	M	R	W
Kulkarni	40.4	3	157	5	19	6	57	1
Nayak	27	8	58	1	7	3	24	—
Shetty	26	4	75	2	19	7	34	3
Patil	3	—	16	—				
Thakkar	49	6	167	2	25	9	54	1
A.V. Mankad	9	1	25	—				

FALL OF WICKETS
1- 27, 2- 57, 3- 138, 4- 186, 5- 298, 6- 329, 7- 462, 8- 493, 9- 534
1- 4, 2- 24, 3- 36, 4- 57

FALL OF WICKETS
1- 51, 2- 225, 3- 227, 4- 237, 5- 273, 6- 293, 7- 447, 8- 470, 9- 526
1- 6, 2- 39, 3- 124, 4- 149, 5- 161

Match drawn. Karnataka won on first innings.

Duncan Fearnley
Cricket Sales Ltd

Perfection in Cricket Equipment

SANSOME PLACE WORCESTER WR1 1UA
Telephone STD 0905 ~~22855~~ 612 98
Telegrams Wickets Worcester
Telex 337300

Tatlow and Pledger (Pty) Ltd
39 Rosettenville Road
Village Main
Johannesburg 2001
Tel: 21-6711

Duncan Fearnley (N.Z.) Ltd
P.O. Box 87
Greytown
New Zealand
Tel: 49302

SECTION H
The Pakistani Season

Quaid-e-Azam Trophy.
P.A.C.O. Pentagular Tournament.
Wills Cup.

*Abdul Qadir. The first bowler ever to take one
hundred wickets in a Pakistan Season. (Adrian Murrell)*

The Australians had not yet completed their tour when the first matches in the Quaid-e-Azam trophy were played. Moreover, the beginning of the Indian tour was only a month away so that once more a vitally important domestic competition was threatened by the plethora of Test matches and one-day internationals which were sure to rob the tournament of its leading players for long periods. As it transpired, Imran Khan was not to appear in a single match so that Lahore were denied his services in the same way that Western Australia were denied the services of Kim Hughes two seasons ago.

The Schweppes County Championship, the Sheffield Shield, the Shell Shields, the Ranji Trophy, the Quaid-e-Azam trophy and the rest are the life-blood of cricket. It is these competitions that test and try cricketers and without them, first-class cricket will die. To deprive them of their best players year after year is to devalue them and to hinder the progress of young and aspiring players who are not being given the opportunity to test their skills against players of international renown.

In 1982–83, for the first time in its twenty-five year history, the Quaid-e-Azam trophy was sponsored. Fujicolor, the photographic film makers, undertook not only to give handsome monetary prizes to the winners and leading performers in the tournament, but also to give prize money of Rs 1,000 to each player who scored a century, took five wickets or assisted in five dismissals in an innings.

Allied Bank for I.D.B.P. was the one change in line-up among the competing sides from the previous season.

10, 11, 12 and 13 October 1982

at National Stadium, Karachi

Habib Bank 274 for 8 dec (Agha Zahid 98, Azhar Khan 52) and 259 for 8 dec (Sultan Rana 78, Azhar Khan 68, Agha Zahid 61, Shahid Mahboob 6 for 107)
Allied Bank 275 (Iqtidar Ali 99) and 152 for 3 (Iqtidar Ali 56)

Match drawn
Habib Bank 8 pts, Allied Bank 6 pts

at Iqbal Stadium, Faisalabad

Rawalpindi 179 for 9 dec (Farrukh Zaman 5 for 54) and 222 (Mohammad Riaz 70, Rafa Afaq 62)
Muslim Commercial Bank 391 for 4 (Azmat Rana 113 not out, Ejaz Faqih 107, Barbar Basharat 77) and 12 for 0

Muslim Commercial Bank won by 10 wickets
Muslim Commercial Bank 17 pts, Rawalpindi 2 pts

Muslim Commercial Bank gained the first victory of the season when they beat Rawalpindi with ease inside three days. Rawalpindi were much troubled by the slow left-arm bowling of Farrukh Zaman, but they declared in the sixty-seventh over with 9 wickets down so denying M.C.B. one bowling point. The M.C.B. batsmen exacted revenge, Babar and Ejaz putting on 105 for the third wicket and Ejaz and Azmat 118 for the fourth.

Rawalpindi offered some resistance in the second innings when Mohammad Riaz and Rafa Afaq added 83 for the fifth

wicket, but, with Ehtesham Khaliq absent ill, the result w never in doubt.

Having gained a place in the competition by virtue having won the B.C.C.P. Trophy in 1982, Allied Bank ga a good account of themselves in their opening match. Alli Bank were strengthened by the inclusion of Saleem Yousu Jalal-ud-Din and Shaid Mahboob who had joined them fro I.D.B.P. and Amin Lakhani, the left-arm spinner, who ha done well with United Bank. Habib Bank sorely miss Mohsin Khan and Javed Miandad who were on Test dut

Agha Zahid was bowled by an off-break from skipp Shoaib Mahboob when two short of his century, and Alli Bank's opener, Iqtidar Ali, suffered a worse fate. He wa stumped on 99. The stumping was one of Zaheer Ahmed five dismissals in the innings.

16, 17, 18 and 19 October 1982

at Bakhtiara Y.C., Karachi

United Bank 260 for 7 (Sadiq Mohammad 109, Tar Nazar 5 for 94) and 346 for 6 dec (Sadiq Mohammad 11 Nasir Valika 65, Siddiq Patni 62, Ashraf Ali 50 not out)
Karachi 315 for 4 (Feroze Najamuddin 92 not out, Um Rasheed 72, Sajid Ali 54) and 137 (Sikhander Bakht 5 f 38, Tauseef Ahmed 4 for 28)

United Bank won by 154 runs
United Bank 15 pts, Karachi 6 pts

at National Stadium, Karachi

Pakistan International Airlines 235 for 9 de (Rizwan-uz-Zaman 112, Azhar 4 for 45) and 195 (Zahi Ahmed 62, Raees Ahmed 4 for 90)
Habib Bank 120 (Saleem Malik 51, Rashid Khan 7 fo 72) and 279 for 8 (Saleem Malik 78)

Match drawn
P.I.A. 7 pts, Habib Bank 3 pts

at Pindi Club, Rawalpindi

Rawalpindi 107 for 8 dec (Shahid Mahboob 6 for 28 and 191 (Shoaib Habib 6 for 70)
Allied Bank 217 for 9 dec (Saleem Yousuf 145 not out and 86 for 3

Allied Bank won by 7 wickets
Allied Bank 14 pts, Rawalpindi 3 pts

at Bagh-e-Jinnah, Lahore

Muslim Commercial Bank 212 (Ejaz Faqih 73) an 365 for 2 (Qasim Umar 203 not out, Anwar-ul-Haq 115
Railways 315 for 7 (Talat Mirza 96, Ejaz Ahmed 66 Shahid Pervez 50, Ilyas Khan 4 for 82)

Match drawn
Railways 8 pts, Muslim Commercial Bank 4 pts

Although trailing by 55 runs on the first innings, Unite Bank gained a most convincing win over Karachi. They wer mostly indebted to Sadiq Mohammad who hit a century in each innings, the third time in his career that he had done this, but the first time that he had managed it in Pakistan. He had considerable support in the second innings when he and iddiq put on 159 for the first wicket.

A combination of pace and spin demolished Karachi when hey batted again, Sikhander Bakht, having lost his Test lace, being particularly effective. United Bank's new recruit rom reigning champions, National Bank, Ehtesham-ud-Din, the experienced seamer, failed to take a wicket on his rst appearance for his new side.

Rizwan-uz-Zaman, the young opening bat who had been hrown into the Test arena a little too soon earlier in the year, ored a fine hundred for P.I.A., and then seam bowler Rashid Khan ripped through the Habib batting, Saleem Malik, in his first season for them being the only batsman to how any confidence.

P.I.A. did not fare too well themselves at the second atempt against the bowling of Liaqat and Raees, and Habib vere set to score 311 to win. Nevertheless, another fine inings by Saleem Malik and some good sense all round took hem to 261 for 5, but then three wickets went down for 16 uns and skipper Abdur Raqeeb settled for a draw.

Allied Bank registered their first win in the championship vhen Rawalpindi were beaten inside three days for the econd time.

The home side struggled against seam bowler Shahid Mahboob who took 6 for 28 in 16 overs. Facing a total of 07, Allied Bank fared little better, losing 6 for 94, but then n innings of great character by Test wicket-keeper Saleem Yousuf swung the game in their favour. His 145 not out was career best, and it represented 67% of his team's score, the ext highest scorer being Shahid Mahboob with 16.

With an unexpected lead of 110, Shoaib Habib attacked Rawalpindi with his off-breaks, capturing a career best 6 for 0 and snatching victory.

In Lahore, the absence of sight-screens delayed the start by ver an hour and then M.C.B. batted laboriously. Railways howed more enterprise, but the game was drifting to a draw vhen M.C.B. went in a second time.

Qasim Umar and Anwar-ul-Haq put on 278 for the first vicket and Qasim reached the season's first double century, ut the cricket had long since become meaningless.

22, 23, 24 and 25 October 1982

at Bakhtiari Y.C., Karachi

Karachi 219 (Kamal Najamuddin 58, Abdul Qadir 5 for 79) and 164 (Feroze Najamuddin 67, Abdul Qadir 9 for 32)
Habib Bank 326 for 4 (Arshad Pervez 109, Agha Zahid 79, Azhar Khan 58 not out) and 58 for 0

Habib Bank won by 10 wickets
Habib Bank 18 pts, Karachi 3 pts

at Qaddafi Stadium, Lahore

Muslim Commercial Bank 282 for 8 dec (Qasim Umar 39, Azmat Rana 81) and 198 (Babar Basharat 60, Shahid Mahboob 7 for 65)
Allied Bank 243 (Shoaib Habib 54, Salman Qizilbash 53, Ejaz Faqih 6 for 107) and 210 (Saleem Yousuf 64, Ejaz Faqih 5 for 57)

Muslim Commercial Bank won by 27 runs
Muslim Commercial Bank 18 pts, Allied Bank 5 pts

Having tormented England and Australia, Abdul Qadir returned to the Habib Bank side and proceeded to inflict misery on the opposition with his leg-breaks and googlies. Quickly into the attack, he undermined Karachi's first innings and bowled nearly 43 overs in the second innings to take 9 wickets. The second wicket to fall had gone to skipper Abdur Raqeeb when he had Umar Rasheed stumped.

Abdul Qadir's bowling brought Habib victory, but they also owed much to openers Agha Zahid and Arshad Pervez who put on 183 for the first wicket.

There was a tense finish at Lahore where Allied Bank, needing 238 to win, passed two hundred with only 6 wickets down, but the wiles of Ejaz Faqih, the M.C.B. skipper, the steadiness of Zaigham Burki and the panic for quick runs led to 4 wickets falling for 8 runs and victory going to M.C.B. who went top of the table.

29, 30, 31 October and 1 November 1982

at National Stadium, Karachi

Pakistan International Airlines 370 for 5 dec (Zaheer Abbas 125, Rizwan-uz-Zaman 121) and 267 for 6 dec (Zaheer Abbas 101, Aftab Baloch 69)
Karachi 302 for 9 (Afzaal Ahmed 98, Umar Rasheed 65, Zafar Ahmed 50, Rashid Khan 4 for 53) and 273 for 8 (Afzaal Ahmed 58, Umar Rasheed 50, Rashid Khan 5 for 83)

Match drawn
P.I.A. 7 pts, Karachi 5 pts

at L.C.C.A. Lahore

Muslim Commercial Bank 356 for 6 dec (Qasim Umar 210 not out) and 271 for 5 dec (Qasim Umar 110, Asif Ali 67 not out)
Lahore 297 for 7 (Saleem Taj 85, Rameez Raja 84) and 161 for 3 (Majid J. Khan 76 not out, Tahir Shah 54)

Match drawn
Muslim Commercial Bank 6 pts, Lahore 6 pts

at Railways Stadium, Lahore

Allied Bank 98 for 8 dec (Mohammad Nazir 4 for 15) and 216 (Iqtidar Ali 66, Salman Qizilbash 52, Mohammad Nazir 7 for 74)
Railways 60 for 9 dec (Shahid Mahboob 5 for 30, Jalaluddin 4 for 25) and 173 (Jalaluddin 6 for 61)

Allied Bank won by 81 runs
Allied Bank 13 pts, Railways 2 pts

The success of Kenyan-born Qasim Umar continued when he hit a career best 210 not out in the first innings against Lahore and followed it with 110 in the second innings. He became the sixth Pakistani player to score a double century and a century in the same match, and this was the third time that the feat had been achieved in the Quaid-e-Azam trophy. What was particularly impressive about the diminutive Qasim was the exciting way in which he went for his shots.

The wicket at Lahore proved to be too good for the bowlers, however, as Saleem Taj and Rameez Raja proved with a second wicket stand of 152. The majestic Majid Khan had no trouble in saving the game for Lahore when they were set the impossible task of making 331 to win.

On an uncertain wicket at the Railways Stadium, Allied Bank won inside three days. The off-breaks of the vastly experienced Railways' skipper, Mohammad Nazir jnr., gave Allied Bank considerable trouble, but an opening partnership of 123 in the second innings between Iqtidar Ali and Salman Qizilbash provided them with a platform for victory.

It was pace rather than spin which was Allied's chief attacking weapon and Jalaluddin had match figures of 10 for 86.

Although the match at Karachi was drawn, it was an historic occasion. It was the eighth time in his illustrious career that Zaheer Abbas has hit a century in each innings, a world record. In the first innings, he shared a third wicket stand of 211 with Rizwan-uz-Zaman who also hit a century and once more emphasised his rich promise.

P.I.A.'s medium pace swing bowler, Rashid Khan, nearly brought his side victory with nine wickets in the match, but Mohiuddin Khan and Mohinder Kumar held out against him and the P.I.A. attack to save the game for Karachi.

4, 5, 6 and 7 November 1982

at National Stadium, Karachi

United Bank 308 for 7 (Sadiq Mohammad 110, Mudassar Nazar 81) and 257 for 6 dec (Ashraf Ali 75 not out, Mudassar Nazar 54, Afzaal Butt 4 for 78)
National Bank 261 for 4 (Saleem Pervez 74, Ali Zia 72 not out) and 159 for 3 (Saleem Pervez 102 not out)

Match drawn
National Bank 6 pts, United Bank 5 pts

at Niaz Stadium, Hyderabad

Habib Bank 250 for 8 dec (Saleem Malik 103) and 307 for 7 dec (Saleem Malik 107, Agha Zahid 51, Arshad Pervez 50)
Muslim Commercial Bank 270 for 8 (Salahuddin 100 not out, Abdul Qadir 7 for 151) and 175 for 4

Match drawn
Habib Bank 6 pts, Muslim Commercial Bank 6 pts

at Qaddafi Stadium, Lahore

Lahore 189 (Jalaluddin 6 for 45) and 329 for 8 dec (Majid J. Khan 101, Pervez Mir 52, Amin Lakhani 4 for 44)
Allied Bank 291 (Shahid Mahboob 110, Sarfraz Nawaz 4 for 73) and 89 for 2

Match drawn
Allied Bank 8 pts, Lahore 5 pts

at Railways Stadium, Lahore

Railways 356 for 7 (Saadat Ali 206 not out, Ijaz Ahmed 51, Rashid Khan 4 for 103) and 248 for 9 dec (Asad Rauf 84, Iqbal Sikander 5 for 91)
Pakistan International Airlines 265 for 5 (Rizwan-uz-Zaman 152, Shoaib Mohammad 69, Mohammad Nazir 4 for 74) and 341 for 6 (Rizwan-uz-Zaman 99, Shoaib Mohammad 69, Zaheer Abbas 57)

P.I.A. won by 4 wickets
P.I.A. 6 pts, Railways 5 pts

The match at Karachi was marred by an unpleasant scen between Mudassar and the National Bank captain, Taslim Arif. Young fast bowler, Afzaal Butt, sent down two quic bouncers which Mudassar ducked under. Evidently, Taslim made some derogatory remarks about Mudassar's inabilit to deal with short-pitched bowling, and the umpires had t intervene when Mudassar went over and threatened Taslim Mudassar also exchanged words with the umpires who chos not to report the incident.

Sadiq Mohammad hit his third century in successive in nings, and he and Mudassar put on 181 for the first wicke on the opening day, but with the batsmen always dominan the match was drawn.

Abdul Qadir produced another outstanding performanc for Muslim Commercial Bank when he took all seven wicket that fell to a bowler in the Habib Bank first innings. Thi brought the teams to parity, and Saleem Malik followed hi 103 in the first innings with 107 in the second when Habi batted again.

There was more good batting from Salahuddin who wa not dismissed in the match, but a draw always seemed inev itable.

It seemed that Allied Bank might force a win over Lahor when, after Shoaib had won the toss and asked Lahore t bat, Jalaluddin again bowled fiercely to take 6 for 45.

Wasim Raja. Although his form at international level deserte him, he had a most successful all-round season for Nation Bank. (Adrian Murrell)

Sadiq Mohammad. A century in each innings for United Bank against Karachi in October was followed by another century in the following match. (Patrick Eagar)

Najamuddin 100 not out, Mogiuddin Khan 51, Iqbal Qasim 4 for 101)
National Bank 339 (Mohammad Jamil 77, Iqbal Qasim 58, Atiq-ur-Rehman 5 for 142) and 308 for 2 (Shafiq Ahmed 104 not out, Saleem Pervez 75, Taslim Arif 56, Ali Zia 56 not out)

National Bank won by 8 wickets
National Bank 16 pts, Karachi 8 pts

at Bahawal Stadium, Bahawalpur

Railways 135 (Ehtesham-ud-Din 6 for 48) and 373 (Abdus Sami 78, Naved Anjum 54, Musleh-ud-Din 54, Tauseef Ahmed 4 for 69, Khurshid Akhtar 4 for 71)
United Bank 347 for 6 dec (Farooq Shera 91, Sadiq Mohammad 65, Haroon Rashid 64 retired hurt, Nasir Valika 56 not out) and 162 for 3 (Mansoor Akhtar 76, Sadiq Mohammad 52)

United Bank won by 7 wickets
United Bank 18 pts, Railways 2 pts

at Qaddafi Stadium, Lahore

Pakistan International Airlines 252 (Naaem Ahmed 63, Zaheer Abbas 57, Shahid Mahboob 5 for 95) and 182 (Jalaluddin 4 for 41, Azeem Hafeez 4 for 41)
Allied Bank 175 (Zafar Mehdi 55 not out, Rashid Khan 7 for 77) and 178 for 7 (Iqtidar Ali 56)

Match drawn
P.I.A. 8 pts, Allied Bank 5 pts

11 and 12 November 1982

at Pindi Club, Rawalpindi

Habib Bank 276 for 8 (Javed Miandad 96, Azhar Khan 50)
Rawalpindi 125 (Abdul Qadir 9 for 49) and 91 (Abdul Qadir 4 for 27)

Habib Bank won by an innings and 50 runs
Habib Bank 18 pts, Rawalpindi 2 pts

Jalal's performance was overshadowed by that of Shahid Mahboob. Shahid had been bowling splendidly throughout the season and is one of Pakistan's brightest young prospects. As Iqtidar Ali was unwell, Shahid was asked to go in first as a night-watchman. He responded by scoring 110 and nursing Allied Bank to a 102-run lead. A century from Majid Khan ended any hopes that Allied had of victory, however.

The match of the round was at Railways Stadium in Lahore where P.I.A. gained a magnificent win.

Railways had batted first and, with Saadat Ali hitting a career best, had reached an impressive 356 in their 85 overs. P.I.A.'s response had come from the increasingly impressive Rizwan who had dominated an opening partnership of 196 with Shoaib Mohammad.

Rizwan had followed this by taking three wickets, but Mohammad Nazir's declaration still left P.I.A. with the mighty task of making 340 to win at well over 5 an hour.

Rizwan and Shoaib gave P.I.A. a fine start with a stand of 163, and Zaheer, Aftab, Zahid and Naeem all maintained the necessary scoring to bring P.I.A. a glorious victory. Rizwan was run out when one short of his second hundred of the match. Four of the six batsmen dismissed were run out in the great dash for victory.

10, 11, 12 and 13 November 1982

at National Stadium, Karachi

Karachi 352 for 7 dec (Afzaaal Ahmed 105, Umar Rasheed 61, Kamal Najanuddin 54, Zafar Ahmed 50 not out, Iqbal Qasim 5 for 133) and 294 for 9 dec (Feroze

A high-scoring match in Karachi ended in a thrilling victory for National Bank. Karachi won the toss and batted first on a placid wicket, declaring at the fall of their seventh wicket when only one ball of their 85 overs remained. Afzaaal Ahmed was the backbone of the innings, but there was solid scoring from most batsmen.

National Bank were struggling at 161 for 7 before wicket-keeper Mohammad Jamil and Iqbal Qasim rallied them with a stand of 94. Jamil then received useful help from Saleem Akhtar and Afzaal Butt so that the last two wickets added 84 and National Bank trailed by only 13 on the first innings.

The game swung in favour of National Bank when Karachi slumped to 117 for 6 in their second innings, but Feroze Najamuddin and Mohiuddin Khan added 95, and with Karachi declaring as soon as Feroze reached his hundred, National Bank were set to make 308 at well over five runs an over.

Taslim Arif and Saleem Pervez attacked the bowling from the start in a stand of 123. Shafiq Ahmed and Ali Zia maintained the momentum and National won a fine victory with time to spare. They did not allow Karachi to bowl a single maiden over in the second innings.

In Bahawalpur, Railways decided to bat first but floundered against the medium pace of Sikhander and Ehtesham. United Bank lost Mudassar and Mansoor, two Test batsmen, for 3, but, with Haroon retiring hurt, the next wicket did not fall until the score had reached 223.

When Railways batted again they succumbed to spin and United Bank moved to a comfortable win.

Allied Bank asked P.I.A. to bat first in Lahore and seemed to have made the right decision when they had their opponents at 41 for 4, but P.I.A. rallied and with Rashid Khan bowling splendidly, they took a first innings lead of 77.

They did not fare well themselves at the second attempt, but they still looked like winners when Rashid and Hasan had Allied Bank at 32 for 4. Sturdy resistance from Iqtidar, Zafar and Shoaib followed and the game was saved.

The revision of the dates of the Indian tour caused the first distress to the competition when the game between Rawalpindi and Habib Bank was transfered to the Pindi Club Ground which, therefore, became a centre for first-class cricket for the first time. Rawalpindi's disasters continued. They asked Habib Bank to bat, saw Javed score 96 and were beaten in two days.

Once more the bowling of Abdul Qadir, unquestionably the world's greatest leg-spinner, destroyed the opposition. He bowled unchanged throughout the match and, in the first innings, he took the first nine wickets to become the first Pakistani to take nine wickets in an innings twice. His 9 for 49 was a career best and in three matches for Habib Bank before joining the national side he had taken 36 wickets.

Following this third successive defeat inside three days, Rawalpindi replaced left-arm fast medium bowler Khatib Rizwan as captain by star batsman Masood Anwar. It was felt that the change would allow Khatib to concentrate on his bowling.

16, 17 and 18 November 1982

at Bakhtiari Y.C., Karachi

Muslim Commercial Bank 225 (Anwar-ul-Haq 54, Qasim Umar 53, Iqbal Qasim 6 for 99, Wasim Raja 4 for 76) and 125 for 9 (Wasim Raja 6 for 66)
National Bank 273 (Taslim Arif 73, Shafiq Ahmed 51, Ilyas Khan 7 for 90)

National Bank were awarded the match
National Bank 18 pts, Muslim Commercial Bank 7 pts

16, 17, 18 and 19 November 1982

at National Stadium, Karachi

Railways 239 (Munawwar Javed 58, Mohinder Kumar 4 for 81) and 329 (Asad Rauf 106, Munawwar Javed 64, Tanvir Ali 5 for 131, Tariq Nazar 4 for 97)
Karachi 236 (Mohammad Nazir 6 for 62) and 209 for 5 (Feroze Najamuddin 52)

Match drawn
Railways 7 pts, Karachi 7 pts

With the Gymkhana Ground in Karachi, the original venu for Quaid-e-Azam matches, unavailable games were switched to the Bakhtiari Youth Centre, a ground where, as the *Pakistan Cricketer* commented, 'even the basic facilities for first-class matches don't exist'. The outcome was the unhappy events of 18 November.

The slow left-arm of Iqbal Qasim and the leg-spin of Wasim Raja had given the National Bank a firm grip on the game with Muslim Commercial Bank, but there was an unpleasant end to the match when, on the third afternoon, some spectators hurled indecent remarks at Babar Basharat, the M.C.B. all-rounder. Babar responded by losing his temper and he left the field and attempting to hit one of the spectators with his bat. A scuffle ensued and Babar was injured.

The match was halted and the umpires decided that play would resume at 3.00 pm, but M.C.B. officials had sent their players home to avoid further injury and National Bank, who were in a commanding position were awarded the match.

The appeal against this decision by Muslim Commercial Bank was rejected, but there was more trouble when National Bank withdrew from the tournament due to disagreement with the Board. The fixtures were thrown into disarray and there was an extension and reorganisation when National Bank returned to the competition on payment of Rs 5,000.

Life was quieter at the National Stadium where Railways recovered from the first morning shock of 17 for 3 and where the spinners, left-arm Tanvir Ali and off-break bowler Tariq Nazar, both of whom had played for Karachi Whites in the under 19 championship, bowled well as did the evergreen Mohammad Nazir jnr.

22, 23, 24 and 25 November 1982

at National Stadium, Karachi

Karachi 246 (Zafar Ahmed 72, Khalid Alvi 58, Ejaz Faqih 6 for 88) and 417 (Feroze Najamuddin 144, Zafar Ahmed 140, Ilyas Khan 5 for 88, Farrukh Zaman 4 for 80)
Muslim Commercial Bank 334 for 7 dec (Qasim Umar 174, Tanvir Ali 5 for 118) and 207 for 1 (Qasim Umar 110 not out, Anwar-ul-Haq 95)

Match drawn
Muslim Commercial Bank 8 pts, Karachi 5 pts

at Niaz Stadium, Hyderabad

National Bank 257 (Taslim Arif 64, Shahid Butt 6 for 110) and 213 (Shafiq Ahmed 79, Mohammad Nazir 4 for 52, Shahid Butt 4 for 81)
Railways 279 (Naved Anjum 53, Taslim Arif 4 for 46) and 195 for 3 (Saadat Ali 92 not out)

Railways won by 7 wickets
Railways 18 pts, National Bank 8 pts

at L.C.C.A., Lahore

Allied Bank 255 for 8 dec (Iqtidar Ali 86, Shahid Mahboob 58) and 90 (Ehtesham-ud-Din 7 for 43)
United Bank 295 for 9 (Siddiq Patni 60, Sadiq Mohammad 53) and 52 for 3

United Bank won by 7 wickets
United Bank 16 pts, Allied Bank 7 pts

Sikhander Bakht lost his place in the Test side, but his bowling had a decisive influence in United Bank winning the Quaid-e-Azam Trophy. (A.S.P.)

at C.M.T. & S.D., Rawalpindi

Pakistan International Airlines 239 (Aftab Baloch 74, Shahid Mohammad 54, Khatib Rizwan 6 for 66) and 276 (Rizwan-uz-Zaman 142, Abdul Wahab 7 for 74)
Rawalpindi 220 (Qazi Khalid 67, Iqbal Sikander 6 for 60) and 187 (Iqbal Sikander 6 for 56)

P.I.A. won by 108 runs
P.I.A. 17 pts, Rawalpindi 6 pts

Muslim Commercial Bank's hold on the top of the table position slipped as Feroze Najamuddin and Zafar Ahmed put on 282 for Karachi's fourth wicket in the second innings at Karachi. Zafar's hundred was particularly pleasing. Unable to hold a regular place in the Pakistan International Airlines' team in 1981–82, he had joined Karachi, the place of his birth, and had quickly established himself as a fluent middle-order batsman.

Karachi lost their last seven wickets for 56 runs, but the stand between Feroze and Zafar had thwarted M.C.B. who batted again needing 330 to win at seven an over. This was clearly impossible, but Qasim and Anwar had their second century opening stand of the match, and Qasim Umar hit a century in each innings for the second time in the season.

Railways inflicted the first defeat of the season on National Bank, the reigning champions, at the same time gaining their first victory of the season. Railways owed much to their new discovery, the left-arm spinner, Shahid Butt, who took ten wickets in the match.

Another success for Railways was their young wicket-keeper Zulqarnian who had seven dismissals in the match, five in the first innings, four of them stumpings.

Left 192 to win, Railways stumbled at the start to lose Abdus Sami and Naved Anjum for 17, but the steadiness of Saadat Ali saw them to victory.

United Bank moved menacingly close to the top when they beat Allied Bank inside three days at Lahore. Nasir Valika won the toss and asked Allied Bank to bat, but his decision looked a poor one when Iqtidar Ali and Shahid Mahboob put on 129 for the first wicket. The later batsmen failed to build on this and a solid second wicket stand and 7 wickets fell for 40 before the declaration.

Sadiq Mohammad and Siddiq Patni began with 110 for United Bank who took a first innings lead of 40, and then Ehtesham-ud-Din produced his finest bowling since joining United Bank, bowling unchanged to take 7 for 43 in 11.1 overs

Intent on an early finish, United Bank hit off the runs at 6 an over.

Rawalpindi's unhappy time continued with their fourth defeat in as many matches. New captain Masood Anwar asked P.I.A. to bat, and deposed captain Khatib Rizwan bowled splendidly, but the first innings ended in virtual stalemate.

Another impressive hundred from Rizwan-uz-Zaman which totally dominated the P.I.A. second innings made things difficult for Rawalpindi who succumbed to Iqbal Sikander's spin for the second time in the match.

The outstanding performance for Railways came from their spinner, Abdul Wahab, who took 7 for 74 in the second innings and, but for Rizwan, might well have won the match for his side.

28, 29, 30 November and 1 December 1982

at L.C.C.A., Lahore

Lahore 248 for 9 (Majid J. Khan 69, Raja Akbar 5 for 79) and 275 for 5 (Aamer Malik 91, Mansoor Rana 62, Majid J. Khan 58)
Pakistan International Airlines 281 for 7 (Aftab Baloch 73, Shoaib Mohammad 56, Sarfraz Nawaz 4 for 81)

Match drawn
P.I.A. 7 pts, Lahore 5 pts

at C.M.T. & S.D., Rawalpindi

United Bank 318 for 8 (Nasir Valika 95, Mahmood Rasheed 85, Farooq Shera 64, Mohammad Sabit 4 for 104) and 313 for 6 dec (Sadiq Mohammad 157, Farooq Shera 50, Abdul Wahab 4 for 79)
Rawalpindi 231 (Maqsood Kundi 59, Shahid Aziz 4 for 40) and 92 for 5 (Ehtesham-ud-Din 4 for 31)

Match drawn
United Bank 8 pts, Rawalpindi 5 pts

Bad weather plagued the game at Lahore where the home side gave some indication that they were finding form, and the rain caused the abandonment of play on the last day at Rawalpindi where the home side, hammered by Sadiq and troubled by Ehtesham were slipping to their fifth defeat.

4, 5, 6 and 8 December 1982

at Punjab University, Lahore

Railways 250 (Musleh-ud-Din 72, Saadat Ali 71) and 242 for 6 (Abdus Sami 97 not out, Asad Rauf 62)
Habib Bank 233 (Anwar Miandad 97, Shahid Pervez 5 for 23)

Match drawn
Railways 8 pts, Habib Bank 7 pts

at L.C.C.A., Lahore

Lahore 301 (Majid J. Khan 101, Rameez Raja 76, Mohammad Naeem 51, Sadiq Mohammad 6 for 84) and 285 for 5 (Majid J. Khan 128 not out, Aamer Malik 120)
United Bank 294 for 9 (Ashraf Ali 111 not out)

Match drawn
United Bank 8 pts, Lahore 7 pts

at Bahawal Stadium, Bahawalpur

Karachi 262 (Munir-ul-Haq 88 not out, Amin Lakhani 5 for 57) and 313 for 4 dec (Munir-ul-Haq 135 not out, Zafar Ahmed 73 not out)
Allied Bank 275 for 8 dec (Talat Masood 89, Moin-ud-Din 61 not out, Mohinder Kumar 6 for 70) and 124 for 5

Match drawn
Allied Bank 8 pts, Karachi 6 pts

Rain washed out any play on the last day of the game between Railways and Habib Bank with Railways, having recovered from 59 for 3, being given the upper hand by a patient innings from Abdus Sami.

There was also no play on the last day at the other match in Lahore which was dominated by Majid Khan who hit a century in each innings. Lahore were in terrible trouble in their second innings at 34 for 4 when Majid joined Aamer Malik. They swung the game completely in favour of Lahore with a stand of 248 before Aamer was run out.

In the United Bank innings, the tail had wagged well, Ashraf Ali scoring 111 not out from number seven and sharing stands of 37 and 62 for the ninth and tenth wickets.

Munir-ul-Haq had a fine match in Bahawalpur where he shared an unbeaten fifth wicket stand of 163 with Zafar Ahmed in the second innings.

Set to make 313, Allied Bank began with a flourish, but the loss of wickets brought the inevitable draw.

11, 12, 13 and 14 December 1982

at C.M.T. & S.D., Rawalpindi

Rawalpindi 268 (Azmat Jalil 62, Qazi Khalid 57, Masood Anwar 54, Mohammad Nazir 5 for 90, Shahid Butt 4 for 103) and 56 (Musleh-ud-Din 6 for 23, Mohammad Nazir 4 for 12)
Railways 278 (Abdus Sami 78, Raja Afaq 6 for 97) and 48 for 5

Railways won by 5 wickets
Railways 18 pts, Rawalpindi 8 pts

at Bagh-e-Jinnah, Lahore

United Bank 278 for 7 (Sadiq Mohammad 59, Mahmood Rasheed 58, Liaqat Ali 4 for 92) and 64 for 1
Habib Bank 252 for 5 dec (Sultan Rana 57 not out, Farooq Shera 5 for 87)

Match drawn
Habib Bank 6 pts, United Bank 5 pts

at Punjab University, Lahore

National Bank 196 (Wasim Raja 66) and 154 for 5 (Shafiq Ahmed 56, Ali Zia 51)
Lahore 273 (Ali Ahmed 61 not out)

Match drawn
Lahore 8 pts, National Bank 5 pts

Once more Rawalpindi were beaten inside three days. A damp wicket prevented play until 2.30 on the opening day when Railways put Rawalpindi in. Mohammad Nazir and Shahid Butt, the spinners, were quickly in operation, but Masood and Asmat put on 94 for the first wicket.

Spinners also provided Railways with problems, but they gained a first innings lead of 10. The pitch was breaking up when Rawalpindi batted a second time, and the medium pace of Musleh-ud-Din and the off-breaks of captain Mohammad Nazir totally destroyed them.

Even so, Railways had to struggle to get the 47 needed to win, and lost five wickets in doing so.

Zulqarnian, the Railways' wicket-keeper, had another fine match with four stumpings and a catch in the first innings.

Rain ruined the match between United Bank and Lahore in which the most notable performance was that of Farooq Shera, the seamer, who took all five Habib wickets to fall.

The match between Lahore and National Bank was also badly mauled by rain with Lahore having slightly the upper hand thanks to a late knock by Ali Ahmed.

This was the only match in the tournament in which no Fujicolor prize money was won.

17, 18, 19 and 20 December 1982

at L.C.C.A., Lahore

Habib Bank 348 for 3 (Tehsin Javed 100, Arshad Pervez 87, Agha Zahid 80, Azhar Khan 54 not out) and 82 for 3
National Bank 183 (Abdur Raqeeb 7 for 77) and 428 for 9 dec (Shafiq Ahmed 118, Saleem Pervez 92, Taslim Arif 69, Saleem Anwar 55, Abdul Qadir 5 for 125)

Match drawn
Habib Bank 8 pts, National Bank 2 pts

at C.M.T. & S.D., Rawalpindi

Lahore 95 for 8 dec (Abdul Wahab 5 for 16) and 346 (Rameez Raja 108, Mansoor Rana 87, Athar 73 not out, Abdul Wahab 4 for 84)
Rawalpindi 220 (Masood Anwar 99, Raja Afaq 71, Pervez Mir 6 for 31) and 223 for 0 (Masood Anwar 108 not out, Azmat Jalil 107 not out)

Rawalpindi won by 10 wickets
Rawalpindi 14 pts, Lahore 4 pts

The other match in Lahore showed a similar shift of fortune. Rashid Khan's bowling and a good all-round performance from captain Naeem Ahmed brought Pakistan International Airlines maximum bonus points and gave them a first innings lead of 96 over Muslim Commercial Bank who slipped to 92 for 5 in their second innings.

There was some solid middle order batting from M.B.C. and the Airlines were left to make 168 at nearly six an over. They went for the runs, stumbled to 15 for 3, lost Shahid Mohammad retired hurt and were happy to settle for a draw in the end.

After a first half of the season of unrelenting gloom Rawalpindi dumbfounded all with a spectacular win over Lahore.

Batting first, Lahore were in pain against the spin of Abdul Wahab and Raja Afaq. Four wickets went down at 67, and Rameez Raja boldly declared at 95 for 8.

Masood Anwar played a captain's innings for Rawalpindi when his side threatened to collapse, and he and Raja Afaq added 139 for the fourth wicket.

A third wicket stand of 184 between Rameez Raja and Mansoor Rana appeared to have given the advantage to Lahore as Rawalpindi were left to score 222 to win the match.

None could have expected them to grasp victory in the way they did. Attacking the bowling from the start, Masood and Azmat showed not the slightest indication that they would be troubled by the Lahore bowlers and they stroked Rawalpindi to a memorable victory by ten wickets at three and a half runs an over.

The outstanding contribution to Lahore's out-cricket came from Pervez Mir whose spin bowling might well have been employed earlier in the first innings.

The win lifted Rawalpindi off the bottom of the table, bringing them level with Karachi and five points ahead of Lahore. United Bank led the table, one point in front of Habib Bank but only nine points separated the first six teams.

Majid J. Khan. His class and composure failed to save Lahore from relegation. (A.S.P.)

18, 19, 20 and 21 December 1982

at Punjab University, Lahore

Muslim Commercial Bank 221 (Rashid Khan 5 for 105, Naeem Ahmed 4 for 32) and 263 (Azmat Rana 89, Rashid Khan 5 for 117)
Pakistan International Airlines 317 for 9 (Naeem Ahmed 61, Feroze Mehdi 55, Rizwan-uz-Zaman 52, Zaigham Burki 4 for 116) and 100 for 7 (Zaigham Burki 5 for 48)

Match drawn
P.I.A. 8 pts, Muslim Commercial Bank 5 pts

There was a remarkable switch in fortunes in the match between Habib Bank and National Bank in Lahore. Habib batsmen scored at four runs an over on the opening day to put their side in total command. The spin of Abdul Qadir and skipper Abdur Raqeeb then destroyed National Bank after Taslim Arif and Saleem Pervez had put on 95 for the first wicket.

Following-on 165 behind, National Bank were given a spirited recovery by their openers who this time put on 169. Raqeeb and Qadir again bowled well, but there was no second collapse and National Bank reached 428 for 9 before a declaration came which was little more than a token, and the match was drawn.

23, 24, 25 and 26 December 1982

at L.C.C.A., Lahore

Railways 313 (Asad Rauf 92, Talat Mirza 61, Nasir Abbas 5 for 108)
Lahore 138 (Mansoor Rana 50 not out, Shahid Butt 5 for 60, Mohammad Nazir 4 for 31) and 154 (Shahid Butt 7 for 60)

Railways won by an innings and 21 runs
Railways 18 pts, Lahore 4 pts

at Punjab University, Lahore

Pakistan International Airlines 315 for 4 (Shoaib Mohammad 109 not out, Asif Mohammad 57, Zahid Ahmed 53 not out, Iqbal Sikander 52) and 120 (Afzaal Butt 9 for 41)
National Bank 234 (Wasim Raja 55, Saleem Pervez 54, Rashid Khan 5 for 105) and 204 for 3 (Saleem Pervez 95, Shafiq Ahmed 55)

National Bank won by 7 wickets
National Bank 14 pts, P.I.A. 8 pts

Lahore became firmly rooted at the bottom of the table when Railways overwhelmed them at the L.C.C.A. ground. After Talat Mirza had left Railways struggled a little, but Asad Rauf had fine support from the last three batsmen, Mohammad Nazir, Zulqarnian and Shahid Butt and the score moved from 168 for 7 to 313 all out. Shahid and Zulqarnian put on 70 for the last wicket.

Lahore twice collapsed before the combined efforts of off-spinner Mohammad Nazir and slow left-arm Shahid Butt, a young man of immense promise, and Railways had won by an innings with more than a day and a half to spare.

Shoaib Mohammad batted throughout the 85 overs of the P.I.A. innings and when Rashid Khan bowled them to a first innings lead of 81, P.I.A. looked to be well in control of the match.

Fast bowler Afzaal Butt, who had had a good season in 1981–82 and who now had greater responsibility since the departure of Ehtesham-ud-Din, shattered P.I.A. with a career best spell of hostile bowling in the second innings which gave him 9 for 41 in 21.4 unchanged overs.

Saleem Pervez and Shafiq Ahmed ensured National Bank of victory when, chasing a target of 202, they added 134 for the second wicket.

Railways win had moved them temporarily into first place, while National Bank, who had beaten P.I.A. and were still striving to retain the title, found themselves still outside the top five.

Javed Miandad led Habib Bank to success in the P.A.C.C Pentagular Tournament. (A.S.P.)

29, 30 and 31 December 1982

at Bahawal Stadium, Bahawalpur

Muslim Commercial Bank 147 (Barbar Basharat 70, Sikhander Bakht 6 for 38) and 123 (Azmat Rana 59, Tauseef Ahmed 4 for 30)
United Bank 176 (Sadiq Mohammad 58, Ilyas Khan 6 for 51) and 98 for 3)

United Bank won by 7 wickets
United Bank 15 pts, Muslim Commercial Bank 4 pts

30, 31 December 1982, 1 and 2 January 1983

at Ibn-e-Qasim, Multan

Karachi 212 for 8 dec (Zafar Ahmed 60 not out, Umar Rasheed 58) and 65 (Khatib Rizwan 6 for 19)
Rawalpindi 137 for 8 dec (Masood Anwar 61, Mohinder 6 for 28) and 142 for 3 (Masood Anwar 70 not out, Sohail Kiani 56)

Rawalpindi won by 7 wickets
Rawalpindi 12 pts, Karachi 4 pts

at L.C.C.A., Lahore

Allied Bank 118 (Talat Masood 50, Afzaal Butt 5 for 44, Iqbal Qasim 4 for 48) and 127 (Iqbal Qasim 5 for 26)
National Bank 162 (Azeem Hafeez 7 for 68) and 87 for 2 (Saleem Pervez 51 not out)

National Bank won by 8 wickets
National Bank 14 pts, Allied Bank 4 pts

at Punjab University, Lahore

Habib Bank 255 (Agha Zahid 82, Azhar Khan 76, A Ahmed 5 for 64)
Lahore 340 (Pervez Mir 73, Aamer Malik 53, Abdu Raqeeb 8 for 80)

Match drawn
Habib Bank 8 pts, Lahore 8 pts

In a low-scoring match in Bahawalpur, United Bank, owin much to the seam bowling of Sikhander and Ehtesham an to the off-spin of Tauseef, defeated Muslim Commercia Bank with more than a day to spare and enhanced thei chances of winning the title.

Babar Basharat, Nadeem Yousuf and Zaigham Burk were the only M.C.B. batsmen to reach double figures in th first innings, but United Bank, too, struggled. Sadiq, in determined mood, gave his side every chance of a lead an he was supported by several who contributed vital run against the immaculate Ilyas Khan, who was leading th M.C.B. side.

United Bank led by 29 on the first innings and this becam a decisive advantage when M.C.B. slipped to 37 for 5 in thei second knock. Azmat Rana and Nadeem Yousuf added 78 but then the last five wickets fell for 8 runs and United Ban strolled to victory.

The rejuvenation of Rawalpindi continued with anothe startling success, this time over Karachi.

Mohinder's bowling gave Karachi a first innings advantage after Masood had put them in. Masood batted with great determination, but he had little support. It was the deposed captain, Khatib Rizwan, who swung the game decisively in Rawalpindi's favour. Gaining some assistance from the conditions, he bowled unchanged to take 6 for 19 with his medium pace left-arm bowling as Karachi were shot out for 65.

Masood Anwar and Sohail Kiani, with a second wicket stand of 120, assured Rawalpindi of their second win of the season, but the threat of relegation still loomed.

A mixture of pace and spin accounted for Allied Bank on the opening day of their match with National Bank. There was no play on the first scheduled day as the wicket was damp and the conditions were exploited fully by Afzaal Butt and Iqbal Qasim.

Dogged batting by National's batsmen, ably led by Taslim Arif, who, returning to his position as wicket-keeper accounted for five batsmen in the first innings, gave them a lead of 54 in spite of some fine pace bowling from Jalal and Azeem.

Allied Bank reached 120 for 6 in their second innings, but lost their last four wickets for 7 runs, three of them to Iqbal Qasim who, in dismissing Shoaib Habib, Jalaluddin and Raees-ur-Rehman with successive deliveries, performed the only hat-trick of the competition.

National Bank's win put them among the leaders of the competition.

The game between Habib Bank and Lahore was a farcical affair. Play was only possible on the last day, and, by mutual consent, the two teams decided to play just for bonus points. 102 overs were bowled in the day and 595 runs were scored as 20 wickets fell. Both sides took maximum points and a record run tally was established for a day's first-class cricket in Pakistan.

The outstanding performance of the day was by the Habib Bank wicket-keeper, Masbod Iqbal, who had seven dismissals, three caught and four stumped, to equal the Pakistan record held by Wasim Bari, Taslim Arif and Shahid Israr.

3, 4, 5 and 6 January 1983

at Gymkhana Ground, Karachi

Pakistan International Airlines 120 (Khurshid Akhtar 6 for 45) and 259 (Aftab Baloch 123 not out, Rizwan-uz-Zaman 58, Khurshid Akhtar 5 for 73)
United Bank 243 (Mahmood Rasheed 65 not out, Siddiq Patni 60) and 137 for 7 (Rashid Khan 4 for 57)

United Bank won by 3 wickets
United Bank 17 pts, P.I.A. 4 pts

4, 5, 6 and 7 January 1983

at Ibn-e-Qasim Bagh, Multan

Lahore 168 (Mohinder Kumar 5 for 53) and 178 (Mohinder Kumar 7 for 73)
Karachi 316 (Zafar Ahmed 100, Feroze Najamuddin 73, Mohsin Kamal 5 for 78, Ali Ahmed 5 for 122) and 33 for 0

Karachi won by 10 wickets
Karachi 18 pts, Lahore 4 pts

Rashid Khan. Seventy wickets in the season gave him a place in Pakistan's World Cup squad and helped Pakistan International Airlines to a successful season. (George Herringshaw)

at C.M.T. & S.D., Rawalpindi

Rawalpindi 288 (Sohail Kiyani 103, Mohammad Riaz 56, Wasim Raja 6 for 106) and 430 (Mohammad Riaz 134, Azmat Jalil 129, Wasim Raja 5 for 154)
National Bank 427 (Shafiq Ahmed 112, Taslim Arif 111, Ali Zia 74, Khatib Rizwan 5 for 78, Mohammad Riaz 5 for 109) and 68 for 2

Match drawn
National Bank 8 pts, Rawalpindi 8 pts

The last round of matches in the tournament arrived with United Bank needing to beat P.I.A. to win the title for the third time. They had last won it in 1981. They could not have had a better start to their ambitions than bowling out the opposition for 120, Khurshid Akhtar being the main destroyer.

Determined, often slow batting gave United Bank a match-winning lead of 123. With P.I.A. on 149 for 8, the match looked over, but Aftab Baloch, who had come in at number six, played a swashbuckling innings, and United Bank found themselves chasing 137 on a wicket that was deteriorating.

They slid to 89 for 7 and the game looked lost, but eminent good sense from Nasir Valika and Tauseef Ahmed saw them home, and the Quaid-e-Azam trophy was theirs.

At the other end of the table, Karachi beat Lahore in three

days so saving themselves from relegation, but condemning Lahore to that fate.

Splendid bowling by Mohinder Kumar, 12 for 126 in the match, was the key to Karachi's victory, but, in truth, they dominated in every phase of the game. Zafar finished the tournament with another innings showing how far his batting had developed, and he and Feroze Najamuddin shared a fifth wicket stand of 163.

The match saw the Karachi wicket-keeper-opening batsman Kamal Najamuddin equal Taslim Arif's national record with ten dismissals in the match. He caught four and stumped one in the first innings and caught five in the second.

One could not help but feel sorry for Lahore who found themselves languishing at the bottom of the table for they had been denied the services of leading players like Imran, Sarfraz and Majid for much, or all, of the season.

The match at Rawalpindi was significant in that Rs 11,000 in Fujicolor prize money was won. There were centuries by Sohail Kiyani, Taslim Arif, Shafiq Ahmed, Azmat Jalil and Mohammad Riaz, who also had five wickets in an innings, and Wasim Raja had eleven wickets in the match with his leg-breaks.

Maqsood Kundi had five dismissals behind the stumps and Ali Zia became the only fieldsman in the competition to hold five catches in an innings.

The outcome of all this was a draw in spite of the mighty performances like Taslim and Shafiq adding 208 for the second wicket for National Bank, and the draw meant that

Iqbal Qasim's spin bowling played an important part in National Bank finishing as runners-up in the Quaid-e-Azam Trophy. (Adrian Murrell)

National Bank finished second and Rawalpindi we relegated.

Quaid-e-Azam Trophy – Final Table

	P	W	L	D	Bonus Bt	Bonus Bl	Pts
United Bank (2)	9	5	–	4	31	25	106
National Bank (1)	9	4	1	4	25	26	91
Railways (6)	9	3	3	3	27	29	86
Habib Bank (3)	9	2	–	7	31	31	82
Pakistan International A.(4)	9	2	2	5	30	32	82
Muslim Commercial Bank (5)	9	2	2	5	27	28	75
Allied Bank (–)	9	2	3	4	22	28	70
Karachi (10)	9	1	4	4	30	22	62
Rawalpindi (7)	9	2	5	2	16	24	60
Lahore (9)	9	–	3	6	20	31	51

The first five teams qualified for the P.A.C.O. Pentagular League. Rawalpindi and Lahore were relegated. Their places in the 1983–4 tournament will be taken by Pakistan Automobile Corporation and House Building Finance Corporation, the finalists in the B.C.C.P. Patron's Trophy, 1982–3.

17, 18, 19 and 20 January 1983

at L.C.C.A., Lahore

United Bank 231 for 8 dec (Nasir Valika 78, Shahid But 4 for 66) and 294 for 7 dec (Nasir Valika 103 not ou Shahid Butt 4 for 129)
Railways 239 for 9 dec (Ijaz Ahmed 61, Tauseef Ahme 5 for 77) and 267 for 9 (Khurshid Akhtar 7 for 101)

Match drawn
United Bank 6 pts, Railways 5 pts

The opening match in the Pentagular Tournament was splendidly contested close affair which ended with Unite Bank one wicket short of victory and Railways only 20 shor of their target.

Generally, the bowling was on top, but United Bank captain, Nasir Valika, had a fine match with the bat, scoring 18 for once out. Khurshid Akhtar had ten wickets in the matc and Shahid Butt began what was to be a fine tournament fo him with eight wickets for 195.

22, 23, 24 and 25 January 1983

at Punjab University, Lahore

National Bank 74 for 8 dec (Tauseef Ahmed 4 for 18 and 224 (Saleem Pervez 102, Ali Zia 70, Tauseef Ahmed 6 for 49)
United Bank 249 (Ashraf Ali 61 not out, Afzaal Butt 4 fo 70, Jahanzeb Khan 4 for 95) and 51 for 1

United Bank won by 9 wickets
United Bank 15 pts, National Bank 4 pts

at L.C.C.A., Lahore

Pakistan International Airlines 209 for 8 (Aftab Baloch 54, Shahid Butt 6 for 90) and 261 (Hasan Jamil 73, Shahid Butt 6 for 128, Mohammad Nazir 4 for 112)
Railways 400 for 9 (Saadat Ali 170, Naved Anjum 81, Zahid Ahmed 4 for 114) and 72 for 2

Railways won by 8 wickets
Railways 16pts, Pakistan International Airlines 5 pts

Nasir Valika won the toss and asked National Bank to bat first on a rain-affected wicket. National were 66 for 3, but five wickets fell for 8 runs, and Shafiq Ahmed declared.

Ashraf Ali, batting at number eight, lifted United Bank to lead of 175, and this proved decisive. In spite of a valiant century from opener Saleem Pervez who shared a third wicket stand of 164 with Ali Zia, National Bank again collapsed to the off-spin of Tauseef and United Bank won with more than a day to spare.

Railways again owed much to the splendid bowling of Shahid Butt, but there was also a magnificent 170 from Saadat Ali who added 175 with Naved Anjum for the third wicket. Consistent contributions all down the order helped Railways to 400 in their 85 overs, and, trailing by 191 on the first innings, Pakistan International Airlines, without Zaheer, had little hope of saving the game.

20, 21 and 22 February 1983

at National Stadium, Karachi

National Bank 266 (Ali Zia 83, Ijaz Ahmed 74, Iqbal Sikander 4 for 63) and 80 for 2 (Ijaz Ahmed 59 not out)
Pakistan International Airlines 292 for 9 (Naeem Ahmed 84 not out)

Match abandoned

at Qaddafi Stadium, Lahore

Habib Bank 272 (Agha Zahid 102, Saadat Ali 4 for 25, Shahid Butt 4 for 94) and 416 for 5 dec (Agha Zahid 119, Mohsin Khan 101 not out, Sultan Rana 127, Shahid Butt 4 for 177)
Railways 268 (Saadat Ali 107, Abdur Raqeeb 5 for 74) and 236 (Naved Anjum 50, Mohammad Nazir 50, Abdur Raqeeb 5 for 94)

Habib Bank won by 184 runs
Habib Bank 18 pts, Railways 8 pts

The match in Karachi was abandoned at lunch time on the third day because of disturbances and a curfew in the city. It was scheduled to be replayed in Lahore, but the statistics of the match remained valid.

Habib Bank's first match in the tournament was completed in three days with Habib Bank easy winners. The first innings ended in stalemate, but then Agha Zahid completed his second hundred of the match. He shared a second wicket stand of 251 with Sultan Rana, and then Mohsin Khan, who batted at number six in the second innings, hit a sparkling hundred to lift the score to 416.

Railways started promisingly enough, but the spin twins,

Raqeeb and Qadir, brought about a mid-innings collapse from which Railways never completely recovered.

17, 18, 19 and 20 March 1983

at Qaddafi Stadium, Lahore

Habib Bank 399 for 4 (Agha Zahid 175, Arshad Pervez 79, Javed Miandad 53)
Pakistan International Airlines 254 for 6 (Shoaib Mohammad 101 not out, Abdur Raqeeb 5 for 93)

Match drawn
Habib Bank 6 pts, P.I.A. 5 pts

at L.C.C.A., Lahore

National Bank 261 for 9 dec (Shafiq Ahmed 92, Ali Zia 52, Mohammad Nazir 7 for 75) and 81 for 1
Railways 212 (Iqbal Qasim 7 for 78)

Match drawn
National Bank 8 pts, Railways 5 pts

No play was possible on the last two days in either of these matches because of rain.

Agha Zahid completed his third hundred in succession, sharing stands of 157 with Arshad Pervez and 122 with Javed Miandad. In the other match, spinners Mohammad Nazir, Man of the Match, and Iqbal Qasim dominated.

22, 23, 24 and 25 March 1983

at Qaddafi Stadium, Lahore

Habib Bank 391 for 7 (Javed Miandad 115, Sultan Rana 110, Iqbal Qasim 5 for 115) and 78 for 2
National Bank 177 (Saleem Pervez 53, Abdur Raqeeb 4 for 56, Abdul Qadir 4 for 89) and 290 (Shafiq Ahmed 84, Saleem Pervez 74, Abdul Qadir 7 for 91)

Habib Bank won by 8 wickets
Habib Bank 18 pts, National Bank 3 pts

at L.C.C.A., Lahore

Pakistan International Airlines 195 (Rizwan-uz-Zaman 61, Feroze Mehdi 51, Shahid Aziz 4 for 38) and 216 (Rizwan-uz-Zaman 69, Shahid Azis 4 for 87)
United Bank 269 for 9 dec (Ashraf Ali 90, Sikhander Bakht 67, Rashid Khan 4 for 63) and 147 for 2 (Haroon Rashid 61 not out)

United Bank won by 8 wickets
United Bank 18 pts, P.I.A. 4 pts

A stand of 213 for the fifth wicket between Javed Mianded and Sultan Rana put Habib Bank in a strong position. When Qadir and Raqeeb spun National Bank out for 177 and Javed asked them to follow-on, that position became impregnable.

Shafiq Ahmed and Saleem Pervez held up Habib Bank's triumphant progress with a second wicket stand of 153 when National bank batted again, but once Raqeeb had broken the stand, Abdul Qadir got to work again and caused havoc

Allied Bank 1982-3
Quaid-e-Azam Trophy

BATTING

Match columns (each with two innings):
1. v. Habib Bank (Karachi) 10-13 October, 1982
2. v. Rawalpindi (Rawalpindi) 16-18 October, 1982
3. v. Muslim Commercial Bank (Lahore) 22-25 October, 1982
4. v. Railways (Lahore) 29-31 October, 1982
5. v. Lahore (Lahore) 4-7 November, 1982
6. v. Pakistan International Airlines (Lahore) 10-13 Nov. 1982
7. v. United Bank (Lahore) 22-24 Nov. 1982
8. v. Karachi (Bahawalpur) 4-8 December, 1982
9. v. National Bank (Lahore) 30 Dec. '82-2 Jan. '83

	1		2		3		4		5		6		7		8		9	
Iqtidar Ali	99	56	0	13	13	20	8	66	41	1	16	56	86	3	16	31		
Shahid Mahboob	20	—	16	—	1	3	0	25*	110	—	0	0	58	16				
Naseer Chughtai	5	3*							0	12*	35	1	32	0	12	—	3	0
Saleem Yousuf	30	41*	145*	9	0	64	20	0	6	22	1	9	0	21			11	35
Shoaib Habib	12	—	0	—	54	13	22	23	46	—	7	29	34*	1	0	21	5	4
Zafar Mehdi			4	—	44*	33	1	0	10	—	55*	33	0	19	42	3	11	17
Farooq Rasheed			5	20*	39	0	0	23	6	—	6	27*	1	0	38	7*	10	38
Moin-ud-Din													14	23	61*	26*	2	21
Amin Lakhani	25*	—	0	—	1	1		0	0	—	11	—	0	4	2	—	0	0
Azeem Hafeez	19	—	—	—	14	1*			0*	—	14	—	6*	0	—	—	1	3*
Raees-ur-Rehman													—	0*	—	—	8*	0
Salman Qizilbash	9	39	15	25	53	12	9	52	44	45*								
Athar A. Khan	27	9	4	9*	16	29	7	4			2	2			0	28		
Talat Masood	3	—	15	—			13*	2							89	0	50	2
Jalaluddin	14	—						12	20	—	10	2*					12	0
Tahir Nisar					0	22												
Byes	5	2					5		1	4	7	9			5		1	
Leg-byes	2		(13)	(10)	4	2	(18)	(9)	3		4	7	(24)	2	8	4	3	4
Wides	1				1						2	2	1		1		2	
No-balls	4	2			4	4			4	3	5	3			2	3	2	
Total	275	152	217	86	243	210	98	216	291	89	175	178	255	90	275	124	118	127
Wickets	10	3	9	3	10	10	8	10	10	2	10	7	8	10	8	5	10	10
Result	D		W		L		W		D		D		L		D		L	
Points	6		14		5		13		8		5		7		8		4	

Catches

27 – Saleem Yousuf (ct 26/st 1)
12 – Iqtidar Ali
11 – Farooq Rasheed
9 – Shoaib Habib
6 – Zafar Mehdi

5 – Amin Lakhani, Athar A. Khan and Moin-ud-Din (ct 4/st 1)
3 – Talat Masood, Shahid Mahboob
2 – Tahir Nisar
1 – Azeem Hafeez, Salman Qizilbash, Naseer Chugtai, Jalaluddin and sub.

BOWLING

	Azeem Hafeez	Shahid Mahboob	Raees-ur-Rehman	Amin Lakhani	Shoaib Habib	Zafar Mehdi	Jalaluddin	Salman Qizilbash
v. Habib Bank (Karachi) 10-13 October, 1982	11–1–50–0 / 14–0–57–0	18–2–59–3 / 30.5–2–107–6		18–5–39–1 / 8–1–17–1	22–3–50–2 / 29–6–60–1		15–3–57–1	
v. Rawalpindi (Rawalpindi) 16-18 October, 1982	9–1–37–1 / 9–2–15–0	16–5–28–6 / 12.5–5–27–2		11–2–24–1 / 26–4–56–1	3–0–6–0 / 29–3–70–6	9–4–9–1		1–1–0–0
v. Muslim Commercial Bank (Lahore) 22-25 October, 1982	13.4–0–52–2 / 27–5–71–2	20–4–60–2 / 33–7–65–7		16–6–42–2 / 22–7–26–0	22–4–87–2 / 4–1–10–0	11–4–27–0 / 1–0–6–0		
v. Railways (Lahore) 29-31 October, 1982		11–2–30–5 / 18–5–39–1			6–2–9–0 / 15–3–56–2		12–2–25–4 / 21.1–5–61–6	
v. Lahore (Lahore) 4-7 November, 1982	11–4–28–0 / 28–5–65–1	18–1–56–0 / 27–7–39–0		20–5–28–1 / 26.4–8–44–4	9–2–20–1 / 23–4–56–3	4–1–7–0	21–6–45–6 / 24–6–91–0	
v. Pakistan International Airlines (Lahore) 10-13 November, 1982	17–5–52–1 / 22–9–41–4	27.2–1–95–5 / 19–3–59–1		5–3–9–0	3–0–18–0 / 3–0–6–0	2–0–10–0 / 0.1–0–0–1	27–10–45–3 / 26–7–41–4	
v. United Bank (Lahore) 22-24 November, 1982	32–5–78–2 / 3.4–0–17–0	27–4–74–2 / 2–0–15–2	14–2–34–1 / 3–0–12–1	7–1–33–1	14–3–30–1	6–1–20–2		
v. Karachi (Bahawalpur) 4-8 December, 1982	10–1–66–1 / 25–3–77–2		11–1–38–1 / 20–7–56–2	32.4–16–57–5 / 35–10–56–0	25–6–64–1 / 38–15–61–0	5–1–13–0 / 14–6–25–0		
v. National Bank (Lahore) 30 Dec., 1982-2 Jan., 1983	20–4–68–7 / 3–0–34–0		5–1–21–0	9–4–13–0	1–0–2–0 / 2–0–7–0	2–0–8–0	15.4–3–44–3 / 7.2–2–32–2	
	255.2–45– / 808–23 / av. 35.13	293–50– / 753–42 / av. 17.92	53–11– / 161–5 / av. 32.20	246.2–74– / 471–17 / av. 27.70	242–50– / 603–19 / av. 31.73	54.1–17– / 125–4 / av. 31.25	169.1–44– / 441–29 / av. 15.20	1–1– / 0–0 / —

Inns	NOs	Runs	HS	Av
16	—	525	99	32.81
11	1	249	110	24.90
11	2	103	35	11.44
16	2	414	145*	29.57
15	1	271	54	19.35
14	2	272	55*	22.66
15	3	220	39	18.33
6	2	147	61*	36.75
12	1	44	25*	4.00
9	4	58	19	11.60
3	2	8	8*	8.00
10	1	303	53	33.66
12	1	137	29	12.45
8	1	174	89	24.85
7	1	70	20	11.66
2		22	22	11.00

Iqtidar Ali

	Byes	Leg-byes	Wides	No-balls	Total	Wkts
	1	2	4	12	274	8
	3	9	5	1	259	8
			(12)		107	8
			(14)		191	10
		3	2	9	282	8
0–2–0	5	1	6	6	198	10
			(5)		60	9
		3	1	4	173	10
		4	1	7	189	10
	2	7	10	8	329	8
	7	3	7	6	252	10
	1	7	5	4	182	10
	15	4	2	5	295	9
	3	3	2		52	3
	2	6	2	14	262	10
0–18–0	2	4	5	9	313	4
	1	5	3	5	162	10
			5	1	87	2

0–
0–0
—

among the remaining batsmen. His seven wickets brought his total for the season to 95, and, with one match remaining, he was in sight of becoming the first Pakistani bowler to take one hundred wickets in a domestic season.

Habib duly won with more than a day to spare.

In the other match, there were strange shifts of fortune. Rizwan and Feroze began with a stand of 116 for P.I.A. who then collapsed to 195 all out. In reply, United Bank were 102 for 6 before Ashraf Ali, Man of the Match for his batting and wicket-keeping, and Sikhander Bakht added 147.

This helped United Bank to an unexpectedly big lead of 74 and with P.I.A. again batting indifferently, they were left to make 143, a task they accomplished with ease.

27, 28, 29 and 30 March 1983

at L.C.C.A., Lahore

National Bank 362 for 7 (Mohammad Jamil 139, Shafiq Ahmed 70) and 407 for 8 dec (Ijaz Ahmed 137, Saleem Pervez 86, Shafiq Ahmed 60, Mohammad Shafiq 54, Naeem Ahmed 4 for 66)
Pakistan International Airlines 277 (Aftab Baloch 59, Rashid Khan 53, Anil Dalpat 50, Iqbal Qasim 4 for 111) and 177 for 3 (Rizwan-uz-Zaman 89)

Match drawn
National Bank 8 pts, P.I.A. 6 pts

at Qaddafi Stadium, Lahore

Habib Bank 305 for 8 dec (Saleem Malik 119, Agha Zahid 75) and 151 (Sikhander Bakht 5 for 58)
United Bank 221 for 9 dec (Nasir Valika 70 not out, Abdul Qadir 5 for 91) and 127 (Abdur Raqeeb 4 for 29)

Habib Bank won by 108 runs
Habib Bank 17 pts, United Bank 4 pts

In a match dominated by batsmen, Mohammad Jamil and Shafiq Ahmed shared a second wicket stand of 154 for National Bank's second wicket in the first innings, and Saleem Pervez and Ijaz Ahmed put on 156 for the second wicket in the second innings. National Bank led most of the way, but a draw always seemed inevitable.

All interest was centred on the Qaddafi Stadium, however, where Habib Bank met United Bank in a game that would decide who won the tournament. At the start of the match, Habib Bank led their rivals by three points, and this was increased when they took maximum batting points and restricted their opponents to two bowling points.

Habib's batting success was founded on a second wicket stand of 150 between Saleem and Agha, and Javed played well before he was run out.

After only six overs, Javed introduced Abdul Qadir into the attack when United batted and he responded by quickly dismissing Siddiq. Nasir and Mansoor Akhtar took the score to 64, but then Abdul Qadir dismissed both batsmen and Haroon, and United Bank were 83 for 4.

Nasir Valika and Ashraf Ali rallied the side with a stand of 63, but Ashraf fell to Raqeeb. It was then that Abdul Qadir took his fifth wicket of the innings, having Sikhander Bakht lbw when he played back. It was his hundredth wicket of the season, a monumental achievement in Pakistani cricket.

United Bank trailed by 84 on the first innings, but fought

Habib Bank 1982-3
First Class Matches

BATTING

	v. Allied Bank (Karachi) 10-13 Oct. 1982	v. Pakistan Internat. Airlines (Karachi) 16-19 Oct. 1982	v. Karachi (Karachi) 22-25 Oct. 1982	v. Muslim Commercial Bank (Hyderabad) 4-7 Nov. 1982	v. Rawalpindi (Rawalpindi) 11-12 Nov. 1982	v. Railways (Lahore) 4-8 Dec. 1982	v. United Bank (Lahore) 11-14 Dec. 1982	v. National Bank (Lahore) 17-20 Dec. 1982	v. Lahore (Lahore) 30 Dec. 1982-2 Jan. 1983	v. Railways (Lahore) 20-22 Feb. 1983	v. Pakistan Internat. Airlines (Lahore) 17-20 March 1983
Agha Zahid	98 61	0 10	79 21*	4 51	0 —	42 —	47 —	80 25	82 —	102 119	175
Arshad Pervez	23* 9	9 35	109 35*	43 50	21 —	0 —	0 —	87 —	21 —	79	—
Sultan Rana	23 78	7 46	38 —	4 29	33 —	1 —	57* —	— 7		19 127	14*
Azhar Khan	52 68	0 4	58* —	31 —	50 —	34 —	44 —	54* 13*	76 —	16 —	—
Tehsin Javed	4 1					0 —	36* —	100 15*	1 —		
Raees Ahmed	24 8	6 32	15* —			39 —	34 —	— 18	0* —		
Zaheer Ahmed	11 9	6 1								0 —	
Anwar Miandad	18 3*	15 6*	— —	31* 12*		97 —	16 —	— 0	36 —	40 30*	
Jamshed Hussain	2 4					2 —					
Abdur Raqeeb	— —	2* 0*	— —	6* —	8* —	4 —			4 —	2 3	
Liaqat Ali	— —	1 —				0* —			0 —	4* 8	
Saleem Malik		51 78	15 —	103 107	10 —					24 14	48 —
Aslam Qureshi		10 44							4 —		
Masood Iqbal			— —	13 5	24* —	2 —		— 14*	21 —		7* —
Abdul Qadir				4 9	0 —						
Mohsin Khan				4 26	13 —					15 101*	
Javed Miandad						96 —				38 —	53 —
Byes	1 3	5 13		3 6		2	2	4 9		4 3	6
Leg-byes	2 9	2 5	(12) 2	2 12	(21)	1	3	2	2	4 8	13
Wides	4 5	1		1			4	2 1	1		2
No-balls	12 1	6 4		1		9	9	5 1		4 3	2
Total	274 259	120 279	326 58	250 307	276	233	252	348 82	255	272 416	399
Wickets	8 8	10 8	4 0	8 7	8	10	5	3 3	10	10 5	4
Result	D	D	W	D	W	D	D	D	D	W	D
Points	8	3	18	6	18	7	6	8	8	18	6

Catches 25 – Masood Iqbal (ct 17/st 8)   17 – Sultan Rana   8 – Agha Zahid, Saleem Malik   6 – Arshad Pervez, Liaqat Ali and Anwar Miandad
21 – Zaheer Ahmed (ct 12/st 9)   9 – Azhar Khan and subs.   7 – Abdur Raqeeb   3 – Javed Miandad

BOWLING

	Liaqat Ali	Jamshed Hussain	Agha Zahid	Abdur Raqeeb	Raees Ahmed	Azhar Khan	Anwar Miandad	Sultan Rana	Arshad Pervez
v. Allied Bank (Karachi) 10-13 October, 1982	16-6-43-2 / 5-0-25-0	6-1-21-0 / 4-2-17-0	21-5-51-1 / 5-1-19-0	13.4-2-54-2 / 17-3-34-0	12-2-39-2 / 4-1-15-1	16-2-55-2 / 14-0-24-2	3-0-10-0	1-0-1-0	1-0-3-0
v. Pakistan International Airlines (Karachi) 16-19 October, 1982	7-2-15-0 / 14-7-22-3		27-8-66-3 / 8-2-13-0	19-5-43-1 / 5-4-3-0	8-1-22-0 / 35-5-90-4	15-0-45-4 / 28-14-33-1	1-0-2-0		
v. Karachi (Karachi) 22-25 October, 1982	4-0-19-0 / 3-1-8-0		11-6-16-1 / 3-2-5-0	24.2-4-59-3 / 29-13-36-1	9-0-21-0 / 3-1-6-0	3-0-10-0 / 11-2-17-0	2-1-1-0		
v. Muslim Commercial Bank (Hyderabad) 4-7 Nov., 1982	7-3-13-0 / 5-1-16-0			34-4-89-0 / 15-4-31-0			3-0-7-0 / 1-1-0-1		
v. Rawalpindi (Rawalpindi) 11-12 November, 1982	1-0-2-0			18.4-1-63-1					
v. Railways (Lahore) 4-8 December, 1982	4-0-18-1 / 26-9-67-3	15-4-42-2	11-2-29-0	7-3-16-2 / 9.2-2-28-1	12-0-56-3		6-0-15-3		
v. United Bank (Lahore) 11-14 December, 1982	22-8-56-2 / 36-13-92-4	11-2-39-1 / 19-4-45-1	10-5-6-1 / 13-3-41-1	23-4-56-1 / 11-2-35-0	13-3-54-1 / 6-1-36-1			3-0-12-0	
v. National Bank (Lahore) 17-20 December, 1982	2-0-21-1 / 4-1-14-0	1-1-0-0			23-3-77-7	2-0-8-0	1-0-2-0	6-1-23-0	
v. Lahore (Lahore) 30 Dec., 1982-2 January, 1983	7-0-25-0 / 2-0-4-0		8-2-12-0 / 2-0-12-0	53-10-151-3 / 15.2-3-80-8	13-1-59-0 / 13-0-83-1	7-1-14-1 / 10-0-81-1	1-0-2-0 / 4-0-24-0	2-0-6-0 / 3-0-21-0	
v. Railways (Lahore) 20-22 February, 1983	7-5-10-0 / 3-0-10-0			14-5-74-5 / 18-2-94-5			8-2-34-0 / 1.1-0-11-1	3-1-10-0	4-2-25-0
v. Pakistan International Airlines (Lahore) 17-20 March, 1983	6-1-10-0			36-7-93-5		3-0-6-0			
v. National Bank (Lahore) 22-24 March, 1983	3-1-6-0 / 6-3-14-0			19.2-4-56-4 / 29-4-109-3		3-0-6-0	13-5-38-0		
v. United Bank (Lahore) 27-30 March, 1983	6-0-15-0 / 8-1-31-2			36-8-88-3 / 16-5-29-4					
	204-62- / 556-18 / av. 30.88	56-14- / 164-4 / av. 41.00	119-36- / 270-7 / av. 38.57	485.4-102- / 1398-59 / av. 23.69	130-15- / 489-13 / av. 37.61	125-21- / 342-14 / av. 24.42	41.1-9- / 140-2 / av. 70.00	10-2- / 53-0 / —	1-0- / 3-0 / —

a Mohsin Khan 1-1-0-0 / 2-1-6-1   b Tehsin Javed 2-1-6-0   d Mohsin Khan 5-3-13-2   f Javed Miandad 2-0-9-0
c Tehsin Javed 2-0-13-0   e Javed Miandad 3-1-10-0

back to dismiss Habib Bank for 151 and so keep themselves in the game.

Needing 235 to win on a wicket which Raqeeb and Qadir exploited to the full, they were dismissed inside 49 overs and Habib Bank had retained the Pentagular League tournament.

Agha Zahid was given the award for the batsman of the tournament, and slow left-arm Shahid Butt took the bowler's award. Zulquarnian, the Railways wicket-keeper, was declared best fielder of the tournament, and another wicket-keeper, Ashraf Ali, was named Man of the Tournament for his 14 dismissals and 220 runs.

P.A.C.O. Pentagular Tournament Final Positions

	P	W	L	D	Bonus Bt	Bonus Bl	Pts
Habib Bank (1)	4	3	–	1	16	13	59
United Bank (2)	4	2	1	1	12	11	43
Railways	4	1	1	2	13	11	34
National Bank (3)	4	–	2	2	9	14	23
Pakistan International Airlines	4	–	2	2	11	9	20

Mudassar Nazar. He could not recapture the form for United Bank that he showed for Pakistan, but he had a splendid season. (Adrian Murrell)

Batting

v. United Bank (Lahore) 27-30 March. 1983		Inns	NOs	Runs	HS	Av
* 75	0	21	2	1152	175	60.63
17	22	18	2	613	109	38.31
25*	15	17	3	633	127	45.21
0	18	16	4	548	76	45.66
		7	1	157	100	26.16
		9	2	176	39	25.14
4	11	8	—	69	27	8.62
13	10	15	5	334	97	33.40
		3	—	8	4	2.66
—	5	9	4	34	8*	6.80
—	3*	6	3	16	8	5.33
119	16	13	—	596	119	45.84
		3	—	58	44	19.33
		7	3	86	24*	21.50
1	28	7	1	47	28	7.83
		5	1	159	101*	39.75
41	2	7	1	354	115	59.00
2	1					
4	3					
2	1					
2	16					
305	151					
8	10					
W						
17						

2 – Abdul Qadir and Tehsin Javed
1 – Raees Ahmed, Mohsin Khan and Jamshed Hussain

Bowling

Aslam Qureshi	Saleem Malik	Abdul Qadir	Byes	Leg-byes	Wides	No-balls	Total	Wkts
			5	2	1	4	275	10
			2			2	152	3
-0-28-0			4	3	1	6	235	9
-2-19-0	1.2-0-1-2		3	6	1	4	195	10
		33-9-79-5	3	7		5	219	10
		42.4-15-82-9	8			1	164	10
		42-6-151-7	5	2		3	270	8a
	15-3-37-0	34-13-67-2	6		1	11	175	4
		19-4-49-9	(11)				125	10
		16-6-27-4	(15)				91	10
			(28)				250	10
			(19)				242	6
			(29)				278	7
			2		1	1	64	1b
		26-5-79-3	2	5		6	183	10
		61-17-125-5	15	6	1	12	428	9
-0-10-0			5		1	6	340	10c
	6-4-6-0	16-6-73-3	14	8		1	268	10d
		20-1-108-3		3			236	10e
	2-0-8-0	36-6-108-1	10	6		4	254	6f
	7-2-13-1	24-5-89-4	5	1	4	3	177	10
	8-1-12-0	31.3-5-91-7	12			8	290	10
	3-2-12-0	38-11-91-5	8	1		6	221	9
		24.1-6-60-3	1	2	2	2	127	10
7-2-	42.2-12-	463.2-115-						
57-0	89-3	1279-70						
	av. 29.66	av. 18.27						

Karachi
Quaid-e-Azam Trophy – 1982-3

Match columns (each match = two innings):
1. v United Bank (Karachi) 16-19 October, 1982
2. v Habib Bank (Karachi) 22-25 October, 1982
3. v Pakistan International Airlines (Karachi) 29 Oct.-1 Nov., 1982
4. v National Bank (Karachi) 10-13 Nov. 1982
5. v Railways (Karachi) 16-19 Nov. 1982
6. v Muslim Commercial Bank (Karachi) 22-25 Nov. 1982
7. v Allied Bank (Bahawalpur) 4-8 Dec. 1982
8. v Rawalpindi (Multan) 30 Dec. 1982-2 January 1983
9. v Lahore (Multan) 4-6 January, 1983

BATTING

Batsman	1	1	2	2	3	3	4	4	5	5	6	6	7	7	8	8	9	9
Afzaal Ahmed	36	0	8	7	98	58	105	20	20	40	3	38	28	41	16	10	4	—
Sajid Ali	54	1	12	7	10	4	6	7	15	48	0	24						
Umar Rasheed	72	1	35	15	65	50	61	30	17	20	15	5	3	—	58	7	7	—
Khalid Alvi	15*	0	0	0							58	15	6	25	8	8	23	17*
Feroze Najamuddin	92*	36	6	67	0	25	44	100*	35	52	4	144	10	15	5	2	73	—
Zafar Ahmed	—	30*	44*	7	50	39	50*	27	42*	18*	72	140	30	73*	60*	0	100	—
Kamal Najamuddin	24	23	58	20			54	11	27	6	23	1			19	4	25	11*
Mohiuddin Khan	—	0	12	17	13	12*	0	51	0	22*	37	7	0	—			44	—
Mohinder Kumar	—	32	6	13*	22	6*	19	2	23	—	5	3	25	—	2	9	5*	
Tariq Nazar	—	0	9	2	11	12			17	—	3	0						
Tanvir Ali	—	0	14	0	1*	—			18	—	3*	7*	9	—	7	3	0	—
Munir-ul-Haq					6	17	—	10					88*	135*	14	0	13	—
Wasim Arif					15*	26							19	4				
Maqbool Haq							—	7					20	—				
Atiq-ur-Rehman							—	22*	12	—						8*		
Zia-ur-Rehman																	6	1 —

	1	1	2	2	3	3	4	4	5	5	6	6	7	7	8	8	9	9
Byes	2		3	8	5	5	2		4		9	14	2	2	4	5	11	
Leg-byes	10	(14)	7		1	14	2	6	2	3	6	13	6	4	11	1	4	5
Wides							1	1	1		2	1	2	5	5	2	4	
No-balls	10		5	1	5	5	8		3		6	5	14	9	3		2	

	1	1	2	2	3	3	4	4	5	5	6	6	7	7	8	8	9	9
Total	315	137	219	164	302	273	352	294	236	209	246	417	262	313	212	65	316	33
Wickets	4	10	10	10	9	8	7	9	10	5	10	10	10	4	8	10	10	0
Result	L		L		D		L		D		D		D		L		W	
Points	6		3		5		8		7		5		6		4		18	

Catches

20 – Kamal Najamuddin (ct 17/st 3)
7 – Wasim Arif
6 – Zafar Ahmed, Mohiuddin Khan, Feroze Najamuddin and Tanvir Ali
4 – Afzaal Ahmed, Mohinder Kumar and Umar Rasheed
3 – Munir-ul-Haq and Atiq-ur-Rehman
2 – Sajid Ali and Tariq Nazar
1 – Khalid Alvi and Zia-ur-Rehman

BOWLING

	Mohiuddin Khan	Mohinder Kumar	Tariq Nazar	Tanvir Ali	Feroze Najamuddin	Afzaal Ahmed	Zafar Ahmed	Umar Rasheed	Sajid Ali
v. United Bank (Karachi) 16-19 October, 1982	6-1-18-0	9-0-28-0	30-4-94-5	29-2-92-0	7-3-6-0	1-0-5-0		3-0-9-0	
	13-0-65-1	14-0-48-0	17-1-71-0	23-1-89-3	9-0-42-1	7-0-18-0			
v. Habib Bank (Karachi) 22-25 October, 1982	15-0-61-1	14-3-41-0	16-2-70-0	24-5-92-0		16-3-50-3			
	4-0-18-0	3-2-6-0		4-1-9-0	4-1-6-0		2-0-14-0		1-0-3-0
v. Pakistan International Airlines (Karachi) 29 Oct.-1 Nov., 1982	9-4-24-0	24-1-95-3	24-2-95-1	21-1-109-0	5-0-28-0	1-0-6-0			
	13-0-34-1	24-1-110-2	19.2-1-75-2	8-1-34-1					
v. National Bank (Karachi) 10-13 November, 1982	15-0-74-2	9-1-25-0			7-1-22-1				
	22-0-115-2	18-0-87-0			4-0-17-0		1-0-3-0		1.3-0-9-0
v. Railways (Karachi) 16-19 November, 1982	11-1-43-2	19.5-2-81-4	10-1-34-3	4-1-23-0	2-0-8-0				
	7-1-30-0	7-0-32-0	34-6-97-4	38-8-131-5		3-0-12-0			
v. Muslim Commercial Bank (Karachi) 22-25 Nov., 1982	9-5-14-0	8-0-32-0	33-3-133-2	29-3-118-5	2-0-2-0	4-0-16-0	2-0-13-0		
	7-0-37-0	7-2-27-0	12-1-37-0	11-0-48-0		6-0-32-1	5-0-24-0		
v. Allied Bank (Bahawalpur) 4-8 December, 1982	20-5-59-0	26.5-6-70-6		11-0-47-2			5-0-25-0		
	6-0-30-1	14-0-57-1		8-2-29-3					
v. Rawalpindi (Multan) 30 Dec. 1982-2 Jan., 1983		11.3-4-28-6		21-5-38-1					
		13-3-47-2		5-1-22-0	1-0-7-0				
v. Lahore (Multan) 4-6 January, 1983	13-3-45-1	21.5-5-53-5		17-5-17-3					
	6-2-17-2	21.2-2-73-7		18-4-51-1	1-0-8-0				

	Mohiuddin Khan	Mohinder Kumar	Tariq Nazar	Tanvir Ali	Feroze Najamuddin	Afzaal Ahmed	Zafar Ahmed	Umar Rasheed	Sajid Ali
	176-22-	265.2-32-	195.2-21-	271-40-	42-5-	38-3-	15-0-	3-0-	2.3-0-
	684-13	940-36	706-17	949-24	146-2	139-4	79-0	9-0	12-0
	av. 52.61	av. 26.11	av. 41.52	av. 39.54	av. 73.00	av. 34.75	—	—	—

a Munir-ul-Haq 1-1-0-0

Inns	NOs	Runs	HS	Av
17	—	532	105	31.29
12	—	188	54	15.66
16	—	461	72	28.81
12	2	175	58	17.50
17	2	710	144	47.33
16	7	782	140	86.88
14	1	306	58	23.53
13	2	215	44	19.54
14	3	172	32	15.63
8	—	54	17	6.75
11	3	62	18	7.75
8	2	283	135*	47.16
4	1	64	26	21.33
2	—	27	20	13.50
3	2	42	22*	42.00
2	—	7	6	3.50

Atiq-uz-Rehman	Maqbool Haq	Zia-ur-Rehman	Byes	Leg-byes	Wides	No-balls	Total	Wkts
			1	7			260	7
				(13)			346	6
				(12)			326	4
				2			58	0
			9	3	1		370	5
			5	3	6		267	6
5-1-142-5-	17-4-68-2		1			7	339	10
-0-41-0	5-0-19-0		9	3	3	2	308	2
-1-27-1			8	4	10	1	239	10
-0-13-0			4	8	1	1	329	10
			1	1	4		334	7
							207	1
	14-2-59-0		5	8		2	275	8
				4	1	3	124	5
-0-30-0-		23-9-34-1	2	3	2		137	8
3-3-40-0		11-4-18-0		(8)			142	3a
		13-4-31-1	12	6	4		168	10
		6-2-22-0	5	2			178	10
9-5-	36-6-	53-19-						
93-5	146-2	105-2						
v. 58.60	av. 73.00	av. 52.50						

Wills Cup – Limited-Over Tournament

Group A

10 February 1983

at Niaz Stadium, Hyderabad

Muslim Commercial Bank 201 for 8 in 45 overs (Qasim Umar 78)
Allied Bank 144 in 35.1 overs (Ejaz Faqih 4 for 29)

Muslim Commercial Bank (4 pts) won by 57 runs

11 February 1983

at Niaz Stadium, Hyderabad

National Bank 271 for 7 in 40 overs (Shafiq Ahmed 79, Ali Zia 71, Saleem Pervez 53)
Pakistan International Airlines 185 in 33 overs (Ali Zia 4 for 42)

National Bank (4 pts) won by 86 runs

at National Stadium, Karachi

Muslim Commercial Bank 257 for 6 in 45 overs (Qasim Umar 52)
Karachi 168 in 37.1 overs (Zafar Ahmed 61, Zaigham Burki 5 for 28)

Muslim Commercial Bank (4 pts) won by 89 runs

12 February 1983

at National Stadium, Karachi

Karachi 151 for 9 in 40 overs (Shoaib Habib 4 for 21)
Allied Bank 152 for 1 in 22.2 overs (Shahid Mahboob 67 not out, Shoaib Habib 61)

Allied Bank (4 pts) won by 9 wickets

14 February 1983

at Niaz Stadium, Hyderabad

Muslim Commercial Bank v **National Bank**

Match abandoned (rain)
Muslim Commercial Bank 2 pts, National Bank 2 pts

at National Stadium, Karachi

Allied Bank 99 in 27.4 overs
Pakistan International Airlines 102 for 0 in 22.4 overs (Rizwan-uz-Zaman 59 not out)

Pakistan International Airlines (4 pts) won by 10 wickets

15 February 1983

at Niaz Stadium, Hyderabad

National Bank v **Karachi**

Match abandoned (rain)
National Bank 2 pts, Karachi 2 pts

Lahore
Quaid-e-Azam Trophy – 1982-3

Matches (BATTING columns, each match = two innings):
1. v. Muslim Commercial Bank (Lahore) 29 Oct.–1 Nov., 1982
2. v. Allied Bank (Lahore) 4–7 November, 1982
3. v. Pakistan International Airlines (Lahore) 28 Nov.–1 Dec., 1982
4. v. United Bank (Lahore) 4–8 December, 1982
5. v. National Bank (Lahore) 11–14 Dec. 1982
6. v. Rawalpindi (Rawalpindi) 17–20 Dec. 1982
7. v. Railways (Lahore) 23–25 Dec. 1982
8. v. Habib Bank (Lahore) 30 Dec. '82–2 Jan. '83
9. v. Karachi (Multan) 4–6 January, 1983

BATTING

Batsman	MCB 1	MCB 2	Allied 1	Allied 2	PIA 1	PIA 2	UB 1	UB 2	NB 1	NB 2	Rawal 1	Rawal 2	Rlys 1	Rlys 2	Habib 1	Habib 2	Kar 1	Kar 2
Tahir Shah	1	54	10	29			10	0	0	—			15	35				
Saleem Taj	85	0	9	34	28	29					15	15	4	7				
Rameez Raja	84	1	48	40			76	27	37	—	27	108	22	21				
Majid J. Khan	33	76*	30	101	69	58	101	128*	1	—			26	6				
Pervez Mir	19	10*	24	52	45	6*	5	5	0	—	1	16	0	2	73	—		
Mohammad Naeem	1	—	38	6	24	25	51	1	46	—								
Sajjad Akbar	15*	—	4*	8*														
Ali Ahmed	16*	—			17	—	7	—	61*	—	22	0	10	3	9	—	10	47
Mohsin Kamal	—	—	3	—	1*	—									0	—	20*	5
Khalid Niazi	—	—									—	5			45*	—	17	16
Mansoor Rana	3	—	5	16	1	62	28	1*	20	—	6	87	50*	38	45	—	21	9
Sarfraz Nawaz			2	—	6	—			24	—								
Akram Raza			4	16					24	—			0	0*	19	—		
Aamer Malik					19	91	15	120	9	—			0	7	53	—	8	1
Anis Siddiqi					17*	2*												
Haroon Rasheed					0	—	2	—			—	1						
Nasir Abbas							1	—	19	—			0	6				
Athar Khan							2*	—	12	—	0	73*	0	16				
Tariq Mansoor											17	15			7	—	36	42
Atif Rauf											0	5			43	—	4	17
Khurram Khurshid											1*	10			0	—	2	6*
Tahir Saqlain															34	—	22	0
Naseer-ud-Din																	1	5
Jalil Ahmed																	5	23
Byes	14	10			2		6		13				2		5		12	5
Leg-byes	15	6	4	7	9	2	1	1	2		(6)	(11)	2	9			6	2
Wides	2	1	1	10			1					2			1		4	
No-balls	9	3	7	8	6		1	2	22				7	4			6	
Total	297	161	189	329	248	275	301	285	273		95	346	138	154	340		168	178
Wickets	7	3	10	8	9	5	10	5	10		8	10	10	10	10		10	10
Result	D		D		D		D		D		L		L		D		L	
Points	6		5		5		7		8		4		4		8		4	

Catches
- 13 – Mohammad Naeem
- 6 – Mansoor Rana
- 4 – Pervez Mir
- 3 – Majid J. Khan, Tahir Shah, Aamer Malik, Tariq Mansoor, Khurram Khurshid and Akram Raza
- 2 – Nasir Abbas, Ali Ahmed and Saleem Taj
- 1 – Jalil Ahmed, Atif Rauf, Athar Khan, Haroon Rasheed and Sajjad Akbar

BOWLING

Match	Mohsin Kamal	Ali Ahmed	Pervez Mir	Khalid Niazi	Sajjad Akbar	Tahir Shah	Sarfraz Nawaz	Akram Raza	Athar Khan
v. Muslim Commercial Bank (Lahore) 29 Oct.–1 Nov., 1982	12-1-67-1; 23-4-70-3	19-2-78-1; 22-5-68-1	20-3-83-2	15-3-52-1; 15-1-52-0	14-1-35-0; 33-12-52-0	4.3-0-16-1; 7-4-16-0			
v. Allied Bank (Lahore) 4–7 November, 1982	15-2-44-0; 10-4-18-0		14-1-58-3; 5-4-4-1		8-0-32-0	7.3-0-27-2	20-2-73-4; 9-0-25-1	16-3-49-0; 5-1-33-0	
v. Pakistan International Airlines (Lahore) 28 Nov.–1 Dec., 1982	15-4-42-0	18-1-77-2	20-6-57-1				32-9-81-4		
v. United Bank (Lahore) 4–8 December, 1982		27-1-100-3				12-4-18-1			16-2-50-2
v. National Bank (Lahore) 11-14 December, 1982		18-3-52-3	7-2-24-1					21-5-49-1	16-6-45-3
v. Rawalpindi (Rawalpindi) 17-20 December, 1982		6-1-15-0; 22-7-50-3	8-1-40-1; 21.1-9-31-6	6-1-27-0; 3-1-8-0		8-1-24-1	1-1-0-0		13-3-35-2; 8-1-35-0
v. Railways (Lahore) 23-25 December, 1982		14-1-43-0; 12-2-47-1	24-4-80-0; 28-8-68-1					4.1-1-22-2	6-0-30-0; 10-1-43-1
v. Habib Bank (Lahore) 30 Dec., 1982–2 Jan., 1983	10.4-3-28-1	12-3-64-5			4-1-22-1			9-1-51-2	
v. Karachi (Multan) 4-6 January, 1983	28-8-78-5; 4-0-11-0	39-8-122-5; 5-1-10-0		19-4-49-0					
Totals	117.4-26-358-10 av. 35.80	214-35-726-24 av. 30.25	147.1-38-445-16 av. 27.81	62-11-210-2 av. 105.00	55-13-119-0 —	39-9-101-5 av. 20.20	61-11-179-9 av. 19.88	56.1-12-204-5 av. 40.80	69-13-238-8 av. 29.75

a Saleem Taj 10-0-23-0 / 3-0-7-0

b Mansoor Rana 1-0-4-0 / Rameez Raja 0.2-0-4-0

c Mansoor Rana 4-0-22-1 / Tariq Mansoor 2-0-12-0 / Atif Rauf 2-0-29-0

d Mansoor Rana 3-0-7-0 / 0.3-0-3-0

e Jalil Ahmed 1-0-5-0 (1) / Atif Rauf 2-0-13-0 (1) / Tariq Mansoor 1-0-4-0 (2)

	Inns	NOs	Runs	HS	Av
	9		154	54	17.11
	10		226	85	22.60
	11		491	108	44.63
	11	2	629	128*	69.88
	14	2	258	73	21.50
	8		192	51	24.00
	3	3	27	15*	—
	11	2	202	61*	22.44
	5	2	29	20*	9.66
	4	1	83	45*	27.66
	15	2	392	87	30.15
	2		8	6	4.00
	6	1	63	24	12.60
	10		323	120	32.30
	2	2	19	17*	—
	3		3	2	1.00
	4		26	19	6.50
	6	2	103	73*	25.75
	5		117	42	23.40
	5		69	43	13.80
	5	2	19	10	6.33
	3		56	34	18.66
	2		6	5	3.00
	2		28	23	14.00

Haroon Rasheed	Nasir Abbas	Aamer Malik	Byes	Leg-byes	Wides	No-balls	Total	Wkts
			4	5	2	14	356	6
			2	5	4	2	271	5
			1	3		4	291	10
			4		2	3	89	2
			4	8	7	5	281	7
2-19-0	24-5-91-3	2-0-3-0	4	6	3		294	9
	7.3-2-13-2		3	4	1	5	196	10
	2-0-13-0	6-2-16-1		4	5	2	154	5
-5-45-1					(9)		220	10a
-2-39-0					(8)		223	0b
		28-1-108-5	5	14	1	5	313	10
		4-1-24-0		2	1		255	10c
		4-0-21-0	11	4	4	2	316	10d
		1-1-0-0			5		33	0e
-9-	61.3-8-	17-4-						
3-1	225-10	64-1						
103.00	av. 22.50	av. 64.00						

at National Stadium, Karachi

Muslim Commercial Bank 218 for 9 in 45 overs
Pakistan International Airlines 219 for 8 in 42.3 overs
(Aftab Baloch 64)

Pakistan International Airlines (4 pts) won by 2 wickets

16 February 1983

at Niaz Stadium, Hyderabad

Pakistan International Airlines 185 for 7 in 35 overs
(Shoaib Mohammad 73)
Karachi 150 for 8 in 35 overs

Pakistani International Airlines (4 pts) won by 37 runs

at National Stadium, Karachi

National Bank 241 for 8 in 45 overs (Ali Zia 54)
Allied Bank 230 for 9 in 45 overs (Salman Qizilbash 67,
Shoaib Habib 55, Afzaal Butt 4 for 42)

National Bank (4 pts) won by 11 runs

Group A – Final Table					
	P	W	L	NR	Pts
Pakistan International Airlines	4	3	1	–	12
National Bank	4	2	–	2	12
Muslim Commercial Bank	4	2	1	1	10
Allied Bank	4	1	3	–	4
Karachi	4	–	3	1	2

Pakistan International Airlines, who were placed first in the group on account of winning the most matches, recovered from a surprise defeat at the hands of National Bank in their opening match. The hero of National Bank's victory was Ali Zia who took four vital wickets with his leg-breaks after hitting a brisk 71. National Bank's scoring throughout the tournament was fast and they headed the run-rate of all teams with 6.02 per over

Zaigham Burki of Muslim Commercial Bank was named best bowler of the tournament, and M.C.B. were again well served by Qasim Umar who had become the first batsman to score a thousand runs in the Quaid-e-Azam Trophy.

Rizwan-uz-Zaman performed splendidly for P.I.A. both as opening batsman and telling leg break and googly bowler. Wasim Bari was outstanding behind the stumps

Wills Cup – Limited-Over Tournament

Group B

10 February 1983

at Qaddafi Stadium, Lahore

Lahore 241 for 6 in 45 overs (Majid J. Khan 88, Aamer Malik 57)
Habib Bank 246 for 6 in 44.2 overs (Javed Miandad 64, Sultan Rana 55, Agha Zahid 50)

Habib Bank (4 pts) won by 4 wickets

Muslim Commercial Bank
Quaid-e-Azam Trophy – 1982-3

BATTING

	v. Rawalpindi (Faisalabad) 10-12 October, 1982		v. Railways (Lahore) 16-19 October, 1982		v. Allied Bank (Lahore) 22-25 October, 1982		v. Lahore (Lahore) 29 Oct.-1 Nov., 1982		v. Habib Bank (Hyderabad) 4-7 November, 1982		v. National Bank (Karachi) 16-18 Nov., 1982		v. Karachi (Karachi) 22-25 Nov., 1982		v. Pakistan Internat. A. (Lahore) 18-21 Dec., 1982		v. United Bank (Bahawalpur) 29-31 Dec., 1982	
Qasim Umar	47	7*	17	203*	89	6	210*	110	25	6	53	21	174	110*				
Anwar-ul-Haq	27	5*	10	115	16	21	29	12	22	9	54	21	43	95	31	22	4	7
Azmat Rana	113*	—	36	—	81	6							20	—	23	89	0	59
Ejaz Faqih	107	—	73	—	7	7	2	0	23	22*	27	13	34	—				
Asif Ali							30	67*	31	49	18	17	29		39	26	0	12
Salahuddin	10*	—	15	16*	4	11	18	38	100*	48*	24	0	18*	—	7	21	2	9
Zaigham Burki	—	—	15	—	4	23	—	—	4	—	25	3	2	—	11	3	14	3*
Ilyas Khan	—	—	17*	—	—	12	—	—	14	—	10	10*	8	—	13	27	2	1
Nadeem Wahab															0*	—		
Shahid Munir											1*	0					1*	2
Farrukh Zaman	—	—	1	—	—	3*	—	—			2	13*	—	—	14	6*	0	0
Babar Basharat	77	—	17	15	46	60	3	7	41	23	0	17			6	12	70	0
Sajid Abbasi	—	—	4	—	0	11	—	—	—	—					20*	9		
Tahir Naqqash							39	24*			0	0						
Tariq Khan															14	0		
Naved Azri																	0	0
Nadeem Yousuf	—	—	1	—	21*	20					0	—			32	24	46	20
Byes			1		5		4	2	5	6	1	4	1	2	5	7		4
Leg-byes	(10)		2	8	3	1	5	5	2	1	4	3	1		2	8	2	3
Wides			2		2	6	2	4					4		2	1		
No-balls			4	5	9	16	14	2	3	11	6	3			2	8	6	3
Total	391	12	212	365	282	198	356	271	270	175	225	125	334	207	221	263	147	123
Wickets	4	0	10	2	8	10	6	5	8	4	10	9	7	1	10	10	10	10
Result	W		D		W		D		D		L		D		D		L	
Points	17		4		18		6		6		7		8		5		4	

Catches

15 – Sajid Abbasi (ct 9/st 6)	6 – Qasim Umar, Ejaz Faqih and Babar Basharat
9 – Nadeem Yousuf	5 – Salahuddin, Shahid Munir (ct 3/st 2) and Zaigham
8 – Ilyas Khan	3 – Asif Ali and Tahir Naqqash
7 – Azmat Rana and Farrukh Zaman	1 – Anwar-ul-Haq and Tariq Khan

BOWLING

	Zaigham Burki	Nadeem Yousuf	Ejaz Faqih	Ilyas Khan	Farrukh Zaman	Azmat Rana	Anwar-ul-Haq	Salahuddin	Tahir Naqqash
v. Rawalpindi (Faisalabad) 10-12 Oct., 1982	4-0-17-1 / 8-1-42-1	4-1-21-0 / 10-3-31-3	21-5-53-1 / 20.2-4-55-1	9-4-27-2 / 26-2-68-2	28.1-10-54-5 / 5-0-17-2				
v. Railways (Lahore) 16-19 October, 1982	7.5-1-29-0	4-1-7-0	31-4-106-1	24-2-82-4	22-4-78-1				
v. Allied Bank (Lahore) 22-25 October, 1982	10-5-18-0 / 8.4-0-42-2	11-5-14-0 / 6-1-27-0	31.5-3-107-6 / 18-3-57-5	8-1-39-1 / 13-0-40-1	26-4-57-2 / 6-1-32-1				
v. Lahore (Lahore) 29 Oct.-1 Nov., 1982	15.3-2-35-2 / 14-3-31-2		18-3-54-1 / 17-2-35-0	16-1-56-0 / 7-1-24-0	13-0-44-0 / 13-1-27-0				23-4-68- / 17-7-24-
v. Habib Bank (Hyderabad) 4-7 November, 1982	20-4-55-3 / 16-1-87-2	6-0-25-1 / 3-0-11-0	16-0-53-0 / 18.4-3-60-1	12-0-36-2 / 14-3-46-0	28.5-5-74-1 / 32-7-85-2				
v. National Bank (Karachi) 16-18 November, 1982	2-0-7-0		35-6-90-3	35-7-90-7	14-2-53-0				2-0-15-0
v. Karachi (Karachi) 22-25 November, 1982	8-2-27-1 / 7-1-24-0		34.3-5-88-6 / 38-5-128-1	20-5-55-0 / 44-11-88-5	11-4-18-0 / 24.4-0-80-4	1-0-5-0	1-0-1-0	1-0-4-0	
v. Pakistan International Airlines (Lahore) 18-21 Dec., 1982	36-6-116-4 / 14-0-48-5	21-4-60-2 / 9-0-28-0		14-1-54-1	16-5-29-0				
v. United Bank (Bahawalpur) 29-31 December, 1982	12-0-47-0 / 3-0-4-0	7-2-16-2 / 2-0-6-0		23.4-6-51-6 / 11-3-30-1	20-4-43-2 / 11-3-32-0			1-0-7-0	3-0-11-0
	186-26-629-23 av. 27.34	83-17-246-8 av. 30.75	299.2-43-886-26 av. 34.07	276.4-47-786-32 av. 24.56	270.4-50-723-20 av. 36.15	1-0-5-0 —	2-0-8-0 —	4-0-15-0 —	42-11-107-4 av. 26.75

† Ehtesham Khaliq absent ill

Inns	NOs	Runs	HS	Av
14	4	1078	210*	107.80
18	1	543	115	31.94
9	1	427	113*	53.37
11	1	315	107	31.50
11	1	318	67*	31.80
16	5	341	100*	31.00
11	1	107	25	10.70
10	2	114	27	14.25
1	1	0	0*	—
4	2	4	2	2.00
8	3	39	14	7.80
15	—	394	77	26.26
5	1	44	20*	11.00
4	1	63	39	21.00
2		14	14	7.00
2		0	0	—
8	1	164	46	23.42

Babar Basharat	Asif Ali	Nadeem Wahab	Byes	Leg-byes	Wides	No-balls	Total	Wkts
				(7)			179	9
			1	7		1	222	9†
			1	7	4	1	315	7
				4		4	243	10
			5	2	1	4	210	10
			14	15	2	9	297	7
			10	6	1	3	161	3
			3	2	1	1	250	8
			6	12			307	7
			5	8		5	273	10
		8–0–35–2	9	6	2	6	246	10
		13–1–54–0	14	13	1	5	417	10
4.4–3–39–2			10	6	2	1	317	9
—0–12–2			9	1		2	100	7
—0–12–0			4			3	176	10
—1–0–1	0.1–0–4–0					2	98	3
.3.4–4–	0.1–0–	21–1–						
3–5	4–0	89–2						
v. 12.60	—	av. 44.50						

at C.M.T. & S.D., Rawalpindi

Rawalpindi 161 for 8 in 45 overs
United Bank 164 for 2 in 36.5 overs (Sadiq Mohammad 80 not out)

United Bank (4 pts) won by 8 wickets

11 February 1983

at C.M.T. & S.D., Rawalpindi

Railways 247 for 9 in 45 overs
Rawalpindi 222 in 43.3 overs

Railways (4 pts) won by 25 runs

12 February 1983

at Qaddafi Stadium, Lahore

United Bank 249 for 6 in 45 overs (Sadiq Mohammad 104, Mudassar Nazar 56)
Habib Bank 218 for 7 in 39 overs (Mohsin Khan 119)

Habib Bank (4 pts) won on faster scoring rate

at C.M.T. & S.D., Lahore

Railways 214 in 42.5 overs (Saadat Ali 53)
Lahore 206 in 44.3 overs (Rameez Raja 60)

Railways (4 pts) won by 8 runs

13 February 1983

at Qaddafi Stadium, Lahore

Rawalpindi 198 in 40 overs (Sohail Kiyani 50)
Lahore 199 for 2 in 33.4 overs (Majid J. Khan 86 not out, Aamer Malik 51 not out)

Lahore (4 pts) won by 8 wickets

14 February 1983

at Qaddafi Stadium, Lahore

Railways *v* **United Bank**

Match abandoned (rain)
Railways 2 pts, United Bank 2 pts

15 February 1983

at Qaddafi Stadium, Lahore

Lahore 130 in 23.3 overs
United Bank 134 for 2 in 18.5 overs (Mansoor Akhtar 52)

United Bank (4 pts) won by 8 wickets

at C.M.T. & S.D., Lahore

Habib Bank *v* **Rawalpindi**

Match abandoned (rain)
Habib Bank 2 pts, Rawalpindi 2 pts

National Bank 1982-3
First-Class Matches

Match key (columns left→right):
1. v. United Bank (Karachi) 4-7 November, 1982 — UB(K)
2. v. Karachi (Karachi) 10-13 Nov., 1982 — K
3. v. Muslim Commercial Bank (Karachi) 16-18 Nov., 1982 — MCB
4. v. Railways (Hyderabad) 22-25 Nov., 1982 — Rly
5. v. Lahore (Lahore) 11-14 Dec., 1982 — Lah
6. v. Habib Bank (Lahore) 17-20 Dec., 1982 — HB
7. v. Pakistan International Airways (Lahore) 23-26 Dec., 1982 — PIA(L)
8. v. Allied Bank (Lahore) 30 Dec., 1982-2 January, 1983 — AB
9. v. Rawalpindi (Rawalpindi) 4-7 January, 1983 — Raw
10. v. United Bank (Lahore) 22-24 January, 1983 — UB(L)
11. v. Pakistan International Airlines (Karachi) 20-22 February, 1983 — PIA(K)

BATTING
(each cell shows both innings)

	UB(K)	K	MCB	Rly	Lah	HB	PIA(L)	AB	Raw	UB(L)	PIA(K)
Taslim Arif	46 —	34 56	73	64 14	35 7	48 69	10 —	49 —	111 37	0 0	14 —
Saleem Pervez	74 102*	5 75	26 —	29 23	10 1	49 92	54 95	20 51*	3 9	3 102	6 0
Shafiq Ahmed	28 —	37 104*	51	43 79	20 56	1 118	1 55	13 —	112 18*	13 0	
Ali Zia	72* 14*	17 56*	30	5 28	12 51	14 17	26 44*	0 —	74	40 70	83 2*
Anwar Khan			24	3 9	0	5 0	8	34	39*	3 4	19 —
Ijaz Ahmed		20 —		29 0					25 17	34	74 59*
Mohammad Shafiq	— 13	30 —	6	13 8	11 14*	3 1	41 2	1 —	4	4 5	
Mohammad Jamil	— 10	77* —	9	3 28	26 8	3 21*					11 13
Afzaal Butt	— —	25 —		21 10	2*	11 2	4 —	0 13*	6	2 2	3 —
Iqbal Butt			5		9* 0*	0 19*	12 —	1*	6	0	6
Jahanzeb Khan			9*		24 0	1	0 0	0*	0	2 7	0 —
Wasim Raja	21 —	15 —	8		66 6*		55 —		30 —		17 —
Saleem Anwar	11* 6				0	36* 55	7 4*				5 —
Iqbal Qasim	— —	58	14					5 —			20* —
Saleem Akhtar		13 —									
Sohail Bhatti									0 0		
Irshadullah											— 0*
Shahid Tanvir											
Afzaal Ahmed											
Byes	9	1	9	5	4 8	3	2 15	2	1	2 1	5 4 5
Leg-byes	(9) 1	3 8	2 1	4 4	5 6	2 2	5	4 3	1 15	5	1
Wides		3	3	5 1	5 1	1	5	3 5	1	1	
No-balls	4	7 2	5	5	5 2	6 12	7	5 1	1 1	5 7	5
Total	261 159	339 308	273	257 213	196 154	183 428	234 204	162 87	437 68	74 224	266 80
Wickets	4 3	10 2	10	10 10	10 5	10 9	10 3	10 2	10 2	8 9†	10 2
Result	D	W	W	L	D	D	W	W	D	L	Ab.
Points	6	16	18	8	5	2	14	14	8	4	

† Wasim Raja absent

Catches 21 – Taslim Arif (ct 18/st 3)   8 – Mohammad Shafiq (ct 7/st 1)
14 – Ali Zia (ct 13/st 1)   6 – Iqbal Qasim and Anwar Khan
13 – Mohammad Jamil (ct 8/st 5)   5 – Saleem Anwar, Iqbal Butt and Shafiq Ahmed

BOWLING
(each cell shows figures; two innings separated by " / ")

Match	Afzaal Butt	Jahanzeb Khan	Shafiq Ahmed	Anwar Khan	Iqbal Butt	Ijaz Ahmed	Taslim Arif	Ali Zia	Mohammad Shafiq
v. United Bank (Karachi) 4-7 November, 1982	13-1-65-0 / 30-12-78-4		8-0-27-1 / 1-0-6-0	17-2-49-2 / 18-2-48-1				5-0-27-0	4-1-3-0
v. Karachi (Karachi) 10-13 November, 1982	20-2-95-2 / 7-3-20-0		23.4-5-66-3			4-1-18-0 / 7-3-13-1	2-0-10-0		1-1-0-0 / 1-0-4-0
v. Muslim Commercial Bank (Karachi) 16-18 Nov., 1982		8-1-16-0 / 2-1-3-0	3-0-6-0 / 1-1-0-0	4-1-17-0 / 1-0-6-0	2-0-7-0				
v. Railways (Hyderabad) 22-25 November, 1982	14-3-22-2 / 14-3-52-1	8-1-53-0 / 1-0-12-0	14-1-48-1 / 17-2-47-1	6-0-24-1 / 4-0-9-0	3-0-29-0 / 5-1-14-1	1-0-6-0	14.3-1-46-4	3-1-25-2 / 2-0-4-0	
v. Lahore (Lahore) 11-14 December, 1982	17.3-3-45-2	17-2-45-3	12-1-41-2	21-5-47-1					2-0-8-0 / 1-0-9-0
v. Habib Bank (Lahore) 17-20 December, 1982	20-2-89-0 / 4-0-17-2	11-1-42-0 / 1-0-9-0	4-0-17-0 / 8-1-23-1	23-7-60-1	20-0-98-1 / 6-1-22-0		7-0-29-0		
v. Pakistan International Airways (Lahore) 23-26 Dec., 1982	25-5-83-2 / 21.4-7-41-9	6-3-10-0 / 17-2-51-1		10-4-34-0 / 4-4-0-0	11-1-45-1				
v. Allied Bank (Lahore) 30 Dec., 1982-2 Jan., 1983	13-3-44-5 / 18-4-64-3		2-0-5-0 / 5-1-13-2		6-0-16-0	2-0-17-0			
v. Rawalpindi (Rawalpindi) 4-7 January, 1983	2-0-5-0 / 28-3-83-2	8-5-5-0	23-8-63-3 / 14-5-28-0	6-0-33-0	11-1-37-1 / 16-5-34-2	3-0-19-0	3-0-22-0	15-2-68-0	
v. United Bank (Lahore) 22-24 January, 1983	29-6-70-4 / 5-0-17-0	5-1-25-1	26.4-4-95-4	5-1-21-0	10-3-34-0			0.2-0-5-0	
v. Pakistan International Airlines (Karachi) 20-22 Feb., 1983	17-2-80-2	18-5-36-3		17-4-55-0		1-0-4-0			
v. Railways (Lahore) 17-20 March, 1983	23-5-64-2				25-11-51-1				
v. Habib Bank (Lahore) 22-24 March, 1983	20-5-72-0				23-5-97-1 / 5-0-29-0			4-0-29-0 / 5-0-26-0	
v. Pakistan International Airlines (Lahore) 27-30 March, 1983	20-2-69-3 / 9-3-37-0				10-2-26-0 / 2-0-4-0			2.5-0-6-2 / 12-1-50-0	
Total	370.1-74- 1212-45 av. 26.93	128.4-26- 402-12 av. 33.50	135.4-25- 390-14 av. 27.85	207-48- 626-8 av. 78.25	86-12- 337-6 av. 56.16	16-4- 60-1 av. 60.00	29.3-2- 110-4 av. 27.50	49.1-4- 240-4 av. 60.00	9-2- 24-0 —

a Saleem Akhtar 6-1-19-0 and 1-0-8-0   b Irshadullah 1-0-1-0   c Saleem Anwar 5-0-21-1 and Mohammad Jamil 1-0-3-

Batting

			v. Railways (Lahore) 17-20 March, 1983	v. Habib Bank (Lahore) 22-24 March, 1983	v. Pakistan International Airlines (Lahore) 27-30 March, 1983	Inns	NOs	Runs	HS	Av
49	45*	53	74	0	86	17	—	667	111	39.23
92	6*	43	84	70	60	27	3	1136	102*	47.33
52	—	28	4	10	36	23	3	1104	118	55.20
0	—	10	4	—	4*	24	5	785	83	41.31
				41	137	16	2	166	39*	11.85
						10	1	436	137	48.44
5	—	4	32	34*	54	20	2	285	54	15.83
5*	—	1	43	139	4	16	3	401	139	30.84
1	—	1	2	—	5*	17	3	110	25	7.85
						10	4	58	19*	9.66
						11	2	43	24	4.77
						8	3	218	66	43.60
12	—	4	2	18	1	13	3	161	55	16.10
—	0*	2	3*	—		7	3	102	58	25.50
						1	—	13	13	13.00
						2		0	0	—
						1	1	0	0*	—
15	—	14	22*	38	6	5	1	95	38	23.75
21	29	6	1			4	—	57	29	14.25
			5	12	5					
5	1	1		3	7					
			4	1						
4		3	8	5	2					
61	81	177	290	362	407					
9	1	10	10	7	8					
		D		L			D			
		8		3			8			

- Ijaz Ahmed
- Afzaal Butt, Jahanzeb Khan, Wasim Raja, Saleem Pervez and subs.
- Saleem Akhtar

Bowling

Wasim Raja	Iqbal Qasim	Shahid Tanvir	Byes	Leg-byes	Wides	No-balls	Total	Wkts
—2-47-0	33-7-102-1		4	3		8	308	7
—1-32-1	26-12-38-0		8	4	6	10	257	6
—2-74-0	35.5-4-133-5		2	2	1	8	352	7a
—0-65-1	44-12-101-4			6	1		294	9
—4-76-4	34-8-99-6		1	4		6	225	10
—1-66-6	24.4-9-33-3		4	3		3	125	9
			8	15	3		279	10
			22		21	3	195	3
—4-42-1			13	2	7	22	273	10
			4	2	2	5	348	3
			9		1	1	82	3
8-5-112-1			10	2	4	15	315	4
			1	10	9	8	120	10
	10.2-2-48-5			3		2	118	10
	15-10-26-5		1	4	2		127	10
—9-106-6			16	10	3	2	288	10
8.1-4-154-5			11	6	10	3	430	10
			1	7	7	13	249	10b
			1	2		1	51	1
—1-33-2	23-3-67-2		6	3		8	292	9
	25.2-7-78-7		5	3	7	4	212	10
	28-3-115-5	10-0-57-0	4	14		3	391	7
	3-0-17-1	2-0-6-0					78	2
	26-1-111-4	10-1-40-0	15	4	3	3	277	10
	9-2-18-1	8-0-29-1	4	2	5	4	177	3c
36.1-33-	337.1-80-	30-1-						
07-27	986-49	132-1						
av. 29.88	av. 20.12	av. 132.00						

16 February 1983

at Qaddafi Stadium, Lahore

Habib Bank 289 for 5 in 45 overs (Javed Miandad 152 not out, Mohsin Khan 62)
Railways 224 in 31 overs (Saadat Ali 62, Abdur Raqeeb 4 for 48)

Habib Bank (4 pts) won by 65 runs

Group B Final Table	P	W	L	NR	Pts
Habib Bank	4	3	–	1	14
Railways	4	2	1	1	10
United Bank	4	2	1	1	10
Lahore	4	1	3	–	4
Rawalpindi	4	–	3	1	2

Railways were placed ahead of United Bank because they had a faster scoring rate in their three matches. They owed much to Saadat Ali who batted with consistent aggression and to skipper Mohammad Nazir jnr. who bowled economically and led the side well.

Javed Miandad and Mohsin Khan saw that Habib Bank dominated the group. Javed was named as the outstanding batsman of the tournament. His 152 not out against Railways came in 153 minutes. Another outstanding performer for Habib Bank was Anwar Miandad who was given the individual award of Rs. 3,000 as the best fielder in the competition.

Rawalpindi's only consolation for a poor season was when Raja Afaq with 3 for 45 and 41 won the Man of the Match award in the game with Railways.

Wills Cup – Semi-Finals

18 February 1983

at National Stadium, Karachi

Habib Bank 199 in 39.5 overs (Saleem Malik 54)
National Bank 148 in 36.1 overs

Habib Bank won by 51 runs

at C.M.T. & S.D., Rawalpindi

Pakistan International Airlines 212 for 9 in 45 overs (Naeem Ahmed 58, Mohammad Nazir 4 for 25)
Railways 128 in 34.5 overs

Pakistan International Airlines won by 84 runs

Wills Cup Final 1983

PAKISTAN INTERNATIONAL AIRLINES v HABIB BANK

The third Wills Cup Final was scheduled for Karachi on Friday, 25 February, but disturbances in the city caused the game to be switched to Lahore where the two previous finals had been played. There was a further hold-up through bad weather and the match was finally played on 27 February

Pakistan International Airlines 1982-3
First-Class Matches

BATTING

Column key (each match shown as two innings columns, (1) first innings, (2) second innings):

- A = v. Habib Bank (Karachi) 16-19 October, 1982
- B = v. Karachi (Karachi) 29 Oct-1 Nov, 1982
- C = v. Railways (Lahore) 4-7 November, 1982
- D = v. Allied Bank (Lahore) 10-13 Nov, 1982
- E = v. Rawalpindi (Rawalpindi) 22-25 Nov, 1982
- F = v. Lahore (Lahore) 28 Nov-1 Dec, 1982
- G = v. Muslim Commercial Bank (Lahore) 18-21 Dec, 1982
- H = v. National Bank (Lahore) 23-26 Dec, 1982
- I = v. United Bank (Karachi) 3-6 January, 1983
- J = v. Railways (Lahore) 22-25 January, 1983
- K = v. National Bank (Karachi) 20-22 February, 1983

BATTING	A1	A2	B1	B2	C1	C2	D1	D2	E1	E2	F1	F2	G1	G2	H1	H2	I1	I2	J1	J2	K1	K2
Rizwan-Uz-Zaman	112	0	121	24	152	99	0	45	30	142			52	1			29	58	37	41	39	—
Asif Mohammad	2	12	21	15					25	20	23	—	24	3	57	0			37	31*	16	—
Shoaib Mohammad	6	0	9	24	69	69	10	24	4	16	56	—			109*	7	2	2			9	—
Shahid Mohammad									54	1	20	—			34	19*	3	2	3	7		—
Aftab Baloch	24	11	2	69	2*	23			74	6	73	—	13	30	2	3	10	123*	54	27	40	—
Zahid Ahmed	34	62	40*	20	2	35	32	39	13	30	35	—	43	10	53*	4	7	7	27*	6	0	—
Naeem Ahmed	3	6	—	—	13	38*	63	10	3	5	—		61	10	—	24	27*	1	1	25	84*	—
Hasan Jamil	19	37	39*	0*			39	7	2	0	1	—	1	2*			8	5	2*	93		
Iqbal Sikander			—	—	2*	3*	10	1	2	17	24*	—			52	18	1	16	6	—		
Anil Dalpat	2*	15	—	—	—	—	11	10*	6	14*	8*					10	3	4	5	6	49	—
Rashid Khan	0	14	—	—	—	—	3*	23	2*	1			13*	1*	—	7	13	17	11	1	0	—
Feroze Mehdi					18	0	4	2			17	—	55	11	11	8	12	17	24	4	32	—
Raja Akbar	—	2*									—	1*			—	3			—	12	0*	—
Rashid Israr	19	22							0	0												
Zaheer Abbas			125	101	—		57	57	4													
Aqeel Memon													1	1								
Ameer Khan															—	8*						
Kamran Rasheed																						
S. M. Iftikhar																						
Byes	4	3	9	5		6	7	1			4		10	9	10	1	1			4	6	
Leg-byes	3	6	3	3	(7)	8	3	7	(24)	(24)	8		6	1	2	10	3		(7)	(8)	4	3
Wides	1	1	1	6		2	7	5			7		2		4	9	1				4	6
No-balls	6	4					1	6	4		5		1	2	15	8					8	
Total	235	195	370	267	265	341	252	182	239	276	281	—	317	100	315	120	120	259	209	261	292	—
Wickets	9	10	5	6	5	6	10	10	10	10	7		9	7	4	10	10	10	8	10	9	

	A	B	C	D	E	F	G	H	I	J	K
Result	D	D	W	D	W	D	D	L	L	L	Ab.
Points	7	7	16	8	17	7	8	8	4	5	

Catches
- 37 – Anil Dalpat (ct 28/st 9)
- 12 – Aftab Baloch
- 10 – Shoaib Mohammad
- 9 – Rizwan-Uz-Zaman
- 8 – Iqbal Sikander
- 7 – Feroze Mehdi
- 6 – Naeem Ahmed, Zahid Ahmed and Rashid Khan
- 5 – Asif Mohammad
- 4 – Raja Akbar

BOWLING

Match	Rashid Khan	Hasan Jamil	Iqbal Sikander	Naeem Ahmed	Aftab Baloch	Rizwan-Uz-Zaman	Raja Akbar	Zahid Ahmed	Ameer Khan
v. Habib Bank (Karachi) 16-19 October, 1982	21.1-4-72-7	9-3-17-1		1-0-1-1			11-2-17-1		
	24-5-71-1	5-1-19-0		17-4-35-1	16-4-47-2	9-3-12-2	7-0-31-0	12-0-41-1	
v. Karachi (Karachi) 29 October-1 November, 1982	16-2-53-4	6-0-44-0	36-3-128-3	20-3-52-2	7-2-10-0	1-0-4-0			
	26-3-83-5	5-0-20-0	19-7-50-2	34-11-79-0	1-1-0-0			13-3-17-1	
v. Railways (Lahore) 4-7 November, 1982	27-2-103-4		16-1-65-0	8-1-23-0	3-0-13-0	14-7-26-3	4-0-16-1	19-1-84-0	
	21-3-48-1		43.3-11-91-5	13-2-46-0			4-1-17-0		
v. Allied Bank (Lahore) 10-13 November, 1982	25-7-77-7	14-3-36-2	2.2-0-9-1	13.4-5-36-1		1-0-4-0		14-2-31-0	
	23-5-57-3	11-2-23-2	20-7-37-1			2-1-1-0		1-0-2-0	
v. Rawalpindi (Rawalpindi) 22-25 November, 1982	21-4-65-2	6-1-27-1	30.4-13-60-6	16-2-44-2	2-0-9-0	2-0-7-0			
	16-3-61-1		20-5-56-6	5.3-3-2-2	5-2-9-0				
v. Lahore (Lahore) 28 November-1 December, 1982		13-6-43-1	30-0-80-3	11-3-25-0		29-5-60-1	31-7-79-5	14-3-39-2	
		14-3-32-1	38-12-88-0				19-4-53-0		
v. Muslim Commercial Bank (Lahore) 18-21 December, 1982	27-4-105-5	8-3-17-0		14.2-4-32-4	7-0-18-0	3-1-3-0	9-0-35-1	8-1-23-1	
	36.4-9-117-5	10-3-33-2		2-2-0-0	4-3-1-0	5-1-6-0	22-4-59-2		
v. National Bank (Lahore) 23-26 December, 1982	27-6-105-5		15.2-5-42-3	2-0-10-0	0.3-0-4-0		18-6-49-2		5-1-22
	15-3-54-0		22-1-62-1				12-5-31-1		1-0-9-0
v. United Bank (Karachi) 3-6 January, 1983	9-2-28-1	3-0-11-0	41.4-11-104-3	10-0-22-0	19-6-37-2	10-1-24-2		12-7-11-1	
	24-10-57-4	8-5-14-0	17-2-40-2		2-2-0-0	7-3-7-1		1-0-5-0	
v. Railways (Lahore) 22-25 January, 1983	9-2-45-1	3-1-9-0		17-0-73-2	23-0-101-0	7-2-23-2	3-1-11-0	23-1-114-4	
	6-2-14-0					1-0-4-0	7-1-15-1	2.5-1-30-1	
v. National Bank (Karachi) 20-22 February, 1983	22-4-86-3		23.4-7-63-4	3-0-6-0	10-2-31-0	10-1-18-1	16-1-48-1		
	5-0-38-1		4-1-10-0	2-1-5-1			7-2-21-0		
v. Habib Bank (Lahore) 17-20 March, 1983	21-0-119-0	10-4-24-0	16-2-65-0	7-1-33-0	6-0-34-0		25-3-101-3		
v. United Bank (Lahore) 22-25 March, 1983	26-8-63-4	2-0-10-0	24-7-68-2		11-3-24-2	3-1-22-0	8-2-26-0	14-4-30-0	
	4-0-17-0		10-1-38-1		5-0-13-1	3.1-0-12-0	2-0-10-0	5-0-18-0	
v. National Bank (Lahore) 27-30 March, 1983	7-0-43-1			15-3-34-0	15-1-54-1	15-0-55-3			12-0-58
	6-0-42-0			20-3-66-4	9-1-21-0	18-2-49-1			26-5-94
Total	464.5-88-1623-65	132-36-397-10	429.1-96-1156-43	233.3-48-626-20	174.3-32-486-9	115.1-23-293-16	209-42-626-18	138.5-23-445-11	44-6-183-3
Average	av. 24.96	av. 39.70	av. 26.88	av. 31.30	av. 54.00	av. 18.31	av. 34.77	av. 40.45	av. 61.00

a Shahid Mohammad 2-0-11-0

17-20 March, 1983		v. United Bank 22-25 March, 1983		v. National Bank 27-30 March, 1983		Inns	NOs	Runs	HS	Av
1	—	61	69	38	89	22	—	1280	152	58.18
						14	1	286	57	22.00
1*	—			24	33*	19	3	574	109*	35.87
		29*	29	0	—	12	2	201	54	20.10
7	—	8	16	59	6*	23	3	682	123*	34.10
0	—	4	5			23	3	538	62	26.90
				16	—	17	3	390	84*	27.85
0	—	0	25			18	4	310	93	22.14
0	—	0	4			15	3	176	52	14.66
		3	14	50	—	16	4	210	50	17.50
		19	32	53	25	18	4	235	53	16.78
5	—	51	0	1	—	18	—	272	55	15.11
		0	1*			7	4	19	12	6.33
				4	—	5	—	45	22	9.00
						5	—	344	125	68.80
						2	1	2	1	1.00
				1	9	3	1	18	9	9.00
		5	2			2	—	7	5	3.50
				6*	—	1	1	6	6*	—

0		2	11	15	4
6		3	4	4	2
		4	1	3	5
4		6	3	3	4
64		195	216	277	177
6		10	10	10	3
D		L		D	
5		4		6	

Hasan Jamil and Aqeel Memon

Shahid Mohammad, Zaheer Abbas, Rashid Israr and subs.

Shoaib Mohammad	S. M. Iftikhar	Kamran Rasheed	Byes	Leg-byes	Wides	No-balls	Total	Wkts
			5	2		6	120	10
			13	5	1	4	279	8
			5	1		5	302	9
			5	14		5	273	8
				(29)			356	7
				(20)			248	9
3-0			7	4	2	5	175	10
			9	7		3	178	7
				17)			220	10
				(32)			187	10
1-0			6	9		6	248	9
				2			275	5
			5	2	2	2	221	10
			7	8	1	8	263	10
30-1			2	2	5	7	234	10
				2		2	204	3
			2	3		1	243	10
				(12)			137	7
				15	1	8	400	9
			4	2		3	72	2
			4	5		5	266	10
			5	1			80	2
			6	13	2	2	399	4
		2-0-12-0	10	4			269	9
		7-1-27-0	6	5	1		147	2
56-1	10-0-53-0		3	1		5	362	7
38-0	15-0-72-0		5	7		2	407	8a
2-	25-0	9-1						
8-2	125-0	39-0						
64.00	—	—						

Zaheer Abbas who led Pakistan International Airlines to triumph in the Willis Cup and scored a mighty 1371 runs in the season at an average of 97.92. (Adrian Murrell)

under a bright winter sun on a lush green wicket, the appearance of which made Javed Miandad ask the opposition to bat when he won the toss.

Unfortunately, the Habib opening attack of Liaqat Ali and Aslam Qureshi proved unable to exploit the conditions and 20 runs came from the first 5 overs. The bowling steadied and the run-rate slowed, but when Agha Zahid joined the attack he saw Rizwan dropped off his bowling, and it was not until the nineteenth over that Habib Bank gained the breakthrough. Shoaib was bowled by Agha Zahid, but there were 76 runs on the board.

Zaheer looked menacingly fluent in his strokes, but he was run out by Mohsin Khan, and Rizwan's good innings came to an end shortly after. Although Zahid Ahmed and Aftab Baloch scored 26 runs in 5 overs, the later batsmen failed to take advantage of the fine start and Habib Bank were set the moderate task of scoring 207 at 4.6 an over.

They could not have had a worse start than losing Mohsin Khan, on whom so much depended, to the third ball of the innings. Rashid Khan struck again when he had Saleem Malik caught behind for 1, and the game was firmly in P.I.A.'s grasp.

Javed Miandad responded with some glorious shots that renewed hope for Habib Bank, but in the fourteenth over, Agha Zahid, who had given sensible support, was run out by Zaheer.

Railways 1982-3
First-Class Matches

BATTING

BATTING	v. Muslim Commercial Bank (Lahore) 16-19 October, 1982		v. Allied Bank (Lahore) 29-31 October, 1982		v. Pakistan International Airlines (Lahore) 4-7 November, 1982		v. United Bank (Bahawalpur) 10-13 Nov. 1982		v. Karachi (Karachi) 16-19 Nov. 1982		v. National Bank (Hyderabad) 22-25 Nov. 1982		v. Habib Bank (Lahore) 4-8 December, 1982		v. Rawalpindi (Rawalpindi) 11-13 Dec. 1982		v. Lahore (Lahore) 23-25 Dec. 1982		v. United Bank (Lahore) 17-20 Jan. 1983		v. Pakistan International Airlines (Lahore) 22-25 Jan. 1983	
Abdus Sami	26	—	0	15	15	18	19	78	7	25	15	0	0	97*	78	0	9	—	40	27	0	4
Saadat Ali			1	9	206*	11	0	45	9	32	40	92*	71	16	11	4	29	—	39	47	170	18
Naved Anjum	28	—			11	31	43	54	46	47	53	3	4	5	29	4	2	—	11	24	81	26*
Munawwar Javed											58	64	12	39	1	4					24	—
Asad Rauf	20	—	4	12	4	84	23	22	0	106	30	15*	2	62	16	3	92	—	14	47	4	—
Mehdi Raza											27	—										
Musleh-Ud-Din	13*	—	6	5	0	34	6	54	38	22	33	—	72	3	4	14*	0	—	13	1	12	—
Shahid Pervez	50	—	16	27	21	2	18	31	0	0	17	—	0	27*	28	—	4	—	3	2		
Mohammad Nazir	—	—	10	39	17*	48	0	2	6*	2*	22	—	24	—	7	—	21	—	31	26	31	—
Zulqarnian	—	—	3*	0	0*		1	20	0	1	2*	—	12	—	6	—	24*	—	4*	0*	0*	—
Shahid Butt			0*	9*	—	—	0	12*			2	—	36*	—	23*	—	38	—			6	24*
Talat Mirza	96		9	36											22	7	61		3	22	20	15*
Gulfraz Khan	3	—	0	10	2	0																
Khalid Javed	0*	—					5*	18	7	0												
Ijaz Ahmed	66	—	6	3	51	0			16	3	45	16	0	9	18	11*	8	—	61	41*	10	—
Byes	1								8	4	8	22					5		1			4
Leg-byes	7		(5)	3	(29)	(20)	(4)	(34)	4	8	15		(28)	(19)	(36)	(5)	14		17	17	15	2
Wides	4		1						10	1	3	21					1				1	1
No-balls	1		4						1	1	3						5		3	5	8	3
Total	315		60	173	356	248	135	373	239	329	279	195	250	242	278	48	313		239	267	400	72
Wickets	7		9	10	7	9	10	10	10	10	10	3	10	6	10	5	10		9	9	9	2
Result	D		L		L		L		D		W		D		W		W		D		W	
Points	8		2		5		2		7		18		8		18		18		5		16	

Catches

- 40 – Zulqarnian (ct 22/st 18)
- 15 – Mohammad Nazir
- 11 – Shahid Butt
- 8 – Naved Anjum
- 7 – Musleh-Ud-Din
- 6 – Asad Rauf and Saadat Ali
- 5 – Abdus Sami and Shahid Pervez
- 3 – Ijaz Ahmed and Munawwar Javed
- 2 – Talat Mirza and subs.
- 1 – Gulfraz Khan

BOWLING

Match	Musleh-Ud-Din	Naved Anjum	Shahid Butt	Shahid Pervez	Mohammad Nazir	Saadat Ali	Khalid Javed	Abdus Sami
v. Muslim Commercial Bank (Lahore) 16-19 October, 1982	21-5-63-3 / 13-1-70-0	2-0-14-0 / 8-0-34-0		11-2-29-2 / 28-6-63-1	31.1-13-37-3 / 48-28-43-1		2-0-14-0 / 22-0-88-0	14-1-49-2 / 13-0-33-0
v. Allied Bank (Lahore) 29-31 October, 1982	12-2-37-2 / 5-1-14-0		9-1-16-2 / 35-11-64-1	4-0-12-0 / 16-6-38-1	14.2-6-15-4 / 49.5-13-74-7	2-0-11-0		1-1-0-0 / 2-0-6-0
v. Pakistan International Airlines (Lahore) 4-7 November, 1982	8-1-34-0 / 5-0-30-0	16-0-87-1	15-2-58-1 / 1-0-11-0	11-5-37-0 / 7-1-29-0	38-8-74-4 / 27-2-109-1			6-0-18-0 / 5-0-35-0
v. United Bank (Bahawalpur) 10-13 November, 1982	7-0-46-1 / 11.2-1-66-2	20-3-81-1 / 5-0-31-0	7-0-34-0	23-2-58-1 / 2-0-32-0	38.3-9-78-1 / 4-0-24-0		5-0-33-0 / 1-0-5-1	
v. Karachi (Karachi) 16-19 November, 1982	3-0-10-0	20-6-70-0 / 10-0-38-1		2-0-6-0 / 1-0-3-0	38-13-62-6 / 59-3-67-3	2-1-4-1 / 31-9-56-1	22-4-69-3 / 17-4-42-0	1-0-5-0
v. National Bank (Hyderabad) 22-25 November, 1982	10-0-32-0 / 9-1-26-1	6-3-9-0	28.4-6-110-6 / 41-13-81-4	5-1-17-1 / 19-6-40-0	26-6-54-1 / 53.4-28-52-4	4-2-21-2		
v. Habib Bank (Lahore) 4-8 December, 1982	22-4-67-3	9-2-30-0	4-0-15-0	10.2-1-23-5	30-9-59-1	9-2-27-0		
v. Rawalpindi (Rawalpindi) 11-13 December, 1982	3-0-13-0 / 13-7-23-6	3-2-6-0 / 2-1-5-0	26-9-103-4		33.2-7-90-5 / 10-4-12-4	7-3-28-1		
v. Lahore (Lahore) 23-25 December, 1982	9-0-36-1 / 2-0-15-0	2-2-0-0 / 4-0-28-1	31-14-60-5 / 24-3-60-7		26.5-12-31-4 / 26.1-10-38-2			
v. United Bank (Lahore) 17-20 January, 1983	7-2-24-0 / 5-0-21-0	3-1-13-0 / 4-1-9-1	19.4-2-66-4 / 69-19-129-4	19-7-26-1	35-7-86-3 / 79-39-90-2	2-0-2-0		1-0-4-0
v. Pakistan International Airlines (Lahore) 22-25 January, 1983	5-0-22-0 / 2-0-2-0	5-0-10-0 / 2-1-1-0	37-10-90-6 / 55-17-128-6		38-10-79-2 / 62.2-28-112-4	6-1-10-0		
v. Habib Bank (Lahore) 20-22 February, 1983	10-0-32-0	8-0-31-1 / 5-2-17-1	30-3-94-4 / 34-3-177-4	5-0-20-0	24-3-78-1	5-1-25-4 / 19-1-99-0		5-0-31-0
v. National Bank (Lahore) 17-20 March, 1983	3-0-12-0 / 4-0-16-0	2-0-25-0 / 3-0-23-0	27.2-2-106-1 / 13-6-29-1		36-5-75-7 / 13-6-12-0	10-0-34-1		
Total	189.2-25-711-19 av. 37.42	139-24-562-7 av. 80.28	506.4-121-1431-60 av. 23.85	163.2-37-433-12 av. 36.08	841.1-269-1451-70 av. 20.72	97-20-317-10 av. 31.70	69-8-251-4 av. 62.75	48-2-181-2 av. 90.50

v. Habib Bank (Lahore) 20-22 Feb. 1983		v. National Bank (Lahore) 17-20 March, 1983		Inns	NOs	Runs	HS	Av
1	2	47	—	23	1	523	97*	23.77
107	34	22	—	22	2	1013	206*	50.65
8	50	35	—	21	1	595	81	29.75
30	15	23	—	10	—	270	64	27.00
41	35			21	1	636	106	31.80
				1	—	27	27	27.00
0	2	12*	—	21	3	344	72	19.11
25	38	1		19	1	310	50	17.22
6	50	13	—	18	5	355	50	23.66
22	5*	0	—	17	8	100	24*	11.11
5	0	1	—	13	6	156	38	22.28
		24	—	11	1	315	96	31.50
				5	—	15	10	3.00
				5	2	30	18	10.00
0*	2	15	—	20	3	381	66	22.41
14		5						
8	3	3						
		7						
1		4						
268	236	212						
10	10	10						
	L	D						
	8	5						

Talat Mirza	Asad Rauf	Byes	Leg-byes	Wides	No-balls	Total	Wkts
			2		4	212	10
3–0–14–0	2–0–4–0	1	8	2	5	365	2
			(18)			98	8
	1–1–0–0		(9)			216	10
	7–0–37–0		(7)			265	5
	2–0–23–0	6	8	2	1	341	6
		5	4	1	7	347	6
			(4)			162	3
		4	2	1	3	236	10
			3			209	5
		4	2	3	5	257	10
		8	1	5		213	10
		2	1		9	233	10
			(28)			268	10
			(16)			56	10
		2	2		7	138	10
			9		4	154	10
		10	3		3	231	8
	8–2–24–0	4	7		4	294	7
			(8)			209	8
		4	4			261	10
		4	4		4	272	10
	11–0–58–0	3	8		3	416	6
		5			4	261	9
			1			81	1
3–0–	31–3–						
14–0	146–0						
—	—						

Anwar joined Javed, but both were dismissed while three runs were scored and at 82 for 5, Habib Bank faced defeat. By the fortieth over, nine wickets were down and 43 runs were still needed. There was no great final flourish and the match ended with 10 balls remaining and 33 runs separating the sides.

Rizwan-uz-Zaman took the Man of the Match award for his batting, the wicket of Javed and some economical bowling, and Pakistan International Airlines took the cup for the third successive year.

WILLS CUP FINAL: PAKISTAN INTERNATIONAL AIRLINES v. HABIB BANK
27 February 1983 at Qaddafi Stadium Lahore

PAKISTAN INTERNAT'L AIRLINES			
Rizwan-uz-Zaman	c and b Agha Zahid		51
Shoaib Mohammad†	b Agha Zahid		31
Zaheer Abbas†	run out		19
Asif Mohammad	lbw, b Abdur Raqeeb		1
Zahid Ahmed	c Mohsin, b Azhar		20
Aftab Baloch	c Agha Zahid, b Azhar		36
Hasan Jamil	b Azhar		18
Naeem Ahmed	run out		2
Wasim Bari*	c Sultan, b Azhar		4
Rashid Khan	not out		1
Raja Akbar	not out		7
Extras	b 4, lb 9, w 2, nb 1		16
(45 overs)	(for 9 wickets)		206

	O	M	R	W
Liaqat Ali	7	1	28	—
Aslam Qureshi	9	1	42	—
Agha Zahid	9	—	43	2
Abdur Raqeeb	9	1	29	1
Saleem Malik	4	—	24	—
Azhar Khan	7	—	24	4

FALL OF WICKETS
1- 76, 2- 97, 3- 102, 4- 110, 5- 139, 6- 175, 7- 186, 8- 197, 9- 197

HABIB BANK			
Mohsin Khan	b Rashid Khan		0
Agha Zahid	run out		9
Saleem Malik	c Wasim Bari, b Rashid Khan		1
Javed Miandad†	c Wasim Bari, b Rizwan-uz-Zaman		51
Anwar Miandad	run out		8
Sultan Rana	c Zaheer, b Naeem Ahmed		28
Azhar Khan	run out		11
Zaheer Ahmed*	b Rashid Khan		30
Aslam Qureshi	run out		1
Abdur Raqeeb	b Rashid Khan		10
Liaqat Ali	not out		1
Extras	b 5, lb 2, w 14, nb 2		23
(43.2 overs)			173

	O	M	R	W
Rashid Khan	8.2	2	27	4
Hasan Jamil	9	1	29	—
Raja Akbar	8	—	36	—
Naeem Ahmed	9	1	30	1
Rizwan-uz-Zaman	9	—	28	1

FALL OF WICKETS
1- 1, 2- 8, 3- 54, 4- 79, 5- 82, 6- 111, 7- 132, 8- 13, 9- 163

Pakistan International Airlines won by 33 runs

Rawalpindi 1982-3
Quaid-e-Azam Trophy

BATTING

Player	v. Muslim Commercial Bank (Faisalabad) 10-12 October, 1982	v. Allied Bank (Rawalpindi) 16-18 October, 1982	v. Habib Bank (Rawalpindi) 11-12 Nov., 1982	v. Pakistan International Airlines (Rawalpindi) 22-25 Nov., 1982	v. United Bank (Rawalpindi) 28 Nov.-1 Dec., 1982	v. Railways (Rawalpindi) 11-13 Dec., 1982	v. Lahore (Rawalpindi) 17-20 Dec., 1982	v. Karachi (Multan) 30 December, 1982-2 January, 1983	v. National Bank (Rawalpindi) 4-7 January, 1983	Inns	NOs	Runs	HS	Av
Azmat Jalil	41 14	21 22	4 11		46 4	62 1	1 107*	16 3	31 129	16	1	513	129	34.20
Shahid Gulrez	0 21	22 16	7 16		27 43	42 0				10		194	43	19.40
Sohail Kiani	21 0		24* 9	2 15		0 0	6 —	18 56	103 14	13	1	268	103	22.33
Mohammad Riaz	13 70	0 1	8 7	0 39	0 17	1 3			56 134	14	—	349	134	24.92
Maqsood Kundi	46 5	8 10	1 3	34 23	59 15*	1 1	0 —	15 5	5 28	17	1	259	59	16.18
Raja Afaq	5 62	19* 40	6 7	16 19	47 0*	1 0	71 —	0 0*	16 1	17	3	310	71	22.14
Ehtesham Khaliq	31 —	0 0					17 —	6* —	18 37	7	1	109	37	18.16
Raja Sarfraz	8 24	4 43	0 8	10 8	6		9 —			11		120	43	10.90
Sabih Azhar	0 12*	1* 0		18 14				0 —	12 12	9	2	69	18	9.85
Imran Khaliq	4* 4									2	1	8	4*	8.00
Khatib Rizwan	3* 1	— 4	11 7	1 0*	17	3* 0	6 —	14	10* 28	14	4	105	28	10.50
Masood Anwar		20 33	29 0	36 19	14 1	54 5	99 108*	61 70*	6 13	16	2	568	108*	40.57
Iqtidar Khwaja		0 8*								2	1	8	8*	8.00
Qazi Khalid			1 4	67 13	4 10	57 12				8		168	67	21.00
Abdul Wahab			23 4*	0* 0	1	0 2*	2		0 0	10	3	32	23	4.57
Yasin Chaudry				19 5		19 16	0 —			5	—	59	19	11.80
Mohammad Sabir					0* —		0* —	— —	0 4*	4	3	4	4*	4.00
Byes	1							2	16 11					
Leg-byes	(7) 7	(12) (14)	(11) (15)	(17) (32)	(10) (2)	(28) (16)	(9) (8)	3 (8)	10 6					
Wides								2	3 10					
No-balls	1								2 3					
Total	179 222	107 191	125 91	220 187	231 92	268 56	220 223	137 142	288 430					
Wickets	9 9†	8 10	10 10	10 10	10 5	10 10	10 0	8 3	10 10					
Result	L	L	L	L	D	L	W	W	D					
·Points	2	3	2	6	5	8	14	12	8					

Catches

20 – Maqsood Kundi (ct 9/st 11)
9 – Masood Anwar
6 – Raja Afaq
5 – Sabih Azhar and Azmat Jalil
4 – Qazi Khalid and Mohammad Riaz

3 – Shahid Gulrez
2 – Abdul Wahab, Khatib Rizwan and subs.
1 – Iqtidar Khwaja, Yasin Chaudry, Sohail Kiani, Raja Sarfraz, and Mohammad Sabir

† Ehtesham Khaliq absent ill

BOWLING

	Khatib Rizwan	Sabih Azhar	Mohammad Riaz	Imran Khaliq	Raja Afaq	Azmat Jalil	Raja Sarfraz	Abdul Wahab
v. Muslim Commercial Bank (Faisalabad) 10-12 Oct., 1982	15-0-48-0	13-0-52-0	46-11-137-3	2-0-14-0	27-2-130-1			
		1-0-1-0		1-0-8-0		1-0-3-0		
v. Allied Bank (Rawalpindi) 16-18 October, 1982	16-4-31-2	11-3-26-1	14.4-0-64-2		21-2-83-3			
	4-1-17-0	4.4-2-6-0	11-2-17-3		12-1-32-0	1-0-1-0		
v. Habib Bank (Rawalpindi) 11-12 November, 1982	16-0-46-1		12-1-40-1		26-0-84-3		2-0-3-0	27-1-83-3
							4-2-2-0	
v. Pakistan International Airlines (Rawalpindi) 22-25 Nov., 1982	17.2-2-66-6	14-4-25-1	21-5-44-1		15-2-36-1			16-2-44-1
	7-0-35-0	3-1-11-0	15-2-47-0		24.5-5-78-1			32.5-6-74-7
v. United Bank (Rawalpindi) 28 November-1 December, 1982	8-0-37-1		8-1-23-1		19-1-69-1		1-0-7-0	19-4-69-1
	9-2-32-0		5-0-30-0		20-2-72-0		4-1-9-0	20-0-79-4
v. Railways (Rawalpindi) 11-13 December, 1982	7-0-33-1		4-1-25-0		23.5-2-97-6		4-0-8-0	22-2-77-3
	8-2-14-3				1-0-3-0			3.4-0-18-1
v. Lahore (Rawalpindi) 17-20 December, 1982	10-2-30-0				12-5-28-3		4-1-13-0	18.3-12-16-5
	16.2-4-43-2				21-1-65-1		8-3-17-0	39-9-84-4
v. Karachi (Multan) 30 Dec., 1982-2 January, 1983	16.4-3-30-3	23-4-67-3			19-3-39-1			21-3-50-1
	13.5-6-19-6	8-1-27-1						
v. National Bank (Rawalpindi) 4-7 January, 1983	14-2-78-5	7-1-13-0	16.3-0-109-5		14-1-68-0			12-1-53-0
	3-0-9-1	1-0-9-0	6-1-23-0		3-1-15-0			1-0-5-1
	181.1-28–	85.4-16–	159.1-24–	3-0–	257.5-28–	2-0–	27-7–	232-40–
	568-31	237-6	559-16	22-0	899-21	4-0	59-0	652-31
	av. 18.32	av. 39.50	av. 34.93	—	av. 42.80	—	—	av. 21.03

First Class Averages

Batting

	M	Inns	NOs	Runs	HS	Av	100s	50s
heer Abbas	13	15	1	1371	215	97.92	7	4
sim Umar	9	18	4	1275	210*	91.07	6	3
udassar Nazar	11	17	4	1110	231	85.38	4	5
ved Miandad	14	16	2	1124	280*	80.28	4	3
far Ahmed	10	18	7	800	140	72.72	2	5
ran Khan	9	8	3	311	117	62.20	1	
gha Zahid	14	23	2	1220	175	58.09	3	8
ajid J. Khan	8	13	2	629	128*	57.18	3	3
ohsin Khan	12	18	4	797	135	56.92	3	4
shraf Ali	14	20	7	719	111*	55.30	1	5
afiq Ahmed	13	23	3	1104	118	55.20	3	8
zwan-uz-Zaman	14	25		1358	152	54.32	4	7
asir Valika	14	24	9	806	103*	53.73	1	5
az Faqih	11	18	7	591	107	53.72	3	2
zmat Rana	6	9	1	427	113*	53.37	1	3
diq Mohammad	11	21	2	1009	157	53.10	4	5
adat Ali	12	22	2	1013	206*	50.65	3	2
az Ahmed	6	10	1	436	137	48.44	1	2
leem Pervez	14	27	3	1136	102*	47.33	2	9
eroze								
Najamuddin	9	17	2	710	144	47.33	2	4
unir-ul-Haq	5	8	2	283	135*	47.16	1	1
leem Malik	18	23	1	1013	124*	46.04	6	2
ultan Rana	13	17	3	633	127	45.21	2	2
aroon Rashid	12	17	2	671	133	44.73	1	5
ameez Raja	8	15	2	579	108	44.53	1	3
li Zia	14	24	5	785	83	41.31		7
asim Raja	13	15	4	443	102*	40.27	1	3
zhar Khan	14	18	4	557	76	39.28		6
asood Anwar	11	20	2	701	125	38.94	2	4
aslim Arif	12	19		728	111	38.31	1	5
rshad Pervez	12	18	2	613	109	38.31	1	3
oaib Mohammad	14	24	3	792	109*	37.71	2	5
oin-ud-Din	3	6	2	147	61*	36.75		1
zmat Jalil	8	16	1	513	129	34.20	2	1
ftab Baloch	13	23	3	682	123*	34.10	1	5
ulman Qizilbash	5	10	1	303	53	33.66		2
nwar Miandad	12	15	5	334	97	33.40		1
tidar Ali	8	16		525	99	32.81		5
sad Rauf	12	21	1	636	106	31.80	1	3
sif Ali	6	11	1	318	67*	31.80		1

Batting cont'd

	M	Inns	NOs	Runs	HS	Av	100s	50s
Mansoor Akhtar	13	22	2	634	130	31.70	2	1
Talat Mirza	7	11	1	315	96	31.50		2
Salahuddin	9	16	5	341	100*	31.00	1	
Mohammad Jamil	10	16	3	401	139	30.84	1	1
Mansoor Rana	9	15	2	392	87	30.15		3
Naved Anjum	12	21	1	595	81	29.75		4
Saleem Yousuf	10	16	2	414	145*	29.57	1	1
Mahmood Rasheed	12	19	3	468	85	29.25		3
Umar Rasheed	9	16		461	72	28.81		5
Anwar-ul-Haq	10	20	1	543	115	28.27	1	2
Afzaal Ahmed	11	21		589	105	28.04	1	2
Naeem Ahmed	13	17	3	390	84*	27.85		3
Farooq Shera	10	15	1	378	91	27.00		3
Munawwar Javed	6	10		270	64	27.00		2
Zahid Ahmed	13	23	3	538	62	26.90		2
Babar Basharat	8	15		394	77	26.26		3
Tehsin Javed	5	7	1	157	100	26.16	1	
Athar Khan	4	6	2	103	73*	25.75		1
Aamer Malik	8	13		333	120	25.61	1	2
Raees Ahmed	7	9	2	176	39	25.14		
Mohammad Riaz	7	14		349	134	24.92	1	2
Talat Masood	5	8	1	174	89	24.85		1
Kamal Merchant	6	10	5	121	38	24.20		
Mohammad Naeem	5	8		192	51	24.00		1
Tahir Naqqash	9	8	3	120	39	24.00		
Abdus Sami	13	23	1	523	97*	23.77		3
Mohammad Nazir	13	18	3	355	50	23.66		1
Kamal Najamuddin	7	14	1	306	58	23.53		2
Nadeem Yousuf	6	8	1	164	46	23.42		
Tariq Mansoor	3	5		117	42	23.40		
Zafar Mehdi	8	14	2	272	55*	22.66		1
Shahid Mahboob	8	12	1	249	110	22.63	1	1
Saleem Taj	5	10		226	85	22.60		1
Ali Ahmed	8	11	2	202	61*	22.44		1
Ijaz Ahmed	12	20	3	381	66	22.41		3
Sohail Kiyani	7	13	1	268	103	22.33	1	1
Shahid Butt	11	13	6	156	38	22.28		
Sikhander Bakht	12	13	2	244	67	22.18		1
Raja Afaq	9	17	3	310	71	22.14		2
Asif Mohammad	8	14	1	286	57	22.00		1
Pervez Mir	8	14	2	258	73	21.50		2
Siddiq Patni	10	19		402	62	21.15		3
Qazi Khalid	4	8		168	67	21.00		2
Hasan Jamil	11	19	4	310	93	20.66		1
Shahid Mohammad	7	12	2	201	54	20.10		1
Mohiuddin Kumar	8	13	2	215	51	19.54		1
Shahid Gulrez	5	10		194	43	19.40		
Shoaib Habib	9	15	1	271	54	19.35		1
Musleh-ud-Din	13	21	3	344	72	19.11		2
Farooq Rasheed	8	15	2	220	39	18.33		
Ehtesham Khaliq	5	7	1	109	37	18.16		
Anil Dalpat	15	19	6	228	50	17.53		1
Khalid Alvi	6	12	2	175	58	17.50		1
Iqbal Qasim	14	10	4	105	58	17.50		1
Shahid Pervez	12	19	1	310	50	17.22		1
Tahil Shah	5	9		154	54	17.11		1
Rashid Khan	15	19	5	239	53	17.07		1
Maqsood Kundi	9	17	1	259	59	16.18		1
Saleem Anwar	8	13	3	161	55	16.10		1
Mohammad Shafiq	13	20	2	285	54	15.83		1
Sajid Ali	6	12		188	54	15.66		1
Mohinder Kumar	9	14	2	172	32	15.63		
Feroze Mehdi	12	19		274	55	14.42		2
Iqbal Sikander	12	16	3	180	52	13.84		1
Ilyas Khan	10	11	2	121	27	13.44		
Athar A. Khan	6	12	1	137	29	12.45		
Anwar Khan	13	16	2	166	39*	11.85		
Abdul Qadir	16	12	2	115	38*	11.50		
Naseer Chughtai	6	11	2	103	35	11.44		
Zulqarnian	13	17	8	100	24*	11.11		
Raja Sarfraz	7	11		120	43	10.90		
Zaigham Burki	9	11	1	107	25	10.70		
Khatib Rizwan	9	14	4	105	28	10.50		

(Qualification – 100 runs, average 10.00)

Mohammad Sabir	Masood Anwar	Byes	Leg-byes	Wides	No-balls	Total	Wkts
			(10)			391	4
						12	0
			(13)			217	9
			(10)			86	3
			(21)			276	8
			(24)			239	10
			(24)			276	10
7-2-104-4			(7)			318	8
1-3-88-2			(4)			313	6
	3-1-10-0		(36)			278	10
	3-0-8-1		(5)			48	5
-0-2-0			(6)			95	8
5-3-121-3	1-0-5-0		(11)			346	10
-0-1-0	1-0-2-0	4	11	5	3	212	8
-1-11-3		5	1	2		65	10
0-0-72-0	4-0-26-0	2	4	1	1	427	10
-1-3-0			3		1	68	2
02-10-	12-1-						
02-12	51-1						
v. 33.50	av. 51.00						

United Bank 1982-3
First-Class Matches

BATTING

BATTING	v. Karachi (Karachi) 16-19 Oct. 1982		v. National Bank (Karachi) 4-7 Nov. 1982		v. Railways (Bahawalpur) 10-13 Nov. 1982		v. Allied Bank (Lahore) 22-24 Nov. 1982		v. Rawalpindi (Rawalpindi) 28 Nov.-1 Dec. 1982		v. Lahore (Lahore) 4-8 Dec. 1982		v. Habib Bank (Lahore) 11-14 Dec. 1982		v. Muslim Commercial Bank (Bahawalpur) 29-31 Dec. 1982		v. Pakistan Int. Airlines (Karachi) 3-6 Jan. 1983		v. Railways (Lahore) 17-20 Jan. 1983		v. National Bank (Lahore) 22-24 Jan. 1983	
Sadiq Mohammad	109	115	110	1	65	52	53	19*	21	157	9	—	59	5	58	25	33	6	33	19	31	29*
Siddiq Patni	15	62					60	3	33	25	37	—	9	29*	7	3	60	13	18	4	27	0
Mahmood Rasheed	15	28	29	3			0	0*	85	11	18	—	58	—	17	—	65*	6	23	47	1	—
Farooq Shera	12	9			91	15*	16	12	64	50	8	—	3	—	5	—	11	25			46	—
Nasir Valika	47	65	17	30	56*	0*	46	—	95	22*	38	—	1	—	14	9*	14	30*	78	103*	15	—
Ashraf Ali	4	50*	19	75*	17	—	46	—			111*	—	35	—	19*	38*	9	8	0	30	61*	—
Kamal Merchant	25*	2*					11	10	1*	1*	6	—	15*	—					38	12		
Imtinan Zamir							19	—	11	4												
Saood Khan							9*	—														
Ehtesham-Ud-Din	—	—	—	—	—	—	0	—	—	—	22*	—	—	—	9	—	0	—	—	—	3	—
Khurshid Akhtar	—	—	—	—	—	—	9*	—	0	—	24	—	—	—	0	—	7	—	—	—	3	—
Sikhander Bakht	19	2	11*	35*	36	—									0	—			14	29	18	—
Tauseef Ahmed	6*	—	—	—	—	—									23	—	0	21*	0*	20*	1	—
Mudassar Nazar			81	54	1	15																
Mansoor Akhtar			21	1	0	76																
Haroon Rashid			5	30	64*	—											17	19	27	15		
Arif-Ud-Din									0	39												
Shahid Aziz									1*	—	2	—										
Waheed Mirza									6	—			21	26*								
Mahmood Ahmed													48*	—			11	11				
Khalid Irtiza																			11	15	15	18*
Nasir Shah																						
Byes	1		4	8	5		15	3			4				4		2		10	4	1	1
Leg-byes	7	(13)	3	4	4	(4)	4	3	(7)	(4)	6		(29)	2			3	(12)	3	7	7	
Wides				6	1		2	2			3				1	2					7	2
No-balls			8	10	7		5								1	3	2	1	3	4	13	1
Total	260	346	308	257	347	162	295	52	318	313	294		278	64	176	98	243	137	231	294	249	51
Wickets	7	6	7	6	6	3	9	3	8	6	9		7	1	10	3	10	7	8	7	10	1
Result	W		D		W		W		D		D		D		W		W		D		W	
Points	15		5		18		16		8		8		5		15		17		6		15	

Catches
34 – Ashraf Ali (ct 25/st 9)
19 – Mahmood Rasheed
17 – Sadiq Mohammad
8 – Tauseef Ahmed
6 – Sikhander Bakht and subs.
5 – Farooq Shera
4 – Mansoor Akhtar and Khalid Irtiza
3 – Siddiq Patni, Nasir Valika, Kamal Merchant and Haroon Rashid

BOWLING

BOWLING	Ehtesham-Ud-Din	Saood Khan	Farooq Shera	Khurshid Akhtar	Kamal Merchant	Sikhander Bakht	Tauseef Ahmed	Sadiq Mohammad	Mudassar Nazar
v. Karachi (Karachi) 16-19 October, 1982	19-4-47-0			15-2-40-2	8-3-19-0	8-1-39-0	31-0-124-1	4-0-24-0	
	8-3-30-0					13.3-2-38-5	12-1-28-4	8-1-27-1	
v. National Bank (Karachi) 4-7 November, 1982	12-2-58-0			24-7-62-0		19-5-57-1	28-4-73-3	2-0-2-0	
	11-2-30-0			14-4-35-1		13-2-35-1	18-6-41-1	1-0-4-0	
v. Railways (Bahawalpur) 10-13 November, 1982	13.5-2-48-6					16-2-58-3	10-3-16-0		3-0-9-0
	27-6-71-1			29.5-6-71-4		22-3-84-0	39-18-69-4	15-3-44-1	
v. Allied Bank (Lahore) 22-24 November, 1982	22-3-76-3	10-3-30-2	3-0-26-0	25-6-58-2	10-0-41-1				
	11.1-4-43-7	2-1-6-0	7-0-38-1	2-2-0-2					
v. Rawalpindi (Rawalpindi) 28 November-1 December, 1982	14-1-51-1		5-0-27-0	21-5-57-2				5-1-18-1	
	11-3-31-4		9-2-50-0	3-1-3-1					
v. Lahore (Lahore) 4-8 December, 1982	13-1-40-0		6-0-23-1	26-0-83-2	5-0-14-0			20-3-84-6	
	9-4-19-2		10-3-45-2	36-10-78-0	10-3-20-0			16-1-57-0	
v. Habib Bank (Lahore) 11-14 December, 1982	24-6-80-0		22.3-3-87-5	13-1-43-0				4-0-14-0	
v. Muslim Commercial Bank (Bahawalpur) 29-31 Dec., 1982	11-2-33-1		7-2-11-0	10-1-33-1		18.3-5-38-6	10-2-24-1		
	9-1-48-3			11-3-29-3		4-2-6-0	9.3-1-30-4		
v. Pakistan International Airlines (Karachi) 3-6 January, 1983	9-3-15-1		5-1-7-0	23.2-6-45-6			20-5-46-2		
	24-4-72-2		4.2-0-21-1	50-20-73-5				33-10-59-1	11-2-27-1
v. Railways (Lahore) 17-20 January, 1983	10-1-20-1			27-6-94-3			5-0-28-0	23.2-6-77-5	
	10-2-37-1			21.4-3-101-7	7-0-31-1		10-0-64-0	3-0-10-0	
v. National Bank (Lahore) 22-24 January, 1983	14-0-39-3			1-0-1-0			8-5-9-1	7.4-2-18-4	
	3-0-22-0		3-0-25-0	7-0-23-0		19-3-77-3	20.1-3-49-6		
v. Pakistan International Airlines (Lahore) 22-25 March, 1983			4-2-7-0	16.2-7-25-1		13-2-49-3	27-7-61-2		
			4-0-14-1	15-1-46-2		9-2-15-0	20-3-35-3		
v. Habib Bank (Lahore) 27-30 March, 1983	14-3-31-1					20.4-3-96-2	17-0-67-3		
	15-2-37-1					18-4-58-5	4-0-16-2		
	314-59-978-38	12-4-36-2	89.5-13-381-11	391.1-91-1000-44	40-6-125-2	216.4-41-751-30	332.4-71-843-46	86-11-301-10	3-0-9-0
	av. 25.73	av. 18.00	av. 34.63	av. 22.72	av. 62.50	av. 25.03	av. 18.32	av. 30.10	av. —

a Mahmood Ahmed 2-0-10-0   † Wasim Raja absent

Left table (batting/bowling by match)

v. Pakistan International Airlines (Lahore) 22-25 March, 1983	v. Habib Bank (Lahore) 27-30 March, 1983	Inns	NOs	Runs	HS	Av
		21	2	1009	157	53.10
4	3	19		402	62	21.15
21 — 22	19*	19	3	468	85	29.25
11 —		15	1	378	91	27.00
6 30* 70*	10	22	8	796	103*	56.85
90 — 32	7	18	6	651	111*	54.25
		10	5	121	38	24.20
		3	—	34	19	11.33
		1	1	9	9*	—
—	0	6	1	34	22*	6.80
		6	1	43	24	8.60
67 — 1	3	12	2	235	67	23.50
7 — 5	2	10	4	85	23	14.16
		4	—	151	81	37.75
6 12 25	35	8	—	176	76	22.00
29 61* 5	24	11	2	296	64*	32.88
		2	—	39	39	19.50
1* — 8	5	5	2	17	8	5.66
		3	1	53	26*	26.50
		3	1	70	48*	35.00
		4	1	59	18*	19.66
17 32 34	12	4	—	95		23.75
10 6 8	1					
4 5 1	2					
1						
6	2					
269 147 221	127					
9 2 9	10					
W	L					
18	4					

2 – Arif-Ud-Din (ct 1/st 1), Shahid Aziz and Nasir Shah
1 – Mudassar Nazar, Imtinan Zamir, Khurshid Akhtar, Waheed Mirza and Ehtesham-Ud-Din

Shahid Aziz	Imtinan Zamir	Nasir Valika	Byes	Leg-byes	Wides	No-balls	Total	Wkts
			2	10		10	315	4
				(14)			137	10
				(9)			261	4
			9	1		4	159	3
				(4)			135	10
				(34)			373	10
				(24)			255	8
			2	1			90	10
7.2-2-40-4	7-1-28-1			(10)			231	10
*-1-6-0				(2)			92	5
3-0-54-0			1	1	1		301	10
0-7-39-0		6-0-24-0	1		2		285	5
			2	3	4	9	252	5a
			2		6		147	10
			4	3		3	123	10
		1-0-2-0	1	3	1		120	10
			(7)				259	10
			17		3		239	9
			1	17	1	5	267	9
			1	1		5	74	8
			5	15	1	7	224	9†
7-3-38-4			2	3	4	6	195	10
*6-4-87-4			11	4	1	3	216	10
32-6-101-0			2	4	2	2	305	8
1-3-19-1			1	3	1	16	151	10
38.2-26-384-13	7-1-28-1	7-0-26-0						
av. 29.53	av. 28.00	—						

Bowling

Bowling	Overs	Mds	Runs	Wkts	Av	Best	10/m	5/inn
Imran Khan	326.4	103	729	53	13.75	8/60	2	4
Rizwan-uz-Zaman	119.1	24	302	17	17.76	3/26		
Khatib Rizwan	181.1	28	568	31	18.32	6/19		3
Shahid Mahboob	293	50	800	43	18.60	7/65		5
Jalal-ud-Din	284	77	784	41	19.12	6/45	1	3
Tauseef Ahmed	365.4	77	956	48	19.91	6/49	1	3
Mohammad Nazir	841.1	269	1451	70	20.72	7/74	1	4
Abdul Wahab	232	40	652	31	21.03	7/74		2
Iqbal Qasim	578.5	161	1477	65	22.72	7/78	1	6
Khurshid Akhtar	391.1	91	1000	44	22.72	7/101	2	3
Abdul Qadir	827.2	184	2367	103	22.98	9/49	4	9
Abdur Raqeeb	485.4	102	1398	59	23.69	8/80	2	5
Shahid Butt	506.4	121	1431	60	23.85	7/60	2	5
Azhar Khan	126	22	342	14	24.42	4/45		
Ilyas Khan	304.4	53	860	34	25.29	7/90		3
Rashid Khan	514.5	95	1772	70	25.31	7/72	2	6
Iqbal Sikander	496.4	110	1362	53	25.69	6/56	1	3
Ehtesham-ud-Din	314	59	978	38	25.73	7/43	1	2
Mohinder Kumar	265.2	32	940	36	26.11	7/73	1	4
Zaigham Burki	186	26	629	23	27.34	5/48		1
Afzaal Butt	400.1	78	1349	49	27.53	9/41	1	2
Nasir Abbas	69.3	9	276	10	27.60	5/108		1
Pervez Mir	147.1	38	445	16	27.81	6/31		1
Shafiq Ahmed	135.4	25	390	14	27.85	3/63		
Sikhander Bakht	291.4	51	1051	36	29.19	6/38		3
Shahid Aziz	138.2	26	384	13	29.53	4/38		
Sadiq Mohammad	86	11	301	10	30.10	6/84		1
Ali Ahmed	214	35	726	24	30.25	5/64		2
Liaqat Ali	204	62	556	18	30.88	4/92		
Naeem Ahmed	233.3	48	626	20	31.30	4/32		
Saadat Ali	97	20	317	10	31.70	4/25		
Shoaib Habib	242	50	603	19	31.73	6/70		1
Amin Lakhani	306	86	651	20	32.55	5/57		1
Sarfraz Nawaz	327.1	76	926	28	33.07	4/63		
Mohammad Sabir	102	10	402	12	33.50	4/104		
Jahanzeb Khan	128.4	26	402	12	33.50	4/95		
Farooq Shera	89.5	13	381	11	34.63	5/87		1
Wasim Raja	297.4	44	1041	30	34.70	6/66	2	3
Raja Akbar	209	42	626	18	34.77	5/79		1
Mohammad Riaz	159.1	24	559	16	34.93	5/109		1
Shahid Pervez	163.2	37	433	12	36.08	5/23		1
Mohsin Kamal	130.4	27	402	11	36.54	5/78		1
Ejaz Faqih	399.2	64	1179	32	36.84	6/88	1	2
Musleh-ud-Din	189.2	25	711	19	37.42	6/23		1
Azeem Hafeez	276.2	48	902	24	37.58	7/68		1
Raees Ahmed	130	15	489	13	37.61	4/90		
Farrukh Zaman	276.4	50	757	20	37.85	5/54		1
Tanvir Ali	271	40	949	24	39.54	5/118		2
Zahid Ahmed	138.5	23	445	11	40.45	4/114		
Tariq Nazar	195.2	21	706	17	41.52	5/94		1
Raja Afaq	257.5	28	899	21	42.80	6/97		1
Tahir Naqqash	221	44	705	16	44.06	4/61		
Hasan Jamil	147	·39	449	10	44.90	2/23		
Mohiuddin Khan	176	22	684	13	52.61	2/17		

(Qualification – 10 wickets)

Leading Fielders

41 Anil Dalpat (ct 30/st 11)
40 Zulqarnian (ct 22/st 18) and Ashraf Ali (ct 30/st 10)
32 Saleem Yousuf (ct 30/st 2)
28 Wasim Bari (ct 22/st 6)
26 Masood Iqbal (ct 18/st 8)
21 Zaheer Ahmed (ct 12/st 9) and Taslim Arif (ct 18/st 3)
20 Kamal Najamuddin (ct 17/st 3) and Maqsood Kundi (ct 9/st 11)
19 Mahmood Rasheed
17 Sadiq Mohammad and Sultan Rana
15 Sajid Abbasi (ct 9/st 6), Mohammad Nazir, Saleem Malik and Ali Zia (ct 14/st 1)
14 Mohammad Jamil
13 Mohammad Naeem
12 Iqtidar Ali and Aftab Baloch
11 Shahid Butt and Shoaib Mohammad
10 Shoaib Habib and Masood Anwar

SECTION I
The Gold Rush

The Season in South Africa

compiled by Robert Brooke

The crowd watching the West Indies XI in Pretoria.

AROSA SRI LANKA TOUR

Early in September 1982, Tony Opatha, the Sri Lankan cricketer, visited South Africa, and a few weeks later, Colin Rushmere of the Eastern Province Cricket Union travelled to Sri Lanka with fourteen contracts. The whole affair was conducted in utmost secrecy. The contracts were signed and on 21 October, the Sri Lankan tourists, captained by Bandula Warnapura, arrived in South Africa.

Warnapura, a former Sri Lankan Test captain, and his players were banned by the Sri Lankan Cricket Board for a period of twenty-five years, but the tour of South Africa was already under way when the ban was announced.

26, 27 and 28 October 1982

at Pretoria

Arosa Sri Lanka 315 (A.N. Ranasinghe 80, G.J.A.F. Aponso 68, J.B.N. Perera 65 not out, H.A. Page 4 for 75) and 123 (B. de Silva 61)
Combined Transvaal XI 313 for 4 dec (B.J. Whitfield 77, V.F. du Preez 71, R.G. Pollock 66) and 127 for 4

Combined Transvaal XI won by 6 wickets

The Arosa XI, named after the initials of their organiser, A. R. Opatha and the initials of the host country, made a good start to their tour when, on winning the toss, they reached 315, Anura Ranasinghe and Flavian Aponso adding 105 for the fifth wicket. The home side batted consistently, but when the Sri Lankans batted again in a heavy atmosphere, they played some injudicious strokes and suffered accordingly. After the Sri Lankan collapse, victory for the Combined XI became a formality.

30, 31 October and 1 November 1982

at Cape Town

Arosa Sri Lanka 275 (J.B.N. Perera 69, L.W. Kaluperuma 67, G.S. Le Roux 4 for 31) and 307 (G.J.A.F. Aponso 92, A.N. Ranasinghe 52, A.P. Kuiper 5 for 60)
Western Province 400 for 7 dec (K.S. McEwan 149, L. Seeff 105, P.N. Kirsten 70 not out) and 106 for 5 (A.R.M. Opatha 4 for 49)

Match drawn

The tourists failed to take advantage of batting first on a perfect pitch and the Currie Cup holders, Western Province, passed their total with only one wicket down. Ken McEwan hit 149 in 167 minutes, including five sixes and fifteen fours, while Seeff's 105 occupied 207 minutes. Their opening stand of 235 was a Western Province record.

The Sri Lankan side batted with more discipline at the second attempt and Flavian Aponso was again impressive. With insufficient time left in which to force victory, Western Province hit furiously, 106 in ten overs, but the match was drawn.

In a two-day match at Stellenbosch against S.A.B. Bowl holders, Boland, Sri Lanka were bemused by Peinaar Anker on a poor pitch and were beaten by five wickets.

South African authority. Captain Peter Kirsten (Western Province) directs his troops. (Adrian Murrell)

First One-Day International

6 November 1982

at Wanderers, Johannesburg

South Africa 291 for 4 (S.J. Cook 120, R.G. Pollock 76 not out, B.A. Richards 71)
Arosa Sri Lanka 102

South Africa won by 189 runs

Second One-Day International

8 November 1982

at Berea Park, Pretoria

South Africa 281 for 5 (S.J. Cook 131, P.N. Kirsten 77)
Arosa Sri Lanka 174 for 5 (N.D.P. Hettiararchy 50)

South Africa won by 107 runs

The Sri Lankans were totally outclassed in both of these matches. Their bowling was plundered by Cook, Richards, Kirsten and Pollock, and the South African bowling was too strong for their batting.

In the second match, Fernanco bowled twelve overs in error.

A two-day game against East Cape Invitation XI at East London ended in a disappointing draw.

, 14 and 15 November 1982

Port Elizabeth

osa **Sri Lanka** 223 (J.F. Woutersz 76) and 321 for 8
c (J.B.N. Perera 96, B. de Silva 73, A.N. Ranasinghe
)

astern Province 287 for 5 dec (D.J. Richardson 134,
. Billison 69) and 162 for 8

atch drawn

ter winning the toss, the tourists struggled against the pace
Watson and Carse. Jerry Woutersz batted for 3½ hours for
s defiant 76 which alone helped the Sri Lankans to respec-
bility.

Wicket-keeper Dave Richardson hit a splendid maiden
ndred for Eastern Province who led comfortably on the
st innings. The Sri Lankans then fought their way back
to the match and, ultimately, the home side were happy to
ttle for a draw in what was the Sri Lankans best perfor-
ance of their tour.

hird One-Day International

7 November 1982

t Kingsmead, Durban

osa **Sri Lanka** 140
outh Africa 143 for 2 (B.A. Richards 74)

outh Africa won by 8 wickets

lthough they batted first in this match and were given a
easonable start by Hettiaratchy and de Silva, the Sri Lan-
ans fared no better than in the previous matches and failed
 last their prescribed number of overs.

South Africa hit off the runs at five an over.

IRST INTERNATIONAL:
OUTH AFRICA v. AROSA SRI LANKA

he first of the two 'Tests' saw the tourists completely over-
helmed by a side superior to them in every department of
he game. It was, in every respect, a mis-match.

A sound 70 by Bandula de Silva and a useful 51 from Jerry
Woutersz helped their side to a reasonable looking total of
13 against some slightly erratic South African bowling.

Jimmy Cook played a fine, if slow, innings of 169 and
hared a fourth wicket stand of 165 with Graeme Pollock.

With the wicket still in perfect condition, there seemed no
eason why the visitors should not make a good score and a
ght of the game, but, lacking the injured Fernando, they
atted lamentably, collapsing before the pace and lift of Jef-
eries and the spin of Kourie to suffer a humiliating innings
efeat.

The saddest aspect of the match was the performance of
eft-arm spinner Ajit de Silva. Arriving in South Africa as the
umber one spinner, he had been quite unable to strike a
ength or find any direction in the important matches. In this
ame he bowled only six overs which cost 33 runs. That tells
ttle of the story, however, for he sent down no fewer than
fteen wides plus a bewildering number of full tosses and
ong hops. He finished the match close to tears.

*Garth Le Roux who constantly disconcerted the West Indian
openers and many other batsmen during the season. (Adrian
Murrell)*

19, 20, 22 and 23 November 1982

at Wanderers, Johannesburg

Arosa Sri Lanka 213 (B. de Silva 70, J.F. Woutersz 51,
G.S. Le Roux 6 for 55) and 141 (A.J. Kourie 5 for 54)
South Africa 378 (S.J. Cook 169, R.G. Pollock 79, L.W.
Kaluperuma 5 for 123)

South Africa won by an innings and 24 runs

Following this match, the tourists went to Pietermaritzburg
where they were beaten in a limited-over match by Natal.
This was followed by a first-class match against Natal.

27, 28 and 29 November 1982

at Durban

Arosa Sri Lanka 129 (K.R. Cooper 6 for 36) and 104
(A.N. Ranasinghe 50, M.D. Clare 6 for 49)
Natal 328 (T.R. Marsden 58, A.J.S. Smith 57, B.A.
Richards 52 retired hurt)

Natal won by an innings and 95 runs

This match followed the now familiar pattern with Sri Lanka
struggling all the way and finally becoming overwhelmed by
the Natal seam attack.

Fourth One-Day International

1 December 1982

at Berea Park, Pretoria

Arosa Sri Lanka 276 for 9 (A.N. Ranasinghe 100)
South Africa 277 for 4 (L. Seeff 141, P.N. Kirsten 100)

South Africa won by 6 wickets

Anul Ranasinghe, who had hit 50 in even time to save his side from complete ignominy against Natal, hit a splendid hundred to help Sri Lanka to their most spirited display of the tour. They reached a commendable 276 in their 55 overs, but a second wicket stand of 220 between Seeff and Kirsten quickly re-established South African supremacy.

4, 5 and 6 December 1982

at Johannesburg

Arosa Sri Lanka 122 (J.B.N. Perera 50, R.W. Hanley 5 for 41) and 200 (N.V. Radford 4 for 56)
Transvaal 362 for 1 dec (H.R. Fotheringham 159 not out, M.S. Venter 132 not out, M. Yachad 50)

Transvaal won by an innings and 40 runs

In their penultimate match, the Sri Lankans were outplayed to an embarrassing degree by a below strength Transvaal side. Only Bernard Perera played the pace attack with any confidence, but 'Spook' Hanley found little resistance as he finished with 5 for 41 in 12.2 overs.

After Mandt Yachad had hit 50 in 84 minutes, Henry Fotheringham joined Venter in an unbeaten second wicket stand of 265 which completely demoralised the Sri Lankans who, at the second attempt reached 200 and again batted without discipline or responsibility. They crashed to an innings defeat in which there were no redeeming features.

SECOND INTERNATIONAL

All Sri Lanka could salvage from the second and final 'Test' was the one first-class century scored for them on the tour, 102 by Bernard Perera, one of the most popular members of the party. All else is best forgotten by the Sri Lankans.

They achieved totals of 282 and 281 at a quick pace, finding little menace in the much-vaunted South African pace bowlers. South Africa replied with 663 for 6 declared, scored at more than four an over, an achievement which speaks for itself.

Larkie Seeff scored 188 on his first-class international debut, but even he did not claim it as anything of great importance. He and Jimmy Cook added 250 for the first wicket, but the most memorable innings was that played by Graeme Pollock. Sixty-one not out out at the end of the second day, he went on to reach his century, scored over a hundred runs before lunch on the third day and was finally caught playing the shot which would have brought him his double century.

His 197 occupied 4½ hours and included five sixes and seventeen fours, a vintage innings from a very great batsman whose absence from the Test scene is one of the tragedies of modern cricket.

Needing 381 to avoid an innings defeat, Arosa Sri Lanka batted with spirit, but they had little hope of avoiding defeat.

Thus ended the saddest of tours. The South Africa Cricket Union deserve full credit for their enterprise and the Sri Lankans must be given full credit for their bravery, but whether the whole exercise was worthwhile remains debatable. The Sri Lankans provided very meagre opposition and were, in no sense, a truly representative side from the weakest of cricketing nations. The players went home to a wealthy exile, but it all did little for cricket.

9, 10, 11 and 13 December 1982

at Newlands, Cape Town

Arosa Sri Lanka 282 (G.J.A.F. Aponso 81, A.N. Ranasinghe 54) and 281 (J.B.N. Perera 102, H.D. Devapriya 53)
South Africa 663 for 6 dec (R.G. Pollock 197, L. Seeff 188, S.J. Cook 112, A.P. Kuiper 66)

South Africa won by an innings and 100 runs

THE WEST INDIAN CRICKETERS IN SOUTH AFRICA

On 12 January 1983, the news that all South African cricket followers had awaited finally broke. A team of West Indian cricketers under the captaincy of Lawrence Rowe was on its way to the republic.

To the official world of international cricket under the auspices of the International Cricket Conference the news was greeted like a major disaster; to the South Africans starved so long of the opportunity of seeing top class international cricket, and desperately disappointed with the showing of the Arosa Sri Lankans it was manna from heaven, a dream finally come true.

The initial moves had been made in July 1982. During the I.C.C. conference in London at that time, Dr Ali Bacher, former South African Test captain, in England hoping to be able to put his country's case for acceptance back into the Test fold, discussed with Surrey's West Indian paceman Sylvester Clarke, whether Clarke would come to South Africa to play for Transvaal. Clarke was interested enough for T.C.C. committee man Don Mackay-Coghill to bring a contract for Clarke a couple of months later. Clarke decided to decline the offer but expressed interest in joining a West Indian team in South Africa.

A further meeting was arranged in October involving Cambridge Blue and Gloucestershire and Transvaal batsman, Ray White, and ex-Glamorgan pace bowler, Greg Armstrong, and after much cloak and dagger work and one false start when plans were leaked to an Australian journalist, the tour finally got under way.

The tour opened on 15 January 1983, to a packed house at the historic Newlands Ground in Cape Town. Small wonder that the West Indians were given a standing ovation with S.A.C.U. president Joe Pamensky leading the applause.

World-wide reaction was immediate and predictable. All the players were banned from Test cricket, some from domestic cricket. Outside the West Indies there were hysterical reactions from such moderate prime ministers as Australia's Malcolm Fraser who wanted all participants

Three men at the centre of cricket in South Africa. ABOVE: *(left) Dr Ali Bacher who made the first moves in the negotiations to get a West Indian side to go to South Africa. (right) Jo Pamensky. The brains behind the tour.* BELOW: *Hassan Howa, the outspoken enemy of apartheid and of the rebel tours. (Adrian Murrell)*

barred from Australia. This blanket condemnation applied to wicket-keeper David Murray who happened to have an Australian wife and daughter, and an Australian home.

On the South African domestic front, Hassan Howa, leader of the S.A.C.U. critics, reaffirmed his policy of 'no abnormal sport in an abnormal society' while admitting to watching the matches on television.

15 January 1983

at Cape Town

West Indies XI 204 for 9 (C.L. King 79 not out, L.G. Rowe 66, S.T. Jefferies 4 for 31)
Western Province 183 (G.A. Gooch 64, E.A. Moseley 4 for 23)

West Indies XI won by 21 runs

The tour opened with a fifty-over match and the highlights of the West Indian innings were a cultured 66 from skipper Lance Rowe and an explosive unbeaten 79 from Collis King. Both West Indian openers, Austin and Alvin Greenidge, had been out for ducks, and King and Rowe shared a fourth wicket stand of 99.

In spite of an assertive 64 from Graham Gooch, Western Province were always struggling, and the West Indies, much to the delight of the crowd, won by 21 runs.

17 January 1983

at East London

Border 100 for 8
West Indies XI 101 for 3 (C.L. King 56 not out)

West Indies XI won by 7 wickets

The tourists were joined by David Murray, now secure in the knowledge that he would be allowed back into Australia to rejoin his wife and family. No border batsman could cope with the pace of Sylvester Clarke who was warned for over-using the bouncer. They could reach only 100 in their fifty overs, a target which the visitors attained in under 23 overs.

19 January 1983

at Port Elizabeth

West Indies XI 243 (C.L. King 71, A.I. Kallicharran 65, J.A. Carse 4 for 31)
Eastern Province 158 (R.L.S. Armitage 58, F.D. Stephenson 5 for 20)

West Indies XI won by 85 runs

Once more the early West Indian batsmen failed, with James Carse doing most damage, but Rowe and Kallicharran, coming together at 35 for 3, took the score to 126, and then King hit hard.

A second wicket stand of 64 between Willey and Armitage was Eastern Province's most significant attempt in their effort to achieve victory, but the target was always well beyond they reach, especially with Franklyn Stephenson in top form.

First International

21, 22, 24 and 25 January 1983

at Newlands, Cape Town

South Africa 449 (R.G. Pollock 100, S.J. Cook 73, A.J. Kourie 69, D.R. Parry 5 for 117) and 108 for 5
West Indies XI 246 (R.A. Austin 93, F.D. Stephenson 56, V.A.P. van der Bijl 4 for 44) and 309 (A.I. Kallicharran 89, S.T. Jefferies 4 for 58)

South Africa won by 5 wickets

The South African players were awarded caps, but in no way could this match, nor indeed any other in which one of the competing teams is not chosen by the official governing body of the game in that country, be regarded as a *bona fide* Test match, and there were few who regarded it as such.

Newcomer Jimmy Cook and veteran Barry Richards gave South Africa a good start, but the feature of the innings was a hundred in 167 minutes off 159 balls by Graeme Pollock. He hit fourteen fours and was at his majestic best.

Kourie batted well, and Garth Le Roux and Steve Jefferies put on 67 for the last wicket to take the South African total to 449.

Apart from a stubborn 93 in 292 minutes, the West Indians were always struggling. They closed the second day at 157 for 7, and in spite of a brisk 56 by Franklyn Stephenson, they followed-on the next day 203 behind.

Kallicharran batted dourly as West Indies struggled to save the game, but a couple of controversial decisions went against the tourists, and South Africa were left needing only 107 to win.

Clarke caused them some discomfort, but Pollock stood firm and nursed his side to victory.

Second International

28, 29, 31 January and 1 February 1983

at Wanderers, Johannesburg

West Indies XI 267 (C.L. King 101, A.J. Kourie 6 for 55) and 176
South Africa 233 (R.G. Pollock 73, P.N. Kirsten 56, S.T. Clarke 5 for 66) and 181 (B.A. Richards 59, S.T. Clarke for 34)

West Indies XI won by 29 runs

Rowe won the toss and elected to bat. Facing an unchange South African side, West Indies had brought in Ray Wynte for the injured Moseley.

They made another bad start, 39 for 3 and Greenidg having retired ill; he was to return at the fall of the eight wicket. King and Kallicharran then added 65 in 53 minute and King went on to a thunderous century. It was scored i 133 minutes off 115 balls and included a six and fifteen four He was mainly responsible for the West Indians 267.

South Africa had an even worse start than West Indies losing both openers and night-watchman Jennings for 8 runs Clarke's pace was decisive in dismissing Richards, but Kir sten and Pollock rallied the side with a stand of 114 unti they, too, succumbed to Clarke's pace, after which th innings declined rapidly and disappointingly.

With neither King nor Greenidge fully fit, the West In dians struggled throughout their second innings and were a out before the end of the third day, leaving South Africa wit a seemingly easy target of 211.

Richards, enjoying some luck, and Cook began with a stand of 87, but then came total collapse before the fas bowling of Sylvester Clarke. 87 for 0 became 124 for 8. Ther was a brave stand between McKenzie, two and a half hours for 26, and Jefferies, but Jefferies was run out by Mattis an Clarke took the final honours.

3 February 1983

at Durban

Natal 202 for 8 (B.A. Richards 54, M.D. Tramantino 50, F.D. Stephenson 4 for 46)
West Indies XI 118

Natal won by 84 runs

Following their deserved win in the international, the West Indian side played a limited-over match against Natal, led by Mike Procter, who was determined to win back his place in the national side for the one-day international series. He batted well, led his side inspiringly and took 1 for 17 in 10 overs, so that Natal gained a surprisingly easy victory.

First One-Day International

5 February 1983

at St George's Park, Port Elizabeth

South Africa 250 for 7 (B.A. Richards 102, R.G. Pollock 66)
West Indies XI 159

South Africa won by 91 runs

ABOVE: *Alan Kourie in action at Cape Town. His spin troubled the West Indian middle order batsmen. Lawrence Rowe is the batsman. (Adrian Murrell)*

BELOW: *(left) Lawrence Rowe, leader of the West Indian side. (right) Collis King. His violent hitting has lost none of its power. (Adrian Murrell)*

The West Indian XI v. South Africa at Johannesburg. (Adrian Murrell)

This was the first of the series of six limited-over matches which would finish the tour.

The match was dominated by a brilliant pre-lunch century by Barry Richards who disdainfully threw off the spell that Clarke had seemed to have cast on him in the previous match. He and Cook shared an opening stand of 95, and there was a magnificent 66 not out from Graeme Pollock who, like Richards, fed avidly on the short-pitched bowling that the West Indians seemed to favour.

The West Indies never came to terms with the task in hand and tight bowling by Kourie destroyed the middle-order.

Second One-Day International

7 February 1983

at Newlands, Capetown

South Africa 194 for 8 (K.S. McEwan 61, P.N. Kirsten 50)
West Indies XI 151

South Africa won by 43 runs

This match was a bitter disappointment for the West Indians. A fine containing spell by Bernard Julien had put them in a good position. Peter Kirsten and Ken McEwan, in his first international, rallied South Africa with a stand of 95 and Garth Le Roux hit lustily, but the final total of 194 did not seem enough to trouble the West Indies.

Jefferies disconcerted the early batsmen, however, a Kourie again did a good job of dismissal and containme with the middle order so that once more the tourists ne came to terms with their target and were all out in under overs.

Third One-Day International

9 February 1983

at Berea Park, Pretoria

South Africa 179 for 9 (E.A. Moseley 4 for 27)
West Indies XI 167

South Africa won by 12 runs

The third match of the series attracted what was stated to the biggest ever crowd to watch a cricket match at Ber Park, Pretoria.

South Africa started slowly after winning the toss, and was only stalwart batting from McEwan and Alan Kou and some big hitting by Ray Jennings that gave their innin any sort of substance.

With a target well within their capabilities, the West dians again struggled against Jefferies with new ball. Dav Murray and Stephenson gave them hope with a use seventh wicket stand of 29. Murray saw 10 runs with Clar and another 10 with Moseley so that when Bernard Juli joined the wicket-keeper only 13 were needed in three ove The ex-Kent man took an agricultural swipe at Le Roux a was caught so ensuring that South Africa could not lose t series.

Fourth One-Day International

1 February 1983

At Wanderers, Johannesburg

South Africa 139
West Indies XI 141 for 3

West Indies XI won by 7 wickets

Another large crowd gathered at the Wanderers for the fourth match in the series, no doubt attracted by the fact that this was a day–night match which started mid-afternoon and finished under floodlights.

Against a full-strength pace attack the South Africans were always struggling. Kirsten fell to Clarke first ball, and both Richards and Pollock found it hard to force the pace. Too much responsibility was placed on the later batsmen, but South Africa were all out in the forty-third over for a meagre 139.

With no pressure on them, the West Indians clipped away at the target. There was the threat of Steve Jefferies, but without the tight spin of Alan Kourie to tax them, the West Indians strolled to a comfortable victory.

Fifth One-Day International

2 February 1983

At Wanderers, Johannesburg

South Africa 228 for 6
West Indies XI 171 (L.G. Rowe 71, A.I. Kallicharran 53, V.A.P. van der Bijl 4 for 25)

South Africa won by 57 runs

ABOVE: *The South African Team v. West Indies XI at Johannesburg.* BELOW: *Franklyn Stephenson in action at Cape Town. He was a constant threat to the South Africans.* (*Adrian Murrell*)

An ungainly shot by wicket-keeper Jennings ends in disaster, bowled Collis King in the fourth one-day international. (Adrian Murrell)

South Africa batted consistently early in the day to ensure that West Indies would face quite a stern task. The match belonged, however, to replacement pace bowler 'Spook' Hanley. He was standing in for Garth Le Roux.

A professional artist, Hanley came on to bowl with the West Indians needing 88 to win with five wickets left. He immediately dismissed Stephenson, but when Murray and Rowe took the score to 164, it seemed that West Indies would win.

Then, in his final over, Hanley held a difficult return catch to dismiss Rowe. Next ball Parry was plumb lbw and, to the astonishment of all, Clarke jabbed the next ball straight back to the bowler to give Hanley his hat-trick. His final delivery just shaved Moseley's off stump, but South Africa were now assured of victory and the series.

Sixth One-Day International

13 February 1983

at Kingsmead, Durban

West Indies XI 155 (C.L. King 60)
South Africa 71 (F.D. Stephenson 6 for 9)

West Indies XI won by 84 runs

The series, and the tour, were concluded at Kingsmead, Durban. Despite a typical innings from Collis King, 60 off 66 balls, including two sixes and five fours, the West Indian total of 155 looked completely inadequate.

However, after rain had reduced the number of overs and freshened the wicket, Clarke and Stephenson destroyed the South African batting. Stephenson, in particular, was devastating, bowling quickly and menacingly. For the first time in

the series, the home side appeared apprehensive against pacemen. Cook played well before he was yorked Stephenson and Rice showed brief aggression, but it wa sorry tale for South Africa. Franklyn Stephenson took last five wickets and finished with the astonishing figures 6 for 9 in 6.5 overs, without, incredibly, bowling a maid

So the first tour of the 'Calypso Cavaliers' came to an en There can be no disputing the success of the tour. The W Indians were received enthusiastically wherever they we and they responded with a cheerfulness and friendlin which won the hearts of the masses. To a man, they seemed to enjoy the tour.

There was confident talk of a further tour in the comi season, involving a team with an even stronger West Indi or international make-up. The effect of such a tour on t structure of world cricket can only be imagined. T S.A.C.U. believe that they have done all that they have be asked to meet the conditions of the I.C.C. and that whatev troubles are caused to I.C.C. members they have broug upon themselves.

From the South African point of view, the match brought forward some interesting points of discussion. On own view is that should future tours come about, every eff should be made by the South Africans to introduce some n blood at international level. Great though the contributio of the likes of Richards, van der Bijl and Rice have been, lit can be gained, in the long term, by their continued retentic

One hears of the determination of Procter to make mark again at international level. This would certainly be mistake, and one is saddened by the news that so great player should wish to return. Perhaps he was in Engli cricket too long where there is a tendency for veteran playe being reluctant to give up, to the detriment of English crick some think.

Rupert 'Spook' Hanley who took a famous hat-trick in the fi one-day international in Johannesburg. (Adrian Murrell)

Everton Mattis in action in the last match of the tour. (Adrian Murrell)

6, 7, 8 November 1982

at De Beers Country Club, Kimberley

Northern Transvaal 'B' 271 (W.F. Morris 51, P. McLaren 4 for 76) and 304 for 7 dec. (K.D. Verdoorn 50)
Griqualand West 319 (K. Sharp 82, H.W. Raath 4 for 82) and 257 for 4 (K. Sharp 125, M.D. Moxon 53)

Griqualand West won by 6 wickets
Griqualand West 19 pts, Northern Transvaal 'B' 7 pts

A career best 144 from Raymond Le Roux put Free State in a strong position on the opening day against Western Province 'B' but Roy Pienaar's maiden century on the second afternoon helped Western's to a first innings lead after early shocks. A disastrous Free State collapse followed a lengthy break for rain on the third afternoon – the seamers of Danie Du Toit providing admirable support for the incisive spin of Omar Henry, whose figures of 6 for 19 were a career best. Free State's pathetic all out 70 left the visitors to score only one for victory. This they achieved without much difficulty.

Meanwhile at Kimberley Northern Transvaal 'B' batted without much conviction until an aggressive 51 by Willie Morris helped them to respectability. Led by a fluent 82 by the skipper, Yorkshireman Kevin Sharp, Griquas achieved a useful lead on the second day and after the visitors set Griquas a target of 257 in 2 hours plus 20 overs, another

A great prize. Bernard Julien is exultant as Kallicharran catches the mighty Graeme Pollock off his bowling at Durban. (Adrian Murrell)

The Currie Cup set-up showed one major change from all previous seasons. It was decided that the five contesting teams should each play eight matches, as in 1981/82, but that the top two teams should then meet in a four-day 'play-off' to decide the championship. Thus it was quite likely that the team finishing top of the table would not be champions, though the leading side would be given the ground advantage. In the event of the match ending in a draw, the top province in the League would be champions.

The SAB Bowl also showed a new formula. The two sections were scrapped and all nine teams would go into the same 'league'. Each played six matches, with a form of 'seeding' devised in an attempt to make the competition stronger. The Bowl final was scrapped. Despite the disruptions caused by the two tours – many matches were re-arranged at fairly short notice and the resultant 'unevenness' sometimes made the competitions difficult to follow – there was some good cricket; unfortunately Transvaal and Western Province in the Currie Cup and Western Province B in the SAB Bowl, were so far ahead of the rest that the really sharp edge of competition was lacking.

SAB Bowl

4, 5, 6 November 1982

at Ramblers, Bloemfontein

Orange Free State 346 for 7 dec (R.A. Le Roux 144, S.M. Hartley 61, R.J. East 52, J.D. Du Toit 3 for 72) and 70 (O. Henry 6 for 19, J.D. Du Toit 4 for 21)
Western Province 'B' 416 (R.F. Pienaar 109, W.G. Kruger 80, J. Seeff 68) and 1 for 0

Western Province 'B' won by 10 wickets
Western Province 'B' 17 pts, Orange Free State 7 pts

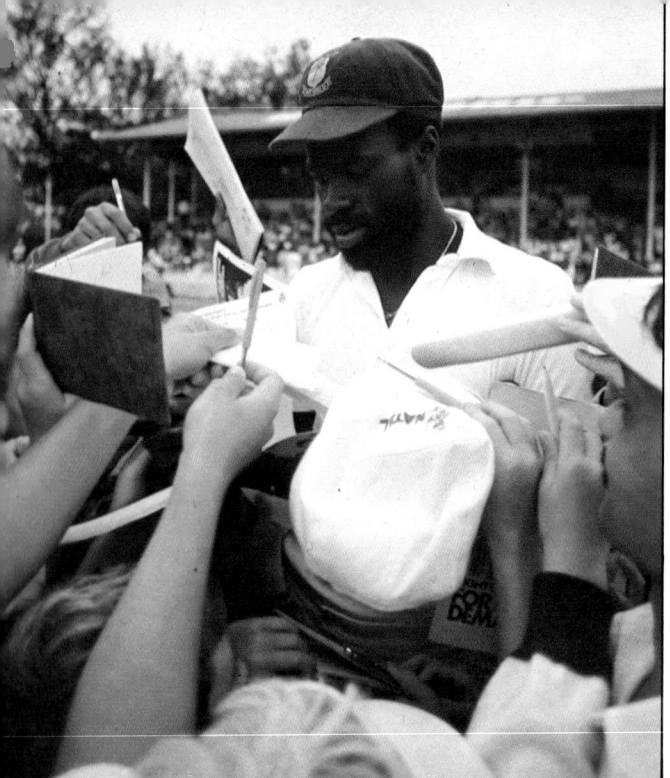

Franklyn Stephenson surrounded by admirers after his devastating 6 for 9 at Kingsmead, Durban, in the sixth and last one-day international. (Adrian Murrell)

superb innings by Sharp (his 128 in 148 minutes was a career best and included 17 fours and 2 sixes), plus good support from fellow-Yorkshireman Martin Moxon, who helped Sharp add 162 for the first wicket in 134 minutes, saw Griquas record their first victory in six seasons.

SAB Currie Cup

12, 13, 15 November 1982

at Berea Park, Pretoria

Northern Transvaal 244 (B.J. Whitfield 69) and 225 for 5 dec (N.T. Day 61 not out, B.J. Whitfield 51)
Natal 248 for 8 dec (R.M. Bentley 62) and 64 for 1

Match drawn
Natal 6 pts, Northern Transvaal 6 pts

SAB Bowl

12, 13, 14 November 1982

at R.J.E. Burt Oval, Constantia

Natal 'B' 200 (T.R. Madsen 68) and 181 (R.R. Lawrenson 4 for 45)
Western Province 'B' 248 (W.G. Kruger 51, M.D. Mellor 50, M.D. Clare 5 for 61) and 134 for 2 (J.P. Ackermann 70 not out, M.D. Mellor 50)

Western Province 'B' beat Natal 'B' by 8 wickets
Western Province 'B' 16 pts, Natal 'B' 3 pts

12, 13, 15 November 1982

at Willowmore Park, Benoni

Orange Free State 175 (D.P. Le Roux 57, T.H.D. Wheelwright 4 for 83) and 340 (R.A. Le Roux 75, R.J. East 73)
Northern Transvaal 'B' 200 (J.W. Furstenburg 76, S.J. Dennis 5 for 54) and 214 (G. Grobler 5 for 59)

Orange Free State won by 101 runs
Orange Free State 16pts, Northern Transvaal 'B' 7 pts

The Currie Cup opened at Pretoria with Northern Transvaal sent in to bat by Natal and grinding out 216 for 6 on a rain interrupted first day. Brian Whitfield was the main contributor with a sound 69, but the scoring was not fast enough for requirements. Natal's batting was also more noticeable for steadiness than fireworks, a steady 62 from Rob Armitage acting as backbone, but some fireworks from Mike Procter ensured a slightly faster rate, if no extra bonus points. Northerns again took few risks on the third morning and the draw was inevitable when Natal showed no interest in going for 222 in one hour plus 20 overs. Two unconvincing teams thus made an indifferent start to the season.

The SAB Bowl continued at Constantia where two drab first innings enlivened only by some good seam bowling from Natal 'B''s Mike Clare, and Natal's second innings collapse saw Western Province to an easy win which they scarcely deserved.

At Benoni attractive batting by Robbie East (73 in 101 minutes) and Raymond Le Roux saw them to a lead of 315 before Northern Transvaal 'B's second innings and Northerns were always struggling to score quickly enough against fine seam bowling from left armer Gerbrand Grobler as they declined to a 101 run defeat. Grobler took 5 for 59 in 22 overs, while Yorkshire's Simon Dennis followed his first innings 5 for 54 with an economical spell of 2 for 33 in 19.1 overs.

SAB Currie Cup

26, 27, 28 November 1982

at Berea Park, Pretoria

Transvaal 367 (S.J. Cook 92, K.A. McKenzie 51, R.G. Pollock 50) and 22 for 0
Northern Transvaal 169 (C.S. Stirk 68, R.W. Hanley 5 for 53) and 219 (N.T. Day 69)

Transvaal won by 10 wickets
Transvaal 22 pts, Northern Transvaal 4 pts

SAB Bowl

26, 27, 28 November 1982

at Oude Libertas, Stellenbosch

Boland 315 (E.J. Barlow 153, A. Du Toit 65) and 193 for 8 dec
Orange Free State 221 (D.P. Le Roux 108 not out) and 186 (P. Anker 4 for 83)

oland won by 101 runs
oland 18 pts, Orange Free State 3 pts

7, 28, 29 November 1982

t Wanderers, Johannesburg

ransvaal 'B' 284 (H.R. Fotheringham 70, W.J. Wilson
for 40) and 246 for 4 dec (H.R. Fotheringham 91, M.
achad 65, W. Kirsch 64)
riqualand West 228 (K. Sharp 113, T.H. Parrymore 4
r 59, I.F.N. Weideman 4 for 80) and 188 (C.D. Mitchley
for 39)

ransvaal 'B' won by 114 runs
ransvaal 'B' 19 pts, Griqualand West 6 pts

ransvaal commenced their Currie Cup campaign with a fast
coring 367 on the opening day of their game with Northern
ransvaal at Pretoria. Jimmy Cook led the way with an
egant 92 and with good backing right down the order there
as little Northerns could do to stem the tide. Only a brave
8 from Craig Stirk did much to keep the Transvaal bowlers
t bay in the first innings, 'Spook' Hanley starring with 5 for
3 and following-on, Noel Day's 69 was in vain as Transvaal
eded only 22 to win.

Champions Boland commenced their Bowl campaign
gainst Free State at Stellenbosch, with a record first wicket
tand of 198 between skipper Eddie Barlow, whose 153 in-
luded three sixes, and Andre Du Toit, but they failed to
uild on this and were out for 315. A gallant 108 not out by
Darryl Le Roux, who carried his bat throughout Free State's
21 saved his side from disaster, but steady batting on the
hird morning put Boland into an impregnable position and
lthough the Free State late order showed spirit they fell 101
hort of the run a minute target of 288. Pienaar Anker bow-
d steadily to take 4 for 83 in 29.4 overs.

Another fine hundred by Kevin Sharp failed to keep
Griqualand West in the game, at Jo'burg, the remaining
Griquas batsmen finding Transvaal 'B' seamers Francois
Weideman and Henry Parrymore too sharp. After a first
nnings lead of 56 an attractive 65 from Mandy Yachad
elped them capitalise on their advantage and a fine 91 from
Henry Fotheringham, supported by Willie Kirsch's 64 put
hem beyond defeat on the third morning. Set 303, Griquas
nade a miserable start, losing 3 for 34, but after an improve-
nent from the middle order, seamer Cyril Mitchley, with
reat support from wicket-keeper Bruce McBride, clinched
ictory.

SAB Bowl

2, 3, 4 December 1982

t UPE Ground, Port Elizabeth

Eastern Province 'B' 322 (R.J.D. Whyte 176) and 249
or 9 dec
Boland 238 (K.J. Barnett 79, S.S. Barnard 57 not out,
M.K. van Vuuren 5 for 53) and 194 for 8 (K.J. Barnett 82
not out, E.J. Barlow 63, I. Howell 4 for 65)

Match drawn
Eastern Province 'B' 10 pts, Boland 8 pts

*Berea Park, Pretoria. The score-board during the third one-
day international. South Africa v West Indies XI. (Adrian
Murrell)*

SAB Currie Cup

4, 5, 6 December 1982

at St George's Park, Port Elizabeth

Eastern Province 373 (R.L.S. Armitage 77, W.K. Watson 99 not out, D.J. Brickett 68, R.G. Fensham 54) and
107 for 2 dec (S.J. Bezuidenhout 60 not out)
Northern Transvaal 230 for 7 dec (B.J. Whitfield 59
and 146 for 7 dec (B.J. Whitfield 53, V.F. Du Preez 52 not
out, D.J. Brickett 4 for 48)

Match drawn
Eastern Province 6 pts, Northern Transvaal 4 pts

at Kingsmead, Durban

Natal 324 (D.R. Bestall 69, G.S. Le Roux 5 for 88) and
124 (J.E. Emburey 6 for 36)
Western Province 121 (K.R. Cooper 5 for 25) and 247
for 4 (G.A. Gooch 87)

Match drawn
Natal 9 pts, Western Province 3 pts

A magnificent 176 in 276 minutes by Eastern Province's Bob
Whyte (his maiden hundred) stopped Boland in their tracks
at Port Elizabeth after paceman Stephen Jones had grabbed
two early wickets and despite a staunch 79 from Derbyshire's
Kim Barnett and a late half century by Solly Barnard,
Boland were 84 short on first innings. Bright batting all down
the order saw Easterns into a good position on the third
morning, and only another splendid innings from Barnett –
he played with all the aplomb and maturity of a future

Alan Kourie. Troubled by injury during the season, he was still South Africa's leading spinner. (Adrian Murrell)

Derbyshire captain – saved Boland from sliding to defeat against the left arm spin of Ian Howell.

A record ninth wicket stand of 151 in 89 minutes between Dave Brickett and Kenny Watson, whose 99 not out in 105 minutes is his best ever score, and who was desperately unlucky to miss his century, changed the course of the Eastern Province first innings after 8 wickets had been lost for 205. Northerns batted stodgily in their own first innings, the consistent Whitfield again top-scoring. Easterns set the visitors a target of 251 in 145 minutes plus 20 overs. Whitfield again gave them a good start but a collapse set in against seamer Dave Brickett and only a dogged unbeaten 52 in nearly 3 hours by Vernon du Preez saved the defeat.

Currie Cup holders Western Province began their defence at Durban and things immediately went wrong. Natal batted on winning the toss and helped by at least four missed chances reached an impressive 324 after Garth Le Roux's pace had seen them struggling at 78 for 3. Natal tightened their grip on the second morning, fine pace bowling by Ken Cooper (5 for 25) and Les Taylor (3 for 35) ensuring a Westerns collapse but then Westerns hit back to have 6 Natal second innings wickets down for 61 by the close of the second day.

Natal again batted badly on the third morning but seemed in with a good chance of victory nonetheless – Westerns needing 328. What followed was a travesty of cricket – in fact

a disgrace to the game. Natal, who included such experienc players as Barry Richards, Chris Wilkins, Les Taylor a John Lever soon showed their only intention was to st Westerns scoring, and to play for a draw. Gooch, combati negative tactics better than anyone, hit a fine 87, Seeff, K sten and McEwan also batted well, but all was to no ava Seamers Lever, Taylor and Cooper all took extraordinar long runs, with equally extraordinarily slow walks back their bowling marks, the last 9 overs before the final 20 we bowled in little under an hour, and for the most part t fieldsmen were scattered around the boundary.

Natal skipper Darryl Bestall, whose negative approa was shown when he failed to enforce the follow-on, w presumably happy with the outcome – and presumably h team-mates supported his tactics. The fact that if all sid adopted similar ideas, cricket would be dead in a ye presumably does not bother the Natal players, most of who have had years in the game and, it seems, no longer ca about cricket.

First Class Friendly Match

13, 14, 15 December 1982

at Potchefstroom

Transvaal 275 (M.S. Venter 80, T.G. Shaw 5 for 73) an 160 for 2 (M. Yachad 102 not out)
Combined Universities 101 (T.H. Parrymore 4 for 8 and 398 (M.D. Logan 129, T.G. Shaw 76)

Match drawn

A splendid century by Mike Logan rescued Universities aft poor batting against the speedy 'Spook' Hanley and t slower attack of Parrymore had forced them to follow-o Transvaal were left to get 225 for victory with time not o their side and despite a brilliant unbeaten 102 in just over tw hours by Mandy Yachad, they fell well short of their targe

SAB Currie Cup

26, 27, 28 December 1982

at St Georges Park, Port Elizabeth

Western Province 444 for 6 dec (K.S. McEwan 10 P.N. Kirsten 81, S.D. Bruce 74 not out, A.P. Kuiper 71 and 8 for 1
Eastern Province 218 (G.S. Cowley 64 not out) an 233 (R.G. Fensham 58, S.T. Jefferies 5 for 56)

Western Province won by 9 wickets
Western Province 21 pts, Eastern Province 5 pts

at Wanderers, Johannesburg

Transvaal 301 for 8 dec (S.J. Cook 121, A.I. Kallicharra 60, L.B. Taylor 6 for 68) and 261 for 3 dec (S.J. Cook 6 A.J. Kourie 57)
Natal 275 (D.R. Bestall 71, T.R. Madsen 57, A.J. Kouri 4 for 88) and 171 for 9 (T.R. Madsen 62, A.J. Kourie 5 f 50)

Match drawn
Transvaal 11 pts, Natal 9 pts

AB Bowl

7, 28, 29 December 1982

t Oude Libertas, Stellenbosch

estern Province 'B' 227 (P.H. Rayner 64, W.G.
uger 58, J. Seeff 53, S.A. Jones 4 for 22) and 150 (P.
nker 4 for 48)
oland 199 (K.J. Barnett 91, O. Henry 5 for 58) and 101
). Henry 6 for 32)

estern Province 'B' won by 77 runs
estern Province 'B' 15 pts, Boland 2 pts

t Jan Smuts Ground, East London

orthern Transvaal 'B' 182 (G.L. Hayes 6 for 57) and
76
order 223 (H.W. Raath 5 for 56) and 136 for 6

order won by 4 wickets
order 16 pts, Northern Transvaal 'B' 5 pts

ast season's champions, Western Province swept to their
st Currie Cup win of the season over a poor Eastern
rovince outfit. Put in by the home team, a splendid century
3¾ hours by Ken McEwan, a sound supporting 81 by
ipper Peter Kirsten and an explosive 71 in 81 minutes, with
x sixes by Adrian Kuiper, saw Western Province amass 444
r 6, with six batting points on the opening day. In reply
asterns attempted enterprising means to push the score
ong but lost wickets steadily and were forced to follow-on.
hey again found the varied Westerns attack, with left arm
aceman Steve Jefferies, outstanding, too much for them,
d Westerns were left to score only 8 for an emphatic 9
icket victory.

Meanwhile, at Jo'burg, Transvaal confirmed themselves as
e early pacemakers, despite being held to a draw by Natal.
ut in to bat by Natal skipper Darryl Bestall, Transvaal
ade a slow start, Alan Kourie spending 44 minutes over his
rst run, but another fine innings by Jimmy Cook, his 121
ccupying 257 minutes, with sound support from Alvin Kal-
charran, helped them to a satisfactory first day score –
espite Graeme Pollock's first Currie Cup 'duck' since 1977.
Jatal, in their turn, batted attractively, and after another
uality innings from Jimmy Cook, Natal just held on for the
raw, finishing with one wicket left and 117 runs short of the
ictory target. For Transvaal, left arm spinner Alan Kourie,
oubled with injury this season, had match figures of 9 for
38 in 50.5 overs.

In the SAB Bowl Western Province 'B' maintained their
00 per cent record with a 77 run win over reigning title
olders Boland. After a sound start Westerns collapsed
gainst the second new ball, going from 212 for 4 to 227 all
ut, but Boland, apart from another fine knock of 91 by Kim
arnett, found runs even harder to come by against the spin
f Omar Henry. Another spinner, Boland's Pienaar Anker,
howed that he too knows his job, tying up the Western
atsmen with figures of 4 for 48 in 29.4 overs but his right
rmed off breaks were no match for Henry's left armers.
econd innings figures of 6 for 32 in 16 overs saw Henry
chieve a match analysis of 11 for 90 and send Boland spin-
ing to defeat.

Border opened their SAB Bowl season on a high note at
East London. Visitors Northern Transvaal 'B' were sent into
bat, on what looked like a batsman's wicket by skipper Ray
Ranger, and a fine spell from medium pacer Greg Hayes
vindicated the gamble. Although the left armed seamers of
Hein Raath picked up 5 for 56, Border achieved a first innings advantage of 41. Northerns again failed to dominate in
the second innings and lack of a major individual innings saw
them give Border a target of only 136. It was far from easy
however. By lunch, they had slumped to 31 for 3, and this
soon became 46 for 5. However, Rodney Ontong and Errol
Laughlin then came together in a match-winning stand of 76
in 92 minutes; these were the last accredited batsmen and the
Jan Smuts Ground was no place for weak hearts.

SAB Currie Cup

31 December 1982, 1, 3 January 1983

at Newlands, Cape Town

Transvaal 196 (H.R. Fotheringham 61, J.E. Emburey 5
for 53) and 328 for 6 dec (K.A. McKenzie 70, C.E.B. Rice
62, H.R. Fotheringham 61)
Western Province 202 (P.N. Kirsten 65, A.I. Kallicharran 5 for 45) and 200 (A.J. Kourie 7 for 79)

Transvaal beat Western Province by 122 runs
Transvaal 16 pts, Western Province 7 pts

1, 2, 3 January 1983

at Kingsmead, Durban

Natal 245 (B.A. Richards 61, R.M. Bentley 55, W.K. Watson 7 for 50) and 192 for 4 (R.A. Smith 75 not out)
Eastern Province 225 for 5 dec (D.J. Richardson 69)

Match drawn
Eastern Province 6 pts, Natal 4 pts

SAB Bowl

1, 2, 3 January 1983

at Jan Smuts Ground, East London

Natal 'B' 211 (G.M. Gower 6 for 44) and 180 (R.C.
Ontong 6 for 61)
Border 176 (E.J. Hodkinson 4 for 40) and 216 for 8 (E.T.
Laughlin 53)

Border won by 2 wickets
Border 15 pts, Natal 'B' 6 pts

at Uitenhage

Eastern Province 'B' 245 (D.H. Howell 59, T.G. Shaw
57) and 265 (I.K. Daniell 96)
Western Province 'B' 385 (P.H. Rayner 162, R.J. Ryall
51, T.G. Shaw 4 for 86, G.L. Long 4 for 92) and 127 for
5

Western Province 'B' won by 5 wickets
Western Province 'B' 18 pts, Eastern Province 'B' 6 pts

1, 3, 4 January 1983

at George Lea Park, Johannesburg

Transvaal 'B' 324 for 9 dec (M.S. Venter 127, M. Yachad 82) and 108 for 6
Orange Free State 123 (K.J. Kerr 4 for 32) and 305 (J.J. Strydom 104, C.J. van Heerden 65, S.N. Hartley 54, B. Roberts 4 for 32)

Transvaal won by 4 wickets
Transvaal 21 pts, Orange Free State 4 pts

Transvaal opened up a formidable Currie Cup lead with a 122 runs triumph over defending champions Western Province. Transvaal won the toss, but were immediately in trouble, losing 2 for 37. Recalled Henry Fotheringham fought with a tenacious 61, but a spell of 3 for 1 in three overs by John Emburey broke the back of the innings and Transvaal were bundled out for 196, their lowest score for some time. Westerns, in their turn, struggled against spin, with Alvin Kallicharran producing a career best 5 for 45. Transvaal, with Fotheringham again batting well for 61, and Rice and McKenzie also reaching half-centuries, found the spinners much less of a problem second time round and then Westerns set to score 323 in 4 hours plus 20 overs, fell before some magnificently incisive left arm spin from Alan Kourie. His second innings analysis of 7 for 79, included the first five wickets and was a major contribution to the 122 run win.

At Durban Natal were involved in another match of slow batting and negative cricket which left their supporters wondering just what was the point of it all. Put in by Eastern Province skipper Gavin Cowley, openers Chris Smith and Brian Whitfield set the scene with a crawl to 21 in the first hour. Smith eventually crept to 31 in nearly three hours (a rate which would surely attract the attention of the selectors to this 'new' Englishman) and only Barry Richards showed much aggressive intent as Natal achieved only a single bonus point. Ken Watson rounded off Natal's first innings with 5 wickets in 59 deliveries on the second morning but another day of excruciating cricket was finished early due to bad light with the first innings still not resolved. The third day saw both sides play through for the inevitable draw; as the batting got slower and slower, and the game more and more pointless, the 'crowd' of 400 resorted to frequent bouts of slow-handclapping. Eight of the participants had experience of the English county game and if ever there was a match which questioned the wisdom of employing such players, this was it. Perhaps the only performance worthy of mention was the wicket-keeping of Dave Richardson, who has *not* played in England.

In the SAB Bowl Border confirmed their promise with a narrow victory over Natal 'B' at East London. Natal never really recovered from a poor start, but their all out 211 seemed useful when Border had lost 3 for 20 by the close, but vigorous tail-wagging on the second afternoon saved them from disgrace against the pace of Evan Hodkinson. The visitors again struggled in the second innings, Rod Ontong (6 for 61) and paceman Gary Gower adding 3 for 56 to his first innings 6 for 44 ensuring an entirely reasonable target of 216. A horrifying start against the pace of Geyer and Hodkinson saw them struggling at 57 for 5, but an 81 run sixth wicket stand by Errol Laughlin and Gavin Hayes saw them turn the corner and finally Gavin Fraser, top scorer in the

first innings, again proved his worth on his recall to the si with a sterling unbeaten 43. Fraser made the winning hit wi three balls left – no wonder he was chaired from the field his supporters.

Western Province 'B' maintained their form at Uitenhag where Eastern Province 'B' did not make the most of winni the toss, though their all out 245 showed a considerab recovery after losing 4 wickets for 59. A maiden first-cla century from the highly promising 20-year-old Paul Rayn (his 162 took 288 minutes and included 20 fours and 5 sixe and a vigorous, if less polished 51 from wicket-keeper Ritch Ryall saw Westerns to a big first innings lead and despite fighting 96 from Ian Daniell, Westerns needed only 127 f victory, with 23 balls left. It was their fourth win in a row ar already their SAB Bowl title seemed assured.

Transvaal 'B' moved into second place, having played on two gaimes against Western's four, with a narrower win ov Free State. The tone was set with an opening stand of 1 between the highly talented young Transvaal openers Man Yachad and Mark Venter. The rest of the innings was an climatic, but Free State collapsed to the spin of Kevin Ke on the second morning, a first innings deficit of 201 ensuri the follow-on and although Joubert Strydom's maiden ce tury in Free States' second knock comfortably saved an i nings defeat, Alan Barrow and Bruce Roberts guided Tran vaal to a 4 wicket win after some early shocks.

SAB Currie Cup

15, 16, 17 January 1983

at Wanderers, Johannesburg

Transvaal 249 (H.R. Fotheringham 64, K.A. McKenz 52) and 162 for 5 dec
Northern Transvaal 142 (N.V. Radford 5 for 39, I.F. Weideman 4 for 29) and 158 (V.F. Du Preez 52, N. Radford 4 for 66)

Transvaal won by 111 runs
Transvaal 18 pts, Northern Transvaal 5 pts

at St Georges Park, Pretoria

Eastern Province 283 (R.L.S. Armitage 79, R.G. Fer sham 66, J.K. Lever 5 for 79) and 321 for 4 dec (W. Larkir 86, R.L.S. Armitage 81, D.J. Richardson 59)
Natal 253 for 7 dec (D.R. Bestall 70, R.A. Smith 51, W. Watson 4 for 48) and 329 for 9 (B.J. Whitfield 117, C. Smith 77, W.H. Watson 4 for 58)

Match drawn
Eastern Province 7 pts, Natal 7 pts

It was top *v* bottom at Wanderers, but Transvaal had surpri ing trouble against their struggling Northern opponent Henry Fotheringham (64 in 169 minutes) and Kevin McKe zie (52 in 109 minutes) ensured a first innings of 249 whe their more celebrated colleagues had failed, and then Fra cois Weideman (4 for 29) took the top off the Norther innings while Neil Radford (5 for 39, and the last 4 for four runs in 31 balls) mopped up the tail. With the pitch suspec Transvaal set Northerns to score 270 in 322 minute plus 20 overs and when Mandy Yachad and Vernon D reez added 69 in 83 minutes the match seemed wide open. achad's enterprising 42 was then ended by Radford, and ith no-one else able to stay and force the pace against the am attack of van der Bijl and Radford, the innings quickly ollapsed, 9 wickets falling for 39 runs and Transvaal winng with more than two hours remaining.

At Port Elizabeth, Eastern Province recovered from a oor start against the Natal seamers, left handed Robbie rmitage and Russell Fensham adding 124 for the fourth icket after early successes by Lever. Lever's final figures of for 79, his best return in a lean season so far, could not revent a total of 283 and after a slow opening stand of 64 y 'Kippy' Smith and Brian Whitfield, Natal declared 30 ehind. An opening stand of 125 between Wayne Larkins d David Richardson, and then another fine innings by obbie Armitage, enabled Easterns to set Natal the huge sk of scoring 352 in 210 minutes plus 20 overs. Surprisingly atal finished within 23 runs of victory, but with only one icket standing. Whitfield and Smith showed unusual ggression in giving their side a splendid start by adding 133 133 minutes for the first wicket, and Whitfield, engaged in ther useful stands, went on to 117 in nearly five hours. owever wickets fell steadily at the other end and after Whiteld's dismissal, Natal were thankful to hold on for a draw. n honourable draw nonetheless.

AB Bowl

4, 15, 17 January 1983

t Pietersburg

Iorthern Transvaal 'B' 87 & 276 (C.P.L. de Lange 82, .D. Mitchley 4 for 84)
ransvaal 'B' 156 (G.E. McMillan 5 for 28) & 141 (B. roctor 5 for 30, G.E. McMillan 4 for 52)

Iorthern Transvaal 'B' won by 66 runs
Iorthern Transvaal 'B' 15 pts, Transvaal 'B' 5 pts

5, 17, 18 January 1983

t Pietermaritzburg

Boland 70 (E.J. Hodkinson 4 for 21) & 139 (PdeV. Geyer for 31)
Iatal 'B' 152 (H. Mansell 69, P.D. Swart 4 for 31) & 59 or 4

Iatal 'B' won by 6 wickets
Iatal 'B' 15 pts, Boland 5 pts

t Ramblers, Bloemfontein

Eastern Province 'B' 293 (D.H. Howell 109, J.D. Ogil-ie 54 not out) & 307 for 9 dec (D.H. Howell 114, R. Le Roux 4 for 43, W.M. van der Merwe 4 for 62)
Orange Free State 320 (R.J. East 69, B. de K. Robey 4 or 56) & 151 for 9 (T.G. Shaw 4 for 33)

Match drawn
Orange Free State 9 pts, E. Province 'B' 9 pts

n the SAB Bowl struggling Northern Transvaal 'B' made a lisastrous start against Transvaal 'B', at Pietersburg. Transaal's pacemen revelled on a rain affected wicket to send

Northern back for 87, and although Transvaal also struggled, they gained a lead of 69. Northerns, with Provincial Rugby player Lourens de Lange hitting 82 from 93 balls, did much better at their second attempt and were able to give Transvaal the none too easy task of getting 208 to win. They failed miserably against seamer Gordon McMillan (4 for 52) and spinner Brett Proctor (5 for 30) and crumbled to a surprise defeat which severely reduced their chances of catching runaway leaders, Western Province 'B'.

Another batting collapse was seen at Maritzburg where fading champions Boland were dismissed before lunch in 32.2 overs after being put in on a soft pitch by Natal 'B'. Natal 'B' reached 82 for 5 before rain caused play to be abandoned in mid-afternoon. Natal's 152 owed much to Henry Mansell's 69 and after Boland had again collapsed to some fine pace bowling by Flippy Geyer, Natal's task of getting 59 to win was a formality, though with 4 wickets falling they received some shocks on the way.

The third SAB Bowl match at this time was at Bloemfontein and was notable for a century in each innings by Eastern Province 'B' opener David Howell. Despite Howell's 109, and a steady half century from Dickie Ogilvie, Easterns were headed on first innings after consistent batting all through the order by Free State. Howell's splendid second innings 114 enabled Easterns to set a target of 281 and although Free State's openers, the Le Rouxs, added 84 in 87 minutes for the first wicket, they were finally glad to hang on for a draw, one wicket to fall, 130 short.

SAB Bowl

20, 21, 22 January 1983

at Country Club, Kimberley

Eastern Province 'B' 264 (M.B. Billson 73) & 260 for 9 dec (V.G. Cresswell 55, D.H. Howell 54, D.G. Emslie 54, A.P. Beukes 4 for 50)
Griqualand West 200 (K. Sharp 60, B. de K. Robey 4 for 45, J.D. Ogilvie 4 for 58) & 282 for 9 (P.L. Symcox 80, K. Sharp 61, M.D. Moxon 57, T.G. Shaw 5 for 59)

Match drawn
Eastern Province 'B' 8 pts, Griqualand West 5 pts

at Jan Smuts Ground, East London

Border 280 for 5 dec (G.C.G. Fraser 105 not out, G.L. Hayes 68 not out, E.T. Laughlin 50) & 227 for 7 (G.L. Hayes 80, G.C.G. Fraser 71, S.A. Jones 4 for 34)
Boland 377 (K.J. Barnett 90, E.J. Barlow 82, R.C. Ontong 6 for 108)

Match drawn
Boland 7 pts, Border 6 pts

At Kimberley Griqualand West had the best of the opening day of their Bowl game with Eastern Province 'B'. Easterns' top order batsmen failed to master the tight Griquas' bowling but middle order aggression enabled them to reach 264. Griquas' openers, Kevin Sharp and Martin Moxon, put on 72 without loss by the close. Griquas suffered a blow on the second morning when star batsman Sharp was run out and they collapsed disappointingly to 200 all out against seamers Dickie Ogilvie (4 for 58) and Brent Robey (4 for 45). Easterns accelerated on the third morning, to set Griquas a target of 325. Sharp and Moxon gave them an ideal start with 105 in 93 minutes, but on Sharp's dismissal the momentum was gradually lost as wickets tumbled and Griquas were finally glad to hang on for a draw after Tim Shaw had created havoc with his left arm spinners.

Two ambitious teams met at East London and when Border lost 4 for 34 on the first morning, Errol Laughlin, supported by Greg Hayes, led the recovery with a sound 60 and then Gavin Fraser put Border on top with a splendid 4½ hour century. Border declared giving Boland 40 minutes batting on the first evening without being able to get the breakthrough. On the second morning a careful stand of 153 between Eddie Barlow and Kim Barnett helped Boland to a 97 run lead, but all dangers of a Border defeat were put out of mind by a sixth wicket stand of 150 between the first innings heroes Gavin Fraser (71) and Greg Hayes (80), after paceman Stephen Jones had taken four early wickets for 12 runs.

SAB Bowl

3, 4, 5 February 1983

at Berea Park, Pretoria

Eastern Province 'B' 262 (D.G. Emslie 78, G.L. Long 59, B. Proctor 6 for 74) & 266 for 7 dec (I.K. Daniell 101)
Northern Transvaal 'B' 245 for 9 dec (S. Vercueil 71 not out, T.G. Shaw 4 for 51) & 189 for 5 (C.S. Stirk 79 not out)

Match drawn
Eastern Province 'B' 7 pts, Northern Transvaal 'B' 4 pts

at Country Club, Kimberley

Griqualand West 174 (G.L. Hayes 4 for 13) & 279 (M.D. Moxon 119 not out, K. Sharp 53, I. Foulkes 5 for 64)
Border 304 (I. Foulkes 110, R.C. Ontong 67) & 138 for 8 (A.P. Beukes 4 for 32)

Match drawn
Border 6 pts, Griqualand West 2 pts

4, 5, 6 February 1983

at R.J.E. Burt Oval, Constantia

Western Province 'B' 434 for 8 dec (S.D. Bruce 176, J.D. Du Toit 63, M.D. Mellor 53, K.J. Kerr 4 for 125)
Transvaal 'B' 166 (O. Henry 5 for 63) & 187 (O. Henry 4 for 50)

Western Province 'B' won by an innings and 81 runs
Western Province 'B' 18 pts, Transvaal 'B' 3 pts

15, 16, 17 February 1983

at Bloemfontein

Griqualand West 200 (K. Sharp 78, W.M. van der Merwe 5 for 49) & 198 (K. Sharp 52, C.J. van Heerden 5 for 56)
Orange Free State 360 (S.N. Hartley 79, R.A. Le Roux 68) & 41 for 1

Orange Free State won by 9 wickets
Orange Free State 18 pts, Griqualand West 5 pts

Northern Transvaal 'B' entertained Eastern Province 'B' [at] Pretoria, neither teams having yet made any impact in t[he] Bowl Log (as with their seniors in the Currie Cup). That t[he] visitors reached 262 in their first knock was due largely [to] skipper David Emslie's 78, and a late aggressive 59 by Gra[eme] Long, and even they had trouble with the spin of Brett Pro[c]tor (6 for 74 in 32.5 overs). Northerns batted very slowly [on] the second day before declaring with 9 wickets down [and] behind, and then Ian Daniell scored a maiden century f[or] Easterns before they declared to give Northerns a victo[ry] target of 284, and ample time. Despite an unbeaten 79 in 1[??] minutes by Craig Stirk the chase was called off with only [??] overs remaining, 95 runs still needed and 5 wickets to fal[l.]

Border hoped to continue their improved form with a w[in] at Kimberley against struggling Griqualand West. Batti[ng] first on a 'green top' Griquas were never able to come [to] terms with the seamers of Fraser and Hayes; they nev[er] recovered from the shock of losing Sharp at 25 and were a[ll] out 174, in 4½ hours. At stumps on the first day Border we[re] 91 for 1 after 2½ hours steady batting and well on the way [to] a lead. 110 in 321 minutes on the second day by Ivor Foulk[es] helped Border to a score of 304 and apparent safety fro[m] defeat but with Sharp playing a fine innings of 53 and Mox[on] carrying his bat for 119 there was little hope of a win and [in] fact though finishing only 12 short of victory, Border on[ly] had two wickets to fall.

At Constantia, leaders Western Province 'B' met secon[d] placed Transvaal 'B' – and a win for the former meant tha[t] barring miracles they could not be caught by any side an[d] were new winners of the SAB Bowl. The match was almo[st] decided on the first day, a brilliant 176 in 204 minutes b[y] Stephen Bruce – a career best for the Currie Cup discard [–] and a record seventh wicket stand between Bruce and Dan [Du Toit (63) helping Westerns to a total of 434 for 8 dec [–] another record. Transvaal showed a disappointing lack [of] fight against Omar Henry's spin on the second day, an[d] Henry (4 for 50) and paceman John During induced a furth[er] Transvaal collapse on the third day to bring an innings wi[n.]

Two disappointing teams met at Bloemfontein, and Fre[e] State, on winning the toss, asked Griqualand West to ba[t.] With Sharp again in fine fettle, the visitors got off to a flyin[g] start, reaching 132 for 2 by lunch. Sharp scored 78 in 13[?] minutes, but on his departure, a collapse set in and Griqua[s] were all out 200 in 4 hours. Free State reached 123 for 2 b[y] the close of the first day and by steady rather tha[n] spectacular batting went on to a 160 run lead on the secon[d] day. No player really cut loose and the Griquas bowler[s] stuck to their task admirably. Sharp gave Griquas a flyin[g] start in their second innings, but following his dismissal fo[r] 52, Carl van Heerden induced another collapse with hi[s] seamers and Free State were left to score 41 to win.

SAB Currie Cup

26, 27, 28 February 1983

at Newlands, Cape Town

Eastern Province 170 (J.E. Emburey 6 for 33) and 22[?] (D.J. Richardson 68, D.L. Hobson 6 for 73)
Western Province 377 (R.F. Pienaar 112, P.N. Kirsten 69, A.P. Kuiper 66, W.K. Watson 6 for 87) and 20 for 0[?]

Western Province won by 10 wickets
Western Province 21 pts, Eastern Province 2 pts

at Kingsmead, Durban

Northern Transvaal 267 (A.M. Ferreira 96, K.D. Verdoorn 81, L.B. Taylor 4 for 45, M.J. Procter 4 for 83) and 97 (M.J. Procter 6 for 52)
Natal 548 for 6 dec (B.A. Richards 123, M.J. Procter 99, R.J.S. Smith 97, T.R. Madsen 87)

Natal won by an innings and 84 runs
Natal 24 pts, Northern Transvaal 6 pts

SAB Bowl
26, 27, 28 February 1983

at Wanderers, Johannesburg

Transvaal 'B' 328 (A. Barrow 70, B. Roberts 70 not out, D.K. Pearse 4 for 50) and 241 for 3 dec (M.S. Venter 100, A. Barrow 91)
Natal 'B' 201 and 247 (C.L. Smith 66, B. Roberts 4 for 56)

Transvaal won by 121 runs
Transvaal 'B' 21 pts, Natal 'B' 7 pts

at Prospect Ground, Grahamstown

Eastern Province 'B' 271 (J.D. Ogilvie 54, I. Foulkes 5 for 73) and 65 for 1
Border 379 for 7 dec (I. Foulkes 135 not out, M.R. Ballantyne 86, R.C. Ontong 56)

Match drawn
Border 7 pts, Eastern Province 'B' 5 pts

The Currie Cup was resumed with champions Western Province entertaining wooden spoon candidate Easterns. Easterns batted poorly when taking first innings. None of the early batsmen could cope with John Emburey's off spin and he finished with the outstanding figures of 6 for 33 from 24.5 overs. Eastern's 170 was never likely to be enough to keep them in the game and this was confirmed on the second day when Westerns, helped by a maiden Currie Cup century by Roy Pienaar, his chanceless 112 occupied 223 minutes and included 3 sixes and 7 fours, and half centuries from skipper Peter Kirsten and Adrian Kuiper, reached a first innings lead of 207. David Richardson (68 in 219 minutes) fought hard for Easterns second time round, but no other batsman could hold off the spin of Denys Hobson (6 for 73 in 33.4 overs) and John Emburey (3 for 62 in 44 overs, 20 maidens) and although the innings defeat was avoided, Westerns needed only 20 to make for victory, so keeping their title hopes alive.

Natal, still without a win though undefeated (a 'tribute' to their mainly negative tactics), entertained lowly Northern Transvaal at Kingsmead. Northerns batted first and started badly against Taylor and Procter, but a record sixth wicket stand of 152 between Anton Ferreira and Kevin Verdoorn enabled them to achieve a respectable 267. Natal however made a fine start, Whitfield and Richards adding 152 for the first wicket in 158 minutes and Richards went on to complete a fine century, his 123 occupying him 207 minutes and including 17 fours. Trevor Madsen (87 in 153 minutes) kept up the

pressure but the Northern bowlers were really put to the sword by Procter. He scored 99 in 80 minutes, with 3 sixes and 13 fours. 'Tich' Smith then thrashed the demoralised bowlers for 97 in 119 minutes, adding 157 in two hours with Robin Smith, and on the former's dismissal Procter finally declared. The Northern batsmen fought well in their second innings but without a major innings, and against the quite lethal off spin of Procter (6 for 52 in 30.1 overs) they never had a hope of saving the game.

Natal's haul of 24 points was a new record for the competition – their success under Procter's more positive leadership left one wondering whether they would now be in with a real chance of Currie Cup success had their earlier games not been played in so negative a fashion.

Transvaal 'B' with almost no hope of catching Bowl leaders Western Province 'B', took on disappointing Natal 'B' at the Wanderers and after an indifferent start gained 6 batting points before declaring at 328 for 9. Natal were always struggling in their reply, though their tail wagged effectively to take them from 59 for 5 to an all out 201, but a magnificent opening stand of 181 in 162 minutes between Alan Barrow (91) and Mark Venter (100) put Transvaal in an impregnable position, and although Natal made a brave attempt to score 369 in 306 minutes plus 20 overs, they were never in with a chance, and a good spell by Bruce Roberts (4 for 56) saw them sink to a 121 run defeat.

Border, retaining hopes of the runners-up spot in the Bowl, travelled to Grahamstown to take on Eastern Province 'B'. Easterns batted unevenly when going in first, but were saved from trouble by two good stands, including a new seventh wicket record of 90 between Dickie Ogilvie and Ian Howell. Their all out 271 was made to look most inadequate however when the in-form Ian Foulkes hit a fine unbeaten 135 in 200 minutes, with 21 fours, to help his side to a lead of 108, but steady rain on the third day destroyed all hopes of a Border win and with it any chances of their achieving the runners-up spot.

SAB Currie Cup
4, 5, 6 March 1983

at Johannesburg

Western Province 349 for 9 dec (P.H. Rayner 121 not out, R.F. Pienaar 61, P.N. Kirsten 55) and 260 for 7 dec (G.A. Gooch 104, N.V. Radford 5 for 116)
Transvaal 286 (A.J. Kourie 72 not out, S.T. Jefferies 6 for 91) and 101 for 0 (S.J. Cook 51 not out)

Match drawn
Transvaal 9 pts, Western Province 7 pts

4, 5, 7 March 1983

at Berea Park, Pretoria

Northern Transvaal 220 (A.M. Ferreira 75, M.K. van Vuuren 5 for 57) and 255 for 6 dec (C.S. Stirk 93, N.T. Day 84)
Eastern Province 162 (S.P. Hughes 4 for 45) and 176 for 2 (R.L.S. Armitage 97 not out, P. Willey 57 not out)

Match drawn
Northern Transvaal 7 pts, Eastern Province 5 pts

SAB Bowl

4, 5, 7 March 1983

at Cude Libertas, Stellenbosch

Boland 244 (E.J. Barlow 82) and 209 for 7 dec
Transvaal 'B' 136 (P. Anker 4 for 39) and 23 for 2

Match drawn
Boland 7 pts, Transvaal 'B' 4 pts

5, 6, 7 March 1983

at Newlands, Cape Town

Western Province 'B' (T.A. Clarke 68) and 258 (O. Henry 54, G.M. Gower 4 for 64)
Border 191 (W.du Plessis 52, E.O. Simons 4 for 56) and 1 for 0

Match drawn
Western Province 'B' 8 pts, Border 6 pts

at Jan Smuts Stadium, Pietermaritzburg

Natal 'B' 382 for 8 dec (C.L. Smith 88, R.M. Bentley 76, S.M. Hedley 54, G.N. Lister-James 51 not out) and 89 fo 4
Griqualand West 209 (P.L. Symcox 53, E.J. Hodkinson 4 for 50) and 261 (F.W. Swarbrook 70, H.J. Liebenberg 61, E.J. Hodkinson 5 for 40, M.D. Makin 4 for 65)

Natal 'B' won by 6 wickets
Natal 'B' 17 pts, Griqualand West 3 pts

Transvaal commenced their home game with reigning Currie Cup holders Western Province knowing that victory would almost certainly confirm them as league winners. They batted first but made a poor start against the Westerns pacemen. Roy Pienaar joined skipper Peter Kirsten in a stand of 63 for the fourth wicket and when another collapse seemed imminent Currie Cup debutant, 21-year-old Paul Rayner came in and hit a splendid century. Rayner's 121 not out, the first hundred on Currie Cup debut since John Clarke's 112 not out for Rhodesia in 1967/68, occupied 257 minutes and included 3 sixes and 14 fours. The 112 he added with John During for the ninth wicket is a Currie Cup record for Westerns. After a declaration at 349 for 9 Transvaal went in for the last 20 minutes and made a disastrous start, finishing the day 9 for 2. Transvaal started badly on the second morning but a useful stand between Fotheringham and Pollock improved matters before Alan Kourie came in and helped add 69 for the seventh and 66 for the ninth wicket, to put his side within striking distance of the Westerns score. With Western captain Kirsten seemingly intent on a draw – in an inexplicable attitude since only victory would give his side a chance of topping the league table, the third day, even Gooch's attractive hundred lacked meaning.

The other game was at Pretoria where neither of the Currie Cup stragglers, Eastern Province and Northern Transvaal could afford to lose. Northern won the toss and immediately struggled against the Eastern pacemen before a sparking 75

in two hours by Anton Ferreira insured the fairly respectab 220 all out. Easterns found the Northern seamers even mo of a handful, giving Middlesex player Simon Hughes t excellent figures of 4 for 45, and slumped to a first innin deficit of 58. Northern quickly lost three second innin wickets, including that of the aggressive Yachad for 45, bu a stand of 149 between Day and Stirk averted all danger a catastrophe. Set to score 314 in 245 minutes plus 20 ove Easterns quickly lost Richardson and Larkins, and Armitas and Willey 'shut up shop', adding 161 before bad ligl finished play with 20 overs and 27 minutes remaining.

At Stellenbosch, deposed Bowl holders Boland ente tained Transvaal 'B', second-placed but with almost n chance of overtaking leaders Western Province 'B'. An in nings of 82 in 3 hours by skipper Eddie Barlow was the bac bone of Boland's 244 all out and then a fine spell of off spi from Pine Anker on the second afternoon caused Transva to slump to an all out 136. Boland tried to force the pace o the third morning before setting the visitors a target of 31 in 285 minutes plus 20 overs but any prospects of an interes ing finish were destroyed by rain. With Transvaal 23 for they were probably thankful to be saved from defeat; the title hopes had gone anyway.

The eight bonus points gained by Western Province wer sufficient to give them the SAB Bowl for the second time three seasons so the game became purely academic. A soun 68 by skipper Bossie Clarke saved Westerns from disaster o the first afternoon and a mid-order collapse by Border on th second day gave Westerns first innings lead. Able to set Bor der 310 to win in 236 minutes plus 20 overs, the champion looked likely to complete a clean sweep with their sixth wi out of six before rain ruined their chances. Still, five out o six was eminently satisfactory, and with a largely young side Western's success was most encouraging. For Border, season of promise had turned rather sour – a comfortabl mid-table position was less than hoped for.

At Maritzburg Natal 'B', without ever really dominating virtually put paid to Griqualand West's hopes of avoidin the wooden spoon with a total of 382 for 8 declared on th first day. Griquas were always struggling against the Nata pacemen and although a sturdy 70 from Fred Swarbroo ensured Natal batted again, Natal, despite having to hurry ran out fairly comfortable winners.

SAB Currie Cup

11, 12, 14 March 1983

at Newlands, Cape Town

Northern Transvaal 237 (K.D. Verdoorn 50, P.J.A Visagie 72, S.T. Jefferies 5 for 85) and 117
Western Province 295 (G.A. Gooch 126, S.T. Jefferies 60) and 60 for 1

Western Province won by 9 wickets
Western Province 17 pts, Northern Transvaal 8 pts

12, 13, 14 March 1983

at Wanderers, Johannesburg

Eastern Province 328 for 6 dec (W. Larkins 64, D.H. Powell 64 not out, D.J. Richardson 56, G.S. Cowley 56) and 114 (V.A.P. van der Bijl 4 for 24, R.W. Hanley 4 for 2)

Transvaal 546 for 8 dec (A.I. Kallicharran 139, H.R. Fotheringham 116, C.E.B. Rice 104, J.A. Carse 5 for 140)

Transvaal won by an innings and 104 runs
Transvaal 21 pts, Eastern Province 4 pts

SAB Bowl

12, 13, 14 March 1983

at Kingsmead, Durban

Northern Transvaal 'B' 243 (S. Vercueil 67) and 315 (M.B. Logan 90, G.E. McMillan 66)

Natal 'B' 441 (C.L. Smith 154, R.M. Bentley 151, S.M. Hedley 51, G.L. Ackermann 4 for 87) and 121 for 0 (M.D. Tramontino 71 not out)

Natal 'B' won by 10 wickets
Natal 'B' 22 pts, Northern Transvaal 'B' 5 pts

Western Province, whose hopes of staying in the championship race depended on their defeating Northern Transvaal at Newlands, started well but let Northerns recover from a first afternoon 118 for 6 to a total of 237. Steve Jefferies bowled splendidly for figures of 5 for 85, but there was a lack of penetrative support from his highly-rated partners. Western's chances were improved with a 4 hour 126 by Graham Gooch, helping them to 5 more bonus points and first innings lead. Le Roux soon dismissed the openers when Northerns batted again and with Jefferies again causing trouble, and getting more spin support than previously, Northerns collapsed to a miserable 117 all out. Westerns strolled to a nine wicket win on the third morning, keeping just in touch with leaders Transvaal, who took on lowly Eastern Province at the Wanderers, and certainly did not find things easy on the opening day.

Consistent, if sometimes stodgy, batting right down the Eastern order kept the champions-elect in the field all day. After a declaration at 328 for 6 Easterns must have had some hopes of at least a draw, but instead found themselves on the end of a hammering which established Transvaal as worthy of the title. A third successive opening stand of more than 100 by Cook and Fotheringham set the scene. Fotheringham went on to 116 in 284 minutes, adding 130 for the second wicket with Kallicharran, a stand which helped Transvaal towards a record number of 9 batting points, before the close of the second day, which saw Kallicharran unbeaten on 138. The carnage continued on the third morning, despite the early loss of the West Indian. Skipper Clive Rice went on to a rapid hundred – his first of the season – and with wicket-keeper Ray Jennings making a quick-fire 49 they reached 546 for 8 by lunch. Rice then declared and the demoralised Easterns collapsed to the pace of van der Bijl and Hanley and a humiliating innings defeat.

At Kingsmead the SAB Bowl competition was completed with Natal 'B'' finishing a disappointing season with a flourish which took them to third spot. A solid 170 minute

67 by Steve Vercuiel ensured a reasonable total for the Northern Transvaal 'B' but their 243 was as nothing when Natal 'B's 'Kippie' Smith and Rob Bentley got going. Their second wicket stand of 304 was a record for any wicket for Natal 'B', and a second wicket record for any Natal side. The stand ensured a first innings lead of 198 and although Northerns batted steadily and well on the third day, they were only able to give Natal a target of 118, which they duly reached with little trouble.

Currie Cup

20, 21, 22 March 1983

at Newlands, Cape Town

Natal 134 (G.S. Le Roux 5 for 34) and 189

Western Province 256 (P.N. Kirsten 70, L. Seeff 63, L.B. Taylor 4 for 59) and 68 for 1

Western Province won by 9 wickets
Western Province 19 pts, Natal 5 pts

at St Georges Park, Port Elizabeth

Eastern Province 201 (A.J. Kourie 4 for 46) and 114 (V.A.P. van der Biji 7 for 42)

Transvaal 404 for 5 dec (S.J. Cook 201 not out, A.I. Kallicharran 95)

Transvaal won by an innings and 89 runs
Transvaal 22 pts, Eastern Province 4 pts

The to date disappointing Natal outfit found themselves struggling against a Western Province side still hoping to retain the championship, some brilliant fast bowling by Garth Le Roux (5 for 34 in 13 overs) skittling the visitors after being put in by the home team on a Newlands pitch conducive to pace. Natal's 134 was very nearly passed on the first evening, Westerns finishing the day four behind with only two wickets down. Westerns, with steady contributions from Kirsten, Larkie Seeff and Gooch eventually won a first innings lead of 122 and another disappointing batting effort by Natal – who admittedly lacked Mike Procter, out with a broken thumb – left Westerns with the formality of scoring 68 for victory on the third morning.

Unfortunately while Westerns were keeping themselves in the championship hunt, pace-makers Transvaal were slaughtering bottom markers Eastern Province to put the league almost beyond doubt. Easterns were asked to bat on a green top and despite a tenacious 45 in 88 minutes by skipper Gavin Cowley they struggled badly to score 201. Transvaal raced to 125 for 1 in 37 overs by the close, and the following day, Cook raced to a career best unbeaten 201 in 404 minutes. He and Kallicharran added 195 for the second wicket and Transvaal declared at tea with a lead of 203. Eastern's attempts to save the match were almost non-existent. Vince van der Bijl achieved his best figures of the season – 7 for 42 in 16.1 overs – and Transvaal ran out innings winners with more than a day to spare. Not for the first time this season Eastern Province showed lack of fight as they assured themselves of the wooden spoon.

Currie Cup

25, 26, 28 March 1983

at Berea Park, Pretoria

Northern Transvaal 284 for 8 dec (V.F. du Preez 78, G.E. McMillan 50) and 191 (G.A. Gooch 4 for 15)
Western Province 304 (K.S. McEwan 100, A.M. Ferreira 4 for 63) and 175 for 6 (R.F. Pienaar 67 not out)

Western Province won by 4 wickets
Western Province 17 pts, Northern Transvaal 8 pts

26, 27, 28 March 1983

at Kingsmead, Durban

Transvaal 331 for 8 dec (K.A. McKenzie 95, J.K. Lever 4 for 124) and 261 for 3 dec (K.A. McKenzie 164 not out, C.E.B. Rice 51 not out)
Natal 264 (D.R. Bestall 80 not out, R.A. Smith 75) and 289 (B.J. Whitfield 83, B.A. Richards 82, D.R. Bestall 52 not out, A.J. Kourie 5 for 111, K.J. Kerr 4 for 92)

Transvaal won by 39 runs
Transvaal 18 pts, Natal 5 pts

Currie Cup Challenge Match

2, 3, 4, 5 April 1983

at Wanderers, Johannesburg

Transvaal 475 (A.I. Kallicharran 151, K.A. McKenzie 92, H.R. Fotheringham 89, O.Henry 4 for 48) and 97 for 1
Western Province 228 (R.F. Pienaar 51, O. Henry 50) and 490 for 7 dec (P.N. Kirsten 168, K.S. McEwan 130 not out, L. Seeff 71, V.A.P. van der Bijl 4 for 109)

Match drawn
Transvaal declared champions

The league part of the 1982/83 Currie Cup competition was completed with games at Pretoria, involving Northern Transvaal and Western Province, and Kingsmead, where Transvaal were the visitors, and hoping to clinch the league leadership, leaving them needing only a draw at home in the challenge match. There were early problems for Western Province at Pretoria when Le Roux left the field injured after only three overs. Vernon Du Preez provided the sheet anchor with 78 in 6¼ hours and with more aggressive support from Gordon McMillan (50) skipper Lee Barnard (39) and Anton Ferreira (32) a fairly satisfactory score of 284 for 8 dec was attained, though only three batting points were gained. Westerns quickly lost Graham Gooch and throughout their innings always struggled against the seamers of Anton Ferreira, but a century, though not one of his best, from Ken McEwan saw them to a narrow lead. A fine spell of seam bowling on the third day by Graham Gooch – his figures of 4 for 15 in 21.2 overs were quite remarkable – swung the game strongly Western's way and although they themselves suffered some shocks as they lost four wickets for 52, they eventually eased their way to a four wicket victory after a century stand by the youngsters Roy Pienaar (67 not out) and Paul Rayner (47).

Westerns were already sure of meeting Transvaal in the final. The latter celebrated their triumph at Durban. Despite a marathon spell by John Lever, who finished with 4 for 124 in 37 overs, Transvaal, having been put in by Natal skipper Mike Procter on a dry pitch, raced to 331 for 8 at more than 3.5 per over and, in reply, Natal, always more tentative, could reach only 264. Darryl Bestall scored 80 in 209 minutes and Robin Smith 75 in 205 minutes but neither really dominated. A brilliant career best unbeaten 164 by Kevin McKenzie – he went from 44 to 164 before lunch – enabled Transvaal skipper Clive Rice to set a target of 329 in 22 minutes plus twenty overs. An opening stand of 156 in hours by Richards and Whitfield gave Natal a cracking start and at the start of the last 20 overs they needed 75 with wickets standing. However, a number of wild shots were played, the batsmen lost their heads and all was lost.

The 'new-fangled' Currie Cup Challenge match involved league winners Transvaal, and runners-up Western Province. The match took place on the Transvaal home arena, the Wanderers ground, Johannesburg, and, under the rules, the home side merely had to draw to win the Currie Cup. Jimmy Cook, scorer of over 1,000 runs during the season helped Henry Fotheringham add 106 for the Transvaal first wicket and then Fotheringham was joined by Kallicharran in a second wicket stand of 108. Already the title was beginning to look pretty safe for Transvaal, and even more so when Kallicharran, whose 151 occupied 3 hours, 4 minutes, added 51 for the fourth wicket with the in-form Kevin McKenzie, who himself completed a quick-fire 92 in little more than two hours. Despite some good spin bowling by Omar Henry, whose figures of 4 for 48 in 16 overs suggested he should have been used more, Transvaal made the game safe when going on to a total of 475.

Western's reply was a disappointing 228. Western did much better second time round, with centuries from skipper Kirsten and Ken McEwan. They put on 181 for the third wicket. Transvaal were eventually set to get 244 in 12 minutes plus 20 overs. For once, they declined a run chase and who could blame them? The draw gave them the Currie Cup; defeat, remote though the possibility was, meant the runners-up spot.

LIMITED OVERS TOURNAMENTS 1982/1983

The two tours meant that the domestic limited overs competitions played during the season to some extent lost their important position. There was, however, some exciting spectator cricket and Transvaal were able to confirm their position as number one domestic team.

In the curtain-raising Computer Sciences Triangular Tournament, held at Durban in October, the three participants were again Natal, the holders, Transvaal and Western Province. The first game of this 50-overs a side tournament was reduced to 35 overs through bad weather. Transvaal batted first to reach 163 and when rain curtailed the game Western Province had reached only 47 for 6 in 19 overs; Transvaal won on faster run rate. Next day Westerns met the holders Natal, who made a good start but wasted it all when going from 91 for 3 to 99 all out, Adrian Kuiper taking 4 for 7 in 6 overs. The Western win, by 6 wickets in 32 overs, was a formality. Transvaal commenced the final match with Natal, knowing that they could lose and still win the title on faster run rate. As it happened the computers were not necessary. Natal again showed little appreciation of the needs of limited-overs cricket, reaching only 142 in 47.3 overs; Transvaal eased past their score in 39 overs with only 3 wickets lost, taking the title for the first time since 1979.

MATCH SCORES

October 8, 1982
Transvaal 163 for 6 (35 overs) (C.E.B. Rice 40) beat
Western Province 47 for 6 (19 overs) on faster scoring rate.

October 9 1982
Natal 99 (39 overs) (A. Kuiper 4 for 7) lost to
Western Province 103 for 4 (32 overs) (P.N. Kirsten 39) by 6 wickets.

October 10 1982
Natal 142 (D.R. Bestall 54, N.V. Radford 4 for 22 (47.3 overs) lost to
Transvaal 144 for 3 (S.J. Cook 73, C.E.B. Rice 42 not out) (39 overs) by 7 wickets.

SAB CURRIE CUP FINAL LOG

	P	W	L	D	Bonus Pts	Total pts
Transvaal	3	6	0	2	77	137
Western Province	8	5	1	2	65	115
Natal	8	1	2	5	59	69
Northern Transvaal	8	0	5	3	48	48
Eastern Province	8	0	4	4	39	39

Transvaal and Western Province drew the Challenge Match so Transvaal were declared Currie Cup Winners

SAB BOWL FINAL LOG

	P	W	L	D	Bonus Pts	Total pts
Western Province 'B'	6	5	0	1	42	92
Transvaal 'B'	6	3	2	1	43	73
Natal 'B'	6	3	3	0	40	70
Orange Free State	6	2	3	1	37	57
Border	6	2	0	4	36	56
Boland	6	1	2	3	37	47
Eastern Province 'B'	6	0	1	5	45	45
Northern Transvaal 'B'	6	1	4	1	33	43
Griqualand West	6	1	3	2	30	40

DATSUN SHIELD

The senior South African Limited overs competition was much interfered with by the tours, but the two leg semi-finals were finally reached with the contestants Western Province, who played Natal, and Transvaal, who had the easier task of meeting Eastern Province. A fine 119 in 204 minutes by skipper Peter Kirsten was the main feature of Western Province's 29 runs first leg victory over Natal at Durban, while Alvin Kallicharran, whose 136 took one minute longer, was the mainspring of Transvaal's easy win over Eastern Province at Johannesburg. Kirsten again, with a sound 82, took the batting honours for Westerns in the second leg as they reached 252 for 8 in their 55 overs and then eased to a 72 run win over too slow Natal while in a run orgy at Port Elizabeth, a Wayne Larkins 117 in 165 minutes inspired Eastern Province to the formidable score of 290 for 5 from their 55 overs, only to see Jimmy Cook (144 in 190 minutes) and Graeme Pollock, whose unbeaten 116 came at almost a run a minute, put on 215 for the Transvaal third wicket and take their side to victory with 6 overs and 8 wickets left.

The final took place at the Wanderers on 19 February and Transvaal once more confirmed their rating as the team of the season with a crushing victory over Western Province.

Transvaal, put in by Peter Kirsten, began with a 135 run opening stand between Jimmy Cook and Henry Fotheringham, equalling the competition record. A further outstanding stand, 87 for the third between Kallicharran and Pollock sealed the Western fate, as they found themselves chasing 304 for victory.

Westerns soon lost openers Graham Gooch and Larkie Seeff and although a stylish 57 in 90 minutes by Ken McEwan gave their fans some brief hopes there was no major innings in support; Westerns collapsed to an all out 194, and a defeat that was frankly almost a slaughter.

DATSUN SHIELD FINAL
19 February 1982 at Wanderers, Johannesburg

TRANSVAAL

S.J. Cook	b Pienaar	70
H.R. Fotheringham	c McEwan, b Gooch	67
A.I. Kallicharran	c Kuiper, b Le Roux	74
R.G. Pollock	c Kuiper, b Le Roux	55
C.E.B. Rice†	not out	11
K.A. McKenzie	b Jefferies	5
R.V. Jennings*	not out	2
A.J. Kourie		
N.V. Radford		
V.A.P. van der Bijl		
R.W. Hanley		
Extras		19
(53 overs)	(for 5 wickets)	303

	O	M	R	W
Jefferies	11	0	54	1
Le Roux	8	1	41	2
Gooch	8	0	35	1
Emburey	11	0	46	0
Kuiper	5	0	23	0
Henry	5	0	43	0
Pienaar	5	0	42	1

FALL OF WICKETS
1- 135, 2- 189, 3- 276, 4- 287, 5- 301

Transvaal won by 109 runs

WESTERN PROVINCE

G.A. Gooch	lbw, b Hanley	12
L. Seeff	c Jennings, b Radford	16
P.N. Kirsten†	c Jennings, b van der Bijl	21
K.S. McEwan	c Fotheringham, b Kourie	57
A.P. Kuiper	c Jennings, b Kallicharran	4
R. Pienaar	st Jennings, b Kourie	36
O. Henry	b Hanley	9
S. Bruce*	c Jennings, b Radford	10
G.S. Le Roux	lbw, b Radford	0
S.T. Jefferies	c and b van der Bijl	7
J.E. Emburey	not out	4
Extras		18
(48·1 overs)		194

	O	M	R	W
van der Bijl	7.1	0	15	2
Hanley	9	2	22	2
Kourie	11	0	38	2
Radford	10	1	40	3
Kallicharran	6	1	26	1
Fotheringham	5	0	35	0

FALL OF WICKETS
1- 27, 2- 36, 3- 88, 4- 93, 5- 159, 6- 160, 7- 177, 8- 178, 9- 183

BENSON & HEDGES NIGHT CRICKET SERIES

The third major domestic limited overs competition was played on a league basis between the five Currie Cup sides. Each team played the others twice, with the side at the bottom of the log dropping out. The four remaining played two semi-final matches, the winners going on to the final.

Natal were the ones to drop out at the end of the League part of the competition, and the semi-finals both played at The Wanderers Ground, Johannesburg were between Eastern Province and Western Province on 2 March, and between Transvaal and Northern Transvaal on 9 March.

The first semi-final was a desperately close-run affair. Graham Gooch's 65 in 110 minutes was the backbone of the Western score of 226 for 9 from their 45 overs, but Easterns wicket-keeping opener David Richardson played even better with a fluent 94 in 142 minutes, Easterns finally needed 12 from the last over, a target which was beyond them, but losing only 6 wickets they had given a splendid account of themselves and Adjudicator Ali Bacher acknowledged the talent of Richardson by awarding him the batting prize.

The second semi-final was something of an anti-climax. Mandy Yachad and Peter Visagie got Northerns off to a fine start with a fast opening stand of 57, and an attacking unbeaten 72 by Anton Ferreira confirmed their challenge before a late collapse limited the score to 223 for 7 from their 45 over allocation. It was never likely to be enough. Cook, who added 165 in 90 minutes with Fotheringham for the first wicket, went on to a brilliant unbeaten 104 as he steered his side to victory with more than 8 overs, and 9 wickets in hand.

The final, on 18 March, at The Wanderers, saw Transvaal complete a clean sweep of the major limited overs trophies; shortly they were to add the Currie Cup to their 'spoils'.

Western Province made a disastrous start, losing 2 for 16 and 3 for 51, but Gooch and Pienaar improved matters with a rollicking fourth wicket stand of 102 in 52 minutes. Gooch obtained 85 in 113 minutes and when Jefferies and Rayner later added 87 in 30 minutes for the sixth wicket to help the side to 275 for 8 in their 45 overs, it seemed the favourite would struggle. Not so; Cook and Fotheringham set thing moving with a quick-fire opening stand of 73, and with Fotheringham going on to 77 in 75 minutes the basis was made for a late sprint. Pollock set things up with a quick 4 and then a devastating unbroken fifth wicket stand of 78 i 32 minutes filled the cup of woe for Westerns. Transva eventually ran out winners with 17 balls and 6 wickets t spare, to complete the most outstanding season ever enjoye by one team in South African Domestic cricket.

First Class Averages

BATTING	M	Inns	NOs	Runs	HS	Av	100
H.R. Fotheringham	10	16	3	974	159*	74.92	2
K. Sharp	6	12	0	760	125	63.33	2
G.G.C. Fraser	5	8	3	315	105*	63.00	1
S.J. Cook	13	21	2	1142	201*	60.11	4
A.I. Kallicharran	11	17	1	822	151	51.38	2
R.J.B. Whyte	5	9	2	356	176	50.86	1
M.D. Logan	4	7	0	350	129	50.00	1
R.G. Pollock	14	20	2	884	197	49.11	2
K.J. Barnett	6	11	1	483	90	48.30	—
K.A. McKenzie	11	16	2	675	164*	48.21	1
K.S. McEwan	10	15	1	654	149	46.72	4
M.S. Venter	8	15	3	556	132*	46.33	3
S.D. Bruce	6	9	1	368	176	46.00	1
R.M. Bentley	9	16	2	639	151	45.64	1
P.N. Kirsten	14	23	4	837	168	44.05	1
A.J.S. Smith	9	15	5	435	97	43.50	—
R.A. Smith	7	13	3	432	75*	43.20	—
J.B.N. Perera	7	14	2	518	102	43.17	1
P.H. Rayner	10	16	3	561	162	43.15	2
E.J. Barlow	6	11	0	472	153	42.91	1
L. Seeff	10	19	3	671	188	41.94	2
D.R. Bestall	9	15	2	540	80*	41.54	—
B.J. Whitfield	9	17	0	705	117	41.47	1
C.E.B. Rice	14	19	3	644	104	40.25	1
G.A. Gooch	9	18	3	597	126	39.80	1
C.L. Smith	9	17	1	628	154	39.25	1
R.A. Le Roux	6	11	0	431	144	39.18	1
G.L. Hayes	6	10	3	271	80	38.72	—
M. Yachad	8	15	1	531	102*	37.93	1

BENSON & HEDGES FINAL
18 March 1982 at Wanderers, Johannesburg

WESTERN PROVINCE			
G.A. Gooch	b Radford		85
A.P. Kuiper	c Rice, b Radford		3
P.N. Kirsten	c Kourie, b Hanley		1
K.S. McEwan	c van der Bijl, b Kourie		11
R.F. Pienaar	lbw, b McKenzie		61
S.T. Jefferies	c Kourie, b van der Bijl		67
P.H. Rayner	b van der Bijl		33
G.S. Le Roux	b van der Bijl		0
O. Henry	not out		2
J. Ryall			
J.E. Emburey			
Extras			12
(45 overs)	(for 8 wickets)		275

	O	M	R	W
McKenzie	9	0	67	1
Kourie	9	0	55	1
Hanley	9	1	35	1
van der Bijl	9	1	52	3
Radford	9	2	54	2

FALL OF WICKETS
1- 15, 2- 16, 3- 51, 4- 153, 5- 186, 6- 273, 7- 273, 8-275

TRANSVAAL			
S.J. Cook	c Rayner, b Pienaar		34
H.R. Fotheringham	c Kuiper, b Gooch		77
A.I. Kallicharran	c Ryall, b Pienaar		31
R.G. Pollock	c Gooch, b Jefferies		45
C.E.B. Rice	not out		44
K.A. McKenzie	not out		37
A.J. Kourie			
R.V. Jennings			
N.V. Radford			
V.A.P. van der Bijl			
R.W. Hanley			
Extras			9
(42.1 overs)	(for 4 wickets)		277

	O	M	R	W
Gooch	9	0	61	0
Emburey	9	0	46	0
Jefferies	9	0	65	1
Le Roux	7	0	43	0
Pienaar	8.1	0	53	2

FALL OF WICKETS
1- 73, 2- 130, 3- 165, 4- 199

Transvaal won by 6 wickets

BATTING cont'd	M	Inns	NOs	Runs	HS	Av	100s
A.J. Kourie	13	17	6	415	72*	37.73	—
C.R. Madsen	7	12	0	452	87	37.67	—
R.F. Pienaar	12	18	1	633	112	37.24	2
B.A. Richards	11	17	1	590	123	36.88	1
M.D. Moxon	6	12	1	393	119*	35.73	1
D.J. Richardson	10	19	1	635	134	35.28	1
J. Seeff	5	8	0	282	68	35.25	—
D.P. Le Roux	5	10	1	320	108*	35.55	1
J.K. Daniell	6	12	1	379	101	34.45	1
J. Foulkes	6	10	1	308	135*	34.22	2
D.H. Howell	9	17	1	541	114	33.81	2
R.L.S. Armitage	9	17	1	534	97*	33.38	—
G.S. Cowley	9	12	4	262	64*	32.75	—
H.J. Liebenberg	6	12	3	293	61	32.56	—
S.T. Jefferies	11	15	2	418	60	32.15	—
N.T. Day	9	18	3	481	84	32.07	—
A.M. Ferreira	9	18	3	480	96	32.00	—
G.E. McMillan	7	12	3	286	66	31.78	—
B. Roberts	6	11	2	277	70*	30.78	—
A. Barrow	6	12	0	365	91	30.42	—
V.F. Du Preez	9	18	1	489	78	28.88	—
J.W. Furstenberg	7	14	1	369	76	28.38	—
M.D. Mellor	6	11	0	312	53	28.36	—
R.J. East	6	11	0	308	73	28.00	—
M.B. Billson	6	11	0	307	73	27.91	—
R.C. Ontong	6	10	1	251	67	27.89	—
D.G. Emslie	6	12	1	300	78	27.27	—
D.J. Brickett	8	9	2	190	68	27.14	—
O. Henry	9	14	2	325	54	27.08	—
P.L. Symcox	6	12	0	325	80	27.08	—
M.C. Tramantino	6	12	1	296	71*	26.91	—
R.G. Fensham	9	15	1	369	66	26.36	—
C.S. Stirk	8	16	1	387	93	25.80	—
W. Larkins	7	12	0	308	86	25.67	—
C.P.L. De Lange	6	12	0	304	82	25.33	—
G.M. Gower	6	8	1	176	40	25.14	—
V.G. Cresswell	6	11	0	273	55	24.82	—
G.L. Long	6	11	0	245	59	24.50	—
T.G. Shaw	6	12	0	293	76	24.42	—
D.L. Hobson	8	8	5	73	35*	24.33	—
P. Willey	8	14	1	314	57*	24.15	—
F.W. Swarbrook	6	11	1	240	70	24.00	—
S. Vercuiel	6	12	2	240	71*	24.00	—
W. Kirsch	6	12	1	263	64	23.91	—
L.J. Barnard	8	16	1	338	47	22.53	—
C.J. van Heerden	4	8	1	156	65	22.29	—
J.D. Ogilvie	5	9	1	176	54*	22.00	—
K.D. Veerdoorn	11	18	1	373	81	21.94	—
R.J. Ryall	10	11	4	153	51	21.86	—
E.T. Laughlin	6	10	0	215	60	21.50	—
D.K. Pearse	6	10	2	171	47	21.38	—
W.K. Watson	9	11	1	212	99*	21.20	—
A.P. Kuiper	11	18	2	335	71	20.94	—
J.J. Strydom	5	9	0	185	104	20.55	1
G.S. Le Roux	11	13	3	205	51*	20.50	—
C.D. Mitchley	9	10	3	142	44	20.29	—
I.F.N. Weideman	8	8	2	121	47*	20.17	—
R.V. Jennings	14	15	6	178	49*	19.78	—
P.H. Williams	8	13	2	217	38	19.73	—
S.A. Jones	6	11	1	197	46	19.70	—
S.J. Dennis	5	9	3	118	37*	19.67	—
C.R. Norris	6	10	2	154	33	19.25	—
S.S. Barnard	6	11	2	169	57*	18.78	—
H.W. Raath	6	10	2	147	32*	18.38	—
P.J.A. Visagie	7	14	1	233	72	17.92	—
N. Mandy	4	8	1	118	45	16.86	—
H.R. Mansell	5	9	0	149	69	16.55	—
A. Du Toit	6	11	0	178	65	16.18	—
A.P. Beukes	5	10	1	144	40*	16.00	—
P.D. Swart	6	11	0	173	38	15.73	—
I.L. Howell	6	10	2	120	44	15.00	—
P.J. Allan	6	10	0	147	35	14.70	—
N.V. Radford	10	8	0	115	45	14.38	—
J. During	7	8	1	98	31	14.00	—
W.J. van der Linden	6	10	1	121	35	13.44	—
G.P. van Rensberg	6	11	1	132	46	13.20	—

BATTING cont'd	M	Inns	NOs	Runs	HS	Av	100s
A.H. Jordan	6	12	0	149	25	12.42	—
M. Michau	5	10	0	117	37	11.70	—
P. Carrick	7	11	1	103	21	10.30	—

(Qualification 8 inns, or 350 runs average 10.00)

First Class Averages

BOWLING	Overs	Mdns	Runs	Wkts	Av	5 inn	10 mtch
P. de V. Geyer	59	27	137	11	12.45	1	—
S.A. Jones	159.4	54	294	23	12.78	—	—
W.M. van der Merwe	88.4	18	269	18	14.94	1	—
T.H. Parrymore	142.1	38	420	26	16.15	—	—
R.R. Lawrenson	137.1	36	330	19	17.37	—	—
P.D. Swart	144.1	40	318	18	17.67	—	—
M.D. Makin	151.4	54	311	16	18.44	—	—
G.M. Gower	205.2	48	487	26	18.77	1	—
V.A.P. van der Bijl	433.5	138	976	52	18.78	1	—
T.G. Shaw	189.2	57	512	27	18.96	2	—
B. Roberts	105.2	26	305	16	19.06	—	—
G.S. Le Roux	519.1	74	907	46	19.72	3	—
E.J. Hodkinson	238	56	624	31	20.13	1	—
J.D. Du Toit	115.1	29	282	14	20.14	—	—
J. During	174	62	343	17	20.18	—	—
G.L. Hayes	116	25	303	15	20.20	1	—
M.J. Procter	110.3	27	247	12	20.58	1	—
R.C. Ontong	160.4	45	440	21	20.95	2	—
O. Henry	375.3	115	866	41	21.12	4	1
B.W. Proctor	130.5	36	381	18	21.17	2	—
D.K. Pearse	185.5	61	388	18	21.56	—	—
D.S. Scott	99.3	28	218	10	21.80	—	—
J.E. Emburey	357.4	109	785	36	21.81	3	—
R.W. Hanley	233	59	671	30	22.37	2	—
I. Foulkes	118	24	307	13	23.62	2	—
S.T. Jefferies	490.2	114	1386	58	23.72	3	—
R.A. Le Roux	115	36	309	13	23.78	—	—
A.J. Kourie	573.1	158	1501	63	23.83	5	—
I.F.N. Weideman	213.5	52	599	25	23.96	—	—
W.K. Watson	257.1	61	770	32	24.06	2	—
S.J. Dennis	170.2	33	507	21	24.14	1	—
A.P. Kuiper	139	27	415	17	24.41	1	—
E.O. Simons	161.1	55	391	16	24.44	—	—
C.S. Mitchley	193.4	35	690	28	24.64	1	—
B. de K. Robey	119	33	301	12	25.08	—	—
W.F. Morris	91	26	286	11	26.00	—	—
N.V. Radford	310.3	52	1145	43	26.63	1	—
K.J. Kerr	201.3	54	566	21	26.95	—	—
H.W. Raath	176	38	543	20	27.15	1	—
P. Anker	241	64	604	22	27.45	—	—
L.B. Taylor	298.1	66	828	29	28.55	1	—
K.R. Cooper	278.4	73	774	27	28.67	1	—
G. Grobler	101.5	21	330	11	30.00	1	—
D.L. Hobson	295.4	75	765	24	31.88	1	—
G.L. Long	192	61	451	15	30.07	—	—
P. McLaren	133	25	457	15	30.47	—	—
G.E. McMillan	144.2	30	458	15	30.53	1	—
D.J. Brickett	206	47	619	20	30.95	—	—
A.M. Ferreira	273.4	72	743	24	30.96	—	—
G.P. van Rensberg	174	33	532	17	31.29	—	—
I.L. Howell	178.1	68	442	13	34.00	—	—
P. Carrick	140	34	411	13	31.62	—	—
C.R. Norris	135.5	30	382	12	31.67	—	—
P.A. Robinson	135.2	24	419	13	32.15	—	—
M.D. Clare	275.4	62	941	28	33.61	2	—
S.P. Hughes	126.3	26	408	12	34.00	—	—
A.P. Beukes	210.5	64	423	17	34.88	—	—
H.J. Liebenberg	135.5	26	429	12	35.75	—	—
J.A. Carse	193.2	40	685	19	36.05	1	—
R.E. Pienaar	188.1	45	580	16	36.25	—	—
P.L. Symcox	131	37	406	11	36.91	—	—
M. van der Vuuren	158.3	31	595	16	37.19	2	—
W. Miller	147	28	488	13	37.54	—	—
T.H.D. Wheelwright	118	18	465	12	38.75	—	—
J.K. Lever	314.4	67	941	23	40.91	1	—

(Qualification – 10 wickets)

SECTION J
The Young Pretenders

The Season in Zimbabwe
The tours of the Sri Lankan
and young Australian teams

Facts and figures compiled by
John R. Ward

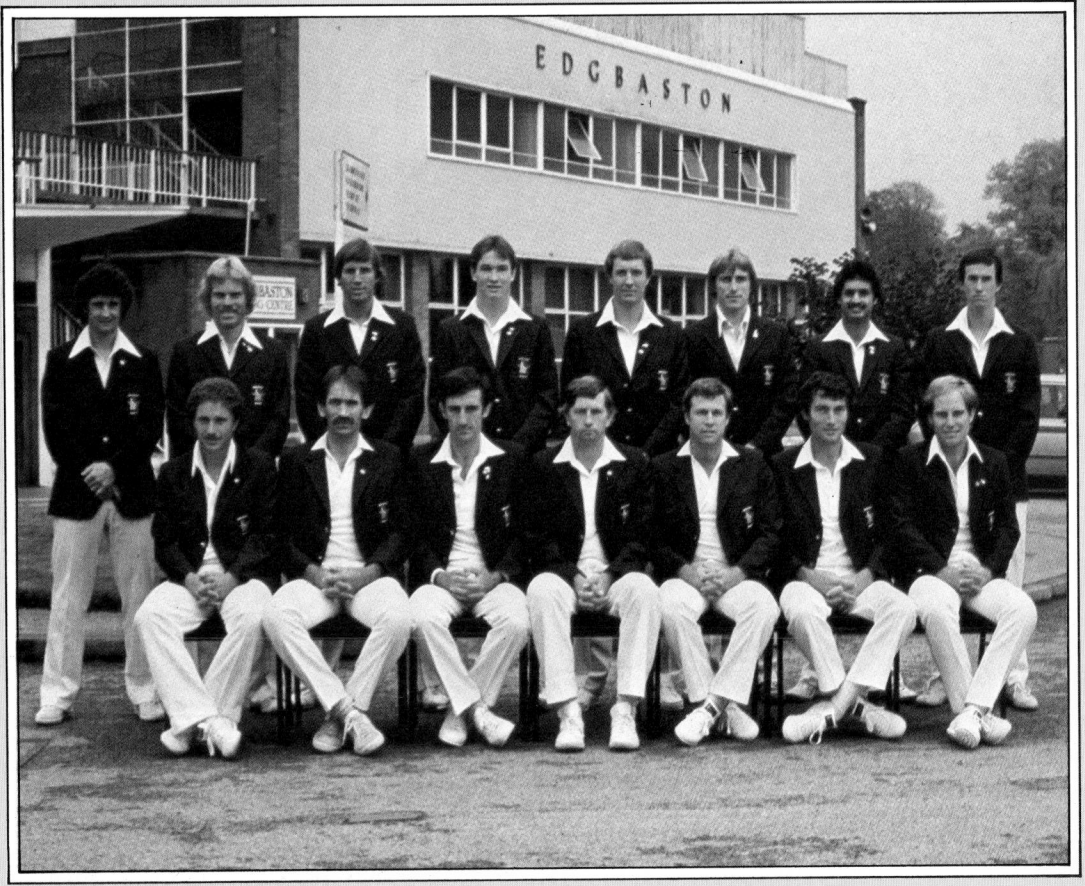

The Zimbabwe team that was chosen for the World Cup. (Ken Kelly)
(Standing, l to r) G. Peckover, C. Hodgson, G. Paterson,
G. Hick, P. Rawson, K. Curran, A. Omarshah, and I. Butchart.
(Sitting, l to r) D. Houghton, V. Hogg, J. Traicos,
D. Fletcher, J. Heron, R. Brown and A. Pycroft.

The 1982–83 season was a highly significant one for cricket in Zimbabwe. Morale has rarely been higher than when Zimbabwe returned triumphant from the I.C.C. Trophy although there were murmurs that most of the opposition had been considerably weaker than First League standard. Now, during the following domestic season, Zimbabwe cricket had to prepare itself for its greatest challenge, competing with the seven Test-playing nations in the Prudential World Cup.

In preparation for this event, Zimbabwe's cricket administrators arranged tours by two powerful visiting teams; Sri Lanka, the latest nation to be granted Test match status, and the Young Australian team. Zimbabwe supporters looked forward to these tours with a mixture of hope and apprehension.

One difficulty which Zimbabwe cricket always has to face is the weather. Cricket is the principal summer sport, and the season takes place between October and March; the timing cannot be changed as the winter sports of soccer, rugby and hockey, which have a large following, dominate the rest of the year. Unfortunately, the main rains of the year come between November and February, right in the middle of the cricket season, and any matches played during that time are liable to be disrupted by rain.

For this reason, it has been necessary since Independence to arrange for one touring side to visit Zimbabwe in October, and another after the rains in March. This leaves the domestic season with two peaks, five months apart. Even in the Currie Cup days, Zimbabwe (then Rhodesia) toured during the months of heavy rainfall.

One of the major handicaps of Zimbabwe cricket is the lack of a first-class internal competition, and this is unlikely to be remedied in the immediate future. During the past ten years, the cricketing strength has tended to converge on Harare. With the exception of Iain Butchart of Bulawayo, Zimbabwe's team in the I.C.C. Trophy was drawn entirely from Harare First League teams. Now that Butchart has transferred to Harare, the whole of the World Cup squad consists of Harare club players. Players like Kevin Curran, Robin Brown and Grant Paterson who, being farmers, play for Mashonaland Country Districts come to the capital at week-ends for League cricket.

Twenty to thirty years ago, the bulk of the national side came from Bulawayo, but as young players like Duncan Fletcher and Jack Heron began to emerge ten years ago, Mashonaland cricket started to become stronger and the drift to the capital began.

Matabeleland cricket has now declined to such an extent that a full Matabele team cannot compete successfully in the National League with any of the top five Harare clubs, and, as support in Bulawayo has declined, representative matches have been centred more and more in Harare.

There has been a similar decline in Gweru, the Midlands, which once boasted mighty national cricketers in Howie Gardiner, a wicket-keeper almost two metres tall, and Richie Kaschula, a slow left-arm bowler, who weighed nearly 120 kilogrammes, and in such a situation a first-class inter-provincial competition is out of the question.

So Zimbabwe's top players play most of their cricket in the one-day National League competition which now consists of four or five Harare clubs. One-day cricket is a poor preparation for Test matches, and the decline in the number of top teams and the lack of depth in those teams are disquieting

features in what is a vital time in Zimbabwe cricket.

Unfortunately, there are no still no top-class Africa cricketers in Zimbabwe. Only in the last ten years has much effort been spent in taking the game to the local Africa population, and now much hard work is being done to make up for lost time, but facilities are usually poor and kit is expensive and difficult to obtain. Nevertheless, many Africans, like the West Indians, show a natural aptitude for the game, but as most have no cricket background whatsoever, it will be years before the present work bears real dividends.

Cricket has always been popular with the Asian population and in the past few years development here has been encouraging. The real star has come to light in 1983 – Ali Omarshah. Always referred to as Ali Shah, he is a determined left-handed opening batsman and a useful slow medium bowler. He was to make his mark against the Young Australians with a century in only his second appearance for the national side.

With the defection to the tour of South Africa by several of Sri Lanka's former Test players, it was feared that the Sri Lankan side to tour Zimbabwe would be a weak one, but, in the event, wicket-keeper Goonatillake was the only player to withdraw from the party originally selected and his replacement, Guy de Alwis, was most impressive behind the stumps. Warnapura, the former Sri Lankan captain, was omitted from the side because of lack of form before he decided to accept the offer to tour South Africa.

The Sri Lankan tour of Zimbabwe began with a high scoring limited over match against Country Districts. Roy

Grant Paterson. Opening batsman. (Ken Kelly)

Dias hit 102 not out, and Sri Lanka won by seven wickets. The local side's bowling was not of the same standard as their batting which saw Brown and Butchart hit fifties.

FIRST ONE-DAY INTERNATIONAL: ZIMBABWE v. SRI LANKA

For the first time Zimbabwe joined the 'Pyjama Game' with the team appearing in pastel green uniforms, apparently because it is done in other countries and for no other reason.

Houghton and Heron gave Zimbabwe a brisk start with 64 off the first eighteen overs, but then three quick wickets fell and Zimbabwe retreated into grim consolidation. Kevin Curran and Duncan Fletcher added 98 for the fourth wicket, but the early impetus had been lost and the final total was a disappointment.

Vince Hogg struck an early blow for Zimbabwe when he had both openers out for 29. Hogg, a thirty-year old fast-medium bowler, had impressed the Young West Indians in 1982 with his fierce in-swing and dip, and he continued to trouble the Sri Lankans with his late movement. Mendis and Madugalle steadied them with a fourth wicket stand of 56, however, and Jeganathan joined Madugalle in another good stand for the sixth wicket. Both became victims of Houghton, his third and fourth catches of the innings, but de Mel and de Alwis had little difficulty in seeing Sri Lanka to victory with ample time to spare.

The only consolation for Zimbabwe after this disappointment was that Kevin Curran was named Man of the Match.

Roy Dias who looked the most accomplished of the Sri Lankan batsmen to tour Zimbabwe. (Adrian Murrell)

FIRST ONE-DAY INTERNATIONAL: ZIMBABWE v. SRI LANKA
30 October 1982 at Harare Sports Club

ZIMBABWE				SRI LANKA		
D.L. Houghton*	c Amerasinghe, b Jeganathan	23		S.R. de S. Wettimuny	c Houghton, b Hogg	9
J.G. Heron	c Amerasinghe, b R.J. Ratnayake	35		P. Amerasinghe	c Rawson, b Hogg	12
K.M. Curran	c Madugalle, b John	59		R.L. Dias	c Curran, b Rawson	16
A.J. Pycroft	c de Alwis, b R.J. Ratnayake	0		L.R.D. Mendis†	c Houghton, b Curran	53
D.A.G. Fletcher†	run out	45		R.S. Madugalle	c Houghton, b Rawson	46
C.A.T. Hodgson	c Madugalle, b D.S. de Silva	2		D.S. de Silva	run out	1
R.D. Brown	not out	4		S. Jeganathan	c Houghton, b Curran	24
P.W.E. Rawson	not out	3		A.L.F. de Mel	not out	16
M.H.E.M. Dudhia				R.G. de Alwis*	not out	12
A.J. Traicos				R.J. Ratnayake		
V.R. Hogg				V. John		
Extras		25		Extras		8
(50 overs)	(for 6 wickets)	196		(45.5 overs)	(for 7 wickets)	197

	O	M	R	W		O	M	R	W
de Mel	10	2	26	—	Hogg	10	1	29	2
John	10	1	36	1	Dudhia	4	1	18	—
R.J. Ratnayake	10	—	38	2	Traicos	10	1	35	—
Jeganathan	10	—	35	1	Rawson	10	—	40	2
D.S. de Silva	10	1	36	1	Curran	7	1	36	2
					Fletcher	4.5	—	31	—

FALL OF WICKETS
1- 64, 2- 71, 3- 72, 4- 170, 5- 177, 6- 189

FALL OF WICKETS
1- 22, 2- 29, 3- 59, 4- 115, 5- 117, 6- 165, 7- 178

Sri Lanka won by 3 wickets

SECOND ONE-DAY INTERNATIONAL: ZIMBABWE v. SRI LANKA

Colin Robertson came into the Zimbabwe side in place of th injured Robin Brown, his first appearance in the nation side, and Eddie Hough replaced Mac Dudhia who had ha a poor game in the first encounter.

Fletcher again won the toss and this time he asked S Lanka to bat. Wettimuny dominated the opening partne ship with Amarasinghe who was out at 34. His dismiss signalled a break-through. Dias was run out for 0 when And Pycroft hit the stumps with his throw, and skipper Mend played a poor shot to be caught in the gully off Hough. 40 fc 3 was a position from which Sri Lanka never effectivel recovered, mainly due to the fact that Zimbabwe continue to bowl aggressively and field superbly.

Zimbabwe's hopes of victory were almost shattered whe Vinothan John, who found both pace and lift in the pitcl dismissed Houghton, Heron and Curran for 18. Neithe Pycroft nor Fletcher found run-getting easy, but they battle on doggedly and when both were missed off relatively eas chances Sri Lanka lost the advantage.

Pycroft and Fletcher extended their stand to 97 befor Pycroft was caught at slip, but Craig Hodgson gave Fletche the necessary support to take Zimbabwe to victory and shar the series.

Fletcher took the Man of the Match award for his battin and his captaincy.

LEFT: *Duncan Fletcher. Captain of Zimbabwe and an ou standing all-rounder.* (*Ken Kelly*)

BELOW: *Eddie Hough bowls to Sidath Wettimuny in th Second One-Day International, 31 October. Amarasinghe the other batsman. Hough lost form and favour in the season*

SECOND ONE-DAY INTERNATIONAL: ZIMBABWE v. SRI LANKA
1 October 1982 at Harare Sports Club

SRI LANKA					ZIMBABWE		
S.R. de S. Wettimuny	lbw, b Traicos			42	D.L. Houghton*	c de Alwis, b John	1
P. Amarasinghe	c Rawson, b Hogg			8	J.G. Heron	c Mendis, b John	3
R.L. Dias	run out			0	K.M. Curran	c de Alwis, b John	2
L.R.D. Mendis†	c Traicos, b Hough			4	A.J. Pycroft	c Amarasinghe, b de Mel	50
R.S. Madugalle	c Hodgson, b Traicos			15	D.A.G. Fletcher†	not out	60
D.S. de Silva	c Robertson, b Fletcher			8	C.A.T. Hodgson	not out	18
S. Jeganathan	b Hough			36	C. Robertson		
A.L.F. de Mel	c Robertson, b Fletcher			11	P.W.E. Rawson		
R.G. de Alwis*	lbw, b Fletcher			2	A.J. Traicos		
R.J. Ratnayake	c Fletcher, b Hogg			20	E.J. Hough		
V. John	not out			1	V.R. Hogg		
Extras				14	Extras		28
(49 overs)				161	(43 overs)	(for 4 wickets)	162

	O	M	R	W		O	M	R	W
Hogg	10	1	32	2	de Mel	10	4	18	1
Hough	7	1	22	2	John	10	3	22	3
Curran	4	—	21	—	R.J. Ratnayake	10	2	30	—
Rawson	10	2	25	—	D.S. de Silva	5	—	36	—
Traicos	10	3	23	2	Jeganathan	7	—	25	—
Fletcher	8	2	24	3	Wettimuny	1	—	3	—

FALL OF WICKETS
1- 34, 2- 34, 3- 40, 4- 74, 5- 83, 6- 87, 7- 109, 8- 118,
9-153

FALL OF WICKETS
1- 6, 2- 17, 3- 18, 4- 115

Zimbabwe won by 6 wickets

Andy Pycroft. A most dependable batsman. (Ken Kelly)

FIRST INTERNATIONAL: ZIMBABWE v. SRI LANKA

With Mendis scoring 87, Sri Lanka beat a Select XI easily in a limited-over game in Mutare shortly before the first of the four-day international matches. This was Zimbabwe's first first-class match against a full Test side and it was sad that skipper Duncan Fletcher had to withdraw from the side with bruised ribs. Former South African Test bowler John Traicos took over the captaincy.

In hot, humid conditions, Zimbabwe took first use of a good wicket when they won the toss. There was a disappointment in the early loss of Heron, but Houghton and Curran prospered in a second wicket stand of 85 although runs never came quickly. Kevin Curran, a talented but impetuous batsman, had won the number three spot in the I.C.C. Trophy matches and with Robin Brown injured, he was able to continue batting in that position in the four-day matches. The responsibility sharpened his game, and he worked for his runs where, in previous years, he was liable to play recklessly.

He was unfortunate to miss a maiden first-class century. He batted confidently into the nineties, but there he became the victim of nerves and was bowled by Jeganathan after a dedicated stay of 4½ hours.

His dismissal ended a stand of 144 with Andy Pycroft who is technically the soundest of Zimbabwe's batsmen, but Pycroft, who has scored nearly 1500 runs in first-class matches against touring sides, had had a poor time since his return from the I.C.C. Trophy, not reaching 20 in a League innings. Now he put failures behind him and produced some batting of quality as he reached his century off 186 balls. He had one piece of fortune when he was dropped on 86, Sri Lanka's only blemish in an otherwise fine fielding display.

Craig Hodgson, an aggressive batsman and a superb fielder, hit 40 off 63 balls and delighted the crowd. 'The

FIRST INTERNATIONAL: ZIMBABWE v. SRI LANKA
5, 6, 7 and 8 November 1982 at Queens Ground, Bulawayo

ZIMBABWE

	FIRST INNINGS		SECOND INNINGS	
D.L. Houghton*	c Jeganathan, b R.J. Ratnayake	45	c Mendis, b John	77
J.G. Heron	lbw, b John	3	c de Alwis, b de Mel	10
K.M. Curran	b Jeganathan	96	b de Silva	18
A.J. Pycroft	c de Mel, b Ratnayake	128	c de Mel, b John	81
C. Robertson	c M. Wettimuny, b de Silva	9	lbw, b Jeganathan	0
C.A.T. Hodgson	b de Mel	40	not out	7
I.P. Butchart	c Madugalle, b Ratnayake	15	st de Alwis, b Jeganathan	22
P.W.E. Rawson	c M. Wettimuny, b Jeganathan	1		
A.J. Traicos†	not out	32		
E.J. Hough	st de Alwis, b Jeganathan	9		
V.R. Hogg	lbw, b Ratnayake	1		
Extras	b 5, lb 16, w 1, nb 15	37	lb 1, w 1, nb 4	6
		416	(for 6 wkts, dec)	221

	O	M	R	W		O	M	R	W
de Mel	20	6	59	1		4	—	29	1
John	20	5	60	1		8	1	29	2
R.J. Ratnayake	29	7	79	4		9	1	34	—
D.S. de Silva	29	3	109	1		19	2	75	1
Jeganathan	33	9	72	3		20.5	5	48	2

FALL OF WICKETS
1- 9, 2- 94, 3- 238, 4- 267, 5- 334, 6- 366, 7- 368, 8- 368, 9- 409
1- 23, 2- 53, 3- 190, 4- 191, 5- 193, 6- 221

SRI LANKA

	FIRST INNINGS		SECOND INNINGS	
S.R. de S. Wettimuny	lbw, b Hogg	2	c Houghton, b Rawson	12
M. de S. Wettimuny	run out	55	c and b Traicos	18
R.L. Dias	c Houghton, b Rawson	85	not out	61
L.R.D. Mendis†	b Rawson	42		
R.S. Madugalle	b Rawson	19		
S. Jeganathan	st Houghton, b Traicos	21	(4) not out	25
D.S. de Silva	c Houghton, b Curran	11		
A.L.F. de Mel	b Rawson	35		
R.G. de Alwis*	b Rawson	40		
R.J. Ratnayake	not out	2		
V. John	b Rawson	1		
Extras	b 2, lb 12, w 3, nb 5	22	b 1, lb 2, nb 7	10
		335	(for 2 wkts)	126

	O	M	R	W		O	M	R	W
Hogg	16	5	51	1		5	1	12	—
Hough	12	3	47	—		5	2	7	—
Rawson	27.5	5	82	6		9	3	11	1
Traicos	27	6	63	1		16.5	5	37	1
Curran	13	2	61	1		5	—	25	—
Butchart	5	2	9	—		3	—	21	—
Hodgson						1	—	3	—

FALL OF WICKETS
1- 10, 2- 127, 3- 163, 4- 203, 5- 226, 6- 246, 7- 246, 8- 324, 9- 331
1- 33, 2- 39

Match drawn

Blond Bomber' is one of those entertaining cricketers who appeal to crowds everywhere.

The later batsmen sacrificed their wickets in the dash for quick runs, essential when two hours were lost to rain.

Jeganathan was the most impressive of the Sri Lankan bowlers. Slow left-arm, he turned the ball sharply and kept an accurate length which frustrated the batsmen.

When Sri Lanka began their reply, Hogg struck a vital blow by dismissing the classy Sidath Wettimuny, but Hough bowled poorly and Sri Lanka climbed back into the game. Mitrah Wettimuny and Dias added 117, and Roy Dias was at his exciting best, punishing Hough severely on his way to 85 off 96 balls. He was by far the most impressive of the Sri Lankan batsmen, and he fell to a fine catch by wicket-keeper Houghton off Rawson.

Rawson bowled with great fire, extracting life where others found only placidity. He prefers not to use the new-ball, but from his easy run, he still generates a good pace. A volatile, but likeable character, he was to enjoy a very good season.

There never seemed a likelihood of a result being obtained, but at 246 for 7, Sri Lanka were still in slight danger of following-on, but de Mel and de Alwis added 78, and Sri Lanka finished 81 runs behind.

Houghton and Pycroft, his return to form complete, batted briskly, and Traicos declared, leaving Sri Lanka three hours in which to make 303. The Wettimuny brothers were out in the first hour, but Roy Dias again batted magnificently, reaching his second fifty of the match off only 53 balls.

Following this match, Sri Lanka beat a Select XI by five wickets at Triangle.

Roger Brown. Opening batsman. (Adrian Murrell)

Roy Dias is caught Hodgson, bowled Rawson for 18, and Zimbabwe are on their way to an innings victory over Sri Lanka. (l to r) Houghton, Traicos, Dias, Rawson and skipper Fletcher. (The Herald)

SECOND INTERNATIONAL: ZIMBABWE v. SRI LANKA

Zimbabwe welcomed back Duncan Fletcher, but Sri Lanka were without de Mel who was reported to have a badly bruised heel, which made it rather a surprise when he appeared as substitute fielder on the first day and held two catches.

Once more Zimbabwe won the toss and Dave Houghton and Jack Heron gave them a magnificent start with 106 in 90 minutes, but this splendid beginning was squandered in mid-afternoon. Curran and Pycroft were beginning to master the attack when a light drizzle started. To the annoyance of the crowd, the umpires led the players off the field and, although the drizzle lasted only a few minutes, play did not start again for an hour, an incredible event which destroyed the impetus of the Zimbabwe innings.

Curran was soon out on the resumption and Fletcher had scored only a single when an appeal for a bat-pad catch was rejected. Practically the whole of the Sri Lankan team threw themselves on the ground in protest and the bowler, de Silva, threw the next ball at the batsman so hard that it beat the wicket-keeper and went through for four no-balls. A sad and disgraceful episode. What a condemnation of the state of the game if this is what Sri Lanka have learned after two years in Test cricket.

Seven wickets were down for 238, but Peter Rawson joined the grafting Andy Pycroft in a century stand which ended when Pycroft was caught in the slips four short of his hundred. It was ironic that he should fall to John because, for most of his innings, he faced the spin combination of slow left-arm Jeganathan and leg-break bowler de Silva.

Rawson gained sufficient support from the tail-enders to reach a maiden fifty in first-class cricket, and the innings closed at 365.

The Sri Lankan reply was as incredible as it was irresponsible. Sense and determination were jettisoned as the batsmen flung their bats at everything. Dias scored ten off ten balls and then gave a simple return catch. Mendis scored 14 off 11 balls and then flashed wildly outside his off stump. Within an hour, they were 34 for 5.

Jeganathan, as he did throughout the tour, batted sensibly, as did de Silva, but there was no stopping Zimbabwe now. Rawson was quick and hostile, and the fielding was electric. In two hours, Sri Lanka were bowled out for 104, and they followed-on 261 runs behind.

Defeat loomed, and when Sidath Wettimuny was caught at slip off the first ball of the innings, it seemed that the match would not last three days. That it did was due to the determination of Mitrah Wettimuny who was resolute, if often strokeless. Mendis scored an aggressive 67, and de Silva was defiant until the end, but nothing could halt the triumph of Zimbabwe.

Vince Hogg's fifteen overs yielded him 6 wickets for 26 runs, and when Curran had John caught by Butchart, Zim-

Heron is beaten by a ball from Jeganathan. Guy de Alwis is the wicket-keeper, Houghton the other batsman.

babwe had beaten a Test-playing country by an innings inside three days. It was their greatest achievement and a tremendous boost to cricket in the country, coming, as it did, so soon after their victory in the I.C.C. Trophy. It was unfortunate that over four months was to elapse before they could again face top-class opposition.

With the departure of the Sri Lankans, the emphasis was

on the National League which was won by Universals, predominantly Asian club which has been strengthened skipper John Traicos, Dave Houghton and Craig Hodgso Universals' outstanding player, however, was Bill Bourn the former Barbados and Warwickshire bowler. Bourne h been coaching regularly in Zimbabwe and has joined wi local coaches in reaching the African population. Much in proved since his Warwickshire days, Bourne finished to bowler in the National League.

It was believed that the Young Australian side would n prove to be such strong opposition as recent touring side Perhaps this was complacency on the part of Zimbabwe wh had not reckoned that the young players chosen had all e joyed excellent seasons in the Sheffield Shield and were ve keen to prove their worth at international level. Wellham ar Ritchie had scored centuries in Test cricket, Phillips ar Macleay had played for Australia in one-day international and Boon and Jones were spoken of as being on the verge the Test side.

The side was quick to demonstrate its talent and ruthle efficiency. Other sides to have toured Zimbabwe had play good quality, cavalier cricket, the Young Australians showe Zimbabwe a new dimension in playing the game hard.

In the opening game in Harare against Zimbabwe Colt the Young Australians made only 165 for 4 on a wicket whic had mistakenly been watered. It was a difficult time for ba ting and the visitors struggled, Greg Shipperd saving the with 72 not out. The Australian difficulties were nothing a compared to those suffered by the home side, however. Ro McCurdy and Mike Whitney tore into the attack, showin a more consistent hostility than Daniel, Marshall an Alleyne had done with the Young West Indian side. The fir

SECOND INTERNATIONAL: ZIMBABWE v. SRI LANKA
12, 13 and 14 November 1982 at Harare Sports Club

ZIMBABWE

FIRST INNINGS

Batsman	Dismissal	Runs
D.L. Houghton*	c M. Wettimuny, b de Silva	50
J.G. Heron	lbw, b de Silva	72
K.M. Curran	c sub (de Mel), b de Silva	26
A.J. Pycroft	c M. Wettimuny, b John	96
D.A.G. Fletcher†	c sub (de Mel), b de Silva	14
C.A.T. Hodgson	c Mendis, b Jeganathan	5
C. Robertson	c and b Jeganathan	12
I.P. Butchart	c de Silva, b Jeganathan	0
P.W.E. Rawson	not out	63
A.J. Traicos	c de Alwis, b R.J. Ratnayake	2
V.R. Hogg	b John	0
Extras	lb 13, w 4, nb 8	25
		365

Bowler	O	M	R	W
John	10.3	2	42	2
J.R. Ratnayake	5	2	26	—
R.J. Ratnayake	13	3	53	1
Jeganathan	42	10	74	3
de Silva	35	3	145	4

FALL OF WICKETS
1- 106, 2- 145, 3- 170, 4- 190, 5- 202, 6- 238, 7- 238, 8- 338, 9- 346

Zimbabwe won by an innings and 40 runs

SRI LANKA

Batsman	FIRST INNINGS		SECOND INNINGS	
S.R. de S. Wettimuny	lbw, b Hogg	5	c Pycroft, b Hogg	0
M. de S. Wettimuny	c Pycroft, b Fletcher	5	c Robertson, b Hogg	38
R.L. Dias	c and b Fletcher	10	c Hodgson, b Rawson	18
A. Ranatunga	c Houghton, b Fletcher	0	(6) c Heron, b Hogg	0
L.R.D. Mendis†	c Houghton, b Hogg	14	(4) c Hodgson, b Hogg	67
S. Jeganathan	b Curran	13	(7) c Hodgson, b Hogg	4
D.S. de Silva	c Traicos, b Rawson	19	(8) not out	37
R.G. de Alwis*	c Fletcher, b Curran	4	(9) c sub, b Curran	3
J.R. Ratnayake	c Heron, b Curran	20	(5) c Houghton, b Hogg	0
R.J. Ratnayake	c Fletcher, b Curran	12	c Pycroft, b Traicos	47
V. John	not out	2	c Butchart, b Curran	0
Extras		0	b 1, lb 5, nb 1	7
		104		221

Bowler	O	M	R	W	O	M	R	W
Hogg	9	3	34	2	15	4	26	6
Fletcher	7	2	30	3	8	5	17	—
Traicos	1	1	0	—	16	2	64	1
Curran	7.2	1	24	4	10.2	3	25	2
Rawson	5	2	16	1	25	7	57	1
Butchart					3	—	25	—

FALL OF WICKETS
1- 6, 2- 20, 3- 20, 4- 34, 5- 34, 6- 58, 7- 62, 8- 90, 9- 102
1- 0, 2- 22, 3- 117, 4- 121, 5- 121, 6- 130, 7- 133, 8- 141, 9- 221

FIRST ONE-DAY INTERNATIONAL: ZIMBABWE v. YOUNG AUSTRALIANS

9 April 1983 at Queens Ground Bulawayo

ZIMBABWE			
R.D. Brown	lbw, b Bennett		9
A.H. Omarshah	c Haysman, b McCurdy		13
C.A.T. Hodgson	run out		10
A.J. Pycroft†	c and b Blizzard		20
D.A.G. Fletcher	c Wellham, b Blizzard		79
D.L. Houghton*	c Ritchie, b Macleay		36
K.M. Curran	not out		19
I.P. Butchart	b Whitney		7
P.W.E. Rawson	c Jones, b McCurdy		22
A.J. Traicos	not out		2
M.P. Jarvis			
Extras			17
(50 overs)	(for 8 wickets)		234

	O	M	R	W
McCurdy	10	—	34	2
Whitney	10	1	54	1
Bennett	10	1	43	1
Macleay	10	1	32	1
Blizzard	10	1	54	2

FALL OF WICKETS
1- 19, 2- 32, 3- 41, 4- 116, 5- 153, 6- 185, 7- 197, 8- 228

YOUNG AUSTRALIANS			
D.M.J. Jones	c Butchart, b Jarvis		21
W.B. Phillips*	c Butchart, b Traicos		75
D.M. Wellham†	b Rawson		8
D.C. Boon	not out		65
G.M. Ritchie	lbw, b Traicos		12
M.D. Haysman	lbw, b Curran		0
K.H. Macleay	c Hodgson, b Rawson		26
M.J. Bennett	not out		1
R.J. McCurdy			
P.A. Blizzard			
M.R. Whitney			
Extras			14
(46.4 overs)	(for 6 wickets)		222

	O	M	R	W
Jarvis	8.4	—	45	1
Fletcher	3	—	15	—
Rawson	8.	3	20	2
Omarshah	4	—	26	—
Butchart	4	—	20	—
Traicos	10	—	37	2
Curran	9	—	45	1

FALL OF WICKETS
1- 34, 2- 53, 3- 132, 4- 154, 5- 155, 6- 220

Young Australians won on faster scoring rate

five batsmen, all internationals, or near-internationals, were shot out for 7 runs, and the change bowlers offered little respite as Zimbabwe Colts were all out for 43.

There was much re-thinking in the Zimbabwe camp before the first international.

FIRST INTERNATIONAL: ZIMBABWE v. YOUNG AUSTRALIANS

Fletcher won the toss and asked the Young Australians to bat first on a wicket that, initially, was lively and uncertain.

Vince Hogg gave both openers a torrid time, but Wayne Phillips batted for survival and his dour fifty was invaluable in that he tired the bowling and laid a foundation on which others could build when the wicket had eased. The decisive partnership was between David Boon and Greg Ritchie, who added 152 for the fifth wicket.

Zimbabwe's fielding was well below its usual high standard and six catches were put down in the course of the innings which did not close until well into the second afternoon. Boon reached his hundred in 317 minutes, and the Australian batting was relentlessly efficient rather than scintillating. For Zimbabwe, it was something of an education.

There was much tension when Zimbabwe began their first innings and it was not eased when Jack Heron was lbw playing across the line to McCurdy's second ball. Robin Brown, returning to the side after injury, was beaten by the pace of the bowling, but new cap Ali Omarshah, who had had a miserable first day in the field, batted with much courage and he and Andy Pycroft restored some pride and hope, and they were still together at the close, 67 for 2.

Pycroft became McCurdy's second victim next morning, and Omarshah was run out in a mix-up with Fletcher who then hit a ball hard at Boon, fielding very close to the bat. Boon caught the ball between arm and thigh and later had to leave the field for treatment.

Dave Houghton. A fine striker of the ball and a wicket-keeper of the highest class. (Ken Kelly)

Ali Omarshah. An Asian player of great promise. The outstanding newcomer in the Zimbabwe season. (Adrian Murrell)

Traicos alone seemed able to play the pace men with confidence, but Zimbabwe trailed by 244 on the first innings and Wellham asked them to follow-on.

They fared little better in the second innings. Heron and Fletcher were both bowled by sizzling deliveries from Whitney. Brown and Omarshah defended doggedly for a time and Houghton made a bright fifty before falling to the second new ball.

There was never any doubt as to how the match would end. Number eleven Hogg scooped McCurdy to third man for two fours to become the fourth batsman in the innings to reach double figures, and Traicos, wastefully at number ten, was left four not out.

Zimbabwe cricket, so high in spirits four months earlier, had now touched rock bottom, and there were scathing criticisms of the national side. Yet, in a midweek Colts match, a team very similar to that which had been bowled out for 43 scored almost 200 against the Young Australians, a brave, if still inadequate effort.

FIRST ONE-DAY INTERNATIONAL: ZIMBABWE v. YOUNG AUSTRALIANS

The signs of recovery which the Colts side had evidenced were given further proof in this match where Zimbabwe having been 41 for 3, rallied to reach 234 off their 50 overs.

The recovery was effected by Duncan Fletcher, the Zimbabwe captain, who, with a brilliant array of strokes, tore the Australian attack apart in what many described as the innings of the season. He had admirable support from Pycroft and Houghton.

Fletcher is such an accomplished player that it remains a

FIRST INTERNATIONAL: ZIMBABWE v. YOUNG AUSTRALIANS
1, 2, 3 and 4 April 1983 at Harare Sports Club

YOUNG AUSTRALIANS

	FIRST INNINGS	
R.B. Kerr	c Butchart, b Rawson	23
W.B. Phillips*	c Fletcher, b Traicos	58
G. Shipperd	lbw, b Rawson	11
D.M. Wellham†	c Butchart, b Hogg	0
D.C. Boon	st Houghton, b Omarshah	148
G.M. Ritchie	c Houghton, b Rawson	69
K.H. Macleay	c Omarshah, b Traicos	31
M.J. Bennett	c Omarshah, b Traicos	24
S.L. Saunders	b Traicos	17
R.J. McCurdy	lbw, b Traicos	1
M.R. Whitney	not out	2
Extras		24
		408

	O	M	R	W
Hogg	26	12	48	1
Fletcher	15	5	34	—
Rawson	41	11	92	3
Butchart	10	3	18	—
Traicos	44.1	10	103	5
Curran	13	2	51	—
Omarshah	11	1	38	1

FALL OF WICKETS
1- 36, 2- 60, 3- 62, 4- 117, 5- 269, 6- 320, 7- 374, 8- 394, 9- 395

ZIMBABWE

	FIRST INNINGS		SECOND INNINGS	
J.G. Heron	lbw, b McCurdy	0	b Whitney	2
A.H. Omarshah	run out	42	c Kerr, b Whitney	55
R.D. Brown	c Ritchie, b Whitney	7	b Saunders	22
A.J. Pycroft	lbw, b McCurdy	33	c Shepperd, b Whitney	6
D.L. Houghton*	c Ritchie, b Macleay	17	c Kerr, b McCurdy	55
D.A.G. Fletcher†	c Boon, b Saunders	0	b Whitney	1
K.M. Curran	c Shepperd, b McCurdy	4	lbw, b Macleay	7
I.P. Butchart	c Macleay, b McCurdy	1	c sub (Hayman), b Bennett	7
P.W.E. Rawson	c Phillips, b Whitney	4	lbw, b Bennett	2
A.J. Traicos	not out	23	not out	4
V.R. Hogg	c McCurdy, b Saunders	9	b Whitney	19
Extras		24		
		164		190

	O	M	R	W	O	M	R	W
McCurdy	19	6	40	4	16	3	43	1
Whitney	19	6	32	2	23.4	10	29	5
Macleay	13	5	28	1	20	10	18	1
Saunders	18.4	7	30	2	18	1	42	1
Bennett	10	6	10	—	16	5	39	2

FALL OF WICKETS
1- 0, 2- 22, 3- 77, 4- 110, 5- 117, 6- 121, 7- 121, 8- 126, 9- 135
1- 6, 2- 48, 3- 77, 4- 96, 5- 100, 6- 119, 7- 139, 8- 153, 9- 177

Young Australians won by an innings and 54 runs

SECOND INTERNATIONAL: ZIMBABWE v. YOUNG AUSTRALIANS
14, 15 and 16 April 1983 at Harare Sports Club

ZIMBABWE

	FIRST INNINGS		SECOND INNINGS	
A.H. Omarshah	c Phillips, b McCurdy	13	c Phillips, b Bennett	105
R.D. Brown	b McCurdy	2	b Whitney	3
J.G. Heron	c and b McCurdy	10	c Bennett, b Whitney	16
A.J. Pycroft	c Kerr, b Bennett	6	c Boon, b McCurdy	35
D.L. Houghton*	lbw, b McCurdy	27	c Phillips, b Whitney	14
D.A.G. Fletcher†	b Whitney	44	b McCurdy	56
C.A.T. Hodgson	c Haysman, b Macleay	9	c Boon, b Bennett	5
I.P. Butchart	c Haysman, b Whitney	1	(9) not out	48
P.W.E. Rawson	c Bennett, b Macleay	1	(10) lbw, b McCurdy	2
A.J. Traicos	not out	4	(8) c Macleay, b McCurdy	0
V.R. Hogg	c Bennett, b Macleay	0	not out	5
Extras		10		19
		127	(for 9 wkts dec.)	308

	O	M	R	W	O	M	R	W
McCurdy	18	4	37	4	23	4	75	4
Whitney	17	4	39	2	23	4	63	3
Bennett	6	4	14	1	20	7	50	2
Macleay	14.1	6	27	3	21	6	68	—
Saunders					7		34	—

YOUNG AUSTRALIANS

	FIRST INNINGS		SECOND INNINGS	
R.B. Kerr	c Houghton, b Rawson	2	(2) c Traicos, b Rawson	12
G. Shipperd	c Houghton, b Rawson	16	(3) lbw, b Rawson	5
D.M. Wellham†	c and b Rawson	8	(4) c Fletcher, b Traicos	16
D.C. Boon	lbw, b Traicos	18	(5) c Houghton, b Fletcher	108
M.D. Haysman	c Traicos, b Rawson	8	(6) c Brown, b Rawson	4
W.B. Phillips*	b Rawson	20	(1) c Hodgson, b Rawson	4
K.H. Macleay	c Fletcher, b Traicos	1	c Pycroft, b Traicos	4
M.J. Bennett	c Traicos, b Rawson	21	lbw, b Rawson	35
S.L. Saunders	c Heron, b Traicos	1	not out	17
R.J. McCurdy	not out	20	c Houghton, b Rawson	0
M.R. Whitney	c Pycroft, b Rawson	2	b Traicos	1
Extras		9		10
		126		216

	O	M	R	W	O	M	R	W
Hogg	13	5	26	—	14	2	34	—
Rawson	18.3	3	55	7	28	6	88	6
Traicos	11	5	22	3	21.5	5	44	3
Butchart	5	1	14	—	1		3	—
Fletcher					10		21	1
Omarshah					5	1	16	—

FALL OF WICKETS
1- 6, 2- 25, 3- 35, 4- 52, 5- 75, 6- 107, 7- 108, 8- 123, 9- 123
1- 3, 2- 33, 3- 128, 4- 160, 5- 239, 6- 247, 7- 247, 8- 252, 9- 275

FALL OF WICKETS
1- 17, 2- 20, 3- 29, 4- 59, 5- 73, 6- 75, 7- 84, 8- 85, 9- 118
1- 8, 2- 17, 3- 24, 4- 50, 5- 51, 6- 70, 7- 195, 8- 197, 9- 197

Zimbabwe won by 93 runs

mystery why, although he has passed fifty nineteen times in first-class matches, he has yet to register a first-class hundred.

A partnership of 89 between Phillips and Boon set the Young Australians on course for victory, but with 13 runs needed and 3.2 overs left, the visitors accepted the umpires offer to end play because of failing light, a decision that did little to win the admiration of the spectators.

The second one-day international scheduled for the following day was cancelled when a heavy overnight storm caused water to seep under the covers and spoil one end of the pitch.

SECOND INTERNATIONAL: ZIMBABWE v. YOUNG AUSTRALIANS

Fletcher won the toss and elected to bat, but Zimbabwe gave another miserable display. Against an Australian side which bowled competitively, fielded immaculately and caught everything, Zimbabwe crumbled. Fletcher alone showed the necessary class as the Young Australians swept all before them.

Hodgson replaced Curran, who had already gone to his Lancashire League side, in the Zimbabwe team, and Haysman replaced the sick Ritchie in the Australian side.

It was expected that the Young Australians, having overwhelmed Zimbabwe with their out-cricket, would achieve a big lead, but Zimbabwe fought back with one of the greatest team performances in their history. Rawson was persuaded to take the new ball and he had both openers caught behind. Then he accepted a sharp caught and bowled chance from

out of form skipper Dirk Wellham and the visitors were 29 for 3.

Haysman also fell to the effervescent Rawson and just as Phillips and Boon appeared to be effecting a recovery, Boon was lbw to Traicos' arm ball. Young Australians finished the day on 97 for 8, but next day, Rawson finished with 7 for 55, and, incredibly, Zimbabwe led by one run.

The magnificent performance in the field seemed to inspire the Zimbabwe batsmen, and although Brown failed and Heron did not last long, Omarshah was all determination. Pycroft scored 35 which, by his high standards, was failure, but Fletcher was in commanding form as Omarshah inched closer to his century. It came after 304 minutes and 213 balls, a splendid achievement by the young man. Drained by his efforts, he was out almost as soon as he had completed his hundred, and the day closed with Zimbabwe on 255 for 8 and the match in the balance.

Next morning, Iain Butchart batted superbly. An attacking batsman, he off-drove the first delivery with the second new ball for 4 and pulled McCurdy over square-leg for 6. His 48 not out was his highest score in first-class cricket and he was deprived of his fifty when Fletcher declared after an hour's play on the third morning, leaving Young Australians five hours in which to make 310.

The tourists went for the runs, but they were soon in trouble as, with Rawson again the spearhead of the Zimbabwe attack, they slumped to 70 for 6.

It was then that Boon and Murray Bennett frustrated Zimbabwe for two and a half hours while they added 125 runs. The Zimbabwe fielding had been quite magnificent, but in

the growing excitement two half-chances were missed.

Boon reached a splendid century and then was caught at the wicket off Fletcher. This gave Zimbabwe the opening that they needed. Rawson returned to remove Bennett and McCurdy with successive balls and last man Whitney came to the wicket with 20 minutes to play.

Stuart Saunders played with great tenacity and took most of the strike, but with seven balls remaining, Traicos beat Whitney with his faster ball and shattered his stumps.

Amid great jubilation, Zimbabwe had won by 93 runs. The hero of the match was Peter Rawson whose 13 wickets for 143 runs had been bettered only once for Zimbabwe, by Joe Partridge.

THIRD ONE-DAY INTERNATIONAL: ZIMBABWE v. YOUNG AUSTRALIANS

Gerald Peckover, having already been named in the World Cup squad, was recalled to the Zimbabwe side, his first match since Independence. He shared a useful stand with Ali Omarshah, but the innings of the match for Zimbabwe was played by Jack Heron who scored 82 of a 132 partnership with Omarshah.

This stand looked to have placed Zimbabwe in a very strong position, but Wayne Phillips, a magnificent striker of the ball, launched a powerful attack on the bowling and led his side to a fine victory.

He had scored only a single when he skied a ball to square-leg, but the simple catch was dropped. Thereafter nothing detracted him from his assault on the bowling. He and Shipperd added 144 for the second wicket before Shipperd retired hurt for 29.

John Traicos. Vice-captain of Zimbabwe. An off-spinner who played Test cricket for South Africa. Born in Egypt of Greek parentage. A truly international cricketer. (Ken Kelly)

THIRD ONE-DAY INTERNATIONAL: ZIMBABWE v. YOUNG AUSTRALIANS
17 April 1983 at Harare Sports Club

ZIMBABWE			
G.E. Peckover*	b Macleay	20
A.H. Omarshah	c Shipperd, b McCurdy	68
J.G. Heron	c Shipperd, b Whitney	82
A.J. Pycroft	b McCurdy	1
D.L. Houghton	c Wellham, b Macleay	32
D.A.G. Fletcher†	c Wellham, b Macleay	5
C.A.T. Hodgson	c Jones, b Macleay	2
I.P. Butchart	not out	8
P.W.E. Rawson	not out	10
A.J. Traicos		
V.R. Hogg		
Extras		14
(50 overs)	(for 7 wickets)	242

	O	M	R	W
McCurdy	10	—	46	2
Blizzard	10	2	32	—
Macleay	10	—	52	4
Bennett	10	2	65	—
Whitney	10	—	33	1

FALL OF WICKETS
1- 45, 2- 177, 3- 182, 4- 190, 5- 198, 6- 203, 7- 231

YOUNG AUSTRALIANS			
D.M.J. Jones	b Rawson	8
W.B. Phillips*	c Omarshah, b Rawson	135
G. Shipperd	retired hurt	29
D.M. Wellham†	c Fletcher, b Traicos	21
D.C. Boon	run out	10
M.D. Haysman	not out	13
K.H. Macleay	not out	9
M.J. Bennett		
R.J. McCurdy		
P.A. Blizzard		
M.R. Whitney		
Extras		21
(49 overs)	(for 4 wickets)	246

	O	M	R	W
Hogg	10	3	36	—
Rawson	10	3	38	2
Fletcher	9	—	40	—
Butchart	8	—	52	—
Omarshah	2	—	17	—
Traicos	10	—	42	2

FALL OF WICKETS
1- 15, 2- 203, 3- 221, 4- 227

Young Australians won by 6 wickets

Phillips continued his onslaught, his 135 coming off 149 deliveries. He was finally caught off Rawson and it was left to Haysman and Macleay to score the final 19 runs. Victory was achieved with an over to spare.

The tour had underlined Zimbabwe's need for more first-class cricket and more top-class opposition. As Brian Taber and Des Rundle, the Young Australian manager, pointed out, the real answer to Zimbabwe's problems is to take the game more extensively to the black population.

Peter Rawson. Twenty-five first-class wickets in Zimbabwe's season and the leading bowler. (Ken Kelly)

BELOW: The Third One-Day International, Zimbabwe v Young Australians. Pycroft is bowled by McCurdy. Wayne Phillips is the wicket-keeper and Houghton the non-striker. (The Herald)

First Class Averages

Batting	M	Inns	NOs	Runs	HS	Av	100s	50s
A.J. Pycroft	4	7		385	128	55.00	1	2
A.H. Omarshah	2	4		215	105	53.75	1	1
D.L. Houghton	4	7		285	77	40.71		3
A.J. Traicos	4	6	4	65	32*	32.50		
K.M. Curran	3	5		151	96	30.20		1
D.A.G. Fletcher	3	5		115	56	23.00		1
C.A.T. Hodgson	3	5	1	66	40	16.50		
J.G. Heron	4	7		113	72	16.14		1
I.P. Butchart	4	7	1	94	48*	15.67		
P.W.E. Rawson	4	6	1	73	63*	14.60		

(Qualification 50 runs, average 10.00)

Bowling	Overs	Mdns	Runs	Wkts	Av	Best	5/inn	10/m
P.W.E. Rawson	154.2	47	401	25	16.04	7/55	3	1
V.R. Hogg	98	32	231	10	23.10	6/26	1	
A.J. Traicos	137	34	333	14	23.79	5/103	1	
K.M. Curran	48.4	8	186	7	26.57	4/21		

(Qualification 5 wickets)

Fielding Figures
13 D.L. Houghton (ct 11 / st 2)
6 D.A.G. Fletcher
5 A.J. Traicos and A.J. Pycroft
4 C.A.T. Hodgson
3 J.G. Heron and I.P. Butchart

SECTION K
Encouraging Signs

Australia in Sri Lanka
Test and one-day Internationals

Roy Dias. (Adrian Murrell)

The Sri Lankan cricketers returned from New Zealand beaten and dispirited. They were soon to entertain the Australians and a quick recovery of fitness and morale was essential for the Australians had chosen a strong party of thirteen for the two and a half week tour.

Kim Hughes was unable to make the trip for domestic reasons and Greg Chappell led the Australian side for what most people believed would be the last time. Graham Yallop, following his record-breaking performances in the Sheffield Shield, was recalled to the side which showed a surprise omission in John Dyson and interesting and worthy inclusions in Roger Woolley, the Tasmanian captain and wicket-keeper, Steve Smith, who had done so well in the finals of the Benson and Hedges World Series, and Tom Hogan, the orthodox left-arm spinner from Western Australia.

FIRST ONE-DAY INTERNATIONAL: SRI LANKA v. AUSTRALIA

The Australians omitted Wessels and Yardley and Roger Woolley made his international debut.

Chappell won the toss and decided to bat on an easy paced wicket. Smith was caught behind off John, but Wood and Yallop added 72 for the second wicket. Wood, who hit six fours, reached 50 off 68 deliveries, but the remainder of the Australian batting, troubled by some accurate bowling, failed to build on the advantage that Wood and Yallop had given them.

Sidath Wettimuny and Susil Fernando gave Sri Lanka just the start that they needed with a stand of 71. Lillee, bowling at half-pace, was still searching for full fitness following his knee operation, and it was spinner Hogan and medium pacer Maguire who brought about a mild mid-innings collapse as Sri Lanka went to 112 for 5.

Sensible batting by Somachandra de Silva and Asantha Mel swung the game in favour of Sri Lanka who achieved their first victory over Australia when de Silva scored the winning run off the first ball of the last over.

It was a good team display from Sri Lanka who bowled well, batted without panic and were brilliantly served behind the stumps where Guy de Alwis took five catches, including a fine diving catch to get rid of Chappell.

SECOND ONE-DAY INTERNATIONAL: SRI LANKA v. AUSTRALIA

Sri Lanka fielded an unchanged side and Australia brought in Yardley and Wessels for Maguire and Smith.

The match followed almost the same pattern as the first match. Wood failed, but Wessels, Yallop and Chappell raised Australia to a commendable, though not daunting, total.

Sri Lanka were given a wonderful start by Wettimuny and Fernando, but both were out at the same total as four wickets fell for 7 runs.

Ranatunge and Madugalle rallied Sri Lanka with a stand of 69. Nineteen-year old Arjuna Ranatunge hit 55 not out off 36 balls and clinched victory for Sri Lanka with ten balls to spare.

17, 18 and 19 April 1983

at Moratuwa

Australians 259 (R.D. Woolley 57, O. Weerasinghe 4 for 48) and 115 for 2 dec
Sri Lankan Board President's XI 131 and 184 for 8

Match drawn

Chappell stood down from the captaincy to give David

FIRST ONE-DAY INTERNATIONAL: SRI LANKA v. AUSTRALIA

13 April 1983 at Colombo

AUSTRALIA				SRI LANKA			
G.M. Wood	b de Silva	50		S.R. de S. Wettimuny	b Hogan	37
S.B. Smith	c de Alwis, b John	1		E.R.N.S. Fernando	st Woolley, b Hogan	31
G. N. Yallop	c de Alwis, b Ranatunge	39		R.L. Dias	lbw, b Chappell	5
G. S. Chappell†	c de Alwis, b John	11		L.R.D. Mendis†	b Hogan	16
D.W. Hookes	c de Alwis, b Ranatunge	0		R.S. Madugalle	c Smith, b Maguire	9
A.R. Border	b de Silva	10		A. Ranatunge	c Hogan, b Hogg	10
R.D. Woolley*	c de Alwis, b de Mel	16		A.L.F. de Mel	c Woolley, b Maguire	27
T. G. Hogan	c R.J. Ratnayeke, b de Mel	27		D.S. de Silva	not out	15
D. K. Lillee	run out	5		R.G. de Alwis*	b Hogg	6
R.M. Hogg	not out	0		R.J. Ratnayeke	not out	
J.N. Maguire				V. John		
Extras	lb 7, w 2	9		Extras	lb 5, w 5, nb 3	13
(45 overs)	(for 9 wickets)	168		(44.1 overs)	(for 8 wickets)	169

	O	M	R	W
de Mel	9	2	35	2
John	9	1	33	2
R.J. Ratnayeke	9	1	44	—
Ranatunge	9	1	26	2
de Silva	9	—	21	2

	O	M	R	W
Hogg	9	—	40	2
Maguire	8.1	—	43	2
Lillee	9	—	25	—
Chappell	9	2	21	1
Hogan	9	1	27	3

FALL OF WICKETS
1- 15, 2- 87, 3- 103, 4- 107, 5- 109, 6- 118, 7- 144, 8- 167, 9- 168

FALL OF WICKETS
1- 71, 2- 82, 3- 82, 4- 102, 5- 112, 6- 139, 7- 157, 8- 168

Sri Lanka won by 2 wickets

SECOND ONE-DAY INTERNATIONAL: SRI LANKA v. AUSTRALIA
16 April 1983 at Colombo

AUSTRALIA				SRI LANKA		
G.M. Wood	lbw, b R.J. Ratnayeke	9		S.R. de S. Wettimuny	b Yardley	56
K.C. Wessels	b R.J. Ratnayeke	39		E.R.N.S. Fernando	run out	34
G. N. Yallop	c Mendis, b Ranatunge	59		R.L. Dias	c Wood, b Yardley	2
G. S. Chappell†	not out	54		L.R.D. Mendis†	b Yardley	2
D.W. Hookes	run out	27		A. Ranatunge	not out	55
A.R. Border	c Dias, b John	6		R.S. Madugalle	b Hogan	37
R.D. Woolley*	not out	3		A.L.F. de Mel	c Wood, b Border	1
B. Yardley				D.S. de Silva	not out	7
T. G. Hogan				R.G. de Alwis*		
D.K. Lillee				R.J. Ratnayeke		
R.M. Hogg				V. John		
Extras	lb 8, nb 2	10		Extras	b 1, lb 15, nb 3	19
(45 overs)	(for 5 wickets)	207		(43.2 overs)	(for 6 wickets)	213

	O	M	R	W		O	M	R	W
de Mel	9	1	29	—	Hogg	7	1	18	—
John	9	—	33	1	Lillee	9	—	30	—
R.J. Ratnayeke	9	—	38	2	Chappell	6.2	—	37	—
Ranatunge	9	—	45	1	Hogan	9	—	62	1
de Silva	9	—	52	—	Yardley	9	1	28	3
					Border	2	—	10	1
					Yallop	1	—	9	—

FALL OF WICKETS
1- 34, 2- 77, 3- 136, 4- 195, 5- 201

FALL OF WICKETS
1- 101, 2- 101, 3- 107, 4- 108, 5- 177, 6- 178

Sri Lanka won by 4 wickets

Hookes the chance to lead the side. The Australians took a commanding lead on the first innings, and Hookes declared his second innings to leave the local side 3½ hours in which to make 244. After another dismal start they were never in a position to look for victory, but some dour batting by the middle order against some good left-arm bowling by Hogan saved the game.

THE INAUGURAL TEST MATCH: SRI LANKA v. AUSTRALIA

Australia gave Test caps to Hogan and Woolley, the first Tasmanian to play for his country for over fifty years, for the first time. Sri Lanka gave a first Test cap to leg-spinner Roshan Guneratne who came in for John from the side that had won the one-day internationals.

Wood laboured at the start, but Wessels was soon driving and cutting profusely. He and Yallop added 170 in 200 minutes for the second wicket, and Wessels reached his second Test century in 173 minutes off 127 deliveries. He was finally out when he mis-pulled into the hands of Roy Dias at mid-wicket. His innings has lasted 252 minutes and he had faced 176 balls, striking twenty-one fours.

Play ended a little early through bad light, but Australia, 258 for 2 at the close, ravished the Sri Lankan attack on the second day. The day belonged to Hookes who was at his brilliant best as he launched a ferocious attack upon the bowling. He hit two sixes and seventeen fours in his 143 not out which took just over three hours. It was exciting stuff and it left the Sri Lankans limp and dejected, a state made worse when Lillee and Hogg removed the first three batsmen for 9 runs.

Mendis alone showed that he had the necessary class and when play ended with Sri Lanka on 65 for 4 he was on 34 not out and no one else had reached double figures.

Ranatunge. A brave effort for Sri Lanka which received insufficient support. He had innings of 90 and 32 in the Test match. (Adrian Murrell)

He and young Ranatunge batted masterfully on the thir▢ day. Their fifth wicket partnership realised 96, and Dule▢ Mendis' sparkling 74 included twelve fours. Ranatunge con▢ tinued to bat well after Mendis had become the second ▢ Yardley's five victims, but the last five wickets went down f▢ 51 runs and Sri Lanka had to follow-on.

Ranatunge who, like his captain, was ever eager to play h▢ shots hit sixteen fours in his 90 which lasted only 16▢ minutes. He is a young man of very rich promise.

Sri Lanka fared little better at the beginning of the▢ second innings than they had done in the first, b▢ Wettimuny, who had done so well in New Zealand, batte▢ with great good sense and was unbeaten at the close of th▢ third day which saw Sri Lanka at 71 for 2.

After the rest day, things began deceptively well for S▢ Lanka. Wettimuny continued to bat finely, and schoolbo▢ night-watchman Rumesh Ratnayeke looked confident an▢ secure as the score moved to 120. Then Ratnayeke was nee▢ lessly run out, emphasising that their suicidal tendenci▢ contributed much to Sri Lanka's downfall.

The spin of Yardley and Hogan now dominated. Neith▢ Mendis nor Madugalle could find form. Ranatunge aga▢ displayed his class and Wettimuny played a brave, defia▢ innings until he was bowled by Hogan four short of h▢ century. The last seven wickets went for 54 runs an▢ Australia won by an innings with more than a day to spar▢

LEFT: *Wood. As eager as ever.* (*Adrian Murrell*)
OPPOSITE: *Bruce Yardley. His off-spin proved decisive in th▢ Test match.* (*Adrian Murrell*)

THE INAUGURAL TEST MATCH: SRI LANKA *v.* AUSTRALIA
22, 23, 24 and 26 April 1983 at Kandy

AUSTRALIA

FIRST INNINGS

Batsman	Dismissal	Runs
K.C. Wessels	c Dias, b D.S. de Silva	141
G.M. Wood	c R.J. Ratnayeke, b Ranatunge	4
G.N. Yallop	lbw, b de Mel	98
G.S. Chappell†	lbw, b de Mel	66
D.W. Hookes	not out	143
A.R. Border	not out	47
R.D. Woolley*		
T.G. Hogan		
B. Yardley		
D.K. Lillee		
R.M. Hogg		
Extras	lb 11, w 1, nb 3	15
	(for 4 wkts, dec)	514

Bowler	O	M	R	W
de Mel	23	3	113	2
R.J. Ratnayeke	28	4	108	—
Ranatunge	19	2	72	1
D.S. de Silva	44	7	122	1
Guneratne	17	1	84	—

FALL OF WICKETS
1- 43, 2- 213, 3- 290, 4- 359

SRI LANKA

Batsman	FIRST INNINGS		SECOND INNINGS	
S.R. de S. Wettimuny	c Woolley, b Lillee	0	b Hogan	9▢
E.R.N.S. Fernando	c Woolley, b Hogg	0	c Woolley, b Lillee	
R.L. Dias	c Border, b Lillee	4	b Hogan	1
L.R.D. Mendis†	c Hookes, b Yardley	74	(5) c Border, b Yardley	
R.S. Madugalle	c and b Yardley	9	(6) b Yardley	
A. Ranatunge	c Lillee, b Yardley	90	(7) b Hogan	3▢
D.S. de Silva	c Hogan, b Yardley	26	(8) c Woolley, b Hogan	
A.L.F. de Mel	c Hookes, b Hogan	29	(9) c Yallop, b Hogan	
R.G. de Alwis*	c Border, b Yardley	3	(10) run out	
R.J. Ratnayeke	c Woolley, b Border	14	(4) run out	3▢
R. Guneratne	not out	0	not out	0
Extras	b 7, lb 5, w 1, nb 9	22	b 6, lb 7, nb 1	1▢
		271		20▢

Bowler	O	M	R	W	O	M	R	W
Lillee	19	3	67	2	11	3	40	1
Hogg	12	4	31	1	3	2	7	—
Chappell	1	—	2	—				
Yardley	23	7	88	5	26	6	78	2
Hogan	11	1	50	1	25.2	6	66	5
Border	4.5	—	11	1				

FALL OF WICKETS
1- 1, 2- 5, 3- 9, 4- 46, 5- 142, 6- 220, 7- 224, 8- 247, 9- 270
1- 17, 2- 59, 3- 120, 4- 151, 5- 155, 6- 155, 7- 162, 8- 164, 9- 191

Australia won by an innings and 38 runs

The Sri Lankan team for the Prudential World Cup which wa selected after the one-day internationals and the Test agains Australia. Back row (l to r) – de Mel; Kuruppu; R.J. Ra nayeke; John; Samarasekera; G. de Silva; de Alwis Ranatunge; Fernando
Front row (l to r) – S. Wettimuny; Dias; Sir Garfield Sober (coach); Mendis; Tamnyah Murugaser (manager); S. d Silva; Madugalle. (Ken Kelly)

Madugalle who had a disappointing time with the bat. (Adria Murrell)

It was a bitter disappointment for Sri Lanka after their fin showing in the one-day internationals. Again they showed lack of durability, of staying power over the arduous days o a Test match. Their tendency to run themselves out was als a factor in their defeat, but Australia had also come back wel from a bad start to the brief tour. They had batted excitingl and their spinners, in particular, had shown an ability to tur the ball and to control length and flight which marked then as players of quality.

THIRD AND FOURTH ONE-DAY INTERNATION ALS: SRI LANKA v. AUSTRALIA

Heavy rain ended a four month drought and caused th abandonment of the last two one-day internationals s giving Sri Lanka the series by 2–0, their first win at interna tional level.

THIRD ONE-DAY INTERNATIONAL: SRI LANKA v. AUSTRALIA
9 April 1983 at Colombo

AUSTRALIA				SRI LANKA	
G.M. Wood	b Ranatunge	35		S.R. de S. Wettimuny	
K. C. Wessels	c Dias, b de Silva	43		E.R.N.S. Fernando	
G. N. Yallop	c de Alwis, b de Silva	51		R.L. Dias	
D.W. Hookes	c de Alwis, b John	23		L.R.D. Mendis†	
A.R. Border	b de Mel	10		R.S. Madugalle	
G. S. Chappell†	not out	9		A. Ranatunge	
R.D. Woolley*	not out	12		D.S. de Silva	
B. Yardley				A.L.F. de Mel	
T. G. Hogan				R.G. de Alwis*	
R. M. Hogg				R.J. Ratnayeke	
J. N. Maguire				V. John	
Extras	lb 8, w 1, nb 2	11			
(39.2 overs)	(for 5 wickets)	194			

	O	M	R	W
de Mel	9	—	44	1
John	6.2	—	23	1
Ranatunge	9	—	42	1
R. J. Ratnayeke	6	—	23	—
de Silva	9	1	51	2

FALL OF WICKETS
1- 60, 2- 105, 3- 151, 4- 172, 5- 172

Match abandoned

In the first match, Wood and Wessels began with a stand of 60 in 67 minutes, and Yallop, dropped on one, kept up the scoring rate, but rain ended play with 5.4 overs of the Australian innings still to be bowled.

The second match was reduced to thirty overs a side by overnight rain. Wessels and Wood fell in a fine opening spell by de Mel, but Yallop and Hookes added 112 in 62 minutes before Hookes was bowled by Rumesh Ratnayeke. The rain came almost immediately after.

Yallop hit two sixes and seven fours in his 60 not out.

So ended Australia's brief tour of Sri Lanka. The home side had been beaten conclusively in the Test match, but their performances in the one-day internationals had given heart to an administration in need of encouragement after the defections to the tour of South Africa and the results in New Zealand.

FOURTH ONE-DAY INTERNATIONAL: SRI LANKA v. AUSTRALIA
10 April 1983 at Colombo

AUSTRALIA				SRI LANKA	
K. C. Wessels	b de Mel	6		S.R. de S. Wettimuny	
G.M. Wood	b de Mel	2		E.R.N.S. Fernando	
G. N. Yallop	not out	60		R.L. Dias	
D.W. Hookes	b R.J. Ratnayeke	49		L.R.D. Mendis†	
S.B. Smith	not out	0		R.S. Madugalle	
A.R. Border				A. Ranatunge	
G.S. Chappell†				A.L.F. de Mel	
R.D. Woolley*				D.S. de Silva	
B. Yardley				B. Kuruppu*	
R. M. Hogg				R.J. Ratnayeke	
J.N. Maguire				V. John	
Extras	b 1, lb 5, w 1	7			
(19.2 overs)	(for 3 wickets)	124			

	O	M	R	W
de Mel	4	—	9	2
John	5	—	15	—
D.S. de Silva	4	—	21	—
Ranatunge	3	—	35	—
R.J. Ratnayeke	2.2	—	16	1
Wettimuny	1	—	21	—

FALL OF WICKETS
1- 3, 2- 12, 3- 124

Match abandoned

SECTION L
The West Indian Season

The West Indies Season
West Indies v India
The Shell Shield and other first-class matches
in the West Indies

*Clive Lloyd. The old warrior who led Guyana to triumph in the Shell Shield
and West Indies to victory over India. (Patrick Eagar)*

The West Indian season was played under a cloud of uncertainty and disillusionment. Some leading players, like Gomes and Holding, had failed to return from Australia where they had been playing in time to represent their islands in the Shell Shield. According to regulations set down by the West Indian authorities, this should have meant that they could not play for West Indies in the Test series against India, but, at Lloyd's insistence the law was ignored so that they could be accommodated, and once more the authority of a controlling body counted for nothing.

More serious to the West Indies, however, was the fact that several leading players, Rowe, King, Croft and Deryck Murray among them, had been tempted to tour South Africa and had, inevitably, been banned. Much emotion was aroused, much political hypocrisy spoken. One fact seemed to get lost and that was that, for the first time in the history of cricket, a team of black cricketers was competing with a team of white cricketers in a representative match in South Africa. Most of us felt that we would never live to see that day. It has not, sadly, meant the end of apartheid, and it was a cosmetic job by the South African politicians who allowed great cricketers who were black to be considered as 'honorary whites', but the meeting of black and white 'international' teams in South Africa could still be regarded as an achievement which future historians may consider to have been a greatly significant one, and one which, hopefully, could begin the integration of all races in the country and the liberation of the black peoples from the servile position which is inflicted upon them at present.

Jones Cup Final

23, 24 and 25 October 1982

at Albion, Berbice

Berbice 307 (L. Baichan 132, S. Persaud 54, D.I. Kallicharran 56, C. Butts 4 for 76) and 257 (L. Baichan 101 not out, T.R. Etwaroo 61, D.I. Kallicharran 54, C. Butts 7 for 56)
Demerara 337 (A.A. Lyte 87, M.A. Harper 60, M.A. Lynch 52, L.A. Lambert 6 for 60) and 73 for 2

Match drawn

Beaumont Cup

7, 8 and 9 January 1983

at Pointe-à-Pierre, Trinidad

North & East Trinidad and Tobago 180 for 9 dec (R.S. Gabriel 103, G.S. Antoine 4 for 42) and 239 for 3 dec (A. Rajah 109 not out, S.A. Gomes 64 not out)
South & Central Trinidad and Tobago 133 (W. Debisette 53, K.C. Williams 4 for 38) and 206 for 8 (R. Sampath 62, G. Mahabir 4 for 66)

Match drawn

The first-class status of the Beaumont Cup, the annual North-East against South-Central match which for many years had been the feature of Trinidad and Tobago's domestic season, had been in grave doubt in 1982 when, following the 'irregularities' of the previous year, the game was further demoted because of the unavailability or unwillingness of several leading players to participate.

In 1983 the teams were more truly representative, and eventually it was the stubbornness of Shamshuddin Jumadeen and Premnath Ramnath which saved South and Central.

Richard Gabriel, who has been playing first-class cricket for fourteen years, was the backbone of the North and East first innings. Simmonds, his opening partner, and S.A. Gomes were the only other players to reach double figures in the match.

South and Central fared even worse, losing their last wickets for 32 runs.

Some bright batting by Gomes and Anmeal Rajah who added an unbeaten 163 put North and East well on top. South and Central, needing 287 to win, lost 3 for 71 before Theo Cuffy and Roland Sampath added 88. Cuffy was run out and five wickets fell while only 37 were added so that Ramnath and Jumadeen were happy to stave off defeat.

21, 22, 23 and 24 January 1983

at Bridgetown, Barbados

Barbados 242 (D.L. Haynes 97, T.R.O. Payne 71) and 256 (M.D. Marshall 71, E.A. Baptiste 4 for 51, A.M.E. Roberts 4 for 55)
Leeward Islands 253 (R.B. Richardson 102, W.W. Daniel 7 for 55) and 189 (A.L. Kelly 55, W.W. Daniel 5 for 33)

Barbados won by 56 runs

at Roseau, Dominica

Guyana 162 (A.A. Lyght 56, W.W. Davis 6 for 54) and 334 (S.F.A. Bacchus 143, N. Phillip 4 for 77, W.W. Davis 4 for 78)
Windward Islands 258 (L.C. Sebastien 88, C. Butts 5 for 81) and 130 (R.A. Harper 4 for 33)

Guyana won by 108 runs

at Kingston, Jamaica

Jamaica 390 (O.W. Peters 82, M.C. Neita 74, H.S. Chang 64, G. Mahabir 5 for 113) and 191 for 7 dec (O.W. Peters 79)
Trinidad and Tobago 262 (R.S. Gabriel 71, K.G. d'Heurieux 59, S.A. Gomes 50, C. Gordon 4 for 46) and 259 for 6 (R.S. Gabriel 96)

Match drawn

The Shell Shield programme opened with reigning champions Barbados beating the young pretenders of Leeward Islands by 56 runs after receiving a dreadful fright.

It was Desmond Haynes and Thelston Payne who provided the substance to the Barbados first innings with a third wicket stand of 140, but there were scant contributions from anyone else.

The Leeward innings was totally dominated by Richie Richardson from Antigua who, in his fifth first-class innings scored his maiden first-class century. He alone withstood the

ery bowling of Wayne Daniel who produced his best bowling figures in the Shell Shield.

Richardson's main helper was Enoch Lewis in a second
icket stand of 80, but Viv Richards was one of Daniel's
ctims, bowled for 0. Nevertheless, Leeward Islands led by
1 on the first innings and when Baptiste and Roberts had
arbados at 83 for 5 and 117 for 7, it seemed that the visitors
ould snatch an historic win. Malcolm Marshall then swung
ie bat to great effect. Daniel and Alleyne gave good support
nd the last three wickets added 139.

With Kelly and Richards batting well, Leeward looked
pable of making the 246 runs needed, but both fell to
hillips and the last 8 wickets went down for 64 runs, Daniel
gain providing the fireworks

After their glorious season in 1982, much was expected of
Vindward Islands and their defeat at Windsor Park was a
itter disappointment. After Lyght and Etward had opened
ith a stand of 73, the game was grasped firmly by Windward
slands. Davis bowled fast and well, Guyana were out for
62, and Lockhart Sebastien and Lance John had an opening
tand of 122. Off-spinner Clyde Butts caused unease to the
niddle order, but a first innings lead of 96 seemed to be
ecisive.

Guyana lost two wickets before clearing off the arrears,
ut Test batsman Fauod Bacchus hit a sparkling 143. Phillip
nd Davis both bowled well, but Kentish and Hinds could
ot prove as effective with their off-breaks as Harper and
Butts did when Windward Islands batted again and crum-
led before them.

*Idine Baptiste who established himself as a valuable all-
ounder in the Barbados side. (George Herringshaw)*

A high-scoring game in Kingston with solid batting performances from most players ended with honours even.
Jamaica, lamenting the loss of their idol, Lawrence Rowe,
one of the very greatest of batsmen whose talents have not
been seen to the full outside his own country, found some
compensation in the performances of newcomer Peters,
while Trinidad had two fine innings from Gabriel and encouraging spin from Mahabir.

28, 29, 30 and 31 January 1983

at Kingston, Jamaica

Jamaica 234 (P.J. Dujon 96 not out, H.L. Alleyne 4 for
46, M.D. Marshall 4 for 49) and 255 (G. Powell 67)
Barbados 435 (T.R.O. Payne 123, C.A. Best 84) and 55
for 1

Barbados won by 9 wickets

at Nevis

Guyana 213 (A.A. Lyght 94, N.C. Guishard 4 for 79) and
318 (A.A. Lyght 100, D.I. Kallicharran 69, S.F.A. Bacchus
56, E.A. Baptiste 46)
Leeward Islands 91 (C. Butts 5 for 23) and 267 (V.A.
Eddy 58, A.L. Kelly 56, R.A. Harper 5 for 95)

Guyana won by 173 runs

at Port of Spain, Trinidad

Trinidad and Tobago 353 (A.L. Logie 138) and 237 for
5 dec (A.L. Logie 79, P.V. Simmonds 75)
Windward Islands 223 and 371 for 8 (S.W. Julien 123,
L.C. Sebastien 123, K.C. Williams 5 for 98)

Windward Islands won by 2 wickets

In spite of a fine innings from Peter Dujon, now adding the
burden of captaincy to his labours as wicket-keeper and leading batsman, Jamaica were outplayed by Barbados for whom
Thelston Payne and Carlisle Best shared a third wicket stand
of 147. Some later hitting by Marshall and Linton consolidated Barbados' lead, and Jamaica failed to master the
pace attack of Marshall, Daniel and Alleyne.

Without Viv Richards, Leeward Islands were beaten in
three days by Guyana. Andrew Lyght played two splendid
innings for Guyana whose bowling strength lay once more in
the off-spin of Harper and Butts.

The most exciting match of the round was at Port of Spain
where Windward Islands brought off a sensational victory
after trailing for most of the match.

Augustine Logie dominated the first day with a fine knock
of 138 which took Trinidad to 353. Windward faltered badly
in reply, losing three men to needless run outs and coming to
within 130 of Trinidad's score, only because of some late
hitting by Phillip and Hinds.

With Logie again batting well and sharing a second wicket
stand of 164 with Philip Simmonds, Trinidad declared at 237
for 5, setting Windward Islands to make 368 at more than
four an over.

Lance John and Lockhart Sebastien gave the visitors a
good start with a stand of 99, and Sebastien and Shane Julien
then added a thrilling 185 for the second wicket. Sebastien hit

his first century in the Shell Shield, and Julien, who plays his club cricket in Barbados, hit a maiden century in first-class cricket.

With an improbable victory now possible, Windward Islands lost 7 wickets for 51 runs, but wicket-keeper Ignatius Cadette and off-break bowler Tom Kentish kept their heads and steered the side to victory so emphasising that the promise that had been shown during 1982 was being realised.

4, 5, 6 and 7 February 1983

at Bridgetown, Barbados

Guyana 230 (A.A. Lyght 112, G.L. Linton 5 for 35) and 420 (C.H. Lloyd 104, M.A. Lynch 75, M.R. Pydanna 72 not out, D.I. Kallicharran 57, A.A. Lyght 53, R. Estwick 4 for 89)
Barbados 403 (T.R.O. Payne 107, D.L. Haynes 79, G.L. Linton 66, R.A. Harper 4 for 89) and 132 for 4

Match drawn

at Kingston, Jamaica

Windward Islands 441 (S.W. Julien 88, L.D. John 80, L.C. Sebastien 73, W.N. Slack 66, N.F. Williams 51 not out, C.U. Thompson 5 for 114) and 211 for 6 (L.C. Sebastien 77, S.W. Julien 50)
Jamaica 440 (P.J. Dujon 102, C.W. Fletcher 99, M.C. Neita 75, W.W. Davis 5 for 98)

Match drawn

at Pointe-à-Pierre, Trinidad

Leeward Islands 459 (V.A. Eddy 124, S.I. Williams 120) and 247 for 9 dec (E.E. Lewis 138)
Trinidad and Tobago 383 (R. Nanan 125, P.V. Simmonds 106) and 100 for 2

Match drawn

A second successive century from Andrew Lyght did little to boost his colleagues who succumbed to the leg-breaks and googlies of George Linton.

Haynes and Payne put Barbados on the way to a substantial lead and although the middle order was undermined by the bowling of Harper, Linton proved his all-round worth and saw Barbados to a first innings lead of 173 and, seemingly, victory.

Resolute batting throughout the order saved Guyana when they batted again. Clive Lloyd hit a century, and there was fine support from Monte Lynch, wicket-keeper Milton Pydanna, hoping for Test recognition, and Derek Kallicharran. Roddy Estwick did the hat-trick when he dismissed Bacchus, Butts and Harper, but time was already beginning to run out for Barbados when he accomplished the feat.

The match in Kingston resolved into a tense struggle for first innings points. Sebastien and John began with a stand of 142 which set the pattern for a big score from Windward Islands.

Jamaica's reply was based on a third wicket stand of 154 between Dujon and Fletcher, and then Mark Neita gave

substance to the rest of the innings as Jamaica drew close and closer to the Windward score.

Windward Islands were without skipper Norbert Philli and were led by Middlesex's Wilf Slack. With Jamaica needing two runs for a first innings lead and with only one wicket to fall, Slack and Winston Davis took six minutes to set the field. Eventually, Davis bowled and C. Gordon gave him return catch. The rest was batting practice.

81 for 4, Leeward Islands recovered through a sixth wicket stand of 158 between Victor Eddy and Shirlon Williams who reached his first century in the Shell Shield. Baptiste and Guishard hit hard and Leeward reached a daunting total of 459.

Trinidad battled bravely and there were maiden first-class centuries for Philip Simmonds and Ranjie Nanan, but they fell 76 short. The fifth century of the match came from Enoch Lewis and a draw became inevitable.

10, 11, 12 and 13 February 1983

at Albion, Berbice, Guyana

Trinidad and Tobago 243 (A.L. Logie 117, L.A. Lambert 7 for 59) and 159 (A.L. Logie 62)
Guyana 395 for 9 dec (C.H. Lloyd 136, R.C. Frederick 103) and 9 for 0

Guyana won by 9 wickets

11, 12, 13 and 14 February 1983

at Plymouth, Montserrat

Jamaica 224 (R.C. Haynes 62, A. Merrick 4 for 76) and 264 (C.W. Fletcher 70, P.J. Dujon 55, A.M.E. Roberts for 65)
Leeward Islands 422 (R.B. Richardson 156, V.A. Eddy 80 not out) and 67 for 2

Leeward Islands won by 8 wickets

at Kingstown, St Vincent

Barbados 243 (T.R.O. Payne 107 not out) and 196 (N.F. Williams 4 for 38)
Windward Islands 307 (L.D. John 110, W.W. Daniel for 73) and 134 for 6

Windward Islands won by 4 wickets

The sensation of the fourth round of matches was the reappearance for Guyana of Roy Fredericks who had last played over two years ago. Fredericks, the Minister of Sport fo Guyana, is the former West Indies and Glamorgan opening batsman. Now in his fortieth year, Fredericks celebrated his return to first-class cricket with a magnificent century, sharing a fourth wicket stand of 163 with Clive Lloyd.

The sensation of the season. Roy Fredericks returned to first-class cricket at the age of 40 to help Guyana to win the Shell Shield. He batted better than ever with innings of 103 and 217. (Patrick Eagar)

Wilf Slack. He helped Windward Islands to second place in the Shell Sheild in spite of a one-match suspension. (Adrian Murrell)

Earlier, Trinidad had struggled against new pace bowler Leslaine Lambert whose 7 for 59 was a career best. Once more Augustine Logie batted splendidly for Trinidad, but his brave efforts were dwarfed by the achievements of Fredericks and Lloyd and he gained little support as Guyana moved to an easy victory. Guyana's win, which coincided with Barbados' defeat in St Vincent, gave them a firm hold of the top place in the Shell Shield.

Jamaica, weakened by the absence of players who chose to go to South Africa more than any other of the sides in the competition, suffered their second defeat when they were overwhelmed by the Leeward Islands.

Only a maiden fifty by eighteen-year Robert Haynes at number seven gave the Jamaican first innings any dignity, and then Richie Richardson hit his second century of the season, a career best 156. Vernon Eddy continued his promising run with 80 not out and Leeward took a first innings lead of 198.

There was no way that Jamaica would survive such a deficit and, in spite of spirited efforts from Colin Fletcher and Jeff Dujon, Leeward Islands strode to a comfortable win.

For Windward Islands there was another historical vic-

tory. They defeated Barbados by 4 wickets in Kingstown s proving that their momentous win in Bridgetown a yea earlier had been no fluke.

Thelston Payne became the first Barbadian to hit thre centuries in the Shell Shield in one season, and his 107 not ou saved the Barbados first innings from complete collapse.

Windward Islands batted with resolution all down th order and took a first innings lead of 64. They owed much t Lance John who again showed his worth as a reliable oper ing batsman with an innings of 110.

Phillip kept up the pressure on Barbados when they batte again, and he, Davis and Middlesex's Neil Williams restric ted them to 196.

Needing 133 to win, Windward Islands lost 5 for 68 a Malcolm Marshall caused uncertainty, but Sebastien, bat ting at number four, stood firm and the task of scoring th runs at nearly five an over was accomplished.

The arrival of the Indian touring team now drew attentio from the Shell Shield. Coming straight from their gruellin and unsuccessful tour of Pakistan, the Indians had only on match prior to the first Test match so that there was little tim for them to become acclimatised.

There had been a considerable shake-up in the India party following the defeats in Pakistan, and Gavaskar wa replaced as captain by Kapil Dev who had been vice-captai in Pakistan. Viswanath and Doshi were omitted from th team altogether and, surprisingly, Gaekwad and Ven kataraghavan, the off-spinner and former captain whos Test career had been thought to be over, were recalled to th party.

17, 18, 19 and 20 February

at Kingston, Jamaica

Indians 185 (C.A. Walsh 4 for 31) and 395 for 6 dec (A.D Gaekwad 89, M.B. Amarnath 82, D.B. Vengsarkar 82, J Arun Lal 77)
Jamaica 306 (P.J. Dujon 104, G. Powell 75, M.B. Amar nath 4 for 26) and 71 for 4

Match drawn

After a miserable first day when they were all out shortly after tea, the Indians recovered well and showed some strength in the drawn game.

It was only a stand of 41 by the young all-rounders Shastr and Sivaramakrishnan that lifted India from 126 for 7, bu even so, Jamaica made short work of passing the Indian total.

Dujon and George Powell both batted well and Dujon took the opportunity to have a long look at the Indian spinners before the first Test. His hundred was full of good sense, but he was missed off Venkataraghavan when 66. The off-spinner's control was immaculate and Dujon uncharac teristically took two and a half hours to reach his fifty.

Amarnath picked up four valuable wickets cheaply and then batted splendidly with six fours and a six in his 82 Vengsarkar and Amarnath added 130 for the fourth wicket and Arun Lal and Gaekwad put on 161 for the first wicket. Certainly an opening partner for Gavaskar had been a main problem for India in Pakistan.

Jamaica lost 3 for 19 and called off the chase for the 27 runs that were needed in 143 minutes.

FIRST TEST MATCH: WEST INDIES v. INDIA

There were strong doubts as to the fitness of Garner and Richards, and it was thought that Payne and Davis might make their Test debuts following the fine performances in the Shell Shield, but both men were passed fit and the only player to win a first Test cap was Augustine Logie of Trinidad who was preferred to Bacchus. Maninder Singh and Gavaskar were the only Indian players in the Test side who had not played in the opening match against Jamaica.

Lloyd won the toss and asked India to bat, and the visitors were soon in trouble. Gaekwad, after his long absence from Test cricket, played Holding with his bat far too far from his body and was caught behind. The same fate befell Amarnath when he edged one of the few balls that Garner got to lift, and Gavaskar who was totally bemused by Marshall when the bowler went round the wicket.

The struggle continued painfully after lunch when Vengsarkar, having been dropped in the gully by Garner, Shastri, Kapil Dev, hooking at Roberts, and Kirmani all perished. At 127 for 7, India had intimations of defeat before tea on the first day.

In a plucky stand, Yashpal Sharma and Sandhu showed a determination lacking in some of their colleagues and took the score to 219 before bad light brought an early close.

They carried their stand to 107, but the final score of 251 on a good batting wicket was very moderate.

Neither of the West Indian openers was in form, but Greenidge played with great application and survived to the end of the day by which time West Indies were 149 for 4. That they had not scored was due to the accurate spin bowling of Shastri and Venkataraghavan. Shastri, in particular, nagged away at the West Indian batsmen, having Richards caught off a beautifully flighted and spun delivery, and also accounting for Gomes. Lloyd straight drove him for six in an attempt to break free, but the game remained nicely balanced. Greenidge's fifty had come in the last over of the day and had taken him four hours.

Had India taken their chances in the field on the third day, West Indies would not have gained their slender first innings lead and seized a slight advantage when Gavaskar was bowled by the first ball of the second innings. Amarnath and Gaekwad added 68, but both were out before the close which came at 81 for 3. Then came the torrents of rain and there was no play on the fourth day so, it seemed, the match would be drawn.

The delay of an hour in starting play on the last day did nothing to alter this opinion. 112 for 4 at lunch. 167 for 6 at tea. India were batting placidly to a draw. Then in one dramatic over after tea, Andy Roberts, recalling the energies and fire of his youth, turned the course of the game and began one of the most remarkable final sessions in Test history.

With his first ball after tea Roberts had Kirmani taken at short-leg off a short pitched delivery. Off the fifth ball, Sandhu was taken in the gully and next ball Venkataraghavan edged to second slip.

Viv Richards in comtemplative mood. It was not the best of seasons for the great man, but his 61 in the second innings of the first Test was a brilliant, match-winning display of hitting.
(Adrian Murrell)

FIRST TEST MATCH: WEST INDIES v. INDIA
23, 24, 26, 27 and 28 February 1983 at Sabina Park, Kingston, Jamaica

INDIA

	FIRST INNINGS		SECOND INNINGS	
S.M. Gavaskar	c Dujon, b Marshall	20	b Holding	0
A.D. Gaekwad	c Dujon, b Holding	1	c Greenidge, b Marshall	23
M.B. Amarnath	c Dujon, b Garner	29	c Greenidge, b Marshall	40
D.B. Vengsarkar	c Richards, b Roberts	30	c Garner, b Marshall	20
Yashpal Sharma	c Haynes, b Garner	63	c Gomes, b Holding	24
R.J. Shastri	c Dujon, b Holding	1	not out	25
R.N. Kapil Dev†	c Marshall, b Roberts	5	c Dujon, b Roberts	12
S.M.H. Kirmani*	c Dujon, b Marshall	5	c Haynes, b Roberts	10
B.S. Sandhu	c Garner, b Roberts	68	c Garner, b Roberts	0
S. Venkataraghavan	hit wkt., b Roberts	0	c Greenidge, b Roberts	0
Maninder Singh	not out	3	c Holding, b Roberts	2
Extras	b 1, lb 15, nb 10	26	b 2, lb 4, w 1, nb 11	18
		251		174

WEST INDIES

	FIRST INNINGS		SECOND INNINGS	
C.G. Greenidge	c Venkat, b Shastri	70	b Dev	4
D.L. Haynes	c Amarnath, b Dev	25	b Dev	34
I.V.A. Richards	c Venkat, b Shastri	29	(4) c Dev, b Amarnath	61
H.A. Gomes	c Sharma, b Shastri	4	(7) lbw, b Dev	10
A.L. Logie	run out	13	(3) c Amarnath, b Dev	3
C.H. Lloyd†	b Venkat	24	(6) not out	17
P.J. Dujon*	lbw, b Dev	29	not out	0
M.D. Marshall	c Sharma, b Dev	23	(5) c Kirmani, b Amarnath	
A.M.E. Roberts	c Sandhu, b Shastri	17		
M.A. Holding	c Kirmani, b Dev	1		
J. Garner	not out	0		
Extras	b 1, lb 8, nb 10	19	lb 5	5
		254	(for 6 wkts)	173

	O	M	R	W	O	M	R	W
Holding	24	5	57	2	17	4	36	2
Roberts	22	4	61	4	24.3	9	39	5
Garner	15.4	4	41	2	13	6	16	—
Marshall	16	4	35	2	24	6	56	3
Gomes	9	—	31	—	7	2	9	—
Richards	1	1	0	—				

	O	M	R	W	O	M	R	W
Kapil Dev	25.3	6	45	4	13	—	73	4
Sandhu	11	4	30	—	3	—	22	—
Venkataraghavan	25	3	66	1	7	—	39	—
Maninder Singh	31	6	51	—				
Shastri	24	8	43	4				
Amarnath					2.2	—	34	2

FALL OF WICKETS
1- 10, 2- 58, 3- 66, 4- 98, 5- 99, 6- 104, 7- 127, 8- 234, 9- 238
1- 0, 2- 68, 3- 69, 4- 112, 5- 118, 6- 136, 7- 168, 8- 168, 9- 168

FALL OF WICKETS
1- 36, 2- 83, 3- 91, 4- 114, 5- 157, 6- 186, 7- 228, 8- 244, 9- 254
1- 46, 2- 65, 3- 131, 4- 132, 5- 156, 6- 167

Umpires: W. Malcolm and D.M. Archer

West Indies won by 4 wickets

Maninder Singh survived for more than two overs so that West Indies needed 172 to win in 30 minutes and 20 overs, a scoring rate of 6.6 an over.

Greenidge and Haynes began a blistering attack, but when Clive Lloyd was out at 65, it appeared that the West Indies would fail in their bid for victory. Then Viv Richards hit 61 from 36 deliveries. He hit four sixes and five fours and fell nobly, caught off a full toss at long-on with two overs remaining and 16 runs needed.

A magnificent victory was achieved with four balls to spare when Dujon clouted Amarnath for 6.

3, 4, 5 and 6 March

at Pointe-à-Pierre, Trinidad

Trinidad and Tobago 193 (P.V. Simmonds 81, Maninder Singh 5 for 48) and 141 (R.S. Gabriel 50, Maninder Singh 7 for 47)
Indians 403 (M.B. Amarnath 114, A.D. Gaekwad 81, S.M.H. Kirmani 74, A. Malhotra 59, G. Mahabir 4 for 71)

Indians won by an innings and 69 runs

at Georgetown, Guyana

Jamaica 149 (D.I. Kallicharran 6 for 60) and 267 (O.W. Peters 89, M.C. Neita 60, C. Butts 5 for 54)
Guyana 517 for 8 dec (R.C. Fredericks 217, C.H. Lloyd 64, S.F.A. Bacchus 57, D.I. Kallicharran 50 not out)

Guyana won by an innings and 101 runs

at Basseterre, St Kitts

Windward Islands 256 (S.W. Julien 68, A.M.E. Roberts 5 for 52) and 182 (A.M.E. Roberts 8 for 62)
Leeward Islands 234 (S.I. Williams 52, W.W. Davis 5 for 60) and 203 (W.W. Davis 4 for 57)

Windward Islands won by 1 run

The Indians gained a welcome victory in three days and so restored some of the confidence shattered by West Indies brilliant Test win. Trinidad collapsed from 84 for 2 to 193 all out, the slow left-arm spin of Maninder Singh proving far too complex for the home batsmen. There was also a welcome two wickets for Madan Lal who was playing his first game since his operation on a heel.

Gavaskar was out cheaply, but Gaekwad and Amarnath added 141 for the second wicket, and then Amarnath, who completed a fine century, and Malhotra added 108 for the third wicket.

Trinidad proved even more inept against Maninder Singh when they batted a second time, and India won by an innings even though they were without Shastri.

Guyana also won in three days and with the win came the Shell Shield for this was their fourth victory in five matches.

Lloyd was quick to employ his spinners in both innings and the off-breaks of Butts and Harper and the leg-breaks of Derek Kallicharran became an unfathomable mystery for the Jamaican batsmen of whom only Fletcher and Powell in the first innings and Fletcher, Peters and Neita in the second showed any real fight.

Guyana had quickly taken the lead in the first innings which was dominated by batting from Roy Fredericks even more brilliant than that which he had shown in his 'come-back' match. Sharing century stands with Bacchus and Lloyd, he hit 217 and completely savaged the Jamaican attack as he brought the Shield to Guyana.

Windward Islands consolidated second place in the table with a thrilling win over Leeward Islands who were again without Viv Richards. Batsmen were never on top against the pace men although, ultimately, it was the off-breaks of Tom Kentish which brought about the dramatic finish.

Windward Islands led by 22 on the first innings, but another magnificent spell of fast bowling from Andy Roberts whose 8 for 62 was his best performance in the Shell Shield turned the course of the match. Windward were 60 for 6, but Phillip and Hinds hit hard to take them to 182 and leave Leeward needing 205 to win.

Kelly and Richardson started confidently with a stand of 63, but both were out in quick succession and a third wicket fell at 85. Just as Leeward seemed to get on top, a wicket would fall, and two wickets by Tom Kentish brought the score to 194 for 9. Williams and Willett hung on bravely, but with only one run separating the sides, Davis had Williams caught and Windward Islands had won.

FIRST ONE-DAY INTERNATIONAL: WEST INDIES v. INDIA

A damp pitch prevented a punctual start and the match was reduced to 39 overs. There were also earth tremors in the early afternoon, but nothing could distract the West Indies who won even more comfortably than the score suggests.

Haynes and Greenidge scored at a brisk rate, Greenidge hitting four fours and four sixes as he showed his true ability for the first time in the season. Kapil Dev's captaincy had

Larry Gomes. Quiet, unassuming, a vital part of the West Indian side. He was greatly missed by Trinidad in the early part of the season. (Patrick Eagar)

FIRST ONE-DAY INTERNATIONAL: WEST INDIES v. INDIA
8 March 1983 at Port of Spain, Trinidad

WEST INDIES				INDIA			
C.G. Greenidge	c Madan Lal, b Maninder Singh		66	S.M. Gavaskar	c Roberts, b Garner		25
D.L. Haynes	c Yashpal Sharma, b Kapil Dev		97	A.D. Gaekwad	b Gomes		22
I.V.A. Richards	c Gaekwad, b Amarnath		32	M.B. Amarnath	run out		27
A.L. Logie	not out		6	D.B. Vengsarkar	c Logie, b Roberts		27
C.H. Lloyd†	c Kirmani, b Kapil Dev		3	R.N. Kapil Dev†	lbw, b Roberts		0
H.A. Gomes				Yashpal Sharma	c Haynes, b Gomes		2
P.J. Dujon*				A. Malhotra	c Holding, b Gomes		21
M.D. Marshall				S.M.H. Kirmani*	not out		13
A.M.E. Roberts				S. Madan Lal	not out		13
M.A. Holding				Maninder Singh			
J. Garner				S. Venkataraghavan			
Extras	b 4, lb 5, w 1, nb 1		11	Extras	b 1, lb 3, w 5, nb 4		13
(38.5 overs)	(for 4 wickets)		215	(39 overs)	(for 7 wickets)		163

	O	M	R	W		O	M	R	W
Kapil Dev	6.5	—	21	2	Holding	5	1	8	—
Madan Lal	7	—	34	—	Roberts	7	2	27	2
Venkataraghavan	9	—	48	—	Marshall	8	—	25	—
Amarnath	7	—	39	1	Garner	9	1	39	1
Maninder Singh	9	—	62	1	Gomes	9	—	50	3
					Logie	1	—	1	—

FALL OF WICKETS
1- 125, 2- 198, 3- 207, 4- 215

FALL OF WICKETS
1- 56, 2- 59, 3- 110, 4- 110, 5- 115, 6- 117, 7- 140

West Indies won by 52 runs

little to commend it, and the Indian batting was somnolent in the face of the required asking rate of five and a half runs an over.

With nearly half their overs gone, India were 58 for 1, but Lloyd allowed Gomes nine overs when three would have sufficed and the Indian batsmen hit 50 runs from them so at least giving the innings some respectability.

SECOND TEST MATCH: WEST INDIES v. INDIA

Only fifty minutes play were possible on the first day, but that was long enough for West Indies to cause India grave problems after Lloyd had asked them to bat.

Gavaskar pushed forward to Holding and went for a quick single, but Holding's reactions were quicker and Gaekwad was run out without facing a ball. In Holding's next over, a short ball reared and swung away to take the edge of Gavaskar's bat. Amarnath and Vengsarkar struggled on until the latter fell to Marshall. Yashpal Sharma batted with Amarnath until rain brought the close, 44 for 3, but Yashpal was concussed by the penultimate ball of the day and it was Shastri who resumed with Amarnath on the second morning.

These two batted right through the first session, but ten minutes after lunch, Amarnath was brilliantly taken at slip, and the rot began. Marshall bowled quickly and accurately and varied his line of attack. 131 for 4 became 175 all out, and by the end of the day, West Indies were 104 for 3, having recovered from the loss of Greenidge, Haynes and Richards with only one run scored.

Gomes and Lloyd continued the recovery on the third day.

Gomes and Greenidge confer (David Cannon)

SECOND TEST MATCH: WEST INDIES v. INDIA
11, 12, 13, 15 and 16 March 1983 at Port-of-Spain, Trinidad

INDIA

	FIRST INNINGS		SECOND INNINGS	
S.M. Gavaskar	c Dujon, b Holding	1	c Dujon, b Garner	32
A.D. Gaekwad	run out	0	c sub (Bacchus), b Gomes	35
D.B. Vengsarkar	c Holding, b Marshall	7	(4) c Dujon, b Roberts	45
M.B. Amarnath	c Lloyd, b Roberts	58	(3) lbw, b Richards	117
Yashpal Sharma	not out	11	b Roberts	50
R.J. Shastri	c Gomes, b Marshall	42	lbw, b Holding	9
R.N. Kapil Dev†	c Haynes, b Marshall	13	not out	100
S.M.H. Kirmani*	b Roberts	7	run out	30
B.S. Sandhu	c Richards, b Marshall	11	not out	0
S. Venkataraghavan	c Richards, b Roberts	1		
Maninder Singh	c Dujon, b Marshall	1		
Extras	b 5, lb 1, w 3, nb 14	23	b 10, lb 20, nb 21	51
		175	(for 7 wkts)	469

	O	M	R	W	O	M	R	W
Holding	13	2	24	1	31	2	104	1
Roberts	22	5	72	3	25	3	100	2
Marshall	19.2	5	37	5	27.1	8	74	—
Garner	10	5	17	—	30	7	81	1
Gomes	2	1	2	—	19	7	45	1
Richards					7	4	14	1

WEST INDIES

	FIRST INNINGS	
C.G. Greenidge	b Sandhu	0
D.L. Haynes	c Kirmani, b Sandhu	0
I.V.A. Richards	c Kirmani, b Dev	1
H.A. Gomes	c Gavaskar, b Venkat	123
C.H. Lloyd†	st Kirmani, b Shastri	143
A.L. Logie	c Dev, b Venkat	13
P.J. Dujon*	lbw, b Dev	31
M.D. Marshall	lbw, b Shastri	14
A.M.E. Roberts	b Dev	9
M.A. Holding	c Vengsarkar, b Maninder	24
J. Garner	not out	21
Extras	b 4, lb 7, w 1, nb 3	15
		394

	O	M	R	W
Kapil Dev	31	6	91	3
Sandhu	19	2	69	2
Venkataraghavan	41	13	97	2
Shastri	21	2	71	2
Maninder Singh	26.3	7	51	1

FALL OF WICKETS
1- 1, 2- 5, 3- 28, 4- 131, 5- 146, 6- 147, 7- 164, 8- 166, 9- 171
1- 63, 2- 132, 3- 206, 4- 312, 5- 325, 6- 329, 7- 463

FALL OF WICKETS
1- 0, 2- 0, 3- 1, 4- 238, 5- 255, 6- 316, 7- 324, 8- 340, 9- 346

Umpires: Sadiq Mohammad and S. Parris

Match drawn

Their stand realised 237 for the fourth wicket, but they never totally dominated the Indian bowling which was of a high standard. Venkataraghavan bowled as well as he has ever done in a Test match and troubled Gomes in particular so that neither batsman was able to force the pace. Clive Lloyd, visibly tiring, eventually became more aggressive, and, in swinging at a wild delivery from Shastri, he overbalanced and was stumped on the leg side.

Gomes' century was his first Test century in front of his home crowd, but when he was caught at slip of Venkataraghavan he had batted for nearly seven and three quarter hours.

West Indies closed on 335 for 7 and in the second over of the fourth morning, Kapil Dev knocked back Roberts' middle stump to record his two hundredth Test wicket. West Indies were finally out for 394, and India faced a daunting task of surviving for nearly two days and scoring 219 to avoid an innings defeat.

They were saved by Mohinder Amarnath who scored his fourth century in eight Tests since his triumphant return to the Indian side. His new found confidence and courage were much in evidence as he seemed completely undisturbed by blows on the body and helmet. Surprisingly, he succumbed to Richards' off-spin and when Yashpal and Shastri quickly followed him India were still in some danger, but Kapil Dev hit about him with vigour and reached a fine hundred with three sixes and thirteen fours.

Joel Garner who returned from a record breaking season in Australia struggled to find the same form in the West Indies. (Adrian Murrell)

Mohinder Amarnath. By far the most successful and tenacious batsmen in the Indian touring team. (Patrick Eagar)

18, 19, 20 and 21 March 1983

at St George's, Grenada

Indians 182 (N. Phillip 5 for 56) and 287 (R.J. Shastri 73, Yashpal Sharma 57, W.W. Davis 5 for 84)
Windward Islands 217 (W.N. Slack 97) and 123 (R.J. Shastri 5 for 22)

Indians won by 129 runs

The Indian tourists recovered from a bad first day to beat Windward Islands with some ease. Norbert Phillip, with three victims in two consecutive overs, destroyed the Indian middle order and it was only a brave ninth wicket stand of 30 between Sivaramakrishnan and reserve wicket-keeper Kiren More that gave India any substance at all.

Wilf Slack batted well for the home side, but the Indian spinners restricted the lead to 35, and the tourists were right back in the game. Shastri batted well as opener in place of the injured Gavaskar until he became one of Davis' five victims. Davis had already set up a Shell Shield record with 33 wickets.

Set to make 253, Windward Islands collapsed before the spin of left-arm Shastri, ably supported by the leg-breaks of young Sivaramakrishnan.

19, 20, 21 and 22 March 1983

at Port of Spain, Trinidad

Barbados 212 (T.R.O. Payne 55, R. Nanan 4 for 46) and 204 (G. Mahabir 6 for 68)
Trinidad and Tobago 153 and 244 (H.A. Gomes 67, H.L. Alleyne 6 for 63)

Barbados won by 19 runs

The Shell Shield came to an end with a tensely fought match between deposed champions, Barbados, and Trinidad and Tobago, who just avoided the wooden spoon. Ganesh Mahabir had bowled Trinidad back into the match after they had trailed by 59 runs on the first innings.

Set to make 264, Trinidad, inspired by skipper 'Larry' Gomes, reached 212 for 5, but Hartley Alleyne finally won the match for Barbados with some fierce bowling. Unfortunately, Barbados' win and Alleyne's bowling were overshadowed by controversy as the pace-man was warned twice on the third day for throwing.

Final Table

	P	W	L	D	Pts
Guyana (4)	5	4	–	1	68
Windward Islands (2)	5	3	1	1	61
Barbados (1)	5	3	1	1	56
Leeward Islands (5)	5	1	3	1	29
Trinidad and Tobago (6)	5	–	3	2	13
Jamaica (3)	5	–	3	2	12

24, 25, 26 and 27 March 1983

at Georgetown

Indians 286 for 3 (M.B. Amarnath 121, R.J. Shastri 75)
Guyana 119 for 6 (T.R. Etwaroo 53)

Match drawn

The first two days were lost to rain, and then the match was reduced to a limited one-innings contest. Amarnath, captaining India, hit a splendid century, but the rain returned.

SECOND ONE-DAY INTERNATIONAL: WEST INDIES *v.* INDIA

In the third limited-over meeting between the two countries, India recorded their first victory and made the highest score hit against the West Indies in a limited-over international.

The Indian innings was founded on a splendid knock by Gavaskar who showed a welcome return to form. He reached 50 in the seventeenth over and shared an opening stand of 93 with Shastri.

Kapil Dev promoted himself to number four and launched a blistering attack on the bowling, hitting three sixes and seven fours in an innings which lasted only 38 balls.

West Indies were handicapped when Marshall was unable to bowl with a pulled groin muscle, and they contributed to their own downfall when Holding dropped Kapil Dev on 37.

India were equally handicapped when Kapil Dev had to leave the field after brilliantly accounting for Greenidge

ABOVE: *Malcolm Marshall. His pace and his line, particularly when bowling round the wicket, troubled the Indians throughout the series. (Adrian Murrell)*

caught and bowled. Richards was at his mightiest, and the score was 98 for 3 in 17 overs before he swung once too often at Madan Lal and was bowled. Bacchus and Dujon both batted well and maintained a good rate of scoring, but they lacked the necessary support and India achieved a famous victory.

THIRD TEST MATCH: WEST INDIES *v.* INDIA

The third Test match was totally ruined by rain. There was no play whatsoever on the second and fourth days, and play did not begin until after lunch on the third day.

Clive Lloyd won the toss and chose to bat first, the first time in the series that they had done so. Greenidge and Haynes began with a stand of 89, but the only impressive batting on the first day came from Richards who finished on 97 not out with the West Indian score at 259 for 5. Richards completed his century on the Sunday, Good Friday having been a rest day and Saturday lost to the weather.

Lloyd and Dujon gave the innings the belligerence that it had lacked, and Dujon provided Venkataraghavan with the one hundred and fiftieth wicket of his long and fragmented

SECOND ONE-DAY INTERNATIONAL: WEST INDIES v. INDIA
29 March 1983 at Albion, Berbice, Guyana

INDIA		
S.M. Gavaskar	run out	90
R.J. Shastri	c Dujon, b Marshall	30
M.B. Amarnath	b Richards	30
R.N. Kapil Dev†	b Roberts	72
Yashpal Sharma	c Greenidge, b Davis	23
D.B. Vengsarkar	not out	18
A. Malhotra	not out	1
S.M.H. Kirmani*		
B.S. Sandhu		
S. Madan Lal		
S. Venkataraghavan		
Extras	b 1, lb 9, w 4, nb 4	18
(47 overs)	(for 5 wickets)	282

WEST INDIES		
C.G. Greenidge	c and b Kapil Dev	16
D.L. Haynes	lbw, b Sandhu	2
I.V.A. Richards	b Madan Lal	64
C.H. Lloyd†	c Amarnath, b Madan Lal	8
S.F.A. Bacchus	c Sharma, b Shastri	52
H.A. Gomes	c Kapil Dev, b Shastri	26
P.J. Dujon*	not out	53
M.D. Marshall	c Sandhu, b Shastri	5
A.M.E. Roberts	b Kapil Dev	12
M.A. Holding	c Malhotra, b Sandhu	2
W.W. Davis	not out	7
Extras	lb 6, w 1, nb 1	8
(47 overs)	(for 9 wickets)	255

	O	M	R	W
Holding	7	—	49	—
Roberts	9	—	44	1
Davis	8	—	40	1
Marshall	7	—	23	1
Gomes	10	—	64	—
Richards	6	—	44	1

	O	M	R	W
Shastri	8	—	48	3
Venkataraghavan	10	—	63	—
Madan Lal	9	—	65	2
Kapil Dev	10	—	33	2
Sandhu	10	—	38	2

FALL OF WICKETS
1- 93, 2- 152, 3- 224, 4- 246, 5- 277

FALL OF WICKETS
1- 6, 2- 22, 3- 62, 4- 98, 5- 154, 6- 181, 7- 192, 8- 228, 9- 232

India won by 27 runs

est career. As West Indies moved to a total which made hem immune from defeat, one of the features of the Indian outcricket was the fine wicket-keeping of Kirmani.

The next event in which India could take pride was the batting of Gavaskar. Dropped at slip by Greenidge off Marshall when 44, Gavaskar hit a six and seventeen fours in his innings of 147. It was his twenty-seventh Test century and left him second only to Sir Donald Bradman with his 29.

THIRD TEST MATCH: WEST INDIES v. INDIA
31 March, 2, 3, 4 and 5 April 1983 at Bourda Oval, Georgetown, Guyana

WEST INDIES	FIRST INNINGS	
C.G. Greenidge	c Kirmani, b Maninder	70
D.L. Haynes	c Sharma, b Venkataraghavan	46
I.V.A. Richards	c Venkataraghavan, b Sandhu	109
H.A. Gomes	c Gaekwad, b Kapil Dev	36
M.A. Holding	run out	0
A.L. Logie	c Kirmani, b Sandhu	0
C.H. Lloyd†	c Kirmani, b Shastri	81
P.J. Dujon*	c and b Venkataraghavan	47
M.D. Marshall	lbw, b Kapil Dev	27
A.M.E. Roberts	c Gavaskar, b Sandhu	36
J. Garner	not out	1
Extras	b 1, lb 14, w 1, nb 1	17
		470

INDIA	FIRST INNINGS	
S.M. Gavaskar	not out	147
A.D. Gaekwad	c Dujon, b Holding	8
M.B. Amarnath	c Richards, b Marshall	13
D.B. Vengsarkar	c Richards, b Garner	62
Yashpal Sharma	not out	35
R.J. Shastri		
R.N. Kapil Dev†		
S.M.H. Kirmani*		
B.S. Sandhu		
S. Venkataraghavan		
Maninder Singh		
Extras	b 1, lb 3, nb 15	19
	(for 3 wickets)	284

	O	M	R	W
Kapil Dev	30	7	68	2
Sandhu	25.4	5	87	3
Shastri	22	3	84	1
Maninder Singh	27	3	90	1
Venkataraghavan	34	2	124	2

	O	M	R	W
Roberts	14	2	38	—
Holding	16	1	72	1
Garner	17	4	57	1
Marshall	13	2	39	1
Gomes	14	5	35	—
Richards	4	—	24	—

FALL OF WICKETS
1- 89, 2- 157, 3- 252, 4- 253, 5- 256, 6- 299, 7- 387, 8- 417, 9- 460

FALL OF WICKETS
1- 24, 2- 68, 3- 180

Umpires: D. Archer and D. Narine

Match drawn

Indians in West Indies 1983
First-Class Matches

BATTING

BATTING	v. Jamaica (Kingston) 17-20 February	First Test Match (Kingston) 23-28 February	v. Trinidad and Tobago (Pointe-à-Pierre) 3-5 March	Second Test Match (Port of Spain) 11-16 March	v. Windward Islands (Grenada) 18-21 March	v. Guyana (Georgetown) 24-27 March	Third Test Match (Georgetown) 31 March-5 April	v. Barbados (Bridgetown) 9-12 April	Fourth Test Match (Bridgetown) 15-20 April	v. Leeward Islands (Brasseterre) 22-24 April	Fifth Test Match (Antigua) 28 April-3 May
A. D. Gaekwad	12 89	1 23	81 —	0 35		5 —	8 —	4 28	3 55	0 0	3 72
J. Arun Lal	1 77		0 —		21 5			5 31		29 1*	
M. B. Amarnath	3 82	29 40	114 —	58 117		121 —	13 —	61 101*	91 80		54 116
D. B. Vengsarkar	42 82	30 20		7 45	4 40	34* —	62 —		15 6	55 —	94 0
Yashpal Sharma	17 24	63 24		11* 50	23 57		35* —	59 11	24 12	45 —	3 20
R. J. Shastri	35 3*	1 25*	— —	42 9	17 73	75 —		58 0	29 19		102 9*
R. N. Kapil Dev	23 —	5 12		13 100*	2 36				0 26		98 0*
S. M. H. Kirmani	0 1*	5 10	74 —	7 30				4 22	11 33		2 —
L. Sivaramakrishnan	21* —				32 6			4 0		29 —	17 —
B. S. Sandhu	13 6	68 0		11 0*					8* 4		
S. Venkataraghavan	0 —	0 0		1 —	12 0				5 0*	14 —	0 —
S. M. Gavaskar		20 0	5 —	1 32		36* —	147* —		2 19		18 1
Maninder Singh		3* 2	14 —	1 —				6* 1*		13* —	
A. Malhotra			59 —		21 12			0 55		9 1*	
S. Madan Lal			45 —		4 37*			13 53	6 0	97 —	35* —
K. More			1* —		23* 11					31 —	
Gursharran Singh			0 —		4 0			15 89		15 —	
Byes	1 6	1 2		5 10	7		1	6	5	5	14 11
Leg-byes	1 6	15 4	(10)	1 20	3	4	3	3 2	1 2	8 4	7 8
Wides	4 1	1		3		1		3		4	1
No-balls	12 18	10 11		14 21	12 7	10	15	11 4	14 16	8	9 10
Total	185 395	251 174	403	175 469	182 287	286	284	246 403	209 277	362 6	457 247
Wickets	10 6	10 10	9†	10 7	10 10	3	3	10 9	10 10	10	10 5
Result	D	L	W	D	W	D[A]	D	D	L	W	D

Catches
14 – S. M. H. Kirmani (ct 12/st 2)
11 – S. Venkataraghavan
10 – K. More (ct 5/st 5)
8 – Yashpal Sharma
7 – Gursharran Singh
6 – M. B. Amarnath, R. N. Kapil Dev and subs.
5 – J. Arun Lal
4 – D. B. Vengsarkar, S. M. Gavaskar and A. D. Gaekwad
3 – S. Madan Lal and Maninder Singh
2 – R. J. Shastri and B. S. Sandhu
1 – L. Sivaramakrishnan

A The match v. Guyana was reduced to a limited-time contest and lost its first-class status. It is not included in the final statistics.

† R. J. Shastri absent hurt.

BOWLING

BOWLING	R. N. Kapil Dev	B. S. Sandhu	M. B. Amarnath	R. J. Shastri	S. Venkataraghavan	L. Sivaramakrishnan	A. D. Gaekwad	Maninder Singh	S. Madan Lal
v. Jamaica (Kingston) 17-20 February	18-2-57-3 / 8-3-11-2	16-5-39-1 / 8-2-25-1	10-2-26-4 / 3-1-10-0	30-4-82-0 / 7-3-11-1	34.5-7-75-2 / 5-2-8-0	3-1-5-0	1-0-2-0		
First Test Match (Kingston) 23-28 February	25.3-6-45-4 / 13-0-73-4	11-4-30-0 / 3-0-22-0	2.2-0-34-2	24-8-43-4	25-3-66-1 / 7-0-39-0			31-6-51-0	
v. Trinidad and Tobago (Pointe-à-Pierre) 3-5 March			11-2-42-1 / 3-0-16-0				16-2-48-2 / 18-4-32-1	21-7-48-5 / 19.2-2-47-7	14.1-0-4- / 4-1-28-1
Second Test Match (Port of Spain) 11-16 March	31-6-91-3	19-2-69-2		21-2-71-2	41-13-97-2			26.3-7-51-1	
v. Windward Islands (St. George's, Grenada) 18-21 March	7-3-18-2 / 10-2-29-1			25-5-47-1 / 18.3-3-22-5	20.1-5-34-3 / 14-6-16-1	20-1-64-2 / 11-2-34-2			11-0-47-1 / 9-1-18-1
v. Guyana (Georgetown) 24-27 March		8-1-44-1		4-2-11-1	5-1-14-2		1-0-2-0		9-0-37-1
Third Test Match (Georgetown) 31 March-5 April	30-7-68-2	25.4-5-87-3		22-3-84-1	34-2-124-2			27-3-90-1	
v. Barbados (Bridgetown) 9-12 April			6-3-14-0	28-5-100-1		31-7-105-3	22-2-94-2	41.5-6-121-2	24-1-71-
Fourth Test Match (Bridgetown) 15-20 April	32.3-7-76-3	5-1-21-0		50-13-133-2	43-6-146-3		1-1-0-0		27-2-96-
v. Leeward Islands (Brasseterre) 22-24 April			23-11-44-1	4.2-2-5-4 / 28-3-97-2	4-1-9-1		23-8-56-2		14-0-68- / 7.1-2-27-
Fifth Test Match (St. John's, Antigua) 28 April-3 May	22-6-71-1			46.4-5-141-1	36-1-114-2	25-1-95-0	1-0-3-0		35-7-105
Total	197-42-539-25 av. 21.56	87.4-19-293-7 av. 41.85	35.2-8-142-7 av. 20.28	272.1-51-734-18 av. 40.77	287.2-58-768-21 av. 36.57	118-15-400-9 av. 44.44	63-10-188-6 av. 31.33	189.4-39-464-18 av. 25.77	145.2-14-504-20 av. 25.20

a Not first-class. Limited-time.   b C. G. Greenidge retired not out

Inns	NOs	Runs	HS	Av
16	—	414	89	25.87
9	1	170	77	21.25
14	1	959	121	73.76
14	—	502	94	35.85
16	2	478	63	34.14
14	3	422	102	38.36
11	1	315	100*	31.50
12	1	199	74	18.09
7	1	109	32	18.16
8	2	110	68	18.33
10	1	32	14	3.55
10	1	245	147*	27.22
7	4	40	14	13.33
7	1	157	59	26.16
9	2	290	97	41.42
4	2	66	31	33.00
6	—	123	89	20.50

ABOVE: *Andy Roberts. His 24 wickets in the Test series was a positive answer to those who thought his Test career was at an end.* (*Patrick Eagar*)

BELOW: *Michael Holding. He struggled against injury, but he was still a force throughout the Test series.* (*George Herringshaw*)

S. M. H. Kirmani	Yashpal Sharma	Byes	Leg-byes	Wides	No-balls	Total	Wkts
		4	6		10	306	10
			6			71	4
		1	8		10	254	10
			5			173	6
		2	3		6	193	10
			(18)			141	10
		4	7	1	3	394	10
		3	3		1	217	10
		1			3	123	10
			6		5	119	6a
		1	14	1	1	470	10
	7-2-22-0	4	11			542	10
		1	11		2	486	10
0-0-0-0					1	1	0
	9-1-26-1		1		3	103	10
	5-1-14-0	4	10		3	264	10
	1-0-6-1	6	5		4	550	9b
0-0	22-4-						
0-0	68-2						
—	av. 34.00						

Barbados 1983
First Class Matches

BATTING

	v. Leeward Islands (Bridgetown) 21-24 January		v. Jamaica (Kingston) 28-31 January		v. Guyana (Bridgetown) 4-7 February		v. Windward Islands (St. Vincent) 11-14 February		v. Trinidad and Tobago (Port of Spain) 19-22 March		v. Indians (Bridgetown) 9-12 April		Inns	NOs	Runs	HS	Av
C. G. Greenidge	8	0	38	20*	3	15	6	15	44	6	237	—	11	1	392	237	39.20
D. L. Haynes	97	38	50	18	79	9	27	18	0	31	25	—	11	—	392	97	35.63
C. A. Best	14	4	84	17*	47	12	20	37	16	16	6	—	11	1	273	84	27.30
T. R. O. Payne	71	0	123	—	107	37*	107*	2	55	15	26	—	10	2	543	123	67.87
L. N. Reifer	0	0	27	—	0	32			1	36			7	—	96	36	13.71
R. L. Skeete	17	48	3	—	0	15*	15	0	2	14			9	1	114	48	14.25
M. D. Marshall	3	71	35	—	34	—	2	36	0	28			8	—	209	71	26.12
G. L. Linton	9	1	43*	—	66	—	6	12	45	3	66	—	9	1	251	66	31.37
N. Phillips	11	18	7	—	5	—	2	25			51	—	7	—	119	51	17.00
H. L. Alleyne	0	24	—	—					0	0*	15*	—	5	2	39	24	13.00
W. W. Daniel	0*	28*	4*	—			1	1*	42	29			7	4	105	42	35.00
N. Broomes					11*	—	7	18					3	1	36	18	18.00
R. Estwick			19	—			0*	18			11	—	4	1	48	19	16.00
G. N. Reifer							26	10			32	—	3	—	68	32	22.66
M. C. Worrell									41	—			1	—	41	41	41.00
J. Garner									17	—			1	—	17	17	17.00
Byes		1	2		4	3	7	3		4							
Leg-byes	3	7	8		6	3	4	6	7	8	11						
Wides	1	2	1		6	1											
No-balls	8	14	10		16	5	13	13									
Total	242	256	435	55	403	132	243	196	212	204	542						
Wickets	10	10	8	1	10	4	10	10	10	10	10						
Result	W		W		D		L		W		D						

Catches

23 – R. L. Skeete (ct 21/st 2)
9 – C. A. Best
6 – M. C. Worrell and C. G. Greenidge
5 – D. L. Haynes and T. R. O. Payne
4 – M. D. Marshall and L. N. Reifer
3 – J. Garner and G. L. Linton
2 – G. N. Reifer and N. Phillips
1 – N. Broomes, H. L. Alleyne and W. W. Daniel

BOWLING

	M. D. Marshall	H. L. Alleyne	W. W. Daniel	G. L. Linton	N. Phillips	R. Estwick	N. Broomes	J. Garner
v. Leeward Islands (Bridgetown) 21-24 January	16-2-57-1	12-2-43-0	13.1-2-55-7	13-3-36-1	16-4-47-1			
	17-5-36-0	8-1-35-0	10-2-33-5	3.5-0-24-2	17-5-45-2			
v. Jamaica (Kingston) 28-31 January	17.2-4-49-4	13-3-46-4	14-0-55-1	8-1-40-0	9-4-26-1			
	18-4-46-3	13.2-3-37-3	14.2-2-53-2	21-5-61-1	15-1-43-1			
v. Guyana (Bridgetown) 4-7 February	15-3-51-2			9.4-2-35-5	14-3-53-1	4-0-31-1	20-6-50-0	
	26.4-5-86-2			14-1-81-1	16-0-74-2	19-0-89-4	22-3-73-1	
v. Windward Islands (St. Vincent) 11-14 February	30-9-68-1		26-3-73-4	19-2-50-1	25-6-53-3		15.5-5-23-1	
	13-0-58-3		7-0-35-0		7.5-0-35-2			
v. Trinidad and Tobago (Port of Spain) 19-22 March	13.4-2-22-2	6-0-21-2	10-0-62-3	1-0-7-0		8-0-29-3		
	30-10-52-2	28-11-63-6	15-2-43-0	12-5-25-0		7-3-23-1		
v. Indians (Bridgetown) 9-12 April		19-4-47-2		10-3-33-2	13-3-50-3	14-4-47-0		16.1-3-52-3
		24-1-106-1		16-3-52-2	13-2-41-1	16-4-46-0		31-4-127-5
	196.4-44-525-20	123.2-25-398-18	109.3-11-409-22	127.3-25-444-15	145.5-28-467-17	68-11-265-9	57.5-14-146-2	47.1-7-179-8
	av. 26.25	*av.* 22.11	*av.* 18.59	*av.* 29.60	*av.* 27.47	*av.* 29.44	*av.* 73.00	*av.* 22.37

THIRD ONE-DAY INTERNATIONAL: WEST INDIES v. INDIA

7 April 1983 at St George's, Grenada

INDIA			
S.M. Gavaskar	c Richards, b Roberts		3
R.J. Shastri	c Dujon, b Marshall		17
M.B. Amarnath	b Gomes		11
D.B. Vengsarkar	c Richards, b Gomes		54
A. Malhotra	c Richards, b Gomes		7
Yashpal Sharma	b Holding		25
R.N. Kapil Dev†	lbw, b Roberts		1
S. Madan Lal	b Gomes		6
S.M.H. Kirmani*	run out		3
B.S. Sandhu	not out		16
S. Venkataraghavan	b Holding		3
Extras	b 5, lb 7, w 5, nb 3		20
(44.4 overs)			166

WEST INDIES			
C.G. Greenidge	c Sandhu, b Shastri		64
D.L. Haynes	c Venkataraghavan, b Amarnath		19
I.V.A. Richards	c Shastri, b Venkataraghavan		28
S.F.A. Bacchus	not out		26
P.J. Dujon*	not out		20
H.A. Gomes			
C.H. Lloyd†			
M.D. Marshall			
A.M.E. Roberts			
M.A. Holding			
J. Garner			
Extras			10
(40.2 overs)	(for 3 wickets)		167

	O	M	R	W
Holding	8.4	2	15	2
Roberts	9	—	38	2
Garner	10	1	30	—
Marshall	7	2	25	1
Gomes	10	—	38	4

	O	M	R	W
Kapil Dev	6	2	21	—
Sandhu	8	2	30	—
Madan Lal	7	1	37	—
Amarnath	4	—	23	1
Venkataraghavan	8	—	24	1
Shastri	5	1	10	1
Yashpal Sharma	2.2	—	12	—

FALL OF WICKETS
1- 9, 2- 36, 3- 47, 4- 74, 5- 109, 6- 114, 7- 127,
8- 138, 9- 153

FALL OF WICKETS
1- 61, 2- 106, 3- 132

West Indies won by 7 wickets

THIRD ONE-DAY INTERNATIONAL: WEST INDIES v. INDIA

Once more Kapil Dev elected to bat first on winning the toss, but this time without the success that India had enjoyed in the second one-day international. The West Indian bowlers extracted both lift and movement from the pitch, and India struggled from the moment that they lost Gavaskar at 9.

Only Vengsarkar, with three fours and two sixes in his 54, showed any competence in dealing with the West Indian pacemen, but he became one of Gomes' four victims. The off-break bowler took 4 for 38 in his ten overs, a best performance in limited-over international cricket.

Greenidge was in belligerent mood from the start and, although Richards fell to Venkataraghavan, West Indies had no difficulty in reaching the target of 167 with time to spare.

9, 10, 11 and 12 April 1983

at Bridgetown

Indians 246 (M.B. Amarnath 61, Yashpal Sharma 59, R.J. Shastri 58) and 403 for 9 (M.B. Amarnath 101 not out, Gursharran Singh 89, A. Malhotra 53, J. Garner 5 for 127)
Barbados 542 (C.G. Greenidge 237, G.L. Linton 66, N.A. Phillips 51)

Match drawn

The Indians were bowled out on the first day for 246 which, as they had lost Gaekwad, Arun Lal and Malhotra for 12, was more than had looked possible in the morning. They owed much to Amarnath and Yashpal Sharma who added 128 for the fourth wicket.

Barbados began tentatively, subdued by the Indian spinners, but, on the third day, Greenidge, batting at number four, routed the Indian bowling and reached his first double century in the West Indies. He hit three sixes and twenty-two fours in an innings which lasted 499 minutes. He shared a fifth wicket stand of 196 with George Linton and a sixth wicket stand of 112 with Mike Worrell, the wicket-keeper. Phillips hit 51 off 40 deliveries.

Batting again with a deficit of 296 on the first innings, India could only bat for a draw, and this was accomplished with Mohinder Amarnath again the Indian hero.

G.N. Reifer	D.L. Haynes		Byes	Leg-byes	Wides	No-balls	Total	Wkts
			3	3	1	8	253	10
				4	1	11	189	10
			2	1	5	10	234	10
			4	5	1	5	255	10
			2	5	1	2	230	10
			5		6	6	420	10
			15	7		18	307	10
				4	2		134	6
			1	1		10	153	10
			5	6	7	20	244	10
			3	3		11	246	10
2-0-8-0	2-0-11-0		6	2		4	403	9
2-0-	2-0-							
8-0	11-0							
—	—							

Guyana 1983
First Class Matches

BATTING	WI (Dominica) 21-24 Jan		Leeward (Nevis) 28-30 Jan		Barbados (Bridgetown) 4-7 Feb		Trinidad (Berbice) 10-13 Feb		Jamaica (Georgetown) 3-5 Mar		Indians (Georgetown) 24-27 Mar		Inns	NOs	Runs	HS	Av
A. A. Lyte	56	23	94	100	112	53	14	5*	36	—	4	—	9	1	493	112	61.62
T. R. Etwaroo	37	46	4	0	0	2					53	—	6	—	89	46	14.83
M. A. Lynch	1	11	6	2	47	75	4	3*	20	—			9	1	169	75	21.12
S. F. A. Bacchus	1	143	25	56	2	37	28	—	57	—	11	—	8	—	349	143	43.62
C. H. Lloyd	28	1	12	40*	27	104	136	—	64	—			8	1	412	136	58.85
M. R. Pydanna	18	34	5	2	11	72*	0	1	28	—	—	—	9	1	171	72*	21.37
R. A. Harper	4	16	20	21	2	1	29	—	0	—	10*	—	8	—	93	29	11.62
D. I. Kallicharran	0	4	20	69	4	57	44	—	50*	—	7	—	8	1	248	69	35.42
C. Butts	7	13	7	0	4	0	2*	—	0*	—			8	2	33	13	5.50
L. A. Lambert	2*	9*	4*	4	9	1	14	—	—	—			7	3	43	14	10.75
R. F. Joseph	4	0			2*	1							4	1	7	4	2.33
G. Charles			0	10			11*	—	13	—			4	1	34	13	11.33
R. C. Fredericks							103	—	217	—			2	—	320	217	160.00
Timur Mohammed											8	—					
W. White											15	—					
Kamal Singh											0*	—					
Byes	3	21			3	2	4		16								
Leg-byes	1	11	12	8	5	5	6		10		6						
Wides						1	6										
No-balls			2	4	3		2	6			6	5					
Total	162	334	213	318	230	420	395	9	517		119						
Wickets	10	10	10	10	10	10	9	0	8		6						
Result	W		W		D		W		W		D[A]						

Catches
12 – M. R. Pydanna (ct 9/st 3)
9 – R. A. Harper
8 – D. I. Kallicharran
7 – S. F. A. Bacchus and A. A. Lyte
4 – L. A. Lambert, M. A. Lynch and subs. (W. White)
3 – C. H. Lloyd and G. Charles
2 – C. Butts
1 – R. C. Fredericks and sub. (T. R. Etwaroo)

A This match was time-limited, one innings, and is not first-class. It is not included in the final statistics.

BOWLING	L. A. Lambert	R. F. Joseph	R. A. Harper	C. Butts	D. I. Kallicharran	G. Charles	M. A. Lynch	Kamal Singh
v. Windward Islands (Dominica) 21-24 January	9-1-26-1	2-0-11-0	35-10-62-2	47.3-15-81-5	22-7-60-2			
	8-1-22-2	7-3-8-1	24-10-33-4	20-7-30-2	11-3-23-0			
v. Leeward Islands (Nevis) 28-30 January	7-3-18-2		6-3-11-0	12.5-4-23-5	10-2-30-1	3-1-4-1		
	12-3-39-1		34-6-95-5	24.2-8-62-3	25-9-49-1	8-5-9-0		
v. Barbados (Bridgetown) 4-7 February	28-5-103-3	18-4-58-2	41.5-11-89-4	25-7-49-0	22-8-65-1		3-1-7-0	
	6-0-27-2	5-1-12-0	18-4-43-1	12-2-34-1			1-0-4-0	
v. Trinidad (Berbice) 10-13 February	23.3-7-59-7		12-1-38-0	25-6-56-2	14-3-31-0	10-1-31-1	6-1-16-0	
	6.5-0-16-2		14-3-30-2	15-2-51-1	10-3-23-2	3-0-15-0	3-1-5-0	
v. Jamaica (Georgetown) 3-5 March	5-0-15-0		17-7-29-3	10-5-18-1	21.5-60-6	4-0-14-0		
	7-1-34-0		21-4-62-2	18-3-54-5	26-4-86-3	2-0-12-0		
v. Indians (Georgetown) 24-27 March	15.2-3-44-1		26-3-61-0	20-3-75-1	9-0-45-0			8-1-46-0
	112.2-21–	32-8–	222.5-59–	209.4-59–	161.5-42–	30-7–	13-3–	
	359-20	89-3	492-23	458-25	427-16	85-2	32-0	—
	av. 17.95	av. 29.66	av. 21.39	av. 18.32	av. 26.68	av. 42.50	—	

a S. Jumadeen absent hurt   b Not first class. One innings limited time

FOURTH TEST MATCH: WEST INDIES v. INDIA
15, 16, 17, 19 and 20 April 1983 at Kensington Oval, Bridgetown, Barbados

INDIA

	FIRST INNINGS		SECOND INNINGS	
S.M. Gavaskar	c Dujon, b Holding	2	c Roberts, b Garner	19
A.D. Gaekwad	c Marshall, b Roberts	3	b Holding	55
M.B. Amarnath	c Dujon, b Marshall	91	c Dujon, b Roberts	80
D.B. Vengsarkar	c Marshall, b Holding	15	lbw, b Holding	6
Yashpal Sharma	c Richards, b Roberts	24	c Greenidge, b Roberts	12
R.J. Shastri	c Richards, b Roberts	29	c Lloyd, b Marshall	19
R.N. Kapil Dev†	c Lloyd, b Marshall	0	(8) c Lloyd, b Marshall	26
S.M.H. Kirmani*	c Haynes, b Roberts	11	(9) run out	33
S. Madan Lal	c Holding, b Garner	6	(10) lbw, b Roberts	0
B.S. Sandhu	not out	8	(7) lbw, b Roberts	4
S. Venkataraghavan	c Dujon, b Garner	5	not out	0
Extras	lb 1, nb 14	15	b 5, lb 2, nb 16	23
		209		277

WEST INDIES

	FIRST INNINGS		SECOND INNINGS	
C.G. Greenidge	c Gavaskar, b Madan Lal	57	not out	0
D.L. Haynes	c Kapil Dev, b Shastri	92	not out	0
I.V.A. Richards	c Gavaskar, b Venkat	80		
H.A. Gomes	c sub, b Venkataraghavan	6		
A.L. Logie	c Amarnath, b Shastri	130		
C.H. Lloyd†	c sub, b Venkataraghavan	50		
P.J. Dujon*	c Vengsarkar, b Dev	25		
M.D. Marshall	c Venkataraghavan, b Dev	8		
A.M.E. Roberts	c Dev, b Madan Lal	20		
M.A. Holding	c Kirmani, b Dev	2		
J. Garner	not out	2		
Extras	b 1, lb 11, nb 2	14	nb 1	1
		486	(for no wkt)	1

	O	M	R	W	O	M	R	W
Holding	14	4	46	2	21	2	75	2
Roberts	16	4	48	4	19.2	3	31	4
Marshall	13	1	56	2	16	1	80	2
Garner	12.2	5	41	2	15	4	48	1
Gomes	2	1	3	—	8	3	20	—

	O	M	R	W	O	M	R	W
Kapil Dev	32.3	7	76	3				
Sandhu	5	1	21	—				
Madan Lal	27	2	96	2				
Shastri	50	13	133	2				
Venkataraghavan	43	6	146	3				
Gaekwad	1	1	0	—				
Kirmani					0.1	—	0	—

FALL OF WICKETS
1- 2, 2- 10, 3- 39, 4- 91, 5- 172, 6- 172, 7- 180, 8- 196, 9- 200
1- 61, 2- 108, 3- 109, 4- 132, 5- 139, 6- 155, 7- 214, 8- 276, 9- 276

Umpires: D.M. Archer and S. E. Parris

West Indies won by 10 wickets

FALL OF WICKETS
1- 98, 2- 220, 3- 230, 4- 262, 5- 395, 6- 454, 7- 458, 8- 481, 9- 483

FOURTH TEST MATCH: WEST INDIES v. INDIA

The determination which Amarnath had shown in the match with Barbados was again in evidence when for the first time in the series the West Indian pace quartet found a wicket which gave them assistance. Gavaskar and Gaekwad were out with only 10 scored, and wickets fell regularly to the speed and aggression of the West Indian bowlers.

Faoud Bacchus. He batted well for Guyana, but he could not force his way back into the Test side. (George Herringshaw)

		Byes	Leg-byes	Wides	No-balls	Total	Wkts
		7	7		4	258	10
		7	3		4	130	10
				1	4	91	10
		3	7		3	267	10
		4	6	6	16	403	10
		3	3	1	5	132	4
			(12)			243	10
			(19)			159	9a
		4	1	1	7	149	10
		3	13	1	2	267	10
			4	1	10	286	3b

Jamaica 1983
First Class Matches

BATTING

	v. Trinidad (Kingston) 21-24 January		v. Barbados (Kingston) 28-31 January		v. Windward Islands (Kingston) 4-7 February	v. Leeward Islands (Montserrat) 11-14 February		v. Indians (Kingston) 17-20 February		v. Guyana (Georgetown) 3-5 March		Inns	NOs	Runs	HS	Av
G. Powell	0	49	38	67	11 —	2	6	75	18	37	6	11	—	309	75	28.09
O. W. Peters	82	79	19	31	27 —	35	23	11	8	15	89	11	—	419	89	38.09
C. W. Fletcher	27	0	0	24	99 —	33	70	28	32*	44	36	11	1	393	99	39.30
H. S. Chang	64	22										2	—	86	64	43.00
M. C. Neita	74	1	0	33	75 —	48	22	15	1	2	60	11	—	331	75	30.09
P. J. Dujon	49	34	96*	30	102 —	5	55	104	6*	4	8	11	2	493	104	54.77
M. A. Tucker	12	0*	3	0								4	1	15	12	5.00
C. Gordon	15	—	2	13	21 —	11*	16					6	1	78	21	15.60
J. A. Williams	0	—	4	20	9 —							4	—	33	20	8.25
C. U. Thompson	28*	2			8* —							3	2	38	28*	38.00
C. A. Walsh	16	—	18	1*		0	1	6	—	6	0	8	1	48	18	6.85
C. Baugh			32	21	22 —	1	5					5	—	81	32	16.20
R. C. Haynes			4	0		62	27*			0	26	6	1	119	62	23.80
C. A. Davidson					26 —			22	0	13	9	5	—	70	26	14.00
J. Gordon					1 —							1	—	1	1	1.00
M. A. Holding						16	6					2	—	22	16	11.00
P. Patterson						0	3	3	—			3	—	6	3	2.00
P. A. O. Francis								2	—	11*	7	3	1	20	11*	10.00
A. G. Daley								18	—	4	5	3	—	27	18	9.00
E. L. Wilson								2*	—	0	1*	3	2	3	2*	3.00
Byes	12		2	4	2	6	4			4	3					
Leg-byes	10	3	1	5	12	1	6	6	6	1	14					
Wides			5	1		2	3			1	1					
No-balls	1	1	10	5	25	8	15	10		7	2					
Total	390	191	234	255	440	224	264	306	71	149	267					
Wickets	10	7	10	10	10	10	10	10	4	10	10					
Result	D		L		D	L		D		L						

Catches
9 – P. J. Dujon (ct 8/st 1)
6 – C. W. Fletcher
5 – O. W. Peters
4 – M. C. Neita
3 – P. A. O. Francis, C. A. Davidson and C. A. Walsh
2 – C. Gordon and subs.
1 – R. C. Haynes, M. A. Tucker, M. A. Holding, P. Patterson, C. U. Thompson, G. Powell and E. L. Wilson

BOWLING

	J. A. Williams	C. A. Walsh	C. U. Thompson	C. Gordon	M. A. Tucker	R. C. Haynes	C. W. Fletcher	M. C. Neita	A. G. Daley
v. Trinidad (Kingston) 21-24 January	17–7–33–1	25–7–79–2	14–3–54–0	15–2–46–4	16–6–32–0				
	13–3–34–2	19–5–49–1	11–0–37–1	17–2–67–2	21–1–65–0				
v. Barbados (Kingston) 28-31 January	18–3–44–0	23–3–53–1		34–5–114–3	28–6–71–2	19–5–45–0	41–9–84–2	1–0–3–0	
	3–0–18–0	7–1–20–0			4.3–0–17–1				
v. Windward Islands (Kingston) 4-7 February	29–3–86–1		41–7–114–5	4.2–0–23–1			30–8–60–1	6–2–9–0	
	9–1–26–0		8–1–28–0	22–3–106–3			13–3–28–0	1–1–0–0	
v. Leeward Islands (Montserrat) 11-14 February		17–0–70–2		21–5–60–0		30–11–63–2	6–1–24–1		
		4–1–23–0							
v. Indians (Kingston) 17-20 February		12–2–31–4							20–2–66–
		22–6–63–0					8–1–27–0	21–6–43–2	30–3–101
v. Guyana (Georgetown) 3-5 March		22–5–57–2				16–1–69–1	1–0–6–0	16–0–71–0	22–2–112
	89–17– 241–4 av. 60.25	151–30– 445–12 av. 37.08	74–11– 233–6 av. 38.83	113.2–17– 416–13 av. 32.00	69.3–13– 185–3 av. 61.66	65–17– 177–3 av. 59.00	99–22– 229–4 av. 57.25	45–9– 126–2 av. 83.00	72–7– 279–5 av. 55.80

a J. Gordon 27–2–121–1   b C. Baugh 4–0–9–1   c M. A. Holding 32.2–7–128–3
2–0–11–0

Gus Logie. A maiden Test hundred in the fourth Test match.
(George Herringshaw)

Only half an hour's play was possible on the first day, but in that time the openers were out. On the second day, Amarnath was quite magnificent as all around him tumbled, he and Yashpal Sharma added 81 for the fifth wicket, but once Amarnath had been caught behind off a lethal delivery by Marshall and Kapil Dev was caught off his glove first ball, the Indian innings disintegrated.

Greenidge and Haynes began with a stand of 98, and West Indies were 172 for 1 at lunch on the third day. They were pegged back by some accurate bowling by Venkataraghavan in the afternoon, and Haynes fell immediately after tea, at 262, to give India renewed hope, but Logie and Lloyd took the score to 355 by the close, and, although the Indian bowlers again contained well on the fourth day, the home side reached 486, a lead of 277.

Augustine Logie, badly missed at slip by Venkataraghavan off Shastri when 7, reached a fine maiden Test hundred and in the later stages of his innings revealed his full range of strokes, prevalent in his batting in the Shell Shield, but hitherto absent in Test cricket. At one stage he hit Venkataraghavan for two massive sixes in the space of three deliveries.

By the close, India were 138 for 4, and with Amarnath retired hurt, they were facing defeat and the loss of the series.

When Marshall came into the attack on the last morning and bowled round the wicket, he immediately had Shastri caught at slip driving. Amarnath returned and batted with great skill and courage, but Kapil Dev suffered the same fate as Shastri.

Kapil Dev, in fact, complained at the number of bouncers that Marshall, in particular, was allowed to bowl, but this was a postscript to the defeat. Kirmani was run out after giving Amarnath good support, Madan Lal went at once, and the magnificent Amarnath was last out, caught at the wicket hooking a Roberts bouncer.

India had just avoided an innings defeat, but the last rites were concluded when Kirmani bowled a no-ball.

22, 23 and 24 April 1983

at Basseterre, St Kitts

Indians 362 (S. Madan Lal 97, D.B. Vengsarkar 55, A. Merrick 5 for 68) and 6 for 1
Leeward Islands 103 (S. Madan Lal 5 for 68, S. Venkataraghavan 4 for 5) and 264 (V.A. Eddy 91 not out, A.L. Kelly 64)

Indians won by 9 wickets

In their penultimate match of the tour the Indians gained a welcome morale boost with a nine wicket victory over Leeward Islands, accomplished with a day to spare. The match did not begin well for the Indians who lost Gaekwad and Malhotra to Merrick for 10, and were indebted to a splendid knock from Madan Lal.

The home side collapsed before the medium pace of Madan Lal and the off-spin of Venkataraghavan, with only two players, Liburd (41) and Merrick (10) reaching double figures. They fared better at the second attempt when skipper Kelly got them off to a good start and Eddy played finely, but they only just averted the innings defeat.

Gaekwad, the acting captain of the Indian side, was again dismissed by Merrick for 0, an unfortunate baptism for a captain, but victory was achieved in the next over, with four leg-byes.

FIFTH TEST MATCH: WEST INDIES v. INDIA

Lloyd once more elected to field when he won the toss and there were quick rewards as Gaekwad lasted only 18 minutes

C. A. Davidson	P. Patterson	E. L. Wilson	Byes	Leg-byes	Wides	No-balls	Total	Wkts
				5		13	262	10
			1	2		4	259	6
			2	8	1	10	435	8
							55	1
				(28)			441	10a
-3-8-0				2		4	211	6b
	17-4-53-1		7	3		14	422	10c
	5-0-26-2		6	1			67	2
	10-1-24-1	22-6-46-2	1	1	4	12	185	10
-0-9-0	6-0-26-0	40-8-95-2	6	6	1	18	395	6
-1-18-1		51.4-7-152-2	16	10		6	517	8
7-4-	38-5-	113.4-21-						
5-1	129-4	293-6						
av. 35.00	av. 32.25	av. 48.83						

Leeward Islands 1983
First Class Matches

BATTING

	v. Barbados (Bridgetown) 21-24 January		v. Guyana (Nevis) 28-30 January		v. Trinidad (Pointe-à-Pierre) 4-7 February		v. Jamaica (Montserrat) 11-14 February		v. Windward Islands (Basseterre) 3-6 March		v. Indians (Basseterre) 22-24 April		Inns	NOs	Runs	HS	Av
A. L. Kelly	7	55	1	56	38	18	18	20	14	41	5	64	12	—	337	64	28.08
R. B. Richardson	102	15	5	28	8	0	156	26	17	39	4	17	12	—	417	156	34.75
E. E. Lewis	40	1	31	8	19	138	26	12*	12	1			10	1	288	138	32.00
I. V. A. Richards	0	45											2	—	45	45	22.50
J. C. Allen	19	21	4	7	50	4	42	2*	14	7			10	1	170	50	18.88
E. Sergeant	28	7	5	14							9	12	6	—	75	28	12.50
E. A. Baptiste	16	5	8	37	44	5	32	—	20	4	9	20	11	—	200	44	18.18
A. C. M. White	8	0									0	6	4	—	14	8	3.50
A. M. E. Roberts	14*	9	8	0	0	4*	6	—	5	16			9	2	62	16	8.85
N. C. Guishard	3	15	17	13	30	19	14	—	3	0			9	—	114	30	12.66
G. Ferris	1	0*	2*	26									4	2	29	26	14.50
V. A. Eddy			4	58	124	0	80*	—	36	35	1	91*	9	2	429	124	61.28
E. T. Willett			1	7*	6*	—	4	—	12	4*	6*	0	8	4	40	12	10.00
R. M. Otto					4	22					5	0	4	—	31	22	7.25
S. I. Williams					120	31	18	—	52	34			5	—	255	120	51.00
A. Merrick							2	—	24*	2	10	30	5	1	68	30	17.00
S. Liburd											41	6	2	—	47	41	23.50
V. C. Newton											9	1	2	—	10	9	5.00
Byes	3			3	4	4	7	6	5	3		4					
Leg-byes	3	4		7	8	2	3	1	9	8	1	10					
Wides	1	1		1	1												
No-balls	8	11	4	3	3		14		11	9	3	3					
Total	253	189	91	267	459	247	422	67	234	203	103	264					
Wickets	10	10	10	10	10	9	10	2	10	10	10	10					
Result	L		L		D		W		L		L						

Catches
10 – E. Sergeant (ct 8/st 2)
9 – R. B. Richardson
8 – S. I. Williams (ct 7/st 1)
7 – A. L. Kelly
6 – N. C. Guishard
4 – V. A. Eddy, E. T. Willett and E. A. Baptiste
3 – E. E. Lewis
2 – A. Merrick, I. V. A. Richards, and A. M. E. Roberts
1 – J. C. Allen, G. Ferris and R. M. Otto

BOWLING

	A. M. E. Roberts	G. Ferris	A. C. M. White	E. A. Baptiste	N. C. Guishard	E. T. Willett	V. A. Eddy	J. C. Allen	R. B. Richardson
v. Barbados (Bridgetown) 21-24 January	14-6-35-1	7-1-34-2	7-0-43-0	18-4-64-3	23.1-3-54-3				
	15-2-55-4	10-0-50-1	4-0-19-0	16-4-51-4	16.3-4-57-1				
v. Guyana (Nevis) 28-30 January	7-2-20-1	5-1-14-0		9.4-2-22-2	28-6-79-4	26-3-47-2	3-0-15-1		
	14-1-43-1	3-0-12-0		13.5-2-46-4	35-4-92-0	37-11-82-3	3-0-29-0		
v. Trinidad and Tobago (Pointe-à-Pierre) 4-7 February	28-3-99-2			16-2-68-2	37-9-85-3	41.3-8-106-2	2-0-8-0		
	7-1-34-0			10-2-23-2	4-1-3-0	4-1-13-0		3-1-6-0	3-1-2-0
v. Jamaica (Montserrat) 11-14 February	14-1-49-0			16-3-38-3	5-1-18-0	15-5-32-3			
	25.5-3-65-6			25-8-88-2	18-5-26-0	20-11-27-2	4-1-9-0		
v. Windward Islands (Basseterre) 3-6 March	17.2-1-52-5			17-2-56-3	11-1-21-1	17-0-61-1			
	20-6-62-8			13.2-2-52-1	7-0-20-0	6-2-4-0			
v. Indians (Basseterre) 22-24 April			17-4-56-0	23-5-61-2		41-14-87-1	4-0-20-0		
			0.2-0-0-0						
	162.1-26-514-28	25-2-110-3	28.2-4-118-0	177.5-36-569-28	184.4-34-455-12	207.3-55-459-14	16-1-81-1	3-1-6-0	3-1-2-0
	av. 18.35	av. 36.66	—	av. 20.32	av. 37.91	av. 32.78	av. 81.00	—	—

a V. C. Newton 29.3-13-45-2

FIFTH TEST MATCH: WEST INDIES v. INDIA
28, 29, 30 April, 1 and 3 May, 1983 at St John's, Antigua

INDIA

	FIRST INNINGS		SECOND INNINGS	
S.M. Gavaskar	c Dujon, b Marshall	18	c Dujon, b Davis	1
A.D. Gaekwad	c Richards, b Roberts	3	lbw, b Marshall	72
M.B. Amarnath	c Lloyd, b Davis	54	c Logie, b Davis	116
D.B. Vengsarkar	c Davis, b Marshall	94	c Dujon, b Marshall	0
Yashpal Sharma	c Gomes, b Roberts	3	c sub, b Gomes	20
R.J. Shastri	st Dujon, b Gomes	102	not out	9
R.N. Kapil Dev†	lbw, b Holding	98	not out	0
S.M.H. Kirmani*	c Greenidge, b Davis	2		
S. Madan Lal	not out	35		
L. Sivaramakrish-nan	c sub, b Marshall	17		
S. Venkataragha-van	b Marshall	0		
Extras	b 14, lb 7, w 1, nb 9	31	b 11, lb 8, nb 10	29
		457	(for 2 wkts, dec)	247

	O	M	R	W	O	M	R	W
Roberts	29	3	110	2	15	3	46	—
Holding	26	3	86	1				
Marshall	27.5	5	87	4	18	7	33	2
Davis	29	1	121	2	23	4	54	2
Richards	11	3	13	—	13	1	36	—
Gomes	4	1	9	1	10	—	49	1

FALL OF WICKETS
1- 5, 2- 28, 3- 119, 4- 131, 5- 337, 6- 376, 7- 419, 8- 457, 9- 457
1- 1, 2- 201, 3- 201, 4- 234, 5- 245

Umpires: D.M. Archer and R. Weeks

Match drawn

WEST INDIES

	FIRST INNINGS	
C.G. Greenidge	retired not out	154
D.L. Haynes	c Shastri, b Sharma	136
W.W. Davis	b Madan Lal	14
I.V.A. Richards	c Gaekwad, b Madan Lal	2
H.A. Gomes	lbw, b Madan Lal	9
A.L. Logie	hit wkt., b Kapil Dev	1
P.J.Dujon*	c Gaekwad, b Venkat	110
C.H. Lloyd†	c Sharma, b Shastri	106
M.D. Marshall	b Venkataraghavan	2
A.M.E. Roberts	not out	1
M.A. Holding	run out	0
Extras	b 6, lb 5, nb 4	15
		550

	O	M	R	W
Kapil Dev	22	6	71	1
Madan Lal	35	7	105	3
Sivaramakrishnan	25	1	95	—
Shastri	46.4	5	141	1
Venkataraghavan	36	1	114	2
Gaekwad	1	—	3	—
Yashpal Sharma	1	—	6	1

FALL OF WICKETS
1- 296, 2- 303, 3- 323, 4- 324, 5- 334, 6- 541, 7- 547, 8- 549, 9- 550

and Gavaskar fell in Marshall's second over with the bowler again slanting the ball across him by bowling round the wicket.

Vengsarkar batted well in dismal conditions, but India were handicapped when Amarnath, who seemed well in control, retired ill with a virus infection. When bad light ended the first day early India were 188 for 4.

On the second day, Kapil Dev dominated play and helped

Desmond Haynes who shared an opening stand of 296 with Gordon Greenidge in the fifth Test. (Patrick Eagar)

R. M. Otto	A. L. Kelly	A. Merrick	Byes	Leg-byes	Wides	No-balls	Total	Wkts
				3	1	8	242	10
			1	7	2	14	256	10
				12		4	213	10
			3	8		3	318	10
			2	8	1	6	383	10
2-1-9-0	1-0-1-0		5		1	3	100	2
		19.5-2-76-4		1	2	8	224	10
		5-1-19-0	6	6	3	15	264	10
		12-1-47-0		7	1	11	256	10
		4-0-20-0		(24)			182	10
		28-5-68-5	5	8	4	8	362	10a
		1-0-2-1		4			6	1
2-1-	1-0-	69.5-9-						
9-0	1-0	232-10						
—		av. 23.20						

Trinidad and Tobago 1983
First Class Matches

BATTING

BATTING	v. Jamaica (Kingston) 21-24 January		v. Windward Islands (Port of Spain) 28-31 January		v. Leeward Islands (Pointe-à-Pierre) 4-7 February		v. Guyana (Berbice) 10-13 February		v. Indians (Pointe-à-Pierre) 3-5 March		v. Barbados (Port of Spain) 19-22 March		Inns	NOs	Runs	HS	Av
R. S. Gabriel	71	96	37	0	32	—			10	30	22	30	9	—	328	96	36.44
P. V. Simmonds	6	31	10	75	106	15	13	13	81	22	26	30	12	—	428	106	35.66
A. L. Logie	5	36*	138	79	46	43*	117	62	7	13	14	0	12	2	560	138	56.00
K. G. D'Heurieux	59	44			0	33*	16	5	18	0			8	1	175	59	25.00
S. A. Gomes	50	16	16	7									4	—	89	50	22.25
T. Cuffy	12	6	36	13*	38	—	24	14	2	2			9	1	147	38	18.37
R. Nanan	33	19	21	—	125	—	16	8	18	5	0	12	10	—	257	125	25.70
J. R. Lyon	0	4*	22*	—									3	2	26	22*	26.00
G. S. Antoine	6	—					0	1	7*	0			5	1	14	7*	3.50
G. Mahabir	0	—	17	—	8		0	0	13	8	17	0	9	—	63	17	7.00
K. C. Williams	2*	—	0	—	0*	—					18*	7*	5	4	27	18*	27.00
A. Rajah			27	15	9	0							4	—	51	27	12.75
R. Sampath				4	17*								2	1	17	17*	17.00
D. Williams					2	—	13*	2*			7	0	5	2	24	13*	8.00
A. E. Daniel						0							1	—	0	0	0.00
W. Debisette							2	28			1	23	4	—	54	28	13.50
P. Moosai							29	7			11	37	4	—	84	37	21.00
S. Jumadeen							1	—			18	0	3	—	19	18	6.33
H. A. Gomes									22	27	7	67	4	—	123	67	31.00
R. Ramparass									3	5			2	—	8	5	4.00
P. Ramnath									1	11*			2	1	12	11*	12.00
Byes		1	2	10	2	5			2		1	5					
Leg-byes	5	2	3	14	8		(12)	(19)	3	(18)	1	6					
Wides					1	1						7					
No-balls	13	4	20	7	6	3			6		10	20					
Total	262	259	353	237	383	100	243	159	193	141	153	244					
Wickets	10	6	10	5	10	2	10	9†	10	10	10	10					
Result	D		L		D		L		L		L						

Catches
6 – G. Mahabir and R. Nanan
5 – P. Moosai
4 – subs
3 – P. V. Simmonds, J. R. Lyon (ct 2/st 1) and T. Cuffy
2 – K. C. Williams and A. Rajah
1 – R. S. Gabriel, R. Sampath, S. A. Gomes, K. G. D'Heurieux, A. L. Logie, D. Williams, R. Ramparass and G. S. Antoine

† S. Jumadeen absent hurt

BOWLING

BOWLING	K. C. Williams	G. S. Antoine	R. Nanan	K. G. D'Heurieux	G. Mahabir	R. Sampath	P. V. Simmonds	A. E. Daniel
v. Jamaica (Kingston) 21-24 January	18-0-78-3 / 4.2-0-31-0	19-3-66-0 / 12-1-51-2	50-11-103-5 / 20-3-55-2	1-0-7-0 / 9-1-37-0	43.1-8-113-5 / 2-0-13-0			
v. Windward Islands (Port of Spain) 28-31 January	16-3-38-0 / 23-3-98-5		35-7-64-3 / 36.4-2-142-3		41-10-91-3 / 20-4-55-0	8-1-19-0 / 4-1-13-0	2.1-1-3-1 / 12-1-44-0	
v. Leeward Islands (Pointe-à-Pierre) 4-7 February	5-0-26-1		54.3-15-116-3 / 33.4-7-71-3	16-0-78-0 / 14-3-34-2	37-12-98-3 / 23-3-74-3		26-2-75-1 / 5-0-24-0	13-3-50-0 / 11-3-38-1
v. Guyana (Berbice) 10-13 February		25-3-112-3 / 1.3-0-9-1	54-12-118-2 / 1-1-0-0	8-0-26-2 / 1-1-0-0	18-3-66-0		1-0-4-0	
v. Indians (Pointe-à-Pierre) 3-5 March		20-1-82-0	41-13-78-2	11-0-44-2	27-5-71-4		4-0-11-0	
v. Barbados (Port of Spain) 19-22 March	11-0-58-1 / 5-1-9-0		21.2-5-46-4 / 31.3-5-76-2		18-5-58-3 / 38-9-68-6		6-2-10-1 / 2-1-8-0	
	82.2-7-338-10 av. 33.80	77.3-8-320-6 av. 53.33	378.4-81-869-26 av. 33.42	69-4-226-6 av. 37.66	267.1-59-707-27 av. 26.18	12-2-32-0 av. —	58.1-7-179-3 av. 59.66	24-6-88-1 av. 88.00

a R.J. Shastri absent hurt

West Indies *v.* India – Test Match Averages

WEST INDIES BATTING

	M	Inns	NOs	Runs	HS	Av	100s	50s
C. G. Greenidge	5	7	2	393	154*	78.60	1	3
C. H. Lloyd	5	6		407	143	67.83	2	2
D. L. Haynes	5	7	1	333	136	55.50	1	1
P. J. Dujon	5	6	1	259	110	51.80	1	
I. V. A. Richards	5	6		282	109	47.00	1	2
H. A. Gomes	5	5		178	123	35.60	1	
A. L. Logie	5	6		167	130	27.83	1	
A. M. E. Roberts	5	6	1	84	36	16.80		
M. D. Marshall	5	6	1	74	27	14.80		
M. A. Holding	5	5		27	24	5.40		

Played in four Tests:- J. Garner 0*, 21*, 1* and 2*
Played in one Test:- W. W. Davis 14

INDIA BATTING

	M	Inns	NOs	Runs	HS	Av	100s	50s
M. B. Amarnath	5	9		598	117	66.44	2	4
R. N. Kapil Dev	5	8	2	254	100*	42.33	1	1
R. J. Shastri	5	8	2	236	102	39.33	1	
Yashpal Sharma	5	9	2	242	63	34.57		2
D. B. Vengsarkar	5	9		279	94	31.00		2
S.M. Gavaskar	5	9	1	240	147*	30.00	1	
B. S. Sandhu	4	6	2	91	68	22.75		1
A. D. Gaekwad	5	9		200	72	22.22		2
S. Madan Lal	2	3	1	41	35*	20.50		
S. M. H. Kirmani	5	7		98	33	14.00		
Maninder Singh	3	3	1	6	3*	3.00		
S. Venkataraghavan	5	6	1	6	5	1.20		

Played in one Test:- L. Sivaramakrishnan 17

WEST INDIES BOWLING

	Overs	Mds	Runs	Wkts	Av	Best	5/inn
A. M. E. Roberts	186.5	36	545	24	22.70	5/39	1
M. D. Marshall	174.2	39	497	21	23.66	5/37	1
M. A. Holding	162	23	500	12	41.66	2/36	
J. Garner	113	35	301	7	43.00	2/41	
W. W. Davis	52	5	175	4	43.75	2/54	
H. A. Gomes		20	203	3	67.66	1/9	
I. V. A. Richards	36	9	87	1	87.00		

INDIA BOWLING

	Overs	Mds	Runs	Wkts	Av	Best	5/inn
R. N. Kapil Dev	154	32	424	17	24.94	4/45	
S. Madan Lal	62	9	201	5	40.20	3/105	
B. S. Sandhu	63.4	12	229	5	45.80	3/87	
R. J. Shastri	163.4	31	472	10	47.20	4/43	
S. Venkataraghavan	186	25	586	10	58.60	3/146	
Maninder Singh	84.3	16	192	2	96.00	1/51	
A. D. Gaekwad	2	1	3	0	—		

Also bowled:- M. B. Amarnath 2.2–0–34–2, L. Sivaramakrishnan 25–1–95–1, Yashpal Sharma 1–0–6–1, S. M. H. Kirmani 0.1–0–0–0

WEST INDIES CATCHES

19 - P. J. Dujon (ct 18/st 1); 8 - I. V. A. Richards; 5 - C. H. Lloyd and C. G. Greenidge; 4 - D. L. Haynes; 3 - J. Garner, H. A. Gomes, M. A. Holding, M. D. Marshall and subs; 1 - W. W. Davis, A. M. E. Roberts and A. L. Logie

INDIA CATCHES

9 - S. M. H. Kirmani (ct 8 st 1); 5 - S. Venkataraghavan; 4 - Yashpal Sharma, R. N. Kapil Dev and S. M. Gavaskar; 3 - M. B. Amarnath and A. D. Gaekwad; 2 - D. B. Vengsarkar and subs; 1 - B. S. Sandhu and R. J. Shastri

take India to a strong position. Amarnath resumed his innings and reached his fifth half-century of the series before becoming Winston Davis' first Test victim when he edged to slip just before tea. The Indians had also introduced a new bowler to Test cricket, leg-spinner Laksham Sivaramakrishnan, who, at 16 years, 118 days, became the second youngest player ever to appear in Test cricket. He failed to take a wicket.

The West Indian wicket-keeper Dujon who claimed nineteen victims in the series and reached a maiden Test hundred in the final match. (Jan Traylen)

S. Jumadeen	P. Ramnath	H. A. Gomes	Byes	Leg-byes	Wides	No-balls	Total	Wkts
			12	10		1	390	10
				3		1	191	7
			2	6			223	10
			3	15	1		371	8
			4	8	1	3	459	10
			4	2			247	9
20–2–59–0			4	6			395	9
							9	1
	14–3–56–0	18–2–51–1		(10)			403	9a
6–1–33–0				7			212	10
14–5–27–2		2–0–8–0		8			204	10
40–8–	14–3–	20–2–						
119–2	56–0	59–1						
av. 59.50	—	av. 59.00						

Windward Islands 1983
First Class Matches

BATTING

	v. Guyana (Dominica) 21-24 January		v. Trinidad (Port of Spain) 28-31 January		v. Jamaica (Kingston) 4-7 February		v. Barbados (St. Vincent) 11-14 February		v. Leeward Islands (Basseterre) 3-6 March		v. Indians (Grenada) 18-21 March		Inns	NOs	Runs	HS	Av
L. C. Sebastien	88	12	5	122	73	77	11	29*	44	9	0	10	12	1	480	122	43.63
L. D. John	56	1	20	42	80	19	110	21	1	15	4	7	12	—	376	110	31.33
C. Elwin	16	30	7	10					12	0			6	—	75	30	12.50
W. N. Slack	11	20	10	27	66	—	20	12			97	32	9	—	295	97	32.77
S. W. Julien	13	14	15	123	88	50	41	13	68	0	37	0	12	—	462	123	38.50
A. D. Tesheira	0	18	39	4	10	48*	2	12	6	16			10	1	155	48*	17.22
N. Phillip	30	17	45	5			12	0	25	49	1	9	10	—	193	49	19.30
I. Cadette	11	1	7	6*	15	7	14	39	35	2	0	15	12	1	152	39	13.81
T. Kentish	0	0	18	13*	8	1*	18	—	2	17*	16	15*	11	4	108	18	15.42
S. J. Hinds	15	2	49*	0	0	—	24	2*	12	20			9	2	124	49*	17.71
W. W. Davis	0*	1*	0	—	0	—	0*	—	0*	11	0*	3	9	5	15	11	3.75
J. Charles					22	0					20	13	4	—	55	22	13.75
N. F. Williams					51*	3	15	—	32	19	13	1	7	1	134	51*	22.33
F. Thorpe											22	14	2	—	36	22	18.00

	Guyana		Trinidad		Jamaica		Barbados		Leeward		Indians	
Byes	7	7	2	3			15				3	1
Leg-byes	7	3	6	15	(28)	2	7	4	7	(24)	3	
Wides				1					1			
No-balls	4	4					4	18	2	11	1	3
Total	258	130	223	371	441	211	307	134	256	182	217	123
Wickets	10	10	10	8	10	6	10	6	10	10	10	10
Result	L		W		D		W		W		L	

Catches
15 – I. Cadette
7 – W. N. Slack
6 – T. Kentish
4 – L. C. Sebastien
3 – C. Elwin, W. W. Davis, A. D. Tesheira and subs.
2 – N. Phillip, N. F. Williams
1 – L. D. John, S. J. Hinds, S. W. Julien and F. Thorpe

BOWLING

	W. W. Davis	N. Phillip	W. N. Slack	T. Kentish	S. J. Hinds	L. C. Sebastien	N. F. Williams	J. Charles
v. Guyana (Dominica)	18-1-54-6	8.3-0-33-2	2-1-4-0	18-3-47-1	7-1-20-0			
21-24 January	30-5-78-4	21.1-2-77-4		19-1-57-1	32-5-87-1	1-0-1-0		
v. Trinidad (Port of Spain)	29-6-98-3	25.5-2-79-2	4-1-14-0	26-4-81-2	21-6-56-2			
28-31 January	15-1-57-4	5-1-26-0		22-1-71-3	24-6-52-0			
v. Jamaica (Kingston)	48.5-15-98-5			38-13-67-2	38-10-82-1	11-2-30-1	17-2-76-0	20-2-48-0
4-7 February								
v. Barbados (St. Vincent)	17-4-69-2	17-2-49-3		11-2-21-0	15-6-27-2		18-3-53-3	
11-14 February	26.1-8-49-2	21-4-39-3		21-8-18-0	21-9-30-1		22-6-38-4	
v. Leeward Islands (Basseterre)	24-7-60-5	14-1-49-0		16.1-5-32-3	5-0-24-0	1-0-12-0	11-3-32-2	
3-6 March	18.1-2-57-4	4-0-18-0		30-8-53-2	7-1-15-1		13-2-40-3	
v. Indians (Grenada)	22.4-4-43-3	17-2-56-5		10-4-14-0			12.2-3-44-2	1-0-6-0
18-21 March	23.5-4-84-5	19-4-52-1	2-1-3-0	22-6-51-0			21-3-84-3	
	272.4-57–	152.3-18–	10-3–	232.1-55–	170-44–	13-2–	114.2-22–	21-2–
	747-41	478-20	21-0	584-14	393-8	43-1	367-17	54-0
	av. 18.21	av. 23.90	—	av. 41.73	av. 49.12	av. 43.00	av. 21.58	—

Shastri reached his century on the third day and India's 457 looked a daunting total, but Haynes and Greenidge quickly dispelled any dreams of an Indian victory with a record opening stand for West Indies against India, passing the previous best of 239 between Rae and Stollmeyer, made in 1948–9. At 296, Haynes was caught off Yashpal Sharma, and the next day Greenidge did not resume his innings. He had batted at a time of great personal distress. His three-year old daughter Rea lay in a coma in hospital, critically ill from a kidney complaint. That night he flew to Barbados to be with her. Tragically, she was to die on 6 May.

The West Indies suffered some set-back when Madan Lal and Kapil Dev restricted them with the second new ball and then quickly accounted for Davis, Richards, Gomes and Logie, but in 224 minutes, Lloyd and Dujon added 207 on an uncertain wicket. Lloyd was violent, Dujon calmer. It was Lloyd's 16th Test century and Dujon's first.

With a lead of nearly 100, West Indies had a chance to force a surprise victory, especially when Gavaskar was caught behind for a single, but Gaekwad and Amarnath added 200 in four hours and Amarnath, the hero of India throughout the tour, reached the sixth century of the match.

Gordon Greenidge. (Patrick Eagar)

W. Davis. Record number of wickets in the Shell Shield. (Dave Cannon)

F. Thorpe		Byes	Leg-byes	Wides	No-balls	Total	Wkts
		3	1			162	10
		21	11		2	334	10
		2	3		20	353	10
		10	14		7	237	5
		2	12		25	440	10
		7	4		13	243	10
		3	6		13	196	10
		5	9		11	234	10
		3	8		9	203	10
		7			12	182	10
3–1–3–0			3		7	287	10
3–1–							
–0							

Star of India
The Prudential World Cup

Kapil Dev lifts the cup in triumph. (Adrian Murrell)

By the time that the Prudential World Cup arrived, the English summer at last showed signs of producing weather that such a festival of cricket deserved. Not only had the rain clouds moved away, but the dark political threats had also receded into the background, at least temporarily, and we could enjoy the cricket.

Before the tournament began, there were controversial selections and sad withdrawals. The most devastating pieces of injury news concerned Australia and Pakistan.

Greg Chappell withdrew from the Australian side because of injury and his place was taken by Macleay. It was generally predicted that the absence of Chappell would reduce the effectiveness of the Australian side by about fifty per cent. His brother Trevor had been a surprise choice for the side and the omission of Yardley was strongly criticised.

It was at first feared that Imran Khan's foot injury would keep him out of the competition altogether, but he remained in the side as a batsman only. His inability to bowl was a grievous loss to Pakistan. Considered by many as favourites to become world champions, the loss of their main strike bowler reduced their attacking potential to meagre proportions. Their selectors, too, had come in for criticism by choosing Mansoor Akhtar instead of Qasim Umar who had such a wonderful domestic season.

The recall of Daniel to the West Indian party caused some surprise, but generally there was little to comment upon in the composition of the West Indian, Zimbabwe, Sri Lankan and Indian sides.

England chose Marks as their defensive spinner, recalled Gatting, rightly, and selected Gould as wicket-keeper, an incomprehensible choice for matches in which fielding, and the inspiration provided by the keeper, could be decisive. The contempt with which the art of wicket-keeping is treated b[y] England selectors, and not by them alone, remains one of th[e] irritants of modern cricket.

ENGLAND v. NEW ZEALAND AT THE OVAL

England were faced with a tough proposition in their open[ing] match – New Zealand, the side who had trounced them so severely only a few months earlier.

England batted first on a friendly day and on a wicke[t] which soon looked just as friendly in spite of the late move[ment] which Cairns achieved to have Fowler well taken a[t] slip. Gower was immediately aesthetically pleasing, dismiss[ing] the ball from his presence with eloquent gestures. H[e] seemed certain to score as many runs as time would allow[,] but suddenly, and unnecessarily, he swotted Coney to mid[-]wicket where Edgar held a good catch on the boundary. Th[e] positive Tavare went the same way and with the sky darken[ing], England were 117 for 3.

Lamb was uncertain, but as rain came closer so his shot[s] became more positive. His shoulders broadened and the run[s] flowed. Gatting was supportive in chunkiness an[d] aggression.

Lamb hit the first four balls of one over from Marti[n] Crowe for 4, 4, 6 and 1, and then there was a shower whic[h] held up play for fifteen minutes. When the over was com[pleted] pleted Gatting hit the last two balls for 4.

New Zealand had a dreadful day in the field. Their throw[ing] was terrible and poor Snedden, looked upon as a[n] economic stock bowler, conceded 105 runs in his 12 overs, a[n] unwanted record for a one-day international. He accounte[d] for both Gatting and Lamb, who had by then made the Mar[

ROUND ONE: ENGLAND v. NEW ZEALAND
9 June 1983 at The Oval

ENGLAND						NEW ZEALAND			
G. Fowler	c Coney, b Cairns		8			G.M. Turner	lbw, b Willis		14
C. J. Tavare	c Edgar, b Chatfield		45			B.A. Edgar	c Gould, b Willis		3
D.I. Gower	c Edgar, b Coney		39			J. G. Wright	c Botham, b Dilley		10
A.J. Lamb	b Snedden		102			G.P. Howarth†	c Lamb, b Marks		18
M.W. Gatting	b Snedden		43			J.V. Coney	run out		23
I.T. Botham	c Lees, b Hadlee		22			M.D. Crowe	run out		97
I.J. Gould*	not out		14			W.K. Lees*	b Botham		8
G.R. Dilley	not out		31			R.J. Hadlee	c Lamb, b Marks		1
V.J. Marks						B.L. Cairns	lbw, b Botham		1
P.J.W. Allott						M.C. Snedden	c Gould, b Gatting		21
R.G.D. Willis†						E.J. Chatfield	not out		9
Extras	lb 12, w 1, nb 5		18			Extras	b 2, lb 4, w 4, nb 1		11
(60 overs)	(for 6 wickets)		322			(59 overs)			216

	O	M	R	W			O	M	R	W
Hadlee	12	4	26	1		Willis	7	2	9	2
Cairns	12	4	57	1		Dilley	8	—	33	1
Snedden	12	1	105	2		Botham	12	—	42	2
Chatfield	12	1	45	1		Allott	12	1	47	—
Coney	6	1	20	1		Marks	12	1	39	2
M.D. Crowe	6	—	51	—		Gatting	8	1	35	1

FALL OF WICKETS
1- 13, 2- 79, 3- 117, 4- 232, 5- 271, 6- 278

FALL OF WICKETS
1- 3, 2- 28, 3- 31, 4- 62, 5- 85, 6- 123, 7- 136, 8- 138, 9- 190

Umpires: B. J. Meyer and D. O. Oslear

England won by 106 runs

of the Match award his, but his rhythm and control escaped him and Dilley plundered him in a sparkling display at the close.

Facing 322, New Zealand's morale was low and they desperately needed a good start to boost them if they were to have any chance of reaching the target. They did not get it. Edgar was splendidly caught by Gould, diving low in front of first slip, Turner pushed forward, missed and was lbw, Wright mis-hit a pull and lofted the ball gently to mid-wicket, and New Zealand were 31 for 3.

The game was, in effect, over. Martin Crowe batted with an air of maturity beyond his years and gave the New Zealand score some dignity. He was last man out, run out off the last ball of the penultimate over when he backed up too far and was sent back. It was a sad end to a fine innings.

England had won with great ease and were already filled with confidence that they could reach the final. There remained little doubt as to their support bowling and the wicket-keeping.

PAKISTAN v. SRI LANKA AT SWANSEA

The Pakistan batsmen swept majestically to a record World Cup score and cast aside, momentarily the doubts that existed about the side since it was realised that Imran would be unable to bowl.

Mudassar left at 88, then Mohsin and Zaheer added 68 in 14 overs before Mohsin fell immediately after lunch. There was no respite for the Sri Lankans as Javed and Imran continued the slaughter with a cascade of elegant shots which caused even the urgency of the Sri Lankan fielding to disappear.

Allan Lamb, Man of the Match, in aggressive mood.(Adrian Murrell)

ROUND ONE: PAKISTAN v. SRI LANKA
9 June 1983 at Swansea

PAKISTAN					SRI LANKA			
Mudassar Nazar	c de Silva, b Ratnayake			36	S.R. de S. Wettimuny	c Rashid Khan, b Sarfraz		12
Mohsin Khan	b John			82	B. Kuruppu	run out		72
Zaheer Abbas	c Kuruppu, b de Mel			82	R.L. Dias	b Rashid Khan		5
Javed Miandad	lbw, b de Mel			72	L.R.D. Mendis[†]	b Tahir		16
Imran Khan[†]	not out			56	A. Ranatunga	c and b Mudassar		31
Ejaz Faqih	run out			2	M.A.R. Samarasekera	run out		0
Tahir Naqqash	not out			0	D.S. de Silva	c Wasim Bari, b Sarfraz		35
Wasim Bari*					A.L.F. de Mel	c Tahir, b Shahid Mahboob		11
Rashid Khan					R.G. de Alwis*	not out		59
Shahid Mahboob					R.J. Ratnayake	c Mudassar, b Sarfraz		13
Sarfraz Nawaz					V. John	not out		12
Extras	b 4, lb 4			8	Extras	lb 8, w 10, nb 4		22
				—				—
(60 overs)	(for 5 wickets)			338	(60 overs)	(for 9 wickets)		288

	O	M	R	W		O	M	R	W
de Mel	12	2	69	2	Sarfraz Nawaz	12	1	40	3
John	12	2	58	1	Shahid Mahboob	11	—	48	1
Ratnayake	12	—	65	1	Tahir Naqqash	8	—	49	1
Ranatunga	9	—	53	—	Rashid Khan	12	1	55	1
de Silva	10	—	52	—	Ejaz Faqih	12	1	52	—
Samarasekera	5	—	33	—	Mudassar Nazar	4	—	18	1
					Zaheer Abbas	1	—	4	—

FALL OF WICKETS
1- 88, 2- 156, 3- 229, 4- 325, 5- 332

FALL OF WICKETS
1- 34, 2- 58, 3- 85, 4- 142, 5- 143, 6- 157, 7- 180, 8- 234, 9- 262

Umpires: K. E. Palmer and D. R. Shepherd

Pakistan won by 50 runs

The Sri Lankan batting is stronger than the bowling, but they could have had little hope of reaching such a massive score. When Wettimuny and Dias, from whom they hoped for much, were both out, any remote chance of victory disappeared. The pugnacious Mendis failed too, but young Kuruppu played very well and at the thirty-over mark, Sri Lanka were 125 for 3, a defiant response. Then came two silly run outs, for which the Sri Lankans have become noted, and all that was left were some fine blows from de Silva and de Alwis who underlined the limitations of the Pakistan attack without Imran.

ZIMBABWE v. AUSTRALIA AT TRENT BRIDGE

The likeable, supremely fit team from Zimbabwe brought about the first upset of the competition when they beat Australia by 13 runs in an enthralling match at Trent Bridge.

Hughes won the toss and asked Zimbabwe to bat, but Omarshah and Paterson gave Zimbabwe a fine start with 55 in 19 overs. They fell to successive balls from Lillee and when the very occasional bowling of Yallop and the gentle left-arm of Border accounted for Heron, Pycroft and Houghton, the heart of the Zimbabwe batting, it seemed that the I.C.C. Trophy winners were doomed to a quick defeat. 94 for 5 at lunch suggested an easy win for Australia by late afternoon.

Fletcher, the Zimbabwe captain, a former Lancashire League professional, rallied his side with an innings of character. In 15 overs, he and Curran added 70, then 75 came in 12 overs with Butchart who hit straight and true. The Australian fielding wilted. Five catches were put down and the bowling looked ragged. One still suspected a lack of discipline in this Australian side.

Ian Butchart who shared an unbeaten stand of 75 in 12 overs with Duncan Fletcher pulls Jeff Thomson to the boundary. (Ken Kelly)

ROUND ONE: AUSTRALIA v. ZIMBABWE
9 June 1983 at Trent Bridge, Nottingham

ZIMBABWE			
A.H. Omarshah	c Marsh, b Lillee	16
G.A. Paterson	c Hookes, b Lillee	27
J.G. Heron	c Marsh, b Yallop	14
A.J. Pycroft	b Border	21
D.L. Houghton*	c Marsh, b Yallop	0
D.A.G. Fletcher†	not out	69
K.M. Curran	c Hookes, b Hogg	27
I.P. Butchart	not out	34
P.W.E. Rawson		
A.J. Traicos		
V.R. Hogg		
Extras	lb 18, w 7, nb 6	31
(60 overs)	(for 6 wickets)	239

	O	M	R	W
Lawson	11	2	33	—
Hogg	12	3	43	1
Lillee	12	1	47	2
Thomson	11	1	46	—
Yallop	9	—	28	2
Border	5	—	11	1

FALL OF WICKETS
1- 55, 2- 55, 3- 86, 4- 86, 5- 94, 6- 164

AUSTRALIA			
G.M. Wood	c Houghton, b Fletcher	31
K.C. Wessels	run out	76
K.J. Hughes†	c Omarshah, b Fletcher	0
D.W. Hookes	c Traicos, b Fletcher	20
G.N. Yallop	c Pycroft, b Fletcher	2
A.R. Border	c Pycroft, b Curran	17
R.W. Marsh*	not out	50
G.F. Lawson	b Butchart	0
R.M. Hogg	not out	19
D.K. Lillee		
J.R. Thomson		
Extras	b 2, lb 7, w 2	11
(60 overs)	(for 7 wickets)	226

	O	M	R	W
Hogg	6	2	15	—
Rawson	12	1	54	—
Butchart	10	—	39	1
Fletcher	11	1	42	4
Traicos	12	2	27	—
Curran	9	—	38	1

FALL OF WICKETS
1- 61, 2- 63, 3- 114, 4- 133, 5- 138, 6- 168, 7- 176

Umpires: D. J. Constant and M. J. Kitchen

Zimbabwe won by 13 runs

Wood began briskly and then prodded vaguely outside his off stump. Hughes' incompatability with England continued when he dipped the ball off his legs and was very well caught. At tea, Australia were 77 for 2 off 25 overs.

Wessels and Hookes paced their stand well and had added 51 in 16 overs and were just gaining momentum when Hookes drove hard at Fletcher only to see Traicos take a spectacular, low diving catch in the covers.

Yallop swung at Fletcher and was very well taken by Pycroft on the square leg boundary. The fieldsman was looking into the sun, but as he juggled with the ball and fell back, he held on to the catch. Australia now needed 93 from 18 overs with six wickets standing. Five runs later Wessels was sent back by Border and was beaten by Heron's throw.

One reason for the Australian rashness was that John Traicos was keeping such a nagging length and bowling with such accuracy that runs were not easy to come by. His spell of bowling was a decisive factor in Zimbabwe's victory.

Rodney Marsh was dropped off a swirling skier with the score at 157, but Border perished at deep square leg at 168. The Australian batting had now become frantic as the run rate required became higher. Lawson swung at a full toss and was bowled. 53 were needed from 5 overs. 41 from 3. 32 from 2.

When the last over began Australia needed a daunting 23. Marsh hit a huge six to reach his 50, but the game was beyond Australia's reach.

Duncan Fletcher had led his men superbly and his own contribution, 69 not out and 4 for 42 in 11 overs, made the job of adjudicator Brian Bolus an easy one in naming the Man of the Match.

INDIA *v.* WEST INDIES AT OLD TRAFFORD

The start of the match was delayed until 1.25 pm and there was an immediate stoppage for bad light, but from then on, the Indian batsmen showed resolution and good sense. There was something of a frenetic start by Srikkanth, but once Yashpal Sharma arrived with the score at 76 for 3, the Indian innings took on a purposeful air.

Kapil Dev stayed only briefly, swishing wildly at Gomes, but he was the only Indian batsman in the first eight who failed to reach double figures. Yashpal Sharma and Roger Binny, in whom the Indian selectors had shown commendable faith as an international player, added 73 in 15 overs of clean, composed hitting. Their stand ended when Binny moved too far across his stumps and was lbw.

By then, however, a good score was in sight, and Yashpal maintained his positive approach until he was too adventurous against the pace of Holding.

There was time for 22 overs before the close and those overs saw Haynes run out in the fourteenth and Greenidge bowled in the eighteenth. Richards played uneasily and the Indians fielded with the enthusiasm of a side who believe that they are winning.

In the second over of the second day, the enthusiasm of the Indian fielders was undisguised when Richards, the most prized wicket, fell to Binny, brilliantly caught by Kirmani. Twenty runs later, Bacchus was wrecked by Madan Lal who bowled most impressively and aggressively.

There was no end to Indian elation. Dujon lifted Binny high to mid-off. Gomes was run out going for a third run

trying to score 106 for the last wicket. There was almost a precedent in the stand between Roberts and Murray against Pakistan at The Oval in 1975, and Roberts and Garner now evoked memories of that stand as they began to hit the ball very hard. Roberts lifted Shastri over mid-wicket. Garner hit the slow left-armer for 4 and 6 off successive balls.

With 12 overs left, 84 were needed. Madan Lal and Binny had both bowled their quota of overs. Kapil Dev returned but Garner glanced dismissively to the boundary. The fifty partnership was reached and when Garner clouted Patil for an enormous 6, the asking rate had dropped to six an over.

Shastri moved in to bowl the fifty-fifth over. He curved the ball gently towards Garner's off stump and as it pitched it turned away, beating the bat. In a flash, Kirmani had whipped off the bails and Garner was out. India had won an historic victory.

ENGLAND v. SRI LANKA AT TAUNTON

For the second time in three days, England reached a big score and Sri Lanka conceded only five runs less than they had done against Pakistan. 78 for 2, Tavare and Fowler having given a meaningful start to the innings, England thrived through Gower and Lamb, and after Lamb had missed a straight ball from Ratnayake and Gatting was run out by Gower who did not heed his call, in came Botham, the local hero. Sadly for the enthusiastic Somerset crowd, Botham was run out by a diving de Mel after he had faced only one ball.

The crowd could console themselves with the beauty of Gower. He had intimated aesthetic pleasure at The Oval now the promise was fulfilled. There seems to be no effort in

The moment of joy. Garner stumped Kirmani, bowled Shastri. India have won. Kirmani throws the ball in the air gleefully. Garner walks away dejected that his brave innings has come to an end. (Dave Cannon)

which the tight bowling of Binny and Madan Lal had made necessary, Marshall was magnificently stumped by Kirmani and, at 130, Lloyd was bowled by Binny.

Holding was dropped on the boundary, but almost immediately, Shastri bowled him. At 157 for 9, West Indies faced defeat, a big defeat which some irresponsible batting and some splendid bowling and fielding had brought about.

Joel Garner joined Andy Roberts in the hopeless task of

ROUND ONE: INDIA v. WEST INDIES
9 and 10 June 1983 at Old Trafford, Manchester

INDIA			
S.M. Gavaskar	c Dujon, b Marshall	19	
K. Srikkanth	c Dujon, b Holding	14	
M.B. Amarnath	c Dujon, b Garner	21	
S.M. Patil	b Gomes	36	
Yashpal Sharma	b Holding	89	
R.N. Kapil Dev†	c Richards, b Gomes	6	
R.M. Binny	lbw, b Marshall	27	
S. Madan Lal	not out	21	
S.M.H. Kirmani*	run out	1	
R.J. Shastri	not out	5	
B.S. Sandhu			
Extras	b 4, lb 10, w 1, nb 8	23	
(60 overs)	(for 8 wickets)	262	

	O	M	R	W
Holding	12	3	32	2
Roberts	12	1	51	—
Marshall	12	1	48	2
Garner	12	1	49	1
Richards	2	—	13	—
Gomes	10	—	46	2

FALL OF WICKETS
1- 21, 2- 48, 3- 76, 4- 125, 5- 141, 6- 214, 7- 243,
8- 246

WEST INDIES			
C.G. Greenidge	b Sandhu	24	
D.L. Haynes	run out	24	
I.V.A. Richards	c Kirmani, b Binny	17	
S.F.A. Bacchus	b Madan Lal	14	
C.H. Lloyd†	b Binny	25	
P.J. Dujon*	c Sandhu, b Binny	7	
H.A. Gomes	run out	8	
M.D. Marshall	st Kirmani, b Shastri	2	
A.M.E. Roberts	not out	37	
M.A. Holding	b Shastri	8	
J. Garner	st Kirmani, b Shastri	37	
Extras	b 4, lb 17, w 4	25	
(54.1 overs)		228	

	O	M	R	W
Kapil Dev	10	—	34	—
Sandhu	12	1	36	1
Madan Lal	12	1	34	1
Binny	12	1	48	3
Shastri	5.1	1	26	3
Patil	3	—	25	—

FALL OF WICKETS
1- 49, 2- 56, 3- 76, 4- 96, 5- 107, 6- 124, 7- 126,
8- 130, 9- 157

Umpires: B. Leadbeater and A.G.T. Whitehead

India won by 34 runs

he man as he pulls, drives and cuts with majesty. Three times he hit the ball over the pavilion with minimum of fuss or exertion and only the consistently committed fielding of the Sri Lankans saved them from total rout. Gould and Dilley, again, hit well and ran fiercely and England's bowlers were left with the simple task of containing their inexperienced opponents to under 333 runs.

The memory of Gower's five sixes and twelve fours was still fresh when Dilley, bowling at a good pace, dismissed Kuruppu and the dangerous Dias, brilliantly caught at slip by a leaping Botham. Mendis batted bountifully and drove through the covers with power and aristocracy, but he fell to Marks whose persistence and accuracy undermined the Sri Lankan middle order. There was another impressive knock from wicket-keeper de Alwis and Sri Lanka died very bravely, but nothing that they did could compete with the beauty that David Gower had exuded earlier in the day.

INDIA v. ZIMBABWE AT LEICESTER

The meeting of the two giant-killers of the first round went conclusively in favour of India. Put in to bat after rain had delayed the start, Zimbabwe scampered with a sense of desperation early on, but Paterson and Heron added 42 runs with orthodox and positive cricket and optimism was growing until Madan Lal dismissed both within three balls.

Fletcher and Houghton ran briskly, restricted by some tight Indian bowling, but aided by some rather lax fielding. It took 34 overs to reach the hundred, however, and as Houghton strove to accelerate, he was caught behind. Curran made a brief assault before he was run out by half the length of the pitch, Fletcher hit across the line and Brown

David Gower has an interruption during his magnificent innings of 130 not out v Sri Lanka. (All Sport)

and Rawson were both caught by Kirmani who established a record for a one-day international with five catches.

Srikkanth was his usual excited belligerence. Gavaskar was out of touch. Amarnath and Patil came together, and with Rawson having retired with a strain, they pillaged the Zimbabwe attack in an effort to get the game over as quickly as possible. They took 15 in one over from Curran, and both of them were out, but by that time, India had victory inextricably in her grasp.

ROUND TWO: ENGLAND v. SRI LANKA
11 June 1983 at Taunton

ENGLAND				SRI LANKA		
G. Fowler	b John	22		S.R. de S. Wettimuny	lbw, b Marks	33
C. J. Tavare	c de Alwis, b Ranatunga	32		B. Kuruppu	c Gatting, b Dilley	4
D.I. Gower	b de Mel	130		R.L. Dias	c Botham, b Dilley	2
A.J. Lamb	b Ratnayake	53		L.R.D. Mendis†	c Willis, b Marks	56
M.W. Gatting	run out	7		R.S. Madugalle	c Tavare, b Marks	12
I.T. Botham	run out	0		A. Ranatunga	c Lamb, b Marks	34
I.J. Gould*	c Ratanunga, b Ratnayake	35		D.S. de Silva	st Gould, b Marks	28
G.R. Dilley	b de Mel	29		R.G. de Alwis	not out	58
V.J. Marks	run out	5		A.L.F. de Mel	c Dilley, b Allott	27
P.J.W. Allott	not out	0		R.J. Ratnayake	c Lamb, b Dilley	15
R.G.D. Willis†				V. John	b Dilley	0
Extras	lb 11, w 8, nb 1	20		Extras	lb 12, w 2, nb 3	17
		—				—
(60 overs)	(for 9 wickets)	333		(58 overs)		286

	O	M	R	W		O	M	R	W
de Mel	12	3	62	2	Willis	11	3	43	—
John	12	—	55	1	Dilley	11	—	45	4
Ratnayake	12	—	66	2	Allott	12	1	82	1
Ranatunga	12	—	65	1	Botham	12	—	60	—
de Silva	12	—	65	—	Marks	12	3	39	5

FALL OF WICKETS
1- 49, 2- 78, 3- 174, 4- 193, 5- 194, 6- 292, 7- 298, 8- 333, 9- 333

FALL OF WICKETS
1- 11, 2- 17, 3- 92, 4- 108, 5- 117, 6- 168, 7- 192, 8- 246, 9- 281

Umpires: M. J. Kitchen and K. E. Palmer

England won by 47 runs

ROUND TWO: ZIMBABWE v. INDIA
11 June 1983 at Leicester

ZIMBABWE			
A.H. Omarshah	c Kirmani, b Sandhu		8
G.A. Paterson	lbw, b Madan Lal		22
J.G. Heron	c Kirmani, b Madan Lal		18
A.J. Pycroft	c Shastri, b Binny		14
D.L. Houghton	c Kirmani, b Madan Lal		21
D.A.G. Fletcher†	b Kapil Dev		13
K.M. Curran	run out		8
I.P. Butchart	not out		22
R.D. Brown	c Kirmani, b Shastri		6
P.W.E. Rawson	c Kirmani, b Binny		3
A.J. Traicos	run out		2
Extras	lb 9, w 9		18
(51.4 overs)			155

	O	M	R	W
Kapil Dev	9	3	18	1
Sandhu	9	1	29	1
Madan Lal	10.4	—	27	3
Binny	11	2	25	2
Shastri	12	1	38	1

FALL OF WICKETS
1- 13, 2- 55, 3- 56, 4- 71, 5- 106, 6- 114, 7- 115, 8- 139, 9- 148

INDIA			
K. Srikkanth	c Butchart, b Rawson		20
S.M. Gavaskar	c Heron, b Rawson		4
M.B. Amarnath	c sub, b Traicos		44
S.M. Patil	b Fletcher		50
R.J. Shastri	c Brown, b Omarshah		17
Yashpal Sharma	not out		18
R.N. Kapil Dev†	not out		2
R.M. Binny			
S. Madan Lal			
S.M.H. Kirmani*			
B.S. Sandhu			
Extras	w 2		2
(37.3 overs)	(for 5 wickets)		157

	O	M	R	W
Rawson	5.1	1	11	2
Curran	6.5	1	33	—
Butchart	5	1	21	—
Traicos	11	1	41	1
Fletcher	6	1	32	1
Omarshah	3.3	—	17	1

FALL OF WICKETS
1- 13, 2- 32, 3- 101, 4- 128, 5- 148

Umpires: J. Birkenshaw and R. Palmer

India won by 5 wickets

PAKISTAN v. NEW ZEALAND AT EDGBASTON

At the end of a grey day in which 3¾ hours had been lost to the weather, New Zealand stood at 211 for 8, and Pakistan were seemingly on their way to a second victory.

The man who had brought them to this position was Abdul Qadir, surely one of the very great leg-spinners, worthy to rank with Mailey, Grimmett, Freeman, Benaud and the rest. Turner and Edgar got off to a blazing start. 22 after three overs. More sedately, the fifty came in the fourteenth over and three overs later, Turner was caught behind off Rashid, a tumbling catch on the leg-side by Wasim Bari who appears to have regained his skill and confidence. His humour and humanity have never deserted him.

It was now that Abdul Qadir dominated the scene, displaying his repertoire with emotion and eagerness. In his second over, Wright was caught behind; in his third, Cairns swatted and was bowled.

In the thirty-second over, Edgar's patience cracked. He charged at Qadir and lofted a simple catch. In the leg-spinner's penultimate over, Howarth too succumbed to frustration and was stumped. Abdul Qadir's 12 overs had given him 4 for 21; the cream of the New Zealand batting had gone.

Coney and Martin Crowe added 46, but Hadlee's threat to flog the bowling was only brief.

The first sign of a New Zealand revival came in the four overs of their innings that remained on the Sunday. Crowe was well caught at extra cover, but Lees and Chatfield hit at everything and ran for almost everything so that 27 invaluable runs were added in those four overs, and the New Zealand total, 238, looked a little healthier than had seemed possible the night before.

Abdul Qadir, Man of the Match, makes an impassioned appeal for lbw against New Zealand skipper Geoff Howarth. Umpire Barry Leadbeater is unmoved. (Ken Kelly)

There have been no more sensational starts to a limited-over international innings than to the start of Pakistan's.

The task of scoring 239 seemed well within the range of the rich talent in the Pakistan batting line-up, and what happened came as a total surprise. The third ball of Hadlee's opening over had Mohsin Khan, Man of the Match at Swansea, lbw. The last ball of the over knocked back Zaheer's off stump. The second ball of Cairn's first over saw Mudassar brilliantly caught low down by Warren Lees and Pakistan were 0 for 3. The whistles had been silenced and the flags had stopped waving as Javed and Imran attempted to salvage something from the wreckage. The batting was uncharacteristically, but understandably grim. It had little effect in stemming the jubilant New Zealanders and Imran departed to an unwise hook in the eleventh over. Apart from a late flourish by Wasim Bari and Abdul Qadir, who took the individual award in his first international of this nature, Pakistan could offer little more resistance and New Zealand's hopes of reaching the semi-final lived again.

AUSTRALIA v. WEST INDIES AT LEEDS

A day of drizzle and dark sky shortened a day at Headingley which was vital to both sides. Most of what there was of the Saturday belonged to Australia. Greenidge flicked Hogg off his legs to Wood at square leg and Richards, after one mighty

LEFT: *Hadlee bowls Zaheer – a bitter blow for Pakistan.* (*Adrian Murrell*)

ROUND TWO: NEW ZEALAND v. PAKISTAN
11 and 12 June 1983 at Edgbaston, Birmingham

NEW ZEALAND				PAKISTAN			
G.M. Turner	c Wasim Bari, b Rashid Khan		27	Mohsin Khan	lbw, b Hadlee		0
B.A. Edgar	c Imran, b Abdul Qadir		44	Mudassar Nazar	c Lees, b Cairns		0
J.G. Wright	c Wasim Bari, b Abdul Qadir		9	Zaheer Abbas	b Hadlee		0
B.L. Cairns	b Abdul Qadir		4	Javed Miandad	lbw, b Chatfield		35
G.P. Howarth†	st Wasim Bari, b Abdul Qadir		16	Imran Khan†	c Chatfield, b Hadlee		9
J.V. Coney	c Ejaz Faqih, b Shahid Mahboob		33	Ejaz Faqih	c Edgar, b Coney		12
M.D. Crowe	c Mohsin, b Rashid Khan		34	Shahid Mahboob	c Wright, b Coney		17
R.J. Hadlee	c Wasim Bari, b Sarfraz Nawaz		13	Wasim Bari*	c Edgar, b Coney		34
J.G. Bracewell	lbw, b Rashid Khan		3	Abdul Qadir	not out		41
W.K. Lees*	not out		24	Sarfraz Nawaz	c M.D. Crowe, b Chatfield		13
E.J. Chatfield	not out		6	Rashid Khan	c and b Cairns		9
Extras	lb 20, w 4, nb 1		25	Extras	b 5, lb 6, w 3, nb 2		16
(60 overs)	(for 9 wickets)		238	(52.2 overs)			186

	O	M	R	W		O	M	R	W
Sarfraz Nawaz	11	1	49	1	Hadlee	9	2	20	3
Shahid Mahboob	10	2	38	1	Cairns	9.3	2	21	2
Rashid Khan	11	—	47	3	Chatfield	12	—	50	2
Mudassar Nazar	12	1	40	—	M.D. Crowe	2	—	12	—
Abdul Qadir	12	4	21	4	Coney	12	3	28	3
Ejaz Faqih	1	—	6	—	Bracewell	11	2	39	—
Zaheer Abbas	3	—	12	—					

FALL OF WICKETS
1- 57, 2- 68, 3- 80, 4- 109, 5- 120, 6- 166, 7- 197, 8- 202, 9- 223

FALL OF WICKETS
1- 0, 2- 0, 3- 0, 4- 22, 5-54, 6- 60, 7- 102, 8- 131, 9- 158

Umpires: H. D. Bird and B. Leadbeater

New Zealand won by 52 runs

ROUND TWO: AUSTRALIA v. WEST INDIES
11 and 12 June 1983 at Headingley, Leeds

WEST INDIES				
C.G. Greenidge	c Wood, b Hogg	4		
D.L. Haynes	c Marsh, b Lawson	13		
I.V.A. Richards	b Lawson	7		
H.A. Gomes	c Marsh, b Lillee	78		
C.H. Lloyd†	lbw, b Macleay	19		
S.F.A. Bacchus	c Wessels, b Yallop	47		
P.J. Dujon*	c Marsh, b Lillee	12		
A.M.E. Roberts	c Marsh, b Lillee	5		
M.A. Holding	run out	20		
W.W. Daniel	not out	16		
W.W. Davis				
Extras	b 1, lb 9, w 10, nb 11	31		
	(60 overs)	(for 9 wickets)	252	

	O	M	R	W
Lawson	12	3	29	3
Hogg	12	1	49	1
Macleay	12	1	31	1
Lillee	12	—	55	2
Yallop	5	—	26	1
Border	7	—	31	—

FALL OF WICKETS
1- 7, 2- 25, 3- 32, 4- 78, 5- 154, 6- 192, 7- 208,
8- 211, 9- 252

AUSTRALIA		
G.M. Wood	retired hurt	
K.C. Wessels	b Roberts	1
K.J. Hughes†	c Lloyd, b Davis	1
D.W. Hookes	c Dujon, b Davis	4
G.N. Yallop	c Holding, b Davis	2
A.R. Border	c Lloyd, b Davis	1
K.H. Macleay	c Haynes, b Davis	
R.W. Marsh*	c Haynes, b Holding	
G.F. Lawson	c Dujon, b Davis	
R.M. Hogg	not out	
D.K. Lillee	b Davis	
Extras	b 1, lb 4, w 5, nb 8	1
	(30.3 overs)	15

	O	M	R	W
Roberts	7	—	14	1
Holding	8	2	23	1
Davis	10.3	—	51	7
Daniel	3	—	35	—
Gomes	2	—	10	—

FALL OF WICKETS
1- 18, 2- 55, 3- 114, 4- 116, 5- 126, 6- 137, 7- 141,
8- 150, 9- 151

Umpires: D. J. Constant and D. G. L. Evans

West Indies won by 101 runs

hook off Hogg, had his off stump knocked out of the ground by Lawson. Haynes became another Lawson victim and Lloyd fell to Macleay. Gomes batted perilously and Bacchus, after an invaluable 47, hit Yallop, surprisingly successful in these matches, straight to Wessels. The day closed with West Indies 160 for 5 off 42 overs, Gomes still there with 51.

The next day West Indies added more runs than Australia would have liked. Gomes took his patchy, but courageous innings to 78, Holding and Daniel struck some lusty blows and 92 runs came in the last 18 overs.

Wessels played back and had his off stump knocked over at 18, and very shortly after, Graeme Wood was hit on the head by a ball from Holding and carried unconscious from the field. It was a nasty blow and a most unpleasant sight. The bowler was not to blame, but the pitch certainly deserved the strictures that it received after the game.

When Daniel and Davis took over the West Indies attack runs came at a furious rate. Daniel could find no length and Davis was equally wayward in both length and direction. Three overs from Daniel cost 35 runs with Hookes the leader of the onslaught. Davis had Hughes caught at slip, and, withstanding a further attack by Hookes and Yallop, he suddenly bowled straighter and faster. The batting continued to be frenzied and Winston Davis began to pick up wickets.

The conditions were in his favour, but, nevertheless, a return of 7 for 51, the best ever in a limited-over international, was a remarkable performance and one which brought him the individual award in his first World Cup match, a game which he had come into only because Marshall and Garner were injured.

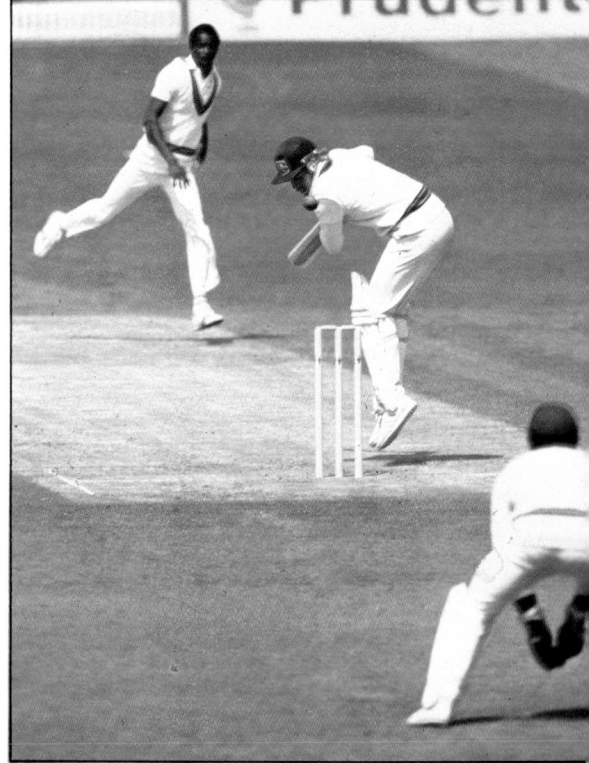

Winston Davis, who took a record seven wickets in the match bowls to David Hookes, scorer of a valiant 45. (All Sport)

ENGLAND v. PAKISTAN AT LORD'S

In one of the least memorable of one-day internationals, England beat Pakistan by 8 wickets with 9 overs and 2 balls to spare. The margin in no way flattered England who totally outplayed a very poor Pakistan side.

England bowled very well. Their pace bowlers maintained line and length and the Pakistan batsmen were frustrated into destruction. Marks plodded away, looked innocuous, but was made to seem unhittable.

In the eleventh over, Mohsin, trying to break free of the shackles imposed upon him, mis-hit Willis to mid-on. Mansoor struggled painfully before he touched Willis, eyes aflame, to Gould. Javed hit Allott for successive fours and then was caught behind off a good delivery from Botham next over. Mudassar mis-hooked just before lunch and Pakistan were 96 for 4.

Imran arrived to join Zaheer and was hit on the foot. He called for a runner, was dropped at the wicket and his runner ran him out. Wasim Raja looked like one with a Test career behind him and Abdul Qadir was run out after he had survived an lbw appeal. Zaheer played some good shots, but seemed reluctant to take on the responsibility which had long since become his.

Imran did not field and Zaheer controlled affairs. Tavare was lbw to the enthusiastic Rashid. Gower looked as if he were still batting at Taunton until he flicked the persevering Mansoor to mid-wicket where Sarfraz held the catch as he fell sideways. Lamb survived a very close call for lbw to Qadir's googly and Fowler survived. He was missed three times but stayed to make 78.

Pakistan looked rudderless and dispirited. Lamb put them out of their misery with a six over long-off.

Javed Miandad is run out while acting as runner for Imran Khan who stands disconsolately at square-leg as Gould removes the bails. (All Sport)

WEST INDIES v. ZIMBABWE AT WORCESTER

On a cloudy day, Zimbabwe, put in to bat, struggled to 70 for 4 off 33 overs at lunch. There was a very brave recovery indeed after lunch when Fletcher and Houghton took the score to 157 before Houghton was caught in the fiftieth over.

Fletcher carried on boldly and the last ten overs produced another 60 runs to suggest that no side could afford to take Zimbabwe lightly.

There was even the suggestion of another surprise when Haynes was caught behind at 3, and, to the jubilation of the

---

ROUND THREE: ENGLAND v. PAKISTAN
13 June 1983 at Lord's

PAKISTAN				ENGLAND			
Mohsin Khan	c Tavare, b Willis	3		G. Fowler	not out		78
Mudassar Nazar	c Gould, b Allott	26		C.J. Tavare	lbw, b Rashid Khan		8
Mansoor Akhtar	c Gould, b Willis	3		D.I. Gower	c Sarfraz,		
Javed Miandad	c Gould, b Botham	14			b Mansoor Akhtar		48
Zaheer Abbas	not out	83		A.J. Lamb	not out		48
Imran Khan†	run out	7		M.W. Gatting			
Wasim Raja	c Botham, b Marks	9		I.T. Botham			
Abdul Qadir	run out	0		I.J. Gould*			
Sarfraz Nawaz	c and b Botham	11		V.J. Marks			
Wasim Bari*	not out	18		G.R. Dilley			
Rashid Khan				P.J.W. Allott			
Extras	b 5, lb 8, w 3, nb 3	19		R.G.D. Willis†			
				Extras	b 1, lb 12, w 2, nb 2		17
(60 overs)	(for 8 wickets)	193		(50.4 overs)	(for 2 wickets)		199

	O	M	R	W		O	M	R	W
Willis	12	4	24	2	Rashid Khan	7	2	19	1
Dilley	12	1	33	—	Sarfraz Nawaz	11	5	22	—
Allott	12	2	48	1	Wasim Raja	3	—	14	—
Botham	12	3	36	2	Mudassar Nazar	8	—	30	—
Marks	12	1	33	1	Abdul Qadir	9.4	—	53	—
					Mansoor Akhtar	12	2	44	1

FALL OF WICKETS
1- 29, 2- 33, 3- 49, 4- 67, 5- 96, 6- 112, 7- 118, 8- 154

FALL OF WICKETS
1- 15, 2- 93

Umpires: B. J. Meyer and A. G. T. Whitehead

England won by 8 wickets

ROUND THREE: ZIMBABWE v. WEST INDIES
13 June 1983 at Worcester

ZIMBABWE				WEST INDIES			
A.H. Omarshah	b Roberts		2	C.G. Greenidge	not out		105
G.A. Paterson	c Dujon, b Holding		4	D.L. Haynes	c Houghton, b Rawson		2
J.G. Heron	st Dujon, b Gomes		12	I.V.A. Richards	lbw, b Rawson		16
A.J. Pycroft	run out		13	H.A. Gomes	not out		75
D.L. Houghton	c Dujon, b Roberts		54	S.F.A. Bacchus			
D.A.G. Fletcher†	not out		71	C.H. Lloyd†			
K.M. Curran	b Roberts		7	P.J. Dujon*			
I.P. Butchart	lbw, b Holding		0	W.W. Daniel			
G.E. Peckover	not out		16	A.M.E. Roberts			
P.W.E. Rawson				M.A. Holding			
A.J. Traicos				W.W. Davis			
Extras	b 1, lb 23, w 7, nb 7		38	Extras	b 1, lb 8, w 9, nb 2		20
(60 overs)	(for 7 wickets)		217	(48.3 overs)	(for 2 wickets)		218

	O	M	R	W			O	M	R	W
Roberts	12	4	36	3		Rawson	12	1	39	2
Holding	12	2	33	2		Curran	10.3	1	37	—
Daniel	12	4	21	—		Butchart	9	1	40	—
Davis	12	2	34	—		Fletcher	4	—	22	—
Gomes	8	—	42	1		Traicos	9	—	37	—
Richards	4	1	13	—		Omarshah	4	—	23	—

FALL OF WICKETS
1- 7, 2- 7, 3- 35, 4- 65, 5- 157, 6- 181, 7- 183

FALL OF WICKETS
1- 3, 2- 23

Umpires: D. G. L. Evans and J. Birkenshaw

West Indies won by 8 wickets

entire Zimbabwe contingent, Richards was lbw at 23.

There had been half an hour's hold up for the light and West Indies were clearly worried as Gomes was beaten several times and it was the nineteenth over before 50 was reached, but the Zimbabwe second string bowling lacked the urgency of Curran and Rawson. Greenidge reached a sombre fifty and then took command. Gomes overcame his earlier misgivings and began to stroke the ball sweetly. There was to be no more giant-killing.

Jack Heron stumped Dujon, bowled Gomes for 12. (Ken Kelly)

AUSTRALIA v. INDIA AT TRENT BRIDGE

The Australians arrived at the half-way stage in the competition without a win and were confronted by an Indian side who had won both of their matches. There were two sad, if not totally unexpected team changes, in that Dennis Lillee was left out of the Australian side for Hogan, the left-arm spinner, and Gavaskar could find no place in the Indian side. The Australians chose, too, to play Chappell in place of the injured Wood, and it was Chappell who dominated the match with a magnificent century.

Wessels, looking very vulnerable, went at 11, but Hughes and Chappell added 144 with some exciting strokes. Chappell's innings included 13 fours, and well as he batted, he profited from two dropped catches. Border was also missed twice in his 26, and the Indian fielding and bowling were well below the standard that one had come to expect.

Apart from Kapil Dev and Madan Lal, who deceived Hookes with a slower ball before the left-hander could go on the rampage, the Indian bowling was wayward and Kapil Dev turned to seven bowlers in an effort to halt the flow of runs.

Srikkanth began the Indian reply with his customary dazzling, if unorthodox, strokes and the score was 38 in the sixth over before Shastri was out. By the twenty-second over, the score was 66 for 6 and the game decided.

Ken Macleay took three wickets in his first four overs and finished with 6 for 39, the second best performance recorded by an Australian bowler in a limited-over international.

So, Australia's hopes of reaching the semi-finals were kept alive, and India, after the euphoria of the first two rounds, were set to do some reassessing of their talents.

ROUND THREE: AUSTRALIA v. INDIA
13 June 1983 at Trent Bridge, Nottingham

AUSTRALIA			
K.C. Wessels	b Kapil Dev		5
T.M. Chappell	c Srikkanth, b Amarnath		110
K.J. Hughes†	b Madan Lal		52
D.W. Hookes	c Kapil Dev, b Madan Lal		1
G.N. Yallop	not out		66
A.R. Border	c Yashpal Sharma, b Binny		26
R.W. Marsh*	c Sandhu, b Kapil Dev		12
K.H. Macleay	c and b Kapil Dev		4
T.G. Hogan	b Kapil Dev		11
G.F. Lawson	c Srikkanth, b Kapil Dev		6
R.M. Hogg	not out		2
Extras	b 1, lb 14, w 8, nb 2		25
(60 overs)	(for 9 wickets)		320

	O	M	R	W
Kapil Dev	12	2	43	5
Sandhu	12	1	52	—
Binny	12	—	52	1
Shastri	2	—	16	—
Madan Lal	12	—	69	2
Patil	6	—	36	—
Amarnath	4	—	27	1

FALL OF WICKETS
1- 11, 2- 155, 3- 159, 4- 206, 5- 254, 6- 277, 7- 289, 8- 301, 9- 307

INDIA			
R.J. Shastri	lbw, b Lawson		11
K. Srikkanth	c Border, b Hogan		39
M.B. Amarnath	run out		2
D.B. Vengsarkar	lbw, b Macleay		5
S.M. Patil	b Macleay		0
Yashpal Sharma	c and b Macleay		3
R.N. Kapil Dev†	b Hogan		40
S. Madan Lal	c Hogan, b Macleay		27
R.M. Binny	lbw, b Macleay		0
S.M.H. Kirmani*	b Macleay		12
B.S. Sandhu	not out		9
Extras	b 1, lb 4, w 3, nb 2		10
(37.5 overs)			158

	O	M	R	W
Lawson	5	1	25	1
Hogg	7	2	23	—
Hogan	12	1	48	2
Macleay	11.5	3	39	6
Border	2	—	13	—

FALL OF WICKETS
1- 38, 2- 43, 3- 57, 4- 57, 5- 64, 6- 66, 7- 124, 8- 126, 9- 136

Umpires: D. O. Oslear and R. Palmer

Australia won by 162 runs

Srikkanth hits a ball to leg in his hard-hitting innings of 39. Marsh looks concerned. (Steve Powell)

NEW ZEALAND v. SRI LANKA AT BRISTOL

The Sri Lankan batting, which had proved to be their strength in the first two matches, could not withstand the pace and movement of Richard Hadlee on a damp wicket, and New Zealand won most convincingly.

It was tight bowling by Ewen Chatfield which first frustrated the Sri Lankans, but Mendis and Madugalle lifted their hopes with a stand of 71 in 20 overs. They seemed in a position to quicken the pace towards a big score, but Hadlee returned for a second spell and dismissed Mendis, and the innings fell apart.

With rain expected, New Zealand began briskly and were 120 for 3 off 25 overs at tea. Howarth continued the assault after the break and although five wickets were lost, the New Zealanders swept to victory with more than 20 overs to spare.

ENGLAND v. NEW ZEALAND AT EDGBASTON

Having carried all before them, England stumbled and finally fell at the fourth hurdle when the ghosts of their winter tour walked again. There was no indication of what was to come when Fowler, batting more postively than at any other time in the competition, and Tavare began with 63 in 19 overs before Tavare fell to the reliable Coney, the most naggingly accurate bowler in the tournament.

The first error that England committed was to send in Botham at number three. Gower had been so dominant in the position that it was hard to understand why any change had been made. It seems that the reasoning was that Botham would be able to plunder the gentle medium of Coney and the off-breaks of John Bracewell and, indeed, he did hit

ROUND THREE: NEW ZEALAND v. SRI LANKA
13 June 1983 at Bristol

SRI LANKA			O	M	R	W
S.R. de S. Wettimuny	lbw, b Hadlee	7				
B. Kuruppu	c Hadlee, b Chatfield	26				
R.L. Dias	b Chatfield	25				
L.R.D. Mendis†	b Hadlee	43				
R.S. Madugalle	c Snedden, b Coney	60				
A. Ranatunga	lbw, b Hadlee	0				
D.S. de Silva	b Coney	13				
R.G. de Alwis*	c Howarth, b Snedden	16				
A.L.F. de Mel	c and b Hadlee	1				
R.J. Ratnayake	b Hadlee	5				
V. John	not out	2				
Extras	lb 6, w 1, nb 1	8				
(56.1 overs)		206				

	O	M	R	W
Hadlee	10.1	4	25	5
Snedden	10	1	38	1
Chatfield	12	4	24	2
Cairns	7	—	35	—
Coney	12	—	44	2
M.D. Crowe	5	—	32	—

FALL OF WICKETS
1- 16, 2- 56, 3- 73, 4- 144, 5- 144, 6- 171, 7- 196,
8- 199, 9- 199

NEW ZEALAND		
G.M. Turner	c Mendis, b de Silva	50
J.G. Wright	lbw, b de Mel	45
G.P. Howarth†	c Madugalle, b Ratnayake	76
M.D. Crowe	c de Alwis, b de Mel	0
J.J. Crowe	lbw, b John	23
J.V. Coney	not out	2
I.D.S. Smith*	not out	4
R.J. Hadlee		
B.L. Cairns		
M.C. Snedden		
E.J. Chatfield		
Extras	lb 6, w 3	9
(39.2 overs)	(for 5 wickets)	209

	O	M	R	W
de Mel	8	2	30	2
John	8.2	—	49	1
Ratnayake	12	—	60	1
de Silva	9	—	39	1
Ranatunga	2	—	22	—

FALL OF WICKETS
1- 89, 2- 99, 3- 110, 4- 176, 5- 205

Umpires: H. D. Bird and D. R. Shepherd

New Zealand won by 5 wickets

Bracewell for a six high over long leg, but the young spinner took his revenge by holding a stinging return catch low down.

Gower now came in to play with immediate fluency and command. Beauty and authority are now perfectly wedded in his batting. At 117, however, he lost Fowler to Chatfield, and what followed was a total disintegration. As Gower drove, hooked and cut at one end, so a series of irresponsible, and often technically inadequate, shots at the other end saw the England innings move to a swift decline.

New Zealand were elated by their success, but their joy was subdued when Willis had Turner lbw and then Edgar was adjudged caught behind. The first decision was not well received, the second was greeted with some anger in the New Zealand camp. The ball was taken very low by Gould who claimed a catch. Umpire Birkenshaw asked Palmer if the ball had carried, but the square-leg umpire seemed to indicate that he could not tell. Nevertheless, Birkenshaw gave Edgar out.

Geoff Howarth now played a captain's innings, joining first with Jeff and then with Martin Crowe in valuable stands which helped restore belief in victory, but when Martin Crowe was bowled by Marks in the twenty-seventh over, New Zealand were 75 for 4.

Now came Jeremy Coney. He and Howarth added 71 before Howarth was run out when he attempted a second run and was beaten by Dilley's fine throw from long-leg. Smith, whose wicket-keeping had been disappointing, did not last long, but Richard Hadlee was magnificently belligerent. In

RIGHT: *David Gower walks away in disbelief – left without partners on 92. Ken Palmer is the umpire. (Ken Kelly)*

*Gatting is bowled by Cairns for 1, an England collapse.
(George Herringshaw)*

4 overs, 70 runs were added and New Zealand were on the
threshold of victory, 14 from 23 balls, when Hadlee was
bowled by Willis. Cairns struck a lusty blow before he was
lbw playing across the line and 4 runs were needed off 9 balls.
There were still 4 wanted when Allott began the last over.

Coney drove a single from the first ball and the second ball
went through the wicket-keeper's gloves for two byes.
Bracewell on-drove the fifth ball of the over for 4 and New
Zealand had won a hard-earned victory.

WEST INDIES v. INDIA AT THE OVAL

The poor form which Viv Richards had shown in the competition appeared not to have vanished when, coming to the
wicket at 17 for 1, he struggled against some accurate bowling on a pitch of uneven bounce. It is the mark of the great
player that he can adapt to conditions, throw off the worries
of recent performances and play as the game demands. This
is just what Richards did. He asserted himself slowly and
deemed that this was to be a day when control would be won
by the deftness of the foil rather than the bludgeoning of the
broadsword. His reading of the situation was confirmed
when Haynes fell to a ball which reared awkwardly off a
length.

Lloyd's response to the pitch was to promote himself in the
batting order, and although he did not find it easy to middle
the ball, he did help Richards to add 80 from 14 overs before
he was run out.

Richards was out in the fifty-second over for 119. He had
quickened towards the end, but he had still hit only seven
fours in his innings, a measure of the care and deliberation
which he had brought to his task.

Srikkanth and Shastri went quickly when India began
their reply, but Vengsarkar and Amarnath revived hopes
that India would repeat their victory of the opening match of
the tournament with a stand which took the score to 89 in 21
overs. At this point, however, Vengsarkar was hit in the
mouth by a ball from Marshall which reared from just short
of a length and he was forced to retire. Two overs later,
Amarnath was struck on the elbow by a ball from Marshall
and although he batted on, he never quite played with his
former dominance.

ROUND FOUR: ENGLAND v. NEW ZEALAND
15 June 1983 at Edgbaston, Birmingham

ENGLAND				**NEW ZEALAND**			
G. Fowler	c J.J. Crowe, b Chatfield	69		G.M. Turner	lbw, b Willis	2
C.J. Tavare	c Cairns, b Coney	18		B.A. Edgar	c Gould, b Willis	1
I.T. Botham	c and b Bracewell	12		G.P. Howarth†	run out	60
D.I. Gower	not out	92		J.J. Crowe	b Allott	17
A.J. Lamb	c J.J. Crowe, b Cairns	8		M.D. Crowe	b Marks	20
M.W. Gatting	b Cairns	1		J.V. Coney	not out	66
I.J. Gould*	lbw, b Cairns	4		I.D.S. Smith	lbw, b Botham	4
V.J. Marks	b Hadlee	5		R.J. Hadlee	b Willis	31
G.R. Dilley	b Hadlee	10		B.L. Cairns	lbw, b Willis	5
P.J.W. Allott	c Smith, b Hadlee	0		J.G. Bracewell	not out	4
R.G.D. Willis†	lbw, b Chatfield	0		E.J. Chatfield		
Extras	b 4, lb 10, w 1	15		Extras	b 2, lb 22, w 1, nb 3	28
(55.2 overs)		234		(59.5 overs)	(for 8 wickets)	238

	O	M	R	W		O	M	R	W
Hadlee	10	3	32	3	Willis	12	1	42	4
Cairns	11	—	44	3	Dilley	12	1	43	—
Coney	12	2	27	1	Botham	12	1	47	1
Bracewell	12	—	66	1	Allott	11.5	2	44	1
Chatfield	10.2	—	50	2	Marks	12	1	34	1

FALL OF WICKETS
1- 63, 2- 77, 3- 117, 4- 143, 5- 154, 6- 162, 7- 203,
8- 233, 9- 233

FALL OF WICKETS
1- 2, 2- 3, 3- 47, 4- 75, 5- 146, 6- 151, 7- 221, 8- 231

Umpires: K. E. Palmer and J. Birkenshaw

New Zealand won by 2 wickets

ROUND FOUR: WEST INDIES v. INDIA
15 June 1983 at The Oval

WEST INDIES			
C.G. Greenidge	c Vengsarkar, b Kapil Dev		9
D.L. Haynes	c Kapil Dev, b Amarnath		38
I.V.A. Richards	c Kirmani, b Sandhu		119
C.H. Lloyd†	run out		41
S.F.A. Bacchus	b Binny		8
P.J. Dujon*	c Shastri, b Binny		9
H.A. Gomes	not out		27
A.M.E. Roberts	c Patil, b Binny		7
M.D. Marshall	run out		4
M.A. Holding	c sub, b Madan Lal		2
W.W. Davis	not out		0
Extras	lb 13, w 5		18
(60 overs)	(for 9 wickets)		282

	O	M	R	W
Kapil Dev	12	—	46	1
Sandhu	12	2	42	1
Binny	12	—	71	3
Amarnath	12	—	58	1
Madan Lal	12	—	47	1

FALL OF WICKETS
1- 17, 2- 118, 3- 198, 4- 213, 5- 239, 6- 240, 7- 257, 8- 270, 9- 280

INDIA			
K. Srikkanth	c Dujon, b Roberts		2
R.J. Shastri	c Dujon, b Roberts		6
M.B. Amarnath	c Lloyd, b Holding		80
D.B. Vengsarkar	retired hurt		32
S.M. Patil	c and b Gomes		21
Yashpal Sharma	run out		9
R.N. Kapil Dev†	c Haynes, b Holding		36
R.M. Binny	lbw, b Holding		1
S. Madan Lal	not out		8
S.M.H. Kirmani*	b Marshall		0
B.S. Sandhu	run out		0
Extras	b 3, lb 13, nb 5		21
(53.1 overs)			216

	O	M	R	W
Roberts	9	1	29	2
Holding	9.1	—	40	3
Marshall	11	3	20	1
Davis	12	2	51	—
Gomes	12	1	55	1

FALL OF WICKETS
1- 2, 2- 21, 3- 130, 4- 143, 5- 193, 6- 195, 7- 212, 8- 214, 9- 216

Umpires: B. J. Meyer and D. R. Shepherd

West Indies won by 66 runs

Kapil Dev made a brisk 36 and Patil looked purposeful, but wickets and overs ebbed away. While Kapil Dev lived, there was hope. He was caught off Holding at 212 and 71 runs needed from the last eight overs was too great a task for Madan Lal, Kirmani and Sandhu.

The end of Vengsarkar's World Cup and of India's hopes in this match. Struck in the face by a ball from Marshall. (All Sport)

PAKISTAN v. SRI LANKA AT LEEDS

It seemed that Sri Lanka would register their first victory in the tournament when, with eight wickets in hand, they needed 102 from 20 overs to beat Pakistan, but Abdul Qadir who had earlier dismissed Dias, returned for the last four overs of his quota and caused havoc and panic among the Sri Lankan batsmen.

Pakistan, put in to bat, had been reduced to 43 for 5 as de Mel moved the new ball disconcertingly on an overcast morning. Then Imran Khan and Shahid Mahboob added 144 and Pakistan reached a respectable, if not apparently decisive, score. Well as Imran and Shahid batted, they benefited from a couple of missed chances.

The game was in favour of Sri Lanka until Qadir had Mendis caught behind and in his next over, dismissed Ratnayake and Ranatunga with successive deliveries. It was at this point that fear gripped the Sri Lankan batting, de Silva was recklessly run out and de Alwis was caught at slip to give Qadir three wickets in 8 balls.

The last pair, John and de Mel, came together with 37 required from 6 overs, and the way in which they made 25 of them before de Mel was caught off Sarfraz merely emphasised the folly of what had gone before.

AUSTRALIA v. ZIMBABWE AT SOUTHAMPTON

Australia avenged the defeat that they had suffered at the hands of Zimbabwe in the first round, but once again Zimbabwe gave a splendid performance and the margin between the two sides was small.

Wessels was left out of the Australian side and Wood and

ROUND FOUR: PAKISTAN v. SRI LANKA
16 June 1983 at Headingley, Leeds

PAKISTAN				
Mohsin Khan	c Ranatunga, b de Mel			3
Mansoor Akhtar	c de Alwis, b de Mel			6
Zaheer Abbas	c Dias, b de Mel			15
Javed Miandad	lbw, b Ratnayake			7
Imran Khan†	not out			102
Ejaz Faqih	lbw, b Ratnayake			0
Shahid Mahboob	c de Silva, b de Mel			77
Sarfraz Nawaz	c Madugalle, b de Mel			9
Abdul Qadir	not out			5
Wasim Bari*				
Rashid Khan				
Extras	b 1, lb 4, w 4, nb 2			11
(60 overs)	(for 7 wickets)			235

	O	M	R	W
de Mel	12	1	39	5
John	12	1	48	—
Ratnayake	12	2	42	2
Ranatunga	11	—	49	—
de Silva	12	1	42	—
Wettimuny	1	—	4	—

FALL OF WICKETS
1- 6, 2- 25, 3- 30, 4- 43, 5- 43, 6- 187, 7- 204

Umpires: D. O. Oslear and A. G. T. Whitehead
Pakistan won by 11 runs

SRI LANKA				
S.R. de S. Wettimuny	c Shahid Mahboob, b Rashid Khan			50
B. Kuruppu	b Rashid Khan			12
R.L. Dias	st Wasim Bari, b Abdul Qadir			47
L.R.D. Mendis†	c Wasim Bari, b Abdul Qadir			33
R.J. Ratnayake	st Wasim Bari, b Abdul Qadir			1
R.S. Madugalle	c Abdul Qadir, b Shahid Mahboob			26
A. Ranatunga	c Zaheer Abbas, b Abdul Qadir			0
D.S. de Silva	run out			1
R.G. de Alwis*	c Javed Miandad, b Abdul Qadir			4
A.L.F. de Mel	c Imran Khan, b Sarfraz Nawaz			17
V. John	not out			6
Extras	lb 8, w 17, nb 2			27
(58.3 overs)				224

	O	M	R	W
Rashid Khan	12	4	31	2
Sarfraz Nawaz	11.3	2	25	1
Shahid Mahboob	10	1	62	1
Mansoor Akhtar	1	—	8	—
Ejaz Faqih	12	—	27	—
Abdul Qadir	12	1	44	5

FALL OF WICKETS
1- 22, 2- 101, 3- 162, 4- 162, 5- 166, 6- 166, 7- 171, 8- 193, 9- 199

ROUND FOUR: AUSTRALIA v. ZIMBABWE
16 June 1983 at Southampton

AUSTRALIA				
G.M. Wood	c Rawson, b Traicos			73
T.M. Chappell	c Traicos, b Rawson			22
K.J. Hughes†	b Traicos			31
D.W. Hookes	c Brown, b Fletcher			10
G.N. Yallop	c Houghton, b Curran			20
A.R. Border	b Butchart			43
R.W. Marsh*	not out			35
K.H. Macleay	c Rawson, b Butchart			9
T.G. Hogan	not out			5
D.K. Lillee				
R.M. Hogg				
Extras	lb 16, w 2, nb 6			24
(60 overs)	(for 7 wickets)			272

	O	M	R	W
Hogg	9	2	34	—
Rawson	9	—	50	1
Fletcher	9	1	27	1
Butchart	10	—	52	2
Traicos	12	1	28	2
Curran	11	—	57	1

FALL OF WICKETS
1- 46, 2- 124, 3- 150, 4- 150, 5- 219, 6- 231, 7- 249

Umpires: D. L. Evans and R. E. Palmer
Australia won by 32 runs

ZIMBABWE				
R.D. Brown	c Marsh, b Hogan			38
G.A. Paterson	lbw, b Hogg			17
J.G. Heron	run out			3
A.J. Pycroft	run out			13
D.L. Houghton	c Hughes, b Chappell			84
D.A.G. Fletcher†	b Hogan			2
K.M. Curran	lbw, b Chappell			35
I.P. Butchart	lbw, b Hogg			0
P.W.E. Rawson	lbw, b Hogg			0
A.J. Traicos	b Chappell			19
V.R. Hogg	not out			7
Extras	b 1, lb 10, w 1, nb 10			22
(59.5 overs)				240

	O	M	R	W
Hogg	12	—	40	3
Lillee	9	1	23	—
Hogan	12	—	33	2
Macleay	9	—	45	—
Border	9	1	30	—
Chappell	8.5	—	47	3

FALL OF WICKETS
1- 48, 2- 53, 3- 79, 4- 97, 5- 109, 6- 212, 7- 213, 8- 213, 9- 213

Chappell began with 46 in 10 overs, but after Chappell had fallen to Rawson, only 104 runs came in the next 30 overs. Traicos was particularly economical and it was not until Yallop and Border came together that a more productive session ensued.

Marsh appeared with 6 overs remaining and lashed 35, including two well struck sixes.

Zimbabwe began soundly with 48 off 13 overs, but four

wickets fell in 10 overs for the addition of 56 runs and the game turned Australia's way. Houghton, however, batted heroically, hitting nine fours and a six. He shared a sixth wicket partnership of 103 in 17 overs with Kevin Curran and Zimbabwe had visions of the double, but Hogg and Chappell broke through and four batsmen went as 1 run was scored and the dream was shattered.

AUSTRALIA v. WEST INDIES AT LORD'S

Electing to bat first on a sun scorched day, Australia lost both openers to Marshall, the quickest bowler in the tournament, by the tenth over, but Hughes and Hookes batted finely to add 101. In context, the partnership was a most impressive one, not only because it came at a difficult time for Australia, but because Hughes, suffering from a thigh injury, was forced to resort to a runner.

Hookes was the first to reach fifty, but hit Davis high to Greenidge shortly afterwards, and although catches were dropped, Australia were stumbling again at 176 for 4 when Hughes danced down the wicket to Gomes and was bowled.

Yallop again provided some quick runs, but it was Marsh who dominated the last scene with 37 in 26 balls. His hitting was amazing as he pulled Holding for 6, hooked the next ball into the tavern and then straight drove the next.

Haynes and Greenidge gave the West Indies a firm basis for reply and after Haynes had chopped the slow left-arm Hogan into his stumps, Richards came in and announced his total rehabilitation with a straight six.

The second West Indian wicket did not fall until the score was 203, and by that time victory was already apparent. For the younger spectators, bred on stories of the ferocity of Lillee and Thompson, names to frighten you to sleep at night, there was only the sad spectre of two medium pacers who conjured no images of the giants of yore.

David Hookes lashes a boundary in his innings of 56. (All Sport)

ROUND FIVE: AUSTRALIA v. WEST INDIES
18 June 1983 at Lord's

AUSTRALIA						WEST INDIES					
G.M. Wood	b Marshall				17	C.G. Greenidge	c Hughes, b Hogg				90
T.M. Chappell	c Dujon, b Marshall				5	D.L. Haynes	b Hogan				33
K.J. Hughes†	b Gomes				69	I.V.A. Richards	not out				95
D.W. Hookes	c Greenidge, b Davis				56	H.A. Gomes	b Chappell				15
G.N. Yallop	not out				52	C.H. Lloyd†	not out				19
A.R. Border	c and b Gomes				11	S.F.A. Bacchus					
R.W. Marsh*	c Haynes, b Holding				37	P.J. Dujon*					
T.G. Hogan	not out				0	M.D. Marshall					
J.R. Thomson						A.M.E. Roberts					
D.K. Lillee						M.A. Holding					
R.M. Hogg						W.W. Davis					
Extras	b 1, lb 18, w 6, nb 1				26	Extras	b 3, lb 18, w 1, nb 2				24
(60 overs)	(for 6 wickets)				273	(57.5 overs)	(for 3 wickets)				276

	O	M	R	W			O	M	R	W
Roberts	12	—	51	—		Hogg	12	—	25	1
Marshall	12	—	36	2		Thomson	11	—	64	—
Davis	12	—	57	1		Hogan	12	—	60	1
Holding	12	1	56	1		Lillee	12	—	52	—
Gomes	12	—	47	2		Chappell	10.5	—	51	1

FALL OF WICKETS
1- 10, 2- 37, 3- 138, 4- 176, 5- 202, 6- 266

FALL OF WICKETS
1- 79, 2- 203, 3- 238

Umpires: K. E. Palmer and A. G. T. Whitehead

West Indies won by 7 wickets

ROUND FIVE: ENGLAND v. PAKISTAN
18 June 1983 at Old Trafford, Manchester

PAKISTAN			
Mohsin Khan	c Marks, b Allott	32
Mudassar Nazar	c Gould, b Dilley	18
Zaheer Abbas	c Gould, b Dilley	0
Javed Miandad	run out	67
Imran Khan†	c Willis, b Marks	13
Wasim Raja	c Willis, b Marks	15
Ejaz Faqih	not out	42
Sarfraz Nawaz	b Willis	17
Abdul Qadir	run out	6
Wasim Bari*	not out	2
Rashid Khan		
Extras	b 3, lb 14, w 2, nb 1	20
(60 overs)	(for 8 wickets)	232

	O	M	R	W
Willis	12	3	37	1
Dilley	12	2	46	2
Allott	12	1	33	1
Botham	12	1	51	—
Marks	12	—	45	2

FALL OF WICKETS
1- 33, 2- 34, 3- 87, 4- 116, 5- 144, 6- 169, 7- 204, 8- 221

ENGLAND			
G. Fowler	c Javed Miandad, b Mudassar Nazar	69
C.J. Tavare	c Wasim Raja, b Zaheer Abbas	58
D.I. Gower	c Zaheer Abbas, b Mudassar Nazar	31
A.J. Lamb	not out	38
M.W. Gatting	not out	14
I.T. Botham		
I.J. Gould*		
V.J. Marks		
G. R. Dilley		
P.J.W. Allott		
R.G.D. Willis†		
Extras	b 1, lb 15, w 7	23
(57.2 overs)	(for 3 wickets)	233

	O	M	R	W
Rashid Khan	11	1	58	—
Sarfraz Nawaz	10.2	2	22	—
Abdul Qadir	11	—	51	—
Ejaz Faqih	6	—	19	—
Mudassar Nazar	12	2	34	2
Zaheer Abbas	7	—	26	1

FALL OF WICKETS
1- 115, 2- 165, 3- 181

Umpires: H. D. Bird and D. O. Oslear
England won by 7 wickets

ENGLAND v. PAKISTAN AT OLD TRAFFORD

On a wicket on which the ball tended to keep low and inhibit stroke making, Pakistan were subdued by an England side which bowled tightly and fielded well. Mohsin Khan was reduced practically to immobility as Willis began with a spell of 6 overs which cost only 7 runs. It was his opening partner Dilley, now more disciplined than formerly, who accounted for Mudassar and Zaheer, and when Mohsin fell to Allott Pakistan were 101 for 3 off 33 overs at lunch.

The revival in fortunes had been brought about almost entirely by Javed Miandad who continued to prosper against Marks when others seemed hypnotised by his gentle spin. Imran and Wasim Raja both hoisted him to Willis at deep mid-on, and, sadly, Javed misjudged the power of Botham's throw and was run out.

Ejaz dominated the closing stages of the innings, but the Pakistan batting efforts were soon put into perspective by Fowler and Tavare who began the England challenge with 115 in 30 overs before Fowler was caught in the covers.

All that was needed now was common sense and this was forthcoming as, without histrionics, England moved to victory in the fifty-eighth over.

NEW ZEALAND v. SRI LANKA AT DERBY

With Sri Lanka the only side in the tournament not to have won a match, New Zealand were confidently expected to win and so clinch a place in the semi-final. Their ambitions were thwarted at the start when de Mel, again finding generous movement in the hazy sunshine, and aided by young Ratnayake, had them at 47 for 4.

RIGHT: *The beginning of New Zealand's disaster day. John Wright is caught by de Alwis off de Mel for 0. (Ken Kelly)*

ROUND FIVE: NEW ZEALAND v. SRI LANKA
18 June 1983 at Derby

NEW ZEALAND				
G.M. Turner	c Dias, b de Mel			6
J.G. Wright	c de Alwis, b de Mel			0
G.P. Howarth	b Ratnayake			15
M.D. Crowe	lbw, b Ratnayake			8
B.A. Edgar	c Samarasekera, b de Silva			27
J.V. Coney	c sub, b de Silva			22
R.J. Hadlee	c Madugalle, b de Mel			15
W.K. Lees*	c Ranatunga, b de Mel			2
B.L. Cairns	c Dias, b de Mel			6
M.C. Snedden	run out			40
E.J. Chatfield	not out			19
Extras	b 4, lb 5, w 11, nb 1			21
(58.2 overs)				181

	O	M	R	W
de Mel	12	4	32	5
Ratnayake	11	4	18	2
Ranatunga	10	2	50	—
de Silva	12	5	11	2
Samarasekera	11.2	2	38	—
Wettimuny	2	—	11	—

FALL OF WICKETS
1- 8, 2- 8, 3- 32, 4- 47, 5- 88, 6- 91, 7- 105, 8- 115, 9- 116

SRI LANKA				
S.R. de S. Wettimuny	b Cairns			4
B. Kuruppu	c and b Snedden			62
A. Ranatunga	b M.D. Crowe			15
R.L. Dias	not out			64
L. R. D. Mendis	lbw, b Chatfield			0
R.S. Madugalle	c Lees, b Snedden			6
M.A.R. Samarasekera	c Lees, b Hadlee			5
D.S. de Silva	run out			2
R.G. de Alwis*	not out			11
A.L.F. de Mel				
R.J. Ratnayake				
Extras	b 1, lb 4, w 10			15
(52.3 overs)	(for 7 wickets)			184

	O	M	R	W
Hadlee	12	3	16	1
Cairns	10	2	35	1
Snedden	10.5	1	58	2
Chatfield	12	3	23	1
M.D. Crowe	4	2	15	1
Coney	4	1	22	—

FALL OF WICKETS
1- 15, 2- 49, 3- 129, 4- 130, 5- 139, 6- 151, 7- 161

Umpires: D. J. Constant and B. Leadbeater

Sri Lanka won by 3 wickets

As de Mel retired from the attack and Edgar and Coney settled in, there were hopes of recovery, but de Silva produced a splendid spell in which he took 2 for 11 in his 12 overs of accurate and intelligently varied leg breaks.

A second spell from de Mel gave him three more wickets and New Zealand, at 116 for 9, were beaten, or so it seemed. It was then that Snedden, who had had a disappointing competition with the ball, and Chatfield blended sense and aggression to add 65 runs and give hope where none had been.

This hope was increased when Wettimuny fell to a swinging yorker, but Kuruppu batted with stability and shared a stand of 80 with Dias which ended when Snedden held a fierce return catch to get rid of Kuruppu.

There was now a slump in Sri Lanka's fortunes as four wickets fell and the run rate dropped alarmingly, but they had learned their lesson in the defeat by Pakistan, and de Alwis, an excellent number nine, gave Dias the help he needed to bring victory.

INDIA v. ZIMBABWE AT TUNBRIDGE WELLS

The true significance of the events at Tunbridge Wells could not really be gauged until a week later, but when India, asked to bat, were 17 for 5 after 13 overs, it seemed certain that Zimbabwe were heading for their second victory of the competition, that India would not qualify for the semi-finals, and that we could all be home in time for tea. All of those assumptions were to prove false within the next few hours.

Rawson's first ball of the day lifted sharply and cast doubts upon the wicket, doubts which were confirmed in Gavaskar's mind by the last ball of the first over which had

A beautiful setting for a memorable innings. Kepil Dev on his way to his record 175 not out at Tunbridge Wells. (All Sport)

Heron is run out as Madan Lal breaks the wicket and Kapil Dev leaps out of the way. (*All Sport*)

him lbw as he aimed lamely to leg. Not a run was scored until the third over and, in the fifth, Amarnath was given out caught behind, a decision with which he clearly did not agree. Then Srikkanth, with a stroke of insanity and irresponsibility, lofted Curran high to mid-off where Butchart took a spectacular running catch. Patil was caught behind on the leg-side and Yashpal touched a ball outside the off-stump.

Kapil Dev had come in at 9 for 4 and one sensed immediately that here, at least, was a batsman who recognised the demands of the position. He accepted responsibility and played with great care. He hit the loose ball hard and defended stoutly, taking no undue risk.

Binny, without declaring his personality, joined his captain in a stand of 60 in 14 overs, but Shastri played a wretched shot and India lunched at 106 for 7. The hundred had come in the thirty-sixth over, the same shot had given Kapil Dev his fifty.

There was some purposeful batting after lunch and Madan Lal and Kapil Dev added 62 in 16 overs before Madan Lal became Houghton's fourth victim. This was to be Zimbabwe's last success.

Kirmani bristled with determination and Kapil Dev was hitting firmly all round the ground. Suddenly, one was aware that one was watching one of the very great innings. He had come to the wicket at 9 for 4 in the tenth over. In the forty-ninth he reached his hundred, but he was not done yet. In 13 overs of exciting and brilliant batting, Kapil Dev added a hundred, and the partnership was finally to realise 126, a record for the ninth wicket.

In all, Kapil Dev hit six sixes and sixteen fours. His 175 not out was the highest score ever made in a one-day international, and India's 266 was their best in the competition. It was stunning stuff, a rare delight to fit the beauty of the setting.

Zimbabwe began briskly enough, but Paterson and Heron fell in successive overs and Pycroft left at 61. Brown was stupidly run out and Fletcher fell to a marvellous catch on the boundary.

Kevin Curran then played a superb innings, and at the end of the fifty-fifth over, Zimbabwe were 226 for 8, only 2 runs

---

ROUND FIVE: INDIA *v.* ZIMBABWE
18 June 1983 at the Nevill Ground, Tunbridge Wells

INDIA				ZIMBABWE			
S.M. Gavaskar	lbw, b Rawson	0		R.D. Brown	run out		35
K. Srikkanth	c Butchart, b Curran	0		G.A. Paterson	lbw, b Binny		23
M.B. Amarnath	c Houghton, b Rawson	5		J.G. Heron	run out		3
S.M. Patil	c Houghton, b Curran	1		A.J. Pycroft	c Kirmani, b Sandhu		6
Yashpal Sharma	c Houghton, b Rawson	9		D.L. Houghton*	lbw, b Madan Lal		17
R.N. Kapil Dev†	not out	175		D.A.G. Fletcher†	c Kapil Dev, b Amarnath		13
R.M. Binny	lbw, b Traicos	22		K.M. Curran	c Shastri, b Madan Lal		73
R.J. Shastri	c Pycroft, b Fletcher	1		I.P. Butchart	b Binny		18
S. Madan Lal	c Houghton, b Curran	17		G.E. Peckover	c Yashpal Sharma,		
S.M.H. Kirmani*	not out	24			b Madan Lal		14
B.S. Sandhu				P.W.E. Rawson	not out		2
Extras	lb 9, w 3	12		A.J. Traicos	c and b Kapil Dev		3
				Extras	lb 17, w 7, nb 4		28
(60 overs)	(for 8 wickets)	266		(57 overs)			235

	O	M	R	W		O	M	R	W
Rawson	12	4	47	3	Kapil Dev	11	1	32	1
Curran	12	1	65	3	Sandhu	11	2	44	1
Butchart	12	2	38	—	Binny	11	2	45	2
Fletcher	12	2	59	1	Madan Lal	11	2	42	3
Traicos	12	—	45	1	Amarnath	12	1	37	1
					Shastri	1	—	7	—

FALL OF WICKETS
1- 0, 2- 6, 3- 6, 4- 9, 5- 17, 6- 77, 7- 78, 8- 140

FALL OF WICKETS
1- 44, 2- 48, 3- 61, 4- 86, 5- 103, 6- 113, 7- 168, 8- 189, 9- 230

Umpires: M. J. Kitchen and B. J. Meyer

India won by 31 runs

short of India at the same point, but Curran played a weak uncharacteristic shot and we were left with the glorious memory of Kapil Dev.

ENGLAND v. SRI LANKA AT LEEDS

In a match which had no bearing on the competition, England again bowled tightly and fielded well to restrict Sri Lanka to a meagre score. Willis started with a mean spell and Cowans, in his first appearance in the competition, and Botham bowled very aggressively. Only the late order batsmen gave the Sri Lankan innings any substantial boost.

Tavare left at 68, and after this Fowler payed with great authority to take England to victory with more than 35 overs to spare.

WEST INDIES v. ZIMBABWE AT EDGBASTON

Zimbabwe's brave venture in the tournament came to an end at Edgbaston where Haynes and Bacchus scored the 172 runs that West Indies needed for victory with just under 15 overs to spare.

In the fourth over of the morning, Garner removed Paterson and the unhappy Heron with successive deliveries. The position worsened as Zimbabwe slipped to 42 for 5 and 79 for 6, but Kevin Curran once more batted with great panache and when he was out in the last over of the innings, he had seen 128 runs added and had given another demonstration of the fighting spirit that had made Zimbabwe a force to be reckoned with in the competition.

RIGHT: *Peter Rawson heaves at Wayne Daniel and is bowled.* (*Trevor Jones*)

ROUND SIX: ENGLAND v. SRI LANKA
20 June 1983 at Headingley, Leeds

SRI LANKA				ENGLAND			
S.R. de S. Wettimuny	lbw, b Botham	22		G. Fowler	not out		81
B. Kuruppu	c Gatting, b Willis	6		C.J. Tavare	c de Alwis, b de Mel		19
A. Ranatunga	c Lamb, b Botham	0		D.I. Gower	not out		27
R.L. Dias	c Gould, b Cowans	7		A.J. Lamb			
L.R.D. Mendis†	b Allott	10		M.W. Gatting			
R.S. Madugalle	c Gould, b Allott	0		I.T. Botham			
D.S. de Silva	c Gower, b Marks	15		I.J. Gould*			
R.G. de Alwis*	c Marks, b Cowans	19		V.J. Marks			
A.L.F. de Mel	c Lamb, b Marks	10		P.J.W. Allott			
R.J. Ratnayake	not out	20		R.G.D. Willis†			
V. John	c Cowans, b Allott	15		N.G. Cowans			
Extras	b 5, lb 2, w 3, nb 2	12		Extras	b 1, lb 3, w 3, nb 3		10
(50.4 overs)		136		(24.1 overs)	(for 1 wicket)		137

	O	M	R	W		O	M	R	W
Willis	9	4	9	1	de Mel	10	1	33	1
Cowans	12	3	31	2	Ratnayake	5	—	23	—
Botham	9	4	12	2	John	6	—	41	—
Allott	10.4	—	41	3	de Silva	3	—	29	—
Gatting	4	2	13	—	Ranatunga	0.1	—	1	—
Marks	6	2	18	2					

FALL OF WICKETS
1- 25, 2- 30, 3- 32, 4- 40, 5- 43, 6- 54, 7- 81, 8- 97, 9- 103

FALL OF WICKETS
1- 68

Umpires: B. Leadbeater and R. Palmer

England won by 9 wickets

ROUND SIX: ZIMBABWE v. WEST INDIES
20 June 1983 at Edgbaston, Birmingham

ZIMBABWE				
R.D. Brown	c Lloyd, b Marshall	14		
G.A. Paterson	c Richards, b Garner	6		
J.G. Heron	c Dujon, b Garner	0		
A.J. Pycroft	c Dujon, b Marshall	4		
D.L. Houghton*	c Lloyd, b Daniel	0		
D.A.G. Fletcher†	b Richards	23		
K.M. Curran	b Daniel	62		
I.P. Butchart	c Haynes, b Richards	8		
G.E. Peckover	c and b Richards	3		
P.W.E. Rawson	b Daniel	19		
A.J. Traicos	not out	1		
Extras	b 4, lb 13, w 7, nb 7	31		
	(60 overs)	171		

WEST INDIES		
D.L. Haynes	not out	88
S.F.A. Bacchus	not out	80
A.L. Logie		
I.V.A. Richards		
H.A. Gomes		
C.H. Lloyd†		
P.J. Dujon*		
J. Garner		
M.D. Marshall		
W.W. Daniel		
W.W. Davis		
Extras	lb 1, w 3	4
(45.1 overs)	(for no wkt)	172

	O	M	R	W
Marshall	12	3	19	2
Garner	7	4	13	2
Davis	8	2	13	—
Daniel	9	2	28	3
Gomes	12	2	26	—
Richards	12	1	41	3

	O	M	R	W
Rawson	12	3	38	—
Butchart	4	—	23	—
Traicos	12	2	24	—
Curran	9	—	44	—
Fletcher	8.1	—	39	—

FALL OF WICKETS
1- 17, 2- 17, 3- 41, 4- 42, 5- 42, 6- 79, 7- 104, 8- 115, 9- 170

Umpires: H. D. Bird and D. J. Constant

West Indies won by 10 wickets

NEW ZEALAND v. PAKISTAN AT TRENT BRIDGE

New Zealand's defeat by Sri Lanka had suddenly presented Pakistan with the unexpected chance to redeem their earlier ineptitudes and to reach the semi-final.

Pakistan won the toss and laboured against some accurate bowling and voracious fielding. The first 20 overs produced only 48 runs and Mohsin unwisely tried to lift Coney for six and was caught at long-on. Mudassar chopped the same bowler into his stumps, and Javed performed a similar act to Hadlee so that much depended on Zaheer and Imran.

They did not disappoint. Zaheer reached his hundred in 121 minutes and Imran, driving with great power, hit 79 in 75 minutes. Their partnership of 147 was achieved in 18 overs of powerful batting and gave New Zealand a task far more formidable than had seemed possible earlier in the day.

At tea, New Zealand were 76 for 2 from 25 overs with Howarth well set and only Qadir looking menacing. The turning point came when Zaheer was brought on to bowl. His first delivery was a chest high full toss which Howarth hit straight into the hands of square-leg. The innings then subsided to 152 for 7, and with Cairns and Hadlee gone and only 8 overs left, 75 were still needed and Pakistan were in complete control.

The New Zealand team spirit is their greatest quality, however, and when John Bracewell began to hit furiously, 53 came off 5 overs.

22 were needed off three overs. Six runs came from the first five balls of the fifty-eighth over, but the sixth saw Bracewell hook Sarfraz mightily only to be caught just inside the boundary by Mohsin.

Coney, so brave a player, now had to keep the strike as much as possible as the last over began with 13 needed. The Pakistan fielding had become hysterical and when Javed threw wildly from mid-on there was a chance of an overthrow, but there was a fatal hesitation by both batsmen and Imran retrieved, threw to the wicket-keeper and the valiant Coney was out, as were New Zealand.

Wasim Bari breaks the wicket. Coney is run out. It is the end of a most courageous innings and Pakistan are through to the semi-finals. (Dave Cannon)

ROUND SIX: PAKISTAN v. NEW ZEALAND
20 June 1983 at Trent Bridge, Nottingham

PAKISTAN				NEW ZEALAND		
Mohsin Khan	c Cairns, b Coney	33		G.M. Turner	c Wasim Bari, b Sarfraz Nawaz	4
Mudassar Nazar	b Coney	15		J.G. Wright	c Imran Khan, b Abdul Qadir	19
Javed Miandad	b Hadlee	25		G.P. Howarth†	c Javed Miandad, b Zaheer Abbas	39
Zaheer Abbas	not out	103		M.D. Crowe	b Mudassar Nazar	43
Imran Khan†	not out	79		B.A. Edgar	lbw, b Shahid Mahboob	6
Ejaz Faqih				J.V. Coney	run out	51
Shahid Mahboob				R.J. Hadlee	c Mohsin Khan, b Mudassar Nazar	11
Sarfraz Nawaz				B.L. Cairns	c Imran Khan, b Abdul Qadir	0
Abdul Qadir				W.K. Lees*	c sub, b Mudassar Nazar	26
Wasim Bari*				J.G. Bracewell	c Mohsin Khan, b Sarfraz Nawaz	34
Rashid Khan				E.J. Chatfield	not out	3
Extras	b 1, lb 2, w 2, nb 1	6		Extras	lb 8, w 5, nb 1	14
	(60 overs)	(for 3 wickets) 261			(59.1 overs)	250

	O	M	R	W		O	M	R	W
Hadlee	12	1	61	1	Rashid Khan	6	1	24	—
Cairns	12	1	45	—	Sarfraz Nawaz	9.1	1	50	2
Chatfield	12	—	57	—	Abdul Qadir	12	—	53	2
Coney	12	—	42	2	Ejaz Faqih	6	1	21	—
Bracewell	12	—	50	—	Shahid Mahboob	10	—	37	1
					Mudassar Nazar	12	—	43	3
					Zaheer Abbas	4	1	8	1

FALL OF WICKETS
1- 43, 2- 54, 3- 114

FALL OF WICKETS
1- 13, 2- 44, 3- 85, 4- 102, 5- 130, 6- 150, 7- 152,
8- 187, 9- 246

Umpires: D. G. L. Evans and M. J. Kitchen

Pakistan won by 11 runs

AUSTRALIA v. INDIA AT CHELMSFORD

This contest had now taken on the dramatic significance of a quarter final. Kirti Azad was brought into the Indian side, his off-breaks being an intelligent counter to the abundance of left-handers, and there was shock news for Australia when Kim Hughes was forced to withdraw just before the match because of his thigh injury.

Kapil Dev won the toss and batted. Hookes captained Australia in an international for the first time. The match began with Lawson bowling a wide. It was a sad portent for Australia of what was to come. 37 extras provided India's second highest score. Hogg alone bowled 15 no-balls and three wides, and Australia once more gave their opponents the advantage of extra 'overs'.

The Indians began briskly, but Gavaskar hit loosely to cover. Srikkanth put up the fifty in the eleventh over, but two overs later he pulled Thomson, who had also begun with a wide, to mid-wicket where Border took a good catch at the second attempt.

The Australians bowled at a funereal pace. By lunch only 30 overs had been bowled and India were 119 for 4. Kapil Dev and Yashpal Sharma continued to attack the bowling, but the Indian innings, like Falstaff, promised more than it performed.

The Australian task, in spite of Chappell's early exit caught in the gully, did not look too daunting. Kirmani had had some difficulty in taking the ball and changed his gloves. The change worked wonders. In the sixteenth over, with the score on 46, Roger Binny was introduced into the attack. He found the edge of Wood's bat and Kirmani took a magnificent diving catch. In his second over, Binny bowled Hookes

Yallop is caught and bowled by Binny off a skier. (All Sport)

ROUND SIX: AUSTRALIA v. INDIA
20 June 1983 at Chelmsford

INDIA				AUSTRALIA			
S.M. Gavaskar	c Chappell, b Hogg	9		T.M. Chappell	c Madan Lal, b Sandhu	2
K. Srikkanth	c Border, b Thomson	24		G.M. Wood	c Kirmani, b Binny	21
M.B. Amarnath	c Marsh, b Thomson	13		G.N. Yallop	c and b Binny	18
Yashpal Sharma	c Hogg, b Hogan	40		D.W. Hookes†	b Binny	1
S.M. Patil	c Hogan, b Macleay	30		A.R. Border	b Madan Lal	36
R.N. Kapil Dev†	c Hookes, b Hogg	28		R.W. Marsh*	lbw, b Madan Lal	0
Kirti Azad	c Border, b Lawson	15		K.H. Macleay	c Gavaskar, b Madan Lal	5
R.M. Binny	run out	21		T.G. Hogan	c Srikkanth, b Binny	8
S. Madan Lal	not out	12		G.F. Lawson	b Sandhu	16
S.M.H. Kirmani*	lbw, b Hogg	10		R.M. Hogg	not out	8
B.S. Sandhu	b Thomson	8		J.R. Thomson	b Madan Lal	0
Extras	lb 13, w 9, nb 15	37		Extras	lb 5, w 5, nb 4	14
(55.5 overs)		247		(38.2 overs)		129

	O	M	R	W			O	M	R	W
Lawson	10	1	40	1		Kapil Dev	8	2	16	—
Hogg	12	2	40	3		Sandhu	10	1	26	2
Hogan	11	1	31	1		Madan Lal	8.2	3	20	4
Thomson	10.5	—	51	3		Binny	8	2	29	4
Macleay	12	2	48	1		Amarnath	2	—	17	—
						Kirti Azad	2	—	7	—

FALL OF WICKETS
1- 27, 2- 54, 3- 65, 4- 118, 5- 157, 6- 174, 7- 207, 8- 215, 9- 232

FALL OF WICKETS
1- 3, 2- 46, 3- 48, 4- 52, 5- 52, 6- 69, 7- 78, 8- 115, 9- 129

Umpires: J. Birkenshaw and D. R. Shepherd

India won by 118 runs

with a ball of full length, and in his third, he caught and bowled Yallop off a skier. Marsh was leg before first ball and Macleay slashed at Madan Lal in the last over before tea, Gavaskar held onto the stinging catch at slip. 69 for 5. Good steady, bowling, with some movement allied to woeful batting had reduced an undisciplined Australian side to this sorry plight.

Hogan was taken at cover to provide Binny with his fourth wicket. The flags were waving and the whistles, annoyingly, blowing. Border was bowled, Lawson chopped on and Thomson went first ball. India, to the surprise of most, were in the semi-final.

Final Tables

Group A	P	W	L	Pts	Run rate
England	6	5	1	20	4.67
Pakistan	6	3	3	12	4.01
New Zealand	6	3	3	12	3.93
Sri Lanka	6	1	5	4	3.75
Group B	P	W	L	Pts	Run rate
West Indies	6	5	1	20	4.31
India	6	4	2	16	3.87
Australia	6	2	4	8	3.81
Zimbabwe	6	1	5	4	3.49

Semi-Finals

Winners of Group A v Runners-up of Group B
Winners of Group B v Runners-up of Group A

WEST INDIES v. PAKISTAN: SEMI-FINAL

Any hopes that this would provide a repeat of epic encounters of the past between these two teams were quickly diminished. Javed Miandad withdrew from the Pakistan side with influenza, Lloyd won the toss and Pakistan batted first on a day of glorious sunshine.

Mudassar and Mohsin struggled from the start against the relentless Garner. In the twelfth over, Mudassar was out and in the eighteenth, Ejaz was caught behind off Holding. Only 34 had been scored.

Mohsin batted for survival and Zaheer, the hope of his side, began to play a few shots. With great good sense, Lloyd used his 'fifth' bowler, Richards and Gomes in the half hour before lunch, and Zaheer, still to go, naturally eager to plunder, hit rashly at a ball from Gomes and was bowled off his pads.

Imran and Mohsin effected some sort of recovery, but as it threatened to become positive, Marshall returned to take 3 wickets in 14 balls at a cost of three runs.

Sarfraz was caught off a skier, and, in the fifty-sixth over, Mohsin was bowled as he hit out at Roberts. He had hit only one 4, a misfield.

There was little chance that Pakistan could defend 184 and Greenidge and Haynes added 34 in 11 overs. Greenidge was lbw to one that kept low and Haynes succumbed to the wiles of Qadir, but by now Richards had decided that the match had gone on long enough and began to clout the ball arrogantly to all parts of the field. Batting suddenly looked an easier art than it had done all day, and the one concession that the great man made was to allow Gomes a chance to reach his fifty.

SEMI-FINAL: PAKISTAN v. WEST INDIES
22 June 1983 at The Oval

PAKISTAN				WEST INDIES		
Mohsin Khan	b Roberts	70		C.G. Greenidge	lbw, b Rashid Khan	17
Mudassar Nazar	c and b Garner	11		D.L. Haynes	b Abdul Qadir	29
Ejaz Faqih	c Dujon, b Holding	5		I.V.A. Richards	not out	80
Zaheer Abbas	b Gomes	30		H.A. Gomes	not out	50
Imran Khan†	c Dujon, b Marshall	17		C.H. Lloyd†		
Wasim Raja	lbw, b Marshall	0		S.F.A. Bacchus		
Shahid Mahboob	c Richards, b Marshall	6		P.J. Dujon*		
Sarfraz Nawaz	c Holding, b Roberts	3		A.M.E. Roberts		
Abdul Qadir	not out	10		M.D. Marshall		
Wasim Bari*	not out	4		J. Garner		
Rashid Khan				M.A. Holding		
Extras	b 6, lb 13, w 4, nb 5	28		Extras	b 2, lb 6, w 4	12
(60 overs)	(for 8 wickets)	184		(48.4 overs)	(for 2 wickets)	188

	O	M	R	W			O	M	R	W
Roberts	12	3	25	2		Rashid Khan	12	2	32	1
Garner	12	1	31	1		Sarfraz Nawaz	8	—	23	—
Marshall	12	2	28	3		Abdul Qadir	11	1	42	1
Holding	12	1	25	1		Shahid Mahboob	11	1	43	—
Gomes	7	—	29	1		Wasim Raja	1	—	9	—
Richards	5	—	18	—		Zaheer Abbas	4.4	1	24	—
						Mohsin Khan	1	—	3	—

FALL OF WICKETS
1- 23, 2- 34, 3- 88, 4- 139, 5- 139, 6- 159, 7- 164,
8- 171

FALL OF WICKETS
1- 34, 2- 56

Umpires: D. J. Constant and A. G. T. Whitehead

West Indies won by 8 wickets

West Indian delight as they are comfortably on their way to their third World Cup Final (All Sport)

ENGLAND v. INDIA: SEMI-FINAL

The majority of people had already decided that West Indies and England would meet in the final before Willis won the toss at Old Trafford and decided to bat. When Fowler and Tavare put on 69 in the first 17 overs English optimism seemed totally justified, but after Roger Binny, with new found confidence, had dismissed both openers, England were beset by indecision and disbelief.

In the period around lunch, just as Lloyd did at The Oval,

Kapil Dev introduced his 'fifth' bowler, a combination of the gentle medium pace of Amarnath and the off-breaks of Kirti Azad. They ended by bowling the full quota of 12 overs each and conceded only 55 runs for the wickets of Gower, Gatting and Botham.

Gower played an airy shot outside the off-stump like he used to in the bad old days, Botham was bowled by a shooter and Gatting was bowled through a gap so big that it reopened questions as to the suitability of his technique for international cricket. Two silly run-outs accounted for Lamb and Gould, and only a ninth wicket stand of 25 between Allott and the hard-hitting Dilley took England past 200, a bitterly disappointing score.

India's main worry was that with a realistic chance of victory, they needed a good beginning and for their batsmen to keep calm. The excitability of the Indians had been seen in the last over of the England innings when Kapil Dev bowled four very wild wides and there was a general air of feverishness.

Gavaskar and Srikkanth did give the innings a sound footing with 46, but they were dismissed in successive overs so that Amarnath and Yashpal Sharma had to start afresh. Psychologically, this was a crucial time, and the two batsmen showed admirable temperament. They had a little fortune. Yashpal survived two confident appeals and substitute fielder Derek Randall just failed to catch Amarnath at mid wicket, but their luck was no more than their dedication deserved.

Amarnath straight drove Allott for six when it seemed that India's required run rate was beginning to mount, and as England began to feel the game slipping away, Willis returned, to have his first delivery pulled over mid-wicket for 6

LEFT: *Gower is magnificently caught by the tumbling Kirmani off Amarnath who leaps in appeal. (Ken Kelly)*

ABOVE: *Marks is bowled by Kapil Dev. (Ken Kelly)*

At 142, Amarnath was splendidly run out, but there was to be no reprieve for England. Yashpal Sharma dominated and Patil echoed the batsman who had punished Willis so violently on the same ground a year ago. The calm was maintained and, in the final balance, England were found wanting.

SEMI-FINAL: ENGLAND v. INDIA
22 June 1983 at Old Trafford, Manchester

ENGLAND					INDIA			
G. Fowler	b Binny	33			S.M. Gavaskar	c Gould, b Allott	25
C.J. Tavare	c Kirmani, b Binny	32			K. Srikkanth	c Willis, b Botham	19
D.I. Gower	c Kirmani, b Amarnath	17			M.B. Amarnath	run out	46
A.J. Lamb	run out	29			Yashpal Sharma	c Allott, b Willis	61
M.W. Gatting	b Amarnath	18			S.M. Patil	not out	51
I.T. Botham	b Kirti Azad	6			R.N. Kapil Dev†	not out	1
I.J. Gould*	run out	13			Kirti Azad		
V.J. Marks	b Kapil Dev	8			R.M. Binny		
G.R. Dilley	not out	20			S. Madan Lal		
P.J.W. Allott	c Patil, b Kapil Dev	8			S.M.H. Kirmani*		
R.G.D. Willis†	b Kapil Dev	0			B.S. Sandhu		
Extras	b 1, lb 17, w 7, nb 4	29			Extras	b 5, lb 6, w 1, nb 2	14
(60 overs)		213			(54.4 overs)	(for 4 wickets)	217

	O	M	R	W		O	M	R	W
Kapil Dev	11	1	35	3	Willis	10.4	2	42	1
Sandhu	8	1	36	—	Dilley	11	—	43	—
Binny	12	1	43	2	Allott	10	3	40	1
Madan Lal	5	—	15	—	Botham	11	4	40	1
Kirti Azad	12	1	28	1	Marks	12	1	38	—
Amarnath	12	1	27	2					

FALL OF WICKETS
1- 69, 2- 84, 3- 107, 4- 141, 5- 150, 6- 160, 7- 175, 8- 177, 9- 202

FALL OF WICKETS
1- 46, 2- 50, 3- 142, 4- 205

Umpires: D. O. Oslear and D. G. L. Evans

India won by 6 wickets

The end of the England innings. Bob Willis is bowled by Kapil Dev. (Ken Kelly)

Sharma reached his fifty and fell to a magnificent catch by Allott. Kapil Dev came in to share the final glory. The crowd anticipated victory a ball too soon and had to be cleared away. Willis placed all his fielders on the pavilion side for the last ball and Patil cracked the winning boundary somewhere into the invading horde.

INDIA v. WEST INDIES: THE FINAL

Neither the first nor the second Prudential World Cup Finals had disappointed, and the third was no exception. The tournament, to the very end, was a total triumph for cricket.

There was no disputing that on paper West Indies had the better side and the bookmakers had made them such firm favourites, that to consider an Indian victory seemed a waste of time. Nothing that happened in the early part of the match looked likely to prove the bookmakers wrong.

There was relentless menace in the pace of the West Indian attack after Lloyd had put India in. Survival appeared to be the only possibility against Roberts and Garner, and Gavaskar could not achieve that. In the fifth over he was caught behind off a stroke of indecision and the score was 2.

Srikkanth now decided to play the game that, if it could be sustained for more than two hours, would make him the most exciting player the game has ever known. His first boundary was when he cut Garner over the slips. Roberts was driven to mid-wicket and then hooked over fine leg for 6. One square drive, down on one knee, was breathtaking. It could not last, but it was a brief joy and brought him 38 exciting runs off 57 balls.

At the other end, Amarnath had again proved to be India's rock and he was now joined by Yashpal Sharma in a partnership on which Indian hopes were rested.

At 90, with lunch approaching, Amarnath was bowled between bat and pad by Holding, and 2 runs later, Yashpal Sharma committed the sin of throwing away his wicket when

preservation was most needed. He tried to hit Gomes high over cover and failed to get to the pitch of the ball.

After lunch, Kapil Dev played two fine shots off Gomes and then went for a six, but was caught at long-on. A waste and with him, surely, had gone any chance India had. In the next over, Azad was caught at square-leg and in the thirty-sixth over, Binny went the same way. Five wickets had gone down in 7 overs for 40 runs. This is what we had feared – no contest.

There was a little bit of wagging from the tail, supported by Patil, but India failed to last their overs, and it now seemed just a question of how soon and by how many, West Indies would win.

There was an early shock for West Indies when Greenidge lifted his bat and offered no stroke at a ball from Sandhu which pitched outside off-stump. It came back at him and he was bowled. This brought in Richards. He had an immediate air of disdain. Sandhu was pulled to mid-wicket for 4. Kapil Dev was driven through mid-off and mid-wicket for further boundaries. When Madan Lal appeared Richards hit him for three fours in his first over. In his next over, Madan Lal had Haynes taken at extra cover off a careless drive.

Clive Lloyd came in and pulled a muscle when he went for his first single so that Haynes reappeared to act as runner.

In the fourteenth over, Richards swung Madan Lal over mid-wicket. There was a roar at another great hit, but the ball hovered and sprinting round and back, Kapil Dev took a magnificent catch. This was the moment of truth.

There was now a new urgency in the Indian play, but to do them justice, they had never lost faith. Again Madan Lal ran in from the nursery end. He found the edge of Gomes' bat and Gavaskar took a good catch at slip. Lloyd attempted to thump Binny through the covers, but he hit the ball straight into the hands of mid-off.

At tea, West Indies were 76 for 5 from 25 overs.

The interval, surely, would bring consultation and sanity. If it did, Bacchus did not hear, for in the first over after tea he chased a widish delivery and Kirmani took a catch as brilliant and spectacular as it was important. Now the impossible had become probable.

There followed a period of great tension as Dujon and Marshall batted more sensibly than any of their colleagues and 43 were added.

Madan Lal had done his glorious work and Amarnath was called up to the Nursery End. His first ball was a gentle loosener and Dujon plopped it gently into his wicket. West Indies now needed 65 from the last 18 overs with three wickets standing.

Another innocent looking seamer from Amarnath moved a fraction and there was Gavaskar hanging on to Marshall's edge at slip. Kapil Dev returned for a final onslaught and had Roberts lbw. It was Kapil Dev's only wicket and he had scored but 15 runs, yet his inspirational value to his side was incalculable.

Still Holding and Garner stood between India and glory and the score edged upwards, but then Amarnath beat Holding's shuffle and the umpire's finger went up. The crowd swarmed on to the field and India retired at a jubilant gallop to the pavilion where they began the celebration of the greatest day in their cricket history.

It was a day to savour, a monument to the greatest of games.

ABOVE: *First blood to West Indies. Gavaskar walks away forlornly, caught behind off Roberts.* BELOW: *Srikkanth lashes a boundary in his exciting innings.* ABOVE RIGHT: *Amarnath square cuts for four in his vital innings. (Ken Kelly)* RIGHT: *The beginning of West Indian problems. Greenidge plays no shot to Sandhu and is bowled. (Adrian Murrell)*

PRUDENTIAL CUP

June 9 – 25 1983   FINAL

GROUP A : England; New Zealand; Pakistan; Sri Lanka

GROUP B : Australia; India; West Indies; Zimbabwe

PRIZES

For the team winning the Final: £20,000, the Prudential Cup, and inscribed silver-gilt medals for each player

Losing Finalists: £8,000 and individual silver medals

Losing Semi-Finalists: £4,000

Winner of each Group match: £1,000

Man of the Match Awards: Each of the 24 Group matches: £200; Each Semi-Final: £400; Final: £600.

MARYLEBONE   CRICKET   CLUB

15p   ## INDIA   v.   WEST INDIES   **15p**

at Lord's Ground, Saturday, June 25th, 1983

Any alterations to teams will be announced over the loudspeaker system

INDIA

1 S. M. Gavaskar	Bombay	c Dujon b Roberts	2
2 K. Srikkanth	Tamilnadu	l b w b Marshall	38
3 M. B. Amarnath	Delhi	b Holding	26
4 Yashpal Sharma	Punjab	c sub b Gomes	11
5 S. M. Patil	Bombay	c Gomes b Garner	27
‡6 N. Kapil Dev	Haryana	c Holding b Gomes	15
7 K. B. J. Azad	Delhi	c Garner b Roberts	0
8 R. M. H. Binny	Karnataka	c Garner b Roberts	2
9 S. Madan Lal	Delhi	b Marshall	17
*10 S. M. H. Kirmani	Karnataka	b Holding	14
11 B. S. Sandhu	Bombay	not out	11

B 5, l-b 5, w 9, n-b 1,   ... 20

Total... **183**

FALL OF THE WICKETS

1...2 2...59 3...90 4...92 5...110 6...111 7...130 8...153 9...161 10...193

Bowling Analysis	O.	M.	R.	W.	Wd.	N-b
Roberts	10	2	32	3	2	...
Garner	12	4	24	1	...	1
Marshall	11	1	24	2	1	...
Holding	9.4	2	26	2	6	...
Gomes	11	1	49	2	...	...
Richards	1	0	8	0	...	...

WEST INDIES

1 C. G. Greenidge	Barbados	b Sandhu	1
2 D. L. Haynes	Barbados	c Binny b Madan Lal	13
3 I. V. A. Richards	Antigua	c Kapil Dev b Madan Lal	33
‡4 C. H. Lloyd	Guyana	c Kapil Dev b Binny	8
5 H. A. Gomes	Trinidad & Tobago	c Gavaskar b Madan Lal	5
6 S. F. A. F. Bacchus	Guyana	c Kirmani b Sandhu	8
*7 P. J. Dujon	Jamaica	b Amarnath	25
8 M. D. Marshall	Barbados	c Gavasker b Amarnath	18
9 A. M. E. Roberts	Antigua	l b w b Kapil Dev	4
10 J. Garner	Barbados	not out	5
11 M. A. Holding	Jamaica	l b w b Amarnath	6

B , l-b 4, w 10, n-b ,   ... 14

Total... **140**

FALL OF THE WICKETS

1...5 2...50 3...57 4...66 5...66 6...76 7...119 8...124 9...126 10...140

Bowling Analysis	O.	M.	R.	W.	Wd.	N-b
Kapil Dev	11	4	21	1	2	...
Sandhu	9	1	32	2	5	...
Madan Lal	12	2	31	3	...	...
Binny	10	1	23	1	1	...
Amarnath	7	0	12	3	2	...
Azad	3	0	7	0	...	...

‡Captain   *Wicket-keeper

Umpires— H. D. Bird & B. J. Meyer

Scorers— E. Solomon & R. M. Costan

Toss won by—West Indies who elected to field

RESULT—India won by 43 runs

Adjudicator—J. M. Brearley

Man of the match—M. B. Amarnath

Luncheon Interval 1.00 p.m.—1.40 p.m.   Tea Interval will be 20 minutes and will normally be taken at 4.30 p.m.

The Playing conditions for the Prudential Cup are printed on the back of this score card.

Total runs scored at end of each over :—

India		1	2	3	4	5	6	7	8	9	10	11	12	13	14	15	16	17	18	19	20
	21	22	23	24	25	26	27	28	29	30	31	32	33	34	35	36	37	38	39	40
	41	42	43	44	45	46	47	48	49	50	51	52	53	54	55	56	57	58	59	60
West Indies		1	2	3	4	5	6	7	8	9	10	11	12	13	14	15	16	17	18	19	20
	21	22	23	24	25	26	27	28	29	30	31	32	33	34	35	36	37	38	39	40
	41	42	43	44	45	46	47	48	49	50	51	52	53	54	55	56	57	58	59	60

ABOVE: *Madan Lal the hero receives acclaim. He has taken three wickets in successive overs, including the great Viv Richards.* LEFT: *Clive Lloyd with runner Desmond Haynes.* (*Ken Kelly*)

Man of the Match Awards

Round One
A.J. Lamb, Yashpal Sharma, D.A.G. Fletcher, Mohsin Khan

Round Two
D.I. Gower, S. Madan Lal, W.W. Davis, Abdul Qadir

Round Three
R.J. Hadlee, T.M. Chappell, C.G. Greenidge, Zaheer Abbas

Round Four
J.V. Coney, D.L. Houghton, I.V.A. Richards, Abdul Qadir

Round Five
A.L.F. de Mel, R.N. Kapil Dev, I.V.A. Richards, G. Fowler

Round Six
Imran Khan, R.M.H. Binny, S.F.A. Bacchus, R.G.D. Willis

Semi-Finals
M.B. Amarnath, I.V.A. Richards

Final
M.B. Amarnath

Prudential World Cup Averages

INDIA BATTING

	M	Inns	NOs	Runs	HS	Av	100s	50s
R.N. Kapil Dev	8	8	3	303	175*	60.60	1	
D.B. Vengsarkar	2	2	1	37	32*	37.00		
Yashpal Sharma	8	8	1	240	89	34.28		2
S. Madan Lal	8	6	3	102	27	34.00		
S.M. Patil	8	8	1	216	51*	30.85		2
M.B. Amarnath	8	8		237	80	29.62		1
B.S. Sandhu	8	3	2	28	11*	28.00		
K. Srikkanth	8	8		156	39	19.50		
S.M.H. Kirmani	8	6	1	61	24*	12.20		
R.M. Binny	8	6		73	27	12.16		
R.J. Shastri	5	5	1	40	17	10.00		
S.M. Gavaskar	6	6		59	25	9.83		
Kirti Azad	3	2		15	15	7.50		

INDIA BOWLING

	Overs	Mds	Runs	Wkts	Av	Best	5/inn
S. Madan Lal	83	8	285	17	16.76	4/20	
R.M. Binny	88	9	336	18	18.66	4/29	
R.N. Kapil Dev	84	13	245	12	20.41	5/43	1
R.J. Shastri	20.1	1	87	4	21.75	3/26	
M.B. Amarnath	49	2	178	8	22.25	3/12	
B.S. Sandhu	83	10	297	8	37.12	2/26	
Kirti Azad	17	1	42	1	42.00	1/28	
S.M. Patil	9	—	61	—			

INDIA CATCHES

14 - S.M.H. Kirmani (ct 12/st 2); 6 - R.N. Kapil Dev; 3 - R.J. Shastri, S.M. Gavaskar and K. Srikkanth; 2 - B.S. Sandhu, Yashpal Sharma, S.M. Patil and R.M. Binny; 1 - D.B. Vengsarkar, Madan Lal and substitute S. Valson did not appear in any of the matches.

ENGLAND BATTING

	M	Inns	NOs	Runs	HS	Av	100s	50s
D.I. Gower	7	7	2	384	130	76.80	1	1
G. Fowler	7	7	2	360	81*	72.00		4
A.J. Lamb	7	6	2	278	102	69.50	1	1
G.R. Dilley	6	4	2	90	31*	45.00		
C.J. Tavare	7	7		212	58	30.28		1
I.J. Gould	7	4	1	66	35	22.00		
M.W. Gatting	7	5	1	83	43	20.75		
I.T. Botham	7	4		40	22	10.00		
V.J. Marks	7	3		18	8	6.00		
P.J.W. Allott	7	3	1	8	8	4.00		
R.G.D. Willis	7	2		0	0	0.00		

N.G. Cowans played in one match but did not bat.

ENGLAND BOWLING

	Overs	Mds	Runs	Wkts	Av	Best	5/inn
N.G. Cowans	12	3	31	2	15.50	2/31	
R.G.D. Willis	73.4	19	206	11	18.72	4/42	
V.J. Marks	78	9	246	13	18.92	5/39	1
G.R. Dilley	66	4	243	7	34.71	4/45	
I.T. Botham	80	13	288	8	36.00	2/12	
P.J.W. Allott	80.3	10	335	8	41.87	3/41	
M.W. Gatting	12	3	48	1	48.00	1/35	

ENGLAND CATCHES

12 - I.J. Gould (ct 11/st 1); 6 - A.J. Lamb; 4 - I.T. Botham and R.G.D. Willis; 2 - C.J. Tavare, M.W. Gatting and V.J. Marks; 1 - D.I. Gower, G.R. Dilley, P.J.W. Allott and N.G. Cowans

D.W. Randall and T.E. Jesty did not appear in any of the matches.

WEST INDIES BATTING

	M	Inns	NOs	Runs	HS	Av	100s	50s
I.V.A. Richards	8	7	2	367	119	73.40	1	2
H.A. Gomes	8	7	3	258	78	64.50		3
J. Garner	4	2	1	42	37	42.00		
C.G. Greenidge	7	7	1	250	105*	41.66	1	1
S.F.A. Bacchus	8	5	1	157	80*	39.25		1
D.L. Haynes	8	8	1	240	88*	34.28		1
C.H. Lloyd	8	5	1	112	41	28.00		
A.M.E. Roberts	7	4	1	53	37*	17.66		
P.J. Dujon	8	4		53	25	13.25		
M.A. Holding	7	4		36	20	9.00		
M.D. Marshall	6	3		24	18	8.00		

Also batted – W.W. Daniel 16* (three matches) and W.W. Davis 0* (five matches). A.L. Logie played in one match but did not bat.

WEST INDIES BOWLING

	Overs	Mds	Runs	Wkts	Av	Best	5/inn
M.D. Marshall	70	14	175	12	14.58	3/28	
M.A. Holding	74.5	11	235	12	19.58	3/40	
A.M.E. Roberts	74	12	238	11	21.63	3/32	
J. Garner	43	10	117	5	23.40	2/13	
W.W. Davis	54.3	6	206	8	25.75	7/51	1
W.W. Daniel	24	6	84	3	28.00	3/28	
I.V.A. Richards	24	2	93	3	31.00	3/41	
H.A. Gomes	74	4	304	9	33.77	2/46	

WEST INDIES CATCHES

16 - P.J. Dujon (ct 15/st 1); 5 - C.H. Lloyd and D.L. Haynes; 4 - I.V.A. Richards; 3 - M.A. Holding, H.A. Gomes and J. Garner; 1 - C.G. Greenidge and substitute.

PAKISTAN BATTING

	M	Inns	NOs	Runs	HS	Av	100s	50s
Imran Khan	7	7	3	283	102*	70.75	1	2
Zaheer Abbas	7	7	2	313	103*	62.60	1	2
Wasim Bari	7	4	3	58	34	58.00		
Javed Miandad	6	6		220	72	36.66		2
Shahid Mahboob	5	3		100	77	33.33		1
Mohsin Khan	7	7		223	82	31.85		2
Abdul Qadir	6	5	3	62	41*	31.00		
Mudassar Nazar	6	6		106	36	17.66		
Ejaz Faqih	6	5	1	61	42*	15.25		
Sarfraz Nawaz	7	5		53	17	10.60		
Wasim Raja	3	3		24	15	8.00		
Mansoor Akhtar	2	2		9	6	4.50		

Also batted – Rashid Khan 9 (seven matches); Tahir Naqqash 0* (one match)

PAKISTAN BOWLING

	Overs	Mds	Runs	Wkts	Av	Best	5/inn
Abdul Qadir	67.4	6	264	12	22.00	5/44	1
Mudassar Nazar	48	3	165	6	27.50	3/43	
Sarfraz Nawaz	73	12	231	7	33.00	3/40	
Rashid Khan	71	11	266	8	33.25	3/47	
Zaheer Abbas	19.4	2	74	2	37.00	1/8	
Tahir Naqqash	8	—	49	1	49.00	1/49	
Mansoor Akhtar	13	2	52	1	52.00	1/44	
Shahid Mahboob	52	4	228	4	57.00	1/37	
Ejaz Faqih	37	2	125	1	125.00	1/52	

Also bowled - Mohsin Khan 1–0–3–0

PAKISTAN CATCHES

9 - Wasim Bari (ct 6/st 3); 4 - Imran Khan: 3 - Mohsin Khan and Javed Miandad; 2 - Mudassar Nazar and Zaheer Abbas; 1 - Ejaz Faqih, Tahir Naqqash, Rashid Khan, Shahid Mahboob, Sarfraz Nawaz, Abdul Qadir, Wasim Raja and substitute.

Prudential World Cup Averages

AUSTRALIA BATTING

	M	Inns	NOs	Runs	HS	Av	100s	50s
G.N. Yallop	6	6	2	187	66*	49.75		2
G.M. Wood	5	5	1	144	73	38.00		1
R.W. Marsh	6	6	2	142	50*	35.50		1
T.M. Chappell	4	4		139	110	34.75	1	
K.J. Hughes	5	5		170	69	34.00		2
K.C. Wessels	3	3		92	76	30.66		1
A.R. Border	6	6		150	43	25.00		
D.W. Hookes	6	6		133	56	22.16		1
T.G. Hogan	4	4	2	24	11	12.00		
G.F. Lawson	4	4		24	16	6.00		
K.H. Macleay	4	4		19	9	4.75		

Also batted - R.M. Hogg 19*, 0*, 2* and 8* (six matches); D.K. Lillee 0 (four matches), J.R. Thomson 0 (three matches)

AUSTRALIA BOWLING

	Overs	Mds	Runs	Wkts	Av	Best	5/inn
G.N. Yallop	14	—	54	3	18.00	2/28	
K.H. Macleay	44.5	6	163	8	20.37	6/39	1
R.M. Hogg	67	8	220	9	24.44	3/40	
T.M. Chappell	19.4	—	98	4	24.50	3/47	
G.F. Lawson	38	7	127	5	25.40	3/29	
T.G. Hogan	47	2	172	6	28.66	2/33	
D.K. Lillee	45	2	177	4	44.25	2/47	
J.R. Thomson	32.5	1	161	3	53.66	3/51	
A.R. Border	23	1	85	1	85.00	1/11	

AUSTRALIA CATCHES

8 - R.W. Marsh; 3 – A.R. Border and D.W. Hookes; 2 – T.G. Hogan and K.J. Hughes; 1 - G.M. Wood, K.C. Wessels, D.K. Lillee, K.H. Macleay and T.M. Chappell

ZIMBABWE BATTING

	M	Inns	NOs	Runs	HS	Av	100s	50s
D.A.G. Fletcher	6	6	2	191	71*	47.75		2
K.M. Curran	6	6		212	73	35.33		2
D.L. Houghton	6	6		176	84	29.33		2
R.D. Brown	4	4		93	38	23.25		
I.P. Butchart	6	6	2	82	34*	20.50		
G.A. Paterson	6	6		99	27	16.50		
G.E. Peckover	3	3	1	33	16*	16.50		
A.J. Pycroft	6	6		71	21	11.83		
A. Omarshah	3	3		26	16	8.66		
J.G. Heron	6	6		50	18	8.33		
A.J. Traicos	6	4	1	25	19	8.33		
P.W.E. Rawson	6	4	1	24	19	8.00		

Also batted - V.R. Hogg 7* (two matches)

ZIMBABWE BOWLING

	Overs	Mds	Runs	Wkts	Av	Best	5/inn
P.W.E. Rawson	62.1	10	239	8	29.87	3/47	
D.A.G. Fletcher	50.1	5	221	7	31.57	4/42	
A. Omarshah	7.3	—	40	1	40.00	1/17	
A.J. Traicos	68	6	202	4	50.40	2/28	
K.M. Curran	58.2	3	274	5	54.80	3/65	
I.P. Butchart	50	4	213	3	71.00	2/52	

Also bowled - V.R. Hogg 15–4–49–0

ZIMBABWE CATCHES

7 - D.L. Houghton; 3 - A.J. Pycroft; 2 - I.P. Butchart, A.J. Traicos, P.W.E. Rawson and R.D. Brown; 1 - J.G. Heron, A. Omarshah and substitute

G. Hick did not play in any of the matches.

NEW ZEALAND BATTING

	M	Inns	NOs	Runs	HS	Av	100s	50s
J.V. Coney	6	6	2	197	66*	49.25		2
G.P. Howarth	6	6		224	76	37.33		2
M.D. Crowe	6	6		202	97	33.66		1
M.C. Snedden	3	2		61	40	30.50		
J.G. Bracewell	3	3	1	41	34	20.50		
J.J. Crowe	2	2		40	23	20.00		
W.K. Lees	4	4	1	60	26	20.00		
G.M. Turner	6	6		103	50	17.16		1
J.G. Wright	6	5		83	45	16.60		
B.A. Edgar	5			81	44	16.20		
R.J. Hadlee	6	5		71	31	14.20		
I.D.S. Smith	2	2	1	8	4*	8.00		
B.L. Cairns	6	5		16	6	3.20		

Also batted - E.J. Chatfield 9*, 6*, 19* and 3* (six matches)

NEW ZEALAND BOWLING

	Overs	Mds	Runs	Wkts	Av	Best	5/inn
R.J. Hadlee	65.1	17	180	14	12.85	5/25	1
J.V. Coney	58	7	183	9	20.33	3/28	
E.J. Chatfield	70.2	8	249	8	31.12	2/24	
B.L. Cairns	61.3	9	237	7	33.85	3/44	
M.C. Snedden	32.5	3	201	5	40.20	2/58	
M.D. Crowe	17	2	110	1	110.00	1/15	
J.G. Bracewell	35	2	155	1	155.00	1/66	

SRI LANKA BATTING

	M	Inns	NOs	Runs	HS	Av	100s	50s
R.G. de Alwis	6	6	3	167	59*	55.66		2
B. Kuruppu	6	6		182	72	30.33		2
R.L. Dias	6	6	1	150	64*	30.00		1
L.R.D. Mendis	6	6		158	56	26.33		1
S.R. de S. Wettimuny	6	6		128	50	21.33		1
R.S. Madugalle	5	5		104	60	20.80		1
V. John	5	5	3	35	15	17.50		
D.S. de Silva	6	6		94	35	15.66		
R.J. Ratnayake	6	5	1	54	20*	13.50		
A. Ranatunga	6	6		80	34	13.33		
A.L.F. de Mel	6	5		66	27	13.20		
M.A.R. Samarasekera	2	2		5	5	2.50		

SRI LANKA BOWLING

	Overs	Mds	Runs	Wkts	Av	Best	5/inn
A.L.F. de Mel	66	13	265	17	15.58	5/32	2
R.J. Ratnayake	64	6	274	8	34.25	2/18	
D.S. de Silva	58	6	238	3	79.33	2/11	
V. John	50.2	3	251	3	83.66	1/55	
A. Ranatunga	44.1	2	240	1	240.00	1/65	

Also bowled - M.A.R. Samarasekera 16.2–2–71–0; S.R. de S. Wettimuny 3–0–15–0

NEW ZEALAND CATCHES

4 - W.K. Lees and B.A. Edgar; 3 - B.L. Cairns; 2 - R.J. Hadlee, M.C. Snedden and J.J. Crowe; 1 - J.G. Wright, G.P. Howarth, J.V. Coney, M.D. Crowe, E.J. Chatfield, J.G. Bracewell and I.D.S. Smith

SRI LANKA CATCHES

5 - R.G. de Alwis; 3 - R.L. Dias, R.S. Madugalle and A. Ranatunga; 1 - B. Kurrupu, L.R.D. Mendis, 2 - D.S. de Silva and substitute

J.V. Jeyarajasingham and E.R.N.S. Fernando did not play in any of the matches.

The end of Roberts. (Adrian Murrell)

Sharma and Patil grab stumps in India's moment of triumph (Adrian Murrell)

The Prudential World Cup
by
TONY LEWIS

At 1am on Sunday 26 June 1983 a public holiday was declared in India. The Indian cricket team had just won the Prudential World Cup at Lord's. Only an hour earlier the handsome skipper, Kapil Dev had stepped proudly forward on the balcony of the pavilion and received the Cup from the President of MCC, Sir Anthony Tuke.

Television had taken live pictures of the whole day's play to India for the first time. Soon the stories were returning of how streets were jammed as thousands stood outside banks and stores where sets were put on display. Ox carts stopped in their tracks. Apparently, firemen motoring to put out a fire found a vantage point for seeing the cricket; they stood on top of their fire engine, stopped ringing their bell, removed their protective clothing and settled down for the day, no doubt, while Bombay burned. In Haryana Kapil Dev's name was god. This was the young man, only twenty-three years old, who grew up among them, who had never seen a Test match until he was actually chosen to play in one, now leading his country by instinct and example. Where was the Indian team which could not master one-day cricket? Whither the small men, helpless against the fast men of West Indies? Gone.

This was wonderful for the health of cricket, for its propagation as a world game of honour, skill and of equal opportunity. India were supposed to have no chance of beating the West Indies in this World Cup Final, but they did.

Forget the romance for a moment. India were underrated. As I write, of the last six one-day internationals they have played against West Indies who were rated the best in the world, they have won three. In the group stage of this World Cup they beat them at the start. Also, and much more significantly, they won a match in Berbice on their recent tour.

On the eve of this Lord's final I attended a cocktail party given by the Indian team. The invitations were rushed out, because before the semi-final against England two days before, they must have imagined themselves soon back home. England with all their ground advantage and their run of success in the competition were favourites. It was a typical Indian drinks party. I got there three-quarters of an hour late with Abid Ali, the former Indian cricketer, and we were the first there! I heard how Dileep Sardesai, another former Test player, had heard of the great semi-final win against England and had announced to his wife 'We win semis. I go to London'. A simple enough message. And so Indians flew into Britain from all directions. Four from Belgium paid £70 each for tickets on the black market. On the morning of the match the same £10 tickets were going for £20.

India's success had repercussions outside India. It gave identity to so many expatriots living in this country. In a strange and surprising way it brought out a patriotism for India among the sons of exiles who had never set foot in the land of their fathers. A Sikh raced up to me as I left Lord's on Saturday evening and said in broad London accent 'We wunnit, mate.'

Cricket in this Prudential Cup competition was a unifying factor; there were many more supporters from overseas than there have ever been before. This was because of the arrangement of the elimination matches into groups with league tables. It used to be a straight knock out contest, now each of the eight teams played at least six matches in their group before going out. The great performance of the series was appropriately by Kapil Dev. India were on their way out of the whole competition when, in their last but one group match, they were reduced to 17 for 5 against Zimbabwe. Kapil Dev came and scored 175 not out. He was the last recognised batsman. It is a world cup record: astonishing even allowing that his mammoth hitting was on the small but delightful Tunbridge Wells ground.

What went wrong with England? That was obviously a disappointment to millions. Bob Willis led a successful campaign until a first group match was lost v New Zealand at Birmingham. Then, the shifting of Botham up the batting

The crowd swarms over Lord's at the end of the match. (Adrian Murrell)

order did not help, neither Botham or his team. There were careless moments, untidy wicket-keeping and a needless sacrificing of the innings before the sixty overs were up. Tremors of the undisciplined Australian winter tour shook the nuts and bolts loose again. Sure enough by the time the semi-final came around when the pressure was on, when it required high skills performed in a tight match, England flopped. There is no doubt that the two finalists were the best sides in the competition.

It was surprising how much teams depended on the success of one player. New Zealand for example, who had beaten England in all five out of five previous one-day internationals, found that their medium fast bowlers did not get the bounce on English pitches which they had got in New Zealand and Australia. They needed some fine innings by Glenn Turner. He failed and so did they.

England were waiting for Botham to fire. His bowling is now expensive, he was pulled out of the front line of attack; the big, bludgeoning innings never came. Pakistan were a major disappointment but showed how much they depend on the bowling spearhead of Imran Khan to give the whole team a cutting edge. His inability to bowl because of a stress fracture to his left ankle, was the neutering of Pakistan.

In their way, despite the army of fast bowlers, West Indies knew that if Viv Richards got a long innings they would win the match. His form got better and better through the competition, but on Final day, he threw his wicket away and the cluster of youngsters, Gomes, Bacchus and Dujon were left in gentle confusion in the middle order.

Zimbabwe's important player, the former league professional, Duncan Fletcher did have a wonderful series of individual performances, but he lacked the all round support. Zimbabwe played good cricket, they beat Australia, but never fired on all cylinders.

Sri Lanka proved that they could bat. Mendis, the skipper, was the man with the flashing blade, Wettimuny the solid anchor, but only de Mel was a threat as a bowler. Lack of depth in the bowling department made them unlikely winners. Australia had looked to several individuals to help them repeat their one-day triumphs of the winter. Two famous ones failed, Lillee and Thomson. Dennis admitted that he should not have toured Sri Lanka with Australia just before the World Cup. He should have stayed at home to build up his injured knee. As it was, he was never fully fit and never happy. Thommo looked as if he needed a month's practice to get line and length into his system. He bowled an Australian length, short, looking for high bounce. English pitches do not help that approach.

So we come to reason for India's great triumph. Sunil Gavaskar their finest batsman, failed. They brusquely dropped him. Immediately, the depth of Indian batting was to be seen. Every one made contributions. Apart from Kapil Dev's blinding world record innings, it was a team effort. They all came off, Amarnath, Srikkanth, Patil, Vengsarkar, Yashpal Sharma.

The World Cup ended with the loss of a sponsor, Prudential who have achieved their marketing ends. There is the likelihood of another one stepping in quickly and next time there might also be a change of venue. Australia with its sophisticated television coverage would be the favourite.

SECTION N
The English Season

Schweppes County Championship.
John Player League. Nat. West. Trophy.
Benson and Hedges Cup.
England v New Zealand.
Full season's results and form charts.
Review of the season by David Lemmon.
Selling cricket by Peter Lush.
Book reviews.

The new pavilion at Taunton. (Adrian Murrell)

And so we turned to the English season. Dismayed somewhat by the happenings in Australia and New Zealand, convinced that English cricket had been lowered into another trough, the English supporter, nevertheless, returned as eagerly as ever to the game where he could renew old friendships and talk again 'of sunshine and of song, And summer days, when we were young.'

The English Ladies Cricket Team, deprived of their tour of the West Indies by authorities who had invoked the South African connection, sought the sun early as a compensation and visited the golf and cricket complex at La Manga, Spain, where they played against a team led by Don Wilson. Surrey and Middlesex were to follow them a few weeks later and Roger Knight could claim that he made the first 'duck' of the English season.

His county, like many others aware of the need for a sensible economic structure for the game, announced ambitious and praiseworthy plans for the development of The Oval where much has already been done to improve the lot of the spectator.

The Ken Barrington Indoor Cricket Centre, incorporating leisure facilities for the local community, is to be built at the Vauxhall End and an appeal for £1.25 million was launched at the start of the season.

Hospitality boxes are planned for the Taverners and

La Manga Sports Complex. A prelude to the English season (Adrian Murrell)

Cricket in March. Don Wilson appeals for lbw against his rival captain Rachel Heyhoe-Flint, La Manga, Spain. (Adrian Murrell)

Mound Stands and should be in use in time for the 1984 season.

The whole of The Oval perimeter wall is to be rebuilt and hospitality rooms are planned for the space under the terraces which, at present, is wasted.

Such enterprise deserves success.

Kent and Essex are other counties to show similar economic foresight. Essex, having transformed the County Ground at Chelmsford into a comfortable and well appointed centre, received the backing of the Suffolk brewers Tolly Cobbold who announced a sponsorship worth £40,000 over a period of three years.

Meanwhile we waited for the rain to stop.

There were the customary pre-season moves and changes. Mike Selvey became the latest captain of Glamorgan where leadership is becoming as dangerous as football management. Derbyshire signed the Danish quick bowler, Ole Mortensen, and were initially thwarted in their attempt to sign Mike Holding. The T.C.C.B. later relented and so we had the prospect of Derbyshire's bowling being opened by a Dane and a West Indian.

Gifford and Old moved to Warwickshire after receiving some discourtesy from the counties that they had served so long. Jefferies, the South African pace bowler who had had one game for Derbyshire in 1982, joined Lancashire, and the likeable David Surridge left Gloucestershire and first-class cricket.

Surrey would no longer have Jackman and Roope in their

Janette Brittain, English Ladies' batsman. (Adrian Murrell)

...ide, and another to leave The Oval was Hugh Wilson who went to Somerset. Geoff Arnold retired after long and distinguished service with Sussex and Surrey, but there were still many familiar faces around waiting for the rain to stop.

To the general delight of all those concerned with first-class cricket in England, the National Westminster Bank announced an increase in its sponsorship from £280,000 to £324,000 while Benson and Hedges, as announced by Len Owen, a director of the company, gave the T.C.C.B. a much needed long term guarantee and sponsorship of nearly two million pounds over the next five years, a magnificent boost to the game.

20, 21 and 22 April

at Cambridge

Cambridge University 180 for 5 dec (R.J. Boyd-Moss 83) and 48 for 4
Glamorgan 184 for 4 dec (R.C. Ontong 51 not out)

Match drawn

Naturally, there was no play on the first day of the English season, and it seemed that there was little hope of play on the other two days, but the groundsman worked wonders and the season was delayed for only a day. There was never likely to be a result, but Boyd-Moss played pleasantly, Pollock bowled well and Curtis showed technical soundness for the

University. For Glamorgan, Alan Jones, in the fifty minutes play possible before lunch on the last day, passed 35,000 runs, leaving only Boycott and Amiss, of those still playing, ahead of him. It does not bear thinking what an English season would be like without him.

23, 25 and 26 April

at Cambridge

Cambridge University 192 for 7 dec and 105 for 6 (P.B. Clift 5 for 20)
Leicestershire 310 for 6 dec (D.I. Gower 124, R.W. Tolchard 61)

Match drawn

at Oxford

Oxford University 145 (S.T. Jefferies 5 for 15)
Lancashire 39 for 0

Match drawn

A thunderstorm ended play shortly after lunch on the last day in The Parks, and, as there had been only limited play on

The season's first centurion. David Gower, 124 v Cambridge University, 24 April. (Adrian Murrell)

the first day and none at all on the Monday, it was a miserable beginning to the season for both sides. There was time enough, however, for Stephen Jefferies, with his brisk pace left-arm over the wicket bowling, to assert that he would be a force for Lancashire during the season although it would not be possible for both he and Clive Lloyd to play in the same side. Two other points of interest in the Lancashire side were that Abrahams was named captain in the absence of Lloyd and we saw the first of leg-spinner Zaida.

At Cambridge, though the game was similarly disrupted, David Gower gave a most handsome display in scoring the season's first century. As he had just been named as captain of M.C.C. in place of Bob Willis who had influenza, it seemed a most appropriate distinction. Gower has retained all the charm and freshness that he displayed when he first appeared some eight years ago, but now there is a certainty, a maturity which has added substance to the early ingenuousness.

Paddy Clift, whose prowess is all too frequently undervalued, began the season with match figures of 8 for 56. Boyd-Moss again played well for Cambridge in a match in which they had little chance to distinguish themselves.

27, 28 and 29 April

at Lord's

M.C.C. v. Middlesex

Match abandoned

at Cambridge

Essex 375 for 4 dec (G.A. Gooch 174, B.R. Hardie 129) and 278 for 7 dec (K.S. McEwan 86, D.R. Pringle 83, T.A. Cotterell 5 for 89)
Cambridge University 165 (T.S. Curtis 50, J.K. Lever 7 for 63) and 93 for 4

Match drawn

at Oxford

Oxford University v. Somerset

Match abandoned

The great event which always begins the season at Lord's, M.C.C. v. The Champion County, was abandoned because the ground was sodden. Oxford University and Somerset attempted to salvage something from their rain-ruined match at Oxford by playing a limited-over game on the Friday, but even that was ended by rain.

At Fenner's, however, Gooch and Hardie began Essex's season with a stand of 263 in 183 minutes. It was only 7 short of the Essex first wicket record set up by Dodds and Avery against Surrey at The Oval in 1946. Gooch, who reached a century before lunch, hit three sixes and twenty-five fours in his three-hour innings and left all mumbling sadly and discontentedly that he would not be in England's side for the World Cup. Hardie began his benefit season in fine style, and another banned Englishman, John Lever, bowled splendidly on the second day to put the game beyond the reach of Cambridge.

In order to give his batsmen necessary practice, Fletcher did not invoke the follow-on and McEwan and Pringle emulated Gooch and Hardie in their attack on the University bowling. Their opening stand was worth 165 in 113 minutes. Left-arm spinner Cotterell, who had impressed with his flight and control in the first two matches of the season, gave another good performance and was rewarded with five wickets. Inevitably, the rain returned.

30 and 31 April, 1 May

at Derby

Gloucestershire 343 for 4 (A.W. Stovold 181, Zaheer Abbas 82 v. **Derbyshire**

Match drawn
Gloucestershire 3 pts, Derbyshire 0 pts

at Leicester

Hampshire 252 for 5 dec (C.L. Smith 129 not out, D.R. Turner 62) v. **Leicestershire**

Match drawn
Hampshire 3 pts, Leicestershire 2 pts

at Trent Bridge

Nottinghamshire 181 for 6 v. **Somerset**

Match drawn
Somerset 2 pts, Nottinghamshire 1 pt

at The Oval

Surrey 126 for 6 (R.D.V. Knight 52 not out) v. **Kent**

Match drawn
Kent 2 pts, Surrey 0 pts

at Worcester

Worcestershire 79 for 3 v. **Yorkshire**

Match drawn
Yorkshire 1 pt, Worcestershire 0 pts

at Oxford

Sussex 280 (I.A. Greig 147 not out, J.R. Turnbull 4 for 51)
Oxford University 21 for 0

Match drawn

30 April, 1 and 2 May

at Old Trafford

Lancashire 429 for 8 dec (D.P. Hughes 153, G. Fowler 133, J.G. Thomas 5 for 103)
Glamorgan 63 for 7 (P.J.W. Allott 4 for 28)

Match drawn
Lancashire 7 pts, Glamorgan 3 pts

at Lord's

Essex 160 for 2 (G.A. Gooch 72 not out) v. Middlesex

Match drawn
Essex 1 pt, Middlesex 0 pts

at Edgbaston

Northamptonshire 193 (P. Willey 53, A.M. Ferreira 4 for 31) and 9 for 0
Warwickshire 281 (G.W. Humpage 67, K.D. Smith 59, B.J. Griffiths 4 for 55)

Match drawn
Warwickshire 7 pts, Northamptonshire 5 pts

The first round of matches in the Schweppes County Championship was ruined by rain. A start was made in all matches on the Saturday, but no play was possible anywhere on Sunday or Monday. This meant that only 37 championship points were won in the eight matches. There were, however, some encouraging performances.

Andy Stovold, whose 181 took 6 hours, 20 minutes, shared a third wicket stand of 154 with Zaheer Abbas at Derby. Knight and Lynch brought Surrey from 13 for 4 to 71 for 5 at The Oval, and Knight found another good partner in Thomas before the close. Chris Smith, who would become 'English' on 11 May, scored a fine hundred at Leicester. His hundred came in 273 minutes. There was welcome support from the likeable David Turner who had had a poor season in 1982.

Mike Gatting began the unenviable job of succeeding Mike Brearley as captain of Middlesex in the game with Essex at Lord's where Gooch once more demonstrated the power denied to England in the two and a half hours play which constituted the match.

The English season begins. Bernard Flack at Edgbaston in May. (Ken Kelly)

Andy Stovold, Gloucestershire. A splendid start to the season with centuries in successive matches. (Adrian Murrell)

More encouraging for England was the news from Old Trafford where Fowler helped his side to recover from 19 for 2 with an innings of 133. He and David Hughes, whose innings was a career best, put on 245 for the third wicket. On the last day, Allott made an early claim for an England recall when he and the impressive Jefferies reduced Glamorgan to 63 for 7.

Ian Greig also hit a career best, 147 not out against Oxford University. Sussex, at one time, were 57 for 4 to Turnbull and Smail.

Warwickshire, who had a look of rejuvenation, bowled out Northants on the Saturday and flagged a little in the chase for batting bonus points on the Tuesday. The best of the Warwickshire bowlers was the much improved Anton Ferreira. Humpage hit with his customary vigour, but Warwickshire slumped from 180 for 3 to 281 all out.

Warwickshire were without Bob Willis, recovering from influenza, but he was named as England's captain for the World Cup.

4, 5 and 6 May

at Cardiff

Essex 325 for 6 dec (K.W.R. Fletcher 151 not out, K.S. McEwan 107)
Glamorgan 255 for 5 dec (Javed Miandad 89, M.W.W. Selvey 63)

Match drawn
Essex 6 pts, Glamorgan 5 pts

at Bristol

Gloucestershire 333 for 7 dec (A.W. Stovold 122, A.J. Hignell 50 not out, P.I. Pocock 4 for 70)
Surrey 252 for 4 (G.S. Clinton 105, D.M. Smith 90)

Match drawn
Surrey 6 pts, Gloucestershire 5 pts

at Leicester

Leicestershire 302 for 3 dec (B.F. Davison 84 not out, D.I. Gower 81, J.C. Balderstone 69) and 54 for 1
Derbyshire 265 for 8 dec (J.G. Wright 60, J.H. Hampshire 52)

Match drawn
Leicestershire 7 pts, Derbyshire 4 pts

at Lord's

Middlesex 331 for 6 dec (G.D. Barlow 128, M.W. Gatting 64 not out, W.N. Slack 56)
Lancashire 98 for 7 dec (N.F. Williams 4 for 47)

Match drawn
Middlesex 6 pts, Lancashire 2 pts

at Northampton

Northamptonshire 346 for 8 dec (P. Willey 175 not out, S.J. Malone 4 for 93)
Hampshire 177 (C.L. Smith 55) and 204 for 5 (T.M. Tremlett 59, T.E. Jesty 53 not out)

Match drawn
Northamptonshire 7 pts, Hampshire 4 pts

at Taunton

Somerset 325 for 7 dec (P.M. Roebuck 81, J.W. Lloyds 58, A.P. Pridgeon 5 for 58)
Worcestershire 253 for 7 (M.J. Weston 92)

Match drawn
Somerset 7 pts, Worcestershire 5 pts

at Hove

Sussex 115 (A.C.S. Pigott 63, R.J. Hadlee 4 for 25, M. Hendrick 4 for 28) and 175
Nottinghamshire 322 for 9 dec (R.J. Hadlee 103, J.D. Birch 55)

Nottinghamshire won by an innings and 32 runs
Nottinghamshire 24 pts, Sussex 4 pts

at Leeds

Yorkshire 61 for 1 v. **Warwickshire**

Match drawn
No points

at Cambridge

Kent 324 for 5 dec (N.R. Taylor 114, M.R. Benson 105) and 157 for 2 dec (C.S. Cowdrey 103 not out)
Cambridge University 140 and 76 for 0

Match drawn

The first result in the Schweppes County Championship was achieved in the match at Hove. On a damp and cold day Sussex were asked to bat and they lost three wickets before a run was scored. They progressed to 5 for 5, and then to 19 for 8 before Phillipson and Pigott made nonsense of what had gone before with a flurry of shots. The afternoon was lost to drizzle and when they batted in the evening session the conditions were certainly better than they had been in the morning, but 19 for 8 was inexplicable even allowing for the excellence of Hadlee, Hendrick and Cooper in exploiting the pitch and the atmosphere.

Hadlee, completely recovered from his hamstring injury, demonstrated his all-round ability on the second day with a fierce century. His innings lasted 147 minutes and a fifth wicket stand of 78 with Birch occupied only 17 overs.

On the last day, Sussex crumpled again before the pace attack and Notts won with two hours to spare.

Essex flourished on the first day at Cardiff when McEwan and Fletcher, in regal form, shared a third wicket stand of 179. Glamorgan found their own hero in new captain Selvey. Coming in as night-watchman, he stayed to score 63, his highest score in first-class cricket in England, and thwart the Essex bowlers in partnership with Javed Miandad.

Andy Stovold scored his second century in successive innings. He and Broad began the Gloucestershire innings with a stand of 143 in 44 overs after Knight had put them in. Hignell and Zaheer both batted briskly and well to see the

Richard Hadlee's all-round cricket was the vital factor in making Notts the first winners of a Schweppes County Championship match during the season. Here he appeals for lbw against Alan Wells. Bruce French supports him. (Adrian Murrell)

Mike Hendrick, 4 for 28 in the first innings, was decisive in the rout of Sussex. (Adrian Murrell)

An unhappy beginning to the Sussex season. The scoreboard shows them at 19 for 8 on the first day against Nottinghamshire. (Adrian Murrell)

home side to four points, and Childs had Butcher stumped by the immensely promising Russell before the close, but next day Clinton and Smith took their second wicket stand to 191. Clinton scored the ninth century of his career on his thirtieth birthday and then the rain returned.

Peter Willey joined the long list of players whose non-availability frustrated the England selectors. Abandoning his usual pugnacious methods, he played a watchful innings of 175 not out, and, surprisingly, the most productive stand he shared was one of 82, unbroken, with Carse, the South African for the ninth wicket. Both men were then prominent in the Northants attack which forced Hampshire to follow-on. Tremlett and Jesty denied the home side any further glories.

Roebuck and Lloyds began brightly for Somerset with a stand of 143 and the Taunton crowd was well pleased with the first day's 325 for 7. Restricted play on the second day made a draw inevitable. Neale and the strong driving Weston added 121 in 44 overs for the visitors, but then Popplewell caused some uncertainty with his outswingers before Younis batted Worcestershire out of further trouble.

A reluctance to play won Abrahams and Lancashire few friends at Lord's on the first day, and Barlow punished them on the second with an innings better than any he has played for three years. He settled quickly into the role of opener and obviously responded to the trust that new captain Mike Gat-

ting showed in him. Gatting himself quickly established authority in the Middlesex side, and Lancashire were soon struggling. Fowler was run out after a dreadful mix-up with David Lloyd who then retired with a neck injury. There had been a plan to forfeit innings, but the rain ruined even this ploy and doomed the match to a draw.

Kent used the match at Cambridge to establish batting form. Taylor and Benson in the first, and Cowdrey in the second, scored impressive hundreds. Cowdrey was particularly forceful, his 103 was scored out of 153 made while he was at the wicket.

David Gower warmed English hearts with another elegant innings. He and the dependable Balderstone added 137 for the second wicket, and Brian Davison, a superb striker of the ball, played a robust knock at the close. Sadly, from an England point of view, Paul Newman, one of the young fast bowling hopes, bowled erratically. Derbyshire countered well with fifties from Hampshire and John Wright before the rain.

Following this game, Barry Wood resigned as Derbyshire's captain, saying that the role was too demanding. Wood became the fifth Derbyshire captain to quit during a season. In the past nine years, Bolus, Taylor, Steele and Miller had all done the same thing, and Derbyshire were now forced to find their seventh new captain since 1975. Miller agreed to lead the side until a new captain was appointed.

Benson and Hedges Cup

7 May

---

at Chesterfield

Derbyshire v. **Yorkshire**

Match abandoned
Derbyshire (1 pt), Yorkshire (1 pt)

at Southampton

Essex 260 for 6 (G.A. Gooch 68, K.W.R. Fletcher 59)
Hampshire 147

Essex (2 pts) won by 113 runs
(Gold Award – K.W.R. Fletcher)

at Old Trafford

Lancashire 127 for 6 v. **Warwickshire**

Match abandoned
Lancashire (1 pt), Warwickshire (1 pt)

at Northampton

Northamptonshire 191 (P. Willey 71, G.E. Sainsbury 4 for 28)
Gloucestershire 192 for 8 (Zaheer Abbas 65)

Gloucestershire (2 pts) won by 2 wickets
(Gold Award – P. Willey)

at The Oval

Middlesex 273 for 6 (R.O. Butcher 85, M.W. Gatting 53)
Surrey 64 for 2

Middlesex (2 pts) won on faster scoring rate
(Gold Award – R.O. Butcher)

at Worcester

Leicestershire 198 (D.I. Gower 67)
Worcestershire 81 (J.F. Steele 5 for 11)

(Gold Award – J.F. Steele)

7 and 9 May

---

at Taunton

Somerset 251 for 7 (I.V.A. Richards 83, J.W. Lloyds 51)
Sussex 192

Somerset (2 pts) won by 59 runs

at Cambridge

Kent 276 for 9 (N.R. Taylor 100, A.P.E. Knott 55)
Combined Universities 212 (S.P. Henderson 82, G.R. Dilley 4 for 32)

Kent (2 pts) won by 64 runs
(Gold Award – N.R. Taylor)

With the exception of the matches at Chesterfield and Old Trafford, the matches in the first round of the Benson and Hedges Cup achieved a result although Surrey could feel a little aggrieved. In dismal conditions Middlesex batted well at The Oval. Barlow and Slack gave them a fine start, but Radley went quickly and they were 85 for 3 in the twenty-fifth over. Gatting and Butcher joined in a thrilling stand of 123 in 23 overs, 62 coming in 9 overs after tea when the Surrey bowlers forgot completely the virtues of length. Gatting has authority to his pugnacity and Butcher was lissome and lethal, a remembrance of the man who was an England player a very short time ago.

There was time for only 20 overs before the close during which time Surrey scored 63 which, as there was no play possible on Monday or Tuesday, was insufficient to give them the match on the faster scoring rate.

Hampshire chose to field against Essex and then mocked their decision by dropping simple chances and, Emery in particular, bowling raggedly. After a quiet start Gooch was lordly and Fletcher was cultured. Hampshire never looked like approaching the Essex total. The middle order fell to Turner, and all the Essex bowlers came away with credit.

The most thrilling struggle was that at Northampton where John Childs hit the winning run off the last ball of the match at eight o'clock in the evening.

Northants had started splendidly, Larkins and Cook took 69 from the first 15 overs and then Willey gave further evidence that this was to be a season of accomplishment. But the Northants middle order disintegrated and the last six wickets fell for 9 runs.

Gloucestershire owed much to Zaheer for he scored 56 of the 86 which were added with Broad for the third wicket in 19 overs. When Zaheer fell to Tim Lamb Northants looked capable of snatching victory, but Graveney played sensibly before the last ball drama.

The slow left-arm of John Steele was devastating at Worcester, his 5 for 11 in 10 overs winning the match for Leicestershire and the Gold Award for himself. Earlier, David Gower had continued his golden form with 67 and a stand of 103 for the second wicket with Balderstone. Like Northants and Gloucestershire, Leicestershire managed a collapse, losing their last six wickets for 28 runs. Their 198 was far too many for Worcestershire, however, who had the look of a side which may be in for a couple of lean years.

In the two matches that were completed on the Monday. Somerset, the holders, beat Sussex with some ease, Viv Richards being as lordly as ever, and Kent, with an accomplished hundred from Taylor, about whom England selectors must be thinking, accounted for Combined Universities for whom Steve Henderson played a valiant innings.

John Player League

8 May

---

at Southampton

Hampshire 214 for 6 (T.E. Jesty 100)
Essex 199 for 8 (B.R. Hardie 51)

Hampshire (4 pts) won by 15 runs

at Canterbury

Kent 208 for 6 (C.J. Tavare 82)
Surrey 80 (D.L. Underwood 5 for 14)

Kent (4 pts) won on faster scoring rate

at Old Trafford

Lancashire v. **Derbyshire**

Match abandoned
Lancashire 2 pts, Derbyshire 2 pts

at Leicester

Leicestershire v. **Worcestershire**

Match abandoned
Leicestershire 2 pts, Worcestershire 2 pts

at Lord's

Middlesex v. **Glamorgan**

Match abandoned
Middlesex 2 pts, Glamorgan 2 pts

at Northampton

Northamptonshire 210 for 7 (R.N. Kapil Dev 66)
Nottinghamshire 74 for 2

Nottinghamshire (4 pts) won on faster scoring rate

at Taunton

Somerset 213 for 5 (I.V.A. Richards 96 not out, P.M. Roebuck 50)
Sussex 124

Somerset (4 pts) won by 89 runs

at Edgbaston

Warwickshire 175 for 5 (D.L. Amiss 55 not out)
Yorkshire 176 for 4 (C.W.J. Athey 72 not out)

Yorkshire (4 pts) won by 6 wickets

The weather was once more the greatest adversary. Three matches were abandoned and at Northampton, after Kapil Dev and Allan Lamb had put on 109 for the third wicket and Kapil Dev had hit 66 off 50 balls in his first match of the season, rain interrupted play for 90 minutes, and Notts were left the easier task of making 74 in 14 overs. Rice, with 45 not out, led them to victory with two balls to spare.

Viv Richards hammered the Sussex bowlers for the second day running, sharing stands of 90 and 81 with Roebuck and Rose respectively on a slow wicket.

Four interruptions for rain at Canterbury could not stop Kent overwhelming Surrey. Chris Tavare was in his jubilant Sunday best mood. Without a flicker of emotion he crashed the Surrey bowling to all parts of the field, dominating a second wicket stand of 114 in 14 overs with Taylor. Surrey were handicapped when Clarke could bowl only 4 of his 8 overs because of a side strain.

The Kent innings lasted only 29 overs, and the Surrey target was reduced to 194 in 27 overs, a very difficult task. They started disastrously and maintained a consistent mood of despair as Underwood nagged them to destruction.

The game at Edgbaston was reduced to 24 overs and Yorkshire won with 8 balls to spare. Yorkshire, who had played only four hours of cricket since the season began, bowled through the rain in order to finish some sort of match. The Warwickshire innings was interrupted and they returned to score 89 from the last 8 overs. One over from Athey cost 21

ABOVE: *Peter Willey began the season in magnificent form for Northants. His 175 in the Championship match against Hampshire was followed with 71 against Gloucestershire in the Benson and Hedges match three days later.* BELOW: *Neil Taylor. Two centuries in a week for Kent at the beginning of May. (Adrian Murrell)*

runs, and one from Sidebottom 22. When Yorkshire batted, however, Athey became the hero. His 72 were superbly struck runs, and Yorkshire raced to victory with 84 runs coming in 8 overs at the close.

Heavily defeated in the Benson and Hedges Cup on the previous day, Hampshire reversed positions with Essex at Southampton. Hampshire were 14 for 2 and then Trevor Jesty hit an effortless century, no panic, no violation of the text book, but brisk efficient runs and crisp shots.

Essex, in contrast, were laboured. Hardie scored an unadventurous fifty and Fletcher could not find the fluency of the previous day. Stuart Turner and Keith Pont suddenly gave hope with 41 belligerent runs in 4 overs, but the return of Malcolm Marshall brought an end to both and victory to Hampshire.

The saddest event concerning the first Sunday of the John Player League was not revealed until two days later. Following allegations that Younis Ahmed had placed a bet of £100 on Leicestershire to beat his own county Worcestershire in the John Player League match, an emergency meeting of the county committee considered all the available evidence, including representations by the player, and decided that Younis was guilty of gross misconduct and that his contract was to be terminated immediately.

Worcestershire County Cricket Club, not the strongest of sides, badly needed Younis' services, but they were left with no option but to dismiss him. In the light of some of the flabby leadership of which cricket authorities have been guilty in recent years, it was a brave decision and, refreshingly, one of integrity.

11, 12 and 13 May

at Chesterfield

Derbyshire 51 for 2 v. **Lancashire**

Match abandoned
No points

at Chelmsford

Essex 320 (K.R. Pont 105, K.W.R. Fletcher 55, G.R. Dilley 5 for 70) and 0 for 0 dec
Kent 0 for 0 dec and 321 for 4 (C.J. Tavare 94, M.R. Benson 78, R.A. Woolmer 63)

Kent won by 6 wickets
Kent 19 pts, Essex 3 pts

at Gloucester

Gloucestershire v. **Sussex**

Match abandoned

at Southampton

Hampshire 216 for 6 dec (C.L. Smith 81 not out, M.D. Marshall 79)
Warwickshire 207 (C. Lethbridge 73 not out, A.I. Kallicharran 53, T.M. Tremlett 4 for 53)

Hampshire won by 9 runs
Hampshire 12 pts, Warwickshire 0 pts

at Lord's

Middlesex v. **Yorkshire**

Match abandoned

at The Oval

Surrey 170 for 4 (M.A. Lynch 69 not out) v. **Leicestershire**

Match abandoned
Surrey 1 pt, Leicestershire 1 pt

at Worcester

Worcestershire 329 for 9 dec (C.L. King 123, V.J Marks 4 for 101)
Somerset 301 for 5 dec (I.T. Botham 107, N.F.M Popplewell 58 retired hurt)

Match drawn
Somerset 8 pts, Worcestershire 6 pts

at Oxford

Oxford University 163 (R.G.P. Ellis 103 not out, M.W.W. Selvey 6 for 47) v. **Glamorgan**

Match abandoned

Rain so destroyed the cricket programme that a few overs at Worcester were all that was possible on the second day. Two matches were abandoned without a ball being bowled and only 25 overs were played at Chesterfield and 51 at The Oval. The game at Oxford ended at close of play on the first day, but the one day's play possible had produced a remarkable achievement. In a rain-affected day, Richard Ellis, the University's opening batsman, batted for 3½ hours to carry his bat for 103 out of a total of 163. Only two other batsmen, Franks (15) and Rawlinson (11), reached double figures. It was the second century of Ellis' career. Most of his innings was spent in contest with the Glamorgan captain Mike Selvey who had his best figures for his new side and took six wickets with his late swing on a damp day.

Another newcomer, Collis King, on a year's contract with Worcestershire, made a brilliant start, hitting six sixes and twelve fours in his 123. After a watchful start he was at his most explosive, at one time scoring fifty off 25 deliveries. Ian Botham responded on the last in characteristic fashion of one who will not be overshadowed. He hit 107 off 166 balls in 122 minutes. He is a man of power.

Hampshire and Warwickshire were restricted to play on the last day, and Hampshire won a thrilling one-innings match by 9 runs. Hampshire were 56 for 5 when Marshall joined Chris Smith. The West Indian was soon into his stride with some fine shots and with Smith accelerating, Hampshire reached 216 for 6, leaving Warwickshire 102 minutes plus 20 overs in which to get the runs. The stand between Marshall and Smith was worth 158.

Warwickshire began with a polished half-century from Kallicharran, and Lethbridge and Old bludgeoned 65 off 8 overs, but the Hampshire bowlers were gnawing away at the Warwickshire wickets and Hogg was run out with two balls left giving Hampshire victory.

On the opening day at Chelmsford, Gooch was bowled by

Under Tavare's firm leadership, Kent looked an impressive side. He is a quiet and cultured man, but he is a positive man and he had quickly established a discipline and sense of commitment in the Kent side.

Friday, 13 May, and Ian Botham once more scorns superstition by hitting the twenty-first century of his career off 116 deliveries. He hits Patel for six. Collis King, who also hit a violent century in the match, is at slip. (Ken Kelly)

the first ball of the match by Dilley, but Essex recovered, mainly through a majestic century by Keith Pont. He first played for Essex thirteen years ago, but he is still looked upon as a promising youngster. Perhaps the early promise has not been fulfilled, though one could argue that he has not been given the encouragement, nor the chances, that he has deserved, but this was a majestic, powerful innings, and he became the fifth Essex batsman to score a century in the season. From the Kent, and England, point of view, the bonus was the bowling of Dilley, who had speed, fluency and control, the result, happily, of application and hard work.

Kent forfeited their first innings and Essex their second in an effort to achieve a result. Needing 321 to win, Kent lost Taylor at 55 and Woolmer, after a hard-hit 63, at 114, but then Benson joined Tavare and at tea, Kent were 141 for 2.

After tea they scored at five an over, Tavare showing that runs could be achieved quickly without violating technique and constantly trying to lash the ball to the boundary. When he was out, after a splendidly efficient innings, Kent needed 74 from 15 overs. Kent faltered a little as Pringle, who had lost all rhythm and reason, tightened up, but after Benson's fine innings had ended, Cowdrey and Knott made the rest look easy and the visitors won with 9 balls to spare.

Benson and Hedges Cup

14 May

at Chelmsford

Essex 225 for 8 (G.A. Gooch 99)
Somerset 172 (I.V.A. Richards 63)

Essex (2 pts) won by 53 runs
(Gold Award – G.A. Gooch)

at Gloucester

Gloucestershire v. **Leicestershire**

Match abandoned
Gloucestershire (1 pt), Leicestershire (1 pt)

at Canterbury

Kent 190 for 7 (G.W. Johnson 72 not out)
Middlesex 191 for 5 (C.T. Radley 88 not out, R.O. Butcher 50)

Middlesex (2 pts) won by 5 wickets
(Gold Award – C.T. Radley)

at Hove

Minor Counties 183 for 4 (D. Bailey 51 not out)
Sussex 184 for 5

Sussex (2 pts) won by 5 wickets
(Gold Award – D. Bailey)

at Cambridge

Glamorgan 225 (Javed Miandad 95)
Combined Universities 59 (M.W.W. Selvey 4 for 10)

Glamorgan (2 pts) won by 166 runs
(Gold Award – Javed Miandad)

14 and 16 May

at Edgbaston

Warwickshire 287 for 5 (A.I. Kallicharran 119, K.D. Smith 75)
Derbyshire 226 (J.H. Hampshire 83, R.G.D. Willis 5 for 37)

Warwickshire (2 pts) won by 61 runs
(Gold Award – R.G.D. Willis)

15 May

at Aberdeen

Scotland 105
Worcestershire 106 for 5 (M.J. Weston 56)

Worcestershire (2 pts) won by 5 wickets
(Gold Award – M.J. Weston)

16 May

at Leeds

Nottinghamshire 195 for 8 (C.E.B. Rice 86 not out)
Yorkshire 170

Nottinghamshire (2 pts) won by 25 runs
(*Gold Award* – C.E.B. Rice)

The second round of Benson and Hedges Cup matches were, inevitably, plagued by the weather, but Essex and Middlesex, in winning their second matches, emerged as clear leaders in groups C and D.

Essex were indebted to a spanking innings by Graham Gooch. It was clinical in application, severe in execution. He did not make a mistake until he was one short of his century, and then he was out. He took 16 runs in one over from Garner, including hoisting him in to the pavilion for 6, and then drove at Wilson, but Rose, at mid-off, leapt high and wide to his right and held a spectacular catch. That was at 176 in the forty-seventh over, and he was sixth out.

Richards scored 63 in 27 overs and then gave himself room to punch Ray East through the off-side, missed, and was bowled. It was his lowest score of the season to date. Botham, with only a single to his name, tried a back-handed sweep,

LEFT: *Viv Richards drives mightily in his innings of 63 v Essex.*
BELOW: *The end of his innings, bowled attempting to cut Ray East. David East is the wicket-keeper.* (*Adrian Murrell*)

ABOVE *(left)*: *Graham Gooch drives Vic Marks for four in his magnificent innings of 99 for Essex v Somerset in the Benson and Hedges Cup match at Chelmsford, 14 May.* ABOVE *(right)*: *Ian Botham survives David East's appeal for run out, but he was not to survive much longer. He was bowled attempting a reverse sweep. (Adrian Murrell).* RIGHT: *Kim Barnett, at 22 the youngest captain in Derbyshire's history. He revived a sagging side. (George Herringshaw)*

missed and was also bowled. After that Somerset fell apart. Three men were run out, Dredge was marvellously caught by the impressive David East, and Somerset were well beaten.

Kent found the all-round Middlesex bowling, even without the injured Phil Edmonds, too restricting. Graham Johnson, far too low at number seven, and Alan Knott resuscitated them after they had been 43 for 5, but Middlesex were rarely troubled even though they lost 3 for 61, and Radley saw them to victory with 3.2 overs to spare.

Javed Miandad led the Glamorgan attack on the Universities' bowling, and he and Eifion Jones added 117 for the seventh wicket after 6 men had been lost for 91. Then Nash and Selvey bowled their overs without rest and at the end of 22 overs, Combined Universities were 21 for 8, in danger of a record low score. They avoided that indignity, mainly through a defiant and sensible 32 from Doggart, Ellis and Cullinan each made 8.

A rather drab game at Hove saw runs hard to come by and Sussex win with 6½ overs to spare. Scotland managed only one boundary, by their West Indian Desmond Haynes, run out for 21, and Worcestershire had few problems.

Kallicharran hit a fine hundred for Warwickshire on the Saturday, sharing a second wicket stand of 108 with David Smith. The home side's total was formidable, and the game closed on Saturday evening with Derbyshire 72 for 3 off 20.3 overs, both openers having failed to score. On the Monday, Hampshire and Hill led a revival and after 40 overs,

Derbyshire were 170 for 4, but Willis turned the game back in Warwickshire's favour when he dismissed Hampshire and Miller in successive overs.

Chasing 196 for victory, Yorkshire lost 4 for 38, and then recovered to 110, only to slump again to 133 for 8. Sidebottom and Illingworth took the score to 170, but in the fifty-first over, Hendrick accounted for Sidebottom and Dennis, and Yorkshire were left to contemplate the catch that Carrick had dropped off Illingworth's bowling when Clive Rice had scored 1.

John Player League

15 May

at Derby

Derbyshire 201 for 5 (J.G. Wright 67)
Northamptonshire 123

Derbyshire (4 pts) won by 78 runs

at Chelmsford

Essex v. **Lancashire**

Match abandoned
Essex (2 pts), Lancashire (2 pts)

at Swansea

Glamorgan 5 for 0 v. **Warwickshire**

Match abandoned
Glamorgan (2 pts), Warwickshire (2 pts)

at Gloucester

Gloucestershire v. **Leicestershire**

Match abandoned
Gloucestershire (2 pts), Leicestershire (2 pts)

at Lord's

Middlesex v. **Hampshire**

Match abandoned
Middlesex (2 pts), Hampshire (2 pts)

at Trent Bridge

Somerset 279 for 3 (I.V.A. Richards 117 not out, I.T. Botham 85)
Nottinghamshire 32 for 1

Somerset (4 pts) won on faster scoring rate

at Hove

Sussex v. **Kent**

Match abandoned
Sussex (2 pts), Kent (2 pts)

at Leeds

Yorkshire v. **Surrey**

Match abandoned
Yorkshire (2 pts), Surrey 2 pts

Only at Derby was a full match possible. John Wright batted well and he and Barry Wood gave Derbyshire a splendid start with 104 for the first wicket. John Hampshire and acting captain Geoff Miller added 54 at the end, and Northants, needing 202, had a wretched start when Newman captured both openers for 9. The visitors never recovered and wickets fell regularly to an accurate Derbyshire attack.

Viv Richards, six sixes and nine fours, and Ian Botham, three sixes and ten fours, added 138 in 13 overs of breathtaking hitting at Trent Bridge. Hemmings, who had taken the wicket of Roebuck, conceded 88 runs in his 8 overs, and the usually economic Hendrick was hit for 62 in his quota. The Notts innings lasted only 11 overs before rain brought play to an end and gave Somerset the victory which their rich batting deserved.

Benson and Hedges Cup

17 May

at Leicester

Leicestershire 171 for 7
Northamptonshire 174 for 2 (A.J. Lamb 106 not out, P. Willey 54 not out)

Northamptonshire (2 pts) won by 8 wickets
(Gold Award – A.J. Lamb

at Uxbridge

Middlesex v. **Glamorgan**

Match abandoned
Middlesex (1 pt), Glamorgan (1 pt)

at Trent Bridge

Nottinghamshire 226 for 8 (C.E.B. Rice 68, J.D. Birch 50, P.G. Newman 4 for 55)
Derbyshire 175 for 9

Nottinghamshire (2 pts) won by 51 runs
(Gold Award – R.J. Hadlee)

at Leeds

Lancashire 222 for 6
Yorkshire 87 for 5

Lancashire (2 pts) won on faster scoring rate
(Gold Award – S.J. O'Shaughnessy)

at Glasgow

Scotland 90
Gloucestershire 91 for 7

Gloucestershire (2 pts) won by 3 wickets
(Gold Award – R.C. Russell)

at Slough

Minor Counties 140 for 9
Essex 141 for 1 (K.W.R. Fletcher 62 not out)

Essex (2 pts) won by 9 wickets
(Gold Award – K.W.R. Fletcher)

17 and 18 May

at Canterbury

Kent 150
Surrey 122 (G.R. Dilley 4 for 29)

Kent (2 pts) won by 28 runs
(Gold Award – G.R. Dilley)

at Taunton

Hampshire 138 (I.T. Botham 4 for 27)
Somerset 116

Hampshire (2 pts) won by 22 runs

Middlesex changed the venue of their game from Lord's to Uxbridge, but still there was no play because of the weather. This was rather surprising as, only a few miles away, at Slough, the great efforts of the local club made play possible. Not only was cricket played on a damp day, but the stewards and gate-people at Slough were a model of courtesy. Not surprisingly, Essex won the match. Minor Counties batsmen can survive against first-class bowling, but they find it very difficult to score runs quickly. Kennedy, Plumb, Bailey, Lewis, Ian Pont and Surridge had all had recent first-class experience, but it was Frank Collyer who demonstrated that the ball could be thumped. Hardie could not imitate him and spent 41 overs in making 30, but Fletcher struck the ball gleefully and the match was won.

Although Yorkshire's seam attack pinned Lancashire down for a spell, the Yorkshire batting could not cope with the Lancashire bowlers. They were 87 for 5 off 35 overs when play was abandoned.

Gloucestershire had a fright at Hamilton Crescent, that lovely Glasgow ground, when, after bowling out Scotland for 90, they were 45 for 6 against de Neef and Morton. Russell led the revival in a stand of 42 with skipper Graveney, and the young wicket-keeper, who had also had a stumping and a catch, won the Gold Award for his 36 not out.

Kim Barnett, at twenty-two the youngest captain in Derbyshire's history, had an unhappy start to his leadership when Derbyshire, with three men needlessly run out, including Barnett himself, were well beaten by Notts.

The appointment of Barnett as captain was a brave one on the part of the Derbyshire committee, and one wishes the young man every success. He is an intelligent, likeable, enthusiastic and hard-working cricketer, and such men deserve our support and our good wishes.

Allan Lamb, who had been out of form in the early, sodden weeks of the season, reasserted himself with a splendid hundred at Leicester. He hit one six and thirteen fours in what was his best score in the Benson and Hedges Cup, and he and Willey added an unbeaten 164 to give Northants an overwhelming victory with 11 overs to spare.

Kent and Surrey went into the second day and in a match dominated by bowlers, it was Graham Dilley who took the honours with fiery and accurate quick bowling.

Hampshire, not renowned for success in the Benson and Hedges tournament, achieved the outstanding victory of the round when they beat Somerset at Taunton even though they had scored a modest 138.

Hampshire resumed on the Wednesday at 78 for 3 in 33 overs, but Botham took four wickets in 14 balls at no cost, and they went from 112 for 3 to 138 all out.

Lloyds went at 12, and Richards, to the greatly improved Malone, at 39, but Roebuck and Rose seemed to have the situation under control until Roebuck was caught at slip. Popplewell caught at the wicket and Rose bowled. There was no recovery. Pocock handled his men with care and intelligence, never allowing them to become over-excited. Cowley bowled his 11 overs for 12 runs and the wickets, both

bowled, of Rose and Botham. Malone took the last two wickets and Hampshire had won a notable victory.

Somerset's second defeat meant that their chances of reaching the quarter-finals were very slim. Essex, Gloucestershire and Middlesex were assured of places in the last eight.

Benson and Hedges Cup

19 and 20 May

at Derby

Lancashire 68 for 4 v. **Derbyshire**

Match abandoned
Lancashire (1 pt), Derbyshire (1 pt)

at Chelmsford

Sussex 208 for 8 (I.J. Gould 55)
Essex 173

Sussex (2 pts) won by 35 runs
(Gold Award – I.J. Gould)

at Cardiff

Surrey 142 for 5 v. **Glamorgan**

Match abandoned
Glamorgan (1 pt) Surrey (1 pt)

at Bournemouth

Minor Counties 168 for 9 (S.J. Malone 4 for 25)
Hampshire 169 for 4 (T.E. Jesty 76 not out)

Hampshire (2 pts) won by 6 wickets
(Gold Award – T.E. Jesty)

at Leicester

Leicestershire v. **Scotland**

Match abandoned
Leicestershire (1 pt), Scotland (1 pt)

at Lord's

Middlesex v. **Combined Universities**

Match abandoned
Middlesex (1 pt), Combined Universities (1 pt)

at Trent Bridge

Nottinghamshire v. **Warwickshire**

Match abandoned
Nottinghamshire (1 pt), Warwickshire (1 pt)

at Worcester

Worcestershire 43 for 5 v. **Northamptonshire**

Match abandoned
Worcestershire (1 pt), Northamptonshire (1 pt)

So unrelenting was the rain that only the two matches in Group C produced a result. At Chelmsford, Essex, looking like winners until after tea on the Thursday, collapsed against the accuracy of the Sussex attack and the guileful captaincy of Barclay. Sussex had been saved from disgrace by Ian Gould who hit fiercely and ran ferociously with Phillipson to take them from 140 for 7 to 208. Essex had bowled well and fielded superbly and then they fell apart. Only Pringle showed the necessary flair with the bat.

At Bournemouth, Hampshire were 42 for 3 against the Minor Counties for whom Surridge and Plumb bowled particularly well, but Jesty made the batting look charming and easy, and Hampshire had a chance of a place in the quarter finals. Earlier, Malone, though not always accurate, bowled with great hosility.

The rain had, in effect, washed Leicestershire out of the competition and the hopes of Derbyshire, Yorkshire, Surrey, Scotland and Minor Counties had also gone.

Combined Universities 1983
Benson and Hedges Cup

BATTING	v. Kent (Cambridge) 9 May	v. Glamorgan (Cambridge) 14 May	v. Middlesex (Lord's) 20 May	v. Surrey (The Oval) 21 and 23 May
R.G.P. Ellis	8	8		5
T.S. Curtis	16	1		2
R.J. Boyd-Moss	0	0		34
S.P. Henderson	82	0		0
G. Pathmanathan	4	0		
P.G. Roebuck	23	1		16
J.G. Varey	35*	4		
M. Cullinan	0	8		
S.J.G. Doggart	14	32		22
K.I. Hodgson	0	3		
A.J. Pollock	2	0*		10
K.A. Hayes				0
J.D. Carr				42*
A.G. Davies				1*
M. Petchey				—
Byes	5			6
Leg-byes	18	2		6
Wides	5			9
No-balls				2
Total	212	59		155
Wickets	10	10		8
Result	L	L	Ab.	L
Points	0	0	1	0

Catches 3 – S. P. Henderson and M. Cullinan
2 – R. G. P. Ellis
1 – G. Pathmanathan, K. I. Hodgson, T. S. Curtis, M. Petchey and sub.

BOWLING	A.J. Pollock	P.G. Roebuck	K.I. Hodgson	J.G. Varey	S.J.G. Doggart	S.P. Henderson	M. Petchey	J.D. Carr	T.S. Curtis
v. Kent (Cambridge) 7 May	11-2-50-2	7-1-25-0	11-3-52-3	11-2-58-2	11-1-45-0	4-1-21-1			
v. Glamorgan (Cambridge) 14 May	11-2-51-2	11-0-32-1	11-3-30-3	11-0-49-2	11-1-43-1				
v. Surrey (The Oval) 21 and 23 May	11-2-25-1	5-0-20-0			11-3-20-0	3-0-16-2	8-1-28-0	11-4-34-0	0.2-0-4-0

Benson and Hedges Cup

21 and 23 May

at Swansea

Kent 30 for 1 *Abandoned*
Glamorgan 148 for 8
Kent 149 for 2 (C.J. Tavare 80 not out)

Kent (2 pts) won by 8 wickets
(Gold Award – C.J. Tavare)

at Old Trafford

Nottinghamshire 13 for 1 *Abandoned*
Nottinghamshire 154 for 8 (M. Watkinson 4 for 39)
Lancashire 157 for 3 (G. Fowler 59 not out)

Lancashire (2 pts) won by 7 wickets
(Gold Award – G. Fowler)

at The Oval

Combined Universities 155 for 8 (S.T. Clarke 5 for 25)
Surrey 156 for 3 (G.S. Clinton 63)

Surrey (2 pts) won by 7 wickets
(Gold Award – S.T. Clarke)

at Slough

Minor Counties v. **Somerset**

Match abandoned
Minor Counties (1 pt), Somerset (1 pt)

23 May

at Bristol

Worcestershire 197 for 6 (C.L. King 51)
Gloucestershire 198 for 3 (Zaheer Abbas 70)

Gloucestershire (2 pts) won by 7 wickets
(Gold Award – Zaheer Abbas)

at Northampton

Scotland 135
Northamptonshire 141 for 3 (G. Cook 63 not out)

Northamptonshire won by 7 wickets
(Gold Award – G. Cook)

at Hove

Sussex 171
Hampshire 174 for 7 (C.L. Smith 63 not out, G.S. Le
Roux 4 for 22)

Hampshire (2 pts) won by 3 wickets
(Gold Award – C.L. Smith)

at Edgbaston

Yorkshire 224 for 5 (C.W.J. Athey 94 not out)
Warwickshire 225 for 5 (D.L. Amiss 64)

Warwickshire (2 pts) won by 5 wickets
(Gold Award – C.W.J. Athey)

The last round of matches in the Benson and Hedges qualifying tournament saw all the winning sides except Surrey reach
the last eight.

In Group A, there were easy wins for Northants and
Gloucestershire. Northants, inspired by a fine innings from
Geoff Cook, won with nearly 19 overs to spare, and, at
Bristol, in a match reduced to 37 overs, Zaheer Abbas
flogged a rather limp Worcestershire attack for 70 in 16
overs. He shared a crucial stand of 95 in 12 overs with
Bainbridge after Stovold and Broad had given the home side
a good start with 69 in the first 18 overs. In the end, Gloucestershire won with four balls to spare.

The match at Old Trafford was restricted to 45 overs, the
first match having been abandoned, but Lancashire needed
only 40.3 overs to reach the target of 155. Fowler and Hughes
shared an unbeaten stand of 71. The other match in Group
B saw Bill Athey play a splendid innings, but all to no avail.
Again the match was limited to 45 overs. Carrick bowled
economically, but Lloyd, Amiss, Smith and Kallicharran
took runs freely from the Yorkshire medium pacers and won
the match with 17 balls to spare.

The decisive match was in Group C where Hampshire
confirmed their Benson and Hedges resurgence with an exciting win. Hampshire bowled well. Malone was fiery again.
Marshall, as ever, was very hard to score from, and Nicholas,
the bowling discovery of the season, Tremlett and Cowley
provided no easy runs. Greenidge was out to the second ball
of the Hampshire innings, but the visitors kept their heads,
and the most recent 'Englishman', Chris Smith, played a
knock of sense and substance which made victory possible
with 7 balls to spare.

Group D saw the first match at Swansea abandoned and
Kent win the rescheduled 39-over match by eight wickets and
more than 6 overs. Once more it was the unruffled, calm and
briskly acquired runs of Chris Tavare which brought victory.

All who feel that quick runs can only be obtained by hitting
across the line or stepping outside the leg stump to carve the
ball through the off-side should be made to watch Tavare
and see how efficiency can prevail.

Benson and Hedges Cup – Group Tables					
GROUP A	P	W	L	NR	Pts
Gloucestershire	4	3	–	1	7
Northamptonshire	4	2	1	1	5
Leicestershire	4	1	1	2	4
Worcestershire	4	1	2	1	3
Scotland	4	–	3	1	1
GROUP B	P	W	L	NR	Pts
Lancashire	4	2	–	2	6
Warwickshire	4	2	–	2	6
Nottinghamshire	4	2	1	1	5
Derbyshire	4	–	2	2	2
Yorkshire	4	–	3	1	1
GROUP C	P	W	L	NR	Pts
Essex	4	3	1	–	6
Hampshire	4	3	1	–	6
Sussex	4	2	2	–	4
Somerset	4	1	2	1	3
Minor Counties	4	–	3	1	1
GROUP D	P	W	L	NR	Pts
Kent	4	3	1	–	6
Middlesex	4	2	–	2	6
Glamorgan	4	1	1	2	4
Surrey	4	1	2	1	3
Combined Universities	4	–	3	1	1

The county at the top of each group is automatically
drawn at home in the quarter-finals.

John Player League

22 May

at Chelmsford

Essex v. **Derbyshire**

Match abandoned
Essex (2 pts), Derbyshire (2 pts)

at Southampton

Northamptonshire 172 for 7 (P. Willey 67)
Hampshire 173 for 3 (D.R. Turner 56 not out)

Hampshire (4 pts) won by 7 wickets

at Leicester

Leicestershire v. **Kent**

Match abandoned
Leicestershire (2 pts), Kent (2 pts)

at The Oval

Surrey v. **Somerset**

Match abandoned
Surrey 2 pts, Somerset 2 pts

	Byes	Leg-byes	Wides	No-balls	Total	Wkts
	4	9	12		276	9
		10	7	3	225	10
	1	4	4		156	3

Minor Counties 1983
Benson and Hedges Cup

BATTING	v. Sussex (Hove) 14 May	v. Essex (Slough) 17 May	v. Hampshire (Bournemouth) 19 and 20 May	v. Somerset (Slough) 23 May
A. Kennedy	43	2	7	
J.G. Tolchard	8			
J.D. Claughton	40			
D. Bailey	51*	27	5	
W.M. Osman	5	11	36	
S.G. Plumb	16*	13	6	
S.A. Clements	—			
N.T. O'Brien	—	17		
F.E. Collyer	—	28	19	
I.L. Pont	—	13*	5	
D. Surridge	—	0*	2*	
R.V. Lewis		1	0	
N.A. Riddell		10	24	
S. Greensword		0	23	
S.P. Davis			7*	
Byes	5		1	
Leg-byes	11	8	16	
Wides	4	2	16	
No-balls		8	1	
Total	183	140	168	
Wickets	4	9	9	
Result	L	L	L	Ab.
Points	0	0	0	1

Catches I. L. Pont, S. G. Plumb and F. E. Collyer each took one catch.

BOWLING	I.L. Pont	D. Surridge	N.T. O'Brien
v. Sussex (Hove) 14 May	9–3–22–0	11–0–48–0	8–0–28–2
v. Essex (Slough) 17 May	8–1–37–0	6–0–24–0	9–4–18–1
v. Hampshire (Bournemouth) 19 and 20 May	9.5–2–42–1	10–3–30–1	

at Edgbaston

Warwickshire 10 for 0 *v.* **Lancashire**

Match abandoned
Warwickshire (2 pts), Lancashire (2 pts)

at Worcester

Worcestershire *v.* **Gloucestershire**

Match abandoned
Worcestershire (2 pts), Gloucestershire (2 pts)

at Hull

Middlesex 127 (R. Illingworth 4 for 6)
Yorkshire 80 for 6

Yorkshire (4 pts) won on faster scoring rate

The rain was still firmly at the top of the Sunday League. Only the match at Southampton went the full distance. Northants faded after a good start and Hampshire batted consistently and convincingly to win with two overs remaining.

At Hull, where runs were never easy to come by, Ray Illingworth took the wickets of Radley, Barlow, Emburey and Edmonds at a cost of 6 runs in his 8 overs. He has kept a quiet role since his reappearance, but the old man of English cricket still showed that he held to the virtues of basic bowling techniques. Rain reduced the Yorkshire target to 80 in 25 overs, and they managed this, with some discomfort and an over to spare.

25, 26 and 27 May

at Southampton

Worcestershire 237 (D.N. Patel 53, M.C.J. Nicholas 5 for 45) and 197 (M.D. Marshall 6 for 58)

BOWLING	B. De Neef	D.L. Snodgrass	W.A. Morton
v. Worcestershire (Aberdeen) 15 May	4–1–16–0	2–1–6–0	11–5–29–2
v. Gloucestershire (Glasgow) 17 May	6–1–14–3		11–4–17–3
v. Northamptonshire (Northampton) 23 May	3–0–33–0		11–1–44–1

Scotland 1983
Benson and Hedges Cup

BATTING	v. Worcestershire (Aberdeen) 15 May	v. Gloucestershire (Glasgow) 17 May	v. Leicestershire (Leicester) 20 May	v. Northamptonshire (Northampton) 23 May
D.L. Haynes	21	7		44
W.A. Donald	11	12		13
R.G. Swan	13	3		9
R.S. Weir	13	6		9
A. Brown	0	22		4
G.D. Halliday	2	1		
H.G.F. Johnston	16	4		
D.L. Snodgrass	2			
B. De-Neef	18*	10		0
G.F. Goddard	3	4		6*
W.A. Morton	0	11*		5
J.E. Ker		0		9
E.T.N. Pollock				6
A.B.M. Ker				21
Byes		1		2
Leg-byes	2	8		5
Wides	2	1		
No-balls	2			2
Total	105	90		135
Wickets	10	10		10
Result	L	L	Ab.	L
Points	0	0	1	0

Catches 2 – A. Brown, W. A. Donald, W. A. Morton and D. L. Haynes
1 – R. G. Swan, R. S. Weir and E. T. N. Pollock

	A. Kennedy	S. A. Clements	D. Bailey	S. G. Plumb	S. Greensword	S. P. Davis	Byes	Leg-byes	Wides	No-balls	Total	Wkts
	9–1–31–0	5–0–23–0	3–0–18–0	3.3–0–3–2				2	4	5	184	5
	0.1–0–1–0			11–3–22–0	7–0–28–0		1	9	1		141	1
	1–0–7–0			11–3–27–1	6–1–18–0	10–0–37–1	3	1		4	169	4

Hampshire 235 (N.E.J. Pocock 60 not out) and 202 for 3 (C.G. Greenidge 116)

Hampshire won by 7 wickets
Hampshire 22 pts, Worcestershire 6 pts

at Leicester

Essex 283 (B.R. Hardie 62, K.R. Pont 53, N.G.B. Cook 4 for 53) and 230 (K.S. McEwan 151)
Leicestershire 300 for 3 dec (J.C. Balderstone 82, B.F. Davison 82 not out, D.I. Gower 74) and 214 for 6 (J.C. Balderstone 97 not out, N.E. Briers 55)

Leicestershire won by 4 wickets
Leicestershire 24 pts, Essex 4 pts

at Lord's

Middlesex 376 for 4 dec (W.N. Slack 140, M.W. Gatting 94, C.T. Radley 59)
Glamorgan 154 (A. Jones 57) and 143 (J.A. Hopkins 54)

Middlesex won by an innings and 79 runs
Middlesex 24 pts, Glamorgan 2 pts

at Taunton

Sussex 408 for 6 dec (P.W.G. Parker 79, G.D. Mendis 65, C.M. Wells 63, A.P. Wells 61 not out, I.A. Greig 59) and 8 for 0
Somerset 224 (B.C. Rose 52) and 190 (I.T. Botham 81, A.C.S. Pigott 4 for 44)

Sussex won by 10 wickets
Sussex 24 pts, Somerset 4 pts

at The Oval

Surrey 305 (D.J. Thomas 76, G.P. Howarth 66, P.J.W. Allott 4 for 68) and 183 for 5 dec (A.R. Butcher 100)

Lancashire 172 (P.I. Pocock 5 for 70, D.J. Thomas 4 for 41 and 142 for 4 (G. Fowler 73 not out)

Match drawn
Surrey 8 pts, Lancashire 5 pts

Phil Edmonds. Unending success for Middlesex in June won him back his Test place. (Adrian Murrell)

	G. F. Goddard	H. G. F. Johnston	G. D. Halliday	D. L. Haynes	J. E. Ker	W. A. Donald	Byes	Leg-byes	Wides	No-balls	Total	Wkts
	11–2–22–1	10.5–4–17–1	3–1–4–0	4–0–9–1			1	2			106	5
	3.5–2–8–0	2–0–8–0	2–1–6–0	11–3–18–0	9–4–11–1		2	3	4		91	7
	9.1–2–31–1			3–1–5–0	4–1–7–0	6–1–13–1	4	2	2		141	3

ABOVE: *Steve O'Shaughnessy batting for Lancashire against Surrey at the Oval, 26 May. Richards is keeping wicket. Knight is at slip. Smith at silly point.* BELOW: *(left): Jack Simmons is bowled out at the Oval, 26 May. (right): Mike Selvey. A positive approach to the job of leading Glamorgan from the doldrums. (Adrian Murrell)*

at Edgbaston

Warwickshire 213 (A.M. Ferreira 50, J.N. Shepherd 7 for 50) and 414 for 2 (T.A. Lloyd 208 not out, D.L. Amiss 142)

Gloucestershire 362 for 8 dec (J.N. Shepherd 168, D.A. Graveney 94)

Match drawn
Gloucestershire 8 pts, Warwickshire 5 pts

at Bradford

Northamptonshire 257 (R.N. Kapil Dev 81, R.G. Williams 59, P. Carrick 5 for 54) and 218 for 7 (R.G. Williams 104 not out)

Yorkshire 157 (D.S. Steele 5 for 48)

Match drawn
Northamptonshire 7 pts, Yorkshire 5 pts

Wins by Hampshire, Leicestershire and Middlesex gave them the first three places in the embryo Schweppes County Championship.

Hampshire recovered from a moderate first innings performance to win in style over Worcestershire at Southampton. On the opening day, the visitors passed the hundred for the loss of one wicket, but the medium pace of Mark Nicholas again proved effective for Hampshire and the last nine wickets went down for 129. Nicholas had bowled only rarely for Hampshire until this season. He had wintered in South Africa where he had developed his bowling considerably, determining a smoother action and winning better control and more movement. The result had been that by the end of May, he had become established as the indispensable all-rounder in a happy and workman-like Hampshire side.

The drying wicket which had helped Nicholas and Marshall on the first day gave Pridgeon equal assistance on the second, and, in spite of a determined innings from their captain and a few belligerent blows from Marshall, Hampshire finished two runs behind on the first innings.

99 for 3 overnight and in an advantageous position, Worcestershire were defeated on the last day when Marshall raised his pace. Hampshire needed 200 in four hours, but they lost time to a thunderstorm. They were launched to success by Gordon Greenidge. He and the watchful Smith opened with a stand of 104 of which the South African scored 16. Greenidge was out to a magnificent diving catch at deep mid-wicket by d'Oliveira when 11 runs were still needed, but Jesty and Nicholas saw that there were no further problems.

In spite of sound batting from Hardie and Pont and an innings of heroic stature from Ken McEwan, Essex suffered their second reversal when Leicestershire reached the target of 214 in 140 minutes. Essex had batted unevenly in their first innings and then their bowlers, lacking the injured Pringle, had been demolished by the combined assault of Gower, Balderstone and Davison.

Batting again, Essex had been 23 for 2, quickly to become 25 for 3, when McEwan came in. He scored 151 out of 207 in four hours with a six and twenty-one fours. It was an innings of majesty. There is none in the world better to watch when he bats like this. It was a brave, unavailing innings. Leicestershire lost Gower and Davison quickly, but though

denied the comfort of their two firmest strikers of the ball, they continued to attack the Essex bowling which was further handicapped by the absence of Lever who had been struck on the ankle. Balderstone's calm and experience, and Briers' controlled aggression gave the home side victory with five balls to spare.

There was no such close finish at Lord's where Middlesex routed Glamorgan who looked desperately like a team of support bowlers. Slack gave the Middlesex innings substance and then Gatting, oozing confidence, purpose and authority, hit 94 in under two hours to provide the necessary elements of flourish and command.

Even without Phil Edmonds, nursing a back injury, the Middlesex attack was far too strong for some poor Glamorgan batting on a blameless wicket and the game barely went into the third day. Glamorgan suffered another disappointment when Rowe injured a thumb.

A massive first innings total to which five batsmen contributed fifties made Sussex immune from defeat on the first day at Taunton. On the second, the variety of the Sussex attack and the indifference of the Somerset batting led to the home side following on, but it still seemed that they could save the match. Their hopes vanished on the last morning. They lunched at 122 for 7 and only a defiant 81 from Ian Botham gave Sussex the frustration of having to go to the wicket again.

A late spurt helped Surrey to reach four batting points at The Oval, and they appeared to be moving to a position where they could enforce the follow-on when Pocock and Thomas reduced Lancashire to 90 for 7, but O'Shaughnessy, highly rated by his county, and the indestructable Jack Simmons added 59, and Maynard stayed long enough to thwart Surrey.

Butcher quickly ran to a fine century on the last morning and Lancashire were set to make 317 in 280 minutes, a task that they never looked like accomplishing. Fowler batted with belief, but his various partners did little before a thunderstorm ended play early.

At Edgbaston, the first two days belonged entirely to John Shepherd. Nearing his fortieth birthday, the former Kent player swung the ball appreciably to record his best figures in the county championship. The following day he shared a sixth wicket stand of 268 with David Graveney. They had come together with Gloucestershire in some disarray at 83 for 5. Shepherd hit 168, only two short of his career best and his first century for Gloucestershire.

The visitors were in a commanding position, and with Kallicharran unwell, Warwickshire had problems, but Andy Lloyd and Dennis Amiss stayed together while 289 runs were added for the second wicket. Lloyd hit the first double century of his career and Amiss, one of the most prolific and best of English batsmen whose virtues have been too often ignored and even dismissed, reached the eighty-third century of his dignified career.

Three years ago, one considered Richard Williams to be one of the most exciting of young English cricketers. He was very close to selection for the England side that went to the West Indies in 1980–81, but since then he has floundered somewhat. It was refreshing to see him return to form with two good innings at Bradford where David Steele displayed his teasing left-arm spin and rain prevented play on the final day.

ABOVE *(left): Andy Lloyd hits a boundary off Phil Bainbridge during his innings of 208 not out, the first double century of his career, for Warwickshire against Gloucestershire at Edgbaston on 27 May. Robert Russell is the wicket-keeper. (right): Dennis Amiss who shared a second wicket partnership of 289 with Lloyd against Gloucestershire. Amiss hit the eighty-third century of his career. Russell is keeping wicket, Andy Stovold is at slip.* LEFT: *The ever-green John Shepherd who had a marvellous all-round match for Gloucestershire against Warwickshire. On 25 May, he took 7 for 50, the next day he scored 168. He hits out during that innings with Tedstone behind the stumps and Amiss at slip. (Ken Kelly)*

28, 30 and 31 May

at Chelmsford

Essex 287 (K.W.R. Fletcher 110)
Surrey 14 (N. Phillip 6 for 4, N.A. Foster 4 for 10) and 185 for 2 (R.D.V. Knight 101 not out, G.S. Clinton 61 not out)

Match drawn
Essex 7 pts, Surrey 4 pts

at Swansea

Glamorgan 250 for 5 dec (J.A. Hopkins 116, A. Jones 79) and 175 for 6 dec (D.A. Francis 66)
Gloucestershire 125 for 0 dec (A.W. Stovold 69 not out, B.C. Broad 52 not out) and 304 for 7 (Zaheer Abbas 116, M.W.W. Selvey 4 for 125)

Gloucestershire won by 3 wickets
Gloucestershire 18 pts, Glamorgan 3 pts

at Canterbury

Hampshire 228 (C.G. Greenidge 68, T.E. Jesty 50) and 125 for 2 dec (M.C.J. Nicholas 51 not out)
Kent 0 for 0 dec and 243 for 5 (C.J. Tavare 70)

Match drawn
Kent 4 pts, Hampshire 2 pts

at Old Trafford

Lancashire 301 for 4 dec (G. Fowler 156 not out, F.C. Hayes 116) and 24 for 0
Yorkshire 228 (P. Carrick 83, S.J. O'Shaughnessy 4 for 73)

Match drawn
Lancashire 8 pts, Yorkshire 3 pts

at Lord's

Middlesex 275 for 8 dec (M.W. Gatting 118, R.O. Butcher 52) and 114 for 6 dec (I.A. Greig 4 for 42)
Sussex 151 for 2 dec (J.R.T. Barclay 56 not out) and 168 for 6 (G.D. Mendis 86)

Match drawn
Sussex 4 pts, Middlesex 3 pts

Neil Foster who took 4 for 10 in the Essex devastation of Surrey at Chelmsford on 30 May. Surrey were dismissed for 14. (Ken Kelly)

Graeme Fowler, a career best 156 not out v Yorkshire at Old Trafford, 28 May. (Adrian Murrell)

at Northampton

Leicestershire 219 (J.C. Balderstone 51, B.J. Griffiths 4 for 46, T.M. Lamb 4 for 49) and 111 for 3 dec
Northamptonshire 74 for 3 dec and 227 for 9 (G. Cook 66, W. Larkins 52, N.G.B. Cook 4 for 65)

Match drawn
Northamptonshire 4 pts, Leicestershire 3 pts

at Trent Bridge

Nottinghamshire 232 for 4 dec (P. Johnson 65 not out, D.W. Randall 52 not out)
Derbyshire 235 for 4 (A. Hill 57 not out)

Derbyshire won by 6 wickets
Derbyshire 12 pts, Nottinghamshire 0 pts

at Worcester

Warwickshire 159 (A.P. Pridgeon 4 for 37, R.M. Ellcock 4 for 70) and 152 for 8 (K.D. Smith 63)
Worcestershire 118 (A.M. Ferreira 4 for 19)

Match drawn
Warwickshire 5 pts, Worcestershire 4 pts

The rain returned in such quantities on the Saturday as to ruin completely the holiday programme. Only at Swansea was any cricket played on the first day and there only 56 overs were bowled. It was significant that this was the only match in which a definite result was obtained. Alan Jones and Hopkins had an opening stand of 160 for Glamorgan and Gloucestershire declared their first innings closed at the end of the second day when they were 125 behind. Selvey set the visitors to make 301 in 3¼ hours. Broad and Stovold, now one of the most efficient opening pairs in county cricket, gave the necessary impetus at the start, but it was the fluency of Zaheer that made victory possible for Gloucestershire. When he left Barry Dudleston, alternating between playing when Gloucestershire needed him and umpiring when the T.C.C.B. required him, called upon reserves of experience to see his side to victory. He on-drove Lloyd high for 4 with four balls remaining and the match was won.

The only other victory went to Derbyshire who beat Notts in a one-innings, last day encounter. Randall and Johnson added an unbeaten 122 for Notts, but Alan Hill played the anchor role and Wright, Barnett and Hampshire the panache to give Derbyshire the twelve points. Barry Wood was dropped from the Derbyshire side and once more his future became cloudy.

The forfeiture of an innings, a sporting declaration and a brisk knock from Chris Tavare could bring no result at Canterbury while the bowlers prospered and the batsmen batted dourly in an ultimately drab game at Worcester.

Mike Gatting again hit well at Lord's, but Sussex came back well and it was sad that this traditionally fine match should be ruined by the weather. It was equally sad in the north where the Roses Match was destroyed by rain. Illingworth elected to field and then watched Fowler, quickly asserting his position as England's number one, and Frank Hayes, a vigorous and stylish batsman who once promised so much, add 222 for the second wicket. Both reached hundreds which benefited from the Yorkshire fielding, but were nevertheless exciting and worthy efforts. Fowler's 156 was a career best. Yorkshire batted lamely before Bairstow and Carrick raised morale and the score.

The most exciting draw was at Northampton where Northants, needing 257 in 220 minutes, were given a splendid start by Cook, Larkins and Willey and reached 163 for 2 with 80 minutes left. They then lost 7 wickets for 42 runs, mostly to some strokes of self-sacrifice, and ended with nine wickets down, 30 runs short of their target, and nine men clustered round the bat to the slow left-arm guile of Cook and John Steele.

There was a sensation at Chelmsford. The charm and forcefulness of the batting of Fletcher and McEwan had lifted Essex to 287 in 89.5 overs and left Surrey with an hour's batting at the end of the day. Phillip and Neil Foster, who was replacing the injured John Lever, opened the Essex attack and in 14.3 overs they bowled Surrey out for 14. At one time, Surrey were 8 for 8 and in danger of recording the lowest ever score in first-class cricket, but Clarke hit a four and he and Monkhouse added 6 to take the score past the dreaded 12. Clinton (6) and Butcher (2) were the only other Surrey batsmen to score. The collapse was inexplicable although the bowling was excellent, fast and controlled. Norbert Phillip had 6 for 4, and Neil Foster, whose career had been in some doubt due to a back injury, had 4 for 10, a career best.

The Essex bowlers were not to find such success when Surrey followed-on and Clinton and Roger Knight batted grimly for most of the last day in match-saving innings.

John Player League

29 May

at Swansea

Glamorgan 253 for 4 (J.A. Hopkins 76, Javed Miandad 61 not out)
Lancashire 232 for 8 (F.C. Hayes 72, J.G. Thomas 4 for 49)

Glamorgan (4 pts) won by 21 runs

at Canterbury

Kent 198 for 7 (C.J. Tavare 67)
Hampshire 133 (R.M. Ellison 4 for 15)

Kent (4 pts) won by 65 runs

at Lord's

Middlesex 216 for 6 (W.N. Slack 69, G.D. Barlow 52)
Sussex 98 for 6

Sussex (4 pts) won on faster scoring rate

at Northampton

Leicestershire 103 for 9 (T.M. Lamb 4 for 9)
Northamptonshire 106 for 6

Northamptonshire (4 pts) won by 4 wickets

at Trent Bridge

Nottinghamshire v. **Surrey**

Match abandoned
Nottinghamshire 2 pts, Surrey 2 pts

at Bradford

Yorkshire 164 for 8
Somerset 147 for 4

Somerset (4 pts) won on faster scoring rate

Somerset's victory at Bradford took them clear at the top of the John Player League. Rain reduced the Somerset target and although Botham had at first been contained by an accurate spell from Sidebottom, he hit 17 runs in one over from Carrick, the thirtieth of the innings, and two overs and one ball later, after Botham's dismissal with one run needed Somerset had won.

Kent moved into second place by defeating Hampshire who had been joint leaders of the table with Somerset Tavare was once again the pulse of the Kent innings, his 67 came off as many balls, and there is now a glamour allied to the quietness and charm. He is a courteous batsman, and like some of his colleagues he was grateful for being dropped. It was not a good day for Hampshire in the field, and it was not much better with the bat. Knott had improvised at the end of the Kent innings when they had threatened to lose their way and then he caught Greenidge from a fine glance off Jarvis, always a vital wicket to get. By the seventeenth over, Hampshire were 65 for 4 and sinking. Their end was spectabular. In the thirty-fourth over, Ellison knocked back Tremlett's off stump and Parks edged his next ball to Knott Malone is probably every bowler's dream of the batsman he ould most like to see coming to the wicket when he is on a at-trick. He did not disappoint. He just touched the ball and Knott took off to make one of his thrilling flying catches.

Middlesex could feel themselves a little aggrieved at Lord's. Barlow and Slack put on 116 for their first wicket, nd they reached 216 off their 40 overs, a rather disappointng score. Bad light reduced the Sussex target to 98 in 18 vers which, though the Middlesex bowling always looked etter than the Sussex batting, Mendis apart, was accomlished with 4 balls to spare.

Glamorgan's Sunday success continued in that they won heir first match, having had the first two rained off, and so vere unbeaten. Clive Lloyd put them in, but Hopkins, Javed nd Ontong punished some rather loose bowling. Javed and Ontong took 86 from the last nine overs. Ontong gave more good service to Glamorgan when he brilliantly caught and owled Clive Lloyd just as he and Hayes were threatening to un riot. Hayes hit two sixes and six fours in a fluent innings, ut Greg Thomas gnawed away at the middle order and there vas no late flourish from Lancashire.

Northants dominated Leicestershire. Tim Lamb took the vickets of Gower, Butcher, Davison and Tolchard and the isitors were 27 for 5, a position of adversity from which they ever recovered. Northants won with 13 overs and 2 balls to pare after Jon Steele had caused a minor alarm.

Benson and Hedges Cup
Quarter Finals

1 and 2 June

at Canterbury

Kent 198 for 9 (M.D. Marshall 4 for 26)
Hampshire 193 for 9 (V.P. Terry 72, C.G. Greenidge 60)

Kent won by 5 runs
(Gold Award – R.M. Ellison)

2 and 3 June

at Chelmsford

Essex 231 for 8 (K.W.R. Fletcher 87, G.A. Gooch 67)
Warwickshire 168 (N. Phillip 4 for 33)

Essex won by 63 runs
(Gold Award – D.R. Pringle)

1 and 3 June

at Old Trafford

Lancashire 290 for 5 (G. Fowler 97, F.C. Hayes 75, C.H. Lloyd 55)
Northamptonshire 183

Lancashire won by 107 runs
(Gold Award – G. Fowler)

1 June

at Bristol

Gloucestershire 12 for 0
v. Middlesex

Match abandoned. Middlesex won on toss of coin.
(Gold Award – Gloucestershire)

The quarter finals of the Benson and Hedges Cup were mutilated by rain. After 4 overs at Bristol the players retreated to the pavilion where they sat for three days in hope that the game could be restarted or a shorter match arranged. They were not to be lucky. Sadly, and unsatisfactorily, the outcome of the match was settled by the toss of a coin. Gatting called correctly and Gloucestershire had 'lost' their first match of the season. As a token of sympathy, they were given the gold award.

The match at Old Trafford was played on the Wednesday and the Friday. It was at the insistence of the umpires, Oslear and Meyer, that play began on the Wednesday, and Lancashire should have been well pleased that they were forced into action. There was a second wicket stand of 146 in 29 overs between Fowler and Frank Hayes. The stand was ended when Fowler, who had batted without inhibition and with a great flourish, was well caught and bowled by Tim Lamb. No play was possible on the Thursday and when Lancashire resumed on the Friday morning, at a formidable 186 for 2, they plundered 104 from their twelve remaining overs. Clive Lloyd and Hughes hit 87 in 38 minutes and Northants were left with a daunting task. With rain still threatening, they required 106 from their first 20 overs to give them victory on the faster scoring rate. It did not come to this. In the search for quick runs, they lost 3 wickets for 46

Derek Pringle, a maturing cricketer, whose all-round performance brought him the Gold Award in the Benson and Hedges Quarter-Final between Essex and Warwickshire, 2 and 3 June. (George Herringshaw)

runs and when Kapil Dev's bold hitting was ended by a Fowler catch in the covers, the game was virtually over.

A commanding innings by Keith Fletcher established the superiority of Essex after Lilley, substituting for the injured Hardie, had been caught behind for nought. Fletcher joined Gooch in a second wicket stand of 152 and it was the Essex captain who was the dominant partner. Slow to assert themselves, the pair had taken the Essex total to only 79 after 29 overs, but eleven overs later, when Gooch drove Gifford to Old at extra cover, the score was 157.

There was now a minor collapse as Fletcher, McEwan, Pont, Phillip and Turner were out before the score reached 200, but Derek Pringle played a firm and sensible innings which left Warwickshire requiring 232 in their 55 overs.

They had reached 30 in the twelfth over when play was suspended. On the final morning, Pringle struck immediately. He dismissed Smith, Kallicharran and Humpage in 23 deliveries at a cost of four runs, and the match swung emphatically in favour of Essex.

The great excitement was at Canterbury where Hampshire contrived to lose a match on the second day which they had seemed to have won on the first, and, indeed, for much of the time on the Thursday. Kent were in total disarray at 119 for 7 against the bowling of Marshall, but Dilley and Ellison, the two left-handers, drove and pulled 65 runs in 15 overs and gave Hampshire some sort of challenge.

In the field, Hampshire had been, on occasions, their own worst enemies. Woolmer was dropped at slip off the first ball of the match, and the Hampshire bowlers amassed 23 wides between them. Jesty echoed his start in Australia with 8 wides, Nicholas, who replaced him, bowled 6, Malone had 5 and Marshall, who bowled very quickly, sent down one.

On what was now a blameless pitch, Terry and Greenidge began Hampshire's attempt to score 199 with a stand of 131. It occupied 43 overs and although Kent, without Dilley who was injured, bowled tidily and fielded magnificently, the Hampshire openers were guilty of not accelerating after the early period of solidifying. 68 from 12 overs, however, was not an impossible task, and Jesty hit briskly, but he, Turner and Nicholas fell in 11 balls. When Nicholas was out, 29 were needed from 5½ overs.

The last over began with Hampshire needing 10 to win with four wickets in hand. Ellison bowled Marshall with his first ball, Cowley with his third and Parks with his fifth so adding to the lustre of his Sunday League hat-trick against the same opponents four days earlier. He is a strong young man, eager in his run to the wicket, positive in his delivery and with that engaging aura that he is striving his hardest with every ball that he bowls.

4, 6 and 7 June

at Derby

Derbyshire 170 (G. Miller 58, J.W. Southern 5 for 60) and 299 for 6 (K.J. Barnett 68, I.S. Anderson 59)
Hampshire 454 for 7 dec (C.L. Smith 193, T.E. Jesty 187, O. Mortensen 4 for 59)

Match drawn
Hampshire 8 pts, Derbyshire 1 pt

at Dartford

Kent 350 for 6 dec (R.A. Woolmer 118, A.P.E. Knott 9 not out) and 87 (J.E. Emburey 6 for 13, P.H. Edmonds for 37)
Middlesex 287 (R.O. Butcher 110, D.L. Underwood for 80) and 154 for 6 (G.D. Barlow 53, D.L. Underwoo 6 for 44)

Middlesex won by 4 wickets
Middlesex 21 pts, Kent 8 pts

at Trent Bridge

Leicestershire 101 (M. Hendrick 6 for 17) and 283 fo 9 dec (J.C. Balderstone 108, N.E. Briers 60, E.E. Hem mings 4 for 85)
Nottinghamshire 225 (D.W. Randall 74) and 32 for (J.F. Steele 4 for 3)

Match drawn
Nottinghamshire 6 pts, Leicestershire 4 pts

at Taunton

Essex 262 (G.A. Gooch 60, K.S. McEwan 54, C.F Dredge 5 for 64) and 242 for 9 dec (D.E. East 77, I.T Botham 4 for 49, V.J. Marks 4 for 103)
Somerset 250 for 7 dec (P.M. Roebuck 69, N.F.M Popplewell 66 not out, D.L. Acfield 4 for 106) and 11 (D.L. Acfield 6 for 34)

Essex won by 141 runs
Essex 22 pts, Somerset 7 pts

at Hove

Worcestershire 223 (J.A. Ormrod 50, A.C.S. Pigott for 74) and 291 for 6 (M.J. Weston 115, D.N. Patel 9C
Sussex 336 for 5 dec (G.D. Mendis 132, J.R.T. Barcla 64, C.M. Wells 51 not out)

Match drawn
Sussex 8 pts, Worcestershire 3 pts

at Edgbaston

Warwickshire 396 for 4 dec (A.I. Kallicharran 209 nc out, T.A. Lloyd 126) and 197 for 3 dec (G.W. Humpage 8 not out, K.D. Smith 68 not out)
Lancashire 250 for 4 dec (N.H. Fairbrother 94 not ou S.J. O'Shaughnessy 68) and 250 (G. Fowler 58, N. Gif ford 6 for 92)

Warwickshire won by 93 runs
Warwickshire 21 pts, Lancashire 4 pts

at Middlesbrough

Glamorgan 289 for 9 dec (R.C. Ontong 112, S.J. Denn 4 for 34) and 162 for 7 (A. Jones 87)
Yorkshire 125 (M.W.W. Selvey 5 for 37) and 408 for dec (C.W.J. Athey 77, J.D. Love 76 not out, D.L. Bairstov 75 not out, G. Boycott 69, R.G. Lumb 56, B.J. Lloyd 4 fc 132)

Match drawn
Glamorgan 6 pts, Yorkshire 2 pts

Chris Smith, a prolific scorer. He hit a career best 193 against Derbyshire at Derby. (Adrian Murrell)

When Frank Hayes, who was batting at number ten because of a stomach upset, swung at Gifford and was caught off a top edge, Warwickshire had beaten Lancashire and so recorded their first win at Edgbaston for nearly four years. A.G. Steel asserted that a captain who wins the toss and puts the other side in when there are no exceptional circumstances deserves to lose, and John Abrahams proved the great Edwardian right. Smith was lbw to Jefferies at 4, and when the next man was out, Lloyd, the score was 297. Lloyd, in fine form, reached his hundred in 266 minutes, and Alvin Kalicharran, displaying the same eagerness for runs that he had shown in 1982, hit two sixes and thirty-four fours in his double century.

Abrahams received more criticism on the Monday when, having reached a tacit agreement with Willis early in the day, he declared the Lancashire innings closed at 5.00 pm, 156 runs in arrears. His action deprived nineteen-year old Neil Fairbrother, playing in his first championship game, of a hard-earned century. He had come to the wicket at 67 for 3. It was difficult to understand the rigidity of an agreement which thwarted the natural aspirations of the young debutant.

Willis made his gesture on the last day when he set Lancashire to make 344 in 278 minutes, an asking rate of about four runs an over on a perfect wicket. Unhappily for the Red Rose, their batsmen played some rash strokes and the old head of Gifford came in to play. He teased Lancashire to destruction and moved Warwickshire, bottom in 1982, to sixth in the table.

The lead in the Schweppes County Championship went to defending champions, Middlesex. Woolmer and the bubbling Knott controlled the game on the first day, and Knott was left in a position similar to Fairbrother's at Edgbaston when Tavare decided to declare and give his bowlers a chance for a few overs before the close. Woolmer's innings was impressive, both for the astuteness of his defence and the variety of his shots. He hit two sixes and sixteen fours and batted with a broken toe.

Butcher responded in his usual entertaining manner, but Middlesex were 63 behind on the first innings. That they got as close to the Kent score was due mainly to a sixth wicket stand of 68 in 13 overs between Butcher and Emburey, and then Emburey produced an inspired spell of bowling which left Kent floundering at 69 for 6. On the last day, in company with fellow spinner Edmonds, recovered from his back trouble, Emburey finished off Kent who were handicapped by injuries to Woolmer and Cowdrey. Needing 151 to win in more than five hours, Middlesex were indebted to the patience of Barlow and the determination of Gatting who stood resolute when Underwood was poised to win the game for Kent.

Trevor Jesty. A magnificent all-rounder who hit a career best 187 v Derbyshire and shared a third wicket partnership of 321 with Chris Smith, 6 June (George Herringshaw)

Dennis Amiss runs behind wicket-keeper Tedstone to catch Frank Hayes off Norman Gifford. The Warwickshire players leap in joy as they record their first home win for over three years. (Ken Kelly)

Hampshire were thwarted at Derby where Bob Taylor and Geoff Miller held out after Kim Barnett and Alan Hill had done much to take the home side away from the danger of an innings defeat. The Hampshire score was founded on a partnership of 321 between Chris Smith and Trevor Jesty who had come together with the score at 16 for 2. Both men hit career best scores. Smith was the more defensive of the two

and his innings lasted 443 minutes, but Jesty was fluent and powerful and played with all the sweetness that he had shown in 1982. It was a splendid achievement by both batsmen and the Danish seam bowler, Mortensen, also revealed his talent.

Essex moved into third place with their first championship victory of the season. The first innings had left the game balanced evenly, but with Essex at 146 for 5 in their second innings, Somerset had taken a slight grip on the match. David East, that splendidly agile and enthusiastic wicket-keeper, was then joined by Norbert Phillip in a stand of 7. in as many minutes. It was at this point that Somerset lost their hold on the game. They were left to make 255 for victory.

3½ hours, but Lloyds fell quickly to Phillip and Slocombe was taken at slip off Foster. David Acfield now came into the attack and soon asserted his authority. Bowling with intelligence, as always, and flighting the ball well, he reduced Somerset to a dishevelled rabble as they swung across the line of the ball or simply played down the wrong one. With Rose unable to bat because of disc trouble, Somerset were beaten with an hour to spare and David Acfield had match figures of 10 for 140.

At Trent Bridge and Middlesbrough, there were great shifts of fortune. Glamorgan batted tediously on the opening day, Ontong's century being their only redeeming feature, but their 289 still proved large enough to force Yorkshire to follow-on after Selvey had found some life and bounce hidden to others. At their second attempt, Yorkshire batted with purpose which they had lacked before. Boycott, whose season had been one of anonymity, hit a brisk 69, and Lumb, Athey, Love and Bairstow all played with controlled aggression so that Glamorgan were ultimately indebted to a superb knock by Alan Jones and a stubborn one by John Derrick for saving the game.

On a restricted first day, Leicestershire finished at 93 for 9 against the movement of Hendrick, the master bowler for the conditions. They added 8 more on the Monday and then saw Notts gain a first innings lead of 125.

Davison went early on the last morning, caught at short-leg off a fierce lifter from Hendrick, but Balderstone settled in for one of his 'they shall not pass' innings, and Notts were left to make 159 in 19 overs. They set about this task as if it would be accomplished with ease and then found themselves in dreadful trouble against Cook and Steele who found slow help for their combined left-arm spin in the wicket. Hendrick and Cooper held on at the end for an embarrassed draw.

A first century of the season by Mendis helped Sussex to a lead of 113 at Hove, but Martin Weston, a young man who likes to hit the ball, hit a maiden first-class hundred on the last day and shared a third wicket partnership of 171 with Dipak Patel. The draw was finally achieved by the doggedness of McEvoy and Humphries.

John Player League

5 June

at Bristol

Gloucestershire v. **Surrey**

Match abandoned
Gloucestershire 2 pts, Surrey 2 pts

at Old Trafford

Northamptonshire 130 for 7
Lancashire 131 for 2 (D.P. Hughes 50 not out)

Lancashire (4 pts) won by 8 wickets

at Lord's

Worcestershire 89
Middlesex 90 for 3

Middlesex (4 pts) won by 7 wickets

at Trent Bridge

Glamorgan 200 for 7 (Javed Miandad 62)
Nottinghamshire 189 (D.W. Randall 75, J.G. Thomas 4 for 41)

Glamorgan (4 pts) won by 11 runs

at Taunton

Somerset v. **Essex**

Match abandoned
Somerset 2 pts, Essex 2 pts

at Coventry

Warwickshire 220 for 7 (Asif Din 52)
Derbyshire 223 for 5 (J.G. Wright 108)

Derbyshire (4 pts) won by 5 wickets

at Middlesbrough

Hampshire 255 for 9 (C.G. Greenidge 89, M.C.J. Nicholas 68)
Yorkshire 257 for 4 (J.D. Love 82 not out, S.N. Hartley 67 not out)

Yorkshire (4 pts) won by 6 wickets

With Somerset's game abandoned, Yorkshire, Glamorgan and Derbyshire moved up on the leaders with good wins. Hampshire suffered another setback when, after scoring what seemed a winning total of 255 and having Yorkshire at 111 for 4 after 25 overs, they were demolished by Hartley and Love who hit 146 in 13 overs and 5 balls.

In spite of Asif Din and Chris Old scoring 61 in 19 minutes, Warwickshire lost to Derbyshire. John Wright hit 108 in 33 overs, but when Willis dismissed him and Wood in the same over, Derbyshire appeared to have lost the match. Miller and Tunnicliffe revived the visitors' fortunes, however, and won the game with three balls to spare.

Glamorgan batted indifferently at Trent Bridge and owed much to Javed Miandad. First he added 63 in 8 overs with Greg Thomas whose 37 was his best score in the John Player League and then he hit the stumps from 25 yards to run out Randall when he looked as if he would win the game for Notts.

Lancashire had an easy win over Northants. Clive Lloyd and David Hughes added 86 in 19 overs and won the match with 5 overs to spare. Middlesex were equally convincing at Lord's. They bowled out Worcestershire in 31.3 overs, Gatting taking three wickets, and then won with 15 overs to spare.

8, 9 and 10 June

at Chelmsford

Nottinghamshire 171 (P. Johnson 54, D.L. Acfield 4 for 24) and 278 (S.B. Hassan 112, J.D. Birch 56, R.E. East 5 for 45)
Essex 351 (K.S. McEwan 79, K.W.R. Fletcher 76, K.R. Pont 62, E.E. Hemmings 4 for 107) and 104 for 2

Essex won by 8 wickets
Essex 23 pts, Nottinghamshire 3 pts

at Bristol

Gloucestershire 375 for 8 dec (A.W. Stovold 84, B.C. Broad 84, P.W. Romaines 73) and 231 for 5 dec (B.C. Broad 92)
Somerset 277 (G.V. Palmer 78, P.W. Denning 73, F.D. Stephenson 4 for 74) and 174 for 0 (R.L. Ollis 99 not out, P.M. Roebuck 74 not out)

Match drawn
Gloucestershire 8 pts, Somerset 6 pts

at Bournemouth

Hampshire 357 for 3 dec (R.A. Smith 100 not out, C.L. Smith 100, V.P. Terry 66, N.E.J. Pocock 57 not out) and 232 for 3 dec (V.P. Terry 114, C.L. Smith 61)
Lancashire 301 for 6 dec (J. Abrahams 117 not out, N.H. Fairbrother 50) and 122 for 4

Match drawn
Hampshire 5 pts, Lancashire 5 pts

at Leicester

Yorkshire 202 (C.W.J. Athey 58) and 281 for 6 dec (D.L. Bairstow 69, G. Boycott 63, J.D. Love 53)
Leicestershire 177 (J.F. Steele 50) and 193 for 7 (N.E. Briers 63, J.C. Balderstone 50, P. Carrick 5 for 69)

Match drawn
Yorkshire 6 pts, Leicestershire 5 pts

at Uxbridge

Derbyshire 238 (A. Hill 89) and 256 (I.S. Anderson 76 not out, R.J. Finney 55, N.F. Williams 4 for 67)
Middlesex 419 for 8 dec (R.O. Butcher 179, W.N. Slack 69) and 79 for 1

Middlesex won by 9 wickets
Middlesex 24 pts, Derbyshire 5 pts

at Hove

Sussex 277 (A.P. Wells 92, E.A. Baptiste 5 for 45) and 225 for 6 dec (A.P. Wells 60)
Kent 226 for 6 dec (D.G. Aslett 55) and 277 for 4 (D.G. Aslett 111, E.A. Baptiste 102 not out)

Kent won by 6 wickets
Kent 20 pts, Sussex 5 pts

at Worcester

Worcestershire 191 (P.A. Neale 52, S.T. Clarke 4 for 45) and 278 (D.B. d'Oliveira 82, G. Monkhouse 4 for 55, P.I. Pocock 4 for 83)
Surrey 451 for 9 dec (M.A. Lynch 112, A.R. Butcher 92) and 19 for 0

Surrey won by 10 wickets
Surrey 23 pts, Worcestershire 3 pts

at Cambridge

Warwickshire 315 for 4 dec (S.H. Wootton 104, R.I.H.B. Dyer 93, G.W. Humpage 63) and 212 for 5 dec (K.D. Smith 79, G.A. Tedstone 67 not out)

Cambridge University 287 for 7 dec (S.P. Henderson 90, G. Pathmanathan 53) and 121 for 5 (S.P. Henderson 56)

Match drawn

at Oxford

Northamptonshire 353 for 9 dec (G. Sharp 89, N.A. Mallender 71 not out, R.G. Williams 50) and 213 for 3 dec (D.J. Capel 51 not out, D.S. Steele 51)
Oxford University 146 (J.G. Varey 69 not out, T.M. Lamb 4 for 27, N.A. Mallender 4 for 41) and 139

Northamptonshire won by 281 runs

The departure of Gatting, Cowans and Daniel to the World Cup appeared to have no effect on Middlesex's bid to retain the championship. The all-round strength of their bowling was too much for Derbyshire on the first day at Uxbridge and on the second, Roland Butcher cut loose with one of his characteristic displays of sustained stroke play. His 179 came in 181 minutes with four sixes and twenty-nine fours. His innings put Middlesex in a commanding position and although Ian Anderson, who retired hurt on 61, and Alan Hill batted courageously, Derbyshire were well beaten. Roger Finney also batted well until falling to Phil Edmonds. Williams bowled quickly and menacingly for Middlesex.

Essex moved into second place when they beat Notts with fourteen balls to spare. Notts had floundered on the first day but the Essex innings had taken longer to assert itself than usual and it was the middle order of Fletcher, McEwan and Pont which provided the substance. With a lead of 180, Essex seemed set for an easy win, but Hassan batted with great determination and with that inelegant, eccentric style of his accumulated match-saving runs. Shortly before tea on the last day, Notts were 250 for 4 and seemed immune from defeat, but a spectacular collapse was brought about by Ray East and six wickets went down for 28 runs in 19 overs. The left-arm spinner had 5 for 29 in his last 16 overs.

Hampshire's failure to beat Lancashire cost them second place, but the match had its compensations for them. Chris Smith gave a further demonstration of his technical ability and powers of concentration with his second century in successive matches, but place of honour went to his nineteen year old brother Robin who was making his championship debut. He reached his hundred in 142 minutes with two sixes and thirteen fours and justified the claims made by those in Hampshire who consider him to be the most exciting prospect to have arrived in English cricket for several years.

At 52 for 4, Lancashire appeared to be heading for great trouble, but Abrahams played a captain's innings to stabilise the situation. The last day saw more reason for Hampshire rejoicing as the vastly improved Paul Terry reached his maiden hundred in first-class cricket. Sadly, the game ended dully after these challenging innings with Lancashire batting out for a draw.

Gary Palmer was another young man to show his developing ability with a career best 78 for Somerset against Gloucestershire. Stovold and Broad again showed their dependability, but Somerset showed no interest in the invitation to make 330 in 217 minutes and ended on 174 with Richard Ollis making a career best 99 not out, but the young left-hander showed his inexperience when failing to score the

Roland Butcher, 179 versus Derbyshire at Uxbridge, 9 June.
(Adrian Murrell)

Steve Malone, a fierce competitor, who had a fine start to the
season for Hampshire. (George Herringshaw)

one run he needed for his century in the final over of the day.

Leicestershire found Phil Carrick's left-arm spin too sub-duing to achieve a target of 307 in 220 minutes where Boycott showed further signs of emerging from his poor patch and Bairstow continued with his happy aggression.

Kent, weakened by injury, gained a thrilling victory at Hove and owed much to their young players. Alan Wells, a fit and positive young cricketer, hit a career best in the first innings, a feat which, in the clamour of the World Cup, went almost unnoticed. He batted well in the second innings too, but it was Kent who took the final honours. Baptiste had bowled well, but Kent had limped rather painfully with the bat and Barclay's invitation for them to make 277 seemed beyond them on the evidence of their first innings showing. This opinion was confirmed when they slumped to 80 for 3, but Baptiste joined Aslett in a thrilling partnership of 191 and although Aslett was bowled with six runs still needed, victory was achieved with three balls left.

Surrey gained their first win of the season when they troun-ced Worcestershire for whom the young d'Oliveira again showed much promise. As one of his opponents said of him, 'He seems to have all the shots, complete technical ability and confidence. He'll be a very, very good player.' Surrey's mix-ture of young, and not so young, Lynch, Butcher, Clarke and Monkhouse were the game's heroes, however.

Warwickshire's reserve batsmen, Wootton and Dyer, grasped the opportunities given them with a second wicket stand of 186 against Cambridge, but Oxford, in spite of defiance by Henderson and Varey, succumbed to the older

head of Tim Lamb who had match figures of 7 for 64 in what was his second first-class game of the season.

11, 13 and 14 June

at Derby

Leicestershire 251 for 9 dec
Derbyshire 79 (G. Ferris 5 for 29) and 168 (P.B. Clift 4 for 58)

Leicestershire won by an innings and 4 runs
Leicestershire 23 pts, Derbyshire 4 pts

at Cardiff

Glamorgan 202 for 6 dec and 206 for 2 dec (R.C. Ontong 61 not out)
Warwickshire 116 for 1 dec (K.D. Smith 54 not out, D.L. Amiss 54 not out) and 293 for 5 (G.W. Humpage 79, K.D. Smith 58, B.J. Lloyd 4 for 93)

Warwickshire won by 5 wickets
Warwickshire 18 pts, Glamorgan 2 pts

at Tunbridge Wells

Kent 287 (M.R. Benson 72, N.R. Taylor 64) and 289 for 5 dec (N.R. Taylor 116 not out, E.A. Baptiste 61 not out)
Essex 285 (K.S. McEwan 142, E.A. Baptiste 5 for 108, R.M. Ellison 4 for 58) and 54 for 2

Match drawn
Kent 7 pts, Essex 6 pts

at Old Trafford

Lancashire 220 for 8 dec (I. Cockbain 52) and 0 for 0 dec
Nottinghamshire 0 for 0 dec and 109 for 3 (R.T. Robinson 53 not out)

Match drawn
Nottinghamshire 3 pts, Lancashire 2 pts

at Northampton

Northamptonshire 371 (D.S. Steele 60, G. Cook 59, D.J. Capel 52, D.A. Graveney 6 for 88) and 125 for 1 dec (G. Cook 77 not out)
Gloucestershire 224 (J.N. Shepherd 69, R.G. Williams 4 for 37) and 131 (R.G. Williams 4 for 18)

Northamptonshire won by 141 runs
Northamptonshire 22 pts, Gloucestershire 4 pts

at The Oval

Middlesex 372 for 9 dec (W.N. Slack 107, R.O. Butcher 81, G. Monkhouse 4 for 59) and 97 for 0 (G.D. Barlow 54 not out)
Surrey 214 (D.J. Thomas 62, J.E. Emburey 4 for 59, P.H. Edmonds 4 for 74) and 254 (D.M. Smith 106 not out, M.A. Lynch 61, P.H. Edmonds 6 for 87)

Middlesex won by 10 wickets
Middlesex 24 pts, Surrey 6 pts

at Hove

Somerset 181 (R.L. Ollis 67) and 112 (G.S. Le Roux 5 for 17)
Sussex 178 and 118 for 3

Sussex won by 7 wickets
Sussex 21 pts, Somerset 5 pts

at Oxford

Oxford University 268 (R.G.P. Ellis 99, T.M. Tremlett 4 for 42, S.J. Malone 4 for 64) and 230 for 3 dec (A.J.T. Miller 127 not out, R.P. Moulding 58 not out)
Hampshire 198 for 4 dec (D.R. Turner 51) and 301 for 2 (D.R. Turner 122 not out, M.C.J. Nicholas 158)

Hampshire won by 8 wickets

Middlesex extended their lead at the top of the table to 30 points with a ten wicket, maximum-point victory over Surrey at The Oval. Middlesex scored at more than 3½ runs an over on the opening day with Slack and Radley giving the innings its foundation in a second wicket stand of 127. There were contributions from nearly all the later batsmen, emphasising the essential team-quality behind the success of Middlesex.

On the Monday, Edmonds and Emburey were quickly into action and sent down 61.2 of the 78.2 overs in which Surrey were bowled out. The Surrey score of 214 would have been much less but for Thomas who, coming in at 105 for 7, hit a lusty 62 before being run out. His effort, and those of Clarke and Pocock, could not save the follow-on, and Surrey were soon 23 for 2 in their second innings. Smith and Lynch threatened to deny Middlesex with a fine stand of 131, but Edmonds brought that to an end and then took five more

Phil Bainbridge of Gloucestershire. Twice left on 99 in mid-June. (George Herringshaw)

wickets as Surrey slumped to 254 all out. Smith was left unbeaten for a valiant and accomplished 106.

Slack and Barlow scored the runs required at a run a minute, and Middlesex, with Edmonds and Emburey the best pair of spinners in the land, looked very likely to retain the Schweppes County Championship.

Essex lost ground in a very dull draw at Tunbridge Wells. The weakened Kent side batted solidly on the Saturday, and on the Monday, Richard Ellison, with a career best, and Eldon Baptiste had Essex struggling. Ken McEwan kept the game alive with his third hundred of the season. He alone shone in a jaded pack.

On the last day, Kent batted tediously. Taylor reached his hundred, but the game died.

Attempts to keep the game alive at Old Trafford and beat the weather by each side forfeiting an innings were finally thwarted by a gale which blew over the sight-screens and brought rain with it.

At Cardiff, enterprise was better rewarded. Only four overs were possible on the Saturday – none was bowled at Old Trafford – and on the Monday Glamorgan declared as soon as they reached 200. Warwickshire scored 116 before the close and declared the next morning.

On the last afternoon, the teams agreed to omit tea and Warwickshire were set to make 293 in 200 minutes. 41 in 6 overs by David Smith and Lloyd was a good beginning, particularly as the slow outfield meant that most of them were run, and although Selvey slowed the rate down, the first after 100 overs had seen them on 207 for 5. On the Monday, Shepherd stood between Gloucestershire and complete collapse. His attacking innings of 69 brought his side closer to avoiding the follow-on, but that indignity was finally avoided by the last wicket pair, Lawrence and Sainsbury, in their stand of 11.

Set to make 273 in 258 minutes on the last afternoon, Gloucestershire were soon in trouble and finally collapsed before the combined spin of Williams, Steele and Willey.

Oxford batted commendably against Hampshire with Ellis caught behind after an impressive 99 and Miller reaching a maiden first-class hundred which virtually assured him of a blue.

Hampshire were left a stiff target of 301 in 165 minutes, but such is the spirit of Hampshire cricket these days that they attacked with confidence. Terry was caught behind for 0, but Turner and Nicholas added a breathtaking 290 in 135 minutes of violence on the Oxford bowling. Nicholas was out with 11 still needed so that much maligned number eleven, Steve Malone, promoted to number four, came in and helped finish the game with a six in which he gloried greatly.

David Steele. His prime function for Northants was as a slow left-arm bowler. (George Herringshaw)

wicket realised 87. Barry Lloyd took three quick wickets, but Geoff Humpage found an equally aggressive partner in Asif Din and the two added 76 in 16 overs. Old helped in a ferocious stand of 78 in 11 overs, and although Humpage departed, Warwickshire were home with 23 balls to spare.

Sussex, who were without Ian Greig who had broken an ankle when falling from a ledge at his home during the previous match, bowled out Somerset for 187 on the opening day, but then conceded a first innings lead of 3 on the Monday. However, Le Roux then tore Somerset apart again, and there was an impressive spell from newcomer Dermot Reeve, who owed his place to Greig's injury.

Needing 116 to win, Sussex ground to victory on the last day with Green proving rocklike as his side completed the double over Somerset.

At 82 for 5 in the limited day on Saturday, Leicestershire were brought to the respectability of 251 by some late contributions of vigour from Clift, Cook and Taylor. Then George Ferris, the eighteen-year old fast bowler from Antigua who was making his championship debut, led a fierce assault on the Derbyshire batting which saw them routed twice in two days. Poor Derbyshire, for whom Barry Wood, out of the side, was complaining of victimisation since giving up the captaincy, were without Anderson, suffering from a stomach virus in the second innings.

Northants won well against Gloucestershire. Even batting, though very slow, saw them 301 for 7 on the Saturday, David Steele and Capel giving the innings late substance

John Player League

12 June

at Derby

Derbyshire 150 (P.B. Clift 4 for 20)
Leicestershire 154 for 5 (R.W. Tolchard 57)

Leicestershire (4 pts) won by 5 wickets

at Chelmsford

Essex 250 for 6 (B.R. Hardie 66, G.A. Gooch 58)
Kent 197 (C.S. Cowdrey 52, N. Phillip 4 for 24)

Essex (4 pts) won by 53 runs

at Cardiff

Glamorgan 167 (G.B. Stevenson 4 for 43)
Yorkshire 155 for 9 (J.G. Thomas 5 for 38)

Glamorgan (4 pts) won by 12 runs

at Old Trafford

Nottinghamshire 154 for 3
Lancashire 155 for 3

Lancashire (4 pts) won by 7 wickets

at Northampton

Northamptonshire 198 for 6 (W. Larkins 102, G. Sharp 51 not out)
Gloucestershire 181 for 6 (A.J. Hignell 70)

Northamptonshire (4 pts) won by 17 runs

at The Oval

Surrey 164 for 7
Middlesex 161 for 7

Surrey (4 pts) won by 3 runs

at Hove

Sussex 263 for 3 (C.M. Wells 104 not out, P.W.G. Parker 104)
Warwickshire 211 for 8

Sussex (4 pts) won by 52 runs

Glamorgan found themselves in the unaccustomed heights of top of the league when they defeated fellow-contenders Yorkshire at Cardiff. Run-getting was never easy, but Alan Lewis Jones played well for the home side and there was an invaluable boost from Greg Thomas at the end. It was Thomas who turned the match Glamorgan's way with five wickets in mid-innings after Love, Hartley and Stevenson had threatened to snatch the game for Yorkshire.

Leicestershire beat Derbyshire with seven balls to spare to record their first win of the season and Lancashire moved into third place with a well-paced victory over Notts, the runs being scored with 10 balls remaining.

Hardie and Gooch started with a stand of 116 to put Essex on their way to their first John Player League win of the season. Phillip and Lever bowled Essex into a strong position, but there was some spirited resistance from Cowdrey, Baptiste and Johnson, wasted at number eight.

Middlesex seemed to be sailing to victory at The Oval, but Radley ran out his partner, Barlow, and was caught behind himself next ball and Middlesex never recovered the momentum given them by Barlow and Slack in an opening stand of 57 in 14 overs. They reached the last over needing 11 to win, but Clarke's pace was too much for James and Williams who strove hard but could only manage 7.

Wayne Larkins scored a century at Northampton and was dismissed by the penultimate ball of the innings. He hit three sixes and six fours and shared a sixth wicket stand of 113 with George Sharp. Gloucestershire made a brave reply and Hignell's 70, which included three sixes, brought them close after a middle order collapse. It was Gloucestershire's first Sunday result.

The best batting of the day was at Hove where Parker and Wells, who hit his best John Player score, scored centuries and added 189 for Sussex's second wicket. Colin Wells reached his hundred in 73 minutes, and the last 10 overs produced 112 runs for the loss of two wickets, one of them Parker, the other, sadly, Colin's brother Alan for 0.

Warwickshire had little hope of reaching the Sussex total and therefore remained at the bottom of the table with Worcestershire.

15, 16 and 17 June

at Derby

Derbyshire 92 (J.K. Lever 4 for 42) and 243 (R.J. Finney 71, J.K. Lever 4 for 76, N.A. Foster 4 for 90)
Essex 360 for 9 dec (K.S. McEwan 178, G.A. Gooch 83)

Essex won by an innings and 25 runs
Essex 24 pts, Derbyshire 4 pts

at Swansea

Somerset 323 for 9 dec (N.F.M. Popplewell 64, D. Breakwell 55 not out, T. Gard 51, J.G. Thomas 5 for 78)

Glamorgan 154 (G.V. Palmer 4 for 58) and 193 for 3 (A.L. Jones 99, J.A. Hopkins 65)

Match drawn
Somerset 7 pts, Glamorgan 4 pts

at Tunbridge Wells

Sussex 191 (P.W.G. Parker 58, C.M. Wells 52, E.A. Baptiste 4 for 46) and 132 (E.A. Baptiste 5 for 39, R.M. Ellison 4 for 35)
Kent 263 (C.S. Cowdrey 94, M.R. Benson 56, G.S. Le Roux 5 for 59, A.C.S. Pigott 4 for 73) and 63 for 1

Kent won by 9 wickets
Kent 23 pts, Sussex 5 pts

at Old Trafford

Lancashire 216 (C.M. Old 4 for 31) and 249 (F.C. Hayes 85, N.H. Fairbrother 68, N. Gifford 5 for 31)
Warwickshire 328 (D.L. Amiss 88, Asif Din 65, C.M. Old 62, J. Simmons 4 for 71, S.T. Jefferies 4 for 121) and 138 for 4 (K.D. Smith 53)

Warwickshire won by 6 wickets
Warwickshire 23 pts, Lancashire 5 pts

at Leicester

Gloucestershire 366 for 7 dec (J.N. Shepherd 95 not out, A.W. Stovold 63, R.C. Russell 55) and 178 for 4 dec (P. Bainbridge 99)
Leicestershire 246 for 9 dec (I.P. Butcher 103, N.E. Briers 68, F.D. Stephenson 5 for 56) and 161 for 9 (I.P. Butcher 76 not out, D.A. Graveney 5 for 34)

Match drawn
Gloucestershire 7 pts, Leicestershire 4 pts

at Uxbridge

Hampshire 176 (V.P. Terry 61, S.P. Hughes 5 for 48) and 121 (P.H. Edmonds 5 for 42)
Middlesex 361 (G.D. Barlow 105, K.P. Tomlins 77)

Middlesex won by an innings and 64 runs
Middlesex 24 pts, Hampshire 4 pts

at Trent Bridge

Surrey 369 for 8 dec (M.A. Lynch 85, D.M. Smith 68, R.D.V. Knight 60, G.S. Clinton 57, K.E. Cooper 6 for 89) and 12 for 0
Nottinghamshire 218 (S.B. Hassan 83, P.I. Pocock 4 for 49) and 161 (R.T. Robinson 94, A. Needham 5 for 52, D.J. Thomas 4 for 33)

Surrey won by 10 wickets
Surrey 23 pts, Nottinghamshire 3 pts

at Cambridge

Cambridge University 307 for 6 dec (T.S. Curtis 92, D.W. Varey 65, S.J.G. Doggart 59 not out) and 244 (R.J. Boyd-Moss 97, A. Walker 4 for 70)
Northamptonshire 260 for 3 dec (M.J. Bamber 77, P.

Villey 52 not out) and 240 for 7 (M.J. Bamber 59, R.G.
Williams 56 not out)

Match drawn

t Oxford

Worcestershire 342 for 8 dec (D.A. Banks 100, S. Wat-
kins 77, M.S. Scott 53, H.T. Rawlinson 5 for 123) and 228
or 8 dec (D.A. Banks 53, D.B. d'Oliveira 52)
Oxford University 285 for 6 dec (A.J.T. Miller 90,
R.G.P. Ellis 61, R.P. Moulding 53 not out) and 137 (R.K.
Illingworth 4 for 37)

Worcestershire won by 148 runs

Middlesex and Essex emphasised their challenges for the
Schweppes County Championship with innings victories in-
ide two days. Young Neil Foster combined with John Lever
o rout Derbyshire on the opening morning and then Ken
McEwan and Graham Gooch shared an Essex third wicket
tand of 181 in 37 overs, McEwan reaching his century in 131
ninutes. Essex increased their lead to 268 on the second
norning and then their seam attack bowled out Derbyshire
or a second time. Derbyshire, with Wood complaining and
ontesting off the field, had one solace on the field when
Roger Finney hit a career best 71.

Middlesex relied on the pace of Hughes and James in the
rst innings and the spin of Edmonds and Emburey in the
econd to overwhelm Hampshire. Tomlins held six catches in
he match and Barlow, totally recovered from the traumas of
he previous season, hit a sturdy hundred. Even without
Gatting's authority, Middlesex looked a very accomplished
ide.

Kent held third place with a good win over Sussex at
Tunbridge Wells where the wicket had been described as
feless. Baptiste, in both innings, and Ellison in the second
xtracted enough life, however, to bowl out Sussex twice for
inder two hundred. Kent were greatly indebted to Chris
Cowdrey who played a typically pugnacious knock before he
ecame one of Pigott's three wickets in 19 balls. Cowdrey
nd Benson put on 133 for Kent's fifth wicket after four
vickets had fallen for 74. It was the decisive stand of the
natch.

There was quite a lot of tedium at Swansea where Breakwell, out of retirement, scored 53 not out and Gary Palmer
gave further evidence of his promise as a seam bowler.
Following-on, Glamorgan were helped to survival by an
pening stand of 120 in 49 overs from Hopkins and Alan
Lewis Jones who hit a career best 99. He was caught behind
off Lloyds, but by that time the game was safe.

Warwickshire moved into fourth place in the table when
hey beat Lancashire with three balls to spare. Old had a fine
natch. He was mainly responsible for Lancashire's collapse
on the first day and then hit a brisk 62 and added two slip
catches on the second. Amiss and Asif Din rescued Warwickshire with a fifth wicket stand of 143 and on the last day,
Gifford bowled 35 overs which brought him 5 wickets. Warwickshire were held up by stands between Hayes and
Abrahams and Hayes and Fairbrother, but in the end they
cored at five and a half runs an over to win. It was the double
over Lancashire and their third championship victory in a
row.

Surrey had their second success of the season when they

beat a limp looking Notts side with considerable ease. Solid
rather than inspired batting took Surrey to a good score and
then the spin of Pat Pocock was mainly instrumental in bowling out Notts before they could save the follow-on. In the
second innings, only Robinson withstood the Surrey attack,
just as in the first only Hassan had shown any determination.
Surrey were handicapped when Pocock strained a groin muscle, but Andrew Needham proved a most adequate substitute
with a career best 5 for 52.

There were some remarkable performances at Leicester
where the home side just hung on to their unbeaten record.
Gloucestershire were given a fine start of 85 in 18 overs by
Stovold and Broad, Ferris being particularly harshly treated,
but they then dwindled into decline until Shepherd restored
positivity with some good blows late in the day. The second
was dominated by Ian Butcher who hit a maiden first-class
century in 284 minutes. Tolchard surrendered a first innings
lead of 120, and then Bainbridge hit fourteen fours in 97
minutes as he reached 99 before being caught at short extra
cover off Steele. David Graveney left Leicestershire 221
minutes in which to get 299. They had reached 143 for 5 when
Graveney himself performed the hat-trick. He bowled Clift
and Steele and had Parsons caught at silly point by
Romaines. Only Butcher stood between Gloucestershire and
victory after that, and he added an innings of great maturity
to his century in the first innings.

Tim Curtis made a career best 92 on the opening day at
Fenner's and shared an opening stand of 123 with David
Varey. Bamber played well for Northants who saw Boyd-
Moss, one of their own men, score 97 against them. Cam-
bridge had the better of the argument in the end.

The same could not be said of Oxford against whom David
Banks hit a century on his debut for Worcestershire. Scott
and Watkins, another newcomer, began with a partnership
of 122, but 6 wickets fell for 61 runs before Banks reasserted
Worcestershire's superiority. Miller, stumped off d'Oliveira
at 90, and Ellis kept the University in the match, but on the
last day they crumbled to the spin of Illingworth.

18, 20 and 21 June

at Bristol

Gloucestershire 370 (P.W. Romaines 135, J.N.
Shepherd 112, D.L. Underwood 5 for 93) and 230 for 4
dec (P. Bainbridge 99 not out, A.W. Stovold 57)
Kent 252 for 8 dec (A.P.E. Knott 83, D.G. Aslett 52) and
272 for 9 (A.P.E. Knott 56, L. Potter 50, J.N. Shepherd 4
for 42)

Match drawn
Gloucestershire 6 pts, Kent 4 pts

at Southampton

Hampshire 83 (A. Sidebottom 5 for 6) and 420 (M.C.J.
Nicholas 97, C.L. Smith 75, R.J. Parks 52)
Yorkshire 432 for 7 dec (C.W.J. Athey 90, D.L. Bairstow
60 not out, R.G. Lumb 60, P. Carrick 54 not out, G.B.
Stevenson 52) and 72 for 3

Yorkshire won by 7 wickets
Yorkshire 23 pts, Hampshire 2 pts

at Northampton

Warwickshire 351 (T.A. Lloyd 97, Asif Din 56, R.G. Williams 4 for 30) and 168 for 6 dec
Northamptonshire 199 (C.M. Old 4 for 48, N. Gifford 4 for 53) and 154 (C.M. Old 5 for 50)

Warwickshire won by 166 runs
Warwickshire 23 pts, Northamptonshire 3 pts

at Bath

Derbyshire 289 (G. Miller 84, W.P. Fowler 59, C.J. Tunnicliffe 51) and 166
Somerset 141 (O. Mortensen 5 for 43, R.J. Finney 4 for 34) and 191 (P.W. Denning 85)

Derbyshire won by 123 runs
Derbyshire 23 pts, Somerset 4 pts

at Horsham

Lancashire 312 for 6 dec (F.C. Hayes 149, D.P. Hughes 53) and 172 (A.C.S. Pigott 5 for 55)
Sussex 230 (M. Watkinson 6 for 51) and 200 (P.W.G. Parker 75, J. Simmons 5 for 47)

Lancashire won by 54 runs
Lancashire 24 pts, Sussex 4 pts

at Worcester

Middlesex 314 for 9 dec (P.R. Downton 87, P.H. Edmonds 65, N.F. Williams 63, W.N. Slack 50) and 221 for 5 dec (G.D. Barlow 58)
Worcestershire 216 (P.A. Neale 55, P.H. Edmonds 4 for 29) and 244 (D.B. d'Oliveira 102, D.N. Patel 88, P.H. Edmonds 5 for 56)

Middlesex won by 75 runs
Middlesex 24 pts, Worcestershire 6 pts

at Cambridge

Nottinghamshire 127 (P. Johnson 73, K.I. Hodgson 4 for 58) and 347 for 8 dec (C.W. Scott 78, J.D. Birch 75, R.T. Robinson 66, C.C. Ellison 4 for 36)
Cambridge University 97 (M.K. Bore 4 for 29) and 192 (S.J.G. Doggart 70, K.E. Cooper 5 for 53, M.K. Bore 4 for 30)

Nottinghamshire won by 185 runs

18 and 19 June

at The Oval

Oxford University 112 (A. Needham 6 for 30) and 103 (I. J. Curtis 6 for 28)
Surrey 313 for 4 dec (A.J. Stewart 118 not out, G.S. Clinton 68)

Surrey won by an innings and 98 runs

While most attention was being captured by the World Cup there were several performances of significance in the first-class programme. Yorkshire gained their first win of the season in somewhat startling circumstances at Southamp-

ton. Hampshire were bowled out half an hour before lunch on the first morning when the swing bowling of Arnold Sidebottom, five catches behind the stumps by David Bairstow and the general poorness of their own batting made life very difficult for them. Yorkshire had gained a lead of 11 before the close and on the second day solid batting increased their lead to 349 runs. They had moved rather sedately at first, but towards the end Bairstow and Carrick added 115 in 26 overs. Hampshire had little to bat for but survival, and survive they nearly did, with the two Smiths and Nicholas giving the innings a firm foundation and Parks and Southern sharing an eighth wicket stand of 89 which meant that Yorkshire would have to bat again. Parks, an elegant young man in all he does, made one wonder, not for the first time, why he does not score more runs. Malone held out valiantly for half an hour, and, in the end, Yorkshire had to score at five an over to win.

Middlesex completed their fifth consecutive championship victory with two hours to spare at Worcester. The champions were 91 for 5 on the first day, but Downton and Edmonds led a recovery which Williams finished with some withering pulls and drives which took him to his 50 in 56 minutes.

Worcestershire threatened to match Middlesex, but Edmonds, and his close catchers, saw the last five wickets go down for 30 runs, 3 to Edmonds in 13 balls. Middlesex then attacked briskly, Emburey's leadership following Gatting's pattern, and left themselves a day in which to bowl out the home side. 8 for 3, Worcestershire recovered admirably through Patel and Damian d'Oliveira who reached a magnificent first hundred for the county. It was an innings of great maturity, scored at a most difficult time. The pair added 180, but there followed another decline and Middlesex led the table by 48 points.

In second place were Warwickshire who gained their fourth win, an emphatic one, over Northants. Sound, if not particularly bright, batting was the foundation of Warwickshire's success coupled with fine intelligent bowling from Old and Gifford whose impact on the Warwickshire side had been immense.

There was a first win of the season for Lancashire for whom Frank Hayes batted well on the opening day and for whom Watkinson bowled quickly and splendidly on the second. Sussex were bowled back into the game by Pigott and Barclay who found Zaidi and Simmons their biggest stumbling blocks. Sussex were left needing 255 to win and when Parker and Le Roux hit a furious 75 in 40 minutes for the sixth wicket to lift them from 92 for 5 to 167, they looked as if they might do it, but Jack Simmons showed all his old wiles and Lancashire won with 5.4 overs to spare.

There was a welcome win for Derbyshire after their recent harrowing defeats. It was the bowling of the Dane, Ole Mortensen, and the left-arm seamers of Roger Finney which accounted for Somerset on the second day after some solid batting on the Saturday. With the wicket deteriorating it was only a defiant 85 in 220 minutes by Peter Denning that almost thwarted Derbyshire who finally won with an hour and a half to spare.

Romaines and Shepherd shared a fourth wicket stand of 221 for Gloucestershire who had lost Broad injured. Gloucestershire had batted slowly at first, but Kent responded with some fierce hitting and good running by Knott and Aslett and Cowdrey conceded a lead of 118 to keep the game open. In his turn, Graveney did the same thing, and there was some brisk batting which ended with Bainbridge and Hignell adding 97 boisterous runs. Bainbridge was left on 99 not out by the declaration, the second time in successive championship matches that he had been on this score. Kent needed 349 in 260 minutes and with Knott punishing the bowling, they looked for a while as if they would get the runs, but in the end, Kevin Jarvis survived 13 overs with Graham Johnson to save the game. As Jarvis is noted as being one of the worst batsmen in the country with a career best of 12, it was a brave and remarkable performance.

Notts and Cambridge struggled in the first innings at Fenner's and recovered in the second, but Simon Doggart's career best was not enough to stave off defeat.

At The Oval, Surrey beat Oxford in two days and there were three career best performances in their victory. Spinners Andrew Needham and Ian Curtis took the bowling honours and Alec Stewart, son of the Surrey manager, hit a pugnacious maiden hundred in what was only his fourth firstclass match.

John Player League

19 June

at Bristol

Kent 244 for 9 (C.S. Cowdrey 66, M.R. Benson 65, D.G. Aslett 56, J.N. Shepherd 6 for 52)
Gloucestershire 189 for 9 (R.J. Doughty 50 not out)

Kent (4 pts) won by 55 runs

at Basingstoke

Leicestershire 179 for 8 (I.P. Butcher 59)
Hampshire 180 for 1 (V.P. Terry 100 not out, C.L. Smith 55)

Hampshire (4 pts) won by 9 wickets

at Luton

Northamptonshire 298 for 2 (W. Larkins 172 not out, P. Willey 84)
Warwickshire 264 for 8 (T.A. Lloyd 84, R.G. Williams 5 for 30)

Northamptonshire (4 pts) won by 34 runs

at Bath

Glamorgan 235 for 4 (J.A. Hopkins 130 not out)
Somerset 237 for 5 (N.F.M. Popplewell 84)

Somerset (4 pts) won by 5 wickets

at Horsham

Sussex 202 for 8 (P.W.G. Parker 52)
Lancashire 200 (J. Abrahams 79 not out)

Sussex (4 pts) won by 2 runs

at Worcester

Essex 207 for 7 (K.S. McEwan 65)
Worcestershire 208 for 7 (P.A. Neale 83 not out)

Worcestershire (4 pts) won by 3 wickets

Wayne Larkins. 172 not out for Northants in the John Player League match against Warwickshire at Luton, 19 June. This record was to last only a month. (George Herringshaw)

This was a Sunday to stir the hearts. At Luton, Wayne Larkins hit the league record score, 172 not out against Warwickshire. He and Peter Willey put on 213 for the second wicket. Warwickshire gave a spirited reply with Lloyd at the beginning and Gifford at the end hitting lustily. Richard Williams was the bowler of the day with his off-spin. Larkins' innings included six sixes and twelve fours.

Paul Terry, with eight fours and four sixes, hit a maiden century in the John Player League and took Hampshire to an emphatic win while John Hopkins hit a Sunday best at Bath, but he saw his side beaten and Somerset go top of the table. Nigel Popplewell was Somerset's match-winner, celebrating the award of his county cap.

Kent moved into second place with strong middle order batting being too much for Gloucestershire for whom John Shepherd took six wickets, his Sunday best and a rare feat.

Lancashire needed 13 runs from the last over to beat Sussex, but Folley was run out off the penultimate ball when they were still 3 short. It was the batting of skipper Abrahams which had brought Lancashire so close.

There was an even tighter finish at Worcester where Illingworth hit the last ball up in the air close to a fielder but managed to give Worcestershire their first success of the season. Once more, it was the captain, Phil Neale, who had made victory possible.

22, 23 and 24 June

at Ilford

Northamptonshire 197 (J.K. Lever 5 for 59) and 81 (J.K. Lever 6 for 36)
Essex 329 (R.E. East 80 not out, K.S. McEwan 69, B.R. Hardie 51, B.J. Griffiths 6 for 92)

Essex won by an innings and 51 runs
Essex 24 pts, Northamptonshire 4 pts

at Abergavenny

Worcestershire 394 for 6 dec (P.A. Neale 135, M.J. Weston 79, J.A. Ormrod 78)
Glamorgan 76 for 2

Match drawn
Worcestershire 3 pts, Glamorgan 1 pt

at Basingstoke

Sussex 218 (G.D. Mendis 91, K. Stevenson 5 for 81) and 276 for 7 dec (G.S. Le Roux 80, J.R.T. Barclay 65, P.W.G. Parker 58)
Hampshire 287 for 4 dec (R.A. Smith 104 not out, C.L. Smith 83)

Match drawn
Hampshire 7 pts, Sussex 3 pts

at Leicester

Leicestershire 349 for 5 dec (R.W. Tolchard 80 not out, P.B. Clift 63, B.F. Davison 60) and 139 for 6 dec
Surrey 209 and 22 for 2

Match drawn
Leicestershire 8 pts, Surrey 4 pts

Phil Neale. He led Worcestershire from the front. A fine batsman. (George Herringshaw)

at Trent Bridge

Nottinghamshire 238 (C.E.B. Rice 98, D.L. Underwood 7 for 88) and 158 (D.L. Underwood 6 for 73)
Kent 260 (P.M. Such 6 for 123) and 137 for 4

Kent won by 6 wickets
Kent 23 pts, Nottinghamshire 6 pts

at Bath

Somerset 238 (J.W. Lloyds 81, J.N. Shepherd 5 for 80) and 299 for 3 dec (N.F.M. Popplewell 143, P.M. Roebuck 51, N.A. Felton 51)
Gloucestershire 232 for 7 dec (A.J. Hignell 103, P.H.L. Wilson 4 for 77) and 198 for 8 (A.J. Hignell 57)

Match drawn
Gloucestershire 6 pts, Somerset 5 pts

at Sheffield

Derbyshire 225 (K.J. Barnett 95, P. Carrick 5 for 45) and 148 (J.E. Morris 58, P. Carrick 7 for 44)
Yorkshire 118 (O. Mortensen 6 for 27, D.G. Moir 4 for 45) and 233 (G. Boycott 112 not out, O. Mortensen 5 for 62, D.G. Moir 5 for 114)

Derbyshire won by 22 runs
Derbyshire 22 pts, Yorkshire 4 pts

at Cambridge

Cambridge University 146 (K.D. James 5 for 28) and 133 (P.H. Edmonds 6 for 49)
Middlesex 309 for 3 dec (W.N. Slack 138 not out, C.T. Radley 76, K.P. Tomlins 55 not out)

Middlesex won by an innings and 30 runs

at Edgbaston

Oxford University 310 for 5 dec (R.P. Moulding 80 not out, A.J.T. Miller 76, R.M. Edbrooke 71) and 48 for 1
Warwickshire 388 for 8 dec (P.A. Smith 114, D.M. Smith 100 not out, D.L. Amiss 63, K.A. Hayes 6 for 58)

Match drawn

With Middlesex engaged in beating Cambridge University in two days, thanks to the left-arm seam bowling of the highly promising Kevan James and the left-arm slow bowling of Phil Edmonds, now back to a standard as good as when he played for England allied to the batting of the dependables, Slack and Radley, Essex were able to gain ground on them at the top of the table. Warwickshire were also engaged against a university side though there was no play on the last day at Edgbaston. The first two days, however, saw good batting from the Oxford side and an exhilarating hundred from that eager cricketer Paul Smith. He shared a stand of 155 with David Smith, a young left-hander, before Kevin Hayes claimed Paul Smith as one of his career best six victims. Both of the young Warwickshire batsmen had not scored a first-class century before.

However, the important action was at Ilford. Northants were bowled out by Lever and Foster for 197, and Essex closed the day on 141 for 2. Ken McEwan had come in with 40 minutes remaining and needing 47 to become the first

atsman to reach a thousand runs, a task he had accomplished before the close. Next day, Essex faltered to 185 for
but Ray East played a highly responsible innings and
ored 80 not out as he saw his side to maximum batting
oints. Phillip, Lever and Foster reduced Northants to 57 for
before the end of the day, and on the last morning only 50
inutes play were necessary for Essex to complete an innings
ctory. In the heavy atmosphere, the ball had moved con-
derably as Griffiths had demonstrated on the second day,
nd this made Ray East's knock a most commendable and
ucial one.

Kent were able to move into third place when their eager
lend of youth and experience proved too much for Notts for
hom Hemmings was well below form and Such showed his
ck of experience when Aslett, Cowdrey and Knott attacked
im on the vital last afternoon. The wicket had always given
ncouragement to the spinners, and Derek Underwood is
ne who needs little encouragement. He gnawed away at
Jotts in the first innings, only Clive Rice's three-hour innings
f power and character withstanding him after Hassan and
obinson's brisk opening, and he destroyed them in the
econd.

Rain ruined the last day at Leicester after the home side
ad moved into a good position and rain ruined most of the
st two days at Abergavenny. On the first day, Ormrod and
Veston had begun with a stand of 136 and Phil Neale, in a
in of good form, had hit three sixes and fifteen fours in a
parkling innings. The consolation for Glamorgan was the
eturn of Charles Rowe, playing his first match since fractur-
ig a thumb at Lord's.

Another who welcomed a return was Keith Stevenson of
Iampshire. His outings have been few over the past two
easons, but he bowled Hampshire into a good position on
he first day when Mendis, curbing his natural tendency to
ttack, played a calm innings as all about him squandered
heir talents. On a shortened second day, Chris Smith gave
irther evidence of his run-accumulating powers and youn-
er brother Robin hit his second championship hundred in
uch a manner as to confirm the estimates of the Hampshire
rophets who say that here is a very great batsman. The last
ay provided a dreary draw when Sussex failed to respond to
ocock's enterprising overnight declaration. The only bright
pot was Le Roux's 80 in 70 minutes, including eight sixes,
ve in eight balls off Cowley.

There was champagne in the Derbyshire dressing room at
heffield. It was ordered by Bob Taylor and drunk at 2.30 on
he last afternoon when Derbyshire had beaten Yorkshire for
he first time since 1957. For the young Derbyshire captain,
Lim Barnett, it was especially pleasing in that nine of his
redecessors had failed to beat the near neighbours. Barnett
ad played a watchful and mature innings on the first day on
wicket which always gave the bowlers help and which was
eported as unfit. It was Barnett's tenacity and support from
inney and others which lifted Derbyshire to 225. The com-
ination of Mortensen's enthusiasm, lift and pace and
Moir's slow left-arm, plus Taylor's catching, saw Yorkshire
ollapse to 118 after an opening stand of 63.

Derbyshire fared little better when they batted again. Phil
Carrick's left-arm spin was the wrecker of the visitors for
vhom the nineteen-year old Morris chose brief glory with 58
ff 37 balls. Later Taylor nudged 33 invaluable runs and
Yorkshire were left to make 256. Carrick's 12 for 89 was a

*Nigel Popplewell. 100 in 41 minutes off 60 balls. Bath, 24 June.
(Adrian Murrell)*

career best as was Mortenson's bowling for Derbyshire.

The beginning of the Yorkshire second innings was
bizarre. The first ball of the second over, bowled by Moir,
accounted for Lumb. Athey then hit three fours before being
stumped off the last ball of the over. At the close, Yorkshire
were 194 for 7, Boycott 92 not out. Next day, Boycott's
magnificent innings, mighty even by his standards, was extended to over four hours and brought Yorkshire closer to
their target, but Derbyshire won when Mortensen produced
a kicker and Dennis fell to a diving catch in the gully by
Fowler. Dennis had helped Boycott add a valiant 35 for the
last wicket.

The first day at Bath had Somerset rescued by Jeremy
Lloyds, batting at number seven, and Gloucestershire
staggering at 87 for 5 before some quick and controlled bowling by Hugh Wilson. On a gloomy second day when only 34
overs were possible, Alastair Hignell battered the Somerset
attack with some blistering drives which brought him two
sixes and thirteen fours in his 144-minute innings. Graveney
declared overnight, six runs behind, and on the last morning, as
Somerset sought quick runs, he used Dudleston and himself
in the main. When Nigel Popplewell arrived at 88 for 1 he
immediately attacked the bowling and reached his hundred
in 41 minutes off 60 balls. It was the fourth fastest hundred
in history. In all, he hit nine sixes and seventeen fours.

Set to make 306 in 194 minutes, Gloucestershire reached
104 for 1 very quickly and then crumbled so that it took sterling defence from Doughty and Russell to save the match.

25, 27 and 28 June

at Chesterfield

Derbyshire 151 and 137 (P.H. Edmonds 6 for 38, J.E.
Emburey 4 for 50)
Middlesex 241 (N.F. Williams 50 not out, S. Oldham 4
for 72) and 48 for 1

Middlesex won by 9 wickets
Middlesex 22 pts, Derbyshire 5 pts

Ken McEwan of Essex. The first batsman to reach a thousand runs in first-class cricket during the season. He did so on 22 June versus Northants at Ilford. (Adrian Murrell)

at Ilford

Essex 281 (K.W.R. Fletcher 79, D.R. Pringle 68 not out) and 69 for 1
Sussex 100 (N.A. Foster 6 for 46) and 249

Essex won by 9 wickets
Essex 23 pts, Sussex 4 pts

at Bristol

Hampshire 363 for 7 dec (M.C.J. Nicholas 110, C.L. Smith 68, N.E.J. Pocock 50 not out, G. Sainsbury 5 for 71) and 272 for 9 dec (R.A. Smith 100, J.H. Childs 4 for 66)
Gloucestershire 302 for 5 dec (A.J. Hignell 109 not out, D.A. Graveney 57 not out) and 215 (A.J. Hignell 61)

Hampshire won by 118 runs
Hampshire 22 pts, Gloucestershire 6 pts

at Hinckley

Leicestershire 253 (B.F. Davison 101, R.C. Ontong 6 for 64) and 266 for 3 dec (D.I. Gower 108 not out, B.F. Davison 91)
Glamorgan 109 (G. Ferris 7 for 42) and 230

Leicestershire won by 180 runs
Leicestershire 23 pts, Glamorgan 4 pts

at Trent Bridge

Nottinghamshire 86 (S.T. Jefferies 8 for 46) and 294 (J.D. Birch 95, S.B. Hassan 51)
Lancashire 158 (F.C. Hayes 52, M. Hendrick 6 for 55, E.E. Hemmings 4 for 54) and 65 (E.E. Hemmings 7 for 23)

Nottinghamshire won by 157 runs
Nottinghamshire 20 pts, Lancashire 5 pts

at The Oval

Northamptonshire 280 for 8 dec (A.J. Lamb 108, P Willey 52) and 203 for 7 dec
Surrey 217 (D.J. Thomas 52, B.J. Griffiths 4 for 66) and 163 for 6

Match drawn
Northamptonshire 7 pts, Surrey 5 pts

at Edgbaston

Yorkshire 239 (S.N. Hartley 69, J.D. Love 58, C.M. Old 4 for 63) and 184 for 9 dec
Warwickshire 125 (G.B. Stevenson 5 for 35) and 302 for 9 (G.W. Humpage 141 not out)

Warwickshire won by 1 wicket
Warwickshire 20 pts, Yorkshire 6 pts

at Worcester

Worcestershire 339 for 8 dec (J.A. Ormrod 84, M.S. Scott 76, D.B. d'Oliveira 58, A.J. Pollock 5 for 107)

Cambridge University 162 and 108 (J.D. Inchmore 5 or 47)

Worcestershire won by an innings and 69 runs

Essex and Middlesex gave emphatic evidence of their dominance of the Schweppes County Championship when both counties won inside two days.

On the Saturday, Essex relied on a second wicket stand of 109 between Hardie and Fletcher and some late runs by Pringle to give their innings any substance, but they took complete control of the game on Monday morning when Neil Foster continued his impressive quick bowling with a career best 6 for 46 which forced Sussex to follow-on. Sussex batted only marginally better in the second innings and it was only a late flourish from Gould and Reeve that made Essex bat again. Victory was a formality, but there was an attendant mishap when Hardie had his nose and cheek bone broken by a lifting ball from Colin Wells.

Middlesex, too, lost a player when Barlow retired hurt as they cantered to victory. Derbyshire were twice destroyed by spin, Emburey again emphasising that he had no rival as an off-break bowler and Edmonds continuing his amazing run of success which he had enjoyed since his return from a back injury. Edmonds also impressed with the bat when runs were needed on Monday morning and he and Williams, a rapidly maturing cricketer, got them.

If Middlesex and Essex were in danger of becoming complacent, then they needed only to look at the form of Warwickshire who gained a most remarkable fifth consecutive championship victory. A dour Yorkshire innings on the first day was held together by a third wicket stand of 115 from Hartley and Love. The Yorkshire score of 239 looked very big indeed on the Monday when Dennis and Stevenson bowled out the home side for 125. Illingworth declared at his overnight score, leaving Warwickshire the last day in which to make 299, or, more realistically, leaving his bowlers a day in which to bowl the home side out on a wicket which was unpredictable and getting slower.

With 8 men out for 180, Yorkshire seemed to be moving to their expected victory. It was then that Norman Gifford joined Geoff Humpage who had combined his usual belligerence with justifiable caution. The partnership began 20 minutes before tea and lasted into the last hour before Gifford, who had brought the wisdom of his years to the situation, missed a full toss from Jarvis. The pair had added 58. Humpage was on 95 and victory was still 61 runs, a dream, away. Willis joined Humpage.

Willis has no equal in his courage and belief that a game is never lost until the last ball is bowled. He played his two famous shots and stuck at it while Humpage let fly with a flurry of boundaries. Yorkshire were now on the defensive and they attacked with the second new ball and then defended with eight men round the boundary, but Warwickshire were not to be denied. Humpage extended what was undoubtedly the finest innings of his career to 264 minutes and with seventeen fours achieved a famous victory.

There were sensations, too, at Trent Bridge. On the Saturday, Steve Jefferies routed the home county with the season's best bowling figures of 8 for 46. Hendrick and Hemmings kept Notts in the game by restricting the Lancashire lead to 72, and Hassan, Birch and Rice then made batting look considerably easier than it had been hitherto. On the last morning, Hemmings found ample turn and exploited the pitch to full advantage as he bowled unchanged for 25.3 overs to take 7 for 23, bringing him match figures of 11 for 77.

Two splendid innings by Brian Davison, a century by David Gower, who shared a stand of 173 with Davison in the second innings, and some ferocious fast bowling by the eighteen-year old George Ferris of Antigua were too much for bottom of the table Glamorgan. Ferris had matches figures of 10 for 104 and gave further indication that the West Indies had another fast bowler on the verge of international class.

Hampshire's fine team work saw them to a very good victory over Gloucestershire. Mark Nicholas and Chris Smith gave the Hampshire innings substance on the first day and there was a good knock from Nick Pocock, whose achievements in welding together this fine Hampshire side have been remarkable. Gloucestershire, through the positive Hignell who hit his second hundred in five days, reached 300 in 75 overs on the Monday and Graveney declared 61 runs behind. Chris Smith became the second batsman to reach a thousand runs for the season, but once more it was Robin Smith who took the honours with his third admirable hundred of the year. Pocock left Gloucestershire 334 in 247 minutes, and Stovold and Romaines began as if they would reach the target in half the time, but Pocock marshalled his resources intelligently, Hampshire fielded well and snatched victory with 23 balls to spare.

The only match not to achieve a result was at The Oval where a match that had been slightly in Northants' favour ended with Surrey settling for a draw. The visitors were happy that Allan Lamb had returned to them with his England form intact.

Cambridge suffered the wrong kind of preparation for the varsity match, an innings defeat and an injury to acting skipper Steve Henderson. For Worcestershire, it was another welcome win in an otherwise barren summer.

John Player League

26 June

at Chesterfield

Derbyshire 160 (J.E. Morris 61, N.F. Williams 4 for 40)
Middlesex 162 for 6

Middlesex (4 pts) won by 4 wickets

at Ilford

Essex 188 for 9 (K.W.R. Fletcher 55)
Sussex 190 for 6

Sussex (4 pts) won by 6 wickets

at Canterbury

Kent 270 for 4 (C.J. Tavare 70, D.G. Aslett 51, R.A. Woolmer 50)
Nottinghamshire 221 for 9 (C.E.B. Rice 97, R.T. Robinson 51)

Kent (4 pts) won by 49 runs

at Leicester

Glamorgan 156 (L.B. Taylor 5 for 41)
Leicestershire 157 for 6

Leicestershire (4 pts) won by 4 wickets

at Bath

Somerset 254 for 6 (P.M. Roebuck 105, I.T. Botham 73, D.V. Lawrence 4 for 41)
Gloucestershire 238 for 6 (A.W. Stovold 57, P. Bainbridge 53)

Somerset (4 pts) won by 16 runs

at East Moseley

Surrey 232 for 6 (M.A. Lynch 70, A.R. Butcher 68, N.A. Mallender 4 for 46)
Northamptonshire 234 for 5 (A.J. Lamb 72, M.J. Bamber 71)

Northamptonshire (4 pts) won by 5 wickets

at Edgbaston

Warwickshire 241 for 7 (A.I. Kallicharran 66, A.M. Ferreira 52)
Hampshire 235 for 8 (T.E. Jesty 76, C.L. Smith 62)

Warwickshire (4 pts) won by 6 runs

at Worcester

Worcestershire 127
Yorkshire 128 for 6

Yorkshire (4 pts) won by 4 wickets

Somerset continued their unbeaten run with Peter Roebuck hitting his first Sunday League century. Botham, who batted with a runner in the latter part of his innings because of a groin strain, gave him fine support in a third wicket stand of 127. Stovold, Romaines and Zaheer gave Gloucestershire an enthusiastic start in their chase for runs, but the rate could not be maintained.

Kent moved into second place with a decisive win over Notts. With the elegant Woolmer and Benson giving Kent a start of 93 and Tavare hitting freely, the home side reached a daunting 270. Notts lost Hassan in the first over, but Clive Rice hit two sixes and six fours in a splendid 97. He and Robinson added 130 in 24 overs, but the later batsmen failed to give the necessary support.

Sussex, aided by some lax Essex bowling, scored an improbable victory at Ilford. The wicket never looked easy and Essex were rescued by a stand of 55 between Hardie and Fletcher for the fifth wicket. With Parker seemingly unable to make contact with the ball, Sussex slipped to 40 for 3. Gould and Imran, playing his first match of the season for Sussex, added 53, but when Alan Wells was out cheaply, Phillipson and Le Roux needed to score 67 in under 7 overs. That they got the runs with 8 balls to spare says little for the accuracy of Essex's concluding bowlers, but both batsmen hit freely.

Middlesex recovered from 78 for 5 to beat Derbyshire, a stand of 59 in 13 overs between Emburey and Downton being crucial, and Yorkshire, in a match restricted to 31

overs, beat Worcestershire with 4 balls to spare.

Glamorgan lost ground when they were well beaten in rather anonymous game at Leicester.

Trevor Jesty hit five sixes in his innings of 76 in 57 minutes for Hampshire at Edgbaston, but he could not bring his side victory. Alvin Kallicharran made an elegant and easy 66 for the home side and Anton Ferreira hit 52 in 24 minutes, but when Smith and Terry began with a stand of 98 and Jesty played his whirlwind innings, it looked as if Hampshire would win. Then Willis bowled Jesty, who had hit 26 off one over from Thorne, and the rest of the Hampshire batting struggled to give Warwickshire their first John Player League win of the season.

Larkins and Sharp were delayed in a traffic jam and arrived too late to play for Northants against Surrey at Imber Court. Allan Lamb took over as wicket-keeper and conceded five runs when he gathered a return from the boundary with his floppy hat in his hand. Butcher and Lynch set Northants a formidable target, Lynch being particularly belligerent, but Allan Lamb hit 72 off 43 balls and the impressive newcomer Mike Bamber batted well to give the visitors a surprisingly easy victory with nine balls to spare.

NatWest Bank Trophy – Round One

29 June

at Reading

Berkshire 128 for 9 (G.B. Stevenson 5 for 27)
Yorkshire 131 for 3

Yorkshire won by 7 wickets
(Man of the Match – G.B. Stevenson)

at Wisbech

Cambridgeshire 172 (N.T. Gadsby 63)
Middlesex 174 for 2 (K.P. Tomlins 80, W.N. Slack 60)

Middlesex won by 8 wickets
(Man of the Match – N.T. Gadsby)

at Bournemouth

Dorset 111
Essex 117 for 3 (K.S. McEwan 73 not out)

Essex won by 7 wickets
(Man of the Match – K.S. McEwan)

at Chester-le-Street

Lancashire 211 for 8 (D.P. Hughes 71, J. Abrahams 51 not out, S. Davis 7 for 32)
Durham 105 (J. Simmons 4 for 25)

Lancashire won by 106 runs
(Man of the Match – S. Davis)

at Bristol

Gloucestershire 297 for 8 (A.W. Stovold 82, P. Bainbridge 75, W.A. Morton 4 for 47)
Scotland 209 for 6 (T.B. Racionzer 61)

Gloucestershire won by 88 runs
(Man of the Match – P. Bainbridge)

Paul Romaines. Given his chance by the injury to Chris Broad, he batted splendidly and kept his place in the Gloucestershire side. (George Herringshaw)

Jack Richards, the excellent Surrey wicket-keeper, who hit a magnificent century in the first round NatWest Trophy game against Lincolnshire. (Adrian Murrell)

at Hitchin

Hertfordshire 159 for 6 (F.E. Collyer 58 not out)
Hampshire 163 for 1 (C.L. Smith 66 not out, C.G. Greenidge 55)

Hampshire won by 9 wickets
(Man of the Match – F.E. Collyer)

at Dublin

Sussex 265 for 7
Ireland 141 (M. Masood 69)

Sussex won by 124 runs
(Man of the Match – M. Masood)

at Canterbury

Kent 237 for 8 (C.J. Tavare 99, C.S. Cowdrey 52)
Cheshire 101 (R.M. Ellison 4 for 19)

Kent won by 136 runs
(Man of the Match – C.J. Tavare)

at Leicester

Leicestershire 253 for 6 (R.W. Tolchard 71 not out)
Devon 121

Leicestershire won by 132 runs
(Man of the Match – R.W. Tolchard)

at Sleaford

Surrey 297 for 6 (C.J. Richards 105 not out, I.R. Payne 56 not out)

Lincolnshire 168 (K.G. Brookes 51, I.R. Payne 5 for 36)
Surrey won by 129 runs
(Man of the Match – C.J. Richards)

at Norwich

Glamorgan 202 for 9
Norfolk 177 (R.C.Ontong 4 for 49)

Glamorgan won by 25 runs
(Man of the Match – R.C. Ontong)

at Bury St Edmunds

Suffolk 164 for 8 (S.M. Clements 59)
Derbyshire 167 for 4 (A. Hill 52)

Derbyshire won by 6 wickets
(Man of the Match – A. Hill)

at Wellington

Somerset 246 (I.V.A. Richards 74, B. Perry 4 for 39)
Shropshire 159

Somerset won by 87 runs
(Man of the Match – B. Perry)

at Edgbaston

Warwickshire 274 for 7 (A.I. Kallicharran 70, K.D. Smith 60, D.L. Amiss 54)
Oxfordshire 256 (F.P. Fowler 119, M.D. Murton 58, R.G.D. Willis 4 for 25, N. Gifford 4 for 47)

Warwickshire won by 18 runs
(Man of the Match – F.P. Fowler)

at Swindon

Northamptonshire 285 for 6 (A.J. Lamb 75, W. Larkins 65)
Wiltshire 120

Northamptonshire won by 165 runs
(*Man of the Match* – A.J. Lamb)

at Worcester

Nottinghamshire 169
Worcestershire 167

Nottinghamshire won by 2 runs
(*Man of the Match* – D.B. d'Oliveira)

The round of the minor counties versus the giants provided no Davids although there were some heroic failures. The games at Wellington and Bury St Edmunds had to go into a second day, and the match at Wellington was one of the six instances in which a minor county player, in this case skipper Brian Perry took the individual award.

Simon Davis put in a magnificent spell of bowling for Durham against Lancashire. The Australian pace man, who will be remembered for his feat against Leicestershire in the previous season, took seven wickets, a remarkable achievement in 12 overs and Lancashire were saved by the combined efforts of Hughes and Abrahams.

Ken McEwan demonstrated why he was currently the most exciting batsman in England when, with Essex at 12 for 2, he hit 73 of the remaining 105 runs.

Frank Collyer raised Hertfordshire's hopes from the lunch score of 65 for 5 off 38 overs, but Greenidge and Chris Smith responded with 94 for the first Hampshire wicket.

Phil Bainbridge had consolation for his recent 99s with 75 and three wickets at Bristol, and Chris Tavare and Chris Cowdrey halted Cheshire's progress at Canterbury. Kent were indebted to excellent bowling by Richard Ellison.

Surrey were tottering at 137 for 6 against Lincoln before Richards and Payne established a seventh wicket record for the competition with an unbroken stand of 160 in 17 overs. It was thrilling stuff with Jack Richards quite magnificent. He reached fifty from 17 balls and his 105 came off 75 balls. The last five balls of the innings were hit for 4, 6, 6, 6, and 4.

Glamorgan had a fright from Norfolk, but the only first-class county to go out was poor Worcestershire, beaten by Notts in the only all first-class encounter. It was a tensely fought match with Saxelby bowling the last over and Worcestershire needing eight to win. He bowled Warner with his second ball, conceded a no-ball, but then had Ellcock caught at long-on by Robinson off the last ball of the day as he went for the intended winning boundary.

If one could give a man-of-the-round award, it would go to Paul Fowler of Oxfordshire. Facing Warwickshire's huge 274, Fowler and Murton opened with a stand of 152. Fowler batted superbly and while he was there, Oxfordshire were winning, but Willis returned to bowl him and Oxfordshire collapsed, losing their last 7 wickets for 33 runs. It was the old hands who saved the day for Warwickshire.

Bob Willis enjoying his best season for many years. He clings tenaciously to his position as England's leading fast bowler. No man has a bigger heart. (Ken Kelly)

Oxford University 1983
First Class Matches

BATTING

	Lancashire (Oxford) 23-26 April	Sussex (Oxford) 30 April-3 May	Glamorgan (Oxford) 11-13 May	Northamptonshire (Oxford) 8-10 June		Hampshire (Oxford) 11-14 June		Worcestershire (Oxford) 15-17 June		Surrey (The Oval) 18-21 June		Warwickshire (Edgbaston) 22-24 June		Cambridge University (Lord's) 29 June-1 July	
R.G.P. Ellis	26	11*	103*	15	13	99	20	61	26	13	34	7	22	18	83
A.J.T. Miller	28	10*	6	7	4	26	127*	90	0	11	22	76	20*	62	48
R.M. Edbrooke	0											71	—		
K.A. Hayes	3											3	—	45	11
G.J. Toogood	4		1	18	6									14	5
J.G. Varey	8					69*	31	11	6	13	0	9*		40*	0
R.P. Moulding	41		0	3	35	34	58*	53*	35	16	0	80*		66	27
M.R. Cullinan	14*		0	2	2	27	—	4	4			—	—	—	2*
J.D. Carr	0		2	9	18	0	—							16*	0
A.H.K. Smail	0		3			0	—	—	0	8	13*				
R.P. Gibaut	7		0												
J.R. Turnbull			0	0	0*	5*	—	—	0*	0*	0	—	—		
H.T. Rawlinson			11	7	4	0	—	0*	24	21	6	—	—		18*
M.P. Lawrence		—													
J.G. Franks			15	4	13	21	11	5	29						
P.G. Heseltine						36	4	40	3	5	3	39	4*	13	29
M.D. Petchey				2	0	0	—	—	0	18	1	—	—	—	—
J.R. Chessher												0	11		
D. Harrison												1	8		
Byes	10		8	5	4					3	3	13		1	
Leg-byes	4		1		3	4	1	7	4	3	2	10		7	7
Wides			4	1		11	4	1				2	1	1	1
No-balls			9	4	6	5	5	13	6				1		5
Total	145	21	163	146	139	268	230	285	137	112	103	310	48	283	236
Wickets	10	0	10	10	10	10	3	6	10	10	10	5	1	6	8
Result	D	D	D	L		L		L		L		D		D	

Catches

14 – M.R. Cullinan
6 – J.R. Turnbull
5 – P.G. Heseltine and J.D. Carr
3 – R.G. Ellis and M.D. Petchey
2 – H.T. Rawlinson and J.G. Franks
1 – M.P. Lawrence, J.G. Varey, A.H.K. Smail, R.P. Moulding, A.J.T. Miller, D. Harrison and R.M. Edbrooke

The match v. Somerset, 27-29 April was abandoned without a ball being bowled.

BOWLING

	J.G. Varey	A.H.K. Smail	J.R. Turnbull	H.T. Rawlinson	J.D. Carr	M.P. Lawrence	M.D. Petchey	R.G.P. Ellis
v. Lancashire (Oxford) 23-26 April	5-0-21-0	5-2-17-0						
v. Sussex (Oxford) 30 April-3 May		20-8-49-3	22-5-51-4	23-7-63-1	30-11-73-1	6-1-36-0		
v. Northamptonshire (Oxford) 8-10 June	1-0-9-0		21-5-60-2	18.5-3-90-3	25-7-71-2		21-3-73-2	8-2-30-0
			13-3-46-2	7-1-41-0	15-6-46-1		9-1-36-0	10-2-36-0
v. Hampshire (Oxford) 11-14 June		10-2-34-0	22-10-40-2		21-7-59-2		20.1-8-62-0	
		4-0-24-0	6-0-47-1	6-0-49-0	11-0-69-0		14-1-85-1	1-0-8-0
v. Worcestershire (Oxford) 15-17 June	10-1-33-0	17-4-42-1	13-1-58-0	30-7-123-5			25.1-5-79-2	
	18-4-69-3	9-1-40-1			12-1-48-2		17-1-61-1	2-2-0-0
v. Surrey (The Oval) 18-21 June	18-3-73-0	5-1-16-0	14-3-59-1	21-6-63-1			25-7-82-1	
v. Warwickshire (Edgbaston) 22-24 June	16-1-74-0		19-7-63-0	17-2-74-0			24-4-70-2	1-0-8-0
v. Cambridge University (Lord's) 29 June-1 July	9-1-37-0			11-3-43-0	25-7-43-1		26-3-127-2	
				9-1-32-2	28-7-84-2		25-3-129-1	
	77-10- 316-3 av. 105.33	70-18- 222-5 av. 44.40	130-34- 424-12 av. 35.33	154.5-31- 626-14 av. 44.71	155-45- 445-9 av. 49.44	6-1- 36-0 —	206.2-36- 804-12 av. 67.00	22-6- 82-0 —

† C.M. Wells absent ill

Inns	NOs	Runs	HS	Av
15	2	551	103*	42.38
15	3	537	127*	44.75
2	—	71	71	35.50
4	—	62	45	15.50
6	—	48	18	8.00
10	3	187	69*	26.71
13	3	448	80*	44.80
8	2	55	27	9.16
7	1	45	18	7.50
6	1	24	13*	4.80
2	—	7	7	3.50
7	4	5	5*	1.66
9	2	91	24	13.00
—				
7	—	98	29	14.00
10	1	176	40	19.55
6	—	21	18	3.50
2	—	11	11	5.50
2	—	9	8	4.50

R.P. Moulding	K.A. Hayes	Byes	Leg-byes	Wides	No-balls	Total	Wkts
					1	39	0
		2	4	2		280	9†
		2	2	4	12	353	9
			2	2	4	213	3
		2			1	198	4
2.3-0-7-0		7	4	1		301	2
		3	1		3	342	8
		1	5	2	2	228	8
		8	2	2	8	313	4
6.1-0-13-0	18-6-58-6	14	8	2	4	388	8
	9.5-1-57-1	4	4	2	5	322	4
1-0-2-0	6-3-9-1		4	2	2	264	6
9.4-0-	33.5-10-						
22-0	124-8						
—	av. 15.50						

Paul Fowler of Oxfordshire. His brave 119 against Warwickshire at Edgbaston, 29 June, came close to giving the minor county victory in the first round of the NatWest Trophy. (Ken Kelly)

29 and 30 June, 1 July

at Lord's

Cambridge University 322 for 4 dec (R.J. Boyd-Moss 139, T.S. Curtis 75, S.P. Henderson 51 not out) and 264 for 6 dec (R.J. Boyd-Moss 124, G. Pathmanathan 64)
Oxford University 283 for 6 dec (R.P. Moulding 66, A.G.T. Miller 62) and 236 for 8 (R.G.P. Ellis 83, R.J. Boyd-Moss 5 for 27)

Match drawn

The Varsity Match, once the highlight of the season, now a fixture looking for a spot on the calendar, produced one of the best games in recent years. Oxford won the toss and asked Cambridge to bat on a grey morning and had an early success when David Varey was caught behind for 6, but against a moderate attack, Boyd-Moss and Curtis added 215 for the second wicket. Boyd-Moss was the dominant partner and, indeed, was to dominate the match. Curtis, in his first University match, had the encouragement of an overthrown 8 and batted very solidly.

Oxford University made an encouraging response, although some of their batsmen, like skipper Toogood, who had a wretched season and played little because of examinations, were short of practice. Miller again showed his fine ability and Moulding, for whom the fixture has become a regular part of his life, batted well.

Cambridge University 1983
First Class Matches

BATTING

BATTING	v Glamorgan (Cambridge) 20-22 April		v Leicestershire (Cambridge) 23-26 April		v Essex (Cambridge) 27-29 April		v Kent (Cambridge) 4-6 May		v Warwickshire (Cambridge) 8-10 June		v Northamptonshire (Cambridge) 15-17 June		v Nottinghamshire (Cambridge) 18-21 June		v Middlesex (Cambridge) 22-24 June		v Worcestershire (Worcester) 25-28 June		v Oxford University (Lord's) 29 June-1 July	
A. Odendaal	1	0	17	10	7	21*														
D.W. Varey	33	10	11	3	0	17	19	28*	23	0	65	18	14	12	4	0	40	7	6	32
R.J. Boyd-Moss	83	3	44	48	15	5	3	—	45	30	45	97	2	4	20	21	5	0	139	124
S.P. Henderson	15	5	13	0	6	36	21	—	90	56	4	0	11	16	27	23	2	25*	51*	8*
T.S. Curtis	24*	18*	33	38	50	0	7	44*	18	13	92	5	16	5	31	24	8	5	75	0
S.J.G. Doggart	3	8*	4	1	29*	—	2	—	17	1*	59*	28	9	70	0	21	19	3	31*	18
K.I. Hodgson	4*	—	19	4*	26	—	7	—	2*	—	14	45	26*	28	0	23	47	21	—	6*
P.G. Roebuck	—	—	31*	0*	19	11*	12	—	9	0										
T.A. Cotterell	—	—	16*	—	4	—	5	—	10*	—	—	5	0	9*	0	1	22	5	—	4
A.G. Davies	—	—	—	—	0	—	0	—												
A.J. Pollock	—	—	—	—	4	—	0*	—	—	—	—	14*	4	12	1	0	3	0	—	—
G. Pathmanathan							48	—	53	18*	10	13	0	6	27	1	2	16	5	64
S.P. Hewitt									—	—	—	3	6	0	0	0*	0*	0	—	—
R.W.M. Palmer											—	0								
C.C. Ellison													1	21	15*	0	1	11*	—	—
Byes	4					1	3		3		5		5	5	5	8	6		4	
Leg-byes	2			4		2	8	1	15	1	17	10	2	4	1	5	2	3	4	4
Wides	1											1		1	3		1	5	2	2
No-balls	10	4				1	3	2	5	3	2	2	1	1	12	6	4	7	5	2
Total	180	48	192	105	165	93	140	76	287	121	307	244	97	192	146	133	162	108	322	264
Wickets	5	4	7	6	10	4	10	0	7	5	6	10	10	10	10	10	10	9†	4	6
Result	D		D		D		D		D		D		L		L		L		D	

Catches

9 – S.P. Henderson

7 – T.S. Curtis and S.P. Hewitt (ct 6/st 1)

4 – R.J. Boyd-Moss, A.J. Pollock, C.C. Ellison and S.J.G. Doggart

3 – D.W. Varey

2 – A.G. Davies, K.I. Hodgson, G. Pathmanathan, and T.A. Cotterell

1 – R.W.M. Palmer and P.G. Roebuck

† S.P. Henderson retired hurt.

BOWLING

BOWLING	P.G. Roebuck	K.I. Hodgson	S.J.G. Doggart	T.A. Cotterell	A.J. Pollock	T.S. Curtis	S.P. Henderson	R.J. Boyd-Moss
v. Glamorgan (Cambridge) 20-22 April	15-6-48-0	13-4-27-0	9-2-25-0	16-2-39-0	15-4-21-3	2-0-11-1		
v. Leicestershire (Cambridge) 23-26 April	8-1-29-1	16-4-55-0	16-2-48-0	23-5-73-2	13-1-69-2	4-0-19-0	4-1-9-0	
v. Essex (Cambridge) 27-29 April	18.5-2-74-2	22-6-81-0	32-2-109-1	10-0-44-1	20-6-53-0			
	9-1-42-0	33-12-71-0	10-3-27-0	29-9-89-5	6-0-36-2	1-0-5-0		
v. Kent (Cambridge) 4-6 May	13-3-44-2	28-5-85-1	11-2-32-1	22-2-82-0	31-6-74-0			
		19-5-57-0	4-1-17-0	12-1-46-1	12-4-35-1			
v. Warwickshire (Cambridge) 8-10 June	2-1-8-0	18-8-35-0	27-6-74-1	30-10-85-0	19-5-69-3		2-1-9-0	9-1-28-0
	10-3-24-1		25-4-81-2	8-1-18-0	18-4-44-2			9-2-38-0
v. Northamptonshire (Cambridge) 15-17 June		22-2-71-2	12-2-53-0	5-1-25-0	17-2-38-0			2-0-12-0
		5-0-25-0	31-4-69-2	23-6-48-3	13-4-47-2			
v. Nottinghamshire (Cambridge) 18-21 June		28-13-58-4	4.2-2-3-3		8-2-27-0			
		12-1-53-0	21-6-66-0	29-14-42-1	10-2-33-0	23-4-58-2	4-1-25-1	9-2-25-0
v. Middlesex (Cambridge) 22-24 June		16-4-46-0	13-2-58-0	20-3-51-1	15-1-67-1	2-0-23-0		9-0-46-1
v. Worcestershire (Worcester) 25-28 June		24-4-82-2	21-7-60-1	7-2-16-0	28-6-107-5		3-0-23-0	
v. Oxford University (Lord's) 29 June-1 July		15-2-61-1	35-11-74-1	23-7-57-2	7.2-1-24-0	1-0-11-0		20-9-41-2
		26-5-64-2	14-4-48-0	16-4-43-1	4-1-6-0	6-2-9-0		12-4-27-5
	75.5-17-269-6 av. 44.83	297-75-871-12 av. 72.58	285.2-60-844-12 av. 70.33	273-67-758-17 av. 44.58	236.2-49-750-21 av. 35.71	40-6-144-3 av. 48.00	13-3-66-1 av. 66.00	60-18-217-8 av. 27.12

Inns	NOs	Runs	HS	Av
6	1	56	21*	11.20
20	1	342	65	18.00
19	—	733	139	38.57
19	3	409	90	25.56
20	3	506	92	29.76
18	5	323	70	24.84
15	5	272	47	27.20
7	3	82	31*	20.50
12	3	81	22	9.00
2	—	0	0	—
9	2	38	14*	5.42
13	1	263	64	21.91
7	2	9	6	1.80
1	—	0	0	—
6	2	49	21	12.25

R.W. Palmer	C.C. Ellison	Byes	Leg-byes	Wides	No-balls	Total	Wkts
		4	4	3	2	184	4
		1	3	2	2	310	6
		3	10		1	375	4
		3	3	1	1	278	7
			5	1	1	324	5
			2			157	2
		2	4	1		315	4
		5		2		212	5
8-0-48-1		4	2	5	2	260	3
4-0-27-0		5	10		1	240	7
	17-7-35-3	3	1			127	10
	8.4-0-36-4		5	2	2	347	8
	5-1-10-0	4		2	2	309	3
	17-7-40-0		8	3		339	8
	3-2-6-0	1	7	1		283	6
	6-0-26-0		7	1	5	236	8
12-0-	56.4-17-						
75-1	153-7						
av. 75.00	av. 21.85						

On the last day Robin Boyd-Moss became the first batsman ever to score two hundreds in a university match, and, with 489 runs, he also became the most prolific scorer in these encounters. When Oxford, inspired by Ellis, went boldly for the runs, they were halted by Boyd-Moss's spin. He had a career best and a fine match, which will undoubtedly go down in history as 'Boyd-Moss's match', was drawn.

2, 3 and 4 July

at Taunton

New Zealanders 544 for 9 dec (G.P. Howarth 88, J.G. Wright 85, R.J. Hadlee 82, E.J. Gray 72, B.L. Cairns 60, P.H.L. Wilson 4 for 109) and 46 for 0 dec
Somerset 267 (J.W. Lloyds 84, P.A. Slocombe 66, E.J. Gray 4 for 24, J.G. Bracwell 4 for 91) and 221 for 9 (P.W. Denning 99, J.G. Bracewell 5 for 73)

Match drawn

2, 4 and 5 July

at Derby

Derbyshire 344 for 8 dec (A. Hill 137 not out, W.P. Fowler 63, A.E. Warner 4 for 72) and 203 for 2 (I.S. Anderson 85)
Worcestershire 136 (J.A. Ormrod 63 not out, C.J. Tunnicliffe 4 for 30, O. Mortensen 4 for 46) and 407 (D.N. Patel 98, P.A. Neale 83, M.S. Scott 57 not out)

Derbyshire won by 8 wickets
Derbyshire 24 pts, Worcestershire 3 pts

at Canterbury

Glamorgan 265 (A. Jones 93, G.R. Dilley 4 for 52) and 216 for 4 (A.L. Jones 58 not out, D.A. Francis 50 not out)
Kent 422 (R.A. Woolmer 97, C.J. Tavare 68, C.S. Cowdrey 50, C.J.C. Rowe 4 for 64)

Match drawn
Kent 7 pts, Glamorgan 5 pts

at Liverpool

Hampshire 323 for 6 dec (C.L. Smith 118, C.G. Greenidge 104) and 246 for 1 dec (C.G. Greenidge 100 not out, M.C.J. Nicholas 89 not out)
Lancashire 305 for 7 dec (G. Fowler 73, F.C. Hayes 66, C. Maynard 61 not out, N.G. Cowley 4 for 76) and 138 for 8 (M.D. Marshall 5 for 64)

Match drawn
Hampshire 7 pts, Lancashire 6 pts

at Trent Bridge

Essex 211 and 285 for 3 dec (K.S. McEwan 81 not out, G.A. Gooch 73, A.W. Lilley 61)
Nottinghamshire 123 (D.R. Pringle 4 for 13, J.K. Lever 4 for 65) and 172

Essex won by 201 runs
Essex 22 pts, Nottinghamshire 4 pts

at The Oval

Gloucestershire 117 (D.J. Thomas 4 for 22) and 143 (I.R. Payne 5 for 13)
Surrey 344 (M.A. Lynch 76, D.M. Smith 53, J.N. Shepherd 4 for 83)

Surrey won by an innings and 84 runs
Surrey 24 pts, Gloucestershire 4 pts

at Hove

Northamptonshire 300 (W. Larkins 93, G. Cook 58, C.M. Wells 4 for 69, D. Reeve 4 for 80) and 223 for 5 dec (P. Willey 80, G. Cook 67, C.E. Waller 4 for 58)
Sussex 250 for 3 dec (G.D. Mendis 121 not out) and 154

Northamptonshire won by 119 runs
Northamptonshire 21 pts, Sussex 7 pts

at Edgbaston

Warwickshire 113 (P.H Edmonds 5 for 26) and 206 (D.L. Amiss 57, P.H. Edmonds 5 for 46)
Middlesex 78 (A.M. Ferreira 5 for 19) and 74 (N. Gifford 6 for 22)

Warwickshire won by 167 runs
Warwickshire 20 pts, Middlesex 4 pts

at Harrogate

Leicestershire 352 for 7 dec (N.E. Briers 97, B.F. Davison 81, I.P. Butcher 66) and 194 for 5 dec (N.E. Briers 55 not out)
Yorkshire 251 (J.D. Love 53, D.L. Bairstow 50) and 206 (D.L. Bairstow 57, G. Ferris 4 for 63, P.B. Clift 4 for 84)

Leicestershire won by 89 runs
Leicestershire 23 pts, Yorkshire 4 pts

The New Zealanders had already played a two-day game against the Combined Services, but their tour proper began with the match at Taunton. With five batsmen passing fifty, they ran up an encouragingly massive 544 against a weakened Somerset attack and then spinners Gray and Bracewell disposed of Somerset by the end of the second day. Howarth chose not to enforce the follow-on, but, as Franklin and Edgar then occupied 18 meaningless overs, it was difficult to understand why. In spite of an attractive innings from Denning and some late fireworks from Garner, Somerset faced defeat at 215 for 9, but Wilson and Davis held out for the last six overs.

Derbyshire lost 4 wickets for 36 runs against Worcestershire, but a watchful, solid innings by Alan Hill, enjoying a good season since gaining batting responsibility in the absence of Wood and Wright, not only rescued the side, but saw them to maximum batting points. Hill's innings, which lasted almost six hours, was Derbyshire's first championship century of the season. He and Miller added 85 in 84 minutes for the fifth wicket, and then Fowler joined Hill in a sixth wicket stand of 121 in 31 overs, Fowler reaching a career best 63.

Worcestershire, who had asked Derbyshire to bat and seen their decision justified in the early morning, lost Weston before the close and crumpled to 136 all out before

Tunnicliffe and Mortensen on the Monday. Following-on, they batted with tremendous resolution and survived until there were only two hours remaining on the last afternoon. Needing 200 in 55 minutes and 20 overs, Derbyshire attacked from the first ball. Morris and Anderson put on 64, Hill and Anderson 119. Anderson's 85 came in 107 minutes, but when he was caught at mid-off he had already assured his side of victory.

There was no such excitement at Canterbury where Kent failed to press home the advantage that they had gained over Glamorgan. They simply could not score runs quickly enough and, although the visitors lost 4 wickets for 91 in their second innings, Kent's bowling posed no problems for Francis and A.L. Jones.

Hampshire nearly snatched victory on the perfect wicket of Liverpool, a bowler's graveyard. Greenidge and Chris Smith began the match with a partnership of 191. It was one of Greenidge's more sedate innings, but the authority of his batting and the grace and ease of his hitting still brought him 104 in 200 minutes. His partner, Chris Smith, continued to gather runs. In his first full season as an Englishman he reminded one of the young Glenn Turner who, in his early days, accumulated runs but left one with no memory of a single shot. As one critic described Smith, he is a Boycott rather than a Gooch, but then that is very high praise indeed and the young man's application and technical ability bode well for a prosperous future.

Lancashire countered Hampshire on the Monday, and then Greenidge hit his second century of the match, although Nicholas' 89 took the eye in the second innings, and his third in four days. Hampshire asked Lancashire to make 265 on a wicket that was still good, but Marshall's fierce bowling was too much for the home side who rushed to 67 for 6, and it was left to the sturdy Jack Simmons and the less probable figures of Radford and Zaidi to save the game.

Surrey beat Gloucestershire in two days at The Oval. Surrey already had a first innings lead by Saturday evening after Clarke and Thomas had bowled out Gloucestershire for 117. They hit freely on the Monday and then Ian Payne had a career best 5 for 13 to rout the visitors for a second time.

A century by Gehan Mendis brought Sussex to within 50 of Northants on the first innings and caused Barclay to declare. In return, Northants, with Cook and Willey adding 110 for the second wicket, extended their lead to 273 before declaring ten minutes after lunch on the last day. Heath immediately fell to Mallender, and although Mendis and Barclay prospered for a while, there was a total disintegration of the middle order. As the wicket began to turn so Sussex's chances of survival became slimmer and the game ended with an hour and twenty minutes to spare.

In spite of a failure by David Gower, Leicestershire compiled a formidable total on the opening day at Harrogate, Davison and Briers sharing a fourth wicket stand of 133. Yorkshire were in some trouble on the Monday, but Jim Love and David Bairstow, who continue to fight and never give less than 100 per cent through all Yorkshire's trials and tribulations, saved the follow-on and Yorkshire ended 101 behind. Leicestershire then scored briskly and set Yorkshire the task of making 296 in 215 minutes. They started poorly, the first four batsmen taking nearly two hours to make 60. Inevitably, Bairstow raised Yorkshire hopes, but, with Illingworth absent due to illness, Ferris finished the innings and

ABOVE: *David Smith is caught at slip by Butcher off Edmonds on the second day.* BELOW: *Andy Lloyd is bowled by Phil Edmonds. Paul Downton keeping wicket.* RIGHT: *Phil Edmonds is bowled by Norman Gifford. Humpage, Amiss and Asif Din are also in the picture. The two slow left-arm bowlers dominated the match.* RIGHT (below): *Wayne Daniel steers Gifford to Kallicharran at second slip and Warwickshire have beaten Middlesex; 2-5 July. (Ken Kelly)*

Gifford and Amiss relax with Buck's Fizz after Warwickshire beat Middlesex. (Ken Kelly)

Leicestershire moved into fourth place.

In third place were Warwickshire who continued their marvellous run of success with a win over Middlesex, the leaders, in one of the most discussed games of the season. When Edmonds and Emburey bowled out Warwickshire on the Saturday it seemed to be just another stage of the champions steam roller moving on, but by 5.40, Middlesex had been bowled out in 50 overs for 78 so conceding a lead of 35 runs. Willis had taken the first three wickets and the medium pace of Ferreira had proved too much for the later batsmen. Only Gatting (15) and Emburey (23) reached double figures. Middlesex had been further handicapped by the absence of Barlow and Slack. Ellis had been called as a late replacement, but, held up by traffic on the M1, he had not arrived until the afternoon when he had been rushed out to bat and got 0.

Warwickshire lost Lloyd and Kallicharran before the close on Saturday, but K.D. Smith and Gifford stayed together while 58 runs were added, in the context of this match a mammoth stand. It was followed by one of 55 between Amiss and Smith which was ended when Smith was caught by Butcher off Edmonds for 32. He had batted for 189 minutes. In the wealth of statistics, it is an innings that will become lost as insignificant. For those who saw it, it was an innings of great character, played for the team, in the most difficult of circumstances. Humpage hit strongly to help Amiss in a stand of 49, and then Amiss himself fell to Emburey, caught at mid-wicket by Edmonds. In scoring 57, Dennis Amiss had given the perfect example of the power of technique on a doubtful wicket. Here was a very great batsman displaying his art, learned by hard work in a hard school and tempered by years of practice. He is a man of substance and it should be obligatory that young batsmen who aspire to great things should have a course in studying him closely. Edmonds finished with match figures of 10 for 72, but Middlesex were set to make 242 to win, the highest score of the match.

They lost 4 for 49 before close on the Tuesday and the following day Norman Gifford whose arrival at Edgbaston had revitalised Warwickshire finished them off. It was a great triumph in a memorable match which did cricket much good, in spite of all the complaints about the wicket.

Seizing the chance offered by Middlesex's defeat, Essex closed the gap to 11 points. 124 for 8 on the Saturday, they were miraculously taken to two batting points by Ray East supported by Lever and Foster.

The Monday saw a complete transformation in the match as Lever, Pringle and Foster routed Notts, and Essex, mocking the vagaries of the wicket, raced to 285 for 3 declared at nearly five an over. Alan Lilley, substituting for the injured Hardie, began the ferocious assault, and McEwan was frantic in his devastation of the bowling. Poor young Such, the off-spinner, conceded 101 in 12 overs.

Notts began the last day at 23 for 1, and they never looked as if they would save the match which ended in early afternoon.

John Player League

3 July

at Derby

Worcestershire 225 for 7 (M.J. Weston 64)
Derbyshire 229 for 6

Derbyshire (4 pts) won by 4 wickets

at Old Trafford

Hampshire 268 for 4 (C.G. Greenidge 162 not out)
Lancashire 210 for 9 (J. Abrahams 65, T.E. Jesty 5 for 43)

Hampshire (4 pts) won by 58 runs

at Lord's

Middlesex 270 for 5 (R.O. Butcher 100, M.W. Gatting 85)
Gloucestershire 272 for 4 (Zaheer Abbas 106 not out)

Gloucestershire (4 pts) won by 6 wickets

at Trent Bridge

Essex 306 for 2 (K.S. McEwan 162 not out, G.A. Gooch 116)
Nottinghamshire 217 for 9 (D.W. Randall 107)

Essex (4 pts) won by 89 runs

at Hastings

Sussex 231 for 3 (P.W.G. Parker 121 not out)
Northamptonshire 143 for 8

Sussex (4 pts) won by 88 runs

at Scarborough

Leicestershire 160 for 8
Yorkshire 161 for 3

Yorkshire (4 pts) won by 7 wickets

It was a Sunday of spectacular batting. At Old Trafford, Gordon Greenidge played what Victor Isaacs described as the finest one-day innings he has ever played. It took him 12 overs to reach double figures, and then he made a violent assault on the Lancashire bowling which took him to 162, including five massive sixes and fourteen fours, by the end of the fortieth over Lancashire made a spirited reply, but Jesty moved the ball about to good effect, and the task was always really beyond them.

Sussex moved to within two points of Somerset with a comfortable win over Northants. Parker reached his second John Player League century of the season off 112 deliveries. He and Colin Wells added 90 in 19 overs for the second wicket and then he shared a third wicket stand of 112 in 13 overs with Imran Khan who was firmly re-establishing himself though still troubled by injury.

Yorkshire stayed level on points with Sussex with a purely competent, no fuss win over Leicestershire, and Derbyshire maintained their challenge with a fine team-effort win over Worcestershire.

At Lord's, Gatting and Butcher made a violent onslaught on the Gloucestershire bowling, scoring 85 off 78 balls, Butcher a thrilling century off 72 balls. Middlesex looked in a good position, but Zaheer batted with total command as he and Hignell scored 113 off 14 overs. Still, when Shepherd came in at number six, 63 were wanted off 25 deliveries. Shepherd hit runs from each of the 12 balls he faced, including two sixes and three fours. So fierce was his attack, so positive was Zaheer's batting, that Gloucestershire reached their target with 4 balls to spare, a mighty win.

At Trent Bridge, Graham Gooch and Ken McEwan hit 273 off 33 overs in a record partnership, not only for the second, but for any, wicket. The partnership was rich in fine strokes. 110 runs came from McEwan in boundaries, seven sixes and seventeen fours, while Gooch struck nine fours and three sixes with his usual nonchalant aggression. McEwan batted for 34 overs, Gooch for 38. It was glorious stuff. Derek Randall hit a hundred for Notts in reply, but the home side were always chasing a lost cause.

Benson and Hedges Cup: Semi-Finals

6 July

---

at Canterbury

Kent 128
Essex 130 for 1 (B.R. Hardie 58 not out)

Essex won by 9 wickets
(Gold Award – S. Turner)

at Lord's

Lancashire 90 (N.G. Cowans 4 for 33)
Middlesex 91 for 4

Middlesex won by 6 wickets
(Gold Award – N.G. Cowans)

Both semi-finals of the Benson and Hedges Cup were won with some ease. At Canterbury, Fletcher won the toss and, on a sticky morning, asked Kent to bat. However sultry the atmosphere and brown the pitch, the movement seemed minimal and the bounce even, but Benson was uncomfortable and suspicious and, at 19, he played tentatively at Lever and was bowled. Tavare now joined Woolmer, who looked quite at ease, for an innings which was to last 35 overs.

Stuart Turner. Gold Award winner at Canterbury. His nagging accuracy frustrated Kent into disaster. (Adrian Murrell)

Pringle and Turner replaced Lever and Foster. Pringle surrendered two fours and a no-ball in his first over and it seemed that the economy which the opening bowlers had exerted might be frittered away. Tavare moved down the wicket to drive the last ball of Turner's first over through the covers, a sweet shot, but it was to be the last positive scoring shot off the forty-year old medium pacer whose appetite for the game is as strong as ever. He was to concede only another 11 runs in his next ten overs and so great was the stranglehold on the Kent batsmen that they chose their own method of destruction.

Woolmer and Tavare had added 43 and had begun to take fretful runs in an attempt to elude Turner's tight grip. Tavare nudged a ball backward off square leg and set off on a run. Woolmer was slow to respond, and Ray East, moving and throwing quickly, hit the one stump that he could see. It was the first evidence of a brilliant day in the field for Essex.

The next was when Aslett was brilliantly caught, one-handed at slip by Gooch off Turner. Gooch had now joined Turner in the attack and gained eccentric movement with his swing bowling. He was just being baited by the Kent supporters for bowling two wides when he had Cowdrey groping in bewilderment and caught behind.

Turner now found the edge of Baptiste's bat in classical fashion and David East took a superb diving catch behind the stumps. His wicket-keeping throughout the innings drew praise from match adjudicator Tom Graveney. Here, surely, is an England player of the very near future.

Five men out at lunch, Kent were to lose a sixth, Knott, to a flying catch by David East before they reached 100.

Tavare played across the line at Gooch in desperation and was lbw. It was the fortieth over and he had scored only 32. Lever, Foster, a handsome, tall, impressive fast bowler, and Pringle saw that the tail did not wag and Kent were out with four overs of their allocation unused.

The Essex outcricket had been totally exhilarating; their batting was less so. With little challenge, they moved to 44 before losing Gooch and then Hardie and Fletcher saw them home. Hardie deserves every praise, returning to the side for this vital match only nine days after breaking his nose and cheekbone against Sussex.

The Essex innings was, in truth, an anti-climax. The batsmen did what they had to do, and without risk. Dilley took an interminable time to bowl an over. Three catches, none of them difficult, were dropped, and Kent drooped from the field on a day that they would like to forget.

At Lord's, on a very grey day, which threatened to take the match into a second day, Lancashire lost the toss and with it, any hope of giving Middlesex a fight. They were without Clive Lloyd, injured, and very soon they were without both openers. Fowler was caught behind off Cowans, bowling very quickly, for 1, and O'Shaughnessy was bowled behind his legs by Daniel. Frank Hayes, beaten for speed, was bowled off his pads by Cowans, and Abrahams was taken at slip off the same bowler. 23 for 4 after 8 overs.

After 13 overs, it was 39 for 5. Hughes and Simmons conjured something from their depths of experience, scoring 27 and 25 respectively, and Lancashire reached 90, Radford also making double figures, 14.

Middlesex were never likely to be facing defeat, but they did not have an easy time. Their innings had two interruptions, for bad light and for a thunderstorm, and the contest finished in the gloom of a near-deserted Lord's at 7.45.

Tilcon Trophy

6 July

at Harrogate

Northamptonshire 171 for 9 (G. Ferris 4 for 32)
Leicestershire 168

Northamptonshire won by 3 runs
(Man of the Match – R.G. Williams)

7 July

Nottinghamshire 265 for 3 (C.E.B. Rice 82 not out, R.T. Robinson 56, D.W. Randall 52)
Yorkshire 268 for 6 (C.W.J. Athey 76, S.N. Hartley 56 not out)

Yorkshire won by 4 wickets
(Man of the Match – C.W.J. Athey)

The Final

8 July

Yorkshire 178 (A. Sidebottom 79, W. Larkins 4 for 20)
Northamptonshire 182 for 2 (W. Larkins 104, P. Willey 64 not out)

Northamptonshire won by 8 wickets
(Man of the Match – W. Larkins)

This was the first time in the eight years of the competition that a county had retained the trophy. Yorkshire recovered from 32 for 6 in the final thanks to 79 off 88 balls by Arnold Sidebottom.

6, 7 and 8 July

at Bristol

Gloucestershire 120 (A.W. Stovold 58, E.J. Chatfield 6 for 40) and 305 for 8 (P. Bainbridge 146)
New Zealanders 338 for 6 dec (J.G. Wright 136, M.D. Crowe 61 not out, G.P. Howarth 60)

Match drawn

Sadly, the tourist's match was once more treated with less respect than it deserved and Gloucestershire fielded a side that included neither Shepherd nor Zaheer. They looked as if they would pay dearly when Chatfield found his best form to destroy them on the opening day, the last eight wickets falling for 41 runs. The New Zealanders, who lost an hour's batting on the first evening, batted strongly on the second day. Wright, much the more dominant partner, and Edgar opened with a stand of 122 although both enjoyed some luck. Howarth and the impressive Martin Crowe also batted well in the afternoon, and Howarth declared overnight with a lead of 218.

On the last day, the tourists were thwarted by Phil Bainbridge who stayed 4¼ hours and hit twenty boundaries.

9, 10 and 11 July

at Lord's

Middlesex 386 for 4 dec (M.W. Gatting 216, C.T. Radley 119)
New Zealanders 234 (G.P. Howarth 72, P.H. Edmonds 6 for 93) and 302 for 5 (M.D. Crowe 134 not out)

Match drawn

9, 11 and 12 July

at Cardiff

Glamorgan 244 (A. Jones 105, A.C.S. Pigott 4 for 48) and 179 for 6 dec (C.J.C. Rowe 52)
Sussex 163 (M.W.W. Selvey 5 for 51) and 224 for 7 (Imran Khan 63, G.D. Mendis 55, M.W.W. Selvey 4 for 61)

Match drawn
Glamorgan 6 pts, Sussex 3 pts

at Bristol

Gloucestershire 236 (J.N. Shepherd 80, R.C. Russell 58, O. Mortensen 4 for 52) and 240 for 7 dec (A.J. Hignell 86, P.W. Romaines 71, D.G. Moir 4 for 93)
Derbyshire 178 (G. Miller 59) and 192 for 9 (A. Hill 64, J.H. Childs 6 for 81)

Match drawn
Gloucestershire 5 pts, Derbyshire 5 pts

t Southampton

ampshire 371 for 6 dec (M.D. Marshall 100 not out, .G. Greenidge 83) and 309 for 4 dec (C.G. Greenidge 54, A.R. Butcher 4 for 123)

urrey 339 for 6 dec (M.A. Lynch 119, C.J. Richards 85 ot out, R.D.V. Knight 57) and 177 for 5 (R.D.V. Knight not out)

Match drawn
ampshire 6 pts, Surrey 6 pts

t Maidstone

ent 349 for 6 dec (R.A. Woolmer 129, C.S. Cowdrey 01 not out, D.G. Aslett 56) and 236 for 3 dec (R.A. Woolmer 92, N.R. Taylor 67, C.J. Tavare 50)

ancashire 310 (J. Abrahams 105, R.M. Ellison 5 for 73) nd 204 for 6 (D.P. Hughes 75 not out, F.C. Hayes 52, E.A. aptiste 4 for 38)

Match drawn
ent 7 pts, Lancashire 5 pts

t Leicester

eicestershire 180 (J.C. Balderstone 52, I.T. Botham 5 or 38) and 277 (D.I. Gower 73, R.W. Tolchard 71, V.J. Marks 5 for 105)

omerset 528 (I.V.A. Richards 216, I.T. Botham 152, .M. Roebuck 51)

omerset won by an innings and 71 runs
omerset 24 pts, Leicestershire 4 pts

t Northampton

orthamptonshire 234 (G. Sharp 98, S.J. Dennis 4 for 2) and 236 for 4 dec (A.J. Lamb 107 not out, G. Cook 1)

orkshire 199 and 190 (D.L. Bairstow 80, D.S. Steele 5 or 67)

orthamptonshire won by 81 runs
orthamptonshire 22 pts, Yorkshire 5 pts

t Nuneaton

Warwickshire 379 for 9 dec (D.L. Amiss 111, T.A. Lloyd 9, N. Phillip 4 for 80, R.E. East 4 for 85) and 36 for 0

ssex 110 (N. Gifford 5 for 2) and 301 (N. Phillip 80, .W.R. Fletcher 62, K.S. McEwan 54, N. Gifford 4 for 84)

Warwickshire won by 10 wickets
Warwickshire 24 pts, Essex 3 pts

t Worcester

ottinghamshire 176 (J.D. Inchmore 5 for 45) and 285 or 8 dec (R.T. Robinson 110, S.B. Hassan 50)

Worcestershire 69 (K.E. Cooper 7 for 33) and 177 (M. Hendrick 5 for 24)

ottinghamshire won by 215 runs
ottinghamshire 21 pts, Worcestershire 4 pts

Mike Gatting, dropped from the England side, gave the best possible reply to the selectors when he hit four sixes and

Dennis Amiss hits 111 on the first day against Essex. The 84th century of his career. (Ken Kelly)

twenty-eight fours in an innings which lasted under four hours and brought him the first double century of his career. He enjoyed some fortune against Bracewell's off-spin, but generally he was in total command of the situation and routed the New Zealand bowling. He and the durable Radley added 318 after the first two wickets had fallen for 46.

On the Sunday, Edmonds, recalled to the England side, celebrated with some splendidly controlled spin bowling which, in harness with Emburey, that constantly thinking bowler, had the New Zealanders bemused. The tourists seemed to be facing their first defeat of the tour on the eve of the first Test, but Martin Crowe once more displayed a maturity beyond his years and with enviable application steered his side to safety.

In the Schweppes County Championship, there was a first win for Somerset. Botham and Garner humbled Leicestershire on the first day. The last 7 Leicestershire wickets went down for 43 runs and Clift retired hurt. Botham, recipient of much advice from the press, moved the ball appreciably and appeared to have rediscovered his outswinger.

On the Monday, he dropped to number nine in the batting order because of a stomach upset, but his form showed no signs of sickness. He made his highest score of the season and shared a record eighth wicket stand of 172 with Viv Richards. Richards was at his arrogant best. In an innings of controlled and sustained aggression, he hit a six and twenty-six fours against an attack that was commendably accurate throughout a long day.

Leicestershire had little hope of saving the game, but Gower and Tolchard batted defiantly until they both fell to Richards. At the other end, Vic Marks nagged away for nearly forty-two overs and gained ultimate reward.

Brilliant as were the performances of Richards and Botham at Leicester, the pride of place still went to Warwickshire and Norman Gifford. Having humbled top place Middlesex, they now destroyed second place Essex and put themselves firmly in contention for the title, two points behind Essex, ten behind Middlesex. They were lucky to win an important toss, but led by the master craftsman Dennis Amiss and aided by some uncharacteristic bad fielding and bowling by Essex, they exploited their fortune well and reached a daunting 379 by Saturday evening.

Gooch and Hardie began smartly for Essex on the Monday morning, 53 runs coming in 10 overs, but then the innings underwent a complete transformation as 7 wickets fell in 27 overs and 49 runs. 107 for 5 at lunch, Essex had succumbed to a sustained spell from Old, ably supported by Ferreira, but it was Gifford who brought about the final disintegration as he took five wickets for 1 run in 11 balls. Following-on 269 runs in arrears, Essex lost Gooch and Hardie with only 4 scored. Fletcher and McEwan added 89 for the third wicket, but Gifford and Ferreira joined forces to nibble away at the middle order so that the score was 209, an innings defeat for Essex looming, when Foster joined Phillip for the last wicket. They took the game into a third day, saved an innings defeat and added 92 before Phillip was stumped off the relentless Gifford who had match figures of 9 for 86 and was once more the central figures in Warwickshire's victory.

Norman Gifford in action in his spell of 5 for 2 which was instrumental in Warwickshire adding second place Essex to their long list of victims. (Ken Kelly)

At the other end of the table, Glamorgan, hampered by no-balls from Winston Davis, took a first innings lead over Sussex, but nearly surrendered the match when Sussex came close to making the 261 they were set. The visitors were denied by Mike Selvey's accuracy. The Glamorgan captain had match figures of 9 for 112. The other Glamorgan hero was Alan Jones who hit 105 on the Saturday in a slow Glamorgan innings on an uneasy wicket. Sussex lost the services of Le Roux in the second innings with a groin injury.

In blazing sun, Gloucestershire were thwarted of victory over Derbyshire for whom Mortensen came in to face the last ball of the match with Childs on a hat-trick. Gloucestershire, thanks to Shepherd and Russell, had recovered from 63 for 5 on the Saturday and snatched a first innings lead of 58 on the Monday. This had been consolidated by Hignell and Romaines, who had prospered when given his extended run because of Broad's injury, when they added 142 for the third wicket when Gloucestershire batted again. John Childs nearly brought victory to the home side, but Hill's dogged batting made salvation possible for Derbyshire.

After Hampshire had made a customary solid start Malcolm Marshall hit strongly for his first century of the season which lifted them fiercely to 371 off 92.5 overs. Marshall then accounted for Pauline and Smith before the close and hit Monkhouse on the toe so that he had to retire hurt. Lynch, Knight and Richards balanced the match on Monday, however, with some excellent batting in scorching heat. Greenidge hit his fifth century in six innings as Hampshire scored ferociously in an attempt to force a win, but the wicket was still fine and there was little hope of bowling out Surrey.

A very good day's cricket at Maidstone on the first day saw

ABOVE: *The last Essex wicket falls on the third morning. Phillip is stumped by Humpage off Gifford, giving the former England spinner match figures of 9 for 86. (Ken Kelly)*

RIGHT: *Mike Gatting. Dropped from the England side, he responded with 216 against the New Zealanders at Lord's on 9 July. His leadership of Middlesex throughout the season was outstanding. (Adrian Murrell)*

Bob Woolmer confirm his recent fine form with a cultured century. He breathes permanence and grace when he is at his best. He countered Lancashire alone in the morning when Taylor and Tavare went cheaply, but Aslett gave him good support and, later in the day, Cowdrey played one of his forceful innings.

Lancashire, through Skipper Abrahams, came back from 97 for 5 on the second day after Ellison had caused problems, and, in the end, in spite of another fine innings from Woolmer, Kent were thwarted.

George Sharp raised Northants with a spirited 98 against Yorkshire. He lifted the home side from 117 for 7, and Yorkshire failed to reach 200. Allan Lamb hit a century which must have heartened the England selectors, and Yorkshire were left to make 271 in 260 minutes. They never got to terms with the task. Inevitably, Bairstow batted with a sense that victory was still possible, but David Steele's slow left-arm was probing away at the other batsmen. Dennis and Booth resisted for 10 overs, and Dennis and Taylor for almost 6, but Taylor was caught off Steele and Northants won with three minutes to spare.

A career best 7 for 33 by Kevin Cooper bowled Notts back into the match and shattered Worcestershire, all out for 69, after the home side had bowled out Notts for 176. Robinson batted with great patience and authority on the Monday to put Notts in an impregnable position. Worcestershire threatened to survive, and even win, on the last day, but Mike Hendrick, in a brilliant spell of bowling, took 5 for 0 in 19 balls, leaving Worcestershire still without a victory in the championship and with only Glamorgan below them.

John Player League

10 July

at Cardiff

Glamorgan 162 for 8
Sussex 164 for 5 (C.M. Wells 63)

Sussex (4 pts) won by 5 wickets

at Bristol

Gloucestershire 174 for 6
Derbyshire 176 for 7 (G. Miller) 52)

Derbyshire (4 pts) won by 3 wickets

at Portsmouth

Hampshire 292 for 1 (C.G. Greenidge 108 not out, T.E. Jesty 166 not out)
Surrey 188 for 5 (A.R. Butcher 65, N.G. Cowley 4 for 42)

Hampshire (4 pts) won by 104 runs

at Maidstone

Kent 217 for 7 (C.J. Tavare 59 not out)
Lancashire 154 (D.L. Underwood 5 for 31)

Kent (4 pts) won by 63 runs

at Leicester

Somerset 196 for 9 (I.T. Botham 64, P.W. Denning 55)
Leicestershire 197 for 2 (N.E. Briers 77 not out)

Leicestershire (4 pts) won by 8 wickets

at Tring

Northamptonshire 131 for 9
Yorkshire 132 for 0 (G. Boycott 64 not out, C.W.J. Athey 63 not out)

Yorkshire (4 pts) won by 10 wickets

at Edgbaston

Essex 230 for 7 (K.W.R. Fletcher 54 not out, N. Phillip 51)
Warwickshire 229 for 9 (G.W. Humpage 65)

Essex (4 pts) won by 1 run

at Hereford

Nottinghamshire 195 for 4 (S.B. Hassan 71, C.E.B. Rice 71)
Worcestershire 195 for 9 (P.A. Neale 86)

Match tied
Nottinghamshire 2 pts, Worcestershire 2 pts

Worcestershire needed 6 from the last over bowled by Kevin Cooper in order to beat Notts. Phil Neale's fine innings came

to an end off the first ball of the over when he was run out by Robinson's throw from the boundary and Cooper's accuracy frustrated Moores so that Pridgeon was run out off the last ball in attempting what would have been the winning run.

Sussex and Yorkshire moved into joint position at top of the table with comfortable victories. Yorkshire overwhelmed Northants at Tring, losing no wickets and winning with 5. overs to spare.

Somerset suffered their first defeat of the season and dropped to third place on level terms with Kent. Briers, in an innings full of flourish, and Davison with 46 not out saw Leicestershire to victory with 23 balls to spare.

Kent maintained their challenge when Underwood's unflagging length proved too formidable for Lancashire who fell further and further behind the asking rate of 5.4 an over and sank finally with one ball remaining.

Derbyshire's improvement was given more evidence by win over Gloucestershire. It was a fine team performance in which Miller's all-round cricket was, perhaps, the key factor. Sainsbury bowled the last over with Derbyshire needing 1 to win, but a six over square-leg by Bob Taylor relieved the pressure and victory was achieved with a ball to spare.

Put in to bat at Portsmouth, Hampshire lost Smith at 2. but Greenidge and Jesty then savaged Surrey mercilessly. For once Greenidge was overshadowed as Jesty scored 64 of the last 99 runs which were made in 11 overs. Jesty hit three sixes and eighteen fours in his spectacular innings, and Greenidge hit one six and nine fours. It was majestic stuff and the Surrey innings was, inevitably, an anti-climax.

A wonderful game of cricket at Edgbaston went eventually in favour of Essex. Phillip played a few lusty shots and Fletcher dabbed and pushed to effect, but it was Derek Pringle's innings of 47 which was breathtaking in its immediate and complete dominance of the bowling. He faced only 17 deliveries and 57 runs came in under 15 minutes.

Pringle's bowling was less successful, but he still played a crucial part in the Essex win. Led by Humpage, Warwickshire were moving to success, but some fine fielding and a little bit of panic stopped them short. They needed 23 off the last 3 overs and this proved beyond them, the game being decided before Hogg hit Pringle's last one-pace delivery for six. The outstanding feature of the game was the wicket keeping of David East. He stumped Asif Din off Pringle quite brilliantly on the leg-side and when Lethbridge played forward and 'lost' the ball when it hit his pad East rushed round from behind the stumps and ran him out. It was a lightening reaction and one could remember seeing only Godfrey Evans do something of this nature.

13, 14 and 15 July

at Southend

Essex 202 (B.R. Hardie 67, M.D. Marshall 6 for 73, T.M. Tremlett 4 for 65) and 340 for 6 dec (K.S. McEwan 142, D.R. Pringle 102 not out, M.D. Marshall 4 for 51)
Hampshire 136 (S. Turner 5 for 30, D.R. Pringle 5 for 66 and 410 for 6 (C.L. Smith 163, M.C.J. Nicholas 72, N.E.J. Pocock 52)

Hampshire won by 4 wickets
Hampshire 20 pts, Essex 6 pts

John Abrahams led Lancashire for much of the season in the absence of Clive Lloyd and enjoyed his best year with the bat. (George Herringshaw)

at Swansea

Lancashire 193 (J. Simmons 104, W.W. Davis 5 for 64, M.W.W. Selvey 4 for 48) and 367 for 8 dec (J. Abrahams 85, C. Maynard 55)
Glamorgan 243 (M. Watkinson 6 for 69) and 206 for 6

Match drawn
Glamorgan 6 pts, Lancashire 5 pts

at Bristol

Gloucestershire 176 (P.W. Romaines 59, W.W. Daniel 7 for 61) and 129 (S.P. Hughes 6 for 32)
Middlesex 374 (M.W. Gatting 93, G.D. Barlow 90, P.R. Downton 58)

Middlesex won by an innings and 69 runs
Middlesex 24 pts, Gloucestershire 3 pts

at Maidstone

Somerset 256 (P.M. Roebuck 99) and 173 (I.V.A. Richards 82, G.W. Johnson 5 for 67)
Kent 150 (R.A. Woolmer 64, J. Garner 6 for 37) and 280 for 7 (R.A. Woolmer 110, M.R. Benson 66 not out)

Kent won by 3 wickets
Kent 20 pts, Somerset 6 pts

at Trent Bridge

Nottinghamshire 124 (R.N. Kapil Dev 4 for 24, A. Walker 4 for 61) and 98 (B.J. Griffiths 4 for 37)
Northamptonshire 293 (P. Willey 108, G. Cook 69, K. Saxelby 5 for 57, E.E. Hemmings 4 for 97)

Northamptonshire won by an innings and 71 runs
Northamptonshire 23 pts, Nottinghamshire 1 pt

at Edgbaston

Derbyshire 365 (A. Hill 121, K.J. Barnett 53, N. Gifford 6 for 77) and 41 for 0
Warwickshire 169 (P.A. Smith 57, D.G. Moir 5 for 44, S. Oldham 4 for 56) and 234 (A.M. Ferreira 66, P.A. Smith 65, R.J. Finney 5 for 58)

Derbyshire won by 10 wickets
Derbyshire 22 pts, Warwickshire 2 pts

at Hereford

Worcestershire 228 (R.K. Illingworth 55) and 205 (D.N. Patel 54, P.A. Neale 50)
Leicestershire 198 (J.C. Balderstone 100 not out, D.N. Patel 5 for 57) and 238 for 5 (J.C. Balderstone 63)

Leicestershire won by 5 wickets
Leicestershire 21 pts, Worcestershire 6 pts

at Leeds

Sussex 185 (A.C.S. Pigott 57 not out, N.S. Taylor 5 for 49) and 238 (Imran Khan 83)
Yorkshire 197 (A.C.S. Pigott 5 for 63) and 162 for 7

Match drawn
Yorkshire 5 pts, Sussex 5 pts

Tim Tremlett of Hampshire. His advance as a seam bowler and reliable late order batsman had much to do with Hampshire's success. He enjoyed a magnificent season and played a vital part in Hampshire's historic victory over Essex at Southend, 13–15 July. (George Herringshaw)

Chris Balderstone. 100 not out and 63 for Leicestershire against Worcestershire at Hereford, 13–15 July, and left out of Leicestershire's next match for disciplinary reasons. (George Herringshaw)

At Southchurch Park, Southend, Pocock won the toss and asked Essex to bat first on a good wicket. On a steamy day, with the estuary tide coming in, Malcolm Marshall and Tim Tremlett gave sense to Pocock's decision as Essex tumbled from 137 for 1 to 202 all out against some first rate seam bowling. Marshall, a highly intelligent bowler, cut down his run and his pace to exploit the conditions and Tremlett, an equally intelligent and courteous young man, found the scene eminently suited to him. By the end of the day, however, Stuart Turner, a wily old fox himself, and Derek Pringle, learning rapidly under good tutelage, had bowled Essex into command as Hampshire closed on 88 for 8.

The next day belonged entirely to Essex. McEwan, with the panache expected of him, and Pringle, much more laboriously, reached centuries of different character and Fletcher declared leaving Hampshire a target of 407.

When Turner had Greenidge lbw early on the last day it seemed that Essex would cruise to victory, but Smith and Nicholas, at first stoically and then with more adventure, added 188. Smith went on to reach his fifth championship century of the summer and when he was out in the third of the last twenty overs Hampshire were only 83 runs short of victory. Pocock played a fierce innings and Hampshire won a memorable victory with five deliveries to spare.

It was the first time since the second world war that a side had scored 400 in the fourth innings to win a championship match and the first time that Hampshire had ever achieved such a feat.

Warwickshire too stumbled in their pursuit of Middlesex and suffered their first defeat in eight matches. The match hinged on a relentless century from Alan Hill on the opening day, an innings which failed to please the locals, but which certainly gave Derbyshire a basis for victory. In spite of more fine bowling by Gifford, Derbyshire batted into the second

day. The first hundred overs of their innings had produced only 213 runs.

Warwickshire batted on a wicket that was crumbling and failed to withstand Moir's slow left arm spin so that they followed-on 196 runs behind. They avoided the indignity of an innings defeat, but Finney, with his left-arm medium pace, produced a career best performance and Derbyshire needed only 39 runs to win.

Meanwhile, Middlesex took advantage of the slips by their challengers to increase their lead to 26 points. They took command of the game at Bristol from the start. Daniel bowled a firm line on off-stump, moved the occasional ball away and was quick. Only Romaines and Wright offered any serious resistance to him and the home side were out for 176. By the end of the day, Middlesex had lost Slack and Radley, but the Gloucestershire lead was only 26. Next day, Barlow and Gatting hammered their way into the nineties, Downton and Williams made late flourishes and Middlesex took maximum batting points. Hughes and Daniel swept Gloucestershire aside more contemptuously in the second innings than they had done in the first, and the Schweppes County Championship looked very much as if it would stay at Lord's.

Glamorgan had dreams of their first win in the match with Lancashire, but ultimately, it was Arthur Francis who fought to stave off defeat. Winston Davis and Mike Selvey bowled with a combination of pace and accuracy to reduce Lancashire to 74 for 8. Forty-two year old Jack Simmons then hit the fourth century of his sixteen-year career in first-class cricket. It was a rumbustious knock, his 104 coming off 132 balls in 124 minutes. Facing 193, more than they had expected, Glamorgan managed a lead of 50, but Lancashire were not to be rushed out a second time and solid batting throughout the order led them to leave Glamorgan a target of 318 in 210 minutes, hardly generous, but Abrahams had been overcautious for most of the summer. Glamorgan flirted dangerously for a time and then Francis, Rowe, Eifion Jones and sense prevailed.

Worcestershire, also in search of a victory, recovered from 97 for 6 to reach 228 at Hereford, and the next day they took an unexpected lead as Patel and Illingworth spun their overs away at a rate of more than 26 an hour. Throughout this effort to avoid being fined, Balderstone batted with grim determination and carried his bat through an innings for the first time in his career which has now lasted for 23 seasons. Worcestershire buoyantly extended their lead to 143 for the loss of only two wickets by the close, but the next day they disintegrated against Ferris and Taylor. Needing 236 to win, Leicestershire reached the last twelve overs needing 73 which were obtained by Whitaker and Clift. Whitaker, a hard-hitting eighteen-year old Yorkshireman, was replacing Gower, on Test duty, in the Leicestershire side.

Northants overwhelmed Notts for whom nothing seemed to be going right. Kapil Dev returned from the World Cup celebrations in India to join with young Walker in routing Notts on the first day and after Willey and Cook had played watchful innings, Notts succumbed more readily at the second attempt than they had done at the first. Well as Griffiths bowled, Notts' lack of application contributed much to their defeat in two days. Their sole bit of encouragement in a match from which they took only one point was Saxelby's career best of 5 for 57.

Roebuck batted dourly for six hours at Maidstone only to fall to a catch on the square-leg boundary one short of his century. Kent surrendered a first innings lead of 106 when Joel Garner tore them apart on the second day, only Bob Woolmer, with sound technique and unrelenting concentration, showing the application necessary to withstand the West Indian. Even though Johnson and Underwood bowled out Somerset a second time, Richards alone defying them, it seemed that the task of scoring 280 to win would be too much for Kent especially as they lost Taylor before the close. On the last day, however, Bob Woolmer played another innings of judgement and calm as Kent's rock, Mark Benson gave more evidence of his maturity and Somerset fielded very badly and bowled only marginally better so that the home side reached victory with three wickets in hand, a most commendable effort.

A slow moving game at Headingley seemed to be moving Yorkshire's way before Imran Khan batted with a positivity lacking elsewhere and the home side were left to make 227 in 250 minutes. Boycott and Moxon were out for 11, two of the fourteen lbw decisions given in the match, and a rather melancholy game ended with Yorkshire 65 runs and Sussex 3 wickets short of victory.

THE FIRST TEST MATCH: ENGLAND v. NEW ZEALAND

England called up Neil Foster, the young and very promising Essex fast bowler as a replacement for the injured Graham Dilley, but it was Foster who was left out on the first morning when it was decided to play both spinners.

England won the toss and Fowler and Tavare began cautiously in fine weather. In the seventh over, Fowler played half back when he would have been better forward and was lbw. Gower gave hint of beauties to come with two elegant leg-side boundries and then, to his obvious chagrin, chopped a ball from Hadlee into his stumps when it lifted more than he had expected. After 40 minutes, England were 18 for 2 and would have been in a worse position had Coney not dropped a straightforward catch at second slip offered by Lamb off the bowling of Cairns.

Lamb and Tavare, who had taken half an hour to open his score, added 49 and then Lamb was bowled by a ball from Cairns which straightened late at him. Tavare was hit in the mouth and retired, bleeding, for treatment. 85 for 3 at lunch.

Botham looked in good form, but he aimed a vicious square drive at Hadlee and dragged the ball back into his stumps. In the next over, Marks, not looking as if this was a situation compatible to his abilities, was caught behind off his glove. 116 for 5, and Tavare returned.

He showed growing confidence and a willingness to hit the ball in partnership with Randall, but when he drove Martin Crowe into the covers Wright made a brilliant stop and return to run him out before he could regain his ground.

Howarth had marshalled his resources splendidly and Hadlee bowled quite magnificently although some of the batting was below what one expects at Test level. Bracewell got some turn with his off-breaks and helped Hadlee to mop up the tail, Randall remained undefeated and belligerent on 75.

With a real opportunity to inflict defeat on England, New Zealand's nerve failed. Off the third ball of the innings,

Wright was superbly caught by Gower in the gully as Willis made a straight ball lift fiercely. Jeff Crowe was caught at slip in Willis' next over off a poor shot and Howarth was bowled by Cowans who, like his captain, bowled very quickly. At 6.10 bad light stopped play and New Zealand were 17 for 3 off 17 overs and 2 balls, their two best batsmen were gone.

Willis began the next day as he had finished the first. He beat Martin Crowe for pace and knocked his off stump out of the ground without a run added.

Edgar had battled on without ever looking convincing and, at 41, he was fifth out when he unwisely tried to cut a lifting ball from Willis.

This brought together Coney and Hadlee, a fine blend of practical common sense and fierce aggression. Hadlee drove Edmonds from the attack and was hard on Botham's early stint. 84 runs came in 15 overs, a stark contrast to what had gone before, before Coney pushed the ball to Willis at mid-on and the England skipper, with unexpected athleticism, hit the one stump he could see. Coney had paid the price for underestimating Willis in the field.

Hadlee continued to blast away and had good support from Warren Lees until he was well caught and bowled by Botham. Hadlee had hit 84 from 78 deliveries. To their surprise, England had a first innings lead of 13.

This was soon extended into match-winning size by Fowler and Tavare who were still there at the close, 146 for 0, achieved in 54 overs.

Richard Hadlee. Man of the Match. 8 for 152 and innings of 84 and 11. (Adrian Murrell)

ABOVE: *The England side for the first Test match at The Oval. (l. to r.) Fowler, Marks, Tavare, Cowans, Edmonds and Lamb. (front row) Taylor, Gower, Willis (captain), Botham and Randall.* BELOW: *Chris Tavare is run out, one of five run outs in the match. He was the victim of brilliant work by John Wright.* RIGHT: *Ian Botham's look of horror at dragging a ball from Richard Hadlee on to his wicket.* (Ken Kelly)

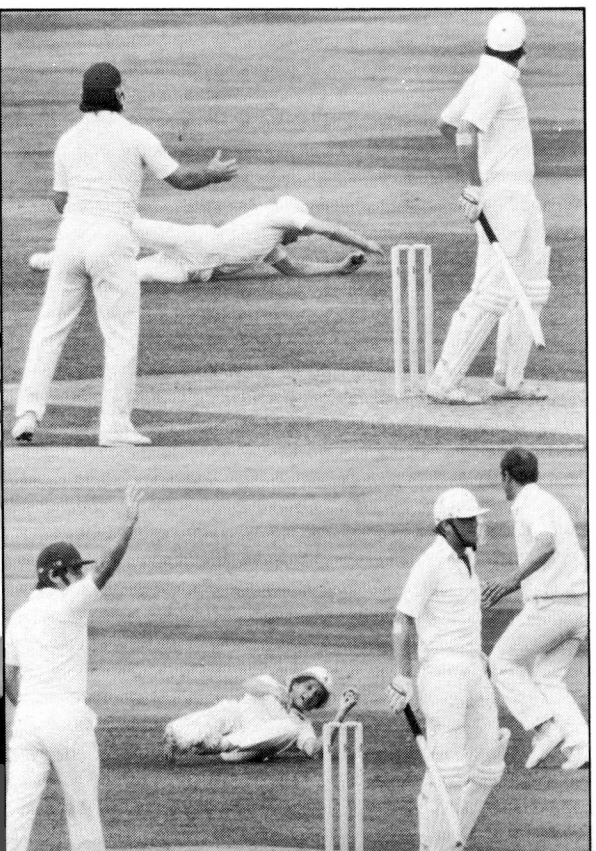

ABOVE: *New Zealand on top. Bob Taylor is batting surrounded by eager fielders.* LEFT: *John Wright is brilliantly caught by the diving Gower off Bob Willis and the New Zealanders have begun disastrously.* BELOW: *Chris Tavare hits to leg during his innings of 109 in his record partnership of 223 with Graeme Fowler. (Ken Kelly).*

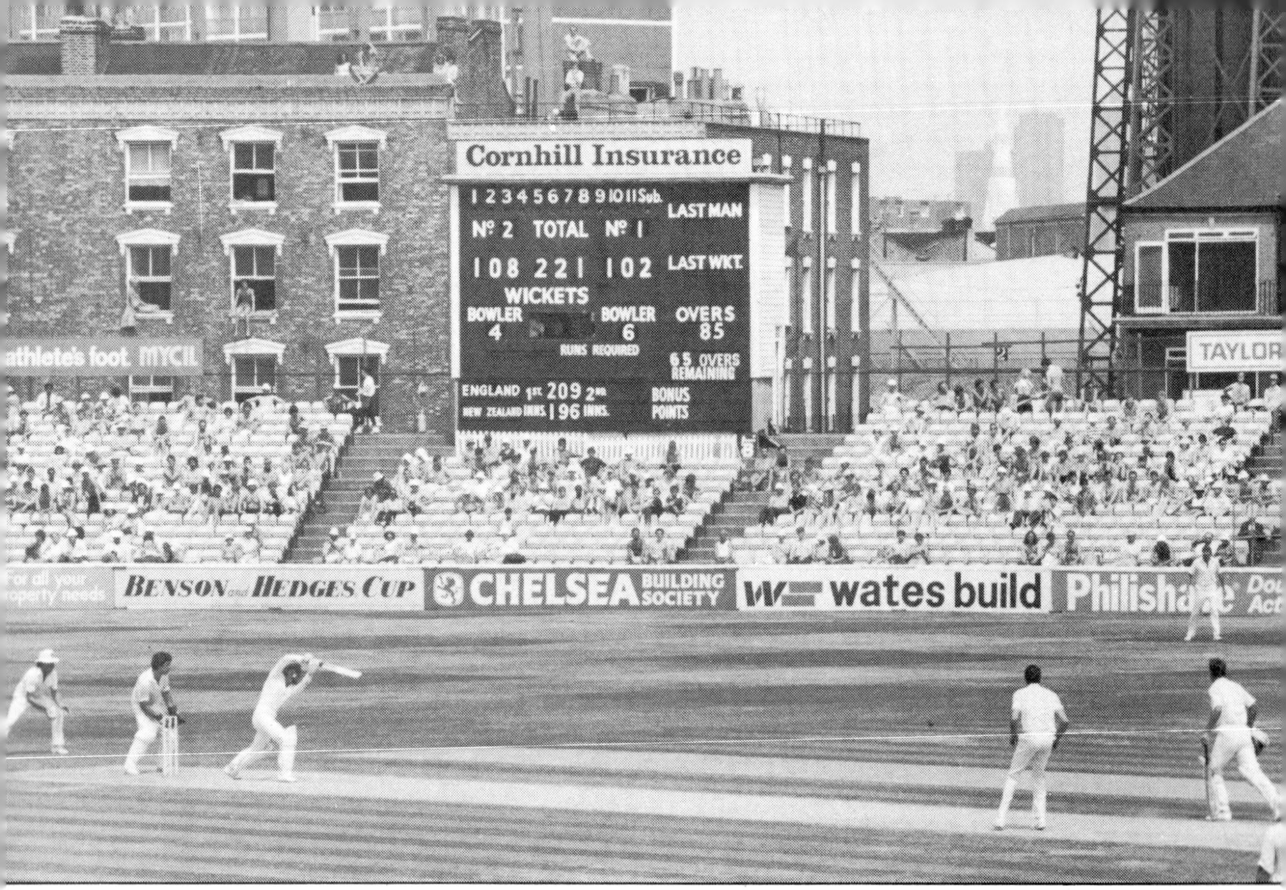

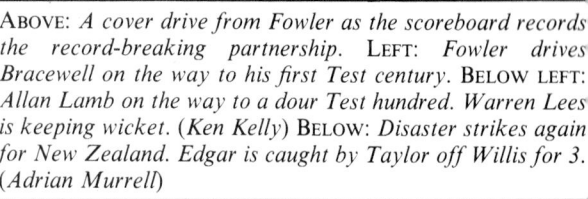

Cornhill Insurance
1 2 3 4 5 6 7 8 9 10 11 Sub.
LAST MAN
No 2 TOTAL No 1
108 221 102
LAST WKT.
WICKETS
BOWLER 4
BOWLER 6
OVERS 85
RUNS REQUIRED
65 OVERS REMAINING
ENGLAND 1st INNS. 209 2nd INNS.
NEW ZEALAND 196
BONUS POINTS
athlete's foot MYCIL
TAYLOR
BENSON and HEDGES CUP
CHELSEA BUILDING SOCIETY
wates build

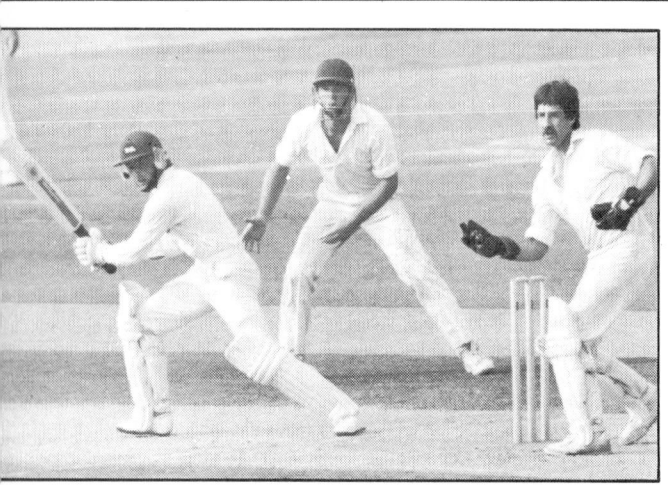

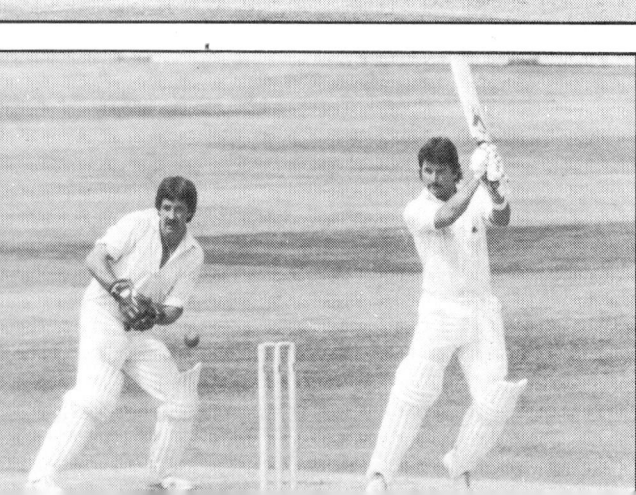

ABOVE: *A cover drive from Fowler as the scoreboard records the record-breaking partnership.* LEFT: *Fowler drives Bracewell on the way to his first Test century.* BELOW LEFT: *Allan Lamb on the way to a dour Test hundred. Warren Lees is keeping wicket.* (*Ken Kelly*) BELOW: *Disaster strikes again for New Zealand. Edgar is caught by Taylor off Willis for 3.* (*Adrian Murrell*)

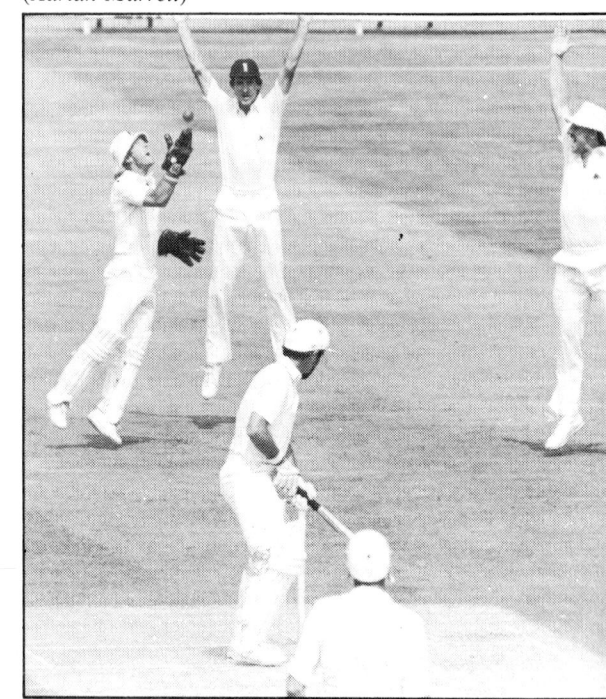

Next day they became the first England openers for twenty-three years to score centuries in the same innings. Tavare was first out, having batted 312 minutes for his 109 in the stand of 223. Fowler departed 12 minutes later. The stage was set for a thrilling afternoon of strokes; sadly, what we saw was dross.

Gower was out of touch and Botham was foolishly run out by Lamb who played an innings of the utmost tedium and one which was likely to drive away more paying customers and so put county cricket in further jeopardy. On a gloriously hot Saturday, with the biggest crowd of the match anticipating pleasure, England scored only 194 runs. It was unforgivable.

Lamb reached his century on the Sunday and Willis declared at 446 for 6 so setting New Zealand a target of 460, by history and in the context of the match impossible. Such views were confirmed when Edgar and Jeff Crowe fell to the magnificently combative Willis with only 25 scored.

Wright and Howarth gave hope with batting of composure, but the next day, having added 16 to the overnight score, they were concerned in a dreadful piece of indecision which saw Wright run out by Tavare for a valiant 88.

Howarth and Martin Crowe countered the wiles of Marks and Edmonds with some relish, but Howarth made a rare mistake when he pushed forward limply at Edmonds and was caught behind. Coney was lbw offering no stroke and Martin Crowe was beaten by one that turned and took the outside edge. Hadlee went the same way to what was to him a leg-break and but for Cairns' last mighty blows of defiance that was the end of New Zealand.

Their consolation was that Hadlee, rightly, was named Man of the Match, but they must have wondered whether ever again they would be in such a good position as they were on the first afternoon when, on a fair wicket, they had bowled England out for 209.

ABOVE: *Howarth in dejection. Wright gives him a consoling pat. (Adrian Murrell)*

Martin Crowe is caught by Taylor off Edmonds for 33. (Adrian Murrell)

The end is nigh. Coney lbw, bowled Marks for 2. (Adrian Murrell)

FIRST TEST MATCH – ENGLAND v. NEW ZEALAND
14, 15, 16, 17 and 18 July 1983 at The Oval

ENGLAND

	FIRST INNINGS		SECOND INNINGS	
G. Fowler	lbw, b Hadlee	1	run out	105
C.J. Tavare	run out	45	c Howarth, b Bracewell	109
D.I. Gower	b Hadlee	11	c Howarth, b Hadlee	25
A.J. Lamb	b Cairns	24	not out	102
I.T. Botham	b Hadlee	15	run out	26
D.W. Randall	not out	75	c Coney, b Hadlee	3
V.J. Marks	c Lees, b Hadlee	4	c M. Crowe, b Bracewell	2
P.H. Edmonds	c and b Bracewell	12	not out	43
R.W. Taylor*	lbw, b Hadlee	0		
R.G.D. Willis†	c J. Crowe, b Bracewell	4		
N.G. Cowans	b Hadlee	3		
Extras	b 6, lb 6, nb 3	15	b 8, lb 23	31
		209	(for 6 wkts dec)	446

	O	M	R	W	O	M	R	W
Hadlee	23.4	6	53	6	37.2	7	99	2
Chatfield	17	3	48	—	35	9	85	—
Cairns	17	3	63	1	30	7	67	—
Bracewell	8	4	16	2	54	13	115	2
M.D. Crowe	5	—	14	—	3	—	9	—
Coney					27	11	39	—
Howarth					3	2	1	—

FALL OF WICKETS
1- 2, 2- 18, 3- 67, 4- 104, 5- 116, 6- 154, 7- 184, 8- 191, 9- 202
1- 223, 2- 225, 3- 269, 4- 322, 5- 329, 6- 336

NEW ZEALAND

	FIRST INNINGS		SECOND INNINGS	
J.G. Wright	c Gower, b Willis	0	(2) run out	88
B.A. Edgar	c Taylor, b Willis	12	(1) c Taylor, b Willis	3
J.J. Crowe	c Randall, b Willis	0	c Lamb, b Willis	9
G.P. Howarth†	b Cowans	4	c Taylor, b Edmonds	67
M.D. Crowe	b Willis	0	c Taylor, b Edmonds	33
J.V. Coney	run out	44	lbw, b Marks	2
R.J. Hadlee	c and b Botham	84	c Taylor, b Marks	11
J.G. Bracewell	c and b Botham	7	(9) c Gower, b Marks	0
W.K. Lees*	not out	31	(8) run out	8
B.L. Cairns	c Lamb, b Botham	2	c Willis, b Edmonds	32
E.J. Chatfield	c Willis, b Botham	0	not out	10
Extras	lb 6, nb 6	12	b 3, lb 1, nb 3	7
		196		270

	O	M	R	W	O	M	R	W
Willis	20	8	43	4	12	3	26	2
Cowans	19	3	60	1	11	2	41	—
Botham	16	2	62	4	4	—	17	—
Edmonds	2	—	19	—	40.1	16	101	3
Marks					43	20	78	3

FALL OF WICKETS
1- 0, 2- 1, 3- 10, 4- 17, 5- 41, 6- 125, 7- 149, 8- 182, 9- 188
1- 10, 2- 26, 3- 146, 4- 197, 5- 202, 6- 210, 7- 228, 8- 228, 9- 228

Umpires: H.D. Bird and D.G.L. Evans

England won by 189 runs

at Old Trafford

Worcestershire 280 (P.A. Neale 139) and 254 for 5 (P.A. Neale 64, D.N. Patel 53)
Lancashire 440 (J. Abrahams 178, D. Lloyd 79)

Match drawn
Lancashire 6 pts, Worcestershire 4 pts

at Lord's

Middlesex 292 (R.O. Butcher 62, M.W. Gatting 54, W.N. Slack 52) and 191 for 4 dec (J.E. Emburey 73 not out, W.N. Slack 55)
Leicestershire 160 (J.E. Emburey 4 for 8, W.W. Daniel 4 for 50) and 143 (J.E. Emburey 4 for 14)

Middlesex won by 180 runs
Middlesex 23 pts, Leicestershire 4 pts

at Taunton

Somerset 342 for 6 dec (I.V.A. Richards 142 not out, P.M. Roebuck 58) and 223 for 7 dec (I.V.A. Richards 76, P.I. Pocock 7 for 79)
Surrey 253 (M.A. Lynch 78, R.D.V. Knight 52) and 252 for 9 (R.D.V. Knight 64, J.W. Lloyds 5 for 120)

Match drawn
Somerset 8 pts, Surrey 5 pts

A valiant and intelligent skipper. Geoff Howarth. (Adrian Murrell)

16, 17 and 18 July

at Derby

Northamptonshire 439 for 4 dec (W. Larkins 236, R.J. Boyd-Moss 80, R.G. Williams 73 not out)
Derbyshire 251 (K.J. Barnett 103) and 196 for 3 (I.S. Anderson 91, K.J. Barnett 53 not out)

Match drawn
Northamptonshire 8 pts, Derbyshire 3 pts

16, 18 and 19 July

at Southend

Essex (K.R. Pont 125 not out, K.S. McEwan 104)
Glamorgan 116 (D.R. Pringle 4 for 22, N.A. Foster 4 for 32) and 240 (R.C. Ontong 79)

Essex won by an innings and 3 runs
Essex 24 pts, Glamorgan 4 pts

at Bournemouth

Nottinghamshire 233 (C.E.B. Rice 79, M.D. Marshall 4 for 70) and 238 (C.E.B. Rice 68, S.B. Hassan 53, J.W. Southern 5 for 75)
Hampshire 404 for 6 dec (V.P. Terry 106 not out, T.E. Jesty 86, C.G. Greenidge 63, N.E.J. Pocock 59) and 68 for 2

Hampshire won by 8 wickets
Hampshire 24 pts, Nottinghamshire 4 pts

Graham Gooch. 176 for Essex against Glamorgan at Southend, 17 July. The highest score ever hit in the John Player League. (George Herringshaw)

Nick Pocock. An inspiring captain who led Hampshire to exciting victories at Southend and Bournemouth. (George Herringshaw)

Paul Terry. His 106 not out for Hampshire against Notts a Bournemouth, 18 July, was the second century of his career an further testimony to his growing powers as a batsman. (Georg Herringshaw)

at Sheffield

Kent 424 for 5 dec (E.A. Baptiste 136 not out, C.S. Cowdrey 113, R.A. Woolmer 61)
Yorkshire 270 (G. Boycott 101, R.M. Ellison 4 for 59) and 121 for 6

Match drawn
Kent 8 pts, Yorkshire 3 pts

Middlesex continued their winning way, but they paid a terrible price for the victory over Leicestershire. In the second innings, Roland Butcher was hit in the face by a ball from George Ferris and taken to hospital with a fractured cheek bone, a fractured bone around the eye and shock. It was deemed as unlikely that he would play again during the season. His loss to Middlesex as batsman and fielder, 37 catches already during the season, was immense. He had been top scorer in the first innings as Middlesex groped their way a little, but the spin of Emburey and the pace of Daniel had proved too much for Leicestershire who decided to omit Balderstone 'for disciplinary reasons'. Emburey proved himself with the bat at the second attempt, and it was he, supported by Daniel and Williams, who bowled Middlesex to victory.

Essex reasserted their challenge when, after two successive defeats, they swamped Glamorgan at Southend. They lost Gooch, Hardie and Fletcher on the opening morning for 61 runs, but McEwan and Pont added 118 and both batsmen

went on to reach centuries. Runs came briskly and Hopkin fell to Foster before the close.

On the Monday, even without the injured Lever, they took 18 more Glamorgan wickets and the match lasted only te minutes on the third day when an obstinate last wicket stand of 59 between Francis and Davis was ended by Foster who had 7 for 82 in the match.

Wayne Larkins led a massive attack on the Derbyshire bowling at Derby. Kim Barnett won the toss and put North ants in. Larkins responded with a career best 236, the highes score of the summer. Cook was able to declare at 439 for after only 98 overs. Kim Barnett's valiant century on th Sunday failed to save the follow-on, but Anderson's tenacity another good knock from Barnett and a storm eventuall saved the game for Derbyshire.

Once more Nick Pocock chose to give the opposition firs use of the wicket when he won the toss at Bournemouth an Malcolm Marshall justified his captain's decision wit another fine spell of bowling. The Notts' batting, Rice apart looked feeble and Hampshire quickly consolidated thei strong position on the Monday when Paul Terry hit th second century of his career and savaged the Notts attac along with Greenidge, Jesty and Pocock. Terry's hundre was the nineteenth hit for Hampshire in the season, testi mony to their great batting strength.

Southern's left-arm spin wore down Notts on the last da and the visitors slumped from 160 for 2 to 238 all out. On wearing wicket, Hampshire scored the 68 runs they neede for victory in just over an hour.

Phil Neale played two fine captain's innings for Worcestershire at Old Trafford, joining with Patel to save them from defeat. Lancashire, 264 for 3 after 100 overs, scored 176 in another 42 in an effort to force an innings win. John Abrahams, enjoying a fine season, reached a career best 178 in 384 minutes, hitting a six and twenty fours.

Somerset were also frustrated. Viv Richards led them to a good first innings score and they bowled out Surrey to lead by 89. Richards again scored briskly, but Pat Pocock took the honours when he captured all seven wickets to fall before the declaration. Surrey needed 313 to win, and there was an early hint that they could achieve that target, but the spin of Lloyds and Richards, and Richards' astute captaincy, brought wickets so that in the end Curtis and Mackintosh held out for a draw through 4 very tense overs.

A change in the weather which brought rain and cloud thwarted Kent at Abbeydale, Sheffield. A glorious stand of 228 in 50 overs for the fifth wicket between Cowdrey and Baptiste who both hit career bests asserted Kent's authority on the opening day. Thereafter, in spite of a typical Boycott hundred, Yorkshire were always struggling and were thankful for the bad light and the rain.

John Player League

17 July

at Southend

Essex 310 for 5 (G.A. Gooch 176, D.R. Pringle 52 not out)
Glamorgan 254 for 4 (R.C. Ontong 73 not out, Javed Miandad 68)

Essex (4 pts) won by 56 runs

at Moreton-in-Marsh

Warwickshire 174 for 9
Gloucestershire 178 for 4 (Zaheer Abbas 64 not out, P.W. Romaines 57)

Gloucestershire (4 pts) won by 6 wickets

at Portsmouth

Hampshire 242 for 6 (C.G. Greenidge 80)
Nottinghamshire 186 for 6 (R.T. Robinson 74)

Hampshire (4 pts) won by 56 runs

at Old Trafford

Lancashire 142 for 8 (C.H. Lloyd 52)
Worcestershire 142 for 5 (D.B. d'Oliveira 51 not out)

Match tied
Lancashire 2 pts, Worcestershire 2 pts

at Lord's

Middlesex 231 for 5 (M.W. Gatting 56)
Leicestershire 204 (B.F. Davison 71, W.N. Slack 5 for 32)

Middlesex (4 pts) won by 27 runs

at Scarborough

Kent 8 for 0 v **Yorkshire**
Match abandoned
Kent 2 pts, Yorkshire 2 pts

Only one over was possible at Scarborough and at Old Trafford rain restricted the match to 19 overs an innings. There was some fine batting by Clive Lloyd and Frank Hayes, and they were matched by Damian d'Oliveira who was dropped, crucially, in the sixteenth over. He and Inchmore scrambled a bye off the last ball of the match to level the scores and give Worcestershire their second tie in successive weeks.

Wilf Slack bowled top scorer Brian Davison and turned the whole course of the game at Lord's with his best figures in the competition. Leicestershire were cruising to victory but collapsed from 147 for 2 to 204 all out, losing by 27 runs with eight balls to spare.

The formidable Hampshire batting was too strong for Notts in spite of Robinson's 74 off 86 balls, and Warwickshire fell again with Zaheer and Romaines continuing recent form for Gloucestershire.

It was Southend, however, where events dominated. In a magnificent display of controlled aggression, Graham Gooch beat Wayne Larkins' month old John Player League record with an innings of 172 which included a six and twenty-eight fours and lasted for 126 minutes. He faced only 117 deliveries and was run out by his partner Pringle on the ball after he had hit his record breaking four. Pringle ran out Stuart Turner without facing a ball, but compensated by scoring fifty and taking Essex to 310, the highest score ever made in the John Player League. Javed Miandad and Ontong scored fifties in Glamorgan's lost cause innings, and the seven days cricket at Southchurch Park, Southend, confirmed what many had felt in 1982 that Cedric Simpson, the curator, provides one of the very best wickets in the country.

20, 21 and 22 July

at Worcester

New Zealanders 246 (R.J. Hadlee 68, M.D. Crowe 65, J.D. Inchmore 5 for 82) and 210 for 6 dec
Worcestershire 200 (D.B. d'Oliveira 77, M.S.A. McEvoy 54) and 156 (R.J. Hadlee 4 for 42)

New Zealanders won by 100 runs

The New Zealanders gained their first win of the tour, but their joy was somewhat tempered by complaints about the Worcester wicket. The tourists were 71 for 7 on the first day, but Martin Crowe added to his growing reputation with an innings of great concentration and Richard Hadlee, in more flamboyant style, added 122. Cairns and Snedden also hit well and the tourists' 246 proved too much for Worcestershire for whom d'Oliveira again showed an admirable temperament and for whom McEvoy played with commendable good sense. New Zealanders added 115 before lunch on the last morning and then declared leaving the home side 4 hours in which to make 257. Hadlee, bowling quite fiercely, reduced them to 88 for 6, but Humphries and Inchmore followed the promising Banks in hitting strongly. After tea, however, the innings folded, and with Curtis injured, the New Zealanders won comfortably.

Chris Cowdrey. His 122 not out for Kent against Essex at Chelmsford in the second round of the NatWest Trophy was an innings of excitement, courage and quality and brought him the Man of the Match award. (Adrian Murrell)

NatWest Trophy – Round 2

20 July

at Chelmsford

Kent 274 for 8 (C.S. Cowdrey 122 not out)
Essex 270 for 9 (G.A. Gooch 122, B.R. Hardie 61, R.M. Ellison 4 for 54)

Kent won by 4 runs
(Man of the Match – C.S. Cowdrey)

at Swansea

Hampshire 294 for 5 (C.G. Greenidge 108, T.E. Jesty 84)
Glamorgan 138 (N.G. Cowley 4 for 21)

Hampshire won by 156 runs
(Man of the Match – T.E. Jesty)

at Old Trafford

Lancashire 163 for 6
Somerset 164 for 2 (N.F.M. Popplewell 68 not out)

Somerset won by 8 wickets
(Man of the Match – N.F.M. Popplewell)

at Leicester

Leicestershire 302 for 5 (D.I. Gower 138 not out, B.F. Davison 68)
Gloucestershire 306 for 6 (Zaheer Abbas 158)

Gloucestershire won by 4 wickets
(Man of the Match – Zaheer Abbas)

at Derby

Middlesex 240 for 8 (G.D. Barlow 62)
Derbyshire 210 (K.J. Barnett 88, N.F. Williams 4 for 36)

Middlesex won by 30 runs
(Man of the Match – K.J. Barnett)

at The Oval

Surrey 138
Warwickshire 143 for 1 (T.A. Lloyd 55 not out)

(Man of the Match – T.A. Lloyd)

at Hove

Sussex 227 for 7 (Imran Khan 114 not out)
Nottinghamshire 151 for 8

Sussex won by 76 runs
(Man of the Match – Imran Khan)

at Leeds

Northamptonshire 211 for 7 (A.J. Lamb 76)
Yorkshire 185 (C.W.J. Athey 54, B.J. Griffiths 5 for 33)

Northamptonshire won by 46 runs
(Man of the Match – B.J. Griffiths)

The second round of the NatWest Trophy saw the exit of the holders, Surrey. Willis won the toss and asked Surrey to bat on a morning that was helpful to seam bowling. The Warwickshire bowlers exploited the conditions well, Surrey batted poorly, with Clinton being run out in a ghastly mix-up, and Kailicharran held three catches at second slip. Warwickshire won with the same ease that they had lost the final the previous year to the same opponents.

Hampshire also gained an easy win. Greenidge set them on the way to success with a six and thirteen fours in his 108, but he was dropped off Malcolm Nash when 9. Trevor Jesty completed the rout of Glamorgan with three sixes and eight fours in his 84 which was scored off 91 deliveries. He followed this with the wickets of Ontong, Francis and Rowe to take the individual award.

An uneven batting display from Northants who owed much to Allan Lamb's fierce 76 and some equally valuable hitting at the close by George Sharp still proved too much for Yorkshire. The home county lost 3 for 21 before Athey and Hartley revived hope with 79 in 25 overs, but Griffiths returned to take three wickets in seven balls and win the match.

At Old Trafford, Lancashire called up coach Peter Lever and he bowled a most economic spell, but Lancashire's batting, after Botham had put them in, was pretty poor, and Somerset won with contemptuous ease by eight wickets with 7.1 overs to spare. Popplewell made the final flourish, but the Somerset bowling really won the day.

A responsible and firmly struck hundred from Imran Khan, benefiting from Hassan missing a simple catch when he was on 20, rescued Sussex from 29 for 3, and, with Colin Wells and Gould giving good support, took them to 227. Nottinghamshire never approached the target. They lost wickets at regular intervals and ended in rather spiritless fashion.

Middlesex had to struggle to beat Derbyshire. They got off to a fine start with a stand of 113 with Holding bowling off a short run and still, seemingly, far from fit. Then they slumped to 139 for 4, but Tomlins and Emburey stopped the slide and there were minor contributions from Downton, Edmonds and Daniel so that Derbyshire faced 240.

Barnett and Anderson began with a stand of 72, then Barnett and Hampshire added 58 for the third wicket. As long as Barnett survived, Derbyshire had a chance of winning, but when the young man who has done so much to restore his county's fortunes was caught off Williams, Middlesex were home in the gloom.

At Chelmsford, Essex relived ghosts from the haunted past of failure. Kent had made a steady start and then slumped to 75 for 3 and the batsmen struggling against searching bowling by Turner and Phillip. Tavare and Cowdrey revived fortunes with a stand of 70 in 19 overs, but then there was a dramatic collapse before Foster's speed and Gooch's accuracy, and with Kent at 182 for 7, Essex were very much on top. But 72 runs came off the last 15 overs with Pringle sprinkling no-balls about liberally. Cowdrey was splendid. He took on responsibility, hit hard and reached his highest score for Kent in any competition with three sixes and fifteen fours.

Gooch and Hardie soon reasserted Essex authority in an opening stand of 147. Gooch was as solid and forceful as he had been the previous Sunday. He moved down the wicket to drive with the greatest power and there seemed no halting him. He and Fletcher took the score to 210 before Gooch, aiming a too adventurous drive, was caught behind off Baptiste. Essex, however, were still firmly in command. With the departure of Gooch, who hit eighteen fours, however, things

Zaheer Abbas in training. His innings of 158 in the NatWest Trophy second round match at Leicester devastated the home side and brought Gloucestershire a memorable victory. (Adrian Murrell)

Jim Griffiths, Man of the Match at Headingley. Three wickets in seven balls against Yorkshire gave the match to Northants. (George Herringshaw)

began to go wrong. Fletcher was bowled by Underwood in the forty-ninth over. Two overs later McEwan also fell to Underwood and Pont went to Ellison without scoring, but still only 31 were needed from 7 overs with five creditable wickets left.

Phillip and Pringle scraped towards the target, and on 262, Phillip was caught driving at Ellison. Thirteen runs were needed and fourteen balls were left. Ellison bowled a maiden.

When the last over started, Essex needed 6 to win with 3 wickets standing. Ellison bowled David East with the third ball and Pringle, swinging despairingly, with the last. Ellison had taken 4 for 12 in his last four overs and Kent had won a dramatic victory.

There was an equally dramatic win at Leicester where the home side seemed safe after Gower, with a magnificent hundred, had shared a third wicket stand of 113 with Davison and later taken Leicestershire past 300.

Gloucestershire lost Romaines and Stovold for 23, but Zaheer Abbas took over in a blistering attack upon the bowling. He shared stands of 117 with Bainbridge and 94 with Hignell. He was fifth out at 274 which left Gloucestershire needing 29 in 7.2 overs. The loss of Graveney for 0 caused concern, and they reached the last two overs needing 8. Russell hit six off the penultimate over, by Parsons, and Shepherd drove the third ball of the last over to the boundary to win the match, one of the great wins in Gloucestershire's history.

BENSON and HEDGES CUP 1983

MARYLEBONE CRICKET CLUB

FINAL

15p

ESSEX v. MIDDLESEX

15p

at Lord's Ground, Saturday, July 23rd, 1983

Any alterations to teams will be announced over the loudspeaker system

ESSEX

1 G. A. Gooch	c Downton b Williams	46
2 B. R. Hardie	c Downton b Cowans	49
3 K. S. McEwan	c Cowans b Edmonds	34
‡4 K. W. R. Fletcher	c Radley b Edmonds	3
5 K. R. Pont	hit wicket b Williams	7
6 D. R. Pringle	l b w b Daniel	16
7 S. Turner	c sub b Cowans	9
*8 D. E. East	c Gatting b Cowans	5
9 R. E. East	run out	0
10 N. A. Foster	b Cowans	0
11 J. K. Lever	not out	0
	B , l-b 12, w 3, n-b 8, ...	23
	Total...	192

FALL OF THE WICKETS
1...79 2...127 3...135 4...151 5...156 6...185 7...187 8...191 9...192 10...192

Bowling Analysis	O.	M.	R.	W.	Wd.	N-b
Daniel	11	2	34	1	2	2
Cowans	10.1	0	39	4	1	...
Williams	11	0	45	2	...	5
Emburey	11	3	17	0	...	...
Edmonds	11	3	34	2	...	1
....	...	...	...	...		
....	...	...	...	...		

MIDDLESEX

1 G. D. Barlow	b Foster	14
2 W. N. Slack	c Gooch b Foster	1
3 C. T. Radley	not out	89
‡4 M. W. Gatting	run out	22
5 K. P. Tomlins	l b w b Gooch	0
6 J. E. Emburey	c D. East b Lever	17
*7 P. R. Downton	c Fletcher b Foster	10
8 P. H. Edmonds	b Pringle	9
9 N. F. Williams	c and b Pringle	13
10 W. W. Daniel	not out	2
11 N. G. Cowans		
	B 3, l-b 9, w 4, n-b 3, ...	19
	Total...	196

FALL OF THE WICKETS
1...10 2...25 3...74 4...74 5...123 6...141 7...171 8...191 9... 10...

Bowling Analysis	O.	M.	R.	W.	Wd.	N-b
Lever	11	1	52	1	...	...
Foster	11	2	26	3	...	...
Pringle	11	0	54	2	2	3
Turner	11	2	24	0	2	...
Gooch	11	2	21	1	...	...
....	...	...	...	...		
....	...	...	...	...		

‡Captain *Wicket-keeper

Umpires—H. D. Bird & B. J. Meyer

Scorers—C. F. Driver, H. P. Sharp & E. Solomon

Toss won by—Essex who elected to field

RESULT— Middlesex won by 4 runs

The playing conditions for the Benson & Hedges Cup Competition are printed on the back of this score card.

Total runs scored at end of each over :—

Essex

1	2	3	4	5	6	7	8	9	10	11	12	13	14	15	16	17	18	19	20
21	22	23	24	25	26	27	28	29	30	31	32	33	34	35	36	37	38	39	40
41	42	43	44	45	46	47	48	49	50	51	52	53	54	55					

Middlesex

1	2	3	4	5	6	7	8	9	10	11	12	13	14	15	16	17	18	19	20
21	22	23	24	25	26	27	28	29	30	31	32	33	34	35	36	37	38	39	40
41	42	43	44	45	46	47	48	49	50	51	52	53	54	55					

BENSON AND HEDGES CUP FINAL: ESSEX v. MIDDLESEX

As Sir Anthony Tuke, President of M.C.C., wrote on the eve of the Benson and Hedges Cup Final, 'The competition has gone from strength to strength over the years.' None would disagree with him.

When the competition began in 1972 it was, like all innovations in cricket, received with some scepticism and reluctance. There were those who complained that it made too great an intrusion into the county championship and distorted the programme, but critics were quickly silenced when the first Benson and Hedges tournament got under way, for here, it was seen, was a competition that offered the best of both worlds, a league basis which meant that defeat did not mean instant extinction and a knock-out section once the best eight teams had been decided.

There were those who recognised the appeal of such a tournament from the start. Mike Denness assessed Kent's strength as being more suitable to the limited-over game than to the county championship, and he set his sights on the Benson and Hedges Cup which Kent won twice in four years under his leadership. Ray Illingworth was another who turned his county's ambitions towards it and he captained Leicestershire in three finals in four years, two victories and one defeat.

It is interesting to look at the sides in that first Benson and Hedges Final in 1972. Of the Yorkshire side, only Lumb and Bairstow remain with the county while Old and Hampshire are playing their cricket elsewhere. Tolchard, Davison, Balderstone and Steel are still regular members of the Leicestershire side while Illingworth and Dudleston are ending their playing days with Yorkshire and Gloucestershire respectively.

The competition has provided many memorable moments; the victory of the Combined Universities over York-

Gatting dives in vain. Foster's throw has beaten him. David East has broken the wicket and umpire Bird's finger goes up. (Patrick Eagar)

shire, again minus Boycott, at Barnsley in 1976; Simon Davis, an Australian pace bowler, routing Leicestershire for 56 at Wellington in 1982; the batting of Gooch and Lilley at Chelmsford in 1979, and of Rose and Gavaskar at Canterbury a year later, but, in most cases the final itself has been disappointingly one-sided with counties, like Notts in 1982, failing to do themselves justice.

There have, of course, been dramatic and emotional finals. In 1976, d'Oliveira limped his way painfully through a courageous, but vain fifty against Kent for whom Johnson scored 78 and took four magnificent catches. 1979 was the sun-baked final in which Essex, to the delight of their supporters, won something for the first time in their 103 year his-

Barlow bowled by Foster for 14. (Patrick Eagar)

Essex exultant. Tomlins lbw to Gooch first ball. (Patrick Eagar)

Graham Gooch on-drives in his imperious innings. Downton keeping wicket. (Patrick Eagar)

tory. Those who were at Lord's that day will never forget the reception that greeted Gooch and Denness as they came down the pavilion steps to open the Essex innings, nor the batting of Gooch and McEwan, which has never been bettered in a big match anywhere.

Yet, what had ultimately been denied the Benson and Hedges Cup was a truly great final. When Len Owen, Director of Benson and Hedges with concern for special events, was asked at a press lunch on the eve of the match what he wished for, he replied 'A great final'. Perhaps in reward for all he has done in furthering the sport and, indeed, in giving support to so many sports in Britain, in 1983 he got it.

It was the first time that the two best sides in the country, currently first and second in the Schweppes County Championship, had reached a cup final at Lord's, but the weather that awaited them, after so much recent sunshine, was a frustrating and disappointing drizzle. Essex included John Lever after his recent surgery on a stomach abscess and omitted Norbert Phillip. Middlesex had Tomlins for the injured Butcher.

Fletcher won the toss and after much deliberation asked

Ken McEwan maintains the Essex surge. Here he cuts Edmonds. (Patrick Eagar)

Middlesex to bat, fifty minutes after the scheduled start in steaming damp. Barlow began confidently, crashing Lever through the off-side for three fours in the bowler's first two overs and so raising doubts as to Lever's real fitness. But the doubts soon transferred to the Middlesex side.

Foster had bowled very quickly in his first over, the smooth run, positive and aggressive, the high and handsome delivery, all breathed menace. In the fourth over of the innings, Slack edged a very fast delivery to slip where Gooch took a mighty right-handed catch low down, comparable to the one he had taken with his left hand in the semi-final at Canterbury. 10 for 1.

Radley, the workman, joined Barlow and began an innings which was to last 56 overs, most of them spent on the front foot, and which was to save Middlesex from total collapse

Fletcher pushes forward to Edmonds and is caught, bat-pad by Radley. (Patrick Eagar)

and, ultimately, bring him the Gold Award. In the tenth over he lost Barlow. The left-hander had just hit Foster for 2 to mid-off, but the next ball was again very fast and moved back at him to knock over his middle stump, a very impressive piece of bowling.

Now came the Middlesex hope, skipper Gatting. Foster and Lever were replaced after bowling seven overs and putting Essex firmly in control. That control was momentarily threatened when Pringle bowled two overs that lacked fire and accuracy. After his recent spate of no-balls he seemed to be afraid in his run to the wicket and he was replaced by Gooch as Turner's partner.

Now began a spell of bowling which should have won the match for Essex. The two medium pacers, swinging the ball, seam up, just short of a length, frustrated Middlesex to the point of suffocation. By the twenty-ninth over, the score was only 72. Gatting turned Gooch to square-leg boundary. Foster set off in pursuit and stopped the ball inches from the rope as Gatting scampered for an improbable third run. He had chosen the wrong fielder. In one movement he had clasped the ball, turned and thrown straight over the top of the stumps where the exuberant David East collected and broke the wicket with a flourish as Gatting dived despairingly for the crease. Tomlins was lbw first ball and Middlesex were 74 for 4.

Turner's splendidly economic spell ended with the thirty-sixth over. His eleven overs had cost only 24 runs and Middlesex were still seven short of the hundred. Emburey was struggling to put bat to ball, but Radley soldiered on, pushing here, nudging there, crouching low and presenting an image of defiance.

Radley reached his fifty in the fortieth over, the hundred was up and Emburey had just been dropped by Fletcher at mid-off. Some Middlesex supporters accused Fletcher of Machiavellian principles in wanting to keep Emburey at the wicket. He survived Gooch's magnificent spell, but he perished in the forty-fourth over when he attempted to drive Lever, now bowling from the Nursery End, and skied the ball to the wicket-keeper. More significantly, Radley, on 59, had been dropped by Pont the over before.

Radley cajoled Downton, Edmonds, Williams and Daniel to help him to add 73 from the last 11 overs. Pringle and Lever were the main sufferers. Lever was palpably not himself and once Pringle had erred, it was difficult to understand why Ray East had been chosen if he were not to be allowed to bowl.

Still, 196 was a meagre total. Essex, who had fielded magnificently, yet ironically had missed their half chances, should find it no problem. This view was quickly confirmed. Hardie crashed Daniel through the covers in the opening over and the second over, for Middlesex and Norman Cowans, was traumatic. Gatting had set an attacking off-side field. Three times Gooch bludgeoned Cowans to leg for four, twice he hit him for two. They were shots of great majesty and Lord's shook to them.

After two overs Cowans was replaced by Williams who was immediately despatched wide of mid-on for another four. In the eighth over, Williams bowled a no-ball which put up the fifty. After 10 overs, Essex had scored 71, Gooch was on 40, Hardie 25. It was stunning batting.

Williams moved in to bowl the twelfth over. Gooch hit him straight and imperious to the Nursery End sight screen. The next ball he again aimed to drive, edged and Downton took a low catch. 79 for 1 at six and a half an over.

The thirteenth over of the innings was the first maiden. McEwan, troubled by an injured wrist, was finding it hard to settle, and the run rate dropped as Hardie had ceased to hit the ball with his early vehemence. Edmonds had applied a break, but, at tea, off 25 overs, Essex were 113 for 1, Hardie 34, McEwan 26, a very healthy position.

Five overs after tea, McEwan drove Edmonds low to Williams at mid-off where Williams swooped and claimed a catch, a claim which the umpire supported.

Eight runs came in the next two overs, four of them extras. Fletcher, needing to play a positive innings to lead his side to a victory which was still theirs for the taking, dithered. He prodded forward at Edmonds and was taken bat-pad at silly mid-off. Hardie's score had advanced only 13 in the past 20 overs, but with 7 wickets in hand, Essex needed only 61 for victory and had 23 overs in which to get them.

Pont was dropped by Cowans in the thirty-fifth over, but he was less fortunate three overs later. The 150 had just been passed and Williams was operating from the Nursery End.

Disaster for Essex. Agony for Pont. He is struck on the head by a ball from Williams and drops his bat, dislodging a bail. (Patrick Eagar)

The dramatic climax. Foster is bowled by Cowans and Middlesex have snatched a sensational victory. (Patrick Eagar)

ABOVE: *Mike Gatting receives the cup from Mr W. D. K. Wilson, Deputy Chairman of Gallaher Tobacco Ltd and a Director of Benson and Hedges. Jack Bailey, Secretary of M.C.C. looks on. Sir Anthony Tuke, President of M.C.C. and Mr Len Owen, Director of Benson and Hedges were also in the presentation party.* BELOW: *Clive Radley receives the Gold Award, Champagne and a copy of* Benson and Hedges Cricket Year. *(Patrick Eagar)*

He bowled a bouncer which Pont took on the side of the helmet. Evidently the impact pressed a helmet stud into the temple and stunned, Pont recoiled and dropped his bat. In doing so, he dislodged the off bail and was out, hit wicket. Essex needed 46 from 17 overs with six wickets remaining.

Hardie had remained flat footed against Edmonds and Emburey. He was totally becalmed. After the departure of Gooch he had virtually ceased to bat. In the forty-first over, perhaps in desperation, he flashed at Cowans, who had returned at the pavilion end, heartened no doubt by the fact that Gooch was no longer there, and was caught behind. His 22 runs since Gooch's dismissal had occupied 29 overs. In sixteen overs since tea he had scored 15.

Turner and Pringle now found themselves faced by an enemy who, under the inspiring leadership of a captain who refuses to admit failure, had refound self-belief. Emburey had induced strokelessness and Gatting had changed bowlers and field-placings to move into the attack. Still the odds were against him. Pringle and Turner nudged, ran and showed good sense and temperament. Runs did not come as quickly as they had done at the start, but in 9 overs, they added 24 runs and at the end of the fiftieth over Essex stood only 17 short of victory and five batsmen still remained to be dismissed.

Pringle had managed two refreshing fours and Turner one when, with the first ball of the fifty-second over, Daniel had

Happy winners. Radley and Gatting with the cup. (Patrick Eagar)

Pringle lbw for 16. 12 needed off 23 balls.

David East managed one and there was a wide, but Turner, who had chosen to survive Emburey when he might have hit, now chose to hit at Cowans in the gathering gloom. He clouted him to deep mid-on where John Carr, fielding as substitute for Williams, and acting as twelfth man through special dispensation as he had already represented Combined Universities in the tournament, took a fine catch.

David East touched a ball down the leg-side to the fine-leg boundary and Essex were 191 for 7, six needed and more than two overs and three men to get them. Next ball East tried to hit over mid-wicket for what would have been a crucial four. Gatting leapt and just got a hand to the ball, breaking its speed. Spinning round, he caught it as it dropped behind him. It was a splendid catch by a fine cricketer and a man who, in half a season, had established himself as a very great captain.

We now had Ray East and Neil Foster together. Foster, who had not been to the wicket in a limited-over match all season, and Ray East, temperamentally unsuited for an occasion such as this. Daniel bowled a wide – 192. On the fifth ball of the over, East was struck on the pad. As the ball squirted out on the off side, he charged down the wicket in search of an impossible leg-bye. Before he could regain his ground, Radley had thrown down the wicket from point, so completing a good day for him.

Lever played out the last ball of the over and so left five runs needed for victory from the final over. With his first delivery, Norman Cowans yorked Foster and Middlesex had won a famous victory.

Foster, for whom the game had held such rich promise earlier in the day, stood forlornly at the crease as the crowd swept on to the field. Gatting, the master tactician had snatched victory where none existed. Cowans, ravaged by Gooch, had come back to take three wickets in his last four balls. Essex, many of their players on the verge of tears, had suffered their second heart-breaking defeat inside four days. In the Stygian glom of Lord's at 8.50 in the evening, the Essex supporters were aware that the ghosts that haunted them before 1979 had not been laid. They trudged sadly home, but more than one was heard to say, 'What a game of cricket!'

The crowd swarm on to the pitch at the end of a great final. (Patrick Eagar)

23, 25 and 26 July

at Edgbaston

New Zealanders 335 for 6 dec (J.V. Coney 68, J.J. Crowe 63, G.P. Howarth 55) and 158 for 3 dec (J.J. Crowe 79)

Warwickshire 195 for 5 dec (D.L. Amiss 78, A.M. Ferreira 55 not out) and 126 (B.L. Cairns 7 for 46)

New Zealanders won by 172 runs

In a rain-interrupted match which Willis kept alive with a meaningful declaration, the New Zealanders gained their second success of the tour. Jeff Crowe played two good innings, and there were also pleasant knocks from Coney, Howarth and Edgar for the tourists. Their match-winner, however, was Lance Cairns who gave by far his best performance in England when, on the last day, on a batsman's wicket, he took 7 wickets for 46 runs in 17 overs during which he consistently moved the ball late. He troubled all batsmen and four of his wickets were bowled. Ian Smith had a good match behind the stumps for the New Zealanders and pulled off a very smart stumping to dismiss Paul Smith off Gray.

John Player League

24 July

at Derby

Nottinghamshire 86 for 2
Derbyshire 87 for 7 (M.K. Bore 4 for 38)
Derbyshire (4 pts) won by 3 wickets

at Canterbury

Middlesex 227 for 5 (M.W. Gatting 69, K.P. Tomlins 55)
Kent 171 (M.R. Benson 59)
Middlesex (4 pts) won by 56 runs

at Leicester

Leicestershire 110 for 5
Essex 66 for 2
Essex (4 pts) won on faster scoring rate

at Northampton

Northamptonshire 196 for 6 (G. Cook 59 not out)
Glamorgan 162 for 8
Northamptonshire (4 pts) won on faster scoring rate

at Taunton

Hampshire 93 for 7 (I.T. Botham 4 for 22)
Somerset 97 for 3
Somerset (4 pts) won by 7 wickets

at The Oval

Surrey 186
Lancashire 187 for 6 (D.P. Hughes 87 not out)
Lancashire (4 pts) won by 4 wickets

at Hove

Sussex 135
Yorkshire 141 for 4 (G. Boycott 75 not out)
Yorkshire (4 pts) won by 6 wickets

at Edgbaston

Worcestershire 208 for 8 (P.A. Neale 83)
Warwickshire 52 for 0
Match tied
Warwickshire 2 pts, Worcestershire 2 pts

With rain scattered about the country, matches in several places were restricted. At Taunton, in a vital match, Hampshire elected to bat, not suspecting rain, but there was a long interruption which reduced the match to 21 overs. Botham bowled well and batted well, and the situation was well suited to the punishing hitting of Richards so that the home side won with 8.2 overs to spare.

Derbyshire and Notts played a match reduced to 17 overs and Derbyshire won with one ball to spare. At Leicester, Essex's target was reduced to 64 off 10 overs, and, with Gooch scoring 30 of the last 38 runs, they won with 9 balls to spare.

Glamorgan suffered badly from the weather at Northampton. Chasing 197, they were 89 for 3 off 20 overs, but rain readjusted the target to 79 in the next 14 overs which, in poor light, became beyond them.

Middlesex celebrated their Benson and Hedges Cup Final win with a convincing victory at Canterbury, their spinners again proving decisive, and Lancashire recovered from 64 for 5 to beat Surrey. As O'Shaughnessy had also retired hurt with a damaged finger, Lancashire's plight was great, but David Hughes, well supported by the very promising Fairbrother, stirred memories of past deeds with a marvellous 87 not out which thumped his side to victory with 8 balls remaining.

Yorkshire swept aside the challenge of Sussex to go 4 points clear at the top of the league. Sussex never established the base for a worthwhile score and Boycott steered Yorkshire home with 10 balls to spare. He shared a second wicket stand of 93 with Sharp and stunned the packed audience by finishing the match with a straight six off Barclay.

After Worcestershire had batted their full 40 overs, rain hampered proceedings at Edgbaston. Rain was falling as Pridgeon began the crucial tenth over. Warwickshire were 34 for 0 off 9. Amiss hit a six and a single. Lloyd hit a six, a four and a single. The rains came more forcefully, and Warwickshire were 52 for 0 off 10. Worcestershire had tied their third John Player League match in succession.

27, 28 and 29 July

at Portsmouth

Derbyshire 319 (C.J. Tunnicliffe 91, J.H. Hampshire 84, M.D. Marshall 4 for 66) and 188 (K.J. Barnett 65, T.M. Tremlett 6 for 82)
Hampshire 250 for 4 dec (M.C.J. Nicholas 100 not out, C.G. Greenidge 72) and 260 for 4 (C.L. Smith 76, C.G. Greenidge 57)

Hampshire won by 6 wickets
Hampshire 23 pts, Derbyshire 5 pts

at Southport

Gloucestershire 201 (P.W. Romaines 79, J. Simmons 5 for 60) and 255 (Zaheer Abbas 112, P. Bainbridge 50, J. Simmons 7 for 73)
Lancashire 330 (J. Abrahams 86, C.H. Lloyd 86, N.H.

Mark Benson. A century in each innings against Warwickshire at Egbaston was just part of a splendid feast of run-getting. (Adrian Murrell)

Brian Hardie of Essex. Thoughtful and dependable in his benefit year. (Adrian Murrell)

Fairbrother 73) and 130 for 5 (N.H. Fairbrother 54 not out)

Lancashire won by 5 wickets
Lancashire 23 pts, Gloucestershire 4 pts

at Northampton

Northamptonshire 336 for 9 dec (D.J. Capel 109 not out, D.S. Steele 54, P. Willey 52, W. Larkins 50, J. Garner 4 for 58) and 273 for 5 dec (R.J. Boyd-Moss 90 not out, G. Cook 82)
Somerset 337 for 7 dec (I.V.A. Richards 117 not out, J.W. Lloyds 100) and 110 for 0 (P.M. Roebuck 55 not out)

Match drawn
Northamptonshire 7 pts, Somerset 6 pts

at The Oval

Nottinghamshire 221 (R.T. Robinson 92, G. Monkhouse 7 for 51) and 197 (R.T. Robinson 82, P.I. Pocock 6 for 74)
Surrey 378 for 9 dec (D.J. Thomas 119, M.A. Lynch 67) and 42 for 1

Surrey won by 9 wickets
Surrey 24 pts, Nottinghamshire 5 pts

at Hove

Sussex 217 (I.J. Gould 59 not out, J.K. Lever 5 for 40) and 127 (Imran Khan 50, J.K. Lever 7 for 55)
Essex 397 (G.A. Gooch 96, D.E. East 91, B.R. Hardie 56, C.E. Waller 6 for 126)

Essex won by an innings and 53 runs
Essex 24 pts, Sussex 5 pts

at Edgbaston

Kent 364 (M.R. Benson 102, A.P.E. Knott 92, N.R. Taylor 51, W. Hogg 5 for 63) and 299 for 6 dec (M.R. Benson 152 not out, D.G. Aslett 68)
Warwickshire 359 for 6 dec (G.W. Humpage 105) and 162 for 8 (D.L. Amiss 69 not out, D.L. Underwood 4 for 30)

Match drawn
Warwickshire 7 pts, Kent 6 pts

The nineteen-year old Neil Fairbrother of Lancashire who, in his first championship game, scored 94 not out

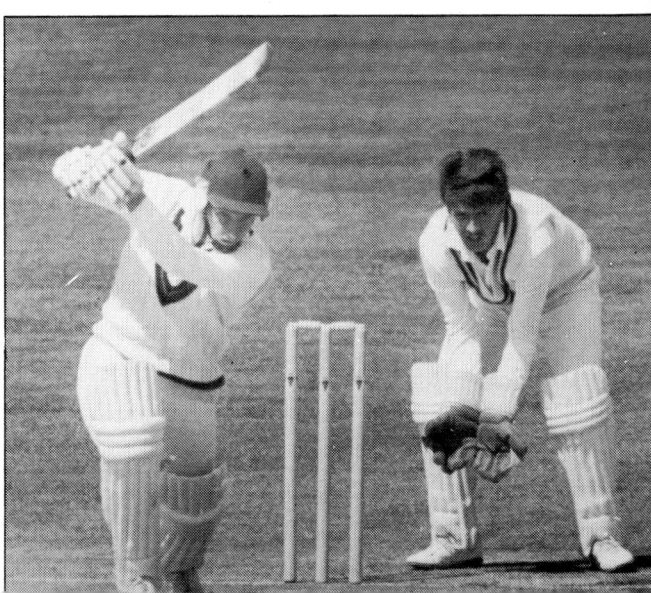

David Thomas. He was called to the England party as a bowler, but his great advance was as a batsman. A lordly maiden century came against Notts at The Oval, 28 July. (Adrian Murrell)

at Worcester

Worcestershire 127 (S.R. Barwick 8 for 42) and 234 (P.A. Neale 77, D.B. d'Oliveira 56, R.C. Ontong 4 for 11, W.W. Davis 4 for 76)
Glamorgan 258 (A.L. Jones 62, A.P. Pridgeon 4 for 68) and 106 for 3

Glamorgan won by 7 wickets
Glamorgan 22 pts, Worcestershire 2 pts

With Middlesex idle, Essex closed the gap at the top of the Schweppes County Championship to one point. Fletcher put Sussex in and Lever and Pringle prised them out for 217. Before the close Essex had reduced the difference to 74 thanks to a display of tremendous power by Gooch who hit 16 off Pigott's first over and continued to bat brilliantly until two overs before time. David East came in as nightwatchman and next day reached a career best. He then held six catches as Essex raced to victory only 50 minutes into the

last day. John Lever produced another devastating spell, 6 for 9 in 5.2 overs, and had match figures of 12 for 95.

There were three centuries in the drawn game at Northampton, by far the most significant coming from David Capel who reached the first hundred of his career. It was refreshing for the twenty-year-old whose season had been marred by injury.

Another career best, 6 for 84 by Tim Tremlett, one of the most charming young men in first-class cricket, set up Hampshire's third championship success in a row. Colin Tunnicliffe bludgeoned ten fours and four sixes on the first day to sustain a Derbyshire recovery, but Mark Nicholas hit a fine hundred to keep Hampshire in the match before Tremlett's bowling left them 227 minutes in which to make 258 to win.

Mark Benson hit a career best 152 not out in 134 minutes to add to his first innings 102 and confirm his ever developing power and authority, but Amiss thwarted Kent and Underwood of victory.

The old and the new in the shape of Jack Simmons and Neil Fairbrother welded Lancashire's victory over Gloucestershire. At forty-two, Simmons continued his recent run of fine all-round form with bowling which brought him 12 for 133. Fairbrother had two fifties in the match and his second took Lancashire from 37 for 5 to victory.

There was another career best bowling performance at The Oval where Graham Monkhouse's medium pace earned 7 for 51 and dismembered Notts. On the second day David Thomas hit a lordly maiden century and then Pat Pocock spun Notts to defeat. Once more, only Tim Robinson offered serious resistance for the visitors.

Pride of place, however, must go to Glamorgan who gained their first championship victory of the season. Remarkably, it was Steve Barwick, who had been totally out of form and favour, who returned his career best, and the season's best figures of 8 for 42 on the opening day to set up Glamorgan's victory at Worcester. They scraped to a lead of 131, and, in spite of some nerves, never really lost their grip on the match.

In his 100 not out for Hampshire against Derbyshire in the first innings at Portsmouth, Mark Nicholas passed 1000 runs for the season, the first English-born player to reach this target.

THE SECOND TEST MATCH

As is now becoming the prevalent custom, Geoff Howarth asked England to bat when he won the toss, but he had quick evidence that he had done the right thing. Fowler was soon caught behind by Smith, who had replaced Lees in the side, off Chatfield, and Gower, the prize catch, went at slip off Cairns.

With Tavare solid and Lamb in full cry after lunch, 40 in 11 overs, England appeared to have weathered the early storm and to be heading for a good score, but Lamb gave himself room to crash a short ball from Cairns through the off-side and edged the ball on to his wicket. Botham looked a mixture of concentration and the willingness to hit the bad ball, but he was deceived by Cairns' change of pace and well caught at slip. Tavare was victim to Coney's deceptive movement and the England innings disintegrated, the last seven wickets falling for 50 runs. The destroyer was Lance Cairns

ABOVE: *England* v *New Zealand at Headingly*. (*Ken Kelly*)
BELOW: *Randall is caught by Coney off Cairns. Jeff Crowe is delighted.* (*Ken Kelly*)

who, in exploiting the conditions admirably and using his leg-cutter to such effect that it bemused most England batsmen like a secret weapon, became the first New Zealander to take 7 wickets in a Test match against England. As he had taken 7 wickets against Warwickshire on the Tuesday, it had become a week for him to remember.

It was imperative that New Zealand, having once more seized the initiative by bowling out England for 225, should not lose a wicket and should build from a firm base. Edgar and Wright survived. They survived the following morning, too, until Edgar, having been hit on the hip bone by Botham, was forced to retire hurt with the score at 26.

Lance Cairns, 7 for 74, and Man of the Match, appeals for lbw against Dilley. (*Adrian Murrell*)

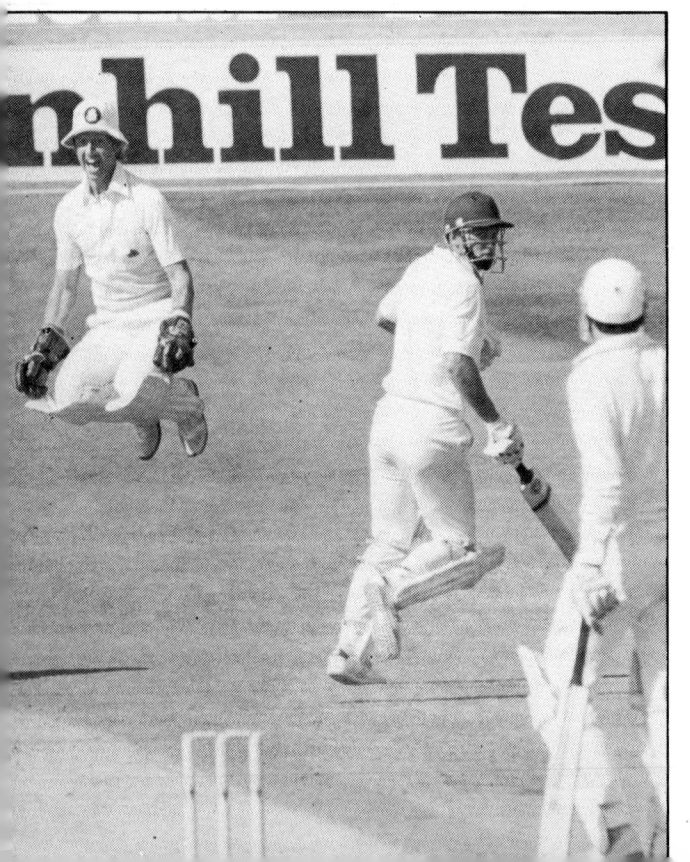

ABOVE: *John Wright edges a ball from Edmonds past Botham in his innings of 93. (Adrian Murrell)*
LEFT: *Bob Taylor jumps for joy as Jeff Crowe is run out following a misunderstanding with John Wright. (Adrian Murrell)*

John Wright, however, stayed and played an innings which had much of his characteristic charm and power off the back foot and some dogged defence. Admirable as his innings was, it had two great blemishes in that he was responsible for running out both Howarth and Jeff Crowe, and when Wright himself surrendered his wicket with a rash, wild shot, New Zealand had lost 3 wickets for 1 run and were in danger of collapse. Coney is most reliable in such situations, a wonderfully level-headed player who mixes dedication and enjoyment in equal quantities, the right blend. Perhaps more importantly, Hadlee quickly found his touch and when Coney left at 218, there was Edgar returning, with a runner to start afresh. He had increased his score to 28 by the close, Hadlee was on 52 and New Zealand had a lead of 27.

They did not fritter away their advantage on the Saturday morning. They extended their lead to 152 and batted until after lunch. Hadlee, a superb cricketer, took his score to 75 before mis-hooking Cowans and getting a bottom edge onto his stumps. It was the only wicket to fall in the morning.

Bracewell went on the second ball after lunch, Edmonds only wicket as he pursued an unchanging policy in search of close catches. Willis finished the innings with a good spell from the Football Stand End, but not before Cairns had played a few entertaining blows. Willis was the best of the

ABOVE: *The end of a magnificent fighting innings. Edgar is bowled by Willis for 84. (Adrian Murrell)*

RIGHT: *Chatfield is lbw to Willis for . (Adrian Murrell)*

England bowlers, for he has a mighty heart, but he, like the others, bowled far too short.

England began uneasily. Both openers survived chances and then Fowler was caught behind again and Tavare, to the amazement of all, had his off-stump knocked flat by Chatfield. There seemed no danger with Gower and Lamb together, but Lamb is still a batsman in search of an identity and he gave himself room to hit Coney and lost his off-stump.

Botham survived a confident appeal for a bat-pad catch first ball, then drove Coney majestically through the covers before hitting at a leg-side ball and lifting it gently over the wicket-keeper's head for Howarth, running round from slip, to catch him. Randall hit three fours and then received a fierce lifter from Chatfield. Dilley lasted the last half-hour with the commanding Gower, but on Saturday evening, England were 154 for 6, 2 runs ahead, and New Zealand had a day in which to contemplate the prospect of a first victory over England in England.

Dilley always looked vulnerable, but he stayed until the score reached 190 when, inevitably, he was caught behind. Taylor showed positive defence in support of Gower, but in one vital and dramatic over, Cairns, destined to be Man of the Match, removed both him and Willis.

ABOVE: *Lamb is bowled by Coney. (Adrian Murrell)*
BELOW: *Botham finds a new way to get out. Howarth catches him behind Smith off Coney. (Adrian Murrell)*

OPPOSITE: *Lance Cairns took ten wickets in the match. Taylor is bowled for 9, and Cowans, the last man, is taken at short-leg for 10. (Ken Kelly)*

Cowans, who had won the support of the Yorkshire crowd, batted bravely and above his capabilities in a last wicket stand of 31 which not only frustrated New Zealand and took their target into three figures, but helped Gower to reach a century of beauty and bravery which shamed his colleagues. His concentration never wavered. He sacrificed singles which could have given him a personal triumph earlier because he put the needs of the side first, and never once, in all the tension in an innings which lasted nearly five hours, did he profane the eloquence of his style.

Two things now stood between New Zealand and victory, Bob Willis and their own nerves. Both came close to denying them. In Willis' third over, Edgar steered a catch to gully, but Howarth's response was to attack. He recognised that to become bereft of scoring shots was the way to the tomb and he assaulted the bowling. He was caught at mid-wicket, but by then he had reduced New Zealand's target to 59 with 8 wickets in hand.

There was a violent alarm when Willis accounted for Wright, taken at short extra cover, and Martin Crowe, bat-pad, in the same over. 61 for 4 and signs of a lack of belief. It was Coney's calm and Jeff Crowe's accumulation of 13 which steadied them.

The elder Crowe was bowled through 'the gate' and Willis had taken 300 Test wickets, but Hadlee and Coney were determined that this was to be New Zealand's finest hour and none could begrudge them. They won shortly after tea and there was great emotion in the New Zealand camp and among their supporters. It was an historic victory, bravely earned by men who love the game and its traditions.

It was right that at the end they should be confronted by the England captain bowling at his fastest and his best. He has never believed in defeat and if there have been greater tactical captains and ones more adept at speaking to the press, there has never been one with a bigger heart. At times, the man's endeavour seems almost more than the human spirit can bear. Only Lillee, Gibbs and Trueman now stand above him in the list of wicket-takers in Test cricket.

ABOVE: *Randall is caught behind by Smith off Chatfield.* (*Adrian Murrell*)
BELOW: *Dilley falls on the last morning. Caught behind off the elated Chatfield.* (*Adrian Murrell*)

OPPOSITE: *Bob Willis takes his 299th and 300th Test Wickets.*
ABOVE: *Allan Lamb dives forward to catch Martin Crowe.*
BELOW: *Jeff Crowe has his middle stump knocked out of the ground.* (*Ken Kelly*)

ABOVE: *Gower in all his glory. 112 not out at Headingley.* (*Adrian Murrell*)
RIGHT: *Three hundred Test Wickets. Bob Willis – a Man for All Seasons.* (*Adrian Murrell*)

OPPOSITE: *New Zealand joy. The champagne bubbles in celebration of the first Test victory in England.* (*Adrian Murrell*)

SECOND TEST MATCH – ENGLAND v. NEW ZEALAND
28, 29, 30 July and 1 August 1983 at Headingley, Leeds

ENGLAND

	FIRST INNINGS		SECOND INNINGS	
G. Fowler	c Smith, b Chatfield	9	c Smith, b Chatfield	19
C.J. Tavare	c Smith, b Coney	69	b Chatfield	23
D.I. Gower	c Coney, b Cairns	9	not out	112
A.J. Lamb	c M. Crowe, b Cairns	58	b Coney	28
I.T. Botham	c Howarth, b Cairns	38	c Howarth, b Coney	4
D.W. Randall	c Coney, b Cairns	4	c Smith, b Chatfield	16
P.H. Edmonds	c Smith, b Cairns	8	c Smith, b Chatfield	0
G.R. Dilley	b Cairns	0	c Smith, b Chatfield	15
R.W. Taylor*	not out	10	b Cairns	9
R.G.D. Willis†	c J. Crowe, b Cairns	9	c Coney, b Cairns	4
N.G. Cowans	c Bracewell, b Cairns	0	c M. Crowe, b Cairns	10
Extras	b 4, lb 7	11	b 8, lb 3, w 1	12
		225		252

	O	M	R	W	O	M	R	W
Hadlee	21	9	44	—	26	9	45	—
Chatfield	22	8	67	1	29	5	95	5
Cairns	33.2	14	74	7	24	2	70	3
Coney	12	3	21	2	8	1	30	2
Bracewell	1	—	8	—				

FALL OF WICKETS
1- 18, 2- 35, 3- 135, 4- 175, 5- 185, 6- 205, 7- 205, 8- 209, 9- 225
1- 39, 2- 44, 3- 116, 4- 126, 5- 142, 6- 142, 7- 190, 8- 217, 9- 221

Umpires: B.J. Meyer and D.J. Constant

NEW ZEALAND

	FIRST INNINGS		SECOND INNINGS	
J.G. Wright	c Willis, b Cowans	93	c Randall, b Willis	26
B.A. Edgar	b Willis	84	c Edmonds, b Willis	2
G.P. Howarth†	run out	13	c Randall, b Willis	20
M.D. Crowe	lbw, b Cowans	37	c Lamb, b Willis	1
J.J. Crowe	run out	0	b Willis	13
J.V. Coney	c Gower, b Willis	19	not out	10
R.J. Hadlee	b Cowans	75	not out	6
J.G. Bracewell	c Dilley, b Edmonds	16		
I.D.S. Smith*	c Tavare, b Willis	2		
B.L. Cairns	not out	24		
E.J. Chatfield	lbw, b Willis	0		
Extras	b 1, lb 4, w 1, nb 8	14	b 8, lb 7, nb 10	25
		377	(for 5 wickets)	103

	O	M	R	W	O	M	R	W
Willis	23.3	6	57	4	14	5	35	5
Dilley	17	4	36	—	8	2	16	—
Cowans	28	8	88	3	5	—	23	—
Botham	26	9	81	—	0.1	—	4	—
Edmonds	45	14	101	1				

FALL OF WICKETS
1- 52, 2- 168, 3- 169, 4- 169, 5- 218, 6- 304, 7- 348, 8- 351, 9- 377
(B.A. Edgar retired hurt at 26 for 0 (19 n.o.) and returned at 218 for 5
1- 11, 2- 42, 3- 60, 4- 61, 5- 83

New Zealand won by 5 wickets

30 July, 1 and 2 August

at Chesterfield

Kent 437 for 9 dec (D.G. Aslett 168, M.R. Benson 66, E.A. Baptiste 63, R.M. Ellison 63, O. Mortensen 4 for 73) and 261 for 4 dec (D.G. Aslett 119)
Derbyshire 368 for 9 dec (I.S. Anderson 112, K.J. Barnett 106) and 253 for 7 (K.J. Barnett 68, R.J. Finney 68)

Match drawn
Kent 8 pts, Derbyshire 7 pts

at Swansea

Surrey 303 (M.A. Lynch 90, R.C. Ontong 4 for 35) and 340 for 4 dec (D.M. Smith 131 not out, A.R. Butcher 128)
Glamorgan 362 (A.L. Jones 56, T. Davies 55 not out, S.T. Clarke 5 for 83) and 282 for 5 (R.C. Ontong 109, A.L. Jones 77 not out)

Glamorgan won by 5 wickets
Glamorgan 23 pts, Surrey 6 pts

at Portsmouth

Hampshire 362 for 4 dec (C.L. Smith 125, M.C.J. Nicholas 76, C.G. Greenidge 71)
Gloucestershire 153 and 306 (A.W. Stovold 106, Zaheer Abbas 87, A.J. Hignell 65, S.J. Malone 4 for 39)

Match drawn
Hampshire 8 pts, Gloucestershire 2 pts

BELOW: *Ian Anderson enjoyed a fine season as Derbyshire's opener. 112 v Kent at Chesterfield. (John Grainger)*

at Old Trafford

Somerset 185 (J. Simmons 4 for 54) and 155 (D. Lloyd 5 for 22, J. Simmons 5 for 41)
Lancashire 355 (J. Simmons 75, D. Lloyd 63, J. Abrahams 52, Nasir Zaidi 51, N.H. Fairbrother 50)

Lancashire won by an innings and 15 runs
Lancashire 22 pts, Somerset 3 pts

at Leicester

Leicestershire 356 for 5 dec (B.F. Davison 85, J.C. Balderstone 82, I.P. Butcher 59)
Sussex 120 (A.M.E. Roberts 5 for 26) and 133 (P.B. Clift 4 for 59)

Leicestershire won by an innings and 103 runs
Leicestershire 24 pts, Sussex 2 pts

at Lord's

Warwickshire 253 (K.D. Smith 103, J.E. Emburey 4 for 48) and 210 (A.I. Kallicharran 55, W.W. Daniel 4 for 33)
Middlesex 385 for 8 dec (M.W. Gatting 116, G.D. Barlow 83, W.N. Slack 81, J.E. Emburey 61) and 81 for 2

Middlesex won by 8 wickets
Middlesex 24 pts, Warwickshire 4 pts

at Northampton

Worcestershire 273 (P.A. Neale 92, N.A. Mallender 6 for 48) and 225 for 4 dec (J.A. Ormrod 71 not out, P.A. Neale 52 not out)
Northamptonshire 200 for 6 dec (R.G. Williams 85, A.P. Pridgeon 4 for 48) and 300 for 3 (P. Willey 117 not out, W. Larkins 80, R.G. Williams 51 not out)

Northamptonshire won by 7 wickets
Northamptonshire 22 pts, Worcestershire 5 pts

at Worksop

Yorkshire 434 for 5 dec (G. Boycott 214 not out, M.D. Moxon 68) and 131 for 4 dec (M.D. Moxon 50)
Nottinghamshire 316 (J.D. Birch 60, R.T. Robinson 56, P. Carrick 5 for 69)

Match drawn
Yorkshire 5 pts, Nottinghamshire 2 pts

Middlesex responded to the Essex challenge with a resounding victory over Warwickshire at Lord's although for much of the last day the match had appeared to be destined for a draw. With the visitors' leading run-getters failing to make contributions of significance on the Saturday, it was left to David Smith to bolster the innings with his first championship hundred of the season. Middlesex surged ahead on the Monday when Barlow and Slack began with a stand of 168 and Gatting, in his usual pugnacious manner, hit a century and shared a fine partnership with Emburey. Nevertheless, the Middlesex bowling on the last afternoon looked uninspired and the side had a jaded look which suggested that Warwickshire would have no difficulty in holding out, particularly as there were stoppages for rain. It took all Gatting's drive to make his side keep at the task, and it was

Derek Aslett – a century in each innings against Derbyshire at Chesterfield and a county cap. (Kent C.C.C.)

Emburey and, ultimately, Daniel who disposed of some late limp resistance to make victory possible, the runs coming in 16 overs.

Glamorgan were left to make 282 in just over 3 hours and they got the runs with 22 balls to spare. They owed much to Ontong who hit 109 off 107 balls and to Alan Lewis Jones who reached a storming 77 off only 43 deliveries, another indication of his new style aggression. The stand of 111 for the third wicket between Ontong and Henderson came in 25 overs and did much to make the late charge possible.

John Player League

31 July

at Chesterfield

Derbyshire 146 for 4 (G. Miller 55 not out) v **Kent**

Match abandoned
Derbyshire 2 pts, Kent 2 pts

at Swansea

Surrey 204 for 7 (D.J. Thomas 72)
Glamorgan 118 for 3 (A.L. Jones 77 not out)

Glamorgan (4 pts) won on faster scoring rate

at Bournemouth

Hampshire 145 for 2 (C.L. Smith 56, C.G. Greenidge 52 not out)
Gloucestershire 148 for 2 (P.W. Romaines 80 not out)

Gloucestershire (4 pts) won by 8 wickets

at Old Trafford

Lancashire 132 (I.V.A. Richards 6 for 24)
Somerset 7 for 0

Match abandoned
Lancashire 2 pts, Somerset 2 pts

at Leicester

Sussex 105 for 7
Leicestershire 12 for 0

Match abandoned
Leicestershire 2 pts, Sussex 2 pts

at Lord's

Middlesex 163 for 8
Warwickshire 82 (J.E. Emburey 5 for 36)

Middlesex (4 pts) won by 10 runs

at Trent Bridge

Yorkshire 106 for 6
Nottinghamshire 107 for 1 (C.E.B. Rice 66 not out)

Nottinghamshire (4 pts) won by 9 wickets

at Worcester

Northamptonshire 147 (W. Larkins 53, D.N. Patel 5 for 27)
Worcestershire 96 for 4 (D.N. Patel 52)

Worcestershire (4 pts) won on faster scoring rate

The heroics of Phil Neale were unable to save Worcestershire from defeat at Northampton. He suffered the jeers of the crowd as he delayed his declaration and set Northants to score 299 at 6 runs an over, but his knowledge of the inadequacies of his attack were soon shown when the home side reached victory with 11 balls to spare, Willey hitting 117 in 113 minutes.

No such finish at Worksop where Boycott hit a double century which lasted into the second day, and Notts responded with a crawl to safety. It resulted in a dreadful draw for which neither side deserved a point.

It was quite different at Chesterfield where Kent scored at 4½ runs an over on the first day. Derek Aslett recorded a career best and emphasised what a fine player he is while Benson, Baptiste and Ellison batted excitingly after Mortensen had done early damage. Derbyshire responded in kind on the Monday with Barnett reaching a century in two hours and sharing an opening stand of 158 with Anderson whose batting was more restrained than his captain's. Aslett hit his second hundred of the match and Cowdrey left the home side 214 minutes in which to score 331, an improbable task though Barnett and Anderson again began briskly with 109. Quick wickets then fell and it was left to Finney and Miller to save the day.

There was some controversy at Portsmouth where, after another hundred from Chris Smith, Stovold, Zaheer, Hignell and the weather thwarted Hampshire. When the last Gloucestershire wicket fell the umpires decreed that there were only five overs remaining although the rule book clearly

interpreted that eight should have been bowled. In the event, Hampshire declined a task which, with 8 overs, they would have attempted.

Troubled by injury, the very sorry, deflated Sussex side crashed to a two-day defeat at Leicester. Little can be said in favour of Sussex. They bowled mundanely and batted dreadfully to succumb twice in a day to the eager Leicestershire side.

The success of Jack Simmons continued. Aided by another veteran, David Lloyd, who had announced that this was to be his last season, he twice routed Somerset for under two hundred. He was encouraged by a sticky wicket in the second innings, but, for good measure, he was also Lancashire's top scorer in their third championship win of the season. He even disposed of Viv Richards, a little unwell, for 0 in the second innings, caught by the impressively active cricketer Nasir Zaidi.

For Glamorgan, there was the excitement of their second successive win. Monte Lynch had struck well for Surrey on the Saturday, but an even, if rather dour batting performance on the Monday had taken Glamorgan to a 59-run lead. A second wicket stand of 122 between Butcher and Smith, who both made centuries, seemed to reassert Surrey's supremacy. Butcher was in fine form and hit 128 off 134 balls. The second wicket stand occupied only 18 overs.

A soggy day meant three abandonments and reduced overs everywhere. At Lord's, Warwickshire needed 92 off 18 overs, scored 26 from the first 7 and then folded up before Emburey. Alan Lewis Jones hit 77 off 36 deliveries to help Glamorgan to their target of 118 off 15 overs. In fact, they got to victory in 12 overs. Romaines led Gloucestershire to victory with 3 balls to spare in the 20-over match at Bournemouth, and Clive Rice led Notts to victory in 12.2 of the 13 overs allowed against League-leaders Yorkshire. Worcestershire were reduced to 22 overs by rain, but Patel's fine all-round cricket ensured that they needed only 19.5 overs in which to beat Northants.

From the abandoned matches, the most noteworthy performance was Richards' six wickets at Old Trafford, a Somerset record.

Nat West Trophy Quarter Finals

3 August

at Bristol

Gloucestershire 252 for 8 (P.W. Romaines 82)
Hampshire 256 for 4 (C.L. Smith 101 not out, M.C.J. Nicholas 51)

Hampshire won by 6 wickets
(Man of the Match – C.L. Smith)

at Canterbury

Kent 251 for 8 (C.S. Cowdrey 56)
Warwickshire 146 (K.B.S. Jarvis 4 for 19)

Kent won by 105 runs
(Man of the Match – K.B.S. Jarvis)

at Northampton

Northamptonshire 198 for 9
Middlesex 199 for 3 (G.D. Barlow 77, C.T. Radley 63)

Middlesex won by 7 wickets
(*Man of the Match* – G.D. Barlow)

at Hove

Sussex 65 (J. Garner 4 for 8, I.T. Botham 4 for 20)
Somerset 69 for 3

Somerset won by 7 wickets
(*Man of the Match* – T. Gard)

Larkins and Cook launched the Northants innings with a
flourish against Middlesex. Cowans was despatched with the
same contempt that Gooch had shown for him in the Benson
and Hedges Final and Williams followed after only one over,
but Gatting is a captain of resource who never allows batsmen to become complacent. Where his quick bowlers had
failed, Slack succeeded, and allied to him was the relentless
accuracy of Phil Edmonds. Cook hit across the line and was
bowled after frustration. In the twentieth over, Larkins skied
a return catch to the bowler and Lamb was brilliantly caught
on the leg-side, second ball, by Downton who was standing
up to Slack. Willey and Williams played some positive shots,
but Willey, whose stance is now completely square on to

*Trevor Guard. Five catches behind the stumps and the Man of
the Match award in Somerset's rout of Sussex at Hove.
(Adrian Murrell)*

suggest that he is playing on another wicket, hit Gatting high
to deep point. Downton added an excellent stumping to his
catch to get rid of Kapil Dev, and, in spite of Capel's elegant
promise, Northants were finished.

Middlesex lost Slack, run out by the bowler Kapil Dev, but
then Radley and Barlow with that assurance that stamps all
that Middlesex do added 149 in 40 overs and left the home
side little hope. Gatting finished the game with a straight six
off Willey, and one felt that the most productive part of the
afternoon for Northants had been the fathers who were in-
formed throughout the day that their wives had added to the
population in the local hospital. It brought some joy over the
public address system.

Willis won the toss and asked Kent to bat. There was
immediate success when the Warwickshire skipper had
Woolmer caught, but from that point on, the game went
totally in Kent's favour. There were positive contributions
from everybody and they reached 251. Jarvis then had Smith
taken at second slip and Kallicharran at first and there was
no contest. The visitors dissolved as rapidly as they had done
in the 1982 Final and Jarvis, only playing because Dilley was
unfit, picked up two more wickets and the individual award.

The recent troubles at Hove gained further publicity with
a dreadful batting display against Somerset for whom Garner and Botham were at their buoyant best and Gard took
five catches behind the stumps. The ball moved appreciably
and it made for a dramatic morning and a very one-sided
match.

It was very different at Bristol where Gloucestershire were
put in and, with Romaines punching well, reached 149 for 2
at lunch off 35 overs. They seemed set for a big score, but
Zaheer, who had suggested ease and longevity, was bowled
by Stevenson in mid-stroke and although there were useful
contributions from Hignell and Bainbridge, 252 for 8 was a
disappointment.

It seemed enough when the dangerous Greenidge was

*Kevin Jarvis. Left out of the Kent side for much of the season,
he returned to take the Man of the Match award in the Nat
West Trophy Quarter Final against Warwickshire. (Adrian
Murrell)*

Graham Barlow steered the Middlesex machine towards further honours in the convincing win at Northampton. (George Herringshaw)

bowled at 13, but Nicholas hit cleanly and Smith took root and 86 were added. Then Jesty helped Smith to add 90 and Hampshire were moving solidly towards their target. Smith was now in total command. He had paced the innings perfectly and although Terry was caught off Shepherd with ten still needed, Hampshire strolled home with 10 balls to spare.

Gloucestershire were handicapped by an injury to Childs which prevented him bowling, but Smith's innings had put the issue beyond all dispute.

4 August

at The Oval

New Zealanders 222 for 9 (J.V. Coney 51)
Surrey 166

New Zealanders won by 56 runs

6, 7 and 8 August

at Bournemouth

Hampshire 149 and 154
New Zealanders 244 (M.D. Crowe 70) and 60 for 1

New Zealanders won by 9 wickets

6, 8 and 9 August

at Chelmsford

Middlesex 83 (D.R. Pringle 7 for 32) and 634 for 7 dec (M.W. Gatting 160, J.E. Emburey 133, G.D. Barlow 132, C.T. Radley 67, P.R. Downton 67)
Essex 289 (C. Gladwin 61, N.G. Cowans 4 for 72)

Match drawn
Essex 7 pts, Middlesex 4 pts

at Cheltenham

Gloucestershire 376 (J.N. Shepherd 98 not out, A.W. Stovold 83, Zaheer Abbas 50)
Glamorgan 204 (R.C. Ontong 81, J.H. Childs 5 for 77) and 163 (J.N. Shepherd 7 for 64)

Gloucestershire won by an innings and 9 runs
Gloucestershire 23 pts, Glamorgan 4 pts

at Canterbury

Worcestershire 376 for 9 dec (T.S. Curtis 84, D.J. Humphries 59, P.A. Neale 56, D.L. Underwood 7 for 103) and 141 (D.L. Underwood 7 for 55)
Kent 276 (C.J. Tavare 93, M.R. Benson 53, J.D. Inchmore 4 for 32, R.K. Illingworth 4 for 86) and 199 for 7 (M.R. Benson 57, D.N. Patel 4 for 88)

Match drawn
Worcestershire 6 pts, Kent 5 pts

at Leicester

Leicestershire 226 (G.J. Parsons 56, M. Hendrick 4 for 47) and 292 for 8 dec (I.P. Butcher 139, M. Hendrick 5 for 25)
Nottinghamshire 212 (B.N. French 59, L.B. Taylor 4 for 29) and 256 (D.W. Randall 94, L.B. Taylor 7 for 73)

Leicestershire won by 50 runs
Leicestershire 22 pts, Nottinghamshire 6 pts

at Weston-super-Mare

Northamptonshire 405 for 5 dec (R.N. Kapil Dev 120, R.G. Williams 75 not out, P. Willey 71, A.J. Lamb 51) and 182 for 4 dec (P. Willey 56)
Somerset 267 for 7 dec (I.V.A. Richards 61, N.F.M. Popplewell 52, N.A. Mallender 4 for 69) and 278 for 8 (I.V.A. Richards 128 not out, R.N. Kapil Dev 4 for 76)

Match drawn
Northamptonshire 7 pts, Somerset 4 pts

at The Oval

Warwickshire 230 (T.A. Lloyd 124 not out, S.T. Clarke 7 for 53) and 323 for 3 dec (A.I. Kallicharran 173 not out, D.L. Amiss 76)
Surrey 301 for 9 dec (A.R. Butcher 75, D.B. Pauline 52, N. Gifford 6 for 94) and 188 for 6 (M.A. Lynch 59 not out, N. Gifford 4 for 82)

Match drawn
Surrey 7 pts, Warwickshire 5 pts

at Eastbourne

Sussex 320 for 5 dec (Imran Khan 82, G.D. Mendis 59, A.P. Wells 54 not out) and 186 for 5 dec
Derbyshire 257 (I.A. Anderson 87, C.E. Waller 4 for 60, C.M. Wells 4 for 72) and 219 for 9 (I.S. Anderson 79, A. Hill 54, K.J. Barnett 51, A.C.S. Pigott 6 for 22)

Match drawn
Sussex 8 pts, Derbyshire 5 pts

ABOVE: *Neil Foster opens the Essex attack against Middlesex in the vital Schweppes County Championship game at Chelmsford. He made his debut for England five days later in what proved to be his last match of the season because of his back injury which necessitated an operation to remove metal plates. (Patrick Eagar).* BELOW: *Richard Ellis is lbw offering no shot at Pringle who had a career best 7 for 32. (Patrick Eagar)*

Downton becomes another Pringle victim. (Patrick Eagar)

at Leeds

Lancashire 344 (D. Lloyd 73, J. Simmons 52) and 256 for 3 dec (S.J. O'Shaughnessy 100 not out, G. Fowler 75, J. Abrahams 50)
Yorkshire 305 for 4 dec (M.D. Moxon 153, J.D. Love 67 not out, C.W.J. Athey 63) and 90 for 7

Match drawn
Yorkshire 7 pts, Lancashire 4 pts

The top-of-the-table clash between Essex and Middlesex began in high drama and ended in something close to farce. Essex, intent on playing to their strengths, asked Middlesex to bat on a green wicket under a lowering sky. The first ball of the morning was a bye; the second saw Slack caught behind by the bounding David East off John Lever. This was the first in a series of Middlesex catastrophes brought about by Derek Pringle, operating from the Writtle end, and some poor batting. The ball moved menacingly all morning. There was some fine catching and Pringle returned career best figures as Middlesex were out shortly before lunch for 83, Barlow, technique and determination in equal measure, was unbeaten on 44. Chris Gladwin, the young left-hander introduced to open the Essex innings, batted with great power and maturity and by the end of the day, with six wickets in hand, Essex led by 105. They failed to capitalise on this on the Monday morning until David East and Foster raised their lead to 206.

Batting again, Middlesex lost Slack at 44. Barlow, however, was badly missed, twice, and he and Radley began sound repair work. It continued into the third day with a stand of 210. Essex had three quick successes before lunch, but Gatting and Emburey added 268 for the fifth wicket. They saved the game for Middlesex, and Essex resorted to saving themselves from being fined for slow over-rate by having Gooch and Pont bowling off two paces to send down 48 overs an hour. The only ones not to be saved were the paying public who voiced some frustration as Middlesex became the first side to score as many as they did for 36 years. Essex lost Pringle with a broken finger to add to their disappointment.

Glamorgan's short run of success was ended when John Shepherd, who had earlier scored 98 not out, caught them on a worn wicket at Cheltenham. It was a very welcome second championship win of the season for Gloucestershire.

A splendidly contested drawn game at Canterbury saw Underwood take 14 wickets for 158 and both sides with a chance of victory at the close. Those two fine young batsmen, Benson and Aslett, both completed a thousand runs for the season, and there was encouragement for Worcestershire in the efforts of Illingworth, Curtis and Patel.

Hampshire chose to field a weakened side against the tourists and lost early on the third day while Sussex showed an encouraging reawakening at Eastbourne. Without a championship win for two months, Sussex set Derbyshire to make 250 in 3 hours on the last afternoon. For a long time Derbyshire looked like winning as Anderson, Barnett and Hill saw them to 187 for 1 with 11 overs remaining. Then Pigott, bowling quite briskly, took 6 for 14 in 7 overs and Derbyshire were thankful to Taylor and Mortensen who batted out the last nine deliveries to save the game for them.

With Kapil Dev in magnificent all-round form, Northants had Somerset at 88 for 5 on the last day, but Viv Richards, batting at number six because of a stomach disorder, reached a hundred off 99 balls and brought Somerset to the brink of victory. Kapil Dev and Willey, however, bowled Northants back to parity.

A punishing century from Ian Butcher who had taken his chance in the Leicestershire side so eagerly set up Leicestershire's victory over Notts. Needing 307 in 273 minutes, Notts had hopes of winning when Randall was batting, his 94 was his best of the season, but Les Taylor claimed seven wickets on a pitch where the bounce was uneven and the home side snatched victory with 6 overs left.

Andy Lloyd carried his bat through the Warwickshire innings on the Saturday and earned a call to the England party, but, in spite of more fine bowling from Gifford, Surrey led on the first innings. The home side appeared to have every chance of winning, but excellent batting from Kallicharran and Amiss turned the match and Surrey were left with little to gain but a draw.

Moxon hit a vigorous career best in the Roses Match and then Steve O'Shaughnessy reached a maiden century to justify the confidence shown in him by the Lancashire selectors. Yorkshire were asked to make 296 in 155 minutes on a crumbling wicket and after McFarlane had dismissed Boycott and Athey they struggled against O'Shaughnessy who took 3 wickets in 17 balls. Moxon, however, stood firm and later Love and Carrick saved the match.

John Player League

7 August

at Chelmsford

Essex 184 for 8 (K.W.R. Fletcher 55 not out)
Middlesex 187 for 6 (G.D. Barlow 56)

Middlesex (4 pts) won by 4 wickets

at Cheltenham

Glamorgan 187 for 7 (Javed Miandad 81)
Gloucestershire 190 for 5 (Zaheer Abbas 80)

Gloucestershire (4 pts) won by 5 wickets

at Canterbury

Kent 228 for 8 (C.S. Cowdrey 95, R.M. Ellcock 4 for 43)
Worcestershire 120 (E.A. Baptiste 4 for 29)

Kent (4 pts) won by 108 runs

at Leicester

Leicestershire 240 for 3 (N.E. Briers 101 not out, D.I. Gower 57)
Nottinghamshire 214 for 5 (R.T. Robinson 68)

Leicestershire (4 pts) won by 26 runs

at Weston-super-Mare

Northamptonshire 123 for 9 (J. Garner 4 for 22)
Somerset 125 for 0 (P.W. Denning 62 not. out, P.M. Roebuck 51 not out)

Somerset (4 pts) won by 10 wickets

at The Oval

Surrey 157
Warwickshire 160 for 5 (D.L. Amiss 60)

Warwickshire (4 pts) won by 5 wickets

at Eastbourne

Sussex 148 (G.D. Mendis 50, S. Oldham 4 for 21)
Derbyshire 146 for 7

Sussex (4 pts) won by 2 runs

at Leeds

Lancashire 162 for 8
Yorkshire 163 for 6

Yorkshire (4 pts) won by 4 wickets

Two new county caps, Aslett and Dennis, had celebratory victories with their sides. Yorkshire won easily at Headingley to stay top of the table and Kent, for whom Chris Cowdrey hit a blistering 95 in 69 minutes, won with 7.2 overs to spare so staying 4 points behind the leaders. Somerset overwhelmed a limp Northants to stay second, and Sussex, in a remarkable match at Eastbourne, won by 2 runs to keep level with Kent.

On a wicket which aided the seamers, Sussex reached 82

without loss and then disintegrated slowly. Derbyshire moved smoothly, if not quickly, and reached 120 for 4 at which point Greig, obviously still far from fit, took wickets with successive balls. Six were needed off the last over, but Reeve bowled straight on a length and thwarted them.

Glamorgan's hopes faded further at Cheltenham and Surrey, who were not enjoying Sundays, were beaten with 15 balls to spare at The Oval. Nigel Briers hit 101 not out in 96 minutes and enabled Leicestershire to reach 240 at Grace Road. Robinson and Rice added 100 in 15 overs for Notts, but they fell short of their target, frustrated by Andy Roberts' accuracy.

Essex lost touch with the leading group when, David East, Pringle and Fletcher apart, they batted moderately and then saw exciting knocks from Barlow and Downton give Middlesex victory with an over to spare.

10, 11 and 12 August

at Chelmsford

Leicestershire 301 (B.F. Davison 106, N.E. Briers 58, N. Phillip 6 for 92)
Essex 129 (G. Ferris 6 for 43) and 394 (G.A. Gooch 110, K.S. McEwan 51)

Match drawn
Leicestershire 7 pts, Essex 4 pts

at Ebbw Vale

Nottinghamshire 245 (J.D. Birch 88, W.W. Davis 7 for 70) and 286 for 9 dec (D.W. Randall 70, C.J.C. Rowe 4 for 29)
Glamorgan 187 (K. Saxelby 5 for 52) and 279 for 9 (A.L. Jones 84 not out, C.J.C. Rowe 61)

Match drawn
Nottinghamshire 6 pts, Glamorgan 5 pts

at Cheltenham

Gloucestershire 356 for 5 dec (A.W. Stovold 164 not out, Zaheer Abbas 109) and 217 for 6 dec (A.J. Hignell 51 not out, N. Gifford 4 for 52)
Warwickshire 303 for 9 dec (K.D. Smith 109, D.L. Amiss 52) and 271 for 6 (K.D. Smith 66)

Warwickshire won by 4 wickets
Warwickshire 21 pts, Gloucestershire 7 pts

at Canterbury

Kent 343 for 8 dec (R.A. Woolmer 120, E.A. Baptiste 91) and 121 for 7 dec
Surrey 233 (R.D.V. Knight 53, A.R. Butcher 52, E.A. Baptiste 4 for 73) and 235 for 6 (M.A. Lynch 76 not out, D.B. Pauline 60)

Surrey won by 4 wickets
Surrey 21 pts, Kent 6 pts

at Northampton

Middlesex 223 (D.S. Steele 4 for 46) and 210 (P.R. Downton 61, P. Willey 4 for 51, R.G. Williams 4 for 74)

Northamptonshire 332 (G. Cook 79, G. Sharp 55 not out, P. Willey 52, J.E. Emburey 4 for 70) and 102 for 1

Northamptonshire won by 9 wickets
Northamptonshire 24 pts, Middlesex 5 pts

at Weston-super-Mare

Yorkshire 286 (G. Boycott 83, M.D. Moxon 55, V.J. Marks 6 for 79) and 177 for 8 dec (P. Carrick 72)
Somerset 164 (R. Illingworth 4 for 48) and 153 for 6

Match drawn
Yorkshire 6 pts, Somerset 3 pts

at Eastbourne

Sussex 263 (Imran Khan 101, A.C.S. Pigott 63, M.D. Marshall 4 for 58) and 269 for 7 dec (G.D. Mendis 76, Imran Khan 55, R.S. Cowan 50)
Hampshire 250 for 6 dec (T.E. Jesty 75, V.P. Terry 68) and 285 for 7 (V.P. Terry 115, C.E. Waller 5 for 96)

Hampshire won by 3 wickets
Hampshire 23 pts, Sussex 5 pts

at Worcester

Lancashire 209 (C.H. Lloyd 84, A.P. Pridgeon 5 for 21, D.N. Patel 4 for 54) and 196 (D. Lloyd 78, N.H. Fairbrother 51, D.N. Patel 5 for 52)
Worcestershire 199 (J. Simmons 5 for 55) and 207 for 5 (J.A. Ormrod 72 not out)

Worcestershire won by 5 wickets
Worcestershire 21 pts, Lancashire 6 pts

Middlesex, leaders in the Schweppes County Championship, confirmed their recent sluggish form by surrendering conclusively to Northants. Reduced by Test calls and injury, they batted poorly on the opening day and never really recovered. Northants, on the other hand, having lost Larkins at 5, batted with purpose throughout the order and took a first innings lead of 109. Middlesex, who had missed a vital bowling point with a dropped catch, fared no better at the second attempt than they had at the first. Initially, it had been the slow left-arm of David Steele that had caused them the most difficulties, now it was the combined off-spin of Willey and Williams, enjoying a fruitful period, which tantalised them. Downton, Williams and Ellis effected something of a middle order recovery, but it was insufficient to trouble Northants.

Essex failed to prosper from Middlesex's defeat. Leicestershire were 157 for 6, but Brian Davison thwarted Essex and took the visitors to a fourth batting point. The early damage had been done by Norbert Phillip who made his point about being omitted from the Benson and Hedges Final. Essex floundered badly even though Leicestershire had been deprived of Cook, called to the Test match, Agnew substituting; they found Ferris' pace far too much for them and, Gladwin and McEwan apart, they batted very badly. Following-on, it was a different matter. There was application and resolution that had been lacking earlier. Gooch hit his first championship hundred of the season, but it took him 5 hours, and the Chelmsford crowd suffered another saving draw as Essex batted out the third day.

Alan Lewis Jones, who batted for three hours, and Steve Barwick batted through the last four overs to save Glamorgan from defeat against Notts. Winston Davis had bowled finely on the first day, but Saxelby, Randall and Rice grasped the iniative for the visitors, and, in spite of Alan Lewis, Rowe and Henderson giving Glamorgan a glimpse of victory, they never really lost it.

There were three very exciting victories. The cultured Woolmer and the effervescent Baptiste had begun the match well for Kent and on Ladies' Day Surrey had dawdled so that when Cowdrey set them to get 232 in 205 minutes on a wicket that was turning it seemed thay had little hope. Lynch, however, hit four sixes and seven fours in an exhilarating 76 not out which, allied to Pauline's responsible 60, set up the Surrey win.

After Stovold, sadly missed in the NatWest Quarter Final, and Zaheer had dominated the first day, David Smith hit the ninth first-class century of his career to keep Warwickshire in touch at Cheltenham. Ultimately, Warwickshire needed 271 in 190 minutes and Smith, Humpage and Kallicharran launched them well. The last ball arrived with one needed for victory and a ball down the leg-side was only parried by wicket-keeper Russell so that Thorne and Asif Din went through for a winning bye.

Equally sensationally at Eastbourne, Hampshire survived Imran Khan's first hundred of the season to score 283 in 187 minutes. Tremlett hit the fifth ball of the last over for 4 to win the match, but the victory was made possible by a chanceless 115 from Paul Terry who hit a six and 13 fours.

Yorkshire and Somerset could contrive no such excitement at Weston-super-Mare where injury to Viv Richards reduced Somerset's hopes of victory.

Ten runs behind on the first innings, Worcestershire, with Patel bowling well, relied on the application and unswerving concentration of Alan Ormrod to take them to their first championship win of the season. On a pitch favouring the spinners, he batted for 280 minutes for 72 not out and took the home side to a much desired victory.

THIRD TEST MATCH

England showed four changes from the side which had lost at Headingley, and three of the replacements, Smith, Foster and Cook, were new to Test cricket. Fowler had reported a slight injury and the selectors had immediately replaced him with Andy Lloyd, who did not play, while Edmonds injured his back on getting out of his car and Cook was called from Leicestershire's match at Chelmsford to take his place. Gatting came back in place of Randall and Foster, with barely a season of first-class cricket behind him, replaced Dilley. Foster had shown great promise, but as the Essex committee reported, he was not fully fit, and it was surprising that the selectors chose to disregard the club's advice. New Zealand introduced Gray to Test cricket.

Howarth won the toss and asked England to bat, a doubtful decision which gained support in the opening over when Chris Smith was lbw to his first ball in Test cricket.

Gower and Tavare survived for an hour at which point, to the surprise of most, Howarth introduced Martin Crowe into the attack. In his first over, Gower mishooked and the ball soared high to square-leg where Cairns missed the simplest of catches. In the next over, bowled by Chatfield, Gower edged the ball to slip where Cairns stood rooted as the 'catch' flew past him.

Rarely can two missed catches have proved so costly in a Test match. Gower found fluency and timing and stroked the ball to the boundary with effortless charm. In the previous

Chris Smith walks away sadly, lbw to Richard Hadlee to his first ball in Test cricket. (Ken Kelly)

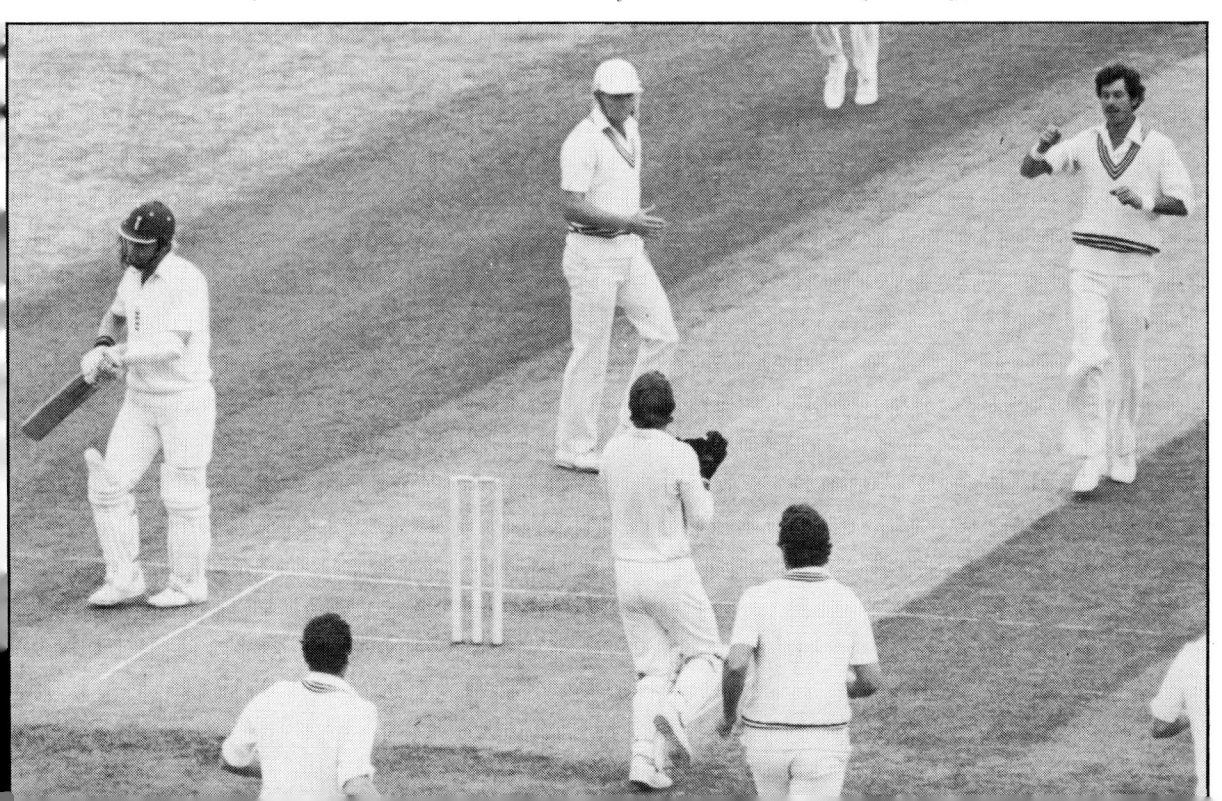

ABOVE: *David Gower prospers after being dropped by Cairns. Gray is at short-leg.* (*Ken Kelly*)

BELOW: *Joy for New Zealand. Tavare is bowled by Martin Crowe for 51.*

county match he had scored 0 and 0, now he hit sixteen fours in his innings of 108 off 198 deliveries. He and Tavare added 149 for the second wicket and were both out to Martin Crowe within half an hour of each other.

Lamb still seemed a mixture of confident shots and uncertain role until he took a lifter from Chatfield and Botham scratched miserably, casting cursing eyes at the wicket. Gatting, however, was forceful, asserting his right to a Test place with some bounding, thumping drives and hooks, but he too was befriended by some poor New Zealand fielding and catching. Taylor also escaped and England closed at 279 for 5. Had New Zealand held their catches, England would not have reached 200. It had been a bad day for the visitors.

Hadlee made short work of the remaining English wickets on the second morning, the last five wickets falling for 47 runs in 20 overs. Gatting, who had given hints of a maiden Test century, was the first to go when he was caught mishooking.

Willis who, contrary to all predictions, seems to get better and quicker with the years bowled fiercely and dismissed Wright with a brute of a ball which lifted sharply. The England captain handled his young newcomers with great sensitivity, encouraging Foster with the new ball and soon introducing Cook into the attack.

The slow left-armer had not enjoyed the best of seasons and he began nervously, but he settled quickly and bowled Howarth when the New Zealand skipper unwisely tried to cut.

ABOVE: *Botham in dejection. Tense and uneasy, he is lbw to Cairns for 8. (Ken Kelly)*

BELOW: *Mike Gatting has an escape. The ball hits the wicket, but he is well home. (Adrian Murrell)*

ABOVE: *New Zealand's troubles begin. Wright is caught off*
fierce lifter from Willis. Smith is at short-leg. (Adrian Murrell

LEFT: *Wickets for Hadlee.* ABOVE: *Taylor is bowled for 16*
MIDDLE: *Foster is caught behind for 10.* BELOW: *Willis falls t*
a diving catch for 7 (Ken Kelly)

BELOW: *Nick Cook's first wicket in Test cricket. Howart*
plays back and is bowled. Taylor reacts joyfully. (Ken Kelly

Close encounters of the Test match kind. Gray plays forward. Gower swoops. Botham and Gatting hover like vultures. (Ken Kelly)

Crowe and Edgar batted with sense and confidence and added 98, but Botham produced a good ball to break the stand. Edgar's splendidly concentrated and defiant innings ended when he lofted Cook tamely to mid-off, and the same bowler then beat Coney on the back foot. Night-watchman Bracewell was caught bat-pad, and New Zealand had stumbled to 176 for 6 at the end of a fine day's cricket.

Hadlee was caught at slip in the first over of the third morning and the last five wickets added only 15 runs. Cook had five wickets on his Test debut, well earned, and Botham

Another wicket for Cook. Jeremy Coney is bowled. (Adrian Murrell)

retorted to the criticism of recent weeks with four.

He was to make a more positive retort later in the day. Howarth, who was outcaptained by Willis in this match, belatedly introduced the slow left-arm of Gray and he bowled impressively to dismiss Gower, Lamb and Gatting whom he had frustrated into rashness. Botham ended New Zealand's hopes with a fine knock of determination and vigour. He hit 61 in just over two hours, faced 101 deliveries and hit seven fours. He bowed elaborately to the press box on reaching his fifty and then took the warmth of applause from a packed and happy Lord's to whom he was still the national hero.

England were out quickly on Monday morning, adding only 5 to their overnight score. Needing 347 to win on a wicket that was now of doubtful quality, New Zealand struggled against the fire of Willis and the accuracy and turn of Cook. Coney batted bravely until he became Foster's first

ABOVE: *Allan Lamb catches Gray off Botham. (Adrian Murrell)* BELOW: *Botham gives a Saturday afternoon display. A fine knock of 61 is punctuated by big hits. Gray evades, Smith looks on in wonder. (Ken Kelly)*

Chris Smith hits past Bracewell in a happier second innings.
(*Adrian Murrell*)

Test wicket, and there was a typical flourish from Hadlee that magnificent all-rounder. Cowans, too, bowled well and England won with a day to spare.

On reflection, New Zealand might consider that when Cairns dropped Gower with the score at 40 for 1, like Citizen Kane's leaving behind of his sleigh, something vital was lost from their lives.

Evan Gray – an impressive first bowling spell for New Zealand.
(*Ken Kelly*)

THIRD TEST MATCH – ENGLAND v. NEW ZEALAND
11, 12, 13 and 15 August 1983 at Lord's

ENGLAND

	FIRST INNINGS		SECOND INNINGS	
C.J. Tavare	b M.D. Crowe	51	c M.D. Crowe, b Hadlee	16
C.L. Smith	lbw, b Hadlee	0	c Coney, b Hadlee	43
D.I. Gower	lbw, b M.D. Crowe	108	c M.D. Crowe, b Gray	34
A.J. Lamb	c sub (J.J. Crowe), b Chatfield	17	c Hadlee, b Gray	4
M.W. Gatting	c Wright, b Hadlee	81	b Gray	15
I.T. Botham	lbw, b Cairns	8	c Coney, b Chatfield	61
R.W. Taylor*	b Hadlee	16	c and b Coney	7
N.A. Foster	c Smith, b Hadlee	10	c Wright, b Hadlee	3
N.G.B. Cook	b Chatfield	16	c Bracewell, b Chatfield	5
R.G.D. Willis†	c Smith, b Hadlee	7	not out	2
N.G. Cowans	not out	1	c Smith, b Chatfield	1
Extras	b 3, lb 3, w 2, nb 3	11	b 5, lb 6, w 9	20
		326		**211**

	O	M	R	W	O	M	R	W
Hadlee	40	15	93	5	26	7	42	3
Chatfield	36.3	8	116	2	13.3	4	29	3
Cairns	23	8	65	1	3	—	9	—
M.D. Crowe	13	1	35	2				
Bracewell					11	4	29	—
Gray					30	8	73	3
Coney	8	7	6	—	6	4	9	1

FALL OF WICKETS
1- 1, 2- 152, 3- 174, 4- 191, 5- 218, 6- 288, 7- 290, 8- 303, 9- 318
1- 26, 2- 79, 3- 87, 4- 119, 5- 147, 6- 195, 7- 199, 8- 208, 9- 210

NEW ZEALAND

	FIRST INNINGS		SECOND INNINGS	
J.G. Wright	c Lamb, b Willis	11	c Taylor, b Botham	12
B.A. Edgar	c Willis, b Cook	70	c Lamb, b Cowans	27
G.P. Howarth†	b Cook	25	c Taylor, b Willis	0
M.D. Crowe	b Botham	46	c Foster, b Cowans	12
J.V. Coney	b Cook	7	c Gatting, b Foster	68
E.J. Gray	c Lamb, b Botham	11	c Lamb, b Cook	17
J.G. Bracewell	c Gower, b Cook	0	(8) lbw, b Willis	4
R.J. Hadlee	c Botham, b Cook	0	(7) b Willis	30
B.L. Cairns	c Lamb, b Botham	5	b Cook	16
I.D.S. Smith*	c Lamb, b Botham	3	not out	17
E.J. Chatfield	not out	5	c and b Cook	2
Extras	lb 5, nb 3	8	b 3, lb 4, nb 7	14
		191		**219**

	O	M	R	W	O	M	R	W
Willis	13	6	28	1	12	5	24	3
Foster	16	5	40	—	12	—	35	1
Cowans	9	1	30	—	11	1	36	2
Botham	20.4	6	50	4	7	2	20	1
Cook	26	11	35	5	27.2	9	90	3

FALL OF WICKETS
1- 18, 2- 49, 3- 147, 4- 159, 5- 176, 6- 176, 7- 176, 8- 183, 9- 184
1- 15, 2- 17, 3- 57, 4- 61, 5- 108, 6- 154, 7- 158, 8- 190, 9- 206

Umpires: D.J. Constant and D.G.L. Evans

England won by 127 runs

Derbyshire C.C.C.
Limited-Over Matches – 1983

BATTING

Match column key:

1. v. Lancashire (Old Trafford) 8 May (J.P.)
2. v. Yorkshire (Chesterfield) 9 May (B.&H.)
3. v. Warwickshire (Edgbaston) 14 May (B.&H.)
4. v. Northamptonshire (Derby) 15 May (J.P.)
5. v. Nottinghamshire (Trent Bridge) 17 May (B.&H.)
6. v. Lancashire (Derby) 19 May (B.&H.)
7. v. Essex (Chelmsford) 22 May (J.P.)
8. v. Warwickshire (Coventry) 5 June (J.P.)
9. v. Leicestershire (Derby) 12 June (J.P.)
10. v. Middlesex (Chesterfield) 26 June (J.P.)
11. v. Suffolk (Bury St Edmunds) 29 June (N.W.)
12. v. Worcestershire (Derby) 3 July (J.P.)
13. v. Gloucestershire (Bristol) 10 July (J.P.)
14. v. Middlesex (Derby) 20 July (N.W.)
15. v. Nottinghamshire (Derby) 24 July (J.P.)
16. v. Kent (Chesterfield) 31 July (J.P.)
17. v. Sussex (Eastbourne) 7 August (J.P.)

Batsman	1	2	3	4	5	6	7	8	9	10	11	12	13	14	15	16	17
J.G. Wright			0	67	5		108										
B. Wood			0	36	26	—	10	17									
K.J. Barnett			30	7	5	—	11	0	20	35	14	10	88	4	29		11
J.H. Hampshire			83	36*	—									35	15		21
A. Hill			35	4	39	—	3	20	12	52	30	30	8	26	3		13
G. Miller			41	26*	16		27*	0		1*	2	52	55*				23
R.W. Taylor			10*		4*	—		7	—	—	10*	11	0				1*
P.G. Newman			4	3	11*	—											
C.J. Tunnicliffe			2	—	5		14*	4	8	—		33*	13*	6	4*		18*
D.G. Moir			3														
S. Oldham			2	—	0		—	4	5	—	—	—	6	2*			—
I.S. Anderson				—	32		33	35	7	47	39	0	28	0	6		30
R.J. Finney					21			7	14*	46*	2	5	29	31*	6		
O. Mortensen								1*	0*	—	—	—	2*				—
J.E. Morris								21	61	7	6	22			16		
W.P. Fowler								26	28	—	37	24	7	0	—		0
B.J.M. Maher								6									—
M.A. Holding														0			
Byes					1		5				4	1		1			
Leg-byes			12	11	4		10	7	3	7	10	10	8	6	4		13
Wides			3	9	4		1	2			6	2	1	4	2		9
No-balls			1	2	2		1	2			5	1	4	1	1		1
Total			226	201	175		223	150	160	167	229	176	210	87	146		146
Wickets			10	5	9		5	10	10	4	6	7	10	7	4		7
Result	Ab.	Ab.	L	W	L	Ab.	Ab.	W	L	L	W	W	W	L	W	Ab.	L
Points	2	1	0	4	0	1	2	4	0	0	—	4	4	—	4	2	0

Catches

13 – R.W. Taylor (ct 12/st 1)
9 – G. Miller
8 – K.J. Barnett
6 – A. Hill
5 – C.J. Tunnicliffe and B.J.M. Maher (ct 4/st 1)
4 – I.S. Anderson and M.A. Holding
3 – J.H. Hampshire and J.G. Wright
2 – R.J. Finney, J.E. Morris and O.H. Mortensen
1 – P.G. Newman and W.P. Fowler

BOWLING

	P.G. Newman	C.J. Tunnicliffe	S. Oldham	D.G. Moir	B. Wood	G. Miller	I.S. Anderson	O. Mortensen	R.J. Finney
(B.&H.) v. Warwickshire (Edgbaston) 14 May	11–1–56–0	11–2–30–2	11–0–58–2	3–1–21–0	11–0–59–0	8–0–44–0			
(B.&H.) v. Northamptonshire (Derby) 15 May	8–3–15–2	2–0–18–0	8–1–16–0		8–0–35–3	8–0–19–2	5–1–15–2		
(B.&H.) v. Nottinghamshire (Trent Br.) 17 May	11–0–55–4	11–1–54–1	11–2–53–2		11–2–29–0	11–1–19–1			
(B.&H.) v. Lancashire (Derby) 19 May	5–3–8–0		5–3–4–1		11–2–26–2	10–1–28–0			
(J.P.) v. Warwickshire (Coventry) 5 June	8–1–47–3	8–0–34–0	8–0–51–3		8–3–29–1			7–1–40–0	
(J.P.) v. Leicestershire (Derby) 12 June		8–1–34–1	8–0–29–0		8–0–32–1			8–0–15–1	3.5–0–28–0
(J.P.) v. Middlesex (Chesterfield) 26 June		8–0–24–2	7–0–35–0			4.1–0–23–1		8–1–30–3	8–1–40–0
(N.W.) v. Suffolk (Bury St Ed.) 29–30 June		12–1–33–0	12–1–47–2			12–2–28–3		12–5–16–3	12–3–32–0
(J.P.) v. Worcestershire (Derby) 3 July		8–0–38–0	8–0–66–2			8–1–27–0		8–0–40–3	8–0–35–1
(J.P.) v. Gloucestershire (Bristol) 10 July		8–0–23–1	8–0–50–2			8–2–12–2		8–0–47–1	8–1–30–0
(N.W.) v. Middlesex (Derby) 20 July		12–1–46–1	12–1–32–2					12–2–51–1	12–1–46–1
(J.P.) v. Nottinghamshire (Derby) 24 July								4–0–33–1	5–2–9–0
(J.P.) v. Kent (Chesterfield) 31 July									
(J.P.) v. Sussex (Eastbourne) 7 August		8–0–35–0	7–1–21–4			8–0–29–1		7.3–0–33–2	8–1–20–2
(J.P.) v. Somerset (Heanor) 14 August		7–0–60–2				8–1–49–1		8–0–19–1	8–1–37–3
(J.P.) v. Glamorgan (Swansea) 21 August		5–0–30–3				5–0–19–1		5–0–27–0	5–0–45–0
(J.P.) v. Yorkshire (Bradford) 28 August	8–3–16–0					8–0–34–2		7.2–0–39–2	2–0–10–0
(J.P.) v. Hampshire (Derby) 4 September	8–2–21–4					8–1–39–0		7–2–17–0	8–0–27–3
Wickets	13	13	20	0	7	14	2	18	10

v. Somerset (Heanor) 14 August (J.P.)	v. Glamorgan (Hove) 21 August (J.P.)	v. Yorkshire (Bradford) 28 August (J.P.)	v. Hampshire (Derby) 4 September (J.P.)	v. Surrey (The Oval) 11 September (J.P.)	Runs
					180
					89
100*	12	29	5		411
					160
19	25	5	7		331
30*	27	8	14		322
	0		13*		56
		6	3		27
—	3				110
					3
					19
54	1	40	12		364
—	21*	41*	11		241
—	3*	—	1*		7
—	6	3	33		175
—	5	8	15		150
—		13*			19
—	7	—	12		19
		2	3		
11	16	9	8		
4	3	3	5		
2	3	1	1		
220	133	168	143		
2	9	7			
W	L	L	W		
4	0	0	4		

W.P. Fowler	M.A. Holding	Byes	Leg-byes	Wides	No-balls	Total	Wkts
		12	4	3		287	5
		3	2			123	9
		9	7			226	8
		2				68	4
		9	9	1		220	7
3–1–2–2		11	1	2		154	5
		4	3	3		162	6
		4	3	1		164	8
		4	7	5	3	225	7
		10	2			174	6
	12–1–50–2	1	11	2	1	240	8
	8–2–27–1	2	4		11	86	2
				Match Abandoned			
		9	1			148	10
1–0–2–0	8–3–32–0	3	9	7	1	219	8
	5–0–21–2		9	3	1	155	7
6–0–24–0	8–0–25–3	4	13	3	3	171	8
	7.4–1–19–3		7	5		135	10
2	11						

Man of the Match Nick Cook. (Ken Kelly)

English Counties Form Charts

The statistics of all limited-over cricket matches follow in pages 428 to 463. The games covered are:

John Player League (J.P.)   Tilcon Trophy (T.T.)
Benson and Hedges Cup (B.&H.)   Asda Trophy (Asda)
National Westminster Bank Trophy (N.W.)

Once again averages are not produced as it is felt that they have little relevance in limited-over cricket where batsmen often sacrifice their wickets for quick runs and bowlers are ordered to contain rather than capture wickets.
In the batting tables a blank indicates that a batsman did not *play* in a game, a dash (—) that he did not *bat*.

13, 15 and 16 August

at Derby

Somerset 273 (J.W. Lloyds 55, R.L. Ollis 50, T. Gard 50, G. Miller 5 for 71) and 233 for 5 dec (P.M. Roebuck 94)
Derbyshire 199 (J.H. Hampshire 74, A. Hill 56, M.R. Davis 4 for 34) and 186 for 4 (B.J.M. Maher 52)

Match drawn
Somerset 7 pts, Derbyshire 4 pts

Essex C.C.C.
Limited-Over Matches – 1983

BATTING

	v. Hampshire (Southampton) 7 May (B.&H.)	v. Hampshire (Southampton) 8 May (J.P.)	v. Somerset (Chelmsford) 14 May (B.&H.)	v. Lancashire (Chelmsford) 15 May (J.P.)	v. Minor Counties (Slough) 17 May (B.&H.)	v. Sussex (Chelmsford) 19 and 20 May (B.&H.)	v. Derbyshire (Chelmsford) 22 May (J.P.)	v. Warwickshire (Chelmsford) 2 and 3 June (B.&H.)	v. Somerset (Taunton) 5 June (J.P.)	v. Kent (Chelmsford) 12 June (J.P.)	v. Sussex (Ilford) 26 June (J.P.)	v. Dorset (Bournemouth) 29 June (N.W.)	v. Nottinghamshire (Trent Bridge) 3 July (J.P.)	v. Kent (Canterbury) 6 July (B.&H.)	v. Warwickshire (Edgbaston) 10 July (J.P.)	v. Glamorgan (Southend) 17 July (J.P.)	v. Kent (Chelmsford) 20 July (N.W.)
G.A. Gooch	68	14	99		38	6		67		58	22	14	116	18	38	176	122
B.R. Hardie	34	51	23	30*	22					66	35			58*	13		61
K.W.R. Fletcher	59	37	3		62*	12		87		41*	55	0	—	33*	54*	1*	31
K.S. McEwan	28	8	1	—	25			3		13	5	73*	162*	—	7	32	17
N. Phillip	20*	1	8		—	0		1		35	4		2*	51		31	10
K.R. Pont	5	17	13	—	18	4		7		6	20*	—	—	—	4	0	0
S. Turner	3	25	11	—	3	9		3*		9	—	—	—			0	0
D.R. Pringle	13*		42*		—	49		31*		8	—	—	—		47	52*	19
D.E. East	—	14*	3	—	12	15		—		1	—	—	—				0
R.E. East	—	7*	10*	—		7*		2*			2*	—	—	—			1*
J.K. Lever			—	—	—	0					7*						
A.W. Lilley		8						0			28	8	13		7		
N.A. Foster								—									—
C. Gladwin																8	
P.J. Prichard																	
D.L. Acfield																	
Byes		1	4					1		1			2	2	1	1	2
Leg-byes	4	13	6		9	13		11		13	10	1	9	4	8	7	7
Wides	21	3			1	3				3	1	1	1	5			1
No-balls	5		2			2				3	·1		1	11		1	1
Total	260	199	225		141	173		231		250	188	117	306	130	230	310	270
Wickets	6	8	8		1	10		8		6	9	3	2	1	7	5	9
Result	W	L	W	Ab.	W	L	Ab.	W	Ab.	W	L	W	W	W	W	W	L
Points	2	0	2	2	2	0	2	—	2	4	0	—	4	—	4	4	—

Catches

30 – D.E. East (ct 26/st 4)
14 – G.A. Gooch
9 – R.E. East
8 – K.W.R. Fletcher

7 – D.R. Pringle
3 – K.S. McEwan, J.K. Lever and S. Turner
2 – N.A. Foster, N. Phillip and A.W. Lilley
1 – B.R. Hardie, K.R. Pont and C. Gladwin

BOWLING

	J.K. Lever	N. Phillip	S. Turner	D.R. Pringle	G.A. Gooch	R.E. East	N.A. Foster	K.R. Pont	A.W. Lilley
(B.&H.) v. Hampshire (Southampton) 7 May	7.3–3–12–1	10–0–27–1	11–2–33–3	6–0–17–2	3–0–11–0	11–0–33–3			
(J.P.) v. Hampshire (Southampton) 8 May	8–2–24–2	8–0–53–2	8–1–48–1			8–1–43–0	8–0–38–1		
(B.&H.) v. Somerset (Chelmsford) 14 May	7–0–16–1	8–1–36–1	11–0–39–1	9.3–0–27–2		11–0–40–2			
(B.&H.) v. Minor Counties (Slough) 17 May	10–3–27–2	10–4–25–1	11–2–24–3	11–3–26–2	6–2–14–0	7–3–6–0			
(B.&H.) v. Sussex (Chelmsford) 19 May	11–5–36–2	6–1–26–0	8–1–26–2	11–1–57–0	9–0–23–1	10–1–25–1			
(B.&H.) v. Warwickshire (Chelmsf'd) 2–3 June		9.3–1–33–4	11–0–31–1	9–2–14–3	4–0–15–0	7–0–27–1	10–0–39–1		
(J.P.) v. Kent (Chelmsford) 12 June	7.2–1–15–3	7–0–24–4	8–0–52–1	8–0–36–0	4–0–28–0	4–0–26–1			
(J.P.) v. Worcestershire (Worcester) 19 June	8–2–32–0	8–0–33–2	8–0–48–3	8–0–53–1		8–0–28–0			
(J.P.) v. Sussex (Ilford) 26 June	7.4–0–39–1	7–0–47–1	8–0–30–0		8–2–17–2	8–0–42–2			
(N.W.) v. Dorset (Bournemouth) 29 June	11.4–2–27–2		12–5–21–1	12–3–19–2		12–4–12–2	12–4–19–3		
(J.P.) v. Nottinghamshire (Trent Br.) 3 July		6–0–19–1	8–0–50–2	5–0–20–1	1–1–0–1	5–0–10–1	4–0–9–0	8–0–43–0	2–0–19–1
(B.&H.) v. Kent (Canterbury) 6 July	11–2–29–3		11–5–15–2	7–1–22–1	11–1–25–2	5–0–11–0	6–2–9–1		
(J.P.) v. Warwickshire (Edgbaston) 10 July		6–1–16–1		8–0–60–2	8–0–36–2	8–0–36–1	6–0–39–1	4–0–32–0	
(J.P.) v. Glamorgan (Southend) 17 July		8–1–29–0	8–0–49–1	8–0–54–1		8–0–47–1	7–0–47–1		
(N.W.) v. Kent (Chelmsford) 20 July		10–1–43–2	10–1–56–2	11–1–54–0	12–3–30–1	5–0–23–0	12–0–44–3		
(B.&H.) v. Middlesex (Lord's) 23 July	11–1–52–1		11–1–24–0	11–0–54–2	11–2–21–1	11–2–26–3			
(J.P.) v. Leicestershire (Leicester) 24 July		3–0–16–2	4–0–35–1	3–0–22–1	5–0–16–1	2.2–0–13–0			
(J.P.) v. Middlesex (Chelmsford) 7 August	8–0–33–1	7–0–34–1	8–0–29–1	8–1–27–1	4–0–26–0	4–0–17–0			
(J.P.) v. Northamptonshire (Wellingborough) 14 August	8–2–22–0	8–0–18–1	8–1–37–0		8–1–49–3	8–1–23–1			
(J.P.) v. Gloucestershire (Colchester) 21 Aug.	8–1–42–3	8–0–44–1	8–0–26–0		8–0–46–2	8–0–52–1			
(J.P.) v. Surrey (The Oval) 28 August		4–1–13–0	7–1–30–2	8–1–20–1	4–0–23–0	8–1–20–2			
(Asda) v. Hampshire (Scarborough) 5 Sept.	8–0–42–1	10–1–31–3	6–3–8–2	8–0–43–1	7–0–24–0	10–2–41–1			
Wickets	23	28	29	23	16	21	13	0	1

v. Middlesex (Lord's) 23 July (B.&H.)	v. Leicestershire (Leicester) 24 July (J.P.)	v. Middlesex (Chelmsford) 7 August (J.P.)	v. Northamptonshire (Wellingborough) 14 August (J.P.)	v. Gloucestershire (Colchester) 21 August (J.P.)	v. Surrey (The Oval) 28 August (J.P.)	v. Hampshire (Scarborough) 5 September (Asda)	v. Yorkshire (Chelmsford) 11 September (J.P.)	Runs
46	41*	18	38	19	10	32		1060
49	—	2	9	25	12	0		490
3		55*	15	19	26	7		600
34		19	12	21	8	9		477
	6*	5	9	95	21	2		301
7			8					109
9	—	7	18*	33	1	10		141
16	15	34			2	9		337
5	—	24	0	0	1	2		77
0		—	3*	1*	8	3*		44
0*		—	—	—		2		9
					6			70
0	—							0
		1	1	36	7	18	100	171
				9*				9
		1	4	1	2	1		
12	1	6	7	5	5	12		
3	2	6			4	5		
8		6		1		1		
192	66	184	159	233	127	195		
10	2	8	8	9	10	10		
L	W	L	W	W	L	L	Ab.	
—	4	0	4	4	0	—	2	

K.W.R. Fletcher	B.R. Hardie	D.L. Acfield	Byes	Leg-byes	Wides	No-balls	Total	Wkts
				12	1	1	147	10
				6	1	1	214	6
			2	8	2	2	172	10
				8	2	8	140	9
				8	2	5	208	8
				7		2	168	10
				6	9	1	197	10
			1	11	2		208	7
				12	2	1	190	6
				7	3	3	111	10
1-0-26-0			2	8	6	5	217	9
				5	8	4	128	10
				8		2	229	9
	1-0-5-0		1	13	2	7	254	4
			1	11	5	7	274	8
			3	9	4	3	196	8
				6	1	1	110	5
				9	6	6	187	6
				3	1	5	158	5
				7	1	2	220	7
		8-3-14-1	4	1		3	128	7
				11	4	1	205	9
0	0	1						

at Cardiff

Glamorgan 336 for 3 dec (R.C. Ontong 105 not out, C.J.C. Rowe 82, D.A. Francis 63, A. Jones 60) and 247 (T. Davies 69 not out)
Kent 301 for 4 dec (M.R. Benson 111, S.G. Hinks 87, C.S. Cowdrey 58 not out) and 283 for 3 (N.R. Taylor 155 not out, M.R. Benson 50)

Kent won by 7 wickets
Kent 20 pts, Glamorgan 5 pts

at Cheltenham

Yorkshire 344 for 5 dec (G. Boycott 140 not out, K. Sharp 121) and 239 for 8 dec (G. Boycott 97)
Gloucestershire 307 for 6 dec (P.W. Romaines 100 not out, J.N. Shepherd 93) and 280 for 5 (B.C. Broad 100, Zaheer Abbas 75)

Gloucestershire won by 5 wickets
Gloucestershire 21 pts, Yorkshire 5 pts

at Old Trafford

Lancashire 193 (W.W. Daniel 4 for 37) and 193 (G. Fowler 59, J.E. Emburey 5 for 64)
Middlesex 120 (G.D. Barlow 50, P.J.W. Allott 5 for 45) and 33 for 0

Match drawn
Lancashire 5 pts, Middlesex 4 pts

Paul Allott had a good week-end to disturb Middlesex. (George Herringshaw)

Glamorgan C.C.C.
Limited-Over Matches – 1983

BATTING

BATTING	v. Middlesex (Lord's) 8 May (J.P.)	v. Comb. Univ. (Cambridge) 14 May (B.&H.)	v. Warwickshire (Swansea) 15 May (J.P.)	v. Middlesex (Uxbridge) 17 May (B.&H.)	v. Surrey (Cardiff) 20 May (B.&H.)	v. Kent (Swansea) 21 and 23 May (B.&H.)	v. Kent (Swansea) 23 May (B.&H.)	v. Lancashire (Swansea) 29 May (J.P.)	v. Nottinghamshire (Trent Bridge) 5 June (J.P.)	v. Yorkshire (Cardiff) 12 June (J.P.)	v. Somerset (Bath) 19 June (J.P.)	v. Leicestershire (Leicester) 26 June (J.P.)	v. Norfolk (Norwich) 29 June (N.W)	v. Sussex (Cardiff) 10 July (J.P.)	v. Essex (Southend) 17 July (J.P.)	v. Hampshire (Swansea) 20 July (N.W.)	v. Northamptonshire (Northampton) 24 July (J.P.)
A. Jones	5	1*	—	—			22	13	34	1			7	38	16	22	
J.A. Hopkins	31	4*	—	—			26	76	23	6	130*	46	32	0	27	0	4
A.L. Jones	22	—	—	—			1	49	0	49	17	19	26	15	13	36	24
Javed Miandad	95	—	—	—			23	61*	62					40	68		19
C.J.C. Rowe	6	—	—	—			25*				25	19	12	—	2	10	
R.C. Ontong	0	—	—	—			5	35	12	25	8*	15	45	8	73*	23	37
M.W.W. Selvey	0	—	—	—			8	—	0*	9*	—	4	8*	2*	—		
E.W. Jones	38	—	—	—			0	—	0*	12	—	7	13	0	—	2	0
B.J. Lloyd	0	—	—	—			18	—	1*	0	—	5	0	13*	—	2	32
M.A. Nash	5	—	—	—			10*	—	0							0*	0*
A.H. Wilkins	3*	—	—	—									—				
D.A. Francis								4*	15	25	11	13	24			12	4
J.G. Thomas								—	37	26	0	3	15		34*	24	
J. Derrick											2			12	—		18*
H. Morris													37	5			
W.W. Davis														0*	1*	0	
S.R. Barwick																	
S.P. Henderson																	
T. Davies																	
G.C. Holmes																	
Byes								1			1				1		3
Leg-byes	10						9	9	10	7	25	10	2	14	13	10	11
Wides	7							3	4	4	6		2	7	2	5	
No-balls	3						1	2	2	1		4	8	1	7		
Total	225	5					148	253	200	167	235	156	202	162	254	138	162
Wickets	10	0					8	4	7	10	4	10	9	8	4	10	8
Result	Ab.	W	Ab.	Ab.	Ab.	Ab.	L	W	W	W	L	L	W	L	L	L	L
Points	2	2	2	1	1	—	0	4	4	4	0	0	—	0	0	—	0

Catches 10 – T. Davies (ct 6/st 4)   7 – E.W. Jones   3 – R.C. Ontong and J.G. Thomas
9 – M.W.W. Selvey and A.L. Jones   6 – W.W. Davis   2 – M.A. Nash, D.A. Francis, G.C. Holmes and Javed Miandad
8 – J.A. Hopkins   5 – B.J. Lloyd   1 – C.J.C. Rowe, A.H. Wilkins and S.P. Henderson

BOWLING

BOWLING	M.W.W. Selvey	M.A. Nash	R.C. Ontong	A.H. Wilkins	B.J. Lloyd	C.J.C. Rowe	J.G. Thomas	J. Derrick	W.W. Davis
(B.&H.) v. Comb. Univ. (Cambridge) 14 May	11-6-10-4	11-7-9-3	6-1-22-1	2-0-4-0	4-1-12-0				
(J.P.) v. Warwickshire (Swansea) 15 May									
(B.&H.) v. Surrey (Cardiff) 20 May	8-2-18-1	11-2-21-2	5.4-0-26-0	5-0-10-0	9-0-31-0		6-1-20-1		
(B.&H.) v. Kent (Swansea) 21 and 23 May	6-1-7-0	5-2-16-1		0.3-0-2-0					
(B.&H.) v. Kent (Swansea) 23 May	8-1-29-1	8-1-33-1	8-1-21-0	4.5-1-26-0	4-0-27-0				
(J.P.) v. Lancashire (Swansea) 29 May	8-0-56-1	8-0-32-0	8-0-43-2		8-0-33-1		8-0-49-4		
(J.P.) v. Nottinghamshire (Trent Br.) 5 June	7-0-37-0	8-0-21-0	8-0-35-3		8-0-39-1		7.4-0-41-4		
(J.P.) v. Yorkshire (Cardiff) 12 June	8-3-16-0	8-2-19-2	8-0-30-1				8-0-38-5	8-0-33-0	
(J.P.) v. Somerset (Bath) 19 June	8-1-27-0	5-0-23-1	7-0-52-1		6-0-39-1		5-0-42-0		8-0-32-2
(J.P.) v. Leicestershire (Leicester) 26 June	7-1-20-0		6.4-0-29-1		3-0-17-0	5-0-13-1	8-0-27-2		8-0-29-2
(N.W.) v. Norfolk (Norwich) 29 June	12-5-20-1		9-1-49-4		12-7-17-1	10-1-34-1	3-0-16-0		10.5-1-26-3
(J.P.) v. Sussex (Cardiff) 10 July	8-1-…-2		8-1-36-2	6-0-38-2	7-0-32-1			6.3-1-20-0	
(J.P.) v. Essex (Southend) 17 July	7-0-56-0		8-0-37-2		8-0-55-0	1-0-10-0	8-0-78-0	8-0-64-1	
(N.W.) v. Hampshire (Swansea) 20 July		12-2-40-1	12-3-58-1		11-1-33-1	5-0-32-1	8-0-56-0		12-2-53-1
(J.P.) v. Northants. (Northampton) 24 July		8-2-20-2	8-0-40-1		8-1-26-1	2-0-17-0		8-1-29-1	
(J.P.) v. Surrey (Swansea) 31 July	6-0-53-1		6-0-52-1		6-0-37-1			2-0-23-1	
(J.P.) v. Gloucestershire (Cheltenham) 7 Aug.	8-0-37-0		7-0-30-2		8-1-20-0	8-1-42-2		1-0-9-0	
(J.P.) v. Kent (Cardiff) 14 August	8-1-56-3		8-0-35-3	8-0-40-0	8-0-37-0				
(J.P.) v. Derbyshire (Swansea) 21 August	5-0-34-3		5-0-17-0	5-0-19-0	5-0-18-1				5-0-23-3
(J.P.) v. Worcestershire (Cardiff) 28 August	8-0-37-1		5.4-0-17-3	8-1-13-3	8-0-26-1				6-0-29-2
(J.P.) v. Hampshire (Bournemouth) 11 Sept.	8-1-24-2			8-1-32-0	8-3-14-2		7-1-29-1		6-1-23-0
Wickets	20	13	28	5	12	7	15	5	11

a Match declared void

v. Gloucestershire (Swansea) 31 July (J.P.)	v. Kent (Cheltenham) 7 August (J.P.)	v. Derbyshire (Cardiff) 14 August (J.P.)	v. Worcestershire (Swansea) 21 August (J.P.)	v. Hampshire (Cardiff) 28 August (J.P.)	(Bournemouth) 11 September (J.P.)	Runs
					12	171
1	2		52	37	13	510
77*	6	20	36	30	45	485
1	81	22				472
—	2	14		35	22	172
29	27	3	23	14		382
—	—	—	—		5*	36
						72
—	—	22*	0	—	12	105
						15
			—		5	8
		3			18	129
			3			142
—	4					36
						42
			—	—	2*	3
						—
4*	48	15	19	26	0	112
—	2*	46*	1	17*	7	73
		4	8*	23*		35
	5			6	2	
4	8	8	9	15	10	
2	2	8	3	9	5	
		4	1	4		
118	187	169	155	216	158	
3	7	7	7	5	9	
W	L	L	W	W	L	
4	0	0	4	4	0	

Nigel Briers, a career best 201 not out for Leicestershire against Warwickshire at Edgbaston. (George Herringshaw)

S.R. Barwick	G.C. Holmes	S.P. Henderson	Byes	Leg-byes	Wides	No-balls	Total	Wkts
				2			59	10
			Match Abandoned					
				12	3	1	142	5
				1	2	2	30	1a
			4	6	2	1	149	2
			1	14	2	2	232	8
				7	7	2	189	10
				13	5	1	155	9
			1	11	9	1	237	5
				16	3	3	157	6
			1	7	1	6	177	10
			2	9	2	2	164	5
			2	7		1	310	5
				9	5	8	294	5
6-0-39-0			2	11	7	5	196	5
6-0-29-1				9	1		204	7
6.4-0-43-1				5	4		190	5
	8-0-46-0		5	11			230	7
				16	3	3	133	9
			1	8	1	1	133	10
		1.4-0-17-0	4	13	5		161	9
2	0	0						

at Wellingborough

Essex 282 (G.A. Gooch 60, W. Larkins 4 for 30) and 236 for 7 dec (K.W.R. Fletcher 71, B.R. Hardie 69)
Northamptonshire 247 for 7 dec (R.J. Boyd-Moss 60, J.K. Lever 5 for 68) and 143 (N. Phillip 4 for 54)

Essex won by 128 runs
Essex 22 pts, Northamptonshire 6 pts

Mark Nicholas of Hampshire, the first English-born batsman to reach a thousand runs in the season. (Adrian Murrell)

Gloucestershire C.C.C.
Limited-Over Matches – 1983

BATTING

BATTING	v. Northamptonshire (Northampton) 7 May (B.&H.)	v. Leicestershire (Gloucester) 15 May (J.P.)	v. Leicestershire (Gloucester) 16 May (B.&H.)	v. Scotland (Glasgow) 17 May (B.&H.)	v. Worcestershire (Worcester) 22 May (J.P.)	v. Worcestershire (Bristol) 23 May (B.&H.)	v. Middlesex (Bristol) 2 June (B.&H.)	v. Surrey (Bristol) 5 June (J.P.)	v. Northamptonshire (Northampton) 12 June (J.P.)	v. Kent (Bristol) 19 June (J.P.)	v. Somerset (Bath) 26 June (J.P.)	v. Scotland (Bristol) 29 June (N.W.)	v. Middlesex (Lord's) 3 July (J.P.)	v. Derbyshire (Bristol) 10 July (J.P.)	v. Warwickshire (Moreton-in-Marsh) 17 July (J.P.)	v. Leicestershire (Leicester) 20 July (N.W.)	v. Hampshire (Bournemouth) 31 July (J.P.)
A.W. Stovold	6		12	1		32	11*	12	15	57	82	37	27	30	9		
B.C. Broad	39		23*	2		31	1*	30	24								33
P. Bainbridge	17		14*	4		40*			4	53	75	4	13	3	49		
Zaheer Abbas	65		—	13		70	—			32	39	106*	21	64*		158	1
A.J. Hignell	17		—	4		5*	—	70	16	8	9	47	41*	6		26	20*
J.N. Shepherd	2		—	0*		—		4	3	35	7	34*	5	11*	25*		
D.A. Graveney	28		—	13		—		27*	38	7*	23	—	26	—	0	—	
R.J. Doughty	0									50*	0*	5*	—				
R.C. Russell	10*		—	36*				—	3		4			1*		14*	
J.H. Childs	1*		—					—	5	—	—	—	—	—	—	—	—
G.E. Sainsbury	—		—					1*	—		2*	—	—	—	—	—	—
P.W. Romaines								—	9	20	30	28	30	28	57	9	80*
B. Dudleston								—									
D.V. Lawrence								—									
A.J. Wright								0	1								
F.D. Stephenson								18*									
E.J. Cunningham																	
Byes				2		9		1			2	5	2				6
Leg-byes	2			3		6		12	10	12	5	8		10	5	7	3
Wides	1			4		2		1	3		2	7	4	2		5	5
No-balls	4					3		2				6			2		4
Total	192		59	91		198	12		181	189	238	297	272	174	178	306	148
Wickets	8		1	7		3	0		6	9	6	8	4	6	4	6	2
Result	W	Ab.	Ab.	W	Ab.	W	Lt	Ab.	L	L	L	W	W	L	W	W	W
Points	2	2	1	2	2	2	—	2	0	0	0	—	4	0	4	—	4

Catches
16 – R.C. Russell (ct 8/st 8)
11 – A.J. Hignell
6 – J.H. Childs, A.W. Stovold and D.A. Graveney
5 – B.C. Broad
4 – P. Bainbridge and P.W. Romaines
3 – G. Sainsbury
2 – J.N. Shepherd
1 – Zaheer Abbas, R.J. Doughty, A.J. Wright and sub.

† Lost on toss of coin

BOWLING

BOWLING	G.E. Sainsbury	R.J. Doughty	J.N. Shepherd	P. Bainbridge	J.H. Childs	D.A. Graveney	B.C. Broad	F.D. Stephenson	D.V. Lawrence
(B.&H.) v. Northants. (Northampton) 7 May	10.4-3-28-4	3-0-20-0	10-1-42-3	11-1-22-2	11-2-29-0	4-0-13-0	5-0-26-1		
(B.&H.) v. Leicestershire (Gloucester) 16 May									
(B.&H.) v. Scotland (Glasgow) 17 May	11-2-22-2		10.3-2-22-2	11-3-9-2	11-4-14-0	11-6-13-3			
(B.&H.) v. Worcestershire (Bristol) 23 May	8-2-30-1		8-0-39-1	5-0-32-0	7-0-32-2	6-1-22-1	3-0-27-0		
(B.&H.) v. Middlesex (Bristol) 2 June									
(J.P.) v. Northants. (Northampton) 12 June	8-0-50-1		8-0-30-2	8-0-35-0	8-0-18-3			8-1-51-0	
(J.P.) v. Kent (Bristol) 19 June	6-1-29-0	5-0-40-1	8-0-52-6	8-0-42-0	6-0-44-0	6-0-26-1			
(J.P.) v. Somerset (Bath) 26 June	8-0-41-0	8-0-62-0	8-0-50-0	8-1-34-2					8-0-41-4
(N.W.) v. Scotland (Bristol) 29 June	6-4-4-0	6-1-28-1	12-5-25-1	12-2-49-3		12-2-42-0			6-1-16-0
(J.P.) v. Middlesex (Lord's) 3 July	8-1-36-1	7-0-69-0	8-1-17-3	4-0-54-0	8-1-36-1	5-0-45-0			
(J.P.) v. Derbyshire (Bristol) 10 July	7.5-0-39-0		8-0-29-2	3-0-18-1	5-0-21-1	8-0-30-1			8-0-26-2
(J.P.) v. Warwickshire (Moreton) 17 July	7-0-31-0		8-0-24-3	5-0-18-1	8-5-11-3	5-0-29-0			7-0-41-2
(N.W.) v. Leicestershire (Leicester) 20 July	12-2-45-1		12-0-60-1	11-1-66-1	12-0-48-0	1-0-8-0			12-1-51-2
(J.P.) v. Hampshire (Bournemouth) 31 July	6-0-36-0			7-1-41-0					7-0-54-2
(N.W.) v. Hampshire (Bristol) 3 August	12-3-51-1		11-0-58-1	12-2-31-0		12-0-54-1			10.5-2-40
(J.P.) v. Glamorgan (Cheltenham) 7 August	8-1-29-2		8-0-40-3	8-0-31-0	8-1-35-0	8-0-37-2			
(J.P.) v. Yorkshire (Cheltenham) 14 August	8-0-32-1		7.1-0-43-0	8-0-46-1	6-0-49-0	8-2-21-2			
(J.P.) v. Essex (Colchester) 21 August	8-1-41-2		8-0-49-3	8-0-58-1	8-1-44-0	8-0-34-2			
(J.P.) v. Lancashire (Bristol) 28 August	7-0-33-0	8-0-57-0	8-1-18-3		6.1-1-33-0				
(J.P.) v. Sussex (Hove) 4 September	4-0-24-0	4.4-0-23-1	6-0-29-2	4-1-11-0					
Wickets	16	3	36	14	10	13	1	0	13

Batting

v. Hampshire (Bristol) 3 August (N.W.)	v. Glamorgan (Cheltenham) 7 August (J.P.)	v. Yorkshire (Cheltenham) 14 August (J.P.)	v. Essex (Colchester) 21 August (J.P.)	v. Lancashire (Bristol) 28 August (J.P.)	v. Sussex (Hove) 4 September (J.P.)	v. Nottinghamshire (Trent Bridge) 11 September (J.P.)	Runs
	29	47	67		13		487
36	1	96	10	81			407
21	21*	4*	55	6	39		422
33	80	8					690
28	13	26	13	32			381
6	13*	11*	16	3	21		196
3	—	—	20*	2			187
					13	13*	81
1	—	—	1*	9*	1		80
14*	—	—	—	—	1		21
	—	—	—	—		4*	7
82	24	36	5	31	1		470
—							—
			23		1	7	32
							18
					4	7	11
19	5	4	7	6	5		
9	4	1	1	1	1		
		2					
252	190	233	220	187	115		
8	5	5	7	8	9		
L	W	L	L	L	L	Ab.	
—	4	0	0	0	0	2	

Bowling

Zaheer Abbas	E.J. Cunningham	A.J. Wright	Byes	Leg-byes	Wides	No-balls	Total	Wkts
			1	9	1		191	10
				Match Abandoned				
			1	8	1		90	10
			2	12	1		197	6
				Match Abandoned				
			7	5		2	198	6
			2	6	3		244	9
				15		11	254	
			14	4		2	209	6
			1	10	2		270	5
				10	2	1	176	7
			14	4		2	174	9
			4	12	3	5	302	5
			2	7	5		145	2
0.3–0–5–0			1	6	8	2	256	4
			5	8	2		187	7
2–0–11–1			9	21	2		234	6
			1	5		1	233	9
	8–0–35–0		4	5	6		191	3
		4–0–18–0	1	8			116	3
2	0	0						

(6–0–25–1 Zaheer Abbas)

at Trent Bridge

Hampshire 194 and 243 for 9 dec (D.R. Turner 94 not out, K. Saxelby 4 for 49)
Nottinghamshire 239 (R.T. Robinson 50) and 28 for 0

Match drawn
Nottinghamshire 6 pts, Hampshire 5 pts

at Guildford

Surrey 363 for 7 dec (A.R. Butcher 122, A.J. Stewart 82, R.K. Illingworth 4 for 76) and 246 for 6 dec (A.R. Butcher 85, D.B. Pauline 69)
Worcestershire 264 (D.N. Patel 105, P.A. Neale 58, S.T. Clarke 4 for 39) and 118 (P.I. Pocock 4 for 13, D.J. Thomas 4 for 33)

Surrey won by 227 runs
Surrey 24 pts, Worcestershire 5 pts

at Edgbaston

Leicestershire 150 (C.M. Old 5 for 56) and 438 for 3 dec (N.E. Briers 201 not out, B.F. Davison 66, J.C. Balderstone 64, J.J. Whitaker 56 not out)
Warwickshire 249 (T.A. Lloyd 75, G.J. Parsons 5 for 51) and 194 for 6 (A.I. Kallicharran 88)

Match drawn
Warwickshire 6 pts, Leicestershire 5 pts

Depleted by injuries and Test calls and suffering a crisis of confidence, Middlesex enticed Mike Brearley from retirement to play at Old Trafford. He scored 17, but Middlesex had a miserable time after they had bowled out Lancashire for 193. Barlow and Williams were the only others to reach double figures as Allott and Watkinson exploited the wearing pitch well. Emburey bowled Middlesex back into contention, but rain prevented any play on the last day and Middlesex had taken only 4 points.

Meanwhile, at Wellingborough, Essex gained a thrilling victory over Northants to come within five points of Middlesex at the top of the Schweppes County Championship. On a slow and untrustworthy pitch, Gooch and Gladwin, who had firmly asserted himself in the Essex side, put on 98 for the first wicket, but the later batsmen failed to capitalise fully on the good start. Larkins came in with 4 surprise wickets, but he fell to Lever before the close as did Cook who had kept wicket after Sharp had injured his back in the first over.

Lever took three more wickets on the Monday as Northants batted dourly and Cook declared 35 runs in arrears. It was the sixth time in the season that Lever, who had missed several matches through injury, had taken five or more wickets in an innings. Essex scored briskly at the second attempt, a 114-run partnership in even time between Fletcher and Hardie for the fourth wicket being vital, and they left Northants 200 minutes in which to make 272.

Lever and Turner made early inroads, aided by some spectacular wicket-keeping from David East, and then Norbert Phillip dismissed Steele with the last ball of one over and had Mallender caught bat-pad off the first ball of the next. Griffiths, last man in as Sharp was absent, was bowled off his pads first ball to give Phillip the first hat-trick of his career and Essex 22 points.

Hampshire C.C.C.
Limited-Over Matches – 1983

BATTING

BATTING	v. Essex (Southampton) 7 May (B.&H.)	v. Essex (Southampton) 8 May (J.P.)	v. Middlesex (Lord's) 15 May (J.P.)	v. Somerset (Taunton) 17 and 18 May (B.&H.)	v. Minor Counties (Bournemouth) 19 and 20 May (B.&H.)	v. Northamptonshire (Bournemouth) 22 May (J.P.)	v. Sussex (Hove) 23 May (B.&H.)	v. Kent (Canterbury) 29 May (J.P.)	v. Kent (Canterbury) 1 and 2 June (B.&H.)	v. Yorkshire (Middlesbrough) 5 June (J.P.)	v. Leicestershire (Basingstoke) 19 June (J.P.)	v. Warwickshire (Edgbaston) 26 June (J.P.)	v. Hertfordshire (Hitchin) 29 June (N.W.)	v. Lancashire (Old Trafford) 3 July (J.P.)	v. Surrey (Portsmouth) 10 July (J.P.)	v. Nottinghamshire (Portsmouth) 17 July (J.P.)	v. Glamorgan (Swansea) 20 July (N.W.)	v. Somerset (Taunton) 24 July (J.P.)
D.R. Turner	28	30		0	13	56*	17	3	4	7								
V.P. Terry	11	2							72	17	100*	37	—	34	—	37	5	11
M.C.J. Nicholas	8	2		27	16	10*	27	7	2	68	—	2	37*	24	—	3	19	12
T.E. Jesty	20	100		20	76*	17	37	4	17	16		76	—	4	166*	39	84	10
R.A. Smith	9										22*	13						
N.E.J. Pocock	17	17		0	43*	—	6	16	6	21		2		0*	—	5	20*	5*
N.G. Cowley	10	15		0	—	—	2	6	0	4		6		—	—	0*	—	0
T.M. Tremlett	4	—		6	—	—	4*	9	1*	1		8		—	—	—	—	11*
R.J. Parks	4			5	—	—	—	0	0	0*								
K.St D. Emery	6*																	
S.J. Malone	16			0*	—	—	—	0	2*									
M.D. Marshall		25*		9	—	—	2	27*	8	18						27*	15*	1
J.W. Southern		15*																
C.G. Greenidge				45	13	34	0	22	60	89			55	162*	108*	80	108	29
C.L. Smith				14	0	44	63*	31			55	62	66*	31	5	43	21	3
J.J.E. Hardy											—							
K. Stevenson											—	4*						
Byes									2			2	2	1				1
Leg-byes	12	6		4	3	9	9	3	13	10	2	21	1	7	5	8	9	8
Wides	1	1		6	1	1	6	2	5	2	1	2	1	3		5		1
No-balls	1	1		2	4	2	1	3	1	2		.		1	2	1	8	1
Total	147	214	Ab.	138	169	173	174	133	193	255	180	235	163	268	292	242	294	93
Wickets	10	6		10	4	3	7	10	9	9	1	8	1	4	1	6	5	7
Result	L	W	Ab.	W	W	W	W	L	L	L	W	L	W	W	W	W	W	L
Points	0	4	2	2	2	4	2	0	—	0	4	0	—	4	4	4	—	0

Catches
- 39 – R.J. Parks (st 33/st 6)
- 13 – N.E.J. Pocock
- 11 – V.P. Terry
- 10 – M.C.J. Nicholas
- 9 – N.G. Cowley
- 8 – C.G. Greenidge
- 6 – T.E. Jesty and M.D. Marshall
- 4 – T.M. Tremlett
- 3 – D.R. Turner
- 2 – R.A. Smith and J.J.E. Hardy
- 1 – S.J. Malone, C.L. Sm. K.St D. Emery and sub

BOWLING

BOWLING	K.St D. Emery	S.J. Malone	T.M. Tremlett	T.E. Jesty	N.G. Cowley	M.C.J. Nicholas	M.D. Marshall	K. Stevenson	C.G. Greenidge
(B.&H.) v. Essex (Southampton) 7 May	8-0-32-0	6-0-25-0	11-1-45-3	9-1-31-0	11-1-46-0	10-0-51-3			
(J.P.) v. Essex (Southampton) 8 May		4-0-21-1	5-0-34-0	8-0-24-1	8-0-38-2	7-0-43-2	8-2-22-2		
(B.&H.) v. Somerset (Taunton) 19 May		8.1-2-24-3	5-1-18-0	9-2-23-2		11-4-12-2	11-2-22-3		
(B.&H.) v. Min. Cos. (Brnmth) 19 and 20 May		11-2-25-4	11-4-17-2	8-1-24-0	11-2-22-0	3-0-8-0	11-1-38-2		
(J.P.) v. Northants. (Bournemouth) 22 May		8-0-36-1	8-0-31-2	4-1-19-1	8-1-30-1	4-0-31-2	8-0-17-0		
(B.&H.) v. Sussex (Hove) 23 May		11-3-34-3	11-0-31-2			11-2-34-1	10-0-33-2	10-3-21-0	
(J.P.) v. Kent (Canterbury) 29 May		8-1-54-1	8-0-33-0	6-0-37-3	2-0-19-0	8-1-30-3	8-0-18-0		
(B.&H.) v. Kent (Canterbury) 1 and 2 June		8-1-28-1	11-3-22-1	4-1-14-0	11-3-34-2	10-2-42-0	11-4-26-4		
(J.P.) v. Yorkshire (Middlesbrough) 5 June		7.5-0-41-0	7-0-70-0		8-1-39-3	8-0-67-1	8-0-23-0		
(J.P.) v. Leicestershire (Basingstoke) 19 June		8-0-43-2	8-3-24-1		8-0-34-0	8-0-32-3		8-0-37-1	
(J.P.) v. Warwickshire (Edgbaston) 26 June		8-0-55-2	8-1-29-1		8-1-32-1	8-0-43-3		8-0-56-0	
(N.W.) v. Hertfordshire (Hitchin) 29 June		12-4-40-2	12-4-18-1	12-3-45-0	12-7-17-0		12-2-23-1		
(J.P.) v. Lancashire (Old Trafford) 3 July		8-0-38-2	8-0-33-1	8-0-43-5	8-0-49-0		8-0-22-1		
(J.P.) v. Surrey (Portsmouth) 10 July		7-0-26-1	8-0-39-0		8-1-42-4	8-0-51-0	7-2-14-0		1-0-4-0
(J.P.) v. Notts. (Portsmouth) 17 July		8-0-29-3	8-0-35-0	8-1-31-1	8-0-49-0	2-0-7-0	6-0-15-0		
(N.W.) v. Glamorgan (Swansea) 20 July		9-1-21-1	7-1-29-1		11-2-46-3	8.5-4-21-4	6-3-6-1		
(J.P.) v. Somerset (Taunton) 24 July		2-0-32-1	4.4-0-28-1				6-0-35-1		
(J.P.) v. Gloucestershire (Brnmth) 31 July		4-0-36-0	8-0-63-1				7.3-0-35-1		
(N.W.) v. Gloucestershire (Bristol) 3 August			12-1-47-2	12-0-65-0	12-3-31-2		12-4-37-2	12-1-44-2	
(N.W.) v. Kent (Canterbury) 17 August		12-4-26-1	12-1-38-4	12-2-34-0	6-0-22-0	5.2-0-25-1	12-6-15-4		
(J.P.) v. Worcestershire (Worcester) 21 Aug.		5-0-11-1	1.2-0-3-1		1-0-3-0		4-1-6-0		
(J.P.) v. Sussex (Southampton) 28 August		8-0-56-0	8-0-28-0	8-0-34-1	8-0-41-0		8-2-19-3		
(J.P.) v. Derbyshire (Derby) 4 September		8-1-34-2	8-2-18-2	7-0-36-1	8-1-26-2	1-0-1-1	8-2-11-1		
(Asda) v. Essex (Scarborough) 5 September		10-2-23-2	10-0-43-1	10-0-43-3	5-0-35-0	5-1-18-1	9-6-14-1		
(Asda) v. Lancashire (Scarborough) 6 Sept.		8-0-42-0	10-0-32-2	6-1-33-0	8-0-51-0	8-1-44-1	10-1-32-2		
(J.P.) v. Glamorgan (Bournemouth) 11 Sept.		6-0-19-1	8-0-25-3	4-0-15-2	8-1-27-2	8-0-29-1		6-0-26-0	
Wickets	0	39	32	23	26	24	29	3	0

David Turner, out of the Hampshire side for much of the season, he played a fine innings of 94 not out against Notts on 16 August. (Adrian Murrell)

v. Gloucestershire (Bournemouth) 31 July (J.P.)	v. Gloucestershire (Bristol) 3 August (N.W.)	v. Kent (Canterbury) 17 August (N.W.)	v. Worcestershire (Worcester) 21 August (J.P.)	v. Sussex (Southampton) 28 August (J.P.)	v. Derbyshire (Derby) 4 September (J.P.)	v. Essex (Scarborough) 5 September (Asda)	v. Lancashire (Scarborough) 6 September (Asda)	v. Glamorgan (Bournemouth) 11 September (J.P.)	Runs
				53*	8	13	14	18	264
0*	21	0	39*	26	48*	11	6	7	484
—	51	28	5	27	11	5	82	2	475
23	49	1	61	9	22	3	61	3	918
									44
—	8*	4	0*	4			36		210
—	—	4	—	5*	3	13	22*	34	124
—	—	11	—	—	2	25	3*	0	85
—	—	3	—	—	11	13*	—	23*	59
									6
—		4*	—		0	7*	—	8*	37
—		0	17	35	0	4	1		189
									15
52*	9	7	21	15	16	45	5	33	1008
56	101*	25	71	2	50			10	753
									—
								1	5
2	1		5	2		1		4	
7	6	6	13	10	7	11	11	13	
5	8	7	5	8	5	4	2	5	
	2	2	2			1	1		
145	256	102	239	194	135	205	245	161	
2	4	10	5	6	10	9	7	9	
L	W	L	W	W	L	W	L	W	
0	—	—	4	4	0	—	—	4	

N.E.J. Pocock

1-0-1-0

0

Byes	Leg-byes	Wides	No-balls	Total	Wkts
	4	21	5	260	6
1	13	3		199	8
	9	7	1	116	10
1	16	16	1	168	9
	2	6		172	7
1	13	3		171	10
	4	2	1	198	7
	9	23		198	8
1	9	6	1	257	4
	8		1	179	8
5	10	11		241	7
5	9	2		159	6
	7	18		210	9
	5	4	2	188	5
	10	8	2	186	6
	10	5		138	10
	2			97	3
6	3	5		148	2
	19	9		252	8
1	5	5	2	173	10
	2	3	1	29	2
	6	8	1	193	8
3	8	5	1	143	9
1	12	5	1	195	10
2	7	1	1	245	5
2	10	5		158	9

Rain thwarted Somerset and Derbyshire at Derby, and, after an absorbing match at Trent Bridge, Notts declined Hampshire's offer of 199 in 125 minutes. The outstanding performance in the match was David Turner's 94 not out in the second Hampshire innings, a knock which reshaped the game when Notts were getting well on top through Saxelby and Hendrick.

Rain brought an end to the game at Edgbaston. Chris Old bowled well and, in spite of Parsons' best bowling of the season, Warwickshire took a good first innings' lead. Nigel Briers then hit a career best 201 not out in 354 minutes and with Whitaker also reaching a maiden first-class fifty, Leicestershire were well on top. Briers' innings included a six and twenty-nine fours.

Kent had a fine win at Cardiff with three and a half overs and three wickets to spare. Glamorgan had batted dazzlingly on the Saturday with each of their four batsmen reaching fifty. Ontong hit two sixes and twelve fours in a fine hundred, and, in the second innings passed a thousand runs for the season. By then, however, Kent had bustled back with Benson again in mighty form and Hinks hitting a career best. Selvey, Davies and Wilkins hit freely at the end of Glamorgan's second innings, Davies making a career best 69 not out, and Kent were left to make 283 in just over four hours. Neil Taylor's career best 155 was the basis of a fine victory. He and Benson began with a stand of 115.

There were thrills, too, at Cheltenham. On the first day, Kevin Sharp hit a welcome and excellent century, and one hopes that Yorkshire will now sustain the confidence of this fine cricketer and pleasant young man. Boycott also reached a hundred, but it was one that drew censure from his captain for its slowness. Romaines and Shepherd lifted Gloucestershire from the despair of 76 for 5 to 247 for 6 on the Monday, and Romaines confirmed a fine season with 100 not out in

BATTING

	v. Combined Univ. (Cambridge) 7 and 9 May (B.&H.)	v. Surrey (Canterbury) 8 May (J.P.)	v. Middlesex (Canterbury) 14 May (B.&H.)	v. Sussex (Hove) 15 May (J.P.)	v. Surrey (Canterbury) 17 May (B.&H.)	v. Glamorgan (Swansea) 21 and 23 May (B.&H.)	v. Leicestershire (Leicester) 22 May (J.P.)	v. Glamorgan (Swansea) 23 May (B.&H.)	v. Hampshire (Canterbury) 29 May (J.P.)	v. Hampshire (Canterbury) 1 and 2 June (B.&H.)	v. Essex (Chelmsford) 12 June (J.P.)	v. Gloucestershire (Bristol) 19 June (J.P.)	v. Nottinghamshire (Canterbury) 26 June (J.P.)	v. Cheshire (Canterbury) 29 June (N.W.)	v. Essex (Canterbury) 6 July (B.&H.)	v. Lancashire (Maidstone) 10 July (J.P.)	v. Yorkshire (Scarborough) 17 July (J.P.)	v. Essex (Chelmsford) 20 July (N.W.)	v. Middlesex (Canterbury) 24 July (J.P.)
N.R. Taylor	100	36	26		4	19*		17	32	47	17	15					5*		
R.A. Woolmer	7	19	4		8	0		6	26	7			50	14	33	31	2*	40	20
C.J. Tavare	46	82	2		9	6*		80*	67	18			70	99	32	59*		43	20
M.R. Benson	17	9	3		10			33*	3	11	21	65	43	7	10	45	—	18	59
C.S. Cowdrey	8	38*	0		49	—		—	17	15	52	66	38*	52	5	7	—	122*	4
A.P.E. Knott	55	8	43		1	—		—	32	1	1	1	—	4	2	1	—	0	21
G.W. Johnson	9	7	72*		25	—		—	13	0	33	—	22*	15*	3	—		3	8
R.M. Ellison	0	0*	12		4	—		—	1*	28	5*	2	—	4*	2	1*	—	10	2*
G.R. Dilley	7	—	16*		0	—		—	—	37*	—	—	2	5	—			7*	4
D.L. Underwood	2*	—	—		27	—		—	2		0	0*	—		0		—		3
K.B.S. Jarvis	0*	—	—		1*	—		—		0*	2	1*							
L. Potter											1	21							
D.G. Aslett											2	56	51	17	6	38		0	19
E.A. Baptiste											47	4	1*	6	1	24	—	7	4
C. Penn												2					—		
Byes	4	1						4			2	3	1			1		1	1
Leg-byes	9	7	3		7	1		6	4	9	6	6	10	7	5	5		11	5
Wides	12		6		3	2		2	2	23	9	3	2	2	8	1	1	5	1
No-balls		1	3		2	2		1	1		1		2		4	1		7	
Total	276	208	190		150	30		149	198	198	197	244	270	237	128	217	8	274	171
Wickets	9	6	7		10	1		2	7	9	10	9	4	8	10	7	0	8	10
Result	W	W	L	Ab.	L	Ab.	Ab.	W	W	W	L	W	W	W	L	W	Ab.	W	L
Points	2	4	0	2	0	—	2	2	4	—	0	4	4	—	—	4	2	—	0

29 – A.P.E. Knott (ct 26/st 3)
14 – G.W. Johnson
11 – R.A. Woolmer
10 – C.J. Tavare

7 – C.S. Cowdrey and E.A. Baptiste
6 – M.R. Benson
5 – R.M. Ellison

4 – N.R. Taylor, G.R. Dilley and D.G. Aslett
2 – K.B.S. Jarvis

1 – L. Potter and D.L. Underwood

BOWLING

	G.R. Dilley	K.B.S. Jarvis	D.L. Underwood	R.A. Woolmer	R.M. Ellison	G.W. Johnson	C.S. Cowdrey	E.A. Baptiste	C. Penn
(B.&H.) v. Comb. Univs. (C'bge.) 7 & 9 May	10.4-0-32-4	11-3-31-1	11-4-19-2	11-0-47-0	9-1-41-1	2-0-14-1			
(J.P.) v. Surrey (Canterbury) 8 May	5-1-22-1	5-0-24-1	5.4-1-14-5	5-0-11-2					
(B.&H.) v. Middlesex (Canterbury) 14 May	10.4-1-31-0	10-1-34-1	10-2-38-2	11-1-33-2	9-2-30-0		1-0-9-0		
(B.&H.) v. Surrey (Canterbury) 17 & 18 May	11-2-29-4	10.3-1-19-2	11-2-22-2	4-1-9-0	11-0-30-0				
(B.&H.) v. Glamorgan (Swansea) 21 & 23 May	8-2-33-0	8-1-29-1	8-2-28-0	7-1-26-3	8-1-22-1				
(J.P.) v. Hampshire (Canterbury) 29 May	5-0-22-0	6-1-22-1	8-0-28-3	4-1-11-1	4.4-0-15-4		6-0-27-1		
(B.&H.) v. Hampshire (Canterbury) 1 & 2 June	3-0-12-0	11-1-42-3	11-2-30-2	11-0-27-0	11-3-22-3		8-0-39-1		
(J.P.) v. Essex (Chelmsford) 12 June		8-1-56-2	8-0-53-1		8-1-44-1		8-0-39-2	8-0-39-0	
(J.P.) v. Gloucestershire (Bristol) 19 June		8-1-29-1	8-0-32-0		8-0-49-2			8-0-28-1	7-0-38-3
(J.P.) v. Notts. (Canterbury) 26 June	8-1-15-2		8-0-36-3	6-0-38-0	5-0-23-0	8-0-50-2		5-0-30-1	
(N.W.) v. Cheshire (Canterbury) 29 June	11-3-19-3		6-3-8-1	12-7-11-1	12-3-19-4		6-2-7-0	10-3-22-0	
(B.&H.) v. Essex (Canterbury) 6 July	11-1-35-0		6-1-12-0	4-2-5-0	11-4-23-1		3-0-6-0	11-2-28-0	
(J.P.) v. Lancashire (Maidstone) 10 July	8-1-25-1		7.5-1-31-5	4-0-26-0	6-0-18-0		6-0-23-0	8-1-19-2	
(J.P.) v. Yorkshire (Scarborough) 17 July									
(N.W.) v. Essex (Chelmsford) 20 July	12-2-45-0		12-1-40-2	12-0-52-1	12-3-54-4			12-0-70-2	
(J.P.) v. Middlesex (Canterbury) 24 July	8-0-39-1		8-0-63-2	8-1-33-1	8-0-33-1			8-0-44-0	
(J.P.) v. Derbyshire (Chesterfield) 31 July		6-0-23-0			8-0-35-0	4-0-20-1	2-0-17-0	8-1-18-2	3.3-0-27-4
(N.W.) v. Warwickshire (Canterbury) 3 Aug.		7.5-2-19-4	12-5-20-2	12-1-35-1	13-2-27-1			8-1-25-2	
(J.P.) v. Worcestershire (Canterbury) 7 Aug.		5.4-0-20-3	6-0-22-1	8-1-30-1	5-0-15-1			8-0-29-4	
(J.P.) v. Glamorgan (Cardiff) 14 August	8-0-25-2	8-1-42-0	8-1-24-1		8-0-32-2			8-0-26-2	
(N.W.) v. Hampshire (Canterbury) 17 August		7-0-17-0	3.4-1-3-1		5-0-11-0		12-3-36-4	12-5-20-5	
(J.P.) v. Warwickshire (Folkestone) 21 Aug.	7-0-30-0		8-0-50-2		6.2-0-34-2		8-0-39-1	8-0-52-3	
(J.P.) v. Somerset (Taunton) 28 August		7.3-0-57-0	8-0-44-0	8-0-42-1	7-0-27-2			8-0-43-0	
(N.W.) v. Somerset (Lord's) 4 September	10-2-29-4	10-0-43-1			10-1-35-0		10-2-29-2	10-1-37-1	
Wickets	22	21	37	14	31	3	11	25	3

	v. Derbyshire (Chesterfield) 31 July (J.P.)	v. Warwickshire (Canterbury) 3 August (N.W.)	v. Worcestershire (Canterbury) 7 August (J.P.)	v. Glamorgan (Cardiff)	v. Hampshire (Canterbury) 14 August (J.P.)	v. Warwickshire (Folkestone) 17 August (N.W.)	v. Somerset (Taunton) 21 August (J.P.)	v. Somerset (Lord's) 28 August (J.P.)	v. Northamptonshire (Canterbury) 3 September (N.W.)	11 September (J.P.)	Runs
					67	0	0	47			432
	—	2	22					21			312
		34	16		64	122*		39			908
	—	33	3	29	16	23	5	0			463
	—	56	95	46	5	13	1	0			689
	—	13	23*	1	7	7*	4	17			242
	—	26*	9	14	10	—	6*	27			302
	—	11	0	1*	0	—	0*	21			104
					9*		—	19			106
		2*	0*		—	5		5*			46
	—		—			5*	—	3			12
	—										22
		29	16	5	42	77	100	14			472
		22	27	42	6	13	25	16			245
	—										2
		4			5	1		2	6		
		11	10	11	5	12		7	1		
		1	7			5	3	3			
		7			2	11		1			
Total		251	228	230	173	281	221	169			
Wkts		8	8	7	10	5	7	10			
	Ab.	W	W	W	W	W	L	L	Ab.		
	2	—	4	4	—	4	0	—	2		

D.G. Aslett 0·5-0-0-1

Byes	Leg-byes	Wides	No-balls	Total	Wkts
5	18	5		212	10
	7	1	1	80	10
1	10		5	191	5
	10	2	1	122	10
	9		1	148	8
	3	2	3	133	10
2	13	5	1	193	9
	13	3	3	250	6
	10	3		189	9
	18	3	8	221	9
5	3	2	5	101	10
1	4	5	11	130	1
	4	2	6	154	10
			Match Abandoned		
	7	1	1	270	9
	12	2	1	227	5
	4	2		146	4
4	11	2	3	146	10
	4			120	10
	8	8	4	169	7
	6	7	2	102	10
2	11	5		223	10
4	5	1	1	224	4
1	17	2		193	9

1

four hours. Boycott batted more purposefully at the second attempt, and Gloucestershire were asked to make 277 in 188 minutes. They won with 11 balls to spare. Broad and Bainbridge put on a solid 93 for the second wicket, and then Zaheer and Broad added 124 fluent runs to make victory possible. It was Zaheer's last innings of the season for Gloucestershire.

Alan Butcher, in his August form, and Alec Stewart, forthright and rich in promise, shared a second wicket stand of 185 on the opening day at Guildford. Patel and Neale responded bravely for lowly Worcestershire, but Butcher and Pauline, seizing his prolonged opportunity in the Surrey side, made 141 for Surrey's first wicket in the second innings. Eventually, Worcestershire were overwhelmed as first Thomas, with pace, and then Pocock, with spin, left them disorganised and in pain.

John Player League

14 August

at Heanor

Somerset 219 for 8
Derbyshire 220 for 2 (K.J. Barnett 100 not out, I.S. Anderson 54)

Derbyshire (4 pts) won by 8 wickets

at Cardiff

Kent 230 for 7 (N.R. Taylor 67)
Glamorgan 169 for 7

Kent (4 pts) won by 61 runs

at Cheltenham

Gloucestershire 233 for 5 (B.C. Broad 96)
Yorkshire 234 for 6 (K. Sharp 53)

Yorkshire (4 pts) won by 4 wickets

at Old Trafford

Middlesex 166 (P.J.W. Allott 4 for 29)
Lancashire 167 for 3 (D. Lloyd 50)

Lancashire (4 pts) won by 7 wickets

at Wellingborough

Northamptonshire 158 for 5 (P. Willey 62)
Essex 159 for 8

Essex (4 pts) won by 2 wickets

at Trent Bridge

Nottinghamshire 197 for 6 (J.D. Birch 92)
Sussex 164 (K.E. Cooper 4 for 26, K. Saxelby 4 for 37)

Nottinghamshire (4 pts) won by 33 runs

at Guildford

Surrey 270 for 6 (R.D.V. Knight 87, D.B. Pauline 84, M.A. Lynch 54)
Worcestershire 242 (C.L. King 127)

Surrey (4 pts) won by 28 runs

Lancashire C.C.C.
Limited-Over Matches – 1983

BATTING

	v. Warwickshire (Old Trafford) 7 May (B.&H.)	v. Derbyshire (Old Trafford) 8 May (J.P.)	v. Essex (Chelmsford) 15 May (J.P.)	v. Yorkshire (Leeds) 17 May (B.&H.)	v. Derbyshire (Derby) 19 May (B.&H.)	v. Nottinghamshire (Old Trafford) 21 and 23 May	v. Warwickshire (Edgbaston) 22 May (J.P.)	v. Nottinghamshire (Old Trafford) 23 May (B.&H.)	v. Glamorgan (Swansea) 29 May (J.P.)	v. Northamptonshire (Old Trafford) 1–3 June (B.&H.)	v. Northamptonshire (Old Trafford) 5 June (J.P.)	v. Nottinghamshire (Old Trafford) 12 June (J.P.)	v. Sussex (Horsham) 19 June	v. Durham (Chester-le-Street) 29 June (N.W.)	v. Hampshire (Old Trafford) 3 July (J.P.)	v. Middlesex (Lord's) 6 July (B.&H.)	v. Kent (Maidstone) 10 July (J.P.)	v. Worcestershire (Old Trafford) 17 July (J.P.)
G. Fowler	45			31	37	—	—	59*	27	97	31			31	22	1	42	
S.J. O'Shaughnessy	0			27	5	—	—	5	1	8	—	—	14	1	3	0	7	12
F.C. Hayes	16			37	21	—	—	5	72	75	2	4	1	18		3	0	23
D.P. Hughes	19			28	2	—	—	42*	3	37*	50*	31*	8	71	0	27	22	
C.H. Lloyd	20*			18	1*	—	—	35	21	55	39*							52
J. Abrahams	16			37*	0*	—	—		18	0	—	—	79*	51*	65	4	21	10
J. Simmons	0			1	—	—	—		38	4*	—	—	7	0	13	25	14	7
C. Maynard	0*			17*	—	—	—		13	—	—	46	24	0	22	1	8	11
M. Watkinson	—			—	—	—	—		15*	—	—		1	0	27*	3	2	5*
P.J.W. Allott	—			—	—	—	—		5*					6*	3	0	1*	—
I. Folley	—			—	—	—	—					—	1		6*	1*		
I. Cockbain									—			25	3	7				
S.T. Jefferies												37*	34		17			
N.H. Fairbrother									—				19			25	0*	
N.V. Radford														14		14		
L.L. McFarlane																	0	—
D. Lloyd																		8
P. Lever																		
K.A. Hayes																		
M. Chadwick																		
J. Stanworth																		
Byes				4				9	1	3		4		1				4
Leg-byes	5			16	2			14	4	5	6	7	11	7		1	4	10
Wides	3			6				2	4	1	2	2		4	18	2	2	
No-balls	3							2	2	3	3			3			8	6
Total	127			222	68			157	232	290	131	155	200	211	210	90	154	142
Wickets	6			6	4			3	8	5	2	3	10	8	9	10	10	8
Result	Ab.	Ab.	Ab.	W	Ab.	Ab.	Ab.	W	L	W	W	W	L	W	L	L	L	Tie
Points	1	2	2	2	1	—	2	2	0	—	4	4	0	—	0	—	0	2

Catches

18 – C. Maynard (ct 13/st 5)
6 – J. Abrahams
5 – J. Simmons and S.J. O'Shaughnessy

4 – G. Fowler
3 – J. Stanworth (ct 2/st 1) and D.P. Hughes

2 – M. Watkinson, C.H. Lloyd, M. Chadwick and N.H. Fairbrother

1 – N.V. Radford, I. Folley, I. Cockbain, P.J.W. Al[l]ott and L.L. McFarlane

BOWLING

	P.J.W. Allott	I. Folley	M. Watkinson	S.J. O'Shaughnessy	J. Simmons	S.T. Jefferies	N.V. Radford	L.L. McFarlane	J. Abrahams
(B.&H.) v. Warwickshire (Old Trafford) 7 May									
(B.&H.) v. Yorkshire (Leeds) 17 May	7–1–14–2	11–3–27–1	5–0–15–0	11–4–14–2	1.4–0–8–0				
(B.&H.) v. Derbyshire (Derby) 20 May									
(B.&H.) v. Notts. (Old Trafford) 21 & 23 May	5–3–2–0	4.5–1–9–1							
(J.P.) v. Warwickshire (Edgbaston) 22 May	2–1–3–0	1–0–5–0							
(B.&H.) v. Notts. (Old Trafford) 23 May	9–1–28–1	9–4–16–1	9–2–39–4	9–3–30–2	9–0–28–0				
(J.P.) v. Glamorgan (Swansea) 29 May	8–0–48–2	8–1–35–0	8–0–46–2	8–0–54–0	8–0–55–0				
(B.&H.) v. Northants. (Old Trafford) 1–3 June	7.1–2–25–2	11–1–34–2	7–0–32–1	11–0–46–2	11–1–40–0				
(J.P.) v. Northants. (Old Trafford) 5 June	8–0–20–2	8–0–16–0	8–0–35–1	8–0–27–1	8–1–22–2				
(J.P.) v. Notts. (Old Trafford) 12 June		8–0–26–2	8–1–21–0	8–0–37–0	8–0–27–1	8–2–29–0			
(J.P.) v. Sussex (Horsham) 19 June		8–0–39–1	8–0–25–1	8–1–35–0	8–0–41–2	8–1–40–1			
(N.W.) v. Durham (Chester-le-Street) 29 June	6–1–6–1	5.3–1–10–2	12–2–27–1	6–2–21–2	12–4–25–4			5–2–4–0	
(J.P.) v. Hampshire (Old Trafford) 3 July	8–1–51–0	3–0–20–0	8–1–52–0	8–0–53–2	5–0–45–0	8–0–34–0			
(B.&H.) v. Middlesex (Lord's) 6 July	11–3–23–2	3–0–7–0	7–2–14–0	5–1–15–0			4.2–0–27–2		
(J.P.) v. Kent (Maidstone) 10 July	8–1–41–2		8–1–49–3	7–0–44–0	8–0–31–1			8–1–34–0	1–0–10–0
(J.P.) v. Worcestershire (Old Trafford) 17 July	8–1–42–3		4–0–27–1		1–0–13–0			6–0–50–1	
(N.W.) v. Somerset (Old Trafford) 20 July			8–0–20–0	4–0–24–0	12–0–32–1			12–4–18–1	2–0–19–0
(J.P.) v. Surrey (The Oval) 24 July		8–0–25–0		8–0–45–2	8–0–37–3			7.4–0–19–3	8–0–44–1
(J.P.) v. Somerset (Old Trafford) 31 July		1–0–6–0							
(J.P.) v. Yorkshire (Leeds) 7 August	6–0–28–0		6.5–1–24–1	6–1–23–0	8–0–21–2			8–0–35–0	
(J.P.) v. Middlesex (Old Trafford) 14 August	8–1–29–4		8–0–31–3	5–0–23–0	8–1–26–0			5–0–20–0	
(J.P.) v. Gloucestershire (Bristol) 28 August	8–0–40–1		8–0–34–3	8–0–41–0	8–0–21–0				7–0–42–1
(Asda) v. Yorkshire (Scarborough) 4 Sept.	7–2–13–3		7–0–32–0	7–1–14–1	8–1–38–3	7–1–31–2			
(Asda) v. Hampshire (Scarborough) 6 Sept.	8–1–34–1		9–0–54–2	6–0–31–0	10–1–41–2	9–1–39–1			8–0–31–0
Wickets	26	10	23	14	21	4	2	5	2

v. Somerset (Old Trafford) 20 July (N.W.)	v. Surrey (The Oval) 24 July (J.P.)	v. Somerset (Old Trafford) 31 July (J.P.)	v. Yorkshire (Leeds) 7 August (J.P.)	v. Middlesex (Old Trafford) 14 August (J.P.)	v. Gloucestershire (Bristol) 28 August (J.P.)	v. Yorkshire (Scarborough) 4 September (Asda)	v. Hampshire (Scarborough) 6 September (Asda)	v. Leicestershire (Old Trafford) 11 September (J.P.)	Runs
29	1		16	33	18	18	10		548
49*	1*	16	30	31	—	8	51		269
16					2	4	4		303
	87*	18	7						452
6	11	46	31	29*	81*	29	41		515
21	6	8	6	14*	65*	15	69*		505
6*	3*	2	2	—	—	6	57*		185
16	16	9	7	—					190
—		0	8*	—	—	—	—		61
			32*	—	—	—	—		47
		11*							19
									35
						19*	—		107
	44	1		—		31*	2		122
									28
—	—	2	—	—					2
3		2	17	50					80
	5								5
					10				10
3	2	1		1	4		2		
10	5	11	5	5	5	9	7		
1	3	4		1	6	2	1		
3	3	1	1	3			1		
163	187	132	162	167	191	141	245		
6	6	10	8	3	3	6	5		
L	W	Ab.	L	W	W	W	W	Ab.	
—	4	2	0	4	4	—	—	2	

P. Lever	D. Lloyd	C.H. Lloyd	Byes	Leg-byes	Wides	No-balls	Total	Wkts
				Match Abandoned				
			6	2		1	87	5
				Match Abandoned				
			2				13	1
					1	1	10	0
			5	8			154	8
			1	9	3	2	253	4
				6			183	10
				9		1	130	7
			1	9			154	3
			1	15	5	1	202	8
				4	4	4	105	10
			1	7	3	2	268	4
				2	3		91	4
			1	5	1	1	217	7
				2	8		142	5
7.5–2–17–0	7–0–18–0		1	9	3	3	164	2
				13	1	2	186	10
						1	7	0
	4–0–15–2			11	4	2	163	6
6–0–20–1			1	15		1	166	10
		1–0–2–1		6	1		187	8
			1	7	2	1	139	9
			1	11	2	1	245	7
0	3	1						

at Edgbaston

Leicestershire 179 for 8
Warwickshire 181 for 2 (A.I. Kallicharran 80 not out, G.W. Humpage 73 not out)

Warwickshire (4 pts) won by 8 wickets

Somerset and Sussex lost ground in the race for the John Player League title when they both suffered surprising defeats. Kim Barnett and Ian Anderson began Derbyshire's chase of 220 with a stand of 105. Barnett, whose maturity of leadership of Derbyshire had been one of the season's outstanding qualities, reached his hundred with the single that brought his side victory with 16 balls to spare. After Birch and Randall had batted well for Notts, Sussex performed lamely at Trent Bridge and succumbed to Saxelby and Cooper.

Yorkshire maintained their lead over Kent with Boycott, Sharp and Athey all responding positively to Gloucestershire's 233, founded on an opening stand of 80 between Stovold and Broad. Kent edged two points ahead of Somerset with a comfortable win at Cardiff.

Warwickshire and Lancashire won with considerable ease, Warwickshire had 14.5 overs to spare, and Essex won with one ball to spare thanks to the undying endeavour of Stuart Turner who had seen his side collapse after Gooch and Gladwin had put on 70 for the first wicket.

There were fireworks at Guildford where Surrey hit their highest score in the John Player League. Pauline and Knight put on 145 for the second wicket in 23 overs, and then Pauline and Lynch put on 82 in 8 blistering overs.

At 33 for 3, Worcestershire had no hope, but Collis King, in one of his rare appearances allowed by his contract with Colne, reached a century off 69 balls, and, in all, hit six sixes and ten fours and a five in his 127 which came in 100 minutes off 83 deliveries. He was superbly caught at long on by Graham Monkhouse, and with him went any hopes of a sensational victory.

Nat West Trophy – Semi-Finals

17 August

at Canterbury

Kent 173 (C.J. Tavare 64, M.D. Marshall 4 for 15, T.M. Tremlett 4 for 38)
Hampshire 102 (E.A. Baptiste 5 for 20, C.S. Cowdrey 4 for 36)

Kent won by 71 runs
(Man of the Match – E.A. Baptiste)

at Lord's

Middlesex 222 for 9 (K.P. Tomlins 58, W.N. Slack 57)
Somerset 222 for 8 (I.T. Botham 96 not out)

Somerset won on losing fewer wickets
(Man of the Match – I.T. Botham)

Hampshire's hopes of reaching a Lord's final were very high and when Marshall had Taylor caught behind in the first

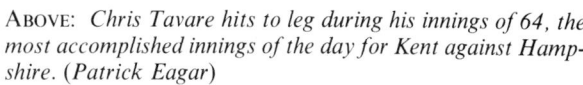

ABOVE: *Chris Tavare hits to leg during his innings of 64, the most accomplished innings of the day for Kent against Hampshire. (Patrick Eagar)*

BELOW: *Chris Cowdrey clenches his fist in the delight of accomplishment. The mighty Greenridge has been bowled. (Patrick Eagar)*

ABOVE: *Derek Aslett hits out during his third wicket stand with Tavare which realised 73 in 23 overs and was a decisive factor in Kent's victory. Bobby Parks looks thoughtful behind the stumps. (Patrick Eagar)*

BELOW: *Man of the Match Eldine Baptiste. (Adrian Murrell)*

Jubilation for Middlesex as Jeremy Lloyds is out. Gatting, Downton and Emburey in ecstasy. (Adrian Murrell)

over, they rose even higher. Kent, without Woolmer and Dilley, struggled against an attack which exploited movement from pitch and atmosphere. Jesty was a little wayward, but the Hampshire attack maintained relentless pressure, and Tremlett gave Marshall magnificent support with an accurate spell of seam bowling which meant that if the batsman took liberties, he was courting disaster. Tavare batted

Man of the Match Botham hits Emburey into the road during his magnificently controlled innings of 96 not out. (Adrian Murrell)

quite magnificently. He combined defence, watchful and responsible, with a pugnacity and purposeful driving, which brought him 64 in 37 overs, a mighty innings in the heavy atmosphere and on the uncertain wicket. Derek Aslett gave him fine support in a third wicket stand of 73 in 22 overs, but Marshall, Tremlett and Malone came out as clear winners as the rest of the Kent batting steered the ball to Pocock at slip or drove undecidely.

Hampshire seemed set for an easy victory, emphasised when Greenidge and Smith began with effortless scoring against Jarvis and Ellison. Smith hit Baptiste for two thunderous fours and then misjudged a third delivery and was splendidly caught at cover by Taylor. Greenidge made a hash

Less happy. A chance from Popplewell evades Edmonds. Gatting and Downton are concerned. (Adrian Murrell)

Leicestershire C.C.C.
Limited-Over Matches – 1983

BATTING

BATTING	v. Worcestershire (Worcester) 7 May (B.&H.)	v. Worcestershire (Leicester) 8 May (J.P.)	v. Gloucestershire (Gloucester) 15 May (J.P.)	v. Gloucestershire (Gloucester) 16 May (B.&H.)	v. Northamptonshire (Leicester) 17 May (B.&H.)	v. Scotland (Leicester) 20 May (B.&H.)	v. Kent (Leicester) 22 May (J.P.)	v. Northamptonshire (Northampton) 29 May (J.P.)	v. Derbyshire (Derby) 12 June (J.P.)	v. Hampshire (Basingstoke) 19 June (J.P.)	v. Glamorgan (Leicester) 26 June (J.P.)	v. Devon (Leicester) 29 June (N.W.)	v. Yorkshire (Scarborough) 3 July (J.P.)	v. Northamptonshire (Harrogate) 6 July (T.T.)	v. Somerset (Leicester) 10 July (J.P.)	v. Middlesex (Lord's) 17 July (J.P.)	v. Gloucestershire (Leicester) 20 July (N.W.)
J.C. Balderstone	35			—	30									33	29			24
N.E. Briers	0			—	5			29	32	34	24	40	4	40	77*	20	4
D.I. Gower	67			—	13			5			0	25	24	15	12		138*
B.F. Davison	32			—	0			0		9	25	14	35	14	46*	71	68
M.A. Garnham	2			—	19			0	2	10	6		29*			11	
R.W. Tolchard	27			—	26			6	57	36	33*	71*	5	12		14	16
A.M.E. Roberts	0			—	5			9			18*	32*				5	—
J.F. Steele	15			—	28*			29	9*	6*			0	6		4	
P.B. Clift	0							14	25	12	24	24	3	11		14	16*
G.J. Parsons	3			—	29*			0*		0			13			3	
J.P. Agnew	0*			—	—												
N.G.B. Cook				—	—				0*					2		0	
I.P. Butcher								2	9	59	5	4	24	24	43	43	12
L.B. Taylor								1*	—	—	—	—	8*	0	—	1*	—
T.J. Boon									6*	4							
R.A. Cobb																	
G. Ferris														—	2*		
J.J. Whitaker																	
J. Addison																	
Byes	1							1							4	2	4
Leg-byes	11				15			3	11	8	16	4	7	4	11	10	12
Wides								4	1		3	6	5	8	2	5	3
No-balls	5				1			2	1		3		3	1	2	1	5
Total	198				171			103	154	179	157	253	160	168	197	204	302
Wickets	10				7			9	5	8	6	6	8	10	2	10	5
Result	W	Ab.	Ab.	Ab.	L	Ab.	Ab.	L	W	L	W	W	L	L	W	L	L
Points	2	2	2	1	0	1	2	0	4	0	4	—	0	—	4	0	—

Catches

9 – M.A. Garnham (ct 7/st 2)
8 – J.F. Steele and D.I. Gower

6 – P.B. Clift, R.W. Tolchard (ct 5/st 1) and N.G.B. Cook

4 – I.P. Butcher and L.B. Taylor
3 – A.M.E. Roberts and N.E. Briers

BOWLING

BOWLING	A.M.E. Roberts	G.J. Parsons	J.P. Agnew	J.F. Steele	P.B. Clift	N.G.B. Cook	L.B. Taylor	J.C. Balderstone	G. Ferris
(B.&H.) v. Worcestershire (Worcester) 7 May	7.4-1-25-2	7-3-10-1	5-1-15-2	10-2-11-5	5-0-15-0				
(B.&H.) v. Gloucestershire (Gloucester) 16 May		1							
(B.&H.) v. Northants. (Leicester) 17 May	10-1-28-1	9-1-48-1	7-1-32-0	7-2-30-0			11-1-32-0		
(J.P.) v. Northants. (Northampton) 29 May	8-0-31-1	2-0-9-0		6-3-16-3		2.4-0-17-0	8-1-24-2		
(J.P.) v. Derbyshire (Derby) 12 June		8-1-29-1		8-0-49-2		6.3-1-20-4	8-0-28-2	7-2-15-1	
(J.P.) v. Hampshire (Basingstoke) 19 June		7-1-19-0		8-0-68-0		8-0-25-1	7.2-1-37-1	7-2-28-0	
(J.P.) v. Glamorgan (Leicester) 26 June	8-2-20-0	8-0-25-1				8-1-21-1	8-0-35-2	7.5-0-41-5	
(N.W.) v. Devon (Leicester) 29 June	6-5-3-0	8-2-27-1		12-6-13-2	4-0-9-0	12-2-45-1		5.1-3-9-3	
(J.P.) v. Yorkshire (Scarborough) 3 July		6.1-0-14-0		8-1-29-0	8-0-35-1		7-0-38-2		8-0-23-0
(T.T.) v. Northamptonshire (Harrogate)				11-4-38-0	11-1-37-1	11-3-36-2	11-3-17-1		11-4-32-4
(J.P.) v. Somerset (Leicester) 10 July	8-2-17-1	8-1-36-3			8-2-41-2	8-1-39-1	7-1-47-1		
(J.P.) v. Middlesex (Lord's) 17 July	8-1-42-0	4-0-18-0			6-0-35-1	8-0-34-2	7-1-44-0	7-0-45-2	
(N.W.) v. Gloucestershire (Leicester) 20 July	12-0-39-2	12-0-84-0				11.3-0-69-0	12-2-53-1	12-1-45-3	
(J.P.) v. Essex (Leicester) 24 July	4.3-0-24-1		1-0-13-0		3-0-26-1				
(J.P.) v. Sussex (Leicester) 31 July	7-2-11-2	1-0-9-0		4-0-7-2	8-1-25-1		8-0-34-1	6-1-14-1	
(J.P.) v. Nottinghamshire (Leicester) 7 Aug.	8-0-24-0	3-0-11-1			5-0-50-1	8-0-36-1	8-0-36-1	8-0-37-1	
(J.P.) v. Warwickshire (Edgbaston) 14 Aug.	6-2-33-2		2-0-19-0	6-0-44-0	6-0-33-0		4.1-0-25-0		
(J.P.) v. Surrey (Leicester) 4 September		8-0-54-2		5-0-39-0	8-0-47-0	8-0-55-0			8-0-38-2
Wickets	12	10	4	16	15	12	19	3	6

v. Essex (Leicester) 24 July (J.P.)	v. Sussex (Leicester) 31 July (J.P.)	v. Nottinghamshire (Leicester) 7 August (J.P.)	v. Warwickshire (Edgbaston) 14 August (J.P.)	v. Surrey (Leicester) 4 September (J.P.)	v. Lancashire (Old Trafford) 11 September (J.P.)	Runs
			45			196
50	0*	101*	10	14		484
16		57		78		450
5	—		25			344
1*	—					80
4	—	—	12	0*		319
—	—	—	10			79
—	—	—	22*	—		119
22*	—	31*	7	35		238
—	—	—	—			48
—	—	—	—	—		0
—	—	—	—			2
4	10*	8		28		275
—	—	14*				24
—	—		20			30
—		12				12
—						2
—		27		65*		92
—			10			10
	2	4	2			
6	10	7	12			
1	1	1	4			
1	1	2	2			
110	12	240	179	258		
5	0	3	8	5		
L	Ab.	W	L	L	Ab.	
0	2	4	0	0	2	

2 – B.F. Davison and G.J. Parsons
1 – J.C. Balderstone and J.J. Whitaker

J. Addison	N.E. Briers	Byes	Leg-byes	Wides	No-balls	Total	Wkts
		2	3			81	10
						59	1
		1	1		2	174	2
		5	3	1		106	6
				7	2	150	10
		2	1			180	2
			10		4	156	10
		4	3	6	2	121	10
		1	17	3	1	161	3
			4	6	1	171	9
		5	6	3	2	196	9
			12	1		231	5
			7	5	4	306	6
			1	2		66	2
		1	4			105	7
		2	12	4	2	214	2
1-0-16-0		4	4	2	1	181	2
	3-0-14-2	5	3		6	261	6
0	2						

of a ball from Cowdrey and was bowled. Baptiste beat Jesty and hit his off stump and then had Terry lbw as he stumbled across his wicket. Pocock, Marshall and Cowley followed in quick succession and Hampshire sighed for the stability of David Turner in the middle order. There was some resistance from Tremlett and Nicholas, who batted doggedly as wickets tumbled, but Hampshire were a beaten side, and Kent had once more proved their bogey team.

There had been some splendid catching by Parks, Cowley, Knott and Johnson, and Tavare and Aslett had batted well. Marshall and Tremlett had bowled superbly, but Baptiste took the individual award for his match-winning spell. A special award should have gone to Chris Cowdrey. Pressed in to action in the absence of Woolmer, he had taken the wickets of Greenidge, Nicholas, Marshall and Cowley for 36 runs, a marvellous bonus for Kent.

At Lord's, Middlesex seemed to be set for their second final of the season until Ian Botham came to the wicket. In a grinding innings, Middlesex had reached 222 for 9, thanks to a good fifty from Tomlins and a typically hard-hitting innings from Gatting. Slack, who had survived rather luckily against the awkward Garner, reached a tenacious fifty, and, on a wicket of uneven bounce, Middlesex could be well satisfied with their score.

Cowans had Lloyds well caught behind by Downton and then he bowled Denning first ball. Richards prospered for a while and then fell to a catch at mid-off by Daniel off Williams. Downton pulled off another good catch to dismiss Slocombe off the impressive Williams and when Roebuck was taken at slip off Cowans, Somerset were 52 for 5. Popplewell joined Botham in a purposeful and confident stand of 104. Popplewell, enjoying his best season, was Downton's third victim, but Vic Marks stayed with Botham while 62 were added.

Botham played one of the most disciplined innings of his career. He batted for 50 overs, an innings lasting 4½ hours. He fashioned everything to the needs of his side even to the extent of playing out the last over from Embury without attempting a scoring shot so that Somerset went through on losing fewer wickets. He once swept Embury out of the ground for six, but most of the time it was a restrained figure, guiding his team to victory with a discipline which was an example to all. This was a very great innings, and Basil d'Oliveira could have no doubt as to whom to name Man of the Match.

17, 18 and 19 August

at Chelmsford

New Zealanders 321 for 4 dec (G.P. Howarth 144, M.D. Crowe 116 not out) and 220 (M.G. Hughes 4 for 71)
Essex 233 (K.R. Pont 81, M.C. Snedden 5 for 68) and 260 (C. Gladwin 89, G.A. Gooch 54, J.G. Bracewell 6 for 111)

New Zealanders won by 48 runs

Essex, like Hampshire and others before them, chose to field a weakened side against the tourists. Andy Golding, slow left-arm, was given his first-class debut, and Merv Hughes, the Victorian pace bowler who had been playing for Woodford Wells, was also included, a strange choice reflecting

Middlesex C.C.C.
Limited-Over Matches – 1983

BATTING

BATTING	Surrey (The Oval) 7 May (B.&H.)	Glamorgan (Lord's) 8 May (J.P.)	Kent (Canterbury) 14 May (B.&H.)	Hampshire (Lord's) 15 May (J.P.)	Glamorgan (Uxbridge) 17 May (B.&H.)	Com. Univs. (Lord's) 20 May (B.&H.)	Yorkshire (Hull) 22 May (J.P.)	Sussex (Lord's) 29 May (J.P.)	Gloucestershire (Bristol) 2 June (B.&H.)	Worcestershire (Lord's) 5 June (J.P.)	Surrey (The Oval) 12 June (J.P.)	Derbyshire (Chesterfield) 26 June (J.P.)	Cambridgeshire (Wisbech) 29 June (N.W.)	Gloucestershire (Lord's) 3 July (J.P.)	Lancashire (Lord's) 6 July (B.&H.)	Leicestershire (Lord's) 17 July (J.P.)	Derbyshire (Derby) 20 July (N.W.)	Essex (Lord's) 23 July (B.&H.)
G.D. Barlow	37		15				11	52		—	11	35	13		8	19	62	14
W.N. Slack	36		11				30	69		—	0	25	28	60	8	19	40	1
C.T. Radley	1		88*				14	23*		—	38	4	27	17*	18	32*	11	89*
M.W. Gatting	53		7				13	9		—	30	0	13*	85	18	56	3	22
R.O. Butcher	85		50				0	31		—	1*	4	4	—	100	12	37	
J.E. Emburey	12		1*				3	—		—	27	30*		38*	0*	40*	28	17
N.F. Williams	12*		—				7	6*		—	10*	—		—			1	13
P.R. Downton	11*		—				31	3		—	4	35	—		7*	43*	12	10
K.D. James	—		3							—	11*	—						
N.G. Cowans	—						2*											
W.W. Daniel	—		—				4	—		—							4*	2*
P.H. Edmonds							2	—				15*	—				18*	9
K.P. Tomlins								6			31		80	0	16	0	46	0
W.G. Merry											—					—		
S.P. Hughes										—				—				
R.G.P. Ellis															9			
J.D. Carr																		
J.F. Sykes																		
C.R. Cook																		
G. Rose																		
C.P. Metson																		
Byes	2		1				2	15			3					1	1	3
Leg-byes	14		10				5			1	6	4	4	10	2	12	11	9
Wides	5		5				2	2		4	1	3		2	3	1	2	4
No-balls	5		5				1			5	3	3					1	3
Total	273		191				127	216		90	161	162	174	270	91	231	240	196
Wickets	6		5				10	6		3	7	6	2	5	4	5	8	8
Result	W	Ab.	W	Ab.	Ab.	Ab.	L	L	Wt	W	L	W	W	L	W	W	W	W
Points	2	2	2	2	1	1	0	0		4	0	4				0	4	—

Catches

36 – P.R. Downton (ct 30/st 6)	6 – R.O. Butcher, G.D. Barlow and N.G. Cowans	2 – S.P. Hughes, W.W. Daniel and R.G.P. Ellis
9 – C.T. Radley	5 – J.E. Emburey	1 – K.P. Tomlins, J.D. Carr, G. Rose,
7 – W.N. Slack and M.W. Gatting	3 – P.H. Edmonds and K.D. James	C.R. Cook and sub.

BOWLING

BOWLING	W.W. Daniel	N.G. Cowans	K.D. James	N.F. Williams	J.E. Emburey	M.W. Gatting	W.N. Slack	S.P. Hughes	W.G. Merry
(B.&H.) v. Surrey (The Oval) 7 May	3–0–10–0	5–0–20–1	7–0–22–0		5–1–5–1				
(B.&H.) v. Kent (Canterbury) 14 May	11–2–27–2	7–0–34–1	11–3–31–2	7–2–17–1	8–0–43–0	11–2–26–0			
(J.P.) v. Yorkshire (Hull) 22 May	8–0–17–1	4–0–18–0				8–2–19–3	4–0–21–2		
(J.P.) v. Sussex (Lord's) 29 May	6–0–38–2			2–0–20–1	8–0–28–1	1.2–0–6–1			
(B.&H.) v. Gloucestershire (Bristol) 2 June									
(J.P.) v. Worcestershire (Lord's) 5 June	6–0–15–2	8–0–22–2			5.3–1–10–2	4–2–9–1	6–0–13–3	2–0–6–0	
(J.P.) v. Surrey (The Oval) 12 June				8–0–31–0	8–1–38–0	8–0–21–2		8–0–37–3	8–0–29–2
(J.P.) v. Derbyshire (Chesterfield) 26 June		8–1–29–0	8–1–23–1		8–1–40–4	3–0–21–0	1.5–0–7–2		
(N.W.) v. Cambridgeshire (Wisbech) 29 June	11.4–3–31–2	12–3–22–1			10–3–33–2	12–2–27–2	1–0–2–0		
(J.P.) v. Gloucestershire (Lord's) 3 July		8–1–50–0	8–0–68–1		8–0–33–1	6.2–0–49–1	1–0–13–0		
(B.&H.) v. Lancashire (Lord's) 6 July	9–1–28–3	11–4–33–4			4.5–1–10–1	7–3–8–2			
(J.P.) v. Leicestershire (Lord's) 17 July				6–0–29–1	8–0–33–1		6.4–0–32–5	7–1–36–0	3–0–25–1
(N.W.) v. Derbyshire (Derby) 20 July	11.2–0–35–3	10–0–41–1		9–1–36–4		12–1–36–0	3–2–4–0	1–0–6–0	
(B.&H.) v. Essex (Lord's) 23 July	11–2–34–1	10.1–0–39–4		11–0–45–2		11–3–17–0			
(J.P.) v. Kent (Canterbury) 24 July	6–0–26–2	2–0–15–0	8–0–29–2			8–1–26–3		6–0–28–1	
(J.P.) v. Warwickshire (Lord's) 31 July	8–0–29–2			1–0–3–1		7.5–1–36–5		1–0–8–1	
(N.W.) v. Northants. (Northampton) 3 Aug.	12–2–42–3	3–0–16–0		1–0–8–0		12–4–25–0	8–0–33–1	12–1–37–3	
(J.P.) v. Essex (Chelmsford) 7 August	7–0–37–2	8–0–36–3		7–0–22–0		8–0–27–0		2–0–10–0	
(J.P.) v. Lancashire (Old Trafford) 14 August			8–0–20–0	7–1–32–0		8–3–29–0		5–0–31–1	
(N.W.) v. Somerset (Lord's) 17 August	12–2–32–1	12–2–48–3		10–0–54–2		3–1–9–0	9–1–26–1		
(J.P.) v. Somerset (Lord's) 21 August			8–2–19–0	7–0–47–2	8–0–13–1	8–0–44–1		7–1–28–0	
(J.P.) v. Northants. (Milton Keynes) 28 Aug.			8–0–48–0		8–3–27–2			8–0–39–2	8–0–37–1
(J.P.) v. Notts. (Cleethorpes) 4 September			7.2–0–25–2	8–0–48–2		8–1–25–1			8–0–24–0
Wickets	26	20	10	27	23	12	13	6	4

a J.F. Sykes 2–0–11–0

n toss of coin

Batting (one-day matches)

	v. Kent (Canterbury) 24 July (J.P.)	v. Warwickshire (Lord's) 31 July (J.P.)	v. Northamptonshire (Northampton) 3 August (N.W.)	v. Essex (Chelmsford) 7 August (J.P.)	v. Lancashire (Old Trafford) 14 August (J.P.)	v. Somerset (Lord's) 17 August (N.W.)	v. Somerset (Lord's) 21 August (J.P.)	v. Northamptonshire (Milton Keynes) 28 August (J.P.)	v. Nottinghamshire (Cleethorpes) 4 September (J.P.)	Runs
		2	77	56	32	8	19	68*	1*	513
	35	26	5	0	9	57				459
	31	17	63	15	41	12	11	1	32	608
	69	47	28*	31		49	28		7	568
										324
	21*	8	—	6	15	1	6	—		253
		4	—	—	3	2	13*		31*	102
	—	20	—	35*	0	12	13		2	238
	—	6*	—		4		7*		25	56
	—					0*				2
	—	—				0				10
	—			5*			7*			56
	55				4	58	16	51*	12	375
								—		—
			9			—				9
	1	18	15*	18	30		19	52	8	170
		0*								0
					2*					2
							6		18	24
							—		33	33
										—
		1	2		1			2		
	12	10	9	9	15	11	17	8		
	2	4		6		5	2	1		
	1			6	1		1			
	227	163	199	187	166	222	158	183		
	5	8	3	6	10	9	8	2		
	W	W	W	W	L	L	L	W		
	4	4	—	4	0	—	0	4		

Bowling (continued)

P.H. Edmonds	C.T. Radley	G. Rose	Byes	Leg-byes	Wides	No-balls	Total	Wkts
					3	3	63	2
				3	6	3	190	7
			3	1	1		80	6
				2	2	2	98	6
							12	0
				7	6	1	89	10
				5	2	1	164	7
6-0-35-1				3		2	160	10
12-3-41-1			5	9		2	172	10
8-0-45-1			2	8	4		272	4
				1	2	8	90	10
			2	10	5	1	204	10
12-2-38-1			1	8	1	4	210	10
11-3-34-2				12	3	8	192	10
8-1-38-1	0.4-0-2-1		1	5	1		171	10
			1	5			82	10
12-3-24-1				6	2	5	198	9
8-0-33-2			1	6	6	6	184	8
			1	5	1	3	167	3a
12-4-33-0				6	4	10	222	8
				3	2	3	159	6
		8-0-26-0	1	3		1	182	6
		8-0-41-1		7	9	7	186	6
10	1	1						

Geoff Howarth. 144 against Essex, the highest score of the tour by a New Zealander. (Adrian Murrell)

Essex's lack of faith in their own talent. Howarth hit New Zealand's highest score of the tour and Martin Crowe gave further evidence of his talent on the opening day. Keith Pont, so wrongly underrated, batted well and Sneddon bowled himself into Test contention. Eventually, Essex needed 309 in 240 minutes, and Gooch and Gladwin batted splendidly. Chris Gladwin hit a career best and showed that he had become a vital part of the Essex challenge, but John Bracewell plugged away to give the tourists victory.

20, 21 and 22 August

at Leicester

Leicestershire 281 for 5 dec (B.F. Davison 123 not out, N.E. Briers 57, J.P. Addison 51) and 198 (J.G. Bracewell 5 for 80)
New Zealanders 265 for 8 dec (T.J. Franklin 61, B.A. Edgar 54, P.B. Clift 4 for 35) and 216 for 2 (T.J. Franklin 98 not out)

New Zealanders won by 8 wickets

Northamptonshire C.C.C.
Limited-Over Matches – 1983

BATTING

BATTING	v. Gloucestershire (Northampton) 7 May (B.&H.)	v. Nottinghamshire (Northampton) 8 May (J.P.)	v. Derbyshire (Derby) 15 May (J.P.)	v. Leicestershire (Leicester) 17 May (B.&H.)	v. Worcestershire (Worcester) 20 May (B.&H.)	v. Hampshire (Bournemouth) 22 May (J.P.)	v. Scotland (Northampton) 23 May (B.&H.)	v. Leicestershire (Northampton) 29 May (J.P.)	v. Lancashire (Old Trafford) 1-3 June (B.&H.)	v. Lancashire (Old Trafford) 5 June (J.P.)	v. Gloucestershire (Northampton) 12 June (J.P.)	v. Warwickshire (Luton) 19 June (J.P.)	v. Surrey (East Moseley) 26 June (J.P.)	v. Wiltshire (Swindon) 29 June (N.W.)	v. Sussex (Hastings) 3 July (J.P.)	v. Leicestershire (Harrogate) 6 July (T.T.)	v. Yorkshire (Harrogate) 8 July (T.T.)
G. Cook	33	20	20	6	—	40	63*	0	25	26	13	3*	29*	31	2	3	0
W. Larkins	36	18	3	4	—	30	24	1	18	1	102	172*	—	65	3	10	104
P. Willey	71	36	1	54*	—	67	18	2	—	39	10	84	15	32	2	5	64*
A.J. Lamb	14	42	10	106*	—	11	10	33	13	4			72	75	12	25	2*
R.G. Williams	16	1	3	—	—	0	—	22	0	16	2	—	3	23*	45*	43	—
D.J. Capel	6	5	—	—	—	4	—	11*	28	1	4	—	—	—	—	22	—
G. Sharp	3	8*	22	—	—	7*	—	0*	16	0	51*	—	—	—	29	23	—
T.M. Lamb	0	0*	13	—	—	4*	—	—	4	13*	0*	—	—	—	0	1	—
J.A. Carse	0	—	4	—	—	—	—	—	—	—	—	—	—	—	4*	3	—
N.A. Mallender	0	—	4*	—	—	—	—	—	5	—	—	—	—	—	2	—	—
B.J. Griffiths	1*	—	0*	—	—	—	—	—	3	—	—	—	—	—	—	0*	—
R.N. Kapil Dev	—	66	—	—	—	1	18*	28	49	—	—	—	—	18	—	—	—
D.S. Steele	—	—	38	—	—	—	—	—	16*	—	—	—	—	5*	25*	—	—
D.J. Wild	—	—	—	—	—	—	—	—	—	—	20*	—	0*	—	—	—	—
R.J. Boyd-Moss	—	—	—	—	—	—	—	—	—	—	—	2	—	—	—	—	—
R.J. Bailey	—	—	—	—	—	—	—	—	—	—	—	—	27	19	21	36	—
M.J. Bamber	—	—	—	—	—	—	—	—	—	—	—	—	71	—	—	—	—
A. Walker	—	—	—	—	—	—	—	—	—	—	—	—	—	—	—	—	—
D. Boyle	—	—	—	—	—	—	—	—	—	—	—	—	—	—	—	—	—
Byes	1			1			4	5					6	2	1		
Leg-byes	9	12	3	1		2	2	3	6	9	7	9	12	4	6	4	
Wides	1	1	2			6	2	1		1	5		7	7	1	6	6
No-balls		1		2								2	3		2	1	6
Total	191	210	123	174		172	141	106	183	130	198	298	234	285	143	171	182
Wickets	10	7	9	2		7	3	6	10	7	6	2	5	6	8	9	2
Result	L	L	L	W	Ab.	L	W	W	L	L	W	W	W	W	L	L	W
Points	0	0	0	2	1	0	2	4	—	0	4	4	4	—	0	—	—

Catches
24 – G. Sharp (ct 20/st 4)
8 – G. Cook, T.M. Lamb and W. Larkins
7 – R.G. Williams
6 – A.J. Lamb
5 – P. Willey
3 – N.A. Mallender and B.J. Griffiths
2 – D.S. Steele and D.J. Wild
1 – R.J. Boyd-Moss, R.J. Bailey, D.J. Capel, M.J. Bamber, D. Boyle and sub.

BOWLING

	J.A. Carse	B.J. Griffiths	P. Willey	T.M. Lamb	R.G. Williams	N.A. Mallender	R.N. Kapil Dev	D.S. Steele	D.J. Capel
(B.&H.) v. Glos. (Northampton) 7 May	11–1–38–3	10–1–46–1	11–1–26–1	11–4–26–2	2–0–12–0	10–0–37–1			
(J.P.) v. Notts. (Northampton) 8 May					5.4–0–41–1	1–0–7–0	7–0–23–1		
(J.P.) v. Derbyshire (Derby) 15 May	7–1–15–1	6–0–22–0	8–0–36–1	8–0–55–1		7–0–27–2		3–0–24–0	
(B.&H.) v. Leicestershire (Leicester) 17 May		11–3–35–1	1–0–4–0		11–3–28–3	10–0–33–0	11–3–31–0		11–2–24–3
(B.&H.) v. Worcestershire (Worcester) 20 May		3.4–2–10–0				7–2–12–3	9–3–10–2		2–1–6–0
(J.P.) v. Hampshire (Bournemouth) 22 May		7–1–38–1	8–0–24–0	8–0–40–1	7–1–33–1	4–0–15–0	4–0–11–0		
(B.&H.) v. Scotland (Northampton) 23 May		11–2–28–3	11–3–18–2	6–1–23–1	5–2–13–0	5–2–15–0	5.3–3–6–1	11–4–23–3	
(J.P.) v. Leicestershire (Northampton) 29 May		8–2–28–1	8–2–12–1	8–2–9–4		7–2–17–2	8–1–24–1		1–0–5–0
(B.&H.) v. Lancashire (Old Trafford) 1–3 June		11–0–55–0			11–0–54–2	11–1–41–1	9–0–47–1	5–0–21–0	
(J.P.) v. Lancashire (Old Trafford) 5 June	8–0–25–0	7–0–26–1	8–2–22–1	7–1–25–0					
(J.P.) v. Glos. (Northampton) 12 June		8–0–30–1	8–0–22–3	8–0–58–1	8–0–21–0	8–1–34–1			
(J.P.) v. Warwickshire (Luton) 19 June		3–0–41–0	8–1–35–1	8–0–48–0	8–0–30–5	8–0–47–2			
(J.P.) v. Surrey (East Moseley) 26 June		5–0–33–0	8–1–34–1	8–0–64–0	2–0–16–0	8–0–46–4			
(N.W.) v. Wiltshire (Swindon) 29 June				12–3–31–1	7–3–16–3	6–0–22–1		8–3–13–2	12–4–31–3
(J.P.) v. Sussex (Hastings) 3 July	8–0–45–0	8–0–80–2	8–1–35–0		8–0–30–0	8–1–34–1			
(T.T.) v. Leicestershire (Harrogate) 6 July	4–0–20–0	11–0–31–1	11–3–25–2	11–0–38–3	6–0–26–0			11–4–14–1	
(T.T.) v. Yorkshire (Harrogate) 8 July		10–3–55–1	6–1–14–0	9–1–19–2	9.3–1–38–2			9–4–18–1	
(J.P.) v. Yorkshire (Tring) 10 July		8–1–14–0	8–0–24–0	7–0–30–0	8–1–28–0		1–0–7–0		
(N.W.) v. Yorkshire (Leeds) 20 July		10–4–33–5	4–0–17–0	10–1–38–0		12–1–34–3	11.2–5–17–2		
(J.P.) v. Glamorgan (Northampton) 24 July		8–0–35–2	5–0–26–0	6–0–25–0		8–0–27–3	7–0–35–1		
(J.P.) v. Worcestershire (Worcester) 31 July		4.5–0–18–3	2–0–21–0	2–0–3–0		3–0–17–0	8–1–24–1		
(N.W.) v. Middlesex (Northampton) 3 August		8–0–32–0	11.4–1–53–0	3–1–8–0	10–0–37–0	12–1–37–2	9–4–21–0		
(J.P.) v. Somerset (Weston-super-Mare) 7 Aug.		8–2–31–0	4–0–17–0	7–1–21–0		5–1–18–0	4–1–13–0		
(J.P.) v. Essex (Wellingborough) 14 August		3–0–19–0	8–1–23–1			4.5–0–32–1	8–2–23–3		
(J.P.) v. Middlesex (Milton Keynes) 28 Aug.				8–0–23–0	7–0–52–0	5.1–1–22–1			2–0–21–0
Wickets	4	23	15	21	12	27	15	8	3

a G. Cook 1–0–6–0   b R.J. Bailey 5–0–49–0

(inning) 10 July (J.P.)	v. Yorkshire (Leeds) 20 July (N.W.)	v. Glamorgan (Northampton) 24 July (J.P.)	v. Worcestershire (Worcester) 31 July (J.P.)	v. Middlesex (Northampton) 3 August (J.P.)	v. Somerset (Weston-super-Mare) 7 August (J.P.)	v. Essex (Wellingborough) 14 August (J.P.)	v. Middlesex (Milton Keynes) 28 August (J.P.)	v. Kent (Canterbury) 11 September (J.P.)	Runs
6	2	59*	10	29	16	29			485
3	39	18	53	30	0	16	47		797
1	0	0	24	41	32	62	23		693
6	76	22		0	5				538
1	16	16		33	9	16	47		312
	15	0	6	27	1	19*	16*		165
2	41*	34*	1	14	22		—		273
23*	—	—	1*	9*	2*				70
									11
4	11*	—	6	0	22	—	—		64
—		—	0	—	—	—			4
	0	22	12	2	0	1			217
									84
			13			—	6		39
			6			6*	25		39
4							13		117
						—	13		84
3							—		13
4	1	2					1		
7	3	11	9	6	10	3	3		
4	4	7	6	2	1	1			
3	3	5		5	3	5	1		
1	211	196	147	198	123	158	182		
9	7	6	10	9	9	5	6		
L	W	W	L	L	L	L	L	Ab.	
0	—	4	0	—	0	0	0	2	

D.J. Wild	W. Larkins	A. Walker	Byes	Leg-byes	Wides	No-balls	Total	Wkts
				2	1	4	192	8
			1	2			74	2
				11	9	2	201	5
				15		1	171	7
				4		1	43	5
				9	1	2	173	3
			2	5		2	135	10
			1	3	4		103	9
			3	4	4	3	290	5
4-0-18-0				5	1	3	131	2a
			1	12	1	2	181	6
				11	1	2	264	8b
		8-0-24-1		8	7		232	6
			1	6			120	10
				5		1	231	3
	0.2-0-1-1			4	8	1	168	10
	11-2-20-4		3	4		7	178	10
		2.3-0-24-0		4		1	132	0
	8-0-18-0			6	2		165	10
			3	11			162	8
				10	3		96	4
			2	9			199	3
			5	5		2	125	0
			4	7			159	8
8-0-17-2	8-0-34-1			2	8	1	183	2
7-0-29-1		6-0-25-0						
3	6	1						

at Colchester

Gloucestershire 82 (N. Phillip 6 for 19) and 265 (B.C. Broad 109, J.K. Lever 4 for 90)
Essex 384 for 6 dec (K.S. McEwan 181, K.R. Pont 78 not out, B.R. Hardie 62)

Essex won by an innings and 37 runs
Essex 24 pts, Gloucestershire 2 pts

at Swansea

Glamorgan 221 for 9 dec (A.L. Jones 57, R.C. Ontong 50) and 240 (J.A. Hopkins 109 not out, A.L. Jones 53, C.J. Tunnicliffe 4 for 48, O. Mortensen 4 for 65)
Derbyshire 285 (K.J. Barnett 67, M.A. Holding 63, W.P. Fowler 61) and 177 for 8

Derbyshire won by 2 wickets
Derbyshire 23 pts, Glamorgan 6 pts

at Folkestone

Warwickshire 470 for 8 dec (D.L. Amiss 164, A.I. Kallicharran 111, D.L. Underwood 5 for 113) and 31 for 0
Kent 268 (G.W. Johnson 79 not out, N. Gifford 6 for 85) and 344 for 8 dec (A.P.E. Knott 80, D.G. Aslett 78, C.J. Tavare 62, M.R. Benson 52, N. Gifford 4 for 111)

Match drawn
Warwickshire 8 pts, Kent 5 pts

at Lord's

Somerset 249 (J.E. Emburey 5 for 54) and 119 (P.H. Edmonds 5 for 19, J.E. Emburey 4 for 28)
Middlesex 242 (M.W. Gatting 105, J.E. Emburey 63) and 93 (S.C. Booth 4 for 26)

Somerset won by 33 runs
Somerset 22 pts, Middlesex 6 pts

at Northampton

Northamptonshire 381 for 2 dec (W. Larkins 187, P. Willey 147 not out) and 213 for 7 dec (R.J. Boyd-Moss 78, D. Lloyd 4 for 53)
Lancashire 331 for 3 dec (D. Lloyd 123, G. Fowler 107) and 115 for 7 (D.S. Steele 4 for 40)

Match drawn
Northamptonshire 4 pts, Lancashire 4 pts

at Hove

Surrey 357 for 6 dec (D.J. Thomas 103 not out, R.D.V. Knight 57, D.B. Pauline 51) and 198 for 5 dec (M.A. Lynch 101 not out, C.J. Richards 52 not out)
Sussex 252 for 7 dec (Imran Khan 71) and 120 for 5

Match drawn
Surrey 7 pts, Sussex 5 pts

at Worcester

Hampshire 365 (C.G. Greenidge 95, N.E.J. Pocock 57, S.P. Perryman 4 for 91, R.K. Illingworth 4 for 104)
Worcestershire 175 and 146 (N.G. Cowley 4 for 38)

Hampshire won by an innings and 44 runs
Hampshire 24 pts, Worcestershire 4 pts

Nottinghamshire C.C.C.
Limited-Over Matches – 1983

BATTING

BATTING	v. Northamptonshire (Northampton) 8 May (J.P.)	v. Somerset (Trent Bridge) 15 May (J.P.)	v. Yorkshire (Leeds) 16 May (B.&H.)	v. Derbyshire (Trent Bridge) 17 May (B.&H.)	v. Warwickshire (Trent Bridge) 20 May (B.&H.)	v. Lancashire (Old Trafford) 21 and 23 May (B.&H.)	v. Lancashire (Old Trafford) 23 May (B.&H.)	v. Surrey (Trent Bridge) 29 May (J.P.)	v. Glamorgan (Trent Bridge) 5 June (J.P.)	v. Lancashire (Old Trafford) 12 June (J.P.)	v. Kent (Canterbury) 26 June (J.P.)	v. Worcestershire (Worcester) 29 June (N.W.)	v. Essex (Trent Bridge) 3 July (J.P.)	v. Yorkshire (Harrogate) 7 July (T.T.)	v. Worcestershire (Hereford) 10 July (J.P.)	v. Hampshire (Portsmouth) 17 July (J.P.)	v. Sussex (Hove) 20 July (N.W.)
C.E.B. Rice	45*	11*	86*	68							97	0	2	82*	71	11	10
R.J. Hadlee	17	—	6	37	—		43		25								
J.D. Birch	2	—	4	50	—		9		7	42*	10	11	1	13*	15	12	28
D.W. Randall	7*	—	8	27	0*		28		75	10	11		107	52		12*	25
R.T. Robinson	—	13*	18	0	10*		0	28	32	51	26	6	56	4	74	4	3
S.B. Hassan	—	7	36	7	1		15		1	38	0	22	33		71	39	3
B.N. French	—	—	1	9	—		10	5	21*	5	11	6	—	—		17*	11
M.K. Bore	—	—	—	0*				1		—	1	3*					4*
E.E. Hemmings	—		19	2	—		0		1		10*	15	34		2*	3	9
K.E. Cooper	—				—		25*		4		4	9	0*				
M. Hendrick	—	—	—	—				0*			—	4*	18				
K. Saxelby		—	0	10*			6*		—		0	12	5		—	—	5*
P. Johnson							5	26	7								
M.A. Fell									—							5	
N.J.B. Illingworth													2			—	2
P.M. Such													0*				
R.B. Kerr														36			
R.A. Pick																—	34*
Byes	1		1				5				1		3	2		3	2
Leg-byes	2	1	8	9	2		8		7	9	18	8	8	16	5	10	4
Wides			5	7					7	4	3	1	6	5	4	8	14
No-balls			3						2		8	6	5	5	8	2	1
Total	74	32	195	226	13		154		189	154	221	169	217	265	195	186	151
Wickets	2	1	8	8	1		8		10	3	9	10	9	3	4	6	8
Result	W	L	W	W	Ab.	Ab.	L	Ab.	L	L	L	W	L	L	Tie	L	L
Points	4	0	2	2	1	—	0	2	0	0	0	—	0	—	2	0	—

Catches

15 – B.N. French	5 – C.E.B. Rice and S.B. Hassan	2 – M. Hendrick
8 – R.T. Robinson and J.D. Birch	4 – P. Johnson	1 – R.J. Hadlee, K. Saxelby, K.E. Cooper,
6 – D.W. Randall	3 – E.E. Hemmings and M.K. Bore	M.A. Fell, R.A. Pick and sub.

BOWLING

BOWLING	R.J. Hadlee	M.K. Bore	K.E. Cooper	M. Hendrick	E.E. Hemmings	K. Saxelby	P.M. Such	N.J.B. Illingworth	S.B. Hassan
(J.P.) v. Northants. (Northampton) 8 May	8-3-29-0	8-1-55-0	8-0-55-2	8-1-16-1	8-0-41-2				
(J.P.) v. Somerset (Trent Bridge) 15 May	8-0-48-0	8-2-31-1		8-0-62-1	8-0-88-1	8-0-42-0			
(B.&H.) v. Yorkshire (Leeds) 16 May	9-3-20-3	11-2-36-1		10-1-34-2	11-1-26-1	11-1-26-1			
(B.&H.) v. Derbyshire (Trent Bridge) 17 May	11-3-25-3	11-2-36-0		11-1-33-1	11-1-26-2	11-0-44-1			
(B.&H.) v. Lancs. (Old Trafford) 22-23 May	8.3-2-16-1		9-1-24-0	8-3-23-1	8-0-43-0	7-0-40-0			
(J.P.) v. Glamorgan (Trent Bridge) 5 June	8-0-40-1	8-0-28-0	8-0-42-3	7-1-29-1	8-0-45-1				
(J.P.) v. Lancashire (Old Trafford) 12 June		7-0-32-1	8-2-23-0	7.2-0-22-0	8-1-21-2	8-0-45-0			
(J.P.) v. Kent (Canterbury) 26 June		8-0-48-0	8-1-64-1	8-1-59-1	8-0-37-1	8-1-45-1			
(N.W.) v. Worcestershire (Worcester) 29 June		12-3-26-0	12-4-18-3	12-3-31-2	12-4-22-1	12-0-46-3			
(J.P.) v. Essex (Trent Bridge) 3 July			8-0-45-1		8-0-41-0	8-0-48-1	7-0-66-0	7-0-65-0	2-0-28-0
(T.T.) v. Yorkshire (Harrogate) 7 July		11-0-65-1	10-0-51-1		11-2-28-2	10.4-2-62-0			
(J.P.) v. Worcestershire (Hereford) 10 July		8-1-40-1	8-3-17-1	8-0-39-2	8-0-33-1	8-0-47-1			
(J.P.) v. Hampshire (Portsmouth) 17 July		8-0-28-0			8-0-49-2	8-0-46-2		8-0-55-1	
(N.W.) v. Sussex (Hove) 20 July		12-2-54-1		12-4-35-1	12-5-24-2			12-5-40-0	
(J.P.) v. Derbyshire (Derby) 24 July		7.5-0-38-4		1-0-4-2					
(J.P.) v. Yorkshire (Trent Bridge) 31 July		6-0-41-3	5-0-35-1		2-0-17-0	2-0-17-0			
(J.P.) v. Leicestershire (Leicester) 7 August		8-1-35-0	8-0-47-0		8-1-35-0	8-0-34-2		8-0-73-1	
(J.P.) v. Sussex (Trent Bridge) 14 August			6.5-0-26-4		8-1-14-0	8-1-37-4		7-0-39-0	
(J.P.) v. Warwickshire (Edgbaston) 28 August		8-0-31-1	8-1-43-0		8-0-37-0	8-0-29-4			
(J.P.) v. Middlesex (Cleethorpes) 4 Sept.		8-1-37-1	8-2-31-1		8-0-51-3	8-0-29-3			
Wickets	8	15	18	12	23	25	0	2	0

v. Derbyshire (Derby) (J.P.) 24 July	v. Yorkshire (Trent Bridge) (J.P.) 31 July	v. Leicestershire (Leicester) (J.P.) 7 August	v. Sussex (Trent Bridge) (J.P.) 14 August	v. Warwickshire (Edgbaston) (J.P.) 28 August	v. Middlesex (Cleethorpes) (J.P.) 4 September	v. Gloucestershire (Trent Bridge) (J.P.) 11 September	Runs
4*	66*	48	9	0	48		658
							128
7*	26		92	10	24		363
		4	40		23		442
34	1*	68	14	48	0		487
24	—	14		10			321
—	—	2	15	7	4		124
—	—			0*	—		9
—	—	23*	3*	0	39*		160
				1	—		43
							22
—	—			5	23*		66
		35*	6	44	2		125
							5
							4
—	—	—			—		0
							36
—	—		—	4			38
2		2		1			
4	10	12	12	7	7		
	3	4	3	1	9		
11	1	2	3	1	7		
86	107	214	197	139	186		
2	1	5	6	10	6		
L	W	L	W	L	W	Ab.	
0	4	0	4	0	4	2	

A. Pick	Byes	Leg-byes	Wides	No-balls	Total	Wkts
		12	1	1	210	7
	2	5		1	279	3
		6	1	1	170	10
	1	4	4	2	175	9
	9			2	157	3
		10	4	2	200	7
	4	6	2		155	3
	3	10	2	2	270	4
	4	15	1	4	167	10
	2	9	1	1	306	2
11–0–41–2	3	12	3	3	268	6
	1	12	2	4	195	9
8–0–56–1		8			242	6
12–2–60–2	1	7	4	2	227	7
8–0–38–1		6		1	87	7
	1	7	5		106	6
	4	10	1	1	240	3
8–0–35–2	2	4	5	2	164	10
8–0–43–2	1	14	1	1	200	7
3–0–21–0		11	1		181	8

10

at Bradford

Yorkshire 316 for 3 dec (G. Boycott 163, A.A. Metcalfe 122) and 283 for 3 dec (G. Boycott 141 not out, J.D. Love 75 not out, C.W.J. Athey 56)
Nottinghamshire 303 for 7 dec (B.N. French 91, J.D. Birch 85, R.T. Robinson 50) and 149 for 3 (R.T. Robinson 70 not out)

Match drawn
Yorkshire 7 pts, Nottinghamshire 5 pts

On Monday, rain fell at Lord's in such quantity that the Long Room was flooded and the pitch under water. By then, Middlesex, thanks entirely to the unquenchable spirit and pugnacity of Gatting and some hearty support from Emburey, had come within 7 of the Somerset first innings and had taken one Somerset second innings wicket for 72. Troubles haunted Middlesex. Slack was injured in a benefit match on the previous Friday and his place was taken by Miller. Gatting ran through his bowlers like a quick change artist, but catches were missed and only Emburey, inevitably, was at his best. When Edmonds found a spot on Tuesday morning, however, to bowl in tandem with Emburey, Somerset were routed, adding only 47 more runs to their overnight score. This left Middlesex 127 to win in two hours, twenty minutes. There was a lengthened tea interval due to rain, however, and, on a wicket that was now turning alarmingly, the task became a great one. Gatting was run out by Popplewell with a back flick from short leg and Middlesex went to 39 for 4.

John Emburey – a splendid all-round season and a decisive contribution to Middlesex as captain in the absence of Mike Gatting. (George Herringshaw)

Somerset C.C.C.
Limited-Over Matches – 1983

BATTING

BATTING	v. Sussex (Taunton) 7 and 9 May (B. & H.)	v. Sussex (Taunton) 8 May (J.P.)	v. Essex (Chelmsford) 14 May (B. & H.)	v. Nottinghamshire (Trent Bridge) 15 May (J.P.)	v. Hampshire (Taunton) 17 and 18 May (B. & H.)	v. Surrey (The Oval) 22 May (J.P.)	v. Minor Counties (Slough) 23 May (B. & H.)	v. Yorkshire (Bradford) 29 May (J.P.)	v. Essex (Taunton) 5 June (J.P.)	v. Glamorgan (Bath) 19 June (J.P.)	v. Gloucestershire (Bath) 26 June (J.P.)	v. Shropshire (Wellington) 29 June (N.W.)	v. Leicestershire (Leicester) 10 July (J.P.)	v. Lancashire (Old Trafford) 20 July (N.W.)	v. Hampshire (Taunton) 24 July (J.P.)	v. Lancashire (Old Trafford) 31 July (J.P.)	v. Sussex (Hove) 3 August (N.W.)
J.W. Lloyds	51	2	10	22	8			14						5	—	—	28*
P.M. Roebuck	29	50	19	46	21			7		30*	105	37	7	43*	0	1*	8
I.V.A. Richards	83	96*	63	117*	16			34			2	74	13	32	28		23
B.C. Rose	25	42	0	1*	20			33*					3				23
I.T. Botham	14	0	1	85	3			45			73	16	64	—	25		—
N.F.M. Popplewell	18	3	21	—	5			0*		84	7	14	1	68*	5*		4*
V.J. Marks	18	10*	29	—	5			—				29	20	—	—	—	—
C.H. Dredge	1*	—	2	—	0			—		25*	—	7	6				
J. Garner	2*	—	6	—	11			—			4*	3	2*				
T. Gard	—	—	7	—	10			—				17	8				
P.H.L. Wilson	—	—	0*	—	0*			—				9*	1*				
G.V. Palmer		—								—						—	
P.W. Denning									—	30	16	5	55	—	37*	5*	0
R.L. Ollis										0				—			
P.A. Slocombe										46	21	16					1*
D. Breakwell										0							
M.R. Davis										—							
Byes	1		2	2						1		4	5	1			
Leg-byes	8	7	8	5	9			6		11	15	6	6	9			1
Wides		2	2		7			2		9	11	6	3	3	2	1	
No-balls	1	1	2	1	1			6		1		3	2	3			4
Total	251	213	172	279	116			147		237	254	246	196	164	97	7	69
Wickets	7	5	10	3	10			4		5	6	10	9	2	3	0	3
Result	W	W	L	W	L	Ab.	Ab.	W	Ab.	W	W	W	L	W	W	Ab.	W
Points	2	4	0	4	0	2	1	4	2	4	4	—	0	—	4	2	—

Catches

29 – T. Gard (ct 25/st 4)
9 – V.J. Marks
8 – I.T. Botham, N.F.M. Popplewell and J. Garner
6 – P.W. Denning and I.V.A. Richards
5 – J.W. Lloyds
4 – P.M. Roebuck, B.C. Rose and P.A. Slocombe
3 – C.H. Dredge
2 – P.H.L. Wilson and G.V. [Palmer]
1 – R.L. Ollis

BOWLING

BOWLING	J. Garner	I.T. Botham	G.V. Palmer	V.J. Marks	C.H. Dredge	I.V.A. Richards	P.H.L. Wilson	N.F.M. Popplewell	M.R. Davis
(B.&H.) v. Sussex (Taunton) 7 May	9-0-49-1	9.2-3-26-2		11-0-38-3	10-1-30-0	1-0-6-0	11-2-30-2		
(J.P.) v. Sussex (Taunton) 8 May	5-0-12-0	5.3-0-14-2	8-0-23-1	8-1-10-1	4-0-22-3	6-1-32-2			
(B.&H.) v. Essex (Chelmsford) 14 May	11-2-47-1	10-1-51-1		11-3-34-3	11-4-22-1		9-0-40-2	3-0-19-0	
(J.P.) v. Nottinghamshire (Trent Br.) 15 May	4-0-7-0	4-0-9-0		2-0-7-1	1-0-8-0				
(B.&H.) v. Hampshire (Taunton) 17-18 May	11-1-20-0	11-4-27-4		11-2-21-2	8.5-2-26-3	1-0-4-0	10-1-28-1		
(J.P.) v. Yorkshire (Bradford) 29 May	8-1-38-1	8-0-40-1		8-1-21-2	8-0-27-2			8-1-27-2	
(J.P.) v. Glamorgan (Bath) 19 June			8-0-48-0		8-0-25-2		8-0-40-1	7-1-38-0	4-0-23-0
(J.P.) v. Gloucestershire (Bath) 26 June	8-1-40-0			8-1-32-1	8-0-41-1	4-0-22-1	6-0-49-0	6-0-38-3	
(N.W.) v. Shropshire (Wellington) 29-30 June	9-2-19-3			12-1-47-2	12-2-34-2	2-0-13-0	12-6-16-1	8.2-3-11-1	
(J.P.) v. Leicestershire (Leicester) 10 July	8-2-23-1	6-0-38-0		8-0-30-0	7-0-48-1	0.1-0-1-0	6-0-38-0		
(N.W.) v. Lancashire (Old Trafford) 20 July	12-6-25-2	11-3-33-0		12-4-22-0	11-1-30-2	10-2-23-2			
(J.P.) v. Hampshire (Taunton) 24 July	8-0-30-1	8-2-22-4		1-0-3-0	4-0-27-1				
(J.P.) v. Lancashire (Old Trafford) 31 July	7-2-6-0		7-0-41-2	8-0-26-0	5-1-8-2	8-0-24-6		3-0-10-0	
(N.W.) v. Sussex (Hove) 3 August	11-7-8-4	9.4-4-20-4		2-1-1-0	7-3-11-1	11-1-21-1			
(J.P.) v. Northants (Weston-s'r-Mare) 7 Aug.	8-3-22-4	8-1-27-0		8-1-24-2	8-1-18-1	8-1-18-1			
(J.P.) v. Derbyshire (Heanor) 14 August	7-1-29-0		6-0-34-0	6-0-37-0	6-0-35-0	6.2-0-32-1		6-0-36-1	
(N.W.) v. Middlesex (Lord's) 17 August	11-3-23-3	12-2-33-1		8-0-45-1	9-0-48-0	12-3-23-0		8-0-34-3	
(J.P.) v. Middlesex (Lord's) 21 August	8-0-17-1	8-0-34-1		8-0-33-1	8-0-23-2	8-0-31-2			
(J.P.) v. Kent (Taunton) 28 August			8-0-58-2	8-1-20-0	8-0-39-0	4-0-15-2		4-0-35-0	
(N.W.) v. Kent (Lord's) 3 September	9-2-15-2	10-0-29-2		10-0-30-3	8.1-0-50-2	9-1-28-1		1-0-9-0	
(J.P.) v. Worcestershire (Worcester) 4 Sept.	8-0-41-0	8-0-29-3		8-1-45-2	8-1-25-1	8-0-44-1			
(J.P.) v. Warwickshire (Taunton) 11 Sept.	8-0-27-0	8-0-42-0		8-1-23-3	8-1-35-1	8-0-35-2			
Wickets	24	25	5	27	28	22	7	10	0

Tomlins played bravely, but Booth and Marks took a grip on the game and five wickets fell in 21 balls without a run being added. It was Somerset's second championship of the season, and for Booth a career best 4 for 26 in his fifth first-class match.

Essex did not need three days in which to beat Gloucestershire who elected to bat on a green wicket in a heavy atmosphere. They were all out just after lunch to the combined seam of Lever, Turner and Phillip whose return to the side had been marked with great success. By the end of the day, with McEwan at his imperial best, Essex had already collected three batting points, and with Pont driving well, they extended their lead to 302 on the Monday morning. With fielders clustered round the bat, Gloucestershire found runs coming at a furious rate when they batted again, but wickets fell almost as furiously to Lever, Phillip and Acfield. At tea, Gloucestershire were 146 for 2, but then the last eight wickets fell for 65 runs in 85 minutes. Broad hit a good hundred before falling to Lever, but Essex gleefully collected maximum points and a day off in which to reflect that though they played a game more than Middlesex, they were now at the top of the Schweppes County Championship, thirteen points clear.

This excitement at the top tended to overshadow events elsewhere. Hampshire crushed bottom of the table Worcestershire and moved into third place because Warwickshire were thwarted by solid Kent batting throughout the order after the home side had been asked to follow-on at Folkestone. Kallicharran and Amiss had plundered centuries and shared a third wicket stand of 133. Warwickshire had batted into the second day, looking for an innings victory which Gifford's bowling nearly brought them. Eventually, it was a stand of 149 in 127 minutes between Knott and Aslett which denied Warwickshire.

A run feast at Northampton, where only one bowling point was gained, saw Lancashire put Northants in and Lar-

v. Northamptonshire (Weston-s-Mare) 7 August (J.P.)	v. Derbyshire (Heanor) 14 August (J.P.)	v. Middlesex (Lord's) 17 August (N.W.)	v. Middlesex (Lord's) 21 August (J.P.)	v. Kent (Taunton) 28 August (J.P.)	v. Kent (Lord's) 3 September (N.W.)	v. Worcestershire (Worcester) 4 September (J.P.)	v. Warwickshire (Taunton) 11 September (J.P.)	Runs
	17	7	26		10	4*	2*	206
51*	32	7	37	60	11	23	7	631
—	15	23	30	86	51	20	4	810
								124
—		96*	1		9	16	49	497
—	3	46	3	13	35	16	23	369
—	38	21	6*	4*	29	2	44	255
—	—	—	—	—	3*	4	—	48
—	12	0	—	0*	4	9	14*	67
—	14*	0*	—	—		4	—	60
								10
	13*			—				13
62*	48	0	15	50	1	28	5	357
—				—				0
—	7	2	33*	—	20	0	9	155
								0
5	3			4	1	2	9	
5	9	6	3	5	17	8	6	
	7	4	2	1	2	1	2	
2	1	10	3	1			1	
125	219	222	159	224	193	137	175	
0	8	8	6	4	9	10	7	
W	L	W	W	W	W	L	W	
4	0	—	4	4	—	0	4	

D. Breakwell

5-0-29-0

	Byes	Leg-byes	Wides	No-balls	Total	Wkts
		9	2	2	192	10
		9	1	1	124	10
	4	6		2	225	8
		1			32	1
		4	6	2	138	10
		7	2	2	164	8
	1	25	6		235	4
	2	12	2		238	6
	1	11	3	4	159	10
	4	11	2	2	197	2
	3	10	1	3	163	6
	1	8	1	1	93	7
	1	11	4	1	132	10
		1	3		65	10
		10	1	3	123	9
		11	4	2	220	2
		11	5		222	9
		17	2	1	158	8
	2	7	3		221	7
	6	1		1	169	10
		7	1		192	9
	1	10		1	174	7

0

Ken McEwan. Two centuries in Colchester week and the first man to two thousand runs. (George Herringshaw)

BATTING

BATTING	v. Middlesex (The Oval) 7 May (B.&H.)	v. Kent (Canterbury) 8 May (J.P.)	v. Yorkshire (Leeds) 15 May (J.P.)	v. Kent (Canterbury) 17 and 18 May (B.&H.)	v. Glamorgan (Cardiff) 20 May (B.&H.)	v. Combined Universities (The Oval) 21 and 23 May (B.&H.)	v. Somerset (The Oval) 22 May (J.P.)	v. Nottinghamshire (Trent Bridge) 29 May (J.P.)	v. Gloucestershire (Bristol) 5 June (J.P.)	v. Middlesex (The Oval) 12 June (J.P.)	v. Northamptonshire (East Moseley) 26 June (J.P.)	v. Lincolnshire (Sleaford) 29 June (N.W.)	v. Hampshire (Portsmouth) 10 July (J.P.)	v. Warwickshire (The Oval) 20 July (N.W.)	v. Lancashire (The Oval) 24 July (J.P.)	v. Glamorgan (Swansea) 31 July (J.P.)	v. Warwickshire (The Oval) 7 August (J.P.)
A.R. Butcher	6	14		9	20	22				46	68	22	65	1	41	5	4
G.S. Clinton	18	4		6	0	63					—	6		11			
D.M. Smith	26*			14	14	40				28		19	20	20	41	37	
R.D.V. Knight	7*	9		7	10	9*				6		26	11*	9	1	4	
M.A. Lynch	—	16		39	30	—				7	70	22	33	6	26	22	11
C.J. Richards	—	6		15	7*	—				19	26	105*	43	13	2	8	
D.J. Thomas	—	4		1		—				12	39	5	0	37	12	72	13
I.R. Payne	—	9								5*	7*	56*	5*	4	16	33*	23
G. Monkhouse	—	3*		2	—	—				—	—			7	0	4*	6
S.T. Clarke	—	0		2	—	—				8	7			7	0*	9	22
P.I. Pocock	—	2		0*	—	—								0*			
G.P. Howarth		4		14	45*	13*											
A. Needham										25*	0*				19	—	7
A.J. Stewart											0					—	8
M.A. Feltham															—		
K.S. Mackintosh															12		12
D.B. Pauline																	35
I.J. Curtis																	0*
P. Waterman																	
Byes						1						1					
Leg-byes		7		10	12	4				5	8	20	5	12	13	9	10
Wides	3	1		2	3	4				2	7	15	4	1	1	1	5
No-balls	3	1		1	1					1		2	10	2			1
Total	63	80		122	142	156				164	232	297	188	138	186	204	157
Wickets	2	10		10	5	3				7	6	6	5	10	10	7	10
Result	L	L	Ab.	L	Ab.	W	Ab.	Ab.	Ab.	W	L	W	L	L	L	L	L
Points	0	0	2	0	1	2	2	2	2	4	0	—	0	—	0	0	0

Catches

13 – C.J. Richards (ct 11/st 2)
9 – D.M. Smith
8 – A.J. Stewart
5 – S.T. Clarke

4 – G. Monkhouse, A.R. Butcher, A. Needham and R.D.V. Knight
3 – M.A. Lynch and P.I. Pocock
2 – I.R. Payne and D.J. Thomas
1 – G.P. Howarth and P. Waterman

BOWLING

	S.T. Clarke	D.J. Thomas	G. Monkhouse	R.D.V. Knight	I.R. Payne	P.I. Pocock	A.R. Butcher	A. Needham	M.A. Lynch
(B.&H.) v. Middlesex (The Oval) 7 May	11–0–52–0	11–0–66–3	4–0–24–0	11–2–32–2	11–0–44–1	7–2–29–0			
(J.P.) v. Kent (Canterbury) 8 May	4–0–19–0	7–1–34–2	6–0–40–2	4–0–38–1	2–0–24–0	6–0–44–1			
(B.&H.) v. Kent (Canterbury) 17 May	11–3–20–2	10–3–34–0	11–2–20–2	11–1–26–3		9.4–4–21–3	2–0–17–0		
(B.&H.) v. Glamorgan (Cardiff) 20 May									
(B.&H.) v. Comb. Univ. (Oval) 21 and 23 May	11–1–25–5	11–2–25–0	11–1–44–1	11–3–23–0		11–5–15–1			
(J.P.) v. Middlesex (The Oval) 12 June	8–1–21–3	8–0–32–2	8–0–31–0		5–0–24–0	8–0–31–1		3–0–12–0	
(J.P.) v. Northants (East Moseley) 26 June	8–0–30–0	6.3–0–53–0	8–0–26–2			8–0–46–3	7–0–54–0		
(N.W.) v. Lincolnshire (Sleaford) 29 June	6–3–3–0	4–1–16–0	7.5–1–26–3		12–0–36–5	12–4–14–0	12–1–45–1		6–1–25–1
(J.P.) v. Hampshire (Portsmouth) 10 July	8–0–57–0	7–0–47–1			8–0–31–0	5–0–46–0	4–0–37–0		
(N.W.) v. Warwickshire (The Oval) 20 July	10.5–1–32–0	7–1–30–0	5–1–33–0	7–1–13–0	5–2–14–1	8–4–14–0			
(J.P.) v. Lancashire (The Oval) 24 July	7–1–18–2	8–0–29–2	8–1–17–1	5–1–30–1	5–0–29–0				
(J.P.) v. Glamorgan (Swansea) 31 July	5–0–22–1	3–0–40–2	1–0–23–0	3–0–27–0					
(J.P.) v. Warwickshire (The Oval) 7 August	8–1–18–1	7–0–32–2	5–1–21–0			8–0–37–2			
(J.P.) v. Worcestershire (Guildford) 14 August	8–0–54–2	6.3–0–43–2	8–0–28–2	6–0–40–0			8–0–59–2		
(J.P.) v. Sussex (Hove) 21 August	8–1–15–0	8–0–46–0	8–0–38–2				8–1–22–3		
(J.P.) v. Essex (The Oval) 28 August		8–2–23–2			8–1–15–1	6.4–0–33–3	8–1–18–3		
(J.P.) v. Leicestershire (Leicester) 4 September		8–0–49–1			8–0–42–4	8–0–50–0	8–0–51–1		
Wickets	16	19	15	12	15	14	1	0	1

A M.A. Feltham 8–0–61–0

	v. Worcestershire (Guildford) 14 August (J.P.)	v. Sussex (Hove) 21 August (J.P.)	v. Essex (The Oval) 28 August (J.P.)	v. Leicestershire (Leicester) 4 September (J.P.)	v. Derbyshire (The Oval) 11 September (J.P.)	Runs
	1	17	63*	111		515
						108
						259
	87	11	5	65		267
	54	1	10	43		390
	6	0	7	17		274
	3	9	8	4		219
			0	0*		158
	—	27				49
	20*	0		—		75
	—	4	12*			18
						76
						51
	5*	36	4	5*		58
						—
						24
	84	32	11	2		164
	—	0*	—	—		0
		—		—		

	1	1	4	5
	5	3	1	3
	3	2		
	1	1	3	6

	270	144	128	261	
	6	10	7	6	
	W	L	W	W	Ab.
	4	0	4	4	2

Geoff Boycott. A century in each innings against Notts at Bradford and close to a thousand runs in August. (George Herringshaw)

P. Waterman	K.S. Mackintosh	I.J. Curtis	Byes	Leg-byes	Wides	No-balls	Total	Wkts
			2	14	5	5	273	6
			1	7		1	208	6
			7		3	2	150	10
					Match Abandoned			
			6	6	9	2	155	8
			3	6		1	161	7
			6	12	7		234	5
				2	1		168	10
				5	7	1	292	1A
				1	2	4	143	1
	5.4–0–51–0		2	5	3	3	187	6
				4	2		118	3
	5.3–0–26–0	4–0–16–0		4	6		160	5
				11	3	4	242	10
		8–1–35–1	7	13	17	3	196	7
8–1–25–1	1–0–2–0		2	5	4		127	10
5–0–19–0		3–0–29–0		12	4	2	258	5
1	0	1						

kins and Willey add 342 for the second wicket. Fowler and David Lloyd responded with an opening stand of 179, but on the last day, with the pitch taking spin, Lancashire did well to hold out against Steele and Williams.

Surrey cancelled the contract of David Smith for disciplinary reasons, a brave and correct decision, and had David Thomas celebrate his call to the England squad with a fiercely hit century at Hove. There was more fierce hitting in the second innings from Lynch, but Knight delayed his declaration too long and the match was drawn.

Boycott scored a century in each innings against Notts and his second century included a hundred before lunch on the last morning. The limelight had been taken from him in the first innings by Ashley Metcalfe who was making his debut for Yorkshire at the age of 19 and became the youngest player in the club's history to score a hundred on his debut. Bruce French hit a career best 91 on the Monday, but skippers Rice and Hartley could not manufacture a result in spite of positive declarations.

John Hopkins carried his bat through Glamorgan's second innings in scoring 109 in 5½ hours, but his heroic innings proved in vain. Needing 177 in 150 minutes, Derbyshire struggled badly and it was left to the ninth wicket pair, Miller and Holding, profiting from a dropped catch, to score 23 in the last three overs and win the match with 2 balls to spare. It was Holding's hitting in the first innings which had given Derbyshire the lead.

In the tourists' match, New Zealand won with ease, but lost the services of Wright with a broken toe and Smith with a broken finger. Franklin, Wright's deputy, played two good innings and Bracewell prospered. Addison batted well on his Leicestershire debut at the age of 17.

BATTING

BATTING	v. Somerset (Taunton) 7 May (B.&H.)	v. Somerset (Taunton) 8 May (J.P.)	v. Minor Counties (Hove) 14 May (B.&H.)	v. Kent (Hove) 15 May (J.P.)	v. Essex (Chelmsford) 19 May (B.&H.)	v. Hampshire (Hove) 23 May (B.&H.)	v. Middlesex (Lord's) 29 May (J.P.)	v. Warwickshire (Hove) 12 June (J.P.)	v. Lancashire (Horsham) 19 June (J.P.)	v. Essex (Ilford) 26 June (J.P.)	v. Ireland (Dublin) 29 June (N.W.)	v. Northamptonshire (Hastings) 3 July (J.P.)	v. Glamorgan (Cardiff) 10 July (J.P.)	v. Nottinghamshire (Hove) 20 July (N.W.)	v. Yorkshire (Hove) 24 July (J.P.)	v. Leicestershire (Leicester) 31 July (J.P.)	v. Somerset (Hove)
G.D. Mendis	11	24	46		9	27	41	34	25	2	11	11	13	8	20	2	4
I.J. Gould	19	14	2*		55	4	6			30	46	—	39*	32	9	14	4
P.W.G. Parker	11	15	8		25	20	9	104	52	11	14	121*	1	7	8	0	5
C.M. Wells	32	1	49		0	43	28	104*	7	23	11	42	63	28	5	46	0
I.A. Greig	4	33	0*		11	24	2*										
C.P. Phillipson	10	0	—		30*	4	0*	1*	15	23*	40*	—	4*		1		13
G.S. Le Roux	36	16	—		6	3	4	—	16	46*	22	1*	21	12	26		2
J.R.T. Barclay	18	8*	42		32	5	—	—	11		48	—	—	4	5	0	2
C.E. Waller	4*	2			—	3*										—	0
A.C.S. Pigott	4	0	—		—	4	—	—	9*			—		0		1*	17
A.M. Green	30		26		25												
A.P. Wells		0				16	2	0	38	16		—		8	22	24	9
R.S. Cowan			—													9*	
A.N. Jones							—										
D.J. Smith							—	5*									
D.A. Reeve								—		2	16*			—	1*	—	6*
Imran Khan										24	41	49	8	114*	28	4	1
Byes						1		4	1		1		2	1		1	
Leg-byes	9	9	2		8	13	2	9	15	12	6	5	9	7	7	4	
Wides	2	1	4		2	3	2		5	2		1	2	4			1
No-balls	2	1	5		5	1	2	7	1	1	1		2	2	3		3
Total	192	124	184		208	171	98	263	202	190	265	231	164	227	135	105	65
Wickets	10	10	5		8	10	6	3	8	6	7	3	5	7	10	7	10
Result	L	L	W	Ab.	W	L	W	W	W	W	W	W	W	W	L	Ab.	L
Points	0	0	2	2	2	0	4	4	4	4	—	4	4	—	0	2	—

Catches

11 – I.J. Gould	6 – A.C.S. Pigott, A.P. Wells and P.W.G. Parker	3 – I.A. Greig, C.E. Waller and Imran Khan
8 – J.R.T. Barclay	5 – C.M. Wells and D.A. Reeve	2 – G.S. Le Roux
7 – C.P. Phillipson	4 – G.D. Mendis	1 – A.M. Green and D.J. Smith

BOWLING

BOWLING	G.S. Le Roux	A.C.S. Pigott	I.A. Greig	J.R.T. Barclay	C.E. Waller	C.M. Wells	R.S. Cowan	A.N. Jones	D.A. Reeve
(B.&H.) v. Somerset (Taunton) 7 May	11–0–65–0	11–0–52–1	11–1–54–2	11–1–25–1	11–1–45–1				
(J.P.) v. Somerset (Taunton) 8 May	8–0–45–2	8–0–34–1	7–0–37–0	8–0–36–1	3–0–25–0	6–0–26–1			
(B.&H.) v. Minor Counties (Hove) 14 May	11–0–38–1	11–1–21–0	11–0–34–2	11–4–28–		5–0–21–0	6–1–21–1		
(B.&H.) v. Essex (Chelmsford) 19 and 20 May	8.3–1–27–1	9–1–33–1	11–1–30–2	11–2–33–2	11–1–31–0				
(B.&H.) v. Hampshire (Hove) 23 May	11–3–22–4	11–1–29–2	11–1–41–0	11–3–24–1	8.5–0–35–0	1–0–7–0			
(J.P.) v. Middlesex (Lord's) 29 May	8–1–32–2	8–0–46–0	6–0–36–2	8–0–35–1		4–0–16–0		6–1–34–0	
(J.P.) v. Warwickshire (Hove) 12 June	8–0–45–3	8–0–45–1		8–0–36–2	2–0–17–1	8–0–26–0			6–0–31–0
(J.P.) v. Lancashire (Horsham) 19 June	8–0–33–3	8–0–31–3		7.5–0–42–0		8–0–28–1			8–1–57–1
(J.P.) v. Essex (Ilford) 26 June	8–0–30–3	8–0–31–1		8–0–49–1		8–0–21–1			8–1–26–1
(N.W.) v. Ireland (Dublin) 29 June	6–3–11–1	2–0–11–0		12–1–28–3	12–2–31–1	8–1–25–0			12–1–26–2
(J.P.) v. Northamptonshire (Hastings) 3 July	8–0–36–2	8–1–23–3		8–0–22–2		8–1–28–0			8–1–26–0
(J.P.) v. Glamorgan (Cardiff) 10 July	8–0–31–1	8–0–27–2		4–0–19–0	4–0–17–0	8–1–21–2			8–0–25–3
(N.W.) v. Nottinghamshire (Hove) 20 July	7–3–15–0	4–1–3–0		12–5–18–3	12–3–19–1	10–0–31–1			12–3–17–2
(J.P.) v. Yorkshire (Hove) 24 July	8–1–19–0	8–1–26–1		5.2–0–32–1		8–1–15–1			8–0–28–1
(J.P.) v. Leicestershire (Leicester) 31 July									1–0–1–0
(N.W.) v. Somerset (Hove) 3 August		8–1–21–0				7–2–15–1			8.5–4–28–
(J.P.) v. Derbyshire (Eastbourne) 7 August		8–0–27–2				8–0–22–1			8–1–21–1
(J.P.) v. Nottinghamshire (Trent Br.) 14 Aug.		8–0–41–0	5–0–28–1		7–0–35–1	4–0–15–1			8–0–38–1
(J.P.) v. Surrey (Hove) 21 August			4.2–0–27–2	8–0–23–1	8–0–24–1	3–0–16–0			8–0–34–1
(J.P.) v. Hampshire (Southampton) 28 August		7–0–37–1		8–2–31–0		6.2–0–24–0			8–0–45–1
(J.P.) v. Gloucestershire (Hove) 4 September		6–0–24–2	5–0–30–2			5–0–18–1			5–0–21–2
(J.P.) v. Worcestershire (Worcester) 11 Sept.		1–0–9–1		1–0–9–0		4–0–15–4			1–0–11–0
Wickets	23	24	15	19	6	15	1	0	19

v. Derbyshire (Eastbourne) 7 August (J.P.)	v. Nottinghamshire (Trent Bridge) 14 August (J.P.)	v. Surrey (Hove) 21 August (J.P.)	v. Hampshire (Southampton) 28 August (J.P.)	v. Gloucestershire (Hove) 4 September (J.P.)	v. Worcestershire (Worcester) 11 September (J.P.)	Runs
50	36	52	2	25	21	474
3	2	19	2	44*	9	353
46	6		24	35*	5	527
0	14	4	6	0	10	516
0	18	35	4	—	24	155
19		32*	0	—		192
						209
2*		4*	9*	—	—	190
	1					10
4	6		3*	—	3	51
					3*	84
3	23	1	38	—	6	206
	2					11
						—
						5
0	0*		—	—	—	25
11	45	7	90	1	30	453
	2	7		1		
9	4	13	6	8	5	
1	5	17	8	2	3	
	2	3	1		2	
148	164	196	193	116	121	
10	10	7	8	3	8	
W	L	W	L	W	L	
4	0	4	0	4	0	

C.P. Phillipson	Imran Khan	P.W.G. Parker	Byes	Leg-byes	Wides	No-balls	Total	Wkts
			1	8		1	251	7
				7	2	1	213	5
			5	11	4		183	4
			1	13	3	2	173	10
				9	6	1	174	7
			15		2		216	6
			1	6	4		211	8
				7	2		200	10
0.3–0–0–1			2	10	1	1	188	9
				4	3	2	141	10
			1	6	1		143	8
				14	7	1	162	8
	2–0–17–0	1–0–10–1	2	4	14	1	151	8
		1–0–6–0		7	5	3	141	4
1.5–0–9–0			2				12	0
				1		4	69	3
	8–0–25–1		13	9	1		146	7
	8–1–22–1		12	3	3		197	6
	6–1–13–3		1	3	2	1	144	10
	8–0–37–2		2	10	8		194	6
	6–1–16–1			5	1		115	9
	3–0–13–1			5	2		64	7
1	9	1						

John Player League

21 August

at Colchester

Essex 233 for 9 (N. Phillip 95)
Gloucestershire 220 for 7 (A.W. Stovold 67, P. Bainbridge 55)

Essex (4 pts) won by 13 runs

at Swansea

Glamorgan 155 for 7 (J.A. Hopkins 52)
Derbyshire 133

Glamorgan (4 pts) won by 22 runs

at Folkestone

Kent 281 for 5 (C.J. Tavare 122 not out, D.G. Aslett 77)
Warwickshire 223 (T.A. Lloyd 62)

Kent (4 pts) won by 58 runs

at Lord's

Middlesex 158 for 8
Somerset 159 for 6

Somerset (4 pts) won by 4 wickets

at Hove

Sussex 196 for 7 (G.D. Mendis 52)
Surrey 144

Sussex (4 pts) won by 52 runs

at Worcester

Hampshire 239 for 5 (C.L. Smith 61, T.E. Jesty 61)
Worcestershire 29 for 2

Hampshire (4 pts) won on faster scoring rate

Under 25 Final

at Edgbaston

Worcestershire 198 for 8
Leicestershire 198 for 5 (T. Boon 88 not out)

Leicestershire won on losing fewer wickets

Kent scored their highest total in the John Player League to beat Warwickshire and go level at the top of the table with Yorkshire. Kent's victory was founded on a third wicket stand of 170 between Aslett and Tavare which rescued them from 38 for 2 in 12 overs.

Somerset and Sussex maintained their challenges, Sussex with a comfortable win over Surrey just before the skies darkened and the rain fell, and Somerset thanks to a good stand between Slocombe and Lloyds when they appeared to be stumbling in a low-scoring match at Lord's. With a match in hand and only two points short of the joint leaders, Somerset seemed ideally placed to win the title.

Hampshire still had a mathematical chance of winning the league. Chris Smith and Trevor Jesty, who passed 500

Warwickshire C.C.C.
Limited-Over Matches – 1983

BATTING

BATTING	v. Lancashire (Old Trafford) 7 May (B.&H.)	v. Yorkshire (Edgbaston) 8 May (J.P.)	v. Derbyshire (Edgbaston) 14 May (B.&H.)	v. Glamorgan (Swansea) 15 May (J.P.)	v. Nottingham (Trent Bridge) 20 May (B.&H.)	v. Lancashire (Edgbaston) 22 May (J.P.)	v. Yorkshire (Edgbaston) 23 May (B.&H.)	v. Essex (Chelmsford) 2 and 3 June (B.&H.)	v. Derbyshire (Coventry) 5 June (J.P.)	v. Sussex (Hove) 12 June (J.P.)	v. Northamptonshire (Luton) 19 June (J.P.)	v. Hampshire (Edgbaston) 26 June (J.P.)	v. Oxfordshire (Edgbaston) 29 June (N.W.)	v. Essex (Edgbaston) 10 July (J.P.)	v. Gloucestershire (Moreton-in-Marsh) 17 July (J.P.)	v. Surrey (The Oval) 20 July (N.W.)	v. Worcestershire (Edgbaston) 24 July (J.P.)
K.D. Smith	16	75	—			2*	30	13	23	24	18	21	60			37	
T.A. Lloyd	13						43	25	10		84	9	32	9	15	55*	19*
A.I. Kallicharran	11	119	—	—			48	0	6		33	66	70	36	1	44*	—
D.L. Amiss	55*	27	—			6*	64	49	12	35	6	14	54	30	31	—	24*
G.W. Humpage	17	7	—			—	4	8	36	25	10	11	0	65	10	—	—
Asif Din	21	26	—			—	13*	16	52	10	19	13	3	15	2	—	—
A.M. Ferreira	34*	10*	—			—	0*	14	17	12	24	52	8*	5	0	—	—
C. Lethbridge	—	4*	—			—									1	8*	—
C.M. Old	—	—	—			—		27	45*	10	11			28	5		
R.G.D. Willis	—	—	—			—		0						3*	7*		
W. Hogg	—	—	—			—								7*			
N. Gifford			—			—		1*	0*	13*	32*	19*	4*	7	5*		
G.C. Small								6									
R.I.H.B. Dyer									43								—
S.H. Wootton									18								
P.A. Smith										10*	13*			41	35		—
D.A. Thorne												10*				42	
G.J. Lord																	
Byes								4			1		5	1			
Leg-byes	8	12					6	7	9	6	11	10	8	8	14	1	4
Wides		4				1	10		9	4	1	11	4		4	2	2
No-balls		3				1	3	2	1		2		2	2	2	4	3
Total	175	287				10	225	168	220	211	264	241	274	229	174	143	52
Wickets	5	5				0	5	10	7	8	8	7	7	9	9	1	0
Result	Ab.	L	W	Ab.	Ab.	Ab.	W	L	L	L	L	W	W	L	L	W	Tie
Points	1	0	2	2	1	2	2	—	0	0	0	4	—	0	0	—	2

Catches

22 – G.W. Humpage (ct 17/st 5)
7 – R.G.D. Willis
5 – D.L. Amiss
4 – A.I. Kallicharran

3 – A.M. Ferreira and N. Gifford
2 – W. Hogg, K.D. Smith, D.A. Thorne, R.I.H.B. Dyer and Asif Din
1 – C.M. Old, T.A. Lloyd, C. Lethbridge, G.C. Small and G.J. Lord

BOWLING

BOWLING	R.G.D. Willis	C.M. Old	A.M. Ferreira	W. Hogg	C. Lethbridge	N. Gifford	G.C. Small	P.A. Smith	A.I. Kallicharran
(B.&H.) v. Lancashire (Old Trafford) 7 May	7–1–25–0	7–0–16–0	11–2–15–3	7.4–2–22–1	9–1–38–1				
(J.P.) v. Yorkshire (Edgbaston) 8 May	7–0–48–0	8–0–54–2	7.4–0–56–0						
(B.&H.) v. Derbys. (Edgbaston) 14 & 16 May	11–1–37–5	9–0–54–2	10–1–42–1	11–0–40–1		10–0–37–0			
(J.P.) v. Glamorgan (Swansea) 15 May	1–0–5–0								
(J.P.) v. Lancashire (Edgbaston) 22 May									
(B.&H.) v. Yorkshire (Edgbaston) 23 May	9–1–37–3	9–0–45–1	9–1–49–0	9–2–27–1		9–1–47–0			
(B.&H.) v. Essex (Chelmsford) 2 June	11–1–51–3	11–2–27–0	11–0–50–2			11–0–61–3	11–3–30–0		
(J.P.) v. Derbyshire (Coventry) 5 June	8–0–31–2	7.3–0–37–1	8–0–35–0	7–0–49–0		8–0–54–2			
(J.P.) v. Sussex (Hove) 12 June		8–0–61–0	8–0–45–2	8–0–44–0		8–0–55–0		8–0–38–1	
(J.P.) v. Northamptonshire (Luton) 19 June		7–0–47–0	8–0–44–0	6–0–55–0		7–0–45–2		6–0–62–0	6–0–33–0
(J.P.) v. Hampshire (Edgbaston) 26 June	8–0–34–2		7–0–37–0	8–1–26–0		8–0–42–2			6–0–34–2
(N.W.) v. Oxfordshire (Edgbaston) 29 June	11–0–25–4	2–0–16–0	12–1–40–1	10–2–58–1		11–0–47–4			12–0–42–0
(J.P.) v. Essex (Edgbaston) 10 July	8–0–32–2		8–0–22–1	7–0–64–2	8–0–34–0	3–0–33–0		6–0–36–1	
(J.P.) v. Glos. (Moreton-in-Marsh) 17 July		7–0–36–1	8–0–19–0		7.3–0–34–0	6–0–31–1		2–0–19–1	
(N.W.) v. Surrey (The Oval) 20 July	10.1–3–23–3	10–4–19–0	8–1–25–3		10–3–26–2	10–2–22–1			
(J.P.) v. Worcestershire (Edgbaston) 24 July	8–0–39–3	8–0–31–1	8–0–44–1			8–0–27–0		6–0–40–1	2–0–12–1
(J.P.) v. Middlesex (Lord's) 31 July			5–0–22–2		5–0–15–1	7–0–46–1	7–0–21–2		8–0–44–0
(N.W.) v. Kent (Canterbury) 3 August	12–1–44–2	12–0–38–0	12–0–43–3	12–2–48–1		12–3–55–2			
(J.P.) v. Surrey (The Oval) 7 August	8–1–17–1		8–2–30–1		8–1–27–3	7–0–34–2			
(J.P.) v. Leicestershire (Edgbaston) 14 August		7–1–22–2	8–0–46–2			8–1–31–1		8–0–32–0	6–2–11–2
(J.P.) v. Kent (Folkestone) 21 August	8–0–58–2	8–0–58–1			8–0–35–0	8–0–67–0			
(J.P.) v. Nottingham (Edgbaston) 28 August		5.5–1–14–4		7–0–20–2		6–0–23–0		8–2–23–4	2–0–13–0
(J.P.) v. Somerset (Taunton) 11 September	7.2–2–19–2				3–0–15–0	8–2–16–1		8–1–32–2	4–0–26–0
Wickets	34	15	21	10	8	22	2	10	5

v. Middlesex (Lord's) 31 July (J.P.)	v. Kent (Canterbury) 3 August (N.W.)	v. Surrey (The Oval) 7 August (J.P.)	v. Leicestershire (Edgbaston) 14 August (J.P.)	v. Kent (Folkestone) 21 August (J.P.)	v. Nottinghamshire (Edgbaston) 28 August (J.P.)	v. Somerset (Taunton) 11 September (J.P.)	Runs
1	5						325
10	23	11	13	62	57	22	512
7	8	25	80*	8	26	38	626
24	21	60	4	17	29	28	590
7	31	15	73*	32	3	8	362
		9	—	20	8	10	237
8	6*	5*					195
		—	—	0		0*	13
	5			10	—		141
	3			7	—		13
9*	4						20
3	5			8*	—		97
0							6
5	15	25*		27			115
							18
2					6*	26*	133
		—	—	14	14	29	109
				40	1		41
1	4		4	2	1	1	
5	11	4	4	11	14	10	
	2	6	2	5	1		
	3		1		1	1	
82	146	160	181	223	200	174	
10	10	5	2	10	7	7	
L	L	W	W	L	W	L	
0	—	4	4	0	4	0	

D.A. Thorne	Byes	Leg-byes	Wides	No-balls	Total	Wkts
		5	3	3	127	6
		17		1	176	4
		12	3	1	226	10
				5	Match Abandoned	
		16	1	2	224	5
	1	11			231	8
	5	10	1	1	223	5
	4 ,	9		7	263	3
				9	298	2
3-0-37-1	2	21	2		235	8
	4	14	5	5	256	10
	1	8			230	7
4-0-32-0		5		2	178	4
		12	1	10	138	10
	4	8	1	2	208	8
	1	10		4	163	8
	4	11	1	7	251	8
7.5-0-33-2		10	5	1	157	10
3-0-25-0	2	7	1	2	179	8
8-1-37-1		12	3	11	281	5
6-0-36-0	1	7	1	1	139	10
8-0-49-1	9	6	2	1	175	7
5						

League runs for the season, added 105 for the second wicket, and rain halted Worcestershire's reply at 29 for 2 off 11.2 overs.

Glamorgan revived early season memories with a good win over Derbyshire whose faint hopes of the title vanished with this defeat, and Norbert Phillip raged to the conclusion of his storming end to the season with a six and twelve fours in his best-ever score in the Sunday League, 95.

Tim Boon rose from a sick bed to hit 88 off 89 deliveries and bring victory to Leicestershire in the under-25 competition.

24, 25 and 26 August

at Colchester

Worcestershire 84 (N. Phillip 6 for 38, J.K. Lever 4 for 43) and 271 (D.N. Patel 95)
Essex 413 for 8 dec (K.S. McEwan 189 not out, G.A. Gooch 103)

Essex won by an innings and 58 runs
Essex 24 pts, Worcestershire 3 pts

at Bournemouth

Somerset 76 (M.D. Marshall 7 for 29) and 173 (P.W. Denning 61 not out)
Hampshire 211 (M.D. Marshall 50, N.F.M. Popplewell 4 for 69) and 39 for 0

Hampshire won by 10 wickets
Hampshire 22 pts, Somerset 4 pts

at Folkestone

Leicestershire 206 (P.B. Clift 70 not out) and 152 (D.L. Underwood 7 for 55)
Kent 337 (C.S. Cowdrey 123, M.R. Benson 80) and 25 for 0

Kent won by 10 wickets
Kent 24 pts, Leicestershire 6 pts

at Blackpool

Lancashire 315 for 9 dec (J. Simmons 101 not out, N.H. Fairbrother 55, G. Miller 5 for 98) and 247 for 8 dec (F.C. Hayes 127 not out, D.G. Moir 4 for 102)
Derbyshire 294 for 6 dec (A. Hill 106, I.S. Anderson 68) and 119 for 2 (I.S. Anderson 54 not out)

Match drawn
Derbyshire 6 pts, Lancashire 5 pts

at Lord's

Middlesex 295 for 9 dec (G.D. Barlow 113, I.R. Payne 4 for 56) and 181 for 7 dec (A.J.T. Miller 59, I.J. Curtis 4 for 14)
Surrey 233 (N.F. Williams 4 for 41) and 140 (J.E. Emburey 5 for 38)

Middlesex won by 103 runs
Middlesex 23 pts, Surrey 5 pts

Worcestershire C.C.C.
Limited-Over Matches – 1983

BATTING

BATTING	v. Leicestershire (Worcester) 7 May (B.&H.)	v. Leicestershire (Leicester) 8 May (J.P.)	v. Scotland (Aberdeen) 15 May (B.&H.)	v. Northamptonshire (Worcester) 20 May (B.&H.)	v. Gloucestershire (Bristol) 23 May (B.&H.)	v. Gloucestershire (Worcester) 22 May (J.P.)	v. Middlesex (Lord's) 5 June (J.P.)	v. Essex (Worcester) 19 June (J.P.)	v. Yorkshire (Worcester) 26 June (J.P.)	v. Nottinghamshire (Worcester) 29 June (N.W.)	v. Derbyshire (Derby) 3 July (J.P.)	v. Nottinghamshire (Hereford) 10 July (J.P.)	v. Lancashire (Old Trafford) 17 July (J.P.)	v. Warwickshire (Edgbaston) 24 July (J.P.)	v. Northamptonshire (Worcester) 31 July (J.P.)	v. Kent (Canterbury) 7 August (J.P.)	v. Surrey (Guildford) 14 August (J.P.)
J.A. Ormrod	5		8	2						0							1
M.J. Weston	12		56	0		10	23	48	36	21	64	9	9	29	9*	5	
D.N. Patel	8		9	0		36	2	14	4	24	23	44	3	34	52	15	9
Younis Ahmed	10																
P.A. Neale	5		18	17*		24	2	83*	12	1	47	86	39	83	0	11	21
M.S.A. McEvoy	15		11*			24	1							17	17		17
J.D. Inchmore	3						1		0			7*	2	12*	1*	13	
D.J. Humphries	4		1	12*		17*	20	5	32	10				13		24	24
R.K. Illingworth	11*		—	—		—	0	3*		8	0*	—	—	—	—	11*	1
A.E. Warner	3		—	—		7*		1	1	2	14	1		1			13
A.E. Pridgeon	0		—	—		—	0			1		1				0	3
D.B. D'Oliveira			0*	3		13	19	26	1	48	31	3	51*	11	5	1	0
R.M. Ellcock			—				5*	—	1*	6				—		0	
C.L. King			4			51							20	16			127
M.S. Scott							2	14	14	23	9	0					
D.A. Banks								0	18		11		2	4	0*		
P. Moores											—	10*	—				
S. Watkins																24	
T.S. Curtis																12	
S.P. Perryman																	8*
P.J. Newport																	
Byes	2		1			2		1	1	4	4	1	2	4			
Leg-byes			2	4		12	7	11	3	15	7	12	8	8	10	4	11
Wides	3					1	6	2	3	1	5	2		1	3		3
No-balls				1			1			4	3	4		2			4
Total	81		106	43		197	89	208	127	167	225	195	142	208	96	120	242
Wickets	10		5	5		6	10	7	10	10	7	9	5	8	4	10	10
Result	L	Ab.	W	Ab.	Ab.	L	L	W	L	L	L	Tie	Tie	Tie	W	L	L
Points	0	2	2	1	2	0	0	4	0	—	0	2	2	2	4	0	0

Catches

21 – D.J. Humphries (ct 12/st 9)
6 – C.L. King
4 – D.N. Patel and R.K. Illingworth
3 – J.A. Ormrod, D.B. D'Oliveira, T.S. Curtis, A.P. Pridgeon and M.J. Weston
2 – J.D. Inchmore and P. Moores (ct 1/st 1)
1 – R.M. Ellcock, M.S.A. McEvoy, P.A. Neale and S.P. Perryman

BOWLING

BOWLING	A.E. Warner	A.P. Pridgeon	J.D. Inchmore	D.N. Patel	R.K. Illingworth	R.M. Ellcock	D.B. D'Oliveira	C.L. King	M.J. Weston
(B.&H.) v. Leicestershire (Worcester) 7 May	9.2-0-40-2	10-0-46-2	11-1-38-1	11-2-33-2	11-3-24-3				
(B.&H.) v. Scotland (Aberdeen) 15 May	11-0-26-2	5-0-15-0		11-4-13-2	11-4-15-2	7-1-17-1	7-2-13-2		
(B.&H.) v. Northants. (Worcester) 20 May									
(B.&H.) v. Gloucestershire (Bristol) 23 May	6-0-27-0	7-1-37-1	4.2-0-23-0	8-1-36-1	8-0-37-0			3-0-18-0	
(J.P.) v. Middlesex (Lord's) 5 June		5-1-16-1	3-0-15-0	3-0-8-1	7-0-27-0	7-0-14-1			
(J.P.) v. Essex (Worcester) 19 June	8-1-26-3	8-0-45-3			7-0-40-0	8-0-38-0	7-1-25-1		2-0-15-0
(J.P.) v. Yorkshire (Worcester) 26 June	5-0-18-1	4-0-18-0		3-0-8-1	7-1-28-3		5.2-1-18-0	6-0-23-0	
(N.W.) v. Notts. (Worcester) 29 June	8-0-38-1	6-2-13-0		12-7-9-0	12-4-14-2	10-2-49-3	12-4-28-2		
(J.P.) v. Derbyshire (Derby) 3 July	7.2-1-37-0	6-0-30-0		7-0-39-1	7-0-44-0	6-1-34-1	5-2-23-3		
(J.P.) v. Nottinghamshire (Hereford) 10 July	8-0-40-2	5-0-14-1	8-0-32-1	8-0-55-0	8-1-13-0			3-0-21-0	
(J.P.) v. Lancashire (Old Trafford) 17 July	6-1-35-2	7-0-45-1	3-0-23-1	3-0-25-2					
(J.P.) v. Warwickshire (Edgbaston) 24 July	5-0-14-0	5-0-29-0							
(J.P.) v. Northants. (Worcester) 31 July		5-0-18-1	5-1-21-0	6.4-0-27-5	7-0-27-3	5-2-12-0			5-0-27-0
(J.P.) v. Kent (Canterbury) 7 August		8-0-54-1	5-0-34-0	8-1-35-3	8-1-25-0	8-0-43-4	3-0-20-0		
(J.P.) v. Surrey (Guildford) 14 August	8-0-32-2	8-0-52-3		5-0-53-1	2-0-28-0			8-0-51-0	
(J.P.) v. Hampshire (Worcester) 21 August	8-0-41-2	8-0-51-1			7-0-46-1		7-0-37-1		
(J.P.) v. Glamorgan (Cardiff) 28 August	8-0-27-1	8-0-37-0	8-0-42-1	6-0-24-1			1-0-13-0		2-0-12-0
(J.P.) v. Somerset (Worcester) 4 September	4-0-8-0	5-0-20-0		7.3-0-32-2	7-1-24-5			5-1-15-0	
(J.P.) v. Sussex (Worcester) 11 September	3-0-22-1	2-0-13-1		3-0-28-2	4-0-14-1			4-0-18-1	
Wickets	19	16	6	25	20	10	8	1	0

v. Hampshire (Worcester) 21 August (J.P.)	v. Glamorgan (Cardiff) 28 August (J.P.)	v. Somerset (Worcester) 4 September (J.P.)	v. Sussex (Worcester) 11 September (J.P.)	Runs
7				23
	5	18	16	370
7	1	29	9	323
				10
0*	8	11	1*	469
9*	0			111
	12			51
—	20	8	3	193
—	0	2	—	36
—	3	1	0*	47
—	12	4*		21
—	29	28*	14	283
				12
		48	5	271
				62
				35
				10
				24
—	32*	26	5	75
—				8
		9	4	13
	1			
2	8	7	5	
3	1	1	2	
1	1			
29	133	192	64	
2	10	9	7	
L	L	W	W	
0	0	4	4	

S.P. Perryman	P.J. Newport	Byes	Leg-byes	Wides	No-balls	Total	Wkts
		1	11		5	198	10
			2	2	2	105	10
		Match Abandoned					
		9	6	2	3	198	3
			1	4	5	90	3
			10	7	1	207	7
		5	3	3	4	128	6
		3	8	1	6	169	10
		1	10	6	5	229	6
		3	5	4	8	195	4
		4	10			142	8
			4	2	3	52	0
			9	6		147	10
			10	7		228	8
6-0-44-0		1	5	3	1	270	6
7-0-39-0		5	13	5	2	239	5
		6	15	9	4	216	5
	7-0-27-2	2	8	1		137	10
	4-0-16-1		5	3	2	121	8
0	3						

at Northampton

Northamptonshire 284 (W. Larkins 145, R.C. Ontong 5 for 52) and 229 for 7 dec. (R.G. Williams 77 not out, W.W. Davis 5 for 58)
Glamorgan 311 (S.P. Henderson 61, A.H. Wilkins 54, N.A. Mallender 4 for 62) and 117 for 5

Match drawn
Glamorgan 7 pts, Northamptonshire 6 pts

at Edgbaston

Warwickshire 300 for 4 dec (A.I. Kallicharran 152) and 218 (A.I. Kallicharran 118 not out, D.L. Amiss 54, Imran Khan 6 for 6)
Sussex 300 for 7 dec (Imran Khan 94, C.M. Wells 71) and 197 (Imran Khan 64, N. Gifford 4 for 33)

Warwickshire won by 21 runs
Warwickshire 23 pts, Sussex 5 pts

at Scarborough

Yorkshire 333 (K. Sharp 73, D.L. Bairstow 57, G.E. Sainsbury 5 for 102) and 193 for 7 dec (P. Bainbridge 4 for 67)
Gloucestershire 261 and 196 for 9 (J.N. Shepherd 73 not out, G.B. Stevenson 5 for 47)

Match drawn
Yorkshire 6 pts, Gloucestershire 5 pts

Once again Essex completed victory inside two days at Colchester. Winning the toss, they asked Worcestershire to bat on a green wicket under heavy cloud. Phillip and Lever bowled unchanged and the visitors, in spite of some missed catches, were all out two overs after lunch. The clouds lifted almost immediately and the sun shone. Gladwin and Hardie were out for 65, but then came batting of the very highest quality as Gooch and McEwan, with restrained power and dignity. In his sixties, McEwan was badly dropped off a skier by wicket-keeper Humphries, but there were few blemishes in a glorious afternoon. They added 161 in 40 overs before Gooch was lbw sweeping across the line. He had fourteen effortless fours. McEwan stayed until the end, passing his two thousand runs for the season, the first batsman to do so, and hit two sixes and twenty-five fours, all of them aesthetically pleasing. Worcestershire were 329 runs behind on the first innings and faced total humiliation. They had dropped d'Oliveira and were without Neale who was injured, but Patel played well to restore some dignity after they had lost 4 wickets for 38 runs. Nevertheless, Essex were not to be denied another rest day and with men clustered round the bat, Lever, Phillip and Acfield bowled them to victory on the second evening.

Middlesex had a tougher fight at Lord's. Miller, a fine replacement for the injured Slack, helped Barlow to put on 91 for the first wicket, and Barlow reached a typically determined hundred, a mixture of watchful defence and forceful shots. Unfortunately, the later Middlesex batsmen disappointed and they finished short of their fourth batting point. Williams and Emburey combined to bowl Middlesex into a 60-run lead, Ian Payne, who had a good all-round match, being the biggest stumbling block as he helped to revive Surrey from 128 for 6. Emburey finally asked Surrey to make

Yorkshire C.C.C.
Limited-Over Matches – 1983

BATTING

BATTING	v. Warwickshire (Edgbaston) 8 May (J.P.)	v. Derbyshire (Chesterfield) 9 May (B.&H.)	v. Surrey (Leeds) 15 May (J.P.)	v. Nottinghamshire (Leeds) 16 May (B.&H.)	v. Lancashire (Leeds) 17 May (B.&H.)	v. Middlesex (Hull) 22 May (J.P.)	v. Warwickshire (Edgbaston) 23 May (B.&H.)	v. Somerset (Bradford) 29 May (J.P.)	v. Hampshire (Middlesbrough) 5 June (J.P.)	v. Glamorgan (Cardiff) 12 June (J.P.)	v. Worcestershire (Worcester) 26 June (J.P.)	v. Berkshire (Reading) 29 June (N.W.)	v. Leicestershire (Scarborough) 3 July (J.P.)	v. Nottinghamshire (Harrogate) 7 July (T.T.)	v. Northamptonshire (Harrogate) 8 July (T.T.)	v. Northamptonshire (Tring) 10 July (J.P.)	v. Kent (Scarborough) 17 July (J.P.)
K. Sharp	17			1	8	26	20	22	40	7	16	24*	24	20	5	—	—
G. Boycott	18			12	13	6	2	32	8		32	48	31	13	13	64*	—
C.W.J. Athey	72*			18	5	15	94*	2	29	12	18	34	39	76	3	63*	—
G.B. Stevenson	25			5	1*	3	7*	2	14	27	10	—	—	29	12	—	—
D.L. Bairstow	0			0	4	7*	14	25		1	8			36	6		—
S.N. Hartley	26*			48	33*	4	24	18	67*	20	8	1	33*	56*	0	—	—
J.D. Love	—			37	14	0	44		82*	34	19*	8*	12*	15	0	—	—
P. Carrick	—			0		14*	—	11		3	2*			2*	38		—
A. Sidebottom	—			32	—	—		31		5	—	—	—	—	79		—
R. Illingworth	—			9*	—	—		—		8*	—	—	—	—			—
P.W. Jarvis	—							8*		3					0		—
S.J. Dennis				0						16*					8*		
A. Ramage					—		—	2*									
M.D. Moxon																	
S.D. Fletcher																	
Byes						3			1		5	4	1	3	3		
Leg-byes	17			6	6	1	16	7	9	13	3	2	17	12	4	4	
Wides	1			1	2	1	1	2	6	5	3	7	3	3			
No-balls				1	1		2	2	1	1	4	3	1	3	7	1	
Total	176			170	87	80	224	164	257	155	128	131	161	268	178	132	
Wickets	4			10	5	6	5	8	4	9	6	3	3	6	10	0	
Result	W	Ab.	Ab.	L	L	W	L	L	W	L	W	W	W	W	L	W	Ab.
Points	4	1	2	0	0	4	0	0	4	0	4	—	4	—	—	4	2

Catches

19 – D.L. Bairstow (ct 14/st 5)
8 – S.N. Hartley
7 – G. Boycott
5 – S.J. Dennis, P. Carrick, C.W.J. Athey and R. Illingworth

4 – J.D. Love, K. Sharp
3 – G.B. Stevenson
2 – P.W. Jarvis and A. Sidebottom

BOWLING

BOWLING	G.B. Stevenson	P.W. Jarvis	A. Sidebottom	C.W.J. Athey	P. Carrick	S.J. Dennis	G. Boycott	R. Illingworth	A. Ramage
(J.P.) v. Warwickshire (Edgbaston) 8 May	8-1-39-1	8-0-39-3	4-0-45-1	1-0-21-0	3-0-23-0				
(B.&H.) v. Nottinghamshire (Leeds) 16 May	7-2-40-0		11-3-23-3		10-1-44-1		6-0-16-0	11-2-18-2	
(B.&H.) v. Lancashire (Leeds) 17 May	11-0-42-0		11-4-29-1			11-2-52-0		11-2-33-3	11-2-40-2
(J.P.) v. Middlesex (Hull) 22 May	8-0-28-1	8-0-37-2	3-0-13-0		8-0-18-0		4-0-15-3	8-3-6-4	
(B.&H.) v. Warwickshire (Edgbaston) 23 May	8-0-56-1		9-0-48-3		9-1-23-0	9-1-46-0			7.1-0-29-1
(J.P.) v. Somerset (Bradford) 29 May	8-1-30-2	6-0-22-0	8-2-23-0		3.1-0-32-0			2-1-8-1	5-0-18-0
(J.P.) v. Hampshire (Middlesbrough) 5 June	8-2-57-2	8-0-58-1	8-0-41-1			8-0-38-0		8-0-47-2	
(J.P.) v. Glamorgan (Cardiff) 12 June	8-2-43-4	8-1-25-1	8-1-28-1		4-0-16-0	8-2-19-1		4-0-24-0	
(J.P.) v. Worcestershire (Worcester) 26 June	4.1-0-25-3	6-0-30-2			7-1-20-3	6-1-13-0	1-0-5-0	6-0-27-2	
(N.W.) v. Berkshire (Reading) 29 June	12-2-27-5		12-5-11-1	6-0-21-0		8-3-14-1	12-5-18-1	10-2-22-0	
(J.P.) v. Leicestershire (Scarborough) 3 July	8-0-33-1		8-0-33-3		8-0-23-1	8-1-32-0		8-1-24-2	
(T.T.) v. Nottinghamshire (Harrogate) 7 July	11-2-52-0	8-2-25-0	8-0-40-0	8-0-30-2	11-2-26-0	9-1-66-0			
(T.T.) v. Northamptonshire (Harrogate) 8 July	5-0-35-0	7-1-66-1	4-1-18-0		9.2-2-25-0	4-0-26-1			
(J.P.) v. Northamptonshire (Tring) 10 July	5-0-14-2		7-0-28-1		8-1-8-1	8-1-31-1	4-0-15-0	8-1-17-3	
(J.P.) v. Kent (Scarborough) 17 July						1-0-7-0			
(N.W.) v. Northamptonshire (Leeds) 20 July	7-1-24-0				12-1-27-3	10-1-45-2	8-2-19-0	12-0-41-0	11-1-44-1
(J.P.) v. Sussex (Hove) 24 July	8-0-35-3		8-1-22-2		8-0-24-0	7.3-0-31-2		8-4-13-2	
(J.P.) v. Nottinghamshire (Trent Br.) 31 July			1-0-19-0		8-0-31-0	6.2-0-31-0			5-0-43-0
(J.P.) v. Lancashire (Leeds) 7 August	8-1-35-2				8-0-17-0	8-1-36-2	4-0-15-0	8-0-36-1	
(J.P.) v. Glos. (Cheltenham) 14 August	8-1-50-0				8-0-61-0	8-0-49-3	8-0-38-0	8-0-30-2	
(J.P.) v. Derbyshire (Bradford) 28 August	6-0-28-1		4-0-20-0		8-1-13-4	8-1-33-0	6-0-32-1	8-0-27-1	
(Asda) v. Lancashire (Scarborough) 4 Sept.	6-1-32-2				7-0-27-1	7-2-14-1		7-0-29-2	
Wickets	30	10	17	2	14	14	5	28	4

	v. Northamptonshire (Leeds) 20 July (N.W.)	v. Sussex (Hove) 24 July (J.P.)	v. Nottinghamshire (Trent Bridge) 31 July (J.P.)	v. Lancashire (Leeds) 7 August (J.P.)	v. Gloucestershire (Cheltenham) 14 August (J.P.)	v. Derbyshire (Bradford) 28 August (J.P.)	v. Lancashire (Scarborough) 4 September (Asda)	v. Essex (Chelmsford) 11 September (J.P.)	Total
		38	8	38	53	56	5		428
	6	75*	11	16	39	8	0		447
	54	10	40	28	42	21*			675
	34	—	9	21	18	0	8		225
	11	2*	24	13*	18*	18	15		202
	37	0	1	15	6	0	13		410
	1	1	0*	11	16	19	38		351
	0	—			10*	5	28*		113
						5			152
	0*	—					3*		20
									11
	0	—	—	—		16*	15		55
	14	—	—						16
	0		4*	—			3		7
	0								0
			1		9	4	1		
	6	7	7	11	21	13	7		
	2	5	5	4	2	3	2		
		3		2		3	1		
	165	141	106	163	234	171	139		
	10	4	6	6	6	8	9		
	L	W	L	W	W	W	L	Ab.	
	—	4	0	4	4	4	—	2	

M. D. Moxon	S. D. Fletcher	Byes	Leg-byes	Wides	No-balls	Total	Wkts
			8			175	5
		1	8	5	3	195	8
		4	16	6		222	6
		2	5	2	1	127	10
		4	6	10	3	225	5
			6	2	6	147	4
			10	2	2	255	9
			7	4	1	167	10
		1	3	3		127	10
			11	2	2	128	9
			7	5	3	160	8
			16	5	5	265	3
			6	6		182	2
		4	7	4	3	131	9
			1			8	0
		1	3	4	3	211	7
			7		3	135	10
			10	3	1	107	1
4-0-17-1			5		1	162	8
			4	1		233	5
	6-1-28-0	2	9	3	1	168	7
			9	2		141	6
1	0						

Paddy Clift. An excellent all-round season for Leicestershire. (George Herringshaw)

244 in 200 minutes, but they never looked like getting the runs against the lethal spin combination of Edmonds and Emburey, and Middlesex won with 19 minutes to spare. They trailed Essex by 14 points with a game in hand.

Third-place Hampshire won inside two days. A weakened Somerset side were routed by Marshall on the opening day, and it was Marshall's brisk fifty that revived a sagging Hampshire batting display. Somerset collapsed again to the home side's seam attack, only Denning and Richards offering resistance, and Hampshire moved easily to victory.

Alvin Kallicharran's magnificent run of form continued with a century in each innings against Sussex, but he was almost out-manoeuvred by an outstanding all-round performance from Imran Khan. The Pakistani captain took 6 for 6, including the hat-trick, and hit 94 and 64, but Norman Gifford's slow left-arm gave the home side victory by 21 runs, the last eight Sussex wickets going down for 95 runs.

More left-arm bowling, this time by Derek Underwood, gave Kent a firm grip on the match with Leicestershire after Chris Cowdrey had hit a career best in what was undoubtedly his best-ever season. He and Benson added 106 entertaining runs in 100 minutes, and Cowdrey's leg-side play was particularly impressive. Kent's win moved them into fifth place.

Jack Simmons rescued Lancashire with his second century of the summer, ably supported by another good knock from young Fairbrother. Alan Hill and Ian Anderson for whom 1983 had been a splendid year brought Derbyshire to parity, but after a glorious century by Frank Hayes, the game subsided to a draw.

Derbyshire C.C.C. — First-Class Matches — Batting, 1983

Batsman	v. Gloucestershire (Derby) 30 April–2 May	v. Leicestershire (Leicester) 4–6 May	v. Lancashire (Chesterfield) 11–13 May	v. Nottingham (Trent Bridge) 31 May	v. Hampshire (Derby) 4–7 June	v. Middlesex (Uxbridge) 8–10 June	v. Leicestershire (Derby) 11–14 June	v. Essex (Derby) 15–17 June	v. Somerset (Bath) 18–21 June	v. Yorkshire (Sheffield) 22–24 June	v. Middlesex (Chesterfield) 25–28 June	v. Worcestershire (Derby) 2–5 July	v. Gloucestershire (Bristol) 9–12 July
B. Wood	— —	18 —	4 —										
J.G. Wright		60 —	6 —	41 —									
K.J. Barnett		20 —	21* —	39 —	4 68	25 0	17 25	1 0	13 35	95 2	22 18	4 12*	21 36
J.H. Hampshire		52 —		22 —									10 23
G. Miller		27 —	—	30* —	58 22*	0 —			84 10	4 2	35 3	49 —	59 10
A. Hill		31 —	14* —	57* —	0 46	89 42	3 0	3 1	5 34	12 4	36 12	137* 47*	4 64
S. Oldham		— —			9 —	19 37	8 15	6 0			7 3*	9* —	
P.G. Newman		12 —			0 1								
C.J. Tunnicliffe		16 —				1 5	8 11	28 29	51 0	18 21	0 2	18 —	7 20
R.W. Taylor		6* —			3 41*	20 5	8		5 31	17 0*	13* 33*	0 22	25 5
D.G. Moir		13* —			17 —	9 6	2 20	3 34	4 0	0 0	4* 12		3 0
I.S. Anderson				35	15 59	3 76*	2* —	4 10	1 33	14 4	3 27	18 85	10 25
O.H. Mortensen					6* —	7* 0	1 4*	4* 4*	0* 0		2 0		0* 0*
J.E. Morris					20 27	38 0	4 29	6 14	23 27	0 58	0 33		1 35
R.J. Finney					30 3	6 55	8 39	14 71	17 13	23 14	6 1	0 —	29 0
W.P. Fowler							5 12	0 28	59 2	16 8	25 0	63 —	4 7*
B.J.M. Maher								2 4					
A. Watts													
M.A. Holding													
Byes				3	3 4	10	5 1		1 2	3	1 3	2 3	2
Leg-byes		6	2	5	1 8	9 9	7	10 7	12 7	13 2	4	12 11	6
Wides		1	4	1	2 11	1	3 2		2 1	6	1	3	
No-balls		3	4	2	2 9	11 11	4 6	8 14	2	6	7 1	7 10	
Total		265	51	235	170 299	239 256	79 168	92 243	289 166	225 148	151 137	344 203	178 192
Wickets		8	2	4	10 6	10 9†	10 9‡	10 10	10 10	10 10	10 10	8 2	10 9
Result	D	D	D	W	D	L	L	L	W	W	L	W	D
Points	0	4	0	12	1	5	4	4	23	22	5		5

Catches 39 – R.W. Taylor (ct 37/st 2) 16 – B.J.M. Maher (ct 13/st 3) 13 – K.J. Barnett and G. Miller
21 – I.S. Anderson   14 – D.G. Moir   8 – W.P. Fowler

English Counties Form Charts

The statistics of all first-class matches are given on pages 464 to 543. The games covered are:

Schweppes County Championship.
Matches against touring and representative sides.

In the batting tables a blank indicates that a batsman did not *play* in a game, a dash (—) that he did not *bat*. A dash (—) is placed in the batting averages if a player had 2 innings or less, and in the bowling figures if no wicket was taken.

RIGHT: *Imran Khan. 6 for 6, 94 and 64 and still on the losing side for Sussex against Warwickshire at Edgbaston. (Adrian Murrell)*
OPPOSITE (*left*): *Gary Sainsbury. A good first year with Gloucestershire. 5 for 102 v Yorkshire at Scarborough, 24 August. (Right): Ray Illingworth. Constantly plagued by off-field politics. (Adrian Murrell)*

v. Warwickshire (Edgbaston) 13–15 July		v. Northamptonshire (Derby) 16–19 July		v. Hampshire (Portsmouth) 27–29 July		v. Kent (Chesterfield) 30 July–2 August		v. Sussex (Eastbourne) 6–9 August		v. Somerset (Derby) 13–16 August		v. Glamorgan (Swansea) 20–23 August		v. Lancashire (Blackpool) 24–26 August		v. Yorkshire (Chesterfield) 27–30 August		v. Nottinghamshire (Derby) 7–9 September		v. Surrey (The Oval) 10–13 September		Inns	NOs	Runs	HS	Av
																						2		22	18	11.00
																						3	—	107	60	35.66
53	—	103	53*	16	65	106	68	22	51	0	47	67	15	8	34	6	—	47	63	121	—	40	3	1423	121	38.45
		84	20	11	3							74	—	6	33	47	13*	32	—	6	—	19	2	485	84	28.52
31*	—			40	12	5	24	5	1	4	0*	22	22*	8*	—	0	—	23	63	46*	—	30	7	699	84	30.39
121	—	4	23	0	7	5	8	19	54	56	36*	0	10	106	10	64	—	5	31	111	—	40	5	1311	137*	37.45
7	—	39	—	15	0					3*	0											17	4	177	39	13.61
										0*	—							1	—	0	—	5	—	14	12	2.80
				91	12	42	1	40	2	28	—	10	0	—	—							25		461	91	18.44
						2	1*					5	3			9	—					21	6	267	41*	17.80
7	—	19	—	16	2*	112	48	87	79	1	33	19	39	68	54*	62	—	7	—	6	—	21	3	224	53	12.44
39	16*	28	91													14*	—	12*	—			37	4	1233	112	37.36
		4	—	0*	5*	1*	—	3	0*	0	—	9*	—									23	15	76	14*	9.50
15	21*	6	4													53	—					20	1	361	58	19.00
15	—	0	3*	25	0	19	68	16	4	12	7	6	21	12	—	17	—	19	5*	0	—	35	2	578	71	17.51
6	—	6	—	15	41			40	3	3	—	61	3	15*	—	91	—	6	—	72	—	26	2	591	91	24.62
24	—	0	—	2	0	28*	13*	11	52					8	—	6	—	6	—			12	2	150	52	15.00
6	—	33*	—															0	—			2	1	39	33*	39.00
				1	—					63	18*					8	—	8	—			5	1	90	63	22.50

Extras:

	4	1	11	4		1	4	4	8			4		6	4			1	1	11	
24		6	6	16	6	14	8	3	1	5	10	4	7	12	2	3			2	7	
7			5	6			4		4			1	1	1		2			1	4	
10		2		4	1	7	4	5	2	5	1	8	5	3	2	10		6	5	1	

365	41	251	196	319	188	368	255	257	219	199	186	285	177	294	119	368		137	202	385	
10	0	10	3	10	10	9	7	10	9	10	4	10	8	6	2	10		10	3	7	
W		D		L		D		D		D		W		D		D		W		D	
22		3		5		7		5		4		23		6		7		20		8	

† G. Miller absent hurt
‡ I.S. Anderson absent ill

5 – O.H. Mortensen and J.H. Hampshire   3 – S. Oldham and A. Hill   1 – sub.
4 – J.E. Morris and R.J. Finney   2 – C.J. Tunnicliffe, M.A. Holding and P.G. Newman

Derbyshire C.C.C. First-Class Matches – Bowling, 1983	P. G. Newman	C. J. Tunnicliffe	S. Oldham	G. Miller	D. G. Moir	A. Hill	O. H. Mortensen	I. S. Anderson	R. J. Finney
v. Gloucestershire (Derby) 30 April–2 May	17–2–70–0	21–5–62–0	20–5–46–2	21–6–52–2	22–4–61–0				
v. Leicestershire (Leicester) 4–6 May	14–2–71–2	17–5–48–0 3–0–17–0	20–2–66–0 6–1–15–0	5–1–10–0 4–2–4–1	15–2–50–1 6–2–14–0				
v. Lancashire (Chesterfield) 11–13 May									
v. Nottinghamshire (Trent Bridge) 31 May	11–4–28–0		9–0–32–0	18–2–70–1	20–4–65–3		7–2–24–0		
v. Hampshire (Derby) 4–7 June	10–1–32–0		30.3–5–105–1	7–1–32–0	38–13–106–1		22–6–59–4	12–2–36–0	12–1–54–1
v. Middlesex (Uxbridge) 8–10 June		16–4–75–1 9–1–29–1	18–3–54–1	16–3–34–1	27–4–110–2	1.2–1–4–0	18–5–48–0 7–0–24–0	6–0–45–1	7–0–18–2 3–0–13–0
v. Leicestershire (Derby) 11–14 June		27–7–77–3	16–5–47–2		3.2–0–7–0		24–2–72–2		9–3–22–2
v. Essex (Derby) 15–17 June		18.3–4–78–3	19–2–62–2		15–2–68–1		24–3–103–3		5–1–23–0
v. Somerset (Bath) 18–21 June		13–5–31–1 18–4–41–3		13–6–15–0 18.4–9–20–2	1–0–4–0 8–6–6–1		22.1–9–43–5 14–2–65–2		9–3–34–4 12–0–49–2
v. Yorkshire (Sheffield) 22–24 June		10–2–23–0 11–2–37–0		1–0–7–0	17–6–45–4 34–7–114–5		16.4–5–27–6 24.1–3–62–5		
v. Middlesex (Chesterfield) 25–28 June		16–4–49–0	33–6–72–4	12–2–28–0 8–3–15–0	18–7–50–2 9.5–5–20–1				11.5–2–31–3‡
v. Worcestershire (Derby) 2–5 July		16.2–7–30–4 25–3–88–2	10–3–23–2 27–6–84–3	33–9–91–3			13–1–46–4 27–5–73–1		6–0–29–0 7.3–2–17–1
v. Gloucestershire (Bristol) 9–12 July		23–5–66–3 13–3–32–2		7–0–25–0 18–4–42–0	9–2–30–0 28–5–93–4		18.4–3–52–4 17–3–47–0		14–1–54–3 6–1–18–0
v. Warwickshire (Edgbaston) 13–15 July			24–9–56–4 13–3–44–1	7–3–13–0 4–2–9–2	23.4–7–44–5 25–8–63–2	1–1–0–0			8–4–10–0 16.3–1–58–5
v. Northamptonshire (Derby) 16–19 July			23–2–96–1		24–4–97–1		16–1–71–1	3–0–26–0	15–4–41–0
v. Hampshire (Portsmouth) 27–29 July		17–4–47–2 15–1–85–1	22.5–6–56–1 11–3–41–0	7–1–30–0 6–0–26–1			23–1–76–1 18–1–74–1	1–0–8–0	14–3–40–0 5–0–20–1
v. Kent (Chesterfield) 30 July–2 August		12–2–51–1 12–0–60–0		39–7–117–2 11–0–56–1	13–0–65–1 4–0–33–0		16–2–73–4 13–2–54–2		10–0–63–0 7–0–51–1
v. Sussex (Eastbourne) 6–9 August		19–2–65–1 21–4–54–2	29–6–80–2 13–5–34–1	9–1–37–1			27–5–89–1 14–6–29–0		27–5–69–1 6–2–19–1
v. Somerset (Derby) 13–16 August		17–7–49–0 7–0–34–1	26–7–71–3 18–6–36–1	25.4–9–71–5 21–5–61–1			20–8–35–2 16–3–70–1		15–3–35–0 6–0–21–0
v. Glamorgan (Swansea) 20–23 August		11–3–29–3 18.5–7–48–4		19–5–42–1 21–5–49–1			17–4–43–2 23–10–65–4		7–1–36–0 4–1–9–0
v. Lancashire (Blackpool) 24–26 August		15–4–46–0 7–0–21–1		45–14–98–5 24.3–4–61–2	24–8–49–1 36–10–102–4				6–1–24–1
v. Yorkshire (Chesterfield) 27–30 August				8–0–38–2 51–19–104–2	15–7–32–0 27–8–57–1	4–1–11–0	7–2–26–2 18–8–28–1	6–1–31–0	6–2–14–0 14–2–48–1
v. Nottinghamshire (Derby) 7–9 September	2–2–0–3 12–0–67–0						11–3–25–4 7.5–1–28–3		6–0–27–1
v. Surrey (The Oval) 10–13 September	22.5–9–53–2			13–6–21–1			17–2–74–1		7–0–23–0
	88.5–20– 321–7 av. 45.85	428.4–95– 1372–39 av. 35.17	388.2–85– 1120–31 av. 36.12	492.5–129– 1278–37 av. 34.54	462.5–121– 1385–40 av. 34.62	6.2–3– 15–0 —	517.3–108– 1605–66 av. 24.31	28–3– 146–1 av. 146.00	281.5–43– 970–30 av. 32.33

a B. Wood 15–4–39–0   c J.E. Morris 2–2–0–0   † C.W.J. Athey absent injured   ‡ A.J. Stewart retired hurt
b B. Wood 5–0–35–0   d K.J. Barnett 1–0–1–0   e K.J. Barnett 2–0–12–0; J.H. Hampshire 2–0–4–0

A. Watts	M.A. Holding	W.P. Fowler	Byes	Leg byes	Wides	No balls	Total	Wickets
			3	2		8	343	4a
			10	4		8	302	3b
				2		2	54	1
Match Abandoned								
			8	3		2	232	4
			10	14	1	5	454	7
			8	17	2	8	419	8
			2	1		6	79	1c
			2	11	1	12	251	9
				2	2	22	360	9
			1	5		8	141	10
				9		1	191	10
	3-0-12-0		2	4		5	118	10
				5	5	3	233	10
	2-0-10-0		5	1		5	241	10
				3			48	1
	7-2-27-0			3		5	136	10
			2	10	2	13	407	10
			2	1		6	236	10
				6		2	240	7
28-1		7-3-11-0	3	1		2	169	10d
16-0		4-1-22-0	11	5	1	5	234	10
2-43-0		7-0-49-1	1	10	3	2	439	4
				1			250	4
			1	2	1	2	260	4
	11-1-49-1		8	6	2	3	437	9
				3		4	261	4
			1	11	2	3	320	5
				8		5	186	5
			4	1		7	273	10
			4	4		3	233	5
	18.3-3-41-3		5	15	2	8	221	9
	24-6-53-0		4	1	1	10	240	10
	17-4-55-0	11-2-26-1		7		10	315	9
	8-3-21-0	11-2-33-0	5	2		2	247	8
	16.3-3-48-5				1	1	160	9†
	26-8-54-0	8-3-24-0	9	6	4	4	396	5e
	9-3-23-2		1	2	1	1	53	10
	15-3-53-5			2		9	186	10
	24-7-54-5		8	11			244	9†
4-	169-41-	60-13-						
1	451-21	214-2						
87.00	av. 21.47	av. 107.00						

There was a quiet draw at Northampton where Glamorgan, needing 203 in 2 hours, went from 73 for 0 to 90 for 5 against Willey, Williams and Steele so that Henderson and Holmes settled for a draw. Earlier, Wayne Larkins had continued recent impressive run-getting with his third hundred in five weeks.

Sadly, Yorkshire made more news off the field than on when Ray Illingworth threatened to resign following the latest demands for special meeting and debate about the handling of the Boycott censure after his first innings at Cheltenham. Yorkshire batted solidly to get their four batting points, and looked set for victory when 9 Gloucestershire wickets went down for 171, but Sainsbury, who had bowled well, joined Shepherd to defy the home side for the last six overs.

FOURTH TEST MATCH

Thomas was omitted from the England side so that Randall for Foster was the only change from Lord's. Thomas, who had had an indifferent season, was a surprise choice ahead of Pigott and others, but his omission left the England bowling rather thin. New Zealand made three changes, Lees and Franklin coming in for Smith and Wright, both injured, and Snedden, surprisingly, replacing Chatfield.

Snedden, however, could not have had a better start, for he had Tavare superbly caught at slip by Cairns in his first over. Smith and Gower repaired the damage, but Gower, struck on the head when he ducked to a short ball from Hadlee that did not bounce, was not at his best, and the batting was uncertain.

Smith was taken at silly-point and Lamb, after a promising start, was given out caught bat-pad. Cairns had knocked back Gower's off-stump, and when Gatting, bristling with aggression, hit across the line England were 169 for 5 and in trouble. Botham and Randall, the last two recognised batsmen, were together, and in short space of time they moved on to the attack aided a little by Howarth's reluctance to maintain pressure. Bracewell was driven from the attack, proving that however much you spin the ball, it is necessary to maintain line and length. In line particularly, he erred.

In the Lord's Test, Botham had played well; in the Nat-West semi-final, he had batted magnificently. What superlatives were left? Initially, he was restrained, responding to the situation, sighting the ball; then he attacked. Off 99 balls he reached his hundred. It was an innings of massive authority. There were three sixes and fourteen fours, huge drives and hooks, reverse sweeps which were not really needed, and a sense of total command.

Nor should one forget Randall. Impish as ever, responsibility allied to a great sense of fun. He exudes a love of the game. They added 186 in 32 overs. It was cricket of joy. England closed the day on 362 for 7, Botham having swept forgetfully across the line and Randall driving loosely to cover, and their position was impregnable.

Taylor and Willis took England beyond 400 on the second morning, and New Zealand's troubles began quickly when Franklin, in his first Test, was well caught, bat and pad, one-handed by Smith diving forward.

Howarth and Edgar prospered for a while, but Cook threatened to stifle scoring and Howarth, anxious to break out, drove too soon and was well caught and bowled. Coney

Gower is hit on the head by Hadlee. His response was positive. (Adrian Murrell)

Snedden and Lees in eager anticipation appeal for lbw against Lamb. (Adrian Murrell)

perished in a similar way when he drove to short extra cover and Edgar, in a moment of indecision, scooped to short mid-wicket. Hadlee was struck on the pad and Gray called for an insane leg-bye to be run out by three yards, and then Hadlee was taken off a lifter which he fended off. Lees was lbw offering no stroke and New Zealand began Saturday with Martin Crowe batting at number eight because of a hand injury suffered while fielding and their only ambition to save the follow-on.

This they failed to do, but Willis decided that England would bat again. Nick Cook had once more taken five wickets in a Test innings.

There was some relaxed, rather indifferent batting from England on the Saturday afternoon, and New Zealand struggled on nobly, but Allan Lamb totally dominated the proceedings. It had been thought that he would have been left out of the side, and certainly his place was in jeopardy, but now he asserted himself and found the personality in his

Luckier this time. Lamb is caught by Howarth off Bracewell. Lees is joyful. (Adrian Murrell)

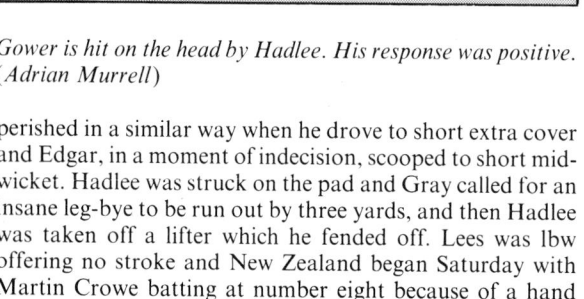

ABOVE: Botham rules. Gray is hit for 6. (Ken Kelly)

BELOW: Randall at home. He hooks a four as Cairns looks on. (Ken Kelly)

troke play for which he had been searching all summer. It was exquisite and powerful batting.

It continued on to the Sunday when Hadlee took the last two wickets in one over to bring his total of Test wickets to 00.

All that remained for New Zealand, required to make 511 to win, was courage. They showed it in plenty, Edgar and Coney in particular.

Edgar's was a remarkably disciplined innings, but his ultimate downfall was due as much to his unwillingness to attack Cook as anything else. Smith had a first Test wicket when Gray was caught at short leg.

The match ended mid-afternoon on the last day when Bracewell was caught behind by the irrepressible Taylor. In a last wicket stand with Hadlee, he had added 55, a stand symbolic of New Zealand's undying spirit.

Hadlee, Man of the Series, finished with 92 not out.

It had been an excellent series in which Willis had shown maturity as a captain and had given the impression that he was ripening with the years as a bowler, now better than he had ever been. He is a remarkable man.

New Zealand must have been a little disappointed. True, they had won their first Test in England, but they were still guilty of a timidity and of an inability to grasp the initiative when it was theirs for the taking. They lost golden opportunities in all three Tests in which they were beaten, but would that all sides could play cricket with their openness and lack of rancour. They contributed much to a joyful summer, and they demand the greatest respect.

ABOVE: *Mixed emotions. Gray is caught off Cook. Gower and Taylor are happy. Gray shuts his eyes in self-reproach. (Adrian Murrell).* BELOW: *Tavare is caught by Jeff Crowe (sub), bowled by Bracewell for 13. (Ken Kelly)*

ABOVE: *Cairns puts a ball past Botham.* (*Ken Kelly*)   BELOW: *Snedden is brilliantly caught by Taylor.* (*Adrian Murrell*)

**The new Ford Orion.
A modern variation on
a classical theme.**

The Orion is a splendidly comfortable, classically styled little saloon. But with front wheel drive, a five-speed gearbox* and all Ford's latest electronic technology, its engineering is strictly contemporary.

The Orion is a brand new addition to the Ford line up. A compact five seater with four doors and a conventional boot, its styling is traditional.

But, although its shape is orthodox, the Orion is no throw-back to the past.

For its size, it's one of the most advanced and refined cars you can buy.

The Orion is available with GL or Ghia interior trim. You can also have a Ghia with a 1.6 fuel injected engine which does 116 mph, and reaches 60 mph from rest in only 8.6 seconds. It also has slightly firmer suspension than its stablemates, which are tuned more for comfort than out and out performance.

But let's look round the model that's most typical of the range: the Ghia.

When you open the door, the first thing you notice is that air of calm that comes from cut pile carpet and tasteful cloth upholstery. You're back in civilisation.

The front seats, a new design, are padded generously and hold you firmly. They even have an adjustable support for the small of your back.

Look around and you'll find the latest equipment at your fingertips, power adjusted, heated mirrors for instance.

The dashboard bristles with switches, and warning lights for everything from low oil level to worn brake pads. You hardly ever need open the bonnet.

Depending on which model you choose, you can specify 4- or 5-speed manual gearboxes or an automatic. (The automatic contains a mechanical bypass which takes over from the hydraulic drive as your speed rises, a feature which makes it very economical.)††

There's a two layer ventilation system that keeps you fresh as well as warm. And such is the attention to sound deadening that even the holes that carry wiring from the engine compartment into the car are sealed against noise.

Another advanced feature – the radio aerial is built into the back window, so it's vandal proof. Signals are received by the heating elements in the glass.

A stereo radio cassette with four speakers and a 'joystick' balance control is standard. So are central locking, a tilting/sliding sun roof, electric front windows and tinted glass.

As for your passengers, one of the best features of the Orion is the way you can stretch out in the back. The Orion has more back seat knee room, leg room and head room than any car in its class. Not only that, but efficient use of space has enabled us to recline the back seat to a comfortable 27 degrees, so you can really sit back and enjoy the ride.

Such thoughtful touches as an illuminated vanity mirror, delayed action courtesy lights and seat back map pockets are all standard in the Ghia. So are the rear seat head rests.

Luggage space? That boot, which incidentally has a remote control release, is huge (13.5 cu ft). Also, two hatches in the back seat fold down. (They're split 60/40.) So you can push long, awkward loads through. It's the next best thing to having a hatchback.

You've a choice of engines, 1.3 or 1.6 litres in the GL and 1.6 or 1.6 with fuel injection in the Ghia.

They are, of course, mounted transversely and drive the front wheels, which partly explains why there's so much space inside the Orion in spite of its compact dimensions.

And with such engineering features as self adjusting tappets, electronic ignition and hemispherical combustion chambers, their low running costs and fuel efficiency are already proven. The figures in the table speak for themselves.††

You can see the new Orion at your local Ford dealer now. We think you'll agree, it's a modern classic.

Cut pile carpet and cloth upholstery: you're back in civilisation.

		††GOVERNMENT FUEL ECONOMY TEST FIGURES – MILES PER GALLON (LITRES/100KM)		
		56 MPH (75 KMH)	75 MPH (120 KMH)	URBAN CYCLE
1.3 4-speed		47.9 (5.9)	36.7 (7.7)	33.2 (8.5)
1.6 5-speed		54.3 (5.2)	40.4 (7.0)	33.2 (8.5)
1.6 Auto		43.5 (6.5)	34.0 (8.3)	27.7 (10.2)
1.6i 5-speed		47.1 (6.0)	36.7 (7.7)	27.7 (10.2)

Over 54 mpg from a 1.6 litre 5-speed at 56 mph.

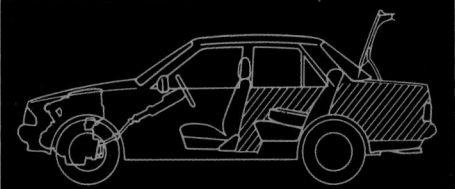

Hatches in back seat fold down to increase luggage capacity.

5-speed gearbox standard on 1.6 and 1.6i models. Automatic an option on the 1.6.

Comprehensive instrumentation and stratified ventilation.

*Standard with 1.6 engines, optional with 1.3. †Ford computed figures. Car illustrated has optional metallic paint and rear seat belts.

 FORD ORION

FOURTH TEST MATCH – ENGLAND v. NEW ZEALAND
25, 26, 27, 28 and 29 August 1983 at Trent Bridge, Nottingham

ENGLAND

	FIRST INNINGS		SECOND INNINGS	
C.J. Tavare	c Cairns, b Snedden	4	c sub (J.J. Crowe), b Bracewell	13
C.L. Smith	c Howarth, b Bracewell	31	c Howarth, b Snedden	4
D.I. Gower	b Cairns	72	c Cairns, b Bracewell	33
A.J. Lamb	c Howarth, b Bracewell	22	not out	137
M.W. Gatting	lbw, b Bracewell	14	c Lees, b Cairns	11
I.T. Botham	lbw, b Snedden	103	c Edgar, b Gray	27
D.W. Randall	c Edgar, b Hadlee	83	b Hadlee	13
R.W. Taylor*	b Bracewell	21	b Hadlee	0
N.G.B. Cook	c Lees, b Snedden	4	c Lees, b Cairns	26
R.G.D. Willis†	not out	25	b Hadlee	16
N.G. Cowans	c Bracewell, b Cairns	7	b Hadlee	0
Extras	b 11, lb 14, nb 9	34	b 6, lb 10, w 1	17
		420		297

	O	M	R	W	O	M	R	W
Hadlee	30	7	98	1	28	5	85	4
Snedden	28	7	69	3	8	1	40	1
Cairns	33.4	9	77	2	20	9	36	2
Bracewell	28	5	108	4	21	2	88	2
Coney	2	—	10	—				
Gray	3	—	24	—	15	4	31	1

FALL OF WICKETS
1- 5, 2- 94, 3- 136, 4- 156, 5- 169, 6- 355, 7- 356, 8- 379, 9- 407
1- 5, 2- 58, 3- 61, 4- 92, 5- 149, 6- 188, 7- 188, 8- 252, 9- 297

NEW ZEALAND

	FIRST INNINGS		SECOND INNINGS	
T.J. Franklin	c Smith, b Botham	2	b Willis	7
B.A. Edgar	c Gatting, b Cook	62	c Gower, b Cook	76
G.P. Howarth†	c and b Cook	36	c Tavare, b Cowans	24
J.V. Coney	c Gatting, b Cook	20	(5) c Taylor, b Cook	68
E.J. Gray	run out	7	(6) c Gatting, b Smith	3
R.J. Hadlee	c Smith, b Cowans	3	(8) not out	92
W.K. Lees*	lbw, b Cook	1	(7) c Lamb, b Cowans	7
M.D. Crowe	c and b Cook	34	(4) c Taylor, b Cowans	0
M.C. Snedden	b Cowans	9	c Taylor, b Cook	12
B.L. Cairns	c Gower, b Cairns	26	b Cook	11
J.G. Bracewell	not out	1	c Taylor, b Smith	28
Extras	lb 5, nb 1	6	lb 2, w 1, nb 14	17
		207		345

	O	M	R	W	O	M	R	W
Botham	14	4	33	1	25	4	73	—
Willis	10	2	23	—	19	3	37	1
Cowans	21	8	74	3	21	2	95	3
Cook	32	14	63	5	50	22	87	4
Gatting	5	2	8	—	2	1	5	—
Smith					12	2	31	2

FALL OF WICKETS
1- 4, 2- 80, 3- 124, 4- 127, 5- 131, 6- 135, 7- 135, 8- 157, 9- 201
1- 16, 2- 67, 3- 71, 4- 156, 5- 161, 6- 184, 7- 228, 8- 264, 9- 290

Umpires: H.D. Bird B.J. Meyer

England won by 165 runs

Another Taylor victim. Coney is caught. (Adrian Murrell)

Cornhill Test Match Averages

ENGLAND BATTING

	M	Inns	NOs	Runs	HS	Av	100s	50s
A.J. Lamb	4	8	2	392	137*	65.33	2	1
D.I. Gower	4	8	1	404	112*	57.71	2	1
C.J. Tavare	4	8		330	109	41.25	1	2
D.W. Randall	3	6	1	194	83	38.80		2
I.T. Botham	4	8		282	103	35.25	1	1
G. Fowler	2	4		134	105	33.50	1	
M.W. Gatting	2	4		121	81	30.25		1
P.H. Edmonds	2	4	1	63	43*	21.00		
C.L. Smith	2	4		78	43	19.50		
R.G.D. Willis	4	7	2	67	25*	13.40		
N.G.B. Cook	2	4		51	26	12.75		
R.W. Taylor	4	7	1	63	21	10.50		
N.G. Cowans	4	7	1	22	10	3.66		

Played in one Test: V.J. Marks 4 and 2; G.R. Dilley 0 and 15; N.A. Foster 10 and 3

ENGLAND BOWLING

	Overs	Mds	Runs	Wkts	Av	Best	5/inn
R.G.D. Willis	123.3	38	273	20	13.65	5/35	1
N.G.B. Cook	135.2	56	275	17	16.17	5/35	2
I.T. Botham	112.5	25	340	10	34.00	4/50	
N.G. Cowans	125	25	447	12	37.25	3/74	
P.H. Edmonds	87.1	30	221	4	55.25	3/101	

Also bowled: V.J. Marks 43–20–78–3; G.R. Dilley 25–6–52–0; N.A. Foster 28–5–75–1; M.W. Gatting 7–3–13–0; C.L. Smith 12–2–31–2

ENGLAND CATCHES

11 - R.W. Taylor; 10 - A.J. Lamb; 6 - D.I. Gower; 4 - M.W. Gatting and R.G.D. Willis; 3 - I.T. Botham, N.G.B. Cook and D.W. Randall; 2 - C.J. Tavare and C.L. Smith; 1 - G.R. Dilley, P.H. Edmonds and N.A. Foster

NEW ZEALAND BATTING

	M	Inns	NOs	Runs	HS	Av	100s	50s
R.J. Hadlee	4	8	2	301	92*	50.16		3
B.A. Edgar	4	8		336	84	42.00		4
J.G. Wright	3	6		230	93	38.33		2
J.V. Coney	4	8	1	238	68	34.00		2
G.P. Howarth	4	8		189	67	23.62		1
M.D. Crowe	4	8		163	46	20.37		
B.L. Cairns	4	7	1	116	32	19.33		
W.K. Lees	2	4	1	47	31*	15.66		
I.D.S. Smith	2	3	1	22	17*	11.00		
E.J. Gray	2	4		38	17	9.50		
J.G. Bracewell	4	7	1	56	28	9.33		
E.J. Chatfield	3	5	2	17	10*	5.66		
J.J. Crowe	2	4		22	13	5.50		

Played in one Test: T.J. Franklin 2 and 7; M.C. Snedden 9 and 12

NEW ZEALAND BOWLING

	Overs	Mds	Runs	Wkts	Av	Best	5/inn
J.V. Coney	63	26	115	5	23.00	2/21	
R.J. Hadlee	232	65	559	21	26.61	6/53	2
M.C. Snedden	36	8	109	4	27.25	3/69	
B.L. Cairns	184	52	461	16	28.81	7/74	1
M.D. Crowe	21	1	58	2	29.00	2/35	
E.J. Gray	48	12	128	4	32.00	3/73	
J.G. Bracewell	123	28	364	10	36.40	4/108	
E.J. Chatfield	153	37	440	11	40.00	5/95	1

Also bowled: G.P. Howarth 3–2–1–0
B.L. Cairns took ten wickets in the second Test match.

NEW ZEALAND CATCHES

10 - I.D.S. Smith; 7 - J.V. Coney and G.P. Howarth; 5 - M.D. Crowe; 4 - W.K. Lees, J.G. Bracewell and J.J. Crowe (2 as subs); 2 - J.G. Wright, B.L. Cairns and B.A. Edgar; 1 - R.J. Hadlee

Man of the Series Richard Hadlee. (Adrian Murrell)

27, 29 and 30 August

at Chesterfield

Derbyshire 368 (W.P. Fowler 91, A. Hill 64, I.S. Anderson 62, D.G. Moir 53, P. Carrick 5 for 122)
Yorkshire 160 (A. Sidebottom 61, G.B. Stevenson 51, M.A. Holding 5 for 48) and 396 for 5 (G. Boycott 169 not out)

Match drawn
Derbyshire 7 pts, Yorkshire 4 pts

at Bristol

Nottinghamshire 308 (S.B. Hassan 90, P. Johnson 52, B.N. French 51) and 278 for 4 dec (P. Johnson 125, C.E.B. Rice 100 not out)
Gloucestershire 300 for 3 dec (B.C. Broad 145, P. Bainbridge 51) and 208 for 6 (A.J. Wright 56 not out)

Match drawn
Gloucestershire 7 pts, Nottinghamshire 4 pts

at Bournemouth

Kent 162 and 319 (C.S. Cowdrey 73, A.P.E. Knott 64, S.J. Malone 4 for 74)
Hampshire 359 (M.D. Marshall 112, V.P. Terry 54) and 125 for 2

Hampshire won by 8 wickets
Hampshire 24 pts, Kent 4 pts

Essex C.C.C.
First-Class Matches — Batting, 1983

	v. Cambridge University (Cambridge) 27–29 April		v. Middlesex (Lord's) 30 April–3 May		v. Glamorgan (Cardiff) 4–6 May		v. Kent (Chelmsford) 11–13 May		v. Leicestershire (Leicester) 25–27 May		v. Surrey (Chelmsford) 28–31 May		v. Somerset (Taunton) 4–7 June		v. Nottinghamshire (Chelmsford) 8–10 June		v. Kent (Tunbridge Wells) 11–14 June		v. Derbyshire (Derby) 15–17 June		v. Northamptonshire (Ilford) 22–24 June		v. Sussex (Ilford) 25–28 June		v. Nottinghamshire (Trent Bridge) 2–5 July	
G.A. Gooch	174	—	72*	—	13	—	0	—	37	13	1	—	60	33	13	31	38	—	83	—	15	—	11	13	21	73
B.R. Hardie	129	—	0	—	0	—	15	—	62	4	16	—	4	39	42	20	13	31*	2	—	51	—	41	27*		
K.S. McEwan	8	86	40*	—	107	—	29	—	1	151	45	—	54	6	79	27*	142	—	178	—	69	—	7	11*	31	81*
K.W.R. Fletcher	34	17	37	—	151*	—	55	—	15	25	110	—	46	12	76	16*	0	—	—	7	33	—	79	—	5	39
K.R. Pont	16*	15			12	—	105	—	53	0	12	—	1	22	62	—	—	17	7	—	22	—	25	—	19	27*
D.R. Pringle	—	83			3	—	19	—	37	6			21	—					9	—			68*	—	36	—
S. Turner	—	16									20	—			3	—	12	2							0	—
D.E. East	—	18					12	—	25	6	17	—	10	77	17	—	18	10	26	—	0	—	2	14*	0	—
R.E. East	—	23*					2	—	25	0	19	—	5	16	19	—	1	7*			80*	—	15	—	45	—
J.K. Lever	—	4					26	—	6	4									8*	—	12	—	9	—	18	—
D.L. Acfield	—	8*					0*	—	4*	1*	0	—	4*	1*	0*	—	1	—			2	—	1	—		
N. Phillip					25	—	40	—	4	4	8	—	36	29	20	—			3	—	0	—				
N.A. Foster											19*	—	4	1	11	—	20*	—	0	—	22	—	2	—	25*	—
A.W. Lilley																									2	61
C. Gladwin																										
A.K. Golding																										
M.G. Hughes																										
Byes	3	3			2		1			4	4		6	1	2						11		1	4		
Leg-byes	10	3	7		6		13		7	7	10		8	4	6	9	9	1	2		5		10		5	1
Wides			1		1		3			1			1	1	1				2		1		6		1	
No-balls	1	1	1		3		3	3	6	5	6		2	1	1		9	3	22		6		4		4	2
Total	375	278	160		325		320	0	283	230	287		262	242	351	104	285	54	360		329		281	69	211	285
Wickets	4	7	2		6		10	0	10	10	10		10	9	10	2	10	2	9		10		10	1	10	3
Result	D		D		D		L		L		D		W		W		D		W		W		W		W	
Points	—		1		6		3		4		7		22		23		6		24		24		23		22	

Catches 68 – D.E. East (ct 63/st 5)   30 – B.R. Hardie   16 – K.W.R. Fletcher   9 – R.E. East   7 – S. Turner, J.K. Lever and D.L. Acfield
35 – G.A. Gooch   18 – K.S. McEwan   12 – D.R. Pringle   8 – N. Phillip   5 – N.A. Foster

at Leicester

Northamptonshire 219 (R.G. Williams 76, D.J. Capel 56) and 279 (R.J. Boyd-Moss 101, R.G. Williams 58, L.B. Taylor 5 for 59)
Leicestershire 399 (I.P. Butcher 107, B.F. Davison 67, D.S. Steele 4 for 59) and 100 for 5

Leicestershire won by 5 wickets
Leicestershire 24 pts, Northamptonshire 5 pts

at Taunton

Glamorgan 218 (R.C. Ontong 74, C.H. Dredge 5 for 51) and 236 (J.A. Hopkins 53)
Somerset 214 (J.G. Wyatt 59, R.C. Ontong 5 for 87) and 241 for 7

Somerset won by 3 wickets
Somerset 22 pts, Glamorgan 6 pts

at The Oval

Essex 300 for 9 dec (K.S. McEwan 72, S.T. Clarke 5 for 63) and 143 (S.T. Clarke 6 for 48)
Surrey 322 (D.B. Pauline 64, D.J. Thomas 51, J.K. Lever 4 for 83) and 124 for 3 (A.J. Stewart 52 not out)

Surrey won by 7 wickets
Surrey 24 pts, Essex 8 pts

at Hove

Sussex 383 for 8 dec (G.D. Mendis 105, C.M. Wells 65, D.K. Standing 56 not out, A.P. Wells 56, S.P. Hughes 4 for 69) and 197 for 4 dec (Imran Khan 62, A.M. Green 53)
Middlesex 302 for 9 dec (K.P. Tomlins 132 not out, A.J.T. Miller 86) and 195 for 6 (K.P. Tomlins 54 not out, C.E. Waller 4 for 61)

Match drawn
Sussex 7 pts, Middlesex 5 pts

at Edgbaston

Worcestershire 402 for 6 dec (D.N. Patel 112, M.S.A. McEvoy 103, N. Gifford 4 for 77) and 230 for 5 dec (P.A. Neale 82 not out, D.N. Patel 80)
Warwickshire 303 for 7 dec (D.L. Amiss 84, A.P. Pridgeon 4 for 63) and 174 for 4 (D.L. Amiss 59 not out, A.I. Kallicharran 53)

Match drawn
Worcestershire 7 pts, Warwickshire 6 pts

v. Warwickshire (Nuneaton) 9-12 July		v. Hampshire (Southend) 13-15 July		v. Glamorgan (Southend) 16-19 July		v. Sussex (Hove) 27-29 July		v. Middlesex (Chelmsford) 6-9 August		v. Leicestershire (Chelmsford) 10-12 August		v. Northamptonshire (Wellingborough) 13-16 August		v. New Zealanders (Chelmsford) 17-19 August		v. Gloucestershire (Colchester) 20-23 August		v. Worcestershire (Colchester) 24-26 August		v. Surrey (The Oval) 27-30 August		v. Lancashire (Old Trafford) 31 Aug-2 Sept.		v. Yorkshire (Chelmsford) 10-13 September		Inns	NOs	Runs	HS	Av
34	3	25	39	16	—	96	—	12	—	9	110	60	5	26	54	7	—	103	—	42	4	17	7	111		38	1	1481	174	40.02
26	1	67	7	12	—	56	—	38	—	18	45	37	69	4	13	62	—	13	—	28	23	17	0	10		37	2	1042	129	29.77
28	54	0	142	104	—	5	—	17	—	32	51	37	0	26	5	181	—	189*	—	72	25	17	30	9		39	5	2176	189*	64.00
0	62	39	12	8	—	10	—	32	—	0	49	10	71			1	—	2	—	3	12	8	1*	0		36	3	1077	151*	32.63
2	10	1	3	125*	—	21	—	5	—					81	32	78*	—	29	—							27	4	802	125*	34.86
8	7	14	102*	17	—	46	—	15	—											7	33*	18	7*	30		21	4	586	102*	34.47
2	0	14	2*	7	—	12	—	12	—	0	8	16	8			14*	—	30	—					11		19	2	177	30	10.41
5*	5	18*	—	0	—	91	—	43	—	1	11	0	14*	36	16			2	—	38	2	61	—	40	—	32	4	635	91	22.67
0	19	4	—	4	—					8	25	6	10*	19	23					31*	0	0	—			27	5	420	80*	19.09
				16	—	1	—			1	28	17*	—							5	2	44	—	10*	—	17	3	211	44	15.07
		0	—	12	—	1*	—	4*	—	1*	1*	9	—							2*	16	6*	—	0	—	22	13	74	16	8.22
4	80	6	9							6	20	29	15	4	3	0	—	18	—	26	5	15	—	4	—	26		413	80	15.88
0	40*			29	—	17	—	29	—					7	0											14	4	219	40*	21.90
																										4		70	61	17.50
								61	—	35	25	33	34	6	89	35	—	20	—	27	5	31	38	31		14		470	89	33.57
														2*	6*											2	2	8	6*	—
														10	0											2		10	10	5.00
1	2			8		7		4		1				12	2	1		6		1	1	8	13	9						
16		12	9	8		4		9		7	6	7	3	7	8	2		5		5	2	6	6	16						
		1	5	8				3		1	1	1		4	5					4										
2		1	2	2		18		19		10	14	8	5			3		1		2	1	5	2	7						
110	301	202	340	359		397		289		129	394	282	236	233	260	384		413		300	143	245	91	288						
10	10	10	6	10		10		10		10	10	10	7	10	10	6		8		9	10	10	4	10						
L		L		W		W		D		D		W		L		W		W		L		D		D						
3		6		24		24		7		4		22		—		24		24		8		6		7						

4 – C. Gladwin   3 – A.W. Lilley
1 – sub.

The leaders in the Schweppes County Championship, Essex and Middlesex, suffered set-backs in the August Bank Holiday matches. Middlesex toiled all day in the field at Hove on the Saturday and could gather only two bowling points as Mendis, the Wells brothers and young Standing, in his first match, ground Sussex to a mammoth score. Middlesex, led by Tomlins, an underrated player who was at last awarded his county cap, and Miller, the Oxford opener who had quickly established himself in the absence of Slack, reached maximum batting points, but they had little hope of forcing a win.

David Acfield helped Ray East in a last wicket stand of 14 to give Essex four batting points at The Oval. Essex had stumbled badly after Ken McEwan's fine knock, but David East raised hopes of points. Surrey responded fiercely on the second day through their middle order and hopes of an Essex victory were shattered by Sylvester Clarke's bowling on the final morning. Essex took eight points and increased their lead over Middlesex, but they had played poorly and once more Fletcher's selection policy which saw a half-fit Pringle and an out-of-form Ray East preferred to Pont, two good scores in the two previous matches, and Turner was incomprehensible.

Hampshire held on to third place with a maximum point win over Kent. Malcolm Marshall and Tim Tremlett added 146 for Hampshire's eighth wicket on the Monday, Marshall hitting a thrilling hundred, and although Cowdrey and Knott battled well when Kent batted again, Hampshire never really lost their grip on the game.

Norbert Phillip. His bowling inspired Essex's late run in the Schweppes County Championship. (Adrian Murrell)

Essex C.C.C. First-Class Matches — Bowling, 1983

	J.K. Lever	D.R. Pringle	S. Turner	R.E. East	D.L. Acfield	G.A. Gooch	N. Phillip	N.A. Foster	K.R. Pont
v. Cambridge University (Cambridge) 27–29 April	22–9–63–7 / 6–1–16–1	14–4–32–0 / 7–2–24–1	15.1–5–22–2 / 7–2–19–1	12–7–16–1 / 10.4–4–15–0	15–8–21–0	2–1–6–0 / 8–4–16–1			
v. Middlesex (Lord's) 30 April–3 May									
v. Glamorgan (Cardiff) 4–6 May	28–9–61–3	12–2–22–1		17–6–38–0	10–0–30–1	10–2–29–0	17–1–50–0		
v. Kent (Chelmsford) 11–13 May	19.3–1–84–1ʹ	20–1–81–2		8–2–27–0	12–0–49–0	3–1–12–0	12–1–40–1		
v. Leicestershire (Leicester) 25–27 May	26–6–80–3			19–3–53–0 / 7.1–0–44–2	20–1–71–0 / 12–1–66–2	7–2–22–0 / 1–0–10–0	17–3–64–0 / 20–1–74–2		
v. Surrey (Chelmsford) 28–31 May			7–3–16–0	1–0–5–0	17–7–23–0	22–6–45–0	7.3–4–4–6 / 13–2–39–1	7–3–10–4 / 13–2–33–1	5–1–10–0
v. Somerset (Taunton) 4–7 June		4–2–9–0		27–7–48–0 / 17–4–35–1	34–6–106–4 / 18.3–5–34–6		14–5–24–3 / 6–1–14–1	19.3–3–49–0 / 7–1–24–1	
v. Nottinghamshire (Chelmsford) 8–10 June			5–2–23–0 / 18–5–33–1	31.2–14–45–5	15–2–24–4 / 47–18–79–1		13–2–52–3 / 12–3–25–0	18–4–57–3 / 30–9–69–3	
v. Kent (Tunbridge Wells) 11–14 June			27–4–83–2 / 20–6–23–1	1–0–8–0	10–4–18–0	32–8–67–2 / 5–0–17–0	18.5–6–44–3 / 25–6–63–1	14–2–43–2 / 23–6–81–0	24–8–51–3
v. Derbyshire (Derby) 15–17 June	11–2–42–4 / 18–4–76–4	8–5–8–3 / 16–4–47–1			3–0–9–1			13–4–24–3 / 27.3–3–90–4	
v. Northamptonshire (Ilford) 22–24 June	21.2–5–59–5 / 15.4–4–36–6			13–4–26–1	5–0–15–0	2–1–2–0	14–2–38–1 / 10–1–16–1	17–4–48–3 / 13–3–23–3	
v. Sussex (Ilford) 25–28 June	15–3–46–2 / 17–2–53–3	4–0–7–2 / 12–1–46–2		1–0–1–0	24–5–61–2			14.1–2–46–6 / 16.1–2–64–3	
v. Nottinghamshire (Trent Bridge) 2–5 July	19–3–65–4 / 11–0–46–2	6.3–1–13–4 / 10–1–43–2	8–4–6–2	7–1–20–2				12–0–42–2 / 14–2–42–0	
v. Warwickshire (Nuneaton) 9–12 July			17–1–55–0 / 3–1–18–0	21–1 51–0	30–10–85–4		18–0–80–4	22–1–85–1 / 3–0–10–0	1–0–2–0
v. Hampshire (Southend) 13–15 July		17.2–4–66–5 / 21–2–92–1	17–7–30–5 / 19–6–41–1	40.1–6–161–3	11–4–28–0	2–0–13–0	5–2–16–0 / 13–2–42–1		
v. Glamorgan (Southend) 16–19 July		18–7–22–4 / 11–1–49–2	12–2–28–1 / 3–0–9–0	6–2–16–0	21–7–50–2	8–2–14–1 / 11–1–40–3		17.5–6–32–4 / 11.5–2–50–3	
v. Sussex (Hove) 27–29 July	17.4–6–40–5 / 17.2–4–55–7	19–3–68–3 / 2–0–21–0	10–6–13–0		5–3–7–1 / 2–0–13–0			19–1–73–1 / 13–5–33–3	
v. Middlesex (Chelmsford) 6–9 August	7–3–17–2 / 40–12–94–3	9.5–1–32–7 / 10–0–49–0			38–19–88–1	56–9–173–1		11–1–27–1 / 33–7–86–0	26–6–71–1
v. Leicestershire (Chelmsford) 10–12 August	13–3–34–1		20–3–48–1	9.4–2–27–1	28–9–70–1		33–9–92–6		
v. Northamptonshire (Wellingboro) 13–16 August	34–11–68–5 / 17–9–48–3		22–7–47–2 / 11–2–26–2	15–3–29–0	15–6–38–0 / 7–2–10–0	8–4–5–0	13–1–48–0 / 9.2–0–54–4		
v. New Zealanders (Chelmsford) 17–19 August				7–0–44–0 / 16–5–37–2		8–4–19–0 / 7–0–17–2	12–1–36–0 / 11–2–35–1		18–2–77–1
v. Gloucestershire (Colchester) 20–23 August	14.3–1–41–3 / 22–2–90–4		10–3–16–1 / 10–3–29–0		34.5–11–67–3		15–4–19–6 / 18–2–68–3		
v. Worcestershire (Colchester) 24–26 August	17–7–43–4 / 13–2–80–3		6–1–22–1		16–0–88–3		16.5–3–38–6 / 15–2–69–3		
v. Surrey (The Oval) 27–30 August	27–7–83–4 / 8–0–30–1	11–2–36–0 / 3–0–12–0		11–3–47–1 / 2–0–12–0	12.3–2–26–3 / 8–4–20–1	20–1–65–1	18–4–45–1 / 8–0–19–1		
v. Lancashire (Old Trafford) 31 August–2 September	20–6–53–5 / 18–2–60–0	1–0–4–0		29–13–50–2	2–2–0–0 / 49.2–14–100–7		23–7–54–5 / 19–3–51–1		
v. Yorkshire (Chelmsford) 10–13 September	26–8–78–7 / 28–3–85–4	23–8–47–1 / 9–0–25–0	5–1–8–0 / 9–3–31–4		5–0–11–0		13.2–2–53–2 / 17.3–3–43–2		
	569–135– 1726–106 av. 16.28	288.4–53– 928–41 av. 22.63	282.1–76– 624–27 av. 23.11	338–96– 889–25 av. 35.56	497.1–140– 1222–43 av. 28.41	212–46– 572–11 av. 52.00	477.2–85– 1409–69 av. 20.42	389–73– 1141–51 av. 22.37	74–17– 211–5 av. 42.20

† B.C. Rose absent hurt   ‡ G. Sharp absent hurt
a C. Gladwin 3–0–15–0   b M.G. Hughes 16–0–91–2 and 15.2–2–71–4

K.J. McEwan	K.W.R. Fletcher	A.K. Golding	Byes	Leg byes	Wides	No balls	Total	Wickets
				2		3	165	10
			1			2	93	4
				Match Abandoned				
			2	8		15	255	5
							0	0
			1	14	1	12	321	4
			2	4	1	3	300	3
			4	14	1	1	214	6
							14	10
			1	8	2	3	185	2
			4	6		4	250	7
				3		3	113	9†
			4	11			171	10
			2	18	2	5	278	10
-20-0				14	4	6	287	10
			2	23	1	8	289	5
				10		8	92	10
				7		14	243	10
				8		1	197	10
			4			2	81	10
							100	10
			5	10		10	249	10
				3			123	10
			1			14	172	10
			2	5	2	12	379	9
	1-0-5-0					3	36	0
				2	1	21	136	10
			2	11		20	410	6
				4		16	116	10
	1-0-10-0		2	6		8	240	10
			2	7		7	217	10
				2	2	1	127	10
			1			6	83	10
-8-1	3-0-15-0		10	12	6	11	634	7a
			1	17		12	301	10
			4	4	1	3	247	7
				2		3	143	9†
		14-2-44-1		3		7	321	4b
		14-1-53-1	3	1		3	220	10
				5		1	82	10
				10		1	265	10
				1		2	84	10
				4		8	271	10
			1	12		7	322	10
	3.3-0-27-0			2		2	124	3
			1	4	1	5	122	10
			1	16	1	5	284	10
			7	7	2	2	204	10
			6	14		5	220	10
–	8.3-0-	28-3-						
1	57-0	97-2						
28.00	—	av. 48.50						

ABOVE: *Chris Broad. A career best 145 and then a parting with Gloucestershire in acrimonious circumstances.* (George Herringshaw)
BELOW: *Sylvester Clarke came to form late in the season and wrecked Essex at the Oval.* (Adrian Murrell)

Glamorgan C.C.C. First-Class Matches — Batting, 1983

Opponents (venue, dates), left to right: v. Cambridge University (Cambridge) 20-22 April · v. Lancashire (Old Trafford) 30 April-3 May · v. Essex (Cardiff) 4-6 May · v. Oxford University (Oxford) 11-13 May · v. Middlesex (Lord's) 25-27 May · v. Gloucestershire (Swansea) 28-31 May · v. Yorkshire (Middlesbrough) 4-7 June · v. Warwickshire (Cardiff) 11-14 June · v. Somerset (Swansea) 15-17 June · v. Worcestershire (Abergavenny) 22-24 June · v. Leicestershire (Hinckley) 25-28 June · v. Kent (Canterbury) 2-5 July · v. Sussex (Cardiff) 9-12 July

	Camb 1	Camb 2	Lancs 1	Lancs 2	Essex 1	Essex 2	Oxf 1	Oxf 2	Middx 1	Middx 2	Gloucs 1	Gloucs 2	Yorks 1	Yorks 2	Warws 1	Warws 2	Som 1	Som 2	Worcs 1	Worcs 2	Leics 1	Leics 2	Kent 1	Kent 2	Sussex 1	Sussex 2
A. Jones	39	—	2	—	13	—	—	—	57	0	79	8	18	87	3	37*	—	—	—	—	3	38	93	46	105	19
J.A. Hopkins	36	—	25*	—	25	—	—	—	34	54	116	7	29	9	44	34	12	65	8	—	1	0	1	24	22	6
A.L. Jones	2	—	—	—	—	—	—	—	6	21*	2	11	3	15	18	17*	0	99	31*	—	37	40	16	58*	0	5
C.J.C. Rowe	39	—	1	—	31*	—	—	—	6	—	—	—	—	—	—	—	—	—	—	—	2	33	26	5	16	52
R.C. Ontong	51*	—	0	—	9*	—	—	—	3	0	19*	31*	112	13	38	61*	0	12*	—	—	6	27	21	3	24	17
J. Derrick	4*	—	—	—	—	—	—	—	—	—	—	—	19	5*	24*	—	0	—	—	—	—	—	—	—	—	—
E.W. Jones	—	—	9	—	—	—	—	—	2	0	9*	0	32*	0	15*	—	16	—	—	—	4	39	15	—	18	21*
J.G. Thomas	—	—	5*	—	—	—	—	—	—	—	—	—	23	0	18	—	12	—	—	—	13	0	—	—	—	—
M.W.W. Selvey	—	—	—	—	63	—	—	—	8*	6	—	—	1	—	—	—	—	—	—	—	11	2	25	—	3	—
M.A. Nash	—	—	—	—	—	—	—	—	—	—	—	—	—	27*	—	—	—	—	—	—	—	—	—	—	—	—
B.J. Lloyd	—	—	4	—	—	—	—	—	3	1	—	—	24	6*	—	—	38	—	—	—	7	22*	10	—	—	—
D.A. Francis	—	—	0	—	0	—	—	—	9	19	5	66	11	17	18	40	28	9	7	—	6	6	23	50*	6	46*
Javed Miandad	—	—	9	—	89	—	—	—	0	3	0	13	—	—	—	—	—	—	—	—	—	—	—	—	—	—
A.H. Wilkins	—	—	—	—	—	—	—	—	1	20	—	—	—	—	—	—	—	—	—	—	0*	6	15	—	0	—
S.R. Barwick	—	—	—	—	—	—	—	—	—	—	—	—	0*	—	—	—	22*	—	—	—	—	—	—	—	—	—
G.C. Holmes	—	—	—	—	—	—	—	—	—	—	—	—	—	—	—	—	10	1*	—	—	—	—	—	—	—	—
H. Morris	—	—	—	—	—	—	—	—	—	—	—	—	—	—	—	—	—	—	7*	—	—	—	—	—	24	0
W.W. Davis	—	—	—	—	—	—	—	—	—	—	—	—	—	—	—	—	—	—	—	—	—	—	4*	—	0*	—
T. Davies	—	—	—	—	—	—	—	—	—	—	—	—	—	—	—	—	—	—	—	—	—	—	—	—	—	—
S.P. Henderson	—	—	—	—	—	—	—	—	—	—	—	—	—	—	—	—	—	—	—	—	—	—	—	—	—	—
Byes	4				2				6	9			1	4			9		4		6	7	2	2	3	2
Leg-byes	4		3		8				6	3	14	6	5	1	10	8	4	5	3		6	7	3	12	11	3
Wides	3		1						1		2	4			1	1	1	1	3				1		3	1
No-balls	2		4		15				12	7	4	2	11	5	13	8	1		13		7	3	11	15	9	7
Total	184		63		255		—		154	143	250	175	289	162	202	206	154	193	76		109	230	265	216	244	179
Wickets	4		7		5				10	9†	5	6	9	7	6	2	10	3	2		10	10	10	4	10	6
Result	D		D		D		D		L		L		D		L		D		D		L		D		D	
Points	—		3		5		—		2		3		6		2		4		1		4		5		6	

Catches 25 – E.W. Jones (ct 24/st 1) 15 – J.A. Hopkins and A.L. Jones 8 – C.J.C. Rowe 6 – D.A. Francis and S.P. Henderson
20 – T. Davies (ct 18/st 2) 14 – R.C. Ontong 7 – A. Jones and H. Morris 5 – Javed Miandad and M.W.W. Selvey

A career best 91 from Fowler put Derbyshire in a strong position at Chesterfield and Yorkshire, with Athey injured, struggled against Holding and Mortensen and were forced to follow-on, but Boycott continued his prolific run of scoring with an eight-hour innings to save his side.

Chris Broad hit his third century in four matches and the highest score of his career at Bristol and then parted with Gloucestershire following a newspaper article in which he talked of differences with senior players and a desire to play for a county where England selectors would more readily recognise his talents. Paul Johnson scored a maiden century and the match was drawn.

Somerset beat Glamorgan with three overs to spare in a generally mundane match at Taunton. Leicestershire won with 10 balls to spare against Northants for whom Boyd-Moss and Williams fought a stubborn rearguard action. In the first innings, Ian Butcher had given yet another impressive display for Leicestershire.

Patel continued his good batting form as Worcestershire dominated the early stages of the match at Edgbaston, but the honours went to Mike McEvoy who reached a maiden hundred in his first season with Worcestershire. McEvoy had previously been with Essex. Neale and Patel again plundered quick runs for Worcestershire in the second innings, but Amiss destroyed their hopes of victory.

John Player League

28 August

at Cardiff

Glamorgan 216 for 5
Worcestershire 133

Glamorgan (4 pts) won by 83 runs

at Bristol

Gloucestershire 187 for 8 (B.C. Broad 81)
Lancashire 191 for 3 (C.H. Lloyd 81 not out, J. Abrahams 65 not out)

Lancashire (4 pts) won by 7 wickets

at Southampton

Sussex 193 for 8 (Imran Khan 90, S.J. Malone 4 for 56)
Hampshire 194 for 6 (D.R. Turner 53 not out)

Hampshire (4 pts) won by 4 wickets

at Milton Keynes

Northamptonshire 182 for 6

v Lancashire (Swansea) 9-12 July	v Essex (Southend) 16-19 July	v Worcestershire (Worcester) 27-29 July	v Surrey (Swansea) 30 July-2 August	v Gloucestershire (Cheltenham) 6-9 August	v Nottinghamshire (Ebbw Vale) 10-12 August	v Kent (Cardiff) 13-16 August	v Derbyshire (Swansea) 20-23 August	v Northamptonshire (Northampton) 24-26 August	v Somerset (Taunton) 27-30 August	v Northamptonshire (Cardiff) 31 August-2 Sept	v Warwickshire (Edgbaston) 7-9 September	v Hampshire (Southampton) 10-13 September	Inns	NOs	Runs	HS	Av
43	20 2	1		44 0		60 7	18 0	8 41	15 48	36 36*	20	9 4	37	2	1059	105	30.25
21 23	1 2	44 11	27 22	15 9	29 4		7 109*	44 24	21 53	44 1	32	3 25	43	2	1123	116	27.39
23 31	17 0	62	56 77*	30 24	12 84*	— 1	57 53	2 5	5 12	0	44 24*	36	40	7	1036	99	31.39
8 43	3 33	5 23*	32 0	9 20	39 61	82 13	0 15	43 6	12 43	0	3	17	33	2	721	82	23.25
20 6	12 79	16 22	39 109	81 46	4 12	105* 11	50 6	0 5	74 20	21*	37	50 38*	43	9	1310	112	38.52
													5	3	52	24*	26.00
33 37*	6 0												18	5	256	39	19.69
	18 7												9	1	96	23	12.00
6	4 6	9	0	6* 24	5 0	— 22	1* 30	7	0 3			8	24	3	250	63	11.90
													2	1	29	27*	27.00
12				1 7									12	2	135	38	13.50
43 45*	1 27	36 27	41 11	13 23	10 33	63 22	2 0			11 11*	89*	29	39	5	903	89*	26.55
													6		114	89	19.00
						— 45	17 2	54	14* 6	4		1 0*	15	3	185	54	15.41
		0*	0		0 9*								7	4	31	22*	10.33
								46 21*	18 20				6	2	116	46	29.00
9 4	13 29	27 9*	34 21*		26 7	— 18		0*	10 0	8		37*	14	3	228	54	20.72
0*	1* 39*	1	15		5* 5	— 2		0*	10 0	8		41	18	9	135	39*	15.00
	20		55*		2 0	12 4	69*	12 0	3	17 11*	14	0*	15	4	260	69*	23.63
			17 32		0 0	36 40	— 26	27 5	61 6*	17 9	0 135*	0	16	2	411	135*	29.35

† C.J.C. Rowe absent hurt

Lan	Ess	Wor	Sur	Glo	Not	Ken	Der	NorN	Som	NorC	War	Ham
5	2	10 2	13 1	1 4	1 4		1	5 4	12		6	6
9 5	4 6	23 6	19 8	2	7 12	8 5	15 1	10 8	3 11	6 1	20	9 9
8 2		4	2		1	3 1	2 1	4		2	1	6
8 5	16 8	4 2	12 1	2	4	15 4	8 10	17 1	6	12 1	8	
243 206	116 240	258 106	362 282	294 163	187 279	336 247	221 240	311 117	218 236	163 50	389 24	252 76
10 6	10 10	10 3	10 5	10 10	10 9	3 10	9 10	10 5	10 10	10 1	5 0	10 2
D	L	W	W	L	D	L	L	D	L	D	L	D
6	4	22	23	4	5	5	6	7	6	4	3	5

4 – B.J. Lloyd and W.W. Davis   2 – M.A. Nash
3 – A.H. Wilkins and J. Derrick   1 – J.G. Thomas, G.C. Holmes, S.R. Barwick and sub.

Middlesex 183 for 2 (C.T. Radley 68 not out, R.G.P. Ellis 52, K.P. Tomlins 51 not out)

Middlesex (4 pts) won by 8 wickets

at Taunton

Kent 221 for 7 (D.G. Aslett 100)
Somerset 224 for 4 (I.V.A Richards 86, P.M. Roebuck 60, P.W. Denning 50)

Somerset (4 pts) won by 6 wickets

at The Oval

Essex 127
Surrey 128 for 7 (A.R. Butcher 63 not out)

Surrey (4 pts) won by 3 wickets

at Edgbaston

Warwickshire 200 for 7 (T.A. Lloyd 57, K. Saxelby 4 for 29)
Nottinghamshire 139 (C.M. Old 4 for 14, P.A. Smith 4 for 23)

Warwickshire (4 pts) won by 61 runs

at Bradford

Derbyshire 168 for 7 (P. Carrick 4 for 13)
Yorkshire 171 for 8 (K. Sharp 56)

Yorkshire (4 pts) won by 2 wickets

Yorkshire maintained their two-point lead at the top of the table with a dramatic win over Derbyshire at Bradford. After Carrick's four wickets, three of them stumpings by Bairstow, Maher and Finney had an unbroken eighth wicket stand of 42 which gave Yorkshire a target of 169. Athey, injured in a car crash on Saturday evening, opened with Boycott, but he collapsed in pain and was led from the field after facing one delivery. Sharp batted finely for the home side, but when he was run out Yorkshire were 123 for 6. Athey returned and hit three 4's off Mortensen in the 36th over, scored 21 not out and took Yorkshire to victory with 4 balls to spare.

Somerset, with Roebuck and Denning putting on 99 for the first wicket, and Richards scoring 86 off 50 deliveries, beat Kent with surprising ease after Aslett had hit a magnificent hundred. Victory in their two remaining matches would now give Somerset the title while Sussex, like Kent, had fallen back in the race by losing at Southampton.

Butcher led Surrey to a surprise win over a limp Essex at The Oval and Warwickshire, with Paul Smith continuing his

Glamorgan C.C.C.
First-Class Matches — Bowling, 1983

	M.A. Nash	J.G. Thomas	M.W.W. Selvey	B.J. Lloyd	R.C. Ontong	C.J.C. Rowe	A.H. Wilkins	Javed Miandad	S.R. Barwick
v. Cambridge University (Cambridge) 20–22 April	6–2–12–0 / 10–5–12–1	4–2–17–1 / 7–3–19–3	12–4–42–0	9–3–21–1 / 7–4–5–0	17–3–46–2	11–2–25–1 / 5–3–8–0			
v. Lancashire (Old Trafford) 30 April–3 May	11–4–27–1	24–7–103–5	23–5–93–2	12–1–56–0	15–2–84–0	11–6–34–0			
v. Essex (Cardiff) 4–6 May		6–1–33–0	10–0–44–1	28.5–4–81–2	30–6–72–0	14–2–30–2	15–4–40–1	2–0–11–0	
v. Oxford University (Oxford) 11–13 May		4–1–21–0	20–8–47–6	11–4–8–2	17–6–29–0	2–1–11–0	8–0–25–2		
v. Middlesex (Lord's) 25–27 May			25–2–76–0	25–0–87–1	22–6–63–0	23.2–3–85–2	14–1–38–1		
v. Gloucestershire (Swansea) 28–31 May	8–2–29–0 / 14–3–56–0		5–1–21–0 / 24–2–125–4	3.4–0–13–0 / 3.2–0–17–2	11–1–38–0 / 14–1–56–1		4–0–20–0 / 8–0–39–0		
v. Yorkshire (Middlesbrough) 4–7 June		10–2–25–2 / 16.4–5–47–0	20–6–37–5 / 29–9–74–0	47–8–132–4	19–7–33–2 / 19–6–37–0				4–0–24–0 / 23–5–85–0
v. Warwickshire (Cardiff) 11–14 June		8–2–28–1 / 11.1–0–62–1	3–0–13–0 / 11–3–33–0	4–0–8–0 / 21–3–93–4	9–0–35–0 / 15–0–78–0				6–2–15–0 / 2–0–17–0
v. Somerset (Swansea) 15–17 June	28–10–69–1	26–6–78–5		2–1–5–0	26–12–47–2				27–5–85–0
v. Worcestershire (Abergavenny) 22–24 June	14–3–45–1		27–8–70–1	26–4–76–0	28–6–98–3	24–3–95–0			
v. Leicestershire (Hinckley) 25–28 June		9–1–25–0 / 4–1–10–0	21–6–68–2 / 14–4–38–1	1–0–2–0 / 5–0–28–0	24.2–4–64–6 / 12–1–52–0	21.5–7–73–2	19–0–82–2 / 10–1–56–0		
v. Kent (Canterbury) 2–5 July			18–1–76–1	23–2–87–1	29–6–73–1	23.2–6–64–4	9–2–34–1		
v. Sussex (Cardiff) 9–12 July			13.5–1–51–5 / 19–3–61–4		15–5–45–2 / 20–5–70–1		1–0–3–0 / 8–1–29–0		
v. Lancashire (Swansea) 13–15 July			18–5–48–4 / 25–6–101–1	14–2–41–0 / 21–6–65–3	11–5–24–1 / 24–4–65–1	5–0–17–0			
v. Essex (Southend) 16–19 July		15–3–61–1	18.2–2–56–3		4–0–17–0	33–7–119–3			
v. Worcestershire (Worcester) 27–29 July			12–5–30–0 / 24–8–79–2		2–1–4–0 / 5.5–2–11–4	3–1–20–0			14.3–3–42–8 / 6–1–28–0
v. Surrey (Swansea) 30 July–2 August			21–3–94–3 / 10–3–41–0		8.5–1–35–4 / 6–3–6–0	7–0–48–2 / 11–3–30–1			7–1–38–0 / 4–0–34–1
v. Gloucestershire (Cheltenham) 6–9 August			33.3–7–92–3	25–5–51–1	32–11–70–3	11–4–27–0			
v. Nottinghamshire (Ebbw Vale) 10–12 August			15–3–72–2 / 11–4–19–1		15–2–38–1 / 14–0–68–0	14–4–29–4			5–0–28–0 / 20–3–59–1
v. Kent (Cardiff) 13–16 August			16–5–38–1 / 19–6–55–1		17.3–1–96–2 / 8.3–0–45–1	19–2–67–0 / 22–4–77–1	8–0–34–1 / 12–1–48–0		
v. Derbyshire (Swansea) 20–23 August			18–3–58–2 / 11–4–27–1		13–3–66–2 / 7–1–23–3	16–2–50–3 / 20.4–0–89–1	10–1–35–1		
v. Northamptonshire (Northampton) 24–26 August			15–1–56–0 / 1–0–1–0		18.5–6–52–5 / 26–6–49–1	29–8–58–2 / 12–2–45–0	8–1–46–0 / 18–4–44–1		
v. Somerset (Taunton) 27–30 August			11–5–21–1 / 10–3–20–2		27.1–5–87–5 / 13–1–48–1	10–2–27–2 / 25–5–72–2	12–3–32–1 / 6–0–33–0		
v. Northamptonshire (Cardiff) 31 August–2 September					23–0–113–1	23–0–123–3	16–3–90–1		11–1–77–1
v. Warwickshire (Edgbaston) 7–9 September			10–1–39–0		25–2–116–0	40.3–8–139–0	14–1–70–0		
v. Hampshire (Southampton) 10–13 September			35–4–87–3			37–6–110–3	5–1–22–0		
	91–29–250–4 av. 62.50	144.5–34–529–19 av. 27.84	628.4–141–2003–62 av. 32.30	288.5–47–876–21 av. 41.71	644–131–2053–56 av. 36.66	473.4–91–1572–38 av. 41.36	205–24–820–12 av. 68.33	2–0–11–0 —	129.3–21–532–11 av. 48.36

a A.L. Jones 3–0–25–0; H. Morris 3.5–0–23–0; D.A. Francis 4–0–25–0; J.A. Hopkins 4–0–23–0.

J. Derrick	W.W. Davis	S.P. Henderson	Byes	Leg byes	Wides	No balls	Total	Wickets
			4	2	1	10	180	5
						4	48	4
			·4	13	2	13	429	8
			2	6	3	3	325	6
			8	1	4	9	163	10
			4	15		8	376	4
				1	1	2	125	0
			4	6	1		304	7
			1			5	125	10
▮–17–0			2	3		11	408	4
0–14–0						2	116	1
			1	4	1		293	5
			5	13	4	17	323	9
			1	3	1	5	394	6
			2	9		1	253	10
				6		3	266	3
	27–10–62–2		5	16	1	4	422	10
	19–7–41–3			2		21	163	10
	16.4–1–48–1		8	2		6	224	7
	22–9–64–5			2	2	16	193	10
	25.5–5–82–3		6	10	2	19	367	8
	30–9–81–3		7	8	8	2	359	10
	16–7–33–2		7	1	1	9	127	10
	25–5–76–4		1	4		15	234	10
	15–5–56–1		2	12	6	12	303	10
	11–1–66–0	6–0–48–2	4	3	1	11	340	4a
	34–5–112–3		14	7	3		376	10
	22.5–4–70–7		2	1	3	31	245	10
	22–3–92–2		1	5		13	286	9
	11–3–32–0	2–0–17–0		6		11	301	4
	11–0–50–0		2	4		2	283	3
	17.2–5–59–2		4	4	1	8	285	10
	6–1–25–1			7	1	5	177	8
	24–6–56–3		2	5	1	8	284	10
	25–9–58–5		7	16	1	8	229	7
	21–7–36–0		2	3		6	214	10
	19–5–48–2			3	9	8	241	7
	17–1–93–2			7		26	529	8
							0	0
	8–1–36–1		8	6	1	2	417	2
	7–1–13–0			13		6	251	6
–1–	452.4–110–	8–0–						
1–0	1389–52	65–2						
–	av. 26.71	av. 32.50						

eager all-round form, swamped Notts at Edgbaston.

Middlesex and Glamorgan each won with more than four overs to spare, and Clive Lloyd and Abrahams took Lancashire from 34 for 3 to 191 and victory at Bristol.

31 August, 1 and 2 September

at Cardiff

Northamptonshire 529 for 8 dec (W. Larkins 252, A.J. Lamb 119)
Glamorgan 163 (J.A. Carse 5 for 43) and 50 for 1

Match drawn
Northamptonshire 8 pts Glamorgan 4 pts

at Bristol

Gloucestershire 351 for 4 dec (P.W. Romaines 121, P. Bainbridge 56, A.J. Wright 56) and 204 for 5 dec (R.C. Russell 64 not out, P. Bainbridge 50)
Worcestershire 253 (D.J. Humphries 53 not out, T.S. Curtis 50, J.N. Shepherd 4 for 76) and 81 for 3 (D.N. Patel 53 not out)

Match drawn
Gloucestershire 8 pts, Worcestershire 3 pts

at Old Trafford

Lancashire 122 (J.K. Lever 5 for 53, N. Phillip 5 for 54) and 284 (S.T. Jefferies 75 not out, D.P. Hughes 68, D.L. Acfield 7 for 100)
Essex 245 (D.E. East 61) and 91 for 4

Match drawn
Essex 6 pts, Lancashire 4 pts

at Leicester

Kent 289 (N.R. Taylor 111, D.G. Aslett 58, N.G.B. Cook 4 for 94) and 113 (D.G. Aslett 53, P.B. Clift 4 for 42)
Leicestershire 310 (J.C. Balderstone 112, R.W. Tolchard 61, D.L. Underwood 5 for 101) and 96 for 2

Leicestershire won by 8 wickets
Leicestershire 24 pts, Kent 7 pts

Jim Carse, 5 for 43 against Glamorgan. (George Herringshaw)

Gloucestershire C.C.C. — First-Class Matches — Batting, 1983

Match key (each match shown as two innings columns):
Der = v. Derbyshire (Derby) 30 April-2 May · SurB = v. Surrey (Bristol) 4-6 May · War = v. Warwickshire (Edgbaston) 25-27 May · Gla = v. Glamorgan (Swansea) 28-31 May · SomB = v. Somerset (Bristol) 8-10 June · Nor = v. Northamptonshire (Northampton) 11-14 June · Lei = v. Leicestershire (Leicester) 15-17 June · Ken = v. Kent (Bristol) 18-21 June · Bath = v. Somerset (Bath) 22-24 June · Ham = v. Hampshire (Bristol) 25-28 June · Oval = v. Surrey (The Oval) 2-5 July · NZ = v. New Zealanders (Bristol) 6-8 July · DerB = v. Derbyshire (Bristol) 9-12 July

Player	Der 1	Der 2	SurB 1	SurB 2	War 1	War 2	Gla 1	Gla 2	SomB 1	SomB 2	Nor 1	Nor 2	Lei 1	Lei 2	Ken 1	Ken 2	Bath 1	Bath 2	Ham 1	Ham 2	Oval 1	Oval 2	NZ 1	NZ 2	DerB 1	DerB 2
B.C. Broad	24	—	49	—	14	—	52*	32	84	92	32	14	32	20	8*	—			46	35	0	7	58	21	21	10
A.W. Stovold	181	—	122	—	47	—	69*	39	84	35	7	0	63	15	13	57	5	6	46	35	0	7	58	21	21	10
P. Bainbridge	34	—	11	—	18	—	—	13	37	18	31	40	45	99	43	99*	5	27	3	13	16	1	3	146	19	0
Zaheer Abbas	82	—	44	—	0	—	—	116											10	18	21	42			0	21
P.W. Romaines	5*	—	4	—	—				73	15*	19	29	23	25*	135	12	10	47	40	23	14	1	23	30	13	71
A.J. Hignell	4*	—	50*	—	—				41	13	26	1	23	5	19	35	103	57	109*	61	10	46	10	0	0	86
D.A. Graveney	—		9		94	—	—	35	4	—	7	11*			7	—	49*	1	57*	14	1	4	3	27*	5	—
J.N. Shepherd	—		5		168	—	—	20	14	4*	69	3	95*		112		22	4	23	8	1	8			80	3
G.E. Sainsbury	—		—		1*	—			—		5	0	0		0	—	—	0*			10	4*	1	8*	0*	—
R.C. Russell	—		9*		13	—	—	0	1*	44	8	6	55		13*	2	0	12	—	5	11	2	8	30	58	25*
J.H. Childs	—		—		—		—	3*			0	0	0		3	—			—	3			0*	3	8	—
A.J. Wright	—		—		0	—							17										0	26	23	16
D.V. Lawrence	—		—		—		—				7*	0			0	—	—	—			0*	1				
B. Dudleston							—	35*									11	12								
F.D. Stephenson									21																	
R.J. Doughty																	8*	16*	—	25*	1	8	10	2		
S.R. Tracy																							0			
E.J. Cunningham																										
Byes	3		6		2			4	6	4		10		4			4	5		2	17	7	1	4	2	
Leg-byes	2		6		20		1	6	4	4	6	11	10	10	7	8	10	10	8	7	5	5	3	5	1	6
Wides			2				1	1	5		1						2	1	4	1	1	1	1			
No-balls	8		16		5		2		1	2	6	6		3	10	17	3			2	9	6		2	6	2
Total	343		333		382		125	304	375	231	224	131	366	178	370	230	232	198	302	215	117	143	120	305	236	240
Wickets	4		7		8		0	7	8	5	10	10	7	4	9†	4	7	8	5	10	10	10	10	8	10	7
Result	D		D		D		W		D		L		D		D		D		L		L		D		D	
Points	3		5		8		18		8		4		7		6		6		6		4		—		5	

Catches 63 – R.C. Russell (ct 46/st 17)   15 – D.A. Graveney   9 – P.W. Romaines   5 – J.H. Childs and A.J. Wright
16 – J.N. Shepherd and A.W. Stovold   14 – P. Bainbridge   6 – B.C. Broad and A.J. Hignell   4 – E.J. Cunningham

at Trent Bridge

Warwickshire 180 (T.A. Lloyd 70, G.J. Lord 61, K.E. Cooper 5 for 48) and 256 for 7 (D.L. Amiss 60, T.A. Lloyd 50, P.A. Smith 50 not out)
Nottinghamshire 449 for 6 dec (R.T. Robinson 207, J.D. Birch 90)

Match drawn
Nottinghamshire 8 pts, Warwickshire 2 pts

at Taunton

Somerset 321 for 6 dec (P.M. Roebuck 106 not out) and 86 (M.D. Marshall 6 for 46, N.G. Cowley 4 for 10)
Hampshire 253 for 3 dec (M.C.J. Nicholas 83, C.G. Greenidge 70, T.E. Jesty 61) and 41 for 1

Match drawn
Hampshire 5 pts, Somerset 4 pts

at The Oval

Surrey 388 (D.B. Pauline 115, R.D.V. Knight 75, M.A. Lynch 53) and 209 for 1 dec (D.B. Pauline 79 not out, A.R. Butcher 76)
Sussex 308 for 4 dec (Imran Khan 124 not out, G.D. Mendis 53 retired hurt) and 299 for 7 (Imran Khan 78)

Sussex won by 3 wickets
Sussex 24 pts, Surrey 5 pts

at Leeds

Yorkshire 293 (D.L. Bairstow 86, A. Sidebottom 78, N.F. Williams 5 for 77) and 252 for 5 dec (D.L. Bairstow 100 not out, P. Carrick 59 not out)
Middlesex 206 for 4 dec (M.W. Gatting 100 not out) and 125 for 2 (G.D. Barlow 58)

Match drawn
Yorkshire 4 pts, Middlesex 4 pts

at Scarborough

New Zealanders 292 (B.A. Edgar 100) and 247 for 6 dec (M.D. Crowe 110 not out, J.J. Crowe 65)
D.B. Close's XI 155 (D.B. Close 51, S.R. Tracy 5 for 29, M.C. Snedden 4 for 41) and 265 (J.H. Hampshire 85, Mushtaq Mohammad 60)

New Zealanders won by 119 runs

As the glorious summer waned, some were frustrated by the break in the weather, others thankful. Captaining Glamorgan for the first time in the absence of Mike Selvey, Rodney

v. Middlesex (Bristol) 13-15 July		v. Lancashire (Southport) 27-29 July		v. Hampshire (Portsmouth) 30 July-2 August		v. Glamorgan (Cheltenham) 6-9 August		v. Warwickshire (Cheltenham) 10-12 August		v. Yorkshire (Cheltenham) 13-16 August		v. Worcestershire (Worcester) 7-9 September		v. Essex (Colchester) 20-23 August		v. Yorkshire (Scarborough) 24-26 August		v. Nottinghamshire (Bristol) 27-30 August		v. Worcestershire (Bristol) 31 August-2 Sept		Inns	NOs	Runs	HS	Av
		35	19	10	7	27	—	4	39	17	100	0	109	44	9	145	43					27	2	1061	145	42.44
15	16	5	15	16	106	83	—	164*	38	37	2	2	26	6	1			43	38	51*	66	42	3	1671	181	42.84
19	6	19	50	18	2	21	—	14	6	9	39	11	29	26	2	51	20	56	50	41*	7	43	2	1217	146	29.68
		3	112	25	87	50	—	109	42	10	75											19	—	867	116	45.63
59	30	79	27	6	2	46	—	12	15	100*	16	12	32	36	1	46	6	121	3	25	0	41	4	1286	135	33.84
0	2	19	13	13	65	2	—	11	51*	0	24*	0	0	37	37	31*	40				3	37	6	1044	109*	33.67
6	9	4	0*			5	—			—	12*	25*	—	8	1	26*	0					28	8	427	94	21.35
1	6	8	3	10	4	98*	—	16*	10	93	13*	1	14	1	73*	—	11				24	34	6	1025	168	36.60
1	5	0*	1	0	3	13	—					4*	6	4	4*						0	23	8	70	13	4.66
21*	14	9	5	34*	1	5	—					4	15*	4	16				64*		13*	32	9	507	64*	22.04
3	0	14	5	19	14	2	—					5	0								0	18	2	82	19	5.12
23	11											29	22	40	19	10*	56*	56	5	—	27	17	2	380	56*	25.33
9	5*																					9	4	22	9	4.40
																						3	1	58	35*	29.00
																						1	—	21	21	21.00
																—	2*	32*	31*	—	0	11	6	135	32*	27.00
																						1	—	0	0	0.00
				0	0*							10	20			—	23	29*	0	—	1	6	1	83	29*	16.60

		1				1	9	14				11	1	1	4			4	5	1	5	3	3		4
6	2	2	1			4		7				11		9	4	5	10	9	1	13		9	6	2	4
		1						2	3										1						1
13	21			4		1						4	3	6	2	1	1	12	8	3	2	2	3	2	6

Right-side note:
The match v. Sussex (Gloucester) 11–13 May was abandoned without a ball being bowled
†B.C. Broad retired hurt

176	129	201	255	153	306	376		356	217	307	280	82	265	261	196	300	208	351	204	121	157
10	10	10	10	10	10	10		5	6	6	5	10	10	10	9	3	6	4	5	1	10
L		L		D		W		L		W		L		D		D		D		L	
3		4		2		23		7		21		2		5		7		8		3	

3 – Zaheer Abbas and subs. 1 – D.V. Lawrence
2 – F.D. Stephenson

Ontong asked Northants to bat and saw them score 529 for 8 in 90 overs. Wayne Larkins, in majestic form, hit a career best 252, the highest individual score of the season. Larkins and Lamb, who maintained his England form, added 242 for the third wicket in only 133 minutes. Glamorgan were bowled out on the second day as Jim Carse had his best return for Northants. The home side followed-on and Alan Jones passed a thousand runs for the season for the 23rd year running. Then came the rain and Glamorgan's blushes were spared.

Somerset were saved by rain at Taunton after Malcolm Marshall had done the hat-trick, and four wickets in five balls. The fierce wind and rain brought an early end at Bristol. Paul Romaines, in his new lease of life as a cricketer, scored a fine hundred on the opening day, and Gloucestershire were always on top.

The strong winds and dark clouds helped Warwickshire to avoid defeat at Trent Bridge where they had been outplayed for most of the match. Tim Robinson hit a career best 207 and was awarded his county cap for an excellent season's work.

Neil Taylor's accomplished century and two very good innings from Derek Aslett could not save Kent at Leicester. The combination of Clift and Steele was too much for Kent in the second innings after a typically professional hundred

from Balderstone had put Leicestershire on top. The worst part of the match for Kent was the inability of Woolmer to bat in the second innings because of a recurrence of his back injury, an injury that was to keep him out of the NatWest Final the following day.

Centuries from Edgar and Martin Crowe and good bowling by Sean Tracy in England on a scholarship, gave New Zealand victory in their final game of the tour.

Duncan Pauline reached a maiden first-class century against Sussex at The Oval. It was an innings of great charm and confirmed the advance that he has shown since being established as Butcher's opening partner after Clinton had lost form. Imran, however, responded majestically for Sussex, and, in the second innings, inspired them to a fine, and totally unexpected victory as they scored 299 in 200 minutes.

In the two vital matches, neither Essex nor Middlesex could force victories. Middlesex struggled on a slow wicket at Headingley where Sidebottom and Bairstow won them to two bowling points. Gatting played quite magnificently after a delayed start on the second morning and declared the Middlesex innings closed after 44.4 overs and the completion of his century in an effort to force a win, but Bairstow and Carrick on the last day took the game beyond Middlesex's reach. Bairstow was at his bounding best and reached not

Gloucestershire C.C.C.
First-Class Matches — Bowling, 1983

Match	J.N. Shepherd	G.E Sainsbury	J.H. Childs	D.A. Graveney	P. Bainbridge	D.V. Lawrence	Zaheer Abbas	E.J. Cunningham	B. Dudleston
v. Derbyshire (Derby) 30 April–2 May									
v. Surrey (Bristol) 4–6 May	25-3-77-1	15-3-35-0	18-4-57-3	19-4-38-0	6-1-33-0				
v. Warwickshire (Edgbaston) 25–27 May	28-12-50-7 19-6-47-0	26-6-81-1 31-7-108-2		23-7-51-0	13-2-25-0 30-9-89-0	11-2-41-2 17-2-78-0	3-0-21-0		
v. Glamorgan (Swansea) 28–31 May	34-9-83-3 6-2-13-0	15-1-46-0	10.2-3-34-1		17-8-24-0 23-6-67-3	11-1-43-0			17.5-3-83-3
v. Somerset (Bristol) 8–10 June	27-10-67-1 10-3-16-0	19-2-58-3 9-5-18-0	10-4-32-0 16-3-55-0	5.3-0-29-1 16-7-28-0	12-4-24-0				
v. Northamptonshire (Northampton) 11–14 June	25-5-68-0 11-0-47-1	12-2-44-0 2-0-15-0	45-13-104-3	47.4-23-88-6	6-1-18-1	9-3-27-0 12-0-59-0			
v. Leicestershire (Leicester) 15–17 June	29-6-77-3 15-5-46-1		35-15-69-0 26-13-47-1	17-4-34-1 20-7-34-5					
v. Kent (Bristol) 18–21 June	23-8-54-1 20-5-42-4	17.5-2-67-2 14-3-48-2	6-0-31-1 2-0-21-0	16-2-61-2	5-0-17-1	16-0-62-3 22-4-84-1			
v. Somerset (Bath) 22–24 June	27-7-80-5 7-7-0-0	19-5-52-2 10.4-2-55-1		5-3-3-0 17-2-85-0	5.5-2-10-2 8-2-40-1	19-5-52-0			10-1-81-1
v. Hampshire (Bristol) 25–28 June	19-4-70-1	25-6-71-5 14-2-73-2	10-2-31-0 33.1-9-66-4	18-7-43-0 9-1-14-2	21-3-46-0 4-0-20-0				
v. Surrey (The Oval) 2–5 July	29.5-8-83-4	24-6-70-2		16-5-53-2	24-3-77-2	4-0-16-0			
v. New Zealanders (Bristol) 6–8 July		23-8-55-0	17-6-70-0	14-3-38-2	16-6-39-1				
v. Derbyshire (Bristol) 9–12 July	28.5-4-52-3 10-5-20-1	20-6-38-2 6-2-16-0	21-10-28-2 35-11-81-6	34-14-42-0 28-6-64-0	8-3-12-1 3-0-9-1				
v. Middlesex (Bristol) 13–15 July	27-5-61-1	21-3-66-2	9-3-37-0	14-3-25-2	33-10-75-3	20-2-82-1			
v. Lancashire (Southport) 27–29 July	33-5-77-3 15.5-2-50-2	29-11-60-3 6-3-7-1	35.4-10-91-2 18-5-35-2	21-8-50-1			13-4-35-0 9-2-23-0		
v. Hampshire (Portsmouth) 30 July–2 August	20-1-69-0	16-3-39-0	33-9-89-2		15-3-69-1	16-2-69-0			
v. Glamorgan (Cheltenham) 6–9 August	23-9-56-2 32-10-64-7	8-4-19-1 2-1-1-0	30.2-10-77-5 21.2-7-67-2	17-5-49-2 12-4-14-1	4-1-11-0		1-1-0-0		
v. Warwickshire (Cheltenham) 10–12 August	26.4-9-54-3 13-2-56-1	33-10-101-3 13-2-54-1	27-9-69-3 17-2-75-2	10-0-41-0 17-0-71-2	10-5-18-0				
v. Yorkshire (Cheltenham) 13–16 August	25-9-52-0 18-6-34-2	25-5-86-2 20-3-67-2	20-4-67-0 14-2-61-1	12-0-43-0 18-4-45-3	33-4-79-1 1-0-5-0				
v. Essex (Colchester) 20–23 August	12-1-84-0	18-4-.67-1	19-0-81-1	20-8-36-1	26.5-6-110-3				
v. Yorkshire (Scarborough) 24–26 August	28-9-79-1 20-5-48-1	30-8-102-5 17.2-4-68-2		14-2-48-0	39-15-79-3 18-5-67-4				
v. Nottinghamshire (Bristol) 27–30 August	24-7-78-1 18-4-49-1	29-7-76-3 8-1-29-0	23-6-51-2 34-8-99-1		12-2-30-1			13-7-20-0 17-0-70-1	
v. Worcestershire (Bristol) 31 August–2 September	25-6-76-4 7-3-19-2	16.2-4-53-1 6-2-12-1	31-10-52-2 8-3-14-0	22-12-24-2	9-2-29-0 4-1-7-0			4-1-13-1 4-0-23-0	
v. Worcestershire (Worcester) 7–9 September	13-6-33-0 6-1-14-0	23.3-6-66-6 5-1-16-0	36-18-64-2 4-1-6-0	30-15-47-2	3-1-27-0 7-0-43-1			11-2-55-2	
	780.1-209-2045-67 av. 30.52	628.4-150-1939-58 av. 33.43	664.5-200-1761-48 av. 36.68	512.1-156-1198-37 av. 32.37	416.4-105-1199-30 av. 39.96	157-21-613-7 av. 87.57	26-7-79-0 av. —	49-10-181-4 av. 45.25	27.5-4-164-4 av. 41.00

a A.J. Wright 1-0-3-0   b S.R. Tracy 21-5-55-2

F.D. Stephenson	A.J. Hignell	R.J. Doughty	Byes	Leg byes	Wides	No balls	Total	Wickets
						Match Abandoned		
			3	8	1		252	4
			4	9		3	213	10
				13	2	2	414	2a
				14	2	4	250	5
				6	4	2	175	6
4–74–4			3	8		6	277	10
	6–1–32–0			1			174	0
			6	11	1	4	371	10
				2		2	125	1
4–4–56–5				7		3	246	9
5–10–2	1–0–14–0		2	4	1	3	161	9
			1	5	1	14	252	8
			4	5	5	2	272	9
		8–4–18–1	4	16	1	2	238	10
		5–0–25–0	5	7	1		299	3
		17–3–69–1	4	17	4	8	363	7
		19–2–80–1	5	3	3	8	272	9
		4–0–24–0	6	13	1	1	344	10
		13–0–66–1	1	8	3	3	338	6b
				6			178	10
			2				192	9
			8	13	1	6	374	10
			4	10		3	330	10
			10	3		2	130	5
			4	12	2	9	362	4
			1			2	204	10
			4	2			163	10
			8	9	1	2	303	9
			1	9	1	4	271	6
			8	8	1		344	5
			13	11		3	239	8
			1	2		3	384	6
			4	17	1	3	333	10
			3	3		4	193	7
		16.5–2–43–2	2	7		1	308	10
		7–0–26–0	3	2			278	4
			2	2		2	253	10
				5	1		81	3
			1	9			247	10
			1	2			137	3
4–13–	7–1–	89.5–11–						
0–11	46–0	351–6						
12.72	—	av. 58.50						

David Bairstow. Unquenchable enthusiasm and a thousand runs in a season for the second time, a Yorkshire record for a wicket-keeper. (Adrian Murrell)

only a fine century, but his thousand runs for the season. Needing to score 340 to win in 90 an hour, Middlesex showed courage in the attempt, but rain decided the issue.

Essex finished 19 points ahead of them on the Friday evening, but must have cursed themselves for not having beaten Lancashire and thereby virtually clinching the title. Lever and Phillip bowled out a depleted Lancashire side on the opening morning. Essex struggled to 160 for 8 in reply, but on the second morning, David East, named wicket-keeper of the year, hit a brilliant 61 as he and John Lever added 58 for the ninth wicket and then Lever and Acfield added 27 for the last wicket. Lancashire were 7 for 2, but Hughes roused them with a very fine 68. Still, at the end of the day, they were 208 for 9 and Essex scented victory. They were denied by rain, which cost 70 minutes play in the morning, and by Jefferies and Allott who were not separated until 2.15 by which time they had added 77 for the last wicket. Jefferies' innings was the highest of his career. David Acfield bowled splendidly for Essex who missed a couple of vital chances. Needing 162 in 195 minutes, Essex began easily, but were on course for victory when rain ended play.

When John Emburey bowled Arnold Sidebottom for 21 on the second day at Headingley it was his hundredth wicket of the season. He was the first bowler to reach this target.

New Zealanders in England 1983
First-Class Matches

BATTING

BATTING	v. Somerset (Taunton) 2-4 July	v. Gloucestershire (Bristol) 6-8 July	v. Middlesex (Lord's) 9-12 July	First Test Match (The Oval) 14-18 July	v. Worcestershire (Worcester) 20-22 July	v. Warwickshire (Edgbaston) 23-26 July	Second Test Match (Leeds) 28 July-1 August	v. Hampshire (Bournemouth) 6-8 August	Third Test Match (Lord's) 11-15 August	v. Essex (Chelmsford) 17-19 August	v. Leicestershire (Leicester) 20-22 August
T. J. Franklin	0 34*		45 12		2 35	33 17		22 25*		41 47	61 98
B. A. Edgar	34 11*	39 —		12 3	13 36	17 46*	84 2	12 8	70 27		54 33
J. G. Wright	85 —	136 —		0 88		15 —	93 26		11 12		32
G. P. Howarth	88 —	60 —	72 11	4 67	55 —		13 20	26 —	25 0	144 7	
J. J. Crowe	27 —	8 —	8 34	0 9	4 41*	63 79	0 13		11 24*	0 42	22
E. J. Gray	72 —		5 42		7 7	28* —			38	11 17	0* 3*
R. J. Hadlee	82 —			84 11	68 —		75 6*		0 30	— 26	
J. G. Bracewell	38 —	0 —	23 3*	7 0	20 30*		16 —	1 —	0 4	— 12	0
W. K. Lees	42* —		35* —	31* 8						5 16	0* 12
B. L. Cairns	60 —		0 —	2 32	29* —	— 7	24* —			— 25	
M. C. Snedden		— —	11 —		14 29			35 —		21	4 —
M. D. Crowe		61* —	10 134*	0 33	65 —		37 1	70 —	46 12	116* 13	25* 22
J. V. Coney		0 —	3 38	44 2	1 2		68 0*		19 10*	7 68	37 50*
I. D. S. Smith		19*			0 4	32* —		2 —	3 17*	10 5	9 —
E. J. Chatfield			13 —	0 10*			0 —		13* —	5* 2	— —
S. R. Tracy								4 —			
Byes	1	1	1 8		5 5	7	1 8	5 1	3	3	4
Leg-byes	12 1	8	4 6	6 1	9 15	13 1	4 7	4 1	5 4	3 1	5 12
Wides	1	3			5 3	1	1		3 1		2
No-balls	2	3	4 14	6 3	4 3	10 1	8 10		3 7	7 3	10 1
Total	544 46	338	234 302	196 270	246 210	335 158	377 103	244 60	191 219	321 220	265 216
Wickets	9 0	6	10 5	10	10 6	6 3	10 5	10 1	10 10	4 10	8 2
Result	D	D	D	L	W	W	W	W	L	W	W

Catches
- 20 – I. D. S. Smith (ct 18/st 2)
- 14 – J. V. Coney
- 13 – M. D. Crowe
- 12 – W. K. Lees and G. P. Howarth
- 11 – J. J. Crowe
- 10 – J. G. Bracewell
- 7 – E. J. Gray
- 6 – B. A. Edgar, J. G. Wright, B. L. Cairns, and T. J. Franklin
- 5 – Substitutes
- 3 – R. J. Hadlee
- 1 – E. J. Chatfield

BOWLING

BOWLING	R. J. Hadlee	M. C. Snedden	B. L. Cairns	J. G. Bracewell	E. J. Gray	G. P. Howarth	E. J. Chatfield	J. V. Coney	M. D. Crowe
v. Somerset (Taunton) 2-4 July	16-3-49-0 10-1-40-0	14-5-50-0 8-3-29-3	19-9-36-2 7-2-19-0	28-9-91-4 23-9-73-5	13-8-24-4 20-6-48-1	3-2-4-0			
v. Gloucestershire (Bristol) 6-8 July	14-7-25-3 20-9-31-2	8-0-42-0 20-2-74-2		29-4-87-3			17.3-6-40-6 18-4-51-0	4-1-9-1 11-1-50-0	
v. Middlesex (Lord's) 9-12 July		7-1-18-0	26-5-78-1	19-3-82-0	13-1-78-0		24-3-69-1	17-4-56-2	
First Test Match (The Oval) 14-18 July	23.4-6-53-6 37.2-7-99-2		17-3-63-1 30-7-67-0	8-4-16-2 54-13-115-2		3-2-1-0	17-3-48-0 35-9-85-0		5-0-14-0 3-0-9-0
v. Worcestershire (Worcester) 20-22 July	16-2-53-3 13-3-42-4	15-3-47-2 5-0-21-1	16-6-44-0 8.3-3-28-2				5-1-31-2	6.5-2-19-3	4-1-19-0
v. Warwickshire (Edgbaston) 23-26 July		14-1-52-0 10.2-0-45-1	17-5-41-1 17-5-46-7		9-5-4-1 3-1-3-1		19-4-60-2 6-2-13-1	6-0-22-0 7-4-9-0	
Second Test Match (Leeds) 28 July-1 Aug	21-9-44-0 26-9-45-0		33.2-14-74-7 24-2-70-3	1-0-8-0			22-8-67-1 29-5-95-5	12-3-21-2 8-1-30-2	
v. Hampshire (Bournemouth) 6-8 August		17-1-53-3 11-1-51-2		8.1-1-26-2	2-1-1-1		20-9-42-2 6-4-3-1		5-2-9-2 6-2-13-1
Third Test Match (Lord's) 11-15 August	40-15-93-5 26-7-42-3		23-8-65-1 3-0-9-0	11-4-29-0	30-8-73-3		36.3-8-116-2 13.3-4-29-3	8-7-6-0 6-4-9-1	13-1-35-2
v. Essex (Chelmsford) 17-19 August	14-2-30-2 10.1-3-26-1	19-3-68-5 10-4-38-0	8-3-18-0 15-3-41-2	22.4-3-68-2 15-1-111-6					6-1-37-1 5-1-25-1
v. Leicestershire (Leicester) 20-22 August		10-2-39-1 12-0-46-1	20-8-55-0 3.4-0-10-1	26-6-95-2 24-7-80-5			20-5-48-2 14-0-44-2	2-0-22-0 3-1-6-1	4-0-7-0
Fourth Test Match (Trent Bridge) 25-29 August	30-7-98-1 28-5-85-4	28-7-69-3 8-1-40-1	33.4-9-77-2 20-9-36-2	28-5-108-4 21-2-88-2	3-0-24-0 15-4-31-1			2-0-10-0	
v. D. B. Close's XI (Scarborough) 31 Aug.-2 Sept.		11-1-41-4 9-2-22-1			8-1-24-1 27-5-88-3	11-0-36-1	6-3-8-0		9-2-36-0 16-2-72-3
	345.1-95- 855-36 av. 23.75	236.2-37- 845-30 av. 28.16	341.1-101 877-32 av. 27.40	325.5-73- 1095-41 av. 26.70	143-40- 398-16 av. 24.87	17-4- 41-1 av. 41.00	303.3-77- 818-28 av. 29.21	124.5-40- 339-14 av. 24.21	76-12- 284-12 av. 23.66

a T. S. Curtis absent hurt

Fourth Test Match (Trent Bridge) 25–29 August		v. D. B. Close's XI (Scarborough) 31 Aug.–2 Sept.		Inns	NOs	Runs	HS	Av
2	7	43	15	18	3	539	98*	35.93
62	76	100	3	21	2	742	100	39.05
				10	—	498	136	49.80
36	24	34	11*	18	1	697	144	41.00
		20	65	19	2	470	79	27.64
7	3	30	10	15	3	280	72	23.33
3	92*			11	2	477	92*	53.00
1*	28			16	3	183	38	14.07
1	7			9	4	136	42*	27.20
26	11	0	17	14	2	254	60	21.16
9	12	19	—	9	—	154	35	17.11
34	0	30	110*	19	5	819	134*	58.50
		20	68	17	3	437	68	31.21
		2	1	12	3	104	32*	11.55
		2*	—	8	4	45	13*	11.25
		0	—	2	—	4	2	2.00
			7					
5	2	9	4					
		1	1	1				
1	14	2	3					
207	345	292	247					
10	10	10	6					
	L		W					

S. R. Tracy	B. A. Edgar	Byes	Leg-byes	Wides	No-balls	Total	Wkts
		7	7	1	2	267	10
		4	2	1	1	221	9
		1	3			120	10
		4	5	1	2	305	8
			2		3	386	4
		6	6		3	209	10
		4	10	1	4	200	10
		2	4	2	7	156	9a
			8	7	1	195	5
		4	2	1	3	126	10
		4	7			225	10
		8	3	1		242	10
			11		5	149	10
10.4–3–29–2–		10			6	154	10
8–1–36–0		3	3	2	3	326	10
		5	6	9		211	10
		1	7		4	233	10
		6	8		5	260	10
		9	4		2	281	5
			6		6	198	10
		11	14		9	420	10
6.3–0–29–5		4	6	2	5	155	10
8–1–21–1	5–0–17–1		4		5	265	10
33.1–5–	5–0–						
115–8	17–1						
14.37	17.00						

NatWest Trophy Final

A dull, grey and very windy day delayed the start of the final until eleven o'clock so that the umpires reduced the match to fifty overs an innings, and, thankfully, it was completed in the day.

Kent made a strange and, in the end, very unwise decision when they replaced the unfit Woolmer by Jarvis instead of Taylor so reducing the power of their batting to a dangerous level. As neither Underwood, the leading wicket-taker in the country in limited-over cricket, nor Johnson was called upon to bowl, the decision bordered upon lunacy.

Tavare won the toss and asked Somerset to bat. Dilley bowled a splendid opening spell and his venomous swing accounted for Denning and Roebuck who was comprehensively bowled by the blond giant. Slocombe, with care and determination, and Richards, with initially uncertain panache, restored the innings. The fifty was raised on the first ball of the fifteenth over when Slocombe hit Jarvis, wayward in direction, to leg for four.

The hop county comes to Lord's. The Kent dressing-room balcony at the NatWest Final. (Adrian Murrell)

ABOVE: *Kent in frustration. Knott, Tavare and Johnson peer in disbelief as the ball flies through the slips to the boundary.* LEFT: *An unusual sight. The ball slips out of Knott's glove as he dives in an attempt to catch Popplewell. Johnson looks on.* BELOW: *Garner is run out by Cowdrey who bowled splendidly. (Adrian Murrell)*

National Westminster Bank Trophy 1983

The County winning the Trophy will receive a prize of £13,000, the losing Finalist £6,500, the losing Semi-finalists £3,750 each and the losing Quarter-finalists £2,000 each.

MARYLEBONE CRICKET CLUB

NatWest Bank Trophy Final

15p

KENT v. SOMERSET

15p

at Lord's Ground, †Saturday, September 3rd, 1983

KENT		
1 M. R. Benson	c Lloyds b Garner	0
2 G. W. Johnson	b Marks	27
‡3 C. J. Tavare	c Roebuck b Marks	39
4 D. G. Aslett	st Gard b Richards	14
5 C. S. Cowdrey	st Gard b Marks	0
6 E. A. E. Baptiste	b Botham	16
*7 A. P. E. Knott	c Roebuck b Dredge	17
8 R. M. Ellison	b Garner	21
9 G. R. Dilley	b Botham	19
10 D. L. Underwood	not out	5
11 K. B. S. Jarvis	c Botham b Dredge	3
	B 6, l-b 1, w , n-b 1, ...	8
	Total...	169

FALL OF THE WICKETS

1...0 2...60 3...73 4...73 5...89 6...112 7...132 8...160 9...162 10...169

Bowling Analysis	O.	M.	R.	W.	Wd.	N-b
Garner	9	2	15	2	...	1
Botham	10	0	29	2	...	...
Dredge	8.1	0	50	2	...	...
Popplewell	1	0	9	0	...	...
Marks	10	0	30	3	...	...
Richards	9	1	28	1	...	...
	...	...	...	...	...	...

SOMERSET		
1 P. M. Roebuck	b Dilley	11
2 P. W. Denning	l b w b Dilley	1
3 P. A. Slocombe	c Johnson b Baptiste	20
4 I. V. A. Richards	c Knott b Dilley	51
‡5 I. T. Botham	c Johnson b Cowdrey	9
6 N. F. M. Popplewell	c Cowdrey b Dilley	35
7 J. W. Lloyds	l b w b Jarvis	10
8 V. J. Marks	c Benson b Cowdrey	29
9 J. Garner	run out	4
10 C. H. Dredge	not out	3
*11 T. Gard		
	B 1, l-b 17, w 2, n-b , ...	20
	Total...	193

FALL OF THE WICKETS

1...10 2...20 3...89 4...95 5...112 6...146 7...176 8...190 9...193 10...

Bowling Analysis	O.	M.	R.	W.	Wd	N-b
Dilley	10	2	29	4	...	...
Ellison	10	1	35	0	2	...
Jarvis	10	0	43	1	...	...
Baptiste	10	1	37	1	...	...
Cowdrey	10	2	29	2	...	...
	...	...	...	...	...	...

Any alterations to teams will be announced over the public address system

RULES—1 The Match will consist of one innings per side and each innings is limited to 60 overs.

2 No one bowler may bowl more than 12 overs in an innings.

3 Hours of play: 10.30 a.m. to 7.30 p.m. In certain circumstances the Umpires may order extra time.

Luncheon Interval 12.45 p.m.—1.25 p.m.   Tea Interval will be 20 minutes and will normally be taken at 4.00 p.m.

‡Captain   * Wicket-keeper

Umpires—D. J. Constant & D. G. L. Evans   Scorers— C. Lewis, D. Oldam & E. Solomon

†This match is intended to be completed in one day, but three days have been allocated in case of weather interference

Kent won the toss and elected to field

Somerset won by 24 runs in a match reduced to 50 overs due to weather conditions

Total runs scored at end of each over:

First Innings	1	2	3	4	5	6	7	8	9	10	11	12	13	14	15	16	17	18	19	20
	21	22	23	24	25	26	27	28	29	30	31	32	33	34	35	36	37	38	39	40
	41	42	43	44	45	46	47	48	49	50	51	52	53	54	55	56	57	58	59	60

Second Innings	1	2	3	4	5	6	7	8	9	10	11	12	13	14	15	16	17	18	19	20
	21	22	23	24	25	26	27	28	29	30	31	32	33	34	35	36	37	38	39	40
	41	42	43	44	45	46	47	48	49	50	51	52	53	54	55	56	57	58	59	60

Hampshire C.C.C. — First-Class Matches — Batting, 1983

	v. Leicestershire (Leicester) 30 April–2 May		v. Northamptonshire (Northampton) 4–6 May		v. Warwickshire (Southampton) 11–13 May		v. Worcester (Southampton) 25–27 May		v. Kent (Canterbury) 28–31 May		v. Derbyshire (Derby) 4–7 June		v. Lancashire (Bournemouth) 8–10 June		v. Oxford University (Oxford) 11–14 June		v. Middlesex (Uxbridge) 15–17 June		v. Yorkshire (Southampton) 18–21 June		v. Sussex (Basingstoke) 22–24 June		v. Gloucestershire (Bristol) 25–28 June		v. Lancashire (Liverpool) 2–5 July	
T.M. Tremlett	29	—	9	59			15		3	—	4						0	1	3	0			11*	10*		
C.L. Smith	129*	—	55	36	81*	—	37	16	3	4*	193	—	100	61			10	22	0	75	83		68	42	118	42
M.C.J. Nicholas	1	—	44	5	1		0	8*	5	51*	1		21	36	45	158	1	5	5	97	44		110	0	11	89*
T.E. Jesty	2	—	8	53*	36		36	28*	50	14	187	—											40	44	16	—
D.R. Turner	62	—	13	18	1		11	13	35	48*	1				51	122*										
N.E.J. Pocock	12	—	4	0	0		60*		29		9		57*	—	29*	—	37	19	1	23	14		50*	9	17	—
N.G. Cowley	6*	—	2	14*	0				8		18				20*	—	22	10	10	10	22*		29	11	7*	—
J.W. Southern			7	—	0*		5				11*						0	0	7*	45*						
R.J. Parks			15				3		0*								8	3	0	52			7			
K. St.D. Emery			8	—																						
S.J. Malone			0*	—			0		0							9*	1	4	0	12						
M.D. Marshall					79		39	—	15	—															26*	—
C.G. Greenidge							5	116	68	4															104	100*
V.P. Terry													66	114	36	0	61	17	22	25	6		19	29	4	—
R.A. Smith													100*	15*	14	—	10	26	3	42	104*		1	100		
K. Stevenson																	5	7*	25	1					2	1
C.F.E. Goldie																										
Byes			2	4			4	1	1		10				2	7			1	4	1		4	5	3	4
Leg-byes	11		5	13	14		2	9	6	3	14		6	3		4	13	3	1	9	6		17	3	15	8
Wides			1				1	11	1		1		1	1	1				2	4	2		4	3		
No-balls			4	2	4		17		5		5		6	2	1		8		3	21	5		8	8	2	3
Total	252		177	204	216		235	202	228	125	454		357	232	198	301	176	121	83	420	287		363	272	323	246
Wickets	5		10	5	6		10	3	10	2	7		3	3	4	2	10	10	10	10	4		7	9	6	1
Result	D		D		W		W		D		D		D		W		L		L		D		W		D	
Points	3		4		12		22		2		8		5				4		2		7		22		7	

Catches 60 – R.J. Parks (ct 51/st 9) 26 – M.C.J. Nicholas 18 – T.M. Tremlett 15 – V.P. Terry 8 – J.W. Southern
30 – N.E.J. Pocock 21 – C.G. Greenidge 17 – C.L. Smith 12 – T.E. Jesty 7 – N.G. Cowley

BELOW: *Instant joy for Somerset. Jeremy Lloyds clasps the ball firmly as he receives the enthusiastic congratulations of his colleagues after he had caught Benson off Garner in the first over of the Kent innings.* OPPOSITE: *Stumping hero Trevor Gard in ecstatic mood.* (*Adrian Murrell*)

Richards had begun to play some commanding shots and Somerset were creeping into total command when Kent made two decisive blows shortly before lunch. Slocombe was caught at slip off a fierce edge and, in the 25th over, Dilley, having returned for a pre-lunch burst, took the outside edge of Richards' bat for Knott to accept a simple catch. 95 for 4 at lunch, and the game very much back in favour of Kent.

Cowdrey replaced Dilley at the pavilion end and, in the early afternoon, Botham swung him high to the mound stand where Johnson took a well judged catch on the boundary rope. Lloyds and Popplewell kept the momentum going, however, and Somerset were always hovering close to four an over.

The final blast came from Marks who hit about him boldly, falling to the last ball of the innings when he was caught on the boundary rope in front of the grand-stand. There had been no decisive innings for Somerset, but their total of 193 never looked an easy one to reach in the conditions. For Kent, Dilley, broad, quick and imposing, had bowled quite magnificently, and Cowdrey, as in the semi-final, had been a most effective bowler. He had taken the wickets of Botham and Marks and seen Knott drop Popplewell off him. The mystery was why Underwood did not bowl and why Taylor or Potter was not in the side for Jarvis or Underwood himself.

v Surrey (Southampton) 9–12 July	v Essex (Southend) 13–15 July	v Nottinghamshire (Bournemouth) 16–19 July	v Derbyshire (Portsmouth) 27–29 July	v Gloucestershire (Portsmouth) 30 July–2 Aug.	v New Zealanders (Bournemouth) 6–8 August	v Sussex (Eastbourne) 10–12 August	v Nottinghamshire (Trent Bridge) 13–16 August	v Worcestershire (Worcester) 20–23 August	v Somerset (Bournemouth) 24–26 August	v Kent (Bournemouth) 27–30 August	v Somerset (Taunton) 31 Aug.–2 Sept.	v Glamorgan (Southampton) 10–13 September	Inns	NOs	Runs	HS	Av
— —	15 —	— —	— —		10 24	— 12*		10	9* —	39* —			19	5	263	59	18.78
47 26	3 163	16 11	33 76	125	9 5			26			20 17	93	35	3	1845	193	57.65
23 34	4 72	42 20	100* 29	76 —	5 18	8 6	1 34	27	14 —	35 49	83* —	0 —	43	5	1418	158	37.31
12 —		86 6*	2 43	31* —	29 24	75 36	13 6	27	31 —	35 15*	61 —	26 —	30	5	1072	187	42.88
					27 20	41 94*			3 —	38 —			17	3	598	122*	42.71
30 17*	0 52	59 —	9* 11*	10* —	21 24	5 11	22 1	57	38 —	9 —	— —	9 —	35	8	755	60*	27.96
	0 0*	— —	— —		16 13	14* 25*	28 24	10	15 —	4 —	— —	13* —	27	9	351	29	19.50
13* —	37 0	— —					1 20						13	5	146	45*	18.25
— 29	9 —					14* 0		39	0 —	1 —			15	2	180	52	13.84
			— —										1	—	8	8	8.00
100* —	4* —	15 —			1* 0		2 4*	7*	3 —	0 —	— —	— —	16	6	47	12	4.70
	6 4*					26* 13	17 19	37	50 —	112 —	— —	5 —	16	4	563	112	46.91
83 154	34 45	63 31*	72 57	71 —		14 36	26 5	95	13 17*	9 48*	70 21*	77 —	27	5	1438	154	65.36
43 26*	0 41	106* —	33 38*	22 —	20 1	68 115	22 25	17	25 18*	54 4	10* —	9* —	33	6	1096	115	40.59
					12 7								12	3	434	104*	48.22
		10* —			4 22								9	3	77	25	12.83
					6 0*								2	1	6	6	6.00

Lower-order figures:

Surrey	Essex	Notts (B)	Derby	Glouc	NZ	Sussex	Notts (TB)	Worcs	Somerset (B)	Kent	Somerset (T)	Glamorgan
7	2	1		1	4	10	2 7		4	4	2	1
7 7	2 11	5	1 2	12		11	8 3	3 1	8	4 1	13 1	7 3 13
4 4	1	1		1 2	2		2	1		1 2	3	
9 5	21 20	21 20		1 2	9	5 6	1 1	4 9		1 1	5 8	1 6

Team totals:

	Surrey	Essex	Notts (B)	Derby	Glouc	NZ	Sussex	Notts (TB)	Worcs	Somerset (B)	Kent	Somerset (T)	Glamorgan
Runs	371 309	136 410	404 68	250 260	362	149 154	250 285	194 243	365	211 39	359 125	253 41	251
Wkts	6 4	10 6	6 2	4 4	4	10 10	6 7	10 9	10	10 0	10 2	3 1	6
Result	D	W	W	W	D	L	W	D	W	W	W	D	D
Points	6	20	24	23	8	—	23	5	24	22	24	5	7

6 – M.D. Marshal   3 – D.R. Turner and subs.   1 – R.A. Smith
4 – S.J. Malone   2 – K. Stevenson

Hampshire C.C.C. First-Class Matches — Bowling, 1983

	K.St.D. Emery	S.J. Malone	J.W. Southern	T.M. Tremlett	T.E. Jesty	N.G. Cowley	M.C.J. Nicholas	M.D. Marshall	N.E.J. Pocock
v. Leicestershire (Leicester) 30 April–2 May									
v. Northamptonshire (Northampton) 4–6 May	22-3-87-1	27-6-93-4	15-9-12-0	20-10-29-2	14-4-31-0	11-0-30-0	6-0-30-1		
v. Warwickshire (Southampton) 11–13 May		12.4-5-36-2		9-0-53-4	7-0-39-2			19-4-61-1	
v. Worcestershire (Southampton) 25–27 May		20-6-58-0	4-0-22-0	22.3-9-41-1	6-0-19-0		20-6-45-5	21-6-39-3	
		16-5-39-1	2.3-1-10-1	7-3-12-0	9-1-34-1		10-0-39-1	24-7-58-6	
v. Kent (Canterbury) 28–31 May		15-1-40-2		9-2-41-1	11-5-30-0	14-3-39-1	8-1-27-0	14-8-16-0	4-0-31-1
v. Derbyshire (Derby) 4–7 June	2-0-6-0	3-0-11-0	43-20-60-5	10-1-22-2		32-10-63-3			
	16-7-20-0	21-6-59-0	38-15-84-3	11-4-14-1	6-2-19-0	14-9-10-0	15-6-22-1		
v. Lancashire (Bournemouth) 8–10 June	13-4-34-3	16-3-50-0	11-3-42-0	17.5-7-50-2		24-7-62-0	8-3-18-0		
	13-6-24-0	10-3-42-2	16-8-19-2						2-0-9-0
v. Oxford University (Oxford) 11–14 June	9-2-38-0	24-10-64-4	20-4-44-2	33-18-42-4		12-3-29-0	13-4-31-0		
	10-4-20-0	13-3-40-1	22-6-74-1	6-2-12-1		5-2-4-0			11-0-51-0
v. Middlesex (Uxbridge) 15–17 June		22-2-85-3	18-5-53-1	31.5-10-82-2		2-0-14-0	2-1-1-0		
v. Yorkshire (Southampton) 18–21 June		31-8-108-1	31-8-111-2	33-10-48-1		13-3-49-1	11-2-35-0		
		7.2-1-32-0		6-0-26-2					
v. Sussex (Basingstoke) 22–24 June		14-3-52-2		21.2-7-39-3		5-2-6-0	17-6-28-0		
		19-5-43-0		27-6-71-3		8-4-41-0	12-4-28-1		
v. Gloucestershire (Bristol) 25–28 June		15-2-74-0		17-5-56-3	14-4-50-0	8-3-20-0	8-0-36-0		
		11.1-4-31-1		16-2-47-3	7-1-31-1	11-11-0-2	1-0-1-0		1-0-8-0
v. Lancashire (Liverpool) 2–5 July			27-7-69-0	16-6-36-0	8-2-24-0	23-5-76-4		21-4-60-2	
			21-7-47-2	5-1-11-1		5-1-10-0		22-3-64-5	
v. Surrey (Southampton) 9–12 July		15-4-58-1	20-2-91-1	11-3-25-1	8-2-15-0		8-2-24-0	11-4-20-2	2-0-15-0
		9-3-22-0	21-7-52-1	3-3-0-0				10-4-25-1	5-3-6-0
v. Essex (Southend) 13–15 July		7-0-39-0	22-2-78-1	28-7-65-4		15.5-4-74-1	3-1-11-0	28.2-6-73-6	
		12-3-28-0		11-0-33-0			12-1-52-0	17-4-51-4	
v. Nottinghamshire (Bournemouth) 16–19 July			9-3-23-0	23-15-12-2	8-3-24-0		4-1-12-1	31-10-70-4	
			29.2-8-75-5	17-9-21-2	6-0-31-0			20-4-46-3	
v. Derbyshire (Portsmouth) 27–29 July	9-2-33-1			18-6-34-2	18-6-47-1	18.4-2-86-2	4-0-23-0	28-8-66-4	
				27-5-82-6	15-3-48-3			14-2-47-1	
v. Gloucestershire (Portsmouth) 30 July–2 August		11-0-61-1		14-5-30-2	4-1-17-1	4.3-1-14-3		12-4-29-3	
		16-4-39-4		17-2-62-1	14.3-2-62-2	7-5-5-0	2-0-16-0	32-10-107-2	
v. New Zealanders (Bournemouth) 6–8 August		24-5-50-2		4-1-7-0		31-13-55-3	14-4-21-3		
		5-1-23-0					4-0-27-1		
v. Sussex (Eastbourne) 10–12 August		15-2-64-1		18-7-47-1	8-3-12-1	18-4-31-0	15.2-4-34-2	26-5-58-4	1-0-6-0
		13-0-82-1		8-0-25-1	15.2-6-33-1	17-7-43-1	18-4-50-3	9-2-23-0	
v. Nottinghamshire (Trent Bridge) 13–16 August		19-3-51-2			21-6-62-3	14.4-4-26-3	5-1-24-0	25-5-55-2	
		3-0-8-0			2-0-6-0	1-0-1-0		5-0-9-0	
v. Worcestershire (Worcester) 20–23 August		13-3-35-2		13-7-22-0		22.5-11-26-3	14-8-20-3	13-3-34-1	2-0-7-0
		11-6-23-0		5-1-16-0		14.5-3-38-4		19-10-24-3	
v. Somerset (Bournemouth) 24–26 August		7-2-17-1		11-3-18-2	5-4-4-0	9-3-15-2	7-1-22-1	13.3-4-29-7	
		15-1-42-3		8-5-4-0	12-7-32-2			17-4-49-2	
v. Kent (Bournemouth) 27–30 August		8-2-38-1		15.5-6-34-1	7-3-15-2	4.3-1-28-1	6-1-23-2	17-6-33-3	
		14-3-74-4		8-0-38-0	17-0-89-1		4-2-22-1	20-4-51-3	
v. Somerset (Taunton) 31 August–2 September		22-5-64-3			8-3-17-0	24-2-77-0	21-11-34-1	7-0-31-0	
		10-3-22-0				15-10-10-4		12-1-46-6	
v. Glamorgan (Southampton) 10–13 September	-			18-8-30-2	6-2-13-0	24-7-60-2	4-0-18-0	18-7-44-1	1-0-5-0
				4-2-9-0		10-5-11-1		8-4-9-1	
	94-28-265-5 av. 52.40	546.1-123-1797-48 av. 37.43	369.5-115-966-27 av. 35.77	600.2-198-1346-63 av. 21.36	256.5-70-804-21 av. 38.28	440.3-147-1053-41 av. 25.68	274.2-74-774-27 av. 28.66	533.5-143-1327-80 av. 16.58	29-3-138-1 av. 138.00

† C.T. Radley absent hurt   ‡ P.A. Neale retired hurt

C.L. Smith	K. Stevenson	R.A. Smith	Byes	Leg byes	Wides	No balls	Total	Wickets
				Match Abandoned				
			9	9	1	15	346	8
			3	14	1		207	10
			1	9	3		237	10
				3	1	1	197	10
							0	0
			5	8	2	4	243	5
			3	1	2	2	170	10
4–4–39–1			4	8	11	9	299	6
–5–20–1			9	9	2	5	301	6
–2–18–0				4	1	5	122	4
		2–0–19–0		4	11	5	268	10
				1	4	5	230	3
	32–5–111–3		1	9		5	361	9†
	18–4–72–3		1	6	1	1	432	7
	1–0–9–0		1	3	1		72	3
	25–5–81–5			6	5	1	218	10
–1–20–1	18–6–55–2		1	14	3		276	7
	12–4–44–2			8	4	2	302	5
3–3–54–1	8–0–41–1		2	7	1		215	10
–1–17–1			7	17		3	305	7
			3	1	1	1	138	8
0.5–0–76–1			2	6	1	6	339	6
1–7–70–3				2			177	5
				12	1	1	202	10
			8	9	5	2	340	6
	18.5–6–67–2		4	16	1	4	233	10
–2–21–0	11–2–30–0		4	3		7	238	10
			4	16	6	4	319	10
–0–4–0				6		1	188	10
			1			1	153	10
			9	4	2		306	10
–0–4–0	23–2–95–2		5	4	3		244	10
	2–0–7–0		1	1	1		60	1
				7	2	2	263	10
				9	2	2	269	7
				16		5	239	10
						4	28	0
1–5–39–2			3	5		4	175	9‡
			16	4	3	2	146	10
				2		6	76	10
			5	1		3	173	10
				14	3	2	162	10
			9	4	3	1	319	10
2–3–79–1			1	12	1	5	321	6
–1–0–0			2			6	86	10
6.1–5–35–3	11–1–26–1		6	9	6		252	10
–3–20–0	8–4–18–0			9			76	2
55–42– 16–15 v. 34.40	187.5–39– 656–21 av. 31.23	2–0– 19–0 —						

ABOVE: *Man of the Match Vic Marks.* (*Adrian Murrell*)
BELOW: *Derek Underwood who took more wickets in all cricket than any other bowler in the 1983 season and yet did not bowl in the NatWest Final.* (*Adrian Murrell*)

Kent C.C.C. — First-Class Matches — Batting, 1983

Match key (each match shown as two innings columns, 1 / 2):

- Sur = v. Surrey (The Oval), 30 April–2 May
- CamU = v. Cambridge University (Cambridge), 4–6 May
- EssCh = v. Essex (Chelmsford), 11–13 May
- Hants = v. Hampshire (Canterbury), 28–31 May
- Midx = v. Middlesex (Dartford), 4–7 June
- SusH = v. Sussex (Hove), 8–10 June
- EssTW = v. Essex (Tunbridge Wells), 11–14 June
- SusTW = v. Sussex (Tunbridge Wells), 15–17 June
- Glos = v. Gloucestershire (Bristol), 18–21 June
- Notts = v. Nottinghamshire (Trent Bridge), 22–24 June
- Glam = v. Glamorgan (Canterbury), 2–5 July
- Lancs = v. Lancashire (Maidstone), 9–12 July
- Som = v. Somerset (Maidstone), 13–15 July

Batsman	Sur 1	Sur 2	CamU 1	CamU 2	EssCh 1	EssCh 2	Hants 1	Hants 2	Midx 1	Midx 2	SusH 1	SusH 2	EssTW 1	EssTW 2	SusTW 1	SusTW 2	Glos 1	Glos 2	Notts 1	Notts 2	Glam 1	Glam 2	Lancs 1	Lancs 2	Som 1	Som 2
N.R. Taylor	—	—	114		16		49		0	29	22	22	64	116*	7	46*	16	1	29	13			3	67*	8	3
R.A. Woolmer	—	—	21	4	63				118	0*											97		129	92	64	110
C.J. Tavare	—	—	23	44	94		70		31	5											68		0	50		
M.R. Benson	—	—	105		78		24		4	2	20	12	72	9	56		8	12	40	7	39				0	66*
C.S. Cowdrey	—	—	5	103*	31*		45		28	2			94				6	47	20	24	50		101*	17*	0	25
A.P.E. Knott	—	—	42*			11*	7*		92*	6	10	5*	12	11	24*		83	56	11	28*	22		26		9	2
G.W. Johnson	—	—	7*	4*			0*		25*	0	37*		25*		0		4	15*	10		13		14*		3	1*
R.M. Ellison	—	—								0	36*		0		3		40*	0	17		20*				18*	
G.R. Dilley	—	—																			13					
D.L. Underwood	—	—								15	2		16				0*	0	26*		1				5	13
K.B.S. Jarvis	—	—								7	0		9		0					9*	0				0	
L. Potter							29		33	14	31	13	19	19	17	11	22	50								
D.G. Aslett											55	111	47	39	25	3*	52	34	39	45*	46		56	0	3	28
E.A. Baptiste												102*	2	61*	12		0	32	34	13	27		6		37	9
C. Penn																					24					
S.G. Hinks											11	0														
S.N.V. Waterton																										
K. Masters																										
S. Marsh																										
Byes				1		5		1	1	1			2				1	4	4	1	5					12
Leg-byes			5	2		14		8	5	2	8	9	14	23	7	2	5	5	6	6	16		5	10	8	
Wides			1			1			2	2	2		4	1	1				1	5	1		4			9
No-balls			1			12		4	12	4	6	2	6	8	1	1	14	2			4		9		3	3
Total			324	157	0	321	0	243	350	87	226	277	287	289	263	63	252	272	260	137	422		349	236	150	280
Wickets			5	2	0	4	0	5	6	10	6	4	10	5	10	1	8	9	10	4	10		6	3	10	7
Result	D		D		W		D		L		W		D		W		D		W		D		D		W	
Points	2				19		4		8		20		7		23		4		23		7		7		20	

Catches:
47 – A.P.E. Knott (ct 39/st 8)   27 – C.S. Cowdrey   15 – M.R. Benson   10 – C.J. Tavare and E.A. Baptiste
28 – G.W. Johnson   18 – N.R. Taylor and D.G. Aslett   14 – R.M. Ellison   8 – G.R. Dilley

These questions were given greater relevance when Benson was well caught at slip in the first over of the innings. Johnson, to his credit, performed admirably in reverting to his old role as opener. He had been open to much criticism from Kent supporters during the year and there were many who found it hard to understand why he was holding a place in the side, but he countered Garner and Botham with a solidity that Kent now found welcome. He and Tavare added 60, but Somerset gaped in wonder as Richards twice and Garner failed to take straightforward catches at slip and in the gully.

Tavare had two lucky escapes and Garner threatened him with a silly mid-on, but his temperament is of the sternest and it was clear that here is a batsman of quality.

The run-rate was all that was needed at the time, but Botham introduced Marks from the nursery end and Richards from the pavilion end after a flurry of rain had brought an early tea. Johnson was beaten in the flight by Marks and was bowled, and then, in one decisive over, Marks removed both Tavare and Cowdrey.

Tavare had hit well and wisely, but now he made an ill-judged swipe at Marks and was caught at deep mid-wicket. Cowdrey, whose batting is the antithesis of his father's, charged at Marks and was well stumped on the leg side by the leaping Gard. 73 for 4, and, with Johnson having opened, little to come.

Much depended on Aslett, but he could have been stumped off Marks off a leaping delivery which beat Gard too and went for byes. Gard soon made amends with a brilliant leg-side stumping off Richards. It was wicket-keeping of very high quality and one hoped that England selectors were watching and realising how a specialist wicket-keeper can decide a game. East, Parks, Richards, Gard, these are the men who can win matches, not number seven batsmen who can scramble a few runs and field straight slip with gloves on.

Baptiste and Knott suggested hope, but Botham beat Baptiste and Knott, having hit one six, died in the deep. Now came a partnership which threatened sensation. In one over, Dilley took sixteen runs off Dredge and Ellison drove mightily and excitingly.

It could not last, however. Ellison was struck on the knee by Garner, patched up by the physiotherapist and batted on with a runner. He hit one defiant four, but, in obvious pain, was bowled. Dilley essayed one too many drives at Botham and had his stumps knocked back. The target had always been tantalisingly out of reach since Tavare and Cowdrey had gone in the same over.

Jarvis hit to Botham at mid-on and the crowds swarmed on. The old timers raced for the pavilion. Trevor Gard, who had done so much to swing the game in favour of Somerset, faced the nursery end and leapt in private exultation.

v. Yorkshire (Sheffield) 16-19 July		v. Warwickshire (Edgbaston) 27-29 July		v. Derbyshire (Chesterfield) 30 July-2 Aug		v. Worcestershire (Canterbury) 6-9 Aug		v. Surrey (Canterbury) 10-12 Aug		v. Glamorgan (Cardiff) 13-16 Aug		v. Warwickshire (Folkestone) 20-23 Aug				v. Hampshire (Bournemouth) 27-30 Aug		v. Leicestershire (Leicester) 31 Aug-2 Sept		v. Somerset (Taunton) 7-9 Sept		v. Northamptonshire (Canterbury) 10-13 Sept		Inns	NOs	Runs	HS	Av
28	—	51	1	12	1			6	16	24	155*	13	3	23	10*	29	15	111	9	104		18	21*	39	6	1275	155*	38.63
61	—	3	20	5	32	5	3	120	6							15	4	22	—			41	—	22	1	994	129	47.33
						93	13									25	62					81	0	16	—	700	94	43.75
11	—	102	152*	66	46	53	57			111	50	42	52	80	15*	26	38	6	0	8	—	44	2	37	3	1515	152*	44.55
113	—	17	23	2	42*	33	43*	2	28*	58*	15*	123	—			29	73			103*	—	53	—	34	10	1364	123	56.83
9*	—	92	—	30	—	21	1			—	—	27	80	19	—	2	64			38	—	8*	—	30	9	848	92*	40.38
		7	—	4	—	9	9	46*	1			79*	20*	23	—	6	32	1	0	9*	—	9		30	13	413	79*	24.29
		14	22	63	—	18*	0*	29	8*			1	10	12	—			10	22					21	7	343	63	24.50
												23	0*	1	—	29	15					18	—	7	1	99	29	16.50
		24	—	5*	—	1	—	1*	—			6	—	0*	—	0	14	10*	0			3	—	20	6	142	26*	10.14
		5*	—			0	—					—	—	0*	—	4*	4*	5	0*					13	5	43	9*	5.37
																								11		258	50	23.45
41	—	2	68	168	119	5	43	8	29	0	14	1	78	12	—	3	42	58	53	17	—	63	30*	36	3	1437	168	43.54
136*	—	5	2	63	14*	9	13	91	6	4*	—	38	12	3	—					24	—			26	5	755	136*	35.95
																								1		24	24	24.00
								8	16	87	41			16	—					43	21			10	3	253	87	25.30
								8	3															2		11	8	5.50
																		0	1	0	0			4		1	1	0.25
																				5	0			2		5	5	2.50

		2				8		8	6	1	4			2		3	2	6			9	4	6	8		5		†R.A. Woolmer absent hurt
10		16	6	6	3	9	10	16	2	6	4	1	2	9		14	4	9	2	1			1	2				
1		8	1	2		4	1	8				7	2	11	2	9	14	4		3	3	1			4		3	
14		16	4	3	4	8		7	2	11	2	9	14	6		2	1	4		4		10			1			

424		364	299	437	261	276	199	343	121	301	283	268	344	337	25	162	319	289	113	357		313	56					
5		10	6	9	4	10	7	8	7	4	3	10	8	10	0	10	10	10	9†	6		9	2					
D		D		D		D		L		W		D		W		L		L		L		D						
8		6		8		5		6		20		5		24		4		7		7		6						

6 – R.A. Woolmer and subs.   2 – L. Potter, K.B.S. Jarvis, S.G. Hinks and K. Masters
5 – D.L. Underwood   1 – C. Penn

Vic Marks was named Man of the Match, rightly, but there should be honourable mentions for Dilley, who bowled magnificently and batted heroically, for Ellison, for Slocombe, for Popplewell, for Richards, for Cowdrey with the ball and for Gard with the gloves on.

John Player League

4 September

at Derby

Derbyshire 143 for 9
Hampshire 135 (P.G. Newman 4 for 21)

Derbyshire (4 pts) won by 8 runs

at Leicester

Surrey 261 for 6 (A.R. Butcher 111, R.D.V. Knight 65)
Leicestershire 258 for 5 (D.I. Gower 78, J.J. Whitaker 65 not out, R.D.V. Knight 4 for 42)

Surrey (4 pts) won by 3 runs

at Cleethorpes

Middlesex 181 for 8
Nottinghamshire 186 for 6

Nottinghamshire (4 pts) won by 4 wickets

at Hove

Gloucestershire 115 for 9
Sussex 116 for 3

Sussex (4 pts) won by 7 wickets

at Worcester

Worcestershire 192 for 9
Somerset 137 (R.K. Illingworth 5 for 24)

Worcestershire (4 pts) won by 55 runs

Middlesex rested some of their leading players, Barlow batted number ten and they lost in the last over at Cleethorpes. Newman, after a season in the wilderness, returned to take four wickets as Derbyshire raised their hopes of prize money. Roger Knight, who had had a very lean season in limited-over cricket, gave a fine all-round performance at Leicester where the elder Butcher showed his young brother on the home side that he was still the senior player. Gower batted well and the very impressive Whitaker just failed to give Leicestershire victory in a thrilling finish. Sussex kept

Kent C.C.C. First-Class Matches — Bowling, 1983	G. R. Dilley	K. B. S. Jarvis	R. M. Ellison	R. A. Woolmer	D. L. Underwood	C. S. Cowdrey	G. W. Johnson	N. R. Taylor	K. Masters
v. Surrey (The Oval) 30 April–2 May	18–7–35–2	12–6–19–1	11–2–24–2	9–3–13–1	1–1–0–0	6–0–29–0			
v. Cambridge University (Cambridge) 4–6 May	13–6–21–3 5–1–7–0	11–2–25–1 4–0–9–0	13–3–31–2 5–3–5–0	7–3–13–3 3–0–9–0	9–3–15–1 8–6–5–0	6–0–21–0	9–3–19–0 6–3–16–0		
v. Essex (Chelmsford) 11–13 May	21.4–3–70 5	18–4–53–0	26–5–74–2	9–3–26–1	22–8–66–2		8–1–14–0		
v. Hampshire (Canterbury) 28–31 May	15.3–8–27–3 3–2–4–0	12–2–37–1 4–1–9–0	22–6–58–2 7–2–15–2		21–5–37–1 7–1–20–0	5–2–15–0 3–0–19–0	14–2–42–3 15–3–44–0	1–0–10–0	
v. Middlesex (Dartford) 4–7 June		17–10–32–3 6–3–9–0	14–3–69–1 4–3–1–0		38.1–15–80–4 25–13–44–6		30–11–93–2 25.3–6–82–0		
v. Sussex (Hove) 8–10 June		22–5–66–2 11–3–33–0	22–12–32–2 8–4–12–0		19–8–38–1 7–3–14–1		3–0–8–0 6–2–17–0	8–2–30–1	
v. Essex (Tunbridge Wells) 11–14 June		27.4–4–86–1 6–0–19–1	28–13–58–4 6–2–17–0		9–4–16–0		1–0–1–0		
v. Sussex (Tunbridge Wells) 15–17 June		25–7–54–2 18–7–36–1	24–11–38–2 19–6–35–4		12–7–24–2	9–1–18–0 5–3–4–0	1–1–0–0		
v. Gloucestershire (Bristol) 18–21 June		14–2–59–1 11–0 53–2	19–7–53–1 18.1–2–63–2		29.5–7–93–5 26–7–53–0	15–5–47–0 7–1–36–0	39–10–77–1		
v. Nottinghamshire (Trent Bridge) 22–24 June		7–0–44–0	5–1–10–0 8–3–18–1		38–12–88–7 32–8–73–6		24.3–6–62–2 24–3–53–3		
v. Glamorgan (Canterbury) 2–5 July	21.1–6–52–4 6–1–11–0		24–7–49–2 2–1–2–0		18–10–28–0 30–9–57–1	10–0–34–1 2–0–7–0	15–3–43–1 32–10–85–3		
v. Lancashire (Maidstone) 9–12 July		21–2–71–0 7–0–30–0	31.5–8–73–5 8–1–27–0		11–5–22–1 20.3–7–69–2	10–3–34–1	9–5–14–0 11–5–28–0		
v. Somerset (Maidstone) 13–15 July		13–1–37–1 5–1–9–0	18–7–36–1 6–2–11–1		26–11–35–2 22–7–54–3		28–9–56–3 17–2–67–5		
v. Yorkshire (Sheffield) 16–19 July	26–8–66–1 13.1–5–20–2		33–8–59–4 16–3–37–0	6–1–17–2 8–3–14–0	3–3–0–0 12–9–9–1	11–2–37–0 4–1–6–0	3–2–6–1		
v. Warwickshire (Edgbaston) 27–29 July		17–6–48–2 10–1–42–1	16–4–49–0 5–0–23–2		38–15–73–3 22–11–30–4	3–0–25–0	10–0–47–0 5.5–3–16–0		
v. Derbyshire (Chesterfield) 30 July–2 August		28–0–109–2 8–1–22–0	28–5–72–3 11.4–2–22–0	8–0–21–0	7–2–13–0 21–9–38–2		6–0–19–1 12–4–33–2	2–0–24–0	
v. Worcestershire (Canterbury) 6–9 August		20–2–55–0 2–0–6–0	11–1–30–0 7–2–15–0	3–2–4–0	44.4–16–103–7 22–6–55–7		27–6–73–1 16.3–2–37–3		
v. Surrey (Canterbury) 10–12 August		18.1–3–32–1 7–2–23–1	18–7–45–2 15–4–43–1	8–5–9–1	20–10–28–2 24.1–5–84–3	2–0–3–0	13–5–20–0 16–3–66–1		
v. Glamorgan (Cardiff) 13–16 August		13–4–48–0 10–0–45–0	22–6–59–0 17–4–58–3		14–4–33–0 7.1–6–2–2	4–0–8–0 22–3–80–3	31.5–8–101–3 15–9–18–2		
v. Warwickshire (Folkestone) 20–23 August	26–4–77–1 5–2–5–0		20–1–60–0		38–7–113–5 5–2–21–0	9.2–2–37–2	21–7–61–0 1–1–0–0		
v. Leicestershire (Folkestone) 24–26 August	18.5–3–53–3 21–7–41–3		16–3–65–0		18–12–18–1 29–11–55–7	11–2–36–2 7–2–24–0	1–0–3–0		
v. Hampshire (Bournemouth) 27–30 August	4–1–19–0	25–5–78–3 8–1–33–1		17–5–30–1	24–7–92–3 10–6–23–0	9–2–28–1	6.3–2–16–2 4–0–8–0		20–2–71–0 7–1–24–0
v. Leicestershire (Leicester) 31 August–2 September		12–0–49–1 1–1–0–0	14–3–43–0	8–4–14–1	40–15–101–5 17–6–33–2		19–4–48–1 13–2–31–0	1–0–3–0	6–1–26–2
v. Somerset (Taunton) 7–9 September	22.1–3–72–3	33–4–137–1			25–10–79–3	24–0–90–1 17–5–27–0	20–1–56–1	16–6–25–0	
v. Northamptonshire (Canterbury) 10–13 Sept.	6–0–36–0 5–0–13–1	15–3–52–0 2–0–10–0			31–12–60–2 33–17–50–2	19–0–68–1	36–9–96–3 35.3–13–76–7	7–1–16–0	
	250.3–67– 629–31 av. 20.29	500.5–93– 1579–30 av. 52.63	598.4–167– 1491–51 av. 29.23	86–29– 170–10 av. 17.00	936.3–358– 2044–106 av. 19.28	220.2–34– 733–12 av. 61.08	631.1–166– 1652–51 av. 32.39	35–9– 108–1 av. 108.00	33–4– 121–2 av. 60.50

a L. Potter 1–0–6–0   † B.C. Broad retired hurt   d C.J. Tavaré 3–0–3–0; M.R. Benson 1–0–4–0
b L. Potter 3–1–6–0   c L. Potter 2–1–2–0   e M.R. Benson 4–1–12–0

C. Penn	E.A. Baptiste	D.G. Aslett	Byes	Leg byes	Wides	No balls	Total	Wickets
				4		2	126	6
			3	8		5	140	10
				1		3	76	0
			1	13		3	320	10
			1	6		5	228	10
				3	1		125	2
			4	7		2	287	10
				5	2	5	154	6a
9-4-74-0	17.3-5-45-5			7	1	6	277	10
2-24-1	8-4-16-2	10-0-69-1	7	3			225	6
	28-5-104-5			9	2	9	285	10
	4-1-8-1			1		3	54	2b
	22-8-46-4			1	2	8	191	10
	18.2-7-39-5			6	1	11	132	10
	7-1-22-1			7		10	370	9ct
				8		17	230	4
2-18-1				3	1	12	238	10
			3			11	158	10
	16-2-43-1		2	3		11	265	10
	4-2-5-0	6-2-12-0	2	12	1	15	216	4d
	25-7-64-3		4	13	6	9	310	10
	10-3-38-4	1-0-8-0		3		1	204	6
	21.1-5-66-2	1-0-5-0	1	7	1	12	256	10
	5-2-9-0			6	1	16	173	10
	28.2-3-72-3			7		12	270	10
	16-8-21-2			2	2	4	121	6
	18-2-88-1		4	13	2	10	359	6
	9-4-31-0	1-0-8-0		6		6	162	8
	23-1-112-3		1	14		7	368	9
	6-0-30-0	7-2-66-1	4	8	4	4	255	7
	18-0-88-1			9	2	12	376	9
			7	11	10		141	10
	25-10-73-4			9	4	10	233	10
			5	7		7	235	6
	12-1-41-0	4-0-20-0		8	3	15	336	3
	13-2-33-0		1	5	1	4	247	10
	13-2-72-0		4	12		34	470	8
				3		2	31	0
	9.1-3-21-3			7	2	4	206	10
			8	9		12	152	10
		1-0-2-0	2	13	3	5	359	10
		6-1-28-1		1		8	125	2
			9	2		18	310	10
			8	3		6	96	2e
			6	11	1	10	462	10
					2		54	0
				4		5	337	6
5-8- 16-2 v. 58.00	376.3-88- 1187-50 av. 23.74	37-5- 218-3 av. 72.66						

ABOVE: *It was something of a lean season for Alan Butcher but he hit a hundred against Leicestershire at Leicester on 4 September, a match which resulted in a narrow win for Surrey.* (George Herringshaw)

BELOW: *Richard Illingworth whose fine bowling destroyed Somerset at New Road on 4 September and thwarted them in their attempt to win the John Player League.* (Ken Kelly)

Lancashire C.C.C. First-Class Matches — Batting, 1983

Match key (each match has two innings columns unless noted):
- Oxf = v. Oxford University (Oxford) 23–26 April
- Glam = v. Glamorgan (Old Trafford) 30 April–3 May
- Midd = v. Middlesex (Lord's) 4–6 May
- Der = v. Derbyshire (Chesterfield) 11–13 May
- Sur = v. Surrey (The Oval) 25–27 May
- Yor = v. Yorkshire (Old Trafford) 28–31 May
- WE = v. Warwickshire (Edgbaston) 4–7 June
- HB = v. Hampshire (Bournemouth) 8–10 June
- NO = v. Nottinghamshire (Old Trafford) 11–14 June
- WO = v. Warwickshire (Old Trafford) 15–17 June
- Sus = v. Sussex (Horsham) 18–21 June
- TB = v. Nottinghamshire (Trent Bridge) 25–28 June
- HL = v. Hampshire (Liverpool) 2–5 July

Batsman	Oxf	Glam 1	Glam 2	Midd 1	Midd 2	Der 1	Der 2	Sur 1	Sur 2	Yor 1	Yor 2	WE 1	WE 2	HB 1	HB 2	NO 1	NO 2	WO 1	WO 2	Sus 1	Sus 2	TB 1	TB 2	HL 1	HL 2
G. Fowler	16*	133	—	7	—			23	73*	156*	—	23	58									36	36	73	6
D. Lloyd	22*	0	—	9*	—																				
S.J. O'Shaughnessy	—	1	—	25	—			42	—	1*	—	68	23	18	28					20*	19			11	0
F.C. Hayes	—	12	—	6	—			2	10	116	—	—	6	0	13	23	—	6	85	149	28	52	12	66	13
D.P. Hughes	—	153	—	15	—			0	0	6	—	11	0	11	0	23	—	5	3	53	0	0	0	19	14
J. Abrahams	—	39	—	0	—			4	12*	5	16*	13	45	117*	4*	0	—	45	42	49	10	15	1	21	14
C. Maynard	—	3	—					4	—					—	36*	33	—	14	5	4	2	0	2	61*	5
P.J.W. Allott	—			16*	—			2*	—			0	—									4	2	5*	
S.T. Jefferies	—	45*	—	11	—							—	24	37*	—			8	—	7	4	—	5	28*	0
L.L. McFarlane	—																								
Nasir Zaidi	—													7*	—			0	0*	—	47*	0	1	3*	13*
J. Simmons		11	—					28	—			8*	9	41	—	3	—	38	6	—	35	9	0	4	35
I. Folley				0	4*			25	—			—	13*					4*	7						
M. Watkinson																		23*	—	15	4	—	0	8	3
C.H. Lloyd								23	18																
I. Cockbain								4	19	13	6*	31	33	2	31	52	—	23	0	21	20	8	0		
N.H. Fairbrother														94*	17	50	—	42	—	40	68	8	0	4	2*
N.V. Radford																								24	27
K.A. Hayes																									
J. Stanworth																									
M. Chadwick																									
Byes		4							1		1	1		9				4	4	3			4	7	3
Leg-byes	1	13		1				9	4	2	1	10	7	9	4	5		7	8	3	4	2	2	13	1
Wides		2							1	1				2	1	1					1				1
No-balls		13		4				6	4	2		3	5	5	5			8	13	2	1			3	1
Total	39	429		98				172	142	301	24	250	250	301	122	220	0	216	249	312	172	158	65	305	138
Wickets	0	8		7				10	4	4	0	4	10	6	4	8	0	10	10	6	10	10	10	7	8
Result	D	D		D		D		D		D		L		D		D		L		W		L		D	
Points	—	7		2		0		5		8		4		5		2		5		24		5		6	

Catches 29 – C. Maynard (ct 27/st 2)   14 – D.P. Hughes   11 – C.H. Lloyd and J. Abrahams   8 – D. Lloyd and N.H. Fairbrother
17 – J. Simmons   13 – F.C. Hayes   9 – Nasir Zaidi   5 – S.J. O'Shaughnessy

---

their faint hopes alive, but the match which drew all attention was at Worcester.

Put in to bat, Worcestershire reached 192 thanks to a solid start from Weston and Curtis and Patel, a ferocious 48 from King and sensible batting by d'Oliveira.

Denning and Roebuck began with a stand of 55, but both went quickly to Phil Newport who was playing in his first John Player League match. Richards and Popplewell threatened to move into the ascendancy, but the spinners, Illingworth and Patel, completely changed the game. Illingworth's left-arm extracted much turn from the wicket and he gave his best display in the competition in taking 5 for 24 in 7 overs. His bowling destroyed Somerset and left them two points behind Yorkshire with each side having one game to play.

ASDA Cricket Challenge

at Scarborough

4 September

Yorkshire 139 for 9
Lancashire 141 for 6

Lancashire won by 4 wickets

5 September

Hampshire 205 for 9 (C.L. Smith 50)
Essex 195 (C. Gladwin 100)

Hampshire won by 10 runs

Final

6 September

Hampshire 245 for 7 (M.C.J. Nicholas 82, T.E. Jesty 61)
Lancashire 245 for 5 (J. Abrahams 69 not out, J. Simmons 57 not out, S.J. O'Shaughnessy 51)

Lancashire won by losing fewer wickets

The competition saw Chris Gladwin hit his first century in senior cricket and Jack Simmons score 16 off the final over, including two 6's, to win the trophy for Lancashire. Lancashire took £5,000 in prize money and earned a Lancashire home for mentally handicapped children a £15,000 mini-bus. Simmons won Man of the Match and batsman of the competition.

	v. Kent (Maidstone) 9-12 July	v. Glamorgan (Swansea) 13-15 July	v. Worcestershire (Old Trafford) 16-19 July	v. Gloucestershire (Southport) 27-29 July	v. Somerset (Old Trafford) 30 July–2 August	v. Yorkshire (Leeds) 6-9 August	v. Worcestershire (Worcester) 10-12 August	v. Middlesex (Old Trafford) 13-16 August	v. Northamptonshire (Northampton) 20-23 August	v. Derbyshire (Blackpool) 24-26 August	v. Essex (Old Trafford) 31 Aug.–2 Sept.	v. Leicestershire (Old Trafford) 11 September	Inns	NOs	Runs	HS	Av
	46 23		79 —		63 —	29 75	11 78	20 59	107 27	35 14	4 5	85 100	26	3	1269	156*	55.17
		5 4				73 19	6 14		123 1*	9 41	13 46	3 105	15	3	507	123	42.25
				2 4		2 100*	12 0	31 0	44 17		2 19	11 —	28	3	685	105	27.40
	4 52	0 30	0 —		7 2	12 9*	10 0		— 3	19 127*	13 68	0 —	28	1	866	149	32.07
	23 75*				86 4 52	26 50	34 17	22 25	5* 39*	37 4		7 3*	28	2	522	153	20.07
	105 24	6 85	178 —		19 34* 16	49	13 0	28 15	— 0				39	7	1261	178	39.40
	2 2	6 55	1 —	17		26 —	0 13	7 15*		10 6	22 35	4 —	27	3	417	61*	17.37
	41 —		17			26 —	0 13	7 15*		10 6	16 75		18	4	225	41	16.07
											16 75		12	4	260	75*	32.50
	8* —	7* —	0* —	6* —	1* —	1* —	1* 0	16* 0	— 15	0* —	4 2		9	8	24	8*	24.00
				8 —	51	48 —		16* 0	— 15		4 2		16	6	215	51	21.50
	9 0	104 22	0 —	8 —	75	52 —	2 3	7 0		101* 1	5 6	57 —	31	2	679	104	23.41
		10 15*		12 —	12								9	4	102	25	20.40
	6 —		0 25*	29 —			3 19*	0 5	— 0	14 13	0 0	1* —	20	4	168	29	10.50
			76	86 15	6	8	84 0	4 39	36* 4	4 20		24 —	16	1	447	86	29.80
		14 22											15	1	291	52	20.78
	31 4*	4 40	0 —	73 54* 50			26 51	36 1		55 4		4 1*	26	5	759	94*	36.14
													2	—	51	27	25.50
	3 20	21 32	11 —	6 2	8								8	—	103	32	12.87
										14 8*	31* 4	29 4	6	2	90	31*	22.50
										1 1		1 1	2	—	2	1	1.00
	4		6	14	4 10	3		1	4 1		5	4 5	5 1 1	9				
	13 3	2 10	19		10 3	10	12 1	8 10	2 4	4 2	7 2	4 16	1				
	6	2 2	2					1	1		1	1 1	1				
	9 1	12 19	14		3 2	7	6 1	1 4	13 11	8 1	10 2	5 5	1				
	310 204	193 367	440	330 130	355	344 256	209 196	193 193	331 115	315 247	122 284	236 214					
	10 6	10 8	10	10 5	10	10 3	10 10	10 10	3 7	9 8	10 10	10 3					
	D	D	D	W	W	D	L	D	D	D	L	D					
	5	5	6	23	22	4	6	5	4	5	4	3					

4 – P.J.W. Allott, G. Fowler and I. Cockbain   2 – J. Stanworth and M. Watkinson
3 – I. Folley and subs   1 – L.L. McFarlane, K.A. Hayes, S.T. Jefferies and M. Chadwick

7, 8 and 9 September

at Derby

Derbyshire 137 (K.E. Cooper 5 for 32, M. Hendrick 4 for 20) and 202 for 3 dec (K.J. Barnett 63, G. Miller 63)
Nottinghamshire 53 (O. Mortensen 4 for 25) and 186 (R.T. Robinson 79, M.A. Holding 5 for 53)

Derbyshire won by 100 runs
Derbyshire 20 pts, Nottinghamshire 4 pts

at Lord's

Middlesex 330 for 8 dec (G.D. Barlow 99, A.J.T. Miller 74, C.T. Radley 54) and 143 for 1 dec (G.D. Barlow 89 not out)
Northamptonshire 202 for 5 dec (G. Cook 82) and 275 for 3 (W. Larkins 100, A.J. Lamb 79 not out)

Northamptonshire won by 7 wickets
Northamptonshire 21 pts, Middlesex 6 pts

at Taunton

Somerset 462 (N.A. Felton 173 not out, I.V.A. Richards 103, C.H. Dredge 50) and 54 for 0
Kent 357 for 6 dec (N.R. Taylor 104, C.S. Cowdrey 103 not out, V.J. Marks 5 for 134)

Match drawn
Kent 7 pts, Somerset 6 pts

at Hove

Leicestershire 175 and 363 for 3 dec (D.I. Gower 140, P.B. Clift 100 not out)
Sussex 285 (G.D. Mendis 84, Imran Khan 73, L.B. Taylor 5 for 80) and 62 for 3

Match drawn
Sussex 6 pts, Leicestershire 4 pts

at Edgbaston

Glamorgan 389 for 5 dec (S.P. Henderson 135 not out, D.A. Francis 89 not out, N. Gifford 4 for 109) and 24 for 0
Warwickshire 0 for 0 dec and 417 for 2 (A.I. Kallicharran 243 not out, T.A. Lloyd 123)

Warwickshire won by 8 wickets
Warwickshire 18 pts, Glamorgan 3 pts

Lancashire C.C.C.
First-Class Matches — Bowling, 1983

	P.J.W. Allott	S.T. Jefferies	L.L. McFarlane	S.J. O'Shaughnessy	D. Lloyd	D.P. Hughes	Nasir Zaidi	I. Folley	J. Simmons
v. Oxford University (Oxford) 23–26 April	23–11–24–0	21.2–14–15–5	12–6–16–0	9–4–14–3	11–7–11–1	7–1–12–0	21–7–39–1		
v. Glamorgan (Old Trafford) 30 April–3 May	15.1–3–28–4	14–5–23–3						1–0–4–0	
v. Middlesex (Lord's) 4–6 May	26–7–56–1	22–6–50–1		8.4–0–30–0	6–1–15–0	6–0–21–0		13–3–55–0	31–7–73–2
v. Derbyshire (Chesterfield) 11–13 May	9–5–16–0			1–1–0–0				6–4–8–1	4–2–9–0
v. Surrey (The Oval) 25–27 May	24–7–68–4 16–4–58–0			10–2–31–1 10–1–20–2		16–1–62–1		5–1–29–0 7–3–12–0	27.1–6–62–2 19–4–69–3
v. Yorkshire (Old Trafford) 28–31 May	20–7–50–2			19.5–3–73–4				21–2–37–2	10–3–21–1
v. Warwickshire (Edgbaston) 4–7 June	20–7–79–0 4–0–15–0	20–6–87–1 7–2–21–1		12–0–54–0 11–2–34–1				7–3–24–0 9–1–39–1	40–13–81–0 8–0–28–0
v. Hampshire (Bournemouth) 8–10 June		33–10–87–1 24–3–76–0		20–5–93–0 5–1–19–0			17–5–42–1 2–0–11–0	26–7–54–0 28–7–67–1	28–8–68–0 11.5–4–53–2
v. Nottinghamshire (Old Trafford) 11–14 June		15–6–28–2					10–8–6–1	11–5–23–0	11–1–37–0
v. Warwickshire (Old Trafford) 15–17 June		34–3–121–4 4–0–27–0					8–2–27–0	16–5–26–0 5–0–26–0	25.5–5–71–4 5.3–0–21–2
v. Sussex (Horsham) 18–21 June		23–8–56–0 7–1–34–0		19.4–4–46–2 9–1–35–2			12–3–39–1 8–2–27–3		7–2–11–0 12.2–3–47–5
v. Nottinghamshire (Trent Bridge) 25–28 June	14–3–36–2 38–11–87–1	13.5–2–46–8 15–3–49–3				8–2–24–1	10–1–34–1		19–7–28–0
v. Hampshire (Liverpool) 2–5 July	23–9–41–3 20–5–58–0			12–1–54–0 12–2–51–1			5–0–18–0 4–1–16–0		44–10–111–2 15–6–46–0
v. Kent (Maidstone) 9–12 July	24.2–2–74–0 11–3–28–0		17–2–67–1 13–1–64–0			4–0–14–0			26–2–78–3 15–2–81–1
v. Glamorgan (Swansea) 13–15 July			16–2–72–1 14–2–59–2		3–2–1–0 8–4–13–0			9–2–29–0 3–0–18–0	24–15–39–2 19.3–9–25–3
v. Worcestershire (Old Trafford) 16–19 July	11–4–28–2 9–3–31–1		8–5–10–1 8–1–26–1		40–12–94–3 24–8–51–0				24–5–64–2 31–4–80–1
v. Gloucestershire (Southport) 27–29 July			8–1–23–0 10–1–41–1	4–0–24–1 8–0–23–0		6–1–18–0 13–3–35–0	19.4–3–52–3 11–3–36–1	6–2–18–1 8–1–27–0	31–12–60–5 26.5–6–73–7
v. Somerset (Old Trafford) 30 July–2 August			14–3–53–3 11–2–25–0		2–0–5–0 18–6–22–5		13–3–29–2 12–5–34–0	8–3–23–1 2–0–3–0	25.1–8–54–4 38–23–41–5
v. Yorkshire (Leeds) 6–9 August	15–1–53–2 8–2–22–0		13–2–40–0 10.4–2–26–2	12–2–38–1 11–8–14–3	10–2–30–1 5–3–5–0		9–1–25–0 2–1–5–0		21–2–74–0 7–5–8–2
v. Worcestershire (Worcester) 10–12 August	18–4–51–3 14–2–43–1		7–0–45–0 11–1–35–1	3–1–13–0 6–2–21–2	11–3–22–2 7–2–11–0				23.5–8–55–5 15–4–30–0
v. Middlesex (Old Trafford) 13–16 August	24–8–45–5 4–0–18–0			4.1–1–13–1	5–2–3–1				8–3–9–0 6–4–2–0
v. Northants. (Northampton) 20–23 Aug.	17.1–5–60–1 11–2–23–1		15–2–65–0 13–2–41–2	10–0–45–0	21–4–64–0 28–4–53–4		9–2–30–0 10–1–28–0		
v. Derbyshire (Blackpool) 24–26 August	12–6–18–1 3–2–2–0		12–3–22–0 4–0–12–0	12–3–49–1					28–5–69–1 22–5–50–0
v. Essex (Old Trafford) 31 August–2 September	17–4–34–1 6–2–17–1	17–3–61–2 8–2–16–1		4–0–18–0 3–0–18–0			8.5–0–32–2		14–5–22–2 5–3–6–0
v. Leicestershire (Old Trafford) 10–13 Sept.	7–2–15–1					7.5–1–44–0			15–3–51–2
	463.4–131– 1178–38 av. 31.00	278.1–74– 797–32 av. 24.90	216.4–38– 742–15 av. 49.46	235.4–44– 830–25 av. 33.20	199–60– 400–17 av. 23.52	67.5–9– 230–2 av. 115.00	191.3–48– 530–16 av. 33.12	191–49– 522–7 av. 74.57	744–214– 1807–68 av. 26.57

a N.H. Fairbrother 1–0–1–0
b G. Fowler 2–0–7–0; N.H. Fairbrother 2–2–0–0

J. Abrahams	M. Watkinson	N.V. Radford	Byes	Leg byes	Wides	No balls	Total	Wickets
			10	4			145	10
				3	1	4	63	7
0–15–1			4	6	1	5	331	6
	5–1–12–1			2		4	51	2
–3–45–1				8			305	10
0–13–0			1	9	1		183	5
	14–2–42–1		2	3			228	10
–0–55–2			4	5		7	396	4
0–42–0			5	4	4	5	197	3
			6		1	6	357	3
			3		1	2	232	3
							0	0
	6–4–10–0		2	3			109	3
	26–1–71–2		3	6		3	328	10
	11–0–56–1			8			138	4
	25–12–51–6		4	9	2	12	230	10
	12–0–45–0		1	6		5	200	10
				3		1	86	10
	17.1–4–59–3			9		4	294	10
		22–2–79–0	3	15	2		323	6
–1–40–0		3–0–20–0	4	8		3	246	1
1–19–1	24–2–83–1			5		9	349	6
1–13–1	11–1–40–1			10			236	3
4–8–1	27.1–9–69–6			9	8	8	243	10
1–27–0	14–3–47–1		5	5	2	5	206	6
–0–37–0	16.1–4–41–2		1	4		1	280	10
–4–34–1	4–4–0–0		13	14	1	3	254	5a
			4	2			201	10
3–15–1				1		4	255	10
0–18–0				3			185	10
			24	5	1		155	10
–0–35–0			1	5		4	305	4
			4	4	1	1	90	7
	1–0–8–0		5				199	10
–0–12–0	15–4–37–1		8	5		5	207	5
	17–4–40–3		4	1		5	120	10
–1–1–0	5–1–12–0						33	0
9–1–67–0	17–3–32–1		2	8		8	381	2
2–5–39–0	3–0–15–0		8	5		1	213	7
6–5–83–3	10–3–31–0		6	12	1	3	294	6
–11–40–1			4	2		2	119	2b
	18–3–67–3			6		5	245	10
	7–1–26–1			6		2	91	4
	14–3–35–1					5	150	4
16–41–	319.3–69–	25–2–						
58–13	929–35	99–0						
av. 50.61	av. 26.54	—						

Allan Lamb. His magnificent 79 not out against Middlesex at Lord's, together with Larkins' century, made the champions hopes of retaining their title very slim. 9 September. (Ken Kelly)

at Worcester

Worcestershire 247 (D.N. Patel 111, G.E. Sainsbury 6 for 66) and 137 for 3 dec (M.S.A. McEvoy 51)
Gloucestershire 121 for 1 dec (A.W. Stovold 51 not out) and 155 (A.W. Stovold 66, R.K. Illingworth 5 for 26)

Worcestershire won by 108 runs
Worcestershire 18 pts, Gloucestershire 3 pts

at Scarborough

Surrey 178 and 176 for 5 (M.A. Lynch 76 not out)
Yorkshire 329 (K. Sharp 139, P.I. Pocock 5 for 94)

Match drawn
Yorkshire 8 pts, Surrey 5 pts

The season drew to its close amid a return of dampness and much tension with a sprinkle of farce.

Nigel Felton hit a maiden century at Taunton and went on to reach a massive 173 not out. There were also centuries from Viv Richards, Neil Taylor (why was he omitted from the side at Lord's?) and Chris Cowdrey who then brought in the element of farce as he bowled one over in 30 seconds when Kent used the time left to increase their over-rate and avoid being fined.

The pace bowling of Holding and Mortensen brought Derbyshire victory on a green wicket after Cooper and Hen-

Leicestershire C.C.C. — First-Class Matches — Batting, 1983

Each match cell shows the two innings scores (first innings / second innings); "—" = did not bat.

Player	v. Cambridge University (Cambridge) 23–26 April	v. Hampshire (Leicester) 30 April–2 May	v. Derbyshire (Leicester) 4–6 May	v. Nottinghamshire (Trent Bridge) 4–7 June	v. Yorkshire (Leicester) 8–10 June	v. Derbyshire (Derby) 11–14 June	v. Surrey (The Oval) 11–13 May	v. Essex (Leicester) 25–27 May	v. Northamptonshire (Northampton) 28–31 May	v. Gloucestershire (Leicester) 15–17 June	v. Surrey (Leicester) 22–24 June	v. Glamorgan (Hinckley) 25–28 June	v. Yorkshire (Harrogate) 2–5 July
J.C. Balderstone	17	— —	69 31*	— —	82 97*	51 10	1 108	8 50	4 —	0 2	32 18	38 20	30 44
R.A. Cobb	12	— —	1 14	— —	14 —	7 28	0 10	22 2					
D.I. Gower	124	— —	81 5*	— —	74 12	20 2	1 20					26 108*	4 1
B.F. Davison	13	— —	84* —	— —	82* 2	37 39*	28 0	3 34*	20 —	17 3	60 10	101 91	81 1
N.E. Briers	24	— —	45* —	— —	38* 55	37 —	7 60	7 63	22 —	68 9	27 36*	11 —	97 55*
R.W. Tolchard	61				— 10	20 —	0 18	3 5	30 —	17 43	80* 0	7 —	3 27
J.F. Steele	37*				— 2*	0 —	0 10	50 0	38* —	5* 0	— 8*	18 —	15* —
P.B. Clift	14*						25 31	48 10	31 —	20 5	63 20	11 —	22 —
N.G.B. Cook						11 —	1* 6	8* —	32 —	1 12	— —	5 —	7* —
G.J. Parsons				— 1		31 28*	15 7*	5 11*		1 0			
J.P. Agnew						0 —							
A.M.E. Roberts				— —	— 15								
L.B. Taylor							1* —	19 —	4	47 —		6 —	
T.J. Boon								3 2	0 —	4 1			
I.P. Butcher									1	103 76*	35 16	17 38	66 44
G. Ferris										0* —	— 0*	1* —	
J.J. Whitaker											22* 17		
J.P. Addison													
Byes	1		10		2 4		2	4 4	2	2		20 4	2 8
Leg-byes	3		4 2		4 14	2 4	8	11 10	11	7 4	4 1	9 6	7 9
Wides	2				1 1		2		1	1	1		3 2
No-Balls	2		8 2		3 1	2	2 3	1 2	12	3 3	10 8	1 3	9 11
Total	310		302 54		300 214	219 111	101 283	177 193	251	246 161	349 139	253 266	352 194
Wickets	6		3 1		3 6	10 3	10 9	10 7	9	9 9	5 6	10 3	10 5
Result	D	D	D	D	W	D	D	D	W	D	D	W	W
Points	—	2	7	1	24	3	4	5	23	4	8	23	23

Catches 53 – R.W. Tolchard (ct 44/st 9) 17 – B.F. Davison and I.P. Butcher 15 – N.E. Briers
30 – J.F. Steele 16 – J.C. Balderstone 10 – D.I. Gower and P.B. Clift

Norman Gifford who played so big a part in Warwickshire's resurgence during the season. (l to r) Hopkins caught by Kallicharran; Ontong bowled; Alan Lewis Jones bowled. Gifford was to take a hundred wickets in the season for only the fourth time in his 23-year career. (Ken Kelly)

	v. Somerset (Leicester) 9–12 July	v. Worcestershire (Hereford) 13–15 July	v. Middlesex (Lord's) 16–19 July	v. Sussex (Leicester) 30 July–2 Aug.	v. Nottinghamshire (Leicester) 6–9 August	v. Essex (Chelmsford) 10–12 August	v. Warwickshire (Edgbaston) 13–16 August	v. New Zealanders (Leicester) 20–22 August	v. Kent (Folkestone) 24–26 August	v. Northamptonshire (Leicester) 27–30 August	v. Kent (Leicester) 31 Aug–2 Sept.	v. Sussex (Hove) 7–9 September	v. Lancashire (Old Trafford) 10–13 September	Inns	NOs	Runs	HS	Av
	52 25	100* 63		82 —	24 20	25 —	3 64	0 18	22 16	5 24*	112 29	31 18	33 —	41	4	1478	112	39.94
														10	—	110	28	11.00
	41 73				0 0			6 17			4 30*	4 140	56* —	24	4	849	140	42.45
	45 26	12 21	20 12	85 —	10 4	106 —	5 66	123* 16	4 0	67 18	16 —	17 36*	2 —	41	6	1417	123*	40.48
	11 11	15 30	7 2	20 —	6 45	58 —	20 201*	57 2	8 23	43 22	5 —	0 42*		38	6	1289	201*	40.28
	0 71	24 25	8 41*	20* —	46 34*	20 —	22 —	17* 26	8 1	2 1*	61 2*	22 —		35	7	775	80*	27.67
	2 12*	0 —	5 0			13 —	9 —	— 6	26 14*	45 —	0 —	12* —		26	9	327	50	19.23
	11* 15	20 34*	44* 32	34 —	49 8	2 —	11 —	12 22	70* 18	1 16	1 —	17 100*	26* —	33	7	843	100*	32.42
	1 3	11 —	4 5		12* 1	14 —		— 0			12* —	4 —		20	5	150	32	10.00
			— —		56 9		14 —				24 —			15	3	207	56	17.25
								6 —		— 26	5 13			5	—	50	26	10.00
														3	—	22	15	7.33
	3 4							3* —	— 37*		29* —	18 —	6 —	18	6	250	47	20.83
	0* 22	1 —	21 0		4 10*	22								7	—	18	5	2.57
			5 3															
	1 5	3 0	16 16	59 —	9 139	1 —	29 13		29 24	107 2	42 18	43 17	4 —	30	1	973	139	33.55
		1 —	6 0		0 —	10* —			5 0	4 —		11 —		12	4	38	11	4.75
		6 40*	4 24	33* —		0 —	22 56*		15 10	20 2	10 —		24 —	16	4	305	56*	25.41
									51 16					2	—	67	51	33.50

	v. Somerset	v. Worcestershire	v. Middlesex	v. Sussex	v. Notts	v. Essex	v. Warwickshire	v. New Zealanders	v. Kent (F)	v. Northants	v. Kent (L)	v. Sussex (H)	v. Lancashire		
	2 1		12	6	2	1 2	1	1 2	9	8	7	9 8	4		† P.B. Clift retired hurt
	6 2	4 13	3	8	6 11	17	2 18	4 6	7 9	16 12	2 3	5 4	5 4		J.P. Agnew replaced N.G.B. Cook
			3		2 5	2		7							v. Essex, 10–12 August, and bowled
	5 7	1	11 8	10	1 4	12	3 18	2 6	4 12	22 3	18 6	3	5		in the match.

	v. Somerset	v. Worcestershire	v. Middlesex	v. Sussex	v. Notts	v. Essex	v. Warwickshire	v. New Zealanders	v. Kent (F)	v. Northants	v. Kent (L)	v. Sussex (H)	v. Lancashire
	180 277	198 238	160 143	356	226 292	301	150 438	281 198	206 152	399 100	310 96	175 363	150
	9† 10	10 5	10 10	5	10 8	10	10 3	5 10	10 10	10 5	10 2	10 3	4
	L	W	L	W	W	D	D	L	L	W	W	D	D
	4	21	4	24	22	7	5	—	6	24	24	4	5

8 – L.B. Taylor   5 – R.A. Cobb and G.J. Parsons   3 – subs   1 – G. Ferris
7 – N.G.B. Cook   4 – J.J. Whitaker   2 – J.P. Agnew

Dipak Patel. 111 in Worcestershire's victory over Gloucestershire, 7-9 September, and a magnificent last month of the season with the bat. (Ken Kelly)

drick had bundled them out for 137 on the first day. Most encouraging for Derbyshire was Newman's return to the county side with 3 for 0 in the first innings.

Leicestershire's hopes of gaining third place were shattered on the opening day at Hove, but Gower and Clift, with his first century of a splendid season, restored pride in the second innings.

Yorkshire were thwarted both by the weather and by Surrey's stubborn batting after Kevin Sharp had hit fifteen fours in another fine century which emphasised his growing confidence. Yorkshire's failure to beat Surrey left them with only one win in the Schweppes County Championship and at the foot of the table.

Worcestershire moved off the bottom with a good win over Gloucestershire. Patel's late season splendour ripened further with 111 in three hours which took him past 1500 runs in a season for the first time. He has been in the Worcestershire side for seven years, but he is still only 25 and remains an all-rounder of great promise. Gloucestershire had the compensation of some excellent bowling by Gary Sainsbury who has prospered more and more since his move from Essex and could be well satisfied with his first season in the West. The ultimate hero, however, was Richard Illingworth who, after the visitors had been asked to make 264 in 186 minutes, had a career best 5 for 26 as Gloucestershire slum-

Leicestershire C.C.C. First-Class Matches — Bowling, 1983

	J.P. Agnew	G.J. Parsons	P.B. Clift	N.G.B. Cook	J.F. Steele	A.M.E. Roberts	L.B. Taylor	G. Ferris	J.C. Balderstone
v. Cambridge University (Cambridge) 23–26 April	19-4-61-0 8-1-39-1	20-6-57-3 8-2-34-0	13-3-36-3 10-5-20-5	16-10-16-1 9-4-11-0	14-6-18-0				
v. Hampshire (Leicester) 30 April–2 May	19-5-53-1	23-6-71-2	15-5-43-1	26-12-36-1	11.3-2-38-0				
v. Derbyshire (Leicester) 4–6 May	23-5-90-2	21-5-46-1	14-2-51-1	21-7-39-3	21-11-29-1				
v. Surrey (The Oval) 11–13 May	9-1-37-0	21-5-63-2		9-2-30-0		12-3-31-2			
v. Essex (Leicester) 25–27 May	18-5-61-3 19-4-75-2	13-1-54-0 18-9-43-2		28.2-12-53-4 32-14-57-3	20-7-38-0 3.2-1-2-1	22-4-63-3 16-3-37-2			
v. Northamptonshire (Northampton) 28–31 May	3-0-21-1 5-0-42-0	5-1-22-1 4-1-9-1		6-2-14-0 27-6-65-4	21-3-60-2		8-3-14-1 13-1-44-2		
v. Nottinghamshire (Trent Bridge) 4–7 June		20-6-58-1	15-4-37-1	21-9-52-3 9-5-7-3	14.1-2-35-3 7-5-3-4		13-5-33-0 3-0-16-1		
v. Yorkshire (Leicester) 8–10 June		9-6-14-1 9-4-25-0	16-4-47-2 12-8-15-1	31-13-63-3 50-16-100-3	17-7-46-2 32-8-85-1		17.2-6-25-2 14-5-45-1		
v. Derbyshire (Derby) 11–14 June			12-4-9-3 21-5-58-4	20-7-39-1	8-1-18-1		9-5-22-2	17.5-8-29-5 13.5-3-44-3	
v. Gloucestershire (Leicester) 15–17 June		15-1-64-1 8-1-28-2	18.5-4-38-2	44-11-117-2 11-2-43-0	34-11-61-2 5.1-0-31-1			12-0-73-0 6-0-36-0	10-3-26-1
v. Surrey (Leicester) 22–24 June			21-6-34-3	21.1-9-40-3			21-5-67-1 5-2-9-1	î4-3-42-2 4-1-9-1	6-2-11-1
v. Glamorgan (Hinckley) 25–28 June			3-2-1-1 20-6-40-2	19-8-40-3	4.5-2-5-1		20.5-5-47-2 17-3-66-1	21-5-42-7 26-8-62-3	
v. Yorkshire (Harrogate) 2–5 July			21-2-52-3 18-4-84-4	33-18-35-1 17-10-29-0	8-3-28-1 6-3-3-0		21.1-8-59-3 6-1-16-0	19-6-61-1 16.4-2-63-4	
v. Somerset (Leicester) 9–12 July			13-2-45-2	42-6-143-2	20.5-3-90-2	28-3-111-2	34-5-115-2		
v. Worcestershire (Hereford) 13–15 July			18-3-41-3 11-3-36-1	15.2-7-18-1 27-13-43-1	14-5-16-1 25-11-48-2		27-10-53-2 12-6-13-2	21-6-86-3 17.5-3-50-3	1-1-0-0
v. Middlesex (Lord's) 16–19 July			20-5-50-3 9-1-38-0	33-8-65-2 8-3-18-0	25-8-71-1 5-1-21-1		15-2-48-2 11-1-39-2	12-0-41-2 15-3-57-1	
v. Sussex (Leicester) 30 July–2 Aug.		5-1-13-2 6-1-22-0	5.4-1-9-2 14-0-59-4	4-2-9-1		13-4-26-5 10.2-2-26-2	13-1-60-1 11-5-14-3		
v. Nottinghamshire (Leicester) 6–9 August		10-2-29-1	19-5-40-3 16-5-69-2	21-8-49-0			24.1-9-29-4 22.2-8-73-7	17-2-69-2 13-3-40-1	
v. Essex (Chelmsford) 10–12 August	15-6-34-3 16-3-60-1		10-6-14-1 35-15-68-1		36-12-83-1		8-3-20-0 25-8-50-2	12.5-3-43-6 21-2-83-1	21-11-26-2
v. Warwickshire (Edgbaston) 13–16 August	12-2-44-1 6-1-31-1	20-9-51-5 7-1-25-1	24-9-59-1 11-2-48-0		8-2-14-0 12-4-41-0		21.5-3-62-3 12-3-35-3		
v. New Zealanders (Leicester) 20–22 August	28-2-83-3 11-1-35-0		18.1-7-35-4 5-0-20-0	5-2-13-0 17-5-55-1	14-3-42-0 16-4-53-1		20-8-43-0		10-4-28-1 7-0-31-0
v. Kent (Folkestone) 24–26 August	17-1-73-2	21-4-67-3	20-0-72-1 5-1-7-0		18.5-7-66-3			17-5-34-1	
v. Northamptonshire (Leicester) 27–30 August		2-0-9-0 4-1-19-0	24-9-51-3 18-3-48-2		13-3-34-2 22-10-43-0		19-4-60-2 27-10-56-3	15-5-44-3 24-4-89-3	
v. Kent (Leicester) 31 Aug.–2 Sept.			17-6-48-3 15-4-42-4	39-12-94-4 16-4-45-1	24-5-73-1 7.3-3-12-3		11.3-7-17-2 3-2-6-1		9-1-39-0
v. Sussex (Hove) 7–9 September			29-10-54-2 2-1-1-0	27-6-53-1 10-2-19-1	10-2-25-1 1-1-0-0		28.2-5-80-5 11-2-27-2	14-1-64-1 2-0-15-0	
v. Lancashire (Old Trafford) 10–13 Sept.			31-5-73-5	28-10-74-3	16-3-35-1 5-2-13-0		4-0-14-1 1.2-0-1-1	8-1-29-0	4-0-10-2
	228-41- 839-21 av. 39.95	269-73- 823-29 av. 28.37	619.4-167- 1592-83 av. 19.18	742.5-265- 1584-56 av. 28.28	520.1-161- 1280-40 av. 32.00	101.2-19- 294-16 av. 18.37	529.5-151- 1381-69 av. 20.01	360-74- 1205-53 av. 22.73	68-22- 171-7 av. 24.42

† I.S. Anderson absent ill a B.F. Davison 4.4-0-18-0 b D.I. Gower 9-0-102-0 ‡ R. Illingworth absent ill * R.A. Woolmer absent hurt

N. E. Briers	J.J. Whitaker	I.P. Butcher	Byes	Leg byes	Wides	No balls	Total	Wickets
				4			192	7
						1	105	6
				11			252	5
				6	1	3	265	8
				6	1	2	170	4
				7	1	6	283	10
			4	7		5	230	10
				1		2	74	3
			4	1		2	227	9
			6	5			226	10
			4		1	1	32	8
			1	5	1		202	10
			8	1	1	1	281	6
			5	7	3	4	79	10
			1		2	6	168	9†
				10		3	366	7
			4	10			178	4
			5	3	1	6	209	10
			4				22	2
			6	6		7	109	10
			7	7		3	230	10
			1	11		4	251	9‡
			1	4	2	4	206	9
			1	13	3	7	528	10
				9	1	4	228	10
-1-0-0			5	5	2	3	205	10
			5	8	3	1	292	10
			7	6	1	4	191	4
			5	4		3	120	10
				1		2	133	10
			10	4	18	13	212	10
			8	6	1	10	256	10
				7	1	10	129	10
-1-0-0	2-1-1-0	2-0-2-1		6	1	14	394	10
			2	3	1	13	249	10
				2	1	11	194	6
			4	5	2	10	265	8
5-0-9-0				12		1	216	2
			6	9	4	6	337	10
							25	0a
			4	4	6	7	219	10
				4	1	16	279	10
			4	9	1	4	289	10
			6	2			113	9*
			1	3	1	4	285	10
							62	3
			9	1		1	236	10
	8-1-87-0					1	214	3b
5-2-	10-2-	2-0-						
-0	88-0	2-1						
-	—	av. 2.00						

ped from 109 for 2 to 155 all out.

There was stunning stuff at Edgbaston. Steve Henderson scored his maiden championship century on the first day, reaching his hundred in 143 minutes. He and Arthur Francis added 210 for the sixth wicket. There was no play on the second day and Warwickshire forfeited their first innings after Selvey's declaration. Alan Lewis Jones hit six boundaries off the one over bowled by Andy Lloyd and Selvey asked Warwickshire to make 414 in 5 hours, 45 minutes. Smith was out quickly to Winston Davis who then withdrew from the attack unwell. Kallicharran and Andy Lloyd then added 308 in 71 overs. Lloyd hit a six and eighteen fours, and Kallicharran went on to reach a career best and bring Warwickshire to victory with 18.3 overs to spare. Kallicharran hit five sixes and thirty-five fours in a remarkable innings which brought the most amazing win of the season, runs coming at 4.28 an over.

The main event, however, was at Lord's where Middlesex needed victory in order to overtake Essex at the top of the table. They could not have asked for a better start. At lunch on the first day, aided by some indifferent bowling and poor fielding, Barlow and Miller had scored 145. Miller's form was a revelation. He must be the best cutter of a ball to have entered cricket for a decade and he responded well to Barlow's positive leadership. Barlow, twice dropped off relatively easy chances, hit firmly and ran magnificently. He is a splendid cricketer and Middlesex owe him much for their

The Edgbaston score-board records the famous victory. (Ken Kelly)

Middlesex C.C.C. — First-Class Matches — Batting, 1983

	v. Essex (Lord's) 30 April–3 May	v. Lancashire (Lord's) 4–6 May	v. Glamorgan (Lord's) 25–27 May	v. Sussex (Lord's) 28–31 May	v. Kent (Dartford) 4–7 June	v. Derbyshire (Uxbridge) 8–10 June	v. Surrey (The Oval) 11–14 June	v. Hampshire (Uxbridge) 15–17 June	v. Worcestershire (Worcester) 18–21 June	v. Cambridge University (Cambridge) 22–24 June	v. Derbyshire (Chesterfield) 25–28 June	v. Warwickshire (Edgbaston) 2–5 July	v. New Zealanders (Lord's) 9–11 July
G.D. Barlow	— —	128 —	30 —	29 38	41 53	7 14	9 54*	105	2* 58	26	21 18*		
W.N. Slack	— —	56 —	140 —	11 3	2 1	69 39*	107 37*	27	50 13	138*	23 7		22
C.T. Radley	— —	33 —	59 —	10 4	19 20	46 17*	16 —		2 32*	76	32 9*	0 10	119
M.W. Gatting	— —	64* —	94 —	118 0	48 41						49 11*	15 10	216
R.O. Butcher	— —	0 —	26* —	52 7	110 13	179 —	81 —	37	1 35	6	10 —	6 1	5*
J.E. Emburey	— —	29 —		11 35*	40 1	2 —	42 —	0	19 31		0 —	23 0	10*
P.R. Downton	— —	4* —		4 23*	5 4*	18 —	27* —	16	87 —		1 —	8 5*	
P.H. Edmonds	— —				1 —	4* —	12 —	11	65 7*		32	0 0	
N.F. Williams	— —			6 —	1 —	11* —	14 —	39	63 —		50*	0 0	
N.G. Cowans	— —				0* —						10 —	3* 1	
W.W. Daniel	— —											1 7	
K.P. Tomlins	— —	1 —		30* 2	7 9*	19 —	38 —	77	9 27	55*		6 13	9
K.D. James						29 —	0 —	33*	6 —				
S.P. Hughes						— —	0* —	1	0* —	2			
R.G.P. Ellis												0 13	
J.D. Carr													
J.M. Brearley													
J.F. Sykes													
A.J.T. Miller													
Byes		4	4		4	8 2	11	1	4 4	4		4	
Leg-byes		6	15	4 1	7 5	17 1	13 1	9	2 9	4	5 3	9 7	2
Wides		1		1	2	2	1		1	2	1	4	
No-balls		5	8		2 5	8 6	2 4	5	3 5	2	5	3 3	3
Total		331	376	275 114	287 154	419 79	372 97	361	314 221	309	241 48	78 74	386
Wickets		6	4	8 6	10 6	8 1	9 0	9†	9 5	3	10 1	10 10	4
Result	D	D	W	D	W	W	W	W	W	W	W	L	D
Points	0	6	24	3	21	24	24	24	24	—	22	4	—

Catches 59 – P.R. Downton (ct 54/st 5)   23 – J.E. Emburey   17 – W.N. Slack
37 – R.O. Butcher   22 – G.D. Barlow, K.P. Tomlins and C.T. Radley   15 – M.W. Gatting

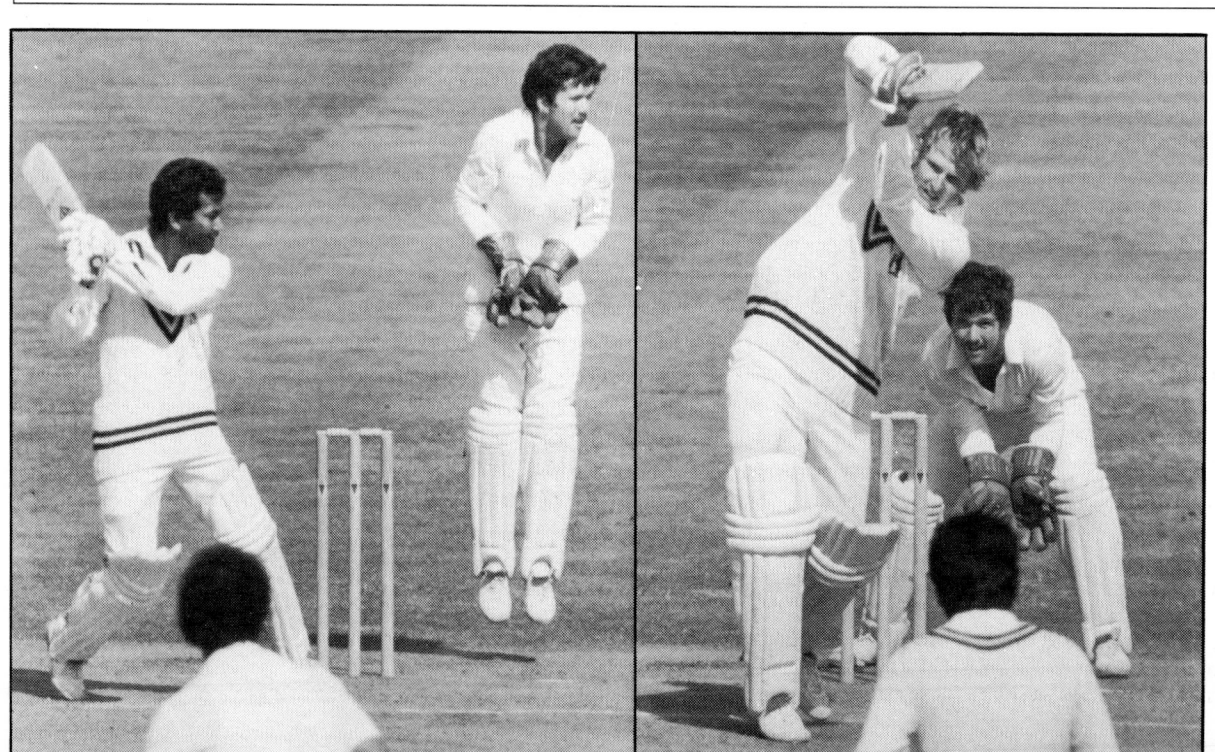

v. Gloucestershire (Bristol) 13-15 July	v. Leicestershire (Lord's) 16-19 July	v. Warwickshire (Lord's) 30 July-2 August	v. Essex (Chelmsford) 6-9 August	v. Northamptonshire (Northampton) 10-12 August	v. Lancashire (Old Trafford) 13-16 August	v. Somerset (Lord's) 20-23 August	v. Surrey (Lord's) 24-26 August	v. Sussex (Hove) 27-30 August	v. Yorkshire (Leeds) 31 Aug.-2 Sept.	v. Northamptonshire (Lord's) 7-9 September	v. Nottinghamshire (Trent Bridge) 10-13 September	Inns	NOs	Runs	HS	Av
90 —	10 7	83 6	44* 132	4 11	50 16*	18 8	113 2	0 38	18 58	99 89*	1 15*	39	7	1545	132	48.28
8 —	52 55	81 14	0 24	5 28	5 17*							28	4	1034	140	43.08
14 —	2 2	4 31*	7 67	29 24	0 —	11 20	27 45	24 37	23 12*	54 5*	1 —	38	6	943	119	29.46
93 —	54 2	116 20*	12 160		105 0				100* 7*	25 —	13 —	24	5	1373	216	72.26
11 —	62 15*											19	3	657	179	41.06
13 —	47 73*	61 —	1 133	4 0	4 —	63 7	11 1	12 6	44* —	19 —	2 38*	33	5	782	133	27.92
58 —	25 19*	6 —	0 67	31 61	8 —	1 0	1 3	5 0	— —	2 —	19* 0	30	7	508	87	22.08
		0 6*				0 0	— —	1 —	— —	6 —	0 —	16	3	145	65	11.15
42 —	6 —	3* —	10 1*	28 23	20 —	4 0	9 1*	4 5*	— —	35* —	32 —	25	7	407	63	22.61
		0 —				6 5*					9 —	8	3	34	10	6.80
4 —	4 —	0 —	2 —	11 8	0* —	17* 9	18 —	— —	— —	7 —	31 —	13	2	88	18	8.00
		0 —		49 5	0 —		4 38	4 45	132* 54*	0 —	6 —	27	5	670	132*	30.45
				34 0			20* —	19 —				8	2	141	34	23.50
4 —	1 —	— —			4* 0*		1* —			0* —		10	6	13	4*	3.25
			0 5	14 34	2 —		27 11	0 1				11	—	107	34	9.72
9* —	12* —	1* —										3	3	22	12*	—
					17 —							1	—	17	17	17.00
					4 —							1	—	4	4	4.00
						6 3	43 59	86 39	5 36	74 44	70 —	11	—	465	86	42.27
8	5 7	5	1 10	1 3	4		5 7		5	4	1 1					
13	8 6	20 6	12	6 4	1	4 3	9 5	12 6	6 7	7 3	8					
1	3 1	1 1	6	1			1		1 1	4 1	1					
6	1 4	4 3	6 11	3 8	5	3	8 2	6 3	5 1	2	8					
374	292 191	385 81	83 634	223 210	120 33	242 93	295 181	302 195	206 125	330 143	201 54					
10	10 4	8 2	10 7	10 10	10 0	10 10	9 7	9 6	4 2	8 1	10 1					
W	W	W	D	L	D	L	W	D	D	L	D					
24	23	24	4	5	4	6	23	5	4	6	4					

The match v. M.C.C. (Lord's), 27-29 April, was abandoned without a ball being bowled.

The match v. Yorkshire (Lord's) 11-13 May, was abandoned without a ball being bowled.

† C. T. Radley absent hurt

14 – P.H. Edmonds   3 – W.W. Daniels and subs.   1 – K.D. James
6 – N.F. Williams   2 – N.G. Cowans, S.P. Hughes and R.G.P. Ellis

LEFT: *A memorable victory. (l to r) Andy Lloyd 123; Alvin Kallicharran a career best 243 not out. They shared a second wicket stand of 308. Davies is the wicket-keeper. (Ken Kelly)*

success in 1983. Sadly, after lunch, Miller had completely lost touch and Barlow was taken at slip by Larkins off Mallender when one short of his century. Gatting could not find his touch and although Radley looked good, the middle order stumbled against Williams and Steele so that Middlesex just reached their fourth point in the hundredth over whereas earlier they had looked set for a score of over 400. Larkins fell before the close and the second day saw Cook play a fine innings before rain halted play.

Cook had to jettison all thoughts of the battle between Essex and Middlesex and treat the match as he would have done normally in the interests of Northants. He declared at the overnight score. Barlow and Miller exploded again with a stand of 118 and Gatting declared in order to leave himself time to bowl out the visitors, but his bowlers erred. The wicket seemed easier now than on the first day as Cook and Larkins plundered 101 for the first wicket. Larkins reached a magnificent hundred in 143 minutes, and then Allan Lamb and Williams took over. Lamb hit Emburey for six over long-on and next over hit Edmonds for six, four and six to win the match. The two spinners who had done so much to lift Middlesex to the top of the table had been mastered and the players left the field in steady rain and Middlesex thirteen points behind Essex with one match remaining.

John Player League

11 September

at Chelmsford

Essex v. Yorkshire

Match abandoned
Essex 2 pts, Yorkshire 2 pts

at Southampton

Glamorgan 158 for 9
Hampshire 161 for 9

Hampshire (4 pts) won by 1 wicket

at Canterbury

Kent v. Northamptonshire

Match abandoned
Kent 2 pts, Northamptonshire 2 pts

Middlesex C.C.C. First-Class Matches — Bowling, 1983	W.W. Daniel	N.G. Cowans	N.F Williams	J.E. Emburey	P.H. Edmonds	M.W. Gatting	W.N. Slack	K.P. Tomlins	R.O. Butcher
v. Essex (Lord's) 30 April–3 May	6–0–31–1	8–2–16–0	12–0–56–0	11–2–23–1	3–0–23–0				
v. Lancashire (Lord's) 4–6 May	5–1–7–0	10–2–26–2	15–4–47–4	4–2–6–0		5–1–7–0	1–1–0–0		
v. Glamorgan (Lord's) 25–27 May	16–6–22–3 13–3–27–3	12–3–40–1 13–3–22–2	18–5–45–3 8–1–31–0	18.3–10–22–3 21–8–29–3		9–5–15–1			
v. Sussex (Lord's) 28–31 May	8–0–40–0 9–0–45–0	7–1–15–0 11–0–38–1	12–3–34–0 9–1–33–1	12–5–24–1 13–4–34–3		8–2–23–0 2–0–9–0		1–1–0–0	1–1–0–0
v. Kent (Dartford) 4–7 June		18–5–48–1 3–1–15–0	22–6–63–2 8–1–15–0	31–8–93–1 17–9–13–6	28.3–5–92–2 22.2–7–37–4	6–1–35–0			
v. Derbyshire (Uxbridge) 8–10 June			16–4–39–2 23–6–67–4	28–12–53–2 16–4–40–1	22.5–7–60–3 18.3–3–54–2		3–2–2–0		
v. Surrey (The Oval) 11–14 June			6–0–19–0 11–1–45–2	30–5–59–4 31–11–61–2	31.2–9–74–4 34.3–7–87–6			1–1–0–0	
v. Hampshire (Uxbridge) 15–17 June			9–1–19–0 6–1–18–0	7–3–18–0 13–4–22–3	15–3–48–2 22.5–6–42–5		1–0–8–0		
v. Worcestershire (Worcester) 18–21 June			20–3–53–2 12–3–43–3	9–0–34–1 23–4–76–2	13.1–4–29–4 22–4–56–5		2–0–5–1 1–1–0–0		
v. Cambridge University (Cambridge) 22–24 June			11–2–44–0 7–3–9–0	29–17–22–3	9–7–2–2 25.3–7–49–6				
v. Derbyshire (Chesterfield) 25–28 June		9–5–14–1 7–1–28–0	9–4–27–1 6–1–17–0	11.1–4–17–3 21–5–50–4	15–3–32–3 21.5–11–38–6	9–1–26–2			
v. Warwickshire (Edgbaston) 2–5 July	5–1–15–0 9–1–33–1	2–0–14–0 3–2–9–0	8–0–24–2 13–5–17–2	20–12–15–3 31–12–63–2	14.3–7–26–5 35.3–16–46–5				
v. New Zealanders (Lord's) 9–11 July	9.1–1–36–1 8–2 30–0	6–5–10–0	3–0–20–0 8–2–15–1	43–16–66–3 30–6–77–1	44–11–93–6 39–6–118–2	1–0–8–0	8–2–13–1		2–0–11–0
v. Gloucestershire (Bristol) 13–15 July	16.2–2–61–7 14–3–46–3		11–5–30–2 7–3–13–0	12–5–17–0 7–4–5–0			8–5–10–1 2–1–1–1		
v. Leicestershire (Lord's) 16–19 July	14–2–50–4 11–4–26–3		13–1–45–1 14–2–58–3	12–8–8–4 9.2–3–14–4		3–1–5–0			
v. Warwickshire (Lord's) 30 July–2 August	15–2–65–2 11.4–1–33–4		12–3–38–2 12–1–56–1	26–12–48–4 23–11–42–3		16–7–28–2 1–0–3–0	3–2–2–0		
v. Essex (Chelmsford) 6–9 August	16.5–1–64–3	24–4–72–4	20–5–59–3	7–1–16–0	9–2–33–0	8–3–13–0	1–1–0–0		
v. Northamptonshire (Northampton) 10–12 Aug.	21–4–68–2 6–0–20–0		12–2–42–1	44–17–70–4 11–1–32–1			10–3–35–1	2–0–11–0	
v. Lancashire (Old Trafford) 13–16 August	9.2–1–37–4 15–3–32–2		22–8–56–3 11.2–1–45–1	25–11–54–2 33–13–64–5			4–2–8–1		
v. Somerset (Lord's) 20–23 August	13.1–2–30–1 8–2–21–0	8–0–37–1 5–1–18–0	18–3–54–2 7–2–21–0	21–8–54–5 23–11–28–4	20–6–54–0 16.5–10–19–5	1–0–1–0			
v. Surrey (Lord's) 24–26 August	11–0–59–1 6–0–26–0		18–8–41–4 9–1–25–2	28–12–40–3 22.1–2–38–5	33–11–48–1 21–9–42–3				
v. Sussex (Hove) 27–30 August			15–3–64–2 8–0–16–0	37–12–72–1 19–5–59–0	45–7–106–1 28–7–54–2				
v. Yorkshire (Leeds) 31 August–2 September	9–3–31–0 10–3–41–1		21–4–77–5 10–3–25–1	34–10–65–1 16–1–58–2	34–10–72–1 24–5–72–0	1–1–0–0 4.2–0–27–0		2–0–8–0	
v. Northamptonshire (Lord's) 7–9 September	7–2–26–1 9–0–31–1		4–0–29–0	27.5–9–60–1 23–6–66–2	26–4–76–3 23.4–2–131–0				
v. Nottinghamshire (Trent Bridge) 10–13 Sept.	13–1–51–0	15–3–43–5	16–2–65–1	5–0–17–0	14.3–4–40–0	8–3–17–0			
	324.3–51– 1104–48 av. 23.08	161–38– 465–18 av. 25.83	532.2–114– 1659–63 av. 26.33	935–325– 1844–103 av. 17.90	733.2–200– 1753–88 av. 19.92	82.2–25– 217–5 av. 43.40	44–20– 84–6 av. 14.00	6–2– 19–0 —	3–1– 11–0 —

† C.J.C. Rowe absent hurt a C.T. Radley 1–0–2–0   c J.F Sykes 8–1–22–0, 13–5–32–1

* G. Miller absent hurt   b G.D Barlow 2–1–2–0; C.T. Radley 1–0–4–0 ‡ P.M. Roebuck retired hurt

S.P. Hughes	K.D. James	J D Carr	Byes	Leg byes	Wides	No balls	Total	Wickets
			7	1		3	160	2
				1		4	98	7
			6	6	1	12	154	10
			9	3		7	143	9†
				2		13	151	2
				6		3	168	6
				5	2	12	350	6
			1	2		4	87	10
-9-57-2	7-5-8-1			9	1	11	238	10
-1-45-1	8-1-18-1		10	9		11	256	9*
-3-44-1			9	3		6	214	10
0-28-0	5-0-11-0		10	6		6	254	10
2-5-48-5	9-1-14-3			13		8	176	10
-5-32-2				3		4	121	10
-4-58-2	5-0-19-0		1	7		10	216	10
-31-0	3-0-17-0		4	8	1	8	244	10
0-51-2	15-7-28-5		5	1	3	12	146	10
-23-1	5-1-11-0		8	5		6	133	10
-22-0			1	4	1	7	151	10
			3			1	137	10
			11	5		3	113	10
			9	21		8	206	10
			1	4		4	234	10
			8	6		14	302	5a
0-39-0				6		13	176	10
-4-6-32-6		3-1-7-0	1	2	1	21	129	10
-2-37-1			6	3		11	160	10
0-32-0						8	143	10
-1-38-0		4-2-7-0	2	7	3	15	253	10
-6-30-2		8-1-17-0	8	1	1	19	210	10
			1	9	3	19	289	10
-4-83-2			5	5	5	19	332	10
-14-0	3-0-9-0		4	3		3	102	1b
				2	1	13	193	10c
			5	4		11	193	10
			4	4	1	11	249	10
			3	3		5	119	9‡
	4-2-10-0		7	7	2	19	233	10
	1-0-1-0			2		6	140	10
3-4-69-4	15-3-41-0		3	6	2	20	383	8
-27-1	9-0-30-1		4	2		5	197	4
-3-34-3				4	1	9	293	10
-6-1				4		11	252	5
				5		6	202	5
2-30-0			2	5		10	275	3
			1	4	1	14	253	6
3-61-	89-20-	15-4-						
-36	217-11	31-0						
25.27	av. 19.72	—						

Yorkshire became John Player League Champions on 11 September when their match at Chelmsford was rained off. It was a mixed season for Yorkshire who finished bottom of the Schweppes County Championship. Phil Carrick was one who could look back on the year with satisfaction. He had a fine all-round season. (Adrian Murrell)

at Old Trafford

Lancashire v. Leicestershire

Match abandoned
Lancashire 2 pts, Leicestershire 2 pts

at Trent Bridge

Nottinghamshire v. Gloucestershire

Match abandoned
Nottinghamshire 2 pts, Gloucestershire 2 pts

at Taunton

Warwickshire 174 for 7
Somerset 175 for 7

Somerset (4 pts) won by 3 wickets

at The Oval

Surrey v. Derbyshire

Match abandoned
Surrey 2 pts, Derbyshire 2 pts

Northamptonshire C.C.C. — First-Class Matches — Batting, 1983

	v. Warwickshire (Edgbaston) 30 April-3 May		v. Hampshire (Northampton) 4-6 May		v. Nottinghamshire (Northampton) 11-13 May		v. Yorkshire (Bradford) 25-27 May		v. Leicestershire (Northampton) 28-31 May		v. Oxford University (Oxford) 8-10 June		v. Gloucestershire (Northampton) 11-14 June		v. Cambridge University (Cambridge) 15-17 June		v. Warwickshire (Northampton) 18-21 June		v. Essex (Ilford) 22-24 June		v. Surrey (The Oval) 25-28 June		v. Sussex (Hove) 2-5 July		v. Yorkshire (Northampton) 9-12 July	
G. Cook	25	—	14	—	71	—	20	9	28	66			59	77*	—	14	29	31	11	12	8	35	58	67	0	51
W. Larkins	4	—	27	—	28	—	13	6	13	52			48	0	—	35	6	6	14	1	2	—	93	0	35	16
P. Willey	53	—	175*	—	52*	—	5	12	8	41			12	44*	52*	11	38	4	49	21	52	2	39	80	13	19
A.J. Lamb	11	—	14	—	43*	—	7	15	21*	8					38*	56*	40	10	20	5	108	39	44	35	24	107*
R.G. Williams	6	—	6	—	—	—	59	104*	—	11	50	—	35	—					40	10	20	5	0	26*	0	27
D.J. Capel	4	—	8	—	—	—	1	24			13	51*	52	—			4	3								
D.S. Steele	9	—	19	—	—	—	12	0	—	1	12	51	60	—			36	30	17	0	36*	30	0	5*	8	—
G. Sharp	39	—	11	—	—	—	36	1*	—	14	89	—	3	—			0	18	6	6*	14	21*	23	—	98	—
N.A. Mallender	24	1*	2	—	—	—	—	—	—	24*	71*	—	23*	—	—	11	3*	2*	1	3	1	4	8	—	11	—
J.A. Carse	8*	8*	36*	—																			6*	—		
B.J. Griffiths	0	—					5*	—											15	0			0	—	1*	—
R.N. Kapil Dev							81	29	—	3																
T.M. Lamb							3	—	1*	0	34	—	21	—			6	2							3	—
M.J. Bamber											17	44			77	59	44	2	35*	17	4	30				
D.J. Wild											13	22	29	—	48	14	19	11	0	5						
R.J. Bailey											5	37*			32	16										
S. Lines											29	—														
R.J. Boyd-Moss													7	—									22	9	17	4*
M. Olley															—	8										
A. Walker																					5*	6*				
Byes			9				1	3		4	2		6		4	5	4			4	7	9	1		1	1
Leg-byes	3		9		4		7	4	1	1	2	2	11	2	2	10	7	4		8	1	8	3		10	3
Wides	1		1				1	6			4	2	1		5		1				7	3	1	1		2
No-balls	6		15				6	5	2	2	12	4	4	2	2	1	2	5	1	2	15	11	2		13	6
Total	193	9	346		198		257	218	74	227	353	213	371	125	260	240	199	154	197	81	280	203	300	223	234	236
Wickets	10	0	8		2		10	7	3	9	9	3	10	1	3	7	10	10	10	10	8	7	10	5	10	4
Result	D		D		D		D		D		W		W		D		L		L		L		W		W	
Points	5		7		1		7		4		—		22				3		4		7		21		22	

Catches: 45 – G. Sharp (ct 40/st 5)   29 – D.S. Steele   11 – D.J. Capel   9 – R.G. Williams and A.J. Lamb
35 – G. Cook (ct 32/st 3)   14 – W. Larkins   10 – R.N. Kapil Dev   7 – N.A. Mallender

---

at Worcester

Sussex 121 for 8
Worcestershire 64 for 7 (C.M. Wells 4 for 15)

Worcestershire (4 pts) won on faster scoring rate

The John Player League had a very wet end. Worcestershire scored 64 in 10 overs to beat Sussex who were pushed into fourth place by the defeat. Parks and Malone added 16 for Hampshire's last wicket to give them victory with 8 balls to spare and Botham and Marks set up Somerset's win with a fifth wicket stand of 59, a win which was finally accomplished by some clouts from Garner.

Somerset's win was all in vain. Rain over the rest of the country halted all cricket and the abandonment of the match at Chelmsford meant that Yorkshire took two points, finished level with Somerset on 46 points and won the title for the first time on more away wins. It was a thoroughly deserved success for they had played capable cricket within the confines of the Sunday League for most of the season. It was also a success which had come at a time when Yorkshire cricket, on and off the field, seemed at a very low ebb and one could only hope that this great county was on the threshold of great things although their record in the county championship hardly suggested this.

John Player League Final Table

	P	W	L	NR	D	Pts
Yorkshire (16)	16	10	3	3	0	46
Somerset (9)	16	10	3	3	0	46
Kent (4)	16	8	3	5	0	42
Sussex (1)	16	9	5	2	0	40
Hampshire (5)	16	9	6	1	0	38
Derbyshire (12)	16	7	5	4	0	36
Essex (5)	16	7	5	4	0	36
Lancashire (10)	16	5	5	5	1	32
Middlesex (2)	16	7	7	2	0	32
Glamorgan (10)	16	6	8	2	0	28
Leicestershire (3)	16	4	7	5	0	26
Surrey (12)	16	4	7	5	0	26
Worcestershire (15)	16	4	7	2	3	26
Gloucestershire (14)	16	4	8	4	0	24
Northamptonshire (8)	16	5	10	1	0	22
Nottinghamshire (5)	16	4	9	2	1	22
Warwickshire (17)	16	4	9	2	1	22

(1982 positions in brackets)

	v Notts (Trent Bridge) 13–15 Jul	v Derby (Derby) 16–19 Jul	v Somerset (Northampton) 27–29 Jul		v Worcs (Northampton) 30 Jul–2 Aug		v Somerset (Weston-s-Mare) 6–9 Aug		v Middlesex (Northampton) 10–12 Aug		v Essex (Wellingborough) 13–16 Aug		v Lancs (Northampton) 20–23 Aug		v Glam (Northampton) 24–26 Aug		v Leics (Leicester) 27–30 Aug		v Glam (Cardiff) 31 Aug–2 Sep	v Middx (Lord's) 7–9 Sep		v Kent (Canterbury) 10–13 Sep		Inns	NOs	Runs	HS	Av
	69	6	0	82	23	18	43	43	79	32*	21	22	29	19	24	21*	—	—	18	82	30	128	36	41	3	1510	128	39.73
	43	236	50	24	9	80	31	11	4	34	10	29	187	7	145	26	13	47	252	13	100	22	2	42	—	1774	252	42.23
	108	15	52	25	7	117*	71	56	52	26*	27	1	175*	22*	2	10	11	2	13	—	—	—	—	40	8	1546	175*	48.31
	—	—	—	—	—	—	51	16	—	—	—	—	—	13	—	—	—	—	119	44*	79*	15	27	21	5	840	119	52.50
	11	73*	35	12	85	51*	75*	20*	33	—	23	21	—	14	17	77*	76	58	20	6	36*	31	2	40	10	1305	104	43.50
	—	—	109*	0*	48	—	8*	—	21	—	31	12	—	12	1	26	56	0	—	19*	—	23	8	24	5	534	109*	28.10
	9	—	54	—	6*	—	—	—	20	—	40*	39	—	13*	3	1	12	7	7	—	—	29*	3	31	6	569	60	22.76
	6	—	0	—	3*	—	—	—	55*	—	—	—	—	—	—	—	16	27*	13	15*	22*	8	—	24	8	536	98	33.50
	—	—	12	—	—	—	—	—	5	—	8	12	—	21	20	0	6*	1	17*	21	—	8	—	27	9	320	71*	17.77
	—	—	—	—	—	—	—	—	—	—	15*	0*	—	—	28*	—	0	12	16*	—	—	—	4	10	8	129	36*	64.50
	0	—	—	—	—	—	—	—	2	—	—	0	—	—	0	—	0	—	0	—	—	—	—	13	2	27	15	2.45
	8	13*	19	26	—	—	120	31*	19	—	—	—	—	—	—	—	—	—	—	—	—	—	—	10	2	349	120	43.62
	—	—	—	—	—	—	—	—	—	—	—	—	—	—	—	—	6	14	8	—	—	—	—	14	1	360	77	27.69
	—	—	—	—	—	—	—	—	—	—	—	—	—	—	—	—	—	—	—	—	—	—	—	9	—	161	48	17.88
	—	—	—	—	—	—	—	—	—	—	—	—	—	—	—	—	—	—	—	—	—	—	—	5	1	94	37*	23.50
	4	—	—	—	—	—	—	—	—	—	—	—	—	—	—	—	—	—	—	—	—	—	—	1	—	29	29	29.00
	12	80	2	90*	12	14	—	—	8	—	—	—	60	2	—	78	22	22	0	101	21	—	6 13	65 37	24	2	704	101	32.00
	—	—	—	—	—	—	—	—	—	—	—	—	—	—	—	—	—	—	—	—	—	—	—	1	—	8	8	8.00
	7*	—	—	—	—	—	—	—	—	—	—	—	—	—	—	—	—	—	—	—	—	—	0	4	3	18	7*	18.00

	Byes/Leg-byes/Wides/No-balls																												
	2	1	1	4		8			5	4	4		2	8	2	7	4				2		10						
	7	10	2	6	7	12	2	5	5	3	4	2	8	5	5	16	4	4	7	5	5	4	5						
	1	3				4	5		1				1	1	6	1				6	10	5	3						
	6	2		4					19	3	3	3	8	1	8	8	7	16	26										
	293	439	336	273	200	300	405	182	332	102	247	143	381	213	284	229	219	279	529	202	275	337	167						
	10	4	9	5	6	3	5	4	10	1	7	9†	2	7	10	7	10	10	8	5	3	6	10						
	W	D	D		W		D		W		L		D		D		L		D	W		D							
	23	8	7		22		7		24		6		4		6		5		8	21		8							

†G. Sharp absent.hurt

5 – P. Willey, R.J. Bailey and M.J. Bamber   3 – A. Walker and M. Olley   1 – S. Lines
4 – R.J. Boyd-Moss and subs (ct 2/st 2)   2 – B.J. Griffiths and D.J. Wild

10, 12 and 13 September

at Chelmsford

Yorkshire 204 (J.D. Love 55, J.K. Lever 7 for 78) and 220 (M.D. Moxon 58, S. Turner 4 for 31, J.K. Lever 4 for 85)
Essex 288 (G.A. Gooch 111, S.D. Fletcher 4 for 71)

Match drawn
Essex 7 pts, Yorkshire 6 pts

at Southampton

Glamorgan 252 (R.C. Ontong 50) and 76 for 2
Hampshire 252 for 6 dec (C.L. Smith 93, C.G. Greenidge 77)

Match drawn
Hampshire 7 pts, Glamorgan 5 pts

at Canterbury

Northamptonshire 337 for 6 dec (G. Cook 128, R.J. Boyd-Moss 65) and 167 (G.W. Johnson 7 for 76)
Kent 313 for 9 dec (C.J. Tavare 81, D.G. Aslett 63, C.S. Cowdrey 53, R.G. Williams 4 for 125) and 56 for 2

Match drawn
Northamptonshire 8 pts, Kent 6 pts

at Old Trafford

Lancashire 236 (G. Fowler 85, J. Simmons 57, P.B. Clift 5 for 73) and 214 for 3 (S.J. O'Shaughnessy 105, G. Fowler 100)
Leicestershire 150 for 4 dec (D.I. Gower 56 not out)

Match drawn
Leicestershire 5 pts, Lancashire 3 pts

at Trent Bridge

Middlesex 201 (A.J.T. Miller 70, R.J. Hadlee 5 for 72) and 54 for 1
Nottinghamshire 253 for 6 dec (C.E.B. Rice 101 not out, R.T. Robinson 56, N.G. Cowans 5 for 43)

Match drawn
Nottinghamshire 7 pts, Middlesex 4 pts

at Taunton

Somerset 219 (J.G. Wyatt 69, N. Gifford 4 for 64) and 117 for 1 (J.G. Wyatt 82 not out)
Warwickshire 300 for 9 dec (T.A. Lloyd 112, G.W. Humpage 71, G.V. Palmer 5 for 38)

Match drawn
Warwickshire 8 pts, Somerset 6 pts

Northamptonshire C.C.C.
First-Class Matches — Bowling, 1983

	B.J. Griffiths	N.A Mallender	J.A. Carse	D.J. Capel	D.S. Steele	P. Willey	R.G. Williams	W. Larkins	R.N. Kapil Dev
v. Warwickshire (Edgbaston) 30-April-3 May	23.1-7-55-4	21-3-74-2	25-9-42-2	9-3-31-0	11-4-17-2	6-1-28-0			
v. Hampshire (Northampton) 4-6 May	17-6-28-2 / 10-2-30-0	15-5-22-2 / 9-3-25-1	18-2-54-3 / 12-2-29-1	/ 4-0-17-0	17-11-21-2 / 19-8-24-3	15-5-26-1 / 14-2-28-0	4-0-14-0 / 11-2-27-0		
v. Nottinghamshire (Northampton) 11-13 May									
v. Yorkshire (Bradford) 25-27 May	17-5-34-2				24-6-48-5	13-6-33-1			19-6-33-2
v. Leicestershire (Northampton) 28-31 May	16.5-3-46-4	18-4-60-1 / 7-2-12-1			2-2-0-0 / 14-3-41-1	15-3-43-0			16-3-60-1 / 7-4-11-1
v. Oxford University (Oxford) 8-10 June		21.3-7-41-4 / 13.4-6-31-2	1.5-0-3-0	1-0-9-0 / 7-3-23-0	20-9-39-1 / 14.4-11-6-1		8-3-17-0 / 24-20-29-3		
v. Gloucestershire (Northampton) 11-14 June		5-0-15-0 / 4-1-9-0			31-11-83-2 / 23-17-15-2	33-10-67-3 / 27.5-9-44-2	16-6-37-4 / 17-10-18-4		
v. Cambridge University (Cambridge) 15-17 June		14-0-50-0 / 11-4-19-2				13-9-11-1 / 12-8-24-0	21.4-8-53-2 / 17-8-31-0	5-2-7-0	
v. Warwickshire (Northampton) 18-21 June		26-4-104-2 / 15-3-36-0		2.5-0-16-0	12.4-5-23-3 / 14-9-14-2	32-6-73-1	12-2-30-4 / 6-3-23-2	4-0-16-0	
v. Essex (Ilford) 22-24 June	39-10-92-6	21.4-1-108-2			7-0-46-1	30-11-40-1	1-0-1-0		
v. Surrey (The Oval) 25-28 June	25-11-66-4 / 22-6-41-3	17.5-6-65-3 / 15-4-63-1				7-4-10-1 / 2-0-4-0	2-1-2-0		
v. Sussex (Hove) 2-5 July	24-4-62-2 / 8.5-0-45-2	17-1-48-0 / 5-0-23-1	17-3-59-0 / 9-0-43-2		24.2-10-42-1 / 7-3-18-3	7-2-21-0 / 6-2-14-2			
v. Yorkshire (Northampton) 9-12 July	6-0-17-0 / 7-2-16-0	18-5-41-3 / 7-2-16-1			41-19-56-3 / 30.4-10-67-5	22-6-50-1 / 29-8-70-0	8.4-3-20-2 / 10-6-13-2		
v. Nottinghamshire (Trent Bridge) 13-15 July	17-7-34-2 / 13.2-3-37-4				2-2-0-0 / 6-2-10-2		2-2-0-0		21.1-11-24-4 / 12-2-18-1
v. Derbyshire (Derby) 16-18 July	21.5-3-54-2 / 18-5-49-1				14-4-35-0 / 8-3-12-0	25-11-27-1 / 9-6-10-0	5-2-13-1 / 10-3-20-0	7-0-21-1	7-1-23-0 / 1-0-3-0
v. Somerset (Northampton) 27-29 July	18-4-55-2 / 5-1-22-0	19-5-47-1 / 4-1-14-0			16-2-76-1 / 13-3-28-0	18-3-49-1 / 1-1-0-0	16-0-65-1 / 4-1-11-0		14-2-33-0 / 7-3-16-0
v. Worcs. (Northampton) 30 July-2 August	22-8-43-0 / 7-3-6-0	24-7-48-6 / 3-0-6-0	20-5-69-3 / 7-1-23-0	2-0-13-0	12-3-32-0 / 25-4-84-3	19-5-48-1	5-2-7-0 / 21-11-35-1		
v. Somerset (Weston-s-Mare) 6-9 August	24-6-49-0 / 7-0-25-0	19-3-69-4 / 11-0-55-1		5-1-20-0	17-9-23-1 / 16-4-67-2	9-2-17-0 / 6-2-7-1	9-0-19-1 / 12-5-29-0		18-5-45-1 / 18.5-4-76-4
v. Middlesex (Northampton) 10-12 August	17-9-27-0	20-8-46-1 / 11-5-22-0		11-1-35-2	23-7-46-4 / 20-9-35-1	8-3-22-0 / 23-5-51-4	1.2-0-6-2 / 30.5-10-74-4		15-3-31-1 / 7-3-12-1
v. Essex (Wellingborough) 13-16 August	19-5-56-0 / 22-6-69-3	19-2-78-3 / 9-1-36-0	21-3-67-2 / 11-5-32-0	7-2-18-0	2-0-5-1 / 9.2-3-41-2		12-0-48-2	14.4-3-30-4	
v. Lancashire (Northampton) 20-23 August	6-1-19-0	2-0-2-0 / 3-1-11-0	11-0-62-0 / 2-0-9-0		26-4-68-1 / 25-15-40-4	40-14-74-2	27-9-90-0 / 20.4-9-33-2		
v. Glamorgan (Northampton) 24-26 August	5-0-17-0 / 3-0-18-0	19.4-3-62-4 / 5-2-19-0	23-6-44-1 / 3-0-13-0		33-16-56-1 / 8-1-23-1	24-6-64-3 / 11-5-26-3	12-4-25-1 / 4-1-9-1		
v. Leicestershire (Leicester) 27-30 August	32-5-85-3 / 5.2-0-38-3	28-6-77-2 / 3-0-36-0	33-6-116-1 / 3-1-11-2	4-0-10-0	27.5-10-59-4				
v. Glamorgan (Cardiff) 31 August-2 September	19-3-44-1 / 6-1-27-0	12-2-43-3 / 6-2-16-1	17-4-43-5 / 5-3-3-0		9-6-3-0		2-1-5-0 / 4-3-2-0		
v. Middlesex (Lord's) 7-9 September	13-4-32-0 / 9-0-47-0	16-2-53-2 / 5-0-27-0		11-5-21-1	23-6-73-2 / 4.4-1-12-0		25-3-77-3 / 6-1-24-1		
v. Kent (Canterbury) 10-13 September	6-0-28-0 / 5-0-11-0	5-1-13-0		2-0-13-0	26.5-5-71-3 / 7-2-11-0		43-7-125-4 / 5-2-4-0		
	536.2-130-1424-50 *av.* 28.48	525.2-112-1642-56 *av.* 29.32	238.5-50-722-22 *av.* 32.81	65.5-15-226-3 *av.* 75.33	678-255-1460-68 *av.* 21.47	484.5-159-991-32 *av.* 30.96	434.1-148-1036-47 *av.* 22.04	30.4-5-74-5 *av.* 14.80	163-47-385-16 *av.* 24.06

a G. Cook 1-0-4-0; A.J. Lamb 1-0-1-0
b G. Cook 2-2-0-0
c R.J. Bailey 1-0-2-0, 14-5-33-3
d R.J. Boyd-Moss 3-1-2-0
e G. Cook 8-1-39-0
f R.J. Boyd-Moss 8-4-13-1

T.M. Lamb	A. Walker	D.J. Wild	Byes	Leg byes	Wides	No balls	Total	Wickets
			17	5	6	6	281	10
			2	5	1	4	177	10
			4	13		2	204	5a
					Match Abandoned			
			4	2		3	157	10
–9–49–4				2		2	219	10
				4			111	3
.1–7–27–4			5		1	4	146	10
–7–37–3			4	3		6	139	10
1–9–1				6	1	6	224	10
–6–18–2			10	11		6	131	10b
–6–47–2	19–4–70–1	13–3–56–0	17	1			307	6c
–1–44–1	23–4–70–4		5	10		1	244	10
.1–7–70–0			4	8	1	6	351	10
1–27–0		20–5–62–2		1	1	4	168	6
0–9–0		3–2–10–0	11	5	1	6	329	10
	15–1–62–2			3	1	10	217	10
	14–4–42–2		1	9	1		163	6
				11		7	250	3
				5	6		154	10
			4	11			199	10
				6	1	1	190	10
	16–2–61–4		1	3		1	124	10
	9–2–27–3		4	1		1	98	10
–7–41–3	15–5–49–2		1	6		2	251	10
–5–38–1	9–4–21–0		11	6	5		196	3
				10	2		337	7
			9	3	5		110	0d
			8	10	1	7	273	10
			8	9		2	225	4e
			6	10		9	267	7
			9	5		5	278	8
			1	6		3	223	10
			3	4	1	8	210	10
			12	7	1	8	282	10
			2	3		5	236	7
			4	4		8	331	3
			5	2	1	1	115	7f
			12	10	4	17	311	10
				8		1	117	5
			7	16	7	22	399	10
				12		3	100	5
			5	6	2	12	163	10
				1		1	50	1
	17.4–2–64–0		1	7		2	330	8
	5–0–28–0		1	3	1		143	1
	16–2–57–2		5	1			313	9
	7–0–27–2			2		1	56	2
8.2–57–	165.4–30–	36–10–						
6–21	578–22	128–2						
19.80	av. 26.27	av. 64.00						

ABOVE: *The last laugh. Keith Fletcher leads Essex to the Schweppes County Championship for the second time in four years. (George Herringshaw)* BELOW: *Keith Pont enjoyed a good season and scored over 800 runs. (Adrian Murrell)*

Nottinghamshire C.C.C. — First-Class Matches — Batting, 1983

	v. Somerset (Trent Bridge) 30 April-2 May		v. Sussex (Hove) 4-6 May		v. Northamptonshire (Northampton) 11-13 May		v. Derbyshire (Trent Bridge) 31 May		v. Leicestershire (Trent Bridge) 4-7 June		v. Essex (Chelmsford) 8-10 June		v. Lancashire (Old Trafford) 11-14 June		v. Surrey (Trent Bridge) 15-17 June		v. Cambridge University (Cambridge) 18-21 June		v. Kent (Trent Bridge) 22-24 June		v. Lancashire (Trent Bridge) 25-28 June		v. Essex (Trent Bridge) 2-5 July		v. Worcestershire (Worcester) 9-12 July	
S.B. Hassan	22	—	3	—			43	—	22	0	11	112	—	9	83	3	15	66	42	0	23	51	25	2	1	50
R.T. Robinson	43	—	12	—			48	—	15	4	14	13	—	53*	16	94	15	66	21	25	3	20	0	22	9	110
D.W. Randall	8	—	43	—			52*	—	74	8											31	11	16	16	10	29
C.E.B. Rice	45	—	37	—															98	45	6	36	16	47	15	3
J.D. Birch	45	—	55	—			2	—	29	2	31	56	—	35*	27	2	4	75	0	11	6	95	23*	5	12	38
R.J. Hadlee	1	—	103	—			9	—																		
B.N. French	9*	—	16	—					28	0	0	15	—	—	19	12	1	40	0	4	2	21	0	8	46	6
E.E. Hemmings	2*	—	11	—					0	4	18	13	—	—					7	27	9	10	29	37	2	9
K. Saxelby			17*	—					11	0	4	1					1	4	18	13	2	8	4	0	35	9
K.E. Cooper			6	—					4	0*	18*	5			29	7	5	4	2	8			1	0	5	16*
M. Hendrick			1*	—					3*	0*	2	2*	—	—	7	12			3*	2	1	9	5	15*	2*	—
P. Johnson							65*	—	29	8	54	1	—	3	0	1	73	15	31	6	0	4				
P.M. Such									0	—	0	1			2*	0*	0	—	0	3*	0	0*	1	5		
C.W. Scott																	2	78								
M.A. Fell											4	32	—	4	0	6	6	41								
M.K. Bore													—	—	0	0	1*	—			1*	24			20	—
N.J.B. Illingworth															17	0	5	15*								
R.A. Pick																										
Byes	1		10				8		6	4	4	2		2	4	1						3	1		1	1
Leg-byes	3						3		5		11	18		3	5	11	3	5	3		3	9	3		3	2
Wides			2								1	2		2	2	6	1	2	1						2	5
No-balls	2		6				2				1	5			7	6		2	12	11	1	4	14		13	7
Total	181		322				232		226	32	171	278	0	109	218	161	127	347	238	158	86	294	123	172	176	285
Wickets	6		9				4		10	8	10	10	0	3	10	10	10	8	10	10	10	10	10	10	10	8
Result	D		W		D		L		D		L		D		L		W		L		W		L		W	
Points	1		24		0		0		6		3		3		3		—		6		20		4		21	

Catches: 52 – B.N. French (ct 49/st 3)   18 – M. Hendrick   13 – C.E.B. Rice   9 – P. Johnson
20 – J.D. Birch   17 – D.W. Randall and S.B. Hassan   11 – E.E. Hemmings   7 – M.K. Bore

Chris Gladwin. His inclusion in the side as Gooch's opening partner coincided with Essex's late run which swept them to the title. A young player of great promise. (George Herringshaw)

at The Oval

Surrey 244 (D.B. Pauline 75, A.R. Butcher 55, M.A. Holding 5 for 54)
Derbyshire 385 for 7 dec (K.J. Barnett 121, A. Hill 111, W.P. Fowler 72)

Match drawn
Derbyshire 8 pts, Surrey 4 pts

at Worcester

Sussex 221 for 2 dec (G.D. Mendis 133 not out, D.K. Standing 60) and 79 for 2
Worcestershire 221 (D.N. Patel 53, D.A. Reeve 4 for 15)

Match drawn
Sussex 6 pts, Worcestershire 2 pts

What had been, after May, a most glorious summer ended in gloom and rain and, in a sense, something of an anti-climax. The match at Old Trafford ended in controversial farce. When Lancashire batted again at 3.05 on the last day, Gower and Whitaker opened the Leicestershire bowling, the main effort being to raise the visitors' over-rate and avoid a fine. Gower bowled 9 overs for 102 runs and Whitaker 8 for 87. 150 was reached in 14 overs. Both Fowler and O'Shaugh-

v. Northamptonshire (Trent Bridge) 13-15 July		v. Hampshire (Bournemouth) 16-19 July		v. Surrey (The Oval) 27-29 July		v. Yorkshire (Worksop) 30 July-2 August		v. Leicestershire (Leicester) 6-9 August		v. Glamorgan (Ebbw Vale) 10-12 August		v. Hampshire (Trent Bridge) 13-16 August		v. Yorkshire (Bradford) 20-23 August		v. Gloucestershire (Bristol) 27-30 August		v. Warwickshire (Trent Bridge) 31 August-2 Sept.		v. Derbyshire (Derby) 7-9 September		v. Middlesex (Trent Bridge) 10-13 September		Inns	NOs	Runs	HS	Av
6	25	3	53	19	28	42	—	7	24	10	44			15	6*	90	14	2	—					34	1	890	112	26.96
22	18	36	29	92	82	56	—	21	8	4	30	50	13*	50	70*	8	11	207	—	0	79	56	—	41	3	1545	207	40.65
				22	94	56				10	70	11	—	1	6			47	—	0	1	23	—	22	1	583	94	27.76
36	16	79	68	39	7	17		9	7	33	47	0	—	23	48	19	18	90		20	2	101*	30	30	2	1026	101*	36.64
0	0	17	20	11	8	60				88	35	1	—	85	5	19	18	90		0	46	30	6	38	2	1086	95	30.16
																						6	—	4	—	119	103	29.75
3	0	23	12	21	22	10	—	59	18	9	15	0	—	91	5*	51	5*	36*		13	4	6	—	38	4	630	91	18.52
9	13	0	5	3	0	18	—	7	33	22	12	38	—	12*		8		2		0	6	11*		32	3	377	38	13.00
0	0	34	15			13	—	5	0	7	6	23	—	0	—	23	—	13*		1*	7			28	3	274	35	10.96
15	12					21*	—	12	15	10	1	30*	—	10*	—	18*	—			0	0			27	7	254	30*	12.70
2*	0*	0	0*					0*	15	14*	7*	14	—			5	—			4	5			26	13	130	15*	10.00
21	1			6	1	19	—	24	5			47	11*			52	125			10	0	0		28	2	612	125	23.53
						0	0			1	—													15	4	13	5	1.18
																								2	—	80	78	40.00
		0	0																					9	—	93	41	10.33
5	7	4	8	6*	17*	6	—			1	12*					20	—							16	5	132	24	12.00
				8	4																			6	1	49	17	9.80
		12*	14	7	4	18	—					4	—							0	25*			8	2	84	25*	14.00

v. Northamptonshire		v. Hampshire (B)		v. Surrey		v. Yorkshire (W)		v. Leicestershire		v. Glamorgan		v. Hampshire (TB)		v. Yorkshire (Brad)		v. Gloucestershire		v. Warwickshire		v. Derbyshire		v. Middlesex	
1	4	4	4	5	11	8		10	8	2	1					2	3			1		1	
3	1	16	3		8	10		4	6	1	5	16		4	6	7	2	9		2	2	4	
				1		1		18	1	3				4						1		1	
1	1	4	7	4	4	17		13	10	31	13	5				12	2	1		21		1	9	14

	Northants		Hants (B)		Surrey		Yorks (W)		Leics		Glam		Hants (TB)		Yorks (Brad)		Glos		Warwicks		Derby		Middx	
Runs	124	98	233	238	221	197	316		212	256	245	286	239	28	303	149	308	278	449		53	186	253	
Wkts	10	10	10	10	10	10	10		10	10	10	9	10	0	7	3	10	4	6		10	10	6	
Result	L		L		L		D				D		D		D		D		D		L		D	
Points	1				4		5		2		6		6		6		5		8		4		7	

6 – P.M. Such and R.T. Robinson   3 – N.J.B. Illingworth and R.J. Hadlee
4 – M.A. Fell, C.W. Scott (ct 3/st 1) and K.E. Cooper   1 – K. Saxelby and sub

nessy hit hundreds. O'Shaughnessy's came in 35 minutes so equalling the fastest first-class hundred ever scored, by Percy Fender in 1920, but it was hard to accept this farce as a record even though it will go down in history as such. It should be said that, whatever the bowling, the runs have to be hit and O'Shaughnessy, five sixes and seventeen fours, is to be commended.

Less fortunate was Alec Stewart whose excellent season came to an end with a broken jaw at The Oval. Barnett and Hill closed very good seasons on a high note and Fowler hit lustily for Derbyshire.

There was no play on the last day at Worcester where Mendis had hit his best score of the season, Standing the best of his short career and Reeve had again bowled well.

There were career bests for Wyatt and Palmer at Taunton where Lloyd was again in fine form and play ended early on the last day.

It was sad that there was no play on the last day at Southampton for this game witnessed the retirement of Alan Jones who was to become county coach. His career lasted 27 seasons and for 23 of them, he has passed 1000 runs. A fine man, a character of wry humour and much wisdom, he will be missed by all who have played against him, but he should benefit Glamorgan well in his new capacity. He has given many of us much pleasure.

In the match itself, Chris Smith and Greenidge dominated with an opening stand of 159.

Graham Johnson finished the match at Canterbury with a career best 7 for 76, but he could not force victory for Kent. Geoff Cook hit his first century of the season for Northants on the Saturday and Kent again batted impressively.

All these events were insignificant, however, as compared to those at Chelmsford and Trent Bridge which were to decide the championship. Middlesex were frustrated to only 6.4 overs on the Saturday during which time they lost Barlow to Hadlee who was reappearing in the Notts side. They struggled to two batting bonus points on the Monday with Miller again eminently impressive. Cowans began a lethal spell with a wicket in his first over, but further wickets evaded him until the score had reached 49. More rain and a century from Rice left Notts 52 runs ahead and Middlesex needing a miraculous turn of events to force the victory that they needed to retain the championship. At 4.15 on the last day, with gloom all over Nottingham and a steady drizzle falling, the match was abandoned.

At Chelmsford, Essex put Yorkshire in to bat and saw Boycott and Moxon bat splendidly on a fierce wicket to score 86 for the first wicket. From that point on John Lever dominated the day. He passed 100 wickets for the season and took 7 for 78 on a wicket of uneven bounce which he ex-

Nottinghamshire C.C.C.
First-Class Matches — Bowling, 1983

	R.J. Hadlee	M. Hendrick	K.E. Cooper	K. Saxelby	E.E. Hemmings	P.M. Such	M.K. Bore	M.A. Fell	N.J.B. Illingworth
v. Somerset (Trent Bridge) 30 April–2 May									
v. Sussex (Hove) 4–6 May	20–11–25–4 19–9–31–3	19.5–10–28–4 16–7–24–2	11–3–20–2 12–5–28–2	6–1–21–0 9–3–31–1	5–4–11–0 20.1–3–55–2				
v. Northamptonshire (Northampton) 11–13 May	10–3–40–1	6–2–10–0	15–5–38–0	11–3–29–1	26–4–77–0				
v. Derbyshire (Trent Bridge) 31 May	12.2–2–37–0		6–1–39–0	7–0–50–1	17–1–68–2	5–0–30–1			
v. Leicestershire (Trent Bridge) 4–7 June		15.3–4–17–6 18–4–49–2	11–3–36–0 18–7–37–1	13–6–44–3 13–3–43–0	44.5–18–85–4	16–5–56–2			
v. Essex (Chelmsford) 8–10 June		15–3–45–0 5–0–19–0	32–7–95–3 10–1–36–1	21–9–52–2 7–0–30–1	45.3–14–107–4	18–7–43–1 1.5–0–9–0			
v. Lancashire (Old Trafford) 11–14 June		22–9–38–2	22–8–45–1	12–2–40–2	16–9–29–2		14–4–51–1	3–0–11–0	
v. Surrey (Trent Bridge) 15–17 June		29–10–65–0	32–9–89–6			27–3–98–1 2–1–4–0	26–6–62–1 2–1–8–0		16–1–46–0
v. Cambridge University (Cambridge) 18–21 June			12–5–27–2 22–10–53–5	12–1–28–3 11–1–44–0		2–1–5–0 18–7–40–1	14.2–4–29–4 26.4–13–30–4		12–4–16–0
v. Kent (Trent Bridge) 22–24 June		8–3–20–1	4–0–6–0	4–0–18–0	29–6–83–3 16.2–1–64–1	29.4–1–123–6 16–2–66–3			
v. Lancashire (Trent Bridge) 25–28 June		22.3–6–55–6 14–4–31–2			25–9–54–4 25.3–15–23–7	3–0–18–0 3–2–1–0	12–5–29–0 9–6–4–1		
v. Essex (Trent Bridge) 2–5 July		14–5–24–2 10–2–32–0	30–15–39–1 22–3–81–0	18.2–3–56–3 18–1–67–2	15–3–31–1	23–8–52–1 12–0–101–1			
v. Worcestershire (Worcester) 9–12 July		9–2–17–2 17–7–24–5	11–0–33–7 11–4–25–0	2.2–0–19–1 5–1–18–1	31–10–85–2		10.3–4–23–2		
v. Northamptonshire (Trent Bridge) 13–15 July		18–5–34–0	19–6–35–0	23.2–8–57–5	35–6–97–4		23–4–54–1		
v. Hampshire (Bournemouth) 16–19 July		16–5–36–2 4–2–6–0		8–0–42–0	37–6–129–1 10–4–31–1		21–4–89–3 4.3–1–18–1		
v. Surrey (The Oval) 27–29 July					28–4–104–2	18.3–5–50–1 3–0–13–1	33–13–80–3		9–1–51–1
v. Yorkshire (Worksop) 30 July–2 August			32–7–120–1 12–4–19–0	24–7–53–1 8–3–16–0	35–8–96–3 14–3–30–0		32–9–80–0 22–11–34–3		
v. Leicestershire (Leicester) 6–9 August		20–6–47–4 19–9–25–5	21–6–59–3 17–2–99–0	11–1–57–1 13–2–53–3	20–7–51–0		16.5–4–53–2 11–2–42–0		
v. Glamorgan (Ebbw Vale) 10–12 August		18–4–43–0 17–6–55–2	12.1–5–22–3 20–4–70–1	23–7–52–5 17–3–45–3	13–4–41–1 18–7–51–2	7–2–20–0 9–0–38–1			
v. Hampshire (Trent Bridge) 13–16 August		20–5–26–1 25–10–50–3	18.5–5–38–3 16–5–47–1	19–3–62–3 20–7–49–4	5–0–11–0 8–2–33–0				
v. Yorkshire (Bradford) 20–23 August		16–8–22–0 12–4–20–0	19–4–70–2 4–2–7–0	15–5–57–0 3–1–9–0	23.1–3–83–1 29–7–128–3		24–2–71–0 17–1–115–0		
v. Gloucestershire (Bristol) 27–30 August		9–2–27–0 11–3–21–1	13–2–32–0 2–0–13–0	11–4–32–0	31.1–6–103–2 24–5–102–5		28–7–89–1 16–4–65–0		
v. Warwickshire (Trent Bridge) 31 August–2 September		18–3–49–3 24–7–63–2	17–2–48–5 13–2–48–0	16.1–5–37–2 19.1–3–76–2	15–6–34–0 29–18–45–2		5–2–6–0 3–1–8–0		
v. Derbyshire (Derby) 7–9 September		20–13–20–4 25–11–46–1	20–9–32–5 28–8–88–1	7–1–40–0 3–1–10–0	1–0–1–0				
v. Middlesex (Trent Bridge) 10–13 September	23–2–72–5 2–1–5–0	12.2–5–22–3 7–4–12–1	14–5–36–1		16–2–43–0 3–0–15–0				
	86.2–28–210–13 av. 16.15	552.1–190–1122–66 av. 17.00	579–164–1610–57 av. 28.24	410.2–95–1337–50 av. 26.74	710.4–195–2000–59 av. 33.89	214–44–767–20 av. 38.35	370.5–108–1040–27 av. 38.51	3–0–11–0 av. —	37–6–113–1 av. 113.00

R.A. Pick	R.T. Robinson	J.D. Birch	Byes	Leg byes	Wides	No balls	Total	Wickets
					Match Abandoned			
				9		1	115	10
				1		5	175	10
				4			198	2
			3	5	1	2	235	4
					2	2	101	10
			2	8		3	283	9
			2	6		1	351	10
				9		1	104	2
				5	1		220	8
			1	6	1	1	369	8
							12	0
			5	2		1	97	10
			5	4			192	10
			4	6			260	10
			1	6			137	4
				2			158	10
			4	2			65	10
				5		4	211	10
				1	1	2	285	3
							69	10
				1		1	177	10
			2	7	1	6	293	10
0–3–101–0			1	5	1		404	6
0–13–0							68	0
4–4–70–0			3	17	1	2	378	9
0–21–0			4	3		1	42	1
6–0–52–0			1	19	2	11	434	5
0–21–1	1–0–1–0	1–0–1–0		7	1	1	131	4
			1	6	2	1	226	10
			2	11	5	4	292	8
			1	7	1		187	10
			4	12		4	279	9
9–4–50–2				3		4	194	10
5.2–2–53–1				1	1	9	243	9
			5	4	1	3	316	3
			1	1		2	283	3
			1	13		3	300	3
			5			2	208	6
				2		4	180	10
			6	3	2	5	256	7
0.2–1–37–1			1			6	137	10
–1–49–1			1	2	1	5	202	3
–1–12–1				8		8	201	10
–0–21–0						1	54	1
44.4–16–	1–0–	1–0–						
00–7	1–0	1–0						
v. 71.42	—	—						

ABOVE: *Alan Jones ended his first-class career for Glamorgan which has lasted for 27 seasons. He will be much missed. (Ken Kelly)* BELOW: *Derek Pringle. A much improved cricketer. (George Herringshaw)*

Somerset C.C.C. — First-Class Matches — Batting, 1983

	v. Nottinghamshire (Trent Bridge) 30 April-2 May		v. Worcestershire (Taunton) 4-6 May		v. Worcestershire (Worcester) 11-13 May		v. Sussex (Taunton) 25-27 May		v. Essex (Taunton) 4-7 June		v. Gloucestershire (Bristol) 8-10 June		v. Sussex (Hove) 11-14 June		v. Glamorgan (Swansea) 15-17 June		v. Derbyshire (Bath) 18-21 June		v. Gloucestershire (Bath) 22-24 June		v. New Zealanders (Taunton) 2-5 July		v. Leicestershire (Leicester) 9-12 July		v. Kent (Maidstone) 13-15 July	
P.M. Roebuck	—	—	81	—	23	—	19	0	69	41	4	74*	2	40	40	—	44	4	10	51	—	—	51		99	9
J.W. Lloyds	—	—	58	—	26	—	12	31	0	0	1	—	0	20	34	—	19	10	81	—	84	14			0	11
P.A. Slocombe			1	—					3	10	5	—			37	—			6	20*	66	13			1	0
B.C. Rose			40	—	4	—	52	5					11	6							34	12				
I.T. Botham			24	—	107	—	27	81	34	19											20	—	152			
N.F.M. Popplewell			37	—	58*	—	9	3	66*	8	6	—	27	9	64	—	19	16	20	143	7	0	0		2	9
V.J. Marks			32	—	27*	—	26	3	12	8											26*	0	23			
T. Gard	—	—			—	—	0	22	29	0	13	—	24	7	51	—	14*	12	7*	—	5	12	10		13	0
C.H. Dredge			30*	—			6	6	—	1*	48*	—	9	—	0	—	13	35					4		16	11
M.R. Davis									16*	0	2	—	19	5*			0	0*								
P.H.L. Wilson					—	—					25	—	0*	1	0*	—			1	—	12	3*	9*		0*	0*
I.V.A. Richards					20	—	2	30															216		32	82
G.V. Palmer					6*	—							78	—	3	1	0	1	8	—						
P.W. Denning							36	4	7	20	73	—	6	3	2	—	9	85	27	21*	0	—	99		19	3
J. Garner							23*	2*													16	26	5		44	25
R.L. Ollis											5	99*	67	17	1	—	0	1			36	—				
D. Breakwell															55*	—	4	13								
N.A. Felton																	5	1			11	51			9	0
N. Russom																					8	—				
J.G. Wyatt																							0	14		
S.C. Booth																										
Byes						5		4		4		3		2		5		1	4	5	7	4	1		1	
Leg-byes		8				11	3	2	6	3	8	1	7	1		13	5	9	16	7	7	2	13		7	6
Wides		1				1		1						1		4			1	1	1	1	3		1	1
No-balls		13				13	4	1	4	3		6	3	2		17	8	1		2	2	1	7		12	16
Total		325		301			224	190	250	113	277	174	181	112		323	141	191	238	299	267	221	528		256	173
Wickets		7		5			10	10	7	9†	10	0	10	10		9	10	10	10	3	10	9	10		10	10
Result	D		D		D		L		L		D		L		D		L		D		D		W		L	
Points	2		7		8		4		7		6		5		7		4		5		—		24		6	

Catches 50 – T. Gard (ct 48/st 2) 12 – J.W. Lloyds 10 – J. Garner and C.H. Dredge 7 – I.T. Botham, G.V. Palmer and S.C. Booth
21 – N.F.M. Popplewell 11 – subs 9 – P.M. Roebuck 6 – P.W. Denning and I.V.A. Richards

---

ploited to the full. Some bold hitting by Love took Yorkshire to a commendable 204 and they gained the upper hand on Monday when Essex slipped to 58 for 4.

Gooch had come in to open on the Saturday evening, but not a ball had been bowled before bad light ended play. It was discovered that he had sustained a hairline fracture in missing a sharp chance on the Saturday and he dropped to number six on Monday. He played a masterful innings. On a spiteful wicket, he hit with that sad brutality which is characteristic of this magnificent player and saw Essex to a position of some strength. Pringle and David East, all energy and enthusiasm, gave fine support and the day ended optimistically.

It was Stuart Turner who broke the Yorkshire resistance on the last day as they went from 136 for 2 to 220 all out. He dismissed Hartley and Moxon in the same over and, like the wonderful Lever, finished with four wickets. Essex were left to make 137 in over an hour and a half, but the rain came and so did the news from Trent Bridge that the Middlesex game had been abandoned. Essex were champions for the second time in their history. It was a well-deserved success although one could not help but spare a thought for Middlesex who had led the table for so long and been cruelly treated by injuries. Gatting had proved to be a mighty captain.

Fletcher had again led Essex admirably on the field even

Schweppes County Championship Final Table

	P	W	L	D	Bonus pts Bt	Bl	Pts
Essex (7)	24	11	5	8	69	79	324
Middlesex (1)	24	11	4	9	60	72	308
Hampshire (3)	24	10	2	12	62	71	289
Leicestershire (2)	24	9	3	12	52	81	277
Warwickshire (17)	24	10	3	11	52	64	276
Northamptonshire (9)	24	7	4	13	63	77	252
Kent (13)	24	7	4	13	68	70	250
Surrey (5)	24	7	4	13	65	70	247
Derbyshire (11)	24	7	5	12	46	45	219
Somerset (6)	24	3	7	14	57	75	180
Sussex (8)	24	3	10	11	50	72	170
Gloucestershire (15)	24	3	8	13	56	61	165
Lancashire (12)	24	3	4	17	56	61	165
Nottinghamshire (4)	24	3	10	11	39	62	149
Glamorgan (16)	24	2	10	12	45	64	141
Worcestershire (14)	24	2	11	11	43	54	129
Yorkshire (10)	24	1	5	18	45	64	125

Hampshire & Derbyshire totals include 12pts for wins in 1 innings matches. (1982 positions in brackets)

v. Surrey (Taunton) 16-19 July	v. Northamptonshire (Northampton) 27-29 July	v. Lancashire (Old Trafford) 30 July-2 August	v. Northamptonshire (Weston-super-Mare) 6-9 August	v. Yorkshire (Weston-super-Mare) 10-12 August	v. Derbyshire (Derby) 13-16 August	v. Middlesex (Lord's) 20-23 August	v. Hampshire (Bournemouth) 24-26 August	v. Glamorgan (Taunton) 27-30 August	v. Hampshire (Taunton) 31 August-2 Sept.	v. Kent (Taunton) 7-9 September	v. Warwickshire (Taunton) 10-13 September	Inns	NOs	Runs	HS	Av
58 42	3 55*	1 11	23 31	4 0	13 94	33 10*		34 21	106* 20		2 13*	38	5	1235	106*	37.42
41 48	100 38*	12 21			55 41	21 32	0 4		0 9	19 18	14 27*	35	2	901	100	27.30
22 0					31 5*		0 4					17	2	224	66	14.93
			40 5			36 10				24	11 —	9	—	184	52	20.44
												13	—	570	152	43.84
46 8	29 —	10 6	52 10	29 26	9 35	25 2	15 7	22 47	0 5*	0 —		39	3	886	143	24.61
14 44		15 42	25 3	27 40	7 0			30 44*	21 0	29 —	26 —	25	3	524	44*	23.81
	20 —	24 3	32* 0	5 4	50 —	23 0	5 8	13 9	32* 0	7 —	23 —	33	4	457	51	15.75
		9 2	0* 8	10 4	0* —		4 2	8 —		50 —		26	5	296	50	14.09
			6*	20		7 —			0	17 —	1 —	17	5	125	20*	10.41
												11	7	60	25	15.00
142* 76	117* —	37 0	61 128*	25 27*		35 20				103 —		20	4	1204	216	75.25
	2			1			5* 0					13	2	116	78	10.54
2 21*	2 —	15 4	10 15	27 44	11 5		12 61*	6 25	39 17	2 —	12 —	36	3	758	99	22.96
		0 —	21* 17*		8 2*	25 2		31 18*				16	6	265	44	26.50
	45 —	38 17	9 14	1 27*	50 —	21 22	13 13	0 21				22	2	517	99*	25.85
												3	1	72	55*	36.00
14 11									41 18	173* —	42 —	12	1	376	173*	34.18
												1	—	8	8	8.00
						7 17	59 27	44 0	8 25*	69 82*	12 —	12	2	352	82*	35.20
	1 0		0*		1* 0*		0* —	0* —		7 —	2* 9	12	5	24	9	3.42
5 5		9		24	6 9	8 7	4 4	4 3		5	2 3	1 2	6		7
5 2	10 3	3 5	10 5	7 4	1 4	4 3	2 1	3 9	12	11	8 2				
1 6	2 5	1			6		1			1 2	1					
6 2			9 5	2 1	7 3	11 5	6 3	6 8	5 6	10	12 3				
342 223	337 110	185 155	267 278	164 153	273 233	249 119	76 173	214 241	321 86	462 54	219 117					
6 7	7 0	10 10	7 8	10 6	10 5	10 9‡	10 10	10 7	6 10	10 0	10 1					
D	D	L	D	D	D	W	L	W	D	D	D					
8	6	3	4	3	7	22	4	22	4	6	6					

The match v. Oxford University (Oxford), 27-29 April, was abandoned without a ball being bowled

† B.C. Rose absent hurt
‡ P.M. Roebuck retired hurt

5 – V.J. Marks, P.A. Slocombe and M.R. Davis
3 – R.L. Ollis and P.H.L. Wilson
2 – B.C. Rose and N.A. Felton
1 – J.G. Wyatt

if his team selections had sometimes bemused. McEwan, Gooch, Lever had performed nobly, but the strength of the side was founded on its great team spirit and the endeavours of Phillip, Acfield, Turner and the rest in the closing weeks had been decisive. On the most encouraging side was the advance of Pringle and Foster, awarded his county cap during this match, and the brilliant wicket-keeping of David East, an heir apparent to Taylor. He was the lynch-pin of a superb fielding side in which Hardie, the beneficiary, and Gooch excelled in close catching positions.

First Class Averages

BATTING

	M	Inns	NOs	Runs	HS	Av	100s	50s
I.V.A. Richards	12	20	4	1204	216	75.25	5	3
C.G. Greenidge	15	27	5	1438	154	65.35	4	9
M.W. Gatting	18	28	5	1498	216	64.95	6	5
J.A. Carse	11	10	8	129	36*	64.50		
K.S. McEwan	26	39	5	2176	189*	64.00	8	8
Imran Khan	13	25	3	1260	124*	57.27	2	12
C.S. Cowdrey	22	34	10	1364	123	56.83	5	5
A.J. Lamb	17	29	7	1232	137*	56.00	5	3
G. Boycott	23	40	5	1941	214*	55.45	7	4
A.I. Kallicharran	22	34	4	1637	243*	54.56	6	4
M.A. Lynch	24	39	10	1558	119	53.72	3	11
C.L. Smith	23	39	3	1923	193	53.41	6	8

Batting	M	Inns	NOs	Runs	HS	Av	100s	50s
G. Fowler	18	30	3	1403	156*	51.96	5	6
P. Willey	23	40	8	1546	175*	48.31	4	9
G.D. Barlow	23	39	7	1545	132	48.28	4	9
R.A. Smith	7	12	3	434	104*	48.22	3	
D.K. Standing	4	8	3	240	60	48.00		2
R.A. Woolmer	14	22	1	994	129	47.33	4	5
M.D. Marshall	16	16	4	563	112	46.91	2	2
D.M. Smith	13	20	4	748	131*	46.75	2	3
J.G. Wright	11	13		605	136	46.53	1	4
D.I. Gower	19	32	5	1253	140	46.40	5	5
R.J. Hadlee	11	15	2	596	103	45.80	1	5
Zaheer Abbas	12	19		867	116	45.63	3	4
T.A. Lloyd	23	41	4	1673	208*	45.21	5	5
R.P. Moulding	8	13	3	448	80*	44.80		4
M.R. Benson	23	37	3	1515	152*	44.55	4	10
D.L. Amiss	26	43	4	1721	164	44.12	4	11
R.N. Kapil Dev	7	10	2	349	120	43.62	1	1
A.J.T. Miller	15	26	3	1002	127*	43.56	1	7
D.G. Aslett	20	36	3	1437	168	43.54	3	8
R.G. Williams	26	40	10	1305	104*	43.50	1	10
W.N. Slack	18	28	4	1034	140	43.08	3	6
C.J. Tavare	15	24		1030	109	42.91	1	9
T.E. Jesty	20	30	5	1072	187	42.88	1	5
A.W. Stovold	23	42	3	1671	181	42.84	4	8
D.R. Turner	12	17	3	598	122*	42.71	1	3
B.C. Broad	16	27	2	1061	145	42.44	3	3
D Lloyd	10	15	3	507	123	42.25	1	4
W. Larkins	25	42		1774	252	42.23	5	4
D.B. Pauline	12	21	2	795	115	41.84	1	7
P.A. Neale	24	40	3	1521	139	41.10	2	11

Somerset C.C.C. First-Class Matches — Bowling, 1983

	I.T. Botham	M.R. Davis	C.H. Dredge	P.H.L. Wilson	N.F.M. Popplewell	V.J. Marks	J.W. Lloyds	G.V. Palmer	J. Garner
v. Notts. (Trent Bridge) 30 April–2 May	13–4–37–1	8–2–35–2	13–1–55–1	15–6–30–1	5–2–13–1	1–0–5–0			
v. Worcestershire (Taunton) 4–6 May	7–3–11–0	15–2–51–1	22–9–36–2	12–0–52–1	7.1–1–26–3	19–7–49–0	3–0–10–0		
v. Worcestershire (Worcester) 11–13 May	11.3–5–28–1		20–2–90–2	9–0–40–0	4–0–28–0	31–8–101–4		12–0–28–1	
v. Sussex (Taunton) 25–27 May	6–0–25–0		11–1–44–0		6–0–13–0	37–9–112–3	27–6–108–1		20–4–49–2
v. Essex (Taunton) 4–7 June	17–3–61–0 18–6–49–4	17–2–55–1 4–0–20–0	24.5–5–64–5 15–5–35–1		11–3–21–1	14–2–36–2 39.5–10–103–4	4–1–8–0 11–2–29–0		
v. Gloucestershire (Bristol) 8–10 June		15.4–2–62–3 14–4–42–1	14–1–59–1 16–1–44–2	12–2–64–1 12–3–43–1	9–2–32–1 6.2–0–18–1		23–7–86–1 10–5–32–0	16–3–56–1 14–4–42–0	
v. Sussex (Hove) 11–14 June		11–3–19–1 6–1–25–1	17–7–42–3 14–4–24–0	10.5–0–44–2 15–7–21–0	8–2–31–1 3–1–12–0		2–0–5–0 1–0–10–0	14–3–31–2 10–3–18–2	
v. Glamorgan (Swansea) 15–17 June			23–10–38–1 9–3–12–0	13.4–4–25–2 8–3–21–0	5–3–6–1 16–3–32–0		13–8–13–2 28–12–50–2	19–5–58–4 11–3–27–0	
v. Derbyshire (Bath) 18–21 June		22–5–55–3	18–7–42–1 8–3–11–1		9–0–25–2 19.4–3–54–3		20.3–8–54–3 13–3–26–1	21–1–62–1 15–6–19–1	
v. Gloucestershire (Bath) 22–24 June				25–5–77–4 23–2–83–3	7–0–33–0 14–0–34–2		5–1–9–1 5.5–2–14–1	20–1–94–2 9–1–27–1	
v. New Zealanders (Taunton) 2–5 July		26–2–123–2 2–1–4–0		29–6–109–4 6–2–11–0	7–1–50–0	35–10–125–1 2.5–0–7–0	16–2–89–1		15–6–32–1 6–1–17–0
v. Leicestershire (Leicester) 9–12 July	14–3–38–5 3–2–9–0		4–1–25–0 12–3–31–2	11–1–44–1 6–1–7–0	1–0–8–0	6–3–18–0 41.4–15–105–5			15.3–4–42–3 12–2–32–1
v. Kent (Maidstone) 13–15 July			9–1–27–0 15–1–37–2	5–1–9–0 8–0–38–2	9–0–40–1 7–0–39–0		2–1–6–0 14–3–40–2		16.1–4–37–6 19–4–61–1
v. Surrey (Taunton) 16–19 July			12–3–39–2 5–1–20–1				28.5–8–89–3 35–6–120–5	10–1–46–0	19–7–41–3 19–5–43–0
v. Northamptonshire (Northampton) 27–29 July			17.1–7–56–1 14–2–45–1	12–0–55–1 14–2–64–1	5–2–22–0		7–3–26–0 4–1–6–0		18–2–58–4 16–5–34–2
v. Lancashire (Old Trafford) 30 July–2 August			21–7–44–2			45–22–72–1	21–9–49–2		26–10–52–3
v. Northamptonshire (Weston-s-Mare) 6–9 Aug.	10–1–56–0 6–0–22–0	5–1–24–0 7–2–29–1	18–6–40–2 9–2–28–0		3–0–22–0	33–9–123–1 25–6–66–2			
v. Yorkshire (Weston-s-Mare) 10–12 August		10–1–39–0 14–3–36–3	10–5–25–2 16–2–33–2			44.2–24–79–6 22–8–61–1		9–2–31–0 4–2–13–0	
v. Derbyshire (Derby) 13–16 August		11–3–34–4 13–2–37–0	13–3–39–1 11–0–38–0		10–2–31–0 4.3–1–20–1	18–7–34–0 16–1–53–2	7–2–23–3 2–0–8–0		16.3–7–28–2 7–1–19–1
v. Middlesex (Lord's) 20–23 August	6–1–23–0 1–0–2–0	13–3–69–2				16.5–2–59–3 6–3–17–3	6–2–18–1		15–4–63–2 7–1–27–1
v. Hampshire (Bournemouth) 24–26 August			15–2–23–3 4–0–11–0		22–4–69–4 1.2–1–5–0		8–2–11–1	8–2–26–0 4–0–14–0	
v. Glamorgan (Taunton) 27–30 August			21.3–7–51–5 15–2–31–1		7–3–14–0	27–10–64–3 21–9–52–2	4–0–10–0 17–2–47–2		14–5–22–1 15.5–2–51–2
v. Hampshire (Taunton) 31 August–2 September		8–1–35–0	13–5–22–0 5–0–26–1		10–4–24–0 4–0–12–0	13–4–40–0	17–2–72–3		
v. Kent (Taunton) 7–9 September	7–0–27–1	10–3–31–0	8–0–36–0			31–7–134–5	3–0–11–0		
v. Warwickshire (Taunton) 10–13 Septemer		9–0–48–0			11–0–52–1	27–3–105–2		12.3–2–38–5	
	119.3–28–388–12 av. 32.33	240.4–43–873–25 av. 34.92	492.3–119–1323–48 av. 27.56	246.3–45–837–24 av. 34.87	232–38–786–23 av. 34.17	572.3–179–1620–50 av. 32.40	357.1–98–1079–35 av. 30.82	208.3–39–630–20 av. 31.50	277–74–708–35 av. 20.22

a P.M. Roebuck 2–0–15–0

b T. Gard 0.2–0–8–0

c P.M. Roebuck 1–0–4–0

d P.A. Slocombe 2–1–1–0; R.L. Ollis 1–0–2–0

e P.M. Roebuck 2–0–6–0; N. Russom 5–1–18–0

f C. Rose 1–0–6–0

† P.B. Clift retired hurt

I.V.A. Richards	S.C. Booth	D. Breakwell	Byes	Leg byes	Wides	No balls	Total	Wickets
			1	3		2	181	6
			2	5	1	10	253	7
			6	8			329	9
2-4-32-0			1	2	2	5	408	6a
						8		0b
			6	8	1	2	262	10
			1	4	1		242	9
			6	4	5	1	375	8
			4	4		2	231	5
				5		1	178	10
				3		1	118	3c
		1-1-0-0	9	4		1	154	10
		28-10-41-1		5	1	1	193	3d
		9-3-36-0	1	12	2		289	10
		16-3-44-3	2	7	1	2	166	10
			4	10	2	3	232	7
			5	10	1		198	8e
			1	12	1	2	544	9
				1			46	0f
			2	6		5	180	9†
29-13-75-2			1	2		7	277	10
10-5-28-2						3	150	10
13-3-42-0			12	8		3	280	7
14-6-29-2			1	4	1	3	253	10
28-8-56-3			4	7	1	1	252	9
1-4-23-0	37-12-93-3		1	2			336	9
18-0-56-1	18-6-54-0		4	6		4	273	5
15-3-41-1	24.3-5-77-1		3	10		7	355	10
18-10-27-0	38-4-107-2			2	4		405	5
	18-10-32-1			5			182	4
10-3-12-0	35-11-94-1			5		1	286	10
1-0-4-0	15-7-23-2		3	4			177	8
				5		5	199	10
				10		1	186	4
	12-2-21-3			4		3	242	10
	7.4-2-26-4			3			93	10
13-2-32-1	12-6-40-1		4	4	1	1	211	10
1-0-5-0				1	2	1	39	0
	22-9-42-1		6	3		6	218	10
	13-2-44-1			11			236	10
	15.1-6-51-0		1	7		1	253	3
				3			41	1
	18-1-105-0		8	2		3	357	6
	11-2-40-1		2	6	3	6	300	9
193-61-	296.2-85-	49-17-						
462-12	849-21	121-4						
av. 38.50	av. 40.42	av. 30.25						

Batting	M	Inns	NOs	Runs	HS	Av	100s	50s
R.O. Butcher	15	19	3	657	179	41.06	2	3
R.T. Robinson	25	41	3	1545	207	40.65	2	11
G.D. Mendis	24	46	6	1624	133*	40.60	4	8
V.P. Terry	20	33	6	1096	115	40.59	3	4
I.T. Botham	14	21		852	152	40.57	3	2
B.F. Davison	26	41	6	1417	123*	40.48	3	8
A.P.E. Knott	23	30	9	848	92*	40.38		6
A.J. Stewart	10	17	4	525	118*	40.38	1	2
N.E. Briers	25	38	6	1289	201*	40.28	1	8
G.A. Gooch	26	38	1	1481	111	40.02	4	7
J.C. Balderstone	25	41	4	1478	112	39.94	3	9
G. Cook	24	41	3	1510	128	39.73	1	11
J. Abrahams	24	39	7	1261	178	39.40	3	4
G.P. Howarth	15	23	2	820	144	39.04	1	6
N.R. Taylor	23	39	6	1275	155*	38.63	5	3
R.D.V. Knight	24	38	6	1235	101*	38.59	1	9
R.C. Ontong	26	43	9	1310	112	38.52	3	7
D.N. Patel	26	44	2	1615	112	38.45	3	10
K.J. Barnett	24	40	3	1423	121	38.45	3	9
D.L. Bairstow	23	35	6	1102	100*	38.00	1	8
A. Hill	24	40	5	1311	137*	37.45	4	6
P.M. Roebuck	22	38	5	1235	106*	37.42	1	9
I.S. Anderson	22	37	4	1233	112	37.36	1	8
M.C.J. Nicholas	26	43	5	1418	158	37.31	3	6
C.E.B. Rice	19	30	2	1026	101*	36.64	2	3
J.N. Shepherd	23	34	6	1025	168	36.60	2	6
N.H. Fairbrother	16	26	5	759	94*	36.14		8
D.J. Thomas	23	31	5	937	119	36.03	2	4
I.A. Greig	9	10	1	324	147*	36.00	1	1
E.A. Baptiste	17	26	5	755	136*	35.95	2	3
J.G. Wyatt	6	12	2	352	82*	35.20		3
R.J. Boyd-Moss	25	43	2	1437	139	35.04	3	7
A. Sidebottom	16	21	7	490	78	35.00		2
K.R. Pont	21	27	4	802	125*	34.86	2	4
D.R. Pringle	17	21	4	586	102*	34.47	1	2
N.A. Felton	7	12	1	376	173*	34.18	1	1
M.D. Moxon	12	23		780	153	33.91	1	4
P.W. Romaines	22	41	3	1286	135	33.84	3	4
A.J. Hignell	20	37	6	1044	109*	33.67	2	6
C. Gladwin	9	14		470	89	33.57		2
I.P. Butcher	17	30	1	973	139	33.55	3	3
G. Sharp	23	24	8	536	98	33.50		3
A.R. Butcher	25	44	3	1350	128	32.92	3	6
J.D. Love	23	38	7	1020	76*	32.90		7
P.A. Smith	13	17	3	458	114	32.71	1	3
K.W.R. Fletcher	25	36	3	1077	151*	32.63	2	4
S.T. Jefferies	10	12	4	260	75*	32.50		1
P.B. Clift	23	33	7	843	100*	32.42	1	2
F.C. Hayes	20	28	1	866	149	32.07	3	4
J.H. Hampshire	15	21	2	601	85	31.63		4
A.L. Jones	23	40	7	1036	99	31.39		8
G.W. Humpage	26	42	6	1116	141*	31.00	2	5
K.P. Tomlins	20	27	5	670	132*	30.45	1	3
G. Miller	21	30	7	699	84	30.39		4
A. Jones	22	37	2	1059	105	30.25	1	5
D.A. Banks	7	13	1	363	100	30.25	1	1
J.D. Birch	24	38	2	1086	95	30.16		8
D.W. Randall	18	28	2	777	94	29.88		6
K. Sharp	12	21	1	597	139	29.85	2	1
C.H. Lloyd	11	16	1	447	86	29.80		3
B.R. Hardie	25	37	2	1042	129	29.77	1	6
M.S. Scott	7	12	2	297	76	29.70		3
P. Bainbridge	24	43	2	1217	146	29.68	1	6
K.D. Smith	27	47	4	1272	109	29.58	2	8
C.T. Radley	25	38	6	943	119	29.46	1	4
P. Carrick	23	32	8	697	83	29.04		4
D.J. Capel	17	24	5	534	109*	28.10	1	3
N.E.J. Pocock	26	35	8	755	60*	27.96		3
J.E. Emburey	24	33	5	782	133	27.92	1	3
I.J. Gould	18	23	6	474	59*	27.88		1
C.J. Richards	25	35	8	751	85*	27.81		2
A.P. Wells	16	28	4	665	92	27.70		5
M.J. Bamber	7	14	1	360	77	27.69		2
R.W. Tolchard	26	35	7	775	80*	27.67		3
T.S. Curtis	19	37	5	880	92	27.50		5
R.G.P. Ellis	15	26	2	658	103*	27.41	1	3

Surrey C.C.C. — First-Class Matches — Batting, 1983

Match columns (two innings each): K = v. Kent (The Oval) 30 April–2 May; GB = v. Gloucestershire (Bristol) 4–6 May; LO = v. Leicestershire (The Oval) 11–13 May; La = v. Lancashire (The Oval) 25–27 May; E = v. Essex (Chelmsford) 28–31 May; Wo = v. Worcestershire (Worcester) 8–10 June; Mi = v. Middlesex (The Oval) 11–14 June; No = v. Nottinghamshire (Trent Bridge) 15–17 June; Ox = v. Oxford University (The Oval) 18–21 June; LL = v. Leicestershire (Leicester) 22–24 June; Nh = v. Northamptonshire (The Oval) 25–28 June; GO = v. Gloucestershire (The Oval) 2–5 July; Ha = v. Hampshire (Southampton) 9–12 July

	K1	K2	GB1	GB2	LO1	LO2	La1	La2	E1	E2	Wo1	Wo2	Mi1	Mi2	No1	No2	Ox1	Ox2	LL1	LL2	Nh1	Nh2	GO1	GO2	Ha1	Ha2
A.R. Butcher	1	—	14	—	9	—	16	100	2	5	92	14*	14	14	13	7*	8	—	21	0	10	12	33	—	19	16
G.S. Clinton	0	—	105	—	2	—	0	23	6	61*	29	4*	7	4	57	5*	68	—	5	11	9	17	33	—	19	16
D.M. Smith	10	—	90	—			32	2			15	—	8	106*					47*				53	—	18	24
G.P. Howarth	9	—	22*	—	20	—	66	6																		
R.D.V. Knight	52*	—	0	—	40	—	28	2*	0	101*	41	—	45	10	60	—			31	6*	13	38	32	—	57	51*
M.A. Lynch	21	—	9*	—	69*	—	0	39*	0	—	112	—	0	61	85	—			33	1*	2	6	76	—	119	42
C.J. Richards	2	—			21*	—	47	—	0	—	6	—	1	3	13	—	33	—	24	—	0	44*	24	—	85*	14
D.J. Thomas	25*	—					76	—	0	—	48	—	62	0	24*	—			13	—	52	0	49*	—	24	28*
G. Monkhouse							17	—	2	—	23	—	35	5					4	—	41	—	1	—	0*	
S.T. Clarke							11	0	4	—	24*	—	19	6	21	—			12	—	43	—	12	—		
P.I. Pocock							4*	—	0*	—	16*	—	4*	23									8	—		
I.J. Curtis																			2	—						
A. Needham									0	4	18	—	1	0	16	—			2	—	8	16*				
I.R. Payne									0	—							3*	—			28		16	—	2*	
A.J. Stewart																	118*	—			25	19				
D.B. Pauline																	38*	—					19	—	0	0
R.G.L. Cheatle																										
M.A. Feltham																										
K.S. Mackintosh																										
P. Waterman																										
Byes			3					1	1		4	1	9	10	1		8		5	4		1	6		2	
Leg-byes	4		8		6		8	9	8		11		3	6	6		2		3		3	9	13		6	2
Wides			1		1		1		2		4				1		2		1		1	1	1		1	
No-balls	2				2				3		8		6	6	1		8		6		10		1		6	
Total	126		252		170		305	183	14	185	451	19	214	254	369	12	313		209	22	217	163	344		339	177
Wickets	6		4		4		10	5	10	2	9	0	10	10	8	0	4		10	2	10	6	10		6	5
Result	D		D		D		D		D		W		L		W		W		D		D		W		D	
Points	0		6		1		8		4		23		6		23		—		4		5		24		6	

Catches 56 – C.J. Richards (ct 49/st 7)   17 – S.T. Clarke   14 – M.A. Lynch   11 – I.R. Payne   8 – G. Monkhouse and P.I. Pocock
28 – R.D.V. Knight   15 – A.R. Butcher   13 – D.M. Smith   9 – D.J. Thomas

Batting	M	Inns	NOs	Runs	HS	Av	100s	50s
S.J. O'Shaughnessy	18	28	3	685	105	27.40	2	1
J.A. Hopkins	25	43	2	1123	116	27.39	2	3
S.P. Henderson	20	35	5	820	135*	27.33	1	4
J.W. Lloyds	21	35	2	901	100	27.30	1	4
K.I. Hodgson	10	15	5	272	47	27.20		
R.J. Doughty	7	11	6	135	32*	27.00		
S.B. Hassan	21	34	1	890	112	26.96	1	5
J.G. Varey	6	10	3	187	69*	26.71		1
D.A. Francis	23	39	5	903	89*	26.55		4
J. Garner	10	16	6	265	44	26.50		
D.B. d'Oliveira	22	39	2	972	102	26.27	1	5
R.L. Ollis	13	22	2	517	99*	25.85		3
A.M. Ferreira	17	24	6	465	66	25.83		3
J.A. Ormrod	24	41	3	967	84	25.44		6
J.J. Whitaker	10	16	4	305	56*	25.41		1
A.J. Wright	10	17	2	380	56*	25.33		2
S.G. Hinks	6	10		253	87	25.30		1
C.M. Wells	24	40	6	857	95	25.20		4
G.S. Le Roux	13	17	1	401	80	25.06		1
S.J.G. Doggart	10	18	5	323	70	24.84		2
W.P. Fowler	17	26	2	591	91	24.62		5
N.F.M. Popplewell	24	39	3	886	143	24.61	1	4
R.M. Ellison	22	21	7	343	63	24.50		1
C.W.J. Athey	20	32	1	758	77	24.45		4
G.W. Johnson	25	30	13	413	79*	24.29		1
L.L. McFarlane	10	9	8	24	8*	24.00		
I.R. Payne	10	11	4	167	40*	23.85		
T. Davies	10	15	4	260	69*	23.63		2
P. Johnson	16	28	2	612	125	23.53	1	4
K.D. James	7	8	2	141	34	23.50		
L. Potter	6	11		258	50	23.45		1
R.G. Lumb	10	15	1	328	60	23.42		2
J. Simmons	23	31	6	679	104	23.41	3	3
M.J. Weston	22	38	1	862	115	23.29	1	2
C.J.C. Rowe	22	33	2	721	82	23.25		3
G.S. Clinton	13	22	3	439	105	23.10	1	3
P.W. Denning	21	36	3	758	99	22.96		4
Asif Din	14	21	3	411	65	22.83		2
M.S.A. McEvoy	16	26	1	569	103	22.76	1	2
D.S. Steele	25	31	6	569	60	22.76		3
D.E. East	26	32	4	635	91	22.67		2
N.F. Williams	25	25	7	407	63	22.61		2
G. Monkhouse	18	18	5	291	46	22.38		
V.J. Marks	17	27	3	530	44*	22.08		
P.R. Downton	25	30	7	508	87	22.08		4
R.C. Russell	24	32	9	507	64*	22.04		3
G. Pathmanathan	7	13	1	263	64	21.91		2
J.R.T. Barclay	21	37	3	743	65	21.85		3
D.J. Humphries	20	30	4	560	59	21.53		2
Nasir Zaidi	13	16	6	215	51	21.50		1
D.A. Graveney	22	28	8	427	94	21.35		2
J.R.P. Heath	9	18	2	335	39	20.93		
L.B. Taylor	19	18	6	250	47	20.83		
I. Cockbain	8	15	1	291	52	20.78		1
H. Morris	8	14	3	228	34	20.72		
P.W.G. Parker	17	27	2	512	79	20.48		4
B.C. Rose	8	9		184	52	20.44		1
I. Folley	12	9	4	102	25	20.40		
R.I.H.B. Dyer	9	15	3	242	93	20.16		1
D.P. Hughes	19	28	2	522	153	20.07	1	3

	v. Somerset (Taunton) 16-19 July	v. Nottinghamshire (The Oval) 27-29 July	v. Glamorgan (Swansea) 30 July-2 Aug	v. Warwickshire (The Oval) 6-9 Aug	v. Kent (Canterbury) 10-12 Aug	v. Worcestershire (Guildford) 13-16 Aug	v. Sussex (Hove) 20-23 Aug	v. Middlesex (Lord's) 24-26 Aug	v. Essex (The Oval) 27-30 Aug	v. Sussex (The Oval) 31 Aug-2 Sept	v. Yorkshire (Scarborough) 7-9 Sept	v. Derbyshire (The Oval) 10-13 Sept	Inns	NOs	Runs	HS	Av
	40 45	40 23*	29 128	75 9	52 6	122 85	40 5	19 13	16 13	18 76	0 21	55 —	44	3	1350	128	32.92
	4 19	3 0											22	3	439	105	23.10
	2 31	22 11*	35 131*	0 43									20	4	748	131*	46.75
													5	1	123	66	30.75
	52 64	35 —	17 —	45 16	53 16	4 20*	57 5	7 40	42 46	75 —	33 1	0 —	38	6	1235	101*	38.59
	78 34	67 —	90 18	31 59*	12 76*	25 9	24 101*	2 6	13 0*	53 45*	36 76*	28	39	10	1558	119	53.72
	21 14	1 —	2 37*	33 8	16 19*	39 8*	23 52*	24 4	43 —	46 —	20 18*	6	35	8	751	85*	27.81
	18 25	119 —	31 1	16 1	33 14	32 3	103* 0		51 —	41 —	14 34	0 —	31	5	937	119	36.03
		32 —	46 —	8* 4*	7 —	15* 0	39* 12						18	5	291	46	22.38
	0 0	19 —	18 —	0 —	3 0	9* —		37 18*	8* —	7 —	12 —	2 —	24	4	285	43	14.25
	4 1	12* —	0* —	15 —	0 —			0 6	0 —	10 —	0 —	7 —	19	7	110	23	9.16
	7 1*	5* —	0 —		0* —			1 4	2 —		0* —		10	4	22	7	3.66
			3 6					11 3					13	1	88	18	7.33
								40* 13	43 —	0 —	12 —	10* —	11	4	167	43	23.85
				20 25	82 43	0 12*	31 5	20 52*	8 —	17 6	42* —		17	4	525	118*	40.38
			52 37	14 60	17 69	51 4	26 20	64 9	115 79*	32 14	75 —		21	2	795	115	41.84
													—		—		
	18* 5*												2	2	23	18*	—
										6* —		0 —	2	1	6	6*	6.00

	v. Somerset	v. Notts	v. Glamorgan	v. Warwicks	v. Kent	v. Worcs	v. Sussex (Hove)	v. Middlesex	v. Essex	v. Sussex (Oval)	v. Yorkshire	v. Derbyshire					
	1 4	3 4	2 4	4	5	9	2 1	7	1	4		8					
	4 7	17 3	12 3	8 4	9 7	3 8	9 2	7 2	12 2	4 4	1 5	11					
	1 1	1	6 1	1 1	4		2	1		5 1		1					
	3 1	2 1	12 11	17 2	10 7	6 1	9 3	19 6	7 2			1					
	253 252	378 42	303 340	301 188	233 235	363 246	357 198	233 140	322 124	388 209	178 176	244					
	10 9	9 1	10 4	9 6	10 6	7 6	6 5	10 10	10 3	10 1	10 5	9†					
	D	W	L	D	W	W	D	L	W	L	D	D					
	5	24	6	7	21	24	7	5	24	5	5	4					

† A.J. Stewart retired hurt

5 – A.J. Stewart (ct 4/st 1)   2 – A. Needham
3 – D.B. Pauline and I.J. Curtis   1 – G.P. Howarth and R.G.L. Cheatle

Batting	M	Inns	NOs	Runs	HS	Av	100s	50s
A.M. Green	16	30	2	552	53	19.71		1
E.W. Jones	15	18	5	256	39	19.69		
P.G. Heseltine	6	10	1	176	40	19.55		
N.G. Cowley	23	27	9	351	29	19.50		
A.C.S. Pigott	23	29	8	408	63	19.42		3
N.A. Foster	13	16	4	232	40*	19.33		
J.F. Steele	24	26	9	327	50	19.23		1
R.E. East	21	27	5	420	80*	19.09		1
J.E. Morris	10	20	1	361	58	19.00		1
C.M. Old	22	25	4	396	62	18.85		1
T.M. Tremlett	24	19	5	263	59	18.78		1
G.A. Tedstone	13	16	3	243	67*	18.69		1
B.N. French	24	38	4	630	91	18.52		3
C.J. Tunnicliffe	17	25		461	91	18.44		2
J.W. Southern	15	13	5	146	45*	18.25		
D.W. Varey	10	20	1	342	65	18.00		1
D.J. Wild	5	9		161	48	17.88		
N.A. Mallander	23	27	9	320	71*	17.77		1
R.J. Finney	20	35	2	578	71	17.51		3
C. Maynard	22	27	3	417	61*	17.37		2
G.J. Parsons	14	15	3	207	56	17.25		1
J.D. Inchmore	20	26	4	377	51	17.13		1
R.G.D. Willis	17	20	9	183	37	16.63		
G.B. Stevenson	20	25	1	396	52	16.50		2
P.J.W. Allott	17	18	4	225	41	16.07		
R.W. Taylor	21	30	7	366	41*	15.91		
N. Phillip	19	26		413	80	15.88		1
T. Gard	25	33	4	457	51	15.75		
A.H. Wilkins	14	15	3	185	54	15.41		1
R.S. Cowan	5	10		154	50	15.40		1
P. Moores	7	11	1	154	30	15.40		
J.K. Lever	18	17	3	211	44	15.07		
B.J.M. Maher	8	12	2	150	52	15.00		1
P.H.L. Wilson	11	11	7	60	25	15.00		
P.A. Slocombe	11	17	2	224	66	14.93		1
S.N. Hartley	14	19	1	261	69	14.50		1
S.T. Clarke	24	24	4	285	50	14.25		1
G.R. Dilley	12	9	1	114	29	14.25		
C.H. Dredge	21	26	5	296	50	14.09		1
R.A. Pick	5	8	2	84	25*	14.00		
R.J. Parks	25	15	2	180	52	13.84		1
K.A. Hayes	8	12		165	45	13.75		
S. Oldham	14	17	4	177	39	13.61		
B.J. Lloyd	14	12	2	135	38	13.50		
N. Gifford	22	21	6	201	39	13.40		
A.E. Warner	9	15	5	131	26*	13.10		
E.E. Hemmings	23	32	3	377	38	13.00		
P.H. Edmonds	19	20	4	208	65	13.00		1
H.T. Rawlinson	8	9	2	91	24	13.00		
K. Stevenson	7	9	3	77	25	12.83		
D.A. Reeve	17	20	5	192	42*	12.80		
K.E. Cooper	22	27	7	254	30*	12.70		
D.G. Moir	17	21	3	224	53	12.44		1
G.C. Small	6	8	3	62	31	12.40		
M.K. Bore	13	16	5	132	24	12.00		
J.G. Thomas	10	9	1	96	23	12.00		
M.W.W. Selvey	24	24	3	250	63	11.90		1
J.D. Carr	9	10	4	67	18	11.16		
R.M. Ellcock	12	18	4	154	36	11.00		
R.A. Cobb	8	10		110	28	11.00		

Surrey C.C.C.
First-Class Matches — Bowling, 1983

	S.T. Clarke	D.J. Thomas	G. Monkhouse	P.I. Pocock	R.D.V. Knight	A.R. Butcher	M.A. Lynch	A. Needham	I.R. Payne
v. Kent (The Oval) 30 April–2 May									
v. Gloucestershire (Bristol) 4–6 May	23–5–62–2	17–3–78–1	16–3–69–0	32–10–70–4	10–4–24–0				
v. Leicestershire (The Oval) 11–13 May									
v. Lancashire (The Oval) 25–27 May	23–10–33–1 / 10–1–40–1	16–4–41–4 / 12–4–29–0	8–3–12–1	32–12–70–5 / 23–10–30–2	8–3–13–0	2–0–9–0	1.3–0–12–0		
v. Essex (Chelmsford) 28–31 May	20–3–58–2	20–2–78–1	13–2–49–1	19.5–6–49–3	17–6–33–2				
v. Worcestershire (Worcester) 8–10 June	18–6–45–4 / 18–5–55–0	16–3–43–1 / 11–3–36–1	14.2–5–35–3 / 23–7–55–4	19–8–45–2 / 29–8–83–4	3–0–13–0 / 6–4–8–0			2–1–1–0 / 7–1–20–1	
v. Middlesex (The Oval) 11–14 June	18–2–55–1 / 3–0–6–0	13–1–60–1 / 5–2–7–0	26–7–59–4	32.4–6–118–3 / 11–1–28–0	3–0–20–0			8–1–34–0 / 9.3–1–50–0	
v. Nottinghamshire (Trent Bridge) 15–17 June	29.4–11–43–2 / 17–6–37–1	20–5–50–3 / 15–3–33–4		34–15–49–4 / 5.4–2–5–0	9–2–29–1 / 5–3–8–0			9–3–15–0 / 21.2–5–52–5	3–0–14–0 / 3–2–2–0
v. Oxford University (The Oval) 18–21 June			14.4–4–21–2 / 6–1–20–0					19–12–30–6 / 22–9–31–3	8–3–15–0
v. Leicestershire (Leicester) 22–24 June	17.3–1–49–1 / 16–2–44–2	15–1–73–2 / 16–7–27–2	13.4–3–40–1 / 9–1–30–2		8.2–2–23–1			17–2–64–0	
v. Northamptonshire (The Oval) 25–28 June	22–6–61–3 / 21–5–50–2	15.2–3–36–1 / 19–3–56–2	31–10–68–3 / 21–4–51–3	22–6–63–1 / 6–0–15–0	3.4–1–22–0				
v. Gloucestershire (The Oval) 2–5 July	14–10–14–3 / 10–1–35–2	15.3–10–22–4 / 10–2–43–2	14–3–27–3 / 8–1–33–1						9–3–22–0 / 9–4–13–5
v. Hampshire (Southampton) 9–12 July	23–6–67–2 / 6–1–20–0	14–0–87–1 / 7–2–32–0	17–5–59–1	12–4–42–1 / 23–6–89–0	14–2–50–0	23–5–123–4			12.5–3–46–0 / 10–4–22–0
v. Somerset (Taunton) 16–19 July	19.3–1–53–3 / 11–5–21–0	20–3–61–1 / 9–0–42–0		28–7–91–2 / 29.5–10–79–7	9–1–32–0				
v. Nottinghamshire (The Oval) 27–29 July	21–4–50–1 / 17.4–7–26–3	15–3–37–0 / 5–3–10–0	21–5–51–7 / 6–3–16–0	17–6–19–2 / 33–10–74–6	10–3–21–0				
v. Glamorgan (Swansea) 30 July–2 August	35–10–82–5 / 13–1–73–1	23–7–46–1 / 4–0–10–0	16.5–4–71–2	9.5–5–11–0 / 10–3–41–0	10–1–30–1			23.1–11–59–0 / 8–0–63–3	
v. Warwickshire (The Oval) 6–9 August	26–7–53–7 / 15–6–26–1	17–3–52–1 / 10–5–33–0	15–2–39–1 / 8–0–35–0	14–5–21–0 / 18–5–44–1	17–4–39–1	8.3–1–42–1	5–0–29–0		
v. Kent (Canterbury) 10–12 August	23–4–65–3 / 13–3–38–1	13–3–35–1 / 10–2–32–1	28–10–73–3 / 10–4–24–3	15–4–48–0 / 3–0–14–1	14–0–48–0				
v. Worcestershire (Guildford) 13–16 August	18–7–39–4 / 15–3–46–1	15–1–48–3 / 14–5–33–4	11–3–35–1 / 4–2–5–0	21–5–63–2 / 16.4–9–13–4		5–3–5–0			
v. Sussex (Hove) 20–23 August	16–5–50–2 / 10–6–13–0	16–3–52–3 / 9–1–30–3	14–3–57–1 / 5–2–6–0	14–2–34–0 / 14–5–35–2	8–1–23–1	5–0–20–0	1–0–6–0		
v. Middlesex (Lord's) 24–26 August	27.1–5–83–3 / 10–3–23–1			27–9–59–1 / 15–5–34–1	9–3–26–0 / 3–0–21–1			12–4–21–1 / 6–0–30–0	27–4–56–4 / 14–3–45–0
v. Essex (The Oval) 27–30 August	18.1–5–63–5 / 24.1–10–48–6	14–2–89–1 / 17–4–37–2		9–1–23–1 / 3–2–1–0	12–3–33–0				19–2–56–2 / 16–5–41–1
v. Sussex (The Oval) 31 August–2 September	13–1–55–1	16.1–3–54–0 / 12–0–50–2		17–3–50–1 / 16–1–96–2	13–4–37–2 / 12–0–58–3	1.1–0–11–0			12–4–45–0 / 3–0–18–0
v. Yorkshire (Scarborough) 7–9 September	26–7–65–1	21–2–83–2		25.5–5–94–5	9–2–22–0				8–0–18–0
v. Derbyshire (The Oval) 10–13 September	12.2–2–27–1	30–6–116–2		24–4–74–1	23–11–44–2				8–1–37–0
	693.1–183–1773–79 av. 22.44	537–114–1781–57 av. 31.24	373.3–97–1040–47 av. 22.12	681.2–200–1774–68 av. 26.08	236–60–677–15 av. 45.13	44.4–9–210–5 av. 42.00	7.3–0–47–0	164–50–470–19 av. 24.73	161.5–38–450–12 av. 37.50

a K.S. Mackintosh 15–2–47–0   b D.M. Smith 0.2–0–1–0   c D.M. Smith 2–0–19–0

M.A. Feltham	I.J. Curtis	P. Waterman	Byes	Leg byes	Wides	No balls	Total	Wickets
				Match Abandoned				
			6	6	2	16	333	7
				Match Abandoned				
				9		6	172	10
			1	4	1	4	142	4
			4	10		6	287	10
				4		5	191	10
			7	4		10	278	10
			11	13		2	372	9
				1	1	4	97	0
			4	5	2	7	218	10
			1	11	6	6	161	10
1-4-25-1	7-4-15-0		3	3			112	10
7-1-19-1	22.1-13-28-6		3			2	103	10
	31-9-70-0		20			10	349	5
	10-2-24-0		4	2		8	139	6
			7	1	7	15	280	8
			9	8	3	11	203	7
			17	5	1	9	117	10
			7	5	1	6	143	10
				7	4	9	371	6
			7	7	4	5	309	4
16-4-41-0			5	5	1	6	342	6a
20-3-66-0			5	2	6	2	223	7
13-3-34-0			5			4	221	10
19-5-47-1			11	8	1	4	197	10
10-4-17-0			13	19	2	12	362	10
17-5-84-1			1	8		1	282	5b
4-0-9-0			6	8	1	2	230	10
13-1-55-0			13	7	12	8	323	3c
23-9-50-1			1	16		7	343	8
2.2-1-5-1			4	2		2	121	7
13-0-51-0			6	6		11	264	10
11-6-9-1			5			7	118	10
8-4-15-0			5	3	8	5	252	7
9-8-3-0			4	2		1	120	5
9-0-28-0			5	9		8	295	9
3.3-0-14-4			7	5		2	181	7
6-1-17-0			8	5	4	2	300	9
			13	2		1	143	10
	13-2-42-0		1	13	1	4	302	4
	8-0-45-0		5	10		6	299	7
	2-0-8-2		12	19	1	7	329	10
		18-5-64-1	11	7	4	1	385	7
18-5–	269-82–	39-7–						
44-2	690-17	151-1						
av. 22.00	av. 40.58	av. 151.00						

Batting	M	Inns	NOs	Runs	HS	Av	100s	50s
K. Saxelby	21	28	3	274	35	10.96		
N.G.B. Cook	25	24	5	201	32	10.57		
G.V. Palmer	10	13	2	116	78	10.54		1
M. Watkinson	15	20	4	168	29	10.50		
M.R. Davis	14	17	5	125	20*	10.41		
S. Turner	15	19	2	177	30	10.41		
M.A. Fell	5	9		93	41	10.33		
D.L. Underwood	25	20	6	142	26*	10.14		
M. Hendrick	21	26	13	130	30*	10.00		

(**Qualification** – 8 innings, average 10.00)

BOWLING

	Overs	Mds	Runs	Wks	Av	Best	10/m	5/inn
Imran Khan	48.2	12	86	12	7.16	6/6		1
J.K. Lever	569	135	1726	106	16.28	7/55	3	8
F.D. Stephenson	74.4	18	230	14	16.42	5/56		1
M.D. Marshall	533.5	143	1327	80	16.58	7/29	1	5
M. Hendrick	552.1	190	1122	66	17.00	6/17		4
S.R. Tracy	54.1	10	170	10	17.00	5/29		1
R.A. Woolmer	86	29	170	10	17.00	3/13		
J.E. Emburey	935	325	1844	103	17.90	6/13		4
A.M.E. Roberts	101.2	19	294	16	18.37	5/26		1
P.B. Clift	619.4	167	1592	83	19.18	5/20		2
D.L. Underwood	936.3	358	2044	106	19.28	7/55	3	9
K.D. James	89	20	217	11	19.72	5/28		1
T.M. Lamb	188.2	57	416	21	19.80	4/27		
L.B. Taylor	529.5	151	1381	69	20.01	7/73	1	3
J. Garner	277	74	708	35	20.22	6/37		1
N. Phillip	477.2	85	1409	69	20.42	6/4		5
T.M. Tremlett	600.2	198	1346	63	21.36	6/82		1
P.H. Edmonds	820.3	230	1974	92	21.45	6/38	2	9
D.S. Steele	678	255	1460	68	21.47	5/48		2
M.A. Holding	169	41	451	21	21.47	5/48		3
R.J. Hadlee	431.3	123	1065	49	21.73	5/72		2
G.R. Dilley	275.3	73	681	31	21.96	5/70		1
R.G. Williams	434.1	148	1036	47	22.04	4/18		
G. Monkhouse	373.3	97	1040	47	22.12	7/51		1
S.T. Clarke	693.1	183	1773	79	22.44	7/53	1	4
A.E. Warner	210.3	38	608	27	22.52	4/72		
D.R. Pringle	288.4	53	928	41	22.63	7/32		2
G. Ferris	360	74	1205	53	22.73	7/42	1	3
N. Gifford	1043.4	346	2393	104	23.00	6/22	2	7
W.W. Daniel	324.3	51	1104	48	23.00	7/61	1	1
S. Turner	282.1	76	624	27	23.11	5/30		1
N.A. Foster	417	78	1216	52	23.38	6/46		1
D. Lloyd	199	60	400	17	23.52	5/22		1
E.A. Baptiste	376.3	88	1187	50	23.74	5/39		3
R.N. Kapil Dev	163	47	385	16	24.06	4/24		
O.H. Mortensen	517.3	108	1605	66	24.31	6/27	1	3
A. Needham	164	50	470	19	24.73	6/30		2
S.T. Jefferies	278.1	74	797	32	24.90	8/46	1	2
G.B. Stevenson	460.1	103	1400	56	25.00	5/35		2
N.G.B. Cook	878.1	321	1859	73	25.46	5/35		2
S.P. Hughes	268.3	61	910	36	25.27	6/32		2
G.S. Le Roux	362.3	92	950	37	25.67	5/17		2
N.G. Cowley	440.3	147	1053	41	25.68	4/10		
R.G.D. Willis	376.5	98	1058	41	25.80	5/35		1
P.I. Pocock	681.2	200	1774	68	26.08	7/79		4
A.C.S. Pigott	585.5	98	1889	72	26.23	6/22		4
A. Walker	165.4	30	578	22	26.27	4/61		
N.F. Williams	532.2	114	1659	63	26.33	5/77		1
M. Watkinson	319.3	69	929	35	26.54	6/51		2
J. Simmons	744	214	1807	68	26.57	7/73	1	5
W.W. Davis	452.4	110	1389	52	26.71	5/50		3
K. Saxelby	410.2	95	1337	50	26.74	5/52		2
A.P. Pridgeon	699.5	166	1978	72	27.47	5/21		2
C.H. Dredge	492.3	119	1323	48	27.56	5/51		2
A. Sidebottom	361	81	1080	39	27.69	5/6		1
J.G. Thomas	144.5	34	529	19	27.84	5/78		2
P. Carrick	848.1	303	1750	62	28.22	7/44	1	6
K.E. Cooper	579	164	1610	57	28.24	7/33		5
G.J. Parsons	269	73	823	29	28.37	5/51		1
D.L. Acfield	497.1	140	1222	43	28.41	7/100	1	2
B.J. Griffiths	536.2	130	1424	50	28.48	6/92		1
M.C.J. Nicholas	274.2	74	774	27	28.66	5/45		1

Sussex C.C.C. — First-Class Matches — Batting, 1983

Player	v. Oxford University (Oxford) 30 April-3 May		v. Nottinghamshire (Hove) 4-6 May		v. Somerset (Taunton) 25-27 May		v. Middlesex (Lord's) 28-31 May		v. Worcestershire (Hove) 4-7 June		v. Kent (Hove) 8-10 June		v. Somerset (Hove) 11-14 June		v. Kent (Tunbridge Wells) 15-17 June		v. Lancashire (Horsham) 18-21 June		v. Hampshire (Basingstoke) 22-24 June		v. Essex (Ilford) 25-28 June		v. Northamptonshire (Hove) 2-5 July		v. Glamorgan (Cardiff) 9-12 July	
	1	2	1	2	1	2	1	2	1	2	1	2	1	2	1	2	1	2	1	2	1	2	1	2	1	2
G.D. Mendis	16	—	0	30	65	8*	38	86	132	—	18	29	31	20	1	6	4	17	91	29	0	1	121*	18	9	55
A.M. Green	33	—	0	6	12	0*	5	23	48	—	16	25	10	37*	29	18	28	0								
P.W.G. Parker	5	—	4	20	79	—	—	7	—	—	43	0	6	20	58	15	4	75	4	58	22	17	39*	3	5	1
A.P. Wells	1	—			61*	—		12	16	—	92	60	15	11*	11	28	20	18	12	0	10	23				
I.A. Greig	147*	—	0	1	59	—		1	1	—	42	—														
C.P. Phillipson	18	—	23	28																						
I.J. Gould	1	—	3	13	33*	—		4*	—	—											16	29	—	44	47	17*
G.S. Le Roux	22	—	6	27							4	38*	35	—	15	9	49	32	29	80	0	25	—	11	15	4
A.C.S. Pigott	27	—	63	0							5	5*	0	—	1	0	42	4	16	0*	6	8			5*	
C.E. Waller	2	—	0*	4*							0	—	3*	—	1	0	2	0	17*	—	0*	0*	—	21	0	—
C.M. Wells	—		6	4	63	—	37*	22	51*	—	21	25	37	26	52	22	0	0	11	0	11	16	—	0	23	3
J.R.T. Barclay			0	36	26	—	56*	4*	64	—	22	33	6	—	3	14	6	23	1	65	9	49	16	41	7	35
A.N. Jones							—	—																		
A. Willows																							—	1*		
D.J. Smith											0*	—	13	—	0	2	6	0*	1	—						
D.A. Reeve													16	—	9*	0*	42*	19	20	4*	1	31	—	2	6	2*
J.R.P. Heath																			4	22	25	25	39	2	0	28
Imran Khan																					17	0			23	63
R.S. Cowan																										
D.K. Standing																										
Byes	2				1								7		4	1	1				5					8
Leg-byes	4		9	1	2		2	6	12		7	3	5	3	1	6	9	6	6	14	10		11	5	2	2
Wides	2				2						1				2	1			5	3				6		
No-balls			1	5	5		13	3	12		6		1	1	8	11	12	5	1		10	7			21	6
Total	280		115	175	408	88	151	168	336		277	225	178	118	191	132	230	200	218	276	100	249	250	154	163	224
Wickets	9†		10	10	6	0	2	6	5		10	6	10	3	10	10	10	10	10	7	10	10	3	10	10	7
Result	D		L		W		D		D		L		W		L		L		D		L		L		D	
Points			4		24		4		8		5		21		5		4		3		4		7		3	

Catches 45 – I.J. Gould (ct 32/st 13)   11 – A.P. Wells   9 – D.J. Smith   6 – C.E. Waller, D.A. Reeve, Imran Khan and subs
14 – J.R.T. Barclay and A.C.S. Pigott   10 – A.M. Green   8 – C.M. Wells and G.D. Mendis   5 – P.W.G. Parker and J.R.P. Heath

Bowling	Overs	Mds	Runs	Wks	Av	Best	10/m	5/inn
J.D. Inchmore	488.3	104	1369	47	29.12	5/45		3
R.M. Ellison	598.4	167	1491	51	29.23	5/73		1
N.A. Mallender	525.2	112	1642	56	29.32	6/48		1
D.A. Reeve	472.1	131	1233	42	29.35	4/15		
C.M. Old	656.3	153	1824	62	29.41	5/50		2
R. Illingworth	411.5	136	951	32	29.71	4/48		
N.G. Cowans	286	63	912	30	30.40	5/43		1
N.S. Taylor	110.2	23	427	14	30.50	5/49		1
J.N. Shepherd	780.1	209	2045	67	30.52	7/50		3
W. Hogg	384.4	73	1198	39	30.71	5/63		1
S.J. Dennis	526.2	117	1600	52	30.76	4/32		
J.W. Lloyds	357.1	98	1079	35	30.82	5/120		1
P. Willey	484.5	159	991	32	30.96	4/51		
P.J.W. Allott	463.4	131	1178	38	31.00	5/45		1
K. Stevenson	187.5	39	656	21	31.23	5/81		1
D.J. Thomas	537	113	1781	57	31.24	4/22		
G.V. Palmer	208.3	39	630	20	31.50	5/38		
A.M. Ferreira	502.4	130	1277	40	31.92	5/19		1
J.F. Steele	520.1	161	1280	40	32.00	4/3		
V.J. Marks	615.3	199	1698	53	32.03	6/79		3
C.L. Smith	167	44	547	17	32.17	3/35		
M.W.W. Selvey	628.4	141	2003	62	32.30	6/47		3
R.J. Finney	281.5	43	970	30	32.33	5/58		1
D.A. Graveney	512.1	156	1198	37	32.37	6/88		2
G.W. Johnson	631.1	166	1652	51	32.39	7/76		2
J.A. Carse	238.5	50	722	22	32.81	5/43		1
I.T. Botham	232.2	55	728	22	33.09	5/38		1
Nasir Zaidi	191.3	48	530	16	33.12	3/27		
S.J. O'Shaughnessy	235.4	44	830	25	33.20	4/73		
G.E. Sainsbury	628.4	150	1939	58	33.43	6/66		3
E.E. Hemmings	710.4	195	2000	59	33.89	7/23	1	2
N.F.M. Popplewell	232	38	786	23	34.17	4/69		
G. Miller	492.5	129	1278	37	34.54	5/71		2
D.G. Moir	462.5	121	1385	40	34.62	5/44		2
P.H.L. Wilson	246.3	45	837	24	34.87	4/77		
G.C. Small	107.5	22	349	10	34.90	3/13		
M.R. Davis	240.4	43	873	25	34.92	4/34		
C.J. Tunnicliffe	428.4	95	1372	39	35.17	4/30		
C.E. Waller	754	223	1873	53	35.33	6/126		2
J.R. Turnbull	130	34	424	12	35.33	4/51		
C.M. Wells	376.3	82	1135	32	35.46	4/69		
R.E. East	338	96	889	25	35.56	5/45		1
A.J. Pollock	236.2	49	750	21	35.71	5/107		1
J.W. Southern	369.5	115	966	27	35.77	5/60		1
S. Oldham	388.2	85	1120	31	36.12	4/56		
R.C. Ontong	644	131	2053	56	36.66	6/64		3
J.H. Childs	664.5	200	1761	48	36.68	6/81		2
D.N. Patel	687.5	204	1799	49	36.71	5/52		2
R.M. Ellcock	244	39	931	25	37.24	4/70		
S.J. Malone	546.1	123	1797	48	37.43	4/39		
I.R. Payne	161.5	38	450	12	37.50	5/13		1
R.K. Illingworth	661.5	173	1830	48	38.12	5/26		1
T.E. Jesty	256.5	70	804	21	38.28	3/48		
P.M. Such	214	44	767	20	38.35	6/123		1
I.V.A. Richards	193	61	462	12	38.50	3/56		
M.K. Bore	370.5	108	1040	27	38.51	4/29		
P. Bainbridge	416.4	105	1199	30	39.96	4/67		
I.A. Greig	185	27	681	17	40.05	3/36		
P.A. Smith	217.4	29	844	21	40.19	3/56		
S.C. Booth	296.2	85	849	21	40.42	4/26		

v. Yorkshire (Leeds) 13–15 July	v. Essex (Hove) 27–29 July	v. Leicestershire (Leicester) 30 July–2 August	v. Derbyshire (Eastbourne) 6–9 August	v. Hampshire (Eastbourne) 10–12 August	v. Surrey (Hove) 20–23 August	v. Warwickshire (Edgbaston) 24–26 August	v. Middlesex (Hove) 27–30 August	v. Surrey (The Oval) 31 Aug.–2 Sept.	v. Leicestershire (Hove) 7–9 September	v. Worcestershire (Worcester) 10–13 September	Inns	NOs	Runs	HS	Av
22 35	18 14	12 1	59 11	0 76	18 35	41 2	105 3*	53* 40*	84 30	133* 7	46	6	1624	133*	40.60
				19 8	39 0	0 8	38 53	27 24	11 14	16 5	30	2	552	53	19.71
2 19		0 4							1 1*	— —	27	2	512	79	20.48
	49 45	0 7	54* 6	3 18		3 19	56 15*				28	4	665	92	27.70
								38 19	16	— —	10	1	324	147*	36.00
											3	—	69	28	23.00
30 5	59* 0	35 26	— —	11* —		17 22	1 —	5* 33	23	— —	23	6	474	59*	27.88
											17	1	401	80	25.06
57* 0	4 0	4 4	— —	63 16*	0* —	22* 24	0 —	— 0*	32	— —	29	8	408	63	19.42
3 11*	7 2	5* 1	— —	15* —		1*		5*		— —	23	11	100	21	7.69
9 8	7 0	12 0	31* 49*	0 6*	45 47*	71 1	65 10	26 39	1 —	— —	40	6	857	71	25.20
6 17	21 9	8 5	8 40	41 —	15 12*	2 27	2 6	— 8			37	3	743	65	21.85
2 1	0 0*	3 4*									7	3	11	4*	2.75
													—	—	
											7	2	22	13	4.40
0 11	8 0			9 0				— 0	12	— —	20	5	192	42*	12.80
4 9		23 38*	1 27	32 11	32* 14				12		18	2	335	39	20.93
15 83	14 50	28 69	82 5	101 55	71 0	94 64	29 62	124* 78	73 17*	— 43*	25	3	1260	124*	57.27
	14 2	1 9	46 24	0 50	0 8						10	—	154	50	15.40
							56* 37*	10 37	18 0	60 22*	8	3	240	60	48.00

Yorks	Essex	Leic	Derby	Hants	Surrey(H)	Warwicks	Middx	Surrey(O)	Leic(H)	Worcs
1 9	2	5	1		5 4		4	3 4	1 5	1
13 10	7 2	4 1	11 8	7 9	3 2	5 2	6 2	13 10	3	10
4 6		2		2		2 2	1 4	2	1	1
17 14	7 1	3 2	3 5	2 2	5 1	13 5	20 5	4 6	4	2 2
185 238	217 127	120 133	320 186	263 269	252 120	300 197	383 197	302 299	285 62	221 79
10 10	10 10	10 10	5 5	10 7	7 5	7 10	8 4	4 7	10 3	2 2
D	L	L	D	L	D	L	D	W	D	D
5	5	2	8	5	5	5	7	24	6	6

2 – G.S. Le Roux, R.S. Cowan, I.A. Greig and D.K. Standing

1 – C.P. Phillipson

† C.M. Wells absent ill

The match v. Gloucestershire (Gloucester), 11–13 May, was abandoned without a ball being bowled

Bowling	Overs	Mds	Runs	Wks	Av	Best	10/m	5/inn
J.P. Agnew	248	42	930	23	40.43	3/34		
I.J. Curtis	269	82	590	17	40.58	6/28		1
C.J.C. Rowe	473.41	91	1572	38	41.36	4/29		
B.J. Lloyd	288.5	47	876	21	41.71	4/93		
T.A. Cotterell	273	67	758	17	44.58	5/89		1
H.T. Rawlinson	154.5	31	626	14	44.71	5/123		1
R.D.V. Knight	236	60	677	15	45.13	3/58		
J.R.T. Barclay	231.1	53	774	17	45.52	3/30		
S.R. Barwick	129.3	21	532	11	48.36	8/42		1
L.L. McFarlane	216.4	38	742	15	49.46	3/53		
J. Abrahams	216	41	658	13	50.61	3/83		
G.A. Gooch	212	46	572	11	52.00	3/40		
K.B.S. Jarvis	500.5	93	1579	30	52.63	3/32		
S.P. Perryman	253.5	54	750	14	53.57	4/91		
C.S. Cowdrey	220.2	34	733	12	61.08	3/37		
M.D. Petchey	206.2	36	804	12	67.00	2/73		
A.H. Wilkins	205	24	820	12	68.33	2/25		
S.J.G. Doggart	285.2	60	844	12	70.33	3/3		
K.I. Hodgson	297	75	871	12	72.58	4/58		

(Qualification 10 wickets)

LEADING FIELDERS

68 – D.E. East (ct 63/ st 5)
63 – R.C. Russell (ct 46/ st 17)
60 – R.J. Parks (ct 51/ st 9)
59 – P.R. Downton (ct 54/ st 5)
56 – C.J. Richards (ct 49/ st 7)
55 – D.L. Bairstow (ct 47/ st 8)
53 – R.W. Tolchard (ct 44/ st 9)

52 – B.N. French (ct 49/ st 3)
51 – R.W. Taylor (ct 49/ st 2)
50 – T. Gard (ct 42/ st 8)
47 – A.P.E. Knott (ct 39/ st 8)
45 – I.J. Gould (ct 32/ st 13)
45 – G. Sharp (ct 40/ st 5)
37 – R.O. Butcher
36 – D.J. Humphries (ct 27/ st 9)
35 – G.A. Gooch and G. Cook (ct 32/ st 3)
30 – B.R. Hardie, N.E.J. Pocock and J.F. Steele
29 – C. Maynard (ct 27/ st 2), and D.S. Steele
28 – G.W. Humpage (ct 23/ st 5), G.W. Johnson and R.D.V. Knight
27 – G.A. Tedstone (ct 23/ st 4) and C.S. Cowdrey
26 – M.C.J. Nicholas
25 – E.W. Jones (ct 24/ st 1)
23 – J.E. Emburey
22 – D.L. Amiss, G.D. Barlow, C.T. Radley and K.P. Tomlins
21 – I.S. Anderson, N.F.M. Popplewell and C.G. Greenidge
20 – T. Davies (ct 18/ st 2), J.D. Birch and D.W. Randall

Sussex C.C.C. First-Class Matches — Bowling, 1983	G.S. Le Roux	A.C.S. Pigott	C.E. Waller	I.A. Greig	J.R.T. Barclay	C.M. Wells	A.N. Jones	P.W.G. Parker	A.M. Green
v. Oxford University (Oxford) 30 April–3 May	4–2–6–0	5–0–10–0	2–0–5–0						
v. Nottinghamshire (Hove) 4–6 May	17–4–41–2	20–4–81–3	31–10–60–3	18–1–68–0	4–0–23–0	10–1–31–1			
v. Somerset (Taunton) 25–27 May	16–3–44–2 22–5–80–2	20–3–55–2 13.4–1–44–4	22–10–44–3	5–0–15–0 15–3–33–1	26–10–54–2 14–8–30–3				
v. Middlesex (Lord's) 28–31 May	13–5–39–1 18–4–50–2	17–2–54–3 13–4–20–0		16–1–78–2 18–4–42–4	2–0–15–0	2–0–20–0	8.4–0–65–2		
v. Worcestershire (Hove) 4–7 June	21–6–38–1 18–4–41–1	22–4–74–6 21–5–50–0		12–1–57–0 24–6–66–3	4–1–8–0 24–8–58–0	16–4–28–3 9–1–29–0		1–1–0–0	11–3–30–2
v. Kent (Hove) 8–10 June	22–9–44–1 8–0–43–0	20–4–67–1 14–2–62–2	25–9–52–2 15.3–2–60–0		7–0–21–0 12–0–67–2	26–15–27–1 8–0–33–0			
v. Somerset (Hove) 11–14 June	20–9–28–3 15–7–17–5	14–6–29–1 10.2–1–23–2	2–0–5–0 8–5–11–0		15.1–8–21–1 9–2–16–1	17–4–37–2			
v. Kent (Tunbridge Wells) 15–17 June	19.3–5–59–5 6–2–12–0	28–4–73–4 1–0–2–0	6–0–14–1			19–4–70–0 5–1–12–0			3.4–1–15–1
v. Lancashire (Horsham) 18–21 June	21–5–66–2 14–3–24–1	16–2–63–0 18–2–55–5	28–8–70–0 26–16–30–1		4–0–33–0 14.2–3–36–3	21–7–43–3 12–1–21–0			
v. Hampshire (Basingstoke) 22–24 June	22–6–54–2	13–0–67–1	27–9–58–0			17–5–48–1			
v. Essex (Ilford) 25–28 June	21–2–76–2 4–0–18–0	15–1–62–1 1–0–2–0	29–12–55–3		7–0–24–1	5.3–1–13–1 6–2–17–0		1.2–0–14–0	
v. Northamptonshire (Hove) 2–5 July	19–4–49–1 9–0–37–0		21–4–38–0 29–6–58–4		5–0–19–0	17.5–2–69–4 8–1–38–0	13–3–57–1 6–0–37–1		
v. Glamorgan (Cardiff) 9–12 July	20–3–57–2 13–4–27–2	21.3–5–48–4 8–0–35–0	28–10–44–1 38–17–50–1		17–1–38–2	6–4–2–0 8–0–26–0			
v. Yorkshire (Leeds) 13–15 July		27–6–63–5 18.4–6–29–2	2–0–5–0 19–7–38–1		4–1–15–0	11–2–22–1 4–0–11–1	16–3–50–1 8–2–11–0		
v. Essex (Hove) 27–29 July		11–1–56–1	42.1–7–126–6		6–2–12–0	6.1–2–21–0	15–1–69–1		
v. Leicestershire (Leicester) 30 July–2 August		24–4–101–2	34–9–90–2		7–1–30–0		15–1–69–0	2–0–16–0	
v. Derbyshire (Eastbourne) 6–9 August		16–2–45–2 11–2–22–6	35.2–18–60–4 17–2–67–0		6–1–19–0 2–0–15–0	24–4–72–4 12–1–49–0			
v. Hampshire (Eastbourne) 10–12 August		19–6–53–2 11–0–59–0	22–3–56–1 25–3–96–5		10–0–60–1	10–3–41–1 5–2–15–1			3–1–17–0
v. Surrey (Hove) 20–23 August		19–7–66–0	31–7–105–1 9–0–59–1		3–0–23–0 6–0–27–0	15–4–46–0 15–3–46–1			
v. Warwickshire (Edgbaston) 24–26 August		19–4–54–2 7–1–29–2	21.1–5–57–0 13–4–39–0		5–2–31–0	13–2–44–1 7–1–29–2			6–2–31–0 9–0–39–0
v. Middlesex (Hove) 27–30 August		21–2–66–3 9–1–23–1	34–12–70–2 14–2–61–4		15–5–59–1 3–0–20–0	10–2–26–2 8–0–43–0			1–0–1–0 1–0–3–1
v. Surrey (The Oval) 31 August–2 September		15.4–1–66–2 14–0–75–0	24–5–66–3 9–1–50–1	18–1–85–0 4–0–25–0		10–0–60–1			7–0–51–1 2–0–13–0
v. Leicestershire (Hove) 7–9 September		16–4–44–2 10–1–42–1	0.3–0–0–1 26–3–104–1	15–4–58–3 7–0–50–1		6–2–8–1 7–1–38–0			10–2–48–1
v. Worcestershire (Worcester) 10–13 September		6–0–20–0	38.2–17–70–2	33–6–104–3					
	362.3–92– 950–37 av. 25.67	585.5–98– 1889–72 av. 26.23	754–223– 1873–53 av. 35.33	185–27– 681–17 av. 40.05	231.1–53– 774–17 av. 45.52	376.3–82– 1135–32 av. 35.46	81.4–10– 358–6 av. 59.66	4.2–1– 30–0 —	53.4–9– 248–6 av. 41.33

a A. Willows 5–2–9–0, 3–1–2–0   b J.R.P. Heath 5–0–28–0, 3–0–30–0   c D.K. Standing 1–0–5–0; I.J. Gould 2–0–9–0   d D.K. Standing 3.3–0–27

D. A. Reeve	Imran Khan	R.S. Cowan	Byes	Leg byes	Wides	No balls	Total	Wickets
							21	0
			10		2	6	322	9
			4	3	1	4	224	10
				2		1	190	10
				4			275	8
				1	1		114	6
			1	7		1	223	10a
			5	7	1	2	291	6
			1	8		6	226	6
			1	9		2	277	4
9-48-3			2	7	1	3	181	10
3-42-2				1		2	112	10
5-38-0				7	1	1	263	10
9-19-0				2		1	63	1
3-4-29-1			3	3		2	312	6
				4	1	1	172	10
6-46-0			1	6	2	5	287	4
5-30-1			1	10	6	4	281	10
9-14-1			4				69	1
5-80-4			1	3	1	2	300	10
8-33-0					1		223	5
4-29-1			3	11	3	9	244	10
10-28-2			2	3	1	7	179	6
5-14-34-3			2	8	1	12	197	10
9-36-3			4	8	4	6	162	7
5-68-1	4.5-0-16-1	3-1-3-0	4	4		18	397	10
	4-2-3-1	5-1-24-0	2	8	3	10	356	5
3-49-0			4	3		5	257	10
4-33-2	8-1-18-1		8	1	4	2	219	9
4-77-1	5-1-10-0		2	8	2	1	250	6
0-27-0			7	3		1	285	7
4-66-3	6-3-3-2		2	9		9	357	6b
5-23-3	3-0-6-0		1	2	1	3	198	5
6-58-1	5-1-8-0		1	5	5	6	300	4
0-60-0	4.3-1-6-6		9	3	1	3	218	10
5-62-1				12		6	302	9
0-30-0			5	6	1	3	195	6
5-46-3	3-2-5-0			4		5	388	10
0-23-0			4	4		1	209	1c
5-46-2	5-1-11-1			5		3	175	10
2-44-0			4	4	2		363	3d
6-15-4			5	4	1	2	221	10
2.1-131-	48.2-12-	8-2-						
33-42	86-12	27-0						
29.35	av. 7.16	—						

REVIEW OF THE SEASON

by David Lemmon

It was a good year. After May the sun shone and there was some splendid cricket, most of which was played in the best possible spirit so that the summer became a joy.

The Prudential World Cup was, as Tony Lewis has indicated elsewhere, a triumph for all concerned and it produced a final to rank with the most exciting matches in the limited-over game. The match of the season was undoubtedly the Benson and Hedges Final at Lord's when Mike Gatting cajoled his side into believing that victory was still possible when defeat looked imminent.

Gatting was the leader of the year. His captaincy was positive and he led by example as well as by intelligence. In the early stages he had to overcome the inevitable comparisons with Mike Brearley, but so unique was his brand of leadership that comparisons to Brearley were soon forgotten. He brought Middlesex one title and came close to bringing them two more. His side was strong in bowling, particularly in spin where Edmonds, in early season, and Emburey throughout, were magnificent, but there is need of more substance in the middle order where often the superb batting of Barlow, who thrived as an opener, was wasted. Butcher's return will help and Miller is a most exciting prospect.

Essex, having thrown away the Benson and Hedges Cup, made a late burst to win a coveted County Championship for the second time. It was a magnificent and, in spite of some peculiar team selections in the late stages of the season, richly deserved achievement. Fletcher fell away badly with the bat, but he led the side with calm and thought. Gooch was mighty in August and September and Ken McEwan had a year of glory. Pont, wrongly left out of the side at the end, played some useful innings, but it was the young left-hander Chris Gladwin who gave the side the fresh impetus that was needed late in the year. Here is a young batsman to watch. His approach is positive and he hits the ball hard, looking for runs from the start. Pringle improved immensely and Turner and Acfield were always dependable. An Essex side without Turner is hard to picture, but he will be forty-one in 1984, not that there is the slightest sign of any lessening powers in his bowling. Foster flourished until injury brought a premature close to his season and Phillip bounded back with a zest which was vital in the Essex success. To one man they owe much, however, John Lever missed seven championship games through injury but finished with 106 wickets at 16.28 runs each. As Derek Underwood so modestly put it at the Wisden-Gerard dinner, 'For me John was the bowler of the season.' Nor must one forget the efforts of David East, a young wicket-keeper of unbounding energy and enthusiasm, who will, if there is justice, play for England before long.

Hampshire's batting was formidable as was seen in their historic victory over Essex at Southend in July and they must win a major trophy within the next few years. They have a wicket-keeper of grace and charm in Parks who, like East, will surely reach Test level, but they are desperately in need of a top quality spin bowler to help them to attain the top flight. Their attack relied heavily on Marshall and Tremlett who must be considered as the most improved seam bowler of the year. He is a young man of intelligence, graciousness and much ability.

Leicestershire contended for honours again without ever

Warwickshire C.C.C. — First-Class Matches, Batting, 1983

	v. Northamptonshire (Edgbaston) 30 April–3 May	v. Yorkshire (Leeds) 4–6 May	v. Hampshire (Southampton) 11–13 May	v. Gloucestershire (Edgbaston) 25–27 May	v. Worcestershire (Worcester) 28–31 May	v. Lancashire (Edgbaston) 4–7 June	v. Cambridge University (Cambridge) 8–10 June	v. Glamorgan (Cardiff) 11–14 June	v. Lancashire (Old Trafford) 15–17 June	v. Northamptonshire (Northampton) 18–21 June	v. Oxford University (Edgbaston) 22–24 June	v. Yorkshire (Edgbaston) 25–28 June	v. Middlesex (Edgbaston) 2–5 July	v. Essex (Nuneaton) 9–12 July
K.D. Smith	59	— —	10	4 34	3 63	1 68*	4 79	54* 58	7 53	44 30	7	0 2	17 32	10 13*
T.A. Lloyd	6	— —	—	43 208*	7 4	126 12		5 43	12 45	97 25		11 49	19 1	89 20*
D.L. Amiss	37	— —	4	40 142	3 7	0 18		54* 15	88 16	1 7	63	41 15	25 57	111
A.I. Kallicharran	28	— —	53	7 —		209* —			30 4	29 7		9 16	2 3	48
G.W. Humpage	67	— —	1	5 13*	16 4	1 81*	63 24	— 79	17 6*	47 16		0 141*	0 24	10
A.M. Ferreira	12	— —	0	50 —	38 14	43* —			— 4*	0 —	1	36 13	0 9	4
G.A. Tedstone	0	— —	5	7 —	17 32	— 0	8* 67*			11 —	9	4 8		
C. Lethbridge	12	— —	73*	2 —										
C.M. Old	22	— —	36	2 —	12 3*		— 9*	44*		62 6*	1 —	4 2		11
G.C. Small	4			31 —	1									
W. Hogg	0*	— —	4	13 —	0 —	— —			7* —	0* —	12*	1* 3		
Asif Din		— —	1		6 1		36* 0	40	65	56 41*	14	1 2	10 9	38
R.G.D. Willis		— —	2	20* —	10* 9*	—		—				2* 16*	12 1	1* —
N. Gifford				15		—			17 —	20 —		4 14	0 22	2* —
R.I.H.B. Dyer							93 7				7			
S.H. Wootton							104 19				34			
S.P. Sutcliffe							— —							
P.A. Smith											114			34
D. Thorne											0		8 7*	
D.M. Smith											100*			
G.J. Lord														
Byes	17		3	4 4	4 5	2 5	1	3		4	14	7	11 9	2
Leg-byes	5		14	9 13	3 3	5 4	4	2 4	6 8	8 1	8	11 11	5 21	5
Wides	6		1		2	1 2		4	1	1	2	1		2
No-balls	6			3 2	12 5	7 5			1 4	3	6 4	2 5	3 8	12 3
Total	281		207	213 414	159 152	396 197	315 212	116 293	328 138	351 168	388	125 302	113 206	379 36
Wickets	10		10	10 2	10 8	4 3	4 5	1 5	10 4	10 6	8	10 9	10 10	9 0
Result	D	D	L	D	D	W	D	W	W	W	D	W	W	W
Points	7	0	0	5	5	21	—	18	23	23	—	20	20	24

Catches 28 – G.W. Humpage (ct 23/st 5)   22 – D.L. Amiss   12 – T.A. Lloyd   8 – A.M. Ferreira
27 – G.A. Tedstone (ct 23/st 4)   16 – A.I. Kallicharran   10 – N. Gifford and Asif Din   7 – C.M. Old and K.D. Smith

really suggesting that they would win them. Gower was absent for long periods. Davison is retiring and the dependable Balderstone is not growing any younger, but Butcher, Whitaker and Briers all flourished while Ferris indicated that he will frighten batsmen for several years to come. Cook seized his Test chance, Taylor was wonderfully consistent after injury had robbed him of the first weeks of the season and Clift had a marvellous year, but the side is likely to endure a period of reconstruction over the next few years.

Kim Barnett must run Gatting close as the captain of the year. He became captain of Derbyshire before his twenty-third birthday, an unenviable task, and he welded them into a side with discipline and determination. He brought the best out of Hill and Anderson, Finney and Fowler all established themselves. Mortensen, the great Dane, had a wonderful debut year and if the spin department can find better form, Derbyshire could be winners of one of the four trophies in 1984.

Gifford's influence on Warwickshire was significant and their revival was the most heartening story of the year. Andy Lloyd established himself as an opening bat on the eve of Test honours and Amiss looked what he has been for many years – one of the very best batsmen in the world. The brightest prospect among the younger players would seem to be Paul Smith, an all-rounder with infectious enthusiasm.

The departure of Willey was not unexpected by Northants followers and the next few years are likely to see a new side emerge. There are doubts about the quality of the pace bowling, but David Steele had a fine season as a left-arm spinner and the most heartening play of the year came from Richard Williams who had looked an England player three years ago and then had declined.

Notts rarely had a settled side and their batting was, at times, woefully weak. Robinson was the most positive of their batsmen and enjoyed a very good season. Johnson, too, showed signs of realising his potential, but Rice has declined and one wonders if injury has brought his career close to its end. The seam attack is very strong, but Hemmings had a poor year and there is need for some quality spin to support Hendrick, Hadlee, Cooper and Saxelby.

Kent, too, need bowlers. Underwood, as always, was magnificent. Quiet, unassuming, gentle and humorous, he was once more the mainstay and as deadly as ever. Ellison and Baptiste gave youthful hope and Dilley, when not injured, was quick and dangerous, but there is little on the horizon outside these. The batting, on the other hand, was the most delightful in the country, with more in reserve. Benson, Aslett, Cowdrey, Taylor and Tavare all thrived and excited. Tavare led the side well as did Cowdrey in his absence, and there was the dedicated Knott who remains a model to all

v. Derbyshire (Edgbaston) 13–15 July	v. New Zealanders (Edgbaston) 23–26 July	v. Kent (Edgbaston) 27–29 July	v. Middlesex (Lord's) 30 July–2 August	v. Surrey (The Oval) 6–9 August	v. Gloucestershire (Cheltenham) 10–12 August	v. Leicestershire (Edgbaston) 13–16 August	v. Kent (Folkestone) 20–23 August	v. Sussex (Edgbaston) 24–26 August	v. Worcestershire (Edgbaston) 27–30 August	v. Nottinghamshire (Trent Bridge) 31 Aug.–2 Sept.	v. Glamorgan (Edgbaston) 7–9 September	v. Somerset (Taunton) 10–13 September	Inns	NOs	Runs	HS	Av
9 7	10 39	35 34	103 18	4 6	109 66	38 10	13 12*	36 4	31 9	7 14	— 1	5	47	4	1272	109	29.58
13 14	13 1	41 23	0 40	124* 5		75 35	30 14*	33 17	13 14	70 50	— 123	112	41	4	1673	208*	45.21
9 16	78 9	34 69*	5 7	38 76	52 31	4 18	164 —	36 54	84 59*	1 60	— 33*	40 —	43	4	1721	164	44.12
4 14		36 9	7 55	1 173*	16 48	3 88	111 —	152 118*	21 53	5 5	— 243*	30 —	34	4	1637	243*	54.56
16 24	16 10	105 13	22 25	13 3*	6 31	27 9	18 —	20* 5	28 18	10 11		71 —	42	6	1116	141*	31.00
3 66	55* 11*	38* 0	23 21	4 20*									24	6	465	66	25.83
	3* 0												16	3	243	67*	18.69
					1 —	4 0*	20* —				0 —		7	3	110	73*	27.50
6 5				10 —	39 34	0 —	16 —		46 —	5 5		16	25	4	396	62	18.85
	— 3	— 2*	11 0*						10* —				8	3	62	31	12.40
1 0	— 1	—	0 0		— —	27* —			—	3*			17	7	72	27*	7.20
41 1		6 0				15 28*			—			2*	21	3	411	65	22.83
	— 37			0 —		13 —		39 —	4 —			2*	13	7	116	37	19.33
4* 0*	— 0	— 0	27* 0	2 —	13 —	39 —				4 —	0 16*		21	6	201	39	13.40
			3 10	17 —	9 17	13 16*	25 —		6* 0	6 13*			15	3	242	93	20.16·
													3	—	157	104	52.33
													—				
57 65	4 5	35* 0	25 5			0 4		0	48* —	8 50*		4	17	3	458	114	32.71
				23* 1*		23 —		0					7	3	62	23*	15.50
										61 29			1	1	100	100*	—
											1 —		3	—	91	61	30.33

3 11		4	4	2 8	6 13	8 1	2	4	1 9	3		6	8 2
1 5	8 2	13 6	7 1	8 7	9 9	3 2	12 3	5 3	12 7	2 3		6	6
	1 7	1 2		3 1	1 12	1 1	1 1		5 1	1		1	3
2 5	1 3	10 6	15 19	2 8	2 4	13 11	34 2	6 3		1	4 5	2	6

169 234	195 126	359 162	253 210	230 323	303 271	249 194	470 31	300 218	303 174	180 256	0 417	300
10 10	5 10	6 8	10 10	10 3	9 6	10 6	8 0	4 10	7 4	10 7	0 2	9
L	L	D	L	W	D	D	W	D	D	D	W	D
2	—	7	4	5	21	6	23	2	6	18	8	8 ·

5 – W. Hogg and R.I.H.B. Dyer   2 – G.C. Small, R.G.D. Willis and sub
3 – D.A. Thorne   1 – S.P. Sutcliffe, G.J. Lord, P.A. Smith and D.M. Smith

who would wish to become professional cricketers. It will be sad for all of us connected with the game when he no longer graces the fields of Kent and England.

Sussex, in spite of a challenge for the John Player League, had a miserable year. They were plagued by injuries, but Barclay almost ceased to exist as a bowler in first-class cricket, and the batting, Mendis and the marvellous Imran apart, was poor. Parker has lost all form and there is a need for him to re-think his game, and much the same could be said of Colin Wells. There are some bright young players in Sussex as Standing proved in the closing weeks of the season.

Worcestershire struggled for most of the year, but Neale led them well and there were signs in August and September that a young and enthusiastic side is emerging. Patel promises much and so does Illingworth. The batting leans too heavily on Neale and Patel, but it will be interesting to see how young d'Oliveira develops.

Transition is the order at The Oval. Strongly managed, Surrey are an ambitious side and will not be long away from success. Pauline and Stewart established themselves as forceful batsmen and, with more consistency, the bowling could be threatening. It remains a mystery as to why Pocock is no longer considered by the England selectors. He is a better off-spinner than the three who went to Australia and he is a better bowler now than when he played for England.

Gloucestershire's batting flourished, but their bowling struggled. Sainsbury improved greatly over the season and must have relished his move West and John Shepherd, forty years old, had a splendid all-round season, but there was a lack of real pace and the spinners were disappointing. Russell had a fine season behind the stumps.

As is their custom, Somerset won a trophy, the NatWest Trophy, but they had a meagre season. They lost Rose, and Botham, who captained well, Garner and Richards missed much of the season. The batting was very disappointing with Denning, in particular, well below form. They used many players and, among the young newcomers, Booth, a left-arm spinner, looked a fine prospect.

It was difficult to determine the structure of the Lancashire side. Troubled, as always, by injury, they rarely fielded the same eleven. Hughes fell away, David Lloyd retired and one must wonder whether Clive Lloyd is still an advantage to them when his presence keeps Jefferies, a formidable bowler, out of the side. Simmons gets younger, however, and Fowler, who so enjoys his cricket, is a great asset. We still await the best of O'Shaughnessy, but Fairbrother could become a very great player if 1983 was simply a taste of his ability.

Glamorgan said goodbye to Alan Jones and they struggled for most of the season. Alan Lewis Jones at last came good and Ontong worked hard. Selvey bowled well and was an

Warwickshire C.C.C.
First-Class Matches — Bowling, 1983

	W. Hogg	G.C. Small	C.M. Old	A.M. Ferreira	C. Lethbridge	R.G.D. Willis	N. Gifford	D.A. Thorne	Asif Din
v. Northants. (Edgbaston) 30 April–3 May	16-4-52-2 3-2-8-0	11-3-28-2	18-5-37-0	22-10-31-4	9.5-2-35-2 2-1-1-0				
v. Yorkshire (Leeds) 4–6 May	4-2-3-0		12-6-17-0	17.4-10-17-1	9-2-20-0				
v. Hampshire (Southampton) 11–13 May	4-2-8-1		10-0-37-2	23-6-68-1	7-0-35-0	11-1-50-1			
v. Gloucestershire (Edgbaston) 25–27 May	8.1-3-31-3		28-4-110-3	33-8-88-1		15-1-77-1	16-6-49-0		
v. Worcestershire (Worcester) 28–31 May	3-0-20-0	11-4-13-3	1-0-5-0	9.5-2-19-4		15-4-50-3			
v. Lancashire (Edgbaston) 4–7 June	11-0-41-1 5-1-28-0		26-7-43-3 13-5-16-1	20-6-42-0 23-6-57-2		12-3-20-0 11-3-43-1	25.3-8-78-0 27.3-8-92-6		
v. Cambridge University (Cambridge) 8–10 June	17-6-20-2 6-1-17-3		14-5-35-1 3-1-3-0		1-0-4-0		5-2-9-1 6-1-13-0		24-5-77-2 12-3-35-0
v. Glamorgan (Cardiff) 11–14 June	20-4-28-3 8-1-28-0		23-6-58-2 5-3-5-0	16-6-35-0 7-1-24-0			9.3-2-31-0 16-1-57-0		15-0-52-1
v. Lancashire (Old Trafford) 15–17 June	15-5-48-0 15.3-3-50-2		28-9-31-4 17-6-29-2	28-6-76-3 17-3-40-1			24.3-8-42-3 35-22-31-5		12-1-57-0
v. Northamptonshire (Northampton) 18–21 June	7-2-10-0 6-0-19-1		16.4-4-48-4 17.4-4-50-5	21-2-68-1 10-4-28-1			27-8-53-4 25-11-48-3		1-0-6-0
v. Oxford University (Edgbaston) 22–24 June	14-2-32-2							20-4-54-0 4-1-20-0	9-1-30-0
v. Yorkshire (Edgbaston) 25–28 June			26.1-7-63-4 13-3-26-3	23-5-57-2 17-4-41-2		16-5-43-1 14-2-48-1	38-17-52-3 19.5-8-44-3		
v. Middlesex (Edgbaston) 2–5 July	3-1-2-0 3-1-3-0			15.1-9-19-5 14-6-21-0		10-5-8-3 14-5-14-3	22-12-33-2 24.3-11-22-6		
v. Essex (Nuneaton) 9–12 July			14-4-40-3 10-1-46-2	12-5-20-1 13-3-62-3		8-1-47-1 16-2-68-1	5.1-3-2-5 40.2-13-84-4		5-1-17-0
v. Derbyshire (Edgbaston) 13–15 July	12-1-45-0		38-9-90-2 5-1-18-0	29.5-6-79-2			52-25-77-6 5-1-15-0		6-3-13-0 0.1-0-4-0
v. New Zealanders (Edgbaston) 23–26 July	17-4-39-0 6-0-17-1	15-7-28-0 6-0-22-0		17-3-40-1		6-2-13-0	28-4-101-2 13-3-50-2		
v. Kent (Edgbaston) 27–29 July	20.4-2-63-5 10-1-55-1	18-1-62-0 15-1-70-2		35-5-102-2 16-1-90-2			18-3-52-1 8-0-47-0		
v. Middlesex (Lord's) 30 July–2 August	20-4-69-2 6-0-27-1	22-5-95-2 1.5-0-5-1		26-7-66-1 5.1-0-21-0			34-8-113-3 2-0-10-0		
v. Surrey (The Oval) 6–9 August	8-2-23-1 2-1-2-0		18-5-57-0 14-2-54-2	27-6-66-0		14.5-4-35-2 5-0-18-0	36-12-94-6 20-1-82-4		
v. Gloucestershire (Cheltenham) 10–12 August	15-1-53-2 7-3-16-0		20-4-64-1 7-1-24-0		9-0-44-0		41-15-72-0 37.1-19-52-4	10-0-59-1 2-0-12-0	
v. Leicestershire (Edgbaston) 13–16 August	14.2-6-39-2 15-1-65-0		20-5-56-5 30-7-76-1		2-1-6-1 21-3-89-1		4-1-11-0 42-8-93-0		
v. Kent (Folkestone) 20–23 August			21-3-107-3 38-5-138-3		2-0-19-0	12-4-44-1 17-4-44-1	30.5-5-85-6 42.3-12-111-4	5-0-23-0	
v. Sussex (Edgbaston) 24–26 August	12-2-46-2 5-0-28-1		17-2-61-0 15-3-46-1				26.3-8-73-1 24-11-33-4	4-0-21-1	
v. Worcestershire (Edgbaston) 27–30 August	19-3-67-1 3-0-9-0	8-1-26-0	25-8-71-0 21-5-61-2				36-15-77-4 29.5-4-88-1		
v. Notts. (Trent Bridge) 31 August–2 September	17-1-60-0		26-4-67-2			17-1-84-0	43-13-99-2		
v. Glamorgan (Edgbaston) 7–9 September	7-1-27-0		30-6-94-0			18-4-47-1	51-18-109-4		
v. Somerset (Taunton) 10–13 September			10-1-30-1 6-2-11-0		7.2-2-15-2	16-6-20-0 5.3-3-12-0	32-11-64-4 21-8-45-1		
	384.4-73- 1198-39 av. 30.71	107.5-22- 349-10 av. 34.90	656.3-153- 1824-62 av. 29.41	502.4-130- 1277-40 av. 31.92	70.1-11- 268-6 av. 44.66	253.2-60- 785-21 av. 37.38	1043.4-346- 2393-104 av. 23.00	45-5- 189-2 av. 94.50	84.1-14- 291-3 av. 97.00

a G.W. Humpage 3-0-13-0
b G.W. Humpage 13-1-38-1
c D.M. Smith 18-3-44-1
d T.A. Lloyd 7-1-28-0
e T.A. Lloyd 1-0-24-0
f G.J. Lord 3-0-12-0

S. P. Sutcliffe	P. A. Smith	A. I. Kallicharran	Byes	Leg byes	Wides	No balls	Total	Wickets
			3	1		6	193	10
							9	0
			3			1	61	1
			14			4	216	6
			2	20		5	382	8
			1	5		5	118	10
				10		3	250	4a
			1	7	1	5	250	10
8–3–84–0			3	15		2	287	7b
1–5–50–2				1		2	121	5
	9–1–26–0			10	1	13	202	6
	6–0–23–1			8	1	8	206	2
			4	7		8	216	10
		5–0–17–0	4	8		13	249	10
			4	7	1	2	199	10
				4		5	154	10
5–9–57–1	19–4–68–1		13	10	2		310	5c
	4–1–26–1				1	1	48	1
			7	7		10	239	10
			3	19		3	184	9
			4	9		3	78	10
				7	4	3	74	10
			1				110	10
		2–1–4–0	2	16		2	301	10
	8–1–20–0			24	7	10	365	10
			4				41	0
	20–2–90–3			13	1	10	335	6
	6–1–32–0		7		1	1	158	3d
	13–4–43–1		2	16	8	16	364	10
	3.5–0–26–1			6	1	4	299	6
	4–0–12–0		5	20	1	4	385	8
	1–0–8–0			6	1	3	81	2
				8	1	17	301	9
		4–2–21–0	4	4	1	2	188	6
		11–1–38–1	11	11		4	356	5
		35–5–109–2	1			3	217	6
	7–3–32–2	14–4–37–1	1	2		3	150	10
	9–1–40–0		2	18		18	438	3
			3	1		9	268	10
		3–0–10–0	2	2		14	344	8
	18–2–59–3	7–0–21–0		5	1	13	300	7
	11.5–1–56–3	10–3–19–1	4	2	4	5	197	10
	21–1–76–1	10–0–57–0	4	16	1	7	402	6
		13–0–64–2	1	1	1	5	230	5
	15–0–63–1	12–1–46–1		9		21	449	6
	15–3–50–0	10–1–33–0		20	1	8	389	5
							24	0e
	24–4–70–3			8		12	219	10
	3–0–24–0		7	2	1	3	117	1f
*4–17–ⴕ91–3ⴕv. 63.66	217.4–29–ⴕ844–21ⴕav. 40.19	136–18–ⴕ476–8ⴕav. 59.50						

excellent captain, realising the problems that confronted him and trying to meet them honestly and vigorously. He badly needs some spin bowling to support him.

Bottom of the Schweppes County Championship and winners of the John Player League, Yorkshire gained as much attention off the field as on as meeting and counter meeting followed with the interminable Boycott debate. Lumb, Athey and Love have all failed to develop into the players of Test quality that was prophesied – and this must indicate something wrong in the Yorkshire set-up whether it be coaching or administration. Sharp and Moxon gave hope of good things, but he who would be optimistic about young Yorkshire batsmen is a brave, or foolish, man. Carrick bowled well and batted well. Bairstow, the greatest of triers, still shines a light of enthusiasm and hope which others have failed to recognise. Cricket is a better game for having David Bairstow part of it. On the positive side, Yorkshire won a major trophy for the first time in fourteen years and for this, they owe much to Illingworth. If only their troubles could be righted, we might still see them become a power in the land.

When I look back on 1983 I shall try to forget the booted England 'supporters' who tried to gain some kind of victory over their Indian counterparts at Old Trafford and so avenge their side's defeat; and I shall try to forget the Yorkshire (or was it Leeds United?) 'supporters' at Chelmsford on a wet Sunday in September. I shall forget, too, the drunken louts who try to drown the Man of the Match awards with boring chants and the West Indian 'supporter' in the pavilion at The Oval who dedicated his life to insulting all around him and preventing others from enjoying the cricket.

I shall remember instead beautiful days in the sun and Gower in all his glory. I shall think of Kapil Dev at Tunbridge Wells and Madan Lal and Amarnath at Lord's. I shall treasure memories of the tenacity of Gatting, the running between the wickets of Barlow, the grace of McEwan and the wonderful power of Gooch. Then there was Botham at Lord's and at Trent Bridge, and Nick Cook and John Lever and John Emburey and young Kevan James, a Middlesex hope, and Trevor Gard and a feast of summer.

I give thanks to the New Zealanders for their courtesy, discipline, over-rate and cricket, and I reflect that, of the top eight players in line for the Wisden-Gerard awards as the leading run-getters and wicket-takers in all cricket, one, Chris Smith, was South African and six were banned for having played in South Africa.

Worcestershire C.C.C.
First-Class Matches — Batting, 1983

	v. Yorkshire (Worcester) 30 April-2 May	v. Somerset (Taunton) 4-6 May	v. Somerset (Worcester) 11-13 May	v. Hampshire (Southampton) 25-27 May	v. Warwickshire (Worcester) 28-31 May	v. Sussex (Hove) 4-7 June	v. Surrey (Worcester) 8-10 June	v. Oxford University (Oxford) 15-17 June	v. Middlesex (Worcester) 18-21 June	v. Glamorgan (Abergavenny) 22-24 June	v. Cambridge University (Worcester) 25-28 June	v. Derbyshire (Derby) 2-5 July	v. Nottinghamshire (Worcester) 9-12 July	v. Leicestershire (Hereford) 13-15 July
J.A. Ormrod	16 —	22 —	45 —	41 4	2 —	50 12	4 24		12 0	78 —	84 —	63* 31	3 30	0 17
M.J. Weston	32 —	92 —	32 —	38 15	17 —	44 115	5 18	14 15	32 2	79 —	0 —	6 37	3 44	10 11
P.A. Neale	2 —	40 —	4 —	38 49	47 —	24 7	52 29		55 3	135 —	21 —	15 83	11 32	33 50
D.N. Patel	11* —	31 —	26 —	53 37	10 —	45 90	6 17	24 22	24 88	7 —	24 —	32 98	6 33	0 54
Younis Ahmed	10* —	35* —												
M.S.A. McEvoy	— —	0 —	25 —		4 —	6 16*		0 7						
D.J. Humphries	— —	9 —		17 2	4 —	11 26	25 17		10 1		20 —			
R.K. Illingworth	— —	1 —	21 —	8 0	1 —	2* 2*	0 15	4 1	7 0		19* —	6 8	1 13	55 8
J.D. Inchmore	— —	5* —	0 —	3* 21	6 —	0 —	38 43	— 1*			18 —		33* 0	19 22
A.P. Pridgeon	— —	— —		4 7	3 —	6 —	0 0		0* 1			5 1	0 9*	16* 1*
S.P. Perryman	— —	— —												22 0
C.L. King			123 —	8 27										
P. Moores			19 —						27 17			0 23	0 2	12 3
A.E. Warner			20* —	4 0			26* 16*	5 14*	9 —		8* —	0 8	6 12	
D.B. D'Oliveira				10 30*	12 —	26 8	29 82	10 52	40 102	42 —	58 —	1 16	6 0	30 5
R.M. Ellcock					1* —		0 —	23* 5*				0 18	0 0	
M.S. Scott								53 13	12 8	34* —	76 —		0 57*	
S. Watkins								77 28						
D.A. Banks								100 53						17 19
T.S. Curtis														
P.J. Newport														
Byes	1	2	6	1	1	1 5	7	1	1 4	1		2		5
Leg-byes		5	8	9 3	5	7 7	4 4	3 5	7 8	3	8	3 10	1	9 5
Wides	1	1		3 1		1	1	1 2	1	1		2		1 2
No-balls	6	10		1	5	1 2	5 10	3 2	10 8	5		5 13	1	4 3
Total	79	253	329	237 197	118	223 291	191 278	342 228	216 244	394	339	136 407	69 177	228 205
Wickets	3	7	9	10 10	10	10 6	10 10	8 8	10 10	6	8	10 10	10 10	10 10
Result	D	D	D	L	D	D	L	W	L	D	W	L	L	L
Points	0	5	6	6	4	3	3	—	6	3		3	4	6

Catches 36 – D.J. Humphries (ct 27/st 9)   14 – D.N. Patel   9 – P.A. Neale and M.J. Weston
17 – M.S.A. McEvoy   12 – D.B. D'Oliveira, J.A. Ormrod and P. Moores (ct 10/st 2)   8 – A.P. Pridgeon and R.K. Illingworth

SELLING CRICKET

by Peter Lush

Marketing Manager, Test and County Cricket Board

It costs more than eight million pounds a year to run cricket in England, and that figure does not include cricket at Lord's. Of that amount, some twenty-five per cent is at present raised through sponsorship.

The Test and County Cricket Board came into being in 1968 and became responsible for the administration of Test and county cricket. The Board, together with the M.C.C. at Lord's, are the game's chief money-raisers, both directly from Test and television receipts and also by means of sponsorship. The activities of the T.C.C.B. in the above areas provide counties with thirty to forty per cent of what they need to keep going.

The Cornhill Test Matches are obviously a big source of revenue, with the series against Australia and the West Indies providing the greatest surplus which can be shared among the counties.

Over the past few years, there has been an ever-increasing need to gain sponsorship which will benefit the game and, it must be emphasised, the sponsor. The media market is a competitive one, and the recipients of sponsorship must provide excellent value for money if they are to continue to benefit. The sponsor is not simply making a philanthropic gesture, although he is generous, he is undertaking a public relations exercise. He requires his name to be associated with the competition he is sponsoring, and he wishes to entertain players and customers after matches and at other functions as these are an integral part of the public relations exercise. It is essential that players understand that while sponsorship is subsidising the game they have a duty to respond to the undemanding wishes of those who make it possible for them to pursue the profession in which they delight.

I joined the T.C.C.B. from an advertising agency, and we are acutely conscious of the function and importance of public relations in our dealings with the press, radio and television. We attempt to give news as soon as we have any so that Peter May, for example, is made available for comment as soon as an England team is announced, and channels of communication are kept open so that the press may learn all it wishes. This does not stop the late night phone calls at home, but it probably helps.

We handle the perimeter advertising for all grounds except Lord's and Headingley where there are special arrangements, and this is becoming an increasingly important source of revenue. We try to encourage county clubs to arrange local deals and sponsorship and many have responded although,

v. Lancashire (Old Trafford) 16–19 July		v. New Zealanders (Worcester) 20–22 July		v. Glamorgan (Worcester) 27–29 July		v. Northamptonshire (Northampton) 30 July–2 August		v. Kent (Canterbury) 6–9 August		v. Lancashire (Worcester) 10–12 August		v. Surrey (Guildford) 13–16 August		v. Hampshire (Worcester) 20–23 August		v. Essex (Colchester) 24–26 August		v. Warwickshire (Edgbaston) 27–30 August		v. Gloucestershire (Bristol) 31 Aug.–2 Sept.		v. Gloucestershire (Worcester) 7–9 September		v. Sussex (Worcester) 10–13 September		*Inns*	*NOs*	*Runs*	*HS*	*Av*
40	22			27	22	0	71*	46	14	30	72*	2	28	2	6	3	1	4	3			8	23	5	—	41	3	967	84	25.44
8	13	10	0	13	21	7	24	9	5							28	18	21	3*	13	8					38	1	862	115	23.29
139	64			10	77	92	52*	56	38	4	39	58	7	10*	2			40	82*	4	0	14	—	3	—	40	3	1521	139	41.10
14	53	2	6	15	10			30	32	24	2	105	6	12	21	3	95	112	80	38	53*	111	—	53	—	44	2	1615	112	38.45
																										2	2	45	35*	—
		54	24			8	38			49	12	14	13	4	22	15	13	103	23	22	5	11	51	30	—	26	1	569	103	22.76
		3	41	16	15			59	2	32	32*	0	13	11	0	0	34	48*	—	53*	—	12	17*	30	—	30	4	560	59	21.53
0	13*	11	0			25	—	17	1	7	—	2	2	9*	9			—	—	0	—	3*	—	2	—	35	6	273	55	9.41
6	—	4	24	0	2	17	—	41	0							0	51	—	—	11	—			12	—	26	4	377	51	17.13
12	—	2*	2*	5	0	13	—	—	1*	1	—	5	0*	22	23	2*	10	—	20	12	—	4	—	3*	—	32	10	190	23	8.63
0	—	7	8	4*	6*	9*	—			2*	—	2*	1	0	1	3	4*									15	6	69	22	7.66
																										3	—	158	123	52.66
21*	—					30	—																			11	1	154	30	15.40
				3	0																					15	5	131	26*	13.10
10	18	77	0	16	56	31	11	11	0	0	5	22	10	11	19					42	—	8	43*	23	—	39	2	972	102	26.27
								0*	11	13	—	5	7	36	2	0	12					16	—			18	4	154	36	11.00
																23	21									12	2	297	76	29.70
																										2	—	105	77	52.50
24	40*	0	36	0	5	15	10																	44	—	13	1	363	100	30.25
		11	—					84	9	32	27	26	19	46	16*	4	0	5	11	50	9*	25	0			17	2	374	84	24.93
																		41*	—	2	—	25	—	4	—	4	1	72	41*	24.00
1	13	4	2	7	1	8	8		7	5	8	6	5	3	16			4	1	2		1	1	5		†T.S. Curtis absent hurt				
4	14	10	4	1	4	10	9	9	11		5	6	7	5	4	1	4	16	1	2	5	9	2	4		‡P.A. Neale retired hurt				
	1	1	2	1		1		2	10						3			1	1		1			1						
1	3	4	7	9	15	7	2	12			5	11		4	2	2	8	7	5	2				2						
280	254	200	156	127	234	273	225	376	141	199	207	264	118	175	146	84	271	402	230	253	81	247	137	221						
10	5	10	9†	10	10	10	4	9	10	10	5	10	10	9‡	10	10	10	6	5	10	3	10	3	10						
D		L		L		L		D		W		L		L		L		D		D		W		D						
4		—		2		5		6		21		5		4		3		7		3		18		2						

6 – T.S. Curtis 4 – S.P. Perryman 2 – R.M. Ellcock
5 – J.D. Inchmore and subs 3 – D.A. Banks and A.E. Warner 1 – C.L. King

obviously, some are slower to react than others. In the past, there has too often been the attitude that finances have always been rocky, but 'somehow we've got by'. Happily, most counties now realise that their economic viability is dependant upon internal programming and effort. The strong impact of the game at every level is the healthiest way to survival.

The sponsor will keep a sharp eye on the game and there is constant reassessment of what he is providing and what he is receiving. In this area, we are at present discussing a change in the format of the John Player Special League which could see a different finale next year.

The T.C.C.B. negotiates with overseas bodies in regard to terms and conditions of tours and it consults with the Cricketers' Association on the minimum wage level for county cricketers. The responsibility of the Public Relations and Marketing Department is telling people what is going on and selling the game, not simply at the highest price, but to those who will benefit it, cherish it and help it to prosper. We look forward to a time when sponsorship becomes a bonus for cricket, not, as at present, its life-blood.

Book Reviews

All books that have been received by the editor are reviewed in the following pages.

TEA FOR XII. *Nico Craven*: pub by the author, The Coach House, Ponsoby, Seascale, Cumbria: 131 pp, £6.95
This is another offering by Nico Craven, the devotee of Gloucestershire, who makes the pilgrimage each summer from his home in Cumbria to watch the county he loves. Nor is this book restricted to first class cricket. The author drops in on club sides for a cup of tea and records their doings with as much warmth as he does those of Zaheer and the rest of the Gloucestershire side. It makes a delightful book. The essence of an English summer is here, not the mass media coverage of a Test match, but the real life and blood of cricket, the county game with its warmth of friendship, its sociability and its compassion. Don't stop recording these summers, Nico Craven. A lovely book.

LORD HARRIS. *James D. Coldham*: George Allen & Unwin: 171 pp, £10.95
Jim Coldham was moved to write this biography when, on wanting to read one, he found that there was none in existence. Immediately, he is to be applauded. In the days when, to reach the age of 23 and not to have had a book written

Worcestershire C.C.C. First-Class Matches — Bowling, 1983

	A.P. Pridgeon	J.D. Inchmore	D.N. Patel	S.P. Perryman	R.K. Illingworth	A.E. Warner	C.L. King	M.J. Weston	R.M. Ellcock
v. Yorkshire (Worcester) 30 April–2 May									
v. Somerset (Taunton) 4–6 May	29-6-58-5	24-5-68-0	15-1-59-1	15-4-52-0	18-2-66-1				
v. Somerset (Taunton) 11–13 May	18.4-8-33-1	7.2-2-6-0	11-1-48-0		13-1-61-0	16.4-3-54-2	8-1-26-1	9-3-43-1	
v. Hampshire (Southampton) 25–27 May	23-8-61-3 10-2-31-0	23-3-59-3 7-0-17-0	23-5-69-3		8-2-26-1 16.4-2-40-0	19-3-52-3 7-0-24-0	7-1-13-0		
v. Warwickshire (Worcester) 28–31 May	15.2-4-37-4 17-4-30-2	9-1-36-1 12-5-19-2	1-1-0-0 26-10-55-1		22-12-28-3				15-2-70-4 4-0-6-0
v. Sussex (Hove) 4–7 June	21-4-79-1	18.1-3-52-1	21-7-43-0		28-7-85-1				19-1-53-0
v. Surrey (Worcester) 8–10 June	18-1-79-2	21-5-55-1	43-16-110-1		23-6-79-2			3-0-15-1 2.2-0-11-0	21-5-68-2 2-1-4-0
v. Oxford University (Oxford) 15–17 June	22-7-42-1 13-1-26-2	20-3-52-0 9-2-27-1	14-5-35-2 12-7-16-0		30-8-83-2 18-10-37-4	13.3-5-40-0 11.2-4-21-3			
v. Middlesex (Worcester) 18–21 June	16-3-48-1 8-1-32-0		25-3-91-2 17-3-46-1		26-7-78-2 8-1-28-1	16.2-2-38-3 12-0-43-2			16-6-49-1 11-1-54-1
v. Glamorgan (Abergavenny) 22–24 June	0.3-0-2-0					12-4-25-2			12-2-26-0
v. Cambridge University (Worcester) 25–28 June	17-5-47-2 16-9-28-3	12-4-23-2 18.1-4-47-5	5.1-1-8-2 6-4-5-0		3-1-17-1 7-5-13-0	17-4-46-3		4-2-8-0	
v. Derbyshire (Derby) 2–5 July	23-5-63-0 5-0-25-1		7-2-26-0 4-0-29-0		31-6-73-1 8-0-47-0	25-6-72-4 5.4-1-32-1			16-2-55-2 9-0-46-0
v. Nottinghamshire (Worcester) 9–12 July	21.4-9-38-2 17-2-47-1	23-5-45-5 12-2-30-1	4-1-11-0 38-13-91-3		9-2-20-1 36-13-45-2	17-3-43-1 14-0-57-1			
v. Leicestershire (Hereford) 13–15 July	11-4-19-0 5-1-10-0	15-4-33-2 5-1-13-1	32-16-57-5 27-4-71-1	20-6-37-2 8-1-25-0	21.5-5-47-1 19.1-4-94-3				
v. Lancashire (Old Trafford) 16–19 July	27.4-7-86-3	24-6-73-3	43-20-84-2	15-2-38-0	10-1-46-0				
v. New Zealanders (Worcester) 20–22 July	27.4-9-65-3 23-5-83-2	25-8-82-5 20-8-31-2	7-2-14-0 3-0-12-0	23-6-48-2 19-7-58-2				8-1-14-0	
v. Glamorgan (Worcester) 27–29 July	28-7-68-4 12-4-22-1	27.5-8-55-3 10-3-19-0	15-10-13-1 3.5-2-12-0	26-11-41-1 9-0-22-0		16-1-44-0 8-2-17-2			
v. Northants. (Northampton) 30 July–2 August	22-7-48-4 11-0-72-1	24-9-64-1 6-1-47-0		22-6-61-1 3-0-16-0	8-1-20-0 15-0-69-1				
v. Kent (Canterbury) 6–9 August	3-1-6-0 10-2-30-2	11.5-3-32-4	39-14-86-0 28-3-88-4		39-7-86-4 14-3-36-0				13-3-37-1 10-1-28-1
v. Lancashire (Worcester) 10–12 August	15.5-9-21-5 12-0-47-2		27-11-54-4 22.3-8-52-5	8-1-20-0 6-1-22-0	13-4-43-0				12-3-32-1 15-0-60-3
v. Surrey (Guildford) 13–16 August	17-4-43-0 16-1-75-3		22.5-2-76-0	23-1-92-0 5-1-26-1	25-9-76-4 5-0-36-0				16-6-53-3 17-1-100-2
v. Hampshire (Worcester) 20–23 August	23.3-4-77-1			32-6-91-4	35-7-104-4				19-5-80-1
v. Essex (Colchester) 24–26 August	22-1-90-0	18-1-73-2	29-7-99-3	19.5-1-93-1					7-0-51-1
v. Warwickshire (Edgbaston) 27–30 August	18-4-63-4 8-2-29-2	17-0-57-0 10-2-40-0	23.3-5-75-2 16-1-63-2		29-9-81-1 15-4-28-0				
v. Gloucestershire (Bristol) 31 August–2 September	16-3-50-0 16-2-46-2	18-0-67-1 15-4-59-0	23-6-78-1 8-0-24-0		36-6-100-1 6-0-22-0				
v. Gloucestershire (Worcester) 7–9 September	4-1-9-0 6-1-29-0		18-5-38-0 19-6-42-3		18-7-43-1 20.1-11-26-5				5-0-27-0 5-0-32-2
v. Sussex (Worcester) 10–13 September	24-6-54-1 10-2-30-1	20-1-68-0 6.1-1-20-1	9-2-19-0		20-5-40-1 8-5-7-0				
	699.5-166-1978-72 av. 27.47	488.3-104-1369-47 av. 29.12	687.5-204-1799-49 av. 36.71	253.5-54-750-14 av. 53.57	661.5-173-1830-48 av. 38.12	210.3-38-608-27 av. 22.51	15-2-39-1 av. 39.00	26.2-6-91-2 av. 45.50	244-39-931-25 av. 37.24

† S.P. Henderson retired hurt

D.B. D'Oliveira	P.J. Newport	T.S. Curtis	Byes	Leg byes	Wides	No balls	Total	Wickets
					Match Abandoned			
				8	1	13	325	7
			5	11	1	13	301	5
			4	2	1	17	235	10
			1	9	11		202	3
				3	1	12	159	10
			4	3	2	5	152	8
				12		12	336	5
-0-18-0			4	11	4	8	451	9
-0-3-0			1				19	0
-1-12-1				7	1	13	285	6
				4		6	137	10
			4	2	1	3	314	9
			4	9		5	221	5
			4	3	3	13	76	2
			6	2	1	4	162	10
				3	5	7	108	9†
-1-31-1			2	12	3	7	344	8
			3	11		10	203	2
			1	3	2	13	176	10
			1	2	5	7	285	8
				4		1	198	10
			12	13			238	5
2-6-64-0			14	19	2	14	440	10
			5	9	5	4	246	10
			5	15	3	3	210	6
			10	23		4	258	10
			2	6	4	2	106	3
				7			200	6
3-1-76-1			8	12			300	3
			8	9	4	8	276	10
			6	10	1		199	7
5-1-18-0			4	8		1	209	10
			1	10		4	196	10
1-0-5-0			9	3		6	363	7
				8		1	246	6
			4	8	1		365	10
			1	5		1	413	8
	6-0-11-0		3	12	1		303	7
		3-1-6-0		7		1	174	4
7-2-23-1	6-1-19-0		3	9		2	351	4
	14-2-40-3		3	6	1	3	204	5
				2		2	121	1
5-2-12-0			4	4		6	155	10
	11-0-28-0			10		2	221	2
	4-0-20-0					2	79	2
69.1-14-	41-3-	3-1-						
262-4	118-3	6-0						
av. 65.50	av. 39.33	—						

about you is failure, it is incredible to discover how many of our great cricketers and administrators of the past went unchronicled. Lord Harris, of course, wrote his own reminiscences, but Jim Coldham's book fills a gap and fills it solidly.

Harris loomed over the cricket world at the beginning of the century like some wrathful god, but behind the severity there was a compassionate and courageous leader, and, in the closing chapters of his biography, Coldham comes very close to the man.

There are sharp images of the crowd at Canterbury week in 1928 falling back reverently to give pathway to the great man, of his kindness and consideration for the professionals, and of his understanding of the young. His nephew, Nigel Haig, believing his only commercial asset was his cricket ability, shocked his family by intimating that, though an Old Etonian, he was thinking of turning professional. Uncle George was called and his advice was clear. 'Well, Nigel, cricket is a very honourable profession.'

When he lost his wife after 56 years of marriage he was complimented on his bravery at reading the lesson at her memorial service. His reply was again straightforward. 'She never funked anything, and I made up my mind I would not.'

Jim Coldham gives a good picture of a giant of the past. We should be grateful to him.

A FUNNY TURN. *Ray East (with Ralph Dellor)*: George Allen & Unwin: 125 pp, £5.95
One of the difficulties of reproducing in print the visual antics of a cricketing clown is that in the transference something is lost. This book is no exception. I think East had a tale to tell about his early days and sense of social injustice. What he has chosen to tell are anecdotes, not all very funny.

THE WISDEN BOOK OF CRICKET QUOTATIONS. *edited by David Lemmon*: Macdonald Queen Anne Press: 224 pp, £9.95
Unfortunately, it is not customary for authors to review their own books. With over a thousand quotations, this book is an attempt to collate some of the wit, wisdom and elegance written about cricket since its earliest days. The quotations are arranged in themes, and there are key word and author indexes. It must be emphasised that this is a book which draws its sustenance from literature and the literature of the game. It is not a book of anecdotes and apocryphal stories.

THIS CURIOUS GAME OF CRICKET. *George Mell*: Unwin Paperbacks: 127 pp, £1.75
This collection of oddities, with illustrations by Bill Tidy, was reviewed in these pages last year. It is well-suited to be a paperback book as it is the type of book one could browse through and smile at while waiting for the train to arrive or for the rain to stop.

PHOENIX FROM THE ASHES. *Mike Brearley*: Unwin Paperbacks: 189 pp, £1.95
This is the paperback edition of Mike Brearley's account of the memorable Test series of 1981 when he led England back from the depths to win against all odds. The book won the *Jubilee Literary Award* of The Cricket Society, an estimable honour, and a deserved one. Splendid value for all to be able to buy this in a cheap edition.

CRICKET WORLD CUP '83. *edited by Derek Hodgson*: Unwin Paperbacks: 48 pp, £1.95
Published less than a week after the final, this is a splendid

Yorkshire C.C.C. — First-Class Matches — Batting, 1983

Each match cell shows both Yorkshire innings (1st 2nd).

	v. Worcestershire (Worcester) 30 Apr–2 May	v. Warwickshire (Leeds) 4–6 May	v. Northamptonshire (Bradford) 25–27 May	v. Lancashire (Old Trafford) 28–31 May	v. Glamorgan (Middlesbrough) 4–7 June	v. Leicestershire (Leicester) 8–10 June	v. Hampshire (Southampton) 18–21 June	v. Derbyshire (Sheffield) 22–24 June	v. Warwickshire (Edgbaston) 25–28 June	v. Leicestershire (Harrogate) 2–5 July	v. Northamptonshire (Northampton) 9–12 July	v. Sussex (Leeds) 13–15 July	v. Kent (Sheffield) 16–19 July
G. Boycott	—	28 —	7 —	18 —	8 69	14 63	46 22	33 112*	0 28	16 22	34 47	25 7	101 34
R.G. Lumb	—	29* —	13 —	8 —	9 56	32 9	60 19	28 0	5 13				
C.W.J. Athey	—		2 —	2 —	25 77	58 7	90 15	0 12	15 29	27 1	8 17	4 0	2 16
S.N. Hartley	—		0 —	16 —	0 39	21 17	23 2*	2 4	69 11	2 9	1 0		
J.D. Love	—		4 —	36 —	24 76*	24 53	31 9*	3 8	58 45	53 25	39 0	43 34	10 26*
D.L. Bairstow	—		30 —	40 —	0 75*	21 69	60* —	4 44	45 11	50 57	31 80	2 10	6 0
P. Carrick	—		6 —	83 —	12 —	3 45*	54* —	15 1	6 16	15 26	47* 20	39 17	27 4
G.B. Stevenson	—	0* —	19 —	9 —	0 —	8 —	52 —	3 3	0 5	16 27			
A. Sidebottom	—		30* —	10 —	40 —	12 7*	—	7 19		35* 0	14 0	23 5*	44 3*
R. Illingworth	—		5 —	1 —	1 —	2 —	—	12* 0	8 —	8 —		7* —	9 —
S.J. Dennis	—				0* —	0* —	7 —	0 17	4 0	1 0*	0 10*	3 4*	
A. Ramage			32 —	0* —									
P.W. Jarvis									5* 1*				11* —
M.D. Moxon										20 28	10 6	20 46	33 0
P.A. Booth											0 0		
N.S. Taylor											0 2	4 —	4 —
K. Sharp												4 17	4 30
I. Swallow													
A.A. Metcalfe													
S.D. Fletcher													
Byes			4	2	1 2	1 8	1 1	2 7	7 3	1 1	4	8 6	7 2
Leg-byes		3	2	3	3	5 1	6 3	4 5	7 19	11 4	11 6	4	7 2
Wides					1 1	1 1	1 1	5	5	2	2	4	2
No-balls		1	3	3	5 11	1	1	5 3	10 3	4 4	1	12 6	12 4
Total		61	157	228	125 408	202 281	432 72	118 233	239 184	251 206	199 190	197 162	270 121
Wickets		1	10	10	10 4	10 6	7 3	10 10	10 9	9† 9†	10 10	10 7	10 6
Result	D	D	D	D	D	D	W	L	L	L	L	D	D
Points	1	0	5	3	2	6	23	4	6	4	5	5	3

Catches 55 – D.L. Bairstow (ct 47/st 8)   15 – C.W.J. Athey   9 – P. Carrick   6 – R.G. Lumb, S.J. Dennis and K. Sharp
17 – G. Boycott   11 – R. Illingworth   8 – J.D. Love   5 – S.N. Hartley and M.D. Moxon

---

little book, neatly produced, profusely illustrated and well written. It has match reports and score cards of all the matches played in the tournament and captures the growing excitement of a competition which, for those of us covering it, was highly entertaining but ultimately exhausting. Derek Hodgson gathered together contributors, organised their material and, along with the Unwin editor John Newth, produced a splendid record of the third Prudential World Cup. It should be on every cricket lover's shelves.

PLAYFAIR CRICKET ANNUAL. *edited by Gordon Ross*: Macdonald Queen Anne Press: 256 pp, £1.25
The indispensable pocket reference book for all lovers of the game. Neat, compact, accurate, it has statistical biographies of all players in the first-class game in England. Best performances may be noted at a glance, as may dates of birth, previous season's averages, career records and essential information relating to international cricket. My only criticism is that players' records are deleted too quickly, for example, there were no details of A.H. Wilkins and B. Dudleston, both of whom reappeared in 1983. Sponsored by the National Westminster Bank, it is a familiar sight on all cricket grounds. Long may it remain so.

WISDEN ANTHOLOGY, 1963–1982. *edited by Benny Green*: Macdonald Queen Anne Press: 978 pp, £29.50

This is the fourth, and last of Benny Green's *Wisden Anthologies*. It is at once imposing and highly readable. I had thought that perhaps the last edition, dealing with more recent events, would be less stimulating than its predecessors, but I was wrong. Like all anthologies, it has something for everybody. Many may quarrel with some of the county matches included, but few could disagree with the choice of articles. There is the lovely piece by Ian Peebles on *A Middlesex Centenary* and G.O. Allen's *Fifty Years On* which excites one as to Jim Swanton's projected biography of this fascinating man. There is Rowland Ryder's *The Pleasures of Reading Wisden* and much else. It is no substitute for the annuals themselves and it is very expensive, but is lovely to have around.

A QUESTION OF CRICKET. *Derek Lodge*: Unwin Paperbacks: 128 pp, £1.75
Beware of this book. It is a drug. Do not have it near you when you have work to do and you are busy, for it will seduce you into hours of tantalising mind-searching and reminiscence. It is a book of quizzes, 417 questions, all of them good, none of them trivial. It is divided into sections, and it tests not only your knowledge of the game, but makes excellent reading and is a mine of information interestingly presented. Thankfully, Derek Lodge has included the answers. A delight.

	v. Nottinghamshire (Worksop) 30 July–2 August		v. Lancashire (Leeds) 6–9 August		v. Somerset (Weston-super-Mare) 10–12 August		v. Gloucestershire (Cheltenham) 13–16 August		v. Nottinghamshire (Bradford) 20–23 August		v. Gloucestershire (Scarborough) 24–26 August		v. Derbyshire (Chesterfield) 27–30 August		v. Middlesex (Leeds) 31 August–2 Sept.		v. Surrey (Scarborough) 7–9 September		v. Essex (Chelmsford) 10–13 September		Inns	NOs	Runs	HS	Av
214*	16	2	1	83	0	140*	97	163	141*	28	43	1	169*	44	2	3		37	23	40	5	1941	214*	55.45
														15	32					15	1	328	60	23.42
49	27	63	9	39	10	0	36	17*	56	29	16	—	—							32	1	758	90	24.45
																27	—	0	18	19	1	261	69	14.50
4	0*	67*	7*	25	2	22	14		75*	9	31	4	49	21	13	1	—	55	20	38	7	1020	76*	32.90
24*	—	10	18	0	10	6*	40*			57	35	5	42	86	100*	13	—	9	12	35	6	1102	100*	38.00
		0*	0*	21	72	—	4			24*	4*	7	0	9	59*	20	—	26	15	32	8	697	83	29.04
5	—			44	23	11	10	1	—	38	13	51	—	1	—	46	—	0	11	25	1	396	52	16.50
										37	0*	61	44*	78	21					21	7	490	78	35.00
				1	—					2	—	3*	—	1	—	0*	—	16	3	16	4	71	16	5.91
		—	0	4*	0*	—	0			4	—	0	—	0	—	6	—	0	11*	23	8	71	17	6.45
—	14																			3	1	46	32	23.00
																				3	3	17	11*	
68	50	153	39	55	5	27	5			7	22	25	42			23	—	38	58	23	—	780	153	33.91
																				2	—	0	0	0.00
		—	0																	5	—	10	4	2.00
37	15*	—	6	4	37	121	2	—	0	73	19	1	27	24	10	139	—	4	23	21	1	597	139	29.85
				4	11*				4*											3	2	19	11*	19.00
								122	7											2	—	129	122	64.50
														0*	—	12	—	1*	1	4	2	14	12	7.00

	Notts (Worksop)		Lancs (Leeds)		Somerset (W-s-M)		Glos (Cheltenham)		Notts (Bradford)		Glos (Scarborough)		Derbys (Chesterfield)		Middx (Leeds)		Surrey (Scarborough)		Essex (Chelmsford)	
	1		1	4		3	8	13	5	1	4	3	9			12			7	6
	19	7	5	4	5	4	8	11	4	1	17	3		6	4	4	1	19	7	14
	2	1		1	1		1		1	4	1	4	1		1				2	5
	11	1	4	1	1			3	3	2	3		1	4	9	11	7		2	
	434	131	305	90	286	177	344	239	316	283	333	193	160	396	293	252	329		204	220
	5	4	4	7	10	8	5	8	3	3	10	7	9	5	10	5	10		10	10
	D		D		D		L		D		D		D		D		D		D	
	5		7		6		5		7		6		4		4		8		6	

4 – G.B. Stevenson   1 – A.A. Metcalfe, I. Swallow, N.S. Taylor and sub.
2 – A. Sidebottom

The match v. Middlesex (Lord's) 11–13 May was abandoned without a ball being bowled

† R. Illingworth absent ill

BOWLED OVER. *Neil Hawke*: Lansdowne-Rigby: 184 pp, £4.95
This is a thoroughly worthwhile book by an honest cricketer who has enjoyed his cricket and survived an horrific illness with courage and dignity. There is no sentimentality, no verbal grating through style. The story is an interesting one and a chastening one. Of biographies by recent and contemporary cricketers, this is among the very best because the man has something valuable to say to all of us. I am glad to have read this and it is highly recommended.

THE CENTURIONS. *Patrick Murphy*: J.M. Dent: 277 pp, £8.95
This is a well-produced book in every sense; handsomely designed, well-written and eminently readable. It has a simple structure in that it consists of an introduction and profiles of the twenty batsmen who have scored a hundred hundreds from Grace to Zaheer. What makes it distinct is that Pat Murphy has captured the essense of each character. Wherever possible he has drawn on the reminiscences of those who knew or played against men like Hobbs, Compton, Woolley, Hammond and the rest, and the comment becomes both apt and personal. So we have Herbert Sutcliffe telling John Hampshire that his erratic batting would improve if he went to church regularly and Barry Wood that his England career would flourish if he got his hair cut. It is the best book Pat Murphy has done since the memorable 'Tiger' Smith.

THE GUIDE TO REAL VILLAGE CRICKET. *Robert Holles*: Harrap: 96 pp, £4.95
There are some fine illustrations by Roy Raymonde, but most of this book is very disappointing. Village cricket is a genre rich in humour and humanity, and I find that this book lacks both. It falls very flat and one longs for the flavour of authentic anecdote and the sense of afternoons in the sun and pints of beer and the exchange of yarns. The style tends to be pedestrian and lacks the warmth necessary for the subject. Return to Selincourt, Parker and Macdonell.

THE ROSES MATCHES, 1919–1939. *Sir Neville Cardus*: Souvenir Press: 520 pp, £9.95
This is a collection of all the reports that Cardus wrote for the *Manchester Guardian* on the matches between Lancashire and Yorkshire in the years between the two world wars. Some of the reports have not been published in book form before and to have them all under one cover is one of the finest publishing achievements of recent years. What is interesting from the literary point of view is that we are able to trace a development in Cardus' style from the rather high-flown lyricism of the early twenties to the controlled and balanced humour and human understanding towards the end of the period. There is a fine introduction by John Arlott and score-cards of each match. I cannot think that there is a cricket-lover who would want to be without this book.

Yorkshire C.C.C.
First-Class Matches — Bowling, 1983

	A. Sidebottom	G. B. Stevenson	S. J. Dennis	P. Carrick	A. Ramage	R. Illingworth	J. D Love	C. W. J. Athey	G. Boycott
v. Worcestershire (Worcester) 30 April–2 May	10–4–23–3	6–3–11–0	13–2–30–0	3–1–7–0					
v. Warwickshire (Leeds) 4–6 May									
v. Northamptonshire (Bradford) 25–27 May	22–4–70–1 7–0–40–1	19–2–43–1 14–2–44–3		30–11–54–5 19–11–32–1	13–0–67–2 13–3–32–0	2.5–0–8–1 16–7–38–2	7–3–14–0		
v. Lancashire (Old Trafford) 28–31 May	24–4–76–3	20.4–2–72–1		29–7–74–0	6–0–18–0	13–2–39–0	5–1–18–0 3–0–11–0	2–1–2–0	
v. Glamorgan (Middlesbrough) 4–7 June	22–1–70–1 14–4–48–1	23–9–43–1 9–1–24–2	25–10–54–4 8–0–48–1	30–12–59–1 7–6–5–1		12–4–21–1 10–4–27–1		12–4–25–1	
v. Leicestershire (Leicester) 8–10 June	14–6–19–2 7–0–24–0	14–3–33–3 5–1–14–1	11–1–42–2 7–2–16–0	31–17–39–1 33–10–69–5		19.3–8–28–2 25–7–54–1			
v. Hampshire (Southampton) 11–21 June	8.5–6–6–5 29.3–9–93–2	10–2–34–2 25–6–80–3	7–1–19–2 34–8–94–2	51–22–78–2		13–8–18–0		5–1–17–1 2–1–4–0	9–4–15–1
v. Derbyshire (Sheffield) 22–24 June	16–3–32–1	15–5–44–3 13–1–65–2	10–3–24–0 8–1–37–1	23.4–8–45–5 18–7–44–7		14–2–52–1			
v. Warwickshire (Edgbaston) 25–28 June		13.2–2–35–5 20–2–54–2	10–5–24–3 13–4–46–0	4–1–10–0 34–12–64–2		9–2–15–1 37.3–13–71–3			
v. Leicestershire (Harrogate) 2–5 July	25–3–73–2 11.5–2–45–1	21–4–63–1 14–2–47–0	30–6–92–3 18–2–66–3	13–2–41–0 7–1–14–0		10–2–38–1			6–1–18–0
v. Northants. (Northampton) 9–12 July	20–1–73–2 7–0–37–1		17–8–32–4 14–3–41–1	40–21–45–3 27.2–6–64–1					
v. Sussex (Leeds) 13–15 July	19–4–56–3 20.5–7–44–3		16–4–40–2 20–3–47–1	33–15–62–2		4–1–12–2		1–0–5–0	6–4–3–0
v. Kent (Sheffield) 16–19 July	8–0–39–1			39–7–106–0		8–1–31–0		9–1–34–1	
v. Nottinghamshire (Worksop) 30 July–2 August		18–5–46–1	25–6–68–1	43.4–18–69–5	7–1–28–0	32–13–69–3			
v. Lancashire (Leeds) 6–9 August		18–6–38–1 7–0–24–1	27–6–88–2 10–0–39–0	26–7–60–1 15–7–18–0		31–10–61–3 13–4–23–0	7–1–46–1	7–0–23–0	2–1–9–0
v. Somerset (Weston-s-Mare) 10–12 August		10–4–32–3 10–5–19–1	9–4–22–0 10–4–16–1	28–10–26–2 28–13–45–2		22–10–48–4 30–13–42–2			
v. Gloucestershire (Cheltenham) 13–16 August		22–5–83–2 10.1–2–43–0	20–2–80–3 9–2–36–2	33.4–10–76–1 19–0–97–1		12–5–17–0 19–3–78–1			
v. Nottinghamshire (Bradford) 20–23 August	16–5–39–2 12–3–38–0	20–5–72–1 9–1–30–1	25–5–66–1 11–2–36–0	31.3–10–81–3 18–10–35–2					
v. Glos. (Scarborough) 24–26 August	21–9–43–3 11–3–42–1	12.3–3–39–2 13–3–47–5	17–5–40–2 15–5–42–2	37–12–80–2 15–5–41–0		20–9–32–0 4–1–10–0			
v. Derbyshire (Chesterfield) 27–30 August	15–3–50–0	18–6–41–2	21.2–1–68–1	47–12–122–5		13–2–29–0			
v. Middlesex (Leeds) 31 August–2 September		9.4–2–37–1 8.5–1–38–1	13–4–41–1 9–0–45–0	5–1–32–0		8–1–54–0 2–0–7–0			
v. Surrey (Scarborough) 7–9 September		14–5–36–1 4–0–16–1	11–2–28–2 16–4–64–2	14.2–5–29–2 11–6–15–0		5–3–16–3 6–1–11–0			
v. Essex (Chelmsford) 10–13 September		14–3–53–2	17–2–69–3	4–0–12–0		1–0–2–0			
	361–81– 1080–39 av. 27.69	460.1–103– 1400–56 av. 25.00	526.2–117– 1600–52 av. 30.76	848.1–303– 1750–62 av. 28.22	39–4– 145–2 av. 72.50	411.5–136– 951–32 av. 29.71	22–5– 89–1 av. 89.00	38–8– 110–3 av. 36.66	23–10– 45–1 av. 45.00

a D.L. Bairstow 6–3–9–0
b P.W. Jarvis 9–3–28–1, 13–4–43–1
c P.A. Booth 6–0–27–0, 11–3–23–0
d P.W. Jarvis 22–1–84–1
e I. Swallow 11.4–2–19–1, 8–3–13–0
f I. Swallow 9–2–35–0, 2–1–15–1
g S.N. Hartley 6–1–24–0; A.A. Metcalfe 1–0–5–0, 1–0–1–0
h S.N. Hartley 7–2–15–1, 1–0–1–0
i D.L. Bairstow 4–1–18–1

S.D. Fletcher	N.S. Taylor	M.D. Moxon	Byes	Leg byes	Wides	No balls	Total	Wickets
			1	1		6	79	3
					Match Abandoned			
			1	7	1	6	257	10
			3	4	6	5	218	7
				2		2	301	4
			1	1			24	0a
			1	5		11	289	9
			4	1		5	162	7
			4	11		1	177	10
			4	10		2	193	7
			1	1	2	3	83	10
			4	9	4	21	420	10
			3	13	6	6	225	10
				2			148	10
				11		2	125	10b
			7	11	1	5	302	9
			8	7	3	9	352	7
				9	2	11	194	5
	13.5–5–33–1		1	10		13	234	10c
	15–3–59–1		1	3	2	6	236	4
	15.4–3–49–5		1	13	4	17	185	10
	15–4–31–1		9	10	6	14	238	10
	20.5–5–105–2			10	1	14	424	5d
			8	10	1	17	316	10
	13.5–2–70–3			12		6	344	10
	17–1–80–1		1	1		1	256	3
			8	7		2	164	10e
			7	4	6	1	153	6
			1	9		6	307	6f
			4	4	1	2	280	5
				4		12	303	7g
				6	1	2	149	3
			4	9	2	12	261	10
			5	1		8	196	9
		12–1–43–0		3	2	10	368	10
–0–26–2			4	6	1	5	206	4
–0–23–1				7	4	1	125	2
–1–27–0		7–1–25–1		1	1		178	10h
8–4–39–1		6–1–24–0		5		1	176	5
6.4–2–71–4		8–0–31–0	9	16		7	288	10i
5.4–7–	110.2–23–	33–3–						
36–8	427–14	123–1						
v. 23.25	av. 30.50	av. 123.00						

WARRIORS IN BAGGY GREEN CAPS. *Ian Brayshaw*: Lansdowne Rigby: 173 pp, £7.95

This is a study of the Australian team of the Ian Chappell era. It briefly outlines the team's achievements, gives match statistics, comparisons with the past, and, most interestingly, character sketches of the leading players. Its strength is that it recognises that not all of these players have been popular and that there was an arrogance, even bad manners, in their success which made them positively disliked in some quarters. Ian Brayshaw does not seek to excuse this, but what he gives us is a very close look at the players and a clear understanding of a bunch of great professional cricketers. It is quite well balanced and perhaps it should be obligatory reading for all Englishmen.

FAMILY ARGUMENT. *John Hampshire (with Don Mosey)*; George Allen & Unwin: 142 pp, £6.95

I am not the greatest lover of 'ghosted' autobiographies that litter the cricket book market, but this is an exception. With Don Mosey's intelligent help, John Hampshire has written a restrained and sensitive account of how he came to play for Yorkshire, the anti-climax of the award of his county cap and how, ultimately, he moved quietly to Derbyshire. There is no fuss. There is sadness, but no bitterness. Like much that concerns Yorkshire these days, it is a sad story, and we must be grateful that it has been so delicately told.

GLOUCESTERSHIRE ROAD. *Grahame Parker*: Pelham Books: 256 pp, £8.95

This is a lovely book. If you want to read a history of a county, read a history by someone who has been close to that county and preferably someone who is able to write. Grahame Parker has all these qualities. He is a former Gloucestershire player who was secretary/manager of the club for eight years. Gloucestershire County Cricket Club has been his life and his warmth and affection for the club and its players is apparent in his writing. Grace, Hammond, Barnett, Jessop and the rest are here. It is a fine story, well told and gives us the reminder that cricket is not really about winning titles, but about people. Grahame Parker has never forgotten this. One is grateful to him and to the National Westminster Bank for making its publication possible.

THE WAY TO LORD'S: CRICKETING LETTERS TO THE TIMES. *selected and introduced by Marcus Williams*: Collins Willow: 286 pp, £8.95

Marcus Williams is a man of great fun and good humour. I can think of no-one better to compile this book than he, and he has done an admirable job. Inevitably, there are the pertinent comments of the famous like Arlott, Barrie, Fry, Warner and Robertson-Glasgow, but there are some letters from those not known to us which often catch a point more succinctly than those by the better known, such as the comment that we would have had no trouble with the Centenary Test if it had been played at The Oval, its rightful home. Well-organised, good reading, delightful dipping.

RANJI. *Alan Ross*: Collins: 256 pp, £10.95

The only hesitation is to whether this book was really necessary for Ranji's life has been well documented and there are others who have need of chronicling. Having said that, one must accept immediately the strength of this biography. Alan Ross was born in India and lived in Sussex. The book is a labour of love and it is the work of one who, with Alan

Gibson, is the most accomplished writer on the game to-day. It has been meticulously researched and eloquently written.

WISDEN CRICKETERS' ALMANACK 1983. *edited by John Woodcock*: Macdonald Queen Anne Press: 1330 pp, £8.95 (hard cover)

The problem that confronts John Woodcock as editor of *Wisden* is the same one that confronts the present writer, how to find space for all the cricket that is now being played. The answer that he finds is the same that was found for *Benson and Hedges Cricket Year*, the almanack is bigger. It is a fine issue, full of substance and with relevant comment on manners in cricket and the South African question. John Woodcock's editorship has brought a positive moral tone to the problems that plague the game. Under his guidance, *Wisden* has gained in strength. It remains a mine of information and an indispensable reference.

JOHNNY WON'T HIT TO-DAY. *David Lemmon*: George Allen & Unwin: 152 pp, £8.95

This is the first attempt at a study of J.W.H.T. Douglas who led England before and after the first world war and was an amateur soccer international and Olympic boxing champion as well as a cricketer. The author was able to speak to many who had known Douglas and to obtain much new material.

ESSEX COUNTY CRICKET CLUB 1983 HANDBOOK. *edited by Peter Edwards*: 200 pp. £1.25

Few county handbooks are as good as the one produced by Peter Edwards at Essex. There are, of course, accounts and statistics of all Essex matches, but there are also several articles of great worth, such as Mike Marshall's interesting piece on china cricket figures of which he is a great collector. This is a handbook of substance and is a great credit to the editor. It is splendid value and of interest to those outside the county as well as to those within its boundaries.

MIDDLESEX COUNTY CRICKET CLUB REVIEW 1982–83. *edited Alvan Seth-Smith*: 127 pp, £2.95

Brought into existence by the efforts of the editor, this handbook is now in its third year and is rightly thriving. It is neatly produced with pleasing statistical lay-out and some enjoyable contributions from Barry Norman, Mike Brearley, Derek Lodge and others. A credit to its founder.

100 CRICKET TIPS. *Ashley Mallett*: Lansdowne Rigby International: 109 pp, £6.95

The success of any coaching manual must depend upon how attractive it is and this book is very attractive. Each tip is accompanied by an action picture of players like Kim Hughes, Allan Border or Viv Richards which make it a worthwhile picture gallery in itself. It covers a wide field and is certainly among the best of these coaching books.

VINTAGE CRICKETERS. *E.M. Wellings*: George Allen & Unwin: 177 pp, £9.95

The writings of E.M. Wellings have delighted many of us over the years and, in spite of a certain acidity, there is delight in this book. It is a meander through the cricket Wellings has seen and played, and a comment on the people he has known. His life has spanned a rich period in the game, and his comments, if tinged with the regret for past glories, are as perceptive as any who have written on the game. His few sentences on such as Barnett, Strudwick and Charlie Harris tell us more than pages by others. This is a book for those who love the game and value its traditions.

BRADMAN'S FIRST TOUR. Rigby International: 159 pp, £7.95

This is a fascinating publication. It is a compilation of reports from a variety of newspapers covering the Australian tour of England in 1930. To have had the research done and a contemporary picture produced of Bradman during that memorable year is a magnificent achievement. The quality of some of the journalism is not high and, inevitably, some of the pictures are poor, but this is a splendid publication.

THE CAPTAIN'S DIARY. *Bob Willis*: Collins Willow: 187 pp, £8.95

This is a tour book which the England captain wrote in conjunction with Alan Lee. It is a pleasant surprise for it is interesting and reads well. Several books of this nature have been attempted before, but this one gets closer to Willis' mind, and to the state of the England team than its predecessors. One does not always agree as, of necessity, punches have to be pulled, but it is a good venture.

EVERYTHING UNDER THE SUN. *Jeff Stollmeyer*: Stanley Paul: 231 pp, £8.95

What does he know of cricket who only cricket knows? The question was posed by another West Indian. Jeff Stollmeyer's answer is implicit in this autobiography – nothing – for this is a book about life, life in which cricket is an important part, but not the only part. It is a rich life and an absorbing one, and so is the book.

GLOVES OF IRONY. *Rodney Marsh*: Pelham Books: 128 pp, £5.95

Off field Rod Marsh can be a charming man; on it he can rouse people's anger. This is an on field book. The style is pugnacious, if one can call it style, and one could have hoped that he would have chosen a better 'ghost' who would have given us the full Marsh story and not this collection of jibes and insults against the New Zealand prime-minister and others.

BENSON AND HEDGES GOLDEN GREATS – BATSMEN. *devised and researched by David Frith: produced by David Puttnam: directed by Andrew Gillman: commentary by John Arlott and David Frith:* Visnews Video Production: running time approx. 90 minutes: £19.95

Over the past few years David Frith has presented evenings at the National Film Theatre of archive film of old cricketers. In a sense, this video is the final fruition of all his research. The problem, of course, is that the very great, like Grace and Trumper, are inadequately represented on film while even the more recent very great like Bradman, Compton and Hutton are only represented on film of doubtful quality. Accepting this fact, this video is a remarkable achievement and compulsive viewing. It is the work of many talents, from sponsors to commentators, but the main achievement belongs to David Frith for what he has assembled. Ranjitsinhji, Hobbs, Sutcliffe, Hammond, Hendren, Woodfull and Sobers are all here and if one has a criticism, it is that Tavare, David Steele, Hookes, Yallop and the like find their way into this illustrious company. Obviously, one's choice is dictated by what is available, but some can consider themselves lucky. Nevertheless, this is a remarkable piece of work and history, as well as ourselves, should be grateful to David Frith and his team. We are promised the great bowlers next and that will be something else to treasure in the long winter evenings.